Handbook of Research on Acquiring 21st Century Literacy Skills Through Game-Based Learning

Carol-Ann Lane
University of Toronto, Canada

Volume II

A volume in the Advances in Game-Based
Learning (AGBL) Book Series

Published in the United States of America by
IGI Global
Information Science Reference (an imprint of IGI Global)
701 E. Chocolate Avenue
Hershey PA, USA 17033
Tel: 717-533-8845
Fax: 717-533-8661
E-mail: cust@igi-global.com
Web site: http://www.igi-global.com

Library of Congress Cataloging-in-Publication Data

Names: Lane, Carol-Ann, 1966- editor.
Title: Handbook of research on acquiring 21st century literacy skills
  through game-based learning / Carol-Ann Lane, editor.
Other titles: Handbook of research on acquiring twenty-first century
  literacy skills through game-based learning
Description: Hershey, PA : Information Science Reference, 2022. | Includes
  bibliographical references and index. | Summary: "This book offers
  findings in digital technology and multimodal ways of acquiring literacy
  skills in the 21st century, highlighting research in discovering new
  pedagogical boundaries by focusing on ways that youth learn from digital
  sources such as video games"-- Provided by publisher.
Identifiers: LCCN 2021044535 (print) | LCCN 2021044536 (ebook) | ISBN
  9781799872719 (hardcover) | ISBN 9781799872733 (ebook)
Subjects: LCSH: Reading--Computer-assisted instruction. | Video games in
  education.
Classification: LCC LB1050.37 .A38 2022 (print) | LCC LB1050.37 (ebook) |
  DDC 372.4028/4--dc23
LC record available at https://lccn.loc.gov/2021044535
LC ebook record available at https://lccn.loc.gov/2021044536

This book is published in the IGI Global book series Advances in Game-Based Learning (AGBL) (ISSN: 2327-1825; eISSN: 2327-1833)

British Cataloguing in Publication Data
A Cataloguing in Publication record for this book is available from the British Library.

For electronic access to this publication, please contact: eresources@igi-global.com.

Advances in Game-Based Learning (AGBL) Book Series

Robert D. Tennyson
University of Minnesota, USA

ISSN:2327-1825
EISSN:2327-1833

MISSION

The **Advances in Game-Based Learning (AGBL) Book Series** aims to cover all aspects of serious games applied to any area of education. The definition and concept of education has begun to morph significantly in the past decades and game-based learning has become a popular way to encourage more active learning in a creative and alternative manner for students in K-12 classrooms, higher education, and adult education. **AGBL** presents titles that address many applications, theories, and principles surrounding this growing area of educational theory and practice.

COVERAGE

- Curriculum Development Using Educational Games
- Digital Game-Based Learning
- Edutainment
- Electronic Educational Games
- Game Design and Development of Educational Games
- MMOs in Education
- Pedagogical Theory of Game-Based Learning
- Psychological Study of Students Involved in Game-Based Learning
- Role of instructors
- Virtual worlds and game-based learning

IGI Global is currently accepting manuscripts for publication within this series. To submit a proposal for a volume in this series, please contact our Acquisition Editors at Acquisitions@igi-global.com or visit: http://www.igi-global.com/publish/.

Titles in this Series

For a list of additional titles in this series, please visit: www.igi-global.com/book-series

IGI Global
PUBLISHER of TIMELY KNOWLEDGE

701 East Chocolate Avenue, Hershey, PA 17033, USA
Tel: 717-533-8845 x100 • Fax: 717-533-8661
E-Mail: cust@igi-global.com • www.igi-global.com

Editorial Advisory Board

List of Contributors

Table of Contents

Volume I

Section 1
Gamification in Higher Education

Reena Raj, CHRIST University (Deemed), India
Cecil Donald, CHRIST University (Deemed), India
Anand Patil, CHRIST University (Deemed), India
Manjula M. Y., CHRIST University (Deemed), India
Swarnalatha P., CHRIST University (Deemed), India

Menşure Alkış Küçükaydın, Eregli Faculty of Education, Necmettin Erbakan University, Turkey
Burcu Durmaz, Süleyman Demirel University, Turkey

Ankit Dhamija, Amity University, Haryana, India
Deepika Dhamija, Amity University, Haryana, India

Smitha Baboo, CHRIST University (Deemed), India
Yogesh Kanna, CHRIST University (Deemed), India
Cathlyn Niranjana Bennett, CHRIST University (Deemed), India

Section 2
Exploring Literacy in Game-Based Learning

Section 4
Teacher Perceptions of Game-Based Learning

Section 5
Gamification, Mobile Learning, and Education Policy

Section 6
Game-Based Pedagogy for Primary-Elementary Educators

Section 7
Learner Assessment, Motivation, and Behaviors in Game-Based Learning

Section 8
Game-Based Learning: Code and Play

Section 9
Virtual Teaching and Project-Oriented Game-Based Learning

Detailed Table of Contents

Volume I

Section 1
Gamification in Higher Education

> *Reena Raj, CHRIST University (Deemed), India*
> *Cecil Donald, CHRIST University (Deemed), India*
> *Anand Patil, CHRIST University (Deemed), India*
> *Manjula M. Y., CHRIST University (Deemed), India*
> *Swarnalatha P., CHRIST University (Deemed), India*

Games have been an inevitable part of education since the beginning. They have indescribably transformed the educational landscape with a higher emphasis on the learner-centric pedagogy. The educational games can be considered to be a contemporary manifestation of these centuries' old philosophies and practices aimed at imparting strategic and tactical thinking, language, logic, and mathematical skills amongst the learners. This chapter explores the meaning, significance, and scope of game-based learning as an instructional tool. It provides an interesting account of several games that are popularly used to facilitate effective learning in various settings. This chapter also examines the relevance and implications of games in education.

> *Menşure Alkış Küçükaydın, Eregli Faculty of Education, Necmettin Erbakan University, Turkey*
> *Burcu Durmaz, Süleyman Demirel University, Turkey*

In this study, a study was made on the Web of Science index by using the words "game-based learning," "video games," "game-based pedagogy," "digital games," "gamification," and "game." The study was carried out with data obtained from the SCI-E, SSCI, and A&HCI indices covering the years 1975-2021. A total of 1,376 articles were reached in accordance with the inclusion criteria. Retrieved articles were subjected to bibliometric analysis. In line with the relevant analysis, the most influential authors, journals, institutions, and articles were revealed under the title "games in education." In addition, based on the articles examined within the scope of this research, a co-word network structure was visualized in terms of cooperation among institutions and authors. As a result of the research, the trends in topics related to games were revealed, and the changes in this area are subsequently discussed.

Chapter 3

Ankit Dhamija, Amity University, Haryana, India
Deepika Dhamija, Amity University, Haryana, India

In recent years, the teaching-learning process in higher education has undergone unprecedented change. Learners from across the world can enroll in any university using online platforms. This learning freedom is fantastic for all stakeholders, but it raises some serious concerns, such as how to ensure effective learner engagement and make the learning experience meaningful for the learners. While technology has aided learning, it has also become a significant source of distraction for students, as they spend too much time on gadgets solely for entertainment. This necessitates innovative and engaging teaching styles from educators. Designing course content as a game makes learning more engaging as learners get a sense of motivation and accomplishment. However, aligning games with lesson plans, designing assessment criteria, and learning outcomes takes a significant amount of time and effort. Hence, this chapter proposes learner-centered interactive instructional strategies that employ GBL to pique learners' curiosity and recommends popular GBL platforms for creating educational games.

Chapter 4

Smitha Baboo, CHRIST University (Deemed), India
Yogesh Kanna, CHRIST University (Deemed), India
Cathlyn Niranjana Bennett, CHRIST University (Deemed), India

Game-based learning is one of the sustainable education methods for future professionals from the higher education learning environment. To attain these innovative and sustainable teaching pedagogies, the components of games and simulations need to be incorporated into the teaching-learning content. The integration of neuroscience and cognitive concepts has become an essential feature in understanding various phenomena in game-based learning with regard to higher education learning environments. Several neural and cognitive processes are involved while engaging in such activities. These activities have played a pivotal role in the pedagogy and teachers had to think on their feet while engaging students in higher education as well. Game-based learning has proven to be a very effective method of engaging higher education students.

Chapter 5

M. Mahruf C. Shohel, University of Surrey, UK
Md. Ashrafuzzaman, Bangabandhu Sheikh Mujibur Rahman Digital University, Bangladesh
Iffat Naomee, University of Dhaka, Bangladesh
Sanjida Akter Tanni, Jagannath University, Bangladesh
Farhan Azim, University of Melbourne, Australia

Game-based pedagogies use games for achieving learning outcomes by guiding the learners through specific tasks, which can be digital and/or non-digital and can promote deep meaningful learning. Therefore, the design of game-based learning helps learners to engage in the meaning-making process and ensure better participation. As the boundaries of classroom learning become blurred through blended or hybrid learning approaches, game-based learning enhances digital literacies for digital natives to prepare them for building a knowledge economy. By exploring existing literature, this chapter highlights how technology can support teachers and learners to go beyond their existing pedagogical boundaries by focusing on ways games may serve as digital sources of learning. It also explores the role game-based pedagogies and digital learning design frameworks play in enhancing learner engagement, collaboration, and cultural understanding.

Chapter 6

Vikas Salunkhe, CHRIST University (Deemed), India
Seena Thomas Kaithathara, CHRIST University (Deemed), India
Darshan S. M., CHRIST University (Deemed), India
Gowri Shankar R., CHRIST University (Deemed), India
Shabarisha N., CHRIST University (Deemed), India

Game-based learning is widely followed at the school level in India, but the higher education system has been longer in adopting it. The pandemic situation has transformed teaching and learning processes from the traditional to the technical method, which requires a more versatile approach. Because of the rapid change from the offline mode to the online mode in higher education, there is little evidence available on the inefficiency of implementing the traditional system of teacher-centered education on online platforms. There comes a lot of the significance in of adapting technology-based games in order to engage and motivate students throughout their course of study. The aim of this chapter is to provide an overview of the effectiveness of game-based learning strategies over traditional learning methods. Moreover, the results of a cross-sectional study conducted by the authors in South Indian universities at the higher education level is included.

Chapter 7

Karthigai Prakasam Chellaswamy, CHRIST University (Deemed), India
Nagarjuna Gururaj Rao, CHRIST University (Deemed), India
Sharon Varghese, CHRIST University (Deemed), India
Georgy P. Kurien, CHRIST University (Deemed), India
Sreedhara Raman, CHRIST University (Deemed), India
Anand Shankar Raja Manivannan, CHRIST University (Deemed), India

Game-based learning is an exciting and interactive tool used by many teachers across the globe. This research aims to check whether any significant change is found in the learning of the student before and after introducing game-based learning in classroom teaching. MBA students were identified as the target group for this research. The production dice game was used for this experiment. The teacher engaged the first session traditionally and later with the production dice game. Student learning was captured through a Google form before and after the game. The Google form had questions ranging from understanding to analyzing to application-level to capture exactly the effectiveness of game-based learning, Paired sample t-test was applied to check the before and after test results, and it was found that there was a significant change in the learning among the identified target group. Through this study, the authors conclude that game-based learning provides better results in student learning as compared to regular classroom teaching.

Chapter 8

Sunitha Abhay Jain, CHRIST University (Deemed), India
Nilofer Hussaini, CHRIST University (Deemed), India
Sunil John, CHRIST University (Deemed), India
Daisy Alexander, CHRIST University (Deemed), India
Bidisha Sarkar, CHRIST University (Deemed), India

The technological developments and innovations have thrown open many challenges in the field of higher education. We are growing up in a society of digital natives who are exposed to the digital environment from their birth. Of late, the focus has shifted from traditional teaching methods to finding innovative ways and means to engage the students. Competence building instead of rote learning is the need of the hour. In order to prepare the students to face the challenges of the real world and make them future ready, it is important for higher educational institutions to focus on imparting to learners 21st century skill sets such as creativity, problem solving, and critical thinking, amongst others. Game-based learning is gaining momentum and is becoming a popular pedagogical tool as it is learner-centric and fosters creativity.

Chapter 9

Emily Guetzoian, Anderson School of Management, UCLA, USA

This chapter discusses gamification strategies in the context of higher education student worker training. Specifically, it builds on the concepts of gamification in corporate training contexts and gamification in the academic classroom environment. It also considers various options to support gamified training content and methods to support student worker engagement and knowledge retention. It explains how these strategies relate to the concept of information literacy for an adult, higher education population. This chapter is ideal for higher education staff, faculty, or administrators who design training curricula for student workers.

Chapter 10

Patrícia Gouveia, LARSyS, Interactive Technologies Institute (ITI), Faculdade de Belas-Artes, Universidade de Lisboa (FBAUL), Portugal
Luciana Lima, LARSyS, Interactive Technologies Institute (ITI), Faculdade de Belas-Artes, Universidade de Lisboa (FBAUL), Portugal
Anna Unterholzner, LARSyS, Interactive Technologies Institute (ITI), Faculdade de Belas-Artes, Universidade de Lisboa (FBAUL), Portugal

This chapter presents experiences in using gaming and interactive media in higher education environments since 2017 culminating in the 2020/21 years when the COVID-19 pandemic forced teachers and students to adopt different work methodologies. Participatory design strategies merged with a tradition of critical and interdisciplinary studies in humanities mediated by online technologies helped shape these strategies enhanced by the cooperation from three different faculties from Lisbon University in Portugal (Universidade de Lisboa, UL), namely FBAUL, IST, and IGOT. The aim of these experiments was to augment the potential for innovation and research taking advantage of gaming research methodologies to involve teachers and students in a common context. This chapter also shows research done in interactive media, augmented and virtual reality, game art, and gender equity. The year 2020 showed how institutional collaboration can open learning spaces to a more focused approach on the interests of young people and to promote a more sustainable and dynamic future.

Chapter 11

Samantha Taylor, Dalhousie University, Canada
Binod Sundararajan, Dalhousie University, Canada
Cora-Lynn Munroe-Lynds, Dalhousie University, Canada

Using the lenses of Vygotskian constructivism, situated cognition, the antecedents of flow, and a pedagogy interwoven with the multiliteracy framework, the authors present a COVID-19 simulation game. The game has multiple levels, challenges, disrupters, and allows for student player groups to work together (i.e., collaborate within and across player groups) to achieve the strategic objectives of the game. The player groups have an overall goal to minimize loss of life, while other parameters need to be optimized, depending on the stakeholder group that the player group is role-playing. While the game can be digitized, it is presented in a manner that allows instructors to implement the game simulation right away in their classrooms. Assessment rubrics, decision matrix templates, and debriefing notes are provided to allow for student learners to reflect on their decisions (based on course concepts) both individually and as a player group.

Chapter 12

Brian Angus McKenzie, Maynooth University, Ireland

This chapter provides a case study of the use of worldbuilding for role-playing games as the foundation for a first year multiliteracies seminar. The author provides an overview of teaching and learning during the pandemic in the Irish context. The chapter provides practical advice on using a MediaWiki installation as the infrastructure for worldbuilding projects. The author shows how this imparts important digital literacies and allows for a critical apprehension of Wikipedia itself. The author argues that online learning and professional development benefit from a multiliteracies approach and, furthermore, that worldbuilding is a useful strategy for overcoming the limitations of online learning while at the same time achieving rigorous learning outcomes.

Section 2
Exploring Literacy in Game-Based Learning

Chapter 13

Minda Marshall, Lectorsa, South Africa
Marinda Marshall, Lectorsa, South Africa

This chapter foregrounds an online gamified visual intelligence innovation (eyebraingym) developed to enhance visual processing skills, improve memory and vocabulary, and increase reading fluency. The explicit aim of the innovation is to improve comprehension towards visual intelligence. Ninety-eight Grade 8 learners at a South African Boy's School completed their online development during the 2021 academic year. These learners were part of a group of students participating in a whole school reading and literacy intervention program. The innovation is an integral part of this ongoing project. Their interaction with the innovation consists of 15 sessions completed once or twice a week for 20 – 40 minutes over five months. The results of the project are positive. It shows that most participating students improved their perceptual development and reading speed (VPF) and cognitive development and comprehension skills (CDF). In addition, these outcomes transferred to improved relative efficiency when working with information (AIUF).

Chapter 14

Interpretations of the cultural meanings made by each of the boys in the study, based on their individual unique experiences engaging with video games, can provide readers with insights into how to approach adolescent aged boys' literacy development through game-based pedagogy. In this chapter the author describes how these four boys developed their multimodal ways of learning by engaging with visual perspectives of video games. The methodological approach documented what boys are saying, as much as possible, which is currently understudied in the literature surrounding boys and their video gaming practices. This chapter addresses some boys' out-of-school video gaming practices for meaning-making and gaining cultural knowledge. Studying the ways in which boys make meanings through multimodal ways of learning can offer insights into strategies for cyber culture that can potentially reinvent traditional literacy pedagogical boundaries and establish new ways and practices for building knowledge.

Chapter 15

Students in the 21st century are learning by doing and playing. Teachers need to incorporate technology into everyday tasks. Games assist students in the learning process. Once students have learned a task through the playing process, they will remember this much easier and longer than simply doing a worksheet. Research shows students enjoy interactive and engaging activities and will choose these types of activities over pencil and paper types of activities. Teachers must prepare students for the future which involves more critical thinking and technological types of skills. Traditional teaching methods and styles have underused technology tools and pedagogical methods. The 2020 Covid pandemic and remote learning delivery style assisted teachers in developing new tools and methods to reach and teach all students with various and diverse needs.

Chapter 16

The digital storyworld model is conceptualised in this chapter as an innovative digital storytelling that incorporates both transmedia and meaning-making narrative approaches. Working with Aristotelian story elements in a non-linear digital series of mini-worlds, the higher education narrator-as-learner enters real-world situations mirrored in a fictional and fragmented environment. The model encourages a playful engagement in the experiential learning process through a range of points of view, encouraging empathy for differing perspectives that are transferable to real-life environments.

    Sam von Gillern, University of Missouri, USA
    Carolyn Stufft, Berry College, USA
    Rick Marlatt, New Mexico State University, USA
    Larysa Nadolny, Iowa State University, USA

This research examines the perceptions and instructional ideas of preservice teachers as relates to using Minecraft, a popular video game, to facilitate game-based learning opportunities in their future elementary classrooms. The participants were 21 preservice teachers who played Minecraft as part of a teacher preparation program course and then completed essays on their experiences with the game and its potential to support student learning in the elementary English language arts classroom. These essays were coded and analyzed for themes. Three primary results were found in data analysis. First, three groups emerged from the data with each group indicating either no interest, some interest, or high interest in using Minecraft in their future teaching. Second, the preservice teachers illustrated various potential instructional strategies for integrating the game into the classroom, and third, participants identified a variety of ways that Minecraft integration can support English language arts instruction and learning.

    Sharon Peck, State University of New York College at Geneseo, USA

Drawing on a multimodal framework, this chapter looks at the ways engagement and embodiment of learning are mediated through play as sixth graders learn to skin or repurpose board games to represent the story of The Lightning Thief. Studying game design for the purpose of skinning, that is, applying a new theme or skin to a game, provides a literacy learning process that can foster collaborative, creative, and authentic learning. Outcomes demonstrated gains in social skills and interactions, critical thinking, reading comprehension, visual representation, graphic design, and writing for specific purposes. Analysis revealed that students were immersed in the learning process to the extent that they felt comfortable acting informally, responding in the moment, and being playful. This chapter shows a way to foster academic growth, engagement in learning, and collaboration is to engage students in skinning games based on literature and integrated a playful learning environment.

    Hacer Dolanbay, Muş Alparslan University, Turkey

Whether we call it the age of information, the age of digitalization, or the informatics, this century is an era in which rapid technological developments are taking place and will continue without stopping. The importance of using the media consciously and appropriately is increasing by reducing the effects of the media on individuals with many positive and negative characteristics. Having media literacy skills, which is one of the basic skills of the new century, is important in learning how tool live with the media. Becoming a conscious media consumer and producer, the way to realize the reality in the media is to have media literacy skills which is one of the basic skills of the new century. This chapter is mainly aimed at studying the dynamics that makeup media literacy and media literacy skills. How the century has transformed to meet the needs of its students will be highlighted within the context of media literacy. Then, the chapter will be completed by explaining how media literacy is reflected in pedagogy with examples suitable for different courses and levels.

Chapter 20

This chapter discusses the theoretical frameworks for artificial intelligence (AI) teachers and how AI teachers have been applied to facilitate game-based literacy learning in existing empirical studies. While the application of artificial intelligence (AI) in education is a relatively emerging research area, it has received increasing attention in the scientific community. In the future, AI teachers are likely to be able to serve as powerful supplementary tools in classroom teaching in support of human teachers. The main goal here is to provide the readers with new insights on promoting game-based literacy learning from the perspectives of AI teachers. To this end, the authors introduce the readers to the key concepts of AI teachers, the merits and demerits of AI teachers in education, scientific research on AI teachers in literacy learning, and some highlighted examples of AI teachers in literacy classrooms for practical concerns.

Section 3
Culturally-Based Game-Based Pedagogy

Chapter 21

This chapter explores the possibility of enhancing literacy skills using indigenous games played by Vhavenda children at foundation phase. It critically analyses different types of Vhavenda games played by children which are ndode, mufuvha, muravharavha, and tsetsetse or trere-tsere to solicit the possibility to enhance literacy skills. Methodologically, this study aligns with the use of qualitative approach where researchers collected data using interviews and observations. The focus is on Vhavenda indigenous games that can be adopted by other cultures to enhance learning inside and outside the classroom environment. The results found that indigenous games develop several literacy skills inclusive of school, arithmetic, communication, cultural, emotional, and physical literacies which are very important for total development of children. Games are enjoyable and interesting and as such make learning fun.

Chapter 22

Critical thinking skills are fundamental for both undergraduate and postgraduate students in the academic environment. These skills allow students to question and reflect on the knowledge and information presented to them. These skills can be learned differently through various instruments. This chapter explores how this game can contribute towards teaching critical thinking skills. There are various indigenous games played in Vhavenda culture. The researchers focus on an indigenous game, Duvheke. The chapter employs game-based pedagogy as a theory that underpins this study. Methodologically, the chapter assumes a qualitative complexion because it seeks to collect in-depth information about Duvheke and how it can be used in teaching critical thinking skills first entering students in a rural university. The data collection method used is interviews which were collected from first entering students. Preliminary findings suggest that critical thinking is needed to play Duvheke. The chapter suggests that Duvheke can be a valuable tool in teaching critical thinking skills.

Chapter 23

Pamela Jennifer February, University of Namibia, Namibia

This chapter investigates the effectiveness of a digital reading tool, called GraphoGame, that could be employed as one of the solutions to the poor reading results of learners that have been revealed in both national and international assessments in Namibia, specifically, and Sub-Saharan Africa in general. Following a research study, this chapter sets out to demonstrate that, through pre-and post-tests, GraphoGame Afrikaans improved the initial reading skills of Grade 1 learners. The results have implications for the utilization of computer-assisted tools to support reading acquisition in the lower grades. As GraphoGame employs a scaffolded approach by presenting learners with letters and words, it can be utilized to support learners individually in classes with large numbers, as is typical in Africa.

Chapter 24

Jianshu Qiao, Queen Mary University of London, UK
John R. Woodward, Queen Mary Univeristy of London, UK
Atm S. Alam, Queen Mary University of London, UK

Researchers have been exploring the potential of educational video games for learning English vocabulary. The primary focus is on two questions: (1) Can educational video games motivate students to learn English vocabulary (which explores students' attitudes)? and (2) Are educational video games effective in acquiring English vocabulary (which explores learning outcomes)? Good quality empirical research on this is rare because of the shortage of games specific to educational purposes. In addition, although some researchers have contributed to answering these two questions, their methodology is not convincing. Therefore, this chapter aims to provide an overview of their methodologies by introducing participant groups, popular educational video games, pre-test, post-test, and data analysis. Finally, this chapter will inspire researchers to conduct more reliable empirical research, thereby making better-found contributions to the field.

Volume II

Joaquim Dias Soeiro, School of Hospitality, Tourism, and Events, Taylor's University, Malaysia
Puteri Sofia Amirnuddin, Taylor's Law School, Taylor's University, Malaysia

The diversification of pedagogic tools remains essential for a fruitful learning experience among the Gen Z students by embedding technology such as gamification in learning. Recent literature has discussed the acquisition of 21st century skills and the educational challenges generally faced by Asian students due to their cultural traits. Against this background, the findings of this study open reflections relating to the benefit of gamification in acquiring 21st century skills. The objective of this chapter is to identify whether gamification is a suitable pedagogic tool among Malaysian law students in order to support the acquisition of 21st century skills. The respondents are from Year 1 and Year 2 of a three-year Bachelor of Laws degree with the majority being Malaysian students. The data collected showed that gamification helps in the acquisition of 21st century skills. Evidently, it showed that gamification can be a suitable alternative pedagogic tool to support the students to learn skills such as critical thinking, creativity, innovation, leadership, or communication.

Haytham Siala, Business School, Newcastle University, UK
Giuseppe Pedeliento, University of Bergamo, Italy
Daniela Andreini, University of Bergamo, Italy

The multi-disciplinary literature on ethics asserts that the relationship between religiosity and ethical perceptions and judgements is an under-researched topic. Despite its importance, few studies have examined the relationship between religiosity and the learning of business ethics. This research investigates whether religiosity is conducive to the learning of business ethics in a digital learning environment: a serious 3D ethics game. A cross-sectional survey was conducted on 302 final-year students from two different academic institutions based in the UK. The results of a structural equation modelling analysis suggest that religiosity does not inform the ethical perceptions and decisions of religious individuals in digital learning environments. Religious individuals perceive the utilitarian aspects of a serious game such as ease of use to be more important for learning ethics than religion. In contrast, less religious individuals perceive the hedonic aspects of a serious game to be a key catalyst for enhancing the learning of ethics.

Meltem Huri Baturay, Atilim University, Turkey
Ahmet Erdost Yastibaş, Gazi University, Turkey
Gonca Yangin Ekşi, Gazi University, Turkey
Cafer Ahmet Çinar, Çanakkale Onsekiz Mart University, Turkey

Increasing human activities in the environment have created severe effects; therefore, handling such effects by raising environmental awareness through several ways has become significant to sustain the environment, which can enhance 21st century skills including critical thinking and information literacy. Digital games can be used for this because they create an environment for learning with higher engagement, motivation, and excitement besides fostering cognitive attainment and retention. Accordingly, a mobile game-based content and language-integrated learning practice (an educational digital game called ENVglish) was developed to raise EFL students' environmental awareness in this qualitative study. During the design and development phases of the game, students' and teachers' perceptions regarding it were collected with semi-structured interviews. The data were content analyzed. The findings indicated that both students and teachers had positive perceptions about the game and that students could improve their English and have environmental awareness with the game.

Section 4
Teacher Perceptions of Game-Based Learning

Jessica Reuter, GOVCOPP, DEGEIT, University of Aveiro, Portugal

Marta Ferreira Dias, GOVCOPP, DEGEIT, University of Aveiro, Portugal

Marlene Amorim, GOVCOPP, DEGEIT, University of Aveiro, Portugal

Mara Madaleno, GOVCOPP, DEGEIT, University of Aveiro, Portugal

Claúdia Veloso, GOVCOPP, DEGEIT, University of Aveiro, Portugal

Innovative educational methods such as gamification are gaining ground in more formal environments and have great potential to improve learning in education. However, the implementation of this strategy in the classroom is assumed to be a complex practice for beginners and requires the development of new competencies by educators. This chapter aims to contribute to the advancement of knowledge about the main competencies needed for educators to perform as facilitators of educational games. The study was developed through critical literature review, interviews, and questionnaires. The outcome is the development of a framework of competencies of an educator willing to use game-based learning. The study highlights the importance of institutional support to boost the development of pedagogical, technological, and social skills among educators. The conclusions of the chapter are valuable for educators aiming to adopt game-based learning and to higher education decision makers committed to expanding innovative learning contexts on their institutions.

Cristina A. Huertas-Abril, University of Córdoba, Spain

María García-Molina, University of Córdoba, Spain

The consideration that the only goal of games is the achievement of entertainment is still commonly accepted, although there is now an outgrowing perspective that believes in the use of games to promote learning. This exploratory quantitative research examines both in-service and pre-service Spanish teacher perceptions (n = 112) about using digital games in their lessons, paying a special attention to the TPACK model, and comparing the results regarding age, gender, and professional situation. Responses show a positive attitude towards the potential use of video games in their lessons, although there are differences considering the results of the items concerning technological, pedagogical, or content knowledge. The data presented in this study is relevant to guide the design of curriculum and training programs, as well as to develop strategies to support and scaffold pre-service and in-service teachers' knowledge and practical implementation of digital game-based learning (DGBL).

Section 5
Gamification, Mobile Learning, and Education Policy

Chapter 30

Absolom Muzambi, University of South Africa, South Africa
Leila Goosen, University of South Africa, South Africa

In order to provide readers with an overview and summarize the content, the purpose of this chapter is stated as reporting on an investigation around acquiring 21st century skills through e-learning. This study takes place against the background of the factors affecting the successful implementation of an e-education policy and community engagement. In terms of research methodology, a case study is used of a specific high (secondary) school in the Metro North district of the Western Cape province, South Africa.

Chapter 31

Fritz Ngale Ilongo, University of Eswatini, Eswatini

This chapter explores the potentially negative and positive impacts of game-based pedagogy on personality development. The methodology of this chapter is qualitative basic research, while the theoretical framework is critical theoretical analyses, articulated around psychodynamic theory, analytic psychology, and positive psychology. The negative view of game-based personality development presupposes 'learners for technology' or the pessimistic view, while the positive view of game-based personality development considers 'technology for learners' as being a perspective which facilitates media literacy, higher order thinking, higher emotional intelligence, and pro-social behaviors. The conclusion is that the positive view of game-based personality development would facilitate learners' effective and efficient acquisition of 21st century literacy skills, that is, information literacy, media literacy, and technology literacy.

Chapter 32

Ana Nobre, Universidade Aberta, Portugal
Vasco Nobre, Universidade Aberta, Portugal

Gamification has been a very frequent research topic in the area of education in recent years, with some positive results, such as increasing student engagement and motivation. However, studies on gamification as an instructional strategy are recent and need more data to help teachers in its use in the classroom. Thus, this work describes a gamification experience of a social game with graduate students, teachers in primary and secondary education, and discusses how the elements present in games can provide engagement and favor learning. Furthermore, the authors present the Kahoot app as a possibility to stimulate and engage students in the teaching-learning process, analyzing some implications of learning with a mobile device. The results had a positive impact on increasing student engagement in both Game Social and Kahoot. Therefore, gamification and mobile learning can be good alternatives to increase the quality of teaching, generating meaningful experiences in the classroom.

Chapter 33

Astronomy and Space-Themed Mobile Games: Tools to Support Science Education or Learning Barriers Due to the Misconceptions They Generate? 646

Georgios Eleftherios Bampasidis, National and Kapodistrian University of Athens, Greece
Apostolia Galani, National and Kapodistrian University of Athens, Greece
Constantine Skordoulis, National and Kapodistrian University of Athens, Greece

This chapter aims to contribute to the discussion of incorporating mobile games with astronomy and space themes in order to support science learning. One concern is when these games include erroneous science content. In this case, they may build or enhance misconceptions or misunderstandings, which eventually create learning barriers. The authors try to determine the learning strategies or pedagogies which can be used to incorporate such games in science education. Research on which characteristics these games should have is also presented. Game-based learning is in alignment with acquiring and developing 21st century literacy skills. One of these skills, information literacy, is related to domain knowledge learning.

Section 6
Game-Based Pedagogy for Primary-Elementary Educators

Chapter 34

Incorporating Digital Literacy Materials in Early Childhood Programs: Understanding Children's Engagement and Interactions 671

Barbara Ellen Culatta, Brigham Young University, USA
Lee Ann Setzer, Brigham Young University, USA
Kendra M. Hall-Kenyon, Brigham Young University, USA

Use of digital media in early childhood literacy programs offers significant opportunities for interaction, engagement, and meaningful practice of phonic skills—and also a few pitfalls. The purpose of this chapter is to review 1) considerations for use of digital media in early childhood settings, 2) selection of appropriate media to facilitate early literacy learning, and 3) inclusion of digital media as an integral component of early literacy instruction, rather than an add-on. With an emphasis on practical ideas and solutions for instructors, the authors draw on studies in which interactive, personalized ebooks and an early literacy learning app were used in conjunction with face-to-face, hands-on activities drawn from Project SEEL (Systematic and Engaging Early Literacy).

Chapter 35

Acquiring Problem-Solving Skills Through Coding Games in Primary School 697

Gaia Lombardi, Istituto Comprensivo Statale Via dei Salici, Legnano, Italy

Play is a spontaneous and free activity of the child and its role in learning processes has been recognized by pedagogical studies from Piaget onwards. Game-based learning places the pupil at the center of the teaching-learning process, creating a motivating and challenging environment in which the pupil can learn freely, proceeding by trial and error, learning to evaluate their choices and those of other players and monitor a number of variables. Game-based learning therefore stands as an individualized and inclusive learning environment, which allows all students to achieve maximum educational success. In more recent years, the spread of online games, the use of coding as a teaching tool, and distance learning experiences have contributed to spreading game-based didactics. In this chapter, the author proposes a path of coding games for the development of problem solving in primary school with interdisciplinary links and to the mathematics curriculum.

The curriculum is an essential and integral part of the education system for lifelong learning and better children's outcomes. The sum of experience throughout their schooling journey can be defined as an educational curriculum expressed in a much broader sense. The school's type of school, study materials used, teaching methods, available school facilities, and the qualifications of schoolteachers provided at the end of primary schooling often diverge with different educational curricula due to the government policy dilemma. There is no unified primary education curriculum in Bangladesh's case. More than three mainstream educational curricula can be founded, each with its own unique set of traits, benefits, and shortcomings. This chapter explores what factors affect a school's choice, which is linked with the educational curriculum being offered, and how it affects the student's quality of education. This chapter also explores gamification theory's implementation to ensure quality primary education in Bangladesh.

The authors of this study seek to provide practitioners with evidence to support the instructional value of Ignite by Hatch, a digital learning game designed for preschool children. Analyses were conducted using the entire population of three- and four-year-old children who used Ignite during the 2020-2021 academic year (n = 29,417) and included the use of descriptive statistics to explore patterns of growth and the Rasch measurement model to explore item difficulty. This chapter also features a preliminary crosswalk establishing the alignment between the domains, subdomains, and games presented within the Ignite game environment and the learning goals provided by the North Carolina Foundations for Early Learning and Development framework. Results suggest strong preliminary evidence in support of the instructional value of Ignite by Hatch. Further research is recommended to understand how knowledge and skill acquisition within the game environment translate to developmental growth outside of the gaming environment.

The aim of this study was to investigate the effectiveness of Minecraft-game-based learning towards on 21st century skills among primary school students. This study employed quasi-experimental methodology. The dependent variable of this study was the 21st century skills. During Minecraft-game-based learning session, students were given the opportunity to build and recreate a world based on certain themes inside Minecraft world based on their creativity and imagination. The session involved a learning process of different skills and knowledge relevant to school and real world which was imitate inside the Minecraft world. The result shows that the intervention of Minecraft-game-based learning is effective in enhancing and retaining the 21st century skills among students. The implication of the study suggests that the functionality of Minecraft as a digital learning tool should be promoted as it involves students to work in a team to solve problems and have fun while acquiring and sharpening the students' 21st century skills.

Section 7
Learner Assessment, Motivation, and Behaviors in Game-Based Learning

Chapter 39

This chapter presents an empirical research where the authors developed tasks based on a digital game supported by assessment strategies. The study is interpretative in nature, in a case study design. The authors designed tasks with technology and assessment strategies in a collaborative work context implemented in a mathematics classroom with 5th grade students (students 10 years old). The results evidence that the use of a digital game and formative assessment have contributed to the learning of complementary and supplementary angle pairs, giving meaning to their utilization as an effective strategy.

Chapter 40

The design and guidelines for gamification offer designers a range of solutions to provide empowerment and engagement to assist with retention within education. This chapter addresses a knowledge gap around the effective use while improving retention. With gaming mechanics as a driving point, specific design considerations were explored: badges, leader boards, points and levels, and challenges. The educator must think from the learner's perspective and find new ways of creating challenges and motivation techniques to provide value. Gamification, when applied to different disciplines, has the potential to facilitate the individual within learner-centricity. Current research indicates that gaming mechanics can encourage and motivate the learner while enriching their experience when applied to education.

Chapter 41

It is a proven fact that learning with the element of fun and games makes the learning process interesting and also helps in student retention. Especially, in the context of e-learning environment, where learner motivation and engagement level are not easy to monitor, it is required to implement some mechanism which can improve their intrinsic motivation and make them self-motivated. Gamification in education and using game-based formative assessment tools will be of great help to not only motivate learners to opt for e-learning courses, but to complete till the end. The current study, thus, focuses on use of game-based formative assessment to improve learners' motivation in the e-learning environment so that their drop-out rates can be controlled, and their engagement level can be improved. Also, it intends to assess the past literature and identify the essential gaming mechanics which can possibly impact the learner motivation. It will also highlight the theoretical perspective used in previous studies on gamification, engagement, and motivation.

Chapter 42

Annesha Biswas, CHRIST University (Deemed), India
Tinanjali Dam, CHRIST University (Deemed), India
Joseph Varghese Kureethara, CHRIST University (Deemed), India
Sankar Varma, CHRIST University (Deemed), India

In today's world, the concept of the game and game theory is turned into new methods of knowing and understanding some of the human behaviours followed by society. In the 21st century, behavioural economics plays a major role in understanding the concept of the `line' game and hence the strategies followed by it. It is a country game played in many parts of India. It is a two-person game with very simple rules and moves. It can be played indoors. Students play the game during the break-outs. The game keenly and minutely determines the objectivity of the game and the behaviour of the players involved inside the game and the way one starts moving helps the other players to understand what one is trying to portray through the game whether it is winning or losing. The strategies involved can be put forth and looked upon from different perspectives. Referring to one such perspective, it can be looked at from a concept of Pareto efficiency, a microeconomic concept. It helps develop logical skills and learn winning strategies.

Chapter 43

Ji Soo Lim, Dokkyo University, Japan

To understand the influence of video games on the player, several important questions must be answered. First, what accounts for the higher level of engagement in digital games relative to other entertainment media? Furthermore, what kind of experience does the player have during gameplay? Specifically, what does the player think when he or she interacts with other characters in the game? This study examines digital games with a focus on the interaction between the game itself and the person playing it. Among the various social behaviors elicited by digital games, much attention has been given to players' prosocial behavior within the context of a game's virtual world. A multidimensional view of behavior is used to analyze the game's situational contexts and players' interpretation of behavior.

Section 8
Game-Based Learning: Code and Play

Chapter 44

Games have been considered as an important part of child development and can roughly be defined as fictional structures with certain rules to be followed to achieve certain goals. Modern games (ex. Minecraft) sometimes require quite sophisticated skills to move on, and these skills mostly match up with 21st century skills. From this perspective, this chapter tries to explain the relationship between 21st century skills and game playing skills, the design thinking approach where students are game designers, coders, and players.

Chapter 45

This chapter begins by arguing that computational thinking and coding should be included as two more C's in the Partnership for 21st Century Learning's list of essential skills. It does so by examining how coding and computational thinking can be used to manipulate people. It argues that gaming uses all the C's, including the two new ones proposed. It then explores connections between playing video games and computer programming. It claims that game-based learning would be an optimal way to leverage these connections to teach coding and describes ways in which to do so, including specific challenges that could be included in game-based learning and a sequence of introducing them so students can "level up." It briefly examines different coding games and describes ways in which educators can create their own coding games. It concludes by arguing that educators can make the connections between gamer thinking and computational thinking visible, use games designed to teach coding, or create their own coding games to take advantage of near transfer.

Chapter 46

This chapter considers ways in which educators can create their own educational applications to integrate into their teaching. It is argued that interactive uses of technology can aid student engagement and encourage uptake of skills presented to them. Today, tools available allow everyone to create not only static websites, but also functional applications. It is possible to get started without knowing how to code, empowering anyone with an interest in technology to become a creator. While these no and low code solutions may come with some restrictions, they may encourage users to explore more traditional ways to engage with code and its possibilities for teaching. The chapter aims to encourage readers to look at technology as a creative practice to include into their teaching. It suggests strategies to help readers select the most appropriate tool for their projects.

Section 9
Virtual Teaching and Project-Oriented Game-Based Learning

Chapter 47

Pavlo Brin, National Technical University "Kharkiv Polytechnic Institute", Ukraine
Mariia Shypilova, Great Wall School, China

In this chapter, the authors investigate the potential of project-oriented game-based learning in making students of educational institutes more engaged and gain a deep understanding of the curriculum content. The literature review presents the main definitions and benefits of project-oriented game-based learning, followed by its contribution to improving the performance of students' training. The results of the research are based on testing the main statements of project-oriented game-based learning empirically – if it really can provide additional value for learners in higher education. The empirical data have been collected based on Ukrainian case study and allow the authors to prove the influence of project-oriented game-based learning on increasing students' engagement, satisfaction, performance, and improving learning outcomes. The main idea of the teaching project was to take as an object of the research a character from a fairytale and analyze its managerial activities. The chapter also analyzes the e-learning instruments which can be used in remote teaching.

Chapter 48

Anacleto Correia, Naval Academy, Portugal
Pedro B. Água, Naval Aacdemy, Portugal

Virtual reality (VR) is a technology that is becoming more common for applications in the field of education and training. VR can be used to create simulated two- and three-dimensional scenarios, promoting interactions between the user and the environment, which allows experiencing virtual training situations very close to real actions. The aim of this text is to describe the development of a teaching and training tool using VR technology for scuba divers' operations within the aquatic context for enhancing critical thinking. To this end, a survey of requirements based on real procedures was carried out in order to transpose them into a synthetic environment. After the construction of the artefact, it was tested and evaluated by qualified users, and the results are promising.

Preface

Over the past few decades, pedagogical trends have mainly focused on e-learning, digitizing learning, multiliteracies, and multi-modal learning. These trends have been synonymous with planning goals for twenty-first century learning. Global scholars and many educators embraced these trends with optimism and total conversion, while others preferred hybrid learning models and maybe even relying on or reverting to traditional learning models. However, the global pressures of policy makers and covid-19 worldwide lockdowns required an immediate dramatic shift in ways learners could consume information. Solutions were necessary to fulfil learners' needs whether in educational, management, retail or healthcare. Digital learning was here to stay, and traditional literacies was becoming a thing of the past. The race was real to embrace technology from k-12 to higher education institutions, workplace training, government, and health care providers. The needs were high to ensure synchronous and asynchronous learning was successful. Technological demands for virtual, digital, multimodal, gamification, e-learning, zoom sessions, have steadily intensified to meet learners' needs, especially for k-12 and higher ed. Let's be clear, gamification and/or game-based learning (GBL) can be digital or non-digital and is based on applying game-based principles to real settings or scenarios to enable learner or user engagement, motivation, and learning. GBL is not a theory which integrates games for students to play as a reward for finishing their homework, or having good behavior, but it is used to increase learner engagement by designing learning activities that can incrementally introduce concepts, and guide users towards an end goal (Pho & Dinscore, 2015).

Scholars and educators have acknowledged the need to address the gaps currently facing today's learners. Recent trends indicate many educators and policy makers have responded by revising pedagogical models by including technological/digital designs and framework that support multimodal, multiliteracies and gamification elements. Scholars have acknowledged the potential contribution of video gaming to complex forms of learning, identifying links between gaming and engagement, experiential learning spaces, problem-solving, strategies, transliteracy reflectivity, critical literacy, and metacognitive thinking. Despite this movement toward the inclusion of video gaming in literacy teaching, concerns about certain risks raised by scholars have slowed the adoption of using video games to foster learning. The adoption of video games as an alternative classroom multiliteracies resource is acknowledged in technology and multiliteracies discourses as a strategy for meaning-making and developing cultural knowledge (Cope & Kalantzis, 2009; The New London Group, 2000). These concerns (largely associated with negative identity construction, violent content, distraction, and time commitment for integration), have slowed the adoption of video games for their potential contribution as spaces/media that encourage complex forms of learning (Gee, 2003, 2007; Squire, 2006; Steinkuehler, 2007, 2011).

Emerging technologies such as multiliteracies, learning by design frameworks and gamification are becoming more prevalent in global classrooms. Traditional literacy pedagogies are shifting toward game-based pedagogy which supports the call to addressing 21st century learners (C21 Canada, 2017). Therefore, within this context there remains a need to study ways to engage learners in meaning-making perhaps with some element of visual design. Multimodal ways of learning can offer insights for reinventing traditional literacy pedagogical boundaries and establish new ways and practices for building knowledge. Educators today need to be positioned with a broad perspective of technology enabling a critical understanding of assessing ways in which technology is universally integrated in our knowledge culture.

Today's educators need to be well versed in technological platforms to meet the needs of 21st century learners. To be successful, in k-12 and higher education levels, educators require foundational knowledge and skills in instructional design. When it comes to the topic of positive learning outcomes, educators will readily agree that tools and strategies that create student-centered learning spaces and engage students' interest are beneficial. Principles of instructional design are grounded in cognitive and constructive learning philosophies. Research in pedagogical online delivery included the community of inquiry model, developed by Garrison et al. in 2000, interconnecting elements of teacher presence, cognitive presence, and social presence to initiate successful learning experiences (Lane, 2011). Since that time new models have emerged which aim to facilitate transformational learning by fostering an environment of collaboration, community, and knowledge development. One of the central models was TPACK developed by Punya Mishra and Matthew Koehler in 2006 and updated in 2016. It is used in many higher education settings and is based on technological pedagogical content knowledge which is intricately linked. Lee and Kim in 2014 implemented the model in a multidisciplinary technology course by integrating the 3 core domains (technology tools, pedagogy, and content). They argue preservice teachers were well versed in the content they are teaching but experienced challenges with pedagogical knowledge when it comes to effective use of technology to address learners' needs (such as group and peer discussions, think/pair/share). They found pre-service teachers had a lack of understanding of pedagogy (being a facilitator, student-centered community, active and engaged learning) which hindered learning of integrated knowledge (applying their knowledge such as adaptability across different contexts, persistence, and collaborative problem solving needed, but also being a reflective practitioner). Swan (2005) suggests creating virtual spaces that foster and support active learning for knowledge acquisition.

Knowledge is transformative in nature and socially constructed. Vygotsky (1978) argues cognitive functions are activated when children socially collaborate. When children exchange words and language with their peers, they are collaborating and socially interacting with each other, which, Vygotsky argued, contributes to the ways they actively learn, and gain knowledge from each other. Therefore, constructivism theory underpins the need for both face-to-face and online learning environments to be learner-centered, knowledge-centered, assessment centered, and community-centered (Swan, 2005). One of the challenges for educators is how to link learner needs, pedagogy and technology to construct more engaging and student-centered environments.

Research indicates the potential of digital technology as a learning process can foster collaborative, creative and authentic learning (Cope & Kalantzis, 2009). Lane (2018) focuses on using the Learning by Design framework, which offers multiple modalities of meanings and a range of knowledge processes and allows practitioners to create pedagogical scaffolds, which do not assume every learner is at the same level (Cope & Kalantzis, 2016). For example, the idea of youth learning from video games is echoed by emerging research recognizing benefits and challenges of integrating video games in classrooms as a pedagogical strategy to gain literacy skills (Beavis, Muspratt, & Thompson, 2015; DeCoito & Richardson,

2016; Duret & Pons, 2016). Hommel (2010) also highlighted that many researchers argue meaningful learning, including critical thinking, decision-making in video games may model engaging and effective instructional techniques. Sider and Maich (2014) also suggest effective literacy teaching strategies for some learners include software programs that provide a multimodal experience. Technology supports the universal design learning (UDL) framework because it can increase access meaningful engagement in learning and reduce barriers (Israel, Marino, Delisio, & Serianni, 2014, p. 16). Recently, important research emerged for use of multimodal and multiliteracy models, adaptive technology, and artificial intelligence (AI) for core curriculum to address learners who have exceptionalities. Integrating technology for core curriculum is a positive approach in the right direction to acknowledge the efficacy of GBL. Yet, focusing solely on using gamification for learning exceptionalities may further compartmentalize these approaches and limit the promotion of scholarly focus to broaden integration within k-12 and higher education settings.

Global need for innovation and adoption in multimodal approaches, gamification, GBL, AI, has been the priority at an alarming pace for many institutions since the announcement of covid-19. This growing need for technological adoption and accessibility has surpassed traditional literacy and instructional approaches. Institutions unwilling to adopt technological innovations and adapt to multimodal, GBL approaches to meet the growing needs of 21st century learners, due to lack of funding or unwillingness to change traditional practices, will find themselves further limiting marketability of their institutions as open, barrier-free opportunities for learning. Mindsets need to change for educators and policy makers to become main players in educational innovation. According to Cope and Kalantzis (2009), learners play multiple roles based on their experiences. Todays' learners have grown up with technology and secondary sources of learning such as video games have increasingly shifted to primary sources of learning especially during the global pandemic. Cope and Kalantzis (2009) also recognize the pedagogical weaving between school learning with practical out-of-school experiences that are based on individual interests (Kalantzis & Cope, 2012).

Educators sometimes consider video gaming as students' rich cultural out-of-school practices; however, more research is surfacing about transitioning these practices into in-school literacy experiences (Beavis, 2014; Cope & Kalantzis, 2009; Kalantzis & Cope, 2012). Video games involve complex forms of text, literacy, and action where stories reveal a variety of genres (Beavis, 2014; Gee, 2003, 2007). Beavis (2014) urges educators to recognize the privileged place that students give to video games as a form of popular culture. She also sees video games as emergent cultural forms because they include stories that fuse words and images and other elements to reposition players as readers, writers, interpreters, and creators who play an active role in the stories. Video games have become increasingly rich in multimodal elements. Games are multilayered, intertextual, and exemplify literacy with the combination of words, pictures, sounds, colours, symbols, music, light effects, and movement (Ajayi, 2011; Beavis, 2014). These interrelations of text and visual images within video games form part of a multiple semiotic system, how we use signs. Semiotic systems are relied upon by meaning-makers in their knowledge designing processes (Cope & Kalantzis, 2009; Kalantzis & Cope, 2012). Steinkuehler (2007) views interrelations of text in video games as gateways for meaning makers to rely on for "textually produced verbal interaction and, therefore, on story-telling" (p. 195).

Some of the themes addressed by Freeman, Adams Becker, Cummins, Davis, and Hall Giesinger (2017) in the NMC/CoSN Horizon Report K-12 Edition (Horizon Report) indicate a future focus over the next five years to position pedagogical strategies—including learning and visualization technologies—to foster creative inquiry. Video games are not specifically named in the report which leads me to believe there remains a certain reluctance by educators to adopt these, perhaps due to scholars' reservations about stereotypical themes (such as themes of power, violence, and misogyny) that may be embedded in video game plots and characters. However, scholarly systemic reviews bridging designs for game-based learning or gamification in learning correlated with learner performance have been lacking in literature. Digital learning as a significant tool for learning both in k-12 and higher education has always existed but full adoption in these settings has been slow due to overreaching research about what games and how games are perceived both in terms of media and/or resistance due to technological knowledge gaps for instructors. This adoption hesitancy for game-based pedagogical models has lingered from 2012 and was acknowledged in the 2019 Horizon report (Alexander, et al., 2019) as fading interest and budget funding pressures for institutions who did not foresee the need for experimenting with these models. In addition, Alexander, et al. (2019) emphasized slow adoption of game-based learning was primarily due to a growing concern of privacy issues surrounding game developers tracking user behavior. In addition, concerns were raised about the suitability of commercially based games for classroom experiences and educational based games may too be limited on the market for widespread use (Alexander, et al., 2019). (p. 39). The Horizon Report in education for 2021 by Pelletier et al., tracked some higher education institutions that implemented full open digital courses, including game-based learning to support learner goals and degree requirements. Moreover, Brull and Finlayson (2016) suggest that gamification has been recognized as a powerful instructional method in k-12 education, as well as top colleges and universities. They also explain how some industries remain in the early adoption stages such as health care, which may relate to gaps in knowledge or technological competency.

Yet, Bohyn Kim (2013) provided several examples of how educational institutions, government, and workplaces that successfully integrated game-based learning to increase engagement, motivation, and knowledge acquisition for learners. For example, gamification was used in training and recruitment in America's army, lead generation marketing, public relations, continuous professional development, health professions and development of health skills. Kim (2013) also suggests gamification can increase motivation and engagement in many higher education settings. A professor at Michigan University converted his undergrad class to game-based learning to empower students to achieve learning goals, having them participate in guilds and giving them rapid responses maintained by his teaching assistances. Kim (2013) argued this gamified approach gave students increased autonomy to become more invested in what and how they learn. Similarly, Purdue University developed a digital passport system whereby students could earn and display badges to demonstrate their competencies and achievements (Pho & Dinscore, 2015). Kim (2015) explains digital badges are used in many higher education settings and organizations including MIT, NASA, US Department of Veteran Affairs and Education, and public broadcasting, to name a few. Pho and Dinscore (2015) emphasize digital badges are identified as significant gamification element. However, they caution instructors to consider their students' proficiency with technology so that the technology itself doesn't become a barrier to learning.

It is important to note that game-based trends in educational settings need empirical research that helps to provide a framework for learner engagement but also support mechanisms for design effectiveness. In a comprehensive review Abdul Jabbar and Felicia (2015) aimed to address the lack of empirical evidence of the impact of game design on learning outcomes, identify how the design of game-based activities may affect learning and engagement, and develop a set of general recommendations for GBL instructional design. Their findings illustrate the impact of key gaming features in GBL at both cognitive and emotional levels. Abdul Jabbar and Felicia (2015) also identified gaming trends and several key drivers of engagement created by the gaming features embedded within GBL, as well as external factors that may have influences on engagement and learning.

The findings imply that students need multiple support measures for motivation and learning in gameplay. A lack of support and rewards for improvement decreases students' engagement (Ke & Abras, 2013) because they expect more rewards as recognition of their efforts and achievements (Tzeng & Chen, 2012). From their review, three recommendations were provided by Abdul Jabbar and Felicia (2015) as follows:

1. Promoting gameplay and learning: Game design must be accompanied with multiple learning tools and interesting tasks and materials that facilitate and help students to explore and complete gaming and learning activities in accordance with their needs and abilities. Many of the papers (Admiraal et al., 2011; Barab et al., 2012; Hou, 2012; Hsu, Wu, & Huang, 2008; Huizenga, Admiraal, Akkerman, & ten Dam, 2009; G.-J. Hwang, Wu, & Chen, 2012; Liao et al., 2011; Meluso et al., 2012; Miller et al., 2011; Sadler et al., 2013; Sanchez & Olivares, 2011; Suh et al., 2010) illustrate that multirole-play or collaborative role-play works effectively when coupled with learning tools and interactive elements and materials (Lennon & Coombs, 2007; Liu & Chu, 2010) to motivate and help learning. When presented with such tools, students are encouraged to work collaboratively to understand the learning tools provided (Hung et al., 2012; Sung & Hwang, 2013; Virvou & Katsionis, 2008) and to meet their individual and collective goals within the game.
2. Motivating gameplay and learning: The elements in GBL must be fully incorporated into the learning activities to provide a sense of enjoyment and motivation that is rewarding for students.

Gaming activities must match students' gender, game type preferences, and preferred mode of gameplay, as well as their abilities and the games' learning tasks (Clark et al., 2011). Challenges and conflicts must match students' abilities and knowledge (Bottino et al., 2007); they must provide equal opportunities for self-efficacy (Cheng et al., 2009; Tzeng & Chen, 2012), avoid causing frustration (Ke & Abras, 2013), and keep pupils focused (Rosas et al., 2003).

3. Supporting gameplay and learning: Gameplay must be supported with appropriate feedback and scaffolding; these can be provided in various forms depending on students' learning requirements (Ke, 2013; Sadler et al., 2013; Sun et al., 2011; Wang, 2008) so that the students can complete tasks and solve problems.

Adoption of Game-based learning for core curriculum classes is becoming more widespread in higher education settings. According to the 2021 Horizon Report on education (Pelletier et al., 2021), an American university in Texas is offering a series of short on-line, game-based academic courses to enable students to complete their degree requirements. Similarly, a North-Carolina state university created a gamified design framework for flipped and self-regulated learning, based on cognitive, metacognitive, and motivational theories. Pelletier, et al. (2021) reported that the North Carolina university implemented this gamified framework since the Fall of 2019 and was applied in redesigning four large undergraduate courses in the fields of business, biochemistry, computer science, and math.

This research handbook attempts to address these needs through a comprehensive compilation of game-based pedagogical models in broad-based settings, from education, including k-12 and higher education institutions, to workplace including healthcare, retail, and some government settings. It also includes perspectives from educators, management, and learners. These perspectives emphasize global integration of games to development of artificial intelligence pedagogical models and include culturally rich technological and non-technological approaches that have been successfully implemented. Game-based learning is not always full technological immersion but surprisingly both can have astonishing learner performance outcomes.

Technological innovation has continued to evolve and offers a much wider spectrum of capabilities even reducing the need for human interaction. Artificial intelligence can be developed to drive learner goals, instructional aims, be responsive to learner needs and address overall methods such as assessment and performance. According to Pellas, Fotaris, Kazanidis, and Wells (2019), a significant body of research relating to augmented reality (AR) already exists; however, they contend not with game-based learning (ARGBL) and how it may be applicable to global k-12 settings. Therefore, integrating instructional strategies with ARGBL may offer the potential to impact students' motivation and learning performance. Pellas et al. (2019) argue ARGBL can potentially influence students' attendance, knowledge acquisition, digital experience, and positive behaviors towards learning. In a similar vein, Bakan and Bakan (2018) conducted a meta-analysis, based on a 12-year review, of scientific databases (such as Web of Science (WoS) database in SCI, SSCI and AHCI) of game-based applications in learning and teaching environments. Emphasizing cognitive retention, Bakan and Bakan (2018) found that game studies, as well as cognitive understanding and application-level knowledge of the field are more effective in learning and in student achievements.

Many scholars have focused on the collaborative aspects of video games (Alexander, 2009; Apperley & Beavis, 2011; Huizenga et. al., 2009; Sanford & Madill, 2006), similarities were found from Vogel et al.'s (2006) analysis revealing significant results for cognitive gains from playing the video game. What the study by Vogel et al. (2006) also revealed was that "females showed significant cognitive gains favoring the interactive simulation and game method" (p. 234). Since these studies focused on elementary students and mathematics, there is still a need to explore the use of computer games, specifically focusing on boys, at the high school level. Recent research is also emerging supporting integration of science, technology, engineering, and mathematics (STEM) concepts in digital games (Decoito & Richardson, 2016). A study by Decoito and Richardson (2016) focused on introducing digital games as a pedagogical tool for K-12 science teacher candidates at a Canadian university. The participants explored the use of video games (for example, an online game, History of Biology) for teaching STEM concepts, and Decoito and Richardson (2016) found that teacher candidates expressed an "overwhelming agreement for including digital online games in science teaching" (p. 10). The participants also expressed the importance of using digital online games for science teaching for "engagement, relevance, reinforcement of content areas, and promoting 21st century skills" (p. 10). Decoito and Richardson (2016) also recognized some concerns surrounding learners' lack of expertise in the game, as well as technical challenges which posed frustration when completing the game. Lopez-Morteo and Lopez's (2007) study also focused on improving learning through an "electronic collaborative learning environment based on interactive instructors of recreational mathematics (IIRM), thus establishing an alternative approach for motivating students towards mathematics" (p. 618). They used an online collaborative environment combined with support elements to bridge content and context for the learning experience. The study had positive results as students were more motivated and excited to learn math when using computer games; however, some negative results included issues with computer failures. Researchers indicated that online collaborative games promoted greater interaction among students, even though students preferred to play games that did not support online interaction. Additionally, results showed students found usefulness of math in daily life, which increased their level of confidence and attitudes towards learning math. Research has continued to indicate how video games can be used as an alternative approach to improve learning experiences. According to an investigation by Byun and Joung (2018), digital games can improve students' motivation and performance in mathematics education.

Research is beginning to emerge documenting how video games, a multimodal form, can represent an alternative pathway to learning, both inside and outside of school. Scholars have identified links between gaming and factors that affect the depth of learning: engagement, experiential learning spaces, problem-solving, strategic transliteracy reflectivity, critical literacy, and metacognitive thinking (see for example, Alexander, 2009; Apperley & Beavis, 2011; Cope & Kalantzis, 2009; Sanford & Madill, 2007; Squire, 2013; The New London Group, 1996, 2000; Van Sledright, 2002). These scholars explained the complex forms of interactive visuals—intertextual and multimodal—that are part of video games, and key to inviting players to understand a variety of texts in a variety of circumstances. They also found that these multimodal aspects help to create a rich environment that invites gamers to interact with a variety of significant learning and literacy experiences. Practitioners remain skeptical of GBL as a direct primary method of knowledge acquisition, preferring to perceive GBL as a secondary, leisure activity with little to no educational value (De Freitas, 2006). Yet the reality is digital fluency remains high among 21st century learners, combined with positive levels of motivation, acceptance, and expectation of acquiring knowledge in an innovative way, which in turn, influences the ways in which they self-regulate their learning. To improve adoption and effectiveness in practice, GBL has been widely examined and used not only as an alternative educational resource but in practice for knowledge acquisition in a variety of settings. It is equally important to note that full of adoption of GBL in the educational stream can benefit learners in not only what they learn but how they learn. According to a study conducted by De Freitas (2006), perceptions are changing about GBL as game design and theory courses are being offered widely in higher education settings. Game-based learning is often experienced-based or exploratory, and therefore relies upon experiential, problem-based or exploratory learning approaches. De Freitas (2006) emphasizes that GBL enables learners to role play, to identify with others, to use games for therapy, to rehearse skills, to explore in open-ended spaces, to learn in groups and to develop higher cognitive skills. Learning environments can include game-spaces which are highly immersive and can be collaborative (De Freitas, 2006). According to Duncum (2004), multiliteracies education is concerned with the relationship between written words and images, which is complex and needs to be recognized. Duncum (2004) further explains that images are not just a mirror to the meaning found in the text, but also offer subtle nuances of interpretation and a range of other cognitive functions, including emotional quality of an image, which all contribute to the uniqueness of modality of multiliteracies forms. As such, Squire (2013) argued that many video games are experiential with the aim to engage and immerse players in interactive gameplay. Jenkins (2002) also argued that video game spaces allow players to co-construct, deconstruct, and reconstruct the plot. Jenkins (2002) also explained that game designers over the years have become narrative architects by developing games with narrative potential, enabling the story-constructing activity of players. These game-based immersive approaches help to create "an emotionally compelling context for the player" (Squire, 2013, p. 110). Further to this point, Squire (2013) argued that good games emotionally connect players and invite them into a world of learning. Jenkins (2005) similarly argued that games can imitate different art forms by offering players "new aesthetic experiences and transform the computer screen into a realm of experimentation and innovation that is broadly accessible" (p. 3). Educators sometimes consider video gaming as students' rich cultural out-of-school practices; however, more research is surfacing about transitioning these practices into in-school literacy experiences (Beavis, 2014; Cope & Kalantzis, 2009; Kalantzis & Cope, 2012). Squire (2013) explained that games are now recognized as experiential learning spaces where learners engage in rich collaborative interactions, and where they can utilize a variety of complex tools to develop complex problem-solving skills (see for example, Alexander, 2009; Gros, 2007).

ORGANIZATION OF THE RESEARCH HANDBOOK

This research handbook is organized into 48 chapters. The handbook is organized into nine sections. These sections include gamification in higher education, exploring literacy in game-based learning, culturally based game-based pedagogy, teachers' perceptions of game-based learning, gamification, mobile learning and education policy, game-based pedagogy for primary-elementary educators, learner assessment, motivation and behaviors in game-based learning, game-based learning: code and play, and virtual teaching and project-oriented game-based learning.

A brief description of each of the chapters follows:

Chapter 1 explores the meaning, significance, and scope of game-based learning as an instructional tool. It provides an interesting account of several games that are popularly used to facilitate effective learning in various settings. This chapter also examines the relevance and implications of games in education.

Chapter 2 identifies a trend in digital learning by examining several articles in the Web of Science index by using the words "game-based learning", "video games", "game-based pedagogy", "digital games", "gamification", and "game". As a result of the research, the trends in topics related to games were revealed, and the changes in this area are subsequently.

Chapter 3 emphasizes how designing course content as a game makes learning more engaging as learners get a sense of motivation and accomplishment. It proposes learner-centered interactive instructional strategies that employ GBL to pique learners' curiosity and recommends popular GBL platforms for creating educational games.

Chapter 4 describes how game-based learning reflects sustainable education for future professionals from the higher education environment. To attain these innovative and sustainable teaching pedagogies the components of games and simulations need to be incorporated into the teaching-learning content. The chapter examines neural and cognitive processes of game-based learning.

Chapter 5 highlights how technology can support teachers and learners to go beyond their existing pedagogical boundaries by focusing on ways games may serve as digital sources of learning. It also explores the role game-based pedagogies and digital learning design frameworks play in enhancing learner engagement, collaboration, and cultural understanding.

Chapter 6 provides an overview of the effectiveness of game-based learning strategies over traditional learning methods. Moreover, the results of a cross- sectional study conducted by the authors in south Indian Universities at the higher education level is included.

Chapter 7 explores the efficacy of game-based learning in classroom teaching for MBA students in higher education. Student's learning was captured through a google form before and after a dice game.

Chapter 8 explores technological developments and innovations in the field of higher education. To prepare the students to face real world challenges, it is important for higher educational institutions to focus on imparting to learners creative, problem solving and critical thinking skills.

Chapter 9 discusses gamification strategies in the context of higher education student worker training. Specifically, it builds on the concepts of gamification in corporate training contexts and gamification in the academic classroom environment. It also considers various options to support gamified training content and methods to support student worker engagement and knowledge retention.

Chapter 10 shows research done in interactive media, augmented and virtual reality, game art, and gender equity. The year 2020 showed how institutional collaboration can open learning spaces to a more focused approach on the interests of young people, and to promote a more sustainable and dynamic future.

Chapter 11 uses the lenses of Vygotskian constructivism, situated cognition, the antecedents of flow, and a pedagogy interwoven with the multiliteracy framework, the authors present a COVID19 Simulation game. The game has multiple levels, challenges, disrupters, and allows for student player groups to work together (i.e., collaborate within and across player groups) to achieve the strategic objectives of the game.

Chapter 12 provides a case study of the use of worldbuilding for role-playing games as the foundation for a first year multiliteracies seminar. The author provides an overview of teaching and learning during the pandemic in the Irish context. The chapter provides practical advice on using a MediaWiki installation as the infrastructure for worldbuilding projects. The author shows how this imparts important digital literacies and allows for a critical apprehension of Wikipedia itself.

Chapter 13 foregrounds an online gamified visual intelligence innovation (eyebraingym) developed to enhance visual processing skills, improve memory and vocabulary, and increase reading fluency. The explicit aim of the innovation is to improve comprehension towards visual intelligence.

Chapter 14 addresses some of boys' out-of-school video gaming practices for meaning-making and gaining cultural knowledge. Studying the ways in which boys make meanings through multimodal ways of learning can offer insights into strategies for cyber culture that can potentially reinvent traditional literacy pedagogical boundaries and establish new ways and practices for building knowledge.

Chapter 15 focus on games that assist students in the learning process. Once students have learned a task through the playing process, they will remember this much easier and longer than simply doing a worksheet. Research shows students enjoy interactive and engaging activities and will choose these types of activities over pencil and paper types of activities.

Chapter 16 conceptualizes an innovative digital storytelling that incorporates both transmedia and meaning-making narrative approaches. Working with Aristotelian story elements in a non-linear digital series of mini-worlds, the higher education narrator-as-learner enters real-world situations mirrored in a fictional and fragmented environment. The model encourages a playful engagement in the experiential learning process through a range of points of view, encouraging empathy for differing perspectives that are transferable to real-life environments.

Chapter 17 examines the perceptions and instructional ideas of preservice teachers as relates to using Minecraft, a popular video game, to facilitate game-based learning opportunities in their future elementary classrooms. The participants were 21 preservice teachers who played Minecraft as part of a teacher preparation program course and then completed essays on their experiences with the game and its potential to support student learning in the elementary English language arts classroom.

Chapter 18 shows a way to foster academic growth, engagement in learning, and collaboration is to engage students in skinning games based on literature and integrated a playful learning environment. Analysis revealed that students were immersed in the learning process to the extent that they felt comfortable acting informally, responding in the moment, and being playful.

Chapter 19 studies the dynamics that makeup media literacy and media literacy skills. How the century has transformed to meet the needs of its students will be highlighted within the context of media literacy. It also explains how media literacy is reflected in pedagogy with examples suitable for different courses and levels.

Chapter 20 discusses the theoretical frameworks for Artificial Intelligence (AI) teacher and how AI teacher has been applied to facilitate game-based literacy learning in existing empirical studies. It also introduces key concepts of AI teacher, research on AI teacher in literacy learning, and some highlighted examples of AI teacher in literacy classrooms for practical concerns.

Chapter 21 explores the possibility of enhancing literacy skills using indigenous games played by Vhavenda children at foundation phase. It critically analyses different types of Vhavenda games played by children which are ndode, mufuvha, muravharavha and tsetsetse or trere-tsere to solicit the possibility to enhance literacy skills.

Chapter 22 focuses on an indigenous game duvheke. The chapter employs game-based pedagogy as a theory that underpins this study. Methodologically, the chapter assumes a qualitative complexion because it seeks to collect in-depth information about Duvheke and how it can be used in teaching critical thinking skills first entering students in a rural based university. The chapter suggests that duvheke can be a valuable tool in teaching critical thinking skills

Chapter 23 investigates the effectiveness of a digital reading tool, called GraphoGame. It sets out to demonstrate that, through pre-and post-tests, GraphoGame Afrikaans improved the initial reading skills of Grade 1 learners. As GraphoGame employs a scaffolded approach by presenting learners with letters and words, it can be utilized to support learners individually in classes with large numbers, as is typical in Africa.

Chapter 24 examines whether the intrinsically motivational factors of digital games could motivate students to learn English vocabulary and achieve better learning outcomes. English vocabulary is always a huge hurdle for students in non-speaking English countries because (a) they lack an English environment to practice vocabulary; (b) traditional memory is quite boring, and (c) they unavoidably forget remembered words. Therefore, this chapter aims to provide an overview of how to comprehensively conduct experimental research, which will expedite further research.

Chapter 25 identifies whether gamification is a suitable pedagogic tool among Malaysian law students to support the acquisition of 21st century skills. The respondents are from Year 1 and Year 2 of a 3-year Bachelor of Laws degree with the majority being Malaysian students. The data collected showed that gamification can be a suitable alternative pedagogic tool to support the students to learn skills such as critical thinking, creativity, innovation, leadership, or communication.

Chapter 26 examines the relationship between religiosity and the learning of business ethics. This research investigates whether religiosity is conducive to the learning of business ethics in a digital learning environment: a serious 3D ethics game. A cross-sectional survey was conducted on 302 final-year students from two different academic institutions based in the UK. The results of a structural equation modelling analysis suggest that religiosity does not inform the ethical perceptions and decisions of religious individuals in digital learning environments.

Chapter 27 introduces a mobile game-based content and language integrated learning practice (an educational digital game called ENVglish) to raise EFL students' environmental awareness. During the design and development phases of the game, students', and teachers' perceptions regarding it were collected with semi-structured interviews. The findings indicated that both students and teachers had positive perceptions about the game and that students could improve their English and have environmental awareness with the game.

Chapter 28 aims to contribute to the advancement of knowledge about the main competencies needed for educators to perform as facilitators of educational games. The outcome is the development of a framework of competencies of an educator willing to use game-based learning. The study highlights the importance of institutional support to boost the development of pedagogical, technological, and social skills among educators.

Chapter 29 examines both in-service and pre-service Spanish teachers' perceptions (n = 112) about using digital games in their lessons, paying a special attention to the TPACK model, and comparing the results regarding age, gender, and professional situation. Responses show a positive attitude towards the potential use of video games in their lessons, although there are differences considering the results of the items concerning technological, pedagogical, or content knowledge.

Chapter 30 explores the factors affecting the successful implementation of an e-education policy and community engagement. In terms of research methodology, a case study is used of a specific high (secondary) school in the Metro North district of the Western Cape province, South Africa.

Chapter 31 explores the potentially negative and positive impacts of game-based pedagogy on personality development. The methodology of this paper is qualitative basic research, while the theoretical framework is critical theoretical analyses, articulated around psychodynamic theory, analytic psychology, and positive psychology. The negative view of game-based personality development presupposes 'learners for technology' or the pessimistic view, while the positive view of game-based personality development considers 'technology for learners' as being a perspective which facilitates, media literacy, higher order thinking, higher emotional intelligence, and pro-social behaviors.

Chapter 32 describes a gamification experience of a Social Game with graduate students, teachers in primary and secondary education and discusses how the elements present in games can provide engagement and favor learning. Furthermore, it presents the Kahoot app as a possibility to stimulate and engage students in the teaching-learning process, analyzing some implications of learning with a mobile device. The results had a positive impact on increasing student engagement in both Game Social and Kahoot. Therefore, gamification and mobile learning can be good alternatives to increase the quality of teaching, generating meaningful experiences in the classroom.

Chapter 33 aims to contribute to the discussion of incorporating mobile games, with astronomy and space themes to support science learning. The authors try to determine the learning strategies or pedagogies which can be used to incorporate such games in science education. Research on which characteristics these games should have been also presented.

Chapter 34 reviews, a) considerations for use of digital media use in early childhood settings, b) selection of appropriate media to facilitate early literacy learning, and c) inclusion of digital media as an integral component of early literacy instruction, rather than an add-on. With an emphasis on practical ideas and solutions for instructors, the authors draw on studies in which interactive, personalized ebooks and an early literacy learning app were used in conjunction with face-to-face, hands-on activities drawn from Project SEEL (Systematic and Engaging Early Literacy).

Chapter 35 proposes a path of coding games for the development of problem solving in primary school, with interdisciplinary links and to the mathematics curriculum. Game-based learning places the pupil at the center of the teaching-learning process, creating a motivating and challenging environment in which the pupil can learn freely, proceeding by trial and error, learning to evaluate their choices and those of other players and monitor several variables. Game-based learning therefore stands as an individualized and inclusive learning environment, which allows all students to achieve maximum educational success.

Chapter 36 explores what factors affect a school's choice, which is linked with the educational curriculum being offered, and how it affects the student's quality of education. There is no unified primary education curriculum in Bangladesh's case. More than three mainstream educational curricula can be founded, each with its own unique set of traits, benefits, and shortcomings. This chapter also explores Gamification theory's implementation to ensure quality primary education in Bangladesh.

Chapter 37 provides practitioners with evidence to support the instructional value of Ignite by Hatch, a digital learning game designed for preschool children. This chapter also features a preliminary crosswalk establishing the alignment between the domains, subdomains, and games presented within the Ignite game environment and the learning goals provided by the North Carolina Foundations for Early Learning and Development framework.

Chapter 38 investigates the effectiveness of Minecraft-Game Based Learning towards on 21st Century Skills among primary school students. During Minecraft Game-Based Learning session, students were given the opportunity to build and recreate a world based on certain themes inside Minecraft world based on their creativity and imagination. The result shows that the intervention of Minecraft Game Based Learning is effective in enhancing and retaining the 21st Century Skills among students.

Chapter 39 presents empirical research where we developed tasks based on a digital game supported by assessment strategies. The study is interpretative in nature, in a case study design. The authors designed tasks with technology and assessment strategies in a collaborative work context implemented in a Mathematics classroom with 5th grade students (students with 10 years old). The results evidence that the use of a digital game and formative assessment have contributed to the learning of complementary and supplementary angle pairs, giving meaning to their utilization as an effective strategy.

Chapter 40 addresses a knowledge gap around the effective use of while improving retention. With gaming mechanics as a driving point, specific design considerations were explored: badges, leader boards, points and levels, and challenges. The educator must think from the learner's perspective and find new ways of creating challenges and motivation techniques to provide value. Gamification, when applied to different disciplines, has the potential to facilitate the individual within learner-centricity.

Chapter 41 focuses on use of game-based formative assessment to improve learners' motivation in the e-learning environment so that their drop-our rates can be controlled, and their engagement level can be improved. It highlights the theoretical perspective used in previous research on gamification, engagement, and motivation.

Chapter 42 suggests behavioral economics plays a major role in understanding the concept of the `line' game played in many parts of India. The game keenly and minutely determines the objectivity of the game and the behavior of the players involved inside the game and the way one starts moving, helps the other players to understand what one is trying to portray through the game whether it is winning or losing. The strategies involved can be put forth and looked upon from different genres of perspectives. Referring to one of such perspectives, it can be looked at from a concept of Pareto efficiency, a microeconomic concept. It helps develop logical skills and learn winning strategies.

Chapter 43 examines digital games with a focus on the interaction between the game itself and the person playing it. Among the various social behaviors elicited by digital games, much attention has been given to players' prosocial behavior within the context of a game's virtual world. A multidimensional view of behavior is used to analyze the game's situational contexts and players' interpretation of behavior.

Chapter 44 explains the relationship between 21st century skills, and game playing skills, the design thinking approach where students are game designers, coders, and players. Games have been considered as an important part of child development and can roughly be defined as fictional structures with certain rules to be followed to achieve certain goals.

Chapter 45 examines how coding and computational thinking can be used to manipulate people. It then explores connections between playing video games and computer programming. It briefly examines different coding games and describes ways in which educators can create their own coding games. It concludes by arguing that educators can make the connections between gamer thinking and computational thinking visible, use games designed to teach coding, or create their own coding games to take advantage of near transfer.

Chapter 46 considers ways in which educators can create their own educational applications to integrate into their teaching. Today, tools available allow everyone to create not only static website, but also functional applications. It is possible to get started without knowing how to code, empowering anyone with an interest in technology to become a creator. The chapter aims to encourage readers to look at technology as a creative practice to include into their teaching. It suggests strategies to help readers select the most appropriate tool for their projects.

Chapter 47 investigates the potential of project-oriented game-based learning in making students at educational institutes more engaged and gain a deep understanding of the curriculum content. The empirical data have been collected based on Ukrainian case study and allow the authors to prove the influence of Project Oriented Game Based Learning on increasing students' engagement, satisfaction, performance and improving learning outcomes. The main idea of the teaching project was to take as an object of the research a character from a fairy tale and analyze its managerial activities.

Chapter 48 explores how virtual reality (VR) is a technology that is becoming more common for applications in the field of education and training. VR can be used to create simulated two and three-dimensional scenarios, promoting interactions between the user and the environment, which allows experiencing virtual training situations very close to real actions. The aim of this text is to describe the development of a teaching and training tool using VR technology for scuba divers' operations within the aquatic context for enhancing critical thinking. To this end, a survey of requirements based on real procedures was carried out to transpose them into a synthetic environment. After the construction of the artefact, it was tested and evaluated by qualified users and the results are promising.

REFERENCES

C21 Canada. (2017). *Canadians for 21st Century Learning and Innovation*. Retrieved from: http://c21canada.org/mission/

Abdul Jabbar, A. I., & Felicia, P. (2015). Gameplay engagement and learning in game-based learning: A systematic review. *Review of Educational Research*, *85*(4), 740–779. doi:10.3102/0034654315577210

Ajayi, L. (2011). A multiliteracies pedagogy: Exploring semiotic possibilities of a Disney video in a third grade diverse classroom. *The Urban Review*, *43*(3), 396–413. doi:10.100711256-010-0151-0

Alexander, B., Ashford-Rowe, K., Barajas-Murphy, N., Dobbin, G., Knott, J., McCormack, M., Pomerantz, J., Seilhamer, R., & Weber, N. (Eds.). (2019). EDUCAUSE Horizon Report: 2019 Higher Education Edition. EDUCAUSE.

Alexander, J. (2009). Gaming, student literacies, and the composition classroom: Some possibilities for transformation. *College Composition and Communication, 61*(1), 35–63.

Apperley, T., & Beavis, C. (2011). Literacy into action: Digital games as action and text in the English and literacy classroom. *Pedagogies, 6*(2), 130–143. doi:10.1080/1554480X.2011.554620

Bakan, U., & Bakan, U. (2018). Game-based learning studies in education journals: A systematic review of recent trends. *Actualidades Pedagógicas, 72*(72), 119–145. doi:10.19052/ap.5245

Beavis, C. (2014). Games as text, games as action. *Journal of Adolescent & Adult Literacy, 57*(6), 433–439. doi:10.1002/jaal.275

Beavis, C., Muspratt, S., & Thompson, R. (2015). Computer games can get your brain working': Student experience and perceptions of digital games in the classroom. *Learning, Media and Technology, 40*(1), 21–42. doi:10.1080/17439884.2014.904339

Brull, S., & Finlayson, S. (2016). Importance of gamification in increasing learning. *Journal of Continuing Education in Nursing, 47*(8), 372–375. doi:10.3928/00220124-20160715-09 PMID:27467313

Byun, J., & Joung, E. (2018). Digital game-based learning for K–12 mathematics education: A meta analysis. *School Science and Mathematics, 118*(3-4), 113–126. doi:10.1111sm.12271

Cope, B., & Kalantzis, M. (2009). "Multiliteracies": New literacies, new learning. *Pedagogies, 4*(3), 164–195. doi:10.1080/15544800903076044

Cope, B., & Kalantzis, M. (2016). *A pedagogy of multiliteracies: Learning by design.* Palgrave Macmillan UK. Retrieved from https://books.google.ca/books?id=N6GkCgAAQBAJ

De Freitas, S. (2006). *Learning in immersive worlds: A review of game-based learning.* Academic Press.

DeCoito, I., & Richardson, T. (2016). Focusing on integrated STEM concepts in a digital game. In M. Urban & D. Falvo (Eds.), *Improving K-12 STEM Education* (pp. 1–23). IGI Global.

Duncum, P. (2004). Visual culture isn't just visual: Multiliteracies, multimodality and meaning. *Studies in Art Education, 46*(1), 252–264. doi:10.1080/00393541.2004.11651771

Duret, C., & Pons, C.-M. (2016). *Contemporary research on intertextuality in video games.* IGI Global. doi:10.4018/978-1-5225-0477-1

Freeman, A., Adams Becker, S., Cummins, M., Davis, A., & Hall Giesinger, C. (2017). *NMC/CoSN Horizon Report: 2017 K–* (12th ed.). The New Media Consortium. Retrieved from https://cdn.nmc.org/media/2017-nmc-cosn-horizon-report-k12-EN.pdf

Gee, J. P. (2003). *What video games have to teach us about learning and literacy* (1st ed.). Palgrave Macmillan. doi:10.1145/950566.950595

Gee, J. P. (2007). *Good video games and good learning: Collected essays on video games, learning, and literacy*. P. Lang. doi:10.3726/978-1-4539-1162-4

Gros, B. (2007). Digital games in education: The design of games-based learning environments. *Journal of Research on Technology in Education, 40*(1), 23–38. doi:10.1080/15391523.2007.10782494

Herring, M. C., Koehler, M. J., & Mishra, P. (Eds.). (2016). *Handbook of technological pedagogical content knowledge (TPACK) for educators*. Routledge. doi:10.4324/9781315771328

Hommel, M. (2010). Video games and learning. *School Library Monthly, 26*(10), 37–40.

Huizenga, J., Admiraal, W., Akkerman, S., & Dam, G. (2009). Mobile game-based learning in secondary education: Engagement, motivation and learning in a mobile city game. *Journal of Computer Assisted Learning, 25*(4), 332–344. doi:10.1111/j.1365-2729.2009.00316.x

Israel, M., Marino, M., Delisio, L., & Serianni, B. (2014). *Supporting content learning through technology for K-12 students with disabilities*. CEDAR Document IC-10.

Jenkins, H. (2002). Game design as narrative architecture. In P. Harrington & N. Frup-Waldrop (Eds.), *First Person*. MIT Press.

Jenkins, H. (2005). Art form for the digital age. In J. Goldstein (Ed.), *Handbook for Video Game Studies*. MIT Press.

Kalantzis, M., & Cope, B. (2012). *Literacies*. Cambridge University Press. doi:10.1017/CBO9781139196581

Kim, B. (2013). *Gamification. Keeping Up With....* ACRL. https://www.ala.org/acrl/publications/keeping_up_with/gamification

Kim, B. (2015). *Understanding gamification*. ALA TechSource.

Lane, C. A. (2011). *Social presence impacting cognitive learning of adults in distanced education*.

Lane, C. A. (2018). *Multiliteracies meaning-making: How four boys' video gaming experiences influence their cultural knowledge—Two ethnographic cases*. Academic Press.

Lee, C. J., & Kim, C. (2014). An implementation study of a TPACK-based instructional design model in a technology integration course. *Educational Technology Research and Development, 62*(4), 437–460. doi:10.100711423-014-9335-8

Lopez-Morteo, G., & Lopez, G. (2007). Computer support for learning mathematics: A learning environment based on recreational learning objects. *Computers & Education, 48*(4), 618–641. doi:10.1016/j.compedu.2005.04.014

Mishra, P., & Koehler, M. J. (2006). Technological pedagogical content knowledge: A framework for teacher knowledge. *Teachers College Record, 108*(6), 1017–1054. doi:10.1111/j.1467-9620.2006.00684.x

Pellas, N., Fotaris, P., Kazanidis, I., & Wells, D. (2019). Augmenting the learning experience in primary and secondary school education: A systematic review of recent trends in augmented reality game-based learning. *Virtual Reality (Waltham Cross), 23*(4), 329–346. doi:10.100710055-018-0347-2

Pelletier, K., Brown, M., Brooks, D. C., McCormack, M., Reeves, J., Arbino, N., Bozkurt, A., Crawford, S., Czerniewicz, L., Gibson, R., Linder, K., Mason, J., & Mondelli, V. (2021). *2021 EDUCAUSE Horizon Report Teaching and Learning Edition*. Boulder, CO: EDU. Retrieved November 9, 2021 from https://www.learntechlib.org/p/219489/

Pho, A., & Dinscore, A. (2015). *Game-based learning. Tips and trends*. Academic Press.

Sanford, K., & Madill, L. (2006). Resistance through video game play: It's a boy thing. *Canadian Journal of Education*, *29*(1), 287–306, 344–345. doi:10.2307/20054157

Sanford, K., & Madill, L. (2007). Understanding the power of new literacies through video game play and design. *Canadian Journal of Education*, *30*(2), 432–455. doi:10.2307/20466645

Sider, S., & Maich, K. (2014). *Assistive technology tools: Supporting literacy*. Ministry of Education Learners in the Inclusive Classroom.

Squire, K. (2006). From content to context: Videogames as designed experience. *Educational Researcher*, *35*(8), 19–29. doi:10.3102/0013189X035008019

Squire, K. D. (2013). Video game-based learning: An emerging paradigm for instruction. *Performance Improvement Quarterly*, *26*(1), 101–130. doi:10.1002/piq.21139

Steinkuehler, C. (2007). Massively multiplayer online gaming as a constellation of literacy practices. *E-Learning and Digital Media*, *4*(3), 297–318. doi:10.2304/elea.2007.4.3.297

Steinkuehler, C. (2011). *The mismeasure of boys: Reading and online videogames*. Wisconsin Center for Education Research, University of Wisconsin.

The New London Group. (1996). A pedagogy of multiliteracies: Designing social futures. *Harvard Educational Review*, *66*(1), 60–93. doi:10.17763/haer.66.1.17370n67v22j160u

The New London Group. (2000). A pedagogy of multiliteracies: Designing social futures. In B. Cope & M. Kalantzis (Eds.), *Multiliteracies: Literacy learning and the design of social futures*. Routledge.

VanSledright, B. A. (2002). Fifth graders investigating history in the classroom: Results from a researcher-practitioner design experiment. *The Elementary School Journal*, *103*(2), 131–160. doi:10.1086/499720

Vogel, J. J., Vogel, D. S., Cannon-Bowers, J., Bowers, C. A., Muse, K., & Wright, M. (2006). Computer gaming and interactive simulations for learning: A meta-analysis. *Journal of Educational Computing Research*, *34*(3), 229–243. doi:10.2190/FLHV-K4WA-WPVQ-H0YM

Vygotsky, L. S. (1978). Readings on the development of children. *Mind & Society*, 79–91.

Acknowledgment

The editor would like to acknowledge the help of all the people involved in this project and, more specifically, to the authors and reviewers that took part in the review process. Without their support, this book would not have become a reality.

First, the editor would like to thank each one of the authors for their contributions. My sincere gratitude goes to the chapter's authors who contributed their time and expertise to this handbook.

Second, the editor wishes to acknowledge the valuable contributions of the reviewers regarding the improvement of quality, coherence, and content presentation of chapters. Most of the authors also served as referees; I highly appreciate their double task.

Carol-Ann Lane
University of Toronto, Canada

Chapter 25
Gamification, Learning, and the Acquisition of 21st Century Skills Amongst Malaysian Law Students

Joaquim Dias Soeiro
ⓘ https://orcid.org/0000-0003-4230-7767
School of Hospitality, Tourism, and Events, Taylor's University, Malaysia

Puteri Sofia Amirnuddin
Taylor's Law School, Taylor's University, Malaysia

ABSTRACT

The diversification of pedagogic tools remains essential for a fruitful learning experience among the Gen Z students by embedding technology such as gamification in learning. Recent literature has discussed the acquisition of 21st century skills and the educational challenges generally faced by Asian students due to their cultural traits. Against this background, the findings of this study open reflections relating to the benefit of gamification in acquiring 21st century skills. The objective of this chapter is to identify whether gamification is a suitable pedagogic tool among Malaysian law students in order to support the acquisition of 21st century skills. The respondents are from Year 1 and Year 2 of a three-year Bachelor of Laws degree with the majority being Malaysian students. The data collected showed that gamification helps in the acquisition of 21st century skills. Evidently, it showed that gamification can be a suitable alternative pedagogic tool to support the students to learn skills such as critical thinking, creativity, innovation, leadership, or communication.

DOI: 10.4018/978-1-7998-7271-9.ch025

INTRODUCTION

Background of the Study

Undeniably, the shift from traditional pedagogies to e-pedagogies was necessary to ensure the continuity of learning during the COVID-19 pandemic. Gamification, as an alternative teaching tool, is not new and has been gaining particular attention in the past decade in the field of education (Hallifax et al., 2019; Majuri et al., 2018). Furthermore, gamification as a pedagogic tool had shown its potential in enabling students gain affective and cognitive skills as well as impacting performances, attitudes and behaviors (Majuri et al., 2018; Manzano-León, 2021; Mohamad et al., 2021; Lane, 2021; Sailer & Homner, 2020; Turner et al., 2019). Alongside with other disciplines and in order to answer employment and societal paradigm shifts, education providers moved towards 21st century skills development with an emerging need for digital skills (Latorre-Cosculluela et al., 2020; Van Laar et al., 2020).

Law schools are renowned for developing graduates with ethics, critical thinking, negotiation argumentation, leadership, problem solving and research skills (Giddings & Weinberg, 2020; Kathrani, 2020). However, content and organization of the profession evolve and change rapidly impacting the preparedness and acclimatizing of the students to the modern functions of the profession (Giddings & Weinberg, 2020). Consequently, education providers need to look at pedagogic approaches which allow for more experientiality and immersion during the learning process.

In Malaysia, there are approximately 20 universities and colleges offering law programmes and there are concerns whether legal education offered at higher learning institutes are in line with the 4th Industrial Revolution to reflect the demands of the 21st century skills (Amirnuddin et al., 2020). This study directs the focus on law education and students from a private university in Malaysia studying Bachelor of Laws programme. Recognized by the Legal Profession Qualifying Board, Malaysia, the Bachelor of Laws programme enables the students to become inter alia, but not limited to, advocate and solicitor, legal advisor, legal writer, legal scholar, forensic or criminal investigator. During the three years of studies, the students would need to pass all 21 core modules and 5 elective modules, and undergo a 6-week internship to enable them to fulfil the required programme learning objectives. In addition, the programme had been designed to develop and assess key capabilities during the studies with an emphasis on discipline specific knowledge, problem solving, critical and creative thinking, communication, lifelong learning, personal and social competencies, entrepreneurialism and global perspective. The pedagogies employed vary from authentic to blended approaches and the Bachelor of Laws programme introduced gamification since 2019.

Problem Statement and Aim of the Study

Previous teaching methods on various law modules centered around the teacher-centric approach, where students were taught via lecture sessions, watching videos, listening to presentations by guest speakers and answering quizzes. The emphasis placed by the lecturer was on providing information to students during lectures and ensuring this information was understood by way of student participation and answering of questions in the tutorials. Although student performance on the module was 'good', with student satisfaction levels ranging from 'good' to 'very good', it was observed by staff teaching those students in Year 2 that the academic skills set would have further improved, particularly with regard to critical and creative thinking, critical reasoning, legal writing, legal research and referencing. This teacher-centric approach is arguably less suitable for today's law students who are required to not only interpret and present legal knowledge but to exercise judgement and move beyond assigned parameters to add value to their legal research and in the advice they provide to clients.

This study was carried out in Malaysia, where Asian parents tend to have high expectations, pushing their children to achieve high scores. Indeed, in Asian cultures, parents are generally very concerned with their children's educational development (Rao & Sun, 2010; Zhang et al., 2010). Hence, obtaining good grades in class was regarded as very important, and the students were generally focused on how much they scored rather than how much they learned. According to Zhang, Biggs and Watkins (2010), there is a high level of competitive pressure among students to achieve excellent academic results. Consequently, students will give strong emphasis to the assessments that they need to complete, which involves socio-cultural concerns in relation to academic success and failure (DiasSoeiro, 2021).

The quest to achieve 21st century skills in the era of the COVID-19 pandemic added complication to the learning process by limiting possible experiences. Indeed, educators had to change the way knowledge and skills were being delivered and assessed. Lin and Nguyen (2021) stressed the issues faced by an Asian student when studying fully online. Knowledge acquisition insecurity, lack of confidence and loneliness were the main aspects emanating from the experience. From a social and cultural perspective, Southeast Asian students can face challenges related to self-pressure, self-evaluation, evaluation, results orientation, memorization and inabilities which will be impacting the learning experience (DiasSoeiro, 2021). However, and as expressed by Latorre-Cosculluela et al. (2020), the adaptation of teaching tools to newer generations seemed to impact the learning positively. Reflecting on the eventual educational challenges, this study was aimed at exploring the use of gamification as learning experience amongst law students. The study also investigated the suitability of this method in the acquisition of 21st century skills in learning law.

LITERATURE REVIEW

Cultural Context of the Study

Literature seems to claim the passive learning attitude of Asian students, lacking in critical thinking and creativity skills (Kahl, 2013; Lam, 2016). This generalization might be true and in reference to certain practices in Asia. The educational system seemed to be less flexible, more rigid, too focused on high achievements, and too standardized (Lam, 2016; Othman et al., 2021). However, this perspective of rationality is a western concept. Indeed, Elliott and Tsai (2008) or You (2020), refuted this idea and supported the understanding that the learner is at the center of the learning experience. They indirectly supported various research works such as the ones by Hall and Ames (1987) and Wong (2004), whereas the concepts of spoon-feeding, rote-learning, repetitive learning, teacher-centered learning, and memorization are misconceptions of the Asian style of learning, also known as the Confucian Heritage Culture (CHC). CHC involves rote memorization but not entirely, as there is a difference between rote memorization and memorization with understanding. The teacher has the role of engaging the learner in the learning process to understand its fundamentals and to achieve a clear outcome. The learner has to interpret the meaning to acquire clear knowledge (Elliott & Tsai, 2008; Wong, 2004).

Within Asian learning attitudes, there are patterns among learners and learner-related matters. For instance, Rao and Sun (2010) highlighted the importance of results and achievements in relation to the high expectations of parents. They also highlighted the effect of pressure from peers, school and parents that affect the self. The high collectivist attitude might be explained by the group cohesion and dynamics (Hofstede, 2011) that can be observed during classes. The cohesion and beliefs of the group, therefore, tend to be strong, and are also marked by the need for a hierarchical structure. The sense of belonging to a cultural group is strong, and misbehaving or breaking a norm will lead to shame, loss of face and moral conflicts (Hofstede, 2011). Asian students tend to prefer to be in a group and require the presence of a lecturer to enhance the learning experience and acquisition of skills. When the learning environment varies and students are in individually involved, the learning can be impacted.

21st Century Skills

The term "Twenty-first Century Skills" does not only reflect the set of skills or knowledge but also the behavioral and attitudinal traits that one must have. Also supported by Cope, Kalantzis and Smith (2018), the pedagogical approaches to be adopted by academics to develop multiliteracies and learning should actively place the learner at the center of engagements and production of skills and knowledge. The Partnership for 21st Century Skills (P21, 2007) classified key skills into three categories: (1) learning and innovation skills, (2) life and career skills, information, and (3) media and technology skills. The Assessment and Teaching of 21st Century Skills (AT21CS) resulted in ten skills grouped into four categories: ways of thinking, ways of working, tools for working and living in the world (Binkley et al., 2012). According to Ananiadou and Claro (2009), the Organisation for Economic Co-operation and Development (OECD) had categorized 21st century skills as information, communication, and ethics and social impact. Based on the study by Van Laar (2020), the 21st century skills could be summarized as technical skills, information skills, communication skills, collaboration skills, critical thinking skills, creativity skills, problem-solving skills, and digital skills.

Constructivism and Experiential Learning

Experiential learning, as can be gathered from its name, means learning through experience. It involves the bridging of the inner self with the learning environment through senses and feelings; a learning that will be transformed into knowledge, skills and behaviour (Beard & Wilson, 2013). Experiential learning can create a high impact and meaningful learning experience as the method allows learners to take the initiative, apply what they have learned and integrate their knowledge and skills in real-life environment (Mohamad et al., 2021). *"Experience, in the degree in which it is experienced, is heightened vitality. Instead of signifying being shut up within one's own private feelings and sensations, it signifies active and alert commerce with the world; at its height, it signifies complete interpenetration of self and the world of objects and events"* (Dewey, 1934, p. 19). Learning by doing and thinking how to do are the key elements in experiential learning. Experiential learning involves: firstly, rapport between the individual and the surrounding environment; secondly, cognition and rationality of the self with this surrounding environment; and finally, the awareness of the person who is experiencing this in terms of his/her emotions, perceptions and mindset towards the experience (Beard & Wilson, 2013).

The construction of knowledge depends on self-understanding based on a person's educational background, including the social and cultural aspects, which represent dimensions one and two of the model by Beard and Wilson (2013). This knowledge has its *interpretations* and *meanings* through the communication that takes place during the *learning experience* (Von Glasersfeld, 1995, p. 134). A lack of structure may lead to various challenges that do not create knowledge. The subjectivity of each individual, a lack of direction, and ambiguity of the experience may contribute to a non-optimization of learning. These limitations are particularly important as learning styles vary, and each individual reacts differently. In other words, the lecturer needs to adopt different learning and teaching approaches to ensure an actively involved class as well as to ensure proper verification of learning through assessments *for* and *as* learning.

Contextual Learning Challenges

From a critical educationist lens, online teaching and learning methods seem to not fully fulfill expectations and somehow learning due superficial intended approaches (Liesa-Orus et al., 2020). The unreadiness of the institutions which includes academics, support systems, support staff (ICT), learning environment, and students could jeopardize the use of technologies in current pedagogies. From a situational and contextual lens, the shift towards online education came faster than the transition required for a learner to adapt to an online education (Besser et al., 2020; Kalantzis & Cope, 2020). Even though Generation Z is the generation born in the 21st century, influenced by social media and the digital world (McCrindle, 2021; Othman et al., 2021), the learners had been experiencing coping issues relating to isolation, loneliness, stress, uncertainty, anxiety or ambiguity due to the novelty and unresolved pandemic situation (Besser et al., 2020). Online learners generally choose their learning environment based on flexibilities and preferences but still can be affected by generic challenges expressed by Besser et al.(2020). The disruption of the daily routine impacted the learner's environment, habits, and hence, learning process. Despite the pandemic situation, online learning still showed challenges in technological literacy, self-regulation, procrastination, or technological sufficiency (Rasheed et al., 2020).

However, studies showed that when students demonstrated the aptitude to adapt, they showed abilities to cope and solve problems better (Besser et al., 2020). Personal traits such as autonomy, self-determination, resilience can help to adapt to online learning and the achievement of 21st century skills (Liesa-Orus et al., 2020). Furthermore, the engagement and experientiality employed during the online classes were revealed positive allowing students to adapt and perform better (Besser et al., 2020; Ofosu-Ampong, 2020). As such, Ofosu-Ampong (2020) emphasized incorporating gaming elements as pedagogical strategy to enhance learning. As stressed by Beard and Wilson (2013), the experience of the learner when learning or studying is key to experiential learning. The learner is at the center of the learning process and requires senses and feelings to acquire the knowledge or skills expected. Online tools must be adequately chosen to satisfy the achievement of the expected learning outcomes.

Gamification

Gamification gained attention and interest in academia which led to opportunities and criticism. Questioning the connectivity between learning, gamification and acquisition of 21st century skills and how learning happens has been discussed in literatures for the past decade (Majuri et al., 2018; Manzano-León et al., 2021; Mohamad et al., 2021; Sailer & Homner, 2020). Defined as *"the use of game design elements in non-game contexts"* (Deterding et al., 2011, p. 9), gamification can also be called serious games, edu-games or gamified learning.

The learning experiences created from game-based activities have proven positive outcomes. However, cognitive learning outcomes still require further attention. In their study, Sailer and Homner (2020) identified significant effects from gamification towards motivational learning outcomes and behavioral learning outcomes. Additionally, Lane (2021) revealed that video games used in classrooms enabled learners (boys in her study) to create meaning and cultural knowledge. Perceived as and related to interpersonal activities, gamification helped to enhance collaboration and cooperation in challenging situations (Sailer & Homner, 2020). The competitive nature of games can cause social pressure but used in an educational context, the engagement and immersion required will enable to create positive attributes. Furthermore, the active rather than passive learning involvement seemed to be efficient and sustainable to benefit the learning experience (van Roy & Zaman, 2018; Wouters et al., 2013; Wouters et al., 2008). Hallifax et al. (2019) emphasized two aspects: the educational content; and its adaptation to the learners as well as the context. According to them, employing adaptive gamification and customization of the learning to the learner will provide a better learning experience. Nevertheless, as informed by Lane (2021), Liesa-Orús (2020), and Sailer and Homner (2020), gamification can have certain drawbacks leading to concerns relating to distraction, negative identity construction, time commitment for integration, violence, anxiety, social pressure, competition, pedagogic context as well as learner, institution, and educator readiness.

Sailer and Homner (2020) highlighted the importance of understanding gamification as a *"design process of adding game elements in order to change existing learning processes"* (p. 78). Therefore, as numerous research had already focused on learning and gamification, further research should focus on the creation of knowledge and skills by exploring how learning is happening through gamification. Gamification seemed to enable learners to improve their motivation, commitment and academic performance (Manzano-León et al., 2021; Turner et al., 2019). With the constant evolution of technology; social and cultural change of the learners; and learning expectations of the learners, parents and institutions, the quest towards 21st century skills development should intensify the usage of technologies and e-pedagogies. In alignment with the 4th and 5th Industrial Revolutions, gamification could be one of the strengths in the future of education. New studies are required to provide insights on long term and short-term utilization of gamification as well as understanding how learning is created through game-based learning (Hallifax et al., 2019).

RESEARCH METHODOLOGY

Research Context

This study was aimed at exploring the use of gamification as learning experience amongst law students while also investigating the suitability of this method in the acquisition of 21st century skills. The research not only focused on how likeable was the tools being used but also identified what skills the students were able to develop and how they were able to develop those skills.

Out of 21 core modules, three modules adopted gamification elements into the Bachelor of Laws programme namely LAW64404 Legal Skills and Methods, LAW60704 English Legal System and LAW61504 Land Law I. The selected modules were those assigned to the co-author, the module leader. The first two modules are first year, first semester modules and the third module is a second year, third semester module. Across the three modules, there were five formative assessments (which were assessed fortnightly and constituted 10% of the total marks). The formative assessments were provided during tutorial sessions where the law students' knowledge and skills on a prior topic were assessed to ensure proper comprehension and understanding of the topics taught. The gamified teaching and learning activities integrated in the tutorial sessions included 'Legal Writing using Toothpaste', 'Poker-ing your Ideas', 'Speed-Dating with the Law', 'Advocating the Law using Zappar', 'Presenting using Neuro-Linguistic Programming', 'Amazing Race with Augmented Reality', 'Testing Comprehension Using ClassPoint' and 'Reflective Exercise with FeedbackFruits' to encourage law students to approach law beyond the conventional methods.

The Implementation of Gamification

The gamification was integrated into LAW64404 Legal Skills and Methods, LAW60704 English Legal System and LAW61504 Land Law I since March 2019 through the five formative assessments, namely the tutorial sessions which were assessed every fortnight. The duration of the tutorial session was one hour and thirty minutes. Law students were grouped into four or five tutorial groups, with a maximum of 25 students per group. The capping of number of students for the tutorial sessions was to enable personalized and close-up interactions between the lecturer and the students.

The co-author, being the lecturer who taught the above assigned modules, embedded gamification elements by adopting 'points' system to reward students' efforts in attending tutorial sessions early, completion of the tutorial questions prior to attending the tutorial sessions, contributions by sharing thoughts during discussions and also submission of full written answers. The co-author also utilized a self-designed leader board using Microsoft Excel (see Figure 1 and Figure 2) for each tutorial group. The purpose of embedding points into the leader board is two-fold: first, to heighten students' engagement and interaction during tutorial sessions; and secondly, for the module leader to identify and monitor weaker and/ or passive students during the tutorial sessions. The leader board is displayed during each tutorial session to provide transparency in the awarding of points and also for the students to assess their own participation in each tutorial session.

Upon the completion of all tutorial sessions, the students will be able to view their performance and progress for each tutorial session. The 10% tutorial participation marks will be provided based on the active engagement of students in each tutorial session. As demonstrated in Figure 1, majority of the students obtained 10 out of 10 marks which reflected the effectiveness of integrating gamification in the tutorial sessions.

Research Procedure

A Google Survey was conducted with a total of 183 respondents, which included law students from the first and second year who had previously experienced the use of gamification. The design of the questionnaire used a QR code as a unique way to encourage Bachelor of Laws students to participate and complete the questionnaire via their mobile devices. The use of a QR code proved successful with the sample of 183 respondents which represented a majority of the total available law student population at the university. The purpose of the survey was to collect information relating to the perceived skills developed by the students.

Figure 1.

No.	Student ID	1	2	3	4	5	TOTAL	Participation x times	Tutorial Participation Marks
1	3341XX	10+20+30+8+8+16+13+10+6	20+2+2+2+2+2+2	2+2+2+2+2+4+22	20+2+2+100+30	1000+20+2+2+2+2+50	1427	31	10
3	3402XX	10+20+30+9+13+9+10+9	20+2+2+2+2+4+2+2	20+2+2+2+2+2+8+16	2+2+6+6+50+20	100+2+2-10+22	1366	29	10
4	3415XX	10+20+30+8+9+10+4+6	2+2+2+2	2+2+2+6+6	2+2+2+10	100+20+2+2+20	797	22	10
5	3401XX	10+20+30+6+10+14+7	20+2+2+2+2+2	20+2+2+2+2+2+8+14	2+2+2+18	100+20+2+2+2+20	367	25	10
6	3400XX	10+20+30+11+9+9+8+13	20+2+2+2+2	20+2+2+10+2+2+2+4+8	2+2+2+16	100+20+2+22	362	23	10
7	3402XX	10+20+30+12+12+12+8+12	20+2+2+2+2	2+2+2+2+6+6	20+2+2+2+16	100+20+2+4+22	350	22	10
9	3397XX	10+30+20+9+4+13+11	20+2+2+2+2+4+2+2	2+2+2+2+2+6+12	20+2+2+2+16	100+20+2+2+10+28	349	27	10
10	3412XX	10+20+30+13+11+13+11	20+2+2	20+2+2+4+8	20+2+12	100+4+4+2+20	334	16	10
11	3402XX	10+30+10+11+5+14+11	2+2+2+2	20+2+2+2+4+14	2+18	100+20+2-10+20	311	18	10
13	3417XX	10+20+30+9+13+12+12	2+2+2+2	2+2+2+5+6	20+2+2+2+22	600+20+2+2+2+30	311	22	10
14	3410XX	10+8+10+16+16	2+2+2+2	20+2+2+2+2+8+8	2+2+6+12	100+20+2+2+2+24	306	22	10
15	3405XX	10+30+6+15+6+12+14+8	2+2+2	10+2+4	2+2+18	100+20+2+2+2+10+2+34	291	20	10
16	3404XX	10+20+14+9+10+11	2+2+2	20+2+2+6+14	2+10	1000+20+2+2+2+10+4+4+36	286	20	10
17	3402XX	10+20+30+15+10+10+8	2+2+2	2+2+2+4+8	2+12	100+2+8+20	285	17	10
18	3401XX	10+30+4+12+7+12	2+4+2+2	2+2+2+6+16	2-20+6+20	100+20+2+2+22	265	20	10
19	3407XX	10+30+14+5+14+11+15	2+2	0	2+2+2+10+20	100+20+2+2+20	257	17	9
20	3402XX	10+30+6+14+12	2+2+2	0	2+2+22	100+20+2+2+20	234	12	9
21	3413XX	10+8+10+16+16	2+2+2+2	10+2+4	2+2+6+12	100+20+2+2+2+24	306	22	10

Figure 2.

Legend			
Participating in the discussion	2 points	*Bonus question	X points
Asking Ms Puteri a question	15 points	Late for tutorials	-10 points
Attending class earlier than Ms. Puteri	20 points	Not prepared	-10 points
Answered all questions before attending tutorial sessions	30 points	Lifeline	-10 points
Prepared full answer	100 points	Absent	0 points

As knowledge and experience are continuously being constructed (Jackson, 2013; Mc Gregor & Murnane, 2010), the survey was released towards the end of the semester. The research was limited to the space within the classroom, where the law classes were being held. This study used data collected from over fourteen weeks of observation of the participants of the class by the researcher, who was also the lecturer. The observation data were recorded in a journal, with references to specific fields of observation such as attitude, behaviour, challenges or remarks from the participants. As presented in Table 1, majority of the students are from Malaysia and the demographic details reflect the total number of students present in the different modules.

Table 1. Demographic details

Categories	Details	Number	Percentage
Gender	Females Males Prefer not to reveal	137 45 1	74.9% 24.6% 0.5%
Study cluster	First year Second year Prefer not to reveal	105 77 1	57.4% 42.1% 0.5%
Origin	Malaysians Other countries	172 11	94% 6%

The nature of the qualitative study had led to an important focus on ethical considerations (Guillemin & Gillam, 2010), and involves the researcher as a tool for the gathering of information (Creswell, 2014). The anonymity, confidentiality, disclosure of information and retention period of the data are examples of information contained in the ethics application (Boydell, 2007). The main ethical points for reflection were concerning: (1) the participants, in terms of anonymity and treatment of information; (2) the researcher, due to multiple positions, such as lecturer or researcher; and (3) the relationship between the participants and the researcher, which required neutrality and freedom from bias.

FINDINGS AND DISCUSSION

This literature presented the embedding of gamification in the academic curriculum in a favorable light. However, its positive impact on the law students' learning is an area identified as a gap in the current literature and therefore to better understand students' experience, this research assessed students' perceptions of gamification on three law modules. Following the completion of the modules, a total of 183 students completed a survey (across all 3 modules taught). The first observation made with regards the students' perceptions were that there were no discerning differences in perceptions based upon intake. The second observation was that there was no commonality to the responses.

Following the quantitative survey, majority of the students (73.8%) enjoyed the experience of gamification and cited excitement, capturing attention and the different approach as reasons for this enjoyment. Representative quotes include:

"I love how the way the tutorial is conducted which really encouraged participation"; "Ms. Sofia is truly an amazing lecturer. I have learnt so much from her and the way she incorporated gamification and leader board in the learning system makes me enjoyed her class even more";

"A great learning experience with Ms. Puteri. Notice improvements not only in my legal writing skills but also communication skills as well";

"I love the activities conducted during tutorial. Tutorial helps me to understand this module easily and effectively".

With regards preparation for the employment market, moderately high number of students (60.6%) felt that the use of gamification techniques will prepare them for future employment market. The reason for the moderate high number of student is that students are embracing the integration of gamification into tutorial sessions only for the modules taught by the co-author. Hence, the slight confidence in the effectiveness of the adoption of gamification.

Despite the overall neutral feeling on the effectiveness on the integration of gamification into the tutorial sessions, majority of students (64.5%) thought that embedding gamification in the module improved the skills that they needed to get employment, particularly analytical thinking skills (66.6%), creative skills (76.5%), innovative skills (77.1%) and critical thinking skills (68.3%). From the authors' perspectives, the activities introduced during the tutorial sessions were carefully designed to achieve the module learning outcomes although it appeared as fun and interactive games. For example, the integration of 'toothpaste' into legal writing was aimed at achieving module learning outcomes on ability to conduct legal writing and proper referencing. Another example, the activity on speed-dating was aimed at achieving module learning outcome to deliver effective oral presentation. Hence, whilst students feel the tutorial sessions are unorthodox with various non-law activities introduced during tutorial sessions, it was primarily designed to ensure that students achieved the module learning outcomes through gamification elements.

The students' positive responses on gamification were reflected in the literature, particularly around the mediums on ability to increase confidence in approaching real-life issues (Hamzah et al., 2015) with the majority of students (65%) feeling that incorporating gamification into the modules allowed them to learn better and improved their confidence in learning law where 26.8% felt neutral and 7.7% felt that they did not feel gamification techniques in class developed their confidence to deal with real life legal issues. From the co-author's perspectives, majority of the students who felt that gamification developed their confidence were generally the proactive learners in the classroom and outside the classroom environment. Given that the students had only experienced the gamification techniques in the modules taught by the co-author, more time is needed for students to get accustomed and acclimatized to the new learning techniques. Hence, the results of the survey where students feel neutral or disagree with the statement is attributed to their confidence level in attempting the problem question involving real-life legal issues without the sample answers or answer structure from the lecturers.

These quantitative results indicated that majority of the students felt they learned better using gamification and shed further light on why they enjoyed learning using gamification and how they developed skills centering on analytical thinking skills, creative skills, innovative skills and critical thinking skills. It is worth noting that prior to integrating gamification elements into learning, lecturers need to encompass a deep passion in enhancing student learning experience. Without the necessary level of engagement, explanation, justification and support of the lecturers, expectations may not be met, frustration could arise and learning, negatively impacted. If the concepts of gamification were not explained from the first day of class, students may experience feeling 'confused', 'lost', 'irrelevant' and begin to disengage, particularly if the use of gamification is not the norm. To enhance the value of gamification, universities should consider implementing gamification as part of every module so that students are able to become more familiar with new learning strategies which can develop their employability skills set and work readiness in the future (Mohamad et al., 2021; Amirnuddin & Turner, 2020).

It is also highly recommended for universities to integrate gamification into mooting activities, also known as 'mock trials'. Mooting is a law school co-curricular activity conducted in a moot court which requires participating students to analyse and argue both sides of an appeal from a fictitious lawsuit before law lecturers and/or lawyers who serve as judges (Turner et al., 2019). In some universities, mooting exercise is embedded into academic curriculum as an elective module to facilitate student learning. The learning process for the mooting activity includes reading the brief, conducting legal research, preparing skeleton argument, preparing bundle of submission and conducting the moot itself. In the process of mooting, students are required to incorporate the actual elements of the 'trials' such as dressing in a formal court attire, adhering to court etiquettes in addressing the judges and counsels, presentations and answering questions from the bench (Hammond & Ross, 2014). Integrating gamification in the pre-mooting session and during the mooting exercise would be particularly useful as students tend to view mooting activities as difficult and intimidating. By introducing elements of gamification, it would inject elements of curiosity and interests to excel in the mooting exercise and contribute to the learning process.

CONCLUSION

This book chapter shares the experiences of staff and students in using gamification in law modules. The discussion supports the existing literature on the use of gamification in the education sector, indicating that the majority of students enjoyed the experience of incorporating gamification into their learning and that the use of such technology developed their employability skills set and better prepare them for the future employment market (WEF, 2020). Having adopted gamification elements since March 2019, the authors believe that the embedding of such initiatives is not only beneficial but necessary given the challenges law graduates will face in competing with artificial intelligence and automation later in practice. It is evident that the majority of students were receptive to the idea of learning law beyond the conventional approach. In addition, it was also observed that students who actively engage in gamification as part of their learning appeared to be more motivated in class, more confident in attempting their assignments and performed better.

With regard to areas for further research, it is believed that by pursuing an in-depth investigation on the effectiveness of gamification on current students and the graduates, with a longer study duration (Hallifax et al., 2019), can produce a better understanding on the impact of gamification on employability. A further research which includes the perspectives of other stakeholders such as employers and governing bodies can also provide a more holistic perspective on the impact of gamification on a graduate's work readiness. Another area for future research is to investigate the hard and soft employability skills gamification are capable of engendering, examining in the first instance one institution where the technology is well established and in the second instance, comparing with other institutions where the platforms had recently been introduced. Only through further investigation on the means in which to better prepare graduates for employment can educational institutions develop a future ready graduate who is distinguishable from a conventional and more traditional graduate (Amirnuddin & Turner, 2020).

Gamification promotes students to integrate lifelong learning, which is important for graduate work readiness given the business environment which also have embedded gamification elements at the workplace (Miri & Macke, 2021; Santos et al., 2021). Gamification encourages students to develop a more comprehensive understanding of a particular subject by providing a platform for students to develop students' core skills and also future skills such as empathy, communication, critical thinking, creativity, strategy, technological innovations, physical skills, imagination, vision and self-actualization (Marr, 2018). Some of the notable skills that can be acquired through using gamification to learn include: (1) intuitive interaction, (2) creative and innovative thinking in learning law, (3) collaboration, (4) life-long learning, (5) digital literacy, (6) promotion of global perspectives, (7) enhancement of discipline specific-knowledge, (8) critical thinking, (9) enhancement of collaboration and teamwork skills, (9) increase in confidence levels, (10) enhancement of communication skills, (11) engagement with the real world and (12) sharpening of students' investigative skills (Amirnuddin & Turner, 2020; Kathrani, 2020; Sailer & Homner, 2020; Turner et al., 2019).

ACKNOWLEDGMENT

This research received no specific grant from any funding agency in the public, commercial, or not-for-profit sectors.

REFERENCES

Amirnuddin, P. S., Mohamed, A. A. A., & Ahmad, M. H. (2020). Transforming Legal Education In The Era Of Fourth Industrial Revolution. *Current Law Journal*, *2*, ix–xxiv.

Amirnuddin, P. S., & Turner, J. T. (2020). Learning Law using Augmented Reality and Neuro-Linguistic Programming. In P. Kumar, M. J. Keppell, & C. L. Lim (Eds.), *Preparing 21st Century Teachers for Teach Less, Learn More (TLLM) Pedagogies* (pp. 259–278). IGI Global. doi:10.4018/978-1-7998-1435-1.ch015

Ananiadou, K., & Claro, M. (2009). *21st century skills and competences for new millennium learners in OECD countries.* OECD Education Working Papers 41. OECD Publishing. doi:10.1787/19939019

Beard, C., & Wilson, J. P. (2013). *Experiential learning: a handbook for education, training and coaching* (3rd ed.). Kogan Page Limited.

Besser, A., Flett, G. L., & Zeigler-Hill, V. (2020). Adaptability to a Sudden Transition to Online Learning During the COVID-19 Pandemic: Understanding the Challenges for Students. *Scholarship of Teaching and Learning in Psychology*. Advance online publication. doi:10.1037tl0000198

Binkley, M., Erstad, O., Herman, J., Raizen, S., Ripley, M., Miller-Ricci, M., & Rumble, M. (2012). Defining twenty-first century skills. In P. Griffin & E. Care (Eds.), *Assessment and Teaching of 21st Century Skills: Methods and Approach* (pp. 17–66). Springer. doi:10.1007/978-94-007-2324-5_2

Boydell, K. (2007). *Ethical issues in conducting qualitative research. Research ethics lecture series. Department of psychiatry.* University of Toronto.

Cope, B., Kalantzis, M., & Smith, A. (2018). Pedagogies and Literacies, Disentangling the Historical Threads: An Interview with Bill Cope and Mary Kalantzis. *Theory into Practice*, *57*(1), 5–11. doi:10.1080/00405841.2017.1390332

Creswell, J. W. (2014). *Research design: qualitative, quantitative, and mixed methods approaches* (4th ed.). SAGE Publications.

Deterding, S., Dixon, D., Khaled, R., & Nacke, L. (2011). From game design elements to gamefulness: defining "gamification". In A. Lugmayr (Ed.), *Proceedings of the 15th International Academic Mindtrek Conference: Envisioning Future Media Environments* (pp. 9–15). ACM. 10.1145/2181037.2181040

Dewey, J. (1934). Art as experience. Academic Press.

DiasSoeiro, J. (2021). Studying Wine in Non-Wine-Producing Countries: How Are Southeast Asian Students Coping With Their Learning? In C. Kahl (Ed.), Higher Education Challenges in South-East Asia (pp. 99-117). IGI Global. doi:10.4018/978-1-7998-4489-1.ch005

Elliott, J., & Tsai, C. T. (2008). What might Confucius have to say about action research? *Educational Action Research*, *16*(4), 569–578. doi:10.1080/09650790802445759

Giddings, J., & Weinberg, J. (2020). Experiential Legal Education. Stepping Back to See the Future. In C. Denvir (Ed.), *Modernizing Legal Education* (pp. 38–56). Cambridge University Press. doi:10.1017/9781108663311.004

Guillemin, M., & Gillam, L. (2010). Ethics, reflexivity, and "ethically important moments" in research. *Qualitative Inquiry*, *10*(2), 261–280. doi:10.1177/1077800403262360

Hall, D., & Ames, R. (1987). *Thinking through Confucius. SUNY Series in Systematic Philosophy*. State University of New York Press.

Hallifax, S., Serna, A., Marty, J. C., & Lavou, E. (2019). Adaptive gamification in education: A literature review of current trends and developments. *European Conference on Technology Enhanced Learning (EC-TEL)*, 294-307. 10.1007/978-3-030-29736-7_22

Hammond, M., & Ross, M. (2014). *The Student Guide to Mooting*. Edinburgh University Press.

Hamzah, W. M., Ali, N., Saman, M., Yusoff, M. H., & Yacob, A. (2015). Influence of Gamification on Students' Motivation in using E-Learning Applications Based on the Motivational Design Model. *International Journal of Emerging Technologies in Learning*, *10*(2), 30–34. doi:10.3991/ijet.v10i2.4355

Hofstede, G. (2011). Dimensionalizing cultures: The Hofstede model in context. *Online Readings in Psychology and Culture*, *2*(1). Advance online publication. doi:10.9707/2307-0919.1014

Jackson, E. (2013). Choosing a methodology: philosophical underpinning. *Practitioner Research in Higher Education Journal*, *7*(1), 49-62.

Kahl, C. (2013). A deeper lecturer and student view of a sustainable learning requirement in tertiary education in Malaysia. *International Journal for Cross-Disciplinary Subjects in Education*, *4*(2), 1144–1152. doi:10.20533/ijcdse.2042.6364.2013.0161

Kalantzis, M., & Cope, B. (2020). After the COVID-19 crisis: Why higher education may (and perhaps should) never be the same. *Access: Contemporary Issues in Education*, *40*(1), 51–55. doi:10.46786/ac20.9496

Kathrani, P. (2020). The Gamification of Written Problem Questions in Law. Reflections on the "Serious Games at Westminster's Project. In C. Denvir (Ed.), *Modernizing Legal Education* (pp. 186–203). Cambridge University Press. doi:10.1017/9781108663311.012

Lam, C. M. (2016). Fostering rationality in Asian education. In C. M. Lam & J. Park (Eds.), *Sociological and philosophical perspectives on education in the Asia-Pacific region: issues, concerns and prospects* (Vol. 29, pp. 9–22). Springer. doi:10.1007/978-981-287-940-0_2

Lane, C. A. (2021). Using Digital Technologies in the 21st Century Classroom: How Video Games Support Dynamic Learning Opportunities. In C. A. Lane (Ed.), *Present and Future Paradigms of Cyberculture in the 21st Century* (pp. 109–134). IGI Global. doi:10.4018/978-1-5225-8024-9.ch007

Latorre-Cosculluela, C., Suárez, C., Quiroga, S., Sobradiel-Sierra, N., Lozano-Blasco, R., & Rodríguez-Martínez, A. (2021). Flipped Classroom model before and during COVID-19: Using technology to develop 21st century skills. *Interactive Technology and Smart Education*, *18*(2), 189–204. Advance online publication. doi:10.1108/ITSE-08-2020-0137

Liesa-Orús, M., Latorre-Cosculluela, C., Vázquez-Toledo, S., & Sierra-Sánchez, V. (2020). The Technological Challenge Facing Higher Education Professors: Perceptions of ICT Tools for Developing 21st Century Skills. *Sustainability*, *12*(13), 5339. doi:10.3390u12135339

Lin, Y., & Nguyen, H. (2021). International Students' Perspectives on e-Learning During COVID-19 in Higher Education in Australia: A Study of an Asian Student. *The Electronic Journal of e-Learning*, *19*(4), 241-251. doi:10.34190/ejel.19.4.2349

Majuri, J., Koivisto, J., & Hamari, J. (2018). Gamification of education and learning: A review of empirical literature. *Proceedings of the 2nd International GamiFIN Conference*. Retrieved from: http://ceur-ws.org/Vol-2186/paper2.pdf

Manzano-León, A., Camacho-Lazarraga, P., Guerrero, M. A., Guerrero-Puerta, L., Aguilar-Parra, J. M., Trigueros, R., & Alias, A. (2021). Between Level Up and Game Over: A Systematic Literature Review of Gamification in Education. *Sustainability*, *13*(4), 2247. doi:10.3390u13042247

Marr, B. (2018). *7 Job Skills of The Future (That AIs And Robots Can't Do Better Than Humans)*. Retrieved from: https://www.forbes.com/sites/bernardmarr/2018/08/06/7-job-skills-of-the-future-that-ais-and-robots-cant-do-better-than-humans/#7c1894496c2e

Mc Gregor, S. L. T., & Murnane, J. A. (2010). Paradigm, methodology and method: Intellectual integrity in consumer scholarship. *International Journal of Consumer Studies*, *34*(4), 419–427. doi:10.1111/j.1470-6431.2010.00883.x

McCrindle, M. (2021). Generation Alpha. Academic Press.

Miri, D. H., & Macke, J. (2021). Gamification, Motivation, and Engagement at Work: A Qualitative Multiple Case Study. *European Business Review*. Advance online publication. doi:10.1108/EBR-04-2020-0106

Mohamad, A. A. A., Amirnuddin, P. S., Ahmad, M. H., & Ramalingam, C. L. (2021). Transforming Legal Education Teaching and Learning: The Remote Communication Technology. *Malayan Law Journal*, *2*, cxxxvii.

Ofosu-Ampong, K. (2020). The Shift to Gamification in Education: A Review on Dominant Issues. *Journal of Educational Technology Systems*, *49*(1), 113–137. doi:10.1177/0047239520917629

Othman, M. N. A., Abdul Rashid, M. A., Ismail, I. R., Abd Aziz, M. F., Norizan, S., & Mohamad Saad, S. A. (2021). Predicting Preferred Learning Styles on Teaching Approaches Among Gen Z Visual Learner. *Turkish Journal of Computer and Mathematics Education*, *12*(9), 2969–2978.

Partnership for 21st Century Skills. (2007). *Framework for 21stcentury learning*. Retrieved from: http://www.p21.org/documents/P21_Framework_Definitions.pdf

Rao, N., & Sun, J. (2010). Educating Asian adolescents: a developmental perspective. In L. F. Zhang, J. Biggs, & D. Watkins (Eds.), *Learning and development of Asian students: what the 21st Century teacher needs to think about* (pp. 37–59). Pearson.

Rasheed, R. A., Kamsin, A., & Abdullah, N. A. (2020). Challenges in the online component of blended learning: A systematic review. *Computers & Education, 144*, 103701. doi:10.1016/j.compedu.2019.103701

Sailer, M., & Homner, L. (2020). The Gamification of Learning: A Meta-analysis. *Educational Psychology Review, 32*(1), 77–112. doi:10.100710648-019-09498-w

Santos, S. A., Trevisan, L. N., Veloso, E. F. R., & Treff, M. A. (2021). Gamification In Training and Development Processes: Perception On Effectiveness And Results. *Revista de Gestão, 28*(2), 133–146. doi:10.1108/REGE-12-2019-0132

Turner, J., Amirnuddin, P. S., & Singh, H. (2019). University Legal Learning Spaces Effectiveness in Developing Employability Skills of Future Law Graduates. *Malaysian Journal of Learning and Instruction, 16*(1), 49–79. doi:10.32890/mjli2019.16.1.3

Van Laar, E., Van Deursen, A. J. A. M., Van Dijk, J. A. G. M., & De Haan, J. (2020). Determinants of 21st-Century Skills and 21st-Century Digital Skills for Workers: A Systematic Literature Review. *SAGE Open, 10*(1), 1–14. doi:10.1177/2158244019900176

Van Roy, R., & Zaman, B. (2018). Need-Supporting Gamification In Education: An Assessment Of Motivational Effects Over Time. *Computers & Education, 127*, 283–297. doi:10.1016/j.compedu.2018.08.018

Von Glasersfeld, E. (1995). *Radical constructivism: a way of knowing and learning. studies in mathematics education series: 6*. Falmer Press.

WEF. (2020). *The Future of Jobs Report 2020*. Geneva: World Economic Forum. Retrieved from https://www3.weforum.org/docs/WEF_Future_of_Jobs_2020.pdf

Wong, J. K. K. (2004). Are the Learning Styles of Asian International Students Culturally or Contextually Based? *International Education Journal, 4*(4), 154–166.

Wouters, P., Paas, F., & van Merriënboer, J. J. G. (2008). How to optimize learning from animated models: A review of guidelines based on cognitive load. *Review of Educational Research, 78*(3), 645–675. doi:10.3102/0034654308320320

Wouters, P., van Nimwegen, C., van Oostendorp, H., & van der Spek, E. D. (2013). A meta-analysis of the cognitive and motivational effects of serious games. *Journal of Educational Psychology, 105*(2), 249–265. doi:10.1037/a0031311

You, Y. (2020). Learning experience: An alternative understanding inspired by thinking through Confucius. *ECNU Review of Education, 3*(1), 66–87. doi:10.1177/2096531120904247

Zhang, L. F., Biggs, J., & Watkins, D. (Eds.). (2010). *Learning and development of Asian students: what the 21st Century teacher needs to think about*. Pearson.

ADDITIONAL READING

Amirnuddin, P. S., Mohamed, A. A. A., & Ahmad, M. H. (2020a). Legal Education in Malaysia: Paradigm Shift in the Era of Fourth Industrial Revolution. In A.A.A. Mohamed (Ed.), Malaysian Legal System (pp. 967 - 996). CLJ Publication.

Cope, B., & Kalantzis, M. (2016). *A pedagogy of multiliteracies: Learning by design.* Palgrave Macmillan.

Lane, C. A. (2019). Video Games Support Alternative Classroom Pedagogies to Support Boys' Meaning-Making. In R. M. Reardon & J. Leonard (Eds.), *Integrating Digital Technology in Education: School-University-Community Collaboration* (pp. 199–224). IAP.

Lane, C. A. (2021). Using Digital Technologies in the 21st Century Classroom: How Video Games Support Dynamic Learning Opportunities. In C. A. Lane (Ed.), *Present and Future Paradigms of Cyberculture in the 21st Century* (pp. 109–134). IGI Global. doi:10.4018/978-1-5225-8024-9.ch007

Sailer, M., & Homner, L. (2020). The Gamification of Learning: A Meta-analysis. *Educational Psychology Review*, *32*(1), 77–112. doi:10.100710648-019-09498-w

KEY TERMS AND DEFINITIONS

21st Century Skills: A set of skills determined to allow and enhance the future employability of the graduates and their insertion at the workplace and in the society.

Employability: A set of skills and attributes that contributes to graduates and makes them employable. The employability is aligned to current and future needs of an industry and a society.

Experiential Learning: A learning process which requires the learner to actively be engaged through experiences. The learner is expected to reflect on the experience occurred in order to create a knowledge or a skill.

Gamification: The integration of game-mechanics or game-elements into a non-game environment such as in the physical classroom or virtual classroom.

Learning: The acquisition of knowledge, skills, and behaviours.

Legal Education: A process of learning whereby the learner in required to acquire skills, knowledge, and behaviours related to principles, theories, and practices of law.

Pedagogy: Practices applied to generate learning.

Chapter 26
The Effect of Religiosity on Learning Ethics in Serious Gaming Environments:
Religious Influences in Serious Educational Games

Haytham Siala
Business School, Newcastle University, UK

Giuseppe Pedeliento
University of Bergamo, Italy

Daniela Andreini
University of Bergamo, Italy

ABSTRACT

The multi-disciplinary literature on ethics asserts that the relationship between religiosity and ethical perceptions and judgements is an under-researched topic. Despite its importance, few studies have examined the relationship between religiosity and the learning of business ethics. This research investigates whether religiosity is conducive to the learning of business ethics in a digital learning environment: a serious 3D ethics game. A cross-sectional survey was conducted on 302 final-year students from two different academic institutions based in the UK. The results of a structural equation modelling analysis suggest that religiosity does not inform the ethical perceptions and decisions of religious individuals in digital learning environments. Religious individuals perceive the utilitarian aspects of a serious game such as ease of use to be more important for learning ethics than religion. In contrast, less religious individuals perceive the hedonic aspects of a serious game to be a key catalyst for enhancing the learning of ethics.

DOI: 10.4018/978-1-7998-7271-9.ch026

INTRODUCTION

Most global financial, economic, and environmental crises have historically been caused or exacerbated by poor ethical decisions. Hence, business schools have a strong remit to ensure that graduates leave university with a deep understanding of their role and responsibility towards their prospective employers, community, and society (Felton and Sims 2005). Ethics now constitute a crucial part of the skill-set and knowledge required in management education (Hardy and Tolhurst 2014; Baden and Higgs 2015; Michaelson 2016). However, few studies have assessed or tested learners' effectiveness in applying ethical theory in practice. Serious games such as practice-based managerial learning instruments could address this gap by enabling learners to impart ethical theory, as well as practical ethical skills and knowledge.

Some studies on business ethics contend that religious beliefs and values can significantly shape the cognitive stages of ethical development (Wagner and Sanders 2001; Longenecker, McKinney, and Moore 2004; Vitell 2009; Swimberghe, Sharma, and Flurry 2011; Peifer 2015). However, the effect of religiosity, i.e. the extent to which individuals adhere to the doctrines, beliefs, and ritual practices of religious institutions and are actively involved in congregational practices such as church attendance (Zinnbauer et al. 1997), on ethical decision-making remains an under-researched area (Singhapakdi et al. 2000; Vitell 2009; Craft 2013), despite the purported symbiotic relationship between religiosity and ethical decisions (Swimberghe, Sharma, and Flurry 2011; Salvador, Merchant, and Alexander 2014). For example, prior research suggests that religious individuals will display higher ethical sensitivity compared to non-religious individuals (Siu, Dickinson, and Lee 2000; Weaver and Agle 2002). In light of these prior research findings, this study investigates whether religiosity facilitates the effective learning of practical ethical skills and knowledge, using the unique context of a virtual educational gaming environment, namely, serious 3D ethics games.

The rationale behind choosing a serious gaming environment is twofold: first, serious games are increasingly used to support managerial learning (Salas, Wildman, and Piccolo 2009; Mustar 2009; Jang and Ryu 2011; Hess and Gunter 2013; Tsekleves, Cosmas, and Aggoun 2016; Allal-Chérif and Makhlouf 2016; Newbery et al. 2018; Rossi and Scappini 2014). Second, since virtual gaming environments allow users to experience episodes of immersion (Weibull 1985; Ruggiero 2000; Werner and James Jr 2001; Liu, Li, and Santhanam 2013), they offer researchers the opportunity to examine whether cognitive distractions experienced in virtual gaming environments can attenuate the hypothesised effect of religiosity on the ethical perceptions and judgements of religious individuals.

The findings have several managerial implications for two target audiences: educators and business managers.

LITERATURE REVIEW

A plethora of articles in the management education literature have criticised traditional instructional methods for failing to equip learners with transferable professional skills and knowledge (Pfeffer and Fong 2004; Ashkanasy 2006; Salas, Wildman, and Piccolo 2009; Armstrong 2011; Daspit and D'Souza 2012; Egri 2013). It has been argued that business management graduates who were not exposed to practice-based environments struggle to apply what they have learnt in corporate environments (Mustar 2009; Salas, Wildman, and Piccolo 2009). Amongst the practice-based learning tools, serious games have been lauded for their ability to imbue learners with transferable hard and soft managerial skills

(Garris, Ahlers, and Driskell 2002; Wouters, Van der Spek, and Van Oostendorp 2009). Inspired by the constructivist approach to learning (Kolb 1984), the primary objectives of serious gaming include enhancing learners' engagement, changing learners' attitudes and behaviours (Lavender 2008; Jouriles et al. 2009), and priming learners with the practical, transferable skills and knowledge needed in the workplace (Salas, Wildman, and Piccolo 2009; Crookall 2010; Bridget and Andrea 2011; Newbery, Lean, and Moizer 2016; Newbery et al. 2018). Additionally, serious games are used in corporate environments as a training intervention (Venkatesh and Bala 2008; Salas, Wildman, and Piccolo 2009; Allal-Chérif and Makhlouf 2016).

A recent systematic literature review on the effectiveness of serious games (Boyle et al. 2016) reveals that although serious games have permeated the management education literature, no prior studies to date have investigated their pedagogical effectiveness in teaching business ethics (Hardy and Tolhurst 2014; Baden and Higgs 2015; Michaelson 2016). Despite the lack of consensus on a broad and consistent definition of business ethics (see Seele (2018) for a recent critical review of the concept), we define business ethics as the conduct of business practice that takes ethical dilemmas and issues into account (Michalos 1982). This notion of business ethics applies ethical principles to examine the potential moral or ethical problems that could arise within a business environment. It applies to all aspects of business conduct and outlines the norms and values that govern ethical actions and behaviours of individuals in business organisations. Accordingly, the teaching of business ethics involves instructors facilitating the transfer of information, knowledge, and skills to students to enable them to invoke ethical principles and apply ethical decisions in a corporate environment (De Los Reyes Jr, Kim, and Weaver 2017).

On the topic of religiosity, some studies reported the existence of a reciprocal relationship between religiosity and the ethical attitudes and perceptions held by individuals (Herman 2015; Peifer 2015); a finding that extends to corporate environments where highly religious managers and employees were found to act in a socially responsible manner (Ho 2010; Fernando and Chowdhury 2010; Küng 2015). The terms 'religion', 'religiousness', and 'religiosity' have been used quite interchangeably in the extant literature. For example, Rest et al. (1986) use the term 'religion', while other scholars have adopted and refer more often to the term 'religiosity' (Wilkes, Burnett, and Howell 1986; McDaniel and Burnett 1990; Barnett, Bass, and Brown 1996) or 'religiousness' (Donahue 1985; Rest 1986; Clark and Dawson 1996; Kennedy and Lawton 1998; Siu, Dickinson, and Lee 2000). In general, religiousness or religiosity are the most frequently cited terms used to describe the strength of an individual's religious belief as reflected in their actions and behaviours.

Religiosity is perceived by some scholars as a multi-faceted and somewhat nebulous phenomenon that is difficult to define, measure, and conceptualise (Chaves 2010; Holdcroft 2006; Rossi and Scappini 2014). The complexity in defining religiosity can be ascribed to it becoming a popular interdisciplinary research topic; scholars from each discipline explore religiosity from a different angle, spawning multiple definitions of the topic (Holdcroft 2006). For example, theologians perceive religiosity from the vantage point of faith, while psychologists might address ideas of devotion and piousness. Further, sociologists consider the concept of religiosity to manifest intrinsically or extrinsically through private prayers and supplications, anonymous charity contributions, congregational prayers, church attendance, doctrinal knowledge, and strict adherence to religious tenets or precepts (Glock and Stark 1965). Stark and Glock (1968) describe religiosity as a broad multi-dimensional concept of religious orientation that includes an assortment of ritualistic, ideological, creedal, communal, moral, and cultural dimensions. Specifically, Stark and Glock (1968) defined religiosity as a form of religious commitment where loyal adherents of a religion would practice the religious tenets and lead a lifestyle that is consistent with said tenets. For the purpose of this study, we are adopting Stark and Glock's (1965) definition as it closely aligns with our research objectives.

Although the concept of religiosity has often been used interchangeably with that of spirituality in extant research, these two constructs are indeed different (Mattis 2000).

Spirituality underlies individuals' felt connection to something larger than life in a reverent and sacred manner (e.g. Elkins et al. (1988) and Potts (1991)). Whereas religiosity – as Zinnbauer et al. (1997) noted – is associated with the individual's level of adherence to the doctrines, beliefs, and ritual practices of religious institutions and the level of organisational religious involvement (e.g. church attendance). In a nutshell, religiosity naturally implies spirituality as it deals with the exercise of spirituality within an institutional context in which such spirituality is both individually and collectively practised.

Religiosity is seen to affect all stages of the ethical decision-making process and, in terms of pedagogy, religiosity was found to significantly shape learners' ethical sensitivity and the subsequent decisions they make when facing an ethical dilemma (Conroy and Emerson 2004; Quddus, Bailey Iii, and White 2009). Yet, no study to date has assessed the impact of religiosity on the moral and ethical decisions made by users in game-based learning environments. In light of these research gaps, this study attempts to answer the following two research questions:

Does religiosity influence the ethical attitudes and perceptions of individuals who are exposed to various ethically charged scenarios in a serious game? Does religiosity effectively inform the learning of ethical skills and knowledge in a practice-based virtual educational environment (serious game)?

THEORETICAL FRAMEWORK AND HYPOTHESES

Since the learning process in this research study is technology-mediated (a serious 3D game), specific technological factors must be taken into account when developing the theoretical framework and research hypotheses.

The 'seminal' technology acceptance model (TAM) has been widely applied in contemporary research studies to understand and predict how individuals use technologies and systems (Davis, Bagozzi, and Warshaw 1989; Kim and Malhotra 2005; Malhotra, Kim, and Patil 2006). The first claim of the TAM is that users will adopt a system if it is usable with minimum cognitive effort, i.e. perceived ease of use (Davis, Bagozzi, and Warshaw 1989; Davis 1993). In educational environments, the 'free' cognitive resources can help learners concentrate more on the learning task (Shen and Chu 2014) rather than on how to use a system (Venkatesh 2000; Sun et al. 2008), potentially resulting in prolonged use of the system (Roca and Gagné 2008; Tao, Hongxiu, and Yong 2010). Hence, the following hypothesis is posited:

H1: There is a positive relationship between perceived ease of use and users' perception of a serious gaming environment's effectiveness for learning practical ethical skills and knowledge.

Another antecedent to technology adoption is perceived usefulness. However, perceived usefulness is of limited importance in explaining the adoption or evaluation of a technology that is used for reasons other than its instrumental value. Moon and Kim (2001) contend that, depending on the specific technology being used, perceived usefulness can assume completely different contours and can be expressed by both extrinsic and intrinsic motivations (Ryan and Deci 2000). For example, when a technology is used for non-instrumental (utilitarian) reasons, usefulness can be substituted with playfulness, i.e. the extent to which a user enjoys using the technology (Davis, Bagozzi, and Warshaw 1992; Van der Heijden 2004). Users who enjoy using a system are more likely to perceive it as engaging and useful (Tractinsky, Katz, and Ikar 2000; Van der Heijden 2004; Sun and Zhang 2008). In addition, previous studies suggest that there is a positive association between the extent to which individuals enjoy using a game-based learning environment and their learning performance (Tractinsky, Katz, and Ikar 2000; Mun and Hwang 2003; Lee, Cheung, and Chen 2005). Thus, the following hypothesis is posited:

H2: There is a positive relationship between perceived playfulness and users' perception of a serious gaming environment's effectiveness for learning practical ethical skills and knowledge.

Individuals' motivation to engage with a game also depends on some extrinsic motivation, i.e. the rewards from its usage. In a gaming environment, extrinsic motivations are leveraged through a reward scheme that is part of the gamification concept, which stimulates the gamer's desire to accomplish specific functional results and goals (Marczewski 2013), such as earning points or badges, or leaderboard rankings (Nah et al. 2014; Landers 2014). Prior studies have shown that the presence of a reward scheme is positively related to a virtual game's ability to achieve its learning outcomes (Jagger, Siala, and Sloan 2015; Siala, Kutsch, and Jagger 2019). Thus, the following research hypothesis is posited:

H3: There is a positive relationship between the reward schemes provisioned in a serious game and users' perception of a serious gaming environment's effectiveness for learning practical ethical skills and knowledge.

Prior research suggests that ethical attitudes could translate into behavioural intentions, which involve adopting a specific ethical choice (Singhapakdi et al. 2000; Swimberghe, Flurry, and Parker 2011; Singhapakdi et al. 2013). Additionally, it has been postulated that religiosity can shape the ethical behaviour and decisions made by religious individuals (Wagner and Sanders 2001; Epstein 2002; Longenecker, McKinney, and Moore 2004; Ibrahim, Howard, and Angelidis 2008; Hogg, Adelman, and Blagg 2010; Salvador, Merchant, and Alexander 2014; Herman 2015), which subsequently leads them to make business decisions that resonate with socially responsible behaviour (Forsyth, O'Boyle Jr, and McDaniel 2008; Fernando and Chowdhury 2010; Lu and Lu 2010; Küng 2015; Syed and Van Buren 2015). Religious values can affect all stages of the ethical decision-making process and they can override organisational norms and influences (Longenecker, McKinney, and Moore 2004). Thus, collectively, these findings suggest the following hypotheses:

H4: Religiosity moderates positively the relationship between perceived ease of use and users' perception of a serious gaming environment's effectiveness for learning practical ethical skills and knowledge.
H5: Religiosity moderates positively the relationship between perceived playfulness and users' perception of a serious gaming environment's effectiveness for learning practical ethical skills and knowledge.
H6: Religiosity moderates positively the relationship between a serious game's reward scheme and users' perception of a serious gaming environment's effectiveness for learning practical ethical skills and knowledge.

METHODOLOGY

Serious 3D Ethics Game

Final year undergraduate business management students were asked to evaluate a serious 3D ethics game. The learning activities and tasks in the game were designed to align with the learning outcomes and curriculum of the taught course (Leemkuil and De Jong 2012) by incorporating theories and concepts from existing pedagogical materials used in teaching a business ethics module. Specifically, case studies involving real-life ethical decision-making scenarios were selected to be translated by a team of developers into interactive decision-making scenarios in the game. The game involves a marketing manager as the main character who has to face various ethical dilemmas in the workplace, which he/she needs to address by responding to a number of interactive questions that eventually lead to a decision. The players are presented with a reflective quiz at the end of each game level to enable them to think and consider how the decisions they made in the previous level could impact on different stakeholders. The game uses thought-provoking interactive dialogues to simulate concrete experience and active experimentation to enable the players to apply what they have learnt in practice. The visual settings and main controls for playing the game were designed to be familiar, simple, and intuitive. External motivations for incentivising learners to play and adopt the game include competitive features such as point accumulation, progression levels, and a leaderboard that displays players with the highest scores.

Data Collection

After briefing the participants about the aim of the study and assuring them that all data collected for this research will be anonymised, the participants were asked to sign an informed consent sheet. Each participant received a £10 Amazon voucher as a token of appreciation for his/her time to take part in this research. An online questionnaire was sent to participants of this study after they completed an induction course during the teaching term. The sample of participants consists of 383 final-year business management students who were enrolled in an undergraduate Business Ethics module in two British universities. The pedagogy, learning materials, and assessment types used for teaching the Business Ethics module were similar across the two universities.

Survey Instrument

The online questionnaire comprised of two parts: the first part included demographic questions (i.e. age, gender, religion, and ethnicity), questions about frequency of playing online games, and work experience. The second part included five-point Likert-type rating questions representing the observed variables used to measure the latent constructs, which were drawn from the existing literature and adapted to this article's research context (see Table 1). To address common method bias (CMB), the items on the questionnaire were displayed in a random order and some of the items used 'negatively' worded questions (Podsakoff et al. 2003).

Table 1. Measurement constructs and items used in this research study

Construct	Item label	Measurement*	Source
PESK	U2	The game will make ethical decisions easier in the future	(Jagger et al 2015)
	U3	I find the game useful to practice ethical decisions	
	U4	The game will make me more efficient at making ethical decisions	
	U5	Using this game helps me to make an ethical decision more quickly	
	U6	The game will improve my performance when making ethical decisions	
	TS1	It was easier to retain knowledge learned in this game than in a textbook or lecture	
	TS2	The game helped me appreciate the skills needed in ethical decision-making	
	TS3	From the game I have learned ethical decision-making skills which can apply in different situations	
	TS4	From the game I have acquired new knowledge useful in day to day business decisions	
	SL1	The game motivates me because it deals with real issues	
	SL2	The issues presented in this game helped me to see from others' perspectives rather than just my own	
	SL3	The game is close enough to real-life to be useful to me	
	SL4	I feel that I can make an appropriate ethical decision in the workplace after playing this game	
EOU	EOU1	To use this game, I would need expert help	(Davis et al. 1989, Kim and Malhotra 2005, Malhotra et al. 2006)
	EOU2	Learning how to play this game is easy for me	
	EOU3	It is easy to do what I want to do in the game	
	EOU4	The game was flexible to interact with in most types of play	
	EOU5	I find this game easy to use	
	EOU6	Interacting with the game is clear and understandable	
	EOU7	I could quickly become skillful at the game	
PP	PP1	I enjoyed playing the game	(Lee et al. 2005, Moon and Kim 2001, Tractinsky et al. 2000)
	PP2	I cared what happened to my character	
R	R1	I felt rewarded when I got points	(Yusoff et al. 2010)
	R2	I felt encouraged to learn more when I completed levels	
	R3	Gaining points motivates me to keep on playing	
	R4	I found that the points system was important to my learning	
RELIG	REL1	How important is religion to your way of life and your daily decisions?	(Glock and Stark 1965, Stark and Glock 1968)
	REL2	How often do you attend congregational prayers at your place of worship?	
	REL3	To lead a good life it is necessary to have some religious belief.	
	REL4**	I do not feel particularly attached to my religion/congregation.	

* Items were measured on a five-point Likert scale where 1 represents 'I totally disagree' and 5 represents 'I totally agree'. Items named REL1 and REL2 were measured on a 5-point Likert scale but used different descriptors: REL1 (1- Not important at all. 2 - Not too important. 3 - Fairly important. 4 - Quite important. 5. Extremely Important) REL2 (1 – Never. 2. Once a year or more. 3 - Once a month or more. 4 - Once a week or more – 5. Once a day or more)

**Reversed item

RESULTS

Of the 383 questionnaires sent to the participants, 366 students opted to participate in the survey (a response rate of 95.6%). After discarding missing cases and outliers using the Mahalanobis distance approach (Byrne 2016), there were 302 valid responses. There was a balanced gender representation in the sample, the age was also fairly representative of the type of respondents, and the ethnicity was also well represented (see Table 2). All the respondents were religious, as the first survey question aimed to detect atheists and precluded them from participating further in the survey.

Table 2. Demographic profiles, work and gaming experience of respondents (n=302)

Variable	Description	Frequency	Percentage
Sex	Male	115	38.1%
	Female	138	45.7%
	Not specified	49	16.2%
Age	< 17	1	0.3%
	18 - 24	260	86.1%
	25 - 34	33	10.9%
	35 - 44	4	1.3%
	45 – 54	4	1.3%
Religion	Muslim	42	13.9%
	Christian	97	32.1%
	Jewish	3	1%
	Hindu	9	3%
	Buddhist	14	4.6%
	Other or not specified	126	41.72%
	No religion	11	3.64%
Ethnicity	White	128	42.4%
	Black	30	9.9%
	Asian	125	41.4%
	Middle Eastern	7	2.3%
	Other	12	4.0%
Frequency of playing online games	Never	76	25.2%
	Seldom	66	21.9%
	Occasionally	83	27.5%
	Often	54	17.9%
	All of the Time	23	7.6%
Work experience	None	191	63.2%
	< 2 years	36	11.9%
	2 to 5 years	52	17.2%
	>5 years	23	7.6%

Measurement Model

The measurement model was tested using confirmatory factor analysis (CFA) in AMOS 24. The initial measurement model included all items used to measure the five investigated constructs: the users' perception of the serious gaming environment's ability to facilitate the learning of practical ethical skills and knowledge (PESK), perceived ease of use (EOU), perceived playfulness (PP), reward (R), and religiosity (RELIG). Eleven items were later removed and, subsequently, the reduced measurement model met the common quality guidelines (Byrne 2016). In particular, we discarded four items from the scale measuring RELIG, one item from the users' perception of the serious gaming environment's ability in facilitating the learning of PESK, three items from perceived EOU, and three items from PP. As shown in Table 3, the retained items had standardised loadings of .5 or more, Cronbach's α and Composite Reliability (CR) were both above .7, and AVE was above .5. The retained measures were thus judged to be valid and reliable.

Table 3. Model validity measures

	Cronbach alpha	CR	AVE	PESK	R	RELIG	PP	EOU	VIF[1]
PESK	0.957	0.956	0.757	**0.870**					N/A[2]
R	0.891	0.891	0.804	0.865***	**0.897**				2.046
RELIG	0.807	0.805	0.675	-0.070	-0.019	**0.821**			2.034
PP	0.733	0.731	0.578	0.433**	0.439***	0.122	**0.760**		1.183
EOU	0.897	0.897	0.745	0.816***	0.762***	-0.126	0.329***	**0.863**	1.897

Note: The values on the diagonal (in bold) represent the square root of the AVEs of the individual constructs and the values underneath the diagonal are the correlations between the constructs. 1=VIF values above 10 indicate multicollinearity; 2=VIF is used to test multicollinearity of predictor variables (not criterion variables). Significance of Correlations:

** p < 0.01; *** p < 0.001

The goodness-of-fit measures were satisfactory: χ^2=132.599; df=93; p < 0.01; CFI=0.990; GFI=0.948; AGFI=0.924; NFI=0.967; IFI=0.990; TLI=0.987; RMR=0.023 and RMSEA=0.038 (Hu and Bentler 1999; Byrne 2016). A Harman's one factor test was conducted to test for common method variance and, since the single factor solution accounted for approximately 40% of the variance, we assume that common method variance is not an issue in our data set (Podsakoff et al. 2003).

Multigroup Invariance of the Measurement Model

The measurement model was tested for multigroup invariance by splitting the sample into two groups of respondents based on their degree of religiosity (high and low religiosity). The high ($n = 140$) and low ($n = 162$) religious categories were derived from the sample using the median split method (Iacobucci et al. 2015) and the explained variance R^2 of the research model was compared to the regression results to determine if there are significant effects across the group. Three consecutive analyses were used to test the measurement model for configural invariance and metric invariance (Byrne 2016). According to Table 4, the satisfactory model fit indices of the measurement model (CFI=0.979; RMSEA=0.038) together with the insignificant CFI difference results suggest that the measurement model is multigroup invariant (Cheung and Rensvold 2002).

Table 4. Goodness-of-fit statistics of multigroup invariance for the measurement model

Model	χ^2	df	$\Delta\chi^2$	Δdf	p	CFI	ΔCFI	RMSEA
Original	264.847	186	-	-	.000	.979	-	.038
Model 1[a]	279.687	197	14.84	11	.000	.978	.001	.037
Model 2[b]	323.278	212	58.431	26	.000	.971	.008	.042

Notes: a = factor loadings constrained; b = factor loadings and intercepts constrained; Dc2 = Difference in c2 values between models; Ddf = Difference in number of degrees of freedom between models; DCFI = Difference in CFI values between models (where applicable);

Multigroup Invariance of the Structural Model

Besides testing for measurement invariance we also tested for invariance of the structural model to see if the model replicates consistently across the calibration and validation group (Byrne 2016). The calibration and validation groups were derived using a half-split random sampling method (Cudeck and Browne 1983), which involved splitting our sample ($n = 302$) into two random groups: sample A ($n = 151$) for the calibration group and sample B ($n = 151$) for the validation group. The model fit indices of the structural model were satisfactory (CFI=0.972; RMSEA= 0.05), suggesting that the hypothesised model of causal structure fits the data well (Byrne 2016) (see Table 5).

Table 5. Goodness-of-fit statistics of multigroup invariance for the structural model

Model	χ^2	df	$\Delta\chi^2$	Δdf	p	CFI	ΔCFI	RMSEA
Original	249.127	142	-	-	.000	.972	-	.050
Model 1[a]	253.942	152	4.815	10	.000	.973	.001	.047
Model 2[b]	261.753	155	12.626	13	.000	.972	.000	.048
Model 3[c]	270.246	159	21.12	17	.000	.971	.001	.048

Notes: a = measurement weights constrained; b = measurement weights and intercepts constrained; c = structural weights; Dc2 = Difference in c2 values between models; Ddf = Difference in number of degrees of freedom between models; DCFI = Difference in CFI values between models (where applicable);

Structural Model

SEM was used for testing the hypotheses and examining the relationships between key constructs. The model fit indices suggest that the hypothesised research fits the empirical data well (CFI=0.973; NFI=0.937; IFI=0.973; TLI=0.965; RMSEA=0.049). In addition, the R^2 for the dependent latent variable PESK is 0.898, implying that the predictors of PESK explain 89.8% of its variance.

As predicted, EOU and R have a significant effect on PESK; thus, H1 and H2 are supported. The results also support H3, which postulates that there is a positive association between PP and PESK. The magnitude of the standardised path coefficient values suggests that R (SPC=.563) is a more influential predictor for PESK than EOU (SPC=. 388) (see Table 6).

Table 6. Path analysis of the basic research model.

Direct or Indirect Effect (Hypothesis)	SPC[1]	Outcome
EOU → PESK (H$_1$)	.388***	Accept
R → PESK(H$_2$)	.563***	Accept
PP → PESK(H$_3$)	.071*	Accept

1=standardised path coefficient; * p<0.05; *** p < 0.001

In addition, a Pearson correlation test was conducted between learners' perceived and actual learning performance. Perceived learning is represented by the self-reported PESK construct and actual learning performance manifests in the players' final game scores. The results revealed that learners' perceived and actual learning performance are significantly correlated (r=.389*; p < 0.05); thus, learners who perceived the serious game to be an effective learning instrument have successfully applied the ethical theories and knowledge that they have acquired from classroom teaching.

The Moderating Role of Religiosity

According to Table 7, the structural path results from the SEM multigroup comparison indicate that the low and high religious groups found EOU and R in a serious gaming environment to be conducive to PESK; however, unlike the 'low religious' group, 'highly religious' learners find PP to not contribute significantly to PESK. The R^2 value of this model suggests that the low religious group predict about 22.8% less of the variation in the dependent latent variable PESK than their counterparts in the high religious group; thus, the high religious group explains the variation in the research model better than the low religious group.

Table 7. subgroup analysis of the basic research model (high vs low religiosity)

Effect	High Religiosity	Low Religiosity
EOU → PESK (H$_4$)	SPC=.351***	SPC=.373***
PP → PESK (H$_5$)	SPC=.061(n.s.)	SPC=.090**
R → PESK (H$_6$)	SPC=.633***	SPC=.515***
R^2	0.898 (0.898)	0.670 (0.818)

Note: values in brackets represent the R^2 of the baseline model; ** p<0.01;*** p < 0.001; n.s.: non-significant

DISCUSSION

The aim of this study was to explore (i) whether religiosity influences ethical attitudes and perceptions when individuals are exposed to various ethically charged scenarios in a serious gaming environment and (ii) whether religiosity shapes the learning of practical ethical skills and knowledge in the context of a serious gaming environment. The research model was tested through a cross-sectional survey administered on a sample of final-year business students from two UK academic institutions. The respondents were placed into a 'high religious' or 'low religious' group based on how they scored on the religiosity scale.

The results confirm the three TAM-related hypotheses, i.e. that EOU, PP, and R contribute significantly to users' perception of the effectiveness of a serious game in facilitating the learning of PESK, which concurs with prior research (Smith, Simpson, and Huang 2007; Hwang et al. 2008; Shafer and Simmons 2011; Jagger, Siala, and Sloan 2015). It also confirms the premise that TAM is suitable for a research context that involves technology enhanced learning or, to be more specific, virtual educational learning environments such as serious games.

According to the results, amongst the three hypothesised antecedents of PESK, the reward scheme (R) was the most influential predictor of users' post-hoc assessment of the game. Thus, to be perceived as pedagogically effective, serious games must address the extrinsic motivations of players, such as their desire to be rewarded. However, regardless of the fact that R accounted for the highest variance in PESK, the role of EOU and PP should not be downplayed; if the serious game was not user-friendly or fun to play, EOU and PP would have had a more significant impact on the post-usage evaluations of the game.

The results from the multigroup analysis of the low and high religious group suggest that PP seems to discriminate between these two groups; learners in the low religious group consider PP to contribute significantly to PESK, but this effect does not replicate in the high religious group. Religious individuals may have perceived the 'playful' aspect of the game to be sacrilegious to the substantive role that religion plays in the ethical decision-making process. To elaborate, religiously zealous learners would ensure that 'hedonic' distractions such as playing a game do not overshadow the overarching ethical precepts sourced from spiritual guidance, specifically when a moral or ethical decision is being contemplated. The case of misconstrued perception between playfulness and religion was also illustrated by Droogers et al (2006, 86).

The higher playfulness displayed by the low religious group can also be explained from a motivational perspective. The low religious group displayed higher levels of intrinsic motivation as evidenced by their comparatively higher EOU and PP scores. In contrast, the high religious group displayed higher extrinsic motivation as evidenced by their comparatively higher R score, which suggests that the high religious group perceive the utilitarian point-scoring mechanisms of the serious game to contribute more to learning soft skills such as ethics than the hedonic aspects of the game. Therefore, religious individuals seem to apply the religiously inspired tenet of strictly adhering to virtue and morality to subsequently be rewarded for good deeds (Vitell and Paolillo 2003) by emphasising the collection of points or rewards gained as part of their learning journey and experience. This finding suggests that in the realm of serious games, religiously informed ethical precepts could persevere and affect the ethical perceptions and decisions of religious individuals.

MANAGERIAL AND PRACTICAL IMPLICATIONS

The findings of this article have several managerial implications for two target audiences: educators and business managers. Regarding educators, the findings suggest that when contemplating the use of a virtual educational gaming environment for teaching business ethics, educators should evaluate and choose games that are easy to use, sufficiently entertaining and include features that generally address the extrinsic motivations of learners such as built-in reward schemes. We suggest that educators facilitate training sessions to support learners who may feel apprehended by new and unfamiliar technologies (Daspit and D'Souza 2012), as learners may otherwise invest more effort into learning how to play rather than assimilating the educational learning outcomes represented in the game. The training intervention should involve student peers who are avid gamers, as peer-trainers can attenuate computer anxiety (Galletta et al. 1995; Francescato et al. 2006; Huber and Lewis 2010) and enhance the learning experience of novice learners (Mahar, Henderson, and Deane 1997; Piccoli, Ahmad, and Ives 2001; Hackbarth, Grover, and Mun 2003; Ke 2008; Jasperson, Carter, and Zmud 2005; Francescato et al. 2006; Venkatesh and Bala 2008; Sun et al. 2008; Saadé and Kira 2009; Huber and Lewis 2010).

In addition, although the results have underlined the instrumental role of religiosity as a moderator, other individual-level variables should also be considered. For example, religious individuals seem to be more extrinsically driven by utilitarian aspects of the game, specifically the built-in reward schemes. It could be worthwhile investigating whether the inclusion of religious narratives such as short passages from the Bible, the Quran, or other sacred texts, or religious symbols and cues in the serious game will significantly inform the ethical decisions made by religious individuals. In addition to making the game entertaining, the design of the serious game should take into account cultural differences such as religion, as our findings have demonstrated that for religious individuals, the conscientious role of religiosity overshadows the entertainment aspect of the game.

Finally, we advise business managers to employ serious games as a training platform for the professional development of existing and prospective staff. Our findings suggest that serious games are effective in imbuing individuals with key soft managerial skills such as ethics. Additionally, serious games can be used as a viable, affordable, and entertaining alternative for nurturing an organisational culture that promotes ethical behaviour in its employees.

LIMITATIONS AND FURTHER RESEARCH

The results and implications of this article should be seen in light of its limitations. The first limitation relates to the sampling strategy of this research study. We used convenience sampling, which according to some researchers limits the generalisability of the results; however, this sampling strategy seems to fit the target population (students) of this study. Further studies are needed to test the validity of our proposed empirical model on different populations like graduate students who are working as interns in companies, as well as employees in different stages of their corporate career.

The second limitation pertains to the measurement of religiosity and the related scale that was first developed by Glock and Stark (1965) and Stark and Glock (1968), drawing from the sociology of religion. There are many dimensions that these authors and others have operationalised for the religiosity measurement scale, such as the intellectual, ideological, ritualistic, experiential, public versus private practice, and consequential dimensions. Thus, religiosity is a complex phenomenon to measure for several reasons that are mostly related to identifying the representative dimensions of this phenomenon, the generalizability of the religious content, and parsimony of measurement scales. In this paper, we decided to accentuate the parsimony of the measurement scale by using a set of observed variables (Siala, O'Keefe, and Hone 2004; Azam et al. 2013) to detect the core items of religiosity. This strategy helped to reduce the questionnaire length and maximise the response rate. Future research could use a more extended scale and verify the dimensions of religiosity that are more likely to affect users' perceptions of a serious gaming environment's ability to facilitate the learning of practical ethical skills and knowledge.

Another limitation is that the level of individual ethics was not included in our research framework. Future research should investigate the effect of religiosity on the individual level of ethics and, in turn, the impact that individual ethics can play on users' perception of the serious gaming environment. The inclusion of this additional variable could shed light on whether some serious games are more effective than others in facilitating the learning of practical ethical skills and knowledge.

Finally, a further limitation relates to the number of moderating variables used. The research aimed to look at the role of religiosity as a moderator; however, there is a myriad of possible moderating variables that could subjectively impact on the serious game's ability to fulfil its learning outcomes. For example, a comparison can be drawn between risk-averse individuals versus risk-seekers when they interact with different ethical business scenarios.

REFERENCES

Allal-Chérif, O., & Makhlouf, M. (2016). Using serious games to manage knowledge: The SECI model perspective. *Journal of Business Research, 69*(5), 1539–1543. doi:10.1016/j.jbusres.2015.10.013

Armstrong, S. J. (2011). From the editors: Continuing our quest for meaningful impact on management practice. Academy of Management Learning & Education, 10(2), 181-7.

Ashkanasy, N. M. (2006). Introduction: Arguments for a more grounded approach in management education. *Academy of Management Learning & Education, 5*(2), 207–208. doi:10.5465/amle.2006.21253785

Azam, A., Qiang, F., Abbas, S. A., & Abdullah, M. I. (2013). Structural equation modeling (SEM) based trust analysis of Muslim consumers in the collective religion affiliation model in e-commerce. *Journal of Islamic Marketing, 4*(2), 134–149. doi:10.1108/17590831311329278

Baden, D., & Higgs, M. (2015). Challenging the perceived wisdom of management theories and practice. *Academy of Management Learning & Education, 14*(4), 539–555. doi:10.5465/amle.2014.0170

Barnett, T., Bass, K., & Brown, G. (1996). Religiosity, ethical ideology, and intentions to report a peer's wrongdoing. *Journal of Business Ethics, 15*(11), 1161–1174. doi:10.1007/BF00412815

Boyle, E. A., Hainey, T., Connolly, T. M., Gray, G., Earp, J., Ott, M., Lim, T., Ninaus, M., Ribeiro, C., & Pereira, J. (2016). An update to the systematic literature review of empirical evidence of the impacts and outcomes of computer games and serious games. *Computers & Education, 94*, 178–192. doi:10.1016/j.compedu.2015.11.003

Bridget, B., & Andrea, T. (2011). Do avatars dream of electronic picket lines?: The blurring of work and play in virtual environments. *Information Technology & People, 24*(1), 26–45. doi:10.1108/09593841111109404

Byrne, B. M. (2016). *Structural equation modeling with AMOS: Basic concepts, applications, and programming*. Routledge. doi:10.4324/9781315757421

Chaves, M. (2010). SSSR Presidential Address Rain Dances in the Dry Season: Overcoming the Religious Congruence Fallacy. *Journal for the Scientific Study of Religion, 49*(1), 1–14. doi:10.1111/j.1468-5906.2009.01489.x

Cheung, G. W., & Rensvold, R. B. (2002). Evaluating goodness-of-fit indexes for testing measurement invariance. *Structural Equation Modeling, 9*(2), 233–255. doi:10.1207/S15328007SEM0902_5

Clark, J. W., & Dawson, L. E. (1996). Personal religiousness and ethical judgements: An empirical analysis. *Journal of Business Ethics, 15*(3), 359–372. doi:10.1007/BF00382959

Conroy, S. J., & Emerson, T. L. N. (2004). Business ethics and religion: Religiosity as a predictor of ethical awareness among students. *Journal of Business Ethics*, *50*(4), 383–396. doi:10.1023/B:BUSI.0000025040.41263.09

Craft, J. L. (2013). A Review of the Empirical Ethical Decision-Making Literature: 2004–2011. *Journal of Business Ethics*, *117*(2), 221–259. doi:10.100710551-012-1518-9

Crookall, D. (2010). Serious games, debriefing, and simulation/gaming as a discipline. *Simulation & Gaming*, *41*(6), 898–920. doi:10.1177/1046878110390784

Cudeck, R., & Browne, M. W. (1983). Cross-validation of covariance structures. *Multivariate Behavioral Research*, *18*(2), 147–167. doi:10.120715327906mbr1802_2 PMID:26781606

Daspit, J. J., & D'Souza, D. E. (2012). Using the community of inquiry framework to introduce wiki environments in blended-learning pedagogies: Evidence from a business capstone course. *Academy of Management Learning & Education*, *11*(4), 666–683. doi:10.5465/amle.2010.0154

Davis, F. D. (1993). *User acceptance of information technology: system characteristics, user perceptions and behavioral impacts*. Academic Press.

Davis, F. D., Bagozzi, R. P., & Warshaw, P. R. (1989). User Acceptance of Computer-Technology - A Comparison of 2 Theoretical-Models. *Management Science*, *35*(8), 982–1003. doi:10.1287/mnsc.35.8.982

Davis, F. D., Bagozzi, R. P., & Warshaw, P. R. (1992). Extrinsic and intrinsic motivation to use computers in the workplace. *Journal of Applied Social Psychology*, *22*(14), 1111–1132. doi:10.1111/j.1559-1816.1992.tb00945.x

Donahue, M. J. (1985). Intrinsic and extrinsic religiousness: Review and meta-analysis. *Journal of Personality and Social Psychology*, *48*(2), 400–419. doi:10.1037/0022-3514.48.2.400

Droogers, A. F., van Harskamp, A., Clarke, P. B., Davie, G., & Versteeg, P. (2006). Playful Religion: Challenges for the Study of Religion. Uitgeverij B.V.

Egri, C. P. (2013). From the editors: Context matters in management education scholarship. Academy of Management Learning & Education, 12(2), 155-7. doi:10.5465/amle.2013.0140

Elkins, D. N., Hedstrom, L. J., Hughes, L. L., Leaf, J. A., & Saunders, C. (1988). Toward a humanistic-phenomenological spirituality: Definition, description, and measurement. *Journal of Humanistic Psychology*, *28*(4), 5–18. doi:10.1177/0022167888284002

Epstein, E. M. (2002). Religion and business–the critical role of religious traditions in management education. *Journal of Business Ethics*, *38*(1-2), 91–96. doi:10.1023/A:1015712827640

Felton, E. L., & Sims, R. R. (2005). Teaching business ethics: Targeted outputs. *Journal of Business Ethics*, *60*(4), 377–391. doi:10.100710551-004-8206-3

Fernando, M., & Chowdhury, R. M. M. I. (2010). The relationship between spiritual well-being and ethical orientations in decision making: An empirical study with business executives in Australia. *Journal of Business Ethics*, *95*(2), 211–225. doi:10.100710551-009-0355-y

Forsyth, D. R., O'Boyle, E. H. Jr, & McDaniel, M. A. (2008). East meets west: A meta-analytic investigation of cultural variations in idealism and relativism. *Journal of Business Ethics, 83*(4), 813–833. doi:10.100710551-008-9667-6

Francescato, D., Porcelli, R., Mebane, M., Cuddetta, M., Klobas, J., & Renzi, P. (2006). Evaluation of the efficacy of collaborative learning in face-to-face and computer-supported university contexts. *Computers in Human Behavior, 22*(2), 163–176. doi:10.1016/j.chb.2005.03.001

Galletta, D. F., Ahuja, M., Hartman, A., Teo, T., & Graham Peace, A. (1995). Social influence and end-user training. *Communications of the ACM, 38*(7), 70–79. doi:10.1145/213859.214800

Garris, R., Ahlers, R., & Driskell, J. E. (2002). Games, motivation, and learning: A research and practice model. *Simulation & Gaming, 33*(4), 441–467. doi:10.1177/1046878102238607

Glock, C. Y., & Stark, R. (1965). *Religion and Society in Tension, Rand McNally Sociology Series*. Rand McNally & Company.

Hackbarth, G., Grover, V., & Yi Mun, Y. (2003). Computer playfulness and anxiety: Positive and negative mediators of the system experience effect on perceived ease of use. *Information & Management, 40*(3), 221–232. doi:10.1016/S0378-7206(02)00006-X

Hardy, C., & Tolhurst, D. (2014). Epistemological beliefs and cultural diversity matters in management education and learning: A critical review and future directions. *Academy of Management Learning & Education, 13*(2), 265–289. doi:10.5465/amle.2012.0063

Herman, S. W. (2015). Spirituality, Inc.: Religion in the American Workplace, by Lake Lambert III. New York: New York University Press, 2009. *Business Ethics Quarterly, 21*(3), 533–537. doi:10.5840/beq201121330

Hess, T., & Gunter, G. (2013). Serious game-based and nongame-based online courses: Learning experiences and outcomes. *British Journal of Educational Technology, 44*(3), 372–385. doi:10.1111/bjet.12024

Ho, J. A. (2010). Ethical perception: Are differences between ethnic groups situation dependent? *Business Ethics (Oxford, England), 19*(2), 154–182. doi:10.1111/j.1467-8608.2010.01583.x

Hogg, M. A., Adelman, J. R., & Blagg, R. D. (2010). Religion in the face of uncertainty: An uncertainty-identity theory account of religiousness. *Personality and Social Psychology Review, 14*(1), 72–83. doi:10.1177/1088868309349692 PMID:19855094

Holdcroft, B. (2006). What is religiosity. *Catholic Education: A Journal of Inquiry and Practice, 10*(1).

Hu & Bentler. (1999). Cutoff criteria for fit indexes in covariance structure analysis: conventional criteria versus new alternatives. *Structural Equation Modeling, 6*(1), 1–55.

Huber, G. P., & Lewis, K. (2010). Cross-understanding: Implications for group cognition and performance. *Academy of Management Review, 35*(1), 6–26.

Hwang, D., Staley, B., Te Chen, Y., & Lan, J.-S. (2008). Confucian culture and whistle-blowing by professional accountants: An exploratory study. *Managerial Auditing Journal, 23*(5), 504–526. doi:10.1108/02686900810875316

Iacobucci, D., Posavac, S. S., Kardes, F. R., Schneider, M. J., & Popovich, D. L. (2015). The median split: Robust, refined, and revived. *Journal of Consumer Psychology, 25*(4), 690–704. doi:10.1016/j.jcps.2015.06.014

Ibrahim, N. A., Howard, D. P., & Angelidis, J. P. (2008). The relationship between religiousness and corporate social responsibility orientation: Are there differences between business managers and students? *Journal of Business Ethics, 78*(1-2), 165–174. doi:10.100710551-006-9321-0

Jagger, S., Siala, H., & Sloan, D. (2015). It's All in the Game: A 3D Learning Model for Business Ethics. *Journal of Business Ethics, 137*(2), 383–403. doi:10.100710551-015-2557-9

Jang & Ryu. (2011). Exploring game experiences and game leadership in massively multiplayer online role-playing games. *British Journal of Educational Technology, 42*(4), 616-23. . doi:10.1111/j.1467-8535.2010.01064.x

Jasperson, J. S., Carter, & Zmud. (2005). A comprehensive conceptualization of post-adoptive behaviors associated with information technology enabled work systems. *Management Information Systems Quarterly, 29*(3), 525–557. doi:10.2307/25148694

Jouriles, E. N., McDonald, R., Kullowatz, A., Rosenfield, D., Gomez, G. S., & Cuevas, A. (2009). Can virtual reality increase the realism of role plays used to teach college women sexual coercion and rape-resistance skills? *Behavior Therapy, 40*(4), 337–345. doi:10.1016/j.beth.2008.09.002 PMID:19892079

Ke, F. (2008). Computer games application within alternative classroom goal structures: Cognitive, metacognitive, and affective evaluation. *Educational Technology Research and Development, 56*(5-6), 539–556. doi:10.100711423-008-9086-5

Kennedy, E. J., & Lawton, L. (1998). Religiousness and business ethics. *Journal of Business Ethics, 17*(2), 163–175. doi:10.1023/A:1005747511116

Kim, S. S., & Malhotra, N. K. (2005). A longitudinal model of continued IS use: An integrative view of four mechanisms underlying postadoption phenomena. *Management Science, 51*(5), 741–755. doi:10.1287/mnsc.1040.0326

Kolb, D. (1984). *Experiential learning as the science of learning and development.* Prentice Hall.

Küng, H. (2015). A Global Ethic in an Age of Globalization. *Business Ethics Quarterly, 7*(3), 17–32. doi:10.2307/3857310

Landers, R. N. (2014). Developing a Theory of Gamified Learning:Linking Serious Games and Gamification of Learning. *Simulation & Gaming, 45*(6), 752–768. doi:10.1177/1046878114563660

Lavender, T. J. (2008). *Homeless: It's no game-measuring the effectiveness of a persuasive videogame.* School of Interactive Arts & Technology-Simon Fraser University.

Lee, Cheung, & Chen. (2005). Acceptance of Internet-based learning medium: the role of extrinsic and intrinsic motivation. *Information & Management, 42*(8), 1095-104.

Leemkuil, H., & De Jong, T. O. N. (2012). Adaptive advice in learning with a computer-based knowledge management simulation game. *Academy of Management Learning & Education, 11*(4), 653–665. doi:10.5465/amle.2010.0141

Liu, Li, & Santhanam. (2013). Digital Games and Beyond: What Happens When Players Compete. *MIS Quarterly, 37*(1), 111-24.

Longenecker, J. G., McKinney, J. A., & Moore, C. W. (2004). Religious intensity, evangelical Christianity, and business ethics: An empirical study. *Journal of Business Ethics, 55*(4), 371–384. doi:10.100710551-004-0990-2

Lu, L.-C., & Lu, C.-J. (2010). Moral Philosophy, Materialism, and Consumer Ethics: An Exploratory Study in Indonesia. *Journal of Business Ethics, 94*(2), 193–210. doi:10.100710551-009-0256-0

Mahar, D., Henderson, R., & Deane, F. (1997). The effects of computer anxiety, state anxiety, and computer experience on users' performance of computer based tasks. *Personality and Individual Differences, 22*(5), 683–692. doi:10.1016/S0191-8869(96)00260-7

Malhotra, N. K., Kim, S. S., & Patil, A. (2006). Common method variance in IS research: A comparison of alternative approaches and a reanalysis of past research. *Management Science, 52*(12), 1865–1883. doi:10.1287/mnsc.1060.0597

Marczewski, A. (2013). *Gamification: A Simple Introduction*. Andrzej Marczewski.

Mattis, J. S. (2000). African American women's definitions of spirituality and religiosity. *The Journal of Black Psychology, 26*(1), 101–122. doi:10.1177/0095798400026001006

McDaniel, S. W., & Burnett, J. J. (1990). Consumer religiosity and retail store evaluative criteria. *Journal of the Academy of Marketing Science, 18*(2), 101–112. doi:10.1007/BF02726426

Michaelson, C. (2016). A novel approach to business ethics education: Exploring how to live and work in the 21st century. *Academy of Management Learning & Education, 15*(3), 588–606. doi:10.5465/amle.2014.0129

Michalos, A. C. (1982). Purpose and policy. *Journal of Business Ethics, 1*(4), 331.

Moon, J.-W., & Kim, Y.-G. (2001). Extending the TAM for a World-Wide-Web context. *Information & Management, 38*(4), 217–230. doi:10.1016/S0378-7206(00)00061-6

Mun, Y. (2003). Predicting the use of web-based information systems: Self-efficacy, enjoyment, learning goal orientation, and the technology acceptance model. *International Journal of Human-Computer Studies, 59*(4), 431–449. doi:10.1016/S1071-5819(03)00114-9

Mustar, P. (2009). Technology management education: Innovation and entrepreneurship at MINES ParisTech, a leading French engineering school. *Academy of Management Learning & Education, 8*(3), 418–425.

Nah, F. F.-H., Zeng, Q., Telaprolu, V. R., Ayyappa, A. P., & Eschenbrenner, B. (2014). Gamification of Education: A Review of Literature. Academic Press.

Newbery, R., Lean, J., & Moizer, J. (2016). Evaluating the impact of serious games: The effect of gaming on entrepreneurial intent. *Information Technology & People, 29*(4), 733–749. doi:10.1108/ITP-05-2015-0111

Newbery, R., Lean, J., Moizer, J., & Haddoud, M. (2018). Entrepreneurial identity formation during the initial entrepreneurial experience: The influence of simulation feedback and existing identity. *Journal of Business Research*, *85*, 51–59. doi:10.1016/j.jbusres.2017.12.013

Peifer, J. L. (2015). The Inter-Institutional Interface of Religion and Business. *Business Ethics Quarterly*, *25*(3), 363–391. doi:10.1017/beq.2015.33

Pfeffer, J., & Fong, C. T. (2004). The business school 'business': Some lessons from the US experience. *Journal of Management Studies*, *41*(8), 1501–1520. doi:10.1111/j.1467-6486.2004.00484.x

Piccoli, G., Ahmad, R., & Ives, B. (2001). Web-based virtual learning environments: A research framework and a preliminary assessment of effectiveness in basic IT skills training. *Management Information Systems Quarterly*, *25*(4), 401–426. doi:10.2307/3250989

Podsakoff, P. M., MacKenzie, S. B., Lee, J.-Y., & Podsakoff, N. P. (2003). Common method biases in behavioral research: A critical review of the literature and recommended remedies. *The Journal of Applied Psychology*, *88*(5), 879–903. doi:10.1037/0021-9010.88.5.879 PMID:14516251

Potts, R. (1991). Spirits in the bottle: Spirituality and alcoholism treatment in African-American communities. *Journal of Training & Practice in Professional Psychology*.

Quddus, M., Iii, H. B., & White, L. R. (2009). Business ethics: Perspectives from Judaic, Christian, and Islamic scriptures. *Journal of Management, Spirituality & Religion*, *6*(4), 323–334. doi:10.1080/14766080903290143

Rest, J. R. (1986). *Moral development: Advances in research and theory*. Praeger publishers.

Reyes, D. L. Jr, & Gaston, T. W. K. (2017). Teaching ethics in business schools: A conversation on disciplinary differences, academic provincialism, and the case for integrated pedagogy. *Academy of Management Learning & Education*, *16*(2), 314–336. doi:10.5465/amle.2014.0402

Roca, J. C., & Gagné, M. (2008). Understanding e-learning continuance intention in the workplace: A self-determination theory perspective. *Computers in Human Behavior*, *24*(4), 1585–1604. doi:10.1016/j.chb.2007.06.001

Rossi, M., & Scappini, E. (2014). Church Attendance, Problems of Measurement, and Interpreting Indicators: A Study of Religious Practice in the United States, 1975–2010. *Journal for the Scientific Study of Religion*, *53*(2), 249–267. doi:10.1111/jssr.12115

Ruggiero, T. E. (2000). Uses and gratifications theory in the 21st century. *Mass Communication & Society*, *3*(1), 3–37. doi:10.1207/S15327825MCS0301_02

Ryan, R. M., & Deci, E. L. (2000). Intrinsic and Extrinsic Motivations: Classic Definitions and New Directions. *Contemporary Educational Psychology*, *25*(1), 54–67. doi:10.1006/ceps.1999.1020 PMID:10620381

Saadé, R. G., & Kira, D. (2009). Computer anxiety in e-learning: The effect of computer self-efficacy. *Journal of Information Technology Education*, *8*.

Salas, Wildman, & Piccolo. (2009). Using simulation-based training to enhance management education. *Academy of Management Learning & Education*, *8*(4), 559–573.

Salvador, R. O., Merchant, A., & Alexander, E. A. (2014). Faith and fair trade: The moderating role of contextual religious salience. *Journal of Business Ethics*, *121*(3), 353–371. doi:10.100710551-013-1728-9

Seele, P. (2018). What makes a business ethicist? A reflection on the transition from applied philosophy to critical thinking. *Journal of Business Ethics*, *150*(3), 647–656. doi:10.100710551-016-3177-8

Shafer, W. E., & Simmons, R. S. (2011). Effects of organizational ethical culture on the ethical decisions of tax practitioners in mainland China. *Accounting, Auditing & Accountability Journal*, *24*(5), 647–668. doi:10.1108/09513571111139139

Shen, C.-Y., & Chu, H.-P. (2014). *The relations between interface design of digital game-based learning systems and flow experience and cognitive load of learners with different levels of prior knowledge*. Paper presented at the International Conference on Cross-Cultural Design. 10.1007/978-3-319-07308-8_55

Siala, H., Kutsch, E., & Jagger, S. (2019). Cultural influences moderating learners' adoption of serious 3D games for managerial learning. *Information Technology & People*, *33*(2), 424–455. doi:10.1108/ITP-08-2018-0385

Siala, H., O'Keefe, R. M., & Hone, K. S. (2004). The Impact of Religious Affiliation on Trust in the Context of Electronic Commerce. *Interacting with Computers*, *16*(1), 7–27. doi:10.1016/j.intcom.2003.11.002

Singhapakdi, A., Marta, J. K., Rallapalli, K. C., & Rao, C. P. (2000). Toward an Understanding of Religiousness and Marketing Ethics: An Empirical Study. *Journal of Business Ethics*, *27*(4), 305–319. doi:10.1023/A:1006342224035

Singhapakdi, A., Vitell, S. J., Lee, D.-J., Nisius, A. M., & Yu, G. B. (2013). The influence of love of money and religiosity on ethical decision-making in marketing. *Journal of Business Ethics*, *114*(1), 183–191. doi:10.100710551-012-1334-2

Siu, Dickinson, & Lee. (2000). Ethical evaluations of business activities and personal religiousness. *Teaching Business Ethics, 4*(3), 239-56.

Smith, N., Simpson, S. S., & Huang, C.-Y. (2007). Why managers fail to do the right thing: An empirical study of unethical and illegal conduct. *Business Ethics Quarterly*, *17*(4), 633–667. doi:10.5840/beq20071743

Stark, R., & Glock, C. Y. (1968). *American Piety: The Nature of Religious Commitment*. University of California Press.

Sun, H., & Zhang, P. (2008). An exploration of affect factors and their role in user technology acceptance: Mediation and causality. *Journal of the Association for Information Science and Technology*, *59*(8), 1252–1263.

Sun, P.-C., Tsai, R. J., Finger, G., Chen, Y.-Y., & Yeh, D. (2008). What drives a successful e-Learning? An empirical investigation of the critical factors influencing learner satisfaction. *Computers & Education*, *50*(4), 1183–1202. doi:10.1016/j.compedu.2006.11.007

Swimberghe, K., Flurry, L. A., & Parker, J. M. (2011). Consumer religiosity: Consequences for consumer activism in the United States. *Journal of Business Ethics*, *103*(3), 453–467. doi:10.100710551-011-0873-2

Swimberghe, K. R., Sharma, D., & Flurry, L. W. (2011). Does a consumer's religion really matter in the buyer–seller dyad? An empirical study examining the relationship between consumer religious commitment, Christian conservatism and the ethical judgment of a seller's controversial business decision. *Journal of Business Ethics*, *102*(4), 581–598. doi:10.100710551-011-0829-6

Syed, J., & Van Buren, H. J. III. (2015). Global Business Norms and Islamic Views of Women's Employment. *Business Ethics Quarterly*, *24*(2), 251–276. doi:10.5840/beq201452910

Tao, Z., Li, H., & Yong, L. (2010). The effect of flow experience on mobile SNS users' loyalty. *Industrial Management & Data Systems*, *110*(6), 930–946. doi:10.1108/02635571011055126

Tractinsky, N., Katz, A. S., & Ikar, D. (2000). What is beautiful is usable. *Interacting with Computers*, *13*(2), 127–145. doi:10.1016/S0953-5438(00)00031-X

Tsekleves, E., Cosmas, J., & Aggoun, A. (2016). Benefits, barriers and guideline recommendations for the implementation of serious games in education for stakeholders and policymakers. *British Journal of Educational Technology*, *47*(1), 164–183. doi:10.1111/bjet.12223

Van der Heijden, H. (2004). User acceptance of hedonic information systems. *Management Information Systems Quarterly*, *28*(4), 695–704. doi:10.2307/25148660

Venkatesh, V. (2000). Determinants of perceived ease of use: Integrating control, intrinsic motivation, and emotion into the technology acceptance model. *Information Systems Research*, *11*(4), 342–365. doi:10.1287/isre.11.4.342.11872

Venkatesh, V., & Bala, H. (2008). Technology acceptance model 3 and a research agenda on interventions. *Decision Sciences*, *39*(2), 273–315. doi:10.1111/j.1540-5915.2008.00192.x

Vitell, S. J. (2009). The Role of Religiosity in Business and Consumer Ethics: A Review of the Literature. *Journal of Business Ethics*, *90*(2), 155–167. doi:10.100710551-010-0382-8

Vitell, S. J., & Paolillo, J. G. P. (2003). Consumer ethics: The role of religiosity. *Journal of Business Ethics*, *46*(2), 151–162. doi:10.1023/A:1025081005272

Wagner, S. C., & Lawrence Sanders, G. (2001). Considerations in ethical decision-making and software piracy. *Journal of Business Ethics*, *29*(1-2), 161–167. doi:10.1023/A:1006415514200

Weaver, G. R., & Agle, B. R. (2002). Religiosity and ethical behavior in organizations: A symbolic interactionist perspective. *Academy of Management Review*, *27*(1), 77–97. doi:10.2307/4134370

Weibull, L. (1985). Structural factors in gratifications research. *Media gratifications research: Current perspectives*, 123-47.

Werner, J. S., & James, W. T. Jr. (2001). *Communication Theories: Origins, Methods and Uses in the Mass Media*. Addison Wesley Longman, Inc.

Wilkes, R. E., Burnett, J. J., & Howell, R. D. (1986). On the meaning and measurement of religiosity in consumer research. *Journal of the Academy of Marketing Science*, *14*(1), 47–56. doi:10.1007/BF02722112

Wouters, Van der Spek, & Van Oostendorp. (2009). Current practices in serious game research: A review from a learning outcomes perspective. In Games-based learning advancements for multi-sensory human computer interfaces: techniques and effective practices. IGI Global.

Zinnbauer, B. J., Pargament, K. I., Cole, B., Rye, M. S., Butter, E. M., Belavich, T. G., Hipp, K. M., Scott, A. B., & Kadar, J. L. (1997). Religion and spirituality: Unfuzzying the fuzzy. *Journal for the Scientific Study of Religion*, *36*(4), 549–564. doi:10.2307/1387689

Chapter 27
A Game–Based Content and Language–Integrated Learning Practice for Environmental Awareness (ENVglish):
User Perceptions

Meltem Huri Baturay
https://orcid.org/0000-0003-2402-6275
Atilim University, Turkey

Ahmet Erdost Yastibaş
Gazi University, Turkey

Gonca Yangin Ekşi
Gazi University, Turkey

Cafer Ahmet Çinar
https://orcid.org/0000-0002-3799-4331
Çanakkale Onsekiz Mart University, Turkey

ABSTRACT

Increasing human activities in the environment have created severe effects; therefore, handling such effects by raising environmental awareness through several ways has become significant to sustain the environment, which can enhance 21st century skills including critical thinking and information literacy. Digital games can be used for this because they create an environment for learning with higher engagement, motivation, and excitement besides fostering cognitive attainment and retention. Accordingly, a mobile game-based content and language-integrated learning practice (an educational digital game called ENVglish) was developed to raise EFL students' environmental awareness in this qualitative study. During the design and development phases of the game, students' and teachers' perceptions regarding it were collected with semi-structured interviews. The data were content analyzed. The findings indicated that both students and teachers had positive perceptions about the game and that students could improve their English and have environmental awareness with the game.

DOI: 10.4018/978-1-7998-7271-9.ch027

INTRODUCTION

Teaching a foreign or second language involves more than teaching about the language. Language teaching should be for effective communication. English language teachers do not, or should not, teach English itself, that is, grammar, verbs, conjugation and so on solely. They should focus on other subject matter and bring real world issues into the classroom. They might also foster 21st century skills through learner autonomy, group work, projects and communicative games. To meet the demands of the 21st century and a new generation of digital native learners, language teaching should be incorporated with cross-curricular subjects and be enriched with educational technologies. This study exemplifies an attempt to incorporate digital games and green practices to improve students' awareness and understanding of environmental sustainability.

The current study aims to investigate how English language learning K12 students and their teachers perceive the game developed in terms of its pedagogical and visual design and from the point of students' English language and environmental awareness gains. To this end, an educational digital game was developed in line with the CLIL framework, that is, the game can be used with dual aims of improving English and Science education for the target group learners. Why a game was preferred to be developed instead of other technologies is that games are supposed to have a great potential to build up awareness of the issues. As Dewey (1963) suggests, learning through problem solving and practical applications lead students to take a more active role in society. The hidden agenda in the game developed is to enhance environmental awareness of students while they are studying English language. Besides, students are able to learn with a trial and error based approach which would be more engaging to present the issue to the students.

BACKGROUND

This part explains content and language integrated learning, game-based language learning, and environmental awareness in detail respectively.

Content and Language Integrated Learning

The integration of content into language classes provides a meaningful and contextualized use of target language and thus students improve their language competence and develop content knowledge simultaneously. Content and Language Integrated Learning (CLIL) has been promoted by the European Union since the 1990s and has been widely used with various applications in education systems of several countries. Graddol (2006:86) describes CLIL as the 'ultimate communicative methodology' by highlighting its more holistic way of teaching and learning languages and authenticity. CLIL practices refer to the "educational settings where a language other than the students' mother tongue is used as a medium of instruction... any second or foreign language can become the object of CLIL" (Dalton-Puffer, 2007:1). CLIL instruction improves language comprehension via other content subjects such as Geography, Science, Maths, etc (Dale & Tanner, 2012). CLIL holds "an integrated approach where both language and content are conceptualized on a continuum without an implied preference for either" (Coyle, 2007:545). CLIL practices have become popular especially in the last two decades highlighting its contribution as "dual-focused educational approach" providing "a more holistic educational experience for the learner" and being "flexible" and "content-driven, and this is where it both extends the experience of learning a language, and where it becomes different to existing language-teaching approaches" (Coyle, Hood & Marsh, 2010:1).

Research suggests that CLIL programs help students outperform their non-CLIL counterparts in higher order thinking skills and overall target language competence (Coyle, 2007; Lasagabaster, 2008). CLIL instruction provides a language rich and cognitively challenging environment for students. Learners benefit from CLIL practices in terms of lexical development (Agustin-Llach & Canga Alonso, 2016). CLIL programs, with dual aims of language teaching and content learning, are believed to serve multilingualism, which is one of the main objectives of the Language Policy Division of the Council of Europe. In CLIL practices, the foreign language is not only the object of study but serves as a medium of instruction to teach other subject matter. Language classes might contribute to responsible social action. CLIL practices can also be used to increase awareness and understanding of topics such as environmental sustainability and protection.

CLIL practices can be adopted in diverse contexts. There is no single model for CLIL and the flexibility of models comes from the emphasis put on learning focus and outcomes. Some examples of CLIL models might be: studying a subject topic in the target language to explore the subject from different perspectives and developing foreign language skills simultaneously (e.g. Geography through the medium of English); a cross curricular project in which language teachers and subject teachers plan and implement together (e.g. water cycle); a global project in which teachers in different countries collaborate and students study global topics with their peers in another country through telecollaboration (e.g. renewable energy, global warming). All the sample models above share the same founding principle that language and content learning are integrated.

Game-Based Language Learning

With the advancement in educational technologies, language learning context today is not limited to that of in-class teaching. Quite the contrary, it could be enriched and the effectiveness of it could be enhanced with the use of videos, animations, augmented, virtual reality applications and digital games. These environments provide language learners with an authentic learning context, engaging and motivating learning experience through constructivist, communicative activities and interactive tasks which are beneficial factors to be embedded into the process of language learning. Besides, these multimedia supported supplementary learning environments could provide students with additional opportunities to study and improve their language learning efficiency (Kétyi, 2013).

Digital games have been used to teach a subject matter in a broad range of disciplines for a few decades. They have the potential of offering an engaging and immersive environment where students could experience learning by doing since they learn from their own mistakes with a trial and error based approach (Escudeiro & Carvalho, 2013). From the point of affective learning outcomes, there are studies reporting that digital games increase motivation (Kocaman & Cumaoğlu, 2014) enhance self-efficacy (Yukselturk, Altıok, & Başer., 2018), confidence and learner autonomy; furthermore, students are stated to develop positive attitudes (Yukselturk et al., 2018) and perceptions towards this engaging and enjoyable learning environment (Ebrahimzadeh & Alavi, 2016).

English language learning is one of the disciplines through which digital games provide language learners with advantages such as increased interaction (Lin & Lan, 2015), communication, engagement and motivation (Gozcu, 2016) and lowered anxiety. Consequently, the language and knowledge acquisitions of students augment with the increase of these parameters. According to the systematic analyses of 50 studies carried out by Hung et al. (2018), digital games are reported to augment language learning from the point of affective and psychological states, language and knowledge acquisition and some participatory behaviors and competences. Digital games help learners acquire target language vocabulary (Ebrahimzadeh & Alavi, 2016), grammar (Castaneda & Cho, 2016; Cam & Tran, 2017), pronunciation (Young & Wang, 2014), improve their reading, speaking (Rusman et al., 2018) and writing skills. In their experimental study, Suh et al. (2010) assessed language learners' achievement by comparing the experimental multiplayer online role-playing games group with the control group of students being exposed to traditional f2f in-class teaching and reported that the former group outperformed the latter one in the improvement of listening, reading and writing skills. There are many studies in the literature indicating favorability of digital (video, computer-based etc.) games over in-class teaching of vocabulary with respect to students' achievement, gains, performance (Aghlara & Tamjid, 2011; AlShaiji, 2015; Ebrahimzadeh, 2017; Turgut & Irgin, 2009; Yip & Kwan, 2006) and retention (Franciosi, Yagi, Tomoshige, & Ye, 2016; Salehi, 2017). It is stated that educational games can operate as stand-alone tools for L2 vocabulary acquisition but the learning objectives should absolutely be a part of the game dynamics (Calvo-Ferrer, 2017). Regarding digital game-based learning for the aim of vocabulary acquisition, Thompson and von Gillern (2020) carried out a new dated meta-analysis in which the researchers systematically analysed 19 studies on the issue. The results of their analysis indicated that the overall effect was moderately large for the video-game based learning groups. They stated that by embedding video-games into English language vocabulary teaching, vocabulary acquisition is promoted and the entertainment students experience in the process may as well provoke their learning gains (Thompson & von Gillern, 2020). In different age groups similar results have been gained on behalf of games for teaching vocabulary. In a study by Segers and Verhoeven (2003), kindergarten students were exposed to vocabulary games on the computer and compared to the students who were taught traditionally by following the regular curriculum. The results of the study indicated positive effects on behalf of the vocabulary game-playing group on the curriculum-dependent vocabulary test. Digital games may also help students to improve their communicative and sociolinguistic competence (Peterson, 2012) in the target language. They can augment students' cultural awareness with culture-related language learning tasks (Neville, 2015).

There are a variety of digital games which provide users with different kinds of experience. Tutorial games are the second most popular game for language learning among the others such as immersive games, exer-games, simulation games, adventure games, music games, board games and alternate reality games as listed by Hung et al. (2018). As defined by the researchers tutorial games facilitate learning through drill and practice, question and answer, quizzes or puzzles. Another taxonomy for the games is that they are categorized according to the number of players: single-player games, massively multiplayer online games and classroom multiplayer games (Li & Tsai, 2013).

Commercial off-the shelf (COTS) entertainment games which are comparatively more comprehensive with respect to their form, technical and linguistic content are mostly played today by the youth (Alyaz & Genç, 2016). Educational digital games, on the other hand, are often developed by researchers or practitioners. Educational ones are stated to be developed specifically for the aim of game-based language learning whereas commercial-off-the-shelf games aim to serve for game-enhanced language learning (Reinhardt & Sykes, 2012). With this perspective, commercial ones cannot take the place of educational ones with respect to their potential for teaching.

Not being considered for taking the place of books, digital educational games are suggested to work as complementary or supplementary activities. However, games should be designed with great care. As suggested, the target vocabulary should have an important and explicit role in the game through which it is presented (Ebrehimzadeh, 2017). Besides, the cognitive load should as well be taken into consideration which is mostly a challenge for some students' learning (DeHaan, Reed, & Kuwanda, 2010). Thus, extraneous elements which may increase students' cognitive load in the games should be minimised (Calvo-Ferrer, 2017). Educational digital games should particularly be designed according to the instructional and multimedia design principles in order to achieve their goals of teaching. Besides, as suggested by Alyaz and Genç (2016), teachers should be equipped with the game-based learning pedagogy within teacher education programs both theoretically and practically.

Environmental Awareness

It is significant to know that human and the environment always interact with each other (Tanık Önal, 2020), yet this interaction has started to be negative recently (Yeşilyurt, Özdemir Balakoğlu, & Erol, 2020) due to industrialization (Tanık Önal, 2020; Ziadat, 2010). With industrialization, people started to use the natural resources extensively, so this extensive use of the natural resources resulted in severe environmental problems including air pollution, solid waste, and noise (Ziadat, 2010), which indicates that people have become the main reason for such environmental problems (Yeşilyurt et al., 2020). As a result, the natural balance between people and the environment started to deteriorate (Tanık Önal, 2020) to a certain extent that can not be reversed unless certain precautions are taken, which poses a serious threat to the sustainment of the environment for the future. Therefore, dealing with the environmental problems resulting from human intervention has become essential.

One way to deal with the devastating human impact on the physical environment is education whose main purpose is to raise students as individuals who have environmental awareness. Environmental awareness can be defined as the knowledge people have related to environmental problems and their responses to environmental problems (Ziadat, 2010). As the definition indicates, an individual having environmental awareness is expected to know the existence of environmental problems and their reasons and react to such problems in an environmentally friendly way so that he/she can understand how his/her activities may affect the environment and how he/she can deal with the environmental problems caused by his/her activities.

METHODOLOGY

The study methodology is based on a tutorial game approach that provides a competitive, interactive, individualized CLIL context where the players try to improve target language vocabulary, grammar and their reading skill and environmental awareness while achieving the tasks. The context was prepared according to the needs of the target groups who are K12 students that need to be equipped with information, media and ICT literacies, ethics/social responsibility (global awareness) and critical thinking and problem solving skills defined as some of the 21century skills (Fadel, 2008).

Research Design

Qualitative research design was employed to design the present study because qualitative research enabled the researchers to explore the perceptions of the students and teachers about the game developed for the present study in terms of the pedagogical and visual design of the game, English language gains, and environmental awareness with a complex and detailed understanding of this issue as Creswell (2007) suggested.

Participants

Eight volunteer Turkish EFL students (5 male and 3 female) and three volunteer Turkish EFL teachers (3 female) at a K12 school in Turkey participated in the study. The student participants were 13 years old and B1 level English language learners. The ages of the teacher participants ranged from 30 to 45, and they had between 10 and 20 years of teaching experience.

The Digital Game: ENVglish

A 2D-mobile single player tutorial game deliverable through mobile devices was developed by the researchers. The tutorial game has an educational aim, thus, provides a practice opportunity for students to practice B1 level English language vocabulary proficiency, grammar and reading skills while they are studying environmental awareness. The screenshots of the game are given in Figures 1, 2, 3, and 4. As Hung et al. (2018) stated there were so far no studies specifically conducted to improve L2 learners' reading development and there are few studies exploring the effects of playing digital games to support or improve learners' subject matter knowledge as environmental awareness in the current study. The competence and skills concerning such subjects are called contemporary competence and 21st century skills (Hung et al., 2018).

Figure 1. Home scene

Figure 2. Instruction part of the digital game

Figure 3. Level scene

Figure 4. Screenshot 1 from the practice part of the digital game

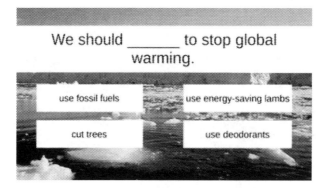

Figure 5. Screenshot 2 from the practice part of the digital game

Figure 6. Screenshot 3 from the practice part of the digital game

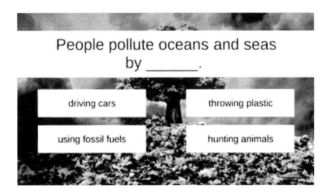

The game features competitive gaming scenarios to enhance basically students' English language vocabulary. The competition here is between the player and the computer and the 'competition against oneself' as Alessi and Trollip (2001) define. Competition is related to challenge and which in turn is related to intrinsic motivation of the players (Malone & Lepper, 1987). The players are expected to answer the questions about global environmental awareness to collect starts so that they could go further levels in the game. The game involves language input and output at three levels of linguistic form, semantic form and pragmatic use (Lan et al., 2018).

The game was developed for Android O.S., and it can be downloaded from the link below.

https://drive.google.com/file/d/1vyAR9v0ynck689v4zGW1uxc6eIxgUqfh/view?usp=drivesdk

Data Collection Tools

The data were collected through two semi-structured interviews, one to collect data from the students and the other one to collect data from the teachers. There were five main questions and three sub-questions in three categories (i.e., technical aspect, English language learning, and environmental awareness) in the interviews (See appendices 1 and 2 for the interview questions). The questions and categories were prepared according to the aim and research questions of the study to find out the perceptions of the students and teachers about the game, which is significant for such studies as the present one as it is stated that how students and teachers perceive a learning context mediates the effect of instruction. In this study, students' and teachers' perceptions are defined as their beliefs regarding an environment's purpose, their expectations about the goals of that environment (Vandercruysse et al., 2013), and how this environment will enhance their learning outcomes as English language and environmental awareness in the present study.

Data Collection Procedure

As the student participants were under 18, the consent of their parents for them to participate in the research was taken in addition to the permission taken from the school to conduct the research. Also, the consent of the teacher participants was taken. Following these, the students and teachers played the game individually, were interviewed by one of the researchers, and the interviews were audio-recorded.

Data Analysis

The collected data were transcribed first and then content-analyzed. In content-analyzing the data, the following framework was followed:

- Deriving codes from the data after reading the data many times,
- Developing themes depending on the similarities and differences between codes,
- Organizing and presenting the data according to the themes and codes,
- Interpreting the data.

The transcriptions of the data were read many times, several codes were derived from the data, the codes were categorized under themes, and the findings were presented by the researchers without adding their comments as suggested.

Trustworthiness

Two strategies suggested by Lincoln and Guba (1985) were used to make the study trustworthy. Firstly, the collected data were content-analyzed separately and compared with each other by three of the researchers. Then, necessary changes were made by the researchers after the comparison in consensus. Secondly, the findings were presented with the students' and teachers' responses from the interviews thickly.

FINDINGS

The findings of the semi-structured interviews were classified according to the collected data.

Students' Perceptions about ENVglish

The semi-structured interviews focused on the perceptions of the students related to the game in terms of the pedagogical and visual design of the game. These perceptions of the students are given in Table 1 below.

Table 1. Students' perceptions regarding the pedagogical and visual design of the game

Themes	Codes	f	%
Pedagogical design	An educative game	8	100
	Effective with its use of trial and error based approach for learning	2	25
	Adding critical thinking questions	1	12,5
Visual design	Clear instructions and buttons	8	100
	Problematic touch event	3	37,5
	Redesigning the game streaming	3	37,5
	Redesigning the use of stars for rewarding	2	25
	Changing font type	1	12,5
Overall design	Good	8	100
	Understandable	8	100
	Easy to use	6	75
	Adding simulations and/or simulated scenes for more comprehensive learning	1	12,5
	Improving the game for other levels of learners	1	12,5
	Adding re-trial opportunity	1	12,5

As Table 1 indicates, all of the participants considered the game as an educative game in terms of the pedagogical design of the game. The quotations below support this assumption.

Participant 5: "I think that it [the game] improved my vocabulary knowledge and my English."
Participant 7: "That the game was in English was a good thing to improve English. At least, we improve our English."
Participant 8: "In my opinion, it is good [for learning English]."

One of the participants suggested adding more critical thinking questions to the game. In addition, two of the participants believed that the use of trial and error based approach in the game was effective for learning as understood from the quotation below.

Participant 1: "... We find the correct answers by answering the questions wrongly. This can help remember easily..."

In terms of the visual design of the game, all of the participants thought that the instructions and buttons in the game were clear. The quotations below reveal this:

Participant 3: "[The instructions and buttons in the game are] clear."
Participant 7: "[The instructions and buttons in the game are] clear."
Participant 8: "Yes, [the instructions and buttons in the game are clear]."

Three of the participants suggested redesigning game streaming. The following quotations show this.

Participant 2: "I spent more time. The game returns to its main page after answering a question instead of passing the next question. It could be better if this is fixed."
Participant 7: "Questions were understandable, but when you answered a question correctly, you returned to the main page instead of passing the next question. If there were a transition to the next question, it could be better."

Similarly, three of the participants reported that the touch event in the game was problematic. The quotations below indicate this:

Participant 1: "There is a detection problem in touching the sides for choosing the sections [of the game]."
Participant 4: "Some buttons did not work when pressed… It was necessary to press twice."

In addition to these, one of the participants recommended changing the font type.
All of the participants considered the game as good in terms of its overall design. The quotations below support this:

Participant 1: "The game is good."
Participant 3: "The game was good."
Participant 4: "The game was really good."

Only a participant proposed adding a re-trial opportunity to the game. Similarly, all of the participants found the game understandable. To illustrate:

Participant 1: "[The game was] understandable. I did not have any difficulty."
Participant 3: "I think it [the game] was understandable. It was not very difficult."
Participant 5: "Yes [the game was understandable]. It [the game] was also easy."

Six of the participants also considered the game easy to use. The quotations below show this.

Participant 1: "Yes [it is easy to use]."
Participant 4: "Yes [it is easy to use]."
Participant 5: "Yes. I think I could use it successfully."

In addition to these, one of the participants suggested adding simulations and/or simulated scenes for more comprehensive learning, and another one recommended improving the game for other levels of learners.
The semi-structured interviews also focused on the perceptions of the students related to the game in terms of English language gains. These perceptions of the students are presented in Table 2 below.

Table 2. Students' perceptions regarding students' English language gains

Themes	Codes	f	%
English language gain	Improving English language	8	100
Vocabulary comprehension	Improving vocabulary	3	37,5
	Including some unknown vocabulary	3	37,5
	Giving definitions of and visuals about unknown vocabulary via a hint button for each word	3	37,5
	Provision of contextual clues	2	25
	Arousing curiosity to search for unknown words	1	12,5
Practice	Revising the distractors of the questions	1	12,5

According to Table 2, all of the participants believed that the game designed and developed in this study could help them to improve their English. To illustrate:

Participant 1: "It teaches [English]. We find the correct answers by answering the questions wrongly. This can help remember easily. We both play and learn."
Participant 5: "I think that it [the game] improved my vocabulary knowledge and my English."
Participant 7: "That the game was in English was a good thing to improve English. At least, we improve our English."
Participant 8: "In my opinion, it is good [for learning English]."

In addition, three of the participants reported that the game helped them to improve their vocabulary. The quotations below point out this finding.

Participant 3: "It [the game] was good in relation to climate, but not every subject. It can teach some words."
Participant 4: "There are unknown words for our class in the game. We learn these words by guessing their meanings from the sentences."
Participant 5: "I think that it [the game] improved my vocabulary knowledge and my English."

Besides one of the participants who thought that the game aroused curiosity to search for the meanings of the unknown words, two of the participants believed that the provision of contextual clues in the questions in the game could help them to learn the meanings of the unknown words as supported by the quotation below:

Participant 4: "There are unknown words for our class in the game. We learn these words by guessing their meanings from the sentences."

According to three participants, unknown words could be problematic for them while playing the game. The quotations below indicate this.

Participant 2: "There were words such as severe that we did not learn and know. I can not remember it well, but there are words like that."

Participant 3: "There were only some words which I did not know. They [their meanings] can be added."

These participants suggested giving definitions of and visuals about unknown vocabulary via a hint button for each word to overcome the unknown vocabulary problem in the game. The quotation of participant 2 shows this.

Participant 2: "If the definitions of the words in some questions appear with a thing such as a question mark or visuals related to the words while answering the questions, you know the words, learn them, and answer the questions according to them, and they [giving the definitions with a thing like question marks and visuals related to the words] become clues."

Also, as the quotation below indicates, one of the participants expressed that the distractors of the questions were challenging for him while playing the game.

Participant 8: "... They [the options of the questions] became a little difficult. The answers of the questions seemed similar to each other, so I had a little difficulty in answering the questions [choosing the correct options]."

In addition, the semi-structured interviews focused on the perceptions of the students related to the game in terms of environmental awareness. Table 3 below indicates these perceptions of the students.

Table 3. Students' perceptions regarding students' environmental awareness gains

Themes	Codes	f	%
Environmental awareness	Enhancing environmental awareness	8	100
	Provision of helpful feedback for retention	2	25
Questions	Adding more comprehensive questions	1	12,5

According to Table 3, all of the participants believed that the game in this study could help them enhance their environmental awareness. The quotations below clearly illustrate this.

Participant 1: "It [the game] enhances environmental awareness because the questions [in the game] give the results [of the environmental problems]. As it [the game] gives the results, it enables us to become more environmentally conscious."

Participant 3: "In my opinion it was logical [the game] because there are still people who are not environmentally conscious, and they can learn something by both playing and having fun."

Participant 4: "We learn new things when we answer the questions. So problems, solutions… Questions change in terms of focusing on the reasons and results. When we learn new things, we become more environmentally conscious."

Participant 5: "I think it [the game] also enhances environmental awareness. For example, for poles, to protect the poles, I learned what I should do and what I should avoid."

Participant 6: "I think it [the game] is good. That is, it explains what we should do, what should be done [to solve the environmental problems in the game]. We choose them [the things to be done to solve the environmental problems in the game]. I think it [the game] was beneficial."

Also, two of the participants stated that the game provided them with feedback that could be beneficial for retention. The following quotation shows this.

Participant 1: "... We find the correct answers by answering the questions wrongly. This can help remember easily. We both play and learn."

In addition, one of the participants reported that the game can enhance environmental awareness more if it is supported with more comprehensive questions. The quotation below clearly supports this.

Participant 2: "There are fill-in-the-blanks questions such as what causes environmental awareness, but if there are questions or a survey such as what people do so that these [environmental problems] occur, what you do, what you are going to do next, it [the game] can enhance environmental awareness more. It [the game] is like answering questions related to climate change. The questions can be extended more by adding questions such as what climate change is, what it is not, what people can do to overcome [it]."

Teachers' Perceptions about ENVglish

The semi-structured interviews made with the teachers focused on their perceptions related to the game in terms of the pedagogical, visual, and overall design of the game, English language gains, and environmental awareness. These perceptions of the teachers are indicated in Table 4 below.

Table 4. Teachers' perceptions regarding the game

Themes	Codes	f	%
Pedagogical design	An educative game	3	100
	Appropriate level	1	33
Visual design	Understandable instructions and buttons	3	100
	Need for a 'next' button for each section	1	33
	Redesigning the game streaming	1	33
Overall design	Easy to use	3	100
	Understandable	3	100
English language gain	Improving students' English language	3	100
	Learning new words	3	100
Environmental awareness	Enhancing environmental awareness	3	100

According to Table 4, while one of the participants found the game appropriate to the English levels of the students, all of the participants considered the game as an educative game in terms of its pedagogical design. The following quotations clearly reveal this.

Participant 1: "I think that it can be beneficial in terms of repeating the words they learn…"
Participant 2: "It is a very effective game [for students] to learn terminological words."
Participant 3: "I find it [the game] very beneficial in terms of their [the students'] learning English. It both presents a vocabulary-based learning…"

In terms of the visual design of the game, all of the participants thought that the instructions and buttons were understandable. The quotations below support this.

Participant 1: "[The instructions and buttons in the game were] understandable."
Participant 2: "[The instructions and buttons in the game were] very understandable."
Participant 3: "[The instructions and buttons in the game were] understandable, and active, and [the instructions and buttons in the game] could work quickly."

One of the participants also mentioned the need for a 'next' button for each section, and another one recommended redesigning the game streaming.

According to all of the participants, the game was easy to use in terms of its overall design. To illustrate:
Participant 1: "Yes, I used it [the game] [successfully]. It was easy to use."
Participant 2: "Yes, I used [the game] [successfully]. I did not have any difficulty while playing the game."
Participant 3: "Yes, I used [the game] [successfully]."

All of the participants also found the game understandable as understood in the following quotations:

Participant 1: "It [the game] was understandable enough. I understood it."
Participant 2: "Yes, it [the game] was very understandable."
Participant 3: "It [the game] was understandable enough."

All of the participants thought that the game could help their students to improve their English and English vocabulary knowledge in terms of English language gains. The following quotations clearly show this.

Participant 1: "I think that it can be beneficial in terms of repeating the words they learn…"
Participant 2: "It is a very effective game [for students] to learn terminological words."
Participant 3: "I find it [the game] very beneficial in terms of their [the students'] learning English. It both presents a vocabulary-based learning…"

In terms of environmental awareness, all of the participants believed that the game could enhance their students' environmental awareness. To illustrate:

Participant 1: "It [the game] is important for environmental awareness. In fact, they [the students] hear lots of this about it [the environment], but supporting it [environmental awareness] with the game they [the students] like a lot can cause them to become environmentally conscious in a way that they can not forget. Because of this, games are important."

Participant 2: "I think it [the game] can enhance their [the students'] awareness."

Participant 3: To answer the questions, they [the students] need to know something [about the questions]. Therefore, the instructions and the target answers of the questions can enhance their [the students'] environmental awareness."

DISCUSSION

All student participants stated that ENVglish is educative, good and understandable and that it improves their English and environmental awareness and found its visual design effective with clear instructions and buttons. Although they liked the game, the students suggested some improvements regarding the touch event, streaming, rewarding system and changing its font type for its visual design which indicate their expectations of such a digital game and learning environment has increased in time in years. They also stated that addition of critical thinking questions and simulations to the game would make it more beneficial to their learning of both the language and the subject matter. This finding is interesting and indicated their preferences for such games. As known todays' students, who are members of the Z generation, like learning experiences which give them an opportunity to learn by doing and applying (Seemiller & Grace, 2017). They like doing experiments and prefer to actively participate in an activity while learning. As reported in the Northeastern University Innovation Survey (2014), these students like to be involved in real-life problems and projects which prepare them for their future lives, this may be the reason why they asked critical thinking questions in the game. This is promising for educators as well since it is reported in the literature that learning experiences that improve students' critical thinking as one the higher-order-thinking skills augments deeper learning and retention.

The teachers who participated in the study, similarly, thought that the digital game was educative, easy to use, understandable and appropriate to the level of their students. They stated that it improves their students' English and environmental awareness. They had few suggestions about the visual design compared to their students which indicated that students are much more interested in visual features and technical characteristics of an application like the game in the current study. Z generation students are known to be net generation (Geck, 2006) member technology-whiz individuals compared to their educators who are also young. These students who are called 'digital natives' (Prensky, 2001) were born to a world of technology and grow in it which probably made them over-sensitive to the design of such environments and also they could criticize effectively based on their long-term experiences with such environments.

According to the student and teacher participants, ENVglish could help students to improve their vocabulary related to environmental problems and their solutions. This finding of the study is in line with the literature which indicates that digital games can improve EFL/ESL students' vocabulary learning (Segers & Verhoeven, 2003; Thompson & von Gillern, 2020). This can result from the fact that students could enjoy playing ENVglish and this enjoyment could stem in the improvement in students' vocabulary learning related to environmental issues and problems as Thompson and von Gillern (2020) found out in their study that the entertainment students experience in the process (playing a digital game) may provoke their learning gains.

Both groups of participants thought that the digital game was helpful to improve the students' English language which was the main aim of the game as reported by Kétyi (2013) in the literature. They stated that it may particularly improve their vocabulary (Ebrahimzadeh & Alavi, 2016). This indicates that there should be digital games like this that could be developed to enrich in-class teaching of language and other subject matter. The findings indicated the researchers the parts to be improved in the game.

According to the findings of the study, both groups of the participants also believed that the game in the study could enhance students' environmental awareness, which may be because of the content of the questions in the game. As Figure 4 indicates, the questions focus on the reasons and solutions of several environmental problems (i.e. global warming, endangered animals, melting ice in the poles, climate change, water pollution, air pollution, and land pollution), so the questions about the causes of these environmental problems could help the student participants to understand how human activities can affect the environment negatively as stated in the literature (Tanık Önal, 2020; Yeşilyurt et al., 2020; Ziadat, 2010), while the other questions about the solutions to these environmental problems could enable them to figure out how they could respond to such problems. Consequently, as Ziadat (2010) explained in his definition of environmental awareness, the game could enable the student participants to have the knowledge related to environmental problems and develop responses to such problems, which could enhance their environmental awareness.

As the participants declared, this CLIL practice environment gave them an opportunity to study new vocabulary, some of which were stated to be challenging and included new terminology. This is in line with the literature which reported that CLIL instruction provides students with a language rich and cognitively challenging environment, which enabled the students in the study to use their higher order thinking skills and improve their English language competence (Coyle, 2007; Lasagabaster, 2008). In addition, the student participants benefitted from this CLIL practice environment as they improved their vocabulary knowledge because Agustin-Llach and Canga Alonso (2016) stated that CLIL practices could contribute to students' lexical development.

FURTHER RESEARCH DIRECTIONS AND CONCLUSION

Digital games provide language learners with an engaging and enjoyable learning environment and thus are promising to use at education. The results of the study are expected to contribute to the concerning literature specifically about digital game-based vocabulary skill improvement and content and language integrated learning. Besides, the findings of the study will contribute to the improvement of the digital game (ENVglish). Thus, the researchers are planning to hold a further study to investigate the learning outcomes of the game after developing the game according to the participants' suggestions.

REFERENCES

Aghlara, L., & Tamjid, N. H. (2011). The effect of digital games on Iranian children's vocabulary retention in foreign language acquisition. *Procedia: Social and Behavioral Sciences*, *29*, 552–560. doi:10.1016/j.sbspro.2011.11.275

Agustin-Llach, M. P., & Canga Alonso, A. (2016). Vocabulary growth in young CLIL and traditional EFL learners: Evidence from research and implications for education. *International Journal of Applied Linguistics, 26*(2), 211–217. doi:10.1111/ijal.12090

Alessi, S. M., & Trollip, S. R. (2001). *Multimedia for learning: Methods and development.* Allyn & Bacon.

AlShaiji, O. A. (2015). Video games promote Saudi children's English vocabulary retention. *Education, 136*(2), 123–132.

Alyaz, Y., & Genc, Z. S. (2016). Digital game-based language learning in foreign language teacher education. *Turkish Online Journal of Distance Education, 17*(4), 130–146. doi:10.17718/tojde.44375

Calvo-Ferrer, J. R. (2017). Educational games as stand-alone learning tools and their motivational effect on L 2 vocabulary acquisition and perceived learning gains. *British Journal of Educational Technology, 48*(2), 264–278. doi:10.1111/bjet.12387

Cam, L., & Tran, T. M. T. (2017). An evaluation of using games in teaching English grammar for first year English-majored students at Dong Nai Technology University. *International Journal of Learning, Teaching and Educational Research, 16*(7), 55-71.

Castaneda, D. A., & Cho, M. H. (2016). Use of a game-like application on a mobile device to improve accuracy in conjugating Spanish verbs. *Computer Assisted Language Learning, 29*(7), 1195–1204. doi :10.1080/09588221.2016.1197950

Coyle, D. (2007). Content and language integrated learning: Towards a connected research agenda for CLIL pedagogies. *International Journal of Bilingual Education and Bilingualism, 10*(5), 543–562. doi:10.2167/beb459.0

Coyle, D., Hood, P., & Marsh, D. (2010). *CLIL - content and language integrated learning.* Cambridge University Press. doi:10.1017/9781009024549

Creswell, J. W. (2007). *Qualitative inquiry & research design: Choosing among five approaches.* Sage Publications.

Dale, L., & Tanner, R. (2012). *CLIL activities: A resource for subject and language teachers.* Cambridge University Press.

Dalton-Puffer, C. (2007). *Discourse in content and language integrated learning (CLIL) classrooms.* John Benjamins Publishing Company. doi:10.1075/lllt.20

DeHaan, J., Reed, W. M., & Kuwanda, K. (2010). The effect of interactivity with a music video game on second language vocabulary recall. *Language Learning & Technology, 14*(2), 74–94.

Dewey, J. (1963). *Experience and education.* Collier Books.

Ebrahimzadeh, M. (2017). Readers, players, and watchers: EFL students' vocabulary acquisition through digital video games. *English Language Teaching, 10*(2), 1–18. doi:10.5539/elt.v10n2p1

Ebrahimzadeh, M., & Alavi, S. (2016). Motivating EFL students: E-learning enjoyment as a predictor of vocabulary learning through digital video games. *Cogent Education, 3*(1), 1255400. doi:10.1080/23 31186X.2016.1255400

Escudeiro, P., & de Carvalho, C. V. (2013). Game-based language learning. *International Journal of Information and Education Technology (IJIET)*, *3*(6), 643–647. doi:10.7763/IJIET.2013.V3.353

Fadel, C. (2008). *21st century skills: How can you prepare students for the new global economy?* https://www.oecd.org/site/educeri21st/40756908.pdf

Franciosi, S. J., Yagi, J., Tomoshige, Y., & Ye, S. (2016). The effect of a simple simulation game on long-term vocabulary retention. *CALICO Journal*, *33*(3), 355–379. doi:10.1558/cj.v33i2.26063

Geck, C. (2007). The generation Z connection: Teaching information literacy to the newest net generation. In E. Rosenfeld & D. V. Loertscher (Eds.), *Toward a 21st-century school library media program* (pp. 236–248). Scarecrow Press.

Gozcu, E., & Caganaga, C. K. (2016). The importance of using games in EFL classrooms. *Cypriot Journal of Educational Sciences*, *11*(3), 126–135. doi:10.18844/cjes.v11i3.625

Graddol, D. (2006). *English next*. British Council Publications.

Hung, H. T., Yang, J. C., Hwang, G. J., Chu, H. C., & Wang, C. C. (2018). A scoping review of research on digital game-based language learning. *Computers & Education*, *126*, 89–104. doi:10.1016/j.compedu.2018.07.001

Kétyi, A. (2013). Using smart phones in language learning – A pilot study to turn CALL into MALL. In L. Bradley & S. Thouësny (Eds.), *20 Years of EUROCALL: Learning from the Past, Looking to the Future. Proceedings of the 2013 EUROCALL Conference, Évora, Portugal* (pp.129-134). Research-publishing.net. 10.14705/rpnet.2013.000150

Kocaman, O., & Cumaoglu, G. K. (2014). The effect of educational software (DENIS) and games on vocabulary learning strategies and achievement. *Eğitim ve Bilim*, *39*(176), 305–316. doi:10.15390/EB.2014.3704

Lan, Y. J., Botha, A., Shang, J., & Jong, M. S. Y. (2018). Guest editorial: Technology enhanced contextual game-based language learning. *Journal of Educational Technology & Society*, *21*(3), 86–89.

Lasagabaster, D. (2008). Foreign language competence in content and language integrated courses. *The Open Applied Linguistics Journal*, *1*(1), 31–42. doi:10.2174/1874913500801010030

Li, M. C., & Tsai, C. C. (2013). Game-based learning in science education: A review of relevant research. *Journal of Science Education and Technology*, *22*(6), 877–898. doi:10.100710956-013-9436-x

Lin, T. J., & Lan, Y. J. (2015). Language learning in virtual reality environments: Past, present, and future. *Journal of Educational Technology & Society*, *18*(4), 486–497.

Lincoln, Y. S., & Guba, E. G. (1985). *Naturalistic inquiry*. Sage Publications. doi:10.1016/0147-1767(85)90062-8

Lowyck, J., Elen, J., & Clarebout, G. (2004). Instructional conceptions: Analysis from an instructional design perspective. *International Journal of Educational Research*, *41*(6), 429–444. doi:10.1016/j.ijer.2005.08.010

Malone, T. W., & Lepper, M. R. (1987). Making learning fun: A taxonomy of intrinsic motivations for learning. In R.E. Snow & M.J Farr (Eds.), Aptitude, learning, and instruction volume 3: Conative and affective process analyses (pp. 223-253). Lawrence Erlbaum Associates, Publishers.

Neville, D. O. (2015). The story in the mind: The effect of 3D gameplay on the structuring of written L2 narratives. *ReCALL*, *27*(1), 21–37. doi:10.1017/S0958344014000160

Northeastern University Innovation Survey. (2014). https://news.northeastern.edu/2014/11/18/generation-z-survey/

Peterson, M. (2012). Learner interaction in a massively multiplayer online role playing game (MMORPG): A sociocultural discourse analysis. *ReCALL*, *24*(3), 361–380. doi:10.1017/S0958344012000195

Prensky, M. (2001). Digital natives, digital immigrants part 2: Do they really think differently? *On the Horizon*, *9*(6), 2–6. doi:10.1108/10748120110424843

Reinhardt, J., & Sykes, J. M. (2012). Conceptualizing digital game-mediated L2 learning and pedagogy: Game-enhanced and game-based research and practice. In H. Reinders (Ed.), *Digital games in language learning and teaching* (pp. 32–49). Palgrave Macmillan. doi:10.1057/9781137005267_3

Rusman, E., Ternier, S., & Specht, M. (2018). Early second language learning and adult involvement in a real-world context: Design and evaluation of the "ELENA Goes Shopping" mobile game. *Journal of Educational Technology & Society*, *21*(3), 90–103.

Salehi, H. (2017). Effects of using instructional video games on teaching English vocabulary to Iranian pre-intermediate EFL learners. *International Journal of Learning and Change*, *9*(2), 111–130. doi:10.1504/IJLC.2017.084609

Seemiller, C., & Grace, M. (2017). Generation Z: Educating and engaging the next generation of students. *About Campus: Enriching the Student Learning Experience*, *22*(3), 21–26. doi:10.1002/abc.21293

Segers, E., & Verhoeven, L. (2003). Effects of vocabulary training by computer in kindergarten. *Journal of Computer Assisted Learning*, *19*(4), 557–566. doi:10.1046/j.0266-4909.2003.00058.x

Suh, S., Kim, S. W., & Kim, N. J. (2010). Effectiveness of MMORPG-based instruction in elementary English education in Korea. *Journal of Computer Assisted Learning*, *26*(5), 370–378. doi:10.1111/j.1365-2729.2010.00353.x

Tanık Önal, N. (2020). Investigation of gifted students' environmental awareness. *International Journal of Curriculum and Instruction*, *12*(2), 95–107.

Thompson, C. G., & von Gillern, S. (2020). Video-game based instruction for vocabulary acquisition with English language learners: A Bayesian meta-analysis. *Educational Research Review*, *30*, 100332. doi:10.1016/j.edurev.2020.100332

Turgut, Y., & Irgin, P. (2009). Young learners' language learning via computer games. *Procedia: Social and Behavioral Sciences*, *1*(1), 760–764. doi:10.1016/j.sbspro.2009.01.135

Vandercruysse, S., Vandewaetere, M., Cornillie, F., & Clarebout, G. (2013). Competition and students' perceptions in a game-based language learning environment. *Educational Technology Research and Development*, *61*(6), 927–950. doi:10.100711423-013-9314-5

Yeşilyurt, M., Özdemir Balakoğlu, M., & Erol, M. (2020). The impact of environmental education activities on primary school students' environmental awareness and visual expressions. *Qualitative Research in Education*, *9*(2), 188–216. doi:10.17583/qre.2020.5115

Yip, F. W. M., & Kwan, A. C. M. (2006). Online vocabulary games as a tool for teaching and learning English vocabulary. *Educational Media International*, *43*(3), 233–249. doi:10.1080/09523980600641445

Young, S. S. C., & Wang, Y. H. (2014). The game embedded CALL system to facilitate English vocabulary acquisition and pronunciation. *Journal of Educational Technology & Society*, *17*(3), 239–251.

Yukselturk, E., Altıok, S., & Başer, Z. (2018). Using game-based learning with kinect technology in foreign language education course. *Journal of Educational Technology & Society*, *21*(3), 159–173.

Ziadat, A. H. (2010). Major factors contributing to environmental awareness among people in a third world country/Jordan. *Environment, Development and Sustainability*, *12*(1), 135–145. doi:10.100710668-009-9185-4

ADDITIONAL READING

Coyle, D., Hood, P., & Marsh, D. (2010). *CLIL - Content and language integrated learning*. Cambridge University Press. doi:10.1017/9781009024549

Dalton-Puffer, C. (2007). *Discourse in content and language integrated learning (CLIL) classrooms*. John Benjamins Publishing Company. doi:10.1075/lllt.20

Gamlo, N. (2019). The impact of mobile game-based language learning apps on EFL learners' motivation. *English Language Teaching*, *12*(4), 49–56. doi:10.5539/elt.v12n4p49

Klimova, B., & Kacetl, J. (2018, January). Computer game-based foreign language learning: Its benefits and limitations. In International conference on technology in education (pp. 26-34). Springer, Singapore.

Lan, Y. J., Botha, A., Shang, J., & Jong, M. S. Y. (2018). Guest editorial: Technology enhanced contextual game-based language learning. *Journal of Educational Technology & Society*, *21*(3), 86–89.

Maley, A., & Peachey, N. (Eds.). (2017). *Integrating global issues in the creative English language classroom: With reference to the United Nations sustainable development goals*. British Council.

Wang, Q. (2020). The role of classroom-situated game-based language learning in promoting students' communicative competence. *International Journal of Computer-Assisted Language Learning and Teaching*, *10*(2), 59–82. doi:10.4018/IJCALLT.2020040104

Xu, Z., Chen, Z., Eutsler, L., Geng, Z., & Kogut, A. (2020). A scoping review of digital game-based technology on English language learning. *Educational Technology Research and Development*, *68*(3), 877–904. doi:10.100711423-019-09702-2

Zhang, R., Cheng, G., & Chen, X. (2020). Game-based self-regulated language learning: Theoretical analysis and bibliometrics. *PLoS One*, *15*(12), e0243827. doi:10.1371/journal.pone.0243827 PMID:33326464

Zou, D., Huang, Y., & Xie, H. (2021). Digital game-based vocabulary learning: Where are we and where are we going? *Computer Assisted Language Learning*, *34*(5-6), 751–777. doi:10.1080/09588221.2019.1640745

KEY TERMS AND DEFINITIONS

Content and Language-Integrated Learning: It is a language learning method which integrates subjects such as mathematics and a language including English with each other and in which students learn both the language and subjects.

Environmental Awareness: It is a kind of awareness that refers to what people know about environmental issues and how they react to environmental issues.

Game-Based Language Learning: It is a language learning method in which students learn a language by playing educational games.

Section 4
Teacher Perceptions of Game-Based Learning

Chapter 28
Educators as Facilitators of Game-Based Learning:
Their Knowledge, Attitudes, and Skills

Jessica Reuter
GOVCOPP, DEGEIT, University of Aveiro, Portugal

Marlene Amorim
(iD) https://orcid.org/0000-0002-0901-0614
GOVCOPP, DEGEIT, University of Aveiro, Portugal

Marta Ferreira Dias
(iD) https://orcid.org/0000-0002-6695-8479
GOVCOPP, DEGEIT, University of Aveiro, Portugal

Mara Madaleno
(iD) https://orcid.org/0000-0002-4905-2771
GOVCOPP, DEGEIT, University of Aveiro, Portugal

Claúdia Veloso
(iD) https://orcid.org/0000-0001-6612-0580
GOVCOPP, DEGEIT, University of Aveiro, Portugal

ABSTRACT

Innovative educational methods such as gamification are gaining ground in more formal environments and have great potential to improve learning in education. However, the implementation of this strategy in the classroom is assumed to be a complex practice for beginners and requires the development of new competencies by educators. This chapter aims to contribute to the advancement of knowledge about the main competencies needed for educators to perform as facilitators of educational games. The study was developed through critical literature review, interviews, and questionnaires. The outcome is the development of a framework of competencies of an educator willing to use game-based learning. The study highlights the importance of institutional support to boost the development of pedagogical, technological, and social skills among educators. The conclusions of the chapter are valuable for educators aiming to adopt game-based learning and to higher education decision makers committed to expanding innovative learning contexts on their institutions.

DOI: 10.4018/978-1-7998-7271-9.ch028

INTRODUCTION

Educators need to be constantly adapting to new technologies and teaching methodologies. For this to occur, continuous skills development and identity reformulation are required. It is a creative adaptation and direction for self-development (Shah & Foster, 2015).

Game-based learning (GBL) practice is considered a new teaching methodology, which aims to challenge educators to adapt the use of games with pedagogical content. This practice also promotes the increase of their professional skills and the educator's motivation, as it promotes engagement in students for learning (Nicholson, 2018) The use of GBL, aims to encourage learning through different types of educational games that have specific learning objectives and outcomes. This strategy involves the repetition of desired results. Through the motivational mechanisms of reinforcement and emotions, the desired results become automatic behavioral processes or habits. This information loop is maintained without great cognitive effort, as this knowledge is obtained gradually throughout the game process (Almeida, 2020).

Educational games are games that have formal objectives, designed to help people learn about particular subjects, expand concepts, reinforce development, or help them learn a skill while playing. This denomination is usually used in a school context, while serious games are more commonly used in companies (Clarke et al., 2017). The difference between GBL and educational games is that GBL is more a method, the way of learning, and educational games are a product in which GBL is possible. Thus, GBL is part of the general concept of educational games and has been used successfully in various fields such as health, management, tourism, and psychology (Chetouani et al., 2018; Carenys & Moya, 2016; Xu et al., 2017; Almeida, 2020).

The implementation of methodologies based on games in the classroom is a practice that has been implemented in educational institutions, at different levels of education, as well as in different countries and environments (Tercanli et al., 2021)Nevertheless, the development of these learning game tools is considered a complex practice for beginners and requires multiple tasks and the presence and development of skills and competencies in the educators themselves (Yi et al., 2020).

Education institutions must create appropriate framework conditions but also educators should be open to new learning approaches such as learner-centered learning. Moreover, the emerging experience in the field suggests that there should be collaboration among colleagues to foster the joint development of such learning environments. Another challenge concerns the existence of technical prerequisites that are necessary to enable the adoption of such innovative approaches and embed them in the constellation of standard learning materials in the future (Buchner & Zumbach, 2020).

In this context, it is essential to identify educators' skills and possible training needs about game-based learning. Once identified, it is necessary to develop and implement teacher training programs to disseminate the use of GBL (Kamışlı, 2019). Different variables such as environment, resources, professional and personal elements are important for the development of these skills. To determine the success of GBL activities, educators should gather knowledge about games, pedagogy, and content (Nousiainen et al., 2018).

When embracing GBL Educators need to conduct several activities including, selecting the adequate game for learning in alignment with their teaching objectives, designing the appropriate instructional practice, guiding and supporting students during the game sessions, providing technical assistance when necessary, and organization reflection and discussion activities, before and afterward, with their students (Veldkamp et al., 2020) The lack of pedagogical and technological knowledge from the teachers is one of the obstacles encountered in the implementation of game-based learning in a more generalized manner. Nevertheless, the effectiveness of this educational approach is, by far, not solely dependent on the technical aspects of the game, but rather on pedagogical issues (Buchner & Zumbach, 2020). According to Karagiannis and Magkos (2021), GBL methods have shown great results, but the usage of GBL methods has not been sufficiently studied for the effectiveness of the learning process.

In this regard, this chapter aims to contribute to the advancement of knowledge about the main skills and competencies needed for educators as facilitators of educational games, to seize all the learning advantages of GBL, namely by promoting synergy, participation, and motivation among students. To this end, this chapter offers a description and characterization of the skills and attitudes needed by educators as facilitators of games in an educational setting. Through a critical literature review, interviews, and questionnaires with educators, the authors seek to identify the necessary skills to be developed as an educator and the challenges that may inhibit the use of this teaching approach.

The chapter advances a framework concerning the canvas of skills and competencies required by an educator willing to adopt GBL in the classroom context. Moreover, this study is of particular importance to the literature about innovative educational methods because it adds to the scientific international literature on the profile of the educator who adopts GBL, a subject that has received little attention from scholars. The chapter's findings are valuable both for educators who intend to adopt GBL in their classrooms as well as for decision-makers in education who are committed to expanding innovative learning in their institutions. For educators, the knowledge about the set of skills or competencies that are relevant to implementing GBL is important to support the development of strategies to expand the adoption of innovative learning approaches.

AN OVERVIEW OF EDUCATORS' COMPETENCIES FOR GBL FACILITATION

Competences for the Integration and Alignment of Games with Curricula and Learning Goals

Building on the literature review conducted in this study, the first step of the research work was to develop a preliminary classification concerning skills and competencies that are relevant for the adoption of GBL. The proposed classification distinguishes among pedagogical skills, technological skills (particularly important in the context of the emerging digital learning environment), social and collaborative skills. The development of such competence groups, and their respective characterization, involved also the classification of competencies that include the knowledge and the emotions of teachers involved with GBL. Educators committed to the adoption of GBL need to find a balance between the conduction of games, their teaching objectives, and students' engagement. Therefore, the development of games needs to consider the preparation of clear guidelines to support teachers in the use of such methodologies. The guidelines and recommendations that complement existing games are very important to support the development of teachers' literacy skills in the use of games, to allow for them to take advantage of all the learning benefits promised by GBL, namely promoting synergy, and stimulating the participation and motivation among students (Linderoth & Sjöblom, 2019). According to Chen et al. (2020), to contribute to the development of an emerging framework on games literacy for teacher education and professional development, it is needed the implementation of GBL.

According to Rowan and Beavis (2017), the pedagogical beliefs of teachers are evidenced in three groups: developing computer skills, delivering curriculum content, and promoting changes in teaching and learning. Since in the light of their belief, they showed confidence in innovation within an existing curriculum and within the limits provided by different educational authorities, schools, and individuals (Chen et al., 2020). To this extent, for Prestridge and Aldama (2016), this means that teachers who engage in digital games depend on their beliefs and roles in the promotion of the acquisition of students' knowledge and skills. It is necessary to train teachers with pedagogical skills in the integration of games in the classroom (Shah & Foster, 2015).

These skills will be necessary to plan meaningful game-based activities (Urh et al., 2015). To understand the strengths and limitations of game-based approaches it is necessary to know them well to know how best to use them (Dabbagh et al., 2015). It is important in addition to getting acknowledged with the use of games and the ability to choose the most appropriate ones for each situation, to ensure synergy between student engagement and games (Foster, 2015; Molin, 2017).

Integrating the GBL approach in the curriculum objectives, and achieving the right alignment with the student's preferences and demographic and socio-cultural differences is one of the most relevant parts of the process. Having the right and targeted approach for a specific audience is what will result in the success of this strategy (Iosup & Epema, 2014). The approach needs to be geared towards the learning process (Bourgonjon & Hanghoi, 2011). The educator needs to find a way and space to embed new pedagogical approaches into a sound educational framework, identifying the types of play methodologies that their agenda and curriculum allow for (Molin, 2017; Frossard, 2013). Furthermore, the GBL facilitator must have the sensitivity to identify learning moments during play, outside of which they have previously defined (Foster & Shah, 2020).

Some studies show that skills and a pedagogical model are necessary to implement games efficiently in schools, guiding teacher intervention and assisting students in learning and evaluating their progress (Gros, 2010). Likewise, educational institutions must create adequate framework conditions. Educators must also be open to new approaches to learning, such as student-centered learning. The need for a pedagogical model to support teachers was also identified as fundamental in studies that prove the usefulness of games by teachers in classes to develop student learning. Authors such as Eastwood and Sadler (2013), Jaipal and Figg (2009) and Silseth (2012) argue that pedagogical skills, in the development of game-based learning, are essential for guiding beginners and senior teachers in bringing together their content and pedagogical experience and adapting the use of games following teaching contexts and needs.

For the approach to be effective, there should be, in addition to planning, the monitoring of the activities to achieve the intended objectives (Raziunaite et al., 2018). Educators should be encouraging and supportive of the activities they are proposing (Arnab et al., 2019). They should be able to explain the new method to the students, but also allow the students to take responsibility during the process (Iosup & Epema, 2014). Knowing how to support and motivate the students, also means granting them the freedom and the trust that the student will learn and develop with this teaching method (Bourgonjon & Hanghoi, 2011). For this trust not to be broken and for the student to feel free to fail and learn from their mistakes, the educator will need to provide prompt support and positive feedback as a form of encouragement and so that boredom does not occur (Urh et al., 2015). Thus, mentoring and monitoring are essential in this process (Rodrigues et al., 2017).

Educators should engage in mediation to promote post-game discussion and encourage student reflection. To this end, careful observation of students' attitudes, choices, and behaviors during the activity is necessary (Arnab et al., 2019). The assessment phase also involves understanding students' different levels of knowledge and personalities and motivation for this type of activity, as measuring individual student performance can be difficult, it is important to focus on the overall performance of the teaching and learning activity (Chen et al., 2020). To acquire or develop these skills, the educator first needs to know the pedagogical content and establish a clear alignment between the game they will develop, the curriculum, and the intended learning and development outcomes (Bourgonjon & Hanghoi, 2011). In GBL activities, the educator needs to play an active role to facilitate learning. For Foster and Shah (2020), regardless of the game approach chosen, a pedagogically competent educator will be able to plan, implement and evaluate game-based learning and link it together to provide the best teaching and learning experience.

Competences to Explore New Technologies and Learning Methods

If, on the one hand, pedagogical competencies are fundamental to adopting GBL in their classrooms, technological competencies assume an identical role in an increasingly digital society. Many educators report a lack of technological skills and digital competencies that are required to develop the games (Hurtado & González, 2017). Likewise, there are several mentions of the importance of being formerly acquainted with the subject, having former experience with educational games, or basic knowledge about the different approaches to GBL (Shah & Foster, 2015).

Kali et al. (2015) argued that teachers should be regarded as designers of digital learning with the support of technology. Likewise, McKenney (2005) summarized the term "ecological" to describe contexts of high complexity and dynamics, in which teachers have to develop their activity to promote and facilitate students' learning. The development of their competencies also implies the ability to flexibly overcome technology-related obstacles (Hurtado & González, 2017). Educators with greater familiarity with digital technologies and media tend to show more competence in-game knowledge (Linderoth & Sjöblom, 2019). Having experience with games, or some instruction about different game approaches, may be indispensable when preparing the curriculum unit (Chen et al., 2020; Guigon et al., 2018). This prior knowledge can be natural if educators enjoy the activities they are proposing. This motivation and knowledge of the tool leave the educator immersed and can provide greater student engagement to enjoy the activity (Nousiainen et al., 2018; Karagiannis & Magkos, 2021).

Another challenge concerns the existence of the necessary technical prerequisites to allow the adoption of such innovative approaches and to integrate them into the constellation of standard learning materials in the future (Buchner & Zumbach, 2020). Teachers must consider that games play an important role as challenging, but important hybrid textual forms that are closely linked to action (Chen et al., 2020). Knowledge about gamification and game-based learning in profound allows educators to demystify the superficial image of the insertion of games in education. Increased knowledge is strategic for the careful analysis of the strengths and weaknesses of this strategy and to know how best to incorporate them into its content in order to maximize learning and make the experience useful for student motivation and development (Chen et al., 2020; Grove et al., 2013).

However, no matter how much preparation and knowledge the educator possesses, in facilitating GBL, unforeseen events may occur, so the educator needs skills to quickly devise a new strategy, improvising and modifying the objectives and tools during the process (Molin, 2017). Thus, it is important for the educator to have a network of supports and to know alternative tools to overcome any unforeseen events (Linderoth & Sjöblom, 2019). In the training process, the educator needs to have access to practical examples on the application to be able to have planning, control, and reconciliation of these activities in the curriculum. It is observed how all competencies need to be interconnected, to engage students in these activities and get better results. Many educators report avoiding this type of tool in education because they do not sufficiently master its use (Marklund & Taylor, 2016).

To obtain this specific knowledge, educators should keep up to date with experts and practitioners of the game (Hurtado & González, 2017). Once training needs have been identified, the creation of a platform for sharing experiences on GBL is needed, where different play processes could be grouped to provide support to educators starting to implement these strategies (Nicholson, 2018; Marklund & Taylor, 2015; Foster & Shah, 2020). Studies such as those developed by Beavis and O'Mara (2010) and Beavis (2013) demonstrated the need and importance of the active and creative dimensions of teachers for the use of digital games in learning and instructions, often referred to as games or GBL. This author states that teachers should look ahead and reimagine curricula to get involved with "old times" texts and literacies (Chen et al., 2020). In addition, the emerging experience in the field suggests that there should be collaboration between colleagues to promote the joint development of such learning environments.

The ability to explore new teaching alternatives and methodologies and to improvise, without worrying about failure, can be fun and motivating for the educator if they are open to new experiences (Chen et al., 2020; Jana, 2016). If the experiments are successful, the educator will increase confidence in their ability to effectively use games to enhance learning (Frossard, 2013; Karagiannis & Magkos, 2021). Thus, social skills such as adaptability, flexibility, and creativity are indispensable skills for all educators who aim to be GBL facilitators (Bourgonjon et al., 2013). It is necessary to have the ability to innovate, be curious and understand game trends that can be useful to collaborate with educational practices (Hanghøj et al., 2020; Pellas et al., 2019).

Adopting the GBL approach in teaching necessitates stepping out of your comfort zone, trying other approaches besides the traditional teaching method, and encouraging new activities (Nicholson, 2018). It is often necessary to learn from mistakes, be persistent, and insist on new activities, which at first may not be as well-received (Jana, 2016).

Competences for Facilitation and Orchestration of Students' Involvement

Encouraging student participation also implies being authoritative when necessary, so that the activity is not only a moment of pleasure but also a moment of learning and skill development among students (Hirumi & Stapleton, 2009; Marklund & Taylor, 2015). This is why the establishment of defined rules and goals is so important (Arnab et al., 2019). Social and creative competence manifests as the ability to take a playful stance, explore and improvise. Having this competence for some educators is something natural and is intrinsically related to their interests (Frossard, 2013).

However, for some educators this process should be developed slowly, testing and inserting small GBL activities at a pace with which they feel comfortable and confident (Weitze, 2016). This process of the educator as a facilitator of games in class will occur in a way that promotes the teacher's creative orientation towards self-development (Hanghøj et al., 2020). Each educator must understand their potential and limitations as a facilitator of GBL, reflect on and reshape their identity as educators (Hunter, 2020). The use of GBL strategies in teaching has challenged educators to rethink and improve their practices to find pedagogical ways of using games in teaching (Weitze, 2016).

In the case of GBL, the teacher assumes the position of the game master, who plans, executes, and evaluates the whole process. In the view of Sánchez-Martín et al. (2020), the emotional analysis of the experience of students using educational games evidence this an effective tool for building a specific vision of science and technology courses, as human constructs, with thinking styles, underpinning all previous approaches. Emotional competencies such as curiosity, the applicability of knowledge, or self-guided learning are linked to scientific values (Kali et al. 2015).

GBL serves the purpose of supporting students to develop an intrinsic learning motivation that is guided by curiosity instead of motivating them with grades. Moreover, grading the students' performance might increase anxiety. So, to grade and maximize the students' experience, the facilitator needs to develop some specific competencies. Knowledge and skill in-game analysis is important so that the educator can draw the right conclusions on each student (Hirumi & Stapleton, 2009). The educator must also foster post-game discussion, and encourage reflection, allowing the students to understand the whole process and the most important takeaways (Jaipal & Figg, 2009). The facilitator will need to help students to see the relevance of this acquired knowledge beyond the classroom, as GBL is an innovative teaching method, and usually, it is expected that the students develop some soft skills beyond the purely academic knowledge (Nicholson, 2018)

GBL can become widely used as it spreads from a small group of teachers to colleagues within and outside teaching environments (Nousiainen et al., 2018). However, fostering cooperation between teachers can be a challenge in institutions (Jana, 2016). Such collaboration needs to be developed to introduce GBL into the culture of teaching and especially to make it a sustainable practice (Ferreiro-González et al., 2019). The ability and willingness to share are still considered an area for improvement among educators (Hurtado & González, 2017). As means to improve collaborative competition, teachers emphasized mutual support, the joint creation of ideas, and the demonstration of concrete practices that facilitate and motivate new teaching approaches (Buchner & Zumbach, 2020). Collaboration among colleagues to jointly create such learning environments is critical for the success, dissemination, and sustainability of this practice in teaching (Kamışlı, 2019).

THE IMPORTANCE OF THE INSTITUTIONAL CONTEXT

Lack of Institutional Support and Collaboration Between Educators

The advancement of GBL and the growth of this methodology in formal education show that institutions are embracing and are more open to experimenting and supporting these activities (Pellas & Mystakidis, 2020). Literature indicates that GBL has received increasing attention, some researchers report that educational games are one of the biggest "hypes" of the last decade in the educational context (Lathwesen & Belova, 2021). In the last decade advances in academia on conceptual, design and pedagogical aspects have grown substantially. However, the introduction of gamification in education can be difficult. Especially if there is no institutional support (Iosup & Epema, 2014). Among the various limitations that may hinder the use of GBL by educators the most cited facts correspond to institutional content (Molin, 2017).

Educators and educational agents face a context of diverse changes with challenges, the advancement of technology, and new forms of engagement, teaching, and learning. The support of the educational institution and the collaboration between educators need to be strengthened. Educators need support to be able to reconcile the various activities with the time available. Implementing a new teaching methodology can be a lengthy process and involves a change of mindset on the part of educators. This is why support networks are so important in this process (Ataide et al., 2019).

The lack of planning and establishment of clear pedagogical objectives, as well as the difficulty in finding suitable games and fitting them into the curriculum, is one of the greatest difficulties encountered by educators (Foster & Shah, 2020). These deficiencies may emerge because of a lack of knowledge about GBL (Becker, 2007; Marklund & Taylor, 2015). But also due to a lack of guidelines to help teachers adapt and adopt pedagogical strategies that foster creativity (Marklund & Taylor, 2016).

Lack of institutional support and institutional pressures ultimately discourage experimentation and the use of this tool in teaching (Bourgonjon et al., 2013; Jana, 2016). Several educators report not having enough time to prepare a game, and to reconcile them with the various other teaching and research activities (Becker, 2007; Kamışlı, 2019). Some games demand time and other support materials, as well as personal and technological resources (Dabbagh et al., 2015; Pinto & Ferreira, 2017).

In addition to these factors, many educators report not feeling the enthusiasm to use technology and games in class (Hanghøj et al., 2020). Such lack of motivation can originate from a variety of factors (Jana, 2016). These include the lack of support from the institution to encourage professional development courses, and the institutions' lack of openness to new ways of teaching (Iosup & Epema, 2014). Other factors include the level of acceptance of GBL from other fellow educators, as well as the apathy of students to engage in new activities, which ends up demotivating the enthusiasts who initiate these activities in the institution (Bourgonjon et al., 2013; Jana, 2016).

According to Gilbert et al. (2021), having institutional support can significantly increase innovation practices, influence the development and maintain the sustainability of this methodology. Institutional support is obtained through a combination of institutional support through guidelines, financial resources, and policies that encourage the use of this methodology in institutions. In addition, it is important to have adequate physical space, physical resources such as tools and materials, and human resources. Human resources can include the help of students in the development and creation of games, researchers, and other colleagues from the institution. Therefore, engaging and motivating others to participate in the whole process is a successful strategy in this methodology.

METHODOLOGY

The methodology adopted to carry out this study is based, on the one hand, on a broad review of the literature related to the skills of educators that adoption of GLB, on the main bibliographic databases, and the other hand, in the application of a questionnaire survey to educators regardless of their level of experience in the adoption of GBL in their educational institutions. In this sense, the study builds on the literature review, that led to the identification of several competencies that are relevant for educators' adoption of GBL, to structure data collection on GBL experiences from educators across several European countries. The data collection was conducted in the scope of the project UNLOCK Creativity through game-based learning at higher education, a European project that aims to provide the context, process, and tools based on a new and innovative learning approach that stimulates the entrepreneurial capacity of both students and educators, aiming to enhance employability, creativity and new professional paths (Unlock Creativity through Game-Based Learning at Higher Education, 2021).

Several case studies have been carried out with educators using GBL in different fields of knowledge and at different educational levels. The case studies have been carried out in Denmark, Germany, the Netherlands, Lithuania, Portugal, and Spain. A total of 37 case studies were conducted. Research shows that educators seek to use GBL methodologies in teaching for different reasons including the fact that it is a new approach to teaching; for being student-centered; for allowing for the acquisition of skills and competencies to use innovative pedagogies; and drivers such as the stimulation of increased enthusiasm, and awareness about issues such as, for example, the academic and cultural diversity of students.

Inhibiting factors reported by interviewees included factors related to educators' skills, institutional barriers, student preparation, and lack of resources. Educators cited as main challenges a lack of technical skills on GBL, institutional bureaucracy to adopt new practices, support from educational institutions, students' unfamiliarity with the concept of games, and a lack of interest from some students and other colleagues in the institution in new methodologies. This chapter also reports a lack of time among facilitators to organize a game and reconcile it with other activities and technical problems where it is always necessary to have greater technical knowledge or have the support of specialized partners.

DATA ANALYSIS AND RESULTS

Advantages and Obstacles Associated with the Implementation of GBL

Regarding the questionnaire applied this was made to educators, regardless of their level of experience in the adoption of GBL in their educational institutions. A total of 20 respondents were selected in Portugal. The data were analyzed in the Stata software. The respondents were aged between 39 and 67 years, with an average of 51 years old. From these, 60% were male and 40% female, all working in public institutions, and their time as an educator ranged from 10 to 48 years. In Table 1, the authors verify a descriptive analysis of the respondents.

Table 1. Descriptive statistics gender and age

Gender N	Min	Max	Mean	SD
Male 12	40	64	50.91667	6.067174
Female 8	39	67	49.125	9.372262
Total 20	39	67	50.2	7.381342

Source: Authors' elaboration

In Table 2, it can be seen that 60% of the respondents are familiar with the concept of GBL, but only 40% have used GBL in their institutions in the classroom. Of those familiar with GBL, only 5 affirm to use it, and four states not ever have used GBL.

Of these educators who have used GBL in class (40% of the total), the authors identified the teaching areas where they have been applied and the types of educational games applied. In the area of marketing (digital games), social sciences (digital games), management (puzzles), humanities (digital games, puzzles, and board games), and language acquisition (digital games). The respondents reported (100%) that they adapted games from other existing games and thus did not have to worry about developing a game totally from zero.

Table 2. Relationship between familiarity and the use of game-based learning

Use_GBL	Familiar_GBL			
	Yes	No	N/A	Total
Yes	5	0	0	5
	41.67	0.00	0.00	25.00
No	7	4	0	11
	58.33	100.00	0.00	55.00
N/A	0	0	4	4
	0.00	0.00	100.00	20.00
Total	12	4	4	20
	100.00	100.00	100.00	100.00

Source: Authors' elaboration

Regarding the reasons that lead educators to use or not to use the GBL approach in teaching. In Table 3 the authors sought to understand the reasons that lead educators to use GBL. The results were grouped according to respondents' answers, whether or not they had already used this methodology. The results refer to the 20 respondents who answered on a 5-point Likert scale their preferences SD (strongly disagree), D (disagree), N (neutral), A (agree), SA (Strongly agree).

Table 3. Advantages associate with the implementation of GBL

Advantages associate with the implementation of GBL	Use Game-Based learning									
	Yes					No				
	SD	D	N	A	SA	SD	D	N	A	SA
Increased student motivation	-	-	-	20%	80%	-	-	27%	46%	27%
Active participation of students in the teaching-learning process	-	-	-	40%	60%	-	-	9%	64%	27%
Possibility of developing transversal competences	-	-	20%	20%	60%	-	9%	19%	36%	36%
Development of teamwork competences	-	-	20%	20%	60%	-	-	9%	64%	27%
Implementation of innovative methods	-	-	20%	20%	60%	-	9%	27%	46%	18%
Better understanding of content	-	-	20%	20%	60%	-	18%	45%	27%	9%

Source: Authors' elaboration

The results indicate that most respondents who have already used GBL in teaching agree (5 points) that the use of GBL is an innovative method in teaching that can help increase students' motivation, improve their participation in the teaching and learning process, develop soft skills and teamwork, and increase knowledge in specific content. About those who have never used GBL, their perception is a little different, as most of them, on a 5-point scale, chose the option "agree", or "neutral", i.e., it is noted that there is some doubt regarding the benefits of this methodology by educators who have never used it.

In Table 4 the authors sought to understand the inhibiting factors in the use of GBL, and which may be an obstacle to some educators in the use of this methodology. The results refer to the 20 respondents who answered on a 5-point scale their preferences SD (strongly disagree), D (disagree), N (neutral), A (agree), SA (Strongly agree).

The results indicate that among respondents who have already used GBL and those who have never used this methodology in teaching the results are similar. Most agree (scale 4) that lack of time, lack of resources, and lack of specific training in GBL are the main difficulties in using educational games. Concerning those who have never used the methodology, the lack of specific training is still pointed out as one of the factors with the greatest impact, along with the size of the class to teach these activities, as factors that may inhibit the use of GBL.

Table 4. Obstacles identify with the implementation of GBL

Obstacles identify with the implementation of GBL	Use Game-based learning									
	Yes					No				
	SD	D	N	A	SA	SD	D	N	A	SA
Lack of framework/adequacy with programmatic contents	-	-	100%	-	-	-	18%	36%	27%	18%
Scarcity of time	-	-	-	60%	40%	9%	-	19%	36%	36%
Lack of resources (e.g. rooms, equipment, utensils, materials, etc.)	-	40%	-	40%	20%	18%	9%	27%	37%	9%
Excessive class size	-	20%	-	40%	40%	-	-	27%	46%	27%
Program/time charge does not allow activities of this nature to be combined	-	20%	60%	-	20%	18%	18%	28%	9%	27%
Lack of specific training in GBL	20%	-	20%	40%	20%	-	9%	18%	27%	46%

Source: Authors' elaboration

These results thus support the relevance of the problems found in the literature on the subject. Institutional support mainly through the encouragement of these teaching methodologies, mobilization of courses and programs that can encourage this practice, acquisition of materials that can be used, and a greater margin of time for these activities in the curriculum is essential to promote the sustainability of this practice. These results will be used in the next section where it is presented a proposal of a conceptual framework.

Proposed Conceptual Framework

Few studies have looked into the development and assessment of teachers' knowledge in GBL, and the aforementioned gaps in filling teachers' competence in GBL (Shah & Foster, 2015). Some studies seek to create pedagogical frameworks to guide educators and institutions with the adoption of game-based learning within a new or existing curriculum, systematically guiding in the process of selecting and integrating games in school contexts.

For example, Nousiainen et al. (2018), has created a pedagogical framework to examine what kind of competencies teachers need in using game-based pedagogy (GBP). In conceptual framework, GBP entails four approaches: using educational games or entertainment games, learning by making games, and using gamification in learning. The results are applicable for developing teacher education and in-service training, as teacher competencies in game-based learning will be more integral to teachers' professional knowledge and skill repertoires (see Figure 1 - A). With a similar objective, Buchner and Zumbach (2020), present a framework for implementing augmented reality (AR) learning environments. This framework suggests that the basic factor determining the use of Augmented Reality is the choice of an appropriate Instructional Strategy.

The model combines the technological perspective (TK, here concerning AR) with the didactic/pedagogical perspective and extends it with a third, enrichment level (see Figure 1 – B). This last aspect may be important for all teachers. Yet, Shah and Foster (2015), in his study created game network analysis (GANA). GANA was conceptualised to provide a methodological framework that teachers need within their ecological context to focus on the pedagogy and content of games, as well as the process of using and applying games in classrooms. This framework empowers teachers with methods desirable for using games to facilitate through the interacting constructs of game analysis, game integration, and the conditions that impact game use in school contexts (see Figure 1 – C).

Figure 1. Examples of models used to create conceptual frameworks.
Source: Nousiainen et al. (2018, pg 94); Buchner & Zumbach (2020, pg 12); Shah & Foster (2015, pg 247).

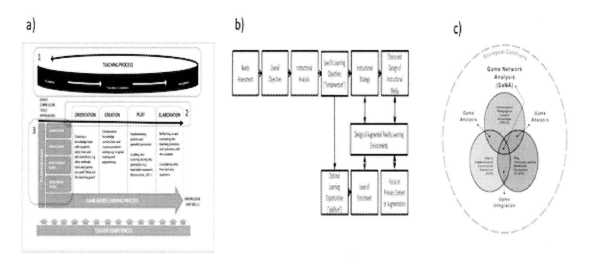

For this chapter, the authors made a conceptual framework with the competencies reported in the study and which are necessary for an educator to be a facilitator of game-based activities. The study revealed that all the competencies referred to as relevant for the adoption of GBL are interconnected. For an educator to become a GBL facilitator, pedagogical, technological, creative, and collaborative competencies must be met (Shah & Foster, 2015). All need to be aligned with the specifically intended teaching and learning objectives. Considering GBL activities, after analyzing the scientific articles, case studies, and questionnaires the authors have highlighted, the necessary competencies that have the greatest impact on GBL activities with grouping these together with the institutional content that the authors have identified among the greatest inhibitors and obstacles cited in the different research.

The conceptual framework can be seen in Figure 2. In pedagogical skills, the main skills identified that are necessary for the GBL facilitator involve the ability to identify new teaching methodologies and the planning and alignment of the chosen game with the pedagogical curriculum. In this process mentoring and tutoring should be carried out by the educator to encourage reflection among learners and a positive attitude during the activity. In addition to the game, assessment activities should be developed according to the objectives initially stipulated in the planning.

Among the main technological competencies is technical and digital knowledge. Experience with games and knowledge of various GBL activities are fundamental for the educator to gain confidence in using this tool in teaching. Self-development and keeping up to date with experts and professionals in GBL are also cited in this research. Social and collaborative competencies will complete the profile of an appropriate GBL facilitator. The ability to innovate and be creative, flexible, and adapt to unexpected situations and out of their comfort zone needs to be inherent to a GBL facilitator. Besides, for the success and sustainability of this practice, the educator must mobilize and work with other colleagues.

Figure 2. A conceptual framework for game-based learning facilitators
Source: Authors' elaboration

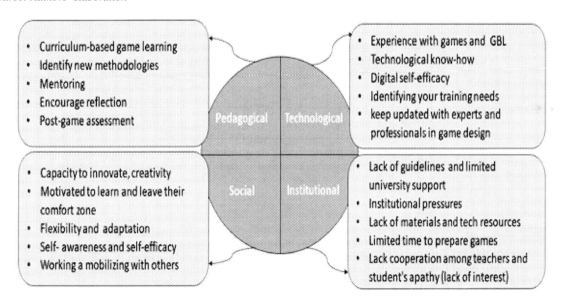

Finally, to complete our framework, the authors highlight institutional content, one of the most important parts for the success of this methodology. Even with the motivation and inclination of several educators for this practice, many report the lack of a guiding thread and support from the institution for the use of GBL. Many educators report feeling lost in how to adapt this practice into their content and feel pressure to follow a traditional teaching method without much openness to innovation. Besides, educators report work overload and too many students in their classes which can limit the use of these practices. When educators do manage to overcome institutional problems, they are also confronted with a lack of cooperation among colleagues and students' apathy for new teaching approaches. Thus, more support and engagement from institutions is needed to include these practices in the programs, to disseminate them among all educators and students so that they adopt and perceive the advantages of using these practices in teaching.

DISCUSSION AND RECOMMENDATIONS

The research results indicate that specific training on GBL should be intensified among educators, and institutional support should be broader so that all educators can grasp the concept of the methodology and begin to insert it into their programs as they understand which of the strategies of the different types of existing GBL may suit their particular case. It is recommended to evaluate the time for the administration of gamified study systems and content development. It is likely that before starting to fully use the gamified system, a lot of time is needed to customize its features and adapt it to the students' working needs and preferences.

It is also recommended to allocate some time to test the gamified systems before applying them at full scale. It is important to expose educators to a wide variety of games that they could try, as teachers needed to be able to experience for themselves what some of these games could do (Becker, 2007). It is also pointed out that not all study subjects are equally easy to gamify. In cases where advanced mechanical skills are required, or on the contrary, highly abstract results are needed, the application of GBL will be more complicated. Before proposing the possibilities of integrating gamified study environments into the study process, consider the occupation aspects of academic staff, as maintaining these systems requires more time and financial resources compared to traditional didactic methods. In the initial stages of integrating gamified systems, increased dissatisfaction, and frustration on the part of academic staff can be expected. This will inevitably affect the workload of the staff responsible for technological support in the higher education institution. Given these aspects, the application of gamification in studies should be applied voluntarily by academic staff and students (*Unlock Creativity through Game-Based Learning at Higher Education*, 2021).

Educators cite several positive skills and attitudes towards GBL. There is a willingness to learn a new methodology and to engage students in new learning experiences. However, the lack of support for teaching and learning at the highest level of the university, the lack of methodological, technological, and institutional support combined with work overload and lack of time to devote to new activities is a major inhibiting factor that can impede the development and sustainability of these practices in teaching, as the results of the chapter expose.

Innovative pedagogies reveal greater professional satisfaction and self-efficacy. One of the biggest challenges nowadays is to find out ways for teachers to build common ground, set together challenges to tackle, and collaborate more deeply to achieve greater impact. When institutions have collaborative power among groups, the development of talent increases. Collaborative cultures create a sense of responsibility and proactivity (Ataíde et al., 2019).

It is recommended that educators keep informed and develop their skills either through online training or external collaborations. Deeper partnerships between the various actors in education, university, community, schools, and stakeholders of the tool are needed, to spread the knowledge about GBL and raise the interest of more educators worldwide. Teachers benefit from a range of collaborative competencies when implementing GBL; these may relate to teamwork within the same school or networking with teachers from other schools and other relevant actors (Nousiainen et al., 2018). Across the countries, many experiments are carried out, but there is a lack of a platform for sharing these activities, specific manuals to guide educators in each of the various GBL modalities that exist. Only after knowing and testing a methodology will educators feel confident to share, disseminate and implement it in the school curriculum.

STUDY LIMITS AND FUTURE RESEARCH DIRECTIONS

The authors identified through the European Unlock project that GBL activities have discrepancies according to region. The project development thus far allows observing that in northern Europe, for example, there are more financial incentives to promote the use of innovative activities in higher education. However, in southern countries, this support must come from the institution's resources or through projects financed by the European Union.

In this sense, for future studies, it is recommended to investigate these practices in other countries and continents to compare institutional resources. It is as well highlighted the need for the support provided by policy agents to encourage new innovative methodologies in education. It is important to investigate in other regions such as America, Asia, and Africa the use of game-based learning in the view of educators and how the lack of institutional support may be limiting the use of these activities. There is little research in the literature on the development of educators' competencies to carry out these activities. Most of the studies focus on the development of students' competencies.

Studies with a larger number of participants are still needed to validate this framework. One of the limitations found in this study was the low number of responses to the questionnaires applied.

CONCLUSION

The use of gamification and game-based learning strategies has a great potential for development among educators to promote student motivation, participation, the development of soft skills, and the review of specific content that can be intensified through this teaching methodology. However, despite a large number of studies in the development of students' skills with these tools, the skills needed by educators are not fully investigated. Understanding the competencies needed by educators and proposing the development of these competencies is fundamental for the success and sustainability of this methodology.

This chapter sought to analyze through the critical review of literature, case studies, interviews, and questionnaires, the main skills needed to the facilitator of game-based learning, these skills were grouped into pedagogical, technological, social, collaborative, and institutional skills. The authors identified the main competencies and designed a conceptual framework to help in the perception of the profile of a GBL facilitator. All these competencies need to be aligned to provide effectiveness in developing these activities in teaching. In this chapter, institutional content stands out, where it is observed that the impact of the support of the educational institution is paramount to provide greater engagement before educators and the dissemination of this practice. As well as the incentive for training programs, webinars, courses and online platforms that disseminate this practice among students and teachers.

Finally, some recommendations are developed at this level, such as the intensification of training for educators, both online and face-to-face in the form of workshops and external collaborations. Further training of educators' technological and pedagogical skills is still needed. Collaboration among university colleagues should be encouraged through practical activities and the online development of these activities should be supported and shared among various actors in education such as the community, university, schools, and other partners interested in GBL practices.

ACKNOWLEDGMENT

This work was co-funded by the Erasmus+ Programme of the European Union Policy (Project Number:612645-EPP-1-2019-1-PT-EPPKA2-KA).

This work was supported by the research unit on Governance, Competitiveness and Public Policy (UIDB/04058/2020), funded by national funds through FCT -Fundação para a Ciência e a Tecnologia.

REFERENCES

Almeida, F. (2020). Adoption of a Serious Game in the Developing of Emotional Intelligence Skills. *European Journal of Investigation in Health, Psychology and Education*, *10*(1), 30–43. doi:10.3390/ejihpe10010004 PMID:34542467

Arnab, S., Clarke, S., & Morini, L. (2019). Co-creativity through play and game design thinking. *Electronic Journal of E-Learning*, *17*(3), 184–198. doi:10.34190/JEL.17.3.002

Ataíde, A., Souto, I., & Pereira, A. (2019). School Problems and Teachers' Collaboration: Before a Collaborative Problem Solving Program. *Education and New Developments*, *1*(July), 222–226. doi:10.36315/2019v1end047

Beavis, C. (2013). Multiliteracies in the wild: Learning from computer games. In G. Merchant, J. Gillen, J. Marsh, & J. Davies (Eds.), *Virtual literacies: Interactive spaces for children and young people* (pp. 57–74). Routledge. http://hdl.handle.net/10536/DRO/DU:30090206

Beavis, C., & O'Mara, J. A. (2010). *Computer games–pushing at the boundaries of literacy. Australian Journal of Language and Literacy, 33(1), 65-76.* http://hdl.handle.net/10072/37372

Becker, K. (2007). Digital game - based learning once removed : Teaching teachers. *British Journal of Educational Technology. SIG-GLUE Special Issue on Game-Based Learning*, *38*(3), 478–488. doi:10.1111/j.1467-8535.2007.00711.x

Bourgonjon, J., De Grove, F., De Smet, C., Van Looy, J., Soetaert, R., & Valcke, M. (2013). Acceptance of game-based learning by secondary school teachers. *Computers & Education*, *67*, 21–35. doi:10.1016/j.compedu.2013.02.010

Bourgonjon, J., & Hanghoi, T. (2011). What does it mean to be a game literate teacher? Interviews with teachers who translate games into educational practice. *Proceedings of the European Conference on Games-Based Learning*, 67–73.

Buchner, J., & Zumbach, J. (2020). Augmented Reality in Teacher Education. a Framework To Support Teachers' Technological Pedagogical Content Knowledge. *Italian Journal of Educational Technology*, *28*(2), 106–120. doi:10.17471/2499-4324/1151

Carenys, J., & Moya, S. (2016). Digital game-based learning in accounting and business education. *Accounting Education*, *25*(6), 598–651. doi:10.1080/09639284.2016.1241951

Chen, S., Zhang, S., Qi, G. Y., & Yang, J. (2020). Games Literacy for Teacher Education : Towards the Implementation of Game-based Learning. *Journal of Educational Technology & Society*, *23*(2), 77–92.

Chetouani, M., Vanden Abeele, V., Leuven, K., Carmen Moret-Tatay, B., Lopes, S., Magalhães, P., Pereira, A., Martins, J., Magalhães, C., Chaleta, E., & Rosário, P. (2018). Games Used With Serious Purposes: A Systematic Review of Interventions in Patients With Cerebral Palsy. *Frontiers in Psychology*, *9*, 1712. doi:10.3389/fpsyg.2018.01712 PMID:30283377

Clarke, S., Peel, D. J., Arnab, S., Morini, L., Keegan, H., Wood, O., Morini, L., & Wood, O. (2017). *escapED : A Framework for Creating Educational Escape Rooms and Interactive Games For Higher / Further Education*. Academic Press.

Dabbagh, N., Benson, A. D., Denham, A., Joseph, R., & Zgheib, M. A. G. (2015). *Learning Technologies and Globalization Pedagogical Frameworks and Applications*. Academic Press.

Eastwood, J. L., & Sadler, T. D. (2013). Teachers' implementation of a game-based biotechnology curriculum. *Computers & Education*, *66*(0), 11–24. doi:10.1016/j.compedu.2013.02.003

Ferreiro-González, M., Amores-Arrocha, A., Espada-Bellido, E., Aliano-Gonzalez, M. J., Vázquez-Espinosa, M., González-De-Peredo, A. V., Sancho-Galán, P., Álvarez-Saura, J. Á., Barbero, G. F., & Cejudo-Bastante, C. (2019). Escape ClassRoom: Can You Solve a Crime Using the Analytical Process? *Journal of Chemical Education*, *96*(2), 267–273. doi:10.1021/acs.jchemed.8b00601

Foster, A., & Shah, M. (2015). The Play Curricular activity Reflection Discussion Model for Game-Based Learning. *Journal of Research on Technology in Education*, *47*(2), 71–88. doi:10.1080/15391523.2015.967551

Foster, A., & Shah, M. (2020). Principles for Advancing Game-Based Learning in Teacher Education. *Journal of Digital Learning in Teacher Education*, *36*(2), 84–95. doi:10.1080/21532974.2019.1695553

Frossard, F. (2013). *Fostering teachers' creativity through the creation of GBL scenarios* [Doctoral thesis, Universitat de Barcelona]. Departament de Didàctica i Organització Educativa. http://hdl.handle.net/10803/130831

Gilbert, A., Tait-MCutcheon, S., & Knewstubb, B. (2021). Innovative teaching in higher education: Teachers' perceptions of support and constraint. *Innovations in Education and Teaching International*, *58*(2), 123–134. doi:10.1080/14703297.2020.1715816

Gros, B. (2010). Game-based learning: A strategy to integrate digital games in schools. In J. Yamamoto, J. Kush, R. Lombard, & C. Hertzog (Eds.), Technology Implementation and Teacher Education: Reflective Models (pp. 365-379). doi:10.4018/978-1-61520-897-5.ch021

Grove, F. De, Cornillie, F., Mechant, P., & Looy, J. Van. (2013). *Tapping into the Field of Foreign Language Learning Games. April 2014*. doi:10.1504/IJART.2013.050690

Guigon, G., Humeau, J., & Vermeulen, M. (2018). A model to design learning escape games: SEGAM. *CSEDU 2018 - Proceedings of the 10th International Conference on Computer Supported Education, 2*(March), 191–197. 10.5220/0006665501910197

Hanghøj, T., Nielsen, B. L., Skott, C. K., & Ejsing-Duun, S. (2020). Teacher agency and dialogical positions in relation to game-based design activities. *Proceedings of the European Conference on Games-Based Learning,* 234–241. 10.34190/GBL.20.033

Hirumi, A., & Stapleton, C. (2009). Applying Pedagogy during Game Development to Enhance Game-Based Learning. *Games: Purpose and Potential in Education,* 127–162. doi:10.1007/978-0-387-09775-6_6

Hunter, J. (2020). *STEAM games are good for learning: A study of teacher professional development in the Philippines.* New orleans, LA: SITE 2020.

Hurtado, M. F., & González, J. (2017). Necesidades formativas del profesorado de Secundaria para la implementación de experiencias gamificadas en STEM. *Revista de Educación a Distancia, 54*(8), 30–36. https://www.um.es/ead/red/54/fuentes_gonzalez.pdf

Iosup, A., & Epema, D. (2014). *An Experience Report on Using Gamification in Technical Higher Education.* Conference paper SIGCSE, Atlanta, GA. 10.1145/2538862.2538899

Jaipal, K., & Figg, C. (2009). Using video games in science instruction: Pedagogical, social, and concept-related aspects. *Canadian Journal of Science Mathematics and Technology Education, 9*(2), 117–134. doi:10.1080/14926150903047780

Jana, M. (2016). Teachers' Views on Game-based Learning (GBL) as a Teaching Method in Elementary Level Education. *Global Journal for Research Analysis, 5*(1).

Kali, Y., McKenney, S., & Sagy, O. (2015). Teachers as designers of technology enhanced learning. *Instructional Science, 43*(2), 173–179. doi:10.100711251-014-9343-4

Kamışlı, H. (2019). On primary school teachers' training needs in relation to game-based learning. *International Journal of Curriculum and Instruction, 11*(2), 285–296.

Karagiannis, S., & Magkos, E. (2021). Engaging Students in Basic Cybersecurity Concepts Using Digital Game-Based Learning: Computer Games as Virtual Learning Environments. In *Advances in Core Computer Science-Based Technologies.* Springer., doi:10.1007/978-3-030-41196-1_4

Linderoth, J., & Sjöblom, B. (2019). Being an Educator and Game Developer: The Role of Pedagogical Content Knowledge in Non-Commercial Serious Games Production. *Simulation & Gaming, 50*(6), 771–788. doi:10.1177/1046878119873023

Marklund, B. B., & Alklind Taylor, A. S. (2016). Educational games in practice: The challenges involved in conducting a game-based curriculum. *Electronic Journal of E-Learning, 14*(2), 121–135.

Marklund, B. B., & Taylor, A. S. A. (2015). Teachers' many roles in game-based learning projects. *Proceedings of the European Conference on Games-Based Learning,* 350–367.

McKenney, S. (2005). Technology for curriculum and teacher development: Software to help educators learn while designing teacher guides. *Journal of Research on Technology in Education, 38*(2), 167–190. doi:10.1080/15391523.2005.10782455

Molin, G. (2017). The Role of the Teacher in Game-Based Learning: A Review and Outlook. Serious Games and Edutainment Applications, 649-674. doi:10.1007/978-3-319-51645-5_28

Nicholson, S. (2018). Creating engaging escape rooms for the classroom. *Childhood Education, 94*(1), 44–49. doi:10.1080/00094056.2018.1420363

Nousiainen, T., Kangas, M., Rikala, J., & Vesisenaho, M. (2018). Teacher competencies in game-based pedagogy. *Teaching and Teacher Education, 74*, 85–97. doi:10.1016/j.tate.2018.04.012

Pellas, N., Fotaris, P., Kazanidis, I., & Wells, D. (2019). Augmenting the learning experience in primary and secondary school education: A systematic review of recent trends in augmented reality game-based learning. *Virtual Reality (Waltham Cross), 23*(4), 329–346. doi:10.100710055-018-0347-2

Pinto, M., & Ferreira, P. (2017). Use of Videogames in Higher Education in Portugal : A Literature Review. In Challenges 2017: Aprender nas nuvens, Learning in the clouds (pp. 605-620). Universidade do Minho – Centro de Competência.

Prestridge, S., & de Aldama, C. (2016). A Classification framework for exploring technology enabled practice-FramTEP. *Journal of Educational Computing Research, 54*(7), 901–921. doi:10.1177/0735633116636767

Raziunaite, P., Miliunaite, A., Maskeliunas, R., Damasevicius, R., Sidekerskiene, T., & Narkeviciene, B. (2018). Designing an educational music game for digital game based learning: A Lithuanian case study. *2018 41st International Convention on Information and Communication Technology, Electronics and Microelectronics, MIPRO 2018 - Proceedings*, 800–805. 10.23919/MIPRO.2018.8400148

Rodrigues, L. F., Costa, C. J., & Oliveira, A. (2017). How does the web game design influence the behavior of e-banking users? *Computers in Human Behavior, 74*, 163–174. doi:10.1016/j.chb.2017.04.034

Rowan, L., & Beavis, C. (2017). Serious outcomes from serious play: Teachers' beliefs about assessment of game-based learning in schools. In C. Beavis, M. Dezuanni, & J. O'Mara (Eds.), *Serious play: literacy, learning and digital games* (pp. 169–185). Routledge. doi:10.4324/9781315537658-16

Sánchez-Martín, J., Corrales-Serrano, M., Luque-Sendra, A., & Zamora-Polo, F. (2020). Exit for success. Gamifying science and technology for university students using escape-room. A preliminary approach. *Heliyon, 6*(7), e04340. doi:10.1016/j.heliyon.2020.e04340 PMID:32671257

Shah, M., & Foster, A. (2015). Developing and Assessing Teachers' Knowledge of Game-based Learning. *Journal of Technology and Teacher Education, 23*(2), 241–267.

Silseth, K. (2012). The multivoicedness of game play: Exploring the unfolding of a student's learning trajectory in a gaming context at school. *International Journal of Computer-Supported Collaborative Learning, 7*(1), 63–84. doi:10.100711412-011-9132-x

Tercanli, H., Martina, R., Dias, M. F., Wakkee, I., Reuter, J., Amorim, M., Madaleno, M., Magueta, D., Vieira, E., Veloso, C., Figueiredo, C., Vitória, A., Gomes, I., Meireles, G., Daubariene, A., Daunoriene, A., Mortensen, A. K., Zinovyeva, A., Trigueros, I. R., . . . Gutiérrez-Pérez, J. (2021). *Educational Escape Room in Practice: Research, experiences and recommendations*. Academic Press.

Unlock Creativity through game-based learning at higher education. (2021). https://www.un-lock.eu/

Urh, M., Vukovic, G., Jereb, E., & Pintar, R. (2015). The Model for Introduction of Gamification into E-learning in Higher Education. *Procedia - Social and Behavioral Sciences, 197*(March), 388–397. doi:10.1016/j.sbspro.2015.07.154

Veldkamp, A., Daemen, J., Teekens, S., Koelewijn, S., Knippels, M. C. P. J., & van Joolingen, W. R. (2020). Escape boxes: Bringing escape room experience into the classroom. British Journal of Educational Technology, 51(4), 1220–1239. doi:10.1111/bjet.12935

Xu, F., Buhalis, D., & Weber, J. (2017). Serious games and the gamification of tourism. In *Tourism Management* (*Vol. 60*, pp. 244–256). 10.1016/j.tourman.2016.11.020

Yi, L., Zhou, Q., Xiao, T., Qing, G., & Mayer, I. (2020). Conscientiousness in Game-Based Learning. *Simulation & Gaming, 51*(5), 712–734. doi:10.1177/1046878120927061

ADDITIONAL READING

Grivokostopoulou, F., Kovas, K., & Perikos, I. (2019). Examining the impact of a gamified entrepreneurship education framework in higher education. *Sustainability (Switzerland), 11*(20), 5623. Advance online publication. doi:10.3390u11205623

Ke, F., Xie, K., & Xie, Y. (2016). Game-based learning engagement: A theory- and data-driven exploration. *British Journal of Educational Technology, 47*(6), 1183–1201. doi:10.1111/bjet.12314

Kiili, K., Lainema, T., De Freitas, S., & Arnab, S. (2014). Flow framework for analyzing the quality of educational games q. *Entertainment Computing, 5*(4), 367–377. doi:10.1016/j.entcom.2014.08.002

Marsh, T. (2011). Serious games continuum : Between games for purpose and experiential environments for purpose. *Entertainment Computing, 2*(2), 61–68. doi:10.1016/j.entcom.2010.12.004

Robson, K., Plangger, K., Kietzmann, J. H., McCarthy, I., & Pitt, L. (2015). Is it all a game? Understanding the principles of gamification. *Business Horizons, 58*(4), 411–420. doi:10.1016/j.bushor.2015.03.006

Werbach, K., & Hunter, D. (2015). *The gamification toolkit: dynamics, mechanics, and components for the win*. Wharton School Press.

KEY TERMS AND DEFINITIONS

Conceptual Framework: A conceptual framework provides a resource to define and illustrate the relevant variables of the study and map out how these may relate to each other.

Educational Games: These are games that have formal objectives, designed to help people learn about particular subjects, expand concepts, reinforce development, or help them learn a skill while playing.

Game-Based Learning (GBL): A pedagogical methodology that focuses on the design, development, and application of games in education/and or training with defined learning outcomes. Can include different types of games such as puzzles, board games, digital games, and others.

Gamification: Using game elements, such as incentive systems, to motivate players to engage with a task they would not otherwise find attractive.

Innovation: Implementation of ideas and practice of creativity that result in the introduction of new teaching methodologies and process improvement.

Institutional Support: Set of policies, practices, physical facilities, software or processes, made available by the organization, which enable successful learning.

Professional Development: The set of tools, resources, and training sessions for educators to improve their teaching quality and effectiveness.

Teacher Competencies: The combination of knowledge, skills, attitudes, values, and personal characteristics, enabling the teacher to act professionally and appropriately in a situation.

UNLOCK: Project UNLOCK - Creativity in HEIs through a game design approach. It aims to provide the context, process, and tools based on an innovative learning approach that stimulates the entrepreneurial skills of both students and educators, aiming to enhance employability, creativity, and new professional paths.

Chapter 29

Spanish Teacher Attitudes Towards Digital Game–Based Learning:
An Exploratory Study Based on the TPACK Model

Cristina A. Huertas-Abril
iD https://orcid.org/0000-0002-9057-5224
University of Córdoba, Spain

María García-Molina
University of Córdoba, Spain

ABSTRACT

The consideration that the only goal of games is the achievement of entertainment is still commonly accepted, although there is now an outgrowing perspective that believes in the use of games to promote learning. This exploratory quantitative research examines both in-service and pre-service Spanish teacher perceptions (n = 112) about using digital games in their lessons, paying a special attention to the TPACK model, and comparing the results regarding age, gender, and professional situation. Responses show a positive attitude towards the potential use of video games in their lessons, although there are differences considering the results of the items concerning technological, pedagogical, or content knowledge. The data presented in this study is relevant to guide the design of curriculum and training programs, as well as to develop strategies to support and scaffold pre-service and in-service teachers' knowledge and practical implementation of digital game-based learning (DGBL).

DOI: 10.4018/978-1-7998-7271-9.ch029

INTRODUCTION

Games play and essential role in our daily life and in our learning, both in nonformal and informal contexts, especially when we are children. However, when society think about formal education, games are still often seen as an "unserious" activity (Pivec, 2007) This consideration in which the only goal of games is perceived as the achievement of entertainment and fun is still widely accepted, although there is now an outgrowing perspective that believes in the use of games to promote learning (Cornellà et al., 2020). In fact, game-based learning can support effective pedagogical methods as long as teachers are given the necessary time, training and tools to implement this approach in their lessons.

The first author to discuss the use of games in education as a tool for learning was Abt, in his book *Serious Games* (1970). Abt considered the use of games to teach the school curriculum as a way of bringing closer "school learning" and "informal learning", and referred to serious games as games that "have an explicit and carefully thought-out educational purpose and are not intended to be played primarily for amusement" (Abt, 1970, p. 9). However, he clarified that that did not mean that those games should not be entertaining, but that being entertaining was not its main purpose. Since that moment on, the use of games in education has been increasingly gaining acceptance.

Three decades later, Prensky (2001) went a step further to delve into the Digital Game-Based Learning (DGBL) methodology, seeing it as the coming together of what he considered two different sides: serious learning and interactive entertainment. This author claimed that the changes in technology had had an influence on students' worlds, styles of learning and capabilities, and considered DGBL as an effective and feasible means to change the learning process in a way that appealed to, and excited, people from the "games generations". It must be borne in mind that digital games do not only refer to video games, but to any other interactive digital media that can be played using computer power and a video display, including console games, computers, tablets or smartphones. In this light, DGBL is broadly defined as "the use of digital games with serious goals (i.e., educational objectives), as tools that support learning processes in a significant way" (EU Lifelong Learning Programme, 2011, p. 10).

DGBL has captured the attention of researchers and practitioners in recent years (Boyle et al., 2016), and it is no surprise that the use of digital games has been widespread across all levels of formal education (i.e., Martín et al., 2019; Gómez-Gonzalvo et al., 2018; Mendez & Boude, 2021). Nevertheless, research on teachers' competences to use digital games in their learning are still limited, especially when considering a holistic framework as the Technological Pedagogical Content Knowledge (TPACK) model, constructivist framework developed by Mishra and Koehler (2006).

After analyzing the role of Game-Based Learning (GBL), paying a special attention to Digital Game-Based Learning (DGBL), and the skills that 21st century teachers need in the light of the TPACK model (Mishra & Koehler, 2006; Koehler et al., 2014), this study aims to explore in-service and pre-service Spanish teachers' perceptions and uses about applying digital games in their lessons, considering the TPACK framework, and to compare the results regarding age, gender, and professional situation. Pre-service and in-service teachers from Spain were chosen as target population due to the impact of the Common Digital Competence Framework for Teachers (INTEF, 2017), and their use of digital technologies in their lessons. INTEF, acronym for the Instituto Nacional de Tecnologías Educativas y de Formación del Profesorado (in English: National Institute of Educational Technologies and Teacher Training) is the Department of the Spanish Ministry of Education and Vocational Training responsible for the integration of educational technologies and teacher training in non-university educational stages in Spain. In 2017, INTEF published the Common Digital Competence Framework for Teachers, in line with the European

Union Framework of Digital Competence of Educators – DigCompEdu (Redecker, 2017), and since then special emphasis has been given to the use and certification of educational technologies, as well as to initial and lifelong teacher training, including DGBL.

Based on the review of existing academic literature on DGBL, four hypotheses were posed

- Hypothesis 1 (H1): Spanish teachers' perceptions regarding the use of digital games in their lessons and DGBL considering the TPACK model are positive.
- Hypothesis 2 (H2): Spanish teachers' perceptions regarding the use of digital games in their lessons and DGBL differ depending on their age.
- Hypothesis 3 (H3): Spanish teachers' perceptions regarding the use of digital games in their lessons and DGBL differ depending on their gender.
- Hypothesis 4 (H4): Pre-service Spanish teachers' perceptions regarding the use of digital games in their lessons and DGBL are significantly better than those of in-service Spanish teachers' perceptions.

BACKGROUND

Digital Game-Based Learning

Education has always evolved in the light of the needs of society, and consequently its direct relation with technology has significantly increased in the last two decades, originating new perspectives (Loveless, & Williamson, 2013; Selwyn, & Bulfin, 2016). Consequently, new approaches have risen, and even though the use of games in education is not new (Casañ-Pitarch, 2018), game-based approaches are gaining importance due to the introduction of technological resources, including digital games, providing students with attractive, new learning possibilities (Eseryel et al., 2014).

Contrary to gamification, which is the process from which games can be adapted to reach specific learning goals (Werbach, 2014), Game-Based Learning (GBL) is an approach that consists of a type of game play with defined learning outcomes, that is, it is designed to balance contents to learn with gameplay, as well as with the ability of the learner/player to understand, retain and apply that content matter to the real world.

GBL is a broad term, involving both digital and non-digital resources (Deterding et al., 2011), and in this case the authors will mainly focus on Digital Game-Based Learning (DGBL), also referred as Digital Game-Based Learning (DGBL), which consists of the GBL approach based on digital games or video games thanks to the use of technological resources. DGBL could be then defined as "the use of digital games with serious goals (i.e., educational objectives), as tools that support learning processes in a significant way" (EU Lifelong Learning Programme, 2011, p. 10). In this context, it is necessary to differentiate between conventional (video) games and serious or applied (video) games. While the main purpose of conventional games in entertainment, serious games primarily aim to teach specific content (Calvo-Ferrer, 2018). This, however, does not entail that serious games should not be entertaining (Casañ-Pitarch, 2018; González-González, & Blanco-Izquierdo, 2012; Oliveira et al., 2009). Although it can be stated that both conventional and serious digital games are educational (Reinders, 2012), the key difference between these two categories lies in the fact that serious games are designed on purpose for teaching (Bellotti et al., 2013).

To facilitate the assimilation of the terms, the difference between gamification, GBL, DGBL and serious (digital) games is summarized in Table 1 below.

Table 1. Gamification, GBL, DGBL and serious (digital) games

	Gamification	**GBL**	**DGBL**	**Serious (Digital) Games**
Definition	Use of game elements in non-gaming contexts.	Process and use of learning by using games.	Process and use of learning by using digital games.	Custom-built (digital) games with explicit learning goals.
Purpose	Not a game, but the implementation of games in non-gaming contexts.	Not a game, but an approach to learning.	Not a digital game, but an approach to learning.	(Digital) game connected with educational goals.
Rationale	Increase of engagement and motivation.	-Increase of engagement and motivation. -Transfer of knowledge. -Acquisition and development of new skills and competences. -Abstract applicable knowledge.		-Increase of engagement and motivation -Transfer of knowledge -Acquisition and development of new skills and competences -Abstract applicable knowledge -Awareness towards the learning process
Focus	User experience.	Learning objectives		Content
Use	Implementation of an extra layer within previous existing environments or learning programs. It can be implementing in both learning and non-learning contexts.	Use of games that can be repurposed for the learning goals. It is advisable to implement it under teachers' supervision.	Use of digital games that can be repurposed for the learning goals. It is advisable to implement it under teachers' supervision.	Use of (digital) games that have been created from scratch to meet specific learning needs in order to reach explicit learning goals. It is advisable to implement it under teachers' supervision.

Source: (Own elaboration)

Regarding (D)GBL, Robson et al. (2015) identified three key characteristics when using (digital) games in education, namely:

- Mechanics: it refers to the objectives, rules settings, context, interactions and boundaries of the game, enhancing action within the digital game and increasing learners'/players' engagement. There are three types of mechanics: setup (where to play it, objects needed, and how these objects are distributed), rules (that shape the goals), and progression (rewards and winnings).
- Dynamics: it "aims at describing the functioning of the rules in the practice and configuring the behavior of the players that participate in the experience" (Casañ-Pitarch, 2018, p. 1149).
- Emotions: it deals with the mental and affective states and reactions evoked and provoked among individual learners/players.

Moreover, following Casañ-Pitarch (2018), four aspects should be borne in mind when designing or using games for education:

- Engagement: the involvement and connection of the learner/player is stronger when the game is set in a specific context and is clearly connected to the learning process.

- Autonomy: as learners/players are the protagonists, they can take control and explore the virtual world at their own pace taking their own decisions, increasing the immersion in their learning process.
- Mastery: by repeating tasks and mechanizing actions, learners gain mastery both in the digital game and in the target content.
- Progression: it is the reward for learners/players for their efforts, as they can witness their progression by gaining points, achieving ranks or unlocking new levels, increasing then their engagement and motivation.

Key Learning Principles of Digital Game-Based Learning

In the light of the above, four key principles behind DGBL can be identified:

Situated learning and task-solving processes: Gee (2013) argued that students do not learn from generalizations and abstractions, but from experiences. Students find patterns in experiences, and they eventually learn to generalize from them, developing generalizations or principles. This author pinpoints that learning must be based on experiences, and these experiences must be well-designed and well-mentored in order to promote effective learning. In numerous occasions, school is usually too focused on students learning facts and data 'to pass tests', while teachers forget to foster students' learning leading to critical thinking and task-solving skills (Susi et al., 2007; Sampson, & Karagiannidis, 2002). Consequently, if learning is based on experience, students should not only learn facts and figures (information), but focus on the facts themselves and apply them. That is, if students do not have any experience associated with that information (i.e., actions, images…), it is possible that they will not be able to fully comprehend the content. This is where digital games come into action: digital games are well-designed experiences to develop task-solving competences and allow students to experience the facts and to make sense out of then in a significant way (Jarvis, 2009; Ziegler, 2016). This is also in line with Gee's principles for GBL (Gee, 2005), "Information on demand and just in time", where it is affirmed that video games give the player the information to solve a problem just when the learners/players need it, so the meaning or purpose of learning is immediately recognizable.

Active Learning: DGBL places the focus on the learners, as they become the center of the teaching-learning process where teachers act as guides. Students develop an active role and become the protagonists of their own learning (Tejederas, 2020), as DGBL is a student-centered approach. Digital games allow students to interact with the world by taking actions and making decisions, participating in the process of learning itself. Students feel a real sense of control of what they are doing. Moreover, most digital games can be customized to match the learning and playing styles of the player, allowing them to solve problems in different ways and, therefore, developing their resilience and problem-solving skills (Gee, 2005).

Risk Taking Processes: Students normally avoid taking risks, as they are usually afraid of making mistakes. In traditional schooling, pointing out students' mistakes in from of the rest of the class can really damage their ego, promoting anxiety and inhibition in future occasions (Tejederas, 2020). However, digital games lower the consequences of failure and present it as a way to gain feedback about the progress made (Gee, 2005). Failure on video games is usually seen as something natural and positive, as it allows players to progress on the game and get closer to reach their goals – it is no longer something to be afraid of, but a common step in the learning process. Digital games favor performance before competence, which means that students are encouraged to try, learning by doing, and to make mistakes before achieving mastery (Gee, 2005).

Motivation and Engagement: DGBL increases students' motivation, as in games they have to face different challenges and work to overcome them (Tejederas, 2020). In words of Gee (2005), games are pleasantly frustrating, which means that challenges presented to learners/players are doable. The objective of games may then be hard to achieve, but not impossible, which increases students' motivation. This author also claimed that digital games present well-ordered problems, meaning that the difficulty of the challenges increased progressively as they built up on each other, which also helped to increase motivation. It is important to notice that motivation has been identified as one of the essential factors that drives learning, as well as a crucial element to achieve students' engagement (Boekaerts, 2010).

TPACK Model

The use of educational technology in general and digital games for education in particular should be subordinated to the teaching methodology or approach employed: educational technology should not condition the teaching work, nor should it be limited to the mere fact of knowing how to use certain digital tools in isolation (Huertas-Abril, 2020). The continuous evolution of educational technology entails evaluating its potential didactic uses for teaching-learning processes, exploring their uses in favor of students' acquisition of knowledge and development of competences.

In this context, it is undeniable the direct bond between educational technology and the Technological Pedagogical Content Knowledge (TPACK) model, constructivist framework developed by Mishra and Koehler (2006), and revised in Koehler et al. (2014). The TPACK model assumes that an appropriate use of technology and pedagogical content knowledge depends largely on teacher's competence. Teacher's competence, therefore, goes beyond subject content knowledge, and must include, together with methodological knowledge, good digital competence (Figure 1).

Figure 1. TPACK model (Mishra, & Koehler, 2006, p. 1025)
Source: Mishra, & Koehler, 2006

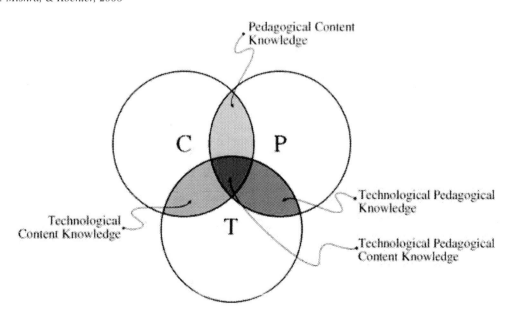

The last revision of the TPACK model (Mishra, 2019) includes ConteXtual Knowledge (XK) (Figure 2):

Figure 2. Revised version of the TPACK image (Mishra, 2019, p. 77)
Source: Mishra, 2019

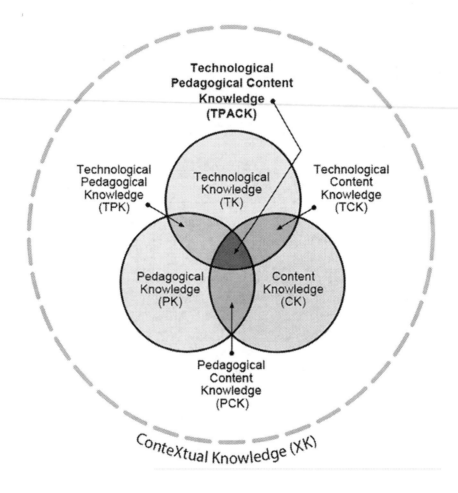

The addition of XK, as stated by Mishra (2019):

...highlights the organizational and situational constraints that teachers work. within. The success of their efforts depends not as much on their knowledge of T, P, C and its overlaps, but rather on their knowledge of the context. This allows us to go beyond seeing teachers as designers of curriculum within their classrooms but rather as intrapreneurs—knowing how their organization functions, and how levers of power and influence can effect sustainable change (p. 77).

The three key areas of the TPACK model (content knowledge, pedagogical knowledge and technological knowledge) must be integrated, so that teachers are able to choose the best digital resources for their lessons. This will have an impact on the use of more appropriate teaching methodologies, which in turn emphasizes the importance of active learning. Fernández et al. (2019) summarize the proposals on which the TPACK model is based as follows:

- Content knowledge: teachers have to know in depth the contents to be taught, as well as the facts, concepts, theories, etc.
- Processes and practices of the teaching method: teachers must know the processes and practices of the teaching method and how they relate to educational thinking and purposes.
- Pedagogical content knowledge: teachers need to know how to teach their subjects, so that it is pedagogical knowledge applied to a particular subject or content.
- Knowledge of technology used for teaching.
- Knowledge of the use of technology for teaching processes.
- Technological pedagogical content knowledge: teaching requires an understanding of the representation of concepts using technology; likewise, teachers should know those techniques and approaches that use technology from a constructivist perspective for teaching content and concepts.

METHODS

The design of this study was developed under an approach of quantitative research, and a method that was both descriptive and correlational.

Context and Participants

A cross-sectional study was designed using a non-probabilistic sample of Spanish pre-service and in-service teachers. For this exploratory study, only pre-service and in-service teachers from Spain were chosen as target population due to the impact of the Common Digital Competence Framework for Teachers (INTEF, 2017), and their use of digital technologies in their lessons.

The results were obtained from a questionnaire designed for teachers to understand their preferences and competencies regarding the use of Digital Game-Based Learning (DGBL) in their lessons. Data were gathered from Spanish teachers (n = 112): 51 pre-service teachers (45.5%), 56 in-service teachers (50.0%), and 5 (4.5) who marked 'other' (i.e., unemployed teachers, inspectors, other stakeholders). The mean age of the participants was 33.40 years old (SD = 14.624), with a range from 18 to 67 years, and 79 were male (70.5%) were male and 33 were female (25.4%). Participants were trained or worked in Early Childhood Education (n = 22, 19.6%), Primary Education (n = 67, 59.8%), Secondary Education (n = 18, 16.1%), Higher Education (n = 4, 3.6%) or other educational stages (n = 1, 0.9%).

Instrument, Data Collection and Data Analysis

A questionnaire (Appendix 1) was designed for both pre-service and in-service teachers regarding the use of digital games in education. The literature review was carried out in the field of DGBL, and three key previous validated questionnaires (i.e., Li, 2017; Martins, & Oliveira, 2019; Takeuchi, & Vaala, 2014) were analyzed and adapted to create the instrument for this research by considering the TPACK model (Mishra & Koehler, 2006; Koehler et al., 2014). This process generated a list of 24 items. Then, a group of experts was selected (2 experts in CALL and 1 expert in Psychopedagogy) to carry out the validation using the Delphi method (Hsu, & Sandford, 2007), and 23 items were finally accepted. The conceptual meaning and the number of items for each construct regarding DGBL, corresponding to the TPACK framework (Questions 07-23), are exhibited in Table 2.

Table 2. Constructs of the questionnaire

Construct	Category	Number of items (content validity confirmed)	Items
Dimension 1	Technological knowledge	3	Q07, Q08, Q09
Dimension 2	Content knowledge	3	Q10, Q11, Q12
Dimension 3	Pedagogical knowledge	3	Q13, Q14, Q15
Dimension 4	Pedagogical content knowledge	1	Q16
Dimension 5	Technological content knowledge	1	Q17
Dimension 6	Technological pedagogical knowledge	3	Q18, Q19, Q20
Dimension 7	Technological pedagogical content knowledge	3	Q21, Q22, Q23

Source: (Own elaboration)

The final questionnaire consisted of two parts: (1) demographic information, (2) use of technology, and (3) DGBL based on the TPACK model. Part 1 was used to obtain participants' demographic information (i.e., gender, age, educational stage). Part 2 included questions about the use of technology (and especially of digital games) in both their personal and professional lives. Part 3 was used to measure their perceptions of DGBL based on the TPACK model. Responses in part 3 were scored on a 4-point Likert scale: "strongly disagree" (1), "disagree" (2), "agree" (3), and "strongly agree" (4).

The questionnaire was administered in the Spring Semester of 2021 (April-June 2021). Due to the partial lockdown derived from the COVID-19 international crisis, the questionnaire was distributed online via Google Forms, considering the advantages stated by Phellas et al. (2011). To reduce potential difficulty in comprehension, the questionnaire was administered in English and Spanish. The questionnaire was voluntary and confidential, results were made anonymous, and all the participants expressed their consent to participate in the study.

The data were analyzed by using IBM SPSS Statistics V24.0 for MacOs. The internal consistency reliability was excellent, as the value of Cronbach's alpha for the scale is 0.914 (Haktanir, et al., 2018; Karaman, et al., 2019).

Finally, to study Spanish teachers' perceptions and uses of DGBL in their lessons, mean comparisons between groups, considering age (H2), gender (H3) and professional situation (H4), were analysed through parametric Student's t test for independent samples. Significance was accepted whenever $p < 0.05$ (Sokal & Rohlf, 1995).

RESULTS

Participants were asked about the technological devices and resources they use or would use in their lessons, being digital boards, Internet, projectors and computers the most utilized appliances (Figure 3).

A total of 47.3% (n = 53) of the respondents play digital games for fun in their spare time. Focusing specifically on the use of video games for educational purposes, respondents have had different key sources to learn about how to apply digital games in their lessons (Figure 4), being the three most frequent answers: (1) from another teacher, coach or supervisor, (2) figured out themselves, and (3) pre-service teacher preparation programs.

Figure 3. Frequency of participants' use of technological devices and resources in their lessons (Own elaboration)
Source: Own elaboration

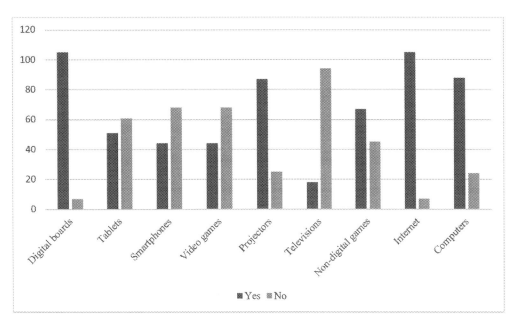

Figure 4. Frequency of participants' key sources to learn how to use digital games in education (Own elaboration)
Source: Own elaboration

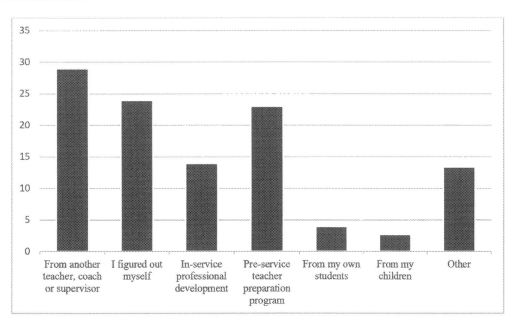

Furthermore, when asked about the frequency they use or would use digital games in their lessons, the participants responses were as shown in Figure 5.

Figure 5. Frequency of participants' estimated time use of digital games in their lessons (Own elaboration)
Source: Own elaboration

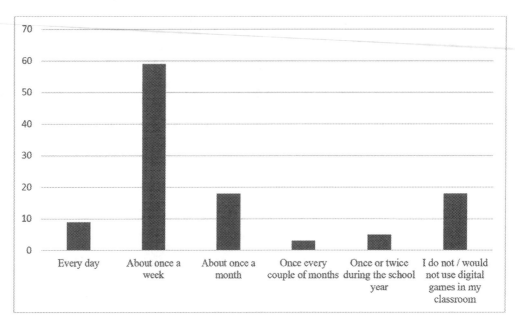

Focusing now on the third part of the questionnaire, DGBL based on the TPACK model, Table 3 below presents the descriptive statistical data considering the different items regarding Spanish teachers' perceptions and uses of DGBL in their lessons.

As presented in Table 2, it should be highlighted that all the respondents show a remarkable positive interest in DGBL, as the most frequent answer is "3 = agree", and most items score higher than 2.5 out of 4 (except for Q13, Q14 and Q18, although they score higher than 2.4), and 3 items even score higher than 3 (Q10, Q11 and Q12).

Differences Regarding Age

The researchers used Student's *t* test for independent samples to examine whether there were statistically significant differences among the participants' perceptions and attitudes regarding the use of digital games in their lessons with regard to their age. For this purpose, two groups were established: 18-27 years old (post-millennial participants) and over 28 years old – post-millennial participants, also known as iGeneration or Generation Z, were born in the period 1994-2010 (Parry, & Urwin, 2017) and are thought to have grown up in a hyper-connected world where technology has always played a key role in their lives (Kasasa, 2020). As shown in Table 4, post-millennial participants scored higher in all Dimensions except for Dimensions 2 and 5, and statistically significant differences between groups ($p < 0.05$) were found in Dimensions 1 and 7.

Table 3. Descriptive statistics per item

Item	N	%				M	SD
		TD	D	A	TA		
Q07	112	8.9	13.4	50.9	26.8	2.96	0.874
Q08	112	14.3	32.1	42.0	11.6	2.51	0.880
Q09	112	8.0	17.9	48.2	25.9	2.92	0.871
Q10	112	0.9	8.0	50.0	41.1	3.31	0.658
Q11	112	0.9	12.5	59.8	26.8	3.13	0.645
Q12	112	0.9	5.4	67.9	25.9	3.19	0.592
Q13	112	12.5	39.3	42.0	6.3	2.42	0.790
Q14	112	10.7	36.6	46.4	6.3	2.48	0.771
Q15	112	7.1	37.5	47.3	8.0	2.56	0.745
Q16	112	2.7	13.4	68.8	15.2	2.96	0.629
Q17	112	12.5	33.9	42.0	11.6	2.53	0.859
Q18	112	10.7	38.4	42.0	8.9	2.49	0.805
Q19	112	5.4	22.3	53.6	18.8	2.86	0.781
Q20	112	6.3	19.6	61.6	12.5	2.80	0.733
Q21	112	8.9	27.7	54.5	8.9	2.63	0.771
Q22	112	12.5	33.9	44.6	8.9	2.50	0.827
Q23	112	8.0	20.5	60.7	10.7	2.74	0.756

Note: TD = Totally disagree; D = Disagree; A = Agree; TA = Totally agree.
Source: (Own elaboration)

Table 4. Student's t test for independent samples (age)

Construct	Age	N	M	SD	t	p*
Dimension 1	18-27 y. o. 28+ y. o.	62 50	3.02 2.51	0.658 0.748	3.771	0.000
Dimension 2	18-27 y. o. 28+ y. o.	62 50	3.14 3.29	0.466 0.620	-1.452	0.150
Dimension 3	18-27 y. o. 28+ y. o.	62 50	2.56 2.39	0.558 0.761	1.328	0.188
Dimension 4	18-27 y. o. 28+ y. o.	62 50	2.98 2.94	0.528 0.740	0.353	0.725
Dimension 5	18-27 y. o. 28+ y. o.	62 50	2.52 2.54	0.825 0.908	-0.146	0.885
Dimension 6	18-27 y. o. 28+ y. o.	62 50	2.82 2.59	0.578 0.739	1.754	0.083
Dimension 7	18-27 y. o. 28+ y. o.	62 50	2.75 2.46	0.600 0.759	2.227	0.028

(*) $p < 0.05$ is recognized as statistically significant.
Source: (Own elaboration)

Differences Regarding Gender

To analyze whether there are statistically significant differences among participants' perceptions and uses considering gender, the researchers used Student's *t* test for independent samples. Table 5 shows that there are statistically significant differences ($p < 0.05$) between groups only in Dimension 1, where women score significantly higher than men.

Table 5. Student's T test for independent samples (gender)

Construct	Gender	N	M	SD	t	p*
Dimension 1	Female Male	33 79	3.08 2.68	0.667 0.741	2.716	0.008
Dimension 2	Female Male	33 79	3.32 3.16	0.468 0.567	1.455	0.148
Dimension 3	Female Male	33 79	2.49 2.49	0.566 0.698	0.071	0.944
Dimension 4	Female Male	33 79	2.94 2.97	0.556 0.660	-0.270	0.788
Dimension 5	Female Male	33 79	2.45 2.56	0.794 0.888	-0.573	0.568
Dimension 6	Female Male	33 79	2.73 2.71	0.684 0.655	0.103	0.918
Dimension 7	Female Male	33 79	2.70 2.59	0.699 0.685	0.714	0.476

(*) p < 0.05 is recognized as statistically significant.

Source: (Own elaboration)

Moreover, even if there were no statistical differences, women also scored higher in Dimensions 2, 6, and 7; while men scored higher than female participants in Dimensions 4 and 5. Similar results were found between both groups for Dimension 3.

Differences Regarding Professional Situation

As illustrated in Table 6, after performing Student's *t* test for independent samples, results demonstrated that there are statistically significant differences ($p > 0.05$) among participants' responses in terms of their professional situation (per-service vs. in-service teachers) for Dimensions 1, 2, 6 and 7. In all cases, except for Dimension 2, pre-service teachers scored higher than in-service teachers.

DISCUSSION

This chapter has aimed to analyze in-service and pre-service Spanish teachers' perceptions and uses about applying digital games in their lessons, considering the TPACK framework (Mishra & Koehler, 2006; Koehler et al., 2014). Teachers are major agents of change and transformation, and they decide whether to integrate DGBL into their instruction (Li, & Huang 2016). Consequently, teachers' attitudes play a key role in determining the extent to which DGBL is used as part of their teaching performance (Hayak, & Avidov-Ungar, 2020), and understanding their perceptions and uses of video games in their lessons at different stages of their career (being pre-service and in-service teachers).

Table 6. Student's T test for independent samples (professional situation)

Construct	Prof. Situation	N	M	SD	t	p*
Dimension 1	pre-service teacher in-service teacher	51 56	3.03 2.54	0.621 0.765	3.655	0.000
Dimension 2	pre-service teacher in-service teacher	51 56	3.08 3.30	0.446 0.605	-2.080	0.040
Dimension 3	pre-service teacher in-service teacher	51 56	2.59 2.38	0.535 0.733	1.757	0.082
Dimension 4	pre-service teacher in-service teacher	51 56	2.98 2.93	0.510 0.735	0.427	0.670
Dimension 5	pre-service teacher in-service teacher	51 56	2.57 2.46	0.855 0.873	0.624	0.534
Dimension 6	pre-service teacher in-service teacher	51 56	2.84 2.58	0.579 0.709	2.085	0.040
Dimension 7	pre-service teacher in-service teacher	51 56	2.76 2.48	0.589 0.746	2.109	0.037

(*) $p < 0.05$ is recognized as statistically significant.

Source: (Own elaboration)

From the self-report questionnaire, it can be highlighted that teachers were well equipped technologically in their classrooms, and most reported they have access to Internet, digital boards, computers and projectors, results in line with other studies (Hébert et al., 2012). Moreover, and despite the use of mobile devices (smartphones and tablets) and (conventional) video games is still limited, more than a third of the participants have access to them in their schools, percentage also similar to findings in previous research (Beavis et al., 2017). This situation, however, does not hinder the use of digital games in the classroom, since they can be played using not only mobile devices or game consoles, but also digital boards and computers. The participants affirm that the average frequency they use video games in their lessons is once a week, and the results show that Spanish teachers' perceptions regarding the use of digital games in their lessons and DGBL considering the TPACK model are positive, corroborating H1 *(Spanish teachers' perceptions regarding the use of digital games in their lessons and DGBL considering the TPACK model are positive).*

The results presented in this chapter, however, emphasize the necessity of lifelong teacher training on DGBL, as participants reported that they have mainly learnt how to implement video games in their lessons from other teachers, self-learning, and pre-service teacher preparation programs. Indeed, and as stated in previous research (Salajan et al., 2010), access to permanent training mat be a larger contribution factor to implement DGBL in education.

An analysis of the research findings suggests that teachers of different ages and at different career stages (pre-service vs in-service teachers) express different attitudes toward integrating DGBL, and there are significant differences in several dimensions, corroborating partially H2 *(Spanish teachers' perceptions regarding the use of digital games in their lessons and DGBL differ depending on their age)* and H4 *(Pre-service Spanish teachers' perceptions regarding the use of digital games in their lessons and DGBL are significantly better than those of in-service Spanish teachers' perceptions)*.

Younger teachers' perceptions and uses of DGBL are more positive than those of older teachers' in all dimensions, except for dimension 2 (content knowledge) and dimension 5 (technological content knowledge), where older teachers score higher – even without statistically significant differences. This result is in line with O'Bannon and Thomas (2014), who found that older teachers are less supportive of using technology, more specifically mobile phones, in the classroom. Moreover, Salajan et al. (2010) support younger teachers' recognition of the instructional usefulness of technologies. Our findings, however, contradict previous studies that have suggested that teachers who are older and have taught for more years tend to incorporate technology into their teaching practices more often than younger and/ or less-experienced counterparts (Giordano, 2007; Wong, & Li 2008), while other research did not find this difference (Niederhauser, & Stoddart 2001).

Regarding H4, the career stage is a differentiating variable in relation to the factors that may difficult, enhance, and motivate teachers to integrate DGBL, as also found in Hayak and Avidov-Ungar (2020). Other research did not find differences: in the study conducted by Chung-Yuan et al. (2017), perceptions toward the integration of DGBL among teachers with less than 10 years of experience were identical to those among teachers with 11-20 years of teaching experience. Considering the TPACK model, previous research state that teachers in later career stages highlighted the pedagogical and the technical factors as hindering the integration of DGBL in their classroom (Hayak, & Avidov-Ungar, 2020).

The study found there are no statistically significant differences between genders, except for dimension 1, refuting almost completely H3 *(Spanish teachers' perceptions regarding the use of digital games in their lessons and DGBL differ depending on their gender)*. It is interesting to highlight that the only dimension with statistically significant differences (dimension 1) refers to technological knowledge, where female participants scored significantly higher than the male counterparts. Our results contradict research that suggested that male teachers use more technology in their teaching and learning processes than female teachers (i.e., Kay, 2006; Wozney et al. 2006).

This research on DGBL is aligned with the TPACK model, which has been widely used to provide a foundation for both teachers and researchers to understand the multiple components of supporting teaching professionals in their teaching practice and the integration of technology in their lessons (Mishra & Koehler, 2006; Koehler et al., 2014). This framework highlights the integrated roles of teachers' technological knowledge, pedagogical knowledge, and content knowledge, and defends that good technology-enhanced teaching practice requires all three (integrated) components. This study focused on DGBL, but we did not measure teachers' knowledge, but teachers' perceptions and uses of DGBL in their lessons considering their pedagogical and technological readiness to effective teaching with technology. As suggested by Li et al. (2019), teachers who are more confident in their technology competence may be more willing to experiment and practice. Consequently, teachers' self-reflection on their teaching performance with the use of technology in general and DGBL in particular can have an active role in transforming their teaching approach and performance over time.

This chapter can have important implications for teacher trainers organizing initial and permanent learning experiences for both pre-service and in-service teachers. Self-reflection and self-confidence are important and difficult factors in research in professional learning (Groff, & Mouza, 2008). Following Li et al. (2019), developing among teachers a culture that includes innovation and experimentation with educational technology and especially with DGBL may be also necessary. Effective and adequate professional teachers' development on DGBL needs to address teachers' competences and skills, and provide sufficient time for experimentation, creation, implementation and reflection, as well as follow-up support for DGBL integration in the classroom.

CONCLUSION

Digital Game-Based Learning offers a wide range of pedagogical possibilities and can support effective teaching methods as long as teachers are given the necessary time, training and tools to implement this approach in their lessons. The TPACK model (Mishra & Koehler, 2006; Koehler et al., 2014) can trigger (self-)reflections on teachers' competences, and help them improve their digital literacy and consequently the quality of their teaching performance. There is no doubt that the development and use of digital games have become a reality nowadays, and technological advances (and affordance) is adequate to implement DGBL in most educational centers at all educational levels, from Early Childhood Education to University Studies.

The findings presented in this chapter, however, should be interpreted in the light of three limitations. First, due to the nature of an exploratory study, only Spanish pre-service and in-service teachers were considered as target population, and therefore the findings may not be applicable to participants from different background or contexts. Future research should consider recruiting participants from different institutions and sociocultural backgrounds to allow further comparisons. Second, the study is only quantitative, and qualitative data could complement these results. Third, the quantitative findings were only based on self-reported data, so they may be affected by respondents' subjective opinions about the phenomena. For this reason, future studies should also consider obtaining information through additional sources to obtain more reliable data. Moreover, further research could move towards an empirical study on the use of digital games in the classroom, analyzing teachers' competences and implementation of digital games in their teaching process.

Finally, to conclude, it shall be acknowledged that future research may also depend on technological advances, as those derived from eye-tracking, artificial intelligence and virtual reality.

Declaration of Conflicting Interests

The authors declared no potential conflicts of interest with respect to the research, authorship, and/or publication of this chapter.

ACKNOWLEDGMENT

This research was partially supported by the Spanish Ministry of Education and Vocational Training ["Becas de colaboración destinadas a estudiantes universitarios para realizar tareas de investigación en departamentos universitarios", BDNS Id. 512590].

REFERENCES

Abt, C. (1970). *Serious Games*. The Viking Press.

Beavis, C., Dezuanni, M., & O'Mara, J. (Eds.). (2017). *Serious Play: Literacy, Learning and Digital Games*. Routledge. doi:10.4324/9781315537658

Bellotti, F., Kapralos, B., Lee, K., Moreno-Ger, P., & Berta, R. (2013). Assessment in and of serious games: An overview. *Advances in Human-Computer Interaction*, *2013*, 1–11. Advance online publication. doi:10.1155/2013/136864

Boekaerts, M. (2010). The crucial role of motivation and emotion in classroom learning. In H. Humont, D. Istance, & F. Benavides (Eds.), *The Nature of Learning: Using Research to Inspire Practice* (pp. 91–112). Centre for Educational Research and Innovation. doi:10.1787/9789264086487-6-en

Casañ-Pitarch, R. (2018). An approach to digital game-based learning: Video-games principles and applications in foreign language learning. *Journal of Language Teaching and Research*, *9*(6), 1147–1159. doi:10.17507/jltr.0906.04

Chung-Yuan, H., Meng-Jung, T., Yu-Hsuan, C., & Liang, J. C. (2017). Surveying in-service teachers' beliefs about game-based learning and perceptions of technological pedagogical and content knowledge of games. *Journal of Educational Technology & Society*, *20*(1), 134.

Cornellà, P., Estebanell, M., & Brusi, D. (2020). Gamificación y aprendizaje basado en juegos. Consideraciones generales y algunos ejemplos para la Enseñanza de la Geología. *Enseñanza de las Ciencias de la Tierra*, *28*(1), 5–19.

Deterding, S., Dixon, D., Khaled, R., & Nacke, L. (2011). From game design elements to gamefulness: defining gamification. In *Proceedings of the 15th international academic MindTrek conference: Envisioning future media environments* (pp. 9-15). Association for Computing Machinery. 10.1145/2181037.2181040

Eseryel, D., Law, V., Ifenthaler, D., Ge, X., & Miller, R. (2014). An investigation of the interrelationships between motivation, engagement, and complex problem solving in game-based learning. *Journal of Educational Technology & Society*, *17*(1), 42–53.

EU Lifelong Learning Programme. (2011). *Production of Creative Game-Based Learning Scenarios: A Handbook for Teachers*. ProActive. https://bit.ly/3tJVKbq

Fernández, E., Ordóñez, E., Morales, B., & López, J. (2019). *La competencia digital en la docencia universitaria*. Octaedro.

Gee, J. P. (2005). Learning by design: Good video games as learning machines. *E-Learning and Digital Media*, 2(1), 5–16. doi:10.2304/elea.2005.2.1.5

Gee, J. P. (2013). Games for learning. *Educational Horizons*, 91(4), 16–20. doi:10.1177/0013175X1309100406

Giordano, V. A. (2007). A professional development model to promote Internet integration into p-12 teachers' practice: A mixed methods study. *Computers in the Schools*, 24(3–4), 111–123. doi:10.1300/J025v24n03_08

Gómez-Gonzalvo, F., Molina Alventosa, P., & Devis, J. (2018). Los videojuegos como materiales curriculares: una aproximación a su uso en Educación Física / Video games as curriculum materials: an approach to their use in Physical Education. *Retos*, 34(34), 305–310. doi:10.47197/retos.v0i34.63440

González-González, C., & Blanco-Izquierdo, F. (2012). Designing social video-games for educational uses. *Computers & Education*, 58(1), 250–262. doi:10.1016/j.compedu.2011.08.014

Haktanir, A., Watson, J. C., Ermis-Demirtas, H., Karaman, M. A., Freeman, P. D., Kumaran, A., & Streeter, A. (2018). Resilience, academic self-concept, and college adjustment among first-year students. *Journal of College Student Retention*, 38, 286–297. doi:10.1177/1521025118810666

Hayak, M., & Avidov-Ungar, O. (2020). The Integration of Digital Game-Based Learning into the Instruction: Teachers' Perceptions at Different Career Stages. *TechTrends*, 64(6), 887–898. doi:10.100711528-020-00503-6

Hébert, C., Jenson, J., & Terzopoulos, T. (2021). "Access to technology is the major challenge": Teacher perspectives on barriers to DGBL in K-12 classrooms. *E-Learning and Digital Media*, 18(3), 307–324. doi:10.1177/2042753021995315

Hsu, C. C., & Sandford, B. A. (2007). The Delphi technique: Making sense of consensus. *Practical Assessment, Research & Evaluation*, 12(1), 1–8. doi:10.7275/pdz9-th90

Huertas-Abril, C. A. (2020). *Tecnologías para la educación bilingüe*. Peter Lang.

INTEF. (2017). *Common Digital Competence Framework for Teachers*. National Institute of Educational Technologies and Teacher Training, Spanish Ministry of Education, Culture and Sport. https://bit.ly/3pkRJdh

Jarvis, P. (2009). Learning from everyday life. In P. Jarvis (Ed.), *The Routledge international handbook of lifelong learning* (pp. 19–30). Routledge. doi:10.4324/9780203870549

Karaman, M. A., Vela, J. C., Aguilar, A. A., Saldana, K., & Montenegro, M. C. (2019). Psychometric properties of U.S.-Spanish versions of the grit and resilience scales with a Latinx population. *International Journal for the Advancement of Counseling*, 41(1), 125–136. doi:10.100710447-018-9350-2

Kasasa. (2021, July). Boomers, Gen X, Gen Y, Gen Z, and Gen A Explained. *Kasasa*. https://bit.ly/3Bm4x5Z

Kay, R. H. (2006). Evaluating strategies used to incorporate technology into preservice education: A review of the literature. *Journal of Research on Technology in Education*, 38(4), 383–408. doi:10.1080/15391523.2006.10782466

Koehler, M. J., Mishra, P., Kereluik, K., Shin, T. S., & Graham, C. R. (2014). The technological pedagogical content knowledge framework. In J. M. Spector, M. D. Merrill, J. van Merrienboer, & M. P. Driscoll (Eds.), *Handbook of research on educational communications and technology* (pp. 101–111). Springer. doi:10.1007/978-1-4614-3185-5_9

Li, C. (2017). *Attitudes towards Digital Game-based Learning of Chinese Primary School English Teachers* [Master's thesis]. University of Edinburgh. https://bit.ly/3yew4UR

Li, S. C. S., & Huang, W. C. (2016). Lifestyles, innovation attributes, and teachers' adoption of game-based learning: Comparing non-adopters with early adopters, adopters and likely adopters in Taiwan. *Computers & Education*, *96*, 29–41. doi:10.1016/j.compedu.2016.02.009

Li, Y., Garza, V., Keicher, A., & Popov, V. (2019). Predicting high school teacher use of technology: Pedagogical beliefs, technological beliefs and attitudes, and teacher training. *Technology. Knowledge and Learning*, *24*(3), 501–518. doi:10.100710758-018-9355-2

Loveless, A., & Williamson, B. (2013). *Learning identities in a digital age: Rethinking creativity, education and technology*. Routledge. doi:10.4324/9780203591161

Martín del Pozo, M., Gómez-Pablos, V. B., Sánchez-Prieto, J. C., & García-Valcárcel Muñoz-Repiso, A. (2019). Review of Game-Based Learning in Secondary Education: Considering the Types of Video Games. Analysis. *Claves de Pensamiento Contemporáneo*, *22*, 1–10.

Martins, A., & Oliveira, L. (2019). Teachers' experiences and practices with game-based learning. *Proceedings of INTED2019 Conference*, 8575-8583. https://bit.ly/3guwMrd

Mendez, M., & Boude, O. (2021). Uso de los videojuegos en básica primaria: Una revisión sistemática. *Espacios*, *42*(1), 66–80. doi:10.48082/espacios-a21v42n01p06

Mishra, P. (2019). Considering contextual knowledge: The TPACK diagram gets an upgrade. *Journal of Digital Learning in Teacher Education*, *35*(2), 76–78. doi:10.1080/21532974.2019.1588611

Mishra, P., & Koehler, J. (2006). Technological pedagogical content knowledge: A new framework for teacher knowledge. *Teachers College Record*, *108*(6), 1017–1054. doi:10.1111/j.1467-9620.2006.00684.x

Niederhauser, D. S., & Stoddart, T. (2001). Teachers' instructional perspectives and use of educational software. *Teaching and Teacher Education*, *17*(1), 15–31. doi:10.1016/S0742-051X(00)00036-6

O'Bannon, B. W., & Thomas, K. (2014). Teacher perceptions of using mobile phones in the classroom: Age matters! *Computers & Education*, *74*, 15–25. doi:10.1016/j.compedu.2014.01.006

Oliveira, L. R., Correia, A. C., Merrelho, A., Marques, A., Pereira, D. J., & Cardoso, V. (2009). Digital games: possibilities and limitations - The spore game case. In T. Bastiaens, J. Dron, & C. Xin (Eds.), *Proceedings of E-Learn: world conference on elearning in corporate, government, healthcare, and higher education* (pp. 3011-3020). Association for the Advancement of Computing in Education.

Parry, E., & Urwin, P. (2017). The Evidence Base for Generational Differences: Where Do We Go from Here? *Work, Aging and Retirement*, *3*(2), 140–148. doi:10.1093/workar/waw037

Phellas, C. N., Bloch, A., & Seale, C. (2011). Structured methods: Interviews, questionnaires and observation. In C. Seale (Ed.), *Research Society and Culture* (3rd ed., pp. 181–205). SAGE.

Pivec, M. (2007). Editorial: Play and learn: potentials of game-based learning. *British Journal of Educational Technology, 38*(3), 387–393. doi:10.1111/j.1467-8535.2007.00722.x

Redecker, C. (2017). *European Framework for the Digital Competence of Educators: DigCompEdu.* Publications Office of the European Union., doi:10.2760/159770

Reinders, H. (2012). *Digital games in language learning and teaching.* Palgrave Macmillan. doi:10.1057/9781137005267

Salajan, F. D., Schönwetter, D. J., & Cleghorn, B. M. (2010). Student and faculty inter-generational digital divide: Fact or fiction? *Computers & Education, 55*(3), 1393–1403. doi:10.1016/j.compedu.2010.06.017

Sampson, D., & Karagiannidis, C. (2002). Personalised learning: Educational, technological and standarisation perspective. *Digital Education Review, 4*(1), 24–39.

Selwyn, N., & Bulfin, S. (2016). Exploring school regulation of students' technology use–rules that are made to be broken? *Educational Review, 68*(3), 274–290. doi:10.1080/00131911.2015.1090401

Sokal, R. R., & Rohlf, F. J. (2015). *Biometry: Principles and practice of statistics in biological research* (4th ed.). W. H. Freeman.

Susi, T., Johannesson, M., & Backlund, P. (2007). *Serious games: An overview.* DiVA.

Takeuchi, L. M., & Vaala, S. (2014). *Level up learning: A national survey on teaching with digital games.* The Joan Ganz Cooney Center at Sesame Workshop. https://bit.ly/38cRQhp

Tejederas, M. (2020). Gamified methodologies in bilingual teacher training. *6th International Conference on Bilingual Education.* https://www.grupo-ebei.es/confbe/2020/

Werbach, K. (2014). ReDefining Gamification: A Process Approach. In A. Spagnolli, L. Chittaro, & L. Gamberini (Eds.), *Persuasive Technology* (pp. 266–272). Springer. doi:10.1007/978-3-319-07127-5_23

Wong, E. M., & Li, S. C. (2008). Framing ICT implementation in a context of educational change: A multilevel analysis. *School Effectiveness and School Improvement, 19*(1), 99–120. doi:10.1080/09243450801896809

Wozney, L., Venkatesh, V., & Abrami, P. C. (2006). Implementing computer technologies: Teachers' perceptions and practices. *Journal of Technology and Teacher Education, 14*(1), 173.

Ziegler, N. (2016). Taking technology to task: Technology-mediated TBLT, performance, and production. *Annual Review of Applied Linguistics, 36*(1), 136–163. doi:10.1017/S0267190516000039

ADDITIONAL READING

Clarke, S. J. (2020). *Developing a Best Practice Approach to the Design Process of Game-based Learning and Gamification Applications* (Doctoral Dissertation, Coventry University). https://bit.ly/2YwIJGI

Hallifax, S., Serna, A., Marty, J. C., & Lavoué, E. (2019). Adaptive gamification in education: A literature review of current trends and developments. In *European conference on technology enhanced learning* (pp. 294–307). Springer. doi:10.1007/978-3-030-29736-7_22

Hilliard, A., & Kargbo, H. F. (2017). Educationally Game-Based Learning Encourages Learners to Be Actively Engaged in Their Own Learning. *International Journal of Education and Practice*, 5(4), 45–60. doi:10.18488/journal.61.2017.54.45.60

Indriasari, T. D., Luxton-Reilly, A., & Denny, P. (2020). Gamification of student peer review in education: A systematic literature review. *Education and Information Technologies*, 25(6), 5205–5234. doi:10.100710639-020-10228-x

Jong, M. S. Y., Chan, T., Hue, M. T., & Tam, V. W. (2018). Gamifying and mobilising social enquiry-based learning in authentic outdoor environments. *Journal of Educational Technology & Society*, 21(4), 277–292.

Putz, L. M., Hofbauer, F., & Treiblmaier, H. (2020). Can gamification help to improve education? Findings from a longitudinal study. *Computers in Human Behavior*, 110, 106392. doi:10.1016/j.chb.2020.106392

Toda, A. M., Valle, P. H., & Isotani, S. (2017). The dark side of gamification: An overview of negative effects of gamification in education. In *Researcher links workshop: higher education for all* (pp. 143–156). Springer., https://bit.ly/3h84wuJ

Van Roy, R., & Zaman, B. (2018). Need-supporting gamification in education: An assessment of motivational effects over time. *Computers & Education*, 127, 283–297. doi:10.1016/j.compedu.2018.08.018

Voulgari, I., & Lavidas, K. (2020). Student Teachers' Game Preferences, Game Habits, and Attitudes Towards Games as Learning Tools. In P. Fotaris (Ed.), *Proceedings of the 14th European Conference on Games Based Learning* (pp. 646–654). Academic Conferences International Limited. https://bit.ly/2VgI36W

KEY TERMS AND DEFINITIONS

Digital Game-Based Learning (DGBL): Learning approach that consists of using interactive digital games with defined learning outcomes. DGBL is designed to balance contents to learn with digital gameplay, as well as with the ability of the learner/player to understand, retain and apply that content matter to the real world.

Game-Based Learning (GBL): Learning approach that consists of a type of game play with defined learning outcomes. GBL is designed to balance contents to learn with gameplay, as well as with the ability of the learner/player to understand, retain and apply that content matter to the real world.

Gamification: Strategic attempt in non-gaming contexts to enhance activities, tasks, projects, etc. to create similar experiences to those undergone when playing games, so that individuals feel motivated and engaged.

In-Service Teacher: Working professional whose occupation is to instruct and who can develop their work at different educational levels and contexts.

Post-Millennial: Demographic cohort born between 1994 and 2010, succeeding Millennials and preceding Generation Alpha. Considered the first generation to have grown up with access to the Internet, alternative names to refer to this cohort include Generation Z, digital natives, and *zoomers*.

Pre-Service Teacher: Trainee teacher.

TPACK Model: Technological Pedagogical Content Knowledge model formulated by Mishra and Koehler (2006), and revised in Koehler et al., 2014, based on the idea that in order for educational technology to be used correctly, teachers need three types of knowledge: technological, pedagogical and content.

Video Game-Based Learning (DGBL): Alternative term to Video Game-Based Learning (DGBL), where the focus is on video games, a narrower term to refer to interactive digital media.

APPENDIX

Questionnaire About Using Digital Games in the Classroom

General Information

Age: ...
Gender: ...
Nationality: ...
Professional situation: ...   Pre-service teacher   In-service teacher   Other
Educational stage I teach/I will teach: ...   Early Childhood Education   Primary Education
    Secondary Education   Higher Education   Other

Q01. What media do you use / would you use in the classroom? (Please choose all that apply)
1. Interactive white board
2. Tablet
3. Handheld devices and/or smartphones
4. Video game devices
5. Projector
6. Television
7. Non-digital games
8. Internet
9. Laptop / desktop computer

Q02. Do you play video / digital games for entertainment or other non-work / non-professional related reasons?
1. Yes
2. No

Q03. How did you first learn about using games in the classroom?
1. From another teacher, coach or supervisor
2. I figured out myself
3. In-service professional development
4. Pre-service teacher preparation program
5. From my own students
6. From my children
7. Other

Q04. How frequently do / would your students use digital games in your classroom?
1. Every day.
2. About once a week.
3. About once a month.
4. Once every couple of months.
5. Once or twice during the school year.
6. I do not / would not use digital games in my classroom.

Q05. What types of digital games do / would your students play most during class time?
1. Entertainment games adapted for education use.
2. Commercial off-the-shelf games.
3. Educational games.
4. Other.

Q06. Indicate video games you know for educational purposes.

_____

_____

_____

Read the following statements and choose the number that best matches your opinion of each statement: (1) "strongly disagree", (2) "disagree", (3) "agree", and (4) "strongly agree".

Technological Knowledge
Q07 I can learn about digital games easily.   1   2   3   4
Q08 I often explore / experiment with digital games.   1   2   3   4
Q09 I have the technical skills I need to use digital games.   1   2   3   4

Content Knowledge
Q10 I have enough knowledge about the curricular area(s) I teach.   1   2   3   4
Q11 I can use an appropriate approach to the curricular area(s) I teach.   1   2   3   4
Q12 I have several ways and strategies to develop my understanding of the curricular area(s) I teach.
        1   2   3   4

Pedagogical Knowledge
Q13 I know how to evaluate student performance in a digital game-based class.
        1   2   3   4
Q14 I can use a wide range of pedagogical strategies in the context of a digital game-based class.
        1   2   3   4
Q15 I know how to organize and maintain classroom management in a digital game-based class.
        1   2   3   4

Pedagogical Content Knowledge
Q16 I can select effective pedagogical strategies to guide the students' thinking and learning in the curricular area(s).   1   2   3   4

Technological Content Knowledge
Q17 I know digital games that I can use to facilitate the understanding and execution of activities in the curricular area(s) I teach.   1   2   3   4

Technological Pedagogical Knowledge

Q18 I can choose appropriate digital games to use in a class to improve student learning.

    1   2   3   4

Q19 I think critically about how to use digital games in the classroom.   1   2   3   4

Q20 I can choose digital games that improve / facilitate / enhance the content of a lesson.

    1   2   3   4

Technological Pedagogical Content Knowledge

Q21 I can determine how digital games combine the curricular area(s) I teach, technology and pedagogical strategies.   1   2   3   4

Q22 I can adapt a digital game for educational use.   1   2   3   4

Q23 I can determine the strengths and limitations of a digital game to teach specific contents.

    1   2   3   4

Section 5
Gamification, Mobile Learning, and Education Policy

Chapter 30

Factors Affecting the Successful Implementation of an E-Education Policy and Community Engagement:
Acquiring 21st Century Skills Through E-Learning

Absolom Muzambi
University of South Africa, South Africa

Leila Goosen
iD https://orcid.org/0000-0003-4948-2699
University of South Africa, South Africa

ABSTRACT

In order to provide readers with an overview and summarize the content, the purpose of this chapter is stated as reporting on an investigation around acquiring 21st century skills through e-learning. This study takes place against the background of the factors affecting the successful implementation of an e-education policy and community engagement. In terms of research methodology, a case study is used of a specific high (secondary) school in the Metro North district of the Western Cape province, South Africa.

INTRODUCTION

This section will describe the general perspective of the chapter and end by specifically stating the objective.

DOI: 10.4018/978-1-7998-7271-9.ch030

The plethora of Information and Communication Technologies (ICTs) around currently have changed the lives of everyone tremendously (Ratheeswari, 2018), especially in education. These emerging technologies, such as *multiliteracies*, introducing learning by design projects and frameworks (Kalantzis & Cope, 2012), as well as gamification, are becoming more prevalent in global classrooms. Since these are leading to an inquiring mindset in school systems and schools, traditional literacy pedagogies are shifting toward game-based pedagogy, which supports the call towards addressing 21st century learners (C21 Canada, 2017).

Likewise, an international journal article on pedagogies by Cope and Kalantzis (2009, p. 164) examined the changing landscape of new literacies teaching and new "learning, revisiting the case for a 'pedagogy of *multiliteracies'* ". It also described "the dramatically changing social and technological contexts of communication and learning".

Therefore, within such contexts, there is a need to study ways for engaging learners in meaning-making, perhaps with some element of visual design. Multimodal ways of learning can offer insights for reinventing traditional literacy pedagogical boundaries and establish new ways and practices for building knowledge. "There is considerable enthusiasm in many quarters for the incorporation of digital games", media and technologies into the classroom as part of the learning process, and the capacity of computer "games to engage and challenge players, present complex representations and" student experiences, as these can get students' brains working and foster perceptions of collaborative, creative and authentic learning, as well as promote deep meaningful learning (Beavis, Muspratt, & Thompson, 2015, p. 21).

For example, the idea of youth learning from video games is echoed by contemporary research on intertextuality in video games (Duret & Pons, 2016), recognizing the benefits and challenges of integrating video games in classrooms as a pedagogical strategy to gain literacy skills (Beavis, et al., 2015). An analysis of three international case studies in the chapter by Uribe-Jongbloed, Espinosa-Medina and Biddle (2016, p. 143) addressed the relationships that existed "between intertextuality and cultural transduction in video game localization." The "former refers to the dual relationship established between texts and previous texts available to" potential readers. By focusing on integrated Science, Technology, Engineering, and Mathematics (STEM) concepts in a digital game, strides can be made towards improving K-12 STEM education (DeCoito & Richardson, 2016).

In a "poster presentation at a scientific meeting" on a new perspective in the cognitive science of effortless attention and action, Hommel (2010, p. 121) "offered a new theoretical framework on stimulus and response representation (the later theory of event coding"), together with supportive data. Hommel (2010) also highlighted that many researchers argued that meaningful learning, including critical thinking, and decision-making in video games may model engaging and effective instructional techniques for grounding attention in action control and the intentional control of selection.

In terms of what works when bringing research into practice regarding differentiation in Ontario classrooms, Sider and Maich (2014, p. 1) suggested that "the reality of implementing classroom-based differentiated instruction can be challenging. One" of the effective literacy teaching strategies that teachers can use for supporting the literacy "learning needs of a range of students" in the inclusive classroom is by using research on technology-supported teaching and learning (Goosen, 2019a; b; c).

Assistive technology tools, information systems and technologies are opening new worlds for learning to children and adolescents with autism spectrum disorders (Goosen, 2022), including software programs that provide a multimodal experience. Content learning can be supported through technology within the universal design learning (UDL) framework, because it can increase access to meaningful engagement in learning and reduce barriers for K-12 students with disabilities (Israel, Marino, Delisio, & Serianni, 2014).

Target Audience

The subject areas and themes presented in this chapter, as part of the edited book, could be of interest to educators in K-12 levels, as well as academics and researchers around the world. Game-based pedagogy is of interest specifically in schools and higher education, but there is also potential for interest from global Ministries of Education and institutions that deliver content for professional practitioners.

Recommended Topics

Highlighting the main theme of the book, and aligned to the **recommended topics** provided, this chapter will especially focus on:

- Acquiring 21st Century Skills Through e-Learning

The following **recommended topics** will also receive particular attention:

- Using game-based learning to improve boys' literacy
- How boys can learn from playing video games
- Game-based pedagogy – using multiliteracies as a lens

However, the following will also be considered in general:

- Secondary sources of learning – using video games for literacy
- Changing teachers' perceptions about using secondary sources of learning
- Framing video games as a mindset change in the classroom
- Beyond classroom textbooks: Using digital learning for meaningful learning
- Video games for meaning making
- Classrooms as multimodal spaces to learn
- Learning by digital design
- Game-based pedagogy reinvents traditional literacy practices
- Game-based pedagogy for creative inquiry

Objective

Game-based pedagogy is gaining significant momentum among global educators, especially with co-vid-19, more post-secondary and K-12 institutions have resorted to e-learning, but often find issues with student engagement. Game-based pedagogy uses games for achieving learning outcomes, which can be digital and non-digital and can promote deep meaningful learning (Beavis, et al., 2015). However, there remains a misconception among some educators that the purpose of digitized learning or game-based pedagogy is to use technologies, such as an iPad, SmartScreen, or computers, in the classroom as a tool for project level student work. Other misconceptions occur when educators use video games on an incentive basis. Students engage in traditional learning and once completed, they are provided with a reward to play games at the end of week. Game-based pedagogy and digital pedagogy is a mindset change. Games have been proven to have a positive outcome on cognitive processes.

Lecturers, who have the **objective** of finding " 'theoretical guidelines or instructional principles that could assist' their students in developing and applying the required skills, seem to prefer 'constructivist learning as the pedagogical engine driving' their teaching" (Goosen & Van Heerden, 2013, p. 159).

Based on the work of the constructivist theorist Vygotsky (1978) on the mind in society, the development of higher mental processes and learning are likely to occur through active engagement and collaboration among learners. This engagement is more reflective of a student-centered environment. However, not all learners learn in the same way – teaching strategies needs to be differentiated. To meet the needs of various learners, a game-based pedagogy can be used as an alternative teaching pathway.

As emerging trends regarding instruction towards performance improvement, video game–based learning and a game-based pedagogy allow learners to discover and engage (Squire, 2013). Secondary sites of learning, especially video games, can provide opportunities for trial and error.

"Interactive digital media, or video games, are a powerful new medium" (Squire, 2013, p. 101). These "offer immersive experiences in which players solve problems" and are what the latter author calls experiential learning spaces, where learners engage in rich collaborative interactions, and where they can utilize a variety of complex tools in order to develop complex problem-solving skills. "Players learn more than just facts—ways of seeing and understanding problems so that they 'become' different kinds of people."

In a journal article on adolescent and adult literacy referring to contemporary "views of literacy, and of English and Language Arts curriculum", Beavis (2014, p. 433) urged educators to recognize "the importance of digital culture and communication forms in many young people's lives and the multiple forms of literacy students engage with as they work, interact and play." The privileged place that students give to video games as a form of popular culture led the latter author to see video games in the English classroom as both textual and action emerging trends in terms of cultural forms, because these include stories that fuse words and images and other elements to reposition players as readers, writers, interpreters, and creators, who play an active role in the stories. Video games have become increasingly rich in multimodal elements.

The authors, who are engaged in game-based pedagogy research and technology; in particular, with learning in educational contexts, respond to an invitation with a chapter proposal aligned to the **recommended topics** provided for the book, but may also discuss projects that exemplify the themes discussed by Kalantzis and Cope (2012), Sider and Maich (2014), Beavis (2014), and/or Squire (2013), or address the overarching question:

- How can a game-based pedagogy influence multiliteracies and meaning-making, as well as foster creative inquiry?

In answer, this chapter scrutinizes theoretical frameworks, empirical evidence, and gap analysis, while being guided by the research purpose as detailed in the abstract.

The purpose of the paper by Vorster and Goosen (2017, p. 119) was "to report on the development of a draft version of a framework for supporting partnership efforts with universities to continually support and enhance the success of e-schools". Government on its own cannot offer sustainable and inclusive quality education, but through research-informed practice on information and communication technologies (Goosen, 2018a), the **policy** goal of the White Paper on **e-Education** (Department of Education, 2004) can be achieved. Departments of education must spearhead programs, which aim at improving information and communication technology skills in e-schools.

Background

This section of the chapter will provide broad *definitions* and discussion of the topic and incorporate the views of others (in the form of a *literature review*) into the discussion to support, refute, or demonstrate the authors' position on the topic.

Before the research is conducted, all terms on the topic must be clearly understood. By understanding the definition of an e-school, a researcher is able to classify those schools, which can be classified as e-schools and those, which are not. This can be a starting point of the research. Goosen and Van der Merwe (2017, p. 115) *defined* e-schools as institutions that have "students who utilize ICT to enhance learning; qualified and competent leaders using ICT for planning, management and administration" and "connections to their **communities**". In an earlier paper, Goosen and Van der Merwe (2015, p. 129) emphasized the latter aspect from the e-education policy, indicating that schools "should work in partnership with families and the wider community in ensuring shared knowledge about e-Learning and creating extended opportunities for community member e-Learning and development through ICTs".

Online learning can be *defined* as "education that uses one or more technologies to deliver instruction to students who are separated from the instructor and to support regular and substantive interaction" between the students (Seaman, Allen, & Jeff Seaman, 2018, p. 5).

Young (2017) stated that a *literature review* in its simplest form is a description of what others have published, offered in the form of a summary. A *literature review* evaluation educates a researcher in the subject matter and helps them to understand the previous facts and writing accomplished earlier, helping to shape an argument or justification (Saunders, Lewis, & Thornhill, 2019).

Theoretical Framework

A theoretical framework provides criteria and guidelines for the selection and implementation of ICTs in high schools in terms of a 'blueprint' for the research being carried out (Adom, Hussain, & Joe, 2018). It can be said that a theoretical framework encompasses what influential scholars in the field of research have published about the research questions and the problem the research intends to investigate, and may even provide ideas on how to solve the problem, including how to understand the findings from data (Kivunja, 2018). An important purpose of the theoretical framework is that it provides the researcher with an opportunity to state theoretical assumptions clearly, so that readers will know what guided data analysis and interpretation (Aldosemani, 2019). A literature review is grounded, or anchored, by a theoretical framework. The theoretical framework supports the rationale for the study, the problem statement, the purpose, and the significance of the study (Osanloo & Grant, 2016). This research is based on the Substitution Augmentation Modification Redefinition (SAMR) model and the Technological Pedagogical Content Knowledge (TPACK) framework.

The Substitution Augmentation Modification Redefinition Model

Technology integration is an important skill that teachers need to acquire to deepen students' learning and support the achievement of instructional objectives. The SAMR model was employed as framework in this research study. It is a four–level taxonomy-based strategy on selecting, using and evaluating the use of technologies in teaching and learning. The model was developed and employed to examine how technological devices, such as computers and mobile devices, are infused into teaching and learning processes (Wahyuni, Mujiyanto, Rukmini, & Fitriati, 2020).The main purpose of the SAMR model is to maximize the use of technology in teaching and learning. The SAMR model consists of four levels of technological integration in teaching and learning which are shown in Figure 1.

The SAMR model indicates that under the substitution dimension, computers are simply used to replace typewriters to produce documents, but with no significant change to their function. Similarly, under the augmentation dimension, computers are, for instance, used to replace typewriters, but with significant functionality increase (e.g. cut and paste, spell checking etc.). Substitution and augmentation play an enhancement role in the teaching and learning process. But when ICTs are used to transform (modify and redefine) teaching and learning processes, a significant redesign of tasks is realized (Jude, Kajura, & Birevu, 2014).

The Technological Pedagogical Content Knowledge Framework

The increasingly ubiquitous availability of digital and networked tools has the potential to fundamentally transform the teaching and learning process. Research on the instructional uses of technologies, however, has revealed that teachers often lack the knowledge to successfully integrate technologies into their teaching and their attempts tend to be limited in scope, variety, and depth (Spector, Merrill, Elen, & Bishop, 2014).

Figure 1. The substitution augmentation modification redefinition model
Based on Wahyuni, et al. (2020, p. 547)

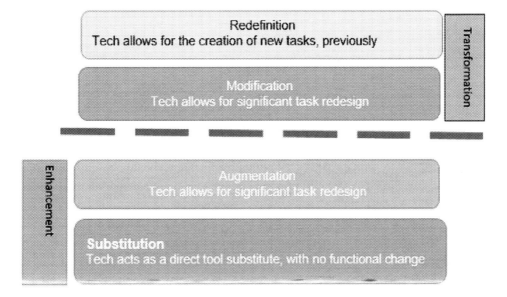

One of the frameworks that has gained momentum in studies of the integration of ICTs into teaching and learning is the TPACK. While Mishra and Koehler (2006), as well as others, have attempted to define and measure TPACK, the framework is not yet fully understood (Angeli & Valanides, 2009). There are three main components of teachers' knowledge: content, pedagogy, and technology (Koehler, Mishra, & Cain, 2013). Mishra and Koehler (2006) identified the following types of teacher knowledge (Anderson, Barham, & Northcote, 2013):

- Content Knowledge (CK) involves the teachers' grasp of the subject content. This would include scientific facts, theories, evidence-based reasoning, as well as discipline specific practices (Goradia, 2018).
- Technological Knowledge (TK) means that an educator must use technology as a teaching tool to support instruction, rather than as a tool for student learning (Tanak, 2020).
- Pedagogical Knowledge (PK) can be understood as teachers' deep knowledge about the processes and practices or methods of teaching and learning.
- Pedagogical Content Knowledge (PCK) *defines* the ability of an educator to pedagogically adapt and customize content for learners of diverse abilities, rather than just delivering subject content knowledge (Abbitt, 2011).

TPACK has been regarded as a potentially fruitful framework that may provide new directions for educators in solving the problems associated with integrating ICTs into classroom teaching and learning (Chai, Koh, Tsai, & Tan, 2011). The study by the latter authors (Chai, et al., 2011) reported that TK, PK and CK have positive influences on TPACK, while TK and PK have positive influences on TPK, leading to TPK positively influencing TPACK.

TPACK helps in the understanding of connections and interactions among content knowledge (of the subject being taught), technological knowledge (computers, the internet, etc.) and pedagogical knowledge (processes, procedures, strategies, etc.) to improve the students' teaching and learning (Archambault & Barnett, 2010). The framework arose in the context of teacher education, with the complex interplay of three primary forms of knowledge that goes beyond seeing these three knowledge bases in isolation (Mishra & Koehler, 2006). One of the reviewed studies (Chai, Koh, & Tsai, 2011) reported TPACK as a multiplicative framework that continues to guide course design and the evaluation of teachers' preparation to integrate ICTs into classrooms (see Figure 2).

The TPACK framework emphasizes technology integration in the classroom. Three major characteristics differentiate ICT frameworks:

1. Learning enhancement capabilities through the use of technologies.
2. As part of technology, technical know-how is used, such as a general understanding of hardware and software.
3. Infrastructure and institutional capacity building, for instance, the availability of computers, software and Internet access devices (Chinaka, 2017).

The TPACK framework further allows teachers to consider what knowledge they need to integrate technologies into their teaching and how they might acquire these (Schmidt, et al., 2009). As a theoretical framework for understanding the teacher knowledge necessary for effective technology integration, TPACK explains the interconnection and complexities among all three components of knowledge (technology, pedagogy, and content) (Celik, Sahin, & Akturk, 2014). In order to develop good content, TPACK proposes that all three must be thoughtfully interwoven together: technology, pedagogy, and content (Mishra & Koehler, 2006).

Figure 2. Pictorial representation of technological pedagogical content knowledge
Based on Archambault and Barnett (2010, p. 1657)

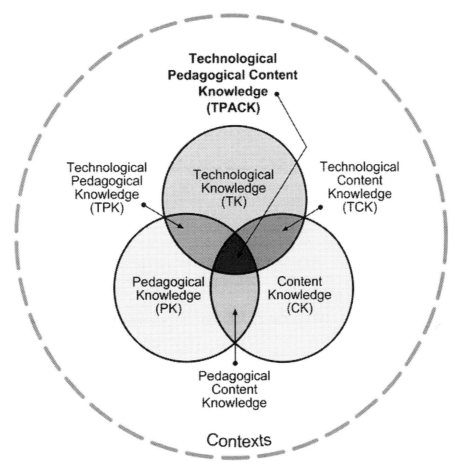

Using Game-Based Learning to Improve Boys' Literacy

Worldwide, it is acknowledged that boys' lower literacy levels need attention. According to Lane (2013, p. 139), in the world Program for International Student Assessment (PISA) "findings 'girls outperform boys in reading in every PISA country", while in Organization for Economic Co-operation and Development (OECD) 'countries, the average gender gap is 39 score points, or over half a proficiency level' ". The focus of the international journal article on technology and inclusive education by Lane (2013) was therefore on using video technology to address boys' literacy gap and connect the male voice in gender dynamics.

"With the ongoing concern of boys' failing in literacy", more recently, the study by Lane (2014, p. 16) explored "ways in which boys' video gaming practices outside of school may have the potential to lead to in school literacy practices. Past research has focused on the themes of violence and misogyny associated with video games. However, there is a misunderstanding of the embedded narratives that exist in video games which needs further attention. The theoretical lenses informing" the research by Lane (2014, p. 16) included post-structural feminism, activity-based "learning (Vygotsky, 1978) and multiple masculinities". A post-structural feminist lens allowed the latter author to better understand "the subjectivity and voice of boys and in which ways they navigate their selection of games along with online collaboration and discussions with peers. Using a multiple" masculinity lens, the latter author explored "the ways in which boys construct their gender. It is important to understand, through their voices, how these boys navigate gender and their identities in school." The latter study also explored activity-based "learning which is inherent in the social aspects of video gaming. Through an ethnographic case study", the latter author employed "deep hanging out with high school boys who engage in video gaming outside of school. Using this approach, the latter author was "able to explore the richness of their stories and how their video gaming practices could be used to improve their" in-school literacy.

How Boys Can Learn from Playing Video Games

"Interpretations of the cultural meanings made by" the boys described in Lane (2018), "based on their individual unique experiences engaging with video games, can provide readers with insights into how to approach adolescent aged boys' literacy development" (Lane, 2021, p. 109).

According to Lane (2019b, p. 199), scholars "have acknowledged the potential contribution of video gaming to complex forms of learning, identifying links between gaming and engagement, experiential learning spaces, problem-solving, strategies", trans-literacy "reflectivity, critical literacy, and meta-cognitive" development. Video games as alternative classroom pedagogies to support boys' meaning making are thus being used by integrating digital technologies into education through school-university-**community** collaboration.

Media-generated headlines, such as those mentioned by Lane (2016, p. 2461), "promote enthusiasm about video games as an alternative classroom strategy but this is" not "frequently underscored in literacy and technology discourses as" the latter seem to be 'wary' "to address boys' literacy underachievement" through these. A literacy information and computer education journal article by the latter author point out that these discourses none-the-less help towards finding ways for boys to make the grade when they 'play, score, engage'!

Game-Based Pedagogy – Using Multiliteracies as a Lens

In two ethnographic cases, Lane (2018) showed how four boys' video gaming experiences influenced their cultural knowledge, using multiliteracies as a lens towards meaning making within a game-based pedagogy. In similar contexts, Kritzinger, Loock and Goosen (2019) looked at cyber safety awareness through the lens of 21st century learning skills and game-based learning.

MAIN FOCUS OF THE CHAPTER

Issues, Problems, Barriers, Challenges

This section of the chapter will present the authors' perspective on the **issues**, **problems**, **barriers**, **challenges**, etc., as these relate to the theme and arguments supporting the authors' position. It will also compare and contrast with what has been, or is currently being, done as it relates to the specific topic of the chapter and the main theme of the book, on acquiring 21st century literacy skills through game-based learning

In terms of advances in technological pedagogical content knowledge, Angeli and Valanides (2009) reported on epistemological and methodological **issues** for the conceptualization, development, and assessment of ICT-TPCK, while with regard to **issues** and ideas in education, Kler (2014) considered ICT integration in teaching and learning for the empowerment of education with technologies.

One of the questions asked by Freeman, Adams Becker, Cummins, Davis, and Hall Giesinger (2017, p. 4) in the New Media Consortium (NMC)/Consortium of School Networking (CoSN) **Horizon** Report, K-12 edition was: "What are the **challenges** that" need to be considered "as solvable or difficult to overcome"?

Closer to the context of the research reported on in this chapter, Mathevula and Uwizeyimana (2014) investigated the **challenges** facing the integration of ICTs into teaching and learning activities at South African (SA) rural secondary schools.

Research Problem: Issues Related to the E-Education Policy and Community Engagement

Some countries lack comprehensive ICT **policies**. For example, South Africa used to "not have a comprehensive ICT **policy**", according to Mathevula and Uwizeyimana (2014, p. 1091), citing and quoting "the South African Information Technology Industry Strategy". There are legislative provisions "scattered throughout the government departments". Aside from "a lack of political will", it is also argued that the absence of a comprehensive **policy** is due to the rapid pace at which the sector is changing, "and the complexity of the **issues** involved". This situation, however, is likely to cause conflict and derail the efforts of the government to integrate ICTs in South Africa.

In an international review of information *ethics*, Wafula-Kwake and Ocholla (2007) pointed out that reports "should also enable readers to understand why *ethics* is important in research relating to e-schools and **community engagement**" (Goosen, 2018d, p. 14). It is important that *ethical* **issues** are considered when conducting any research. The research conducted into e-schools' **community engagement** involves human beings, who have the right to know that their responses and personal information will be kept safely.

The research problem is about e-schools and their engagement with the **community**. The SA government, through the Western Cape Education Department (WCED), has invested a lot of money to try and implement the **policy** goal of the White Paper (Department of Education, 2004), where each school must have access to information and communication technologies. The problem to be solved by this research can be summarized by the following questions, with particular attention to a particular high school in the Metro North district of the Western Cape province. To what extent:

- Does this high school have state-of-the-art information and communication technology 17 years after the White Paper (Department of Education, 2004) was published?
- Can this high school be considered an e-school?
- Are ICTs effectively used at this high school to effectively engage with its **community**?

These questions will be investigated and answers to these questions will form the outcomes of this research.

The "New Partnership for African Development (*NEPAD*) launched the e-Schools Initiative, intended to equip all African high schools with ICT equipment including computers … . It also meant to connect African students to the Internet" (May & Abreh, 2017, p. 116). Evoh (2007) also reported on policy networks and the transformation of secondary education through ICTs in Africa regarding the prospects and **challenges** of the *NEPAD* e-schools initiative. The idea to use and integrate ICTs in schools in South Africa was discussed and crafted after the *NEPAD* conference in 2003. The progress that had been made so far from the inception of the idea must be assessed. There is also a need for research on e-schools' **community engagement**.

The use of ICTs in teaching and learning has seen exponential growth in the Western Cape, in particular at high schools. Historically, it has been almost two decades since the idea was conceptually and contextually documented in the White Paper (Department of Education, 2004). The main reason for the introduction of ICTs into the curriculum was to try and enhance the effectiveness of teaching and learning (Ojo & Adu, 2019) by increasing access to information and communication technologies. The **policy** goal of the White Paper on **e-Education** (Department of Education, 2004) outlined that every learner and teacher at both primary, secondary and tertiary levels must have skills, which portray competence in the use of ICTs (Vorster & Goosen, 2017). This meant that most schools would be turned into e-schools with e-learning replacing the traditional ways of teaching and learning in South Africa. In an effort to live up to its dreams, the government rolled out various programs to spearhead the deployment of ICTs into schools. E-schools were to be centers for **communities**, where they could manage access to ICT skills. Hence, the researcher seeks to explore the extent to which South African schools have been converted to e-schools and the extent to which they interact with their immediate **communities**.

Barriers to Information and Communication Technologies Diffusion in Schools

Technological progress in all spheres of human activity has brought about huge changes in attitudes toward teaching and learning, as well as the way the world is perceived (Tiba, Condy, & Tunjera, 2016). By using ICTs, for instance, conventional teaching methods have been challenged, instructional practices have been transformed, and new instructional methods have emerged (Buabeng-Andoh, 2019). A variety of research on education and ICTs provided explanations as to why new technologies have not changed schools as much as other organizations (Mumtaz, 2000). As a complex process, integrating technologies into teaching and learning may encounter a number of barriers. It is essential to demonstrate the barriers that hamper technologies integration, in order to establish the framework for this research (Schoepp, 2005).

Teachers' unenthusiastic response to ICTs might be driven by a lack of technical knowledge underlying the processes that underpin their planning (Webb & Cox, 2004). It is imperative for teachers to envision the technologies' potential opportunities, obtain support and training just-in-time, and experiment with these so that they can use the tools effectively. Only then can teachers and students feel confident in the use of new technologies (Dzimiri & Mapute, 2013).

According to Zubković, Pahljina-Reinić and Kolić-Vehovec (2017), at the teacher, school, and system levels, there are strong barriers to the successful implementation of ICTs. Buabeng-Andoh (2012) found technical considerations, content characteristics, user characteristics, and organizational capacity as factors that may affect the adoption of ICTs by educators. In several studies, barriers have been divided into extrinsic and intrinsic barriers. However, what these meant by extrinsic and intrinsic differed. The study by Bingimlas (2009, p. 237) referred to extrinsic barriers as "first-order and cited access, time, support, resources and training and intrinsic barriers as second-order and cited attitudes, beliefs, practices and resistance".

In addition, researchers, such as Al-Alwani (2010), categorized groups of barriers to the use of technology that many researchers have also identified. These include nervousness, trauma, feelings of foolishness, fear of the unacquainted, and fear of degrading effects, computer addiction and extreme fear of computers, potentially involving active resistance, and sabotage.

A lack of proper infrastructure and internet connections, teachers not equipped with the skills, knowledge and competence to use ICT, lack of training for teachers, lack of software/hardware, etc. are some of the reasons why teachers fail to embrace and integrate ICTs into teaching and learning (Bhatia & Ilyas, 2016).

Snoeyink and Ertmer (2001) suggested that ICT implementation in schools is hindered by the following types of barriers: Barriers of the first order include equipment, equipment unreliability, technical support, and other resource-related **issues**, whereas barriers of the second order include *organizational* culture, and educator factors. The implementation of innovative technologies and learning in a massive open online course could thus be useful (Goosen, 2019d).

From another perspective, **obstacles** are related to two kinds of conditions: material and non-material. A lack of computers or copies of software may be one of the material conditions. Non-material **obstacles** include teachers' inadequate knowledge and skills in ICTs, the difficulties they face in integrating ICTs into instruction, and the lack of time they have (Bingimlas, 2009).

Barriers at the Teacher Level

Using computers in the classroom is heavily influenced by teachers' attitudes towards technology (Raman & Yamat, 2014). In addition, the latter authors indicated that teachers prefer using traditional methods in their classroom when teaching, because of their lack of motivation, acceptance, and readiness to embrace ICT integration and adoption. Some of the barriers to ICT integration in teaching and learning are outlined next.

Teachers' Attitudes Toward Information and Communication Technologies

A teacher's attitude plays a crucial role in the teaching-learning process that uses computers and internet connections. Although teachers' attitudes toward the use of these technologies are crucial, several observations reveal that they may not be clear about the extent to which these technologies can facilitate and enhance teaching and learning. Despite their positive attitudes toward technology, some teachers may refrain from implementing these in teaching, due to low self-efficacy, which is the tendency to believe that they are not qualified to do so (Mikre, 2011). Attitude, motivation, computer anxiety, and computer self-efficacy are factors affecting teachers' use of computers in their lessons. The use of ICTs in education may also be hindered by resistance from teachers and a lack of enthusiasm. Unless teachers acquire some basic skills and are willing to experiment with students, the use of ICTs in education is at a disadvantage.

Lack of Knowledge and Skills

Teachers' level of confidence in using technologies is one of the most important factors that determine their level of engagement with ICTs. Those, who are not confident using computers in their work, will try to avoid these as much as possible (Jones, 2004). When teachers do not know how to use ICTs in the classroom, they face embarrassment in front of their pupils and colleagues, which results in a loss of status and degradation of their professional skills (Russell & Bradley, 1997). In addition to the degree of confidence that teachers have about employing ICTs, teacher competence is also determined by their perceptions of their competence and how well they are trained (Pina & Harris, 1993). Furthermore, Jones (2004), in the British Educational Communications and Technology Agency study, also stated that many teachers, who did not believe themselves to be well-versed in computer use, felt anxious about using the technology in front of a class of children, who knew more than they did. The effective use of ICT is dependent on teachers' competency with computers. Therefore, teachers, who lack ICT competence, were unable to integrate ICT tools into their lessons (Knezek & Christensen, 2002). There are different levels of technical competence in developing countries that are a significant barrier to the adoption and acceptance of ICTs (Pelgrum, 2001). Due to the huge expansion in South African education, teachers now teach abnormally large classes of over sixty students. It can sometimes be difficult using ICT resources that provide for the needs of all learners to teach in such an environment (Van Heerden & Goosen, 2012).

Lack of Confidence

It has been noted that teachers lack confidence in using ICTs in education. A number of studies have identified reasons why teachers lack confidence in ICTs in education. A lack of confidence among teachers with regard to the effective use of ICTs in education is due to a fear of failure (Beggs, 2000). The teachers' inability to keep up with the latest technologies can also lead to a lack of confidence in the use of ICTs. Teachers, who are confident in using ICTs, want to extend their use of these in the future, because they recognize that technologies are helpful in their teaching and in their personal work (Kler, 2014).

Barriers at the School Level

Barriers at the school level are likely to be more manageable and solvable if government and other key players collectively invest effort and resources to solve these. Some of the barriers to ICT acceptance and integration at school level are outlined next.

Lack of Accessibility

A lack of access to ICTs is not simply a matter of lack of hardware and software or other materials within the school. It can also be a result of inadequate organization, poor quality hardware, incompatible software, or teachers without access to ICTs (Jones, 2004). Mumtaz (2000) pointed out that schools with high quality ICT resources tend to have very good evidence of using ICTs effectively in the classroom; so, a lack of computers and software can seriously hinder what teachers can do with ICTs in the classroom. Additionally, it has also been found that isolating internet access during the day and inadequate hardware inhibited the integration of technologies in Saudi Arabian schools (Al-Alwani, 2010). Recent studies on Syrian schools showed that inadequate computing resources hindered technology integration (Albirini, 2006). For ICTs to be integrated into education, there must be access to ICT resources and infrastructure (Kler, 2014).

Lack of Effective Training

A major obstacle to the successful integration of ICTs in education is a lack of adequate training. Through proper training, teachers can acquire the expertise and efficiency that is required to use ICTs in the classroom. Only then will they be able to use ICTs effectively during the teaching and learning process. However, teachers rarely receive this type of effective training. To be successful in integrating ICTs into classroom teaching, teachers must be trained to do so efficiently (Kler, 2014).

Lack of Technical Support

Teachers cannot be expected to overcome the barriers to using ICTs without both good technical support in the classroom and adequate school resources. One of the top barriers to the use of ICTs in education, according to primary and secondary teachers, was the lack of technical assistance (Pelgrum, 2001). Teaching is often hampered by technical **problems** when using ICTs. The technical barriers may include a lack of accessibility to websites, disconnected Internet connections, printers that are not printing, malfunctioning computers, and teachers working on old computing devices (Kler, 2014).

Lack of Time

Time constraints were one of the factors that hindered teachers' decision to integrate ICTs. ICT-enhanced lesson preparation is a time-consuming process, because one hour of ICT-enhanced instruction requires three to four hours of preparation. Teachers find it either difficult to prepare lessons or to conduct lessons within the limited time (Raman & Yamat, 2014). Despite the fact that teachers are qualified and competent to use ICTs, the lack of time also hinders the successful integration of ICT into education. Teachers complain that planning lessons for a class, exploring different sites, and looking at the various aspects of educational software are time-consuming (Kler, 2014).

Economic and Political Factors

Around 30% of African people have access to the internet, compared to the 77% internet use in European countries. It is evident from these statistics that the distribution of ICT is uneven between developed and less developed nations. For ICTs to be adopted, there are some prerequisites, such as a certain level of education, income, and quality infrastructure. The majority of African people generally fail to meet these conditions (Monsoï, 2017). Many African countries, particularly those suffering from poverty, hunger, and disease, find it difficult to evaluate the benefits of ICTs. ICTs cannot solve all social and economic **problems**, and so **policy** makers may lower the priority of establishing effective national ICT strategies, due to these (Wafula-Kwake & Ocholla, 2007). Schools themselves are under-funded and have little resources to spend on technologies. The absence of policies to regulate the growth and use of ICTs in the country creates a barrier. In many countries, computers and related items are considered luxury items, and the government imposes heavy taxes on them, raising their prices (Minishi-Majanja,

2007). Mutula (2004) cited evidence in support of the idea that educational institutions should receive government subsidies for technologies.

Empirical Evidence of Barriers to Information and Communication Technology Diffusion

There is a rich body of empirical research that has focused on barriers to ICT adoption. Research on the integration of ICTs in education has shown disbelief in ICT benefits as one of the other major barriers to ICT adoption (Al-Senaidi, Lin, & Poirot, 2009). ICTs present many **challenges** to integrating these into education, and generally, in most developing countries. Several physical and cultural factors influence teachers' ICT use, including reliable electricity access, inadequate infrastructure, the language of instruction, demographics, such as population density and size, and geographical factors, such as country size and terrain (Hennessy, Harrison, & Wamakote, 2010). A lack of political will to alleviate the **problems** of access is further compounded by extreme poverty, growing HIV/AIDS prevalence, and poor planning. According to Bwire, Nyagisere, Masingila, and Ayot (2015), in a study conducted by the University of Nairobi in Kenya, teachers, who are integrating ICT in their classrooms, think that technologies will burden them more. It is more difficult for **policy** makers to address the **obstacles** at the teacher level, because it is ultimately up to teachers to make the necessary changes in their own attitudes and alternative approaches to ICTs (Stigler & Hiebert, 2009). Other alternatives, which could be considered in this context, include trans-disciplinary approaches to action research for e-schools, **community engagement**, and ICT for Development (ICT4D), as well as cross-disciplinary approaches to action research and action learning (Goosen, 2018b).

Current technologies used in academic teaching often support traditional didactic modes, such as lecturing - this according to Liu (2011). Apparently, teachers lack an adequate understanding of a technology-assisted pedagogy.

The use of ICTs in education is frequently impeded by corruption, according to a study by Enakrire and Onyenania (2007). In most African countries, corruption rates in all sectors are a major hindrance to progress in the procurement and adoption of ICTs in teaching and learning. In recent years, most countries' Ministries of Education have experienced a lot of corruption scandals involving huge amounts of ICT procurement tenders. Many teachers express concerns and doubts on whether ICT investment projects can survive corruption in their countries (Langat, 2015).

It has been reported by Ghavifekr, et al. (2014) that students and teachers must work together to trust technology, improve uptake, and overcome resistance to technology. Teachers must be confident and competent in integrating different ICT tools into their lessons. Ghavifekr, et al. (2014) went on to indicate that support from administrators is very discouraging. Several teachers felt that school administrators refuse to support them in attending workshops and training programs so they can effectively use ICT integration.

System-level **obstacles** to ICT integration in education also exist. In some countries, the education system and rigid assessment pillars were the primary **obstacles** to ICT integration into everyday teaching. In addition to the variables within the classroom, teacher's control, cultural factors of the institution, leadership, curriculum, and assessments can also impact ICT integration in education (Ndawi, Thomas, & Nyaruwata, 2013).

Research Gaps

While there have been many studies looking at the factors that affect the adoption and integration of ICTs as a pedagogical tool in schools in developed nations, little research is available on the same for developing nations like South Africa. The researcher has to establish some of the **problems**, which are faced in South Africa when turning public schools into e-schools. The progress in the implementation of the **policy** goal of the White Paper (Department of Education, 2004) must be investigated to determine whether South African schools are now e-schools, which can engage with their **communities** for a healthy mutual relationship.

The then South African national Department of Education (2004, p. 6) wanted "to ensure that every school has access to a wide choice of diverse, high-quality communication services which will benefit all learners and local **communities**". This showed that the government initially thought about investing in information communication technologies in schools 17 years ago. The main concern now is whether government has made much progress in this regard. If not, what are the **challenges**? This has to be investigated.

Action Research "is contributing to transformation and equity in the context of e-schools", **community engagement** and ICT4D (Goosen, 2018b, p. 97). All research on **the successful implementation of** the idea of effective use of ICTs in schools and **community engagement** are aimed at working towards bringing Information Technology and development to the classes (Mentz & Goosen, 2007) of those groups, which were marginalized in the past. Do schools help to develop ICT skills in **communities**? This, too, has to be investigated.

SOLUTIONS AND RECOMMENDATIONS

Although information and communication technologies are not the **solution** to all educational **problems**, these are essential to teaching and learning today (Chinaka, 2017). This section of the chapter will discuss possible **solutions** for dealing with the **issues**, **problems** and **challenges** presented in the preceding section, as well as **recommendations** for integrating ICTs into rural South African schools (Dzansi & Amedzo, 2014) – this is in response to Freeman, et al. (2017) asking how effective **solutions** can be strategized to some of the themes addressed by the latter authors.

"Some of the **problems** that boys experience in schools … stem from their natural propensity to (be) more active and aggressive than girls … . Part of the **solution** must therefore be the remasculinization of schooling" (Lane, 2013, p. 146).

Towards Solutions

Towards obtaining **solutions**, paradigmatic "assumptions and perspectives impact significantly on" how methodological selections are made, "and demand a consideration of different research methods" with more focus placed on the limitations of different **approaches** (Maree, 2020, p. 38). "Whereas a nomothetic **approach** is" characterized "by procedures and methods aimed at discovering general laws, an idiographic **approach** is" characterized "by a focus on the individual and on understanding individual" behavior, "with little (if any) emphasis on formulating general laws."

According to the pragmatism **approach**, the researcher must first try to show a brief history of choosing the 'best' in terms of using methods (Goosen, 2008; Goosen, Mentz, & Nieuwoudt, 2007), which work for the kind of research problem that is under investigation (Kaushik & Walsh, 2019). *Ethical* ICT4D **solutions** should also be considered in terms of research integrity for massive open online courses (Goosen, 2018c).

Lane (2016, p. 2462) interpreted her findings reported on in the latter article "as an ongoing concern over boys' literacy and the growing need to explore alternative **solutions** which may alleviate further perpetuation of this **issue**."

Recommendations

Based on strategy **recommendations**, which "included a number of best practices" (Lane, 2018, p. 75) in terms of focusing on digital literacy, Lane (2018, p. 30) explored how some "boys relied on visual spatial skills to demonstrate learning outcomes".

"Video games, such as these, could potentially address boys' underachievement in school and support" **recommendations** at the time "by the Ontario Ministry of Education (MOE) to 'harness' boys' interests in non-traditional literacy sources" (Lane, 2016, p. 2461).

Another **recommendation** from Goosen and Van Heerden (2017), as **solution** to the questions asked by Freeman, et al. (2017), could include taking learning beyond the horizon with educational technologies.

FUTURE RESEARCH DIRECTIONS

This section of the chapter will discuss **future** and **emerging trends** and provide insight about the future of the theme of the book, on acquiring 21st century literacy skills through game-based learning, from the perspective of the chapter focus. The viability of a paradigm, model, implementation **issues** of proposed programs, etc., may also be included in this section. **Future research directions** within the domain of the topic will finally be suggested.

Freeman, et al. (2017, p. 4) indicated a **future** focus over the next five years to position pedagogical strategies - including learning and visualization technologies - and foster creative inquiry, by asking questions, such as:

- "What is on the five-year horizon for K-12 schools worldwide?" and
- Which **emerging** "**trends** and technologies will drive educational change?"

In terms of long-term **emerging trends** driving "technology adoption in K–12 education for five or more years", Freeman, et al. (2017, p. 3) included advancing cultures of innovation. With regard to mid-term **emerging trends** driving "technology adoption in K–12 education for the next three to five years", a "growing focus on measuring learning" was considered, as well as the short-term **trends** driving these.

Lane (2016, p. 2465) indicated that **future research directions** will include examining "the ways boys learn and interact with these types of video games to address their literacy underachievement", as well as "with other gamers in the surrounding networks" (Lane, 2013, p. 147).

Significance of the Research

To the Researcher

The researcher will broaden the understanding of the characteristics of an e-school and its sphere of influence in the **community**. The study will also enable the researcher to gain research skills and experience of conducting research in the **future** and combine academic theories with practical procedures.

Emerging trends in research indicated that the potential of digital technologies as a learning process can foster collaborative, creative and authentic learning (Cope & Kalantzis, 2009).

Lane (2021) looked at how video games support dynamic learning opportunities when using digital technologies in the 21st century classroom in terms of present and **future** paradigms of cyberculture.

Regarding innovative **emerging trends** in flipped teaching and adaptive learning, the "adoption of video games as an alternative classroom resource is acknowledged in technology and multiliteracies discourses as a strategy for meaning-making and developing cultural knowledge." The chapter by Lane (2019a, p. 138) addressed "how educators may be informed about" digitizing learning and how video games can be used as alternative pathways to learning.

CONCLUSION

This section of the chapter will provide a discussion of the overall coverage of the chapter and concluding remarks. The chapter provided an introduction of the topic of **acquiring 21st century skills through e-learning**, before offering background information in a *literature review* on **theoretical frameworks** and empirical evidence in a study of the **factors affecting the successful implementation of an e-education policy and community engagement**. Barriers to the adoption and integration of ICTs as a pedagogical tool in schools also received attention.

REFERENCES

C21 Canada. (2017). *The Spiral Playbook. Leading with an inquiring mindset in school systems and schools*. Canadians for 21st Century Learning and Innovation.

Abbitt, J. T. (2011). An Investigation of the Relationship between Self-Efficacy Beliefs about Technology Integration and Technological Pedagogical Content Knowledge (TPACK) among Preservice Teachers. *Journal of Digital Learning in Teacher Education, 27*(4), 134–143. doi:10.1080/21532974.2011.10784670

Adom, D., Hussain, E. K., & Joe, A. A. (2018). Theoretical and Conceptual Framework: Mandatory Ingredients. *International Journal of Scientific Research, 7*(1), 93–98.

Al-Alwani, A. E. (2010, August). Barriers to effective use of information technology in science education. *International Conference on Enterprise Information Systems and Web Technologies (EISWT)*, 42–49.

Al-Senaidi, S., Lin, L., & Poirot, J. (2009). Barriers to adopting technology for teaching and learning in Oman. *Computers & Education, 53*(3), 575–590. doi:10.1016/j.compedu.2009.03.015

Albirini, A. (2006). Teachers' attitudes toward information and communication technologies: The case of Syrian EFL teachers. *Computers & Education*, *47*(4), 373–398. doi:10.1016/j.compedu.2004.10.013

Aldosemani, T. (2019). Inservice Teachers' Perceptions of a Professional Development Plan Based on SAMR Model: A Case Study. *The Turkish Online Journal of Educational Technology*, *18*(3), 46–53.

Anderson, A., Barham, N., & Northcote, M. (2013). Using the TPACK framework to unite disciplines in online learning. *Australasian Journal of Educational Technology*, *29*(4), 549–565. doi:10.14742/ajet.24

Angeli, C., & Valanides, N. (2009). Epistemological and methodological issues for the conceptualization, development, and assessment of ICT-TPCK: Advances in technological pedagogical content knowledge (TPCK). *Computers & Education*, *52*(1), 154–168. doi:10.1016/j.compedu.2008.07.006

Archambault, L. M., & Barnett, J. H. (2010). Revisiting technological pedagogical content knowledge: Exploring the TPACK framework. *Computers & Education*, *55*(4), 1656–1662. doi:10.1016/j.compedu.2010.07.009

Beavis, C. (2014). Games as text, games as action: Video games in the English classroom. *Journal of Adolescent & Adult Literacy*, *57*(6), 433–439. doi:10.1002/jaal.275

Beavis, C., Muspratt, S., & Thompson, R. (2015). 'Computer games can get your brain working': Student experience and perceptions of digital games in the classroom. *Learning, Media and Technology*, *40*(1), 21–42. doi:10.1080/17439884.2014.904339

Beggs, T. (2000). Influences and Barriers to the Adoption of Instructional Technology. *Mid-South Instructional Technology Conference*, 14.

Bhatia, H. K., & Ilyas, Z. (2016). Barriers of ICT Integration in Teaching Learning. *Jamia Journal of Education, 3*(1). Retrieved from https://www.researchgate.net/profile/Harjeet_Bhatia/publication/319272961_Jamia_Journal_of_Education_An_International_Biannual_Publication_Volume_3_Number_1_November_2016

Bingimlas, K. A. (2009). Barriers to the successful integration of ICT in teaching and learning environments: A review of the literature. *Eurasia Journal of Mathematics, Science and Technology Education*, *5*(3), 235–245. doi:10.12973/ejmste/75275

Buabeng-Andoh, C. (2012, Apr 30). Factors influencing teachers' adoption and integration of information and communication technology into teaching: A review of the literature. *International Journal of Education and Development using ICT, 8*(1), 136–155. Retrieved from https://www.learntechlib.org/p/188018/

Buabeng-Andoh, C. (2019). Factors that influence teachers' pedagogical use of ICT in secondary schools: A case of Ghana. *Contemporary Educational Technology*, *10*(3), 272–288. doi:10.30935/cet.590099

Bwire, A. M., Nyagisere, M. S., Masingila, J. O., & Ayot, H. (Eds.). (2015). *Proceedings of the 4th International Conference on Education*. Academic Press.

Celik, I., Sahin, I., & Akturk, A. O. (2014). Analysis of the relations among the components of technological pedagogical and content knowledge (TPACK): A structural equation model. *Journal of Educational Computing Research*, *51*(1), 1–22. doi:10.2190/EC.51.1.a

Chai, C. S., Koh, J. H., & Tsai, C. C. (2011). Exploring the factor structure of the constructs of technological, pedagogical, content knowledge (TPACK). *The Asia-Pacific Education Researcher, 20*(3), 595–603.

Chai, C. S., Koh, J. H., Tsai, C. C., & Tan, L. L. (2011). Modeling primary school pre-service teachers' Technological Pedagogical Content Knowledge (TPACK) for meaningful learning with information and communication technology (ICT). *Computers & Education, 57*(1), 1184–1193. doi:10.1016/j.compedu.2011.01.007

Chinaka, G. (2017). *Factors affecting the adoption and integration of ICT as a pedagogical tool in rural primary schools* (Dissertation). Midlands State University.

Cope, B., & Kalantzis, M. (2009). "Multiliteracies": New literacies, new learning. *Pedagogies, 4*(3), 164–195. doi:10.1080/15544800903076044

DeCoito, I., & Richardson, T. (2016). Focusing on integrated STEM concepts in a digital game. In M. Urban & D. Falvo (Eds.), *Improving K-12 STEM Education* (pp. 1–23).

Department of Education. (2004, September 2). White Paper on e-Education: Transforming Learning and Teaching through Information and Communication Technologies (ICTs). *Government Gazette,* (26734), 3 - 46.

Duret, C., & Pons, C. M. (Eds.). (2016). *Contemporary research on intertextuality in video games.* IGI Global. doi:10.4018/978-1-5225-0477-1

Dzansi, D. Y., & Amedzo, K. (2014). Integrating ICT into Rural South African Schools: Possible Solutions for Challenges. *International Journal of Educational Sciences, 6*(2), 341–348. doi:10.1080/0975 1122.2014.11890145

Dzimiri, C., & Mapute, L. (2013). Integration of Information and Communication Technology (ICT) with pedagogy. *IOSR Journal of Humanities and Social Science, 16*(3), 86–92. doi:10.9790/0837-1638692

Enakrire, T. R., & Onyenania, O. G. (2007). Causes inhibiting the growth or development of information transfer in Africa: A contextual treatment. *Library Hi Tech News, 24*(4), 20–28. doi:10.1108/07419050710778491

Evoh, C. (2007). Policy networks and the transformation of secondary education through ICTs in Africa: The prospects and challenges of the NEPAD e-schools initiative. *International Journal of Education and Development Using Information and Communication Technology, 3*(1), 64–84.

Freeman, A., Adams Becker, S., Cummins, M., Davis, A., & Hall Giesinger, C. (2017). *New Media Consortium (NMC)/Consortium of School Networking (CoSN) Horizon Report: 2017 K– 12.* The New Media Consortium.

Ghavifekr, S., Razak, A. Z., Ghani, M. F., Ran, N. Y., Meixi, Y., & Tengyue, Z. (2014). ICT integration in education: Incorporation for teaching & learning improvement. *Malaysian Online Journal of Educational Technology, 2*(2), 24–45.

Goosen, L. (2008). A Brief History of Choosing First Programming Languages. In J. Impagliazzo (Ed.), *History of Computing and Education 3* (Vol. 269, pp. 167–170). Springer. doi:10.1007/978-0-387-09657-5_11

Goosen, L. (2018a). Sustainable and Inclusive Quality Education Through Research Informed Practice on Information and Communication Technologies in Education. In L. Webb (Ed.), *Proceedings of the 26th Conference of the Southern African Association for Research in Mathematics, Science and Technology Education (SAARMSTE)* (pp. 215 - 228). Gabarone: University of Botswana.

Goosen, L. (2018b). Trans-Disciplinary Approaches to Action Research for e-Schools, Community Engagement, and ICT4D. In T. A. Mapotse (Ed.), *Cross-Disciplinary Approaches to Action Research and Action Learning* (pp. 97–110). IGI Global. doi:10.4018/978-1-5225-2642-1.ch006

Goosen, L. (2018c). Ethical Data Management and Research Integrity in the Context of e-Schools and Community Engagement. In C. Sibinga (Ed.), *Ensuring Research Integrity and the Ethical Management of Data* (pp. 14–45). IGI Global. doi:10.4018/978-1-5225-2730-5.ch002

Goosen, L. (2018d). Ethical Information and Communication Technologies for Development Solutions: Research Integrity for Massive Open Online Courses. In C. Sibinga (Ed.), *Ensuring Research Integrity and the Ethical Management of Data* (pp. 155–173). IGI Global. doi:10.4018/978-1-5225-2730-5.ch009

Goosen, L. (2019a). Research on Technology-Supported Teaching and Learning for Autism. In L. Makewa, B. Ngussa, & J. Kuboja (Eds.), *Technology-Supported Teaching and Research Methods for Educators* (pp. 88–110). IGI Global. doi:10.4018/978-1-5225-5915-3.ch005

Goosen, L. (2019b). Technology-Supported Teaching and Research Methods for Educators: Case Study of a Massive Open Online Course. In L. Makewa, B. Ngussa, & J. Kuboja (Eds.), *Technology-Supported Teaching and Research Methods for Educators* (pp. 128–148). IGI Global. doi:10.4018/978-1-5225-5915-3.ch007

Goosen, L. (2019c). Information Systems and Technologies Opening New Worlds for Learning to Children with Autism Spectrum Disorders. Smart Innovation, Systems and Technologies, 111, 134-143. doi:10.1007/978-3-030-03577-8_16

Goosen, L. (2019d). Innovative Technologies and Learning in a Massive Open Online Course. In L. Rønningsbakk, T.-T. Wu, F. E. Sandnes, & Y.-M. Huang (Eds.), Lecture Notes in Computer Science (Vol. 11937, pp. 653–662). Springer. doi:10.1007/978-3-030-35343-8_69

Goosen, L. (2022). Assistive Technologies for Children and Adolescents With Autism Spectrum Disorders. In F. Stasolla (Ed.), *Assistive Technologies for Assessment and Recovery of Neurological Impairments* (pp. 1–24). IGI Global. doi:10.4018/978-1-7998-7430-0.ch001

Goosen, L., Mentz, E., & Nieuwoudt, H. (2007). Choosing the "Best" Programming Language?! In E. Cohen (Ed.), *Proceedings of the 2007 Computer Science and IT Education Conference* (pp. 269-282). Informing Science Press.

Goosen, L., & Van der Merwe, R. (2015). e-Learners, Teachers and Managers at e-Schools in South Africa. In C. Watson (Ed.), *Proceedings of the 10th International Conference on e-Learning (ICEL)* (pp. 127 - 134). Nassau: Academic Conferences and Publishing International.

Goosen, L., & Van der Merwe, R. (2017). Keeping ICT in Education Community Engagement Relevant: Infinite Possibilities? Communications in Computer and Information Science, 730, 113 - 127. doi:10.1007/978-3-319-69670-6_8

Goosen, L., & Van Heerden, D. (2013). Project-Based Assessment Influencing Pass Rates of an ICT Module at an ODL Institution. In E. Ivala (Ed.), *Proceedings of the 8th International Conference on e-Learning*. Academic Conferences and Publishing.

Goosen, L., & Van Heerden, D. (2017). Beyond the Horizon of Learning Programming with Educational Technologies. In U. I. Ogbonnaya, & S. Simelane-Mnisi (Ed.), *Proceedings of the South Africa International Conference on Educational Technologies* (pp. 78-90). Pretoria: African Academic Research Forum.

Goradia, T. (2018). Role of educational technologies utilizing the TPACK framework and 21st century pedagogies: Academics' perspectives. *IAFOR Journal of Education, 6*(3), 43–61. doi:10.22492/ije.6.3.03

Hennessy, S., Harrison, D., & Wamakote, L. (2010). Teacher Factors Influencing Classroom Use of ICT in Sub-Saharan Africa. *Itupale Online Journal of African Studies, 2*(1), 39–54.

Hommel, B. (2010). Grounding attention in action control: The intentional control of selection. In Effortless attention: A new perspective in the cognitive science of attention and action (pp. 121-140). Academic Press.

Israel, M., Marino, M., Delisio, L., & Serianni, B. (2014, September). *Supporting content learning through technology for K-12 students with disabilities* (Document No. IC-10). Retrieved from University of Florida, Collaboration for Effective Educator, Development, Accountability, and Reform Center: https://ceedar.education.ufl.edu/tools/innovation-configurations/

Jones, A. (2004). *A review of the research literature on barriers to the uptake of ICT by teachers*. London, UK: British Educational Communications and Technology Agency (BECTA). Retrieved from www.becta.org.uk

Jude, L. T., Kajura, M. A., & Birevu, M. P. (2014). Adoption of the SAMR model to asses ICT pedagogical adoption: A case of Makerere University. *International Journal of e-Education, e-Business, e- Management Learning, 4*(2), 106–115.

Kalantzis, M., & Cope, B. (2012). *Introducing the Learning by Design Project*. University of Illinois.

Kaushik, V., & Walsh, C. A. (2019). Pragmatism as a research paradigm and its implications for Social Work research. *Social Sciences, 8*(9), 255. Advance online publication. doi:10.3390ocsci8090255

Kivunja, C. (2018). Distinguishing between theory, theoretical framework, and conceptual framework: A systematic review of lessons from the field. *International Journal of Higher Education, 7*(6), 44–53. doi:10.5430/ijhe.v7n6p44

Kler, S. (2014). ICT Integration in Teaching and Learning: Empowerment of Education with Technology. *Issues and Ideas in Education, 2*(2), 255–271. doi:10.15415/iie.2014.22019

Knezek, G., & Christensen, R. (2002). Impact of new information technologies on teachers and students. *Education and Information Technologies, 7*(4), 369–376. doi:10.1023/A:1020921807131

Koehler, M. J., Mishra, P., & Cain, W. (2013). What is Technological Pedagogical Content Knowledge (TPACK)? *Journal of Education, 193*(3), 13–19. doi:10.1177/002205741319300303

Kritzinger, E., Loock, M., & Goosen, L. (2019). Cyber Safety Awareness – Through the Lens of 21st Century Learning Skills and Game-Based Learning. *Lecture Notes in Computer Science*, *11937*, 477–485. doi:10.1007/978-3-030-35343-8_51

Lane, C.-A. (2013). Using Video Technology to Address Boys' Literacy Gap and Connect the Male Voice in Gender Dynamics. *International Journal of Technology and Inclusive Education*, *2*(1), 139–150. doi:10.20533/ijtie.2047.0533.2013.0020

Lane, C.-A. (2014, March). How video games affect boys' literacy practices. In *The Robert MacMillan Graduate Research in Education Symposium - Theory to Practice.* Western University.

Lane, C.-A. (2016). 'Play, Score, Engage': Finding Ways for Boys to Make the Grade! *Literacy Information and Computer Education Journal*, *7*(4), 2461–2467. doi:10.20533/licej.2040.2589.2016.0327

Lane, C. A. (2018). *Multiliteracies meaning-making: How four boys' video gaming experiences influence their cultural knowledge—Two ethnographic cases.* The University of Western Ontario. Retrieved from https://ir.lib.uwo.ca/cgi/viewcontent.cgi?article=7128&context=etd

Lane, C.-A. (2019a). Digitizing Learning: How Video Games Can Be Used as Alternative Pathways to Learning. In Innovative Trends in Flipped Teaching and Adaptive Learning (pp. 138-161). IGI Global.

Lane, C.-A. (2019b). Video Games Support Alternative Classroom Pedagogies to Support Boys' Meaning-Making. In Integrating Digital Technology in Education: School-University-Community Collaboration (pp. 199-224). Information Age.

Lane, C.-A. (2021). Using Digital Technologies in the 21st Century Classroom: How Video Games Support Dynamic Learning Opportunities. In Present and Future Paradigms of Cyberculture in the 21st Century (pp. 109-134). IGI Global.

Langat, A. C. (2015). Barriers Hindering Implementation, Innovation and Adoption of ICT in Primary Schools in Kenya. *International Journal of Innovative Research and Development*, *4*(2), 1–11.

Liu, S. H. (2011). Factors related to pedagogical beliefs of teachers and technology integration. *Computers & Education*, *56*(4), 1012–1022. doi:10.1016/j.compedu.2010.12.001

Maree, K. (2020). Planning a research proposal. In K. Maree (Ed.), *First steps in research* (3rd ed., pp. 25–53). Van Schaik.

Mathevula, M. D., & Uwizeyimana, D. E. (2014). The challenges facing the integration of ICT in teaching and learning activities in South African Rural Secondary Schools. *Mediterranean Journal of Social Sciences*, *5*(20), 1087–1097. doi:10.5901/mjss.2014.v5n20p1087

May, E. L., & Abreh, M. K. (2017). Strategies for Achieving ICT Literacy & Proficiency in the Rural Primary and Secondary Schools in Ghana. *Journal of Education & Social Sciences*, *5*(2), 114–126. doi:10.20547/jess0521705203

Mentz, E., & Goosen, L. (2007). Are groups working in the Information Technology class? *South African Journal of Education*, *27*(2), 329–343.

Mikre, F. (2011). The Roles of Information Communication Technologies in Education: Review Article with Emphasis to the Computer and Internet. *Ethiopian Journal of Education and Sciences, 6*(2), 109–126.

Minishi-Majanja, M. K. (2007). Integration of ICTs in library and information science education in sub-Saharan Africa. *World library and information congress: 73rd IFLA general conference and council, 19.*

Mishra, P., & Koehler, M. J. (2006). Technology pedagogical content knowledge: A framework for teacher knowledge. *Teachers College Record, 108*(6), 1017–1054. doi:10.1111/j.1467-9620.2006.00684.x

Monsoï, K. C. (2017). Information Communication and Technology (ICT) diffusion and inequality in Africa. *Journal of Internet and Information Systems, 7*(1), 1–7. doi:10.5897/JIIS2016.0090

Mumtaz, S. (2000). Factors affecting teachers' use of information and communications technology: A review of the literature. *Journal of Information Technology for Teacher Education, 9*(3), 319–342. doi:10.1080/14759390000200096

Mutula, S. (2004). IT diffusion in Sub-Saharan Africa: Implications for developing and managing digital libraries. *New Library World, 105*(7/8), 281–289. doi:10.1108/03074800410551039

Ndawi, V. E., Thomas, K. A., & Nyaruwata, T. L. (2013). Barriers to Effective Integration of Information and Communication Technology in Harare Secondary Schools. *International Journal of Scientific Research, 2*(9), 211–216.

Ojo, O., & Adu, E. (2019). The effectiveness of Information and Communication Technologies (ICTs) in teaching and learning in high schools in Eastern Cape Province. *South African Journal of Education, 38*(Supplement 2), 1–11. doi:10.15700aje.v38ns2a1483

Osanloo, A., & Grant, C. (2016). Understanding, selecting, and integrating a theoretical framework in dissertation research: Creating the blueprint for your "house". *Administrative Issues Journal: Connecting Education, Practice, and Research, 4*(2), 12-26.

Pelgrum, W. J. (2001). Obstacles to the integration of ICT in education: Results from a worldwide educational assessment. *Computers & Education, 37*(2), 163–178. doi:10.1016/S0360-1315(01)00045-8

Pina, A. A., & Harris, B. R. (1993). *Increasing Teachers' Confidence in Using Computers for Education.* Paper presented at the annaul meeting of the Arizona Educational Research Organization, Tucson, AZ.

Raman, K., & Yamat, H. (2014). Barriers Teachers Face in Integrating ICT during English Lessons: A Case Study. *Malaysian Online Journal of Educational Technology, 2*(3), 11–19.

Ratheeswari, K. (2018). Information Communication Technology in Education. *Journal of Applied and Advanced Research, 3*(S1), 45. doi:10.21839/jaar.2018.v3iS1.169

Russell, G., & Bradley, G. (1997). Teachers' computer anxiety: Implications for professional development. *Education and Information Technologies, 2*(1), 17–30. doi:10.1023/A:1018680322904

Saunders, M., Lewis, P., & Thornhill, A. (2019). *Research Methods for Business Students* (8th ed.). Pearson.

Schmidt, D. A., Baran, E., Thompson, A. D., Mishra, P., Koehler, M. J., & Shin, T. S. (2009). Technological Pedagogical Content Knowledge (TPACK): The development and validation of an assessment instrument for preservice teachers. *Journal of Research on Technology in Education, 42*(2), 123–149. doi:10.1080/15391523.2009.10782544

Schoepp, K. (2005). Barriers to Technology Integration in a Technology-Rich Environment. *Learning and Teaching in Higher Education: Gulf Perspectives, 2*(1), 56–79. doi:10.18538/lthe.v2.n1.02

Seaman, J. E., Allen, I. E., & Jeff Seaman, J. (2018). *Grade Increase: Tracking Distance Education in the United States.* Retrieved from Babson Survey Research Group: https://files.eric.ed.gov/fulltext/ED580852.pdf

Sider, S., & Maich, K. (2014, February). Assistive technology tools: Supporting literacy learning for all learners in the inclusive classroom. *What Works? Research into Practice, 50*(1), 1-12. Retrieved from https://oere.oise.utoronto.ca/wp-content/uploads/2014/05/WW_TechnologyTools.pdf

Snoeyink, R., & Ertmer, P. A. (2001). Thrust into Technology: How Veteran Teachers Respond. *Journal of Educational Technology Systems, 30*(1), 85–111. doi:10.2190/YDL7-XH09-RLJ6-MTP1

Spector, J. M., Merrill, M. D., Elen, J., & Bishop, M. J. (Eds.). (2014). *Handbook of research on educational communications and technology.* Springer. doi:10.1007/978-1-4614-3185-5

Squire, K. D. (2013). Video game–based learning: An emerging paradigm for instruction. *Performance Improvement Quarterly, 26*(1), 101–130. doi:10.1002/piq.21139

Stigler, J. W., & Hiebert, J. (2009). *The teaching gap: Best ideas from the world's teachers for improving education in the classroom.* Simon and Schuster.

Tanak, A. (2020). Designing tpack-based course for preparing student teachers to teach science with technological pedagogical content knowledge. *Kasetsart Journal of Social Sciences, 41*(1), 53–59.

Tiba, C., Condy, J., & Tunjera, N. (2016). Re-examining factors influencing teachers' adoption and use of technology as a pedagogical tool. In *South Africa International Conference International Conference on Educational Technologies* (pp. 1-11). Pretoria: African Academic Research Forum.

Uribe-Jongbloed, E., Espinosa-Medina, H. D., & Biddle, J. (2016). Cultural Transduction and intertextuality in video games: An analysis of three international case studies. In C. Duret & C. M. Pons (Eds.), *Contemporary research on intertextuality in video games* (pp. 143–161). IGI Global. doi:10.4018/978-1-5225-0477-1.ch009

Van Heerden, D., & Goosen, L. (2012). Using Vodcasts to Teach Programming in an ODL Environment. *Progressio, 34*(3), 144–160.

Vorster, J., & Goosen, L. (2017). A Framework for University Partnerships Promoting Continued Support of e-Schools. In J. Liebenberg (Ed.), *Proceedings of the 46th Annual Conference of the Southern African Computer Lecturers' Association (SACLA)* (pp. 118-126). Magaliesburg: North-West University.

Vygotsky, L. S. (1978). *Mind in Society: The development of higher mental processes* (M. Cole, V. John-Steiner, S. Scribner, & E. Souberman, Eds.). Harvard University Press.

Wafula-Kwake, A., & Ocholla, D. N. (2007). The Feasibility of ICT Diffusion amongst African Rural Women: A case study of South Africa and Kenya. *International Journal of Information Ethics, 7*(2), 1–20.

Wahyuni, S., Mujiyanto, J., Rukmini, D., & Fitriati, S. W. (2020, June). Teachers' Technology Integration Into English Instructions: SAMR Model. In *International Conference on Science and Education and Technology (ISET)* (pp. 546-550). Atlantis Press. 10.2991/assehr.k.200620.109

Webb, M., & Cox, M. (2004). A review of pedagogy related to information and communications technology. *Technology, Pedagogy and Education, 13*(3), 235–286. doi:10.1080/14759390400200183

Young, M. (2017). Quality of literature review and discussion of findings in selected papers on integration of ICT in teaching, role of mentors, and teaching science through science, technology, engineering, and mathematics (STEM). *Educational Research Review, 12*(4), 189–201. doi:10.5897/ERR2016.3088

Zubković, B. R., Pahljina-Reinić, R., & Kolić-Vehovec, S. (2017). Predictors of ICT Use in Teaching in Different Educational Domains. *European Journal of Social Sciences Education and Research, 11*(2), 145. doi:10.26417/ejser.v11i2.p145-154

KEY TERMS AND DEFINITIONS

E-Learning: Refers to a learning system that we can obtain through the internet using an electronic device.

E-School: A school that teaches students entirely or primarily online or through the Internet.

Information and Communications Technologies (ICTs): Form a global network in which ideas are exchanged, or information and knowledge is shared, through devices such as cell phones or computers, used to connect people.

New Partnership for Africa's Development (NEPAD): Was launched in 2001 as an African-owned and African-led strategic framework for socio-economic development of the African continent. It was a product of outstanding initiatives of the great African minds of President Thabo Mbeki (South Africa) and President Abdoulaye Wade (Senegal).

School Management Team (SMT): As constituted in the new educational dispensation that ushered in the Outcomes Based Education (OBE) system is a structure with the sole function of giving leadership guidance, direction and assistance in the teaching/learning situation.

Chapter 31
Game–Based Pedagogy and Learner Identity Development:
Mechanical vs. Autotelic Identities

Fritz Ngale Ilongo
University of Eswatini, Eswatini

ABSTRACT

This chapter explores the potentially negative and positive impacts of game-based pedagogy on personality development. The methodology of this chapter is qualitative basic research, while the theoretical framework is critical theoretical analyses, articulated around psychodynamic theory, analytic psychology, and positive psychology. The negative view of game-based personality development presupposes 'learners for technology' or the pessimistic view, while the positive view of game-based personality development considers 'technology for learners' as being a perspective which facilitates media literacy, higher order thinking, higher emotional intelligence, and pro-social behaviors. The conclusion is that the positive view of game-based personality development would facilitate learners' effective and efficient acquisition of 21st century literacy skills, that is, information literacy, media literacy, and technology literacy.

INTRODUCTION

The increasingly complex and ceaselessly changing 21st century cultural, social, economic, and political landscapes constitute the nexus requiring simultaneous application of multiple literacy practices to enable learners effectively and efficiently develop literacy skills (Luke & Elkins, 2002; Carrington, 2001). There is an imperative need to develop a pedagogy that entails cooperative learning, a democratic ethos, self-directedness, and technological support (Alloway, Freebody, Gilbert & Muspratt, 2002). To tap into learners' psychological and sociocultural capital while developing multiple literacy practices, requires a philosophical underpinning which coherently integrates the demands of 21st century literacy skills, mastery of technology, self-regulation, and social learning attitudes among learners (Lingard, Martino, Mills & Bahr, 2002).

DOI: 10.4018/978-1-7998-7271-9.ch031

Social constructivism appears to be the most relevant lens through which the socioeconomic, cultural, political, and technological complexities can be matched by an equally complex, autotelic, self-regulated, self-directed, and self-accomplishing and learner psychological-technical prism (Gee, 2003). In other words, guided peer assistance both in formal and informal settings through technology-mediated activities like interactive videogames, constitutes a springboard for acknowledging a broader spectrum of learner literacy competence than was traditionally recognized (Love & Hamston, 2003). Social constructivism emphasises the interconnectedness and mutually determining elements of social learning derived from school based discourse and societal partners and settings in learner identity development and literacy skills' acquisition (Cope & Kalantzis, 2000; Ryan & Anstey, 2003; McCarthey, 2001).

Scaffolding is the integration of learner self-directedness and interdependence with guiding and supportive partners, which in the development of 21st century literacy skills includes technology-mediated activities, through the triggering and facilitating zone of proximal development (ZPD) (Bruner, 1983; Vygotsky, 1986). Thus, game-based pedagogy becomes a scaffolding experience for the development of 21st critical literacy skills, because learners creatively and interdependently co-create new understandings, through their sociocultural capital, interpersonal interactions, mastery of game-based technology, all within their zone of proximal development (Leont'ev, 1981; Rogoff, 1990; Stone, 1993).

It is subsequently a truism that traditional literacy pedagogies are being progressively substituted worldwide by constructivist multiliteracies through learning by design frameworks and gamification (Kalantzis & Cope, 2012). In other words, 21st century learners have as primordial challenges and opportunities, especially in the domain of literacy skills; engagement in meaning making through multimodal approaches, knowledge construction, enhancement of cooperative, creative, critical thinking, decision-making, and authentic learning (Cope & Kalantzis, 2009).

Gamification is an increasingly prevalent educational trend that facilitates the development among learners of new ways of being, knowing, doing, and worldviews, for mediating individual identity transformation, by motivating self-directed thought in learners, in terms of both multimodal approaches, and identification to a multiplicity of roles (Clark, Sengupta, Brady, Martinez-Garza, & Killingsworth, 2015). The former envisages pro-social identity change through identity construction or transformation, which forms a fundamental objective of research for game-based pedagogy (Martin, 2012). Information technology in general and game-based pedagogy in particular are very powerful mediating forces that influence identity formation by fast dissolving geographical boundaries, while creating opportunities and challenges through information dissemination and networking on a global scale (Pirraglia & Kravitz, 2012; Qualman, 2011).

In essence, gamification as a contemporary pedagogical orientation has a sociocultural ethos which emphases ontological and epistemological learner transformations through games which facilitate identity construction and transformation (Squire, 2006; Gee, 2003). Game-based pedagogy adopts a virtual framework for understanding identity and for interpreting both educational and entertainment games through a combination of virtual and non-virtual personas, as the condition sine qua non for effectively and efficiently navigating game-based learning activities (Gee, 2003; Squire, 2006).

The main preoccupation of this chapter is to determine then to what extent learners who are in the process of developing 21st century literacy skills through multiple technology mediated literacy practices, will not experience their identity development compromised through videogames becoming an end in themselves and not only the means to an end. In other words will game-based technology not lead to some learners to experience psycho-social fragmentation, self-absorption, narcissism, and manifest anti-social behaviours? Without being fatalistic, the chapter also posits positively that if game-based pedagogy is accompanied by a homocentric underpinning, learners' identity development will be characterised by; media literacy, higher order thinking, higher emotional intelligence, and pro-social behaviors.

STATEMENT OF THE PROBLEM

This chapter posits that learner acquisition of 21st century literacy skills could be influenced by the role of game-based pedagogy in determining learner identity definition and redefinition (Campbell, 2013, p. 44). To what extent would game-based pedagogy influence learner mechanical or autotelic identity development during the acquisition of 21st century literacy skills?

OBJECTIVES OF THE PAPER

The objectives of the paper are:

1. To determine the influence of game-based pedagogy on learner psycho-social fragmentation.
2. To find out the role of game-based pedagogy on learner media literacy levels.
3. To find out how game-based pedagogy could determine self-absorption or universalistic identities in learners.
4. To determine the impact of game-based pedagogy on learners' self-inflated or inclusive identities.
5. To find out the possible influence of game-based pedagogy on de-socialization or pro-social behaviours in learners.

METHODOLOGY

The methodology of this paper is qualitative basic research, while the theoretical framework is critical theoretical analyses.

Basic Research

Basic research, also called pure research or fundamental research, aims to improve understanding or prediction of natural or other phenomena (National Science Foundation, 2014).

Theoretical Framework

Critical Theoretical Analyses

Critical Theory is a social theory oriented toward critiquing and changing society as a whole, in contrast to traditional theory oriented only to understanding or explaining it. Critical theory basically seeks "to liberate human beings from the circumstances that enslave them" (Horkheimer, 1982). Critical theory involves a normative dimension, either through criticizing society from some general theory of values, norms, or "oughts", or through criticizing it in terms of its own espoused values.

The core concepts of Critical Theory are as follows:

- That critical social theory should be directed at the totality of society in its historical specificity (i.e. how it came to be configured at a specific point in time), and
- That Critical theory should improve understanding of society by integrating all the major social sciences, including geography, economics, sociology, history, political science, anthropology, and psychology.

Reviewing Game-Based Pedagogy through Critical Theory

The preoccupation at this point is centered on the following question: to what extent is gamification personalized to meet specific learner aptitudes? In other words, to what extent are game-based curricula designed *not* for individual learners to construct superimposed identities, as opposed to designing the same curricula *for* identities that learners a priori potentially have? To what extent in other words, do game-based curricula address the following queries; what learners *Can Do*, and what they *Like Doing*?

What Learners Can Do

If 'learning preferences' refer to the conditions, encompassing environmental, emotional, sociological and physical conditions, that an individual learner would choose, if they were in a position to make a choice (Dunn et al. 1989), then without considering preferred learning styles, could that not have a vital bearing on how the development of 21st century literacy skills takes place? Reinforcing this view point, Gardner and Hatch posit that it is primordial for teachers to 'detect the distinctive human strengths and use them as a basis for engagement and learning' (Gardner and Hatch 1990). In other words, do learners have a choice to develop 21st century literacy other than through gamification or game-based pedagogy? If the answer is negative, would that restriction not affect learners' identity development and performance levels in acquisition of literacy skills?

By extension, teachers' a priori awareness of students' learning styles could be a determining factor in the game-based pedagogical approach, in the sense that learning style awareness would help teachers gain a better understanding of the needs of learners, in relation to learning materials, levels of difficulty, in connection to learning styles. The aforementioned is in line with social constructivism which posits that learners would achieve success in the learning process if they are actively involved (Dewar 1996). But involvement levels could be determined by taking into account their learning styles as mediating elements. In addition, learner engagement is seen to improve: a sense of being in control, self-esteem, motivation, metacognition, and improved learning outcomes (Hartman 1995; Leadership Project 1995).

Finally, conclusions of research correlating academic achievement and learning style came out with the following notions (Dunn et al. 1982; Dunn et al. 1986; Lemmon 1985; MacMurren 1985):

- Pupils do learn in different ways to each other
- Pupil performance in different subject areas is related to how individuals learn
- When pupils are taught with approaches and resources that complement their particular learning styles, their achievement is significantly increased.

Game-based pedagogy facilitators who would be aware of their learners' intelligences, learning styles (Dunn et al. 1989), values, and personality profiles, stand a greater chance of: having a majority of their learners benefiting from gamification because of holistically structured teaching-learning approaches that will foster attainment of learning goals, in this case development of 21st century literacy skills.

Can Do could be considered under learners' intelligences and learning styles.

Question - what type(s) of intelligences do learners possess?

Nine intelligences identified by Howard Gardner (1983) which could be used in determining learners' intelligences include:

- Visual/Spatial Intelligence: *Ability to perceive the visual*
- Interpersonal Intelligence: *Ability to relate and understand others*
- Verbal/Linguistic Intelligence: *Ability to use words and language*
- Logical/Mathematical Intelligence: *Ability to use logic, reason and numbers*
- Musical/Rhythmic Intelligence: *Ability to produce and appreciate music*
- Intrapersonal Intelligence: *Ability to self-reflect and be aware of one's inner state of being*
- Bodily Kinesthetic Intelligence: *Ability to control body movements and handle objects skillfully*
- Naturalist Intelligence: *Ability to do with the outdoors*
- Existential Intelligence: *Ability to ability to be sensitive to, or have the capacity for conceptualizing or tackling deeper or larger questions about human existence.*

Question – what are learners' dominant learning styles?

- Visual (spatial). You prefer using pictures, images, and spatial understanding
- Aural (auditory-musical). You prefer using sound and music
- Verbal (linguistic). You prefer using words, both in speech and writing
- Physical (kinesthetic). You prefer using your body, hands and sense of touch
- Logical (mathematical). You prefer using logic, reasoning and systems
- Social (interpersonal). You prefer to learn in groups or with other people
- Solitary (intrapersonal). You prefer to work alone and use self-study.

What Learners Like Doing

It is undeniable that digital media are indispensable in knowledge co-construction, shaping, sharing, and storing within a social constructivist nexus, through and in which digital technologies act as enablers (Landow, 1997). To develop an inclusive game-based pedagogy and technology would entail taking into consideration among other factors, learners' learning styles and personality profiles. The latter would be vital in the design and execution of gamification teaching-learning processes that should adapt to the broadest scope of available learners in order to make their material accessible and comprehensible to the most learners (Draper, 2004).

The fact that not much research has been carried out to determine the correlation between learners' personality traits and digital learning makes the personality variable even more important in the case of game-based pedagogy for developing 21st century literacy skills (Blickle, 1998). Nonetheless, the importance of personality traits (which influence what a learner *likes doing*) has been recorded as having significant impact on students' learning, motivation, and academic performance (Wolk & Nikolai, 1997; Hamburgher & Ben-Artzi, 2003; Ibrahimoglu, Unaldi, Samancioglu, & Baglibel, 2013).

On a specific note, digital E-learning environments have been found to especially propitious for introvert learners, that is, students who can study in isolation from both teachers and peers, since they rely more on nonverbal communication (Atashrouz, Pakdaman & Asgari, 2008). In other words, game-based pedagogy should take cognizance of learner personality traits in the design of learning environments that will not only suit different learning styles but also various personality traits (Siddiquei & Khalid, 2017), in other to have an inclusive ethos (Litzinger, Lee, Wise, & Felder, 2007).

Like Doing could be considered through values, interests, and personality profiles.

Question – what are learners' dominant values?

- Freedom: Search for adventure, control over one's life, pleasure, glamour, popularity
- Knowledge: Determination to learn and grow, gain power, develop rational intelligence, understand the environment and principles of nature
- Idealism: Actively searching for justice, equality, equity, service, self-sacrifice, eternal life, beauty
- Security: passionately desire happiness, self-respect, family and social stability, comfort.

Question – what are leaners' dominant interests?

- Realistic: Working outdoors, using tools, machines
- Investigative: Working with abstract, mathematical ideas
- Artistic: Working with ideas using imagination and intuition
- Social: Working with people
- Enterprising: Working with people and ideas
- Conventional: Working with words and numbers

Question – what are learners' dominant personality profile(s)?

- Extrovert: Directing attention towards the external world and things
- Introvert*:* Directing attention towards the internal world of concepts and ideas
- Sensing: Perceive the world by directly observing the surrounding reality
- Intuitive: Perceive the world through impressions and imagining possibilities
- Thinking: Making decisions through logic
- Feeling: Making decisions by using fairness and human values
- Judging: Viewing the world as a planned and structured environment
- Perceiving: Viewing the world as a spontaneous environment
- Guardian: Looking for security, membership and belonging
- Rational: Seeking knowledge and competence

- Artisan: Looking for freedom and action
- Idealist: Searching for meaning and unique identity.

This paper posits that, without the aforementioned learners' aptitudes being a priori identified and integrated into game-based pedagogy curricula, there could be a mismatch between the latter and learners' intrinsic motivations, aptitudes, and authentic capabilities. The said mismatch could negatively influence learners' identity development and their effective and efficient participation in the avowed collaborative ethos of game-based pedagogy.

BACKGROUND

Technological Media and Identity Development

Technological media and network sites, of which game-based pedagogy is an integral aspect, serve as information and web-based services for allowing individuals and corporations to construct public and private identities (Qualman, 2011). In other words, this research considers technological media as an integral space and place for identity development of learners as they engage in the acquisition of literacy skills through multimodal game-based pedagogy.

Identity

In psychology, identity includes qualities, beliefs, personality, looks and/or expressions that make a person (self-identity) or group (particular social category or social group). The process of identity development can be creative or destructive (Paul, 2015). A psychological identity relates to self-image (one's mental model of oneself), self-esteem, and individuality. In cognitive psychology, the term identity refers to the capacity for self-reflection and the awareness of self (Leary & Tangney, 2003). Psychologists most commonly use the term "identity" to describe *personal identity*, or the idiosyncratic things that make a person unique. Meanwhile, sociologists often use the term to describe *social identity*, or the collection of group memberships that define the individual. For this researcher, learner personality could be conditioned by game-based pedagogy, to become either mechanical or autotelic.

Technological Media Mediated Identities

Technological media and network sites serve as information and web-based services for allowing individuals and corporations to construct a private and public identity (Boyd & Ellison, 2007, p. 211; Qualman, 2011, p. 64). For this chapter, game-based pedagogy could lead to either a techno-centric, mechanical, robotic, or to a homocentric, humane, and pro-social orientation to learner identity development. Technological media mediated identities will subsequently be considered from dual perspectives:

- Learners *for* technological media – serving as an appendage for a techno-centric system.
- Technological media *for* holistic flourishing of learners through a homocentric and pro-human ethos.

MAIN FOCUS OF THE CHAPTER

Learners for Technological Media

The Pessimistic View

The Frankfurt School led by Adorno and Hochheimer (1972) advanced the pessimistic view which considered audiences, in this case learners, as powerless victims of technological media, in that learners are passive receivers of content and could therefore be assaulted and manipulated. For Baudrillard, electronic digitality is accused of distorting the real, and disorienting learners in relation to reference, truth, and objectivity (Lenoir, 2004). The central issues implied here are the status and nature of reality, the situation of the learner as potentially being disembodied, dematerialized, and potentially dehumanized through a technologically deterministic educational pedagogy. The latter could be perceived as a venue for fear and uncertainty, to which the theorist Lev Manovich concurs by attempting to distinguish how technological media is different and illusory, in regard to reality, viewer interaction, and space (Manovich, 2001). Finally, the pessimistic view argues that through technological media, humans in general, and learners in this case would be infantilized and displaced into irrelevancy through passivity and dependence upon technology, which usurps humankind's agency (Carr, 2014).

Consequences of the Pessimistic View of Technological Media in Identity Development

For this chapter, technological media, that is, game-based technology, could lead to negative learner identity development as follows: psycho-social fragmentation, ambiguous parenting style due to technological media literacy deficiency, self-absorption, self-inflation (narcissism), and anti-social behaviours. It is presumed that the latter could negatively affect the acquisition of 21st century literacy skills.

Technological Media and Psycho-Social Fragmentation

Through new technological devices, there is pervasive and invasive breaching of hitherto sacrosanct personal spaces, resulting in the blurring of boundaries between information versus entertainment, comedy versus political news, public versus private, work versus leisure, local versus global, real versus reel, consumption versus civic engagement (Pew research Center, 2010). The challenge for literacy practitioners and policy makers is to rethink their assumptions about learners' engagement with technological media and its possible consequences for identity development and well-being.

For Arnett's (2002), many young people today are developing bicultural identities – one rooted in their local culture and the other in the larger global culture. Hybrid identities or multicultural identities could be one consequence of game-based pedagogy, with the possibility of identity confusion in some young people. Turkle (1995) also paints a rather troublesome picture by speaking of identities in the digital age as fragmented, shifting, and partial. She frames online youth identity practices as acts of identity simulation and draws attention to new levels of identity crisis. The blurring of frontiers could yield what amounts to a new type of human being distinguished by the fragmentation, discontinuity, and fluidity of the self (Rogers-Vaughn, 2012). This sense of fragmentation is associated with a global increase in the full range of what has come to be called mental illness: self-disorders, narcissism, depression, anxiety, addictions, with disruption of human attachment and relationships at every level (Alexander, 2008; Wilkinson & Pickett, 2009). In other words, psycho-social fragmentation might lead to pathologies in identity development, especially when the former is exacerbated by deficiencies in media literacy.

Technological Media and Ambiguous Parenting Style

Parenting styles have seen a shift from authoritarian to a more ambiguous style, because children study longer, start working much later, and remain dependent longer on parents (Arnett, 2002; Livingstone, 2009). But then, simultaneously, children enjoy more autonomy, especially in choosing technological media, leisure time use, and peer network, in which case it becomes challenging for parents to enter and master the worlds of their children. In line with the preceding, Livingstone states, "For children and parents already absorbed in the fraught emotional conflicts of negotiating boundaries of public and private, dependence and independence, tradition and change, this presents a new burden, adding official responsibilities to what were hitherto private struggles" (Livingstone, 2009, p. 178–180).

Throughout development from childhood to adolescence, parents play an important role in the formation of their child's regulation of emotions and behaviors, as well as their child's self-esteem and identity (Shaffer & Kipp, 2010). The ambiguous parenting style characterized by a parent being rejective (Brown & Whiteside, 2008), overprotective (Bögels et al., 2001), and anxious (Muris et al., 2000) could increase children's social anxiety and behavior problems (Fang et al., 2006), exacerbate parental controlling behavior (Greco & Morris, 2002), and negatively impact literacy skills.

Technological Media, Self-Absorption, and Minimal Self-Reflection

The question at this juncture is whether uncritically and unquestioningly immersing learners for example in game-based pedagogy could not negatively affect their identity development, because critical literacy "invites children not only to crack the code, make meaning, and use texts, but also to analyze texts - considering both, how they work and what work they do in the world" (Comber & Nixon, 2005, p.128).

In other words, when learners are not taught to become critically aware of technology media-produced texts, their thinking about such texts go unchallenged (Alvermann & Xu, 2003). By extension, the emphasis on individual responsibility to be media literate creates additional burden for learners, teachers, and parents. Livingstone (2009) correctly points out that the finger will be pointed at the user for being unskilled, incompetent, gullible, or naive instead of at those who provide biased, incoherent, manipulative, and inadequate texts. How then could minimal self-reflection and self-absorption in game-based pedagogy affect learner identity development?

In response to the aforementioned, the sheer volume of technological media exposure of learners is an issue because "in an age of information overload people need to allocate the scarce resource of human attention to quality, high value messages that have relevance to their lives" (Hobbs, 2010, p. 1). Net addiction through infobesity could lead to three attention process parameters of self-absorption in learners (Ingram, 1990): degree parameters, duration parameters, and flexibility parameters. Self-absorption or pathological self-absorption is characterized by a dysfunctional shift in the combination of these mentioned parameters. Excessive internal attention which is outlined as degree parameter corresponds to likelihood of maladaptive functioning (sense of ontological insecurity). Sustained internal attention which is outlined as duration parameter (attributional biases) is another necessary element of self-absorption.

Cognitive intransigence (uncompromising positional stance) which is outlined as flexibility parameter is also a necessary element of self-absorption.

Technological Media and Narcissism

Buckingham (2008) and Livingstone (2009) have both reported the banality of most technological media use by young people. "Recent studies suggest that most young people's everyday uses of the Internet are characterized not by spectacular forms of innovation and creativity but by relatively mundane forms of communication and information retrieval" (Livingstone, 2009, p. 62) and also that "there is little evidence that most young people are using technological media to develop global connections" (Buckingham, 2008, p. 14).

It is this researcher's standpoint that uncritical and unreflective use of social media could lead to the development of narcissism in users. Horney (1939, p. 89-90) regarded narcissism as essentially representing self-inflation, which, "like economic inflation, means presenting greater values than really exist," loving and admiring the self without adequate foundation, and expecting the same from others. Although narcissists use a variety of defence mechanisms, contemporary psychoanalytic accounts stress grandiosity, rationalization, and fantasy. In other words, the pervasiveness of 'information inflation' coupled with psycho-social fragmentation, uncritical and unreflective manipulation of technological media through game-based pedagogy, could lead to the development of narcissistic elements in learner identity development.

Technological Media and Anti-Social Behaviours

Media illiteracy, psycho-social fragmentation, self-absorption, minimal self-reflection, and narcissism are deemed as propitious factors for engagement in cyber bullying. Cyberbullying has become increasingly common, especially among teenagers (Smith et al., 2008). Harmful bullying behavior can include posting rumors, threats, sexual remarks, a victims' personal information, or pejorative labels (US Legal, n.d.). Bullying or harassment can be identified by repeated behavior and an intent to harm (An Educator's Guide to Cyber Bullying, 2011). Victims may have lower self-esteem, increased suicidal ideation, and a variety of emotional responses, including being scared, frustrated, angry, and depressed (Hinduja & Patchin, 2009). It might not be presumptuous to intimate that game-based pedagogy could see some learners engage in anti-social behaviors.

Technological Media for Learners

The Optimistic View

This chapter also emphasizes an optimistic view in relation to technological media and learner identity development through; technological media and media literacy, higher order thinking, emotional intelligence, universalism, and pro-social attitudes.

Media Literacy and Identity Development

Media literacy has been recognized as an empowering set of competencies, skills, and attitudes which facilitate well-being, adolescent developmental tasks, and citizenship training (Call et al., 2002). As Silver (2009) points out, media literacy is built on three main elements: access to media and media content; critical approach, the ability to decipher media messages, and awareness of how media work; and creativity, communication, and production skills. In other words, media literacy among learners could increase the effectiveness of game-based pedagogy, in the acquisition of 21st century literacy skills.

Nonetheless, the fundamental issue is determining to what extent technological media users are privy to and master the aforementioned constellation of skills, core elements, and can respond to the following key questions which could have an impact on identity development as they engage with technological media (Aufderheide, 1993; Center for Media Literacy n.d.):

- Who created this message?
- What techniques are used to attract attention?
- How might different people understand this message differently?
- What lifestyles, values, and points of view are represented in or omitted from this message?
- Why was this message sent?

In addition, the evolution of media literacy has been beset by shortage of funding, near absence of teacher training programs, lack of government recognition, and inadequate policy support amidst many other challenges (Scheuer, 2009). Addressing the latter issues could be decisive in making game-based pedagogy effectively applicable especially in Africa.

Technological Media and Higher Order Thinking

There is increasing emergence of technology as "the other" in the human technology relation, where non-human entities are the primary other party in the majority of interactions (Floridi, 2014). For example game-based pedagogy would not necessarily imply the infantilization of learners, as much as the latter's efforts might be redeployed towards more complex and rewarding activities involving creativity, invention, ideation and problem-solving, as in 21st century literacy skills.

Gainer (2007) further highlights how learners can enjoy the transactional process of everyday literacies when they deconstruct and become self-reflexive with their engagement with texts. In other words, technological media would become tools for both mechanical task relief and cognitive processing offload, and mental offload not just for lower-level tasks like obtaining information, but increasingly for cognitively-relevant tasks like planning and coordination.

Technological Media and Emotional Intelligence

Media theorists assert that technology is capable of transforming the environment and the life of the subject (Vitos, 2014), by providing experiences that allow emotion to be structured quickly and effectively across individuals such that they become group individuals through the individuation of the collective. The structuring of emotion is the necessary genesis of the collective, and the collective will only arise to the extent that an emotion structures itself across grouped individuals (Simondon, 1989). Music, especially EDM (Electronic Dance Music) could facilitate collective structuration of emotion for group individuation (Butler, 2006; Rief, 2009). Media theorists assert that these experiences are transformative because the great potential of technological media is in providing experiences that allow emotion to be structured for individual and collective equilibrium. Game-based pedagogy could then have a therapeutic ethos for emotional transformation through specific video games for example.

Technological Media and a Universalist Ethos

Media literacy and in this case 21st century literacy skills could become an important tool for democracy (Scheuer, 2009), since wider exposure to other cultures could develop multicultural sensitivity. Furthermore, through literacy skills, there could be the expectation of participation and a progression in the magnitude of digital collaboration, from sharing to cooperation to collective action (Shirky, 2009). Through game-based pedagogy, learners would appreciate their status of being simultaneously local and global citizens, whose trans-national identity is influenced by globalization, increased transnational flows of people and media, and learners' participation in online communities (Kipping, 2004). Dahlgren (2007) notes how young people are discovering common interests with a potentially huge network of like-minded peers, developing new critical skills, and building alternative deliberative spaces – all activities that raise the possibility of a virtual public sphere. The collective action-taking capacities afforded by technological media have been recently demonstrated in cases of global crisis response (Hui, 2013) and political action. Social media allowed the coordination of Arab Spring, the Hong Kong university protests featured real-time personalized drone footage, and the "Je suis Charlie" manifestations in France are cases in point.

Technological Media and Pro-Social Attitudes

Media literacy through critical literacy skills can be a powerful tool for voice and empowerment in learners. Shah and McLeod (2009) argue that communication competence is the most crucial foundation for civic competence. The integration of media literacy programs into game-based pedagogy's curricula, could help develop communication competencies and also channel learners' competencies in a civic direction. Youniss et al. (2002) have shown that civic identities can be developed through civic engagement which explores ideologies, develops awareness about civil rights and duties, and encourages learners to see their actions as interdependent and meaningful to the larger society.

A Stuart Foundation study in 2003 claims that through participation in youth technological media practice, learners gained the following skills; a voice and sense of social responsibility, improved basic literacy skills, increased confidence and credibility, positive adult and peer relationships, strengthened career-related skills, successful transitions to adulthood, and life transforming changes. Shah and McLeod (2009) and Shah et al. (2009) argue that communication competence is the most crucial foundation for civic competence.

SOLUTIONS AND RECOMMENDATIONS TO ADDRESS THE PESSIMISTIC VIEW

Solutions and recommendations for effective management of the 'pessimistic view' of learners *for* technological media include; a Human Factor ethos, digital and media literacy life skills, and the development of autotelic personality traits among learners engaged in game-based pedagogy.

Human Factor Ethos

In the context of this chapter, the way forward for game-based pedagogy could entail integrating and harmonizing the exigencies of technological media, media literacy, higher order thinking, emotional intelligence, pro-social behaviors, all centered on a Human Factor ethos. The central tenet of the Human Factor (HF) literature is that qualities such as responsibility, accountability, trustworthiness, integrity, motivation, commitment, emotional maturity, honesty, love, tolerance, loyalty and personal caring hold the key to all forms of development (Adjibolosoo 1999, 1998, 1995, 1994, 1993, Chivaura and Mararike 1998).

In the light of the aforementioned, the following are Human Factor traits which could be developed among learners engaged in game-based pedagogy, as highlighted by Adjibolosoo (2000):

1. Knowledge of one's rights, privileges, duties, and responsibilities as a member in a community.
2. Willingness to contribute to societal integration.
3. Development of the virtue of hard work, commitment, integrity, trustworthiness, responsibility, dedication, loyalty, and self-respect.
4. Development of worthy citizens guided by decent moral precepts, that is, good citizens who can live, work, contend and cooperate in a civilized way, and who are loyal, patriotic, filial, respectful to elders, law-abiding, and humane, caring of family, parents, neighbours, friends, tolerant of all people, clean, neat, punctual, and well mannered.

In other words, character building should precede but be complementary to, and interactive with both media literacy and social media, for authentic identity development of learners engaged in game-based pedagogy. Like Heraclitus was quoted as saying, 'much knowledge does not teach wisdom' (Bryce, 1921, p. 84). Alternatively, technical mastery of technological media even media literacy, without a priori emphasis on Human Factor development, could compromise learner identity development. The HF becomes logically the kingpin of every human endeavour, in the sense that no human undertaking, in this case identity development and acquisition of critical literacy skills, achieves its best results without it (Chivaura & Mararike, 1998, p. 21).

Digital and Media Literacy Life Skills

Hobbs (2010) defines digital and media literacy as a constellation of life skills that is necessary for full participation in media-saturated, information-rich societies. These include the ability to do the following:

1. Make responsible choices and access information by locating and sharing materials and comprehending information and ideas.
2. Analyse messages in a variety of forms by identifying the author, purpose, and points of view and evaluating the quality and credibility of the content.
3. Create content in a variety of forms, making use of language, images, sound, and new digital technologies.
4. Reflect on one's own conduct and communication behaviour by applying social responsibility and ethical principles.
5. Take social action by working individually and collaboratively to share knowledge.

For Silver (2009), media literacy entails: accessing the media, understanding and critically evaluating contents, and creating multimodal communications, which skills are perfectly in line with those posited by game-based pedagogy.

Autotelic Personality Traits

Autotelic is a word composed of two Greek roots: *auto* (self), and *telos* (goal). An autotelic activity is one we do for its own sake because to experience it is the main goal (Csikszentmihalyi, 1997, p. 117). Csikszentmihalyi's concept of an autotelic personality is derived from his flow model. According to his original model (Csikszentmihalyi, 1975/2000), flow is experienced when an actor perceives a balance between the challenge of an activity and his or her own skills. In the context of this book paper, the challenges for learners engaged in game-based pedagogy would entail integrating and harmonizing the exigencies of technological media, media literacy, individuation, higher order thinking, emotional intelligence, pro-social behaviors, all centered on a Human Factor ethos.

Csikszentmihalyi and Csikszentmihalyi (1988) proposed that flow is experienced when both, challenges and skills, are high, and in effect most flow research to date has started from these assumptions and operationally defined flow as experiences of balance (or high/high combinations). In other words, there is an imperative need for a combination of the maximal challenges from 21st century literacy skills, social media exigencies, and autotelic identity development. The latter complex balance would not be easily resolved without the 'low self-centeredness ethos' which characterizes autotelic personalities.

Nakamura and Csikszentmihalyi (2002) further describe core characteristics of autotelic personalities (i.e., curiosity and interest in life, persistence, and low self-centeredness) as metaskills. Csikszentmihalyi et al. (1993) proposed that these complementary (receptive and active) qualities in tandem produce a powerful autotelic combination. The simultaneous presence of complementary or even opposing traits fosters a dynamic, dialectical tension which is conducive to "optimal" personality development and the evolvement of complex individuals (Csikszentmihalyi, 1996; Csikszentmihalyi et al., 1993).

In confirmation of the aforementioned prerequisites of an autotelic personality, Rosen (2010) in his book Rewired, describes the iGeneration that came after the Net generation as having the following distinctly autotelic traits: introduction to technology, literally at birth; constant media diet; adeptness at multitasking; fervor for communication technologies; love of virtual social worlds and anything Internet related; ability to use technology to create a vast array of content; unique learning style; need for constant motivation; closeness to family; confidence; openness to change; need for collective reflection; desire for immediacy. The development of an autotelic or complex identity would become an effective and efficient 'feedback and feed forward driver'. The latter would balance the challenges of Human Factor centrality and technological media on the one hand, and media literacy skills for individuation, higher order thinking through emotional intelligence, universalism, and pro-social behaviors on the other. This delicate balance would be vital in the development of complex, integrated, and adaptable identities in learners involved in game-based pedagogy.

Autotelic personalities have a greater ability to manage the intricate balance between the play of challenge finding and the work of skill building (Csikszentmihalyi et al., 1993). According to Csikszentmihalyi, challenge finding and skill building are supported by the following opposing traits or processes which are simultaneously present in autotelic personalities: pure curiosity and the need to achieve, enjoyment and persistence, openness to novelty and narrow concentration, integration and differentiation, independence and cooperation (Csikszentmihalyi et al., 1993; Nakamura & Csikszentmihalyi, 2002).

Where non-autotelic individuals may see only difficulty in game-based pedagogy, their deep sense of interest aids autotelic individuals to recognize in the latter opportunities to develop their 21st century literacy skills.

FUTURE RESEARCH ORIENTATIONS

Future research orientations should be undertaken under the following rubrics:

1. Determining the extent to which game-based pedagogy leads to effective learning, the latter in this case referring to relatively permanent changes in mental processes and behaviours among learners.
2. Analysing the role of cultural belief systems in learners' degree of acquisition of 21st century literacy skills through game-based pedagogy.
3. Analysing the cultural sensitivity of the philosophical underpinning of game-based pedagogy.

CONCLUSION

The inevitability of the 'technology other' and by extension technology media is seen in that the best 'worker' for many contemporary jobs is a human and a machine in collaboration (Cowen, 2013). Secondly, the impact of technology is pervasive and inevitable, such that technology media increasingly determines the way we conceive reality, human life, and mind (Canan, 2014), and ultimately develop corresponding identities. If we assume that humans want to like, join, participate, share and engage as a means of social belonging and self-actualization, then gamification of the learning process could inherently provide graduated ways to accomplish the latter through escalated action-taking such as liking, subscribing, joining, participating, coordinating and leading. While there are challenges of valorization, selection, information overload and filter failure (Asay, 2009), the essence is that technological media and by extension game-based pedagogy cannot be excluded from extending the possibilities for collective individuation and socialization. The way forward will be to make a hard choice between having 'learners *for* technological media or technological media *for* learners' in which case if the choice is for the former, learners' identities might be reflective of mechanistic tendencies, whereas if the latter is preeminent, technological media could become facilitators of maximal individuation.

This chapter posits like Jenkins (2006) that for game-based pedagogy to be effective and efficient as a medium for the acquisition of 21st century literacy skills, learners a priori and in the learning process should; be able to find their voices and communicate effectively through play, performance, simulation, appropriation, multitasking, distributed cognition, collective intelligence, judgment, transmedia navigation, networking, and negotiation. In addition, there is need to develop media literacy curricula grounded in Human Factor elements, while employing proper guidance and channelling to expand the resources that learners engaged in game-based pedagogy may use toward identity development. Furthermore, ''critical literacy must be broadened to include information searching, navigation, sorting, assessing relevance, evaluating sources, judging reliability and identifying bias" (Livingstone, 2009, p. 187). The aforementioned also implies stressing the abilities to write, produce, participate, and communicate core abilities for authentic identity development (Gainer, 2007; Goodman, 2003; Vasquez, 2003; Buckingham, 2007; Chen & Wu, 2010; Chen et al., 2011; Hobbs, 2010; Kellner, 2002; Kotilainen, 2009).

There is the undeniable need to review and to popularize critical literacy, where the line between the teacher and learner becomes blurred, as they both become learners in the process of "reading the word and the world" (Freire & Macedo, 1987). As Ito et al. (2010) suggest, adults should act as coconspirators and experienced peers rather than authority in the game of developing critical literacy skills. Chavez and Soep (2005) talk about "pedagogy of collegiality" where adults and youth work as collaborators, which perspective aptly suits the cooperative philosophy of game-based pedagogy. Finally, there is need to establish a collective and also an individual sense of social agency and awareness of moral and political responsibility to society, which digital media and especially game-based pedagogy could facilitate at both local and global levels. In line with Hobbs (2010), it is thus imperative to obtain the active support of many stakeholders in this process: educational leaders at local, state and federal levels; trustees of public libraries; leaders of community-based organizations; state and federal officials; members of the business community; leaders in media and technology industries, and the foundation community.

CLOSING REFLECTIONS

Some parting questions for practicing teachers include:

1. To what extent are learners media literate, that is, capable of critical self-reflection, self-regulation, have aptitude for accessing technology media, understanding and critically evaluating contents, and creating multimodal communications, while remaining non-morbid?
2. To what extent is the game-based pedagogy rigorous enough by integrating instruction and practice opportunities that involve interactive experiences and leverage multiple modalities to apply knowledge across settings, learning styles, intelligences, personality traits, and contexts?
3. How far do game-based teaching and assessment use multiple modalities that will provide a variety of exposure types for all students and support deeper and authentic learning?
4. To what extent are game-based learning materials aligned to learners needs, and not only to curriculum based learning objectives?
5. How would you ensure that learners are both intrinsically and extrinsically motivated by game-based materials, in relation to relevance to students' culture, interests, and needs?
6. Do learners have a choice NOT to use game-based pedagogy in developing 21st century literacy skills? If they do not have a choice, how does this impact their 'unique voices', that is, intelligences, learning styles, and personality profiles? In other words, what is the ethical orientation of gamification in game-based pedagogy which 'excludes students' voices'?
7. How would you make sure that ALL learners enthusiastically participate in game-based approach to development of literacy skills, achieve the expected learning goals, and effectively learn, that is, experience relatively permanent changes in mental processes and behaviours?
8. How would you ensure that you respect the facts that: individuals have different strengths, learn in different ways, should be given opportunities to respond in a range of different ways, learners could be rewarded differently for their responses, and that there is more than one way to approach and solve a learning problem?

REFERENCES

Adjibolosoo, S. (1993). The human factor in development. *Scandinavian Journal of Development Alternatives*, *12*(4), 139–149.

Adjibolosoo, S. (1994). The human factor and the failure of economic development and policies in Africa. In F. Ezeala-Harrison & S. Adjibolosoo (Eds.), *Perspectives on Economic Development in Africa*. Praeger Publishers.

Adjibolosoo, S. (1995). *The significance of the human factor in African economic development*. Praeger.

Adjibolosoo, S. (1998). *Global development the human factor way*. Praeger.

Adjibolosoo, S. (1999). *Rethinking development theory and policy. A human factor critiques*. Praeger.

Adjibolosoo, S. (2000). *Pillars of economic growth and sustained human-centred development*. Paper presented at the International Institute for Human Factor Development Conference, Harare, Zimbabwe.

Adorno, T., & Horkheimer, M. (1972). *The dialectic of the enlightenment*. Herder and Herder.

Alexander, B. (2008). *The globalization of addiction: A study in poverty of the spirit*. Oxford University Press.

Alloway, N., Freebody, P., Gilbert, P., & Muspratt, S. (2002). Boys, literacy and schooling: Expanding the repertoires of practice. Commonwealth of Australia, Department of Education, Science and Training.

Alvermann, D., & Xu, S. (2003). Children's everyday literacies: Intersections of popular culture and language arts instruction. *Language Arts*, *81*(2), 145–154.

An Educator's Guide to Cyberbullying. (2011, Apr. 10). Senate.gov

Arnett, J. (2002). The psychology of globalization. *The American Psychologist*, *57*(10), 774–783. doi:10.1037/0003-066X.57.10.774 PMID:12369500

Asay, M. (2009, 14 January). *Shirky: Problem is filter failure, not info overload*. cnet. Accessed from https://www.cnet.com/news/shirky-problem-is-filter-failure-not-info-overload/

Atashrouz, B., Pakdaman, S. H., & Asgari, A. (2008). Prediction of academic achievement from attachment rate. *ZtF. Zeitschrift für Familienforschung*, *4*(2), 193–203.

Aufderheide, P. (1993). *Media literacy: A report of the national leadership conference on media literacy*. Aspen Institute.

Blickle, G. (1998). Personality traits, learning stratigies, and performance. *European Journal of Personality*, *10*(5), 337–352. doi:10.1002/(SICI)1099-0984(199612)10:5<337::AID-PER258>3.0.CO;2-7

Bögels, S. M., van Oosten, A., Muris, P., & Smulders, D. (2001). Familial correlates of social anxiety in children and adolescents. *Behaviour Research and Therapy*, *39*(3), 273–287. doi:10.1016/S0005-7967(00)00005-X PMID:11227809

Boyd, D. (2008). *Taken out of context: American teen sociality in networked publics* (PhD Dissertation). University of California-Berkeley.

Boyd, D., & Ellison, N. (2007). Social network sites: Definition, history, and scholarship. *Journal of Computer-Mediated Communication, 13*(1), 210–230. doi:10.1111/j.1083-6101.2007.00393.x

Brown, A., & Whiteside, S. (2008). Relations among perceived parental rearing behaviors, attachment style, and worry in anxious children. *Journal of Anxiety Disorders, 22*(2), 263–272. doi:10.1016/j.janxdis.2007.02.002 PMID:17383852

Bryce, J. (1921). *Modern democracies.* Macmillan and Co., Ltd.

Buckingham, D. (2007). *Beyond technology: Children's learning in the age of digital culture. Polity.*

Buckingham, D. (2008). *Youth, identity, and digital media (The John D. and Catherine T. MacArthur Foundation series on digital media and learning).* The MIT Press.

Butler, M. (2006). *Unlocking the groove: Rhythm, meter, and musical design in electronic dance music.* Indiana University Press.

Call, K., Riedel, A., Hein, K., McLoyd, V., Petersen, A., & Kipke, M. (2002). Adolescent health and well-being in the twenty first century: A global perspective. *Journal of Research on Adolescence, 12*(1), 69–98. doi:10.1111/1532-7795.00025

Campbell, H. (2013). *Digital religion: Understanding religious practice in new media worlds.* Routledge Taylor and Francis Group.

CananA. (2014) *Philosophy of new media.* Accessed from http://philosophyofnewmedia.com/

Carrington, V. (2001). Literacy instruction: A Bourdieuian perspective. In P. Freebody, S. Muspratt, & B. Dwyer (Eds.), *Difference, silence, and textual practice: Studies in critical literacy* (pp. 265–285). Hampton Press, Inc.

Center for Media Literacy. (n.d.). *CML MediaLit Kit.* Retrieved May 15, 2011 from http://www. medialit. org/bp_mlk.html

Chavez, V., & Soep, E. (2005). Youth radio and the pedagogy of collegiality. *Harvard Educational Review, 75*(4), 409–434. doi:10.17763/haer.75.4.827u365446030386

Chen, D., & Wu, J. (2010). *Deconstructing new media: From computer literacy to new media literacy.* Paper presented at the 8th international conference on education and information systems, Technologies and Applications, Orlando, FL.

Chen, D., Wu, J., & Wang, Y. (2011). *Unpacking new media literacy.* Retrieved on December 3, 2012, from www.iiisci.org/journal/CV$/sci/pdfs/OL508KR.pdf

Chivaura, V., & Mararike, C. (1998). *The human factor approach to development in Africa.* University of Zimbabwe Publications.

Clark, D. B., Sengupta, P., Brady, C. E., Martinez-Garza, M. M., & Killingsworth, S. S. (2015). Disciplinary integration of digital games for science learning. *International Journal of STEM Education, 2*(1), 1–21. doi:10.118640594-014-0014-4

Comber, B., & Nixon, H. (2005). Children re-read and re-write their neighbourhoods: Critical literacies and identity work. In J. Evans (Ed.), *Literacy moves on: Using popular culture, new technologies and critical literacy in the primary classroom* (pp. 127–148). Heinemann.

Cope, B., & Kalantzis, M. (2000). Introduction: Multiliteracies: the beginnings of an ideas. In B. Cope & M. Kalantzis (Eds.), *Multiliteracies: Literacy learning and the design of social futures* (pp. 3–8). MacMillan Publishers.

Cope, B., & Kalantzis, M. (2009). 'Multiliteracies': New literacies, new learning. *Pedagogies, 4*(3), 164–195. doi:10.1080/15544800903076044

Cowen, T. (2013). *Average is over: Powering America beyond the age of the great stagnation*. Dutton.

Csikszentmihalyi, M. (1975). *Beyond boredom and anxiety. Experiencing flow in work and play*. Jossey-Bass.

Csikszentmihalyi, M. (1990). *Flow*. Harper & Row.

Csikszentmihalyi, M. (1996). *Creativity. Flow and the psychology of discovery and invention*. Harper Perennial.

Csikszentmihalyi, M. (1997). *Finding flow*. Basic Books.

Csikszentmihalyi, M. (2000). Positive psychology: An introduction. *The American Psychologist, 55*(1), 5–14. doi:10.1037/0003-066X.55.1.5 PMID:11392865

Csikszentmihalyi, M., & Csikszentmihalyi, I. (1988). *Optimal experience: Psychological studies of flow in consciousness*. Cambridge University Press. doi:10.1017/CBO9780511621956

Csikszentmihalyi, M., Rathunde, K., & Whalen, S. (1993). *Talented teenagers*. Cambridge University Press.

Dahlgren, P. (2007). *Young citizens and new media: Learning from democratic participation*. Routledge.

Dewar, T. (1996). *Adult learning online*. http://www.cybercorp.net/ ~tammy/lo/oned2.html

Down's Syndrome Association. (2008). *Incidence of Down's Syndrome in the UK*. DSA.

Draper, S. (2004). *Learning Styles*. www.psy.gla.ac.uk/~steve/lstyles.html

Dunn, R., Cavanaugh, D., Eberle, B., & Zenhausern, R. (1982). Hemispheric preference: The newest element of learning style. *The American Biology Teacher, 44*(5), 291–294. doi:10.2307/4447506

Dunn, R., Della Valle, J., Dunn, K., Geisert, G., Sinatra, R., & Zenhausern, R. (1986). 'The effects of matching and mismatching students' mobility preferences on recognition and memory tasks'. *The Journal of Educational Research, 79*(5), 267–272. doi:10.1080/00220671.1986.10885690

Dunn, R., Dunn, K., & Price, E. (1989). *The learning style inventory*. Price Systems.

Fang, X. Y., Dai, L. Q., Fang, C., & Deng, L. (2006). The relationship between parent-adolescent communication problems and adolescents' social adjustments. *Xinli Fazhan Yu Jiaoyu*, 2247–2252.

Floridi, L. (2014). *The Fourth Revolution: How the infosphere is reshaping human reality*. Oxford University Press.

Freire, P., & Macedo, D. (1987). *Literacy: Reading the word and the world*. Bergin and Garvey.

Gainer, J. (2007). Social critique and pleasure: Critical media literacy with popular culture texts. *Language Arts*, *85*(2), 106–115.

Gardner, H., & Hatch, T. (1990). *Multiple intelligences go to school: educational implications of the theory of multiple intelligences*. Center for Children and Technology Technical Report. www.edc. org/cct/ccthome/reports/tr4.html

Gee, J. (1996). *Social linguistics and literacies: Ideology in discourses*. Falmer.

Gee, J. (2003). *What video games have to teach us about learning and literacy*. Palgrave Macmillan. doi:10.1145/950566.950595

Giddens, A. (1991). *Modernity and self-identity: Self and society in the late modern age*. Stanford University Press.

Goodman, S. (2003). *Teaching youth media: A critical guide to literacy, video production, and social change*. Teachers College Press.

Greco, A., & Morris, T. (2002). Parental child-rearing style and child social anxiety: Investigation of child perceptions and actual father behavior. *Journal of Psychopathology and Behavioral Assessment*, *24*(4), 259–267. doi:10.1023/A:1020779000183

Hall, S., & Gay, P. (1996). *Questions of cultural identity*. Sage.

Hamburger, Y., & Ben-Artzi, E. (2003). Loneliness and Internet use. *Computers in Human Behavior*, *19*(1), 71–80. doi:10.1016/S0747-5632(02)00014-6

Hartman, V. (1995). Teaching and learning style preferences: Transitions through technology. *VCCA Journal*, *9*(2), 18–20.

Hinduja, S., & Patchin, J. (2009). *Bullying beyond the schoolyard: Preventing and responding to cyberbullying*. Corwin Press.

Hobbs, R. (2010). *Digital media literacy: A plan of action*. The Aspen Institute.

Horkheimer, M. (1982). *Critical theory selected essays*. Continuum Pub.

Ibrahimoglu, N., Unaldi, I., Samancioglu, M., & Baglibel, M. (2013). The relationship between personality traits and learning styles: A cluster analysis. *Asian Journal of Management Sciences and Education*, *2*(3), 93–108.

Ingram, R. (1990). Self-focused attention in clinical disorders: Review and a conceptual model. *Psychological Bulletin*, *107*(2), 156–176. doi:10.1037/0033-2909.107.2.156 PMID:2181521

Ito, M., Gutierrez, K., Livingstone, S., Penuel, B., Rhodes, J., Salen, K., & Schor, J. (2010). Living and learning with new media: Summary of findings from the digital youth project (The John D. and Catherine T. MacArthur Foundation reports on digital media and learning). MIT Press.

Jenkins, H. (2006). *Convergence culture: Where old and new media collide*. New York University Press.

Kalantzis, M., & Cope, B. (2012). *Literacies*. University of Cambridge Press. doi:10.1017/CBO9781139196581

Kaplan, A., & Haenlein, M. (2010). "Users of the world, unite! The challenges and opportunities of social media" (PDF). *Business Horizons*, *53*(1), 61. doi:10.1016/j.bushor.2009.09.003

Karen, H. (1939). *New ways in psychoanalysis*. Norton.

Kellner, D. (2002). New media and new literacies: Reconstructing education for the new millennium. In L. Lievrouw & S. Livingston (Eds.), *The handbook of new media* (pp. 90–104). Sage.

Kietzmann, J., & Kristopher, H. (2011). Social media? Get serious! Understanding the functional building blocks of social media. *Business Horizons*, *54*(3), 241–251. doi:10.1016/j.bushor.2011.01.005

Kipping, P. (2004). Media literacy-An important strategy for building peace. *Peace Magazine*. Retrieved on December 3, 2012, from homes.ieu.edu.tr

Kotilainen, S. (2009). Promoting youth civic participation with media production: The case of youth choice editorial board. In D. Frau-Meigs & J. Torrent (Eds.), Mapping media education policies in the world: Vision,programmes and challenges. New York: UN-Alliance of Civilization.

Landow, G. (1997). *The convergence of contemporary critical theory and technology*. The Johns Hopkins University Press.

Leadership Project. (1995). *Adult Learning Principles & Practice*. Sheridan College.

Leary, M., & Tangney, J. (2003). *Handbook of self and identity*. Guilford Press.

Lemmon, P. (1985). A school where learning styles make a difference. *Principal*, *64*, 26–29.

Lenoir, T. (2004). Foreword. In *M.B.N. Hansen, New Philosophy for New Media*. The MIT Press.

Leont'ev, A. (1981). The problem of activity in psychology. In J. Wertsch (Ed.), *The concept of activity in Soviet psychology*. Sharpe.

Lingard, B., Martino, W., Mills, M., & Bahr, M. (2002). Addressing the educational needs of boys. Commonwealth of Australia, Department of Education, Science and Training.

Litzinger, T. A., Lee, S. H., Wise, J. C., & Felder, R. M. (2007). A psychometric study of the index of learning styles. *Journal of Engineering Education*, *96*(4), 309–319. doi:10.1002/j.2168-9830.2007.tb00941.x

Livingstone, S. (2009). *Children and the internet: Great expectations, challenging realities*. Polity Press.

Love, K., & Hamston, J. (2003). Teenage boys' leisure reading dispositions: Juggling male youth culture and family cultural capital. *Educational Review*, *55*(2), 161–177.

Luke, A., & Elkins, J. (2002). Towards a critical, worldly, literacy. *Journal of Adolescent & Adult Literacy*, *45*(18), 668–674.

MacMurren, H. (1985). *A comparative study of the effects of matching and mismatching sixth-grade students with their learning style preferences for the physical element of intake and their subsequent reading speed and accuracy scores and attitudes* (Doctoral dissertation). St. John's University.

Manovich, L. (2001). *The Language of new media*. The MIT Press.

Martin, C. (2012). Video games, identity, and the constellation of information, video games, identity, and the constellation of information. *Bulletin of Science, Technology & Society*, *32*(5), 384–392. doi:10.1177/0270467612463797

Marwick, A., & Ellison, N. (2012). "There isn't wifi in heaven!" Negotiating visibility on Facebook memorial pages. *Broadcast Education Association of Journal of Broadcasting and Electronic Media*, *56*(3), 378–400. doi:10.1080/08838151.2012.705197

McCarthy, S. (2001). Identity construction in elementary readers and writers. *Reading Research Quarterly*, *36*(12), 122–134. doi:10.1598/RRQ.36.2.2

Muris, P., Meesters, C., Merckelbach, H., & Hulsenbeck, P. (2000). Worry in children is related to perceived parental rearing and attachment. *Behaviour Research and Therapy*, *38*(5), 487–497. doi:10.1016/S0005-7967(99)00072-8 PMID:10816907

Nakamura, J., & Csikszentmihalyi, M. (2002). The concept of flow. In C. R. Snyder & S. J. Lopez (Eds.), Handbook of positive psychology (pp. 89–105). Academic Press.

Obar, J., & Wildman, S. (2015). Social media definition and the governance challenge: An introduction to the special issue. *Telecommunications Policy*, *39*(9), 745–750. doi:10.1016/j.telpol.2015.07.014

Osatuyi, B. (2013). Information sharing on social media sites. *Journal of Computers in Human Behavior*, *29*(6), 2622–2631. doi:10.1016/j.chb.2013.07.001

Paul, J. (2015). Despite the terrors of typologies: The importance of understanding categories of difference and identity. *Interventions*, *17*(2), 174–195. doi:10.1080/1369801X.2014.993332

Pew Research Center. (2010). *Millennials: Confident. Connected. Open to change*. Retrieved August 15, 2011 from www.pewresearc.org/millennials

Pirraglia, P., & Kravitz, R. (2012). Social media: New opportunities, new ethical concerns. *Journal of General Internal Medicine*, *28*(2), 165–166. doi:10.100711606-012-2288-x PMID:23225258

Qualman, E. (2011). *Socialnomics: How social media transforms the way we live and do business*. John Wiley & Sons, Inc.

Rief, S. (2009). *Club cultures: Boundaries, identities and otherness*. Taylor and Francis.

Rogers-Vaughn. (2012). The social trifecta of human misery and problematical constructions of the self: Implications for formation and supervision. *Reflective Practice (Decatur, Ga.)*, *32*, 206–223.

Rogoff, B. (1990). *Apprenticeship in thinking. Cognitive development in social context*. Oxford University Press.

Ryan, M., & Anstey, M. (2003). Identity and text: Developing self-conscious readers. *Australian Journal of Language and Literacy, 26*(1), 9–22.

Scheuer, M. (2009). Foreword. In D. Frau-Meigs & J. Torrent (Eds.), Mapping media education policies in the world: Visions, programmes and challenges (pp. 7–8). New York: The United Nations-Alliance of Civilization.

Sefton-Green, J. (2003). *Digital diversions: Youth culture in the age of multimedia.* Routledge Tailor & Francis Group.

Shaffer, D., & Kipp, K. (2010). *Developmental psychology: Childhood and adolescence* (8th ed.). Wadsworth Cengage Learning.

Shah, D., & McLeod, J. (2009). Communication and political socialization: Challenges and opportunities for research. *Political Communication, 26*(1), 1–10. doi:10.1080/10584600802686105

Shah, D., McLeod, J., & Lee, N. (2009). Communication competence as a foundation for civic competence: Process of socialization into citizenship. *Political Communication, 26*(1), 102–117. doi:10.1080/10584600802710384

Shirky, C. (2009). *Here comes everybody: The power of organizing without organizations.* Penguin.

Siddiquei, N. L., & Khalid, R. (2017). Emerging Trends of E- Learning in Pakistan: Past, Present and Future. *International Journal of Law, Humanities &. Social Science, 2*(1), 20–35.

Silver, A. (2009). A European approach to media literacy: Moving toward an inclusive knowledge society. In D. Frau-Meigs & J. Torrent (Eds.), Mapping media education policies in the world: Visions, programmes and challenges (pp. 11–13). New York: The United Nations-Alliance of Civilization.

Simondon, G. (1989b). *L'individuation psychique et collective.* Aubier.

Simondon, G. (2005). *L'individuation à la lumière des notions de forme et d'information.* Jerome Million.

Smith, K., Mahdavi, J., Carvalho, M., Fisher, S., Russell, S., & Tippett, N. (2008). Cyberbullying: Its nature and impact in secondary school pupils. *Journal of Child Psychology and Psychiatry, and Allied Disciplines, 49*(4), 376–385. doi:10.1111/j.1469-7610.2007.01846.x PMID:18363945

Squire, K. (2006). From content to context: Videogames as designed experience. *Educational Researcher, 35*(8), 19–29. doi:10.3102/0013189X035008019

Stone, C. (1993). What is missing in the metaphor of scaffolding? In E. Forman, N. Minick, & C. Stone (Eds.), *Contexts for learning: Sociocultural dynamics in children's development* (pp. 169–183). Oxford University Press.

The City Reporters. (2013). *REVEALED! Govt plans to read your tweets, Facebook posts, possibly jail you.* Available at http://thecityreporters.com/revealed-govt-plans-to-readyour-tweets-facebook-posts-possibly-jail-you/

Turkle, S. (1995). *Life on the screen: Identity in the age of the Internet.* Touchstone.

Vasquez, V. (2003). What Pokemon can teach us about learning and literacy. *Language Arts, 81*(2), 145–154.

Vitos, B. (2014). *Experiencing electronic dance floors: A comparative research of techno and psytrance in Melbourne* (Unpublished PhD Thesis). Monash University, Clayton, Australia.

Weber, S., & Mitchell, C. (2008). Imaging, keyboarding, and posting identities: Young people and new media technologies. In D. Buckingham (Ed.), Youth, identity, and digital media (pp. 25–48). The MIT Press.

Wilkinson, R., & Pickett, K. (2009). *The spirit level: Why greater equality makes societies stronger.* Bloomsbury Press.

Wolk, C., & Nikolai, L. A. (1997). Personality types of accounting students and faculty: Comparisons and implications. *Journal of Accounting Education, 15*(1), 1–17. doi:10.1016/S0748-5751(96)00041-3

Youniss, Bales, S., Christmas-Best, V., Diversi, M., McLaughlin, M., & Silbereisen, R. (2002). Youth Civic Engagement in the Twenty-First Century. *Journal of Research on Adolescence, 12*(1), 121–148. doi:10.1111/1532-7795.00027

Chapter 32
Gamification and Mobile Learning:
New Pedagogical Strategies

Ana Nobre
ⓘ https://orcid.org/0000-0002-9902-1850
Universidade Aberta, Portugal

Vasco Nobre
Universidade Aberta, Portugal

ABSTRACT

Gamification has been a very frequent research topic in the area of education in recent years, with some positive results, such as increasing student engagement and motivation. However, studies on gamification as an instructional strategy are recent and need more data to help teachers in its use in the classroom. Thus, this work describes a gamification experience of a social game with graduate students, teachers in primary and secondary education, and discusses how the elements present in games can provide engagement and favor learning. Furthermore, the authors present the Kahoot app as a possibility to stimulate and engage students in the teaching-learning process, analyzing some implications of learning with a mobile device. The results had a positive impact on increasing student engagement in both Game Social and Kahoot. Therefore, gamification and mobile learning can be good alternatives to increase the quality of teaching, generating meaningful experiences in the classroom.

INTRODUCTION

Throughout the 20th century, several technological advances were developed, in the eyes of each generation of people who were growing and following (from near or far) this process of complete replacement, improvement or creation of electronic equipment and new technological and digital media. Companies that directly developed this technology provided such advance. Programmers were creating and improving software or applications, in terminology more updated.

DOI: 10.4018/978-1-7998-7271-9.ch032

The spread of the internet and technological developments in multimedia, from desktop computers to notebook and tablet portables and, later, smartphones, combined with lower prices, allowed for the popularization of these products, expanding the possibility and number of people connected to the internet, in a world that demands more and more interactivity, and communication that is fast and efficient, with large storage and memory capacity on the devices.

We intensively use different applications on our mobile devices on a daily basis, performing various functions and facilities for the day to day, from checking the balance at the bank, exchanging messages with distant friends and family, having fun listening to music or playing online, and even learning a new language or studying for a history test. The use of Digital Information and Communication Technologies (DICT) in school life is already a reality.

In the area of education, the game is revealing itself as an important pedagogical tool to improve current teaching and learning (Zampa & Felipe Mendes, 2016). We live in a context that involves the constant inclusion of new teaching methodologies and TDIC tools, mainly because digital natives are more sophisticated in the use of the Internet, smartphones and mobile devices than the previous generation (Akçayır, Dündar, & Akçayır, 2016). Therefore, as Prensky (2012) argues, learning based on digital games is in line with the needs and learning of digital natives, motivating and adapting to all disciplines and skills.

Initially, gamification appears as a technology that uses the traditional elements of a classic game, but applied to other areas, such as marketing, training, among others, in order to encourage engagement in products or services (Kim, Song, Lockee, & Burton, 2018). However, over the years, it began to be used in the field of education, with the specific purpose of engaging students in their learning process. As this is a recent subject, it is interesting to study the possibilities of applying gamification in education, in addition to the digital tools available that can help teachers to work in the classroom. In order to innovate in pedagogical strategies, we created a social game in the Teaching Training Course.

Kahoot software is a free platform accessed by computer or mobile device that enables, through four tools (Quiz, Jumble, Discussion and Survey), the use of some of the concepts related to gamification in the classroom, promoting meaningful learning for students using the game in an educational context (Bicen & Kocakoyun, 2018). Dellos (2015) concluded that Kahoot offers benefits for the teacher and students by providing a fun and competitive environment to promote learning and motivate students. So, proposing a gamified classroom in conjunction with Kahoot can be a very interesting alternative to increase engagement and qualify the students' learning process. In this context, we intend to evaluate the use of gamification in a classroom, using kahoot software, in order to verify whether or not it can contribute to the teaching of business communication.

This chapter aims to: a) define the concept of Gamification and Mobile Learning b) describe the case studies developed c) results d) some conclusions about the study.

BACKGROUND

Gamification

The word gamification appeared in 2003, being given to the computer programmer and inventor Nick Pelling, gaining strength from 2010 and in 2011 it starts to generate reports and statistics on the subject (Alves, 2014).

The definition of what gamification is about can be explained through the idea of using game elements, using their strategies, in contexts that are not considered games. For Nobre (2021), gamification is the process of using game mechanics, game style and game thinking, in a non-game context, as a means to solve problems and engage people. Thus, gamification analyzes the elements present in game design, which make it fun, aiming to include these same elements in non-game situations, such as a classroom, for example.

Complementing this concept, gamification can be understood as the possibility of using digital games to solve social problems and situations, involving the public (Zapata-Rivera & Bauer, 2012).

It is understood that making use of these new strategies in education is a way to engage students and motivate them to the teaching-learning process, in which they are inevitably submitted. As an example, for Gomes at al (2018) the gamification process in education can be using game design elements to reframe and draw from another perspective, that of gamification, the curriculum, practices and the pedagogical mediation processes, which would promote greater engagement of teachers and students.

Thus, having as a reference the context of the emergence of gamification and the objectives of engagement between subjects, whatever the scope, it is considerable to delimit that the creation of a game or a specific virtual environment for gamification to happen is not foreseen, including with a certain educational purpose. What is possible and expected is that all the resources and possibilities that games have to solve real life problems are incorporated in the context of planning and executing gamification. Thus, the choice of key elements will depend on the objectives, that is, the purpose for which gamification will be used.

This strategy, according to Gomes *at al* (2018), can be guided by the reward, with the use of medals or points (PBL – Points, Badges and Leaderboards), or, otherwise, motivating the people involved to give meaning to their characters according to the context in which they are inserted.

What is proposed, with gamification, is a return to the meaning of the teaching-learning experience, noting that experiences can help individuals to reformulate their ideas and conceptions about what is valid or not based on their practice (Nobre, 2021). Accordingly, it is noteworthy that the understanding resulting from each experience will vary from individual to individual, that is, each one has a way of interpreting the world. Thus, the use of game strategies is presented as a potentiator of significant learning, as it makes it possible to adapt the strategies and elements of games in the educational context according to the students' perceived needs.

The emergence of gamification and its application is not only related to education, but in any context that fits the following situation: The use of game elements such as mechanics, aesthetics and thoughts to engage people to take actions, promote learning and resolve problems (Kapp, 2012; Kim, Song, Lockee, & Burton, 2018).

These elements are defined according to Kapp (2012) as:

- Mechanics: are usually the elements used in many games such as levels or stages, badges or medals, ranking, scoring and time control. They are important for the construction of the gamification process, however, they are insufficient to transform a boring experience into something immersive if only these mechanics are used.
- Aesthetics: for gamification to be successful, the experience must be pleasant and this depends a lot on the aesthetics that are used in the user interface. So, the experience must be aesthetically appealing and not difficult for players or students to understand.

- Thoughts: Perhaps the most important element of gamification, thoughts are the ideas that make up the game's story. It's thinking about how the experience will be motivating to make players compete with each other and at the same time cooperate to achieve a common goal. Therefore, it is the thoughts that define the experiences performed by students that lead to the desired learning with gamification.

These game elements are the tools used for the solution, whether digital or not, to lead to gamified learning (Alves, 2014) and, furthermore, their use depends on the context and the desired goals. There are several factors in games that motivate students and can be used to aid teaching and learning. Among these elements, fun, game, rules, interactivity, result and quick feedback are capable of generating engagement like no other media (Gomes *at al*, 2018). In general, the most used elements in gamified applications are feedbacks, ratings, points and levels (Surendeleg, Murwa, Yun, & Kim, 2014). The main advantage of gamification is the possibility to make learning more "delightful" or "interesting" using game elements. In traditional education methodology, classroom or virtual classes are understood as overwhelming by students and gamification has great advantage to minimize this problem (Surendeleg, Murwa, Yun, & Kim, 2014). Therefore, gamification appears as an option to try to bring the teacher closer to the context of students, inserted in the digital age.

Mobile Learning

In the educational field, the main changes observed in recent times are in the attitude of the teacher towards education, that is, the teacher is no longer the sole holder of knowledge to become a mediator of learning. On the other hand, the student is no longer a passive figure, who only receives information, and assumes a more active posture, which does not conceive an education without interaction and pedagogical practice of the knowledge that is being built.

Technologies, if well used, can help the teacher to achieve these educational goals, as they allow a variety of possibilities, as well as offering students the opportunity to see and exercise their knowledge, especially with the help of multimedia resources (Filipe & Nobre, 2019) (sound, image, text, video, animation, etc.).

With the emergence of mobile devices, man started to use these resources to access information more and more. The rapid migration to this new form of access to technological resources is due to a wide range of factors, such as: the reduction in the acquisition cost of a mobile device in relation to a conventional computer, the practicality of using a mobile device, the ease of use access to the Internet in virtually all spaces, the need to connect at all times, among other factors.

If this revolution takes place in society, the school could not remain on the sidelines of this transformation. According to Bottentuit Junior (2012, p. 130), "mobile learning is a concept created for learning that uses mobile resources, that is, equipment and devices that allow the learner to move while accessing the content".

Students in contemporary society, known as digital generation, generation z or generation thumb (because they are always with their fingers on the screens of devices), have mobile technologies with fast reach, since almost all students have cell phones (smartphones) with access Internet and a set of services and applications. Therefore, using these resources in the classroom became easier (Moura, 2009).

Another aspect to consider is that the acquisition and maintenance of computer labs in educational institutions has become costly, as the school does not always have the resources to repair the machines in a quick time. Many schools, being public, require a whole bureaucracy (bidding) to carry out maintenance on equipment. Therefore, providing the school with Wi-Fi Internet access becomes more practical and cheaper than maintaining a computer lab, as the practices can take place anywhere in the institution.

On the other hand, in order to guarantee, in fact, that mobile learning takes place in a productive way, it is necessary to first incorporate the digital culture of the use of these resources by teachers. Then, it is necessary to appropriate resources and tools (mobile phone, tablet, notebook and technological devices), exploring the pedagogical possibilities (Nobre, 2021) of each item (camera, video recorder, audio recorder, calculator, bar code reader, etc.).

After acquiring these basic knowledge of changing to digital culture and appropriating the pedagogical possibilities from the applications, an investment in work methodologies to optimize these resources is also necessary. In this regard, gamification techniques are mentioned, which allow the creation of game environments during the process of using the apps, with challenges and rewards that motivate the student to continue using the App; and the possibility of the inverted classroom, where the teacher can record short videos, podcasts and indicate readings of materials on the Internet, so that students can build their knowledge at home, optimizing time in the classroom, allocating it for the most practical activities and task solving, through your mobile device.

These are just a few examples of active methodologies (Nobre, 2020) for using mobile devices in the classroom. There are other possibilities that can be integrated, such as learning by projects, by problems, by peers, among others. Figure 1 shows a summary of the main steps that must be followed by teachers before starting the use of mobile learning in the classroom.

Figure 1. steps for implementing mobile devices in education, Source: Organized by the author

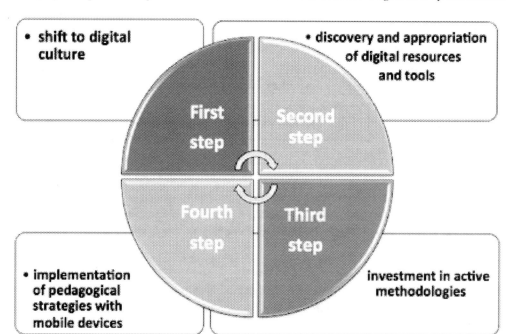

As we can see in Figure 1, there is a path to be followed so that the teacher can take advantage of mobile technologies in the classroom. However, using these resources in the classroom is certainly an asset to the teaching and learning process, as it allows the student to have continuous learning, which goes beyond the limits of the classroom and leads him to develop autonomy in the process of search for information and construction of knowledge.

Observing carefully and researching the options, the teacher will see that nowadays there is practically an application for each content or skill to be developed, which is responsible for planning your class well, integrating the resources in a didactic and motivating way, and involving their students in the learning process.

Mobile Devices and App in Today's Society

We are already at the beginning of the third decade of the 21st century and mobile devices are a reality present in the routine of most Portuguese people. There are hundreds of clicks given daily for the most diverse activities and daily functions.

With the use of mobile devices, new customs were created; by the ease of communication, portability and by the new forms of interaction in social networks and by applications. Applications (app) have created new possibilities for mutual and multiple influences. New applications are launched constantly and with all kinds of functionality, for entertainment, education, communication, shopping, corporate, news, social, relationship and so on. According to Mandel and Long (2017), the smartphone is not only the hardware, he also ushered in a new era for software developers around the world. The opening of the App Store by Apple in 2008, followed by the Android Market, (now Google Play) and other app stores, created a way for IOS and Android developers to write apps that can run on smartphones anywhere.

Every day new app options are appearing to be downloaded on mobile devices (Filipe & Nobre, 2019). Paid or free, they become successful with the consumer public and promise to make life easier and organize routine. However, all this facility or utility that apps can offer brings, as a counterpart, the excessive use of mobile devices, seen as harmful by professionals from different areas. We could make a comparative picture with the benefits and harms that mobile technology, specifically; smartphones bring to the individual's life.

According to Castells (1999), it is up to each society to have the skill of mastering technology, knowing how to use its full potential with maturity, incorporating it into the accelerated transformations that are taking place in society. And this social process takes time to be carried out, as each society has its reality described and its pace to develop the ability to deal with these changes, tracing its own history.

Technologies in the Educational Field

In the educational field, we will focus more on the use of smartphones, as it is more frequent and recurrent among our students.

Teachers cannot turn a blind eye to using DICT as a powerful and fun teaching resource. Teachers, knowing how to use them efficiently, literally have in their hands a variety of tools and applications that are available on the Internet. However, according to Moran (2013), many teachers are not adapted or do not have the necessary skills to use technology in the classroom, because they do not feel safe or because they do not master the technology, a field that students already master, influencing the teaching and learning process.

Knowing how to plan classes using these tools is essential for the teacher to have full control of the class, for that, they must know well the functioning, functions and use that each one will have for a given class. The 21st century teacher cannot be absent from technological progress, nor welfare inattentive to the uses and functions that the Internet can provide for education and for their teaching practice. About this, Carvalho (2015) says that it is never too much to emphasize that being literate, in the 21st century, is not limited to knowing how to read and write, as happened in the past. This concept also integrates the Web and its resources and tools that provide not only access to information, but also ease of publication and sharing online. Being online is essential to exist, learn, give and receive.

The use of DICT in the school environment will expand the development of the knowledge collection for students, who can use tools to make their learning more fun and exciting, and the integration of the teacher with the use of the internet. Using online tools and applications (Filipe & Nobre, 2019) in classes, teachers can update their knowledge and integrate into the web platform like their students, in a world that increasingly demands an online and connected presence.

Therefore, the idea is to transform the school into a collaborative environment, in which students and teachers can study, carry out reading and writing practices, develop research projects, sharpen creativity, in addition to performing playful activities with other artistic and imagery languages with the use of applications and digital tools, all of this combined with the school's own infrastructure, with the availability of electronic equipment for everyone and access to the internet. Without this, unfortunately, the tools are not much use.

The teaching of business communication must awaken in the student, mainly, their critical and autonomous sense and the development of a civic conscience. For this, the teacher must articulate the theory with the chosen methodology.

The application of the media in business communication classes should not only be seen as playful attractions for students, but to prepare them more rigorously to critically assess information and news that emerge daily. Communication has several versions that fit and adapt according to each ideology or party. The aim is to develop in students skills and abilities so that they, used to the world of media and technologies, can expand their research, be able to communicate and carry out critical and constructive assessments about society and the world around them.

One of the justifications of those who defend the use of DICT in the teaching of business communication is that the discipline, being a very broad and interdisciplinary field of study, manages to bring together in itself several resources in the pedagogical action.

The activities are also focused on making students realize the importance that the Communication discipline has for their social and intellectual formation as an individual who lives in a constantly evolving community (Nobre at all, 2021).

The use of digital tools to aid the teacher's praxis, combined with its methodology, seeks to instigate the student to seek new sources and new research objects, with studies that awaken in the student the will to expand their knowledge, including becoming aware of the place that it occupies, of perceiving its participation in society.

Within the diversity of technological resource options as tools available for use in the classroom, it is up to the teacher to choose the one that best assists them within their methodology in the teaching and learning process, allowing them to make their class more interactive and attractive to students, motivating them to participate in the class, facilitating teacher planning "as the process of research, storage and presentation is in the same place, as well as access to a multitude of information, from videos, music, images, documentaries on a certain subject." (Monteiro, 2017, p.44) for teachers and students. Also according to Monteiro (2017); "Emaze, Prezi, Genial.ly, Publisher, Powtoon, Easel, Kahoot, Educaplay are some of the digital tools, with numerous advantages, that the teacher can use in their teaching plans, in order to make them more dynamic and appealing".

Along with the use of applications, some highlighted above, the teacher can also apply methodologies, combined with technology, such as: digital portfolios or web folio, research with collaborative projects, use of Google tools for Educators, such as Google Maps and Google Earth and activities applying Web Quests, fostering students' interest and commitment to their research and study activities.

METHODOLOGY

The problem that gives rise to this chapter can be expressed as follows: How can gamification in learning projects/strategies contribute to the development of active / creative methodologies?

The research design fits into a Mixed-Methods approach (Creswell, 2003) oriented towards the production of useful knowledge and the resolution of real problems in real contexts. However, to answer this question, we used the Development Methodology (Van der Maren, 1996), whose focus, in this case, is to obtain gamified activities, as a product of research development.

At first, we carried out a literature review with a view to substantiating the concepts involved in the investigation, and to obtain a model that serves as a basis for generating the desired activities. The next step is aimed at planning the gamified activities, in light of the studies carried out in the previous phase. The heart of this step is to obtain a roadmap/prototype of activities with the required attributes. To carry out some activities it will be necessary to produce digital resources.

Subsequently, the stage of development and use of tools is passed, if necessary, that allow the operationalization of the generated models. The next phase aims to apply and test the activities produced. Therefore, this work is characterized as a qualitative research, where the collected data were analyzed qualitatively and deepened with interpretative analysis, in order to obtain answers regarding the use of gamification.

The case study elaborated was applied to students from two curricular units, one of 1st cycle and another of the Teaching Training Course. Thus, the organization of the case study was carried out in three stages: (i) the professor of that discipline applied a list of exercises that students should answer in a discursive way. From this list, he identified which points the students had the greatest difficulty; (ii) in order to acclimate students with the Kahoot tool, the teacher elaborated a set of very simple questions/answers, linked to the discipline called "warm-up", where students interacted with the Quiz tool and understood its functioning; (iii) then the teacher systematized a set of questions using the Kahoot platform.

REPORT OF EXPERIENCES

Social Game

In the current scenario, digital native students or even digital immigrants make constant use of computers, smartphones, Internet and games. The culture of passivity (watching) would be replaced by increased interactivity with active participation, because, currently, young people have the need to apply their attention in a distributed manner, alternating between different stimuli (Gomes *at al*, 2018). Gamification is part of this sociocultural transformation, so gamifying a class can motivate students and increase learning.

The choice to build a social game was an attempt to integrate the various types of activities and involve students helping them to experiment with new pedagogical strategies using new technologies. Kapp (2012) presents some gamification strategies and how they can favour student engagement:

- Rules: every game has implicit or explicit rules and often the student's involvement is as much to overcome challenges and even challenge the rules themselves.
- Conflict, competition, and cooperation: every game is based on challenges and participants can compete with each other or collaborate to overcome them.
- Reward and feedback: the player always expects some kind of "score" or score. There are several types of "rewards" and also forms of reinforcement or feedback that aim to encourage the player to continue their participation.
- Levels of difficulty: players are also encouraged to improve their performance with different levels of difficulty
- Story Creation: Narrative is always a motivating and engaging element for many players who like to identify with a certain type of character or plot.

Not all gamification features can be used in all situations. We chose some of Kapp's proposals, but we also included other elements present in the games that we deem important for our experience.

From what was described by Kapp (2012), we highlight the importance of rules and a challenge between groups, to generate both an element of competition and collaboration. Despite having some symbolic elements and creating a fiction in one of the challenges, there was no defined narrative for the entire game. There were also no difficulty levels as we believe it is a factor that works more for individual games.

We also highlight other elements such as:

1. Forms of quantification and scoring: there is no game without some kind of quantification or scoring. But a score doesn't have to be reductive turning every activity into a number indiscriminately. It is possible to create several quantifiable elements to give a qualitative variety to the game. For example, in one of the challenges they had to make a meal that was healthy, tasty and cheap. There were three variables to be quantified. This quantification must be thought out very carefully in the script, defining different weights depending on the degree of difficulty and must always be very explicit in the game rules.
2. Different Learning Paths: Another element of gamification is allowing everyone to choose their path to solve challenges. This was considered in our script as they had a lot of challenges and they could choose the best way to solve them.
3. Flow and Feedback: The challenge was to create a script that would connect the skills previously raised with the gamification techniques that would generate a continuous movement of the participants. We try to make a continuous submission and feedback system using Whatsapp and responding as quickly as possible to each post.

A Social Game was developed with 24 students from the Teaching Training Course, all of whom are also primary and secondary school teachers. The challenge of this activity was to make a didactic sequence that worked on classes to be held outside the classroom. In the group we had teachers who worked with "technical visits", "environmental studies", visits to museums, etc.

The challenges were created in advance and were sent by SMS to the students and they were supposed to publish the result of the actions in the Whatsapp community. In addition, a map was created on Google Maps with all the challenges and their location.

Below is a brief description of the main challenges and competencies worked:

Challenge 1: Meeting in a specific space. Explore space from the references provided.
Challenge 2: Identify and register an element according to its teaching area. This activity worked both the identification of structures, research and comparison.
Challenge 3: Interacting with people in a public place: They should choose a place and make a summary. This challenge included both the ability to interact and the description of the process.
Challenge 4: Production of a video that was a representation of your teaching area. This is an activity of production and reinterpretation.
Challenge 5: Lunch at the mall: Is it possible to eat well for little? They should exemplify with a meal. They should register (photo) and describe the amount spent. There was quantification in the rule about the elements present (nutritional quality), flavour and also the amount paid.
Challenge 6: Create a collective story. Hold an exhibition for the end of the school year. There were six groups that competed with each other. In the end they commented and participated, enjoying the production of their colleagues a lot.

Below is the table with the challenges and the Gamification techniques used:

Table 1. Gamification elements in the social game

Challenge	Gamification Elements
Formation of Groups	Explanation of the Rules
Challenge 1 Meeting	Space Exploration
Challenge 2	Identify and register an element. Different paths in learning
Challenge 3	Interaction - Creation
Challenge 4	Digital resource production
Challenge 5	Lunch
Challenge 6	Final work - Exhibition

Source: Organized by the author

Kahoot App

Game-based learning is a best practice in education. Finding ways to integrate competitive games in the classroom that promote learning is essential for educators in the 21st century (Dellos, 2015). The idea of introducing game concepts into the classroom stems from their ability to engage and motivate students. The structural elements that can be part of a game are rules, objectives, results, feedback, competition, challenge, interaction and plot (Prensky, 2012).

Kahoot is a free game-based Web learning platform that can be used in any subject at different educational levels. A game on Kahoot temporarily turns a classroom into a game show. The teacher plays the role of a game presenter and the students are the competitors. The teacher's computer connected to a large screen shows possible questions and answers, and students give their answers as quickly as possible on their own digital devices.

The app is accessed through https://getkahoot.com/, where users can register to create questions and activities, as well as students can access activities created by their teachers. Kahoot is accessible on any device with an Internet connection. In this sense, the teacher can promote activities inside and outside the classroom.

To conduct the class using the application, it is initially necessary for the teacher to take ownership of the tool. So, the first step is to create your account, which can be registered on Kahoot itself, and only requires basic data, such as name, email and password.

After the account is created in the environment, the teacher must choose what type of activity he intends to design. Among the options, we have:

- Quiz: to create multiple-choice questions, with a timer for each question and a score for each answer (ideal for room games);
- Jumble: set of ordering questions, where students must hit the correct order in each of the questions prepared by the teacher;
- Discussion: to hold debates and open questions;
- Survey: for taking questions with a timer, without scoring the answers given by students (only learning verification).

In the case of this work, the Quiz tool was selected, which allows lively and competitive classes, fostering meaningful learning in students, through games and competition, in an educational context (Bicen & Kocakoyun, 2018).

To perform the activity on Kahoot, the teacher must create a user to configure the Quiz with their questions and answers. Quiz allows several configuration options according to the proposed objective. The teacher can activate the classic version, where all students compete against each other, or even the version where students assemble teams or teams that compete (Bicen & Kocakoyun, 2018). After this step, the game can start with students receiving a PIN (access code) to enter the Quiz with a nickname (nickname). According to Dellos (2015), creating a questionnaire is quick and easy, that is, it facilitates the development of the activity without taking up too much of the teacher's time.

The teacher, during the game, will assume the role of moderator of the activity, being responsible for advancing between the various questions, in addition to providing feedback for each completed question. In the case of the student, he will answer the questions by clicking on the color corresponding to the answer he wants and, at the end of each question, he will be able to see his score with the current ranking (Bicen & Kocakoyun, 2018).

After the Quiz, the podium will be presented with the badges (gold, silver and bronze) and the final ranking with the top five. Since, the classifications of all students, as well as their scores can be saved in the teacher's profile, in addition to allowing these same data to be saved in an electronic spreadsheet or in Google Drive. Another very important aspect of Kahoot is that it allows students to evaluate the Quiz they participated, if they learned something, if they would recommend the tool and how they feel about the activity.

Several gamification features are identified in Kahoot and are summarized in Table 2.

Table 2. Gamification elements identified in Kahoot,

Challenges	Mechanics	Elements
- Answer each question correctly as quickly as possible; - Time expires with each question.	- quick feedback,; - graph with the number of students for each answer in real time; - ranking; - badges.	- collaboration; - competition; - interaction; - discovery; - fun.

Source: Organized by the author

Therefore, kahoot can be applied to gamify classroom teaching.

RESULTS

Social Game

We can say that we have achieved goals of different natures, such as: awareness, mapping, identification, interaction, sharing, production and publication. The collaboration was great. All participated, published and commented on the work of their colleagues.

The following were produced: 10 films, 18 commented texts, 5 audios, 234 photos. The purpose of innovating the strategy and encouraging these students/teachers to expand their activities and their "classrooms" using technology was very highlighted in the evaluation of the process they responded to.

We had some difficulties with quick feedback, as we weren't able to stay online all the time during the activity and the feedback took a little longer than expected, especially in the last challenge that had the collective story built a day after the experience.

Analyzing the questionnaires answered by the students/teachers after the experience, the most mobilizing challenges were the interaction and Production of the digital resource.

The least interesting activity, in the students/teachers' opinion, was lunch. Although the issue involved a complex problematization in terms of cognitive challenge, it was a task that was not performed in real time. Because the most motivating thing for students was to publish, share and enjoy in real time. Fulfilling tasks competitively and in a group generates visible engagement. This engagement is greater when they collaborate, that is, they produce something together, and this elaboration gains more importance when it is added to both symbolic and spatial elements. Another point highlighted by the students/teachers for the success of the activity was the fun. Everyone said it was a fun activity or related words.

Kahoot

The case study elaborated was applied in two classes of Business Communication, in the distance learning modality, of the Applied Languages course at Universidade Aberta, Lisbon, Portugal. This study took place in the first semester of 2021, comprising eighty-three students.

In this discipline, the focus is on communication, therefore it is necessary to identify, analyze and describe the Theories and Formulate the variables that directly or indirectly influence the effectiveness of communication. Traditionally, descriptive exercises are carried out where the student discovers the communication processes and how the elements of the different theories are related. In the case of this work, we chose to use a more dynamic approach and with questions using multiple choice or true/false questions, based on illustrative figures of the previously discursive questions.

Thus, the organization of the case study was carried out in three stages: (i) the professor of that discipline applied a list of exercises that students should answer in a discursive way. From this list, he identified which points the students had the greatest difficulty; (ii) in order to familiarize students with the Kahoot tool, the teacher prepared a set of very simple questions/answers, linked to the discipline called "warm-up", where students interacted with the Quiz tool and understood its operation; (iii) after, the teacher systematized a set of questions using the Kahoot platform. These questions addressed questions that, in a way, had already been included in the list of exercises carried out previously, but the list was adapted, becoming more visual and with multiple choice questions. Students then answered the Quiz, where each student got feedback on their performance when performing the activity.

Upon completing the activity, the final ranking was displayed, as well as the badges obtained with the activity. During this moment, it can be seen that the students were curious to know their classification, and that of other colleagues.

Kahoot will be able to promote the development of various skills, as well as offer advantages and opportunities to teachers, including:

1. Increased motivation: by introducing new elements into the classroom, especially those related to technology, students are more curious and engaged. These stimuli can be converted into motivation for learning, as the use of the application creates a healthy competition environment in the pursuit of learning;
2. Improved reasoning: the quiz scores differentiated (higher) for students who answer faster and more correctly. In this way, it requires quick thinking so that they can remain among the best;
3. Improved concentration of classes: when the teacher communicates to students that they will assess their learning using Kahoot, students tend to pay more attention to the content, as they need to take ownership of the content to participate in a more active and qualitative way in the moment the game;
4. Allows role reversal: the teacher may ask students, individually or in groups, to prepare multiple choice questions for Kahoot. This enables the development of learning in a different way, as they leave the position of student and become 'teachers', as they need to think about issues to be implemented for other students;
5. Collaborative work: Kahoot allows the teacher to use the questionnaire individually or collectively, that is, if the game is played in a class, where not all elements have mobile devices, the teacher can create work groups, making more complexity in questions and increasing response time. Thus, students will have more time to answer each question;

6. Use of DICT in the classroom: there are many critics regarding the introduction of mobile technologies in the classroom, however, by using Kahoot, we were able to prove that the cell phone can become a positive form of integration;

7. Real-time learning assessment: varying assessment techniques can become a way of including the various skills of students (speaking, writing, interpreting, drawing, pointing, etc.). Kahoot, when used as an assessment tool, can favor both students, as they can feel more excited about this modality, and facilitate the teacher's activity, as, at the end of the questions, he/she obtains an electronic report with the grades of each student, as well as the overall performance of the class. This allows for feedback on the teaching and learning process and immediate intervention on the class or group of students who have obtained unsatisfactory results.

In addition to the possibilities mentioned above, Kahoot can also be converted into an inclusion tool, as it allows the insertion of images, videos and sounds in the question's place. If the teacher has students in the class with any limitations, whether visual or auditory, they can choose one of these resources, in order to include all students in the quiz.

CONCLUSION

The article sought to reflect on gamification and present the possibilities of applicability of the use of tools and applications that already exist on the market for mobile devices for teachers, for the practice of the teaching and learning process, breaking with the routine of the traditional classroom.

The use of mobile devices is emerging as a great educational possibility. However, technology alone will not solve any educational problem if the human factor, that is, teachers, are not engaged and involved in the process, reflecting on strategies and methodologies to integrate these resources to their content.

The use of the smartphone in the classroom as a problem and distraction for the student should be reverted in favor of teaching and the teacher as a pedagogical tool that helps in class, it being up to the teacher to choose and fit the best application for each class proposal and elaborated theme planning.

The possibilities for using mobile devices are very wide, students point to an increase in motivation, given the introduction of new methods in the learning process. In addition, teachers have acquired new ways of bringing knowledge to their students, placing them more at the center of the process, ensuring that they develop autonomy and ability to work as a team, and integrating Digital Information and Communication Technologies resources into the process of learning.

It should be noted that the use of mobile devices, as well as any other technology, consists of a certain initial work, but in the long term, it becomes a gain for the teacher, as he/she will be able to reuse the experience in future classes. Experiences that use a more active methodology are always more significant and the results are approved by the students.

Schools are increasingly equipped with modern resources, so it is up to the teacher to seek alternatives that integrate their classes to this reality. Teachers must adapt and level the reality of the school and school practices, creating a panorama that provides efficient and inclusive learning for its true time, with the characteristics and advantages of the 21st century.

Kahoot has incredible potential, all it takes is the teacher's creativity to prepare interesting questions and establish innovative methods and rules of exploration. In this chapter, we highlight the Kahoot! as a possible pedagogical proposal of this applicability in the classroom for teaching-learning. In this scenario, we realize that Kahoot it can be an excellent teaching tool with a methodology to apply different approaches, in addition to being a tool with powerful evaluative potential, as the assessment is instantaneous, allowing the student to expand their knowledge through the interactivity of the class, motivating student learning and the new didactic forms by the teachers. Bringing increasingly closer student and teacher within the teaching and learning process. From the data collected through the questionnaire, it is possible to notice a receptivity in the use of Kahoot and a positive impact, as the students requested that other classes be held using digital games.

The idea of "Fun" was important in the social game experience according to students/teachers. Experiencing a different model of class exploring spaces in another way, leaving the routine and proposing a different dynamic was also very important for the students. Thus, it is possible to increase the student's interest in learning and improve pedagogical practices.

However, gamification cannot be seen as a definitive solution to learning problems, or a "magic formula" for teaching-learning. It is actually another option to be adopted by professors, especially in subjects with a high rate of failure or retention. That is why it is an important topic to be discussed and researched to increase the quality of teaching.

REFERENCES

Akçayır, M., Dündar, H., & Akçayır, G. (2016). What makes you a digital native? Is it enough to be born after 1980? *Computers in Human Behavior, 60,* 435–440. doi:10.1016/j.chb.2016.02.089

Alves, F. (2014). *Gamification - Como criar experiências de aprendizagem engajadoras. Um guia completo.* DVS Editora.

Bicen, H., & Kocakoyun, S. (2018). Perceptions of Students for Gamification Approach. *International Journal of Emerging Technologies in Learning, 13*(02), 72–93. doi:10.3991/ijet.v13i02.7467

Bottentuit, J. B. Jr. (2012). Do Computador ao Tablet: Vantagens Pedagógicas na Utilização de Dispositivos Móveis na Educação. *Revista Educaonline, 6,* 125–149.

Carvalho, L. F. S. (2015). *Utilização de Dispositivos Móveis na aprendizagem da Matemática no 3o Ciclo.* Dissertação de Mestrado em Tecnologias de Informação e Comunicação na Educação. Universidade Portucalense. Departamento de Inovação, Ciência e Tecnologia.

Castells, M. (1999). *La Era de la información: economiá, sociedad y cultura.* Siglo Veintiuno Editores.

Creswell, J. W. (2003). *Research design: qualitative, quantitative, and mixed method approaches.* Sage Publications.

Dellos, R. (2015). *Kahoot! A digital game resource for learning.* Academic Press.

Filipe, A. (2019). Design of a Learning Framework for Open Mobile Applications. *Educ. foco. Juiz de Fora, 24*(1), 529-530.

Gomes, C., Pereira, A., & Nobre, A. (2018). *Gamificação no ensino superior online: dois exemplos. LE@D - Laboratório de Educação a Distância e Elearning.* Universidade Aberta.

Kapp, K. (2012). *The Gamification of Learning and Instruction: Game-based Methods and Strategies for Training and Education*. Pfeiffer.

Kim, S., Song, K., Lockee, B., & Burton, J. (2018). *Gamification in learning and education: enjoy learning like gaming*. Springer. doi:10.1007/978-3-319-47283-6

Mandel, M., & Long, E. (2017). *A Economia de Aplicativos no Brasil*. Washington, DC: PPI Progressive Policy Institute.

Monteiro, T. B. P. (2017). *"História Go": O contributo dos dispositivos móveis para o ensino-aprendizagem nas visitas de estudo. Relatório realizado no âmbito do Mestrado em Ensino de História no 3.o Ciclo do Ensino Básico e Ensino Secundário*. Faculdade de Letras da Universidade do Porto.

Moran, J. (2013). A integração das tecnologias na educação. In A Educação que desejamos: novos desafios e como chegar lá (5th ed.). Campinas: Papirus.

Moura, A. (2009). *Geração móvel: um ambiente de aprendizagem suportado por tecnologias móveis para a "Geração Polegar"*. Universidade do Minho, Centro de Competência.

Nobre, A. (2020). The Pedagogy That Makes the Students Act Collaboratively and Open Educational Practices. In *Personalization and Collaboration in Adaptive E-Learning*. IGI Global. doi:10.4018/978-1-7998-1492-4.ch002

Nobre, A. (2021). Educational Practices Resulting From Digital Intelligence. In *Handbook of Research on Teaching With Virtual Environments and AI*. IGI Global., doi:10.4018/978-1-7998-7638-0.ch003.

Nobre, A. (2021). Open Educational Practices and Resources in the Higher Education Learning Environment. In *Advancing Online Course Design and Pedagogy for the 21st Century Learning Environment*. IGI Global. doi:10.4018/978-1-7998-5598-9.ch006

Nobre, A., Mouraz, A., Goulão, M.F., Henriques, S., Barros, D., & Moreira, J. A. (2021). Processos de Comunicação Digital no Sistema Educativo Português em Tempos de Pandemia. *Revista Práxis Educacional, 17*(45), 1-19.

Prensky, M. (2012). Aprendizagem Baseada. In *Jogos Digitais*. Senac São Paulo.

Surendeleg, G., Murwa, V., Yun, H.-K., & Kim, Y. S. (2014). The role of gamification in education–a literature review. *Contemporary Engineering Sciences, 7*(29), 1609–1616. doi:10.12988/ces.2014.411217

Van Der Maren, J. M. (1996). Méthodes de Recherche pour l'Education (2a ed.). Bruxelles: De Boeck Université.

Zampa, M. P., & Felipe Mendes, L. C. (2016). Gamificação: uma proposta para redução da evasão e reprovação em disciplinas finais da graduação. *Caderno de estudos em sistemas de informação, 3*(2).

Zapata-Rivera, D., & Bauer, M. (2012). Exploring the Role of Games in Educational Assessment. In M. C. Mayrath, J. Clarke-Midura, D. H. Robinson, & G. Schraw (Eds.), *Technology-Based Assessments for Twenty-First-Century Skills: Theoretical and Practical Implications from Modern Research* (pp. 147–169). Information Age Publishing.

Chapter 33
Astronomy and Space–Themed Mobile Games:
Tools to Support Science Education or Learning Barriers Due to the Misconceptions They Generate?

Georgios Eleftherios Bampasidis

ⓘ https://orcid.org/0000-0002-0109-7823

National and Kapodistrian University of Athens, Greece

Apostolia Galani

National and Kapodistrian University of Athens, Greece

Constantine Skordoulis

ⓘ https://orcid.org/0000-0002-8748-1489

National and Kapodistrian University of Athens, Greece

ABSTRACT

This chapter aims to contribute to the discussion of incorporating mobile games with astronomy and space themes in order to support science learning. One concern is when these games include erroneous science content. In this case, they may build or enhance misconceptions or misunderstandings, which eventually create learning barriers. The authors try to determine the learning strategies or pedagogies which can be used to incorporate such games in science education. Research on which characteristics these games should have is also presented. Game-based learning is in alignment with acquiring and developing 21st century literacy skills. One of these skills, information literacy, is related to domain knowledge learning.

DOI: 10.4018/978-1-7998-7271-9.ch033

INTRODUCTION

Mobile-based games are a developing subset of video games that has gained popularity especially among the youngsters through the years (Barlett et al., 2009; Koutromanos, 2020). Most pupils possess portable electronic devices with touch screens, such as smartphones and tablets (Rideout & Robb, 2019), that permit the easy installation of multiple applications, most of which are games (San-Martin et al., 2020). This widespread technology advent gave the game developers the opportunity to launch sophisticated products by adopting all the latest advances in software and hardware. A huge number of mobile games is now available to every user through online repositories and portals, irrespective of the device's operating system. The developers deliver games designed exclusively for portable devices at an affordable cost for most of the users.

The recent school closure and the mandatory quarantine due to the COVID-19 pandemic safety measures (Pullano et al., 2020) forced pupils to widely use their mobile devices, taking advantage of their portability and convenience. Under the circumstances, their leisure activities have been limited and their mobile devices have taken a dominant role in their entertainment. King et al. (2020) claim a higher engagement in digital gaming activities because of the COVID-19 lockdowns.

These arguments are indicative of the influence that mobile-based games have in the learning procedure. Pupils interact with digital gaming virtual environments for many hours per week. Following Mayer (2002), such a game may affect a pupil's knowledge construction schemes as a stimuli source. However, there is a significant factor that one should take into consideration in this case. The game designers focus mainly on providing entertainment products and look at users as potential customers. Because of the extremely hard competition in this market (Kerim & Genc, 2020), they prioritize mainly the user satisfaction (Barnett et al., 2018) and prefer building their scenarios on science fiction instead of scientific facts. As a result, many of them are based on - or contain - repeatable scientific inaccuracies. The study of their impact on science learning is the main scope of this chapter.

Due to their popularity - particularly among pupils - these games may form or increase erroneous understanding of astronomy and space facts or phenomena and construct - or support - nonscientific beliefs. Any misunderstandings or alternative views of science facts still remain, even after the pupil's engagement with pure science courses in formal education (Duit, 1987). The study of these beliefs is very important for educators as well as for curriculum designers. As far as the latter is concerned, these student views should be considered when trying to transform astronomy and space science subjects to school knowledge.

In this framework, games containing inaccurate science information certainly limit learning. But living in the era of mobiles and tablets, these devices and their games are part of modern culture and should be included in educational design. In fact, mobile-based games can significantly contribute to developing student skills through the learning process (Koutromanos & Avraamidou, 2014). In general, the educational dimension of video games and learning science through them have been studied lately, as is described in several review papers (e.g. Anastasiadis et al., 2018). Clark et al. (2016) emphasise the importance of serious games design on providing positive learning outcomes, while Martinez-Garza et al. (2013) mention that these games engage pupils to STEM disciplines. Arango-Lopez et al. (2018) review pervasive games, which illustrate an expansion of the real world (Benford et al., 2005) and report progress on pupils' learning outcomes.

This chapter focuses on mobile-based games with astronomy or space context, which can be downloaded from online repositories, and their design differs from the one of the serious games. As these leisure games are easily accessible and can be played by pupils out of the context of the classroom, their possible impact on the learning process and utilization as educational tools (i.e. in lessons with astronomy concept) is also examined.

This chapter studies the following research questions:

1. Can mobile-based games that focus on astronomy and space themes support science education?
2. Which learning strategies or pedagogies can be used to incorporate space-themed mobile games in education?
3. Which learning barriers may be created by the erroneous science content of mobile games?

The rest of the chapter is structured as follows. The next section is the literature review on the subject, divided into three parts, concerning each one of the research questions. Then, in the Methodology section, the instruments that have been used for this study are described. The research findings are presented in a specific section, which are interpreted in the Discussion. Finally, the authors provide future research recommendations and draw the conclusions of this study.

BACKGROUND

Leisure mobile-based games are a branch of video games, which have been developed for the wider public without any cost and are part of the commercial games. They can be easily downloaded to smart devices from online repositories. Most of these games have simple rules, easy gameplay and undemanding interface, without requiring any prerequisite knowledge or skill. A significant preference for gaming among smart device users has been recorded (Cheng, 2012). The educational value of the space-themed mobile games is twofold: they can be used as educational tools, or they may prevent the learning process by building misconceptions. Since games influence the cognition process of the player (Wouters et al., 2013), they may also affect the player's information literacy skill development, one of the 21st century literacy skills, which is dependent on domain knowledge learning (Kong, 2014).

Space-Themed Mobile Games' Impact in Learning Science

The pupils of the 21st century are characterized as digital natives (Prensky, 2001), as almost every activity of them is based on digital technologies. Due to the widespread use of mobile devices, the educational dimension of their games as well as learning science through them has to be explored. This section examines the leisure mobile games support to science education, concerning the knowledge acquisition and the proper application strategies.

The role of gaming in science learning has been studied extensively. Games may facilitate a pupil's cognitive development since they empower empathy to pupils for academic domains and, through their model-based scenarios, help them acquire scientific knowledge (Gee, 2008). To begin with, the game based learning (GBL) studies indicate games' positive impact in constructing scientific knowledge about fundamental concepts in science, such as motion and force (Chen et al. 2020; Herodotou, 2018), optics (Oh et al., 2017; Wang & Zheng, 2021), electricity (Yasin et al., 2018) and electromagnetism

(Anderson & Barnett, 2013). Similar results are reported for GBL applications that adopt the astronomy concepts of the movements of the Earth and the Moon, as well as the related phenomena (Liou et al., 2017), even in teacher training courses (Susman & Pavlin, 2020). Cardinot & Fairfield (2019) presented an astronomy-based board game, the questions of which have been derived from astronomy facts. Rare exceptions should be mentioned from the three bodies norm. Asai (2010) described a GBL application for desktop PC based on lunar exploration by exploiting Augmented Reality (AR) technology. Thus, in the astronomy field, such digital GBL applications deliver positive results on knowledge construction concerning the Earth-Moon-Sun system, as they offer ideal visual representations. However, the question on the impact of space in learning science beyond the three bodies system still remains unanswered. This chapter argues about the impact of mobile leisure games in transferring the concepts of rocket science and orbital mechanics to school science.

The authors searched for scholar publications and research about mobile games that take advantage of the wealth of recently acquired space science knowledge and data. They queried the keywords of "Astronomy AND mobile AND games", "Astronomy AND mobile AND app", "Space AND mobile AND games", "Space AND mobile AND app" and Astronomy AND "mobile games" AND education through the Education Resources Information Center (ERIC), Scopus, IEEE Xplore, Web of Science, SAO/NASA Astrophysics Data System (ADS) and Google Scholar. To focus on space-themed scenarios, applications unrelated to gaming were excluded and the queries' results of ADS and Scholar were limited to the astronomy domain. The outcome of this research showed that, except for the Earth-Moon-Sun system, other Astronomy-related GBL educational resources designed for mobile devices are quite few in literature.

Table 1 contains the mobile-based games that have a space-themed scenario, different from the Earth-Moon-Sun system. Table 1 also shows the astronomy concept that each game focuses on. The awarded game Kerbal Space Program helps the players learn the basics of rocket science and orbital mechanics (Mallory, 2019; Ranalli & Ritzko, 2013). Its educational version, the KerbalEdu, focuses on Newtonian mechanics, gravity and the concept of energy (Mozelius et al., 2017). Recently, collaboration between LANDKA and European Space Agency and European Southern Observatory produced the KIWAKA (http://landka.com/apps/kiwaka/), an educational game that helps pupils learn about observational astronomy and more specifically about stars and constellations. Two other games ("It's here" and "SolarSystemGO") are solar system-themed that adopt AR technology to represent the planets as celestial objects, but their goal is limited to planet identification (Boonsamuan & Nobaew, 2016; Costa et al., 2020). SpaceMission is a cosmology-themed mobile game that exploits real space data with an impact more in motivating than learning about galaxies (Massimino et al., 2013). It should also be noted that, all the above-mentioned mobile games could be classified as serious.

To sum up, although space science has significantly enriched our perspective about the solar system (and beyond), its unique environments and its mechanisms, very few projects have explored the impact of mobile space-based games in learning science, even in the informal format. The short number of titles can explain this gap in literature. Additionally, the concepts that these space-themed mobile games focus on are orbital mechanics and rocket science. These concepts can be easily linked with the science curricula as they are based in the fundamental concept of force and motion.

Table 1. This table lists the mobile game applications that focus on an astronomy/space exploration topic with an education perspective and also contains their impact in science learning

Game Name	Astronomy concept	Results	Comments	Reference
Kerbal Space Program	Space exploration	The players have to design a space mission using science facts.	Multi-level game in various platforms	Bainbridge, (2018); Mallory, (2019); Ranalli & Ritzko (2013)
KerbalEdu	Space exploration	Educational edition of Kerbal Space Program	Promote tangential learning	Mozelius et al. (2017)
It's here	Solar System	Pupils have to reach the planets with a spacecraft. The research showed improvement in intrinsic motivation and it was interesting and challenging for the engaged pupils.	Role-playing game	Boonsamuan & Nobaew (2016)
SolarSystemGO	Solar System	Pupils discover the planets of the solar system during outdoor activity and enjoy their engagement.	Location-based game with AR technology, currently in Portuguese	Costa et al. (2020)
SpaceMission	Cosmology-Galaxies	Using real images of galaxies to motivate pupils and the general public to science.	It exploits real data. It produces a film by user-defined frames. It Operates on iOS, WINDOWS platforms	Massimino et al. (2013)
KIWAKA	Stars and constellations	The pupils learn about the stars and constellations	Collaboration between LANKA and ESA and ESO. It operates on iOS	http://landka.com/apps/kiwaka

Instructions for Astronomy and Space Science Learning through Mobile-Based Games

The lack of literature about the educational value of space-based leisure or commercial mobile games limits the suggestions for their usage in the learning process. The latter refers to the proper learning context in which a space-themed mobile game could be integrated. Therefore, the authors searched for methodologies and instructions on GBL in general through relevant recent publications.

Table 2 contains strategies for successful implementation of GBL in science learning, as derived from the literature. Games in education have been used to support science learning in different ways, together with traditional strategies. Serious games can be used with problem-solving, collaborative learning, inquiry-based learning and learning by design (Cheng et al., 2015). Koutromanos & Avraamidou (2014) reviewed (mainly serious) mobile games and they mention among others the development of problem solving skills when using games for educational purposes. Of course, the educational setting of these games significantly helps these strategies. On the other hand, the leisure games' design lacks the scenario scripts, puzzles and complexity of serious games and the above mentioned strategies are difficult to be applied to the pupils. Hebert & Jenson (2019) provide a set of nine strategies ("pedagogies") - best practices - on GBL educational applications. The mobile space-based games could help students understand difficult concepts such as rocket science and orbital mechanics through the steps of Engineering Design Process (Bainbridge, 2018; Ranalli & Ritzko, 2013). In addition, games and gaming can be used as a motivator towards science (Gee, 2008). Motivation is related to games' challenges, realism and the chance to investigate new information, based on the user's experience (De Freitas, 2006). The space-themed mobile games could operate as excellent motivators for science (Boonsamuan & Nobaew, 2016; Costa et al., 2020). Alternatively, Martin et al. (2019) suggest establishing a connection between games and science concepts and using analogies.

Each of these strategies can be used according to the preferences and needs of teachers and pupils. However, the choice of one or some of the above mentioned strategies in the classroom framework would have to deal with pupils' perspective of science facts and laws. In the following subsection, the relation between the published misconceptions in astronomy and space and the space-themed mobile games is presented.

Table 2. Strategies/pedagogies as derived from the literature that successfully incorporated game-based learning

Methodology/Strategy	References
Engage with the gameplay and discuss it with the pupils	Hebert & Jenson (2019)
Connect the gameplay with a specific learning activity	Hebert & Jenson (2019)
Encourage collaboration within the game	Hebert & Jenson (2019)
Create activities that support high level skills	Hebert & Jenson (2019)
Link the game with the curriculum	Hebert & Jenson (2019)
Determine the lesson steps and tasks	Hebert & Jenson (2019)
Focus on the purpose and not on technology	Hebert & Jenson (2019)
Use games as supplementary material	Hebert & Jenson (2019); Cheng et al. (2015)
Make cross-curricular connections	Hebert & Jenson (2019)
Engineering Design Process	Bainbridge (2018); Ranalli & Ritzko (2013)
Motivational tool/activity	Gee (2008); De Freitas (2006); Boonsamuan & Nobaew (2016); Costa et al. (2020)
Use with Inquiry-Based Learning	Chen et al. (2020); Cheng et al. (2015)
Flipped Learning	Croxton & Kortemeyer (2018)
Instructional Design	Khan et al. (2017)
Tangential Learning	Mozelius et al. (2017)
Analogies	Martin et al. (2019)

Science Erroneous Content in Space-Related Mobile Games

Astronomy in education was traditionally limited to the study of the Earth as a celestial object (i.e. orbit, seasons) as well as the Moon, the other planets and gravitational interactions. Consequently, the research on pupils' concepts was focused on these topics (Whitaker, 1983; Acker, & Pecker, 1990; Sharp & Kuerbis, 2006; Driver et al., 2014). Research also unveiled numerous alternative conceptions about the solar system and its objects and beyond (Favia et al., 2014). Bampasidis (2019) relates the scientific erroneous contexts of 20 leisure space exploration-themed games with common pupils' misconceptions. Table 3 illustrates these games' erroneous science facts and lists their erroneous concepts on rocket science.

Table 3. Erroneous science facts, especially in rocket science, found in scenario and game play of mobile-based games from the Google Play repository adopted from Bampasidis (2019)

Erroneous science facts	Erroneous concepts in rocket science
• Scale and shape of celestial bodies • No gravity exists in space except for the Earth • Alternative ideas about gravity impact on spaceship trajectories • Asteroids are not a part of the solar system	• Rocket launch and flight control • Flight control within the atmosphere - rocket upgrade during the flight • Interplanetary flights of space shuttle • Spaceship disintegration upon a space rock collision

When pupils play space-related mobile games, they are exposed to a content that is scientific as well as scientifically inaccurate. Pupils' misconceptions that could be related to that content as derived from Table 3 (Bampasidis, 2019) and the relative literature (Whitaker, 1983; Acker, & Pecker, 1990; Sharp & Kuerbis, 2006; Driver et al., 2014; Favia et al., 2014) are:

1. Orbital mechanics
2. Rocket science

By the term rocket science, the authors focus on all the steps of a rocket's launch. It has been shown that mobile-based games show a pattern of erroneous ideas in rocket's lift-off. For instance, the player of these games has the opportunity to pilot the rocket after launch, to upgrade it during the flight.

To conclude, a vast combination of instructional strategies can be used for mobile game implementation to school education. Pupils' alternative views may be a barrier to construct mental representations of nature's laws. The chapter aspires to deliver suggestions on using these games in the real classroom.

METHODOLOGY

The authors' objective was to explore the potential of astronomy and space-themed mobile games to support science education. In this framework, they aimed to justify any possible learning barriers due to erroneous science content in these games. The possibility of using such games as educational tools is explored and educational instructions for this purpose are suggested.

First, one has to select the leisure mobile games that are appropriate for educational purposes. Towards this, the authors have chosen mobile game titles through the following procedure. Space and rocket science were the requested items. In particular, research focuses on mobile games, which represent a rocket and simulate its launch stages and/or refer to interplanetary voyages. These topics are less represented in astronomy-related educational games. The authors search for mobile games that have been designed for the Android operating system, regardless of their game engine. All the selected games are available as apps on Google Play and are free of charge with almost no hardware or software prerequisites. These criteria were adopted since a vast number of modern pupils have access to these games via their mobile devices. The game selection was conducted in the time period between June and August 2021. It should be mentioned that some of the games remained online only for a while and then they were removed. These games were excluded. Additionally, games with a distinct educational aspect were omitted as well as space war games. The serious games were excluded, because, as Mozelius et al. (2017) mention, they fail to catch the players' preference, compared to the commercial ones. Space war games are arcade games without any educational value. Finally, user game reviews and ratings on the Google Play platform were ignored, since it is unreliable information (Stoyanov et al., 2015). The search for space-themed mobile games derived 25 titles listed in Table 4. These titles are representative of the wealth of gaming apps that are available on Google Play which are related to space adventures.

Since these games are designed for entertainment, they fail to fit the criteria and rubrics proposed by researchers for educational games and applications (e.g. Papadakis et al., 2017). Therefore, in order to evaluate each leisure mobile game's educational potential in a classroom framework, the authors used the rubric of Rice (2007). This rubric has been designed to help teachers choose the proper video games to incorporate them in their lessons by a yes or no scoring ("yes" takes one point, while "no" is rated with zero). In brief, it has an assessment list of twenty characteristics that describe when the video game user develops higher order thinking after the interaction with the game. Ideally, the highest score of this ranking is twenty. The general rule is, the higher ranking of this evaluation, the "higher order thinking in its users" (Rice, 2007). This assessment evaluates the game's simplicity, the role of the player in the game, its storyline, the existence of avatars and non-playing characters. Additionally, it evaluates the games' problem-solving procedure and the problem complexity as well as the existence of alternative walkthroughs. This rubric takes into account all the characteristics that the teacher has in mind, when aiming to implement a game in lesson and the assessment results are listed in Table 4, along with the titles.

The next step is to examine if the games with the highest ranking of this assessment (the "Voyager Grand Tour" and the "Spaceflight simulator") could be used as educational tools by school teachers. Table 2 contains a list of successfully applied GBL strategies and instructions to pupils by using serious games. The question is which of them are appropriate when having leisure games.

First of all, the alignment of these game applications and school curricula should be considered (Hebert & Jenson, 2019). Chatzimichali (2020) reported in her Master's thesis that the Earth-Sun-Moon system is found in each one of 17 primary educational curricula around the globe and about half of these include elements of space exploration. Therefore, a relation between the themes of the commercial space-based mobile games and curricula topics is clear as the list mentions. Such games can be used as enablers to pupils' engagement in science and technology (Boonsamuan & Nobaew, 2016; Costa et al., 2020; De Freitas, 2006; Gee, 2008) or as supplementary material (Cheng et al., 2015; Hebert & Jenson, 2019).

Teacher knowledge and training on the subject is also an important factor. There is no official guide from stakeholders to teachers on how to implement video games in schools (Vlachopoulos & Makri, 2017). Teachers avoid using them, or they use them rarely, since they lack formal training (Khan et al., 2017). Moreover, digital GBL requires from the teacher a combination of content knowledge, gaming knowledge and proper integration techniques (Vlachopoulos & Makri, 2017; Wang & Chen, 2021). Consequently, any incorporation of these games requires strategies which teachers are familiar with, such as Inquiry based learning (Pedaste et al., 2015).

One other factor to consider is the available instructional time. Teachers complain that time is not enough (Fitzgerald et al., 2019), while they self-reported that they need about 78% of classroom time to teach (OECD, 2019). So, adding a new tool may be a time-related problem too. In this context, the strategy of flipped learning could be applied where the game can be connected with a specific activity and a specific concept. It seems that flipped learning environments by using mobile phones improved test scores and reduced course failures (McKnight et al., 2016).

Table 4. Mobile games assessment according to the rubric of Rice (2007). The developer's name has been included in the parenthesis just after the game's title. VGCVI is the Video Game Cognitive Viability Index, which ranges from 0 to 20.

Game title	Score (Rice, 2007 rubric)	Scientific topic
Voyager Grand Tour (Rumor games)	15	Interplanetary voyage
Spaceflight simulator (Stefo Mai Morojna)	15	Rocket launch - Interplanetary voyage
Rocket Launch (Mobifoni Technology) Space Rocket Simulator (Aleksandr Turkin)	10	Rocket launch
Space Drone (Positive Imagination Syndrome)	10	Rocket launch - interplanetary voyage
Space agency (Nooleus) Space Rocket Exploration (Genc Sadiku)	8	Rocket launch - Interplanetary voyage
Idle Tycoon: Space Company (Bling Bling Games GmbH) Rocket Sky! (Kwalee LTD) Rocket Mission: Moon (FleiCOM)	8	Rocket launch
Space Rocket Master, a fun scifi Space Flight Simulator (Pulsar Studio Games)	7	Rocket launch
Mission Gravity (Stefan Obergrussberger) Planet Gravity (Humberto Lobos Sucarrat) Feel Gravity (JOCS) Moon Landing (Aleksandr Turkin)	7	Interplanetary voyage
Rocket star - Idle Space Factory Tycoon Games (Pixodust games) 2 Minutes in space: Missiles! (Rarepixels - Indie Games) Go Space - Space ship builder (Preus) Lunar Mission (Puppet Games) Cave FRVR - Spaceship Landing & Galaxy Exploration (FRVR) Space Colonizers Idle Clicker Incremental (CapPlay)	3	Rocket launch - Interplanetary voyage - space exploration
Space mission: Rocket launch (Launchship) Space Frontier (Ketchapp) Space Frontier 2 (Ketchapp) Space Inc (Lion Studios)	3	Rocket launch

To conclude, the instructional strategies with which a teacher incorporates space-themed mobile games in lesson are:

1. The connection with the curriculum
2. The use of the game as a supplementary material
3. The use of the game as an enabler
4. The Inquiry-based learning (IBL)
5. The Flipped learning approach.

FINDINGS

As it has been discussed in the previous section, the games "Voyager Grand Tour" and "Spaceflight simulator" achieved the highest score of the Rice's (2007) rubric. The former game is related to orbital mechanics, while the latter is related to rocket science. These are the main domains that pupils are exposed to, when playing the games of Table 4. Concerning the research questions of this chapter, the following findings are derived from the application of the previously described methodology on space-based mobile games.

RQ 1: Can Mobile-Based Games that Focus on Astronomy and Space Themes Support Science Education?

According to the assessment of Rice (2007), the "Voyager Grand Tour" and the "Spaceflight simulator" games may encourage high order thinking when incorporated in lessons, compared to the similar mobile games. Both games are more complex than the rest ones, have a specific storyline and definite goals. Their puzzles are more complex and need effort to be solved, while the player can accomplish the goals by following different paths. The user has to adjust games' variables to succeed in their tasks and, adjusting these variables differently, gives different results. Both games simulate satisfactory real conditions, requiring interaction with their virtual environment and need information gathering to accomplish each level task. The other games of Table 4 lack these characteristics.

The game "Voyager Grand Tour" focuses on orbital mechanics. It is based on the simulation of the twin spacecraft Voyager 1 and 2 interplanetary journeys. Briefly, the game's main missions focus on data collection from the solar system planets, which was the main goal of the real mission. To achieve these objectives, the player should launch the probe to the planet to be inserted into a proper trajectory. Gravity plays a major role in accomplishing the game missions. In fact, the player, by adjusting the relative angle of launch to the target, tries to get the proper gravity assist for spacecraft's tours, especially from gas giant planets (Figure 1).

There is a definite connection with Newtonian mechanics, a fundamental concept in science formal curriculum. Players interact directly with the environment by adjusting the parameters. This visual representation benefits the instruction time and motivates the pupils to get involved in the lesson by using a real space exploration story.

It should be mentioned that both games do not contain erroneous science facts in orbital mechanics and rocket science, as similar games of Table 4. The basic topic of game "Spaceflight simulator" is rocket science. The purpose of its first levels is to build a rocket from parts, in order to have an operational space vehicle (Figure 2). It has a brief guide during the building phase. Its educational value is that the game has separate sequential phases. Building a rocket by following real specifications is essential for moving to the next game's phase. Thus, it links science and technology via space exploration. The next levels of the game use orbital mechanics.

Figure 1. Screenshot of the game "Voyager Grand Tour". The dotted curve shows the trajectory of the probe. When approaching Saturn, the planet's gravity affection to the spacecraft's velocity is apparent. (Image courtesy of Kevin Tarchenski/Rumor Games, LLC)

Figure 2. Screenshot of the game "Spaceflight simulator". Rocket building (left) and launch (right). (Images credit: Stefo Mai Morojna).

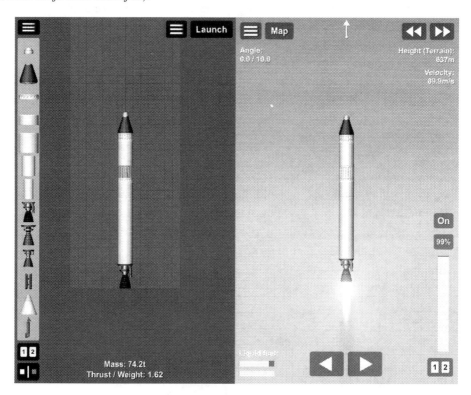

RQ 2: Which Learning Strategies or Pedagogies Can be Used to Incorporate Space-Themed Mobile Games in Education?

Five are the strategies/pedagogies in which a teacher can incorporate space-themed mobile games (connect it with the curriculum, use as supplementary material or as enabler, in inquiry based learning and in flipped learning). The players of the "Voyager Grand Tour" and the "Spaceflight simulator" can directly interact with the game's environment by adjusting parameters, while such actions are missed from the other games. These results are listed in Table 5.

Table 5. Successful teacher strategies/pedagogies to incorporate space-themed mobile games

Strategies/pedagogies	Voyager Grand Tour (Rumor games)	Spaceflight simulator (Stefo Mai Morojna)
Connection with the curriculum	Concepts of Newton's laws	Try and error method (Chen et al., 2020)
Supplementary material	Applications of Newton's laws	Applications of Newton's laws
Enabler	Motivate pupils to investigate the physics of interplanetary journeys	Motivate pupils to work as real scientists and engineers
Inquiry based learning material	By adjusting parameters and decide which is the the proper for a specific mission, pupils seek for relations, formulate hypotheses, test and evaluate their hypotheses (Pedaste et al., 2012)	When the pupils build the rocket by combining parts, they seek for relations, formulate hypotheses, test and evaluate their hypotheses (Pedaste et al., 2012)
Flipped learning materials	Pupils construct knowledge actively. Use game as a quiz on in-class work (Lo & Hew, 2017)	Pupils construct knowledge actively. Use game as a quiz on in-class work (Lo & Hew, 2017)

RQ 3: Which Learning Barriers May be Created by the Erroneous Science Content of Mobile Games?

Several leisure astronomy and space-based mobile games contain scientific content that is erroneous. According to Table 3, one can focus on three concepts that may create or enhance misconceptions or misunderstandings towards scientific beliefs. The main concepts are listed in Table 6.

Table 6. This table lists representative games that contain erroneous science and rocket science. The name of the company is also written in parenthesis.

Erroneous science and rocket science	Game
No gravity exists in space except for the Earth	2 Minutes in space: Missiles! (Rarepixels - Indie Games)
Alternative ideas about gravity impact on spaceship trajectories	Rocket star - Idle Space Factory Tycoon Games (Pixodust games) Space Frontier 2 (Ketchapp)
Flight control and rocket upgrade during the flight	Space mission: Rocket launch (Launchship) Go Space - Space ship builder (Preus) Space Frontier (Ketchapp) Space Rocket Master, a fun scifi Space Flight Simulator (Pulsar Studio Games) Space Colonizers Idle Clicker Incremental (CapPlay)

On the other hand, as far as the concept of gravity is concerned, several games use the gravitational force as a crucial parameter in the gameplay (for example, "Mission Gravity" by Stefan Obergrussberger, "Planet Gravity" by Humberto Lobos Sucarrat and "Feel Gravity" by JOCS). It should be noted that some games include information that differs from the real situation. For instance, the game "Voyager Grand Tour" hints that the Voyagers twin spacecraft visited the inner planets of the solar system, which is false.

DISCUSSION

This section argues about the educational value of mobile-based games that focus on astronomy and space themes, despite their erroneous science content. It also discusses which are the proper instruction strategies for teachers to incorporate space-themed mobile games in science education. Despite the notional explanations, this discussion hopes to assist future research in incorporating mobile space-themed games to science education as an effective alternative teaching tool.

Mobile Space Themed Games that Support Science Education Characteristics

Learning is an active process and pupils build mental representations of natural phenomena based on their experiences and perceptions (Driver, 1989). According to Piaget, playing, a common activity for pupils, influences their mental development, and in this context, video games could influence it too, as a modern form of playing (Herodotou, 2018). Choosing mobile games, a popular branch of video games, for science education is a complex procedure. The safe way is to use serious games, which have a definite educational setting. Mobile-based games help teachers match pupils' interest to science, as other digital resources do (McKnight et al., 2016). As many leisure and commercial space-themed mobile games are very popular among pupils, their scientific accuracy becomes an important factor.

In the astronomy domain, mobile games' topics and scenarios are limited to the system of the Earth, Moon and Sun, while few adopt space exploration scenarios. In order to set up a framework for selecting space-based leisure mobile games for educational purposes, the authors used the assessment proposed by Rice (2007). This rubric evaluates the possibility of a video game to enhance higher order thinking in players. The current assessment by using this rubric delivered the score of 15 as the highest Video Game Cognitive Viability Index (VGCVI) for only two games: the "Voyager Grand Tour" and the "Spaceflight simulator". Rice mentions a ranking of at least 15 for a game to be considered an effective higher order thinking enabler. This performance can be explained by the fact that the selected games miss "Not Playing Characters" and avatars to interact with the player, as the rubric demands. Concerning the interaction with lifelike avatars, both games indeed expand cognitive processing as Rice (2007) argues. Increased opportunities for higher order thinking are achieved in both games by the parameter adjustment. The two high-ranking games have a storyline that encourages the players to make complex thoughts and correlations with previously acquired knowledge. The rest of the games can be separated into two groups, the ones with lower-range performance (rank of 10) and the ones with little or no cognitive viability (ranking below 9). The low scores of these games indicate that they focus on leisure and they lack any educational dimension.

Judging from the assessment, the characteristics of "Voyager Grand Tour" and "Spaceflight simulator" compared to the rest ones are listed below:

1. They contain no scientific inaccuracies on fundamental science concepts.
2. Both are focused on a specific science concept, which are orbital mechanics and rocket engineering respectively.
3. They represent real conditions without exaggerations.
4. The player can change the game's variables to provide different results.
5. The results of each effort are affected by natural laws (e.g. the gravitational pull of a celestial object).
6. Their gameplay is easy.
7. Both can be installed in almost every mobile device.

Therefore, teachers, who wish to incorporate leisure or commercial mobile games in their lessons, can search for titles with the above-mentioned characteristics. Except for orbital mechanics and rocket science, this methodology could be applied to other science concepts too.

Devising Instructional Strategies/Pedagogies for Using Space-Based Mobile Games in School Science

Regarding the instructional strategies that teachers may use games with, there are several choices. Both games "Voyager Grand Tour" and "Spaceflight simulator" promote active learning through their gameplay and scenario. Pupils in traditional classrooms are usually passive receivers, but when playing these games, they act like scientists and engineers, which is common in GBL (Barab et al., 2009). As described in the Methodology section, five strategies/pedagogies fit in the case of leisure games, which may use them as curriculum connection linkers, supplementary material, enablers, with inquiry-based learning or flipped learning. Methods like the IBL need more time for preparation from the teacher (Fitzgerald et al., 2019).

Using both games in the IBL concept is also suggested. Building a rocket and traveling in space seems a problem that in order to be solved pupils have to seek for relations, formulate hypotheses and then test and evaluate them (Pedaste et al., 2012). Both games give the tools and activities towards this direction.

In this context, mobile games may help teachers save both preparation and instructional time effectively. One other aspect of mobile-based games is the fact that the pupil will literally need no time to be familiar with the game. On the contrary, when using computer simulations the teacher has to train pupils to become familiar with the software (Trundle & Bell, 2010).

The "Voyager Grand Tour" has a specific scenario with determined goals to achieve. The sense of gravitational pulling is embedded with its gameplay, a factor that the user should take into account to accomplish the game's missions. This feature is directly related with the concept of gravity and Newton's laws, which are fundamental topics in school science. These concepts are theoretical and abstract (Angell et al., 2004) and a common teaching approach is to begin by the bodies' interaction at a distance. However, this approach rarely helps pupils understand adequately the concept, as it contradicts their everyday experience (Baldy, 2007). Additionally, teachers have limited access to astronomy material (Cardinot & Fairfield, 2019). They also have to overcome the issue of finding space educational resources accessible to every pupil with no cost as well as pupil-friendly resources. NASA and ESA offer a wealth of educational material related to space. In practice, most of them are supplementary to the curriculum and need preparation for team working or can be used only as demonstration experiments in the classroom. On the contrary, the "Voyager Grand Tour" can be used as an alternative pleasant tool to represent the concept and as a simulation of demonstrating how the real world works, which is difficult to observe (Smith & Holmes, 2021).

The "Spaceflight simulator" scenario lacks direct linking with the curriculum. Still, it has "a trial and error" sense in its gameplay. The user decides which rocket components are appropriate for a space flight in order to simulate the launch's real conditions. In this framework, the player conducts a self-directed inquiry to solve the problem (Podolefsky, et al., 2010). On the other hand, the pupils' repeated gameplay efforts for finding a solution make them give little attention to connect or apply knowledge to it (Chen et al., 2020). In addition, this game can be used to introduce pupils to the Engineering Design Process (EDP) as similar projects did (Bainbridge, 2018; Ranalli & Ritzko, 2013), and fosters the pupils' STEM competencies.

Finally, both games can be used in flipped learning approaches, by using them as quizzes on in-class work (Lo & Hew, 2017). It should be noted however, that such pedagogy might lead to wrong conceptions, as Croxton & Kortemeyer (2018) observed when using games. Of course, no teaching strategy is ideal and it is the teacher's privilege to choose or combine effective strategies that activate the pupils and engage them in the learning procedure (Manurung, 2012).

Possible Learning Barriers Caused by Mobile Space-Themed Games

The results of this study indicate that the space-themed games are possible enablers of misconceptions and misunderstandings of the fundamental concept of gravity and rocket science. While the latter seems to have minor importance in compulsory education, the former is a key factor for physics discipline. Recent research reported that at least 25% of the pupils of five countries possess misconceptions of the concept of gravity (Neidorf et al., 2020). Media as sources of misconceptions, as well as pupil's personal experiences, have been documented (Patil et al., 2019). The virtual and interactive world of games, which plays a major role on pupils' daily schedule, may shape their concepts in science facts and nature's mechanisms. Virtual world experiences are as meaningful as the real world ones (Barko & Sadler, 2013). The concern becomes significant since mobile games assist self-learning (Mozelius et al., 2017) and thus, may enhance alternative ideas in pupils. These misconceptions are barriers to understanding science (National Research Council, 1997). By inductive reasoning, mobile games with erroneous science content are also barriers to science education. Prior knowledge of the pupils' misconceptions is an important factor for effective teaching (Osborne, 2014). In these circumstances, the teachers should treat games like those mentioned in Table 6, which have significant incorrect science content on Newton's laws' concept, carefully, if they decide to include them in their lessons. Games like the "Voyager Grand Tour" and the "Spaceflight simulator" may be used to promote conceptual change, as the computer simulation with astronomical concepts did (Trundle & Bell, 2010). This change should be considered for successfully transforming scientific knowledge to school science.

Another idea to put forward for consideration is that the teachers may use games with erroneous science, like those in Table 6, as examples of false information that one can encounter through digital resources. Indeed, through games, pupils are exposed in a virtual environment that contains science or pseudoscience. The learning procedure and its outcome will certainly help pupils develop the competencies of 21st century literacy skills and especially information literacy. Information literacy refers to the ability of understanding facts, separating them from fiction throughout the web (American Library Association [ALA], 2000) and evaluating computer-based information in general (Fraillon et al., 2019). Several studies connect digital games in education and the development of such skills in pupils (Gumulak

& Webber, 2011; DiNardo & Broussard, 2019; Encheva et al., 2020). Pupils through these lessons will have in hand examples derived from their everyday leisure activities.

On the other hand, collaboration and communication skills cannot be developed through this kind of mobile games. Usually they have a single player mode. The goal of its game is simple and the exploratory character of the game is very limited.

FUTURE RESEARCH DIRECTIONS

In this chapter, the authors study the impact leisure mobile games have on science learning. However, a quantitative research mixed with qualitative data will explore the results of space-themed mobile games in science learning in a real educational setting. In such a continuation of research, the pupils' learning outcomes have to be measured by pre- and post-questionnaires. When applied to classrooms, similar assessment methods to those described in literature but with computer simulations can be used (Trundle & Bell, 2010; Wang et al., 2017).

As described previously, mobile-based games can be used as tools to transform concepts from astronomy such as gravity to science for pupils and transfer knowledge into practical application (Manurung, 2012). Since formal teacher training lacks GBL topics in several countries (Khan et al., 2017), the introduction of GBL in tertiary pre-service teacher education or in-service teachers training programs will benefit their professional development.

One other suggestion of this chapter is to game designers and developers. They can provide games with a specific science concept that support learning through the interaction with the pupil which is aligned with Herodotou's (2018) conclusions.

Finally, an online database, containing leisure mobile games can be created as an educational resource for teachers and informal education trainers.

CONCLUSION

The main scope of the chapter is to study the role of space-themed mobile games in science learning. Although there is little research on incorporating mobile games in science learning (Hebert & Jenson, 2019), this study agrees with Herodotou's (2018) conclusion that mobile games without any educational setting can be used in education. In order to help teachers seek for the proper mobile space-themed game for their lessons, the authors implemented an assessment by using a rubric (Rice, 2007).

This evaluation has revealed specific characteristics that can benefit pupils in learning science. These characteristics are the scientific accuracy, the focus on a specific science concept, the representation of real conditions without exaggerations and the player's intervention with the game's variables that produces different results, which are affected by natural laws. Concerning the game's technology, it should have easy gameplay and installation in a great variety of devices.

The mobile games that this study considers can be incorporated into education within a constructed methodology, which fits their particular features. If the teacher decides to use it as a resource, she/he can be used as game motivator or supplementary material. Of course, IBL and flipped learning are the two pedagogies in which these games could match if related with problem solving. In any case, the games should be linked with the curriculum. Such applications may also benefit teachers' instruction time.

Mobile gaming could become a powerful and pupil friendly educational tool. Mobile space-themed games can enable pupils towards science and engineering, break down common misconceptions and reduce science abstractness, which is in alignment with Cardinot & Fairfield's (2019) observations. Such games have another advantage as they easily simulate conditions that are extremely difficult to be experienced in real life, in agreement with Griffiths (2002).

Finally, as these games may facilitate pupils' cognitive development, the authors suggest how such games can be used in formal or informal educational activities to deal with alternative views.

REFERENCES

Acker, A., & Pecker, J. C. (1990). Public misconceptions about astronomy. In *International Astronomical Union Colloquium* (Vol. 105, pp. 229-238). Cambridge University Press. 10.1017/S025292110008684X

American Library Association. (2000). *Information literacy competency standards for higher education.* https://repository.arizona.edu/handle/10150/105645

Anastasiadis, T., Lampropoulos, G., & Siakas, K. (2018). Digital game-based learning and serious games in education. *International Journal of Advances in Scientific Research and Engineering, 4*(12), 139–144. doi:10.31695/IJASRE.2018.33016

Anderson, J. L., & Barnett, M. (2013). Learning physics with digital game simulations in middle school science. *Journal of Science Education and Technology, 22*(6), 914–926. doi:10.100710956-013-9438-8

Angell, C., Guttersrud, Ø., Henriksen, E. K., & Isnes, A. (2004). Physics: Frightful, but fun. Pupils' and teachers' views of physics and physics teaching. *Science Education, 88*(5), 683-706.

Arango-Lopez, J., Collazos, C. A., Velas, F. L. G., & Moreira, F. (2018). Using pervasive games as learning tools in educational contexts: A systematic review. *International Journal of Learning Technology, 13*(2), 93–114. doi:10.1504/IJLT.2018.092094

Asai, K., Sugimoto, Y., & Billinghurst, M. (2010). Exhibition of lunar surface navigation system facilitating collaboration between children and parents in science museum. In *Proceedings of the 9th ACM SIGGRAPH Conference on Virtual-Reality Continuum and its Applications in Industry* (pp. 119-124). 10.1145/1900179.1900203

Bainbridge, W. S. (2018). Computer Simulation for Space-Oriented Strategic Thinking. In *Computer Simulations of Space Societies* (pp. 113–139). Springer. doi:10.1007/978-3-319-90560-0_5

Baldy, E. (2007). A new educational perspective for teaching gravity. *International Journal of Science Education, 29*(14), 1767–1788. doi:10.1080/09500690601083367

Bampasidis, G. (2019). Ψηφιακά παιχνίδια σε συσκευές κινητής τεχνολογίας και κίνδυνοι δημιουργίας επιστημονικών παρανοήσεων: Παραδείγματα από την Αεροδιαστημική Επιστήμη και την Τεχνολογία [Digital games in portable devices and the dangers of creating misconceptions: Examples from Aerospace science and Technology]. *Astrolavos, 32*.

Barab, S. A., Scott, B., Siyahhan, S., Goldstone, R., Ingram-Goble, A., Zuiker, S. J., & Warren, S. (2009). Transformational play as a curricular scaffold: Using videogames to support science education. *Journal of Science Education and Technology, 18*(4), 305–320. doi:10.100710956-009-9171-5

Barko, T., & Sadler, T. D. (2013). Practicality in virtuality: Finding student meaning in video game education. *Journal of Science Education and Technology, 22*(2), 124–132. doi:10.100710956-012-9381-0

Barlett, C. P., Anderson, C. A., & Swing, E. L. (2009). Video game effects—Confirmed, suspected, and speculative: A review of the evidence. *Simulation & Gaming, 40*(3), 377–403. doi:10.1177/1046878108327539

Barnett, L., Harvey, C., & Gatzidis, C. (2018). First Time User Experiences in mobile games: An evaluation of usability. *Entertainment Computing, 27*, 82–88. doi:10.1016/j.entcom.2018.04.004

Benford, S., Magerkurth, C., & Ljungstrand, P. (2005). Bridging the physical and digital in pervasive gaming. *Communications of the ACM, 48*(3), 54–57. doi:10.1145/1047671.1047704

Boonsamuan, S., & Nobaew, B. (2016). Key factor to improve Adversity Quotient in children through mobile game-based learning. In *2016 International Symposium on Intelligent Signal Processing and Communication Systems (ISPACS)* (pp. 1-6). IEEE. 10.1109/ISPACS.2016.7824759

Cardinot, A., & Fairfield, J. A. (2019). Game-based learning to engage students with physics and astronomy using a board game. *International Journal of Game-Based Learning, 9*(1), 42–57. doi:10.4018/IJGBL.2019010104

Chatzimichali, E. (2020). *A comparative analysis between science curricula for primary school from 17 countries regarding the subject of astronomy* [Συγκριτική μελέτη της παρουσίας της αστρονομίας στα αναλυτικά προγράμματα της πρωτοβάθμιας εκπαίδευσης 17 χωρών προερχομένων από τις 5 ηπείρους] (Master's thesis). National & Kapodistrian University of Athens. Retrieved from https://pergamos.lib.uoa.gr/uoa/dl/frontend/el/browse/2916920

Chen, C. H., Huang, K., & Liu, J. H. (2020). Inquiry-Enhanced Digital Game-Based Learning: Effects on Secondary Students' Conceptual Understanding in Science, Game Performance, and Behavioral Patterns. *The Asia-Pacific Education Researcher, 29*(4), 319–330. doi:10.100740299-019-00486-w

Cheng, C. W. (2012). The system and self-reference of the app economy: The case of angry birds. *Westminster Papers in Communication & Culture, 9*(1).

Cheng, M. T., Chen, J. H., Chu, S. J., & Chen, S. Y. (2015). The use of serious games in science education: a review of selected empirical research from 2002 to 2013. *Journal of Computers in Education, 2*(3), 353-375.

Clark, D. B., Tanner-Smith, E. E., & Killingsworth, S. S. (2016). Digital games, design, and learning: A systematic review and meta-analysis. *Review of Educational Research, 86*(1), 79–122. doi:10.3102/0034654315582065 PMID:26937054

Costa, M. C., Manso, A., & Patrício, J. (2020). Design of a mobile augmented reality platform with game-based learning purposes. *Information (Basel), 11*(3), 127. doi:10.3390/info11030127

Croxton, D., & Kortemeyer, G. (2018). Informal physics learning from video games: A case study using gameplay videos. *Physics Education, 53*(1), 015012. doi:10.1088/1361-6552/aa8eb0

De Freitas, S. (2006). *Learning in immersive worlds: A review of game-based learning.* IJSC.

DiNardo, C. O., & Broussard, M. J. S. (2019). Commercial tabletop games to teach information literacy. *RSR. Reference Services Review, 47*(2), 106–117. doi:10.1108/RSR-10-2018-0066

Driver, R. (1989). The construction of scientific knowledge in school classrooms. In R. Millar (Ed.), *Doing science: Images of science in science education* (pp. 83–106). Falmer Press.

Driver, R., Squires, A., Rushworth, P., & Wood-Robinson, V. (2014). *Making sense of secondary science: Research into children's ideas.* Routledge. doi:10.4324/9781315747415

Duit, R. (1987). Research on students' alternative frameworks in science - topics, theoretical frameworks, consequences for science teaching. In J. Novak (Ed.), *Proceedings of the 2nd International Seminar on Misconceptions and Educational Strategies in science and Mathematics* (pp. 151–162). Ithaca, NY: Cornell University.

Encheva, M., Tammaro, A. M., & Kumanova, A. (2020). Games to improve students information literacy skills. *The International Information & Library Review, 52*(2), 130–138. doi:10.1080/10572317.2020.1746024

Favia, A., Comins, N. F., Thorpe, G. L., & Batuski, D. J. (2014). A direct examination of college student misconceptions in astronomy: A new instrument. *J. Rev. Astron. Educ. Outreach, 1*(1), A21–A39.

Fitzgerald, M., Danaia, L., & McKinnon, D. H. (2019). Barriers inhibiting inquiry-based science teaching and potential solutions: Perceptions of positively inclined early adopters. *Research in Science Education, 49*(2), 543–566. doi:10.100711165-017-9623-5

Fraillon, J., Ainley, J., Schulz, W., Duckworth, D., & Friedman, T. (2019). *IEA international computer and information literacy study 2018 assessment framework.* Springer Nature. doi:10.1007/978-3-030-19389-8

Gee, J. P. (2008). Learning and games. In K. Salen (Ed.) The Ecology of Games: Connecting Youth, Games, and Learning. John D. and Catherine T. MacArthur Foundation Series on Digital Media and Learning. Cambridge, MA: The MIT Press. 10.1162/dmal.9780262693646.021

Griffiths, M. D. (2002). The educational benefits of videogames. *Education for Health, 20*(3), 47–51.

Gumulak, S., & Webber, S. (2011). Playing video games: Learning and information literacy. In *Aslib Proceedings.* Emerald Group Publishing Limited. doi:10.1108/00012531111135682

Hebert, C., & Jenson, J. (2019). Digital game-based pedagogies: Developing teaching strategies for game-based learning. *Journal of Interactive Technology and Pedagogy, 15.*

Herodotou, C. (2018). Mobile games and science learning: A comparative study of 4 and 5 years old playing the game Angry Birds. *British Journal of Educational Technology, 49*(1), 6–16. doi:10.1111/bjet.12546

Kerim, A., & Genc, B. (2020). Mobile Games Success and Failure: Mining the Hidden Factors. In *2020 7th International Conference on Soft Computing & Machine Intelligence (ISCMI)* (pp. 167-171). IEEE.

Khan, A., Ahmad, F. H., & Malik, M. M. (2017). Use of digital game based learning and gamification in secondary school science: The effect on student engagement, learning and gender difference. *Education and Information Technologies*, *22*(6), 2767–2804. doi:10.100710639-017-9622-1

King, D. L., Delfabbro, P. H., Billieux, J., & Potenza, M. N. (2020). Problematic online gaming and the COVID-19 pandemic. *Journal of Behavioral Addictions*, *9*(2), 184–186. doi:10.1556/2006.2020.00016 PMID:32352927

Kong, S. C. (2014). Developing information literacy and critical thinking skills through domain knowledge learning in digital classrooms: An experience of practicing flipped classroom strategy. *Computers & Education*, *78*, 160–173. doi:10.1016/j.compedu.2014.05.009

Koutromanos, G. (2020). Primary School Students' Perceptions About the Use of Mobile Games in the Classroom. In Mobile Learning Applications in Early Childhood Education (pp. 230-250). IGI Global.

Koutromanos, G., & Avraamidou, L. (2014). The use of mobile games in formal and informal learning environments: A review of the literature. *Educational Media International*, *51*(1), 49–65. doi:10.1080/09523987.2014.889409

Liou, H. H., Yang, S. J., Chen, S. Y., & Tarng, W. (2017). The influences of the 2D image-based augmented reality and virtual reality on student learning. *Journal of Educational Technology & Society*, *20*(3), 110–121.

Lo, C. K., & Hew, K. F. (2017). A critical review of flipped classroom challenges in K-12 education: Possible solutions and recommendations for future research. *Research and Practice in Technology Enhanced Learning*, *12*(1), 1–22. doi:10.118641039-016-0044-2 PMID:30613253

Mallory, S. (2019). To the Mun: Kerbal Space Program as Playful, Educational Experience. In *International Conference on Human-Computer Interaction* (pp. 320-332). Springer. 10.1007/978-3-030-22602-2_24

Manurung, K. (2012). Creative teachers and effective teaching strategies that motivates learners to learn. *Indonesian Journal of Science Education, 2*(1), 1-8.

Martin, W., Silander, M., & Rutter, S. (2019). Digital games as sources for science analogies: Learning about energy through play. *Computers & Education*, *130*, 1–12. doi:10.1016/j.compedu.2018.11.002

Martinez-Garza, M., Clark, D. B., & Nelson, B. C. (2013). Digital games and the US National Research Council's science proficiency goals. *Studies in Science Education*, *49*(2), 170–208. doi:10.1080/03057267.2013.839372

Massimino, P., Costa, A., Becciani, U., Krokos, M., Bandieramonte, M., Petta, C., Pistagna, C., Riggi, S., Sciacca, E., & Vitello, F. (2013). Learning astrophysics through mobile gaming. *Astronomical Data Analysis Software and Systems XXII*, *475*, 113.

Mayer, R. E. (2002). Multimedia learning. *Psychology of Learning and Motivation*, *41*, 85–139. doi:10.1016/S0079-7421(02)80005-6

McKnight, K., O'Malley, K., Ruzic, R., Horsley, M. K., Franey, J. J., & Bassett, K. (2016). Teaching in a digital age: How educators use technology to improve student learning. *Journal of Research on Technology in Education*, *48*(3), 194–211. doi:10.1080/15391523.2016.1175856

Mozelius, P., Fagerström, A., & Söderquist, M. (2017). Motivating factors and tangential learning for knowledge acquisition in educational games. *Electronic Journal of e-Learning, 15*(4), 343-354.

National Research Council. (1997). *Science Teaching Reconsidered: A Handbook.* The National Academies Press. doi:10.17226/5287

Neidorf, T., Arora, A., Erberber, E., Tsokodayi, Y., & Mai, T. (2020). *Student misconceptions and errors in Physics and Mathematics: exploring Data from TIMSS and TIMSS Advanced.* Springer Nature. doi:10.1007/978-3-030-30188-0

OECD. (2019). *How much time do teachers spend teaching? In Education at a Glance 2019: OECD Indicators.* OECD Publishing. doi:10.1787/62fbb20d-

Oh, S., So, H. J., & Gaydos, M. (2017). Hybrid augmented reality for participatory learning: The hidden efficacy of multi-user game-based simulation. *IEEE Transactions on Learning Technologies, 11*(1), 115–127. doi:10.1109/TLT.2017.2750673

Osborne, J. (2014). Teaching scientific practices: Meeting the challenge of change. *Journal of Science Teacher Education, 25*(2), 177–196. doi:10.100710972-014-9384-1

Papadakis, S., Kalogiannakis, M., & Zaranis, N. (2017). Designing and creating an educational app rubric for preschool teachers. *Education and Information Technologies, 22*(6), 3147–3165. doi:10.100710639-017-9579-0

Patil, S. J., Chavan, R. L., & Khandagale, V. S. (2019). Identification of misconceptions in science: Tools, techniques & skills for teachers. *Aarhat Multidisciplinary International Education Research Journal, 8*(2), 466–472.

Pedaste, M., Mäeots, M., Leijen, Ä., & Sarapuu, S. (2012). Improving students' inquiry skills through reflection and self-regulation scaffolds. *Technology, Instruction. Cognition and Learning, 9*(1-2), 81–95.

Pedaste, M., Mäeots, M., Siiman, L. A., De Jong, T., Van Riesen, S. A., Kamp, E. T., Manoli, C. C., Zacharia, Z. E., & Tsourlidaki, E. (2015). Phases of inquiry-based learning: Definitions and the inquiry cycle. *Educational Research Review, 14*, 47–61. doi:10.1016/j.edurev.2015.02.003

Podolefsky, N. S., Perkins, K. K., & Adams, W. K. (2010). Factors promoting engaged exploration with computer simulations. *Physical Review Special Topics. Physics Education Research, 6*(2), 020117. doi:10.1103/PhysRevSTPER.6.020117

Prensky, M. (2001). Digital Natives, Digital Immigrants. MCB University Press.

Pullano, G., Pinotti, F., Valdano, E., Boëlle, P. Y., Poletto, C., & Colizza, V. (2020). Novel coronavirus (2019-nCoV) early-stage importation risk to Europe, January 2020. *Eurosurveillance, 25*(4), 2000057. doi:10.2807/1560-7917.ES.2020.25.4.2000057 PMID:32019667

Ranalli, J., & Ritzko, J. (2013). Assessing the impact of video game based design projects in a first year engineering design course. In 2013 IEEE Frontiers in Education Conference (FIE) (pp. 530-534). IEEE. doi:10.1109/FIE.2013.6684880

Rice, J. (2007). Assessing higher order thinking in video games. *Journal of Technology and Teacher Education, 15*(1), 87–100.

Rideout, V., & Robb, M. B. (2019). *The Common Sense census: Media use by tweens and teens*. Common Sense Media.

San-Martín, S., Jimenez, N., Camarero, C., & San-José, R. (2020). The path between personality, self-efficacy, and shopping regarding games apps. *Journal of Theoretical and Applied Electronic Commerce Research, 15*(2), 59–75. doi:10.4067/S0718-18762020000200105

Sharp, J. G., & Kuerbis, P. (2006). Children's ideas about the solar system and the chaos in learning science. *Science Education, 90*(1), 124–147. doi:10.1002ce.20126

Smith, E. M., & Holmes, N. G. (2021). Best practice for instructional labs. *Nature Physics, 17*(6), 662–663. doi:10.103841567-021-01256-6

Stoyanov, S. R., Hides, L., Kavanagh, D. J., Zelenko, O., Tjondronegoro, D., & Mani, M. (2015). Mobile app rating scale: A new tool for assessing the quality of health mobile apps. *JMIR mHealth and uHealth, 3*(1), e27. doi:10.2196/mhealth.3422 PMID:25760773

Susman, K., & Pavlin, J. (2020). Improvements in Teachers' Knowledge and Understanding of Basic Astronomy Concepts through Didactic Games. *Journal of Baltic Science Education, 19*(6), 1020–1033. doi:10.33225/jbse/20.19.1020

Trundle, K. C., & Bell, R. L. (2010). The use of a computer simulation to promote conceptual change: A quasi-experimental study. *Computers & Education, 54*(4), 1078–1088. doi:10.1016/j.compedu.2009.10.012

Vlachopoulos, D., & Makri, A. (2017). The effect of games and simulations on higher education: A systematic literature review. *International Journal of Educational Technology in Higher Education, 14*(1), 1–33. doi:10.118641239-017-0062-1

Wang, J. Y., Wu, H. K., & Hsu, Y. S. (2017). Using mobile applications for learning: Effects of simulation design, visual-motor integration, and spatial ability on high school students' conceptual understanding. *Computers in Human Behavior, 66*, 103–113. doi:10.1016/j.chb.2016.09.032

Wang, M., & Zheng, X. (2021). Using game-based learning to support learning science: A study with middle school students. *The Asia-Pacific Education Researcher, 30*(2), 167–176. doi:10.100740299-020-00523-z

Whitaker, R. J. (1983). Aristotle is not dead: Student understanding of trajectory motion. *American Journal of Physics, 51*(4), 352–357. doi:10.1119/1.13247

Wouters, P., Van Nimwegen, C., Van Oostendorp, H., & Van Der Spek, E. D. (2013). A meta-analysis of the cognitive and motivational effects of serious games. *Journal of Educational Psychology, 105*(2), 249–265. doi:10.1037/a0031311

Yasin, A. I., Prima, E. C., & Sholihin, H. (2018). Learning Electricity Using Arduino-Android Based Game to Improve STEM Literacy. *Journal of science Learning, 1*(3), 77-94.

ADDITIONAL READING

Arici, F., Yildirim, P., Caliklar, Ş., & Yilmaz, R. M. (2019). Research trends in the use of augmented reality in science education: Content and bibliometric mapping analysis. *Computers & Education*, *142*, 103647. doi:10.1016/j.compedu.2019.103647

Atwood-Blaine, D., & Huffman, D. (2017). Mobile gaming and student interactions in a science center: The future of gaming in science education. *International Journal of Science and Mathematics Education*, *15*(1), 45–65. doi:10.100710763-017-9801-y

Breuer, J., & Bente, G. (2010). Why so serious? On the relation of serious games and learning. *Journal for Computer Game Culture*, *4*, 7–24.

Flewitt, R., Messer, D., & Kucirkova, N. (2015). New directions for early literacy in a digital age: The iPad. *Journal of Early Childhood Literacy*, *15*(3), 289–310. doi:10.1177/1468798414533560

Fudenberg, D., Drew, F., Levine, D. K., & Levine, D. K. (1998). *The theory of learning in games* (Vol. 2). MIT Press.

Herodotou, C. (2018). Young children and tablets: A systematic review of effects on learning and development. *Journal of Computer Assisted Learning*, *34*(1), 1–9. doi:10.1111/jcal.12220

Hewett, K. J., Zeng, G., & Pletcher, B. C. (2020). The acquisition of 21st-century skills through video games: Minecraft design process models and their web of class roles. *Simulation & Gaming*, *51*(3), 336–364. doi:10.1177/1046878120904976

Mayer, R. E. (2019). Computer games in education. *Annual Review of Psychology*, *70*(1), 531–549. doi:10.1146/annurev-psych-010418-102744 PMID:30231003

Oliveira, A., Feyzi Behnagh, R., Ni, L., Mohsinah, A. A., Burgess, K. J., & Guo, L. (2019). Emerging technologies as pedagogical tools for teaching and learning science: A literature review. *Human Behavior and Emerging Technologies*, *1*(2), 149–160. doi:10.1002/hbe2.141

Westera, W. (2019). Why and how serious games can become far more effective: Accommodating productive learning experiences, learner motivation and the monitoring of learning gains. *Journal of Educational Technology & Society*, *22*(1), 59–69.

KEY TERMS AND DEFINITIONS

Engineering Design Process: The iterative process with specific steps that an engineering team follows to solve a definite problem.

Flipped Learning: The active learning procedure in which the pupils prepare the lesson by studying the material that the teacher has prepared out of the lesson's instruction.

Leisure Games: The games that have been designed without a specific educational setting. They differ from commercials as they can be played without any cost.

Orbital Mechanics: The study of motion of rockets, spacecrafts, and artificial satellites by applying Newton's laws.

Rocket Science: The field of science that encompasses the principles of science and engineering in order to design and build rockets.

Serious Games: Video games that can be used for learning skills competencies, as they have an educational setting.

Tangential Learning: The self-education learning procedure when a person is exposed to new knowledge in an enjoyable and familiar context.

Section 6
Game-Based Pedagogy for Primary-Elementary Educators

Chapter 34
Incorporating Digital Literacy Materials in Early Childhood Programs:
Understanding Children's Engagement and Interactions

Barbara Ellen Culatta
Brigham Young University, USA

Lee Ann Setzer
Brigham Young University, USA

Kendra M. Hall-Kenyon
 https://orcid.org/0000-0001-5960-6566
Brigham Young University, USA

ABSTRACT

Use of digital media in early childhood literacy programs offers significant opportunities for interaction, engagement, and meaningful practice of phonic skills—and also a few pitfalls. The purpose of this chapter is to review 1) considerations for use of digital media in early childhood settings, 2) selection of appropriate media to facilitate early literacy learning, and 3) inclusion of digital media as an integral component of early literacy instruction, rather than an add-on. With an emphasis on practical ideas and solutions for instructors, the authors draw on studies in which interactive, personalized ebooks and an early literacy learning app were used in conjunction with face-to-face, hands-on activities drawn from Project SEEL (Systematic and Engaging Early Literacy).

DOI: 10.4018/978-1-7998-7271-9.ch034

INTRODUCTION

Early literacy skills are the gateway to success in reading and academic performance, and digital media (e.g., apps, computer programs, ebooks, relevant online content and videos) can play a role in supporting these essential skills (National Early Literacy Panel, 2008; Sénéchal, Lefevre, Smith-Chant, & Colton, 2001; Storch & Whitehurst, 2002). For example, digital early literacy activities can give teachers practical ways to increase opportunities for children to be exposed to and solidify literacy skills (Moses, 2013). Combining digital literacy activities with hands-on instructional experiences gives teachers varied and compelling ways to strengthen children's skills. Additionally, incorporating digital media into early childhood programs can activate children's engagement (Hart, 2013; Larson, 2010). However, when digital media is not used effectively, it can distract or confuse students (Chiong, Ree, Takeuchi, & Erickson, 2012; deJong & Bus, 2002). Educators should therefore be in tune with research and exemplary literacy programs that purposefully and effectively incorporate digital media into their early literacy practices.

This chapter will review some of the benefits and practical ways of making digital media an integral part of an early literacy program. It will highlight issues to consider when selecting digital media for use with young children and strategies for ensuring that it contributes to effective literacy instruction. In addition to incorporating research-based guidelines, the chapter will draw upon examples and practical ideas for supporting young children's literacy skills from both the research and an early literacy project, *Systematic and Engaging Early Literacy (SEEL)*. All referenced SEEL activities can be accessed for free at https://education.byu.edu/seel.

BACKGROUND

Learning to use technology as a tool for communication, creation, and instruction is critical for children to be able to effectively engage in the modern world (Suarez-Orozco, 2007). Indeed, "The migration from the physical to the digital world represents a fundamental shift in the lives of our children. The events that take place in the virtual world are not ancillary to their lives but are some of the most important elements of them" (R. Culatta, 2021, p. 5).

Since digital media opens possibilities for a richer learning environment for children, teachers must purposefully consider how to capitalize on technology to facilitate children's development of early literacy skills. Most importantly, teachers must intentionally integrate technology into a comprehensive instructional plan rather than using "computer time" as an add-on or a reward. One useful model for technology integration is TPACK (Technology Pedagogical Content Knowledge), which helps teachers think about how technological, content, and pedagogical knowledge domains can intersect to effectively teach and engage students with technology (Common Sense Media, 2021; Mishra & Koehler, 2006, 2009). Factors teachers should thus consider as they layer the use of digital media into a comprehensive instructional plan include the influence of technology on young children's motivation and engagement, connections to the real world, and recognition of meaning and purpose in literacy learning activities.

Motivation and Engagement

Most digital media tools arrange for users to make active responses; they also capitalize on design features (e.g., animations, music, and hotspots) to keep children's attention. However, some digital app designs tend to activate extrinsic over intrinsic motivation by relying on incentives such as collecting, winning, and competing. Extrinsic motivation in instruction leads to a preference for completing the task, a focus on easier and familiar tasks, and a desire to meet teacher requirements (Elliot, 1999; Guthrie & Knowles, 2001). On the other hand, materials that activate intrinsic motivation draw upon the learner's curiosity, interests, self-expression, and desire to understand and gain competence. These materials capitalize on compelling conceptual themes, social and real-world interactions, and relevant texts (Elliot, 1999; Guthrie & Knowles, 2001; Johnston, 2012). Digital media that successfully activate engagement enable children to interact with impactful content and engage in social interactions around the media (Lauricella, Robb, & Wartella, 2007).

Choice is another key source of motivation for children (Patall, Cooper, & Robinson, 2008). With carefully selected digital media, instructors can allow students to have some control over electronic learning activities and some autonomy in the way they navigate through instruction (Wong, 1996). Some apps include choice-making design features that permit children to select among alternative tasks and activities. Dunn, Gray, Moffett, and Mitchell (2018) showed that it was important for children to have a choice in digital media—not necessarily in terms of which app to use but in terms of how to engage with apps to create and explore. While teachers might want to take advantage of apps that focus on drill and practice, they should keep in mind the differences among apps in regard to capturing attention and achieving a desired purpose.

Since digital media can make electronically-delivered content compelling, teachers must also ensure that an app's game mechanics are not the only thing capturing the children's attention (Chiong et al., 2012). Further, an electronic book that reads the words one at a time or asks children to point to a picture and then responds "well done" cannot simulate the experience of adult-child conversations (Plowman, McPake, & Stephen, 2012). Technological interactivity does not guarantee an educational encounter.

Connections to World Knowledge

While technology should not displace shared experiences or explorations of the real world, coupling technology with hands-on instruction can be helpful in expanding children's experience and knowledge as teachers introduce compelling images, videos, and virtual interactions (Donohue & Schomburg, 2017). Learning experiences from digital and real-world sources can also draw upon and elaborate prior knowledge. Connecting digital and real-world experiences to prior knowledge serves to extend, deepen, and solidify that knowledge, which is essential for learning (Kervin, Mantei, & Herrington, 2009). Visual media and/or interactive and game-based digital apps can situate encounters with targeted content and inputs into compelling and relevant themes and contexts that support skills and comprehension.

Meaning and Purpose

Early childhood educators can use digital media to activate meaning and purpose by ensuring that children make connections between real-life experiences and digital representations of events and by arranging for digital media to serve as a tool for sharing and expressing ideas and understandings (Cowan, 2017, 2019; Trad, 2021). Digital media can permit children to create and communicate their goals, interests, and ideas as they produce ebooks, share photos and drawings, and convey messages via in-class social media or personal-learning networks (Cowan, 2019). Teachers, children, and parents can communicate on restricted, in-class social media and portfolio-creation platforms, such as *Seesaw* (https://seesaw.me), where children can document their experiences, share and respond to entries, and show off their work (Common Sense Media, 2021; Cowan, 2019; Knauf, 2016). Digital tools can also support other communicative functions, allowing children to imagine, make comments, express ideas and emotions, give information and share news, ask and answer questions, convey options and desires, and make requests (Dore, 1979; Halliday, 1973; Tough, 1977). Adults can serve as scribes to record children's dictations and provide interactive writing supports that fit with the Fred Rogers Center (2012) recommendations that adults scaffold children's engagements with digital media. Thus, meaning and purpose can be addressed by "extending the media experience to offline opportunities for learning and development" (p.8). Teachers can use digital media to provide exposure to and experience with motivating and personally-relevant content and then extend that content to hands-on, interactive activities—or vice versa.

In summary, technology affords additional modes of instruction and has some unique advantages, but it does not automatically provide good learning opportunities. Digital media's usefulness depends on the extent to which it is methodically integrated into an overall program and fits with the content and goals of instruction. Planning at the programmatic level, taking advantage of the abilities of digital media to enlarge children's worlds, carefully evaluating the content's motivating features, and ensuring that digital experiences reinforce the meaning and purpose of instruction will help ensure that digital media enhances children's learning.

WAYS TO USE DIGITAL MEDIA TO FACILITATE EARLY LITERACY DEVELOPMENT

Educators who acknowledge the benefits of using digital media in educational programs can evaluate how best to weave the electronic options into education programs to support children's literacy development. Educators should be aware of available digital media, challenges of drawing upon digital media, recommendations for analyzing digital media, and strategies for making the best use of digital media to teach early literacy skills.

Available Digital Tools

Digital tools available to raise interest in literacy and facilitate the development of specific skills can include online content, ebooks, guided story making apps, story creation apps, and early literacy apps designed to teach specific skills.

Online Content

Early childhood educators can incorporate online content, such as YouTube video clips or informational websites, into their programs to bring real-life events, individuals, objects, activities, or creatures into the classroom. Such media can expand or activate children's background knowledge, providing more meaning around the literacy instruction.

Ebooks

Published trade books are often available as ebooks as well as in print version (e.g., *Epic Books for Kids,* 2021). An internet search for "digital books for children" yields an array of children's ebooks, some requiring paid subscriptions, but many available for free. Some ebooks allow children to engage with the text by triggering sound effects and animations and playing character voices with taps and swipes. Others have digitized voices, providing opportunities for even very young children to interact with the text more independently (Gee, 2010).

Guided Story-Making Apps

Guided or constrained story-making apps provide young children with the supported opportunity to create their own digital stories. In guided story-making apps, children select settings, characters, props, and actions from among specified options. Examples of such apps include *Art Maker (*https://www.sesamestreet.org/art-maker*)* and *Puppet Pals* (Polished Play, 2021*)*. These guided story creations resemble cartoons. They allow children to move objects and characters within the scene and make the characters act on objects, interact, and make verbalizations and vocalizations. The story can then be turned into a video dramatization. Young children will require scaffolding from an adult to create a cohesive story rather than a string of random actions and comments.

Open-Ended Story-Making Apps

Some apps for creating ebooks permit open-ended and personalized options, where a young child and adult can collaborate to add audio, video, text, and images to stories they create. The content isn't structured, and the options for creating the text are limitless. Options available in open-ended ebook apps that make the experience personal for children include writing or co-constructing a story about an experience, illustrating the story with photos or drawings uploaded or taken from the app, reading the story, or listening to a text-to-speech narration of the story. Children can engage with the book by swiping to turn pages or pressing buttons to start the narration. They can create stories that include pictures of peers and of themselves in the book, and they can make their own contributions to the book by typing in words. Examples of open-ended apps for creating books include *Pictello* (https://www.assistiveware.com/products/pictello) and *Book Creator* (https://bookcreator.com).

Early Literacy Apps

There are many native mobile apps and web-based programs designed to teach specific literacy skills. The skills addressed in these instructional activities include phonological awareness (blending, rhyming, alliteration), letter-sound associations, letter naming, decoding, spelling of phonic patterns, and reading of leveled or controlled texts. Early literacy apps have the potential to offer playful practice of early literacy skills and can provide meaningful learning moments. The selection and inclusion of engaging and interactive apps increase children's exposure to early literacy skills. Options for early literacy apps include those that focus on practicing skills, teach a skill in a game, or set instruction in a meaningful context such as shopping or growing plants.

- **Skill- or Drill-based Apps** focus on having children practice skills such associating sounds with letters, blending sounds to make words, connecting written with spoken words, and associating words that rhyme with corresponding pictures. The tasks involved can resemble digital worksheets. While the target phonic pattern changes, the activities tend to remain the same. *Phonics Town* (Al Bailey Apps, 2021) is an example of an app that permits children to act on words and letters to practice recognizing phonic patterns, associating letters with sounds, and blending sounds.
- **Game-based Apps** use game mechanics (e.g., collecting, building, exploring, creating spectacles) to permit children to practice targeted early literacy skills in playful ways. Many of these apps allow children to choose how they navigate through the materials (Wong, 1996). The apps use game-like functions, navigational choice, and contingent interactions to highlight a targeted sound or letter pattern. The child can explore how objects interact and can create spectacles by making objects react in funny or unexpected ways. Phonics games such as those in *Fast Phonics* (Reading Eggs, 2021) insert instructional activities into games where players solve puzzles or earn points to complete an objective and earn digital prizes.
- **Theme- or Story-based Apps** aim to provide purpose and meaning for reading and writing by allowing children to encounter target patterns within a story context based on common and concrete events. For example, a theme-based app might highlight *-ub* words within an activity in which children scrub and rub a dirty cub in a tub. Such apps can stimulate interest by connecting texts to prior knowledge or real-life events. The SEEL early literacy program was the foundation for two theme-based apps, *Hideout Early Literacy* and *Flying Kitchen* (Third Rail LLC, 2021; available free of charge on the Apple App Store).

Challenges of Drawing upon Digital Media

While the wealth of available electronic media presents instructors with tremendous opportunities, there are also challenges associated with choosing and implementing digital media to support young children's learning. Making wise selections and interweaving technology seamlessly into the curriculum is a "complex innovation" (Voogt & McKenney, 2017), demanding teachers' time and best effort.

One common challenge in using technology with young children is the oft-expressed concern about too much screen time—particularly passive screen time and exposure to apps or programs that blur the distinction between content and advertising. But not all digital activities are created equal. While limits are appropriate, teachers and parents might consider basing the amount of tech use on the value of individual digital activities, rather than on a predetermined amount of screen time (R. Culatta, 2021). Such factors might include the level to which an app facilitates active rather than passive involvement, the extent to which children creatively and resourcefully interact with the technology, the ways in which the digital activity can connect users, and the degree to which children are engaged in learning or merely motivated by the design features. These considerations are more nuanced and useful than a single measure of time in front of screens (R. Culatta, 2021).

Another challenge in choosing apps or other digital media is the distracting nature of some design elements. Some apps include features that capture children's attention, but actually make it harder for children to focus on the educational content. Teachers and parents choosing and interacting with children around apps can also get distracted by secondary features (Chiong et al., 2012).

Technology sometimes also functions as an add-on or an afterthought, with teachers using "iPad time" as separate from and unrelated to other learning activities, or as a reward. Further, teachers sometimes use technology as glorified worksheets, rather than capitalizing on the unique features of digital media that can allow students to communicate, create, evaluate, and collaborate (R. Culatta (2021). In addition, without adult guidance, children may fail to realize the app's purpose, understand the task, or benefit from exposure to the targeted skill. Children will benefit most as teachers interact with them around the digital media to extend, explain, and discuss the content, demands, and skills targeted.

Recommendations for Analyzing Digital Media

Given the potential impact that digital media can have on young children's lives, educators should follow guidelines for taking advantage of digital media while avoiding possible pitfalls.

National Association for the Education of Young Children (2012) issued guidelines for using technology effectively in early childhood classrooms

- Fit apps to a focused instructional purpose.
- Select media that fit with children's prior knowledge and entering skill-level.
- Arrange for opportunities for adults to interact with children around the media.
- Scaffold the children's knowledge or understanding of the concepts, language, and skill being introduced in the media.
- Balance exposure to digital media with opportunities to engage in active, hands-on, creative encounters with others and with the real world.
- Relate digital content to the classroom curricular content.

Attending to these guidelines can help teachers overcome some challenges related to the use of digital media and carefully analyze specific elements of the media they use.

In addition to paying attention to general guidelines for using digital media with children, educators must analyze specific elements of the media they use. Since educational apps are often marketed as prepackaged early literacy solutions, educators should carefully consider the purpose and design features and the pedagogical soundness of any apps they consider using, with an eye toward enhancing rather than distracting from children's learning (Northrop & Killeen, 2013). The following recommendations for analyzing digital media can help guide teacher's decisions.

Purpose and Design Features

While apps specify the overall area of the curriculum they address (e.g., letter-sound associations, word building, phonics, phonological awareness), teachers must select apps that fit the particular skill being taught as well as the level of instructional difficulty that matches children's entering skills. Teachers will also want to consider design features and the extent to which these features (e.g., collecting, signaling cause/effect relationships, earning prizes, competing) may detract from or support learning.

Pedagogical Soundness

Product descriptions of apps often claim they support early literacy learning, but few provide evidence to support the claim. When choosing digital media for early literacy programs, educators should consider factors that influence the efficacy of apps, making informed decisions in alignment with best practices in literacy instruction (B. Culatta, Hall-Kenyon & Bingham, 2016). Some of the pedagogical features that should be considered include the representation of consonants, silent letters, sequence of sounds in words, order of skills introduced, modeling and feedback, and task clarity.

Representation of Consonants

Be particularly alert to early literacy apps that do not accurately represent the sounds that letters make. Although digraphs such as *sh, ch,* and *ng* consist of two letters that represent one sound, some apps try incorrectly to isolate individual sounds in digraphs. Further, the letter *x* represents *two* sounds, /ks/, and the letters *qu* represent two consonant sounds, /kw/, but some apps don't attach the correct sounds to the letters.

Some apps add additional sounds to letters. For example, the sound of the letter *f* (along with /s/, /sh/, /r/, /z/, and /l/) should be taught by simply continuing the sound (e.g., /ssss/), but many apps add a stressed /uh/ vowel to the letter to produce s**uh**. Even plosive sounds such as /b/, /p/, /t/, /d/, /k/, and /g/ are produced in some apps with an exaggerated *-uh* vowel at the end (e.g., b-**uh**). When producing these sounds in isolation, it is important not to put *additional* stress on the added vowel. When produced in isolation, plosive consonant sounds should be produced by softly repeating an *unstressed* vowel.

Accurately representing English vowels can be tricky. An educator who is selecting early literacy apps must pay particular attention to the way an app treats vowels. Vowels can have more than one sound, and the same vowel sound can have more than one spelling. Some apps assign only one sound to each vowel. One app gives the letter *a* the sound in *at* but then produces that same *a* sound for the *a* in the word *all*, giving the word an unfamiliar, incorrect pronunciation. The words *art, air, any, ant,* and *apron* all start with the letter *a*, but the initial *a* represents different sounds. If the app covers all those instances of the letter *a*, it should present the pronunciation variations in a systematic, comprehensible way.

Silent Letters

While sounds combine to make words, not all letters are produced when blending sounds into words. One app makes the mistake of providing a sound for each letter in a segmented word (such as c-a-k-e) —giving the /eh/ sound to the *e*—and then expecting children to see the letters *c-a-k-e* and blend them into the word *cake*.

Sequence of Sounds in Words

Sounds for letters in words should be accessed in left to right order. Some apps, however, allow users to tap letters in words in any order to hear the sounds. If the sounds are selected in right to left order, they can't possibly be blended into the targeted word. Individual sounds that will be combined into a word should appear or only be allowed to be activated in left to right order, since that is the way readers need to decode them.

Order of Skills Introduced

Learning to read requires building from basic to more advanced skills. For example, children should be taught to read short vowel words (such as *cap, bed, sit, dog,* and *bug*) before long vowel words (like *cape, bite,* and *note*). Further, when instructing first grade children, not all long vowels should be introduced at the same time (National Governors Association Center for Best Practice, Council of Chief State School

Officers, 2010). Some apps, however, intersperse words with short and long vowels and introduce the various spellings for a long vowel sound at the same time.

Modeling and Feedback

Early literacy apps should provide sufficient exposure to sounds and to the letters associated with those sounds. Modeling entails exposing children to the sound patterns that go with letters and highlighting sound patterns such as rhyming and alliteration. For children to recognize printed words and to translate letter patterns into meaningful words, they need to have many opportunities to see and hear the relationship between spoken and written words. For example, to learn to read short vowel words such as *cat, bat, fat,* and *sat*, an app should provide many opportunities to hear and see *–at* in those words. In another example, some apps expect children to recognize rhyming words without first exposing them to examples of rhyming words.

Very few early literacy apps provide corrective feedback for an incorrect response. Rather, the child only receives a generic reply such as "try again." The same is true for a correct response: most apps give generic praise (like "great job!") or make a special sound (like applause). But they do not explain why the answer was correct. Apps should provide specific feedback such as "yes, the words *back* and *sack* rhyme" or "Uh-oh, *track* and *car* don't rhyme—but *track* and *crack* do sound alike". Both moments—when children get it right or when they make a mistake—can become learning opportunities.

Task Clarity: Vocabulary and Content

In selecting early literacy apps, it is important to consider whether the child will be able to understand what is expected. Children who do not understand a task will likely end up randomly pressing buttons to see what will happen. Some early literacy apps use complex or unfamiliar words to illustrate sound or phonic patterns. Obscure words or pictures that are hard to identify can interfere with the child's ability to learn an early literacy skill. For example, one app designed to teach rhyming used a picture of a garbage can labeled as a "bin." For most children in the United States, "bin" is not a common, familiar word. Even if an app focuses on a skill that fits a child's developmental level, educators must carefully review the complexity of the vocabulary, language, and task.

Instructionally sound apps and other technology can enhance early literacy instruction, but educators must be knowledgeable consumers. High ratings or glowing reviews do not necessarily indicate that an app has been evaluated through the lens of solid instructional principles.

Design Features vs. Pedagogical Soundness

When evaluating apps for possible use in their programs, teachers must consider a variety of elements (e.g., literacy skill targeted, design features, and pedagogical soundness). All these elements, however, play an important role in the early literacy apps' overall effectiveness. In one SEEL study, fifteen preschool teachers interacted with three early literacy apps—*Endless Reader* (Originator Inc, 2014)., a game-like phonics app; *Preschool Matching Game: Rhyming Words* (Alligator Apps, 2012), a 'skill and drill' app for matching rhyming words; and *Hideout: Early Reading* (Third Rail LLC, 2014), an app that embeds phonological patterns into a theme-based context. The teachers were asked whether they would consider adopting any of the three apps, along with reasons why (or why not).

Teachers gravitated toward apps they believed would engage the students, commenting frequently on the auditory and visual effects and the game-like features of the *Endless Reader* and *Hideout* apps and the apps' potential to hold children's interest. While some teachers referred to and stated that they preferred apps with sound pedagogical principles, most did not mention pedagogical flaws found in some of the apps. In general, teachers tended to emphasize the design elements embedded in the app that served to capture children's attention. Teachers must take care not to assume that children's interest in and attention to an app's design features automatically results in skill acquisition. They should also realize that engagement with a pedagogically-flawed app could lead to mislearning (e.g., if an app pronounces both letters in a digraph).

Ways to Make Digital Media an Integral Component of Early Literacy Instruction

While the NAEYC guidelines for using digital media with young children provide teachers with a general sense of how to incorporate media, teachers must still devise practical, specific plans for capitalizing on digital resources. Technology should be an integral part of how teachers intentionally teach and arrange for children to practice early literacy skills (NAEYC, 2012) and not simply an isolated classroom activity. Educators can integrate digital media into their early childhood programs to facilitate children's early literacy development as they a) operate within a vision for learning, b) draw upon story-making tools to produce personalized texts, c) connect app content and skills with classroom instruction, d) monitor children's engagement with and around digital media, and e) adopt appropriate scaffolding strategies.

Employ Tech to Support the Learning Vision

Teachers can be intentional in the way they introduce technology to teach and extend targeted skills. They can use media to reinforce students' learning of specific skills rather than viewing the tools as stand-alone instructional options. In so doing, teachers might adopt the following instructional framework for teaching early literacy skills (Northrup and Killeen, 2013):

1. Teach the concept without using a digital device.
2. Explain the purpose of a targeted digital learning activity and model its use.
3. Provide guided practice with the app.
4. Arrange for opportunities for independent practice, both on and off the device.

Using an instructional framework such as this can help ensure that the students are using the media to learn the targeted principle. Adults should provide support and scaffolding as needed (R. Culatta, 2021).

Utilize Story-making Apps to Create Personalized Texts

Effective literacy instruction requires opportunities to systematically teach literacy skills while also contextualizing and personalizing instruction, thus helping to ensure that children realize the meaning and purpose for reading and writing (Kucirkova, 2018). Reading about engaging first-hand experiences activates prior knowledge and personal meaning construction, which can increase motivation and comprehension (B. Culatta, Hall, Kovarsky, & Theadore, 2007; deTemple & Snow, 2001; Kearns, 2021; Tracey & Morrow, 2009).

In several Head Start classrooms, the SEEL project contextualized instruction by conducting theme-based units that revolved around depicting hands-on activities in personalized books. In one unit, children learned about popcorn while also blending and rhyming with -*op* words. They sprouted seeds, helped grind popcorn seeds to use in making cornbread, and learned about the physics involved in popping popcorn. To teach the physical principle of popcorn kernels exploding because of agitating water trapped inside, the children held drops of water and a popcorn seed and were asked to imagine a little bit of water inside the seed. They also watched a video clip of boiling water to illustrate the forceful movement of heated water. The children replicated the seed exploding by turning a cloth model of a kernel inside out and watching a video clip of popcorn popping in slow motion. During the literacy portion of the instruction, the children rhymed with -*op* words as they hopped to a popcorn shop with popcorn seeds, put a top on the popcorn to keep the kernels from hopping out, dropped the popcorn into a popper, watched the popcorn hop and pop, told the popcorn to stop popping, and hopped back with a top on the popped popcorn. Digital photos of the children were taken as they engaged in the activity. These were used to create a digital book via the ebook-creation app *Pictello*. A page from the book is illustrated in Figure 1. The story was read to and with the children to further highlight the -*op* rhyming words and print awareness concepts. The children's own experiences were also associated with a book about popping too much popcorn, *Popcorn* by Frank Asch (2015), which is available in a print or digital version.

Figure 1. A page from an ebook created to illustrate a popcorn activity

In kindergarten classrooms, SEEL activities also engaged students in hands-on experiences and then arranged for them to encounter opportunities to read and write as they created personalized digital books about their experiences (Culatta, Culatta, Frost, & Buzzell, 2004). For example, instructors assisted the children in creating digital texts that focused on the -ap word ending as they created raps by snapping, tapping, clapping, and slapping their hands, tapping their feet, and making up tap-dance routines. During the creation of the digital stories, children engaged in interactive and shared writing about what they had experienced, which permitted additional exposure to the targeted phonic -ap pattern. They also engaged in an interactive reading of the book *Rap a Tap Tap* (Dillon & Dillon, 2002) about tap dancer Bill "Bojangles" Robinson, which includes the repetitive phrase "Rap a tap – think of that." In creating the personalized digital book, children were presented with questions about their rapping and tapping along with cloze or sentence-completion prompts (i.e., partially formulated sentences) so that they could insert ideas that included target words they had heard and used during the activity. These co-constructed personalized books became phonetically-controlled texts that fit the children's reading levels, interests, and experiences. Instructors illustrated the ebooks with photos of the children as they engaged in the instructional activity. Children participated in shared and interactive writing as they helped create the text and selected animated transitions that added elements of creativity and novelty.

Teachers can save time and effort by repurposing previously-developed digital stories for use with a new group of children who have had the same hands-on experience that the personalized digital book is based on. While a good bit of the digital story can stay in place, the new group of children can add their own writings or dictate ideas about what they experienced. In addition, some photos of the current group, taken as they participated in the live instructional activity, can be incorporated into the digital book. When teacher- and child-created books were reused and adapted in the SEEL project, the children enjoyed commenting on images of themselves as well as those of other children who had previously engaged in the same activity. In one study, children used digital tools to take notes or leave messages to share thoughts and opinions about other children's work (Hutchison et al., 2012). The virtual interactions, facilitated by teachers, allowed students to gain early literacy skills while participating in social interactions centered on an app. Even non-readers could dictate notes for an adult to transcribe.

To evaluate the effectiveness of combining Project SEEL's hands-on, interactive lessons with personalized digital books for acquisition of early literacy skills, a single-subject-design study was conducted. Using a multiple-baseline-across-behaviors design, researchers evaluated four kindergarten students' reading across comparable CVC words before and after intervention (Hales, 2012). The children, identified as being 'at-risk' for reading problems, had not met criteria for acquiring expected literacy skills. They received Tier 3 supplemental instruction in dyads using SEEL lessons. Each lesson began with a hands-on activity which targeted a phonic pattern and was followed by the students and instructor creating, reading, and discussing an interactive digital book, created with *Pictello*, about the experience. The students made significant increases in the reading of targeted phonic patterns, once instruction was initiated, in comparison to non-trained phonic patterns.

Connect App Content and Skills to Classroom Instruction

In addition to capitalizing on ebook-creation apps, hands-on SEEL instructional activities can be associated with content and skills in theme-based apps. In instructional settings using SEEL lessons, children participated in a hands-on activity in which they encountered a targeted rhyme or phonic pattern and then came across examples of the same target words in a *Hideout* virtual experience.

To continue the example of popping popcorn, children in Head Start classrooms hopped to a pretend popcorn shop, and stopped to shop, and pop real popcorn. They also popped popcorn virtually via the *Hideout* app, as illustrated in Figure 2. In the *Hideout* activity, children blended initial consonants with the -op ending and were exposed to rhyming -op words (hop, pop, shop, top, stop) as they tapped on images of popcorn kernels to make them hop and pop. Finally, they listened to a brief text about the popcorn activity. Table 1 provides examples in which hands-on instruction was combined with relevant digitally-delivered content.

Figure 2. Children participating in a popcorn activity

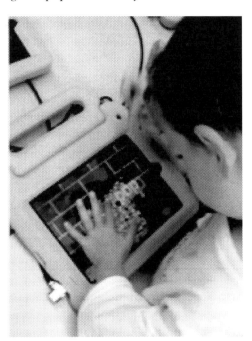

Monitor and Support Engagement and Interactions

Interactive digital media can provide instruction that targets particular literacy skills and is engaging (Marsh & Yamada-Rice, 2013). While research supports the use of digital tablets as a tool to increase child engagement (Couse & Chen, 2010), engagement will not automatically result in learning. For example, children using an app might show interest in its animated videos or cause-effect sequences without increasing proficiency with the targeted skill. Thus, teachers should be aware of different types of engagement and interactions as children encounter the media.

Table 1. Examples of hands-on instruction combined with digitally-delivered content

Target skill	SEEL Activity	Digitally-delivered Content
Read Spanish VCVC words	*¿Que Hay en la Sala?* Children engaged in a treasure hunt and labeled places and objects, with CVCV (consonant-vowel-consonant-vowel) words found around in the room as they searched for a hidden object.	Children used a personalized digital book that involved going on a virtual treasure hunt within their own classroom. They clicked on photos of places in the room where they found notes telling them where to go next in the search for a hidden object. The children then participated in writing a text about the activity that was added to the digital book. The book incorporated branching links to permit children to go from place to place and the branching of pages gave them some choice in navigating through the book.
Rhyme and read with -*ot* word endings	Dots and in a Lot and Spots on a Pot Children trotted on dots that they pretended were hot and trotted on dots in a parking lot (slots in the lot marked off with masking tape in the class). They followed dots to a pot, puts dots and spots on the pot.	The teacher and children created a digital book using *Pictello* about putting dots and spots in slots in and on a pot. They added photos of a paper parking lot where they followed dots to the lot and let cars slip into slots marked with dots and -*ot* words.
Read VCV words with -*ub*	Scrub a Cub Children got to rub and scrub a dirty bear cub (a plastic honey bottle in the form of a bear) and sang a song as they rubbed and scrubbed the cub: "scrub, scrub, scrub a cub in a tub, rub-a-dub, rub and scrub the cub in the tub."	In the *Hideout* app, children got to virtually rub and scrub a "dirty" cub in a tub on the screen. They also dragged initial letters to meet rime endings (e.g.,c—>ub = cub) and read about what they did (e.g., scrub a cub in a tub. rub and scrub the cub. rub-a-dub, etc.).
Rhyme with -*ack*	Pack Snacks in a Backpack Children cracked snacks and packed snacks in snack packs and then in a backpack.	The *Hideout* app includes an activity where children virtually pack snacks in sacks and put snack packs on a rack. They also build -*ack* words and read about what they did.

Cognitive, Social and Emotional Engagement

A useful structure for characterizing the ways that digital media can capture children's attention and motivate participation is one that distinguishes among cognitive, social, and emotional engagement.

- **Cognitive Engagement:** According to Hirsh-Pasek, et al. (2015), engagement at the cognitive level occurs when children are focused and actively involved in responding to tasks and experiences presented throughout the instruction, rather than simply manipulating objects, or watching entertaining graphics. Cognitive engagement refers to a student's effort or investment in learning and involves concentration, contribution, and persistence (Fredricks, Blumenfeld, & Paris, 2004).

- **Social Engagement:** Social exchanges during play enrich children's learning experiences (B. Culatta, Black, & Hall-Kenyon, 2013). Engagement thus involves not only focus and thought, but also the degree of social interaction which occurs during instruction. Vaala, Ly, and Levine (2015) suggest that social engagement in relation to apps can include children interfacing with characters in an app, communicating with other people through the app, commenting about what they are doing or learning, and collaborating with peers while sharing a device.

- **Emotional/Affective Engagement:** Children's emotional response to the learning experience activates the storage of the information in long term memory and facilitates learning (Immordino-Yang, 2016). Just as teacher use of affect (e.g., tone of voice, dramatization) can help children understand stories (Moschovaki, et al., 2007), affective engagement activated via digital delivery can do the same. Affective engagement is a significant factor in virtual learning (Axelrod & Home, 2006).

Interactions During Encounters with Apps

In order to assess children's cognitive, social, and emotional engagement, teachers need to rely on external evidence and observable behaviors. Measurable ways include coding affective behaviors, implementing a behavioral rating scale, and differentiating between positive and negative behaviors.

One method of measuring affective engagement lies in coding behaviors such as facial expressions (Axelrod & Hone, 2006). Ponitz and Rimm-Kaufman (2011) measured cognitive engagement by examining a child's focused attention while using computer software to determine the time spent on task. Moschovaki et al. (2007) determined level of child engagement in shared reading experiences by examining children's affective responses, including repetitions of phrases, dramatizations of scenes, and comments expressing emotions related to the task. Observations of children interacting with personalized digital books in the SEEL project noted that the children produced positive affective behaviors during both the SEEL activities and the interactive ebook creation. In the hands-on activities, the students often asked for multiple repetitions of an activity. They also remembered past activities and would ask if they could "play that again." When creating digital books, children's engagement increased when they were given the opportunity to make their own contributions to the books. Students were eager to type words into the digital book and expressed the desire to interact with the book through comments such as, "I want to press a word," "Could I do another one?" and "I like this part." When interacting with the digital books, students recognized the pictures and phrases in the text that reminded them of activities they had completed; for example, one student said, "That's the song that we sang!" The students often wanted to select books from previous sessions when they saw the title page in the app library. The students also made several comments about the pictures in the books of peers participating in the same activity they completed. Particularly interesting to the students were the pictures of themselves.

Another option for evaluating engagement is to use a behavioral rating scale. In one SEEL study (Hales, 2013), children's engagement during lessons incorporating hands-on SEEL activities and personalized digital books was observed and evaluated using the Direct Behavior Rating (DBR) scale (Chafouleas,

2009). The DBR gives a rating of a child's behavior throughout an entire intervention session, expressed as a percentage in the following domains:

- **Engaged:** Actively or passively participating in the academic activity, e.g., looking at the teacher and contributing a related comment.
- **Respectful:** Displaying compliant and polite behavior in response to adult direction and/or interactions with peers, e.g., following teacher direction or interacting pro-socially with a peer.
- **Disruptive:** Interrupting regular group activity, e.g., arguing with the instructor or running around the room.

(See DBR tutorial at http://www.directbehaviorratings.com/cms/index.php/library/online).

Despite student engagement appearing to decrease slightly from the SEEL activity to the digital book reading on the iPad, students were rated as academically engaged and respectful 75-100% of the time during the intervention session. With the DBR, however, it was not possible to separate levels of engagement for the SEEL hands-on lessons from the digital book interactions.

Different types of engagement and interactions, such as those described above, can be classified as positive or negative. Lyman (2017) observed children interacting with three different iPad apps (one presented in a game format, one situated in a meaningful theme-based context, and one focused on practicing a skill) and recorded children's affective engagement, awareness of the targeted skill, focused attention, and peer interactions. Overall, the children exhibited more positive than negative behaviors and relatively equal proportions of positive and negative behaviors for each app. However, variations in the types of positive and negative behaviors reflected differences in the nature of the apps. For example, the game-based app yielded a lower total number of behaviors, presumably due to stretches of time where children watched animated sequences. With the app that focused on a skill within a meaningful story context, the children demonstrated the most focused attention, along with positive behaviors, such as relevant comments to peers and purposeful actions, such as scrubbing cubs or packing sacks with snacks, in part because each component of the app required active manipulation. The skill-based app yielded the highest numbers of manipulations (children clicking on picture cards in a rhyme matching task), but these matching behaviors were often haphazard and random. This observation illustrates that children are not necessarily learning the skills an app targets, even when they are focused on the app and exhibiting positive affect around it. Table 2 outlines descriptions of observed behaviors during children's use of three different apps for the Apple iPad. The list, although not exhaustive, is intended to display the types of behaviors/engagement teachers might look for when using digital media in early literacy instruction.

Teachers seeking to evaluate an app's effectiveness for learning can glean a variety of cues from children's engagement and the degree to which they are learning what the app purports to teach.

Adopt Appropriate Scaffolding Strategies

Information about children's understanding of desired learning outcomes can come by interacting with them around the digital media and asking questions about the tasks. Since adult modeling and scaffolding is critical to supporting children's literacy learning, teachers should be aware of specific supports to employ (MacKay, 2015; NAEYC 2012). As adults interact with children around digital media, they can adjust scaffolding to meet children's needs, explore children's knowledge of the task and skill, and facilitate comprehension and vocabulary knowledge.

Table 2.

Behaviors	Descriptions
Positive behaviors	
Positive affect	Smiling, laughing, producing positive verbal statements and expressive sounds
Attention	Looking at the screen while manipulating the device, watching the screen while another child plays, leaning towards the game
Purposeful manipulation	Tapping pictures and words, dragging letters and words, manipulating characters and objects
Negative behaviors	
Negative affect	Frowning, expressing frustration or hesitancy towards playing the game
Inattention	Looking around the room, leaning away from the game, disengaging from the game
Random manipulation	Rapidly and repeatedly tapping, incorrectly manipulating the game, haphazardly dragging pictures or objects

Adjust Scaffolding to Meet Children's Needs

When observing children's behaviors and engagement, teachers should provide responsive support as needed. For example, in observing children as they interacted with personalized digital books created as part of the SEEL program to write about hands-on activities, instructors noted that children sometimes initially protested when using the iPad for reading the digital stories that did not incorporate many game-like features (Hales, 2012). Children also appeared to focus on manipulating the device at first, hovering their hands over the on-screen buttons or repeatedly pressing buttons without pausing to listen to the audio segments. However, once the adult helped the children to focus on the content and goal of the digital book activity, observers recorded more student comments that were relevant to the literacy task. Adult modeling of the use of ebooks helped stimulate the children's interest in the literacy material and focus their attention on the phonological and phonic pattern exemplified.

Explore Children's Knowledge of the Task and Skill Being Addressed

When providing meaningful opportunities for children to utilize apps to learn and practice early literacy skills, teachers should be sure to model the skill within the app (Northrop & Killen, 2013). Teachers can provide an overview of what is involved, model the expected behavior, and ask the children to restate what they are supposed to do. Modeling also includes commenting on and asking questions about targeted skills within the context of the app (Neumann & Neumann, 2014). Adults should provide scaffolding in the form of feedback regarding children's successes and struggles with the skills (Northrop & Killeen, 2013; Neumann & Neumann, 2014). When adults provide encouragement and specific feedback as children interact with an app, they motivate children and allow the experience to fit individual children's abilities (Hirsh-Pasek et al., 2015). The use of adult scaffolding and feedback can allow children a personalized experience not possible with the app alone.

Table 3. Supports teachers can offer to facilitate student learning

Child's Behavior	Teacher's Questions and Comments
Cannot identify the purpose of the app	• Let's figure out what this activity is trying to teach. • What does the activity want you to do? • Do you know what you are supposed to do? • You will notice that the game (or story or activity) focuses a lot on words that . . . . . . (e.g., rhyme, begin with the same first sound, have the /e/ short vowel). • Here are some examples of words you will hear (or see). • I'll show you what to do. Watch what I do.
Cannot identify the targeted skill	• Do you notice a pattern (or some similarity) in these words (or letters or sounds)? • The app is trying to teach _____. Here are some examples of what the app is trying to teach _____.
Gives incorrect responses	• What does this part of the word say? • You said or did _____. Does that make sense? • What's wrong with this _____ (the way the child responded)? • You made a mistake. You did or read _____. Can you fix it? • What could be the right answer? • Let's take a closer look at this one. • You got this part right. But let's take another look at this part.
Fails to focus attention; makes random responses	• This first part says _____. You know this part. • Look at this part. What sound does it make? • You're trying to _____ (remind of purpose). • This app is supposed to help you _____. (remind of task). • You read (or found or spelled or made the word) _____. Does it look (or sound) right?
Makes decoding errors; guesses	• Let's look at that word again. Look at the parts. • Don't guess. • Check what you did. Does it look (or sound) right? • You made a mistake. You said (or read or found) _____. Can you fix it? • Does the word you read (or made) fit with the story? • You did or made _____. Does that work? What else would work? • Try that again. Remember, the activity is trying to teach _____. • You did _____. Was that, okay? • You made a mistake. Can you find it? What was the tricky part? • What's wrong with _____?

Facilitate Story Comprehension and Vocabulary Knowledge

As with printed, traditional text, children may not comprehend stories they come across in digital format. Interactive pictures can be highly engaging but can also distract from understanding the text. In a study by Hoel & Jernes (2020), ebook apps' interactive features limited dialogue between the children and the teachers. The groups of children paid more attention to clicking the hotspots and determining whose turn it was than they did to the content of the story. The interactions between teacher and children improved, however, when teachers asserted more control during a second reading. If a teacher's goal is shared dialogue around an ebook, a less interactive ebook is likely the better choice.

Adults can scaffold children's learning by extending and elaborating the information and engaging in language-rich interactions to support comprehension. For example, adults can relate the story content to children's own experiences; paraphrase important ideas; use child-friendly wording to explain complex concepts; and provide explanations, summaries, and overviews. These and other strategies can engage children in interactive or dialogic reading, involving children in a conversation about the text by making comments and asking questions that relate to the children's prior knowledge. Arranging for joint engagement around digital media is beneficial to children's learning (Lauricella, Robb, & Wartella, 2007; Takeuchi & Stevens, 2011).

While key vocabulary in ebooks and apps can be highlighted and hyperlinked to a definition, this elaboration may not necessarily contribute to word knowledge. Discussing key vocabulary in context, relating unfamiliar words to children's own experiences, and giving child-friendly explanations are important ways to teach vocabulary within printed or digital texts (Beck, McKeown, & Kucan, 2015). These strategies were useful in hands-on SEEL activities that were then turned into personalized digital books and in children's encounters with activities presented via the *Hideout* app. For example, in one SEEL activity, experienced in real life and virtually within the *Hideout* app, children rip old pieces of cloth to fit in a rag bag, put tags on the bags and rags, and drag and wag the rags to clean the room. The adult might support children's understanding by demonstrating the meaning of *drag,* talking about the purpose of rags, describing the decision involved in turning a piece of cloth into a rag, and explaining what tags are and why they are used. Table 3 lists supports teachers can offer when children fail to understand a keyword, text, or skill; or struggle to engage successfully with the digital media.

CONCLUSION

Technology, which is ubiquitous in even young children's lives, can serve an important function in literacy learning. As young children grow into literacy, however, the digital media they encounter must support and enrich that journey.

Teachers must choose digital media through careful analysis of its pedagogical appropriateness and its ability to engage children socially, emotionally, and cognitively. Special care must be taken to distinguish between design features that distract versus those that stimulate engagement.

Children's time with technology should not be an isolated event, unrelated to other learning. As educators design the early literacy curriculum, they must layer in appropriate digital media with face-to-face instruction in a purposeful and supported way, connecting the digital media to the curricular content and to hands-on playful experiences. The SEEL examples shared in this chapter illustrate ways in which teachers can creatively and flexibly integrate digital media with classroom experiences in the early literacy curriculum.

When teachers take advantage of the unique features of technology, it can enrich the educational experience in a variety of ways. Digital tools can allow children to interact meaningfully with peers and teachers, make connections between real-life and digitally-represented experiences, and represent hands-on playful experiences. Such interactions around digital media can add variety, support targeted skills, increase engagement, and capitalize on peer-to-peer interactions within a community of early literacy learners.

Digital media cannot, however, substitute for a responsive, knowledgeable adult's attention and guidance. Motivation and engagement can be monitored and enhanced as teachers scaffold children's understanding of the purpose of the digital media and the target skill(s). Teachers can extend, elaborate, and explain to ensure that children understand expectations; comprehend the included ideas, stories or text; and make connections to prior knowledge or experience.

Thus, as teachers choose and employ appropriate technology, intertwining it with curricular decisions, they can build knowledge and skills while offering young children enjoyable and varied experiences with digital media that augment overarching literacy goals.

ACKNOWLEDGMENT

We would like to thank Richard Culatta, CEO of the International Society for Technology in Education, for his expertise and review of the manuscript.

REFERENCES

AssistiveWare. (2020). *Pictello* (Version 3.7.2) [Mobile app]. http://itunes.apple.com

Al Bailey Apps. (2021). *Phonics town* (Version 1.01) [Mobile app]. http://itunes.apple.com

Alligator Apps. (2014). *Preschool matching game: Rhyming Words* [Mobile app]. http://itunes.apple.com

Asch, F. (2015). *Popcorn*. Aladdin.

Axelrod, L., & Hone, K. (2006). Affectemes and allaffects: A novel approach to coding user emotional expression during interactive experiences. *Behaviour & Information Technology*, *25*(2), 159–173. doi:10.1080/01449290500331164

Beck, I., McKeown, M., & Kucan, L. (2013). *Bringing Words to Life: Robust Vocabulary Instruction* (2nd ed.). Guilford Press.

Book Creator. (2021). *Book creator* [Online software]. https://bookcreator.com/2021/07/

Chafouleas, S. M., Riley-Tillman, T. C., & Christ, T. J. (2009). Direct Behavior Rating (DBR): An emerging method for assessing social behavior within a tiered intervention system. *Assessment for Effective Intervention*, *34*(4), 201–213. doi:10.1177/1534508409340391

Chiong, C., Ree, J., Takeuchi, L., & Erickson, I. (2012). *Print books vs e-books. Comparing parent-child co-reading on print, basic and enhanced e-book platforms.* The Joan Ganz Cooney Center at Sesame Workshop. http://www.joanganzcooneycenter.org/wp-content/uploads/2012/07/jgcc_ebooks_quickreport.pdf

Common Sense Media. (2021). *Introduction to the TPACK model.* https://www.commonsense.org/education/videos/introduction-to-the-tpack-model

Couse, L. J., & Chen, D. W. (2010). A Tablet Computer for Young Children? Exploring Its Viability for Early Childhood Education. *Journal of Research on Technology in Education, 43*(1), 75–98. doi:10.1080/15391523.2010.10782562

Cowan, K. (2017). Digital Languages: Multimodal meaning-making in Reggio-inspired early years education. In DigiLitEY: The Digital and Multimodal Practices of Young Children, Short Term Scientific Mission—Final Report. Academic Press. http://digilitey.eu/wp-content/uploads/2015/09/ElisabeteBarros-STSM-FinalReport_FI-1.pdf

Cowan, K. (2019). Digital meaning making: Reggio Emilia-inspired practice in Swedish preschools. *Media Education Research Journal, 8*(2), 11–29.

Culatta, B., Black, S., & Hall-Kenyon, K. (2013). *Systematic and Engaging Early Literacy: Instruction and intervention.* Plural Publishing, Inc.

Culatta, R., Culatta, B., Frost, M., & Buzzell, K. (2004). Project SEEL: Part II. Using technology to enhance early literacy instruction in Spanish. *Communication Disorders Quarterly, 25*(2), 89–96. doi:10.1177/15257401040250020601

Culatta, B., Hall, K., Kovarsky, D., & Theodore, G. (2007). Contextualized approach to language and literacy instruction. *Communication Disorders Quarterly, 28*(4), 216–235. doi:10.1177/1525740107311813

Culatta, B., Hall-Kenyon, K., & Bingham, G. (2016). *Five Questions Everyone Should Ask Before Choosing Early Literacy Apps.* The Joan Ganz Cooney Center at Sesame Workshop. https://www.joanganzcooneycenter.org/2016/01/07/five-questions-everyone-should-ask-before-choosing-early-literacy-apps/

Culatta, R. (2021). *Digital for Good: Raising Kids to Thrive in an Online World.* Harvard Business Review Press.

de Jong, M. T., & Bus, A. G. (2002). Quality of book-reading matters for emergent readers: An experiment with the same book in a regular or electronic format. *Journal of Educational Psychology, 94*(1), 145–155. doi:10.1037/0022-0663.94.1.145

de Temple, J. M., & Snow, C. E. (2001). Conversations about literacy: Social mediation of psycholinguistic activity. In L. Verhoeven & C. Snow (Eds.), *Literacy and motivation: Reading engagement in individuals and groups* (pp. 71–94). Lawrence Erlbaum Associates.

Dillon, L., & Dillon, D. (2002). *Rap a tap tap: Here's Bojangles—Think of that!* Blue Sky Press.

Donohue, C., & Schomburg, R. (2017). Technology and interactive media in early childhood programs. *Young Children, 72*(4), 72–78.

Dunn, J., Gray, C., Moffett, P., & Mitchell, D. (2018). 'It's more funner than doing work': Children's perspectives on using tablet computers in the early years of school. *Early Child Development and Care, 188*(6), 819–831. doi:10.1080/03004430.2016.1238824

Elliot, A. J. (1999). Approach and avoidance motivation and achievement goals. *Educational Psychologist, 34*(3), 169–189. doi:10.120715326985ep3403_3

Epic! Creations. (2021). *Epic books for kids* (version 5.31) [Mobile app]. https://www.getepic.com

Fred Rogers Center for Early Learning and Children's Media at Saint Vincent College. (2012). *A framework for quality in digital media for young children: Considerations for parents, educators, and media creators*. https://cmhd.northwestern.edu/wp-content/uploads/2015/10/Framework_Statement_2-April_2012-Full_Doc-Exec_Summary-1.pdf

Fredricks, J. A., Blumenfeld, P. C., & Paris, A. H. (2004). School engagement: Potential of the concept, state of the evidence. *Review of Educational Research, 74*(1), 59–109. https://doi.org/10.3102/00346543074001059

Gee, J. P. (2010). *New digital media and learning as an emerging area and "worked examples" as one way forward*. MIT Press.

Guthrie, J. T., & Knowles, K. T. (2001). Promoting reading motivation. In L. Verhoeven & C. Snow (Eds.), *Literacy and motivation* (pp. 159–176). Erlbaum.

Halliday, M., & Halliday, M. (1973). *Explorations in the functions of language*. Edward Arnold.

Hales, A. (2012). *Using Systematic and Engaging Early Literacy instruction and digital books to teach at-risk kindergarteners to read target words* [Unpublished master's thesis]. Brigham Young University, Provo, UT, United States.

Hart, A. (2013). *Kindergarteners' incidental learning of words during exposure to systematic and engaging early literacy instruction and digital books* [Unpublished honors thesis]. Brigham Young University, Provo, UT, United States.

Hoel, T., & Jernes, M. (2020). Samtalebasert lesing av bildebok-apper: barnehagelærer versus hotspoter [Dialogue-Based Reading of Picture Book Apps: The Kindergarten Teacher Versus Hotspots]. *Norsk Pedagogisk Tidsskrift, 104*(2), 121–133. doi:10.18261/issn.1504-2987-2020-02-04

Hirsh-Pasek, K., Zosh, J. M., Golinkoff, R. M., Gray, J. H., Robb, M. B., & Kaufman, J. (2015). Putting education in educational apps: Lessons from the science of learning. *Psychological Science in the Public Interest, 16*(1), 3–34. https://doi.org/10.1177/1529100615569721

Hutchison, A., Beschorner, B., & Schmidt-Crawford, D. (2012). Exploring the use of the iPad for literacy learning. *The Reading Teacher, 66*(1), 15–23. https://doi.org/ 10.1002/TRTR.01090

Immordino-Yang, M. H. (2016). *Emotions, Learning, and the Brain*. W. W. Norton & Company.

Johnston, P. (2012). *Opening minds: Using language to change lives*. Stenhouse.

Kervin, L., Mantei, J., & Herrington, J. (2009). Using technology in pedagogically responsive ways to support literacy learners. In T. Wee & R. Subramaniam (Eds.), *Handbook on new media literacy at the K-12 level: Issues and Challenges* (pp. 203–215). IGI Global.

Knauf, H. (2016). Interlaced social worlds: exploring the use of social media in the kindergarten. *Early Years, 36*(3), 254-270. doi:10.1080/09575146.2016.1147424

Kucirkova, N. (2018). *How and why to read and create digital books: A guide for primary practitioners.* UCL Press.

Larson, L. C. (2010). Digital readers: The next chapter in ebook reading and response. *The Reading Teacher, 64*(1), 15–22. https://doi.org/10.1598/RT.64.1.2

Lauricella, A. R., Robb, M. B., & Wartella, E. (2007). Challenges and suggestions for determining quality in children's media. In D. Lemish (Ed.), The Routledge international handbook of children, adolescents, and media (pp. 425–432). https://doi.org/10.4324/9780203366981.CH52.

Lyman, S. (2017). *Comparison of early literacy iPad applications: Children's engagement* [Unpublished master's thesis]. Brigham Young University, Provo, UT, United States.

MacKay, K. (2015). *Does an iPad change the experience? A look at mother-child book reading interactions* [Unpublished doctoral dissertation]. Brigham Young University, Provo, UT, United States.

Marsh, J., & Yamada-Rice, D. (2013). Early literacy in the digital age. In D. Barone & M. Mallette (Eds.), *Best Practices in Early Literacy Instruction* (pp. 79–95). Guilford Press.

Mishra, P., & Koehler, M. (2006). Technological pedagogical content knowledge: A framework for integrating technology in teachers' knowledge. *Teachers College Record, 108*(6), 1017–1054. https://doi.org/10.1111/j.1467-9620.2006.00684.x

Mishra, P., & Koehler, M. (2009). Too cool for school? No way! Using the TPACK framework: you can have your hot tools and teach with them, too. *Learning & Leading with Technology, 36*(7), 14+. link.gale.com/apps/doc/A199794723/AONE?u=byuprovo&sid=bookmark-AONE&xid=6b0decfc

Moschovaki, E., Meadows, S., & Pellegrini, A. (2007). Teachers' affective presentation of children's books and young children's display of affective engagement during classroom book reading. *Instituto Superior de Psicologia Aplicada, 22*(4), 405-420. doi:10.1007/BF03173463

Moses, A. (2013). What, when, and how electronic media can be used in an early literacy classroom. In D. Barone & M. Mallette (Eds.), *Best Practices in Early Literacy Instruction* (pp. 96–118). Guilford Press.

National Governors Association Center for Best Practices & Council of Chief State School Officers. (2010). *Common Core State Standards (English Language Arts).* http://corestandards.org/

National Association for the Education of Young Children. (2012). *Technology and interactive media as tools in early childhood programs serving children from birth through age 8.* http://www.naeyc.org/files/naeyc/file/positions/ PS_technology_ WEB2.pdf

National Early Literacy Panel. (2004, December). *The National Early Literacy Panel: Findings from a synthesis of scientific research on early literacy development* [Paper presentation]. The National Reading Conference, San Antonio, TX, United States.

Neumann, M. M., & Neumann, D. L. (2014). Touch screen tablets and emergent literacy. *Early Childhood Education Journal, 42*(4), 231–239. https://www.learntechlib.org/p/152727/

Northrop, L., & Killeen, E. (2013). A framework for using iPads to build early literacy skills. *The Reading Teacher, 66*(7), 531–537. https://doi.org/10.1002/TRTR.1155

Originator Inc. (2014). *Endless reader* (Version 2.3) [Mobile app]. http://itunes.apple.com

Patall, E. A., Cooper, H., & Robinson, J. C. (2008). The effects of choice on intrinsic motivation and related outcomes: A meta-analysis of research findings. *Psychological Bulletin, 134*(2), 270–300. https://doi.org/10.1037/0033-2909.134.2.270

Plowman, L., McPake, J., & Stephen, C. (2010). The technologisation of childhood? Young Children and technology in the home. *Children & Society, 24*, 63-74. http://dx.doi.org.erl.lib.byu.edu/10.1111/j.1099-0860.2008.00180.x

Ponitz, C. C., & Rimm-Kaufman, S. E. (2011). Contexts of reading instruction: Implications for literacy skills and kindergarteners' behavioral engagement. *Early Childhood Research Quarterly, 26*(2), 157–168. https://doi.org/0.1016/j.ecresq.2010.10.002

Polished Play, L. L. C. (2021). *Puppet Pals* (Version 1.9.8) [Mobile app]. http://itunes.apple.com

Eggs, R. (2021). *Fast phonics* (Version 3.0.4) [Mobile app]. https://readingeggs.com/fast-phonics-games/

Sénéchal, M., LeFevre, J.-A., Smith-Chant, B. L., & Colton, K. V. (2001). On refining theoretical models of emergent literacy: The role of empirical evidence. *Journal of School Psychology, 39*(5), 439–460. https://doi.org/10.1016/S0022-4405(01)00081-4

Workshop, S. (2021). *Art maker* [Online software]. https://www.sesamestreet.org/art-maker

Storch, S. A., & Whitehurst, G. J. (2002). Oral language and code-related precursors to reading: Evidence from a longitudinal structural model. *Developmental Psychology, 38*(6), 934–947. https://doi.org/10.1037/0012-1649.38.6.934

Suarez-Orozco, M. M. (Ed.). (2007). *Learning in the global era: International perspectives on globalization and education.* University of California Press.

Takeuchi, L., & Stevens, R. (2011). *The new coviewing: Designing for learning through joint media engagement.* The Joan Ganz Cooney Center at Sesame Workshop. https://www.joanganzcooneycenter.org/wp-content/uploads/2011/12/jgc_coviewing_desktop.pdf

Third Rail Games, L. L. C. (2014). *Flying kitchen* (Version 2.02) [Mobile app]. http://itunes.apple.com

Third Rail Games, L. L. C. (2014). *Hideout: Early reading* (Version 2.02) [Mobile app]. http://itunes.apple.com

Tough, J. (1977). *The Development of Meaning.* George Allen & Unwin.

Tracey, D., & Morrow, L. (2009). *Best practices for phonics instruction in today's classroom. Sadlier Professional Development Series, 13*, 1–22 .

Trad, R. (2021). *Teachers' and students' experiences using social media as a pedagogical tool within classrooms: A systematic literature review* [Unpublished master's thesis]. https://ir.lib.uwo.ca/etd/7824

Vaala, S., Ly, A., & Levine, M. H. (2015). Getting a read on the app stores: A market scan and analysis of children's literacy apps. *The Joan Ganz Cooney Center at Sesame Workshop.* https://www.joangan-zcooneycenter.org/wp-ontent/uploads/2015/12/jgcc_gettingaread.pdf

Verhoeven, L., & Snow, C. (Eds.). (2001). *Literacy and motivation: Reading engagement in individuals and groups.* Lawrence Erlbaum Associates.

Voogt, J., & McKenney, S. (2017). TPACK in teacher education: Are we preparing teachers to use technology for early literacy? *Technology, Pedagogy and Education, 26*(1), 69–83. https://doi.org/10.1 080/1475939X.2016.1174730

Wong, K. (1996). Video game effect on computer-based learning design. *British Journal of Educational Technology, 27*(September), 230–232. https://doi.org/10.1111/j.1467-8535.1996.tb00690.x

ADDITIONAL READING

Culatta, B., Hall-Kenyon, K., & Bingham, G. (2016). Five Questions Everyone Should Ask Before Choosing Early Literacy Apps. The Joan Ganz Cooney Center at Sesame Workshop. https://www.joangan-zcooneycenter.org/2016/01/07/five-questions-everyone-should-ask-before-choosing-early-literacy-apps/

Culatta, R. (2021). *Digital for Good: Raising Kids to Thrive in an Online World.* Harvard Business Review Press.

Culatta, R., Culatta, B., Frost, M., & Buzzell, K. (2004). Project SEEL: Part II. Using technology to enhance early literacy instruction in Spanish. *Communication Disorders Quarterly, 25*(2), 89–96. doi: 10.1177/15257401040250020601

Dillon, L., & Dillon, D. (2002). *Rap a tap tap: Here's Bojangles—Think of that!* Blue Sky Press.

Guernsey, L., & Levine, M. (2016). Getting Smarter About E-Books for Children. *Young Children,* (May), 38–43.

Westby, C., & Culatta, B. (2017). Telling Tales: Personal event narratives and life stories. *Language, Speech, and Hearing Services in Schools, 48*(3), 135–217. doi:10.1044/2016_LSHSS-15-0073 PMID:28732097

KEY TERMS AND DEFINITIONS

Activate Background Knowledge: To present content that students can readily relate to their existing experiences.

Context- or Theme-Based App: A digital application that provides purpose and meaning for reading and writing by allowing children to encounter target patterns within a context based on common and concrete events.

Digital Media: Educational or entertainment content delivered electronically, with or without the use of the internet. Such media may include videos, games, ebooks, and applications for creative uses including ebook creation.

Engagement: The extent to which an activity captures the intended audience's attention and motivates cognitive, social, and/or emotional participation.

Pedagogical Soundness: Appropriateness of a given product or method for its target audience, according to correct instructional principles.

Personalized Ebook: A digital application made using open-ended ebook creation tools that incorporates children's first-hand experiences, dictations, photographs, and other individualized materials.

Scaffolding: Adult assistance adjusted to support an individual child's learning, including types of questions asked, attention-maintaining procedures, emotional affect, and prompts.

Chapter 35
Acquiring Problem-Solving Skills Through Coding Games in Primary School

Gaia Lombardi

iD https://orcid.org/0000-0002-7618-8586

Istituto Comprensivo Statale Via dei Salici, Legnano, Italy

ABSTRACT

Play is a spontaneous and free activity of the child and its role in learning processes has been recognized by pedagogical studies from Piaget onwards. Game-based learning places the pupil at the center of the teaching-learning process, creating a motivating and challenging environment in which the pupil can learn freely, proceeding by trial and error, learning to evaluate their choices and those of other players and monitor a number of variables. Game-based learning therefore stands as an individualized and inclusive learning environment, which allows all students to achieve maximum educational success. In more recent years, the spread of online games, the use of coding as a teaching tool, and distance learning experiences have contributed to spreading game-based didactics. In this chapter, the author proposes a path of coding games for the development of problem solving in primary school with interdisciplinary links and to the mathematics curriculum.

INTRODUCTION

Play is a natural, spontaneous and fundamental activity for the child, whose importance in childhood development runs through the entire history of pedagogy: this idea has its roots mainly in the European Enlightenment and Romantic eras and the writing of philosophers, educators and pedagogists such as Rousseau, Pestalozzi and Froebel, to get to the medical aprroach of Maria Montessori, who defines playing as "the child's job" (Montessori, M., 1948).

It is mainly with Piaget's studies that play is recognized as having an important role in cognitive development (Piaget, 1951 and 1953). Piaget's theories about learning emphasised the need for children to explore and experiment reality by themselves. For Piaget, play was a means by which children could

DOI: 10.4018/978-1-7998-7271-9.ch035

develop and refine concepts before they had the ability to think in the abstract. At the first stages, sensorimotor play offers the children the opportunity to exercise their skills in movement, fine motor skills and prehension; at the preoperational stage (2 to 7 years) and at the following concrete stage (7 to 11 years), playing allows them, on a cognitive level, to refine their logical skills to elaborate the symbolic thought that will lead to the development of language and, later, the abstract thought (Piaget, 1954).

According to Vygotskij's constructivist studies (Vygotskij, 1966), play is placed in what is called the zone of proximal development, that is the intermediate area between what the child can do on his own and what he can learn if appropriately guided by an adult. While playing, the child surpasses himself, learns to create, to fantasize, and develops his own imagination. It is in this area that new skills are learned and new intellectual abilities develop: the zone of proximal development is the area in which the teacher's intervention can be most significant, especially if it is performed in a stimulating context, which gives space to the natural curiosity of the child and the exploration of knowledge. The zone of proximal development is therefore the "school zone" and, in the school, it can become the ideal place for active game-based learning. In recent years, and in particular with the spread of online games and the need to provide distance learning, the school system has been able to recognize the importance of game-based learning, in particular for the fostering of those basic skills that are now considered indispensable for the 21st Century citizen. Among these there is roblem olving, considered as the ability to pose and solve problematic situations in a creative way, making use of all one's cognitive resources and the different forms of intelligence that the individual is endowed with (Gardner, 1983). In the game the whole body of the child is involved, and all forms of intelligence are exercised, from the visuo-spatial one to the kinesthetic, from the logical-mathematical one to the linguistic, from the intrapersonal to the interpersonal. Furthermore, the play space is a free, rewarding, motivating space in which the child can learn by trial and error; playing also stands as a collaborative activity, in which to learn to cooperate to achieve the result. It is Bruner (Bruner, 1976) who points out that play offers an excellent opportunity for children, driven by his natural curiosity for the world, to try and experience several combinations of behaviors, at the same time minimizing the consequences of their actions by applying them in a situation of minimum risk, thus educating themselves to respect the rules. Bruner also introduces the "scaffolding" as a metaphor for the intervention of the expert person (an adult, or a peer) who helps the less experienced person (the child) in solving a problem or a task that he would not be able to complete on his own. This creates a close link between Bruber's scaffolding and Vygotsky's already mentioned "zone of proximal development", that zone constituted by the distance between the actual level of development of the child (acquired skills) and the potential level (skills that can be acquired). The scaffolding provided by the expert compensates for the difference in level between the required skills and the child's capacity and allows him to operate at a level slightly higher than that of his actual development. When children receive the support they need in the initial phase of learning, it opens up for them the possibility of using the material made available at a later time, independently and effectively. Here is how play, in which the child experiences the world, relationships, objects, becomes a place and an opportunity for learning.

Children at play often reach a state that psychologist Mihaly Csikszentmihalyi (Csikszentmihalyi, 1990) calls "flow": an elusive state of mind where time seems to disappear as children deeply focus on what they're doing. Flow can be also described as a subjective psychological state of maximum positivity and gratification, which can be experienced during the performance of activities and which corresponds to "complete immersion in achievement". The situation that makes it possible to come into contact with this state of being is characterized by the perception, by the individual, of sufficient and adequate opportunities for action (challenges) by the environment and, correspondingly, of personal adequate capacity to act on it. (skills). Entering the flow therefore depends on the balance between these two components. Playing implies high levels of personalization and individualization of activities: each child follows their own times and rhythms and expresses themselves according to the attitudes and preferences that are characteristic of them.

Playing is therefore an all-encompassing and immersive experience for the child, but it must present a challenging component that mobilizes its resources in the activity and in order to complete the game itself. This challenge and resource mobilization mechanism is the same one that is put in place in the learning process.

Game-Based Learning approach (GBL) has therefore entered rightfully among the most applied methodologies in schools, not only with younger children, and in all disciplines: according to Steinmaurer et al. (2020), the GBL approach is a combination of four aspects:

- Curriculum knowledge practices,
- Pedagogical knowledge practices,
- Scenario-based knowledge practices
- Daily knowledge practices.

Basically, the GBL approach will enable students to carry out their own learning in a free and safe learning environment in which they can learn freely without the fear of making mistakes as the GBL provides instant feedback and the operations are often reversible. "Game-based learning occurs when playing a game causes a change in the player's academic knowledge -including cognitive skill-" (Mayer, R. E., 2020).

GBL has found a wider application area in the teaching of mathematics: the use of games has proved particularly useful for the discovery of logical concepts, the activation and exercise of strategy skills and the application of rules and roles, especially in the first years of schooling (kindergarten and primary school), in which the pupils are, according to Piaget's theory, in the stages of concrete preo-operative and operative thinking and, through play, they begin to access symbolic thinking.

In Mathematics learning, the application of GBL is also seen to have many benefits in helping to improve the quality of the teaching and learning process. Setting clear learning objectives in line with curriculum requirements with student-centered implementation has made GBL more effective (Farber, 2015).

CODING, COMPUTATIONAL THINKING AND PROBLEM SOLVING

The terms Coding, Computational Thinking and Problem Solving have acquired a relevant importance in the studies of cognitive psychology applied to teaching and in didactics, and it is perhaps appropriate to give a brief definition suitable for the purpose of this chapter.

In cognitive psychology, Problem Solving is defined as the mental process that the individual puts in place to discover, analyze and solve problems, where the problem can be briefly defined as a situation which is difficult to deal with or control due to its complexity. "Problems have two critical attributes. First, a problem is an unknown in some context. Second, finding or solving for the unknown must have some social, cultural, or intellectual value. [...]" (Jonassen. DH & Wung, W., 2012). Problem Solving involves a series of steps:

- The identification of a situation as problematic;
- The decision to face the problem (problem posing);
- The understanding of the problem.

Problem Solving also involves creativity skills to genereate alternative solutions to the problem, evaluate and select one, and implement and follow up the solution

The term Computational Thinking was historically by Seymour Papert in 1980 as a result o his constructionist approach to education in which the affective and social dimensions of learning are equally important as the technical and disciplinary contents; however, Papert does not come up with a complete definition of Computational Thinking: "Their [of people using computers for providing mathematically rich activities] visions of how to integrate computational thinking into everyday life was insufficiently developed" (Papert, S., 1980).

The term is then taken up with a meaning closer to the computer science community by Jeannette Wing in 2006. According to Wing's definition "Computational Thinking is the thought process involved in formulating a problem and expressing its solution(s) in such a way that a computer—human or machine—can effectively carry out." As Computational Thinking we can therefore define that problem-solving process that first of all involves the analysis of the problem; then the definition of an automatable procedure (algorithm) to solve it and finally the design of the tools suitable for verifying its correct functioning. Implementing the procedure in a programming language is only a later stage. Computational Thinking is a form of procedural thinking with which the subject breaks down a problem into sub-problems that can be easily solved in a number finished steps from an ideal performer. "Computational Thinking is a kind of analytical thinking. It shares with mathematica thinking in the general ways in which we might approach solving a problem. It shares with engineering thinking in the general ways in which we might approach designing and evaluating a large, complex system that operates within the constraints of the real world. It shares with scientific thinking in the general ways in which we might approach understanding computability, intelligence, the mind and humam behaviour" (Wing, J. M, 2008)

This is why Computational Thinking is at the heart of computer science, but it also finds space in teaching practice, from the earliest years of school. Computational Thinking is an essential literacy for all students that combines five cornerstones:

- Problem decomposition (breaking down a complex problem or system into smaller, more manageable parts) ;
- Pattern recognition (looking for similarities among problems);
- Data representation
- Generalization/abstraction (use of the data to develop a solution strategy that can be applied to as many similar cases as possible
- Algorithms (formalization of a process or set of instructions that allow the performer to solve the problem in a finite series of steps.

On the basis of these definitions it might seem that there is no difference between Problem Solving and Computational Thinking, and that Computational Thinking merely constitutes a procedural form of problem solving, which approaches the problem situation by breaking it down and generalizing the solution through an algorithm. It is Jannette Wing herself who specifies how the two terms (and their underlying concepts) are related to each other: Computational Thinking describes the mental activity in formulating a problem to admit a computational solution. The solution can be carried out by a human or machine. This latter point is important; first, human compute; second, people can learn computational thinking without a machine; finally,computational thinking is not just about problem solving, but also about problem formulation. (Wing, J.M., 2014).

Since, as mentioned, the concept of Computational Thinking has entered the terminology of teaching, it is important not only to have given a definition that connects it to the learning processes, but also to define its limits: what Computational Thinking is not? "It's easy to fall into the trap that CT [Computational Thinking] is thinking like a computer. Yet it is a trap conveniently avoided if you keep in mind our "think like a <domain" structure expert> 'for <domain-specific> thinking skills. Thought is inherently human characteristic that implies reasoning. Computers don't think, so CT is NOT 'to think like a computer', rather it is about thinking like a computer scientist. And the problem-solving approaches commonly used by constituting computer scientistscomputational thinking (Grover, S, & Pea, R., 2017). Thinking like the computer is a very common simplification and trivialization of computational thinking and just as wrong, as the computer does not think, but executes a series of instructions. The ideal performer is the one who succeeds in this task without making mistakes and in the shortest possible time.

How does Coding fit into this scenario, and how can it be defined?

According to the clear and exhaustive definition given by Bogliolo (Bogliolo, A., 2008) Coding is the didactic and playful application of the basic principles of programming to contribute in a transversal and natural way to the development of computational thinking. It is the ability to identify and represent the solution to a problem as a concatenation of elementary steps. Coding arises from different perspectives: as an application of Computational Thinking, of which it takes up the logical and operational structures; as a didactic tool for the development of logical thinking; as a real language, suitable for communication purposes before programming constructs. In teaching, therefore, Coding enters according to these three aspects: the formal logic represented by the introduction to Computational Thinking; the playful and creative one in the various activities; finally a communicative aspect that makes it a highly inclusive tool.

Coding therefore has to do with human thought before programming languages; it is a tool for developing the computational landscape rather than a content to be learned. The introduction of coding in schools has not added a study discipline to the curriculum or enriched the technology or mathematics programs: it has instead equipped pupils and teachers with a formidable tool for the development of algorithmic thinking, accessible to all and transversal to all disciplines (as shown by the activities presented by the author and the result of his personal experience as a teacher in primary school).

CODING AS A LEARNING TOOL: CODING UNPLUGGED GAMES

In recent years, the proposal of coding activities as a tool for the development of computational thinking has opened a new field of games, from the use of specific platforms (Code.org, Scratch), to unplugged activities with instruction sets (CodyFeet, CodyRoby, CodyColor), up to the first programming experiences applied to robotics (Trinchero, 2019). Thanks above all to coding literacy campaigns such as the EU CodeWeek (https://codweek.eu/), coding has entered schools of all levels, from kindergarten to Uninversity, as a transversal activity with a strong playful and creative component. The movement of interest towards coding has developed in many cases "from the bottom", i.e. from the interest of teachers in the subject and their ability to see coding not in terms of contents to learn, but of transversal tools to put in their teachers' "toolbox". (Lombardi, G., 2020)

This is the path that the author, a mathematics teacher in primary school for over twenty years and with experience in the use of coding as an interdisciplinary teaching tool, wants to propose in this chapter. Starting from unplugged coding games, suitable for kindergarten and early primary school pupils, and following a growing level of logical complexity, we will arrive at the use of online tools such as Code.org at first as a programming training, then for the realization of autonomous projects, to finally complete the path with simple didactic robotics.

Through this path, students will learn to master some logical concepts and computational thinking; they will experience firsthand by learning to debug and to keep processes under control by predicting the moves of other players and possible alternative moves.

Unplugged games are, as indicated by the definition itself, games which, despite having content strictly linked to coding, computational thinking or programming, do not require the use of technological devices (compuer, tablet, smartphone), but can be performed with pen and paper, or with the help of tools such as dice, chessboards, placeholders, cards or puppets. They are usually games with a high motor component, which can be played o a board or a grid (often prepared on the floor using paint or adhesive tape), in pairs, in groups, or in teams, and which lend themselves to being inserted in interdisciplinary contexts such as role play, storytelling, quizzes and many others.

CODING GAMES: A PATH THROUGH CODYFEET, CODYCOLOR, CODYROBY

CodyFeet, CodyRoby e CodyColor are three unplugged coding games (with the possibility of development on an online platform) born and developed by prof. Alessandro Bogliolo, Professor of Computer Systems at the University of Urbino, and by the group of teachers and researchers of the Summer Schools of Coding and Computational Thinking held at the same University of Urbino in the years 2017-2018-2019. They are very popular games in the Italian school context, especially for the age group 3-11 years, many of their applications have been developed by groups of teachers in their classrooms, in particular during the literacy campaigns of the EU CodeWeek. The reflection on their use for problem solving also developed in a comparison between peers between communities of practice of teachers throughout the Italian territory, with the sharing of teaching materials and ideas in informal groups referring to the site http://codemooc.org/.

Made first in chronological order, CodyRoby is certainly the best known unplugged coding game of the three, and was developed into a game set consisting of a chessboard and a deck of cards.

Similar in structure, which we will see in detail, the three games can be offered to children of different ages according to an increasing order of complexity, starting from CodyFeet (designed for kindergarten children), to get to CodyColor and to CodyRoby, which still have a strong component of movement and at the same time an increasing level of abstraction, and therefore ranks among the coding activities suitable for pupils in the last years of primary school.

All the three games are based on the concept of simple instruction as a piece of information that can be performed uniquely by any player, human or machine . The instructions are represented on cards in a conventional way with oriented arrows and according to a color code. The games require the performer, Roby, to move on a grid or a chessboard, turning 90° to his left or right and advancing one square at a time. The instructions that the programmer, Cody, gives to Roby are differently represented in the three tools, but they share the association between actions and colors according to the following code:

- Yellow: rotation in place to the left by 90°:
- Red: rotation in place to the right by 90°;
- Grey: no rotation
- Green: move forward one square

The basic structure of the game consists of giving and receiving instructions to move along a grid or a chessboard and involves a very clear separation of roles between those who give the instructions (programmer) and those who execute them (performer), who move on different planes. Through this separation of roles and levels, the child (who during the game will have the opportunity to assume both, alternately) begins to learn to take different points of view with respect to the dynamics of the game itself; dynamics that will be then translated into the logical ability to keep several variables under control in a problematic situation.

CodyFeet and CodyColor

In CodyFeet and CodyColor the instructions are represented directly by the boxes that make up the path. So the path is also the program. The performer moves along the path looking at the box on which he is located at each step, reads the instruction, interprets it, executes it and moves on to the next box (and next instruction).

CodyFeet (http://codemooc.org/wp-content/uploads/2018/09/CodyFeet-CC.png) is an unplugged coding method for preschool children, preparatory to the use of CodyRoby and of the visual block programming platform (Code.org, Scratch, Blockly). The peculiar characteristic of CodyFeet is to compound an extreme simplification, which makes it intuitive and correct by construction, with the basic principles of coding and the paradigms of visual block programming. In the CodyFeet instruction set, the movement instructions are provided by the drawing of a pair of small feet in the center of the cards, accompanied by the reference color. The shape of the feet drawn on the card is an icon immediately comprehensible even by very young children and suggests the idea of position and movement together. The instruction given by the single card is not, in this case, a simple instruction, but the combination of two instructions:forward movement (provided by the drawing of the feet) and rotation (provided by the color). This type of instruction seems to be more natural for younger children, for whom the game was designed and realized.

The cards are square in shape, of 25 cm on each side, so that they can be positioned on the ground and used by children as a real "path" on which to physically move, and eare quipped with appropriate joint points that allow them to be positioned sequentially according to different paths.

The color code is inspired by that of the CodyRoby game:

- Yellow: rotation in place to the left by 90°:
- Red: rotation in place to the right by 90°;
- Grey: no rotation

There are also a start card and a finish card, both blue, and some "free" cards (white), designed for the insertion of other instructions or actions consistent with the game activity that is taking place. On the other hand, the forward movement of a square is not indicated by means of a special green card, as it is already encoded by the drawing of the feet.

The programming construct underlying the CodyFeet card structure is the sequence: read the instruction - execute the instruction - go to the next instruction.

CodyFeet therefore proposes itself as the first game with oriented cards to be offered to children from three years onwards, to help them develop lateralization and discrimination between left and right, but of course its potential is not limited to this: the basic structure of the game can be adapted to a variety of didactic contexts and implemented with the use of other elements such as dice, placeholders, characters.

In figure 1 CodyFeet cards are used as a first approach to coding with six-year-old pupils in a Primary School, in and role playing context during a welcome activity.

Figure 1.

As an activity of connection between Kindergarten and Primary School, the teachers proposed the reading of the book "A House for Hermit Crab" by Eric Carl, in clear analogy with the entry of children into the new "home" represented by the Primary School. After the reading, the story was dramatized in a coding role playing in which the children, in pairs, made the journey of Hermit Crab and gradually met the different characters of the story. At each "stage" the children at first threw a large sponge die, then took as many cards from the deck as indicated by the die, then freely composed a path from the starting point (fixed). At the end of the path they placed the arrival card and the character. At this point, each child walked the path (assuming the role of the performer) guided by his partner (programmer), and vice versa.

The cards had previously been "explored" by the whole group of children, guided by the teacher, to identify the "hidden code" represented by the association between color, image and shape of the card, and then to consolidate the left and right topological concepts. This fundamental preliminary work of "discovery" of the cards is an excellent stimulus for the application of heuristic thinking, because it allows children to freely explore the materials, making and sharing hypotheses, and to identify those characteristics, in the different components of the game, which introduce the elements of coding. Despite its simplicity, the game puts children in contact with several concepts such as instruction, code, sequence.

Even the CodyColor cards (http://codemooc.org/wpcontent/uploads/2018/10/CodyColor-CC.pdf) are square in shape, 25 cm per side, designed to be arranged on a path or on a grid, usually of 5 x 5 squares; however, the coupling points between the cards are missing: this, if on the one hand makes the arrangement of the tiles more free, on the other hand it reduces the visual immediacy of the game. The color code is the same as CodyFeet, and also in this game it is nt necessary to indicate tne movement one step ahead, because it is implied in each card (grey only means no rotation, so when on a grey card, the player always moves ahead). There are no Start or End tiles.

Also in this case the cards contain a reading instruction (the color code) and a movement instruction (rotation and movement in the adjacent square), but, eliminating the design of the footprints and the joints, it is only the color to indicate the rotation to be carried out. This allows the player to compose the cards both along a path, as in CodyFeet, or within a grid; it is also allowed to pass twice or more times on the same square, coming from different directions: the rotations, in fact, are always referred to the point of view of the performer on the grid.

In both these gamese, therefore, the instructions are found on the playground and are read and performed by the child in the role of the ideal performer: the fact that the instruction can only be read by being on it makes the idea that the computer (or robot) reads one instruction at a time and executes it immediate and intuitive.

While maintaining a strong movement component, CodyColor stands at a higher level of abstraction than CodyFeet, as the combinations between the cards are based on the instruction of movement implied by the color and the "visual clues" given by the joints and the shape of the feet have been eliminated.

Also the game levels can be different:

- Trace a path given a start point and an end point;
- Optimize a path on a grid;
- Create a path that hinders or crosses that of the opponent;
- Identify the exit point from a grid already filled with cards, given the entry point;
- Find the entry point that allows you to stay longer in the grid.

CodyColor introduces the possibility that a loop or nest is created in a path, thus asking the player to find a strategy to get out of it (otherwise the path cannot be completed). in terms of problem solving, the appearance of loop situations calls into question the ability to retrace one's steps, modify one's strategy and reformulate the path.

CodyColor also had a digital evolution in 2019, once again thanks to research team from the University of Urbino, who created a web game version in which it is possible to arrange different levels of challenges and training matches (https://codycolor.codemooc.net/#!/). Run in this mode, CodyColor transforms from an unplugged activity into an online game; this does not reduce its potential in terms of development of algorithmic thinking, but rather takes the coding game to a higher level of abstraction, eliminating the motor component and introducing remote interaction with a virtual player (human or machine).

In September 2021 an Italian toy manufacturer created, in collaboration with the research group coordinated by Pro. Alessandro Bogliolo, the CodyColor Puzzle, with shaped tiles to be inserted following the color code. It therefore becomes possible to manipulate the instruction-tiles at the level of eye-manual coordination and, following the game instructions, create different figures. In terms of abstraction, the game is placed at an intermediate level between motor activity with floor chessboard and online implementation, maintaining a physical and manipulative component and at the same time making the game a sort of solitaire in which the player can practice. their knowledge of the color code and autonomously identify different solution strategies.

CodyRoby

With CodyRoby, the instruction plan leaves the execution plan for good. While in the previous games the instructions were represented on the cards that made up the game plan, and the performer had to get on them to read the instructions and execute them, in CodyRoby the game plan (chessboard or floor grid) is the plan on the which Roby, the ideal performer moves, while Cody, the programmer, gives him instructions from the outside. The separation of roles between programmer and performer also becomes definitive (roles which, however, during the game, it is advisable to make interchangeable between students or groups). This exchange of roles allows children to understand that digital tools are not "thinking" tools, but skilled, rapid, precise executors of algorithms written by a human mind. In the game it appears evident that the real problem solver is Cody, the programmer, while Roby limits himself to showing the correctness of the solution found and puts it into practice without any possibility of intervening to modify it. This soon introduces the need for debugging into the game, ie correcting programming or execution errors. In doing so, the children soon realize that the programmer has the complete vision of the game, who can intervene by foreseeing any obstacles in order to avoid or remove them, and therefore learning from their mistakes, while this possibility is denied to the performer. that he cannot retrace his steps unless the programmer gives him the instructions to do so. Observations of this type emerge spontaneously during the game and are significant both in terms of participation, motivation and inclusion of the pupils and, above all, in terms of the development of logical and procedural thinking, because they help to elaborate and socialize reasoning. Especially with younger pupils or pupils in difficulty, this "bringing to light" one's own inner logical path, expressing it in words, helps the triggering and development of thought.

CodyRoby therefore takes the unlugged coding game to a higher level of abstraction: the tools (which we will examine in detail shortly) maintain a strong component of visual immediacy and, of course, a formal correctness of language consistent with CodyFeet and CodyColor ; the global motor component also remains high, especially when used on the floor, but it is the very structure of the game that gives the possibility to access procedural thinking strategies that are already partially abstract, as they are formulated on a different level from that of the game itself.

The entire set of cards and other game tools can be downloaded at the site: http://codemooc.org/ codyroby/_, while it is possible to have an overview at the site: http://www.famigliattiva.org/wp-content/ uploads/2019/11/Kit-CodyRoby-fatv-A5-624x440.jpg_

Figure 2.

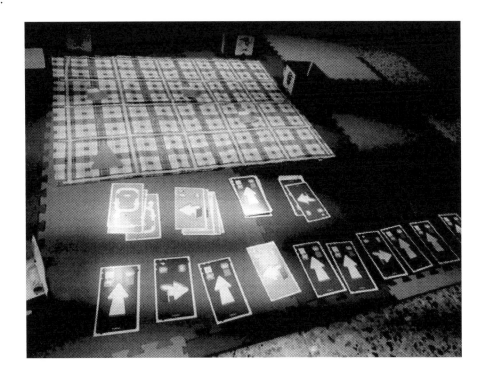

Figure 2 shows a path made with the movement cards and the repetition card. The repetition-card introduces the concept of path optimization, and for children it is very stimulating to ask themselves about the "benefits" brought by this type of card to their game: the reduction of time to carry out a program, for example, and the possibility of reduce errors. In the author's experience, this type of observation has been reported in the class as a reference to the relationship between repeated addition and multiplication.

As mentioned, CodYRoby's color cards carry a simple instruction to rotate or move forward. since these are simple instructions, it is almost superfluous to specify that there is no backward movement card: this is in fact obtained with a double rotation of 90 ° to the right or left and a forward movement. On some educational robots (for example the Bee-Bots, which will also be discussed in this chapter) there is a key for moving backwards: this however would not be consistent with the logic of the CodyRoby language, in which the set of instructions is sufficient to make any kind of movement on the playing space. In the author's experience, this observation is one of the first that children make when they start using the set of cards: from the didactic point of view, an effective strategy is to invite them to discover the answer. This favors their involvement in the game not only on a playful level, but also on a logical level. In the same way, it is children themselves who gradually discover how to "debug" by correcting their mistakes.

When it was conceived, in 2014, for participation in the EU CodeWeek, the CodyRoby set of cards was designed as a board game, for which a chessboard, the silhouettes of the robots, and color / movement cards had been prepared. correspondence has already been indicated here.

Later, other function cards were added to the set: repetition, conditional instructions, universal move, and the possibility of assigning sensors to the robot. In educational use, the meaning of these cards is gradually discovered by children as their difficulties and experience increase. The first to appear is usually the repetition card: in the case of particularly long or complex paths, in fact, it may happen that a type of card runs out, and the need arises to "shorten" the path by collecting the instructions repeated in a single paper. This too is a discovery that children quickly make: the repetition card, as well as the analogous block on the visual programming platforms, allows you to use a single color card to repeat the same movement several times.

Blue cards with conditional instructions can also be introduced later, with higher levels of game complexity. The use of conditional statements is one of the closest points of contact between the semantics of CodyRoby and that of visual block programming. In fact, conditional instruction introduces variability into the game: if ... then ... else. A close relationship can be noted here with elements of the Mathematics Primary School curriculum, in which conditional statements are usually represented by flow charts during problem solving activities.

Figure 3.

The figures 2 and 3 accompanying the chapter show a game realted to some topics of environmental education, carried out as part of the EU CodeWeek 2019 in a third class of an Italian primary school (pupils aged 8/9). The game consisted in correctly differentiating some waste by taking it to the corresponding bin (a box with the indication of the material to be given), avoiding obstacles on the path (orange cones on the grid). The pupils, in pairs, worked out the path using the instruction cards; then, one assumed the role of Cody and read the "program", from left to right, an instruction at a time, giving directions to the companion who, in the role of Roby, was on the game grid. The pupil in the role of performer played the movements (displacements or rotations) one at a time.

As you can see, the programmer / performer roles are now separated, and the program is "written" before it is executed; the instructions are read (and consequently executed) one at a time. In the event of an error, the reading of the program requires to be completed and then debugging is carried out; the execution is finally done from the correction point on. The game is very complex, and requires players to solve problems at different levels: formal correctness in writing, reading and executing the code; choice of the suitable path to reach the desired place; possible correction of errors. The path is therefore first "thought" and visualized on the grid (solicitation of visual and logical intelligence, with the ability to predict the next steps), then "translated" into simple instructions according to a known code (solicitation of linguistic intelligence), physically performed (solicitation of the kinesthetic intelligence) and finally possibly corrected (solicitation of the logical-mathematical intelligence). The problem solving process is applied on multiple levels of abstraction (children often proceed by trial and error), but it is above all socialized and shared in the dialogue between the two players, who act as a collaborative couple. The sharing of reasoning among them, with the class group and with the present teacher elicits the production of questions and hypotheses, of possible variants, urging the use of lateral thinking: "what would happen if ...". This asking questions, making hypotheses, verifying them (first visually and if necessary in practice) is the basis of the scientific method; in daily teaching practice, in classes that regularly carry out coding activities, the cognitive relapse is noted by the tachers precisely in a greater "problem posing", in the ability to "see" the possible problematic situation, to analyze it and to formulate hypotheses for the identification of possible solutions.

A further, interesting evolution of CodyRoby is the possibility to equip the robot with sensors that allow it to identify "if there is a way" in front of, or on the sides of the performer (as happens in the paths of The Harvester on Code.org). The equipment with sensors, on a logical level, introduces the conditional instruction, and allows Roby, traveling the grid according to the program, leaves a trace on the boxes, coloring them in sequence, or alternating the yes/no color states according to the programmer's instructions. The alternation of states resumes by analogy the on/off states of the computer, and therefore the possibility of passing or not passing information, almost as if it were Roby, like Tom Thumb, who "left traces" to help us communicate with him by teaching us his two-digit language. A game conceived in this way becomes a prerequisite for approaching activities to binary code, and for pixel art activities, very common in schools and used for different didactic purposes (deconration, storytelling, listening and precision training, study of coordinates...).

CODING UNPLUGGED AND VISUAL BLOCK PROGRAMMING. THE EVOLUTION OF A LANGUAGE

It is not the purpose of this chapter to go into the examination of platforms for visual block programming such as Code.org or Scratch, but simply to show how the unplugged coding games presented so far can find a natural evolution in visual block programming and they are preparatory to them both in logical terms and in terms of uniformity of language. As seen in the previous examples, in fact, the use of the CodyRoby education set naturally leads children to discover the concepts of repetition, nesting, conditional education and facilitates their use in problem solving activities.

Figure 4shows a situation of this type, in which the CodyRoby cards are flanked by a possible "move" on the chessboard and defined as a "universal move", elaborated starting from the practice with the paths of Code.org. In this class the pupils had experienced both game modes and the visual block programming language was brought to the CodyRoby playground to address a path problem. We can consider it a real "translation" between two ways of using the same language, with two different levels of abstraction and the implication of a high degree of problem solving ability (hypothesis, control of possible variables).

Figure 4.

Cody Color has found its evolution on Scratch in a game by Alessandro Bogliolo, designed especially for remixing by players, already familiar with the Scratch platform, who want to create their own game (https://scratch.mit.edu/projects/250921166_). At this level, CodyColor can be offered at the end of primary school to pupils who already know Scratch. With Scratch, in fact, you exit the games of running paths and enter the real gamification, in which the player is also the creator of the project. In this sense, Code.org can be used as a literacy to block visual programming languages and as a first creative training, as its repertoire of instructions is rather limited.

FROM CODING UNPLUGGED TO ROBOTICS

CodyRoby's set of sitructions constitutes a real programming language, equipped with simple instructions, repetition constructs, conditional instructions. It is a formally and semantically coherent and complete language.

So far it has been used in floor games, in which the roles of programmer and performer were taken by children engaged in the game. All in all, as a complete and coherent language, it can also be applied to non-human ideal performers, such as didactic robots.

Figure 5.

Figure 5 shows the application of the CodyRoby language to the programming of a BlueBot, a bee-shaped robot very common in schools, to which commands can be given by means of buttons placed on the upper part. The proposed game, in particular, was a word search game in English (as a second language) for 3rd graders (7/8 years old), facilitated by the presence of flashcards, for the strengthening and consolidation of the vocabulary.

There is an analogy between the programming mode of the BlueBots (and of the even more well-known BeeBots) and the CodyRoby cards: the programming buttons in fact give simple and univocal instructions, so that each CodyRoby card corresponds to one single pressure of a button; there is no button for repetition (the instructions must all be given, in sequence), while there is a key for moving backwards in a box, which has already been mentioned previously. A game development of this kind is possible in any age group, when children have acquired the concept of simple instruction and are able to master a programming sequence.

Figure 6.

In this last example, the pupils program a toy robot owned by the teacher, first writing the program with CodyRoby cards and then transporting it to the robotic object. The game consists of a team competition of general knowledge: the squares of the chessboard bear a colored sticker corresponding to a material. In turn, each team chooses a child who throws a dice and draws from the deck of simple instructions as many cards as indicated by the dice: with these the team writes a program of their choice starting from the square in which the robot is located (the starting square). is given by the teacher) and programs the robot. When you reach the end of program box, you must answer a question relating to the corresponding subject. The game was proposed as an activity at the beginning of the schoolyear for fourth and fifth grade students (9-11 years), with questions prepared by the teachers and related to the topics studied the previous year. A playful and fun way to carry out the initial review and prepare children for the entrance tests, at the same time resuming the ranks of a literacy path to coding started in previous years.

In this case the coding component acts as a start of the game, but it is essential to earn points (which are lost if programming errors are made) and to program the robot to arrive on the box of the desired subject, in which it is believed to have the better knowledge, or to avoid ending up on that of an unwelcome subject. At the age of 10, in most cases, the pupils show a good ability to visualize the path; they no longer proceed by trial and error, but elaborate it mentally and the writing of the program almost always takes place without hesitation.

CONCLUSION

Problem Solving, Comuptational thinking and Coding are terms that have entered the common use of teaching: the underlying constructs are closely related as they pertain to the development of those forms of human thought, analytical and procedural, which allow the individual to move in reality. With good reason, therefore, they have entered among the fundamental competences for the citizen of the 21st century, and have found space among the didactic activities in every kind of school.

The approach through a playful methodology allows children to be involved in coding activities even in preschool, as all forms of intelligence (visual, kinesthetic, logical ...) are involved and all cognitive resources are mobilized, thus favoring a natural, spontaneous and gradual learning.

In the present chapter, the author presented a possible process of literacy in computational thinking and the development of logical skills starting from three unplugged coding games, in the belief (confirmed by the didactic experience) that the game is the training and development modality more natural and pervasive cognitive for the child, and therefore can and should be used in school as an effective teaching tool that every teacher must have in their ideal "toolbox". Coding games have proved, in daily practice, not only a means of inclusiveness, motivation and interest, but an excellent tool for the development of the cognitive abilities of the students, then found directly and indirectly in the didactic experience, even if not always "measured" with statistical data.The proposal of challenging but at the same time collaborative strategy games promotes the pupils' propensity to "get involved" in the field of learning; urges them to reach thei own zone of proximal development, facilitating them in their new acquisitions; it reassures and provides positive feedback to the weakest pupils, and on the other hand it involves and empowers the more able pupils. Working on game strategies means working on thinking strategies, making them explicit, visible, and training pupils to argue them. Not only logical thinking is favored, but the entire approach to metacognition, which is fundamental for the articulation of a complete, and effective method of study and research.

REFERENCES

Bogliolo, A. (2018). *Coding in your classroom now*. Giunti.

Bruner, J. K. (1976). Play, Thought and Language. *Peabody Journal of Education, 60*(3), 60-69.

Csikszentmihalyi, M. (1990). *Flow: The Psychology of Optimal Experience*. Harper.

Farber, M. (2015). *Gamify your classroom: A field guide to game-based learning*. Peter Lang. doi:10.3726/978-1-4539-1459-5

Gardner, H. (1983). *Frames of Mind: The Theory of Multiple Intelligences*. Basic Books.

Gardner, H. (1993). *Multiple Intelligences: The Theory in Practice*. Basic Books.

Grover, S., & Pea, R. (2017). Computational Thinking: A Competency Whose Time Has Come. Computer science education: Perspectives on teaching and learning in school, 19.

Jonassen, D. H., & Hung, W. (2012). Problem Solving. In N. M. Seel (Ed.), *Encyclopedia of the Sciences of Learning*. Springer. doi:10.1007/978-1-4419-1428-6_208

Lombardi, G. (2020). The role of unplugged coding activity in developing computational thinking in ages 6-11. In Handbook of Research on tools for teaching computational thinking in P-12 education (pp.184-199). Information Science Publishing.

Mayer, R. E. (2020). Cognitive foundations of game-based learning. In J. L. Plass, R. E. Mayer, & B. D. Homer (Eds.), *Handbook of game-based learning* (pp. 83–110). The MIT Press.

Montessori, M. (1948). *The discovery of the child*. Kalakshetra.

Papert, S. (1980). *Mindstorms: Children, computers, and powerful ideas*. Basic Books.

Piaget, J. (1951). *Play, dreams and imitation in childhood*. Heinemann.

Piaget, J. (1953). *Origins of intelligence in the child*. Routledge & Kegan Paul.

Piaget, J. (1954). *Construction of reality in the child*. Routledge & Kegan Paul. doi:10.1037/11168-000

Steinmaurer, A., Pirker, J., & Christian, G. (2020). sCool - Game Based Learning in STEM Education: A Case Study in Secondary Education. *The Challenges of the Digital Transformation in Education, 917,* 614–625. doi:10.1007/978-3-030-11932-4_58

Vygotsky, L. (1966). Igra i ee rol v umstvennom razvitii rebenka [Play and its role in the mental development of the child]. *Voprosy Psihologii, 12*(6), 62–76.

Wing, J. M. (2006). Computational Thinking. *Communications of the ACM, 49*(3), 33-35. https://www.cs.cmu.edu/~15110-s13/Wing06-ct.pdf

Wing, J. M. (2008). Computational thinking and thinking about computing. *Philosophical Transactions Series A, Mathematical, Physical, and Engineering Sciences, 366,* 3717-25. . doi:10.1098/rsta.2008.0118

ADDITIONAL READING

Grover, S. (2018). *The 5th 'C' of 21st Century Skills? Try Computational Thinking (Not Coding).* EdSurge.

Papadakis, S., Kalogiannakis, M., Orfanakis, V., & Zaranis, N. (2016). Using Scratch and App Inventor for teaching introductory programming in secondary education. A case study. *Int.J. Technol. Enhanced Learn.*, *8*(3/4), 217–233. doi:10.1504/IJTEL.2016.082317

Papadakis, S., Kalogiannakis, M., Orfanakis, V., & Zaranis, N. (2017). The appropriateness of Scratch and App Inventor as educational environments for teaching introductory programming in primary and secondary education. *International Journal of Web-Based Learning and Teaching Technologies*, *12*(4), 58–77. doi:10.4018/IJWLTT.2017100106

Plass, J. L., Mayer, R. E., & Homer, B. D. (2020). *Handbook of Game-Based Learning.* MIT University Press.

Resnick, M. (2017). *Lifelong kindergaten: cultivating creativity through projects, passions, peers and play.* MIT Press. doi:10.7551/mitpress/11017.001.0001

Wing, J. M. (2008). Five deep questions in computing. *Communications of the ACM*, *51*(1), 58–60. doi:10.1145/1327452.1327479

Wing, J. M. (2011). *Computational thinking: What and why.* The Link. Retrieved from https://www.cs.cmu.edu/link/research-notebook-computational-thinking-what-and-why

KEY TERMS AND DEFINITIONS

Coding Unplugged: Coding activities, mainly of a playful nature, which do not involve the use of technological devices.

Computational Thinking: Cognitive tool that uses the fundamental concepts of computer science and programming to solve problems, define systems and understand human behavior.

Logical Skills: Skill set that enable to reason logically when posing or solving problems, improving the ability to provide well-reasoned answers to any issues and to make rational decisions.

Multiple Intelligences: Different ways students learn and acquire information. These multiple intelligences range from the use of words, numbers, pictures and music, to the importance of social interactions, introspection, physical movement and being in tune with nature.

Robotics: In the didactic field, use of programmable objects with a playful purpose for the development of computational thinking.

Zone of Proximal Development: In Vygotskji's theory of development, it's the space between what the child can learn on his own and what he can learn under adult supervision.

Chapter 36
Discrete Primary Education Curriculum in Bangladesh:
Implications of Gamification for Quality Education

Md Jahangir Alam
https://orcid.org/0000-0001-6312-5685
University of Dhaka, Bangladesh

Sheikh Rashid Bin Islam
Bangladesh Consulting Services, Bangladesh

Keiichi Ogawa
Kobe University, Japan

ABSTRACT

The curriculum is an essential and integral part of the education system for lifelong learning and better children's outcomes. The sum of experience throughout their schooling journey can be defined as an educational curriculum expressed in a much broader sense. The school's type of school, study materials used, teaching methods, available school facilities, and the qualifications of schoolteachers provided at the end of primary schooling often diverge with different educational curricula due to the government policy dilemma. There is no unified primary education curriculum in Bangladesh's case. More than three mainstream educational curricula can be founded, each with its own unique set of traits, benefits, and shortcomings. This chapter explores what factors affect a school's choice, which is linked with the educational curriculum being offered, and how it affects the student's quality of education. This chapter also explores gamification theory's implementation to ensure quality primary education in Bangladesh.

DOI: 10.4018/978-1-7998-7271-9.ch036

INTRODUCTION

Education has always been credited with helping to minimize population growth, decrease maternal mortality, promote agricultural production, increase labor force participation, and most importantly, promote democratization (Yunus & Shahana, 2018). Bangladesh has made significant progress in education by increasing access to primary educational services, boosting primary school enrollment, and raising the country's overall literacy rate. Despite the development, inequality exists in education due to the difference in the quality of education caused by the discrete primary education curriculums. In Bangladesh, there is no unified educational curriculum that is solely monitored and managed by the country's Ministry of Education (MoE). The government's negligence has created the opportunity for multiple primary education curriculums to arise in the country, each of which follows its own set of guidelines and is often not monitored. Lack of monitoring can cause inequality in terms of quality of education and access to freedom of school choice due to financial limitations of parents, as the institutes following different educational curriculums set their fees freely (Mousumi & Kusakabe, 2017). This difference in the quality of education and feasibility of studying in a particular primary school due to the different curriculums can cause significant inequality (Genoni et al., 2019) and might have different implications for children. The socio-economic conditions of parents and gendered differences are similarly related to the discrete primary education curriculum issues (Asadullah & Chaudhury, 2015). In Bangladesh, wealth is a deciding factor for the quality of educations in the present society. The different education curriculum is making inequality for impoverished students (Parvin & Haider, 2012). While comparing all the comparative implications of the different educational curriculums and the scope of Gamification could be implemented to increase the overall quality of primary education (Surendeleg et al., 2014). It is a digitalized concept that can bring historical change to the present education system not only of Bangladesh but of the whole world. Gamification can engage students more into studies and unify the education curricula by offering a single method of interactive education delivery (Dicheva et al., 2015). Hence, this chapter showcases the implications, benefits, and downsides of having a diverse primary educational curriculum in Bangladesh, as well as, the scope of the theory of Gamification in implementing quality primary education.

BACKGROUND AND CONTEMPORARY STATE OF THE PRIMARY EDUCATION CURRICULUM IN BANGLADESH

In 1974, the first Education Commission in Bangladesh was formed and constituted by Dr. Qudrat-e-Khuda. After that, in 1978, a new Advisory Committee was formed to take a fresh look at education's difficulties and concerns. During the mid-1990s, the education system and curriculum were overhauled once more (MoE, 2004). Bangladesh's education system and curriculum endured final reform in 2009, laying down the foundation for the current primary educational curriculum through the final draft of the National Education Policy 2009 (MoE, 2010).

Table 1 shows the school types and management mechanisms in Bangladesh. The schools are divided into two groups as the mainstream and outside the mainstream. Almost all the types of facilities are available in both the rural and urban areas in Bangladesh. Schools among the types used to follow the government-decided curriculum, but the schools are hardly monitored in practice and do not follow the government's instruction. Bangladesh's current educational system is essentially a legacy of the British colonial era (Blunch & Das, 2015). It is characterized by the conjunction of three distinct streams that run parallel to one another. The mainstream is a vernacular-based secular education system that dates back to the colonial era. There is also a separate religious, educational system. As a result of English as a medium of instruction, another stream of education, fashioned after the British school system and employing the same curriculum, has sprung up in Bangladesh's major cities, especially its capital Dhaka. Chowdhury and Sarkar (2018) explained the differences between general education and religious education in Bangladesh. This difference contributed to existences of different educational curriculums (Nath & Choudhury, 2019).

Table 1. School types and mechanism of primary education in bangladesh

Mainstream (Formal)	Outside Mainstream (Non-Formal)
1. State-owned Schools	1. Non-formal Primary Schools-NGOs or Centers
2. Non-State Schools-Registered non-Governmental Primary Schools (RNGPS)	2. Madrassa (Mainly Ebtedayee known as Ebtedayee Madrassas, Quomi Madrassa and attached with High Madrassas)
3. Community Schools and Others, i.e., High School attached, satellite. 4. Experimental Schools (each district at Primary Training Institute)	3. Kindergartens (KG)-generally the Private Fee Charging Schools

Source: Created by the Authors based on DPE (2019)

Haque and Akter (2013) categorized the education system namely: Bangla Medium, English Version, Madrassa education, and English Medium. English Medium schools offer slightly better facilities and follow the western education system and curriculum. While Madrassa education is more leaned towards religious education and often skipped essential education and the general standard of education, this curriculum is widely selected by the financially challenged families in Bangladesh. English medium being the most expensive, while Madrasa education is often at the bottom. The school types and choice of school exist due to financial availability and lack of government intervention (Mousumi & Kusakabe, 2017; Parvin & Alam, 2016). However, the current curriculum and structure do not allow the scope of learning through physical or computer games. However, if learning such methods were present it can increase students' engagement, eagerness, and overall learning. Figure 1 determines the risk factors related to the medial and final outcome due to Bangladesh's discrete primary education curriculum.

Primary education is now a fundamental human right and is well recognized by the MoE of Bangladesh. This recognition led the country to secure more than 90 percent attendance at primary schools and achieved greater gender parity through implementing the Bangladesh Primary Education (Compulsory) Act of 1990, which required all citizens to have compulsory and free primary education (Mehtab, 2019). Additionally, this encouraged the country to shift its focus to improving the quality of education (Sommers, 2013). Figure 2 indicates the details of the primary education system and management in Bangladesh. Bangladesh government provides one of the world's most extensive primary education management in terms of enrolling children. Furthermore, the figure shows the top-down school management system of primary education in Bangladesh.

Figure 1. Factors and outcomes of discrete primary education curriculum
Source: *Created by the authors based on Huang and Soman, 2013.*

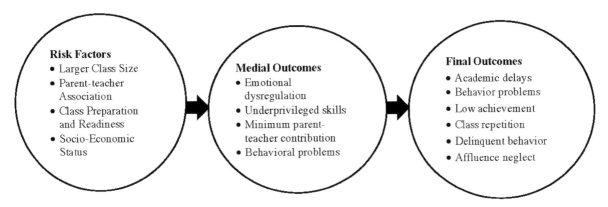

Figure 2. Primary education system in Bangladesh
Source: *Created by the authors based on DPE, 2019.*
Note: *DG-Director General; DPE-Directorate of Primary Education; DPEO-District Primary Education Officer; MOE-Ministry of Education; NFPE-Non-Formal Primary Education; PTA-Parent-Teacher Association; SMC-School Management Committee; UEO-Upazila Education Officer.*

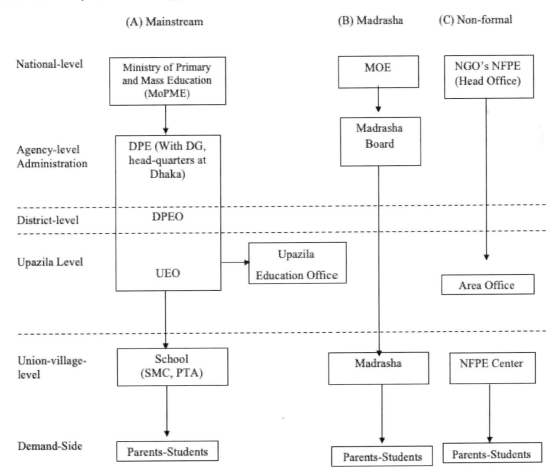

Despite important achievements in ensuring the enrollment rate of primary education in Bangladesh, these are often undermined by the financial restrictions due to the absence of monetary moderateness of parents (Khan et al., 2014). Insolvent parents often need to enlist their children in schools following education curriculums that may not be their best option, henceforth restricting their decision of education curriculum and choice of school (Alam, 2020). There is no obvious indicator or measurement to rank or score the available educational curriculums; it would also be irrational to criticize one education curriculum over the other.

Because of reduced financial costs and government-backed subsidies, the Bangla medium and Madrassa education are more accessible because the government set low school fees. These two educational curricula are strongly result-oriented and leave out essential subjects for primary education, undermining the quality of education. Numerous parents consider the English version and English medium to be following international standards and focusing more on the growth of students. Unfortunately, as they do not have any government fee guidelines, these educational settings are expensive, and due to the financial restrictions, many parents cannot afford them (Kader & Salam, 2018). Here, it makes one wonder, will a unified instructive education curriculum be the answer for eradicating the disparity and ensuring the quality of education.

THEORETICAL FRAMEWORK OF PRIMARY EDUCATION CURRICULUM IN BANGLADESH

Sylva et al. (2010) refine the significance of the primary education curriculum, as most children go into a very long process of pedagogy. The primary educational curriculum lays the groundwork for students to be reinforced and worked upon to advance to higher education. Consequently, the implication of the primary education curriculum is of most extreme significance, as without quality education, students will struggle and will not be able to grasp and utilize the knowledge at a higher level properly. The country's development and education are interlaced, and for a country to flourish and develop, it must put necessary budget resources into education. High emphasis should be on the primary education curriculum, where all starts to shape (Peters et al., 2006). Students' socio-economic condition determines their ability to afford and enroll in any particular primary education curriculum. The students' achievements, objectives, and encouragement are highly influenced based on the enrolled primary education curriculum. Despite multiple pre-enrollment control variables, education curriculum placement has a considerable impact on educational performance in the primary and high school years (Chowdhury, 2010).

Additionally, Mølstad (2015) analyzes a single, unified education curriculum of Norway and Finland. He expresses that a single, unified educational curriculum would diminish disparity and imbalance like the quality of education and allow governments to manage it in more detail. In America, the education curriculum is constantly enhanced by educational reforms. Educations reforms refer to some tests on the students and other related matters to the educational curriculum (Seixas et al., 2016). Alongside a unified educational curriculum or even multiple education curriculum, the introduction of the Theory of Gamification, which involves the engagement of students through the use of video game attributes in non-video game contexts such as education, has proven to be very effective in practical use (Hamari et al., 2014). This theoretical framework suggests that the primary education curriculum is vital for building education and the country's foundation. In addition, a single, unified educational curriculum might be more appropriate, yet it may not be conceivable in all conditions. In such cases, gamification can reduce imbalance and improve the overall quality of primary education in Bangladesh through providing a unified education delivery method that may be as effective or more as a unified educational curriculum.

REIMAGINE THE PRIMARY EDUCATION CURRICULUM THROUGH THE THEORY OF GAMIFICATION

Due to the COVID-19 pandemic, most educational institutes are in peril around the globe, forcing them to shutter; most educational institutions, including primary educational institutes, have moved to online education to keep academic activities alive. Online education is becoming more popular as access to the internet becomes more widespread, and unavoidable circumstances increase the restrictions on physically decimating primary education (Muthuprasad et al., 2021). However, this new form of education has both strengths and weaknesses. Regarding student motivation, well-being, and intercommunication, the online learning environment is vastly different from the typical classroom setting (Bignoux & Sund, 2018). Online education limits interaction and collaboration with teachers and students, and in most cases, cannot reproduce the physical classroom environment (Miller, 2013).

Gamification is the most recent accumulation in the field of education. However, there is a long tradition of using proactive engagement to motivate people and make education more enjoyable (Oyshi et al., 2018; Brull & Finlayson, 2016). The origins of gamification may be traced back to the late 1890s. In the nineteenth century, gamification began to spread its branches, and in the 1990s, it began to take on new dimensions (Stott & Neustaedter, 2013). Finally, in the twentieth century, it was dubbed Gamification, which gained traction and was being accepted by a growing number of people in academia. Kiryakova et al. (2014) talked about how gamification might help with inculcation. Moreover, Huang and Soman (2013) discussed the necessary scholastic approach and strategy for increasing motivation and involvement in the learning process.

The Community of Inquiry paradigm is a valuable beginning point for developing an accessible education platform, including primary education. It claims that building a students' group is the key to resolving pedagogy destroyed by online education platforms (Mou, 2016). Through three interdependent components, learning in this connection is akin to learning in a traditional classroom setting: social presence, cognitive presence, and instructional presence. Here, gamification theory can play a crucial role by providing online education equally as effective as a traditional class because it is well-designed (Landers, 2014).

Children are particularly attracted to visual and colorful objects. They also like interaction and storytelling. Due to these, video games are prevalent among children. As a result, by employing gamification in primary education curriculums for delivering class, children can be engaged to learn and achieve mastery. These unique and interactive game element designs and characteristics can provide a considerably more learning and inspirational environment beyond the education available in the physical classrooms (Roy & Zaman, 2018).

Because gamification is essential and online education is becoming more widespread, it is critical to consider the extent to which gamification can be implemented in all types of educational systems (Hamari et al., 2014; Urh et al., 2015). Bangladesh has a variety of educational curricula. Each of them has a varied level of educational quality, resulting in a disparity. This mismatch could be remedied by introducing gamification, which will ensure that all students receive the same level of education through unifying educational delivery. Gamification is achievable because the learning outcomes of various educational curricula are the same. As a result, primary education will be more uniform and of outstanding quality across all primary education curriculums.

QUALITY EDUCATION AND CURRICULUM: A GLOBAL AGENDA

Halinen (2018) and Airaksinen et al. (2016) recent works also center around primary education curriculums. Only a couple of countries have different historical, social, etymological, religious, and strict impacts as Bangladesh. In this way, it is exceptionally uncommon to discover four unique and assorted primary education curriculums in a country. Accordingly, most literature reviews to date have not effectively depicted the dissimilarity and imbalance that can be brought about by contrasts in primary education curriculum and limited school choices because of the absence of monetary limits.

Several educational roadblocks have hindered progress thus far. Education in Bangladesh has long suffered from a lack of a cohesive curriculum. A single-focus curriculum endeavor and numerous recommendations have been offered. In Bangladesh, students' memorization power is highly evaluated by primary schools and directed mainly by the curriculum. Other areas of academic performance are hardly appreciated as the curriculum follows the rote learning system, and educational evaluation, composition, and appraisal is rarely assessed (Begum & Farooqui, 2008).

Furthermore, the assessment methodology excludes key crucial traits because relying on memorizing skills causes limited social contribution. To address the issues, the holistic development of ambitious learners is inevitable through school-based assessment (Ahsan et al., 2012). Promoting inclusion and inclusive education has been acknowledged as critical for developing nations to provide education for all during the previous decades. Due to Bangladesh's position as a developing country, the nation focuses on different programs such as legislative reform, public awareness, and teacher development to alleviate poverty (Malak, 2013). As a result, education and development have a well-established positive relationship.

Recently, as the popularity of online education has increased, the trendy expression Gamification is on the ascent, and much examination has been done to affirm its capability. A few institutions regularly use gamification in parallel with typical forms of education; most institutions report that gamification is very effective. According to Klock et al. (2020), gamification can motivate and engage students while maintaining a high learning quality. Simultaneously, it can raise educational standards by promoting mastery and lifelong learning. If the educational program is properly organized, gamification may transform how we look at the primary education curriculum in the future (Martí-Parreño et al., 2016; Sailer & Homner, 2020). This chapter will contribute to academia by addressing how to unified primary education curriculum might result in improved quality of education and reduced disparities; simultaneously, by addressing how the correct gamification application may contribute to a similar or better effect.

IMPLICATION OF PRIMARY EDUCATION CURRICULUM IN BANGLADESH

Bangladesh's progress in the education sector, especially in primary education, is commendable. In just half a century, the country has achieved remarkable results, but issues still need to be addressed. The lack of a coherent primary education curriculum is one of several issues that are frequently ignored. The availability of different primary educational curriculum is not necessarily a detriment; when it produces divergences and is ignored, it becomes a barrier for quality education (Young, 2014). The presence of different primary education curriculum, the majority of which heavily focus on grades rather than the quality of learning, is the main reason why Bangladesh has not scored higher on international standardized tests compared to leading OECD countries. Due to financial constraints and a lack of school choice, most people cannot access curriculums that focus on the quality of learning (Alam, 2019).

Subsequently, this chapter presents the disparity and inequality caused by different primary educational curriculums. Simultaneously, this chapter hopes to showcase the idea of the Theory of Gamification, which incorporates games in education (Landers, 2014). This chapter illustrates the possibility of unifying the instructive primary education curriculum and essentially improving the quality of education by implementing gamification in the primary education curriculums in Bangladesh.

This chapter was conducted through qualitative research, using the case study approach, which is exploratory. However, this case study research has taken an essential to explain a specific phenomenon, which might not be similar to other situations, contexts, or perspectives. Several cases were selected in considering the diverse school types in Bangladesh to understand the implication of different education curricula and possible Gamification theory's effect for further policy implementation in Bangladesh.

Further, this chapter is to understand the possible phenomena of the discrete curriculum in Bangladesh's primary school education, and this methodology was adopted to understand the discrete formal and non-formal primary education curriculum in Bangladesh. Through an interview with the schoolteachers and parents with children studying in primary schools to understand the supply and demand-side intervention to explain the discrete curriculum in Bangladesh. The school headteachers and teachers, parents were the unit of analysis for this study. Fifteen schools were chosen based on a purposive sampling of five types of primary schools in Bangladesh. Further, 15 parents with children studying in class were interviewed based on snowball sampling to understand Bangladesh's discrete primary education curriculum and its consequences for a child learning at the primary level. Primary and secondary data sources were used to conduct this study; the authors used two tools to collect the data: in-depth questionnaire interviews and document review.

FINDINGS OF THE STUDY

Human behaviors are linked to improving their socio-economic condition to contribute to society, and educational advancement is unavoidable. When it comes to their child's education, parents emphasize socio-economic factors. This study adds to the growing body of knowledge that social realities, rather than curriculum, significantly impact parents' school selections for their children.

First, this chapter revealed that the school curriculum is the most significant impediment to enrolling in Bangladeshi schools. Because most parents cannot afford to pay for their children's high tuition fees for the diverse curriculum offered by the schools, they are obliged to enroll their children in government primary schools.

Second, access, rights, equity, and self-determination for children's education are all dependent on parental capacities and realities. Parental involvement in their children's education is dependent primarily on government funding policies to ensure social justice in education and increase child equity. This study finds that institutional justice is deemed more important than ensuring an identical curriculum for all pupils, regardless of their parents' socio-economic circumstances. Many Parents emphasized that, although schools were required to follow the government curriculum, many schools did not and pushed their students to follow different curriculums.

Third, high socio-economic conditions determined children's school preparation in developed countries, with a heavy emphasis on the curriculum. This study revealed that children's school preparation is influenced by their parents' engagement with them in Bangladesh, particularly private tutoring. A diverse curriculum has hindered children's education unless parents arrange for private tutoring for their children. Furthermore, due to Bangladesh's diversified primary curriculum, children's school readiness is linked to private tutoring. Gamification theory has the potential to play a significant role in Bangladesh's primary education development. Because most teachers are not properly trained, the school curriculum is mostly used to educate as a rote learning approach, and gamification in learning is not viable. Furthermore, the current curriculum in Bangladesh's primary schools does not follow gamification rules for teaching pupils.

Fourth, gender and vulnerability have an important impact on parents' decisions about their children's education at the primary level. Due to gender inequalities in primary schooling, parents are more inclined to pay for boys' private tutoring than girls. Moreover, religious grounds also played an important role in selecting supplementary private tutoring for their children due to curriculum diversity.

Finally, gamification in education could benefit primary school students. Parents from indigenous communities and socio-economic conditions confront challenges in their children's education during the early stages of primary school because of cultural variety. Because of the increased student-teacher ratio (1:45), most schools do not give adequate time. Furthermore, most parents indicated that the curriculum followed by the schools is repetitive for the children to learn to improve in the future. Parents also believe that schools' curricula should emphasize their children's development of socio-emotional and practical abilities. Table 2 interprets the school types to explain the demand and supply-side issues related to discrete curriculum, denoting that child has a limited scope to learn from school due to discrete curriculum and poor school management. In most cases, the school does not follow gamification, which helps children learn proactively and engages all the children in academic activities.

DISCUSSIONS

The purpose of primary education is to ensure that students develop in various ways, ensuring that they may maximize their cognitive, social, emotional, cultural, and physical talents while preparing them for their school careers (Sallis, 2014). Bangladesh's education system is well acknowledged to be severely disadvantaged. The government placed a strong priority on education to ensure universal access to school, where a significant portion of the budget should be allocated to develop educational improvement (Töremen et al., 2009). However, Bangladesh's educational system has several issues, likely low primary school performances and dropouts are caused by the economic condition of parents, school environment, school lunch, malnutrition, larger class size, teachers training, shortage, and coordination among parents and schoolteachers (Hasan et al., 2018).

Parents make schooling decisions mostly in contexts where the available options are less than ideal. 70 percent of students are enrolled in the primary school attended government or non-governmental organization (NGO) schools, with a minority attending madrasas and private schools. Half of all school-aged youngsters received private tuition in addition to their regular school sessions. Children from wealthier families with more educated parents were more likely to attend school and participate in a private school. However, proximity and the variety of schools available were also considered (Cameron, 2011).

Table 2. Discrete curriculum matrix in primary school class one in Bangladesh

School Types	Demand Side Intervention and Outcome	Supply Side Intervention and Outcomes
Government Primary Schools	a) Long class hours without active learning engagement. However, parents believe that learning through play might be helpful for their children, but the schools do not have the facilities to meet all the parent's demands. b) School lunch facilities are primarily unavailable. c) Difficulties in engaging learning for the lower- and middle-income group of people. d) The discrete curriculum needs private tutoring assistance to prepare for the school. e) In most cases, students are not appropriate ages and high absent rate among the government primary schools. f) Government primary school is the last choice of parents for their child schooling.	a) In most cases, the government education administration hardly monitors the school to address the curriculum and learning outcome issues. b) There are no standard rules to follow, and most of the schools are run by internal management except the government primary schools. c) There is no student-centric learning orientation, and mostly, teachers follow the rote memorization framework. d) Pre-service teacher training is not possible due to the shortage of teachers at government primary schools. e) Training should be organized based on the need-based assessment and standardized to the curriculum. f) Teachers' qualifications and standards are not met in most cases, although the government has specific teacher recruitment rules.
Private Primary Schools and English Medium Schools	a) Mainly, the upper-income parent enrolls their children in English medium schools. b) Middle-income group of parents chooses the private schools as the priority. c) Specific school uniforms are strictly followed, and school meals are not a concern for the parents as most children bring meals from home. d) Comparatively lower-class size in comparison with the government primary schools	a) School management committees are found more active in schooling issues. Although the teachers are not trained and received any formal training, they only have the opportunity for in-service school training. b) The schools followed many supplementary curriculums to attract enrollment in their school. c) In most cases, parents from lower-income groups could not enroll their children due to excess tuition fees, especially the English medium schools.
Primary Education in Madrassa (Aliya and Quomi)	a) The lower-income group of parents and primarily orphan children enroll in Madrassa. b) Parents with more religions believe in enrolling their children for holistic gain. c) Children enrolled mostly stay at boarding facilities, and d) Most of the students are not living with their parents.	a) Teachers are not trained at all, and they hardly follow the curriculum of the government curriculum. b) In most cases, the Madrassa does not follow standard books to teach their students lifelong learning. c) Parents also confined those children with lower ability mostly enroll in Madrassa. d) Most of the curriculum is religious-based. Madrassa used to follow the Qur'an and religious curriculum where additional social skills hardly developed.
Community Primary Schools	a) Primarily available in the rural areas. b) Parents are on the hard poverty lines to provide their children with educational support. Parental income does not meet the criteria for a child's schooling. c) Children have been highly affected by malnutrition since childhood.	a) Primarily, the teachers are not well trained. b) Teachers do not have the skills to teach government curriculum for children's lifelong learning and social skills development c) Parents talked about the quality in the rural areas, Madrassas are the best option for child development due to broken family's economic condition.
NGOs Primary Schools	a) The classes are conducted per the parent's demand and flexible when family members manage times to bring their children to school. b) In most cases, the dropout children and children with particular needs participate in NGO schools. c) Larger class size and most of the students are needed special attention	a) Teachers are not trained at all. b) Teachers are usually recruited locally with very minimum education qualifications to teach children. c) The schools mainly do not impose any expenses, but they charge the school fees to continue students learning due to the growing demand. d) The school environment is not amicable for the students.

Source: Created by the Authors based on Field Study.

Equitable access to education requires more than equal opportunities; it also means offering additional and specialized help to the most marginalized and impoverished students. Equity in education demands measures to ensure that well-targeted programs overcome specific populations' educational barriers. While equal access to education is a heated concern in the United States, it is primarily a physical access issue for underprivileged students in Bangladesh (Lewin, 2007). They result in most government interventions focusing on meeting the family's material and financial requirements rather than on the fundamental learning of the children. The specific types of school assistance that disadvantaged children need are neither identified nor provided (Hossain & Zeitlyn, 2010).

Children are currently very engaged in gaming and related learning activities. Gamification is used extensively in the education sector in many nations across the world. The primary school system in Bangladesh is based on academic teaching, which is not appealing to children who are continuously looking for excitement. The government could not integrate gamification into the primary education curriculum, which may have had a significant impact on the country's future prosperity (Oyshi et al., 2018).

In Bangladesh, the primary education system is highly diverse, with no single balanced and widely followed curriculum. Government schools provide students with some basic knowledge that is not as developed as private school curriculums. The differences in curriculum make a significant impact on the quality of schooling (Ahmed, 2010). In comparison to English medium schools, government and NGO schools are unable to provide high-quality primary education. This lack of consistency in the educational curriculum is creating an unstable situation for disadvantaged students. Competing against private school students becomes complicated with their weak educational skills, often evident in most competitive exams, including public examinations.

CONCLUSION

It has been established that the government's education ministry does not have complete authority and oversight over all the primary education curriculums in Bangladesh. School choice is frequently influenced by the cost of schooling and the quality of education provided, which are determined by the education curriculum. Variations in educational quality and the feasibility of studying at a specific school due to diverse educational curricula could be a significant source of disparity with a variety of implications. A diverse educational curriculum has been developed to compensate for the lack of a unified educational system, resulting in an unequal educational environment for impoverished families. The lack of government intervention in primary education and the lack of oversight in government primary schools are also important factors in creating a discrete education curriculum. Gamification can play a vital role in improving the quality of education for all types of primary education curricula as online education and the use of technology in education becomes more prevalent. Because the learning outcomes of all curriculums are the same, the education delivery of all curriculums may be offered through a single medium using gamification. Gamification can provide students with new ways to learn that are both visually appealing and participatory. Gamification in education encourages students to think more critically while also being more motivated to engage in learning. If implemented effectively, game-based learning, such as gamification, can dramatically improve educational quality, mastery, and life-long learning. As a result, incorporating Gamification into Bangladesh's primary education curriculum would significantly reduce inequality and improve overall educational quality.

REFERENCES

Ahsan, M. T., Sharma, U., & Deppeler, J. M. (2012). Challenges to prepare pre-service teachers for inclusive education in Bangladesh: Beliefs of higher educational institutional heads. *Asia Pacific Journal of Education*, *32*(2), 241–257. doi:10.1080/02188791.2012.655372

Airaksinen, T., Halinen, I., & Linturi, H. (2016). Futuribles of learning 2030 - Delphi supports the reform of the core curricula in Finland. *European Journal of Futures Research*, *5*(1), 2. doi:10.100740309-016-0096-y

Alam, M. J. (2019). Dilemma of Parental Aspiration for Children with Special Needs in Early Childhood Education (ECE) Settings: The Case of Bangladesh. *Asia-Pacific Journal of Research in Early Childhood Education*, *13*(3), 25–43. doi:10.17206/apjrece.2019.13.3.25

Alam, M. J. (2020). Who Chooses School? Understanding Parental Aspirations for Child Transition from Home to Early Childhood Education (ECE) Institutions in Bangladesh. In S. Tatalović Vorkapić & J. LoCasale-Crouch (Eds.), *Supporting Children's Well-Being During Early Childhood Transition to School* (pp. 85–107). IGI Global. doi:10.4018/978-1-7998-4435-8

Asadullah, M., & Chaudhury, N. (2015). The Dissonance between schooling and learning: Evidence from rural Bangladesh. *Comparative Education Review*, *59*(3), 447–472. doi:10.1086/681929

Begum, M., & Farooqui, S. (2008). School based assessment: Will it really change the education scenario in Bangladesh? *International Education Studies*, *1*(2), 45–53. doi:10.5539/ies.v1n2p45

Bignoux, S., & Sund, K. J. (2018). Tutoring executives online: What drives perceived quality? *Behaviour & Information Technology*, *37*(7), 703–713. doi:10.1080/0144929X.2018.1474254

Blunch, N. H., & Das, M. B. (2015). Changing norms about gender inequality in education: Evidence from Bangladesh. *Demographic Research*, *32*(6), 183–218. doi:10.4054/DemRes.2015.32.6

Brull, S., & Finlayson, S. (2016). Importance of gamification in increasing learning. *Journal of Continuing Education in Nursing*, *47*(8), 372–375. doi:10.3928/00220124-20160715-09 PMID:27467313

Cameron, S. (2011). Whether and where to enroll? Choosing a primary school in the slums of urban Dhaka, Bangladesh. *International Journal of Educational Development*, *31*(4), 357–366. doi:10.1016/j.ijedudev.2011.01.004

Chowdhury, F. D. (2010). Dowry, women, and law in Bangladesh. *International Journal of Law, Policy and the Family*, *24*(2), 198–221. doi:10.1093/lawfam/ebq003

Chowdhury, R., & Sarkar, M. (2018). Education in Bangladesh: Changing contexts and emerging realities. In R. Chowdhury, M. Sarkar, F. Mojumder, & M. M. Roshid (Eds.), *Engaging in Educational Research: Revisiting Policy and Practice in Bangladesh* (Vol. 44, pp. 1–18). Springer. doi:10.1007/978-981-13-0708-9_1

Dicheva, D., Dichev, C., Agre, G., & Angelova, G. (2015). Gamification in education: A systematic mapping study. *Journal of Educational Technology & Society*, *18*(3), 75–88. https://www.jstor.org/stable/jeductechsoci.18.3.75

Genoni, M., Bhatta, S., & Sharma, U. (2019). Equity in education outcomes and spending in Bangladesh: Evidence from household income and expenditure surveys. *Bangladesh Development Studies*, *42*(2/3), 217–262. https://www.jstor.org/stable/27031112

Halinen, I. (2018). The new educational curriculum in Finland. In M. Matthes, L. Pulkkinen, C. Clouder, & B. Heys (Eds.), *Improving the quality of childhood in Europe* (Vol. 7, pp. 75–89). Alliance for Childhood European Network Foundation. https://www.allianceforchildhood.eu/files/Improving_the_quality_of_Childhood_Vol_7/QOC%20V7%20CH06%20DEF%20WEB.pdf

Hamari, J., Koivisto, J., & Sarsa, H. (2014). Does gamification work? A literature review of empirical studies on gamification. *2014 47th Hawaii International Conference on System Sciences*, 3025-3034. 10.1109/HICSS.2014.377

Haque, M. S., & Akter, T. (2013). Cultural imperialism in English medium schools: A critical insight. *Stamford Journal of English*, *7*, 98–128. doi:10.3329je.v7i0.14468

Hasan, K., Islam, M. S., Shams, A. T., & Gupta, H. (2018). Total quality management (TQM): Implementation in primary education system of Bangladesh. *International Journal of Research in Industrial Engineering*, *7*(3), 370–380. doi:10.22105/RIEJ.2018.128170.1041

Hossain, A., & Zeitlyn, B. (2010). *Poverty, equity and access to education in Bangladesh.* CREATE. https://files.eric.ed.gov/fulltext/ED517693.pdf

Huang, W. H. Y., & Soman, D. (2013). Gamification of education. *Report Series: Behavioural Economics in Action, 29.*

Kader, M. A., & Salam, M. A. (2018). A comprehensive study on service quality and satisfaction level to the English medium education system in Bangladesh. *International Journal of Contemporary Research and Review*, *9*(7), 20850–20866. doi:10.15520/ijcrr/2018/9/07/541

Khan, M. N. U., Rana, E. A., & Haque, M. R. (2014). Reforming the education system in Bangladesh: Reckoning a knowledge-based society. *World Journal of Education*, *4*(4), 1–11. doi:10.5430/wje.v4n4p1

Kiryakova, G., Angelova, N., & Yordanova, L. (2014). Gamification in education. *Proceedings of 9th International Balkan Education and Science Conference.*

Klock, A. C. T., Gasparini, I., Pimenta, M. S., & Hamari, J. (2020). Tailored gamification: A review of literature. *International Journal of Human-Computer Studies*, *144*, 102495. Advance online publication. doi:10.1016/j.ijhcs.2020.102495

Landers, R. N. (2014). Developing a theory of gamified learning: Linking serious games and gamification of learning. *Simulation & Gaming*, *45*(6), 752–768. doi:10.1177/1046878114563660

Lewin, K. M. (2007). *Improving access, equity and transitions in Education: Creating a research agenda.* Centre for International Education. http://www.create-rpc.org/pdf_documents/PTA1.pdf

Malak, M. S. (2013). Inclusive education in Bangladesh: Are pre-service teachers ready to accept students with special educational needs in regular classes? *Disability, CBR and Inclusive Development*, *24*(1), 56–81. doi:10.5463/dcid.v24i1.191

Martí-Parreño, J., Seguí-Mas, D., & Seguí-Mas, E. (2016). Teachers' attitude towards and actual use of gamification. *Procedia: Social and Behavioral Sciences, 228*, 682–688. doi:10.1016/j.sbspro.2016.07.104

Mehtab, F. H. (2019). *Constitutional responsibility of the Government of Bangladesh for implementing compulsory primary education: Issues and challenges* [Doctoral dissertation, University of Dhaka]. Dhaka University Institutional Repository.

Miller, C. (2013). The gamification of education. *Developments in Business Simulation and Experiential Learning, 40*. https://absel-ojs-ttu.tdl.org/absel/index.php/absel/article/view/40/38

Ministry of Education Bangladesh (MoE). (2004). *National Education Commission Report 2003*. http://lib.banbeis.gov.bd/pdf_view.php?book=National%20education%20Commission%20report-2003.pdf

Ministry of Education Bangladesh (MoE). (2010). National. *Educational Policy, 2010*. https://moedu.gov.bd/sites/default/files/files/moedu.portal.gov.bd/page/ad5cfca5_9b1e_4c0c_a4eb_fb1ded9e2fe5/National%20Education%20Policy%202010%20final.pdf

Mølstad, C. E. (2015). State-based curriculum-making: Approaches to local curriculum work in Norway and Finland. *Journal of Curriculum Studies, 47*(4), 441–461. doi:10.1080/00220272.2015.1039067

Mou, S. (2016). Possibilities and challenges of ICT integration in the Bangladesh education system. *Educational Technology, 56*(2), 50–53. http://www.jstor.org/stable/44430461

Mousumi, M. A., & Kusakabe, T. (2017). Proliferating English-Medium schools in Bangladesh and their educational significance among the "Clientele". *Journal of International Development and Co-operation, 23*(1), 1–13. https://ir.lib.hiroshima-u.ac.jp/files/public/4/42488/20170215110511630423/JIDC_23-1_1.pdf

Muthuprasad, T., Aiswarya, S., Aditya, K. S., & Jha, G. K. (2021). Students' perception and preference for online education in India during COVID-19 pandemic. *Social Sciences & Humanities Open, 3*(1), 100101. Advance online publication. doi:10.1016/j.ssaho.2020.100101 PMID:34173507

Nath, S. R., & Chowdhury, M. A. R. (2019). *State of primary education in Bangladesh: Progress made, challenges remained*. Campaign for Popular Education.

Oyshi, M. T., Saifuzzaman, M., & Tumpa, Z. N. (2018). Gamification in children education: Balloon shooter. *2018 4th International Conference on Computing Communication and Automation (ICCCA)*. 10.1109/CCAA.2018.8777534

Parvin, N., & Alam, M. J. (2016). Empowerment of Women to alleviate Poverty through Education in Bangladesh. *Journal of Governance and Innovation, 2*(2), 49–60. https://osderpublications.com/uploads/1597820877.pdf

Parvin, R., & Haider, M. Z. (2012). Methods and practices of English language teaching in Bangla and English medium schools. *Bangladesh Education Journal, 11*(1), 51–63.

Peters, M. A., Besley, A. C., & Besley, T. (2006). *Building knowledge cultures: Education and development in the age of knowledge capitalism*. Rowman & Littlefield Education.

Roy, R. V., & Zaman, B. (2018). Need-supporting gamification in education: An assessment of motivational effects over time. *Computers & Education, 127,* 283–297. doi:10.1016/j.compedu.2018.08.018

Sailer, M., & Homner, L. (2019). The gamification of learning: A meta-analysis. *Educational Psychology Review, 32*(1), 77–112. doi:10.100710648-019-09498-w

Sallis, E. (2014). *Total quality management in education.* Routledge., doi:10.4324/9780203417010

Seixas, L. R., Gomes, A. S., & Filho, I. J. M. (2016). Effectiveness of gamification in the engagement of students. *Computers in Human Behavior, 58,* 48–63. doi:10.1016/j.chb.2015.11.021

Sommers, C. (2013). *Primary education in rural Bangladesh: Degrees of access, choice, and participation of the poorest.* CREATE. http://www.create-rpc.org/pdf_documents/PTA75.pdf

Stott, A., & Neustadter, C. (2013). *Analysis of Gamification in Education.* Simon Fraser University.

Surendeleg, G., Murwa, V., Yun, H.-K., & Kim, Y. S. (2014). The role of gamification in education - a literature review. *Contemporary Engineering Sciences, 7*(29), 1609–1616. doi:10.12988/ces.2014.411217

Sylva, K., Melhuish, E., Sammons, P., Siraj-Blatchford, I., & Taggart, B. (Eds.). (2010). *Early childhood matters: Evidence from the effective pre-school and primary education project.* Routledge. doi:10.4324/9780203862063

Töremen, F., Karakuş, M., & Yasan, T. (2009). Total quality management practices in Turkish primary schools. *Quality Assurance in Education, 17*(1), 30–44. doi:10.1108/09684880910929917

Urh, M., Vukovic, G., Jereb, E., & Pinter, R. (2015). The model for introduction of gamification into E-learning in higher education. *Procedia: Social and Behavioral Sciences, 197,* 388–397. doi:10.1016/j.sbspro.2015.07.154

Young, M. (2014). What is a curriculum and what can it do? *Curriculum Journal, 25*(1), 7–13. doi:10.1080/09585176.2014.902526 PMID:6909418

Yunus, M., & Shahana, S. (2018). New evidence on outcomes of primary education stipend programme in Bangladesh. *Bangladesh Development Studies, 41*(4), 29–55. https://www.jstor.org/stable/27031081

Chapter 37
Providing Validity Evidence for Ignite by Hatch:
A Digital Game–Based Learning Experience for Preschool Children

Hannah E. Luce
The University of North Carolina at Charlotte, USA

Richard G. Lambert
University of North Carolina at Charlotte, USA

ABSTRACT

The authors of this study seek to provide practitioners with evidence to support the instructional value of Ignite by Hatch, a digital learning game designed for preschool children. Analyses were conducted using the entire population of three- and four-year-old children who used Ignite during the 2020-2021 academic year (n = 29,417) and included the use of descriptive statistics to explore patterns of growth and the Rasch measurement model to explore item difficulty. This chapter also features a preliminary crosswalk establishing the alignment between the domains, subdomains, and games presented within the Ignite game environment and the learning goals provided by the North Carolina Foundations for Early Learning and Development framework. Results suggest strong preliminary evidence in support of the instructional value of Ignite by Hatch. Further research is recommended to understand how knowledge and skill acquisition within the game environment translate to developmental growth outside of the gaming environment.

INTRODUCTION

As digital curriculum materials become ubiquitous and resources remain finite, teachers and schools are required to make choices about which resources they will use to support learning in their classrooms. While well-designed digital learning games provide students with opportunities to actively engage with adaptive and standards-based content, poorly designed digital learning games can consume resources

DOI: 10.4018/978-1-7998-7271-9.ch037

such as time and money with minimal impact on student learning. In this chapter we will explore two key research questions with an aim of providing practitioners with the validity evidence required to make informed decisions regarding the use of Ignite, an adaptive digital learning game designed for preschool children. Although the Ignite game environment provides young children with experiences in seven domains of development, including, Social-Emotional, Social Studies, Language and Communication, Literacy, Mathematics, Science and Technology, and Physical, the focus of this chapter will be the domains of Language and Communication and Literacy.

REVIEW OF LITERATURE

Playful Learning

Play-based learning is not a new concept, but one that has emerged from years of research in the fields of Education and Psychology. For example, Psychologist, Jean Piaget (1962) described how play helped children move through the four stages of cognitive development. As children progressed through the various stages, he described the ways in which play became increasingly abstract. Another noteworthy Psychologist, Lev Vygotsky (1978) recognized the role of play in learning when he examined how play fostered cognitive development by allowing children to practice activities and try-on new behaviors within the context of imaginative play. One way to encourage playful learning in early childhood is to provide opportunities for children to engage with the curriculum through game-based learning experiences. While game-based learning can be defined as game play with specific learning outcomes (Shaffer, Halverson, Squire, & Gee, 2005), for the purpose of this chapter, we will focus on digital learning games, which can be defined as a game or experience that harnesses the entertainment power of a video game and serves a specific educational purpose (All et al., 2015).

Benefits of Game-Based Learning

In recent years researchers and practitioners have become increasingly interested in understanding the benefits of using digital learning games in the classroom. Researchers have identified several positive outcomes associated with learners using digital learning games, including, increased motivation and engagement, active learning, and the adaptability of digital content. Learner motivation can be easily enhanced in the game environment using incentive strategies, such as, collecting stars or earning digital currencies, trophies, or badges for successes in the game environment (Plass et al, 2015). When learners feel rewarded for their efforts, they are more likely to persist with future challenges presented in the game environment. Marone (2016) also found that learners experience increased engagement through carefully designed and dynamic environments that serve as both a challenge and a tutor. He argues that such games can act as the knowledgeable other, providing learners with experiences in their Zone of Proximal Development (Vygotsky, 1978). Another benefit of digital game-based learning is that users engage in active learning processes while engaging in game play (Qian et al., 2016). Active engagement has been shown to be more effective in knowledge and skill retention than traditional lecture-style learning. Additionally, when children are engaged in active learning, they are more likely to develop self-directed learning (SDL) strategies, which assist in future learning and promote autonomy. Finally, the digital game environment allows for rapid change of content and approach. Well-designed digital learning games are rigorously tested during the development process and are continually updated as learning goals and needs change over time (Cahill, n.d.). Adaptability is a unique property of digital curriculum materials and games, as content can be changed easily, unlike print materials that often take years to develop, test, and publish.

Features of Well-Designed Digital Learning Games

Researchers have identified several integral components of well-designed digital learning games. The first element requires that players experience adequate difficulty within the game environment. Marone (2016) contributes that digital learning games must present problems that are both interesting to solve and appropriately challenging for the intended audience. Achieving adequate difficulty can also be operationalized by creating a game-pathway that provides users with easier experiences first and then moves towards more difficult tasks (Cahill, n.d.). This predetermined path allows learners to build more foundational skills and knowledge at lower levels and apply their learning as they proceed through the gaming environment. Finally, well-designed digital learning games are constructed using learning standards and appropriate curriculum materials (Cahill, n.d.). Digital learning games should allow learners to build knowledge and skills in the game environment that help them to meet learning goals outside of the digital environment.

Self-Directed Learning (SDL) and Digital Learning Games

Self-directed learning (SDL) can be defined as "any increase in knowledge, skill, accomplishment, or personal development that an individual realizes through his or her own effort, using any method in any situation at any time" (Toh & Kirshner, 2020, p. 1). SDL has been described as a critical competency in the 21st century, as it allows for learners to adapt to changing demands, learn new skills, and acquire new knowledge in the digital age (Morris & Rohs, 2021). While SDL was conceptualized in the field of adult learning, researchers and practitioners recognize that SDL should be facilitated throughout childhood and adolescence to promote adults who are capable of SDL (Morris & Rohs, 2021). Sarac and Tarhan (2020) posit that preschool children already have many preliminary SDL skills including, the capacity to plan, monitor, evaluate, and reflect on their own learning. However, they also recognize that early childhood learning experiences lay the foundation for lifelong learning habits, therefore teachers should continue to promote the development of SDL strategies in the classroom (Sarac & Tarhan, 2020). Morris and Rohs (2021) explored how SDL could be facilitated with children during the digital age and found that contextualized learning, where children are tasked with solving real world problems, and active learning supported the development of SDL (Morris & Rohs, 2021).

Digital learning games can be used to promote SDL, as they can provide learners with authentic learning environments, where independent learning can be achieved through feedback, guidance, and graceful failure (Plass et al., 2015; Toh and Kirshner, 2020). Within the game environment, some degree of failure is expected. Plass et al. (2015) describe graceful failure as the act of failing in a low-stakes environment. When children experience graceful failure, they are more likely to take risks and try new things. Plass et al. (2015) also found that children who experience graceful failure are more likely to develop self-regulated learning strategies such as, goal setting and monitoring (Plass et al., 2015). Kirshner (2020) conducted a grounded theory study to understand what SDL strategies learners use while engaging with video games and what factors promote SDL in video game environments. Findings indicated that learners employ several SDL strategies while operating within the video game context, including *trial and error, observation and modeling,* and *reflect and improvise* (Toh & Kirshner, 2020). *Trial and error* was described as the lowest-level metacognitive strategy, where learners proceeded through the game environment using an inefficient and unsystematic process. Learners may be more apt to employ a trial-and-error process if their task in the game environment has not been properly scaffolded or clearly defined (Toh & Kirshner, 2020). *Observation and modeling* was described as the second-lowest meta-cognitive strategy where learners imitate the actions of others, without developing a true understanding of process (Toh & Kirshner, 2020). Finally, *reflect and improvise* was defined as the highest-level metacognitive strategy, where learners engaged in a cyclical process of action and reflection to derive new methods and strategies for over-coming challenges (Toh & Kirshner, 2020). Toh and Kirshner found that higher-ability players were more apt to employ higher-level SDL strategies to overcome challenges presented in the game environment.

Validity Evidence

Validity can be defined as "the extent to which the scores from a measure represent the variable they are intended to" (Price et al., 2017). Collecting validity evidence about a measure or learning tool is essential to understanding the interpretations that can be made about learners. Validity can be established through the process of collecting, analyzing, and providing evidence that support certain interpretations of scores under specified conditions of use. In this chapter we will primarily focus on presenting validity evidence in support of content validity and relationships with criteria. Establishing content validity requires that researchers present alignment or correspondence between predetermined learning standards and content presented within the measure (American Educational Research Association et al., 2014). Relationships with criteria evidence will also be provided and can be established when researchers relate scores to predetermined and relevant criteria (American Educational Research Association et al., 2014).

RESEARCH FOCUS

This study uses empirical data collected through the Ignite application during the 2020-2021 school year and aims to provide practitioners with the validity evidence needed to make an informed decision regarding the use of one digital learning game designed to promote kindergarten readiness skills in children ages two through five.

This study seeks to address the following research questions:

1. In what ways does Ignite by Hatch meet the requirements of a well-developed learning game?
2. What is the expected growth for a preschool child who engages with the Ignite application over the course of a school year?

DESCRIPTION OF THE SAMPLE

The analyses outlined in this chapter were conducted using the entire population of three- and four-year-old children who used the Ignite games during the 2020-2021 academic year ($n = 29,417$). For each domain specific analysis, all three- and four-year-old children who attempted at least one game within a given domain were retained. The sample was split almost evenly between boys (49.5%) and girls (50.5%). Three-year-old children comprised 36.8% of the sample and four-year-old children comprised 63.2% of the sample. The racial / ethnic composition of the sample was as follows: White (non-Hispanic) – 43.9%, Black (non-Hispanic) – 25.7%, Asian – 1.4%, Native American – 3.0%, Hispanic – 26.0%. Geographically, the sample was comprised of children from across the entire customer base, and therefore was national in scope.

CONTEXT FOR WELL-DEVELOPED LEARNING GAMES

Each game within the Hatch Ignite gaming environment belongs to an overall developmental domain and skills-based sub-domain. Each game was designed to meet the developmental needs of children at specific skill levels. These skill levels (*Beginning*, *Emerging*, *Intermediate*, *Accomplishing*, and *Proficient*) form an intended developmental pathway. Children make progress through games of increasing difficulty and complexity as they complete games to acquire focal skills. The skills they acquire in this process build upon each other. The first research question seeks to determine whether Ignite by Hatch meets the requirements of a well-designed learning game. Once again, well-designed learning games offer intended users experiences that range in difficulty. Users should encounter more foundational experiences early on and more difficult experiences later, only once they have acquired the necessary skills. In this study, game difficulty was considered in two ways. First, we assumed that four-year-old children should outperform three-year-old children across all games given their expected higher developmental level. To test this assumption, we compared the initial pass rates of the three- and four-year-old age groups across all games. Second, we assumed that initial pass rates would be highest for Beginning games, and then would decline as game difficulty level increased in turn from *Emerging*, to *Intermediate*, *Accomplishing*, and finally to *Proficient* games. To test this assumption, we compared the initial pass rates and game difficulty levels across the skill levels within each domain. These analyses provided preliminary relationships with criteria validity evidence, as four-year-old children should consistently outperform three-year-old children and children should experience lower passing rates as nominal difficulty increases. Finally, well-designed digital learning games feature content that aligns to learning goals or standards. We explored the alignment between domains, subdomains, and games provided in the Ignite game environment and the North Carolina Foundations for Early Learning and Development Framework to provide preliminary content validity evidence.

Comparisons of Performance Across Age Groups

For the Language and Communication Domain, a pattern emerged indicating consistent differences in initial passing rates between three- and four-year old children. Four-year-old children had higher initial pass rates than three-year-old children for almost every game. For three of the most difficult games, no children passed their initial attempt and therefore there were no differences between three-year-old children and four-year-old children. For one very easy game, a very large percentage of both three-year-old children (95.0%) and four-year-old children (93.8%) passed the game on their initial attempt. For the remaining 34 games, the expected advantage in initial passing rates for four-year-old children was clear and ranged up to as much as 14.5 percentage points.

For the Literacy Domain, a consistent pattern also emerged. Four-year-old children had higher initial pass rates than three-year-old children for every game except one. For one very easy game, the overall passing rate was very high (93.4%). The initial passing rate for three-year-old children was 94.5% and 92.8% for four-year-old children. The expected advantage in initial passing rates for four-year-old children was present for the remaining 40 games in the Literacy Domain and ranged up to as much as 14.9 percentage points.

Evidence for Variability in Game Difficulty

To investigate the match between intended and data-driven game difficulty levels, we adopted several specific analytical definitions and methods. First, we examined the initial passing rates for each game, which is the percent of children passing on their first attempt. This method allowed us to evaluate game difficulty independent of practice effects. Next, we examined whether the passing rates tended to decrease in a way that corresponded with increases in nominal game skill level. Specifically, this means that *Beginning* skill level games should be passed at a higher rate than *Emerging* games, which in turn should be passed at a higher rate than *Intermediate games*, followed by *Accomplishing* and finally by games with *Proficient* skill levels.

Next, we used the Rasch measurement model as an exploratory strategy to estimate game difficulty. The games within the Language and Communication Domain met the assumption of the Rasch model with statistical evidence that they were measuring a single underlying trait or ability. We also found sufficient evidence to support using the Rasch model to estimate game difficulty levels for the Literacy domain. This approach used advanced statistical methods to estimate game difficulty relative to all other games within the same domain. We identified a game as "Difficult" if it yielded a model-estimated difficulty of .5 logits or higher, meaning a game location of at least .5 logits above the average game difficulty within the respective domain. We identified a game as "Easy" if it yielded a model-estimated difficulty of -.5 logits or lower, meaning a game location of at least .5 logits below the average game difficulty within the respective domain. Games with locations on the ability scale within .5 logits of the average difficulty level for the respective domain were considered "Average."

Next, we compared the empirical game difficulty levels to the nominal or intended skill level for each game. We labeled a game as a mismatch if it had a nominal skill level of *Beginning* or *Emerging* and a model-estimated difficulty level of Difficult, or conversely, a nominal skill level of *Accomplishing* or *Proficient* and a model-estimated difficulty level of Easy. Finally, we examined the developmental pathway generated by the Rasch model. We used the pathway formed from the easiest game to the most difficult game to evaluate whether the rank order of game difficulty generally followed the expected hierarchy of skill level for each domain.

Language and Communication Results

For the Language and Communication Domain, there were matches between intended and empirical game difficulty levels for almost all the games (32 of 38). The overall pattern was very positive in that the initial pass rates generally became systematically lower as the nominal skill level of the games progressed from *Beginning* to *Proficient*. Specifically, the Language domain analyses included seven *Beginning* level games. Six of them had a model-estimated difficulty level of Easy. The initial pass rates for the *Beginning* games ranged as high as 94.2%. The Language Domain analyses included eight *Emerging* level games. Five of them were classified as Easy and three were classified as Difficult. The initial pass rates for the *Emerging* games ranged as high as 80.1%. The Language Domain analyses included seven *Intermediate* level games. Two of them were classified as Difficult and five were classified as Easy. The initial pass rates for the *Intermediate* games ranged up to 33.1%. The Language Domain analyses included nine *Accomplishing* level games. The model classified two of them as Easy, one as Average, and six as Difficult. The initial pass rates for the *Accomplishing* games ranged up to 23.4%. The Language Domain analyses included seven *Proficient* level games and three of them were classified as Average and four as Difficult. The initial pass rates for all *Proficient* games were less than 16%.

These results demonstrate a relatively clear progression of increasing game difficulty from the *Beginning* skill level to the *Proficient* skill level. The results illustrated a plausible developmental pathway of skills acquisition through which children can progress as they engage with the games in the Language Domain. The Language games were relatively equally represented across the Easy, Average, and Difficult model-estimated difficulty levels. The results showed a full span of game difficulty levels ranging from very easy to very difficult. This finding was evident in both the model estimated game difficulty levels and the initial passing rates which ranged from as high as 94.2% for the easiest game to as low as 0.0% for the most difficult game.

The easiest game was *Classroom Cleanup*, which had a nominal skill level of *Beginning*, a model-estimated difficulty level of Easy, and an initial pass rate of 94.2%. Similarly, the next easiest game, *Moon Mission*, had a nominal skill level of *Emerging*, a model-estimated difficulty level of Easy, and an initial pass rate of 80.1%. The most difficult game was *Use of Less Common Objects*, with a nominal skill level of *Accomplishing*, a model-estimated difficulty level of Difficult, and an initial pass rate of 0.0%. Similarly, the next most difficult game, *Use of Common Objects,* had a nominal skill level of *Accomplishing*, a model-estimated difficulty level of Difficult, and an initial pass rate of 0.0%.

Literacy Results

For the Literacy Domain, there were also matches between intended and empirical game difficulty levels for almost all the games (38 of 41). Again, the overall pattern was very positive in that the initial pass rates generally became systematically lower as the nominal skill level of the games progressed from *Beginning* to *Proficient*. Specifically, the Literacy Domain analyses included six *Beginning* level games and all of them had a model-estimated difficulty level of Easy. The initial pass rates for the *Beginning* games ranged up to 93.4%. The Literacy Domain analyses included six *Emerging* level games. One of them was classified as Easy, three as Average, and two as Difficult. The initial pass rates for the *Emerging* games ranged up to 22.3%. The Literacy Domain analyses included five *Intermediate* level games. One of them were classified as Difficult, three as Average, and one as Easy. The initial pass rates for the *Intermediate* games ranged up to 20.0%. The Literacy Domain analyses included nine *Accomplishing* level games. The model classified five of them as Average and four as Difficult. The initial pass rates for the *Accomplishing* games ranged up to 17.2%. The Literacy Domain analyses included 15 *Proficient* level games. Almost all of them, 12 of the 15, were classified as Difficult. The initial pass rates for all *Proficient* games were less than 20% and was less than 13.0% for 14 of the 15 games.

These results demonstrate a clear progression of increasing game difficulty from the *Beginning* skill level to the *Proficient* skill level for the Literacy Domain. The results illustrated a well-defined developmental pathway of skills acquisition through which children can progress as they engage with the games in the Literacy Domain. The Literacy games were relatively equally represented across the

Easy, Average, and Difficult model-estimated difficulty levels. The results showed a full span of game difficulty from very easy to very difficult. This finding was evident in both the model estimated game difficulty levels and the initial passing rates which ranged from as high as 93.4% for the easiest game to as low as 3.5% for the most difficult game.

The easiest game was *Rhyming*, which had a nominal skill level of *Beginning*, a model-estimated difficulty level of Easy, and an initial pass rate of 93.4%. Similarly, the next easiest game, *Magic Hat 1*, had a nominal skill level of *Beginning*, a model-estimated difficulty level of Easy, and an initial pass rate of 86.5%. The most difficult game, *Teddy Bear Rhyme*, had a nominal skill level of *Proficient*, a model-estimated difficulty level of Difficult, and an initial pass rate of only 3.5%. The next most difficult game, *Blending Word Parts*, had a nominal skill level of *Accomplishing*, a model-estimated difficulty level of Difficult, and an initial pass rate of only 3.6%.

Alignment between Game Content and Learning Standards

Well-developed learning game environments provide children with opportunities to engage with content that is constructed based on learning standards or goals. To demonstrate alignment and provide content validity evidence, we present a preliminary crosswalk between the North Carolina Foundations Framework for Early Learning and Development and content presented in the Ignite game environment. Although the North Carolina Foundations Framework is only one state's standards for young learners, the developmental indicator continuums presented in the framework demonstrate widely held expectations for children from birth to age five across five key developmental and learning domains, including Language Development and Communication (LDC). The framework clearly addresses the interconnected and interrelated nature of learning during the early years and suggests that teachers provide instruction embedded within routine activities (North Carolina Foundations Task Force, 2013). The Ignite game environment provides a scope and sequence of experiences that allow for repeated practice of specific skills needed to communicate, read, and write. The alignment between experiences presented within the Ignite game environment and the early learning framework is crucial to ensure that children are interacting with developmentally appropriate, rigorous, and standards-based content.

The North Carolina Foundations Framework for Early Learning and Development LDC provides seven learning goals in the area of *Learning to Communicate*, five goals in the area of *Foundations for Reading*, and three goals in the area of *Foundations for Writing*. These goals are labeled LDC-1 - LDC-15. Within the Ignite game environment, young children interact with experiences that promote the development of communication, foundations for reading, and foundations for writing through experiences within the Language and Communication Domain and the Literacy Domain (See Figure 1 for alignment). The Language and Communication Domain is organized into five subdomains, which include, *Academic Vocabulary, Conventions of Language, Listening and Understanding, Receptive Language*, and *Vocabulary* and the Literacy Domain includes experiences in nine subdomains, including, *Alliteration, Alphabet Knowledge, Blending, Concepts of Print, Key Ideas and Details, Letter-Sound Correspondence, Rhyming, Segmenting*, and *Writing Development*. Most subdomains listed above contain experiences across the entire game pathway at increasing levels of difficulty. For example, children encounter six unique *Listening and Understanding* experiences and two continued practice experiences. Experiences in this subdomain range from a nominal skill level of one to a nominal skill level of six, with easier games appearing first, moderately difficult experiences appearing in the middle, and challenging experiences appearing toward the end. For example, children first complete experiences with simple directions such as,

Classroom Clean Up and *Moon Mission,* then move to *Two-Step Directions,* and finally follow directions to solve complex problems in experiences such as *Underwater Instructions* and *Building a Spaceship.* Within the game environment, children generally encounter most level one Literacy and Language and Communication experiences before encountering level two experiences. This predetermined pathway approximates the developmental pathway and acknowledges the interconnected and interrelated nature of learning in early childhood, as it allows for communication, reading, and writing skills to develop concurrently (see Table 1 for alignment).

Table 1. Crosswalk between Ignite game environment and NC Foundations Standards

Ignite Domain	Ignite Subdomain	Foundations Standard	Number of Games	Skill Levels
Language & Communication Development	Academic Vocabulary	LDC-7	9	4-6
Language & Communication Development	Conventions of Language	LDC-6	4	3-6
Language & Communication Development	Listening and Understanding	LDC-1-3	8	1-6
Language & Communication Development	Receptive Language	LDC-1-3	8	1-6
Language & Communication Development	Vocabulary	LDC-5,7	8	1-6
Literacy	Alliteration	LDC_11	6	1-6
Literacy	Alphabet Knowledge	LDC-12,13,14	18	2-6
Literacy	Blending	LDC-11	6	1-6
Literacy	Concepts of Print	LDC-10	8	1-6
Literacy	Key Ideas and Details	LDC-9	18	1-6
Literacy	Letter-Sound Correspondence	LDC-11,12,13	11	4-6
Literacy	Rhyming	LDC-11	6	1-6
Literacy	Segmenting	LDC-11	6	1-6
Literacy	Writing Development	LDC-14,15	9	1-6

Experiences within the Ignite game environment also present children with opportunities to solve developmentally appropriate, contextualized, and real-world problems. For young children, learning concepts of print lays the foundation for future reading development. Ignite provides students with eight experiences in the subdomain *Concepts of Print*, including, *Book Orientation, Print versus Pictures, Print versus Pictures Continued Practice, Print Directionality, Print Directionality Continued Practice, Identifying Book Features, Letters or Words*, and *Concepts of Print Six*. Once again, games are presented in an order such that children encounter easier experiences and build foundational skills first, and then proceed to more challenging application-based experiences. After children develop an understanding of what constitutes print, they encounter examples and non-examples to understand nuances and solidify their developing understandings. In this case, the game environment provides children with numerous contextualized and authentic experiences that help to facilitate the acquisition of critical pre-literacy and pre-reading skills. Games such as those presented within the *Concepts of Print* subdomain also support children in developing SDL strategies, as the problems encountered in the game environment mirror those encountered outside of the game environment and require children to be active learners, rather than passive learners.

Within the Ignite game environment, children can engage with 37 experiences, ranging in nominal difficulty levels from one to six, that address LDC *Learning to Communicate* goals. Such games provide opportunities for vocabulary acquisition, learning language conventions, and developing receptive language skills. The game environment also provides children with 79 experiences, ranging in nominal difficulty levels from one to six, that support the LDC *Foundations for Reading* goals. Such experiences include practice with phonological awareness skills, such as, alliteration, blending, rhyming, and segmenting, and concepts about print, alphabet knowledge, and letter-sound correspondence. Finally, the Ignite game environment provides children with 38 experiences, ranging in nominal difficulty levels from one to six, that support the LDC *Foundations for Writing* goals. These experiences include games within the subdomains of alphabet knowledge, letter-sound correspondence, and writing development. While young children form the foundation for writing when they begin to scribble on paper, older children move toward representing their thoughts and ideas with letters. Therefore, as children progress through the game pathway, they are presented with more experiences that allow them to build knowledge of letters and letter-sound correspondence.

After considering the alignment between the North Carolina Foundations Framework for Early Learning and Development LDC goals and the experiences provided within the Ignite gaming environment, there are clear and strong associations between the content covered within the game environment and learning goals for young children. This investigation and crosswalk between developmentally appropriate learning goals for young children and content provide preliminary content validity evidence to support the use of Ignite as an instructional tool.

Summary of Results for Well-Designed Learning Games

The results of this portion of the study outline important validity evidence for the instructional usefulness of the Ignite games. The main focal points were the performance differences between three and four-year-old children, the match or mismatch between intended game skill levels and empirically generated game difficulty levels, and the degree of alignment between experiences encountered within the game environment and the learning goals outlined in the North Carolina Foundations Framework for Early Learning and Development. With respect to the differences in performance by age, four-year-old children outperformed three-year-old children for 74 of the 79 games evaluated. The performance advantage for four-year-old children was often substantial. The difference was usually greater than 10 percentage points, and often approached 15 percentage points. Only five games presented exceptions to this finding. For three of them, the passing rates were 0.0%, meaning that three-year-old children did not outperform four-year-old children. Rather, the games were simply so difficult that no children passed on their first attempt. For the other two games, three-year-old children outperformed four-year-old children by less than two percentage points, and both games were very easy with passing rates greater than 93.0%. These games were easy enough that nearly all children, regardless of age, passed on their first attempt. Therefore, with respect to age differences, the results support a strong validity argument.

Regarding the match or mismatch between intended game skill levels and empirically generated difficulty levels, results indicated a close match between the intended skill level and the initial passing rates and game difficulty levels for most of the games. Of the 79 games evaluated, the results suggested a possible mismatch between intended skill level and game difficulty for only nine (11.4%) of the games. A coherent, well-defined, and sequenced developmental pathway from *Beginning* to *Proficient* games emerged for each domain that ranged from the easiest games to the most difficult games, and the pathway generally corresponded very well to the intended nominal skill levels. A wide range of game difficulty levels from easy to difficult emerged for both domains. This finding demonstrates that the children can be challenged and continue to grow, develop, and learn at all skill levels. Overall, the findings supported the instructional value of the games. Furthermore, the results of this portion of the study demonstrated strong validity evidence for the Ignite learning games by supporting both of our initial assumptions about game difficulty level.

With respect to the alignment, there were strong correspondences between domains, subdomains, and games presented within the game environment and the learning goals outlined in the North Carolina Foundations Framework for Early Learning and Development. This finding provides initial content validity evidence in support of the instructional value of the Ignite game experiences for preschool children. Given the close alignment between learning goals, based on widely held expectations for young children, practitioners can feel more confident that the time children spend within the game environment contributes productively to their knowledge, skills, and understandings of relevant learning standards.

Additionally, children acquire SDL strategies when they engage in contextualized and problem-based learning experiences (Morris & Rohs, 2020). The Ignite game environment challenges children to solve contextualized problems as they engage with developmentally appropriate games. SDL is also accomplished when children actively engage in the learning process. The Ignite game environment presents an opportunity for children to engage in active meaning-making. Using Ignite in the preschool classroom could help children make progress toward learning goals, while also promoting the development of SDL strategies.

CONTEXT FOR EXPECTED GROWTH

Another aim of this study was to use empirical evidence to describe expected growth for preschool children using the Ignite application. If Ignite is a useful digital learning tool, then children should be able to acquire new knowledge and skills within the game environment and achieve higher nominal skill levels over time. Developers of Ignite recommend that children engage with the application for 30 minutes per week and expect that children will, on average, achieve one higher nominal skill level in each domain over the course of the school year. Ideally, three-year-old children move from a nominal skill level of two to three, while four-year-old children move from a nominal skill level of three to four. However, developers understand that children are unique and prioritize growth in nominal skill level over absolute level achieved. Also, with Ignite being a relatively new digital learning game, many children in the sample were first time Ignite users, and therefore had no previous experience with the format or content of the game environment.

Expected Growth

Descriptive statistics were used to look at patterns of growth within the Language and Communication and Literacy Domains, for three- and four-year-old children by months played, average monthly minutes engaged, and gender. In this analysis population data were used, therefore descriptive statistics were appropriate. The highest median level achieved in the first month of game play and the highest median level achieved in the last month of game play were reported for each age, month, and minute group by domain. Median scores were reported because the nominal skill levels are ordinal data. Each child's average number of monthly minutes was calculated by summing all game minutes for the 2020-2021 school year and dividing the number of minutes by the number of months played. Children with zero minutes were eliminated from the sample. Although, Ignite by Hatch recommends that children use the game for 30 minutes per week, most children played significantly more. This is likely a result of the Covid-19 pandemic, where many preschool children were engaged in virtual learning activities. For the purpose of this study, we retained children with average monthly minutes greater than zero and less than 9,600 (approximately 40 hours per week or 160 hours per month). It should be noted that this number of minutes is not recommended by Ignite by Hatch, nor supported by the American Psychological Association (Pappas, 2020), however, was determined to be a plausible value in this study. After average monthly minutes were calculated, children were assigned to categorical time groups, which were, less than 120 minutes per month (< 30 minutes per week), 120 to 360 minutes per month (30 - 90 minutes per week), and greater than 360 minutes per week (< 90 minutes per week). For each categorical minute group, the gender breakdown closely matched the population (less than or equal to +/- 1.4%).

Expected Growth for Three-Year-Old Children

From the data several patterns emerged. For one, groups of children who engaged with the application for more months and a greater number of average monthly minutes gained a greater number of nominal skill levels than those who played fewer months and fewer minutes. Also, children reached more difficult nominal skill levels in Language and Communication, than Literacy, when minutes and months were held constant. To make the same gains in Literacy, as Language and Communication, children had to play for more minutes, more months, or both. Children who played for less than 120 minutes (*M=73.25, SD = 28.82*) gained one nominal skill level within the Language and Communication Domain when they played four-seven months, whereas children who averaged 120-360 monthly minutes (*M=230.00, SD=68.05*) gained one-two nominal skill levels when they played two-six months, and children who averaged greater than 360 monthly minutes (*M=1266.72, SD=1158.73*) gained one nominal skill level after only two months of game play. Children who played for less than 120 minutes per month gained one nominal skill level within the Literacy Domain by playing five-11 months, while children who played 120-360 minutes gained one nominal skill level by playing three-six months, and children who played more than 360 minutes achieved one nominal skill level by playing for three-four months. Children who engaged with the application for more months and a greater number of average monthly minutes attained greater growth in nominal skill levels (see Table 2 and Table 3 for full results).

Table 2. Median level achieved for three-year-old children by months engaged with the games and monthly minutes played

Average Monthly Minutes	Number of Months Engaged	Language and Communication			Literacy		
		Highest Level First Month	Highest Level Last Month	Average Growth in Nominal Skill Level	Highest Level First Month	Highest Level Last Month	Average Growth in Nominal Skill Level
Less than 120	1	1	1	0	1	1	0
	2	1	1	0	1	1	0
	3	1	1	0	1	1	0
	4	1	2	1	1	1	0
	5	1	2	1	1	2	1
	6	1	2	1	1	2	1
	7	1	2	1	1	2	1
	8	1	3	2	1	2	1
	9	1	3	2	1	2	1
	10	1	3	2	1	2	1
	11	1	4	3	1	2	1
120-360	1	2	2	0	1	1	0
	2	1	2	1	1	1	0
	3	1	2	1	1	2	1
	4	1	3	2	1	2	1
	5	1	3	2	1	2	1
	6	2	3	1	1	2	1
	7	1	3	2	1	3	2
	8	1	3	2	1	3	2
	9	1	4	3	1	3	2
	10	1	4	3	1	3	2
	11	*	*	*	*	*	*
More than 360	1	3	3	0	2	2	0
	2	2	3	1	2	2	0
	3	2	4	2	2	3	1
	4	2	4	2	2	3	1
	5	2	4	2	2	4	2
	6	2	4	2	2	4	2
	7	2	4	2	2	4	2
	8	2	4	2	2	4	2
	9	2	5	3	2	4	2
	10	2	5	3	2	5	3
	11	*	*	*	*	*	*

Note. Cells with fewer than 15 children were removed from this table

Table 3. Descriptive statistics for three year old childrens' minutes engaged

Minutes	N	M	SD	Minimum	Maximum
<120	1082	73.25	28.82	3.48	119.99
120-360	2828	230	68.05	120.08	359.91
>360	5760	1266.72	1158.73	360.31	9460.79

Note. 26 extreme cases were removed (minutes >=9600).
26 cases were removed, min: 9628.22-19673.69 mean 12,652 and SD 2657.94
19 three year olds played 11 months

Expected Growth for Four-Year-Old Children

Similar patterns emerged for four-year-old children's use and growth. Groups of children who played a greater number of months and averaged higher monthly minutes, outperformed those with lower monthly minutes and a lower number of months engaged. Except for children who averaged more than 360 monthly minutes, who performed similarly across domains, four-year-old children gained nominal skill levels in Language and Communication more quickly than they gained nominal levels in Literacy. For example, children who averaged less than 120 minutes per month achieved one nominal skill level gain in Language and Communication after three months but didn't achieve one nominal skill level gain in Literacy until after five months of game play. For Language and Communication, children who averaged less than 120 monthly minutes ($M=74.56$, $SD=29.35$) achieved one nominal skill level gain after three months, children who averaged between 120 and 360 monthly minutes ($M=232.21$, $SD=68.14$) achieved two nominal skill levels after three months, and children who averaged greater than 360 monthly minutes ($M=1343.53$, $SD=1184.14$) achieved one nominal skill level gain after two months. Children who engaged with the application for less than 120 monthly minutes, on average, gained one nominal skill level in Literacy after five months of game play, while children who engaged with the application between 120 and 360 minutes and greater than 360 minutes gained one nominal skill level in Literacy after two months. Four-year-old children who played between 120-360 minutes, on average, achieved a level four in Language and Communication after seven months of game play. Children who played more than 360 minutes per month, on average, achieved a nominal skill level of four in Language and Communication after three months, and achieved a nominal skill level of four in Literacy after four months (see Table 4 and Table 5 for full results).

Table 4. Median level achieved for four-year-old children by months engaged with the games and monthly minutes played

Average Monthly Minutes	Number of Months Engaged	Language and Communication			Literacy		
		Highest Level First Month	Highest Level Last Month	Average Growth in Nominal Skill Level	Highest Level First Month	Highest Level Last Month	Average Growth in Nominal Skill Level
Less than 120	1	1	1	0	1	1	0
	2	1	1	0	1	1	0
	3	1	2	1	1	1	0
	4	1	2	1	1	1	0
	5	1	2	1	1	2	1
	6	1	3	2	1	2	1
	7	1	3	2	1	2	1
	8	1	3	2	1	2	1
	9	1	3	2	1	2	1
	10	1	3	2	1	2	1
	11	*	*	*	*	*	*
120-360	1	2	2	0	1	1	0
	2	2	2	0	1	2	1
	3	1	3	2	1	2	1
	4	1	3	2	1	2	1
	5	1	3	2	1	3	2
	6	2	3	1	1	3	2
	7	2	4	2	1	3	2
	8	1	4	3	1	3	2
	9	1	4	3	1	3	2
	10	1	4	3	1	3	2
	11	*	*	*	*	*	*
More than 360	1	3	3	0	2	2	0
	2	2	3	1	2	3	1
	3	3	4	1	2	3	1
	4	2	4	2	2	4	2
	5	2	4	2	2	4	2
	6	2	4	2	2	4	2
	7	2	5	3	2	5	3
	8	3	5	2	2	5	3
	9	3	5	2	2	5	3
	10	2	5	3	2	5	3
	11	2	5	3	1	5	4

Note. Cells with fewer than 15 children were removed from this table.

Table 5. Descriptive statistics for four year old childrens' minutes engaged

Minutes	N	*M*	*SD*	Minimum	Maximum
<120	1404	74.56	29.35	4.20	119.95
120-360	3934	232.21	68.14	120.07	359.99
>360	11874	1343.53	1184.14	360.12	9325.15

Note. 48 extreme cases were removed (monthly minutes >= 9600)
48 extreme cases were removed, min 9667.78, max 24344, mean 13015 max 3403.44
76 children used the application for 11 months, however 404 four year olds played 11 months

Summary of Results for Expected Growth

Ignite by Hatch recommends that children engage with the application for approximately 30 minutes per week or 120 minutes per month. Three-year-old children in the categorical, less than 120-minute per month group, averaged 18 minutes per week of game play and gained on average, one nominal skill level in Language and Communication after four months, and one nominal skill level in Literacy after five months. This finding suggests that this is an appropriate recommendation. However, children who demonstrated prolonged engagement, as defined by greater minutes and months, progressed through, and successfully completed more complex experiences. Similarly, four-year-old children who were assigned to the categorical, less than 120-minute per month group, averaged 19 minutes per week of game play and gained on average, one nominal skill level in Language and Communication after three months, and one nominal skill level in Literacy after five months. This finding suggests that the recommendation is appropriate if the desired outcome is a gain in one nominal skill level, however, four-year-old children who engaged for a greater number of minutes and months successfully completed more complex games.

FUTURE RESEARCH RECOMMENDATIONS

The findings of this study provide initial evidence for the instructional value of the Ignite games. There are several important areas for future research: 1.) the generalizability of skills acquired within the gaming environment to situations outside the gaming environment, 2.) the usefulness of the games for gathering evidence of child developmental growth, specifically to support placements on developmental progressions within formative assessment measures, and 3.) the value of evidence from the gaming environment for instructional planning purposes.

Early childhood teachers face a challenging task as they attempt to meet the unique developmental needs of all the children in their classroom. Differentiating and individualizing instruction is very difficult and time consuming. It will be helpful to investigate whether teachers find the information that the games provide to be useful for instructional planning, and in assessing the children using authentic formative assessment such as *Teaching Strategies* GOLD. If so, the Ignite gaming system could be a valuable and time saving source of meaningful evidence about child progress.

It will be critically important to examine in future studies whether teachers observe generalizations from learning within the gaming environment to behavior in the classroom. Intentional research to establish evidence that the skill and knowledge gains made within the gaming environment transfer to the classroom and other settings. Future research could also use objective, direct assessments of child developmental status to demonstrate that the learning, growth, and development of children using the games as recommended is enhanced beyond what would naturally occur for children who do not engage with the gaming environment. Future research could also focus on child engagement levels within the gaming environment with the goal of producing guidelines for teachers about how to use the games to maximize benefits for young children. Specifically, usability studies could be conducted to further understand exactly what children do when they enter and engage with the gaming environment.

Future research is also needed to investigate whether the positive results from this study extend to all sub-groups of children. For example, such studies could address questions related to potential subgroup differences in performance within the gaming environment related to child ability level, special needs status, or ethnic / racial background. Future research can reach beyond initial passing rates to examine overall passing rates after repeated practice attempts. Finally, the content and structure of each game with a potential mismatch between intended and actual difficulty level could be investigated further with an eye toward potential game enhancements.

While Ignite by Hatch supports SDL in several ways, including exposure to contextualized learning experiences, rooted in solving real-world problems, and encouraging active learning, future research is needed to understand how children employ and develop metacognitive strategies in response to challenges posed in the game environment. Toh and Kirshner (2020) established a model in which they linked ability within the game environment to the complexity of metacognitive responses. Ideally, as children develop familiarity and confidence within the game environment, they also move from basic metacognitive strategies and responses, such as *trial and error*, to more complex and demanding strategies and responses, such as *observation and modeling* and *reflect and improvise*. Future research is needed to understand how teachers can support children in developing and strengthening metacognitive skills within the digital game environment.

REFERENCES

All, A., Nuñez Castellar, E. P., & Van Looy, J. (2015). Assessing the effectiveness of digital game-based learning: Best practices. *Computers & Education, 92-93*, 90–103. doi:10.1016/j.compedu.2015.10.007

American Educational Research Association, American Psychological Association, & National Council on Measurement in Education. (2014). *Standards for educational and psychological testing*. American Educational Research Association.

Cahill, G. (n.d.). *Why game-based learning?* The Learning Counsel.

Marone, V. (2016). Playful constructivism: Making sense of digital games for learning and creativity through play, design, and participation. *Journal of Virtual Worlds Research, 9*(3), 1–18. doi:10.4101/jvwr.v9i3.7244

Morris, T. H., & Rohs, M. (2021). The potential for digital technology to support self-directed learning in formal education of children: A scoping review. *Interactive Learning Environments*, 1–14. doi:10.1080/10494820.2020.1870501

North Carolina Foundations Task Force. (2013). *North Carolina foundations for early learning and development*. Author.

Pappas, S. (2020). What do we really know about kids and screens? *Monitor on Psychology*, *51*(3), 42.

Piaget, J. (1962). *Play, dreams and imitation in childhood*. Routledge and Kegan.

Plass, J. L., Homer, B. D., & Kinzer, C. K. (2015). Foundations of game-based learning. *Educational Psychologist*, *50*(4), 258–283. doi:10.1080/00461520.2015.1122533

Price, P. C., Chiang, I.-C. A., Leighton, D. C., & Cutler, C. (2017). Reliability and validity of measurement. In R. Jhangiani (Ed.), Research methods in psychology. Pressbooks.

Qian, M., & Clark, K. R. (2016). Game-based learning and 21st CENTURY Skills: A review of recent research. *Computers in Human Behavior*, *63*, 50–58. doi:10.1016/j.chb.2016.05.023

Saraç, S., & Tarhan, B. (2021). Preschool teachers' promotion of self-regulated learning in the classroom and role of contextual and teacher-level factors. *International Electronic Journal of Elementary Education*, *13*(2), 309–322. doi:10.26822/iejee.2021.192

Shaffer, D. W., Squire, K. R., Halverson, R., & Gee, J. P. (2005). Video games and the future of learning. *Phi Delta Kappan*, *87*(2), 105–111. doi:10.1177/003172170508700205

Toh, W., & Kirschner, D. (2020). Self-directed learning in video games, affordances and pedagogical implications for teaching and learning. *Computers & Education*, *154*, 1–11. doi:10.1016/j.compedu.2020.103912

Vygotsky, L. S. (1978). *Mind in society: Development of higher psychological processes*. Harvard UP.

ADDITIONAL READING

All, A., Nuñez Castellar, E. P., & Van Looy, J. (2015). Assessing the effectiveness of digital game-based learning: Best practices. *Computers & Education*, *92-93*, 90–103. doi:10.1016/j.compedu.2015.10.007

Marone, V. (2016). Playful constructivism: Making sense of digital games for learning and creativity through play, design, and participation. *Journal of Virtual Worlds Research*, *9*(3), 1–18. doi:10.4101/jvwr.v9i3.7244

Morris, T. H., & Rohs, M. (2021). The potential for digital technology to support self-directed learning in formal education of children: A scoping review. *Interactive Learning Environments*, 1–14. doi:10.1080/10494820.2020.1870501

Plass, J. L., Homer, B. D., & Kinzer, C. K. (2015). Foundations of game-based learning. *Educational Psychologist*, *50*(4), 258–283. doi:10.1080/00461520.2015.1122533

Qian, M., & Clark, K. R. (2016). Game-based learning and 21st CENTURY Skills: A review of recent research. *Computers in Human Behavior*, *63*, 50–58. doi:10.1016/j.chb.2016.05.023

Saraç, S., & Tarhan, B. (2021). Preschool teachers' promotion of self-regulated learning in the classroom and role of contextual and teacher-level factors. *International Electronic Journal of Elementary Education*, *13*(2), 309–322. doi:10.26822/iejee.2021.192

Shaffer, D. W., Squire, K. R., Halverson, R., & Gee, J. P. (2005). Video games and the future of learning. *Phi Delta Kappan*, *87*(2), 105–111. doi:10.1177/003172170508700205

Toh, W., & Kirschner, D. (2020). Self-directed learning in video games, affordances and pedagogical implications for teaching and learning. *Computers & Education*, *154*, 1–11. doi:10.1016/j.compedu.2020.103912

KEY TERMS AND DEFINITIONS

Digital Learning Game: A play-based experience that was developed to help learners meet specific learning goals or learning standards and is accessed using technology.

Game-Based Learning: A play-based experience used to support the acquisition of new knowledge and/or skills and incorporates the use of strategy and skill.

Ignite by Hatch: A digital learning game designed to support preschool children in achieving developmentally appropriate learning goals in seven domains of development.

Language and Communication Domain: A subset of Ignite experiences, which include, experiences with academic vocabulary, vocabulary, conventions of language, listening and understanding, and receptive language.

Literacy Domain: A subset of Ignite experiences, which include alliteration, alphabet knowledge, blending, concepts of print, key ideas and details, letter sound correspondence, rhyming, segmenting, and writing development.

Metacognition: The ability to think about one's thinking.

Self-Directed Learning: The ability to autonomously employ the necessary strategies to meet learning goals.

Validity Evidence: A collection of information that allows researchers and practitioners to make appropriate and relevant interpretations about scores.

Chapter 38
Levelling Up Primary School Students' 21st Century Skills Through Minecraft–Game–Based Learning

Mohd Ali Samsudin
Universiti Sains Malaysia, Malaysia

Goh Kok Ming
SJKC Chi Sheng 2, Malaysia

Nur Jahan Ahmad
Universiti Sains Malaysia, Malaysia

Yogendran Abrose
Universiti Sains Malaysia, Malaysia

ABSTRACT

The aim of this study was to investigate the effectiveness of Minecraft-game-based learning towards on 21st century skills among primary school students. This study employed quasi-experimental methodology. The dependent variable of this study was the 21st century skills. During Minecraft-game-based learning session, students were given the opportunity to build and recreate a world based on certain themes inside Minecraft world based on their creativity and imagination. The session involved a learning process of different skills and knowledge relevant to school and real world which was imitate inside the Minecraft world. The result shows that the intervention of Minecraft-game-based learning is effective in enhancing and retaining the 21st century skills among students. The implication of the study suggests that the functionality of Minecraft as a digital learning tool should be promoted as it involves students to work in a team to solve problems and have fun while acquiring and sharpening the students' 21st century skills.

DOI: 10.4018/978-1-7998-7271-9.ch038

BACKGROUND

Alexander and Ho (2015) assert that game design is a complex process involving art, design, and engineering. Students have the opportunity to develop the concept ideas, characters, and narratives during the game-based learning activities. Students develop professional design standards that are unique to the commercial video game in the market as they translated their narratives into 2D and 3D artwork with interactive elements. The researchers discover that when students apply the game theory and make use of hardware and software, they are able to communicate, collaborate, and solve problem as a team. Alexander and Ho (2015) also discover that:

Game development is an art form that borrows and transforms previous art-making experiences into a new form of participation and collaboration (p. 35).

Salen (2007) agrees that game design creativity manifests itself in a variety of ways, such as through creative problem-solving algorithms or with drawing and 3D modelling programmes to create the game's look. The design and programming of games facilitates student learning and provides an authentic 21st-century learning experience (Navarrette, 2013).

Understanding how to build a successful game requires system-based thinking, iterative critical problem solving, art and aesthetics, writing and storytelling, interactive design, game logic and rules, and programming abilities (Salen, 2007, p. 305).

21st Century Skills

The term "21st century learning" refers to an educational reform that seeks to provide every student with the essential skills to meet 21st century challenges (Beetham & Sharpe, 2013). Malaysia has implemented 21st century education since 2014. It is focusing on four key components, known as the 4 C's which are communication, collaboration, creativity, and critical thinking (ŽivkoviĿ, 2016). One of the most important subjects of this country's educational system is science. For some students, science is a difficult subject to learn (Kamisah et al., 2007). The results are unbalanced in which some students perform exceptionally well, while others tend to be left behind in science subjects.

According to Kamisah et al. (2007), Malaysia has an exam-oriented educational system that does not have a definitive educational environment for culture and science literacy. Teachers are being pressured by the Ministry of Education to complete the content syllabus. As a result, teachers place a greater emphasis on science knowledge while placing less emphasis on other things such as practical knowledge, science process skills, critical thinking skills, and moral values. Furthermore, the 2012 PISA results reveal that the country's educational system is in a crisis. Malaysian students had scored 398 which was below the average score (498) in the reading section, they scored 420 which was below the average score (501) in science and scored 421 which was below the average score (494) in mathematics. Malaysian students were also found to have significant deficiencies in higher order thinking skills (HOTs) such as reasoning and clarification. One of the factors affecting the outcome is the students' internal behaviour (Noor Erma & Leong Kwang En, 2014). Since the evaluation was not relevant to them, the majority of the students did not take the question seriously and did not answer the questions very well. Furthermore, the previous curriculum's lack of focus on higher order thinking skills among students is a contributing factor to this issue. As a result, the students were unable to apply their knowledge to do the questions.

To prepare students with 21st century skills, high-intensity efforts are needed. According to Nurazidawati, Tuan Mastura, and Kamisah (2011), some students, despite having a good idea, do not know how to articulate it. In addition, another 21st century field of perception, moral norms and values have been established and need to be discussed in the Malaysian context. Based on the study entitled "Integration of 21st Century Skills in Science Curriculum" by Osman and Marimuthu (2010), they report that it is important for us to understand how science education contributes to the development of 21st century skills, human resources, and student identities in today's world.

The rapid growth and changes that have occurred in our world today have complicated all our attempts to shape the future. Because of the effects of these developments, people must be ready to adopt the 21st century's trend in tandem with world culture and the globalization period. The transition from the manufacturing industry to the service economy, which includes the shifts in the workplace, individual and family roles, and mass media interaction, as well as the shift from specialization to general knowledge, which include rapidly evolving science and technology in all areas of life (Seele & Lock, 2017) are required. The NEA states that the educational system built in America is no longer exist in the economy and society. Students might think that people have moved from an economy-based on the need to work manually in a globalised economy where the data's assimilation is in the right brains of people (Jones, 2014; Pink, 2006). Blikstein et al. (2017) agree that there is a shift to higher levels of education in society, where the critical and problem-solving skills and technological expertise are needed. Expert employee's technology of the 21st century can design, develop, and manage today's workforce who are highly sought after. However, the managers at work feel that many employees have lack the skills they need in the 21st century and so in school they ought to have studied them. Jonassen (2007) reports the problem of the 21st century solving poorly prepared employees and students can be cognitively challenging.

The National Association for Education (NEA) is a 21st century organization that promotes readiness through the foundation of the Partnership for skills of the 21st century. They provide educators with resources and tools to help students prepare for a world economy and create a skills framework that will address the demand for future innovation (Soulé & Warrick, 2015). Under the student's results of learning and innovation, four special skills are identified and commonly referred to as the "Four Cs" (4Cs) which are important for education (Claymier, 2014; Hunt, 2013). The 4Cs' skills include critical thinking and solving problems, communication, collaboration, creativity, and innovation. The 21st Century Learning, along with the 4 Cs and social awareness involve in acquiring skills in work or life that include technological fluency and literacy. The managers who are seeking competent employees for future work (Sardone & Delvin-Scherer, 2010) regard the 4Cs as critical skills in the workforce. Some executives (about 75.7%) have agreed that in the next three to five years they want to grow in the global economy of today, they need to have these 21st century skills to work in their organizations. The managers (about 80%) thought it would help them prepare for the future by teaching these skills to the students. The staff managers in the study also emphasis how important for the students to build the skills of reading, writing and arithmetic. These skills help the employees to think critically, solve problems, work together and effectively communicate. Ledward and Hirata (2011) agree that critical thought, problem solving, communication and teamwork needed to be proficient. Fandiño (2013) also proposes that such skills will help students flourish in a new global economy that demands effective use of information, synthesis, and communication. They must be able to work together to solve complex problems and find new knowledge through technologies from the 21st century.

A study of the essential qualifications for the 21st century learning is developed by Sardone and Delvin-Scherer (2010) to measure students' abilities to recognize their own motivational factors and learned the skills of digital games from the 21st century. The study examines the undergraduate students, who work with the middle school students on a game-based learning project. Sardone and Delvin-Scherer record the impressions on the motivation and playability of video games from the participants. They record the learning and innovation skills related to skills of the 21st century. They did interview with the focus group and record the experiences and reactions of the participants to game-based learning. They find that the students are indeed:

Capable of recognizing the learning skills incorporated into video games (p. 409).

They also make note that the decision of participants to use video games for instruction of "pair modelling and positive reactions" with middle-school students seemed to have an impact. The results show that the knowledge of the contents and teacher reactions of the participants in video games are important factors. Sardone and Delvin-Scherer (2010) have discovered that games actually teach students and develop skills of the 21st century. These qualifications are similar to the ISTE standards that include creativity and innovation, communication and collaboration, fluence of research and information, thinking, solving problems and making decisions, and digital citizenship that the international society for technology in education has developed for operations and concepts (ISTE)- ISTE) (Higgins, 2014).

Furthermore, the students should be able to articulate their ideas and ideas effectively via various communication instruments (Donovan et al., 2014). The 21st Century Partnership reports that it is important to ensure not only that student are able to articulate ideas through verbal, written and nonverbal communication, but also that they are able to hear the meaning of their ideas. The use of video game chats, voice streaming Websites, playing with friends and different digital tools can help them to develop these communication and collaboration. The ability to listen and effectively communicate affects the results of the teamwork in a video game. These environments provide a rich and immersive learning environment through joint gameplay to apply a variety of literatures of the 21st century (such as visual, technological, and textual).

A study of content analytics conducted by the Learning Games Lab New Mexico State University reports that students in the middle schools are interested in playing video games (Trespalacios et al., 2011). The study examines the acquisition of communication and collaboration skills of the 21st century. The scientists had invited kids in a summer research lab to play video games. The students were asked preferential questions in various settings after each research session. The results show that the students were motivated by companionship and collaboration, competition, and challenge rather than working in groups. Moreover, the data shows that 72% of 72 students prefer multiplayer games instead of single player games. Trespalacios et al. (2011) find that 30% of students who worked with other players to achieve their goals, and 34% of students wanted the multiplayer games because they could play with their friends. During the content analysis phase, the three main subjects had developed company, partnership and competition. These themes are directly affected students' preferences in the study. These results show that the students liked to work as a team and to develop their skills for social collaboration. These collaborative experiences reinforced by different levels of skills or expertise among players. Their expertise or skills are learned and shared between the communities when the roles defined by means of gameplay. The acquisition of information, values, attitudes, and purposes are the key factors in the successful communication with different groups and environments (Partnership for the 21st Century, 2011) and video games with their various cultural spaces are one type of digital tool that enables students to practise these skills on a platform. Economic and social skills are needed to interact with people of different language and cultural backgrounds today (NEA, 2010).

The importance of creativity and innovation is comparable to that of literacy (Robinson, 2006). According to the Partnership for 21st Century Skills, creativity and innovation help students develop their capacity for creative thinking, collaborative problem solving, and implementation of innovations (Donovan et al., 2014; NEA, 2010). Creativity is a critical 21st century skill for resolving today's most pressing global issues (Robinson, 1998; Newton & Newton, 2014). The collection of abilities, skills, motivations, and states that students must acquire in order to deal with these real-world issues (Alismail & McGuire, 2015; Hsiao et al., 2014; Hwang et al., 2015; Molderez, & Fonseca, 2018).

Four researchers at Taiwan National Normal University's Department of Technology Application and Human Resource Development have developed a game-based learning system to foster student creativity. Hsiao et al. (2014) had collected data on two fifth-grade classes. The experimental group consisted of one class, while the control group consisted of the other. The students were completing an "Electrical Science" classroom unit. The study's objective was to ascertain the instructional strategies used in the two classes. The researchers had created ToES, a digital game. One class was taught using the game-based learning system, while the other was taught using traditional classroom methods. The data reveals that when the experimental group immersed in a game-based learning environment, their creativity and performance on manual skills had improved significantly. Hsaio et al. (2014) discover that the digital game was not only an effective learning tool, but also had a positive effect on student creativity and performance. Additionally, they discover that the game environment has aided in the "improvement of practical behaviours pertaining to manual skills" (p. 377). This study demonstrates how the use of a video game could stimulate students' creativity and provide an opportunity for them to practise the 21st century skills. The Partnership for the Twenty-First Century (National Education Association, 2010) concurs with Hsaio et al. (2014) advocate for game-based learning strategies that involve the use of video games to practise skills. They believe that students must be able to generate new ideas through a variety of techniques. Additionally, students must be able to elaborate, refine, analyse, and evaluate their work in order to maximise their creative efforts while demonstrating individual and group originality and inventiveness. According to the research done by Hsaio et al. (2014), creativity is not an innate characteristic of students but can be fostered and nurtured through 21st century learning. This study demonstrates that creative and innovative thinking can be taught. According to the results of the above report, today's thinking skills are not only based on conventional creative and critical skills, but also extended skills that can enhance students 21st century skills. This research had focused on the perceptions of Year 5 pupils at national schools on science subjects and examined the level of 21st century skills among students, which is a highlight of the 21st century changes and challenges. The differential in the pupils' ability levels in the 21st century in terms of gender of the pupils, as well as the relationship between the pupils' expectations of science subjects and 21st century skills are also highlighted in this section.

Game-Based Learning and 21st Century Skills

To prepare students for a 21st century economy, they need to be more creative minded to think deeper and develop their skills (Hilton, 2015; Checa-Romero & Gómez, 2018). Video games, like Minecraft, could be part of that educational mind shift to ensure that students are not merely consumers of media but the creators and designers of future innovations. Thus, they are more prepared for systematic and balanced academic achievement. Minecraft is a 16-bit sandbox video game that can run on most computers and mobile devices unlike other games that demand more hardware and substantial graphics cards. The content of the game is user-friendly. The avatars and the environments look very much like they are made of *Legos*. The enormously popular game boasts over 100 million registered players worldwide for the original PC version alone (Persson, 2014). This does not include players on mobile devices or newer releases of the game. *Minecraft* is a hybrid game with action-oriented learning structures and creative sandbox features. It gives players a choice to build a creative mode with unlimited resources or play in survival mode in which they have to gather their own resources, craft, and fight off attacks from monsters and other players. Other playing modes include hardcore, adventure, spectator, and multiplayer modes each with their own set of rules and player restrictions. In Minecraft, the players are also able to build machines in the game and modify the game's programming.

Minecraft Education for Game-Based Learning

Sandbox video games, such as *Minecraft's* 3D grid, fall under the art education paradigm of game design due to the "aesthetic choices" the students make in order to build and design an infinite number of creations (Overby & Jones, 2015). Additionally, Bergstrom and Lotto (2015) note that there is significant research into "aesthetic computing" which broadens the scope and emphasises the ways in which art can inform computing through creative coding or code bending. Overby and Jones (2015) examine the phenomenon of *Minecraft* through participant observations and interviews in a case study. They observed children participating in the game and interacting with one another while working on construction projects. Overby and Jones wanted to investigate how *Minecraft* could be used to aid in the teaching and learning of art. They conducted interviews with eight children ranging in age from five to eighteen years. Except for one participant, all were family members or acquaintances of the study's authors. Many of the children were female, which the researchers took note of as they considered how video games like *Minecraft* might encourage girls to consider careers in technology. Overby and Jones (2015) concur with Hayes (2008) that males are overrepresented in technology fields and that more females should enter these fields. They explain that *Minecraft* as their platform mean "classroom-friendly programme" capitalises on the educational potential of virtual spaces that support art education. Overby and Jones discover that players frequently acquire knowledge and skills in *Minecraft* by cultivating a culture of "peer teaching." They also discover that *Minecraft* enables children to create, collaborate, and reflect on their knowledge and artwork.

Additionally, Overby and Jones (2015) discover that it is equally engaging for male and female participants and that gaming and computing could be used to encourage more female students to pursue careers in technology. According to the researchers, using *Minecraft* in the classroom serves as a gateway to architecture concepts, 3D modelling software, and collaborative art. Overby and Jones (2015) conclude that:

Learning to programme in Minecraft may lead students to more complex coding activities or pique their interest in learning Photoshop, Maya, or other image and 3D modelling programmes that can assist them in creating new skins and objects for their Minecraft world (p. 24).

This is why educators in the STEAM fields have embraced *Minecraft* to teach engineering, physics, art, and mathematics (Jenkins, 2014). Student collaborations has extended beyond *Minecraft* and frequently result in the creation of modifications ("mods") to the game's programming to enhance content and gameplay (Elkins, 2015; Gee, 2003, 2005, 2012; Gee & Hayes, 2010). According to Myers (2008), the students can also acquire a variety of critical 21st century skills through digital design activities. *Minecraft* is unique in that it motivates students to learn fundamental concepts such as content creation, programming, 3D modelling, and game design through gameplay (Hewett, 2014).

RESEARCH METHODOLOGY

The aim of this study was to investigate the effectiveness of Minecraft-Game Based Learning towards on 21st century skills among the primary school pupils. The independent variable was the teaching method which consisted of Minecraft-Game Based Learning. The dependent variable of this study was 21st century skills. The 21st century skills questionnaire was adapted from Kelley et al. (2019). Examples of questionnaires items adapted from Kelley et al. (2019) are shown in Table 1. Some modifications were made to suit with level of the participants involved in this study. A pilot test was conducted to check the reliability of the questionnaire, and it was found that the reliability coefficient was high with the Cronbach Alpha's value of 0.81.

The questionnaire consisted of 25 items, measuring students' 21st century skills. The maximum score of 21st century skills questionnaire was five marks per response, which gave the total maximum scores of 125. The scale of scores for each questionnaire is based on the Likert scale, which starts from one to five marks. One mark was given for "strongly disagree" option and five marks for "strongly agree" option. The results from the tests were transformed into indexes by using a summated scale approach. The summated scale refers to the total score for the respondent on the scale, which are the sum of their ratings for all the items in the 21st century skills questionnaire. The summated scales of the 21st century skills in Pre-Test, Post-Test, and the extended Post-Test would be used for the data analysis. The results of the data analysis would indicate whether there was a significant change of 21st century skills among the students before and after the intervention of Minecraft-Game Based Learning programme.

The research methodology utilised in this study was a quasi-experimental design with Pre-Test, Post-Test, and an extended Post-Test of 21st century skills (Campbell & Stanley, 1963). The research design is illustrated in Table 2.

Table 1. Example of questionnaires

Examples of questionnaire items for 21st century skills Adapted from Kelley et al. (2019)	
1.	I can accept and respect others' opinions
2.	I can help others when needed.
3.	I can apply information in new tasks.
4.	I can ask questions to solve issues.
5.	I can elaborate and improve on ideas.
6.	I can use creativity and imagination.

Table 2. Quasi-experimental design with pre-test, post-test, and extended post-test

Pre-test	Intervention	Post-test	Extended post-test
O1	X	O2	O3

X the intervention of Minecraft-Game Based Learning
O1 pre-test of 21st century skills
O2 post-test of 21st century skills
O3 extended post-test of 21st century skills

Minecraft is a part of learning activities designed for the lesson of the Design and Technology at the Primary School level in Malaysia. The intervention of this study was carried out during the Movement Control Order (MCO) in Malaysia. The study samples consisted of 33 twelve-year-old pupils studying at one of the primary schools in Penang Island, which is situated in the northern region of Peninsular Malaysia. The school was closed due to the Covid-19 Pandemic from June till September 2021. They had a Minecraft remote learning activity once a week, which took 90 minutes per session. The pupils were involved with Minecraft activities through remote learning as all the participants stayed at home. They used laptops with internet connectivity to participate in a Minecraft multimode setting to collaborate and meet virtually as Minecraft players in the same world of Minecraft. The schoolteacher acted as the host of the virtual world, who provided a code for students to enter the same Minecraft world for a multimode setting.

This study was conducted in 13 weeks as follows:

- The Pre-Test of 21st century skills was given before the intervention that is in week 1.
- Seven weeks of Minecraft Game Based Learning intervention. In this study, the samples had experienced Minecraft-Game Based Learning activities which were: (i) providing an opportunity to mix world building with storytelling while using many of the Minecraft: Education Edition tools, (ii) exploring the concept of sustainable forest in Minecraft world, (iii) practicing observational skills and become honey connoisseurs by exploring honey's wide range of colours and tastes, (iv) learning alternative energy sources by having them build homes that make use of renewable energy in different Minecraft biomes, (v) building a rocket in Minecraft, (vi) building Mars rover in Minecraft (vii) exploring International Space Station (ISS) (viii) building a model of the circulatory system which goes over its major structures, and reviews the flow of blood throughout, and (ix) fun learning through Minecraft scavenger hunt (x) challenging students through Minecraft Esport. It took about 10 weeks to complete the Minecraft-Game Based Learning activities.
- Post-Test of 21st Century skills was given after the intervention in Week 11.
- The extended 21st Century skills was given 2 weeks after the Post-Test to determine the retention effect of Minecraft-Game Based Learning in Week 13.

The Design of Minecraft Activities to Enhance 21st Skills

Providing an Opportunity to Mix World Building with Storytelling while using Many of The Minecraft: Education Edition Tools

Minecraft brings a renewed interest in the educational games by providing educators an opportunity to mix world building with storytelling while using many of the Minecraft: Education Edition tools (Kangas et al., 2016). In Minecraft, students have the ability to build and recreate a fairy tale inside of Minecraft based on their creativity and imagination. They can demonstrate an understanding of digital storytelling and guide visitors of their Minecraft world through a comprehensive and interesting digital story experience. To make their world more interactive, students will use the narrative tools in Minecraft, for example slate, poster, board, signs, and Non-Player Characters (NPCs) to convey their storyline. Acknowledging differences among students, students are encouraged to modify the story they have read before and alter the storyline as long as the learning objectives are achieved. This process of building and recreating promotes reflection and stimulates students' critical thinking. Students are willingly to be creative when the learning opportunity is given. As an extension activity, they will also learn how to use the world builder tools for instance the fill and clone tools and utilize redstone and other elements in the game to combine coding skills with their storytelling. To train students to be future-ready learners, students are encouraged to collaborate on the creation of their project and share responsibilities among a group. With this, Minecraft helps students develop a range of 21st Century skills.

Exploring the Concept of Sustainable Forest in Minecraft World

Games involves learning process of different skills and knowledge relevant to school and real world (Lane & Yi, 2017). The issue of pollution and the increasing use of plastics have had a negative impact on the natural environment. For that, awareness on this issue needs to be created through Education. Minecraft helps students explore the world and learn ways to care for the environment by providing a template world about the natural environment. In this world, students are introduced to concepts and how these concepts relate to forest care. By using the world of Minecraft, students' thinking can be questioned and challenged with a variety of questions so that students can think to answer the questions asked whether in economic, social, and environmental terms. Next, students are also given the opportunity to appreciate the beauty of the natural environment and know the importance of forests to us. To take advantage of the world of templates provided, students can also be challenged with future studies in which students play a role as urban developers and how students can develop the city while they need to ensure the forest is maintained. Students can also be challenged to restore the condition of damaged forests based on creativity and critical thinking so that the balance of the ecosystem is ensured.

Practicing Observational Skills and Become Honey Connoisseurs by Exploring Honey's Wide Range ff Colours and Tastes

Minecraft can train students' observation skills in a fun way. Minecraft has partnered with the American Beekeeping Federation's Kids and Bee Program to build a Minecraft world that helps students become honey connoisseurs by exploring honey's wide range of colours and tastes. Before starting to explore this world, students can be asked about the honey production process as a teaching induction set so that students can start thinking and have the curiosity to explore this world of Minecraft. In the world of Minecraft, students interact with NPCs to find out relevant information and observe the honey production process. In addition, Minecraft can also help students know that geographical factors can affect the production of honey that differs in terms of colour and taste. Furthermore, Minecraft also allows students to build honey collecting machines automatically using Minecraft blocks. Through the process of building this machine, students also need computational thinking to build step by step activity.

Learning Alternative Energy Sources by Having Them Build Homes That Make Use of Renewable Energy in Different Minecraft Biomes

Lumen City Challenge and Lumen Power Challenge in Minecraft are introduced to facilitate students in learning renewable energy. These Minecraft biomes provide a fun way of learning alternative energy sources for students to build homes that make use of renewable energy that exists. With these, students explore their responsibility as good citizen and respond to environmental issues happened. In Lumen City Challenge and Lumen Power Challenge, students can explore and get ideas of how to build a sustainable city in a proper way. Then, students can conduct further learning activities by building their own sustainable city collaboratively. In this instance, students need to repair those damaged buildings and think of their plan to conserve and preserve their environment amidst of rapid development in the city. While repairing the city, students have to make their choices of choosing which renewable energy to be used as the alternative energy resources. Thus, students have to compare the strength and weakness of these renewable resources and find the answers where the energy production comes from. Besides mastering the skill, students will have the opportunities to learn about simple coding to do the repairing or building process faster.

Building a Rocket that can be Launched

Besides of learning space station, students can grab the chance to learn more about rocket and its structures through Minecraft. Learning will be more meaningful if students design and build their own rocket. Through this designing activity, they need to understand that how rockets take off and what blocks are required to make this automation system in Minecraft. Thus, imagination and planning happen among students as they take consideration of the materials needed. They need to place the blocks accordingly in correct position to ensure the automation system runs well. Minecraft trains student to be more patience and observable during their work. In such activity, Minecraft blocks, for example, sticky piston, slime, redstone block and level are used to put up a system. Hence, students are trained and learn about the correct usage of Minecraft blocks, learn to experiment their design and make improvement on it till better result. This is the beauty of Engineering element of STEM in Minecraft. In order to enabling STEM, students can be encouraged to take part in the Spaceships Minecraft Challenge.

Building Mars Rover

Children are born curious and ask many questions as they grow about the world around them. This is how children build their confidence, knowledge and skills that will enable them to adapt in their futures and ours. In Minecraft, they design models, collect information, test and retest, and communicate what they have done and found. To young children, they are simply natural in their behaviours with significant benefits to their habits of mind and their sense of competence. Minecraft enables their natural behaviours by providing a game-based learning environment to build, create, recreate, and examine their own preconceptions, and challenge themselves in Minecraft Challenges. Building Mars Rover is one of the Minecraft Challenges that students need to build their own Mars rover in Minecraft and understand the environment on Mars. Apart from that, it is vital that teachers stimulate students to think scientifically about the weather, growing crops, drinking water, and living situation. Thus, these challenges encourage students to build Mars rover based on criteria set by the teachers and explain their justification about the structures of their Mars rover with different Minecraft blocks. If they believe that students need to build ideas on their own, magic might happen.

Exploring International Space Station (ISS)

Astronomy topic can be introduced to students through Minecraft. Minecraft provides a journey for students to learn and explore space by using its International Space Station (ISS) world template. This astronomical Minecraft experience definitely stimulates students' thinking and visualisation. Besides, students can learn about the history of Astronomy and how the current solar system works. The International Space Station (ISS) provides students a cognitive scheme in which they can model and build their own space station or satellite based on their imagination by using Minecraft blocks and tools. For example, students build their space station or satellite by using iron blocks, grass blocks and it can be powered up by redstone and command blocks. This process requires students' acquisition of a wide range of knowledge and skills. In classroom mode, students can build dan display their Minecraft models to represent their concepts to get their immersive experiences. The knowledge and skills that are learnt through Minecraft will help them to understand the universe and the origin of space. Thus, educators can combine Minecraft with education so that students can have the chances to engage their interests as they learn in a safe and positive learning environment.

Building a Model of the Circulatory System which Goes Over its Major Structures, and Reviews the Flow of Blood Throughout

Minecraft helps students to explore and navigate the path that blood goes through the major parts of the blood circulatory system. Its major parts of the system can be identified through the Minecraft model. Students model the structures by using the Minecraft blocks and power it up by using redstone and command blocks. During the process of modelling, students can be guided to brainstorm on how the blood circulatory system work. Educators or teachers can stimulate students' thinking by questioning the purpose of the heart and lungs in a human body and why do human beings need to breath in oxygen. Students construct their knowledge based on the modelling activity through Minecraft. Besides of building and modelling, Minecraft also offers educators to run a digital escape room by putting Non-Player Characters (NPCs) as the quiz component to challenge and test student understandings of the blood circulatory system. In this digital escape room, those who can answer correctly will be teleported to next level or task till they finish the game. With this, Minecraft will not only help students to visualize but also give them the chance to learn through fun way.

Fun Learning through Minecraft Scavenger Hunt

Minecraft is not only a solo game but involves students to work in a team, to solve problems and have fun to reach the end of the destination in digital scavenger hunt. The scavenger hunt can be organized and carried out in Minecraft by using its unique features. In order to increase the levels of scavenger hunt, teachers can prepare few tasks that require students to solve and get their access codes (in coordinate position) to next level or tasks. Non-Player Characters (NPCs) or any boards can be used to give further instructions and guidance for students to accomplish their missions and teleport themselves (Avatars) to the location that fixed in Minecraft world. The tasks embedded in Minecraft can be taken from any subjects such as Mathematics, Science and Language Arts. Student will also learn to document their products and answers. This Minecraft Scavenger Hunt will probably take students about 45-60 minutes to complete, depending on students' ability levels. Adding competitive element like the time factor is the best way to enhance students' engagement in playing Scavenger Hunt in Minecraft.

Challenging Students through Minecraft Esports

Esports is the one of the new ways to engage students, enhance motivation, and keep them learnt especially during school closures. Minecraft serves as a learning environment that helps student to practice their social emotional learning and student leadership in team. Students collaborate, communicate, and solve problems together on projects in a shared Minecraft world with multiplayer. There are seven new lessons and worlds provided, Pirate Cove, Space Race, Gold Rush, Busy Bees, Binary Builders, Splat Racers, and 3D Print. Based on Esports Educator Framework, students can take part in build battles and use Structure Block to model their 3D builds. Students can export their 3D builds to 3D printers and visualise their build in concrete form. Minecraft provides variety of settings of Esports world to cater student learning needs. To win, students must team up and create their creative Minecraft builds through communication and collaboration. From the perspective of teachers, Esports helps teachers to incorporate creative, collaboration, critical thinking and communication among students. Besides, the values and ethics can be cultivated through learning activities to guide students practice digital citizenship. Hence, Minecraft engages students with competitive and collaborative learning activities which suits the nature of students.

RESULTS

The result of ANOVA with repeated measures test in Table 3 shows that the main effect of Minecraft towards 21st Century Skills was significant, Wilk's lambda $= 0.085$, $F(2, 31) = 166.869$, and Sig < 0.001.

Table 3. Result of multivariate test for 21st century skills

Effect		Value	F	Hypothesis df	Sig.
Skills	Wilks' Lambda	0.085	166.869	2.000	0.001

For the within variable, this result has also been supported by the univariate test. However, to choose and interpret the suitable univariate test, the assumption of the sphericity must be tested by using Mauchly test as shown in Table 4.

Table 4. Result of Mauchly test

Within Subjects Effect	Mauchly's W	Approx. Chi-Square	df	Sig.	Epsilon Greenhouse-Geisser
Skills	.930	2.234	2	.327	.935

The result of Mauchly test indicates that the Sig. value was more than 0.05. Therefore, the assumption of sphericity of variance covariance matrix was met. Therefore, the Sphericity Assumed test is referred as the univariate test for the purpose of the interpretation. It is found that there was a significant effect of test time on 21st Century Skills as shown in Table 5.

Table 5. Result of Sphericity Assumed test

Source		Type III Sum of Squares	df	Mean Square	F	Sig.
21st Century Skills	Sphericity Assumed	7224.434	2	3612.217	191.807	.000

The significant multivariate and univariate test indicate that at least there is a significant difference of the mean score between the tests (Pre-Test, Post-Test, and extended Post-Test). Based on the result of the pairwise comparisons test in Table 6, it shows that there was a significant change of mean scores for 21st Century Skills between Pre-Test and Post-Test and between Post-Test and extended Post-Test.

Table 6. Pairwise comparisons test of 21st century skills

Skills	Skills	Mean Difference	Std. Error	Sig.
Pre Test	Post Test	17.612	1.197	0.001
Post Test	Extended Post Test	0.979	0.966	0.955

Table 7 shows the result of estimated marginal means for 21st Century Skills. The result shows that there was an increase in the mean score between the Pre-Test (126.00) and Post-Test (190.70) of 21st Century Skills. Therefore, it can be concluded that Minecraft is effective in enhancing the 21st century skills learning among the pupils.

Table 7. Estimated marginal means

Skills	Mean	95% Confidence Interval	
		Lower Bound	Upper Bound
Pre Test	78.606	76.556	80.656
Post Test	96.218	95.014	97.422
Delayed Post Test	97.197	95.596	98.798

The similar pattern also was observed on the change of Post-Test to Delayed Post-Test of the group 21st Century skills. Thus, it can be interpreted, although the intervention of Minecraft was removed from the learning process, the students did show some improvement on the 21st century skills. This indicates that the past learning experiences of Minecraft had successfully trained the participants to acquire and internalise the 21st Century skills for a future learning task.

SOLUTIONS AND RECOMMENDATION

This study indicates that Minecraft was able to increase the 21st-century skills of the students (Poiroux et al., 2016). The learning experiences and opportunities created by Minecraft can address the implementation of 21st-century skills in fun ways. The features of Minecraft can set the virtual platform to become a multiplayer setting. Therefore, all players can meet and work together in the same room. As Minecraft provides many challenges, the multiplayer environment can allow the participants to work collaboratively to complete the task (Hewett et al., 2020). One of the Minecraft activities requires the students to build Mars Rovers. As Mars Rover is a sophisticated vehicle with robotic capability thus, the students need to collaborate to ensure all Mars Rovers compartments have been considered in the designing and developing process. Some participants can focus on building the base and the frame structures, whereas others can help by creating the four tyres of the Mars Rovers that were supposed to be sturdy.

Besides building Mars Rovers in Mars through this programme, the pupils had the experience to manifest their creativity through tasks by building their own control center and food supply system in Mars. With such conditions in Mars, students were challenged to imagine creatively and think critically about their creation which can make humans survive with the most effective solution. Students had received wealth of information each day, but they were required to think, analyze, evaluate information received and then make their decision based on facts to create in their virtual learning spaces (Kuhn & Stevens, 2017). Minecraft activities in this project had given them a chance to take information and apply it to solve problems and create solutions or prototypes. For instance, the pupils had combined chemistry elements, such as are hydrogen (H) and oxygen (O), to produce water (H_2O) that are the essential living requirement for humans and crops and made a self-harvesting system by using sticky pistons, redstone, hopper, observer, and dispenser. It was fun and essential to move beyond about Minecraft as it required students to demonstrate their knowledge and thinking during the building process and final product. Thus, the pupils not only had learnt new knowledge, but also practice some chemistry experiment in a safe sandbox environment via Laboratory Table (Lab Table) in Minecraft. Minecraft might be considered as the most user friendliest way to set up custom experiments, where other games are usually lack modifiability (Nebel et al., 2016).

To promote the pupils' creativity in through this project, they should be confident that they had the capability to complete the task. In Minecraft, blocks can be arranged in a way that could reproduce almost every static object or shape, thus providing stimuli for a very different set of education projects (Nebel et al., 2016). It is found that Minecraft has positive effect on increasing students' creativity (Bereczki & Karpati, 2021) and divergent thinking abilities (Blanco-Herrera et al., 2019). This expectation has been cultivated in students in Minecraft as students are able to express their creative behaviors via creations of prototypes that fulfill the common evaluation criteria, namely: 1) originality, 2) usefulness, and 3) novelty (Diedrich et al., 2015). Furthermore, they have worked as a team to start their living project in Mars and be collaborative Martian community. Although students often dislike working in group as they do not have collaboration skills in working on something productively (Tech4Learning, n.d.), but this was not the case in this project. Minecraft had provided a space for students to develop the skills, behaviors and attitude that resulted in a productive and successful teamwork by listening, sharing, clarifying motivating, and showing empathize to each other. Thus, the importance of collaboration is flourished effectively in students (Poiroux, Dahl-Jørgensen, Løyland & Rye, 2016).

Through this project, Minecraft had changed the nature of literacy. To have strong literacy skills, students should have the ability to read and share thoughts and ideas in ways other can understand (Tech4Learning, n.d.). In digital era, the medium of communication has changed from traditional to digital ways, but the literacy ability is still the same regardless of the medium. Acknowledging this, Minecraft activities assist the participants to build communication skills with multimedia forms of communication, transforming from "listening and doing" to "showing and explaining" by using multimedia in Minecraft by offering a variety of task formats (Darling-Hammond et al., 2020). For example, in this study the pupils had used camera to capture their creations and explain it through Book and Quills. They also showed their understandings about music notes by activating the Note Block based on different blocks beneath it in Minecraft. Hence, Minecraft facilitates the process of learning communication skills as technology has changed the way how students communicate (Roztocki et al., 2019).

FUTURE RESEARCH DIRECTIONS

The 21st-century learning design in Minecraft is infinity, meaning it allows educators to design and manipulate the Minecraft world to suit different pedagogical approaches. Future research can expand the concept of Minecraft beyond the game-based learning approach, with the infusion of unsupervised discovery-based learning approach and self-supervised learning with a lot of guiding questions that stimulate students to used higher-order thinking skills such as building models within the game for completing the tasks (Nieto et al., 2021). Instead of seeing the solution of the Minecraft task to be recipe-driven, the task can be designed to be open-ended, with a different route of learning to complete the task. The current study has indicated that playing Minecraft in an educational setting is not purposely designed for knowledge construction for specific subjects only, as the focus is more on enhancing 21st-century skills. Thus, future research can be done to investigate how questions can be formulated to promote students' higher order thinking skills that require complex cognitive processes for the knowledge construction in the Minecraft world. In other words, future research should compare content-free Minecraft activities and subject-based Minecraft activities that incorporate series of higher-order thinking questions. Future research can postulate that infusion of higher-order thinking skills in subject-based Minecraft would provide a context for the students to practice their 21st Century skills meaningfully instead of generic

Minecraft of activities. Therefore, Minecraft can be used as a tool for students or pupils to enhance their ability to analyze, evaluate and create new knowledge. For example, the teachers can integrate Minecraft as the pedagogical tool in Project-Based Learning (PBL) to push the learning in classrooms from instruction to construction. Students could work in groups to solve problem such as improving the landscape to meet the green city requirement by reducing the plastic usage and landfills. This authentic problem will stimulate students to actively brainstorm, plan, model, and experiment using higher order thinking skills to solve problems created in Minecraft. Probably, future research can utilize qualitative data technique used by Stufft and von Gillern (2021) by analyzing students' written reflection on the process of making interpretations and decision making within a game.

CONCLUSION

There are growing numbers of educational games developed to support the teaching of 21st century skills and Minecraft is one of them. The present study has indicated that Minecraft Game Based Learning was able to promote meaningful learning through providing players with opportunities to develop valued 21st century skills such as collaboration, creativity, and critical thinking (Edwards et al., 2021). The collaboration skill is needed to ensure that students work well in team or with others, respect other people's opinion, and try to compromise with one another in order to accomplish goals or shared responsibility. The creativity element can make students more innovative and inventive such as creating new information or create original idea. Also, the critical thinking is needed to reason, solve problem, and make decision. Having said this, Minecraft provides the platform for these skills to be enhanced by giving the players the real agency over the challenge or learning objective they are trying to achieve. As opposed to a question-and-answer format that calls for rote memorization, Minecraft presents systems-based challenges that need to be solved through understanding and experimentation. These challenges are often novel to the students, offering access to experiences that would otherwise be too expensive or too dangerous to accomplish in a classroom. Along those same lines, Minecraft creates an opportunity in which the players can fail safely without any cost on real material to them or anyone else. This allows for reflection and iteration on the part of the player, by thinking critically about their own approach and improving on it. Minecraft works best when it is experienced as a group, and the type of play that takes place in a learning game which is no exception. As mentioned above, Minecraft also imitates the kind of collaborative work style that typifies a modern workplace in which specialized professionals bring together their complementary skillsets to work effectively with each other in the pursuit of a shared goal (Qian & Clark, 2016). Exchanging ideas with other people and having mutual understanding or agreement with one another are very crucial in collaborative work style as well (Callaghan, 2016). Thus, Minecraft does not just teach students what to learn, but also how to learn alongside with other people such as their peers. Minecraft can be considered as a tool for constructivist learning and content creation. The game serves as a blank slate that educators can use to design learning (Kuhn, 2017). The open-ended nature of Minecraft also affords the players the ability to solve a problem in multiple ways (Hewett et al., 2020); meaning that there is not just one way to solve the designed problems encountered but there are other alternatives to find the solutions. The world created by Minecraft illuminates the experiences such as searching, accessing, communicating, and discovering solutions to complex situation. Such experiences are crucial because they reflect solutions to practical, real-life problems that might not have any prescribed solution when they are first confronted. Finally, Minecraft creates the opportunity for the players to use multiple types of reasoning and to make judgments and decisions based on the evidence presented from their activities in the game.

ACKNOWLEDGMENT

The authors would like to thank Microsoft Malaysia for the collaboration opportunities.

REFERENCES

Alexander, A., & Ho, T. (2015). Gaming worlds: Secondary students creating an interactive Video game. *Art Education*, *68*(1), 28–36. doi:10.1080/00043125.2015.11519303

Alismail, H. A., & McGuire, P. (2015). 21st century standards and curriculum: Current research and practice. *Journal of Education and Practice*, *6*(6), 150–154.

Beetham, H., & Sharpe, R. (Eds.). (2013). *Rethinking pedagogy for a digital age: Designing for 21st century learning* (Vol. 711). Routledge. doi:10.4324/9780203078952

Bereczki, E. O., & Kárpáti, A. (2021). Technology-enhanced creativity: A multiple case study of digital technology-integration expert teachers' beliefs and practices. *Thinking Skills and Creativity*, *39*, 39. doi:10.1016/j.tsc.2021.100791

Bergstrom, I., & Lotto, R. B. (2015). Code Bending: A new creative coding practice. *Leonardo*, *48*(1), 25–31. doi:10.1162/LEON_a_00934

Blanco-Herrera, J. A., Gentile, D. A., & Rokkum, J. N. (2019). Video games can increase creativity, but with caveats. *Creativity Research Journal*, *31*(2), 119–131. doi:10.1080/10400419.2019.1594524

Blikstein, P., Kabayadondo, Z., Martin, A., & Fields, D. (2017). An assessment instrument of technological literacies in makerspaces and FabLabs. *Journal of Engineering Education*, *106*(1), 149–175. doi:10.1002/jee.20156

Callaghan, N. (2016). Investigating the role of Minecraft in educational learning environments. *Educational Media International*, *53*(4), 244–260. doi:10.1080/09523987.2016.1254877

Campbell, D. T., & Stanley, J. C. (1963). *Experimental and quasi-experimental design for research*. Cengage Learning.

Checa-Romero, M., & Pascual Gómez, I. (2018). Minecraft and machinima in action: Development of creativity in the classroom. *Technology, Pedagogy and Education*, *27*(5), 625–637. doi:10.1080/14759 39X.2018.1537933

Claymier, B. (2014). Integrating stem into the elementary curriculum. *Children's Technology & Engineering*, *18*(3), 5.

Darling-Hammond, L., Schachner, A., & Edgerton, A. K. (2020). Restarting and reinventing school: Learning in the time of COVID and beyond. Palo Alto, CA: Learning Policy Institute.

Diedrich, J., Benedek, M., Jauk, E., & Neubauer, A. (2015). Are Creative Ideas Novel and Useful? *Psychology of Aesthetics, Creativity, and the Arts*, *9*(1), 35–40. doi:10.1037/a0038688

Donovan, L., Green, T. D., & Mason, C. (2014). Examining the 21st century classroom: Developing an innovation configuration map. *Journal of Educational Computing Research*, *50*(2), 161–178. doi:10.2190/EC.50.2.a

Edwards, B., Edwards, B. B., Griffiths, S., Reynolds, F. F., Stanford, A., & Woods, M. (2021). The Bryn Celli Ddu Minecraft Experience: A Workflow and Problem-Solving Case Study in the Creation of an Archaeological Reconstruction in Minecraft for Cultural Heritage Education. *Journal on Computing and Cultural Heritage*, *14*(2), 1–16. doi:10.1145/3427913

Elkins, A. J. (2015). Lets Play: Why School Librarians Should Embrace Gaming in the Library. *Knowledge Quest*, *43*(5), 58–63.

Fandiño Parra, Y. (2013). 21st century skills and the English foreign language classroom: A call for more awareness in Colombia. *Gist Education and Learning Research Journal*, *7*, 190–208.

Gee, J. P. (2003). What video games have to teach us about learning and literacy. *Computers in Entertainment*, *1*(1), 20–20. doi:10.1145/950566.950595

Gee, J. P. (2005). Learning by design: Good video games as learning machines. *E-Learning and Digital Media*, *2*(1), 5–16. doi:10.2304/elea.2005.2.1.5

Gee, J. P., & Hayes, E. (2012). Nurturing affinity spaces and game-based learning. *Games, learning, and society: Learning and meaning in the digital age, 123*, 1-40.

Gee, J. P., & Hayes, E. R. (2010). Passionate affinity groups. In Women and Gaming (pp. 105-123). Palgrave Macmillan. doi:10.1057/9780230106734_6

Hayes, E. (2008). Girls, gaming and trajectories of IT expertise. In Beyond Barbie and Mortal Kombat: New perspectives on gender and computer games (pp.138-194). Cambridge MA: The MIT Press.

Hewett, K., Zeng, G., & Pletcher, B. (2020). The Acquisition of 21st Century Skills Through Video Games: Minecraft Design Process Models and Their Web of Class Roles. *Simulation & Gaming*, *51*(3). doi:10.1177/1046878120904976

Hewett, K. J. E. (2014). Jump in! A teacher's journey into Minecraft. *TechEdge Magazine*, *2*, 14–17.

Higgins, S. (2014). Critical thinking for 21st century education: A cyber-tooth curriculum? *Prospects*, *44*(4), 559–574. doi:10.100711125-014-9323-0

Hilton, M. (2015). Preparing students for life and work. *Issues in Science and Technology*, *31*(4), 63.

Hsiao, H., Chang, C. C., Lin, C., & Hu, P. (2014). Development of children's creativity and Manual skills within digital game-based learning environment. *Journal of Computer Assisted Learning*, *30*(4), 377–395. doi:10.1111/jcal.12057

Hunt, M. W. (2013). (APP) elite for instruction: 21st-century learners in a video and audio production classroom. *Techniques - American Vocational Association*, *88*(8), 36.

Hwang, G. J., Chiu, L. Y., & Chen, C. H. (2015). A contextual game-based learning approach to improving students' inquiry-based learning performance in social studies courses. *Computers & Education, 81*, 13–25. doi:10.1016/j.compedu.2014.09.006

Jenkins, B. (2014). Don't quit playing: Video games in the STEM classroom. *Techniques, 89*(1), 60–61.

Jonassen, D. H. (2007). Engaging and supporting problem solving in online learning. *Online Learning Communities*, 109-127.

Jones, V. R. (2014). Teaching STEM: 21st century skills. *Children's Technology & Engineering, 18*(4), 11–13.

Kamisah, O., Zanaton, H. L., & Lilia, H. (2007). Sikap terhadap sains dan sikap saintifik di kalangan pelajar sains. *Jurnal Pendidikan, 32*(3), 39–60.

Kangas, M., Koskinen, A., & Krokfors, L. (2017). A qualitative literature review of educational games in the classroom: The teacher's pedagogical activities. *Teachers and Teaching, 23*(4), 451–470.

Kelley, & Knowles, Han, & Sung. (2019). Creating a 21st century skills survey instrument for high school students. *American Journal of Educational Research, 7*(8), 583–590. doi:10.12691/education-7-8-7

Kuhn, J. (2017). Minecraft: Education edition. *CALICO Journal, 35*(2), 214–223. doi:10.1558/cj.34600

Kuhn, J., & Stevens, V. (2017). Participatory culture as professional development: Preparing teachers to use Minecraft in the classroom. *TESOL Journal, 8*(4), 753–767. doi:10.1002/tesj.359

Lane, H. C., & Yi, S. (2017). Playing with virtual blocks: Minecraft as a learning environment for practice and research. In *Cognitive development in digital contexts* (pp. 145–166). Academic Press. doi:10.1016/B978-0-12-809481-5.00007-9

Ledward, B. C., & Hirata, D. (2011). *An overview of 21st century skills. Summary of 21st century skills for students and teachers*. Kamehameha Schools–Research & Evaluation.

Molderez, I., & Fonseca, E. (2018). The efficacy of real-world experiences and service learning for fostering competences for sustainable development in higher education. *Journal of Cleaner Production, 172*, 4397–4410. doi:10.1016/j.jclepro.2017.04.062

Myers, B. (2008). Minds at play. *American Libraries, 39*(5), 54–57.

National Education Association. (2010). *Preparing 21st century students for a global society: An educator's guide to the "Four Cs."* National Education Association.

Navarrete, C. (2013). Creative thinking in digital game design and development: A case study. *Computers & Education, 69*, 320–331. doi:10.1016/j.compedu.2013.07.025

Nebel, S., Rey, G. D., & Schneider, S. (2016). Mining learning and crafting scientific experiments: A literature review on the use of Minecraft in education and research. *Journal of Educational Technology & Society, 19*(2), 355–366.

Newton, L. D., & Newton, D. P. (2014). Creativity in 21st-century education. *Prospects, 44*(4), 575–589. doi:10.100711125-014-9322-1

Nieto, J. J., Creus, R., & Giro-i-Nieto, X. (2021). *Unsupervised Skill-Discovery and Skill-Learning in Minecraft.* arXiv preprint arXiv:2107.08398.

Nor, E. B. A., & Eu, L. K. (2014). Hubungan antara sikap, minat, pengajaran guru dan pengaruh rakan sebaya terhadap pencapaian matametik tambahan tingkatan 4. *JuKu:Jurnal Kurikulum & Pengajaran Asia Pasifik, 2*(1), 1–10.

Nurazidawati, Tuan Mastura, & Kamisah. (2011). *Pengalaman pembelajaran melalui khidmat komuniti pelajar Sains: Tranformasi dan inovasi dalam pendidikan.* Bangi: Penerbit Universiti Kebangsaan Malaysia.

Osman, K., & Marimuthu, N. (2010). Setting new learning targets for the 21st century science education in Malaysia. *Procedia: Social and Behavioral Sciences, 2*(2), 3737–3741. doi:10.1016/j.sbspro.2010.03.581

Overby, A., & Jones, B. L. (2015). Virtual LEGOs: Incorporating Minecraft into the art education curriculum. *Art Education, 68*(1), 21–27. doi:10.1080/00043125.2015.11519302

Partnership for 21st Century Skills. (2011). *21st century skills map.* Partnership for 21st Century Skills.

Persson, M. (2014, February 25). *Minecraft user announcement* [Social media message]. Retrieved from https://twitter.com/notch/status/438444097141882880

Pink, D. H. (2006). *A whole new mind: Why right-brainers will rule the future.* Riverhead Books.

Poiroux, J., Dahl-Jørgensen, T., Løyland, M., & Rye, S. (2016). *Using Minecraft to Enhance Collaboration as a 21st Century Skill in Primary Schools.* University of Oslo.

Qian, M., & Clark, K. R. (2016). Game-based Learning and 21st century skills: A review of recent research. *Computers in Human Behavior, 63*, 50–58. doi:10.1016/j.chb.2016.05.023

Robinson, K. (1998). National Advisory Council for creative and cultural education - NACCCE. *RSA Journal*, (5486), 20.

Robinson, K. (2006, June). *Ken Robinson: Do schools kill creativity?* [Video file]. Retrieved From https://www.ted.com/talks/ken_robinson_says_schools_kill_creativity?language=en#t201246

Robinson, K., & Aronica, L. (2006). *Creative schools: The grassroots revolution that is transforming education.* Penguin Books.

Roztocki, N., Soja, P., & Weistroffer, H. R. (2019). The role of information and communication technologies in socioeconomic development: Towards a multi-dimensional framework. *Information Technology for Development, 25*(2), 171–183. doi:10.1080/02681102.2019.1596654

Salen, K. (2007). Gaming literacies: A game design study in action. *Journal of Educational Multimedia and Hypermedia, 16*(3), 301–322.

Sardone, N. B., & Devlin-Scherer, R. (2010). Teacher candidate responses to digital games: 21st-century skills development. *Journal of Research on Technology in Education, 42*(4), 409–425. doi:10.1080/15391523.2010.10782558

Seele, P., & Lock, I. (2017). The game-changing potential of digitalization for sustainability: Possibilities, perils, and pathways. *Sustainability Science, 12*(2), 183–185. doi:10.100711625-017-0426-4

Soulé, H., & Warrick, T. (2015). Defining 21st century readiness for all students: What we know and how to get there. *Psychology of Aesthetics, Creativity, and the Arts, 9*(2), 178–186. doi:10.1037/aca0000017

Stufft, C., & von Gillern, S. (2021). Fostering Multimodal Analyses of Video Games: Reflective Writing in the Middle School. *Journal of Adolescent & Adult Literacy*, jaal.1198. doi:10.1002/jaal.1198

Tech4Learning. (n.d.). *Creating a 21st century classroom: combining the 3R's and the 4C's*. Author.

Trespalacios, J., Chamberlin, B., & Gallagher, R. R. (2011). Collaboration, engagement & fun: How youth preferences in video gaming can inform 21st century education. *TechTrends, 55*(6), 49–54. doi:10.100711528-011-0541-5

Živkovi, Ł. (2016). A model of critical thinking as an important attribute for success in the 21st century. *Procedia: Social and Behavioral Sciences, 232*, 102–108. doi:10.1016/j.sbspro.2016.10.034

Section 7
Learner Assessment, Motivation, and Behaviors in Game-Based Learning

Chapter 39

How Gaming and Formative Assessment Contribute to Learning Supplementary and Complementary Angles

Elvira Lázaro Santos
Instituto Superior de Lisboa e Vale do Tejo, Portugal

Leonor Santos
Instituto de Educação, Universidade de Lisboa, Portugal

ABSTRACT

This chapter presents an empirical research where the authors developed tasks based on a digital game supported by assessment strategies. The study is interpretative in nature, in a case study design. The authors designed tasks with technology and assessment strategies in a collaborative work context implemented in a mathematics classroom with 5th grade students (students 10 years old). The results evidence that the use of a digital game and formative assessment have contributed to the learning of complementary and supplementary angle pairs, giving meaning to their utilization as an effective strategy.

INTRODUCTION

Game-based learning is regarded as a kind of teaching that is based on the principle that, by their nature, games trigger positive emotional experiences and make the user the protagonist of their learning by developing action strategies (Offenholley, 2012). When the game being used is digital, the action strategies developed are based on decisions that are restricted by a set of rules in a computer program in the context of the game providing immediate feedback and reward (Schuytema, 2008). The active and participative style of learning with digital games therefore breaks away from the traditionally passive lesson. The student develops an interaction with the digital device that even if it was not designed for this purpose, it becomes an instrument with potential for specific learning uses. Therefore, we need to

DOI: 10.4018/978-1-7998-7271-9.ch039

identify the limitations imposed by the device, but also to recognize the new possibilities. Likewise, taking advantage of the new possibilities is very challenging for the teacher and demands a deep reflection on how to use them (Artigue, 2002).

The presence of an entity in the classroom that is emotionally neutral, such as technology can contribute to students being more dynamic and no longer remaining in the position of observers. As such, the teacher's intervention should be an intentionally designed mediation to align the response that the technology provides the student after the interaction, with his/her learning needs, through verbal or written feedback (Santos & Santos, 2019). Thus, formative assessment is of great importance for the students' learning success since the evidence intentionally collected by teachers along with the feedback contributes to the student's reflection process so that they become agents in their own learning (Black & Wiliam, 2009). However, the implementation of formative assessment is far from becoming a classroom reality as it entails a radical change in the way the teacher relates to their students and how they relate to each other in the classroom (Black, 2015), which calls for the need to continue developing these types of studies.

This chapter presents an experimental investigation in which we developed mathematics tasks based on digital game and formative assessment strategies that include the use of assessment criteria and written feedback from the teacher. The task and the game that was introduced to students was designed to understand how one might engage students in tasks of this nature and how these strategies might contribute to the learning of pairs of complementary and supplementary angles. In this context, we intended to understand the contribution of using a digital game and formative assessment in students' learning of supplementary and complementary angles.

TASKS WITH DIGITAL TECHNOLOGY

Regarding the intention towards the use of technology in the classroom, Pierce and Stacey (2013) find that it can be used to support students' work towards finding answers more quickly on problems by developing appropriate strategies. So, these authors present a conceptual framework that specifies educational opportunities from the use of technology that can be adopted by teachers to benefit learning. This concept map does not describe every possible opportunity, but it is organized into three levels which reflect the teachers' perspectives, taking into consideration the tasks they will set for their students; the style of classroom interaction; and the perspectives on the subject they should promote, i.e., mathematics as a whole, or a topic. Regarding the tasks that will be set for the students the map highlights five different types of opportunities to use mathematics software. These different types of tasks range from: a) assisting in mathematical learning using paper and pencil, by encouraging calculations check, thus freeing the student from mechanical work, and allowing him/her to focus his/her attention on other areas of the problem; b) allowing the student to work with real data; c) exploring variance and regularities that can be, for instance, through the use of an applet with sliders; d) analyzing simulated data or collecting data through graphs from real situations; e) or, using different representations of the same mathematical concept, visualized simultaneously.

In Pierce and Stacey's (2013) conceptual framework, we also see the teacher's intent to use technology in mathematics learning. Thus, the teacher may choose to use technology in order to introduce students to mathematics as a subject with a role in society, but he or she may also choose to give emphasis to the understanding of concepts, or even to approach topics in new ways that first allow for a more general overview of the purpose of the topic before focusing on details.

The interest in software is also mentioned by Hoyles and Noss (2003) for its transformative potential for mathematical learning and student engagement. Through this engagement it can allow insights into the students' ideas and practices because by exploring and solving problems with digital technology, their thoughts become both visible and progressively shaped by their interactions with the tool. Laborde et. al., (2006) also mention the exploratory nature of these environments and their contribution to amplify the investigative processes during task solving, enabling the visibility of the student's understanding and the strategies they devise. The meaning of the student's actions is provided by the technology and the technology provides responses to the student's actions.

Since digital games are part of the students' daily lives as a tool for recreation and entertainment, it is possible to use them as motivational factors. With the use of digital games, the user can adapt the rhythm of the game to their own pace of work, as opposed to lectures in which the student is dependent on the teacher's pace. In addition, games also feature information in multiple aspects that help reach users with different learning styles, making them useful for assigning meaning and strengthening information retention. Game-based tasks provide conditions for formulating hypotheses, experimenting with strategies, and understanding the consequences of actions taken, i.e., they are very similar to research-based learning (Mayo, 2009).

Therefore, tasks based on digital games become of great importance to enhance an exploratory type of teaching and learning, solving problems and developing suitable strategies. These tasks are based on challenge and require more focus and dedication (Bissoloti, Nogueira, & Pereira, 2014). These digital games impose new rhythms, new perceptions and different ways of thinking, thus contributing to new ways of learning (Garcia, Rabelo, Silva, & Amaral, 2011).

FORMATIVE ASSESSMENT PRACTICES

Formative Assessment

In order to provide a theoretical framework for the formative assessment Black and Wiliam (2009) mention three key processes in teaching and learning, which are to identify: (i) where the learner is right now; (ii) where the learner is going; and, (iii) how to get there. Traditionally, the teacher is responsible for each of these steps, however, it is necessary to consider the role of students and their peers in this process. By crossing these three processes with the three players (teacher, student, and peers) we get five strategic categories which are consistent with the regulatory assessment of learning. Black and Wiliam (2009) use a table to present the roles of each of the players in formative assessment and their respective steps in the process (Table 1).

Throughout the whole process, the teacher is concerned with encouraging the student's thinking, which makes the student become more active and so the teacher's job is less predictable. Formative assessment is thus concerned with developing and enhancing the existence of moments for reflection and uncertainty in the teaching and learning process aimed at regulating the learning process. As such, formative assessment should be developed during the learning process focusing on both the outcomes and the processes. In this process, the other participants are equally important - the teacher and the student's peers. It is the teacher's responsibility to collect relevant information in order to better get to know the student, and the whole process of interaction between the different participants, thereby generating opportunities for reflection and rethinking the outputs and subsequent new learning (Black & Wiliam, 2009).

Table 1. Aspects of formative assessment

	Where the learner is going	**Where the learner is right now**	**How to get there**
Teacher	**1.** Clarifying learning intentions and criteria for success Understanding and sharing learning intentions and criteria for success	**2.** Engineering effective classroom discussions and other learning tasks that elicit evidence of student understanding	**3.** Providing feedback that moves learners forward
Peer	Understanding learning intentions and criteria for success	**4.** Activating students as instructional resources for one another	
Learner		**5.** Activating students as the owners of their own learning	

Source: (Black & Wiliam, 2009)

In order to ensure effective, quality learning for all students, formative assessment should be used systematically in the classroom rather than emerging as an interruption of classroom activity (Black & Wiliam, 2009; Storeygard, Hamm, & Fosnot, 2010). Teachers should seek evidence from a variety of sources to ensure the converging of that evidence so that each student can display his or her strengths and for which the primary purpose is to obtain information that supports the learning and teaching of Mathematics. Hence, the assessment should not merely be done to the students but, instead, it should be done for the students, in order to guide them and improve their learning (NCTM, 2014).

Assessment Criteria and Feedback

The assessment criteria are a set of rules that guide the entire work and that should be taken into account by all participants, i.e., they are a language which is accepted and used by all players involved, both the assessors and the assessed (Santos, 2019; Vial, 2001).

Thus, the criteria in formative assessment do not follow a rationale of control in which the instructions demand no deviation from the appropriate path, but rather follow a rationale of orientation, and it is therefore up to the individual to find the path to reach a reference point (Vial, 2001). Hence, the assessment criteria are a set of rules which guide students in the preparation of their work and its redesign, but also for the teacher when he/she examines the students' work to understand whether they have acquired a certain knowledge or developed a certain skill (Nunziati, 1990; Santos & Cai, 2016). Also, it assigns feedback to guide the students' efforts in rewriting their outputs.

The feedback is an essential element of formative assessment because without it there is no interaction between the student and the teacher which provides all the essential information for the development of reflection and learning (Sadler, 1989). When the teacher needs to give useful verbal feedback to students it leads the teacher to be more attentive to student responses in class and to acknowledge that the learning process has to involve students in order for them to construct their own learning (Black & Wiliam, 2006). The questions asked are more open-ended in nature and students are also given more time to think about their answer and all of their answers are taken into consideration regardless of whether they are right or wrong (Black, 2015).

Written feedback can be provided through annotations as transmission of information or through annotations in the form of dialogue. Annotations in the form of dialogue are important because they emphasize questions, clues and encourage the student's reflection (Santos, 2008). So in order for feedback to be meaningful to the student and to contribute to his/her learning, it must: (i) be clear, so that it can be understood by the student; (ii) encourage the student to reconsider his/her answer; (iii) suggest clues for further action; (iv) not include the error correction, so as to allow the student to identify it; (v) identify what is already done well, to promote self-confidence and acknowledgement of his/her knowledge (Santos, 2008).

Providing feedback on the students' work enables us to give directions on what paths to pursue in order to overcome challenges. The use of feedback should encourage students' internal dialogue based on external feedback (Santos & Pinto, 2018). In addition to the need to think much more carefully about the feedback that is recorded to guide the student in their improvement, it is also necessary to select tasks that allow for a type of work which encourages students to develop and express their thinking. Black and Wiliam (2018) mention that some teachers have asked questions about what is considered good feedback. The authors state that, even though in the beginning it was not possible to identify a good answer, today we already know that good feedback is that which stimulates thinking (Black & Wiliam, 2018).

METHODOLOGY AND CONTEXT OF THE RESEARCH STUDY

The study is interpretive in nature, following a design of case study. An interpretive methodology focuses on the search for meanings in order to obtain a better understanding of the problem studied through the participants' point of view. Qualitative researchers are interested in clarifying the internal dynamics of situations, which may be invisible to the external observer (Bogdan & Biklen, 1994). It is an investigation that seeks to understand the ways in which teachers and students, in their joint interactions, create environments for each other (Erickson, 1986). The case study design aims to investigate a contemporary phenomenon within its real-life context where the boundaries between what we intend to study and its context are not clearly defined (Yin, 1998). Choosing the qualitative case study design is also supported by the fact that this approach pays special attention to the characterization of a phenomenon in its singularity (Merriam, 1988), where observation has a flexible and open nature (Aires, 2015) that is important to understand a complex practice such as teaching.

This study is informed by a collaborative approach as it is conducted with people who, collaboratively with others, examine their own experience and action carefully, intertwining action with reflection (Heron & Reason, 2006). In a context of collaborative work between the researcher, the first author, and two mathematics teachers, we have designed tasks based on a digital game and assessment strategies that were implemented in the classroom. The data presented in this chapter are related to the practice of one of the teachers in the collaborative work team. João, the teacher, is 37 years old and graduated at a Higher School of Education. He has been teaching for 15 years and sees himself as a person who likes to learn.

The students worked in groups to explore a digital game aimed at developing the competence of estimating the amplitude of angles and problem-solving strategies using pairs of complementary and supplementary angles. There is a screen where the user is prompted to draw, with the help of a slider, an angle with a certain amplitude randomly determined by the game. In order for the user to hit the desired point, it is necessary to devise a strategy that consists of using pairs of supplementary angles or pairs of complementary angles. The mathematical topics involved in this strategy are topics studied in the students' mathematics curriculum, as well as the estimation of the amplitude of angles.

The task designed on paper (Appendix 1), apart from the initial information given to the students about the game that they will be using, contains tables for recording the values of the amplitudes of the angles, both the ones randomly generated by the computer and the values estimated by the students, as well as the reference to the difference between these values. This way, the experiments conducted by the students are recorded in tables that provide the group with a quick overview of the quality of the accuracy of their estimates and also of the evolution of their performance. The questions challenge the students to develop success strategies and to reflect on them to improve their performance.

The task was developed taking into account the need to: (i) Introduce the necessary procedures to use the game; (ii) Encourage the performance of experiments and have them recorded to observe regularities; (iii) Describe and explain the process developed; and (iv) Elaborate a winner strategy.

The presented data collection was made through observation, with audio and video recording, of two lessons (A1 and A2), as well as in collaborative work sessions (S9) and a final interview (E2) with teacher João, also recorded on audio. Data analysis followed content analysis (Bardin, 2011). The categories of analysis were created by focusing on the aspects "The digital game and student´s learning of supplementary and complementary angles" and "The formative assessment and student´s learning of supplementary angle and complementary angle".

LEARNING SUPPLEMENTARY AND COMPLEMENTARY ANGLES WITH DIGITAL GAME AND FORMATIVE ASSESSMENT

The Digital Game and Students' Learning of Supplementary and Complementary Angles

The game provided to students gives the user 10 consecutive attempts to try their accuracy in drawing angles. So, the students were confronted with the rules of the application regarding the difference in the degrees between the amplitude of the given angle and its angle in order for it to be accepted as a valid estimate. Consequently, the concept of precision was a challenge that the students were facing in this game:

Paulo: *We're putting it there, it's close but it says we didn't get it right?*

Teacher: *Just keep experimenting and you'll find out how much tolerance you get, okay? (A1)*

During class some groups were using the application to play but they were not recording their activity, as the interaction of the game was carrying them away. João even said that when he referred to the questions on the worksheet, these students started to respond to what was being asked, namely to the records: '*Several groups were playing and were not recording anything. And many of the challenges faced were related to the fact that they hadn't read the task*' (João, S9). After this initial stage the students revealed some difficulties with the development of strategies involving angles but also with the description and explanation of the strategy they had developed. To help overcome this challenge João provided some blank sheets of paper so that the students could draw the angles involved in the winning strategy, thereby hoping that the students would reflect on what they were doing and would be able to understand the relationship between the angles involved: '*For them to associate the applet with what we were doing in class (which is the construction of angles) I was thinking that if they drew those angles it would naturally get them to then connect them to the complementary angles*' (João, S9). After this first stage the students started using the game as a mathematical learning tool and were able to develop strategies using complementary and/or supplementary angles to be successful in their launches. But they still struggled to write clearly about these strategies. For example, although during lesson 1 the students performed the task with the purpose of receiving written feedback, to reformulate and improve their productions, during the stage of rephrasing the work on lesson 2, many of the teacher's interactions are intended to support the groups' work in understanding the written feedback that was provided on their work. In the following situation, the students mention: "*Yes, we used the auxiliary angles of 0º, 90º and 180º to help us to reach the result*". The teacher in his written feedback asks them: "*How do you used the angles 0º, 90º and 180º to help you to reach the result?*" (Figure 1).

Figure 1. Work performed by the students during the first stage with feedback from the teacher

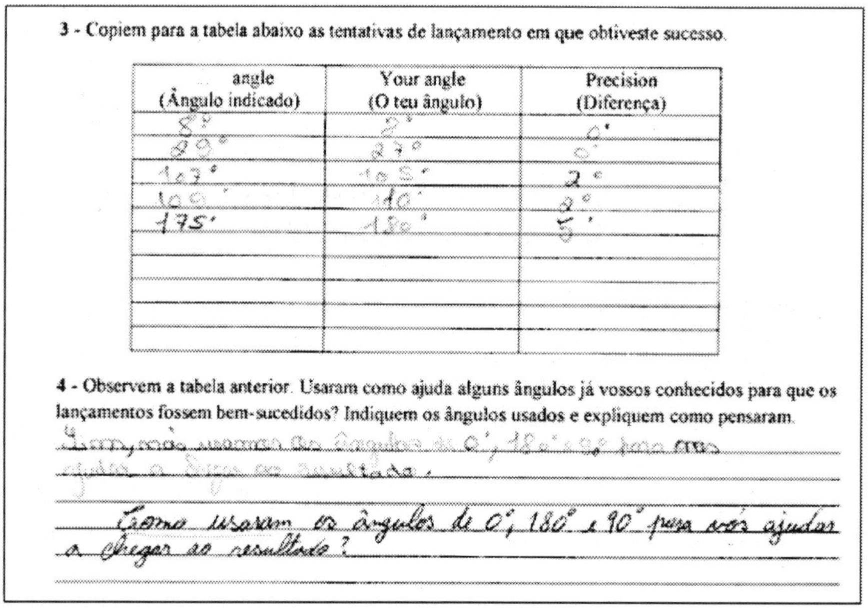

3 - Copiem para a tabela abaixo as tentativas de lançamento em que obtiveste sucesso.

angle (Ângulo indicado)	Your angle (O teu ângulo)	Precision (Diferença)
8°	9°	0°
89°	87°	0°
107°	105°	2°
109°	110°	2°
175°	180°	5°

4 - Observem a tabela anterior. Usaram como ajuda alguns ângulos já vossos conhecidos para que os lançamentos fossem bem-sucedidos? Indiquem os ângulos usados e expliquem como pensaram.

Sim, nós usamos os ângulos de 0°, 180° e 90° para nos ajudar a chegar ao resultado.

Como usaram os ângulos de 0°, 180° e 90° para vos ajudar a chegar ao resultado?

João tries to get students to understand what was intended, by clarifying through verbal feedback, in order for them to explain their reasoning leaving no room for doubt about what they thought and how they did it, comparing it to what they thought at the time and what they didn't record from that reasoning:

Andreia: *We write here the angles that we thought of.*

Teacher: *You need to write down what you did and what you thought. When do you use one and when did you use the other and why. (A2)*

Figure 2. Work performed in the second stage

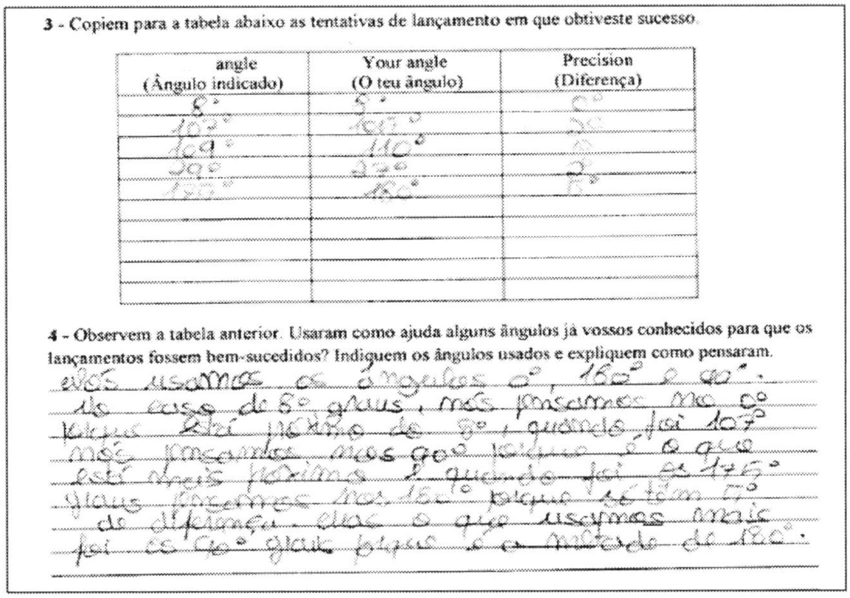

At the end of the assignment, combining the support of the written feedback with the teacher's verbal feedback, the students re-wrote their work, explaining in more detail all their reasoning. As we can see in figure 2, the students added: '*In the case of 8° we thought of 0° because it's close to 8, when it was 107° we thought of 90° because it's the closest one, and when it was 175° we thought of 180° because it's only 5° apart. But the one we used the most was the 90° because it's half of 180°.*'

At the end of the lesson, the teacher engages the students in sharing information regarding how they developed their strategies, confirming that the use of the game was effective in learning the new concepts has helped to develop the communication of those strategies. He uses the game again and invites students to reveal the strategy they would devise for the angle that the application randomly generates (lines 1, 2, and 3). The teacher can see how the game helped to understand the relationship these angles pairs because the students explained how they use another angles more friendlily to draw than the proposed angle (line 4).

Teacher introduce the name´s information regarding pairs of angles that the students have been using, as we can see in the following excerpt for the information regarding pairs of complementary angles (line 5):

1. **Teacher:** *And if I want to get 79°, what angle will I use as my reference?*
2. **Renata:** *The right angle.*
3. **Teacher:** *And how much do I have to take out of 90° to get 79°?*
4. **Renata:** *11°.*
5. **Teacher:** *So the angle I don't want together with the angle I do want form a right angle. These two angles together are called complementary angles.* (A2)

The teacher organizes the identical process to introduce the information regarding the notion of pairs of complementary angles.

THE FORMATIVE ASSESSMENT AND STUDENT'S LEARNING OF SUPPLEMENTARY ANGLE AND COMPLEMENTARY ANGLE

When the teacher planned the activity, he assumed that the students would succeed on more than half the attempts before progressing on to reflect over the strategy they had devised to succeed. Thus, when accompanying the groups, he checks if they comply with the rules stipulated for the task, since at this stage each group may need a different number of times to master the strategy to be used: '*Have you got half of them right, or not yet? You have to keep trying*' (João, A1).

The teacher monitors the groups by interacting when he feels it is necessary or when he is asked to do so. Sometimes João noticed that the students were using alternative strategies to decide in which sector of the screen the ray would be, in order to draw the angle with a certain amplitude. For example, one of the groups used a sheet of paper as an aid which they placed on top of the screen after having drawn the angle using the protractor. These strategies can compromise the proposed objective of the task, which leads the teacher to have to discourage students from using that technique: '*You must use only your thinking. Where do you think the angle side will be with that amplitude?*' (João, A1). Later, the teacher returns to the same group to find out how the work was progressing and discovers that the students had replaced their previous strategy with an alternative one, using their fingers to determine where the moving ray of the angle would be on the screen: '*But how can you figure out how to get it right, without using your fingers on the screen?*' (João, A1).

But there are other groups that seem to be able to think of a strategy but are unable to record it. João realizes that perhaps the students have not yet been able to synthesize the strategy they were using, and tries to help the group in this stage of recording their reasoning:

Teacher: *Your strategy is to think of an angle to help place the ray in order to hit the requested value, right?*

Rui: *Yes.*

Teacher: *So now you just have to think about that strategy. What angle do you know of that can help you?*

Rui: *Oh, I got it!*

Teacher: *How will you figure out how to get it right as many times as possible? (A1)*

Throughout the course of the task, teacher João walks by the groups and intervenes when he notices that there is a question. Sometimes, João offers a clue to help the students in discovering the strategy, like for instance, '*What was the value that you used as a measure that helped you decide where to put the side of the angle?*' (João, A1).

One of the groups showed that they could already explain their strategy verbally for an angle they had chosen, the 168° angle. However, in their records, the group wanted to mention how they had figured it out - first by using the 90° reference angle, and then they decided to use the 180° angle. Since the group was struggling to record the entire process they thought up, the teacher suggested that they represented that process through a diagram:

Teacher: *Which angle did you guys choose?*

Paulo: *We used to use the 90° angle, but the 168° angle was too far from the 90°, and then we thought of using the 180° angle.*

Teacher: *Draw the angle on paper, if it helps to make it clearer (A1).*

Later the teacher came back to the group to follow up on the work and found that the students had already drawn the 168° angle but had not progressed any further. The teacher steps in as if he was bringing a new participant into the class to whom they would have to explain what was happening (line 3), which leads students to think in order to respond to the teacher's challenge, by organizing a diagram with arrows to show the dynamics of their thinking (line 4):

1. **Teacher:** *So how are you doing it?*
2. **Paulo:** *We have drawn the 168° angle.*
3. **Teacher:** *Don't forget that you are explaining how you did it. When someone sees your work, they have to think 'So where did they start?' So you need to record everything so that it's clearly understandable.*

The students wonder for a bit and then Sara comments:

4. **Sara:** *Let's put some arrows here to describe what we did.* (A1)

In the following lesson, students were introduced to the <u>assessment criteria</u> for the first time (Appendix 2). During this lesson, each student received a copy of the assessment criteria, and the teacher involved the class in looking at the description of the assessment criteria by asking the students to read them aloud, and pointing to the differences and similarities of the descriptions on the interactive board, where he projected the criteria sheet, like for instance in parameter 'Use the information and knowledge acquired', while clarifying the meaning of the expressions used:

Teacher: *The information is what is in the activity that you have to follow to do the task. And the knowledge is what you have already learned before you started doing this activity. If you don't remember, you don't use your information or knowledge, and you'll be at level?*

Ricardo: *Zero. (A2)*

When this stage is completed, João distributes the students' work from lesson 1 with <u>teacher's written feedback</u>. João informs the students that they should read the comments and check the assessment criteria to understand what they should improve in their work. So, the students must transcribe the values of the amplitudes of the angles that they need to improve on to a new worksheet, and after considering the teacher's comments and the assessment criteria, they must rewrite their work on the new worksheet.

At times it was necessary to help students experiment with ways of arguing with each other so that each group could be more independent from the teacher's presence, using their knowledge and learning to respect the opinion of others and give them credit when deserved. Instead of answering the question, <u>the teacher engages the students in the discussion</u> through his explanations (lines 6) and, in the end, the discussion was successful (lines 9, 10 and 11):

1. **Rui:** *Teacher, is the 145° angle closer to the right or closer to the straight angle?*
2. **Teacher:** *What do you guys think?*
3. **Renata:** *We think it' s closer to the right.*
4. **Teacher:** *And how about you?*
5. **Rui:** *We think it' s closer to the straight.*
6. **Teacher:** *So how about you explain why you think it's closer to the right and the others explain why they think it's closer to straight? That would be a way for you to come to an understanding.*
7. **Renata:** *So tell me why you think it's the straight?*
8. **Rui:** *Because the 145° is between the 100° and the 180° so it's almost half until 180°.*
9. **Renata:** *And I was thinking that 90° was closer.*
10. **Teacher:** *So his explanation convinced you, did it?*
11. **Renata:** *Yes.* (A2)

DISCUSSION AND CONCLUSION

The students used the interaction of a digital game to draw angles of certain amplitude and through the elaboration of strategies they answered to the challenge posed by the task. The results show that the students tended to use the game exclusively for the playful purpose of entertainment. This behavior is natural because the students did not know the game and it allowed them to have a first contact with it anyway.

Additionally, students revealed difficulties in developing effective and winning strategies involving angles. Because the game providing immediate feedback (Schuytema, 2008) the students considered that there work was finished in each of the plays. Students continued to play through trial and error, but without reflecting on how they played. In this way, a task based on the digital game proved to be a challenge for the students. The task required more attention and dedication from students to develop appropriate strategies (Bissoloti, Nogueira, & Pereira, 2014). The task was also a challenge for the students to overcome the difficulty of explaining their strategies. Therefore, students become protagonists of their learning (Offenholley, 2012).

Moreover, it is also possible to conclude that using a task based on digital game helped student to understand the mathematics involved by exploring variance and regularities, using different representations of the same mathematical concept (Pierce & Stacey, 2013; Hoyles & Noss, 2003) thus contributing to the development of strategies with the contribution of pairs of supplementary and complementary angles, which are mathematical concepts that otherwise tend to be presented to students in a traditional way. With the game used, the student's thoughts became visible and progressively shaped by their interactions with the tool because the exploratory nature of the game enabling the visibility of the student's understanding (Laborde et. al., 2006). The teacher uses the characteristics of working with digital games to conduct the students' mathematical activity, making their strategies visible to them, in a personalized way.

The teacher played a very important role because he was always a mediator between the feedback returned by the game and the students' difficulties to develop and communicate winning strategies involving angles. Throughout the whole process the teacher encourages students to be agents of their own learning in line with the format of formative assessment by engaging them through verbal feedback thus helping to reduce obstacles and guiding students to reflect on their work by assigning an important role to error exploration (Black & Wiliam, 2009; 2006; Black, 2015). Moreover, the use of verbal feedback helped them transform the device into a learning tool and to develop autonomy, both in the appropriation of the rules (Artigue, 2002) as well as the collaboration between the different elements of the group. Regarding the use of written feedback and its relationship with the use of the assessment criteria, not all groups have responded favorably to the intention of written feedback. Yet in the classroom, with the help of verbal feedback, it was possible to get the students to evolve in the recording of their work, which is why this work needs to continue. Hence, we are able to conclude that, when the teacher supports students by asking questions or helping them overcome struggles, this shows the importance of involving students in using formative assessment in the classroom to encourage them to make decisions for their own learning (NCTM, 2014; Nunziati, 1999; Santos, 2019; Vial, 2001).

We conclude that this study contributes to promote this digital game is realizing the interaction between students and the school subjects, favoring the learning process. This way, we create a bridge between playful activities and the school's formal content. They are dynamic alternatives to promote more dialogue and interaction as pedagogical resources. The use of formative assessment and the use of tasks based on a digital game favored the development of strategies and the recording of their conclusions contributed to mathematics learning.

The use of formative assessment with tasks using technology, in particular the use of digital games, thus helping teachers or future teachers to develop assessment strategies with tasks based on a digital game contribute to the educational success of their students.

ACKNOWLEDGMENT

Work financed by national funds through FCT - Fundação para a Ciência e Tecnologia (Foundation for Science and Technology) through a scholarship awarded to the first author (SFRH/BD/117144/2016).

REFERENCES

Aires, L. (2015). *Paradigma Qualitativo e Práticas de Investigação Educacional*. Universidade Aberta.

Artigue, M. (2002). Learning mathematics in a CAS environment: The genesis of a reflection about instrumentation and the dialectics between technical and conceptual work. *International Journal of Computers for Mathematical Learning, 7*(3), 245–274. doi:10.1023/A:1022103903080

Bardin, L. (2011). *Análise de conteúdo*. Coimbra: Edições 70.

Bissoloti, K., Nogueira, H. G., & Pereira, A. T. C. (2014). *Potencialidades das mídias sociais e da gamificação na educação a distância*. Available at: https://seer.ufrgs.br/renote/article/view/53511/33027

Black, P. (2015). Formative assessment – an optimistic but incomplete vision. *Assessment in Education: Principles, Policy & Practice, 22*(1), 161–177. doi:10.1080/0969594X.2014.999643

Black, P., & Wiliam, D. (2006). Developing a Theory of Formative Assessment. In J. Gardner (Ed.), *Assessment and Learning* (pp. 81–100). SAGE.

Black, P., & Wiliam, D. (2009). Developing the theory of formative assessment. *Educational Assessment, Evaluation and Accountability, 21*(1), 5-31.

Black, P., & Wiliam, D. (2018). Classroom assessment and pedagogy. *Assessment in Education: Principles, Policy & Practice, 25*(6), 551–575. doi:10.1080/0969594X.2018.1441807

Bogdan, R., & Biklen, S. (1994). *Investigação Qualitativa em Educação*. Porto Editora.

Erickson, F. (1986). Qualitative Methods in Research on Teaching. In M. C. Wittrock (Ed.), *Handbook of Research on Teaching* (pp. 119–161). Macmillan.

Garcia, M., Rabelo, D., Silva, D., & Amaral, S. (2011). Novas competências docentes frente às tecnologias digitais interativas. *Revista Teoria e Prática de Educação, 14*(1), 79–87.

Heron, J., & Reason, P. (2006). The practice of co-operative inquiry: Research 'with' rather than 'on' people. In P. Reason & H. Bradbury (Eds.), *Handbook of action research: Participative inquiry and pratice*. Sage.

Hoyles, C., & Noss, R. (2003). What can digital technologies take from and bring to research in mathematics education? In A. J. Bishop, M. A. Clements, C. Keitel, J. Kilpatrick, & F. K. S. Leung (Eds.), *Second International Handbook of Mathematics Education* (Vol. 10, pp. 323–349). Springer. doi:10.1007/978-94-010-0273-8_11

Laborde, C., Kynigos, C., Hollebrands, K., & Strässer, R. (2006). Teaching and learning geometry with technology. In A. Guitiérrez & P. Boero (Eds.), *Handbook of Research on the Psychology of Mathematics Education: Past, Present and Future* (pp. 275–304). Sense Publishers.

Mayo, M. (2009). Video games: A route to large-scale STEM education? *Science, 323*(5910), 79–82. doi:10.1126cience.1166900 PMID:19119223

Merriam, S. (1988). *Case study research in education. A qualitative approach*. Jossey-Bass.

NCTM. (2014). *Principles to Actions: Ensuring Mathematical Success For All*. NCTM.

Nunziati, G. (1990). Pour construire un dispositif d'évaluation formatrice. *Cahiers Pedagogiques, 280*, 47–62.

Offenholley, K. H. (2012). Gaming Your Mathematics Course: The Theory and Practice of Games for Learning. *Journal of Humanistic Mathematics, 2*, 79–92. doi:10.5642/ jhummath.201202.07

Pierce, R., & Stacey, K. (2013). Teaching with new technology: Four 'early majority' teachers. *Journal of Mathematics Teacher Education, 16*(5), 323–347. doi:10.100710857-012-9227-y

Sadler, D. R. (1989). Formative assessment and the design of instructional systems. *Instructional Science, 18*(2), 119–144. doi:10.1007/BF00117714

Santos, E., & Santos, L. (2019). O papel do GeoGebra nas práticas de regulação do ensino da área do paralelogramo. Quadrante, 28(1), 6-26.

Santos, L. (2008). Dilemas e desafios da avaliação reguladora. In L. Menezes, L. Santos, H. Gomes & C. Rodrigues (Eds.), Avaliação em Matemática: Problemas e desafios, (pp. 11-35). Viseu: Secção de Educação Matemática da Sociedade Portuguesa de Ciências de Educação.

Santos, L. (2019). Reflexões em torno da avaliação pedagógica. In M. I. Ortigão, D. Fernandes, T. Pereira, & L. Santos (Orgs.), Avaliar para aprender no Brasil e em Portugal: Perspectivas teóricas, práticas e de desenvolvimento (pp. 165-190). Curitiba: Editora CRV.

Santos, L., & Cai, J. (2016). Curriculum and assessment. In A. Gutiérrez, G. Leder, & P. Boero (Eds.), *The Second Handbook in the Psychology of Mathematics Education* (pp. 153–185). Sense Publishers.

Santos, L., & Pinto, J. (2018). Ensino de conteúdos escolares: A avaliação como Fator estruturante. In *F. Veiga (Coord.), O Ensino como fator de envolvimento numa escola para todos* (pp. 503–539). Climepsi Editores.

Schuytema, P. (2008). *Design de Games: uma abordagem prática.* Cengage Learning.

Storeygard, J., Hamm, J., & Fosnot, C. T. (2010). Determining what children know: Dynamic versus static assessment. In National Council of Teachers of Mathematics (Ed.), Models of Intervention in Mathematics: Reweaving the Tapestry (pp. 45-69). Reston, VA: NCTM.

Vial, M. (2001). *Se former pour évaluer. Pédagogies en développement.* De boeck Université.

Yin, R. (1989). *Case study research, design and methods.* Sage.

APPENDIX 1

Task

You have been put in charge of the rescue mission on Planet Geometry. Your job is to set the right angle for the launch that will allow to catch the rocket that will take you to Planet Geometry.

You have 10 chances for your mission to be considered valid.

Let's start the rescue operation. To do so, follow these steps:

1° - Click the "**Start**" button

2° - Check the angle that is displayed by the game

3° - Click the "**Check it**" button

4° - Drag the "**Set the angle**" button so that the ray's opening forms the angle with the required amplitude

1 - Record your entries in the following table:

Angle	Your angle	Precision

If you got **less than half** of the 10 attempts right, ask your teacher for a new table.

If you got **half or more** of the 10 attempts right, move on to question #2

2 - In which boards are the differences less than 6°?

3 - Copy your successful launch attempts onto the below table.

Angle	Your angle	Precision

4 - Did you use any angles that you already know to help your launches be successful? Name the angles you used and explain how you came to think of them.

5 - Choose one of the values that you did not get right at the beginning of the task and explain how you would do it in order to be more successful in the rescue operation.

APPENDIX 2

Criteria for The Assessment of Group Work

Box 1. Use of strategies and exploration process

Does not present the appropriate strategies Does not present an exploration process or presents a totally inadequate exploration process	Presents appropriate strategies Presents a poorly organized and very incomplete exploration process	Presents appropriate strategies Presents an organized and almost complete exploration process	Presents appropriate strategies Presents an organized and complete exploration process

Box 2. Use the information/knowledge studied

Does not use information/ knowledge essential to the exploration of the task	Recognizes information/ knowledge essential to the exploration of the activity, but does not apply it properly	Recognizes and partially applies information/knowledge essential to the exploration	Recognizes and appropriately applies information/knowledge essential to the exploration of the task

Box 3. Description and explanation of the activity developed (communication)

Does not describe the steps of the work performed or the way its elements thought Do not describe or explain the conclusions drawn	Partially describes the steps of the work done and how its elements thought Describes the conclusions reached but does not fully explain them	Describes and explains all the steps of the work and how its elements thought, including the attempts and conclusions reached Describes the conclusions reached, but does not fully explain them	Describes and explains all the steps of the work and how its elements thought, including the attempts and conclusions reached Describes the conclusions reached and explains them in full

Box 4. Written mathematical language

Uses mathematical language	Uses mathematical language with inaccuracies	Uses mathematical language with small inaccuracies	Uses mathematical language revealing a good knowledge of the relationships between the terms and knowledge used

Chapter 40
Gamification Design Principles and Mechanics to Improve Retention

Robert Costello
https://orcid.org/0000-0002-8962-7533
Middlesbrough College, UK

ABSTRACT

The design and guidelines for gamification offer designers a range of solutions to provide empowerment and engagement to assist with retention within education. This chapter addresses a knowledge gap around the effective use while improving retention. With gaming mechanics as a driving point, specific design considerations were explored: badges, leader boards, points and levels, and challenges. The educator must think from the learner's perspective and find new ways of creating challenges and motivation techniques to provide value. Gamification, when applied to different disciplines, has the potential to facilitate the individual within learner-centricity. Current research indicates that gaming mechanics can encourage and motivate the learner while enriching their experience when applied to education.

INTRODUCTION

The design and guidelines for Gamification have always been outstanding for the designers to find a range of solutions to provide empowerment, engagement, and assist with retention within Education. It is essential to think of the learner's perspective and find new ways of creating challenges and motivation techniques to provide value and learner engagement (Gatti, Ulrich & Seele, 2019). To assist with motivation, engagement, and influences, as pointed out by Gatti et al. (2019), Bhatti (2019), and Herman et al. (2020), maintaining the learner attitudes is essential when dealing with learners. This is extremely important when looking at 21st-century skills of literacy and how game-based learning disciplines are supporting the learners (Hung, Yang & Tsai, 2020). This chapter explores design principles associated with Gamification and how different sections can improve the educational experience. Principles of Gamification can be applied not only to Education but also to industries to empower the employees.

DOI: 10.4018/978-1-7998-7271-9.ch040

Types of applications that Gamification applied to are that of Military (Hancock, Sirizzotti & Martin, 2019); Health & Medical (Cotton & Patel, 2019); Disabilities (Shaban & Pearson, 2019); Education (Costello, 2020) and Literacy (Hung, Yang & Tsai, 2020).

Gamification is changing the world in profound ways. Educators, having recognized the contributions that the use of gaming mechanics is having on the learner's growth and wellbeing, are now thinking about how they can strengthen the learning process through creating innovative ways to challenge and support the learner (Costello, Lambert & Smith, 2019; Tolks et al., 2019). Through engagement via MLearning (Costello & Lambert, 2018), the learner with productive media interaction and feedback is used to inspire the individual to gain a sense of accomplishment; educators are spicing up the classroom activities to immerse the learner through adding enjoyment and motivational techniques so that learners can achieve great heights. The main drive of Gamification is to influence the learner's own goal and alter their perception of their educational experience through the use of severe gaming mechanisms. Aspects of long-term engagement should be considered to assist the learner in growing and developing new competencies within a set framework identified by the institution/lecturer (Hammerschall, 2019; Udara & De Alwis, 2019). It is vital when exploring frameworks that institutions explore and embed social-cultural contexts and how work, learning, educators, policy-holders play an essential part in designing skills within the 21st Century and Gamification (Maqsood, 2020).

Prior research has shown that incorporating community-based activities within Gamification has led to the higher success of outcomes relating to performance and integration (Berkling & Neubehler, 2019; Ayastuy et al., 2021). The educator can use gaming elements to systematically map concepts onto the academic subject matter to create a novel instructional approach that can offer problem-solving, collaboration, and communication, as documented through the research conducted by Putz, Hofbauer and Mates (2019) and Costello (2020) who applied gamification techniques to individuals within a situation that involved "*monotonous and non-challenging tasks*". These ideas of bridging ownership of the learning process, as pointed out by Maqsood (2020), as assisted with developing 21st-century skills of literacy in which learners have managed to improve searching for information (Shmelev, Karpova, Kogtikov & Dukhanov, 2016), improving team working (Mesko, Győrffy & Kollár, 2015), and discussions (Hung, Yan & Tsai, 2020). Gamification has remarkable motivational influences to utilize and encourage learners to engage in the learning environment by deploying intrinsic and extrinsic motivational techniques.

Learners could embrace these values and obligations while working in an educational community and use them to develop their principles, competencies, language, and perspectives. González and Mora (2014) indicate that communities build upon competencies and commitment, and ethical behavior. Through education, communities would ensure 21st-century skills are being considered, where literacy within could be supported in collaborative groups (McCauley, Davison, McHugh, Domegan & Grehan, 2021; Hung, Yang & Tsai, 2020). To take advantage of the community environment, the educator, as recommended by Herro et al. (2017), Hu et al. (2017), Zolyomi and Schmalz (2017); Costello (2020), should focus on creating and mapping clear learning objectives; the experience of the learner must involve organized stages; interactive resources; and finally mapping them onto the curriculum. Educational practices must be able to adapt in the future to accommodate the challenges associated with the demanding needs of the learner. The following section focuses on innovative ways the educator uses Mapping within Gamification to explore this avenue to support education learners through innovative techniques.

GAMING MECHANICS

Gaming mechanics plays an essential part within the educational experience, and vital that the educator adapt these to suit the needs of the learners to harness and build upon their knowledge, skills, and abilities (Herro et al., 2017). The educator would identify a generic starting point and recommend a succession of milestones for the learner to reach before each activity and challenge is complete. Educators would select various activities to suit their disciplines to embrace and make the learning as exciting and enjoyable as possible. These skills can range from building up from digital literacy to teamwork to assist with improved practices and skills sets that can be directly applied to immersive learning environments and individuals educational learning styles and traits (McCoy, Lewis & Dalton, 2016; Buckley & Doyle, 2017; Alt & Raichel, 2020)

Legaki, Xi, Hamari and Assimakopoulos, (2019) point out that monitoring performance via control groups can engage learners more. This approach assists with feedback, identifying promising trends, and attendance, which interwoven provides an effective acceptance. Educators must build upon activities that challenge the learner from critical thinking and problem-solving to interpretive analysis and planning when engaging in new topics (Herro et al., 2017). These skills would enable the learner to face real-life problems, in which they would feel confident while finding a suitable solution, too (Taub et al,. 2020). Students on specific tasks can alter their own educational experience and improve their opportunity to succeed within the educational journey. Through self-confidence, the learner would build up new vocabulary and engagement within practical sessions (Hamm et al., 2019; Walsh, O'Brien & Costin, 2021). To achieve these necessary skills, institutions can introduce additional support mechanisms that provide learners with technologies, social support, and connections to assist with positive learning experiences.

ADDITIONAL SUPPORT MECHANISM

Educators within institutions can build upon gamification mechanics to influence tutorials, exercises, and peer reviews from others within the community to engage in interest and attitudes (Chen, Yang, Huang & Fu, 2019). Chu et al. (2017) and Zolyomi and Schmalz (2017) recommend that tutors place intervention measures for students struggling with extra additional support through the use of technology. Students who have SEN, mobility issues, or disability needs can benefit from Gamification, as it enables them, depending on their needs, to engage in a social setting, so they do not feel isolated (Prandi et al., 2015; Cameron & Bizo, 2019). They can create positive connections with other learners (Fichten et al., 2014) and improve their behavior (Bond, 2015). Through bringing in additional supporting mechanisms like creative and critical thinking, extra curriculum reading (Mystakidis & Berki, 2018), and ways of improving individuals attention spans (Buckley & Doyle, 2017) can directly improve the educational experience and, in particular, skills needed within the 21st century, like those of digital literacy (Eryansyah, Erlina, Fiftinova & Nurweni, 2019).

This additional support mechanism can come in aid of technology, activities, and from the community. Perryer et al. (2016) build upon the research from (Chu et al., 2017; Zolyomi & Schmalz, 2017; Fichten et al., 2014; Prandi et al., 2015) and recommend that if the learner has a more positive learning experience, then the individual can construct a more healthy approach from successes and failures within the gamification environment. The tutor can build further exercises into the environment to allow practices and improvements to embed good practices. Gamification provides the students with the experience to engage in collaborative problem solving through fun and enjoyment. Gamification drives the learner to solve problems and improve the "*health and interpersonal relationships*" (Sera & Wheeler, 2017) while adjusting their natural perception of the learning process. Cardador et al. (2016) suggest that focusing on the objectives of the activities would seek to improve performance by the individual through setting achievable goals and having a way of sufficiently checking and measuring progress against objectives. Maican et al. agrees with Sera and Wheeler (2017) and suggests that applying social aspects to Gamification would enable the learner to relax and improve "*one's own mental and physical development*" (Maican et al., 2016).

Several free applications can be used for educational purposes and industry to enable gaming mechanics to freely incorporate within the learning environment, positively affecting the learning experience (Maican et al., 2016; Sera & Wheeler, 2017). Costello and Lambert (2019), Costello (2020) suggest that setting up community activities through Gamification would improve learners' skills and competence independent of and relative to others within the social network. As suggested by Cardador et al. (2016) and Costello, Lambert and Smith (2019), other applications can be used depending on the challenges or activities that are trying to achieve. For example, Pokémon Go, World of Tanks (WoT), is a free-to-play MMO that enables teams of players to battle against computer-controlled opponents on the PC/Mobile. This team-building approach supports knowledge-sharing, culture awareness, and mastery skills (Maican et al., 2016; Carter & Mahoney, 2020). Expanding on free-to-play game likes that of World of Tanks (WoT), and the research carried out by Shen et al. (2020), additional support mechanism like that of team-building enable individuals to build cooperative behavior among individuals to increase future interaction. To assist in gameplay design, teams are not balanced by skills but "*balancing tank tiers and the different tank types*" to make the game more challenging (Shen et al., 2020, P4). A critical difference between WoT and similar games is that it does not balance teams by skill. Thus, the potential for imbalanced matches, and the frustration they create, is relatively high. As Esmaeili and Woods (2016) indicate, WoT provides opportunities for teams to share scenarios where individuals have to share sources, statistics, and experiences to assist in observations throughout the gameplay, to assist in team working challenging/battles. The game offers the individuals the ability to use online chat (voice and text) to assist with interaction and engagement to record achievements. Games like that of Pokémon Go, World of Tanks (WoT), would assist with 21st-century Digital Literacy issues (Hung, Yang & Tsai, 2020) as individuals within educational setting would need to record/track achievements, share thoughts, problems solving techniques, and issues within the community-based activities.

Through the use of interactive classrooms and team-building activities will ensure individuals will develop skills, such as problem-solving (Mantiri, 2019), critical analysis (Buckingham, 2010), engage in their deadlines, and assist with projects to engage with the multidimensionality of digital literacy within the 21st century (Cobo, Zucchetti, Kass-Hanna & Lyons, 2019).

Williams et al. (2012) suggest that the tutor must consider boundaries when applying communities to educational practices as the learner has to negotiate new meanings and interactions and adapt to existing or new practices that emerge. Learners with SEN or disability needs might adjust to new practices and interaction complex, so extra support is needed (Chu et al., 2017; Zolyomi & Schmalz, 2017). These interactions will assist with multidimensionality and problem solving within digital literacy (Buckingham, 2010; Cobo, Zucchetti, Kass-Hanna & Lyons, 2019). Bring in games like Pokémon Go, World of Tanks (WoT) to assist with interactions, where interactions are complex but could improve skills with digital literacy when capturing Pokémon, or even recording current statistics belonging to weekly progress within the classroom will ensure developmental skills are observed (Howell, 2017; Costello & Lambert 2019; Costello 2020).

Planning and being responsive to the learning environment would enable the tutor to adjust their attitudes to activities feedback from the learners. Feedback would allow the learner to gain the necessary skills to progress further within the learning process while positively impacting them. Educators need to create a positive relationship between the educational materials and how the learner interacts. Educational activities could be assigned tasks outside the classroom, from keeping fit to tracking interactive progress within games (Barkley, Lepp & Glickman, 2017).

This particular approach would enable friends to be created based on similar interests and discourage negative behavior (Barkley, Lepp & Glickman, 2017). Determining this balance through the needs of the learner is crucial, and the next section builds upon this, looking at Motivation (Maican et al., 2016), Mastering skills (Bíró, 2014; Behnke, 2015), Behavioural change (Banfield & Wilkerson, 2014; Cavallo et al., 2017; Sailer et al., 2017) and Socialization (Cardador et al., 2016; Rodrigues & Costa, 2016) with mapping.

MAPPING

Gamification within Education can create a positive effect to the learner when addressing issues of stress, dealing with issues of isolation within the classroom/community, and creating relationships for individuals to support each other in times of personal wellbeing issues (Kogan, Hellyer, Duncan & Schoenfeld-Tacher, 2017; Costello, Lambert & Smith, 2019; Costello & Lambert, 2018). Tailoring to the needs of the learners would enable the learning environment to be based around a learner-centricity approach, supporting the individual/community through the module within the education life cycle. These approaches will assist with reconceptualizing digital literacy and the developments needed in creating relationships to recognize understanding and experience within digital technologies (Pangrazio, 2016; Buckingham, 2016).

De Sousa Borges et al. (2014) and Tanouri, Mulcahy and Russell-Bennett, (2019) indicate that mapping gamification mechanics onto the emotional response of the learner would enable new knowledge to be conveyed to the individual within a scenario-based setting, allowing continuous interaction and feedback in real-time. De Sousa Borges et al. (2014) and Schmidt-Kraepelin et al. (2019) suggest that social media and networking can motivate individuals while providing them with interest. This approach would allow the learner to enhance their skills through engagement while undergoing tasks, skills development, assessments, and self-reflection.

Industry experts and academics can harness these approaches by using various approaches like collaborative/individual projects, tutorials, training programs, MLearning, and real-world problems through gaming examples or gaming engines to harness the students' abilities to enable them to master their own skills sets. As Hanbidge, Tin and Sanderson, (2018) point out, MLearning is about maximizing the learning process and enhancing the students learning experience through emerging technologies while exploring different ways within the digital society. Mobile devices can engage and enhance communities and improve direct relationships (Mac Callum and Jeffrey, 2014). Rewarding their progress with various types of intrinsic and extrinsic motivational techniques helps enhance and empower the way they learn and maximize the results from the learning process. This empowerment through Gamification and motivation would provide the learner with the necessary ability to change their behavior through having the proper support and nurture within a community, social setting, or favorable conditions (Bennett et al., 2017; Nuutinen et al., 2017; Jin, 2017).

FHKPS et al. (2021) expand on nurturing the needs of the individual by suggesting that focusing on psychological and behavioral theories would encourage learners to explore and learn more. This approach would drive the learner to engage in more proposing challenges put to them by the tutor and be easier to follow (de Sousa Borges et al., 2014). The use of psychological and behavioral theories would allow industry or academics to provide different mechanisms to support the acquisition of new domain knowledge and reward the learner/staff with the right course of action while helping to build relationships between other individuals on the activity to ensure that the tasks completed on time and improving self-efficiency (Yee et al., 2012; Chong, 2019). Working with others in a community can provide the learner with a sense of fun, engagement, and reward while being supportive within a safe environment to make mistakes. *'Amusement or fun elements'* refers to a learning environment that engages the activities through competitions and awards by status. Academics or management can use various mechanisms to improve productivity or motivation, which would enable individuals to engage with the activities (Demkah & Bhargava, 2019). According to Korn (2012), Gooch et al. (2015), and Gooch et al. (2016), these mechanisms would support learners who have special educations needs/disabilities to enable them to have more empowering learning experiences while focusing on wellbeing. Gamified platforms can be easily adapted to facilitated educational programmes to assist in wellbeing; one example is "nutrition literacy in families" through Gamification. This Gamification platform assisted with improving motivation and shifted behavior in health belonging to the participants within the study of 3-to-5-year-old children (Azevedo, Padrão, Gregório, Almeida, Moutinho, Lien & Barros, 2019).

'Wellbeing-oriented' Gamification through motivation enables the learner to make a more profound connection within the learning process (Nicholson, 2012). Wellbeing-orientation enables the individual to remember memories through learning. Depending on activities chosen by the tutor, wellbeing can bring health benefits through social interaction and collaborative challenges, enabling individuals to share experiences, form bonds, and create relationships (Howard, 2001; So & Brush, 2008; Dawson, 2008).

Pedreira et al. (2015) indicate that mapping would enable academics and industry to effectively implement the domain topic and apply the correct use of motivation and fun aspects through Awards/Points-based systems for activities to support wellbeing. To support wellbeing within Gamification, it is critical to ensure 'Knowledge-base' has been considered.

'Knowledge-base' is essential as this is crucial when setting course structures and feedback to the individual as they rely on judgment and discretion (Taylor, 2017). The course structure would enable the tutor to set learning outcomes to challenge the individuals over time, ensuring that the domain knowledge is scaffolded corrected through the learning process (Strampel et al., 2017). Through using digital solutions to assist with scaffolding learning, can provide learners with the necessary accreditation and endorsement to create suitable strategies needed for personalized learning experiences within the 21st century and, in particular digital literacy (O'connor, Hanlon, O'donnell, Garcia, Glanville & Mair, 2016; Mehtälä, 2018).

MOTIVATION

Gamification has had such a positive effect on the learner, from motivating intrinsically to extrinsically. This research topic has emphasized and facilitated individuals' autonomy, collaborative, and social development while they actively, willingly set goals and needs to achieve competence within their own beliefs and behaviors (Costello, 2020). The learners' abilities have enabled them to create and build relationships to support future progression within their educational and industrial journeys. According to Maican et al. (2016), the success of Gamification is down to the design of the gaming mechanics. Challenges can be set for the student to seek for themselves, in which they can feel a sense of achievement and can demonstrate they can meet targets for mastering skills. Through adopting mastering skills and using motivational models, individuals can be heavily influenced through self-regulation, and learning outcomes, to support self-control and achievement, which can be supported through digital literacy approaches (Pala & Başıbüyük, 2021). Using a combination of techniques and approaches, learners would have a more personalized engagement, which would, in return, impact achievement (Miller, 2021).

Perryer et al. (2016) and Maican et al. (2016) do indicate that using a combination of non-motivational activities in which everyone can contribute, in which no one feels better than everyone else, can lead to endless possibilities (Roth et al., 2015). Motivation within Gamification has revealed a positive effect on the learner, developing skills from group assignments, strategic thinking, problem-solving, and interpretative analysis skills. Rodrigues and Costa (2016) indicate that by incorporating extrinsic and intrinsic motivational techniques within the educational environment, the learner has more desired challenges, and this would mean that the learner would be able to adjust their personal view of the activities and can adopt different strategies for short or long term goals to fit their effort.

By improving the learner's motivation factor, aspects of social elements could be encompassed to make the learning environment more enjoyable in which regular usage would enable communities to be formed. Perryer et al. (2016) highlight that gamification assists in promoting cooperation through effective competition, performance, and engagement as Bista et al. (2012) suggests that for motivation to work within a community, individuals must actively engage and contribute to sustaining a social connection that encourages others to commit to activities and share experiences for learners to achieve. As Miller (2021) points out, social connections are significant within digital technologies, and literacy is vital to ensure engagement and achievement within the learning experience.

Another way to assist the community in engaging motivation is to use competition (Banfield & Wilkerson, 2014). Massung et al. (2013) say that competition encourages engagement and unites learners to achieve a common goal or target (O'Brolcháin et al., 2016). This is an essential factor when assigning activities or challenges for Motivation of Learners (MoL) within a predefined setting like that of Massively Multiplayer Online Role-Playing Games (MMORPGs), or Massively Multiplayer Online Games (MMOs) like Minecraft or even Pokémon Go (Geroimenko, 2019, Costello & Lambert, 2019; Costello, Lambert & Smith, 2019; Lichty, 2019).

Through Gamification, educators can subject individuals to the same rules and outcomes to group settings and enable them to manage resources over a given time frame, monitoring performance and behaviors. Each time an activity is achieved, a reward/point/badge is given to drive them to succeed further until the completion of a task and the quality of the task finished. Such elements are vital within Education for the learner to know. These features would offer the individuals skills and competence to compete within Education and in the industry. Educators can assess the learner's work for the uniqueness and adaptability of the learning platform (Heeter, 1992; Kiili et al., 2012; Eleftheria et al., 2013; Roth et al., 2015). Learning platforms can improve digital learning, not just reading strategies, but engagement (Dalton & Proctor, 2007), motivation (Shopova, 2014), and technical literacy (Al-Qallaf & Al-Mutairi, 2016).

MASTERING SKILLS

Literature has shown that the use of Gamification in the classroom and the industry can enhance the atmosphere of the learner's environment while making the learning experience more appealing (Knautz et al., 2013; Kellinger, 2017*). Applying scaffold instructions on the individual's needs through dynamic customization of personalization engagement activities would capture the learner's freedom (Martí-Parreño et al., 2016). Providing personalized engagement to the learner will assist individuals to understand and apply content in a more interactive design. This can be from video recording materials, introductory lectures, computer-based activities, and multimedia enhancing interactive design tools to assist with mentoring and coaching strategies (Tobin & McInnes, 2008; McLoughlin & Lee, 2010; Huang et al., 2012). Scaffold instructions would give the necessary steps required to enable the learner to construct their learning from decisions based upon successes and failures within the learning environment. The mistakes that the learners had encountered would allow for further practice and improvement, embedding new skills within the learning process. Mastering these new skills would depend on the disciplines they are studying for. This approach of supporting new skills to be embedded and practiced can allow the learner to engulf in an energized learning environment that makes the learning activities interesting (Bíró, 2014; Behnke, 2015; Rosen et al., 2020).

Perryer et al. (2016) suggest that to enable the individual to learn from their decisions, it is essential to incorporate aspects of collaborative development to stimulate the learner by giving groups of people the chance to participate in shared activities. Cutrer et al. (2017) indicate that using a motivational technique to share conversation could assist in the adaptation to explore people's successes and struggles within their learning process as a form of self-regulated learning. To support self-regulated learning, Baek and Touati (2017) indicate the use of collaborative learning, where the learner will experience fun and enjoyment through engaging in social interaction. Community structures and group dynamics can influence learners' experience enjoyment and fun by identifying and considering various instructional methods.

Gonzalez and Kardong-Edgren (2017) build upon the research carried out by Wood and Reiners (2012) and indicates that for learners to master a learning skill set, they must focus on "*effortful activities designed to optimize improvement*" (Ericsson, Krampe & Tesch-Romer, 1993, p. 363). Effortful activities refer to the Deliberate Practice "DP," which involves placing a learner within a controlled setting to allow the students to identify techniques to support performance skills like improving retention, motivation, and performance monitoring. The more the learner is engaged in the activity, the more efficient their skill set be for the future. For DP to work, you need four key areas: 1) to take a baseline of skills associated with the learner (diagnostic of skills); 2) identify objectives and degree of difficulties in which the learner face, passing each scaffold learning phase (Martí-Parreño et al., 2016; Perryer et al., 2016); 3) formative assessments to make sure the learner is achieving over the progression pathways; 4) mastery achieved through practice and sharing through social networking (Hassan, Dias & Hamari, 2019).

Through social interaction, students would be able to gain recognition from the academic and from peers. To master the skills and to demonstrate the knowledge that has been gained, the learners could use social media like YouTube (Costello & Shaw, 2014), Facebook (King et al., 2013), Twitter (Singer, 2012; Raunch, 2013) to share their knowledge for others to gain. Using social media as a way of developing a community of practice, or "emphasis on educational strategies designed to improve cultivation of professional behavior", which in return would support new policies (Livstrom, Szostkowski & Roehrig, 2019), collaborative development, and social interaction (De Coninck, Valcke, Ophalvens & Vanderlinde, 2019). Sharing knowledge through mastery of skills would enable the learner to gain and seek enjoyment associated with the rewarding process. The principles of self-determination theories would enable the learner to improve their behavior and attitudes by creating a positive relationship with technology.

It is clear from the literature that there are multiple ways for a learner to gain mastery skills. However, academics/industry must play a critical role in implementing new practices and innovative techniques to promote enjoyment, retention, and motivation within the learning environment. For the learner to gain mastery skills, exercises must incorporate problem-solving activities that push for freedom to be independent without the worries of failing and have that drive to push the barriers of their abilities (Flores-Morador, 2013; Baek & Touati, 2017).

BEHAVIORAL CHANGE

The development of Gamification has enabled user experience to incorporate new factors into the learning environment that provides us with an opportunity on how the learner induces behaviors and attitudes to examine whether or not these factors lead to more significant usage and involvement. Rodrigues and Costa (2016) and Cardador et al. (2016) indicate that the behaviors of individuals can change due to factors associated with social factors, enrichment of activities and interaction, social cues, trust, friendship, confidence, innovation, enjoyment, and ease-of-use. According to Herzig et al. (2012), behavioral intention can improve the user's participation and engagement by determining the environment's usefulness and ease of use from the individual's perspective. Offering the learner an environment that incorporates enjoyment, simplicity, and usefulness would encourage the individual to improve relationships with activities and promote a greater acceptance of the learning journey. Deterding et al. (2011) indicate that friendliness, interactivity, and much content should play an essential factor when influencing individual behavior within the gamification setting. The use of intrinsic and extrinsic rewards can have a predefined dramatic effect on the behaviors of the learner, in which game design thinking and game mechanics should be well thought out by aligning objectives with rewards and incorporating design elements that create a desire and incentive and challenges the individual within the environment to feel submerged and engulfed with fun and enjoyment.

The idea of mapping gaming mechanics and designs to learning activities to enhance motivation would improve user experience (Hochleitner et al., 2015), beliefs, and values to immerse themselves in the learning environment. Banfield and Wilkerson (2014) and Vicente et al. (2019) suggest that setting goals and objectives would enable the learner to recognize the curriculum to learn performance criteria to assist in self-improvements. Individuals can start to change their behaviors through improving activities, but the learning tasks must be more engaging, like *"capture the flag events, quiz challenges, debates, use of leader boards and point gathering"* (Banfield & Wilkerson, 2014). Cavallo et al. (2017) and Sailer et al. (2017) suggested that it can influence the learner's behavior by allowing them to see real-time responses to their actions, either visual or performance directed by others within the community.

It is essential to harness this as it would facilitate adaptive learning. With the aid of modern technology, feedback can come in a series of ways depending on the capabilities of the gamification environment or features adopted by the tutor, such as augmented and mixed reality, 3D audio and video, virtual worlds, narratives, modeling, and socialization. Socialization would provide the learner with more enjoyable exercises and activities. In contrast, they are being drawn in with others within the community by analyzing tasks and sharing knowledge, skills, resources, and tools with other individuals to complete the learning objectives.

SOCIALIZATION

Through socialization, learners can gain valuable information about their progress towards goals, which helps steer their behavior and improve motivation through sharing achievement so that other individuals can see. This aspect of socialization enables individuals to share their current performance with others to provide information about personal progress and capability to other learners where their performance has improved. According to Hanus and Fox (2015), social comparison theory (SCT) can be applied to the learning environment to aid the learner to evaluate their own opinions, make judgments. They can compare themselves to other individuals to reduce uncertainty while learning from each other. This is vital when exploring digital literacy within the 21st century and how technology is shaping culture and assisting individuals to engage more in create, manage and publishing more materials online (Reynolds, 2016). As Fülöp (2009) indicates, competition within any setting can be motivational, rewarding, joyful, and exciting, contributing to the individual achieving the desired improvement goal. Constructive competition within Gamification enables the learners to see others' learning pace, thus making the individual want to self-motivate and improve within the community while directly asking for guidance on achieving the tasks (Banfield & Wilkerson, 2014).

This particular mechanism gives the learner a sense of goal progression, coupled with helpful feedback, a more desirable learning experience (Koivisto & Hamari, 2019). As Cardador et al. (2016) and Rodrigues and Costa (2016) point out, the use of socialization can improve how individuals can receive feedback by using concepts of Gamification like points, mayorships, volume, and valence (Wang et al., 2017), badges, real-time support and encouragement from others within the classroom or the working environment. Adopting socialization concepts within the learning environment enables the tutor to focus on culture, tradition, and teaching (Costello, 2017) to bring loyalty and personal influences (ease-of-use, pleasure, and usefulness) into the teaching setting. The use of social cues can steer an environment to deploy a more robust, diverse social presence enhancing technologies among the learner/individual. Lotherington and Jenson (2011) mentioned that digital literacy practices ensure complexity is dealt with in the education systems and how to communicate effectively while observing etiquette and dimensions in an underpinning manner while in a social presence (Pietraß, 2009).

Using concepts of social presence like that of social actors or avatars enable the learner to experience a more realistic simulated learning environment that can show or resemble the personality and emotions of other real-life people. Interactive digital media/agents within socialization can encourage learners to interact more by offering them confidence, familiarity, and friendliness. These approaches would give the learner a sense of security for them to form an emotional relationship. Through these personal connections, tutors can ensure that tasks or exercises can challenge the scaffold learning approach (Rodrigues & Costa, 2016; Richard & Calvert, 2017; Wang et al., 2017), while the individual will not feel threatened. When applying socialization to Gamification, the educator would monitor the individual's ability to solve challenges where any difficulties other individuals or other support mechanisms can step in and influence the individual's thought patterns.

Through Gamification, socialization improves the way learners complete tasks, challenges, receive support, and retrieve feedback on how they go about problem-solving. The individuals expect better outcomes and adjust their own experience through engagement within technology (Bernik, Vusić & Milković, 2019).

SUMMARY

This chapter looks at different ways of exploring Gamification & Digital Literacy and the ways to improve retention through enhancing the engagement of the learner. It is critical to explore learner-centricity to provide the learners with rich interactive media and real-time feedback to inspire a sense of engagement and accomplishment, and then this would enhance the atmosphere education life cycle. By offering the learner a freedom choice of techniques, tools, and activities within the abilities to build upon skills, individuals can construct their learning from decisions based upon successes and failures either in a group-based scenario or as an individual task, knowing that a support network is always available. Offering the learner an environment that incorporates enjoyment, simplicity, and Gamification can be perceived as relationships to support activities throughout their learning journeys.

FURTHER READING

Gamification is a rapidly growing field not just within Education, but in other areas, like business (Naraghi-Taghi-Off, Horst & Dörner, 2020), Health and Wellbeing (Jamaludin, Wook, Noor & Qamar 2021), Military and Cyber Security (Abadia Correa, Ortiz Paez & Peña Castiblicanco, 2021). Through integrating Gamification, industries and institutions can bring non-playful fields into the cognitive structure to support emotions (Naraghi-Taghi-Off, Horst & Dörner, 2020) and wellbeing.

Research has indicated that using Gamification and digital literacy tools can influence the motivation of individuals not just in the workplace but also in academia to assist with planning and application to promote individual engagement (Miri & Macke, 2021). Literature does show that Gamification within industry and academia does have a positive impact on individuals' knowledge retention (Jamaludin, Wook, Noor & Qamar 2021). *"independent of age and gender"* (Putz, Hofbauer & Treiblmaier, 2020). The future pathways of Gamification and digital literacy are to fully integrate the mechanics of non-playful fields into the cognitive structure to enhance individuals' engagement to support feelings of achievement, mastery of skills, and competency. Digital literacy would assist in academic achievements and support learners' curiosity using various motivational techniques. Exploring digital literacy within Gamification is vital while breaking down the potential inclusivity that would benefit the academic world, from the team working to deploying a more robust, diverse social presence enhancing technologies tailored towards learner-centricity.

REFERENCES

Abadia Correa, J., Ortiz Paez, L., & Peña Castiblicanco, N. (2021). *Development of a Training Game to Provide Awareness in Cybersecurity to the Staff of the Aviation Military School "Marco Fidel Suárez" of the Colombian Air Force in the city of Cali.* Academic Press.

Al-Qallaf, C. L., & Al-Mutairi, A. S. (2016). Digital literacy and digital content supports learning: The impact of blogs on teaching English as a foreign language. *The Electronic Library.*

Alt, D., & Raichel, N. (2020). Enhancing perceived digital literacy skills and creative self-concept through gamified learning environments: Insights from a longitudinal study. *International Journal of Educational Research*, *101*, 101561.

Ayastuy, M. D., Torres, D., & Fernández, A. (2021). Adaptive Gamification in Collaborative systems, a systematic mapping study. *Computer Science Review*, *39*, 100333.

Azevedo, J., Padrão, P., Gregório, M. J., Almeida, C., Moutinho, N., Lien, N., & Barros, R. (2019). A web-based gamification program to improve nutrition literacy in families of 3-to 5-year-old children: The Nutriscience Project. *Journal of Nutrition Education and Behavior*, *51*(3), 326–334. doi:10.1016/j.jneb.2018.10.008 PMID:30579894

Baek, Y., & Touati, A. (2017). Exploring how individual traits influence enjoyment in a mobile learning game. *Computers in Human Behavior*, *69*, 347–357. doi:10.1016/j.chb.2016.12.053

Banfield, J., & Wilkerson, B. (2014). Increasing student intrinsic motivation and self-efficacy through gamification pedagogy. *Contemporary Issues in Education Research (Online)*, *7*(4), 291–298. doi:10.19030/cier.v7i4.8843

Barkley, J. E., Lepp, A., & Glickman, E. L. (2017). "Pokémon Go!" may promote walking, discourage sedentary behavior in college students. *Games for Health Journal*, *6*(3), 165–170. doi:10.1089/g4h.2017.0009 PMID:28628384

Behnke, K. A. (2015). *Gamification in Introductory Computer Science* (Doctoral dissertation). University of Colorado Boulder.

Bennett, D., Yábar, D. P. B., & Saura, J. R. (2017). University Incubators May Be Socially Valuable, but How Effective Are They? A Case Study on Business Incubators at Universities. In *Entrepreneurial Universities* (pp. 165–177). Springer International Publishing. doi:10.1007/978-3-319-47949-1_11

Berkling, K., & Neubehler, K. (2019). Boosting Student Performance with Peer Reviews; Integration and Analysis of Peer Reviews in a Gamified Software Engineering Classroom. In *2019 IEEE Global Engineering Education Conference (EDUCON)* (pp. 253-262). IEEE. 10.1109/EDUCON.2019.8725247

Bernik, A., Vusić, D., & Milković, M. (2019). Evaluation of Gender Differences Based on Knowledge Adaptation in the Field of Gamification and Computer Science. *International Journal of Emerging Technologies in Learning*, *14*(8), 220. doi:10.3991/ijet.v14i08.9847

Bhatti, N. (2019). CAI and conventional method for retention of mathematics: An experimental study. *Journal of Physics: Conference Series*, *1157*(3), 032079. doi:10.1088/1742-6596/1157/3/032079

Bíró, G. I. (2014). Didactics 2.0: A pedagogical analysis of gamification theory from a comparative perspective with a special view to the Components of Learning. *Procedia: Social and Behavioral Sciences*, *141*, 148–151. doi:10.1016/j.sbspro.2014.05.027

Bista, S. K., Nepal, S., Colineau, N., & Paris, C. (2012). Using Gamification in an online community. In *Collaborative Computing: Networking, Applications, and Worksharing (CollaborateCom), 2012 8th International Conference on* (pp. 611-618). IEEE.

Bond, L. (2015). *Mathimagicians Quest: Applying game design concepts to Education to increase school engagement for students with emotional and behavioral disabilities* (Doctoral dissertation).

Buckingham, D. (2010). Defining digital literacy. In *Medienbildung in neuen Kulturräumen* (pp. 59–71). VS Verlag für Sozialwissenschaften. doi:10.1007/978-3-531-92133-4_4

Buckingham, D. (2016). Defining digital literacy. *Nordic Journal of Digital Literacy,* 21-34.

Buckley, P., & Doyle, E. (2017). Individualising Gamification: An investigation of the impact of learning styles and personality traits on the efficacy of Gamification using a prediction market. *Computers & Education, 106,* 43–55. doi:10.1016/j.compedu.2016.11.009

Cameron, K. E., & Bizo, L. A. (2019). Use of the game-based learning platform KAHOOT! To facilitate learner engagement in Animal Science students. *Research in Learning Technology, 27*(0), 27. doi:10.25304/rlt.v27.2225

Cardador, T. M., Northcraft, B. G., & Whicker, J. (2016). A theory of work gamification: Something old, something new, something borrowed, something cool? *Human Resource Management Review.*

Carter, M. S., & Mahoney, M. C. (2020). Gamification and Training the Technical Workforce. *The Marine Corps Gazette.*

Cavallo, A., Robaldo, A., Ansovini, F., Carmosino, I., & De Gloria, A. (2017). *Gamification of a System for Real-Time Monitoring of Posture. In eHealth 360.* Springer International Publishing.

Chen, S. W., Yang, C. H., Huang, K. S., & Fu, S. L. (2019). Digital games for learning energy conservation: A study of impacts on motivation, attention, and learning outcomes. *Innovations in Education and Teaching International, 56*(1), 66–76. doi:10.1080/14703297.2017.1348960

Cho, M. H., & Castañeda, D. A. (2019). Motivational and affective engagement in learning Spanish with a mobile application. *System, 81,* 90–99. doi:10.1016/j.system.2019.01.008

Chong, D. Y. K. (2019). Benefits and challenges with gamified multimedia physiotherapy case studies: A mixed-method study. *Archives of Physiotherapy, 9*(1), 7. doi:10.118640945-019-0059-2 PMID:31139434

Chu, S. K. W., Reynolds, R. B., Tavares, N. J., Notari, M., & Lee, C. W. Y. (2017). *Assessment Instruments for Twenty-First Century Skills. In 21st Century Skills Development Through Inquiry-Based Learning.* Springer Singapore.

Cobo, C., Zucchetti, A., Kass-Hanna, J., & Lyons, A. (2019). *Leaving no one behind: Measuring the multidimensionality of digital literacy in the age of AI and other transformative technologies.* Academic Press.

Cole, H., & Griffiths, M. D. (2007). Social interactions in massively multiplayer online role-playing gamers. *Cyberpsychology & Behavior, 10*(4), 575–583. doi:10.1089/cpb.2007.9988 PMID:17711367

Costello, R. (2017). *Research on Scientific and Technological Developments in Asia. In Socio-economic challenges facing the Asia and Pacific region in Higher Education. IGI Global.*

Costello, R. (2020). Gamification Strategies for Retention, Motivation, and Engagement in Higher Education: Emerging Research and Opportunities. IGI Global.

Costello, R., & Lambert, M. (2018). Motivational influences for Higher Education (HE) Students. *International Journal of Online Pedagogy and Course Design*, *9*(1), 3.

Costello, R., & Lambert, M. (2019). Pokémon GO as a Cognitive and Societal Development Tool for Personalised Learning. *International Journal of End-User Computing and Development*, *8*(1), 1–30. doi:10.4018/IJEUCD.2019010101

Costello, R., Lambert, M., & Smith, L. (2021). An innovative approach of using Mobile Gaming to bridge, anxiety, depression & isolation. *International Journal of Adult Vocational Education and Technology*.

Costello, R., & Shaw, N. (2014). Personalised Learning Environments, HEA STEM (Computing): Learning Technologies Workshop. University of Hull.

Cotton, V., & Patel, M. S. (2019). Gamification use and design in popular health and fitness mobile applications. *American Journal of Health Promotion*, *33*(3), 448–451. doi:10.1177/0890117118790394 PMID:30049225

Cutrer, W. B., Miller, B., Pusic, M. V., Mejicano, G., Mangrulkar, R. S., Gruppen, L. D., & Moore, D. E. Jr. (2017). Fostering the development of master adaptive learners: A conceptual model to guide skill acquisition in medical Education. *Academic Medicine*, *92*(1), 70–75. doi:10.1097/ACM.0000000000001323 PMID:27532867

Dalton, B., & Proctor, C. P. (2007). Reading as thinking: Integrating strategy instruction in a universally designed digital literacy environment. *Reading comprehension strategies: Theories, interventions, and technologies*, 423-442.

Dawson, S. (2008). A study of the relationship between student social networks and sense of community. *Journal of Educational Technology & Society*, *11*(3), 224–238.

De Coninck, K., Valcke, M., Ophalvens, I., & Vanderlinde, R. (2019). Bridging the theory-practice gap in teacher education: The design and construction of simulation-based learning environments. In *Kohärenz in der Lehrerbildung* (pp. 263–280). Springer VS. doi:10.1007/978-3-658-23940-4_17

de-Marcos, L., Domínguez, A., Saenz-de-Navarrete, J., & Pagés, C. (2014). An empirical study comparing gamification and social networking on e-learning. *Computers & Education*, *75*, 82–91. doi:10.1016/j.compedu.2014.01.012

de Sousa Borges, S., Durelli, V. H., Reis, H. M., & Isotani, S. (2014). A systematic mapping on Gamification applied to Education. In *Proceedings of the 29th Annual ACM Symposium on Applied Computing* (pp. 216-222). ACM. 10.1145/2554850.2554956

Demkah, M., & Bhargava, D. (2019, February). Gamification in Education: A Cognitive Psychology Approach to Cooperative and Fun Learning. In *2019 Amity International Conference on Artificial Intelligence (AICAI)* (pp. 170-174). IEEE. 10.1109/AICAI.2019.8701264

Deterding, S., Dixon, D., Khaled, R., & Nacke, L. (2011). From game design elements to gamefulness: defining Gamification. In *Proceedings of the 15th international academic MindTrek conference: Envisioning future media environments* (pp. 9-15). ACM. 10.1145/2181037.2181040

Deterding, S., Sicart, M., Nacke, L., O'Hara, K., & Dixon, D. (2011). Gamification using game-design elements in non-gaming contexts. In *CHI'11 Extended Abstracts on Human Factors in Computing Systems* (pp. 2425–2428). ACM. doi:10.1145/1979742.1979575

Eleftheria, C. A., Charikleia, P., Iason, C. G., Athanasios, T., & Dimitrios, T. (2013). An innovative augmented reality educational platform using Gamification to enhance lifelong learning and cultural education. In *Information, Intelligence, Systems and Applications (IISA), 2013 Fourth International Conference on* (pp. 1-5). IEEE. 10.1109/IISA.2013.6623724

Eryansyah, E., Erlina, E., Fiftinova, F., & Nurweni, A. (2019). EFL Students' Needs of Digital Literacy to Meet the Demands of 21stCentury Skills. *Indonesian Research Journal of Education*, 442–460.

Esmaeili, H., & Woods, P. C. (2016). Calm down buddy! it's just a game: Behavioral patterns observed among teamwork MMO participants in WARGAMING's world of tanks. In *2016 22nd International Conference on Virtual System & Multimedia (VSMM)* (pp. 1-11). IEEE.

Fhkps, B., Ho, W., Leung, E., Li, P., Mok, B., Shek, V., & Shek, E. (2021). Nurturing leadership qualities under COVID-19: Student perceptions of the qualities and effectiveness of online teaching and learning on leadership development. *International Journal of Child and Adolescent Health*, *14*(1), 89–100.

Fichten, C. S., Asuncion, J., & Scapin, R. (2014). Digital Technology, Learning, and Postsecondary Students with Disabilities: Where We've Been and Where We're Going. *Journal of Postsecondary Education and Disability*, *27*(4), 369–379.

Flores-Morador, F. (2013). *The beam in the eye: ICT, school and broken technologies* [La viga en el ojo: los nuevos medios de comunicación, la escuela y las tecnologías rotas]. Academic Press.

Fülöp, M. (2009). Happy and Unhappy Competitors: What Makes the Difference? *Psihologijske Teme*, *18*(2), 345–367.

Gatti, L., Ulrich, M., & Seele, P. (2019). Education for sustainable development through business simulation games: An exploratory study of sustainability gamification and its effects on students' learning outcomes. *Journal of Cleaner Production*, *207*, 667–678. doi:10.1016/j.jclepro.2018.09.130

Geroimenko, V. (2019). Concluding Remarks: From Pokémon GO to Serious Augmented Reality Games. *Augmented Reality Games*, *2*, 305.

González, C. S., & Mora, A. (2014). Methodological proposal for Gamification in the computer engineering teaching. *Proceeding Computers in Education (SIIE), 2014 International Symposium on*, 29-34. 10.1109/SIIE.2014.7017700

Gonzalez, L., & Kardong-Edgren, S. (2017). Deliberate Practice for Mastery Learning in Nursing. *Clinical Simulation in Nursing*, *13*(1), 10–14. doi:10.1016/j.ecns.2016.10.005

Gooch, D., Vasalou, A., & Benton, L. (2015). Exploring the use of a Gamification Platform to Support Students with Dyslexia. In *Information, Intelligence, Systems and Applications (IISA), 2015, 6th International Conference on* (pp. 1-6). IEEE. 10.1109/IISA.2015.7388001

Gooch, D., Vasalou, A., Benton, L., & Khaled, R. (2016). *Using Gamification to motivate students with dyslexia*. doi:10.1145/2858036.2858231

Hamm, J. M., Perry, R. P., Chipperfield, J. G., Parker, P. C., & Heckhausen, J. (2019). A motivation treatment to enhance goal engagement in online learning environments: Assisting failure-prone college students with low optimism. *Motivation Science*, *5*(2), 116–134. doi:10.1037/mot0000107

Hammerschall, U. (2019). A Gamification Framework for Long-Term Engagement in Education Based on Self Determination Theory and the Transtheoretical Model of Change. In *2019 IEEE Global Engineering Education Conference (EDUCON)* (pp. 95-101). IEEE. 10.1109/EDUCON.2019.8725251

Hanbidge, A. S., Tin, T., & Sanderson, N. (2018). Information Literacy Skills on the Go: Mobile Learning Innovation. *Journal of Information Literacy*, *12*(1).

Hancock, D., Sirizzotti, M. S., Joe, R., & Martin, R. J. (2019). *Methods and systems for gamification.* U.S. Patent Application No. 15/466,379.

Hanus, M. D., & Fox, J. (2015). Assessing the effects of Gamification in the Classroom: A longitudinal study on intrinsic motivation, social comparison, satisfaction, effort, and academic performance. *Computers & Education*, *80*, 152–161. doi:10.1016/j.compedu.2014.08.019

Hassan, L., Dias, A., & Hamari, J. (2019). How motivational feedback increases user's benefits and continued use: A study on Gamification, quantified-self and social networking. *International Journal of Information Management*, *46*, 151–162. doi:10.1016/j.ijinfomgt.2018.12.004

Heeter, C. (1992). Being there: The subjective experience of presence. *Presence (Cambridge, Mass.)*, *1*(2), 262–271. doi:10.1162/pres.1992.1.2.262

Herman, K. C., Prewett, S. L., Eddy, C. L., Savala, A., & Reinke, W. M. (2020). Profiles of middle school teacher stress and coping: Concurrent and prospective correlates. *Journal of School Psychology*, *78*, 54–68. doi:10.1016/j.jsp.2019.11.003 PMID:32178811

Herro, D. C., Lin, L., & Fowler, M. (2017). Meet the (Media) Producers: Artists, Composers, and Gamemakers. *Journal of Applied Research in Higher Education*, *9*(1), 40–53. doi:10.1108/JARHE-04-2015-0029

Herzig, P., Strahringer, S., & Ameling, M. (2012). Gamification of ERP systems -Exploring gamification effects on user acceptance constructs. In *Multikonferenz Wirtschaftsinformatik* (pp. 793–804). GITO.

Hochleitner, C., Hochleitner, W., Graf, C., & Tscheligi, M. (2015). A Heuristic Framework for Evaluating User Experience in Games. In Game User Experience Evaluation. Bernhaupt.

Howard, T. C. (2001). Telling their side of the story: African-American students' perceptions of culturally relevant teaching. *The Urban Review*, *33*(2), 131–149. doi:10.1023/A:1010393224120

Howell, E. (2017). Pokémon GO: Implications for literacy in the classroom. *The Reading Teacher*, *70*(6), 729–732. doi:10.1002/trtr.1565

Huang, Y. M., Liang, T. H., Su, Y. N., & Chen, N. S. (2012). Empowering personalized learning with an interactive e-book learning system for elementary school students. *Educational Technology Research and Development*, *60*(4), 703–722. doi:10.100711423-012-9237-6

Hung, H. T., Yang, J. C., & Tsai, Y. C. (2020). Student Game Design as a Literacy Practice. *Journal of Educational Technology & Society*, *23*(1), 50–63.

Jamaludin, A., & Hung, D. (2017). Problem-solving for STEM learning: Navigating games as narrativized problem spaces for 21st. *Research and Practice in Technology Enhanced Learning*, *12*(1), 1–14. doi:10.118641039-016-0038-0 PMID:30613250

Jamaludin, N. F., Wook, T. S. M. T., Noor, S. F. M., & Qamar, F. (2021). Gamification Design Elements to Enhance Adolescent Motivation in Diagnosing Depression. *International Journal of Interactive Mobile Technologies*, *15*(10), 154. doi:10.3991/ijim.v15i10.21137

Jin, D. Y. (2017). The Emergence of Asian Mobile Games: Definitions, Industries, and Trajectories. *Mobile Gaming in Asia: Politics, Culture and Emerging Technologies*, 3-20.

Kankanhalli, A., Taher, M., Cavusoglu, H., & Kim, S. H. (2012). Gamification: A new paradigm for online user engagement. *Thirty Third International Conference on Information Systems*, 1-10.

Kellinger, J. J. (2017). Let the Games Begin! Teaching Your Game. In A Guide to Designing Curricular Games (pp. 271-311). Springer International Publishing. doi:10.1007/978-3-319-42393-7_8

Kiili, K., Kiili, C., Ott, M., & Jönkkäri, T. (2012). Towards creative pedagogy: Empowering students to develop games. In *6th European Conference on Games Based Learning*. Academic Press.

King, D., Greaves, F., Exeter, C., & Darzi, A. (2013). 'Gamification': Influencing health behaviours with games. *Journal of the Royal Society of Medicine*, *106*(3), 76–78. doi:10.1177/0141076813480996 PMID:23481424

Knautz, K., Orszullok, L., & Soubusta, S. (2013). Game-based IL instruction–A journey of knowledge in four acts. In *European Conference on Information Literacy* (pp. 366-372). Springer International Publishing. 10.1007/978-3-319-03919-0_48

Kogan, L., Hellyer, P., Duncan, C., & Schoenfeld-Tacher, R. (2017). A pilot investigation of the physical and psychological benefits of playing Pokémon GO for dog owners. *Computers in Human Behavior*, *76*, 431–437. doi:10.1016/j.chb.2017.07.043

Koivisto, J., & Hamari, J. (2014). Demographic differences in perceived benefits from Gamification. Computers in Human Behavior, 35, 179-188.

Koivisto, J., & Hamari, J. (2019). The rise of motivational information systems: A review of gamification research. *International Journal of Information Management*, *45*, 191–210. doi:10.1016/j.ijinfomgt.2018.10.013

Korn, O. (2012). Industrial playgrounds: how Gamification helps to enrich work for elderly or impaired persons in production. In *Proceedings of the 4th ACM SIGCHI symposium on Engineering interactive computing systems* (pp. 313-316). ACM. 10.1145/2305484.2305539

Legaki, N. Z., Xi, N., Hamari, J., & Assimakopoulos, V. (2019, January). Gamification of The Future: An Experiment on Gamifying Education of Forecasting. *Proceedings of the 52nd Hawaii International Conference on System Sciences*. 10.24251/HICSS.2019.219

Lichty, P. (2019). The Gamification of Augmented Reality Art. In *Augmented Reality Games II* (pp. 225–246). Springer. doi:10.1007/978-3-030-15620-6_10

Livstrom, I. C., Szostkowski, A. H., & Roehrig, G. H. (2019). Integrated STEM in practice: Learning from Montessori philosophies and practices. *School Science and Mathematics*, *119*(4), 190–202. doi:10.1111sm.12331

Lotherington, H., & Jenson, J. (2011). Teaching multimodal and digital literacy in L2 settings: New literacies, new basics, new pedagogies. *Annual Review of Applied Linguistics*, *31*, 226–246. doi:10.1017/S0267190511000110

Mac Callum, K., Jeffrey, L., & Na, K. (2014). Factors impacting teachers' adoption of mobile learning. *Journal of Information Technology Education*, *13*. doi:10.28945/1970

Maican, C., Lixandroiu, R., & Constantin, C. (2016). Interactive.ro – A study of a gamification framework using zero-cost tools. *Computers in Human Behavior*, *61*, 186–197. doi:10.1016/j.chb.2016.03.023

Mantiri, O., Hibbert, G. K., & Jacobs, J. (2019). Digital literacy in ESL classroom. *Universal Journal of Educational Research*, *7*(5), 1301–1305. doi:10.13189/ujer.2019.070515

Maqsood, S. (2020). *The Design, Development and Evaluation of a Digital Literacy Game for Preteens* (Doctoral dissertation). Carleton University.

Martí-Parreño, J., Seguí-Mas, D., & Seguí-Mas, E. (2016). Teachers' Attitude towards and Actual Use of Gamification. *Procedia: Social and Behavioral Sciences*, *228*, 682–688. doi:10.1016/j.sbspro.2016.07.104

Massung, E., Coyle, D., Cater, K. F., Jay, M., & Preist, C. (2013). Using crowdsourcing to support pro-environmental community activism. In *Proceedings of the SIGCHI Conference on Human Factors in Computing Systems* (pp. 371-380). ACM. 10.1145/2470654.2470708

McCauley, V., Davison, K., McHugh, P., Domegan, C., & Grehan, A. (2021). Innovative Education Strategies to Advance Ocean Literacy. In *Ocean Literacy: Understanding the Ocean* (pp. 149–168). Springer. doi:10.1007/978-3-030-70155-0_7

McCoy, L., Lewis, J. H., & Dalton, D. (2016). Gamification and multimedia for medical Education: A landscape review. *Journal of Osteopathic Medicine*, *116*(1), 22–34. doi:10.7556/jaoa.2016.003 PMID:26745561

McLoughlin, C., & Lee, M. J. (2010). Personalised and self regulated learning in the Web 2.0 era: International exemplars of innovative pedagogy using social software. *Australasian Journal of Educational Technology*, *26*(1). Advance online publication. doi:10.14742/ajet.1100

Mehtälä, S. (2018). *User interface design for children and youth: websites and applications to promote mental health and wellbeing*. Academic Press.

Mesko, B., Győrffy, Z., & Kollár, J. (2015). Digital literacy in the medical curriculum: A course with social media tools and Gamification. *JMIR Medical Education*, *1*(2), e4411. doi:10.2196/mededu.4411 PMID:27731856

Meyer, M., & Wood, L. (2017). A critical reflection on the multiple roles required to facilitate mutual learning during service-learning in Creative Arts education. *Teaching in Higher Education*, *22*(2), 158–177. doi:10.1080/13562517.2016.1221808

Miller, J. Y. (2021). *Digital Literacy: The Impact of a Blended Learning Model on Student Motivation and Achievement* (Doctoral dissertation). Gardner-Webb University.

Miri, D. H., & Macke, J. (2021). Gamification, motivation, and engagement at work: A qualitative multiple case study. *European Business Review*. Advance online publication. doi:10.1108/EBR-04-2020-0106

Mystakidis, S., & Berki, E. (2018). The case of literacy motivation: Playful 3D immersive learning environments and problem-focused Education for blended digital storytelling. *International Journal of Web-Based Learning and Teaching Technologies*, *13*(1), 64–79. doi:10.4018/IJWLTT.2018010105

Naraghi-Taghi-Off, R., Horst, R., & Dörner, R. (2020). Gamification Mechanics for Playful Virtual Reality Authoring. In STAG (pp. 131-141). Academic Press.

Nicholson, S. (2012). A user-centered theoretical framework for meaningful Gamification. *Games Learning Society*, *8*(1), 223–230.

Nuutinen, M., Seppänen, M., Smedlund, A., & Kaasinen, E. (2017). *Seeking New Ways of Innovating in Industry-Research Collaboration Practice. Innovating in practice*. Springer International Publishing.

O'Brolcháin, F., Jacquemard, T., Monaghan, D., O'Connor, N., Novitzky, P., & Gordijn, B. (2016). The convergence of virtual reality and social networks: Threats to privacy and autonomy. *Science and Engineering Ethics*, *22*(1), 1–29. doi:10.100711948-014-9621-1 PMID:25552240

O'Connor, S., Hanlon, P., O'donnell, C. A., Garcia, S., Glanville, J., & Mair, F. S. (2016). Understanding factors affecting patient and public engagement and recruitment to digital health interventions: A systematic review of qualitative studies. *BMC Medical Informatics and Decision Making*, *16*(1), 1–15. doi:10.118612911-016-0359-3 PMID:27630020

Oprescu, F., Jones, C., & Katsikitis, M. (2014). I PLAY AT WORK—Ten principles for transforming work processes through Gamification. *Frontiers in Psychology*, *5*, 5. doi:10.3389/fpsyg.2014.00014 PMID:24523704

Pala, Ş. M., & Başıbüyük, A. (2021). The Predictive Effect of Digital Literacy, Self-Control and Motivation on the Academic Achievement in the Science, Technology and Society Learning Area. *Technology, Knowledge and Learning*, 1-17.

Pangrazio, L. (2016). Reconceptualising critical digital literacy. *Discourse (Abingdon)*, *37*(2), 163–174. doi:10.1080/01596306.2014.942836

Pedreira, O., García, F., Brisaboa, N., & Piattini, M. (2015). Gamification in software engineering–A systematic mapping. *Information and Software Technology*, *57*, 157–168. doi:10.1016/j.infsof.2014.08.007

Perryer, C., Celestine, A. N., Scott-Ladd, B., & Leighton, C. (2016). Enhancing workplace motivation through Gamification: Transferrable lessons from pedagogy. *International Journal of Management Education*, *14*(3), 327–335. doi:10.1016/j.ijme.2016.07.001

Pietraß, M. (2009). Digital literacy as framing: Suggestions for an interactive approach based on E. Goffman s frame theory. *Nordic Journal of Digital Literacy*, *4*(3-4), 131-142.

Prandi, C., Nisi, V., Salomoni, P., & Nunes, N. J. (2015). From Gamification to pervasive game in mapping urban accessibility. In *Proceedings of the 11th Biannual Conference on Italian SIGCHI Chapter* (pp. 126-129). ACM 10.1145/2808435.2808449

Putz, L. M., Hofbauer, F., & Mates, M. (2019). A vignette study among order pickers about the acceptance of Gamification. In GamiFIN (pp. 154-166). Academic Press.

Putz, L. M., Hofbauer, F., & Treiblmaier, H. (2020). Can Gamification help to improve Education? Findings from a longitudinal study. *Computers in Human Behavior*, *110*, 106392.

Raftopoulos, M. (2014). Towards gamification transparency: A conceptual framework for the development of responsible gamified enterprise systems. *Journal of Gaming & Virtual Worlds*, *6*(2), 159–178. doi:10.1386/jgvw.6.2.159_1

Rauch, M. (2013). Best practices for using enterprise gamification to engage employees and customers. In *International Conference on Human-Computer Interaction* (pp. 276-283). Springer Berlin Heidelberg. 10.1007/978-3-642-39262-7_31

Reynolds, R. (2016). Defining, designing for, and measuring "social constructivist digital literacy" development in learners: A proposed framework. *Educational Technology Research and Development*, *64*(4), 735–762. doi:10.100711423-015-9423-4

Rodrigues, F. L., & Costa, C. J. O. A. (2016). Playing seriously – How gamification and social cues influence bank customers to use gamified e-business applications. *Computers in Human Behavior*, *63*, 392–407. doi:10.1016/j.chb.2016.05.063

Rosen, Y., Stoeffler, K., Yudelson, M., & Simmering, V. (2020). Towards Scalable Gamified Assessment in Support of Collaborative Problem-Solving Competency Development in Online and Blended Learning. In *Proceedings of the Seventh ACM Conference on Learning @ Scale* (pp. 369-372). 10.1145/3386527.3405946

Roth, S., Schneckenberg, D., & Tsai, C. W. (2015). The ludic drive as innovation driver: Introduction to the Gamification of innovation. *Creativity and Innovation Management*, *24*(2), 300–306. doi:10.1111/caim.12124

Sailer, M., Hense, J., Mandl, H., & Klevers, M. (2017). Fostering Development of Work Competencies and Motivation via Gamification. In *Competence-based Vocational and Professional Education* (pp. 795–818). Springer International Publishing. doi:10.1007/978-3-319-41713-4_37

Schek, E. J., Mantovani, F., Realdon, O., Dias, J., Paiva, A., Schramm-Yavin, S., & Pat-Horenczyk, R. (2017). *Positive Technologies for Promoting Emotion Regulation Abilities in Adolescents. In eHealth 360*. Springer International Publishing.

Schmidt-Kraepelin, M., Thiebes, S., Stepanovic, S., Mettler, T., & Sunyaev, A. (2019). Gamification in health behavior change support systems-A synthesis of unintended side effects. In *Proceedings of the 14th International Conference on Wirtschaftsinformatik* (pp. 1032-1046). Academic Press.

Sera, L., & Wheeler, E. (2017). Game on: The Gamification of the pharmacy classroom. *Currents in Pharmacy Teaching & Learning*, *9*(1), 155–159. doi:10.1016/j.cptl.2016.08.046 PMID:29180148

Shaban, A., & Pearson, E. (2019). A Learning Design Framework to Support Children with Learning Disabilities Incorporating Gamification Techniques. In *Extended Abstracts of the 2019 CHI Conference on Human Factors in Computing Systems* (p. LBW0284). ACM. 10.1145/3290607.3312806

Shen, C., Sun, Q., Kim, T., Wolff, G., Ratan, R., & Williams, D. (2020). Viral vitriol: Predictors and contagion of online toxicity in World of Tanks. *Computers in Human Behavior, 108*, 106343. doi:10.1016/j.chb.2020.106343

Shmelev, V., Karpova, M., Kogtikov, N., & Dukhanov, A. (2016, October). Students' development of information-seeking skills in a computer-aided quest. In *2016 IEEE Frontiers in Education Conference (FIE)* (pp. 1-4). IEEE.

Shopova, T. (2014). Digital literacy of students and its improvement at the university. *Journal on Efficiency and Responsibility in Education and Science, 7*(2), 26–32. doi:10.7160/eriesj.2014.070201

Singer, N. (2012). You've won a badge (and now we know all about you). *New York Times*, 4.

Slomka, J. (2014). *Toward transdisciplinary professionalism in the teaching of public health*. Establishing Transdisciplinary Professionalism for Improving Health Outcomes.

So, H. J., & Brush, T. A. (2008). Student perceptions of collaborative learning, social presence and satisfaction in a blended learning environment: Relationships and critical factors. *Computers & Education, 51*(1), 318–336. doi:10.1016/j.compedu.2007.05.009

Stamper, L. J. (2015). The LandWarNet School, The Army Learning Model, and Appreciative Inquiry: How is a Centralized Training Organization Improved by Introducing Decentralization. Academic Press.

Tanouri, A., Mulcahy, R., & Russell-Bennett, R. (2019). Transformative gamification services for social behavior brand equity: A hierarchical model. *Journal of Service Theory and Practice, 29*(2), 122–141. doi:10.1108/JSTP-06-2018-0140

Taub, M., Sawyer, R., Smith, A., Rowe, J., Azevedo, R., & Lester, J. (2020). The agency effect: The impact of student agency on learning, emotions, and problem-solving behaviors in a game-based learning environment. *Computers & Education, 147*, 103781. doi:10.1016/j.compedu.2019.103781

Taylor, N. (2017). Monitoring, Accountability and Professional Knowledge. In *Monitoring the Quality of Education in Schools* (pp. 43–52). SensePublishers. doi:10.1007/978-94-6300-453-4_4

Tobin, R., & McInnes, A. (2008). Accommodating differences: Variations in differentiated literacy instruction in grade 2/3 classrooms. *Literacy, 42*(1), 3–9. doi:10.1111/j.1467-9345.2008.00470.x

Tolks, D., Sailer, M., Dadaczynski, K., Lampert, C., Huberty, J., Paulus, P., & Horstmann, D. (2019). ONYA—The Wellbeing Game: How to Use Gamification to Promote Wellbeing. *Information (Basel), 10*(2), 58. doi:10.3390/info10020058

Udara, S. W. I., & De Alwis, A. K. (2019). Gamification for Healthcare and Well-being. *Global Journal of Medical Research*, 25–29. doi:10.34257/GJMRKVOL19IS4PG25

Vicente, E., Verdugo, M. A., Gómez-Vela, M., Fernández-Pulido, R., Wehmeyer, M. L., & Guillén, V. M. (2019). Personal characteristics and school contextual variables associated with student self-determination in Spanish context. *Journal of Intellectual & Developmental Disability*, *44*(1), 23–34. doi:10.3109/13668250.2017.1310828

Walsh, J. N., O'Brien, M. P., & Costin, Y. (2021). Investigating student engagement with intentional content: An exploratory study of instructional videos. *International Journal of Management Education*, *19*(2), 100505. doi:10.1016/j.ijme.2021.100505

Wang, L., Gunasti, K., Gopal, R., Shankar, R., & Pancras, J. (2017). The Impact of Gamification on Word-of-Mouth Effectiveness: Evidence from Foursquare. *Proceedings of the 50th Hawaii International Conference on System Sciences*. 10.24251/HICSS.2017.090

Williams, J., Ritter, J., & Bullock, S. M. (2012). Understanding the complexity of becoming a teacher educator: Experience, belonging, and practice within a professional learning community. *Studying Teacher Education*, *8*(3), 245–260. doi:10.1080/17425964.2012.719130

Wood, L. C., & Reiners, T. (2012). Gamification in logistics and supply chain education: Extending active learning. In P. Kommers, T. Issa, & P. Isaías (Eds.), *IADIS International Conference on Internet Technologies & Society*, (pp. 101–108). Academic Press.

Yee, N., Ducheneaut, N., Shiao, H. T., & Nelson, L. (2012). Through the azerothian looking glass: Mapping in-game preferences to real-world demographics. *Proceedings of the SIGCHI Conference on Human Factors in Computing Systems*, 2811-2814. 10.1145/2207676.2208683

Zolyomi, A., & Schmalz, M. (2017). Mining for Social Skills: Minecraft in Home and Therapy for Neurodiverse Youth. *Proceedings of the 50th Hawaii International Conference on System Sciences*. 10.24251/HICSS.2017.411

Chapter 41

Learner Motivation Through Gamification in E-Learning:
A Study on Game-Based Formative Assessment in E-Learning

Anshita Chelawat

Vivekanand Education Society's Institute of Management Studies and Research, India

Seema Sant

ⓘ https://orcid.org/0000-0002-0024-5556

Vivekanand Education Society's Institute of Management Studies and Research, India

ABSTRACT

It is a proven fact that learning with the element of fun and games makes the learning process interesting and also helps in student retention. Especially, in the context of e-learning environment, where learner motivation and engagement level are not easy to monitor, it is required to implement some mechanism which can improve their intrinsic motivation and make them self-motivated. Gamification in education and using game-based formative assessment tools will be of great help to not only motivate learners to opt for e-learning courses, but to complete till the end. The current study, thus, focuses on use of game-based formative assessment to improve learners' motivation in the e-learning environment so that their drop-out rates can be controlled, and their engagement level can be improved. Also, it intends to assess the past literature and identify the essential gaming mechanics which can possibly impact the learner motivation. It will also highlight the theoretical perspective used in previous studies on gamification, engagement, and motivation.

"The role of a teacher and the role of game rules are roughly equivalent. A teacher wants to exert influence on students to encourage certain behaviours; to reward the positive and discourage the negative. In games, rules are designed to guide players through a level or stage in an intuitive manner." -- Steven Lumpkin, Senior Designer, RollerCoaster Tycoon World

DOI: 10.4018/978-1-7998-7271-9.ch041

INTRODUCTION

The propagation of e-learning in the field of education cannot be ignored in the current scenario when learning through digital modes has become the only feasible option to continue the learning process. The outbreak of COVID-19 has made us realize the need to revamp our education system and policy. Launch of New Educational Policy (NEP) in India, in this respect, on July 28, 2020 after the period of 34 years was the first step in this regard. Apart from promoting *equity, affordability, quality, access, and accountability* in the Indian Educational System, it has specially highlighted the importance of digitalization in the education. Various governmental platforms like SWAYAM, DIKSHA, e-PG Pathshala aims to extends assistive tools to the teachers to monitor the progress of the students (NEP-2020). Additionally, these platforms, including many others, will ensure the equal access to the students along with quality and practical learning experiences through their virtual labs. The ease to access the content from anywhere, anytime, and, any number of times resulted in massive enrolment in various e-learning courses.

With the growing enrolment rate in e-learning, the major challenge is to make **non-active students** (enrolled but not actively involved with the course) active in the studies (Bubou & Job, 2020). Online learning provides learners with independency to learn at their own pace, but **it cannot guarantee that the students will be motivated** (Samir Abou El-Seoud et al., 2014) enough to take such course at their own or to complete it till the end. Online learning or e-learning has been widely used by the students as it provides independency and ability to self-regulate the learning, however it often accompanied by lack of motivation which eventually results in higher drop-out rates as compared to traditional mode of learning (Vogel et al. 2018; Danka, 2020). As per (Kahan, Soffer & Nachmias 2017), it is very essential to understand the needs, interests, experiences, and preferences of learners in any educational setting. Introducing an element in the education system which can boost students' interest and engagement level help in reducing drop-out rates to a great extent. And gamification is one such concept which is increasingly being used by various ed-tech companies, institutions, and instructors to keep the students motivated till the end of the course.

Thus, Gamification and education are no longer a stranger, rather their amalgamation can transform the way a teacher teaches and a student learns. Inclusion of gaming elements in the learning process will make learning more engaging and fruitful. Especially, in the online setting where there is no face-to-face interaction, use of gaming mechanics can help in improving student engagement and motivation level. Kelly Monahan and Cary Har in their Article on 'Gaming away the Leadership Gap: Linking Gamification and Behavioral Science to Transform Leadership Development' highlighted that how gaming mechanisms like conquering a cartoon villain or treasuring the imaginary coins can lead to an intrinsic motivation. Several studies have proved that motivation is an essential ingredient for productive learning and for the acquisition of higher skills (Al-Samarraie et al., 2013). Motivation is not only significantly related to participants' course engagement (Barak et al., 2016; Xiong et al., 2015; Yang, 2014), but also to their intention to complete the course to its end and earn a certificate. As per (Ryan & Deci, 2000), Academic motivation is the key driver for initiation and regulation of activity. (Francis et al., 2019) viewed through their survey on literature that one of the crucial predictors of students' academic success is their academic motivation, or their reason for engaging in a task. Thus, the effect of motivation can be pointedly higher in the online learning environment, as compared to traditional learning environment (Yang, 2014) as there is no one who is supervising the learners directly.

Thus, to motivate the learners (who are opting for any e-learning course with no age bar) gamification techniques can do wonder. It can help learners to not only learn with fun but to monitor their progress, performance, and position. And since several studies have proved that knowledge about their performance can boost their future efforts, it can be a solution to reduce drop-out rates. While traditional method of assessment can check the knowledge level, they are not sufficient to give intermittent feedback to the learners. Formative assessment in this respect not only gives feedback but includes various gaming mechanics which motivates the learners to move ahead and keep their engagement level intact. Current study is divided under several section; first it will explore how gamification in e-learning is making its space; second, it will elaborate on various gaming mechanics used in e-learning setting which improves students' motivation; third, it will highlight the gaming tools for formative assessment, and last, based on past literature and theories it will elaborate on how use of game-based formative assessment tools can result in learner motivation.

The objectives of current study are:

- To study the impact of gamification in education, especially in the e-learning
- To study how gamification can improve learner motivation
- To study various gamification tools and their application in online learning environment
- To study the game-based formative assessment tools and their impact on learner motivation

BACKGROUND

It has been believed that with the increase in gaming population, the inclination of students towards game-based learning tend to increase. Whether its traditional form of learning or e-learning, it is very much required that the motivation of the learner should remain persistent. By persistent it means that their motivation should remain either constant or increases as they proceed with the course opted by them. Any fall in the motivational level will lead to increase in the drop-out rates. Studies have proved that in order to keep the learners motivated the learning process should be made interesting, competing, should facilitate collaboration, and provides learner with autonomy to not only learn at their own pace but to monitor their progress and performance at every stage. This will ultimately improve their engagement and motivational level (Chapman & Rich, 2018). Current study aims to explore the impact of gamification in e-learning and how game-based formative assessment tools can improve student motivation and engagement level. For the purpose of current study, learners include all those individuals who are opting for any online or e-learning course under Massive Open Online Course (MOOCs) platform. The next section defines the key concepts used in current study: e-learning, gamification, learner motivation, & formative assessment.

E-Learning

The concept or the definition of e-learning varies: for some it is related to content, some other link it to communication, and some focuses on technology (e-learning: the key concepts by Robin Mason, Frank Rennie). American Society for Training & Development (ASTD) defined e-learning as a wide set of applications and processes, such as web-based learning, computer-based learning, virtual classrooms, and digital collaboration. It is the effective learning process created by combining digitally delivered content with (learning) support and services (Open and Distance Learning Quality Council, UK). It is considered as an economical method which can facilitate independent learning to the user in a virtual learning environment.

According to the **Technology Standard Committee**, "e-learning system is a learning technology that uses web browsers as a tool for interaction with learners and other systems". Aparicio & Bacao (2013), in their theoretical framework of e-learning concepts, have revealed almost 23 concepts related to use of computer and technology in the learning process. As per them the evolution of e-learning system has been rooted in the concept of Computer-Assisted Instruction. While different time period has given a new name to the e-learning systems like Computer-based Education, Computer-assisted learning, Computer-managed instructions, artificial learning, mobile learning, etc., the basic meaning of e-learning remains the same which is learning through an electronic device. (Mehra & Omidina, 2010) explained online learning as something which facilitate the learners to participate in the learning process regardless of their geographical boundary, through internet. They further defined blended learning as a combination of online learning and traditional learning. As per them, e-learning is a broader term which encompasses both online learning and blended learning.

Existence of e-learning in the field of education has come with ample number of advantages like flexibility to learn at convenience, use of multiple interactive tools to engage learners, efficient transfer of knowledge, learner autonomy, customized and self-paced learning, and most importantly it is not restricted to any age, boundary, or number of students. As mass number of students can enrol and opt for the courses, one of the forms of e-learning is known as Massive Open Online Courses (MOOCs). Massive Open Online Courses (MOOCs) is an e-learning environment where a learners can virtually enrol for the courses and interact with the learning communities around the world. The evolution of MOOC finds its root in the existence of connectivism philosophy which will be discussed further in later part of the chapter. Based on various definition given by authors and researchers, following is the composite definition of the term e-learning:

E-learning system is an IT-enabled model of facilitating the learning, which is either taking place at the real time (synchronous) or in a self-regulated and self-directed environment (asynchronous) to bring changes in the knowledge, skills, and competencies of the learners.

Gamification

Gamification in education is the recent development which is happening around the world. It has been very well defined by Deterding et al. (2011) as the 'the use of video game elements in nongaming systems to improve user experience (UX) and user engagement'. As per them, the intention of using gamification in the learning process is to stimulate motivation, ability, attitude, and performance. Similarly, Kapp (2013) explained gamification as a technique to use game-based mechanics, aesthetics, and game thinking which can engage people, motivate them, promote learning, and develop problem-solving approach. In simple words, gamification is an instructional strategy where game elements are used by teachers/ instructors to pose a challenge in front on players (students) which eventually lead them to the learning experience. Thus, in a gamified environment students are more engaged and motivated towards the learning process (Alsawaier, 2018). (Chapman & Rich, 2018) in their study on impact of gamification on students' motivation has found out that 67.7% of students feel that gamified course was more or much more motivating than the traditional courses.

In the context of education, several researchers have mentioned the use game mechanics and game thinking to motivate the learners and promote learning (Kapp, 2012; Werbach & Hunter, 2012). Game thinking is related to application of game-based concepts to solve problems and creating an engaging learning environment (Bovermann & Bastiaens, 2020). For gamification to help in learner engagement, it is important to understand its two important tools- game mechanics and game dynamics. While game mechanics include the features that compose a game and makes it challenging and rewarding, game dynamics are the learners' interaction with this mechanics.

Learner Motivation

The willingness and readiness of learners to opt for online courses to attain their motive of certification, reskilling, upskilling, etc. is known as learner motivation. (Samir Abou El-Seoud et al., 2014) investigated the effect of e-learning on Higher Education. According to them, self-motivation is one of the crucial factors which can lead to success of e-learning process. (Tankelevičiene & Damaševičius, 2009) believed that there are three components in overall structure of e-learning processes that depend upon learning context; **Learner** (which includes understanding Learners' needs and differences to support them in their growth), **Activity** (includes how things needs to be presented and designed based on differential needs of learner), and **Environment** (includes all sort of support in e-learning processes). Motivation, thus, plays a decisive role in determining the efforts and dedication a learner will put in the learning process. While intrinsic motivation makes learner do something out of fun and enjoyment, extrinsic motivation is more related to external pressure or force like getting a reward.

Formative Assessment

Assessment can be defined as the mechanism to measure the performance and progress of the learner. It is a part of learning process which determines the current knowledge of the student (Lot & Salleh, 2016). While a summative assessment is done after the completion of the courses to gauge the overall learning of the learner, formative assessment is an ongoing measurement of student progress and help them to understand their strengths and weaknesses. Formative assessment aims to provide continuous feedback to the students and work on their knowledge gaps. It acts like a control function which aims to track students' performance and their efforts to attain the goal. So far, whether its MOOCs or virtual classes, summative assessment has been given more weightage. But summative assessment (getting a certificate) alone cannot guarantee the course completion (Danka, 2020). Thus, an introduction of game-based formative assessment tool in e-learning system will not only make the learning interesting, but keep the learners engaged throughout the session. Game-based Formative Assessment (GFA) will eventually boost the learners' motivation as it includes the gaming mechanics and tools where learner can set their goal, monitor their progress, check their knowledge level, interact with peers, involved in peer-to-peer assessment, and earn rewards in the form of badges, points, and certificates. Game-based mechanics helps in learner engagement, increases their motivation level, promote learning, and develop a problem-solving approach (Bovermann & Bastiaens, 2020). In this respect, (Mohd Arif et al., 2019) has cited the work of Black and William (2003) who had predicted that the inclusion of technology will improve the quality of formative and summative assessment.

LITERATURE REVIEW

While many studies have done on the use of gamification in learning process and learner motivation, very few studies have exclusively covered the inclusion of game-based formative assessment in e-learning setting to enhance learner motivation. And since in India, the emergence of e-learning as a serious mode of learning have emerged very recently, studies are required to study how to improve the e-learning success rate (by controlling the drop-out rate and increasing learner motivation). Specifically, self-determination theory, behaviourism, and connectivism philosophy will be discussed in connection with the gamification in education. Self-determination theory has been widely used in the context of e-learning, especially intrinsic motivation. Similarly, connectivism recognizes the need to stay connected in an online learning environment. Finally, Behaviorism philosophy highlighted the human psychology towards certain behavior which are enforced by rewards or penalties. Thus, enforcing a certain behavior by rewards and correcting a misbehavior by lack of rewards or a form of a penalty, are parallel to gamification elements such as rewarding and penalizing through points and badges, or upgrading and demoting in a game setting (Alsawaier, 2018). The literature review has been divided under certain heading which includes:

- Gamification in education with reference to e-learning
- Gamification and learner motivation
- Game-based formative assessment in e-learning and learner motivation

On Gamification in Education with Reference to E-Learning

Gamification, according to Yu-kai Chou (n.d.), keep human motivation at its highest. He considers this as a 'Human-focussed design', as compared to traditional 'function-focussed design'. While function-focussed design is concerned about getting the job done as quickly as possible, human-focussed design takes into consideration learners' feelings, emotions, and reasons, this results into more engaging learners. In simple words, it is the application of game-based fun and engaging elements which can make the learning process more productive. (Mohd Arif et al., 2019) in this respect believes that inclusion of games in the learning scenario promotes student-centered learning experience as they can have a full control over it. "Kahoot' is one such platform which allows learners to compete with each other by means of various challenges. (Kamunya et al., 2020b) opined that gamification in education make the learning enjoyable and students learn by not playing a specific game but they learn as if they are playing a game. Similarly, (Hassan et al., 2021) believes that gaming mechanics and components can make e-learning more engaging and entertaining. As inclusion of gamification in e-learning will be accompanied by competition, challenges, quick feedback, recognition and rewards, it helps in improving interaction between students with platforms, their peers, and instructors (Castro et al., 2018b).

Certain statistics as highlighted by a website finance.com in their article on "54 Gamification Statistics You Must Know: 2020/2021 Market Share Analysis & Data" includes impact of gamification in education. The article cited various literary work to emphasize the positive impact of gamification in education. Some of the citations are as follows:

- An expected growth rate of 15.6% in game-based learning in higher education by 2024 (Metaari, 2019)

- Rise in student performance by 34.7% as a result of challenge-based gamification in education (Science Direct, 2020)
- As compared to students who are receiving traditional lecture-based learning, the performance of student with challenge-based gamification may see rise of 89.45% (Science Direct. 2020)
- Gamified learning is far more motivating and engaging than traditional courses (Intuition, 2019)

On Gamification and Learner Motivation

Games are in existence since decades, thus are capable in understanding human psychology and what motivates them. Apart from fun element, they know how to keep learners engaged till the end by posing them with the challenges and giving rewards for their efforts, thus facilitates immediate feedback. To apply gamification in any field, the core concepts of games should be understood which includes (Glover, 2013):

- **Goal-focussed Activity**: means making efforts to achieve a goal which can range from mastering a topic or skill. It includes facing challenges, levels, or quest.
- **Reward Mechanism**: includes earning rewards once a level is reached in the form of leaderboards, prizes or virtual goods, badges, etc.
- **Progress Tracking**: is to keep the learners' progress updated and giving feedback

As per Yu-kai Chou, who developed an Octalysis Framework for gamification in learning, the reason why gamification is increasingly being used for the purpose of learning and development is its inherent capacity to engage and motivate the learners. Games drive the learners and commit them to certain activities. Several researches have proved that gamification helps in increasing student engagement and motivation along with their learning efficiency (Fischer et al., 2016). Further (Dabbagh et al., 2016) discovered that implementing a system of penalty and reward improves student attendance, performance, and motivation to a great extent. There are several researchers who claim that gaming elements while on one side increases learners' extrinsic motivation by providing them with rewards, they reduces learners' intrinsic motivation (Hassan et al., 2021). In this context, self-determination theory proposed by Deci & Ryan plays an important role which will be discussed in succeeding pages.

(Rozman & Donath, 2019) in their study on 'The Current State of the Gamification in E-Learning: A literature Review of Literature Reviews' have done a meta-analysis on the gamification topics in e-learning. There findings highlighted that there are only a few studies which specializes in gamification in e-learning. And those studies who have specialized in this field have reported positive effect of gamification in e-learning. They have further analyzed that while e-learning has been opted majorly for its affordability, participant's drop-out rate and lack of motivation still persist. One important finding from their research is that majority of studies in the field revolved around learner motivation, their performance and engagement level, attitude, and social interactions.

(Panagiotarou et al., 2020) studied the gamification acceptance for learners with different skills. They examined the users' perception of gamification acceptance in e-learning environment using Technology Acceptance Model (TAM). By studying 188 students who enrolled in a MOOC, they concluded that there is a significant difference between perceived usefulness, perceived ease of use, and actual usage of learners with different digital skills. In simple words, individuals with different level of digital skills have different perceptions towards use, usefulness, and actual usage of online course.

In a case study done by (Bovermann et al., 2018) on online learning readiness and attitude towards gaming in gamified learning environment, concluded that students with technical competencies are more motivated towards e-learning. And despite of some students has a dismissive attitude towards playing games, they supported game-based learning in an online learning environment. Gaming elements like digital badges and progress bars are being positively taken by students. Overall, almost 80% of students who participated in the survey of gamification in online learning have responded positively.

A study on assessing gamification effects on e-learning platforms by (Castro et al., 2018a) through an empirical study on a group of students who have enrolled for an online learning platform have concluded that use of gamification improves the efficiency of online platforms and resulted in decreasing the drop-out rate from 42 to 27%. Additionally, inclusion of gamification increased the time spent by users on the platform. And among various gaming mechanics, battles and scoring table have the maximum visits as it promotes the competitive spirit among the learners.

(Kamunya et al., 2020a) have proposed an adaptive gamification model. As per them, since each individual learner has a unique set of abilities and needs, same set of gaming mechanics cannot be applied on all. Thus, they proposed a model for adaptive gamification in e-learning environment. In the similar context, an ontological study done by (Bennani et al., 2020) on personalized gamification in e-learning has supported the need of adaptive gamification. The core concepts used in their study included gamification, user, learning environment (e-learning), interaction (what individuals do with gamified elements and different users), experience (of using gamified elements in learning), and feedback. (Hassan et al., 2021) in this respect has gone step ahead and explored the learning style of the learners to predict their personalized gaming elements. They believed that adaptive gamification not only increases student motivation but positively impacts the course completion rates. Through their experiment on 185 students enrolled in an e-learning course, they concluded that by designing a personalized gamification experience for the learners based on their learning style, motivation level increased by 25% and drop-out rate decreased by 26%. A snapshot of their study has been present in the Table 1:

Table 1. Gaming element based on learner's learning style (Hassan et al., 2021)

Type of learner	Gaming element	Reason
Active	Leaderboards and challenges	It provides social communication channels to learners
Reflective	Feedback and a progress bar	As they are keen on self-study, they enable them to monitor their progress and assess their level of expertise
Sensing	Challenges, badges, and levels.	As they want to practice the material and are interested in facts, figures, and details,
Intuitive	Multiple content objects	To satisfy their need for innovation in content material and to avoid repetition and assess their mastery levels in concepts
Visual	Progress bar and points	Assist them in monitoring their progress and make learning attractive
Verbal	Challenges and points	As they give importance to textual input
Sequential	Challenges that assessed their level of information absorption.	As they like to learn in steps, a gradual learning process
Global	Feedback	To judge their level of mastery as they tended to skip most of the content and did not prefer to go into detail about the concepts

Game-Based Formative Assessment in E-Learning and Learner Motivation

Learning through digital mode has been largely characterized by learning on MOOCs. They aim to enhance the collaboration and connectivity between the learners. But while connectivist principles succeeded in attracting the students to enrol for e-learning courses (cMOOCs: Connectivist MOOC), it could not assure the completion of the same (Danka, 2020). And the solution lies in implementing motivation techniques in e-learning system, especially the assessment techniques. Enhancing interactivity and implementing summative assessment to e-learning (xMOOC: extended MOOCs) may motivate the learners to complete the course and get the certificate (Danka, 2020). But several studies have proved that MOOCs providing certificate, too, are facing high drop-out rates. It can be resolved by giving autonomy to learners and motivate them intrinsically rather than extrinsic motivation. (Danka, 2020) viewed that if the learners' initial motivation to enrol for the course ends with dropping out without completing the same, there are high chances that the learning experience was not sufficient enough to accomplish their personal goals. (Chapman & Rich, 2018) concluded that more the students spent time with gamified course, more will be their overall motivation to unlock assignments, achievements, leaderboard levels, etc. They have further found out that game elements which enables them to track their progress as well as of others and those providing feedback about their performance motivates them the most.

Formative assessment, in this respect, may prove fruitful as it provides ongoing feedback to the learners and track their progress. Game-based formative tools are increasingly adopted by the instructors and various MOOC platforms to engage the learners till the end. These tools give autonomy to learners to set their goals, progress towards their attainment, check their and others' progress, and most importantly adds a surprise element to learning in the form of points, badges, avatars, virtual goods, etc. Formative assessment relates to motivation because, firstly, it helps in providing intermittent feedback to the learners with respect to their development, areas of improvement, and achievements. Secondly, it informs the instructors about the learners' needs and their progress. Thirdly, formative assessment can best implement the concept of gamification in e-learning setting. Thus, the study will elaborate about how implementation of game-based formative assessment system in e-learning system can create an interest among the learners to complete their online courses.

In this respect, web-based interactive platform 'Kahoot' has been recently popularized for its ability to assess the students' performance and progress formatively. It is helping the educators to revamp their teaching pedagogy and shift their role from sole provider of knowledge to knowledge navigators (Mohd Arif et al., 2019). In their study, based on mixed methodology, they have concluded that use of formative assessment tools like Kahoot helps learners to relate with lectures, recalls the learned concepts in a more enjoyable manner, discover new information, improves their retention power, and monitor their progress. It even motivated them to increase their efforts to perform better than others.

GAMIFICATION TOOLS IN E-LEARNING: OCTALYSIS FRAMEWORK

Gamification in e-learning as per (Rozman & Donath, 2019) includes those methods and technology which motivates and engages the learners to complete their course in the e-learning environment. As per their research on search trend in 'gamification in e-learning', they concluded that it is stable since 2012. (Pastushenko et al., 2018) in their study on 'Increasing students' motivation by using virtual learning environments based on gamification mechanics' have designed an educational gaming platform named bombsQuery. They have created a storyline gaming component to motivate the students to clear the bombs from the field by writing a part of jQuery Code mentioned in the task by marking them with white flags. The platform helped the students see their current progress and the number of levels remaining to complete the assignment. The assessment of coding has been automatically providing them immediate feedback, and if correct, the participant can move to the next level. The surveyed results concluded that learners are more motivated to learn when the gaming elements has been added.

In this context, OCTALYSIS framework, developed by Yu-kai Chou, has been considered as pioneer efforts in implementing gamification in the learning system. In his Octalysis Framework: an octagon shaped model with eight core drivers, he highlighted three aspects as depicted in the Figure 1:

Figure 1. The Octalysis framework

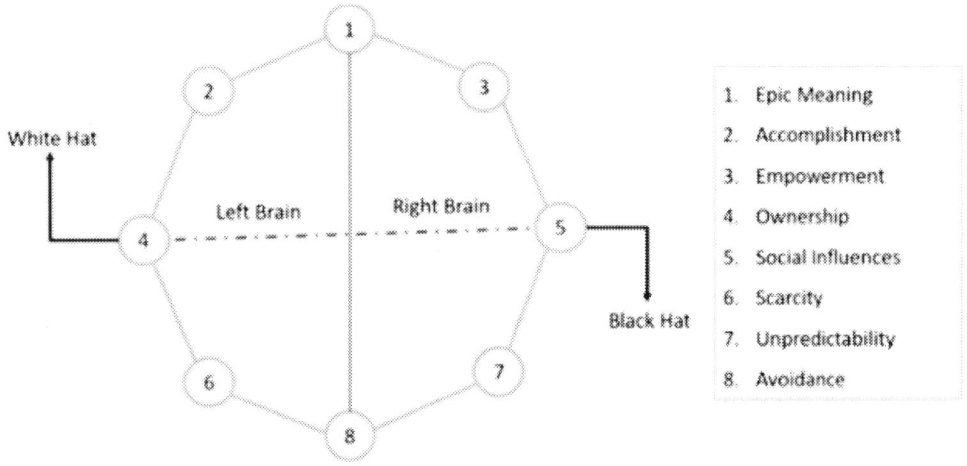

Adapted from Growth Engineering, 2021

Aspects of Octalysis Framework

Aspect 1: Eight Core Drivers

It includes eight key motivators of human behavior that drives them towards a certain task (with respect to this paper, its learning or education).

- **Epic Meaning & Calling**– it drives learners to achieve a higher purpose beyond their personal goals
- **Development & Accomplishment**– includes accepting a challenge and work harder to reach a desired goal and witness their progress.
- **Creative Expression & Feedback**– help learners to experience freedom to express and immerse into the gaming experience to learn. It also includes receiving feedback, as it aids in improving learners' creativity.

- **Ownership**– it gives learner confidence that they possess and own something, triggering their natural desire to take a pride in ownership.
- **Social Influence & Relatedness**– reflects learners' need to interact, seek help, get affiliation, and companionship. This driver triggers learners' competitive nature and their relative status with others. Relatedness is the learners' desire to connect with their social groups with whom they share common interests.
- **Scarcity & Impatience**– reflects the propensity of learners to get what they don't have. And since this is related to human tendency where they get attracted to something which is rare or difficult to obtain, these things drive their behavior.
- **Unpredictability & Curiosity**– are the elements of surprise and excitement to experience something novel.
- **Loss & Avoidance**– are related to preserving the hard-earned things. The desire of learners to minimize the potential loss or risks wherever and whenever we can, drives them.

Aspects 2: Left Brain vs. Right Brain Drivers

This aspect is based on the emotional and logical part of the brain. Table 2 below further explains their relevance in gamification in education and learner motivation.

Table 2. Left brain vs. right brain drivers

	Left Brain Core Drives	**Right Brain Core Drives**
Related to	Logic, calculations, and ownership	Imagination, social connection, and personal expression
Motivation	Extrinsic	Intrinsic
What drive behaviour/ action	Motivation to achieve a goal or receive an award	Motivated to do as the activity or experience is enjoyable and rewarding
Core Elements	Development & Accomplishment, Ownership & Possession, Scarcity & Impatience	Empowerment of creativity & Feedback, Social Influence & Relatedness, Unpredictability & Curiosity

Aspect 3: White Hat vs. Black Hat Drivers

This aspect of Octalysis refer to positive (white hat) and negative (black hat) emotions associated with motivation. Table 3 below explains this aspect in detail.

Table 3. White hat vs. black hat drivers

	White Hat	**Black Hat**
Emotions	Positive emotions like excitement, happiness, and a sense of meaning	Negative emotions like rage, disappointment, and frustration
Place in Octagon	Top half	Bottom half
Core Elements	Epic Meaning & Calling, Development & Accomplishment, Empowerment of creativity & Feedback	Scarcity & Impatience, Unpredictability & Curiosity, Loss & Avoidance

While white hat drivers are viewed as positive, they fail to create a sense of urgency to react (like urgency to complete an online course or completing an assignment on time). Thus, to get learners' movement active in the online learning environment, black hat drivers are required. They create a need to react immediately to avoid any adverse results (like being marked absent, loss in badges earned, etc.)

Gamification in online learning environment is a new trend which aids in learner motivation (Danka, 2020). Inclusion of gaming element in the initial phase of the learning acts like an extrinsic motivation, but can later results into developing an intrinsic motivation. (Szabó and Szemere 2016, 2017). Following are a few of the gaming mechanics that can lead to learner engagement and motivation:

- **Character Generation**: Under this, learners are allocated with different avatars based on their character. It not only reflects the appearance of the avatar or the user information, but in-game-skills and abilities possessed by the learner (Danka, 2020). It ensures learner autonomy as it considers their preference among the available avatars, however it also includes a measurement tool which assigns the character based on users' knowledge and wisdom. Just like real games, the avatars keep on changing based on the level a learner has reached, thus motivates a learner to move up in the ladder to win a new character. This gaming mechanics starts with setting up a profile as the learner logs in (where they get freedom to choose from the characters available based on their preference), and later as they move up in their level of education new characters are assigned to them based on pre-defined criteria by the instructors. Just like role playing activity, it also involves instances where learners have to defend the role assigned to them by the instructor through a debate or a discussion. These kind of mechanics help learners understand others' perspective and situations and make them more openminded (Danka, 2020).

- **Experience Point and Levelling-up System**: They keep a track on the learners' progress by presenting them with challenges. Just like real games where players confront the challenges, earn points, level-up and gain new powers, in an online learning environment learners earn experience points as they progress which they can later redeem to 'level-up' and awarded with new skill-sets to adopt advance learning. These are short-terms goals which ultimately lead learners towards their ultimate aim (completing the course and earn a certificate). Since short terms goals are easily achievable in a short span of time, learners get rewards, and motivation can be maintained by a series of short-term feedback on success (Danka, 2020). It is important to understand that when points are meant to stimulate a competition among learners, they should be used as score; contrary to it, if points aim to give feedback to learner, they should not be revealing to other (Da Rocha Seixas et al., 2016).

- **Progress Bars**: They are visual representation of learners' progress based on experience points gained, badges awarded, level reached, etc. They represent the completion of number of pre-defined activities and actions, and reflect student mastery over the subject.

- **Leaderboards**: They reflects learners' ranking based on various statistics like highest number of experience points, most challenges completed, most badges earned, etc.

- **Scoreboards**: Similar to leaderboard, they reflect the total points earned till the level.

- **Narrative or Storyline**: It includes a small story which can progresses as learners moves up in the level. A human mind always responds positively to the story as they can connect to them more personally, adding a narrative or a story will boost their motivation to complete the next level.

- **Challenges/Quests, Badges/Medals & Accomplishments**: Challenges or quests includes mission or short term goals to accomplish and gain rewards after execution (Da Rocha Seixas et al., 2016). Trophies or badges are the virtual rewards gained by the learner after successfully completing a task.
- **Virtual Goods**: These are the intangible goods which learners can acquire either by progressing up or by redeeming the points earned. They provide learners with the possibilities of personalizing their learning experience and improves their engagement level. They give learners an opportunity to showcase their possessions, prestige, and status, off course in an e-learning environment in terms of their knowledge level.

These game mechanics motivates people as there are dynamics working underneath which stimulate the learners' needs and desires. It triggers their need to get rewarded, attain status, accomplishing a task, self-expression, competition, and altruism. The effective combination of these mechanics stimulates learner to progress in their learning path.

GAME-BASED FORMATIVE ASSESSMENT TOOLS

These gaming mechanics aids in formative assessment in online setting and motivates learner by recognizing their efforts, constantly giving them feedback, and giving them freedom to monitor their progress. Levelling-up system depicts learners' progress towards course completion, introduce them to the in-game possibilities where learner can become a leader, and develops a competitive spirit among the learners to keep progressing. Levelling up is like a hierarchy into the environment reflecting the internal achievement. Considering the Connectivism philosophy, a learner should have autonomy to set their educational goals. And game-based formative assessment tools led them to various tasks and challenges, which eventually help them in accomplishing their goals (without any formal instruction from the instructor). And when learners have freedom to move towards their goals without any force, but through a series of challenges, they will be self-directed and motivated

While addition of visuality and storyline are viewed as external in the online learning environment, immediate feedback, experience points, and levelling-up are the internal elements. Based on Octalysis Framework, Table 4 below include various formative tools that can be used in an online learning environment.

LEARNER MOTIVATION IN E-LEARNING THROUGH GAME-BASED FORMATIVE ASSESSMENT

Introduction of formative assessment in online learning setting intends to increase learner motivation, rather than measuring learning outcome (Danka, 2020). Based on the array of literature reviewed and literature review mentioned under various papers, Table 5 justifies how inclusion of gamification in e-learning can improve learner motivation and highlight the need to develop an adaptive gamification experience for learners to retain their motivation and engagement level:

Table 4. Game-based formative assessment tools based on Octalysis framework

Sr. No.	Octalysis Core Drivers	Formative Assessment Tool derived	Reference Work
1	Epic Meaning & Calling	Creating a **storyline or narrative** in the form of quest or challenges to overcome Rewards or Badges	(Dicheva et al., 2015) (Fitz-Walter, 2015) (Conger, 2016) (Dicheva et al., 2015) (Hamari et al., 2014) (Da Rocha Seixas et al., 2016) (Fitz-Walter, 2015) (Dabbagh et al., 2016) (Bovermann et al., 2018)
2	Development & Accomplishment	**Experience Points**: are earned as learners progress in their course and give them a sense of accomplishment **Badges** **Progress Bar**: showcases the learner where they have reached in their courses and boost their efforts. It helps them understand how close are they towards their goal (course completion or certificate) **Scorecards**: are the complete track records of the learners' accomplishments so far and motivate them to get more **Leaderboard**: reflects learners' position in terms of number of badges earned, points secured, etc. as compared to others	(Conger, 2016) (Hamari et al., 2014) (Da Rocha Seixas et al., 2016) (Fitz-Walter, 2015) (Dabbagh et al., 2016) (Conger, 2016) (Dicheva et al., 2015) (Hamari et al., 2014) (Bovermann et al., 2018) (Castro et al., 2018b) (Conger, 2016) (Da Rocha Seixas et al., 2016) (Conger, 2016) (Hamari et al., 2014)
3	Creative Expression & Feedback	**Levels**: reflects the pathway learner has to take to complete their course **Quizzes**: to check short-term progress of the learner and facilitates instant feedback	(Conger, 2016) (Hamari et al., 2014) (Da Rocha Seixas et al., 2016) (Dabbagh et al., 2016) (Castro et al., 2018b) (Fitz-Walter, 2015)
4	Ownership	**Possession of virtual goods** in exchange of badges or points earned	(Conger, 2016) (Da Rocha Seixas et al., 2016) (Fitz-Walter, 2015)
5	Social Influence & Relatedness	**Discussion boards** to check learners' interactivity and motivation to share knowledge others	(Dicheva et al., 2015)
6	Scarcity & Impatience	Providing a **limited period reward like a virtual badge or goods**. It can assess how a quick a learner is to achieve them. It may also include opening a quiz for a limited time with bonus marks.	(Dicheva et al., 2015)
7	Unpredictability & Curiosity	**Challenges or quest** as learner keep on moving in the curiosity of 'what next'	(Dicheva et al., 2015) (Hamari et al., 2014) (Fitz-Walter, 2015) (Dabbagh et al., 2016)
8	Loss & Avoidance	**Streak Rewards**: includes completing a set of activities within a specific period of time to earn a reward. **Battles**: includes competition between learners	(Dicheva et al., 2015) (Da Rocha Seixas et al., 2016) (Dicheva et al., 2015) (Fitz-Walter, 2015) (Castro et al., 2018b)

It is important to understand the underlying phenomena responsible to motivate learners to opt for e-learning. Three important theories: Self-Determination Theory (SDT), Connectivism Model, and Behaviorism are referred in the current study to understand the role of motivation in e-learning environment. While SDT is related to learners' motivation, connectivism theory has been considered as a base of e-learning environment like MOOCs.

Table 5. Citations based on literature reviews

Citations	Authors
Learner Motivation through Gamification	
Motivation as a key determinant of success in online learning	Lineham, Kirman, Lawson, & Chan, 2011
Use of game-based elements improves learner motivation and their learning behavior	Deterding et al., 2011; Kapp, 2012; Werbach & Hunter, 2012
Acquisition of virtual badges positively impacts learners' behavior, motivation, and encouragement	Hakulinen, Auvinen, & Korhonen, 2015; Hamari, 2015
Gamification elements based on social interaction improves intrinsic motivation	Shi & Cristea, 2014
Gamification aims to create a combine effect of intrinsic and extrinsic motivation	Muntean (2011)
Learner Motivation through Game-based Formative Assessment Tools	
Game dynamics, mechanics, and aesthetics improves individual motivation and helps in reducing drop-out rates	Katherine Andrea Cuartas Castro, Íngrid Paola Hernández Sibo, and I-hsien Ting
Gamification positively impacts personal motivation	Chang, J.W., Wei, H.Y Leaning, Utomo & Santoso, 2015
Gamification in education leads to better learning experience for students	Ryan, R., Deci, E, Albrecht and Green 2008
Use of gamify elements like points, leaderboard, discussion board, etc. influences learners' motivation, retention, and engagement positively	Kuo & Chuang, 2016, Rigole et al., 2017
Giving autonomy to learners to earn points in an online learning setting by uploading and reviewing the document, promotes student engagement and interactivity	Caro-Alvaro et al., 2017
Testifies the use of gamified elements like badges, story-line, leaderboards, etc. to improve learners' participation, performance, and their motivation levels	O'Donovan, 2012, Panagiotis et al. (2016)
Adaptive Gamification in e-learning	
Experimented to analyze student's profile to create a personalized gamified learning environment and concluded that use of personalized gaming elements improves student's collaboration and interactions	Paiva et al., 2016
Each individual interacts differently with different gamified elements	López, C., & Tucker, C. (2018).
Gamification in e-learning/Use of Gaming Elements in e-learning	
Use of games positively impacts psychological characteristics of learners	Souza-Concilio, I.A., Pacheco, B.A
Important aspects to be highlighted while using gamification in education: learners' commitment at different phases of learning, sense of competition, game mechanics, learners' learning style and their level of expertise, and learner motivation	Monterrat, B., Yessad, A., Bouchet, F., Lavoué, E., & Luengo, V. (2017, June)
Use of games in learning: "learning through play"	Arif et. al., 2019
Gamification as a breakthrough in education which has transformed the teaching and learning process	Deterding et al., 2011; Gee, 2003; Prensky, 2001; Blohm & Leimeister, 2013
Gamification converts students from mere passive consumers of information to an active participant	Murphy (2005)
Gamification in education prepares students to handle success and failure, and develops critical thinking & problem-solving skills	Icard, 2014

Theoretical Background

1. Self Determination Theory:

A well-known theory in the context of learners' motivation is Self-determination theory (SDT) given by Deci and Ryan in the year 1985. The theory elaborates about the intrinsic and extrinsic motivational factors which are responsible to energize people and improves their level of engagement. As per SDT, there are three important factors which are responsible for the individual growth and constructive social development- Competence, Relatedness, and Autonomy. These components are related to intrinsic motivation, which is the innate tendency to look out for novelty, challenges, and extending the capacities to explore and learn (Ryan & Deci, 2000). Fulfilment of these components promotes intrinsic motivation which further strengthen learners' engagement level. Table 6 below elaborates these components and how they can be applied in the gamified environment as a tool of assessment to motivate learners. It also differentiates between the type of player based on their motivation type.

Table 6. SDT theory of motivation and formative assessment tools

Intrinsic Motivation Factors	Meaning	Player /User Types	Game Based Formative Assessment Tools
Competence	Desire to gain mastery and achievements	Achiever/Player	Certificates, Badges, Rewards, Points, Leaderboards, Virtual goods,
Relatedness	Need to interact and connect with other	Socializer/ Philanthropist	Leaderboards, Discussion Forum,
Autonomy	Desire to be independent and free	Free Spirit	Avatars/Characters Identification, Quizzes, Challenges/Quest

While intrinsic motivation is related to doing things out of enjoyment or excitement, extrinsic motivation is related to the obligation to do things so as to avoid undesirable consequences like punishment or penalty (Bovermann & Bastiaens, 2020).

2. Connectivism

Most of the e-learning environment like MOOCs, finds their roots in Connectivism model. MOOCs are based on three important components- peer-to-peer interactivity, open access to learning material, and presence of technological equipment to process learning (Danka, 2020) which is line with the connectivist philosophy proposed by George Siemens (2005). He has predicted certain trends in the education system which make the existing theories redundant. It includes non-linearity in knowledge acquisition, existence of technological aid to store and retrieve information, and the impact of chaos and network on learning. He has described Chaos as 'something which lacks order and predictability'. In simple words, learning according to him will no longer be based on a simple meaning-making task only, but a challenge for the learners to recognize the hidden pattern. And a network is how various entities are connected with each other. Thus, meaning-making and forming connections between specialized community is crucial (Duke et al., 1966).

The connectivist pedagogy have promoted democratization in the education where learner autonomy, online education, and life-long learning has taken the front seat (Danka, 2020). The core of connectivism philosophy lies in the enhancing the collaboration and connectivity between the learners. But, while connectivist principles succeeded in attracting the students to enrol for e-learning courses, it could not assure the completion of the same (Danka, 2020). And the solution lies in implementing motivation techniques in e-learning system, especially the assessment techniques. Based on his theory, he had proposed 8 principles of connectivism philosophy (Duke et al., 1966) mentioned in Table 7, which can be applied in the context of e-learning.

Table 7. Connectivism philosophy and gamified e-learning environment

Principles of Connectivism	Application in E-learning Environment (gamified environment)
Learning and knowledge rests in diversity of opinions	Peer-to-peer interactivity and discussion boards
Learning is a process of connecting specialized nodes or information sources	Through gamification (gaming mechanics)
Learning may reside in non-human appliances	Learning Management System: a software application to manage content
Capacity to know more is more critical than what is currently known.	Collaborative efforts to learn from each other
Nurturing and maintaining connections is needed to facilitate continual learning.	Peer-to-peer interactivity and discussion boards
Ability to see connections between fields, ideas, and concepts is a core skill.	Peer-to-peer interactivity and discussion boards
Currency (accurate, up-to-date knowledge) is the intent of all connectivist learning activities.	Discussion forums, externals links
Decision-making is itself a learning process. Choosing what to learn and the meaning of incoming information is seen through the lens of a shifting reality. While there is a right answer now, it may be wrong tomorrow due to alterations in the information climate affecting the decision	Learner autonomy to opt for various challenges, quizzes, etc.

Thus, connectivism focuses on shifting control to the learner (self-organization) and designing of a learning environment where people and system are connected to facilitate the flow of information. It supports the most democratic form of education where learners have autonomy, diversity, and interactivity (Danka, 2020). It has provided a useful insight for learners to flourish in the digital era by developing their learning skills.

3.   Behaviourism

Behaviourism philosophy highlighted the human psychology towards certain behaviour which are enforced by rewards or penalties. Thus, enforcing a certain behaviour by rewards and correcting a misbehaviour by lack of rewards or a form of a penalty, are parallel to gamification elements such as rewarding and penalizing through points and badges, or upgrading and demoting in a game setting (Alsawaier, 2018). In the context of present study, game-based formative assessment tools provide a source of rewards or penalties to learners to stimulate their behaviour. Here, the tools discussed in Octalysis Framework perfectly exemplifies how core drivers like epic meaning, accomplishment, curiosity, loss, etc. can alter the learner behaviour towards the course which they have opted.

CHALLENGES IN GAMIFIED E-LEARNING ENVIRONMENT

- Increasing ***Drop-out Rates*** among learners in an e-learning environment. There are several studies which have concluded that increasing drop-out rates among learners is a real concern in online learning environment, even after inclusion of gamification. Freitas, Morgan, & Gibson (2015) conclude that only 7-10% of students complete the enrolled courses. Some of the reasons for this increasing drop-out rates as cited by Freitas et al. (2015); Khalil & Ebner (2014); Kizilcec, Pérez-Sanagustín, & Maldonado (2017) includes lack of collaboration and communication among students, difference in knowledge level of students, lack on interactivity between learner and instructor, and lack of motivation.

- ***One-size Fits all*** concept in gamification has been criticised by several researchers. Since the elements used under a gamified learning environment are uniform across the different genres of learners, some researchers believe that 'one size does not fit all' as every learner has a unique learning characteristics, abilities, style, and approaches. Thus, they believe that learning should be personalized based on the needs and abilities of the learner. Motivating these different sets of learners to fulfil their individual needs and preferences is a challenge. Gamification elements should be designed in such a way that personal needs of each user can be fulfilled. As per (Hassan et al., 2021), learner community belongs to diverse background and needs customized gamification experience based on their learning style and how they process the information. Providing them same gamification experience might lead to reluctance and boredom.

- In developing countries like India, E-learning is still considered as an ***alternative mode of learning***, thus has not been considered seriously (Hassan et al., 2021)

- ***Lack of readiness among learners*** to face the assessment. The ability of each learner is different, and since an automated formative assessment checks all the learners at the same point it sometimes demotivates the learners who are yet to master the topic before facing such assessment.

- ***Successive fall in motivation***. It has been predicted and put forth by certain studies that as learners move up in the course their motivation level to respond to formative assessments fall. As per one such research done by (Mohd Arif et al., 2019), students feels less excited as they move up and failed to pay close attention to their performance as they are worried about lack of preparations and growing competition. They are unprepared to face such competitive environment.

- Several studies have reflected the ***negative effects of using gamification*** in e-learning like use of scoreboards may pose a threat to affective level of students (Hanus and Fox, 2015), use of competition tools as a negative elements (Charles et al. 2011), diverse abilities among students may result in failure of gamification (Wilson, Calongne, and Henderson, 2015), and presence of students who don't like games or have a negative feelings with respect to gaming elements (Hakulinen, 2015 & Whitton 2012).

- Lack of ***technological infrastructure and poor internet connectivity*** hinders the gamified learning environment.

FUTURE RESEARCH AND DIRECTIONS

Based on the current study, it is understood that gamified learning environment can boost learner motivation. Also, by implementing game-based formative assessment, learners' engagement and motivation level can be improved further. However, further research is required to understand what other factors can motivate learners towards e-learning and the challenges faced by them to adopt gamified learning environment. Additionally, future research should focus on reasons of a smaller number of Learning Management System (LMS) platforms in educational institutions, with an aim to promote gamification in education. Also, there is a need to explore the concept of 'adaptive gamification' to understand the individual needs and expectations. Some studies have suggested that gamified environment should be customized by working more closely on task designing.

CONCLUSION

While e-learning environment like MOOCs, which have facilitated learners with autonomy and control over their learning process, are claiming democratization of education, its participants include people who are more technology-savvy than the marginalized group of people. These marginalized group people are facing the real constraints in accessing the internet due to poor digital infrastructure. And while the research paper talks about motivation through gamification in formative assessment, they are not able to use the internet to access such tools and gaming element. Additionally, as compare to technological advanced countries, developing countries like India also lacks in creating a Learning Management System (LMS), which can serve as a base to implement gamification in education or e-learning. Currently, the use of gaming mechanics is limited to online learning platforms like MOOCs. Inclusion of gamification even in the virtual classes is hard to see in India due to lack of technological infrastructure. Thus, the first step to improve learner motivation in e-learning setting is to implement LMS to support gamification in education. Secondly, there is a need to motivate students to use LMS which can be done using gamification or game-based learning elements which students are familiar with (Fischer et al., 2016). Thirdly, to find out which game-based formative assessment tools motivates the learners, involvement of stakeholders (learners, educators, Ed-tech companies, Government etc.) is required to understand everyone's perception. Lastly, Learner should embrace technology to further their level of education or knowledge and improve their digital skills.

REFERENCES

Al-Samarraie, H., Teo, T., & Abbas, M. (2013). Can structured representation enhance students' thinking skills for better understanding of E-learning content? *Computers & Education*, *69*, 463–473. doi:10.1016/j.compedu.2013.07.038

Alsawaier, R. S. (2018). The effect of gamification on motivation and engagement. *International Journal of Information and Learning Technology*, *35*(1), 56–79. doi:10.1108/IJILT-02-2017-0009

Bennani, S., Maalel, A., & Ben Ghezala, H. (2020). Age-learn: Ontology-based representation of personalized gamification in e-learning. In Procedia Computer Science (Vol. 176, pp. 1005–1014). doi:10.1016/j.procs.2020.09.096

Bovermann, K., & Bastiaens, T. J. (2020). Towards a motivational design? Connecting gamification user types and online learning activities. *Research and Practice in Technology Enhanced Learning, 15*(1), 1–18. doi:10.118641039-019-0121-4

Bovermann, K., Weidlich, J., & Bastiaens, T. (2018). Online learning readiness and attitudes towards gaming in gamified online learning – a mixed methods case study. *International Journal of Educational Technology in Higher Education, 15*(1), 0–17. doi:10.1186/s41239-018-0107-0

Bubou, G. M., & Job, G. C. (2020). Individual innovativeness, self-efficacy and e-learning readiness of students of Yenagoa study centre, National Open University of Nigeria. *Journal of Research in Innovative Teaching & Learning.* doi:10.1108/JRIT-12-2019-0079

Castro, K. A. C., Sibo, Í. P. H., & Ting, I. (2018a). Assessing gamification effects on E-learning platforms: An experimental case. *Communications in Computer and Information Science, 870*, 3–14. doi:10.1007/978-3-319-95522-3_1

Chapman, J. R., & Rich, P. J. (2018). Does educational gamification improve students' motivation? If so, which game elements work best? *Journal of Education for Business, 93*(7), 314–321. doi:10.1080/08832323.2018.1490687

Chou, Y-k. (n.d.) *Wordpress.* Retrieved from https://yukaichou.com/gamification-examples/octalysis-complete-gamification-framework/

Conger, S. (2016). Gamification of Service Desk Work. *The Impact of ICT on Work,* (November), 1–220. doi:10.1007/978-981-287-612-6

Da Rocha Seixas, L., Gomes, A. S., & De Melo Filho, I. J. (2016). Effectiveness of gamification in the engagement of students. *Computers in Human Behavior, 58*, 48–63. doi:10.1016/j.chb.2015.11.021

Dabbagh, N., Benson, A. D., Denham, A., Joseph, R., Al-Freih, M., Zgheib, G., Fake, H., & Guo, Z. (2016). *Learning Technologies and Globalization; Pedagogical Frameworks and Applications.* Springer. https://link.springer.com/10.1007/978-3-319-22963-8

Danka, I. (2020). Motivation by gamification: Adapting motivational tools of massively multiplayer online role-playing games (MMORPGs) for peer-to-peer assessment in connectivist massive open online courses (cMOOCs). *International Review of Education, 66*(1), 75–92. doi:10.100711159-020-09821-6

Dicheva, D., Dichev, C., Agre, G., & Angelova, G. (2015). Gamification in education: A systematic mapping study. *Journal of Educational Technology & Society, 18*(3), 75–88.

Duke, B., Harper, G., & Johnston, M. (1966). *Connectivism as a Learning Theory for the Digital Age.* Academic Press.

Fischer, H., Heinz, M., Schlenker, L., & Follert, F. (2016). Gamifying higher education. beyond badges, points and leaderboards. *Knowledge Communities in Online Education and, Visual Knowledge Management - Proceedings of 19th Conference GeNeMe 2016, as Part of IFKAD 2016*, 93–104.

Fitz-Walter, Z. J. (2015). Achievement unlocked: Investigating the design of effective gamification experiences for mobile applications and devices. School of Information Systems; Science & Engineering Faculty, Queensland University of Technology.

Francis, M. K., Wormington, S. V., & Hulleman, C. (2019). The Costs of Online Learning: Examining Differences in Motivation and Academic Outcomes in Online and Face-to-Face Community College Developmental Mathematics Courses. *Frontiers in Psychology, 10*(September), 1–12. doi:10.3389/fpsyg.2019.02054 PMID:31551886

Glover, I. (2013). Play As You Learn: Gamification as a Technique for Motivating Learners. *Proceedings of World Conference on Educational Multimedia, Hypermedia and Telemcommunications, 1999*–2008. http://shura.shu.ac.uk/7172/

Growth Engineering. (2021). *Growth Engineering.* Retrieved from https://www.growthengineering.co.uk/how-to-use-the-octalysis-framework-for-your-gamified-training-programme/

Hamari, J., Koivisto, J., & Sarsa, H. (2014). Does gamification work? - A literature review of empirical studies on gamification. *Proceedings of the Annual Hawaii International Conference on System Sciences,* 3025–3034. 10.1109/HICSS.2014.377

Hassan, M. A., Habiba, U., Majeed, F., & Shoaib, M. (2021). Adaptive gamification in e-learning based on students' learning styles. *Interactive Learning Environments, 29*(4), 545–565. doi:10.1080/10494820.2019.1588745

Kamunya, S., Mirirti, E., Oboko, R., & Maina, E. (2020a). An Adaptive Gamification Model for E-Learning. *2020 IST-Africa Conference. IST-Africa, 2020,* 1–10.

Kamunya, S., Mirirti, E., Oboko, R., & Maina, E. (2020b). An Adaptive Gamification Model for E-Learning. *2020 IST-Africa Conference, IST-Africa 2020.* https://api.elsevier.com/content/abstract/scopus_id/85094323708

Lot, M., & Salleh, S. M. (2016). Game-based learning as a platform for formative assessment in principles of account. *Information (Japan), 19*(9B), 3971–3976.

Mehra, V., & Omidina, F. (2010). Predicting Factors Affecting University Students' Attitudes To Adopt E-Learning in India Using Technology Acceptance Model. *International Journal on New Trends in Education and Their Implications, 1*(June), 33–43.

Mohd Arif, F. K., Zaireen Zubir, N., Mohamad, M., & Yunus Md, M. (2019). Benefits and Challenges of Using Educational Games. *Humanities & Social Sciences Reviews, 7*(4), 1–15. doi:10.4018/978-1-5225-3398-6.ch001

Panagiotarou, A., Stamatiou, Y. C., Pierrakeas, C., & Kameas, A. (2020). Gamification acceptance for learners with different E-skills. *International Journal of Learning. Teaching and Educational Research, 19*(2), 263–278. doi:10.26803/ijlter.19.2.16

Pastushenko, O., Hruška, T., & Zendulka, J. (2018). Increasing students' motivation by using virtual learning environments based on gamification mechanics. *ACM International Conference Proceeding Series,* 755–760. 10.1145/3284179.3284310

Rozman, T., & Donath, L. (2019). The Current State of the Gamification in E-Learning. *Mednarodno Inovativno Poslovanje = Journal of Innovative Business and Management, 11*(3), 5–19. doi:10.32015/JIBM/2019-11-3-2

Ryan, R. M., & Deci, E. L. (2000). *Self-Determination Theory and the Facilitation of Intrinsic Motivation, Social Development, and Well-Being. 55*(1), 68–78. (https://www2.deloitte.com/us/en/insights/focus/behavioral-economics/gaming-away-leadership-gap-developing-leaders.html)

Chapter 42
Political Economy Inside the Strategy of Line Game

Annesha Biswas
CHRIST University (Deemed), India

Tinanjali Dam
CHRIST University (Deemed), India

Joseph Varghese Kureethara
https://orcid.org/0000-0001-5030-3948
CHRIST University (Deemed), India

Sankar Varma
https://orcid.org/0000-0001-9848-9876
CHRIST University (Deemed), India

ABSTRACT

In today's world, the concept of the game and game theory is turned into new methods of knowing and understanding some of the human behaviours followed by society. In the 21st century, behavioural economics plays a major role in understanding the concept of the `line' game and hence the strategies followed by it. It is a country game played in many parts of India. It is a two-person game with very simple rules and moves. It can be played indoors. Students play the game during the break-outs. The game keenly and minutely determines the objectivity of the game and the behaviour of the players involved inside the game and the way one starts moving helps the other players to understand what one is trying to portray through the game whether it is winning or losing. The strategies involved can be put forth and looked upon from different perspectives. Referring to one such perspective, it can be looked at from a concept of Pareto efficiency, a microeconomic concept. It helps develop logical skills and learn winning strategies.

DOI: 10.4018/978-1-7998-7271-9.ch042

INTRODUCTION

In a time when we all are reduced to our own limited spaces because of a pandemic ruling large, it is perhaps the identification of the intricacies immanent within a game that can perhaps formulate a means towards critical thinking, among the students. This comes not as an exhaustive task for the present, rather this comes as a much-needed methodology that calls to engage students, despite each one of them being far away from their peers. These days, students are bereft of a real-world physical space; i.e., the logic of a classroom has become something intangible. It is in this scenario, a closer network, molded out of a real-world methodology that needs to be identified. This can happen through identifying the online space as a means to carry forward games as interactive and engaging tools for students and the subsequent enhancement of their productivity. This particular characteristic of a real-world engagement and interaction hence can be satiated through using games as a means is the primary argument this study attempts to unfold.

Background

Games are for entertainment, exercise and engagement of time. One of the most important requirements of any game is knowledge about the game. It is impossible for anyone to engage in games without having a sound learning of the rules and strategies of games. Rules are mostly static but strategies are dynamic. Strategies are to be employed to achieve the expectations of the players. Although most of the players intent to win the game or minimize the loss of the result, there are many who get involved in games for other intentions as well. Some players play games for the love of it. Some others expect the intellectual and physical exercise involved around a game. There are some others who use games for various experiments of their strategies. They use games as their test arena. In an academic setting, games are used to train the students to sharpen their intellectual acumen, to provide entertainment, to teach optimization techniques and to develop sportsman spirit.

There are various types of games people are engaged in. One of the types of games is board games. Chess is one of the most popular and at the same time a classical board game played by people of all ages and walks of life. Chess is not a solved game. Hence, it is very challenging even when played by the best brains. A solved game is one in which the outcome at any level can be predicted if the players involved play the game evenly. For a better understanding of it, if the game is played by two computers from any position, the result is easily mapped with the help of a decision tree.

Line Game is a country game played in various parts of Kerala, the southern state of India. It is played on a 3 x 3 grid drawn on a plane surface. Mostly, the Line Game is played between two players with each of the players having three identical pieces each. Line Game has multiple moves formulated to help one identify not just the movements but the strategies hidden behind the movements for a successful win. Academic and pedagogic learning which have been caught up under an online space in this 21st century can use this game to motivate critical thinking. This can also help in the creation of a space that motivates context-laden learning theories, such as situated learning, cognitive apprenticeship, and knowledge building.

However, a major idea that goes mostly unanswered while using the pedagogy of learning through games is the fact that social inequality has had a cultural or symbolic dimension to it. Not everybody might grasp as well as has the know-how to understand the rationale behind many games. However, the Line Game here strikes through the above concern raised quite easily through using a simple logic of moves involved between two parties. The most important aspect of this game that needs a highlight is that the discrimination immanent within this game like in other games too such as chess etc. comes as an understanding for a student into how the first player can dominate the field as well as into how the second player is forced to strategize accordingly. To elaborate the same, it is the understanding that whoever has the first move has a better chance to dominate the game and eventually can lead it to victory. This particular idea hence dominates and at the same time corrupts the entire logic of most of the real-world discourses too. This epistemic position of a first player hence automatically becomes a larger understanding to a society that stands highly disaggregated. Many call it the first mover's advantage. Many indoor games and outdoor games are with the first mover's advantage.

GAMES, STUDENTS AND TEACHERS

Historically speaking, playing has been an impactful and significant aspect of children's early learning. The act of playing different genres of games/music/archeries/art and so forth has always been there in the tradition of games and learning skills. Research indicates that these skills, when given more attention and effort, come out to be the skillful development of a child's later age and also it is seen that the art of knowledge and one's way of reacting to circumstances are far more logical than usual. (Olivia N. Saracho).

Through this impact of children learning better with games, it is highly appreciable to the teachers who play a key role in the development of educating students. It is therefore seen that the awareness and the tendency to train teachers for game-based learning, in the developed countries is way higher than that of the developing countries. The use of Randomized Control Trials (RCT) has been in use more in the developed countries than that of the developing countries, which clearly envisages that the methodology is more advanced. This kind of awareness and tendency to an extent is taking its form in the developing countries too. Different EdTech platforms developed in India like Byju's, Unacademy, Vedantu, Aloha learnings, etc are the best examples that India as one of the developing countries has adopted. On the same note, the teachers we find on such platforms are highly trained and most engaging in the teaching learning process.

Though the idea of games is seen from a cultural lens as something physical, the nearest possibility that the 21st century can think of is to revive old histories and represent them in the form of games in the closest of the ways possible. Video games are seen as instruments in this regard that can catch the hold of attention for a long time. Video games are often seen as instruments and environments to transfer and teach curricular knowledge, mainly Social Sciences (Wouters et al., 2013; Young et al., 2012), Natural Sciences (Steinkuehler & Duncan, 2008) and language (Gee, 2007). Beyond curricular content, some studies attempt to demonstrate that games can act as a motivational tool or driving force to develop transversal and transferable skills, such as improving perception and attention keeping (Green & Bavelier, 2003), collaborative problem-solving strategies (Chen & Hwang, 2017), digital and traditional literacy (Gee, 2007; Steinkeuhler, 2007), IT and informational skills (Hayes, 2008), systematic thinking (Squire, 2005), ethical reasoning (Simkins & Steinkuehler, 2008) or scientific reasoning (Steinkuehler & Duncan, 2008).

Per Roland Landers, CEO, All India Gaming Federation, "varied skills such as critical thinking, creative thinking, decision making and problem-solving are essential for one's growth in life. This study has helped us conclude that gaming is a way to collaborate, engage, and it is becoming a sector where people want to build their careers." The interactive characteristic of games enables the player to enthusiastically connect with the subject matter. According to Garris (2002), 'learning occurs when the learner repeats a desired emotional or cognitive behaviour based on the interaction and feedback they get from the game'. Thus, Digital Game-Based Learning (DGBL) generates a learner-centred, learner-guided setting in which the learner has control over the game and has the flexibility to investigate and experiment within the environment. Digital gaming is a multibillion-dollar industry, and surveys (e.g., 2005 Kaiser Family Foundation Study and 2007 Project Tomorrow Survey, quoted in Johnson 2008; also quoted in Chaudhary 2008) show that children—ages 8–18 years—spend more time (44.5 hours per week) in front of computer, television and game screens than any other activity in their lives except sleeping. According to the latest statistics of Internet & Mobile Association of India (2011), 'Internet usage in the country is driven primarily by young people, with over 75 per cent of the Internet users being school- or college-going kids and young men'. The use of games as one of the mediums for reinforcing and testing knowledge gives the learner a fun ambience, plus an inquisitiveness to attempt the game. It draws the learner's mind space and interest, thereby justifying the purpose of having the online learning module (Business Standard, 2004).

Building a certain kind of a space that draws an affinity in students is hence the primary job of the 21st-century learning process. Games in this regard emerge as the identification of an affinity space. Affinity spaces are an open field for the popular culture of mass media (films, television series, video games, literature). Common among young people's daily lives, digital technologies and social media create new, enhanced opportunities for affinity spaces, fan practices, discourses and dialogues to spread out over the Internet (Gutiérrez-Martín & Torrego-González, 2017). Affinity spaces are a special kind of semiotic social space (Gee, 2005). Semiotic social spaces and affinity spaces share that they are concerned with the way in which people construct and interpret meaning. For instance, in a real-time strategy game like Age of Empires, people may accept warfare tactics as normal practices, but they most probably will not in their daily, non-virtual routine. In popular culture, fans are the members of the affinity space, and the fandom (a portmanteau term of fans and kingdom) is the affinity space around a certain practice holding them together. As Gee (2004) indicates, an affinity group is a space people congregate to share and forward a particular interest with participation ranging from hanging out to publishing artefacts, sharing knowledge, or furthering the collective knowledge of the space. Participating in affinity spaces associated with massively multiplayer online games (MMOs) has been shown to host a veritable "constellation" of literacy practices (Steinkuehler, 2007), while also providing affiliation around interest-driven learning (Hayes & King, 2009) immersed in popular culture. Supporting the development of broader 21st-century literacies, other studies have highlighted the productivity of participatory culture (Jenkins, 1992), and affinity spaces associated with participating in online forums (Steinkuehler & Duncan, 2009) as well as writing and publishing fan fiction (Black, 2005) and taking part in "challenges" associated with The Sims games (Gee & Hayes, in-print). Therefore, the proposed game in this study comes as a mapping out of the space, wherein the map would have been a bit different for each student playing the game, and the spaces and routes continue to change across time. This makes the game practically an executable pedagogy in the 21st century learning too.

In recent years, behavioural science has become more prominent in strategizing society's social and behavioural norms. The concepts of game theory, Prisoner's dilemma, and Nash Equilibrium have provided many critical insights in describing the problems faced by individuals who either profit from cooperation or by defecting against their partners. The strategies implicated in Line Game help to attain the winning position inside the game and address third world issues.

Game-based learning has been an influential factor in acquiring 21st-century literacy skills in recent years. Game-based pedagogy can be defined as a space or environment where game-based activities and content enhance one's knowledge, skill acquisition and learning opportunities (Kirriemuir & McFarlane 2004). The increasing use of literacy skills reflects the rise in technological use and the abilities that enhance learner engagement, collaboration, problem-solving and cultural learning. Castells (2010), describes the 21st century as a period of intense transformation of business operations by emphasizing collaboration, knowledge, and mobility (Dunning, 2000).

Talking about the historical perspectives of game-based learning, Social constructivism has been considered as one of the essential reading-learning theories in identifying, understanding, and refining goals since the 1980s. The earlier works of Social constructivism included approaches of Inquiry-based learning (IBL) (Chu et al. 2007, Kuhlthau et al. 2007, Harada and Yoshina 2004), Project-based learning (PBL) (Harada et al. 2008), Inquiry -Project-based learning (IpBL) (Chu 2009, Chu et al. 2011), Problem-based learning (Hmelo-Silver, 2004) and Constructionism (Papert 1980, Harel and Papert 1991, Kafai 1995, Reynolds and Harel Caperton 2011).

In recent decades, the definition of literacy has been increasingly reflected by the ability to use technology in communicating and gathering information. As per the International Reading Association, the literacy skills used by today's generation is far beyond what it was in 1996. UNESCO's Delors Report (1996) issued by the International Commission on Education for the 21st Century recommended that there are four notable pillars of education: learning to know, learning to do, learning to be and learning to live together.

The applications of gamification promote the learners cognitive, emotional, social and motivational engagements when employed in the classroom (Hammer 2011, Chu et al. 2017). Developing games for educational purposes focus upon two core themes in common: At first, make learning a fun activity, and secondly, learning through doing or solving such as simulations, Line Game, Spell bee, Vocabulary games offers a powerful learning tool. However as characterised by Malone (1980), in the gamification process, the gaming activity should be structured in such a manner that the player can increase or decrease challenges level, in order to replicate one's personal skills with the activity requirements. Also, the activity should help the player to evaluate one's performance and provide feedback on one's criteria of performance. Orwant (2000), categorises the Hertz (1997) taxonomy of gaming into major categories like action games, adventure games, puzzle games, role-playing games, simulations, strategy games etc.

However, Squir (2008) distinguishes the ways in which educational games differ from commercial games. It has been seen that commercial games are inherently motivating but educational games use the game as a reward or incentive for learning educational content and thus becomes an intrinsic factor of motivation (Habgood and Ainsworth, 2011). In Line Game, monopolizing the opponent's decision-making process plays a dominant role. Moves being alternatively made decrease the board options and reduce the opponent's chances to win the game. Nevertheless, the situation of monopoly prevails at every end of the society, whether being household monopoly, political monopoly, institutional monopoly, hierarchical monopoly, and gender-based monopoly. In the pursuit of winning the game, players need to strategize their moves and decisions appropriately. Given the game's preconditions like fair chances, assured rationality, fair moves, equal opportunities, decision enforcement, an assured winning position can be retained.

McCherry et al. (2011) state that with the substantial and growing interest in the virtual spaces of 21st Century skills such as collaboration, communication and problem solving, very little attention has been given to the ways and behaviours in which users are associated with these 21st-century skills. The findings of the study suggested that spatial interactions of games can be bifurcated into five domains of behaviours: Spatial Positioning (navigation), Spatial appropriateness (display orientation), spatial interactivity (artificial intelligence interaction), spatial realisation (system orientation), and socio-spatial interactivity (human-controlled interaction). Based on the above criteria, it could be concluded that novices require time to adjust and get accustomed to the enclosed culture and to get familiar with the environment.

With regards to the evolving scientific education in the 21st century, Morris et al. (2013) argue that games can be used as cultural tools for science education. To engineer and master modern science education in the 21st century, the workforce should incorporate games in the education system and learn about the effectiveness of video games in producing cognitive and behavioural change (McGonigal, 2011). They further suggest that games can improve one's motivation, cognition and metacognition and serve as a cultural tool in making use of the existing capabilities (Greenfield, 1994). However, youngsters spending most of the time in video game arcades were actually not involved in any physical activity nor outdoor games and were using the arcade as one of the social gathering places (Greenfield, 1984).

As per the US Common Core State Standards (CCSS) frameworks to address the 21st-century skills, the application of higher-order thinking skills integrate a range of technology tools for solving word problems and developing rigorous knowledge in the area of English language/Arts, literacy (ELAL) and Mathematics. In the process of reading, writing and research, the students are required to comprehend, evaluate and interpret complex ideas, information and evidence through reading, writing, listening and speaking by engaging with information technology (CCSS 2010). On the other hand, UNESCO in its Learning Metrics Task Force (LMTF) divides the process of learning into seven domains. This holistic framework of LMTF includes the areas of physical wellbeing, social and emotional, Culture and Arts, Literacy and communication, Learning approaches and cognition, Numeracy and mathematics as well as science and technology. Politically, LMTF ensures the adoption of the Sustainable Development Goal (SDG) 4 on education by promoting knowledge sharing across the international community.

In the year 2002, the American Organisation with several educators, business leaders and consultants, conceptualized a 21st-century skills framework (P21, 2009) which became well known in the field of education and information technology. This framework includes three major competencies of learning and innovation skills, information media and technology skills, life and career skills, enhancing critical thinking, communication and interaction as well as collaboration and creativity.

GAMES AS PEDAGOGICAL TOOLS

In today's world, the concept of the game based pedagogy has set the learning and education system into a new method of understanding and discovering some of the key human race behaviours that are followed in society. In this 21st century era, behavioural and new institutional economics plays a major role in understanding the concept of the Line Game and hence the strategies followed by it. The Line Game keenly and minutely determines the objectivity of the game and the behaviour of the players involved in the game. The way one makes the move helps the other player to understand what one is trying to portray through the game; i.e., either winning or losing or the strategies followed at least. Game-based pedagogy allows learners in active engagement and discovering new methods. This process helps to build in the thinking capabilities and ideas. These methods, if introduced with all enthusiasm and awareness, from K-12 and higher education, can definitely create a better rational power as per the motive. If such processes of game theory, new strategies and skills are dealt with on an everyday basis, it will then definitely consider the complex tools and problems existing in the society and will develop complex ways of learning in a much smoother way possible.

While understanding the methods and processes of acquiring game-based learning, it is important to note a concept of the education economy that has come to existence because of the unification and cooperation of economic and educational research. (Sabodash, O.A 2021). In the 21st century too, there lacks a huge state of scientific maturity, but of course, there is an ongoing tendency to shift from the traditional approach of learning to more logical and reason-based learning and this should be considered as the stepping stone to acquire not only the skillful knowledge and understanding but also the development of human capital, human brain and the economic analysis of the results of the educational activities.

SOME FEATURES OF LINE GAME

Line Game is played between two players. In Figure 1, we can see the playing board, and the pieces for both the players.

Figure 1.

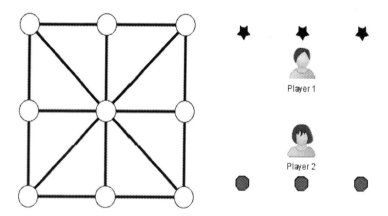

Each player gets three identical pieces. One of the players, say Player 1, begins the movement by placing one of the pieces allotted to that player in any of the points (white circle) on the board. Player 2 and Player 1 alternately place their pieces one after the other. The first player to place all three pieces on a straight line wins the game. See some of the possibilities in Figure 2.

The game has some similarities to the famous 3 x 3 Tic-tac-toe game. If player 2 is really dumb, player 1 can win the game in the fifth move. Similarly, player 2 can win the game in the sixth move. However, if both the players play perfectly choosing the best movement, the game is more interesting. Here, the strategy of each player matters. After the sixth move, if player 2 does not win the game, player 1 and player 2 alternately move the pieces to an adjacent circle that is vacant. Some of the preconditions of Line Game are as follows.

- Given the rules, both players have fair chances
- The rationality of the players is assured
- No external forces in the decision-making of the players

Figure 2.

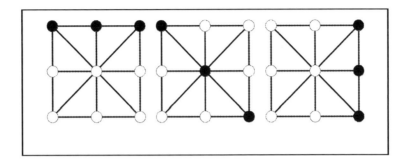

The real complexity of the game is in the number of possible moves for the first six moves themselves. There are 10x9x8x7x6x5 = 151200 possible moves. The game can end in either of the players winning the game or in a draw. Draw happens when both the players strategically move to avoid a defeat. In Figure 3, we can see the winning strategies of player 1 and player 2. In the first game displayed, player 2 (blue) wins the game in the tenth move. In the second game, player 2 wins the game in the seventeenth move.

Figure 3.

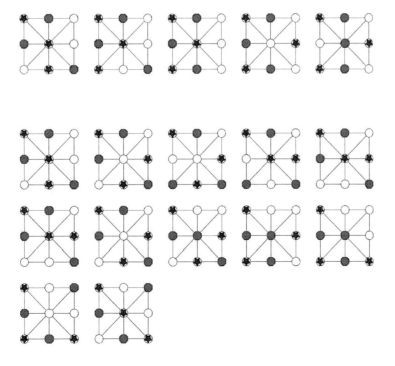

ECONOMIC MODEL OF THE LINE GAME

Practically speaking, the Line Game or any game which specifically involves two players and the strategies involved in it can be put forth and looked upon from different genres of perspectives. Referring to one of such perspectives, it can be looked at from a concept of Pareto efficiency, a microeconomic concept. To understand briefly, we tend to describe the first case of the Line Game strategy where we see that there are two players, player 1 and player 2. Assuming that both the players are equally efficient, player 1 makes the first move, in this regard, player 1 gets the most benefit and all chances of maximizing her/ his benefit and hence utilizes it to the most. Also, it is needless to mention that player 1 is in a better off position and not necessarily making the second player worse off in the process (Pareto efficiency concept). Now, when player 2 moves, player 2 exactly has one chance less than that of player 1 but still tries to maximize and utilize the remaining 8 chances which are available to player 2, without making anyone worse off in the process. And this process continues and the chances of maximizing the resources by both the players followed by the movement made also tends to decline by one chance each time. And finally, when either player tries to take straight consecutive chances in a line, we might see that player 1 having made the movement first wins the game with all the privileges that player 1 holds.

Reversely, sometimes the player 1 might strategically portray her/his movement in a way to block her/ his movement, so that player 2 is set on a complex situation and which makes player 1 win, if player 2 is confused, she/he might lose but then if player 2 is smart enough to show her/his intelligence 2(which represents the skills, ideas and the success of the game-based learning) player 2 might win, although player 1 had moved first. It is to be noted that in such a game the strategies that are followed by both the players need to be closely observed. Generally, a game is all about the set of rules and regulations whereas, there exists a huge difference between a game and the strategy; wherein, the strategy explains the plan that each player thinks and accordingly tends to move their position. It is also expected from the players to be rational in their behaviour while strategizing and playing the game considering the set of beliefs and rules in mind. Through the strategy that each player is willing to put forth while playing the game, helps them to optimize and maximize their payoffs. Playing a mathematical game or any kind of game gives a thrilling kind of experience, and hence in such kind of game, there might be a lot of possible outcomes, producing payoffs for each individual player and because these payoffs sometimes are in the form of monetary or even satisfactory job, hence the players are keen on playing the game while strategizing the entire game. Hence, playing the game with a proper strategy makes one win the game and generate better skills and overall development. (Game Theory Through Examples, Erich Prisner).

Through this, it can be focused under a broader aspect of how the society, in turn, is getting affected by the discrimination, which implies that educators need to recognize and realize their privileges that sometimes the online games and game-based learning can be only accessible to the populist structure or culture of the society. This economic model mainly reflects on the individual's maximizing behaviour that may include discrimination. Here, when we are considering the two players (Player 1 and Player 2), we assume that player 1 having made the movement first, acts as a majority group whereas player 2 acts as a minority group because player 2 loses one chance (chance, which comprises taking a better off position). group whereas player 2 acts as a minority group because player 2 loses one chance (chance, which comprises taking a better off position).

Here, while the firms (player 1 and player 2) will try to maximize, economically, the opportunity cost (a microeconomic concept) will be theorized which implies for someone to gain something, something needs to be sacrificed. But, here the strategy which is being played by the employers being the upper position than the employees' acts as a taste-based discriminating factor. Also, there exist wage differentials among the employers and employees. Therefore, to relate it with the players of the strategy in Line Game, we can tell that player 1 occupies an upper hand because she/he is moving first and plays an important role and tries to maximize and utilize all the resources with all the chances, possibilities and well-equipped strategies, while player 2 acts as a minority and makes the first move with one chance less already. In the same way, player 1 makes the second move with two chances less and again player 2 makes the second move with three chances less, player 1 makes the third move with four chances less and again player2 makes the third move with five chances less with. Thus there occurs the phenomenon of decision tree algorithms.

This very concept while we intend to relate it with the 21st Century game-based learning and pedagogy, can be suggested in a way that, the taste of the parents (considering the employers) which is much common is that they view that game-played (referring to the employees) as a task, meant only for the leisure time or for relaxation of the mood after heavy tiresome work. This very thinking makes the game lose its gravity. But, when such pedagogy and skills can also be useful in daily day learning, the value of it should and will reach a greater height than what the literacy skill is aiming for. Therefore, educating parents along with educating the students should be taken as one of the major steps for fostering creative skills, for this definitely has a major impact on the current education and learning method. Because, an era before 21st century, was not common in learning and acquiring skills through the online game mode of learning hence, with the wake of pandemic too, the concept of online learning and pedagogy stands quite off the mainstream and thus, it has become the immediate need to research and develop strategies that would help one to acquire literacy skills and foster creative inquiry through such mode.

Thus, strategizing the Line Game helps in understanding the game rules and regulations, the rational behaviour of the human race, the specifications and the peculiarities of the society (considering, Indian Society). The Line Game actually reflects the existing different intersectionalities. Studying the Line Game and knowing the strategies of how to play it, actually would help in understanding the behavioural economics working in the markets, institutions and the firms' functioning.

It is known and understood that "Everyone is equal before the law." Thus, while explaining the strategies of the Line Game theory, it follows certain game rules and regulations and the players involved in the game are bound to follow the rules and are expected to be rational. Similarly, when compared or related to real-life incidents, all citizens are equal before the law and should abide by the laws and rules while considering the most rational and logical way of understanding society and circumstances. For, education in any mode aspires for positive, moral and societal values. Nevertheless, the Line Game explains the strategies and reflects on various overwhelming methods which are required and much-needed ailments to live in our day to day life.

Therefore, in the game-based learning pedagogy, the strategies of the Line Game suggest that both players (player 1 and player 2) of the game with different bargaining power can reach the winning position with fair means and equal opportunities. If there is an interest coalition between both parties in the game, then it may not lead to the winning situation for either. Thus, contributing to both formal and informal educational agendas, collaborative activities consisting of discussion, reflection, and planning can support learning in a gaming environment.

ISSUES AND CHALLENGES OF GAME BASED LEARNING

Game based pedagogy has been proven to have a positive outcome on the cognitive development of the learners. According to famous theorist Lev Vygotsky, learning and cognitive development among learners occurs through active engagement and collaboration and is more reflective in a student centered environment. However not all learners learn in the same way. Game based learning includes certain issues and challenges within it. While taking into consideration the example of developed and developing countries, there exists a clear understanding of how the developed countries have taken a good step towards accepting and practicing the game based pedagogy. However, in the developing countries (for example: India) we see that the awareness regarding the game based pedagogy is not much prevalent yet. One of the many reasons could be the social and economic barrier which mostly is visible in the developing countries society. It is evident in the developing countries that only a certain section of the social class can afford the game based learning while for the rest, it becomes a challenging task to support economically. Hence, at this juncture, fruitful policy implication becomes necessary. On the other hand, it also becomes very important for teachers' training and explaining them the methodology by which the best can be delivered to the students. `

Now talking about the challenges related with the game based pedagogy, the excessive use of such learning creates needless competition among the players to reach the winning position. As a result, the learner's (player) focus shifts to winning rather than learning, specifically when rewards or incentives have been allocated to the game. This further causes the risk of leaving behind the real motive of learning and forgetting that the real purpose is to facilitate learning. Another limitation associated with game based learning is that excessive use of game towards learning a concept shifts the focus of the players away from collaboration and diminishes the importance of cooperative learning and sharing of ideas among each other.

Some educational games played using the Internet or computer may increase the cognitive development among learners, but even though it can affect the learner mentally as well as physically. Learners getting addicted to online games creates long term physical effects like repetitive physical strain, eye-stain, fatigues, and mood swings. Therefore, to avoid these physical symptoms, players should be actively encouraged to take enough breaks during the games. On the other hand, educational games can mentally affect a player as well. As per study conducted by Newman university college, Birmingham, England, educational games cause low self-esteem and aggressive behavior, specifically when the player loses the game numerous times. Also due to the addictive nature of the game, overusing or overplaying can result in poor social skills by causing social isolation among the players. Some of the online games create negative effects on the players that encourage violence (Adams, 2017).

CONCLUSION

The Line Game presented here opens a wide variety of possibilities. Its simplicity is a major attraction. It is played on various surfaces such as floor, board or paper. Students play this game during the break hours using paper and pencil. A simple dumb move can cost the game. Hence, at most attention is required from the players. It is not a solved game as nobody had ventured to study it. The game can be played as an online game. Artificial Neural networks, Economics, Investment strategies, Critical

Thinking, Optimization Strategies, resilience, defensive techniques etc. can be developed among the students if we carefully use this game as a pedagogical tool.

REFERENCES

Adams, C. (2017). *The Disadvantages of using games as a Learning tool.* Academic Press.

Castells, M. (2010). *The rise of the network society. The Information age: Economy, society, and culture* (2nd ed., Vol. 1). Wiley-Blackwell.

CCSS. (2010). *Common core state standards initiative.* Retrieved May 6, 2015, from http://www.corestandards.org/the-standards

Chaudhary, A. G. (2010). Educational gaming: An effective tool for learning and social change in India. *Journal of Creative Communications, 5*(3), 135–152. doi:10.1177/0973258612471244

Chu, S. K. W., & Kennedy, D. M. (2011). Using online collaborative tools for groups to co-construct knowledge. *Online Information Review, 35*(4), 581–597. doi:10.1108/14684521111161945

Chu, S. K. W., Tang, Q., Chow, K., & Tse, S. K. (2007). *A study on inquiry-based learning in a primary school through librarian-teacher partnerships.* Academic Press.

Delors, J. (1996). *Learning: The treasure within.* Paris: UNESCO. Retrieved May 11, 2015 from https://unesdoc.unesco.org/images/0010/001095/109590eo.pdf

Dunning, J. H. (2000). Regions, globalization, and the knowledge economy: Issues stated. In J. H. Dunning (Ed.), *Regions, globalization, and the knowledge-based economy* (pp. 7–41). Oxford University Press.

ET. (2008). 21st century learning: Research, innovation and policy. directions from recent OECD analyses. *OECD/CERI International Conference.*

Garris, R., Ahlers, R., & Driskell, J. E. (2002). Games, motivation, and learning: A research and practice model. *Simulation & Gaming, 33*(4), 441–467. doi:10.1177/1046878102238607

Gee, J. P. (2003). What video games have to teach us about learning and literacy. *Computers in Entertainment, 1*(1), 20–20. doi:10.1145/950566.950595

Gee, J. P. (2017). Affinity spaces and 21st-century learning. *Educational Technology,* 27–31.

Greenfield, P. M. (1994). Video games as cultural artefacts. *Journal of Applied Developmental Psychology, 15*(1), 3–12. doi:10.1016/0193-3973(94)90003-5

Greenfield, P. M., Camaioni, L., Ercolani, P., Weiss, L., Lauber, B. A., & Perucchini, P. (1994). Cognitive socialization by computer games in two cultures: Inductive discovery or mastery of an iconic code. *Journal of Applied Developmental Psychology, 15*(1), 59–85. doi:10.1016/0193-3973(94)90006-X

Habgood, M. P. J., & Ainsworth, S. E. (2011). Motivating children to learn effectively: Exploring the value of intrinsic integration in educational games. *Journal of the Learning Sciences, 20*(2), 169–206. doi:10.1080/10508406.2010.508029

Harada, V. H., & Yoshina, J. M. (2004). *Inquiry learning through librarian-teacher partnerships.* Linworth Publishing.

Harel, I. E., & Papert, S. E. (1991). *Constructionism.* Ablex Publishing.

Herodotou, C., Sharples, M., Gaved, M., Kukulska-Hulme, A., Rienties, B., Scanlon, E., & Whitelock, D. (2019, October). Innovative pedagogies of the future: An evidence-based selection. In *Frontiers in Education* (Vol. 4, p. 113). Frontiers. doi:10.3389/feduc.2019.00113

Hmelo-Silver, C. E. (2004). Problem-based learning: What and how do students learn? *Educational Psychology Review, 16*(3), 235–266. doi:10.1023/B:EDPR.0000034022.16470.f3

Jan, M. (2009). *Designing an augmented reality game-based curriculum for argumentation* (Unpublished doctoral dissertation). University of Wisconsin-Madison.

Jan, M., Chee, Y. S., & Tan, E. M. (2010). Learning science via a science-in-the-making process: The design of a game-based learning curriculum. In S. Martin (Ed.), *iVERG 2010 Proceedings - International Conference on Immersive Technologies for Learning: A multi-disciplinary approach* (pp. 13-25). Stockton, CA: Iverg Publishing.

Jan, M., & Tan, E. (2013). Learning in and for the 21st century. Professorial Lecture Series, 4, 13-22.

Kafai, Y. B. (1995). *Minds in play: Computer game design as a context for children's learning.* Routledge.

Kirriemuir, J., & McFarlane, A. (2004). *Literature review in games and learning* (Vol. 8). Futurelab.

Kuhlthau, C. C., Caspari, A. K., & Maniotes, L. K. (2007). *Guided inquiry: Learning in the 21st century.* Libraries Unlimited.

McCreery, M. P., Schrader, P. G., & Krach, S. K. (2011). Navigating Massively Multiplayer Online Games: Evaluating 21st Century Skills for Learning within Virtual Environments. *Journal of Educational Computing Research, 44*(4), 473–493. doi:10.2190/EC.44.4.f

McGonigal, J. (2011). *Reality is Broken: Why Games Make Us Better and How They Can Change the World.* Penguin.

Morris, B. J., Croker, S., Masnick, A., & Zimmerman, C. (2012). *The emergence of scientific reasoning. In Trends in Cognitive Development.* InTech.

Morris, B. J., Croker, S., Zimmerman, C., Gill, D., & Romig, C. (2013). Gaming science: The "Gamification" of scientific thinking. *Frontiers in Psychology, 4*, 607. doi:10.3389/fpsyg.2013.00607 PMID:24058354

National Research Council. (2010). *Exploring the Intersection of Science Education and 21st Century Skills: A Workshop Summary.* Washington, DC: National Academies Press.

National Research Council. (2012). *A Framework for K-12 Science Education: Practices, Crosscutting Concepts, and Core Ideas.* National Academies Press.

Papert, S. (1980). *Mindstorms: Children, computers, and powerful ideas.* Basic Books, Inc.

Peterson, A., Dumont, H., Lafuente, M., & Law, N. (2018). *Understanding innovative pedagogies: Key themes to analyse new approaches to teaching and learning.* Academic Press.

Qian, M., & Clark, K. R. (2016). Game-based Learning and 21st-century skills: A review of recent research. *Computers in Human Behavior, 63*, 50–58. doi:10.1016/j.chb.2016.05.023

Reynolds, R., & Harel Caperton, I. (2011). Contrasts in student engagement, meaning-making, dislikes, and challenges in a discovery-based program of game design learning. *Journal of Educational Technology Research and Development, 59*(2), 267–289. doi:10.100711423-011-9191-8

Saracho, O. N., & Spodek, B. (1995). Children's play and early childhood education: Insights from history and theory. *Journal of Education, 177*(3), 129–148. doi:10.1177/002205749517700308

Shirky, C. (2010). *Cognitive surplus: Creativity and generosity in a connected age*. Penguin.

Simkins, D. W., & Steinkuehler, C. (2008). Critical ethical reasoning and role-play. *Games and Culture, 3*(3-4), 333–355. doi:10.1177/1555412008317313

Smagorinsky, P. (2007). Vygotsky and the social dynamics of classrooms. *English Journal*, 61–66.

Smagorinsky, P. (2013). What does Vygotsky provide for the 21st-century language arts teacher? *Language Arts, 90*(3), 192–204.

Squire, K. (2008). *Video games literacy: a literacy of expertise*. In J. Coiro, M. Knobel, C. Lankshear, & D. J. Leu (Eds.), *Handbook of Research on New Literacies* (pp. 639–673). Lawrence Erlbaum.

Steinkuehler, C., & Duncan, S. (2008). Scientific habits of mind in virtual worlds. *Journal of Science Education and Technology, 17*(6), 530–543. doi:10.100710956-008-9120-8

Trilling, B., & Fidel, C. (2009). *21st Century skills: Learning for life in our times*. Jossey-Bass.

Wouters, P., Van Nimwegen, C., Van Oostendorp, H., & Van Der Spek, E. D. (2013). A meta-analysis of the cognitive and motivational effects of serious games. *Journal of Educational Psychology, 105*(2), 249–265. doi:10.1037/a0031311

Chapter 43

The Process of Prosocial Behavior Between Players/ Characters in Digital Games:
A Multidimensional Approach to the Situational Context and Gameplay

Ji Soo Lim
Dokkyo University, Japan

ABSTRACT

To understand the influence of video games on the player, several important questions must be answered. First, what accounts for the higher level of engagement in digital games relative to other entertainment media? Furthermore, what kind of experience does the player have during gameplay? Specifically, what does the player think when he or she interacts with other characters in the game? This study examines digital games with a focus on the interaction between the game itself and the person playing it. Among the various social behaviors elicited by digital games, much attention has been given to players' prosocial behavior within the context of a game's virtual world. A multidimensional view of behavior is used to analyze the game's situational contexts and players' interpretation of behavior.

These days, it is common to see people of all ages playing digital games on smartphones or portable game consoles while riding the train. According to the infographics released at the Electronic Entertainment Expo 2015 by HIS Technology, consumer spending on games in 2015 was expected to exceed that of movies and recorded music combined. Because digital games are so engaging, some people may become addicted to them (World Health Organization, 2018). For their compelling and competitive contents, digital games have been the scapegoat for youth crime (e.g., "Trump turns spotlight on violent video games in wake of Parkland shootings," Phelps, 2018). On the other hand, some people overcame their mental health problems by turning their recovery processes into motivational games (McGonigal, 2015), while others became or dream of becoming a lawyer like the admired game character Phoenix

DOI: 10.4018/978-1-7998-7271-9.ch043

Wright in *Ace Attorney* (Capcom, 2001) (Katada, 2019). Although many people enjoy playing games, the commuter train is not full of aggressive criminals or righteous heroes. Not all shooting game players are motivated to commit a crime, and not all *Ace Attorney* players become lawyers. What do players think or feel when they interact with other characters in the game?

Since games are popular especially among young people, their effects on players have been a focus of study in areas including media studies, education, and psychology, mostly based on theories of television effects. Many studies on the effects of video games tend to focus on the negative aspects, relating video games to learning of violence, shooting incidents, and youth crime (e.g., Adachi & Willoughby, 2011; Bushman & Anderson, 2002; Dill & Dill, 1998; Funk, Baldacci, Pasold, & Baumgardner, 2004). Similarly, although they are few in number compared to game violence studies, there are studies on the effect of games on prosocial behavior of players (e.g., Gentile et al., 2009; Greitemeyer & Osswald, 2009).

There are also studies on the effects of "prosocial games" on prosocial player behavior. Chambers and Ascione (1987) set up an experiment to look at the difference in the effects of prosocial and aggressive games on donating and helping behaviors of children, yet they failed to show significant effects. Various similar studies have been conducted to suggest the prosocial effects of games. In some studies, questionnaires were used to assess the prosocial behavioral intentions (e.g., Gentile et al., 2009); in others, spontaneous prosocial behaviors were observed (e.g., Greitemeyer & Osswald, 2010). Most results support that playing prosocial games promotes prosocial behaviors. However, compared to the rigorously studied topic of violence in games, the study of prosocial behavior in games is shallow in terms of theoretical background. Relevant methodologies are yet to be developed for this field.

The most critical issue is that prosocial behavior has been loosely defined in previous studies. In many prosocial game studies, the definitions of "prosocial" are not concrete, and many studies view prosocial behavior as a one-dimensional concept. There is also a question of internal validity in the methodologies related to the ambiguity of the definition of prosocial behavior. Since prosocial behavior is not clearly defined, the validity of assessment instruments becomes questionable. Therefore, a clear definition of prosocial behavior must be provided to conduct a valid study on the effects of prosocial games. Also, studies on the effects of prosocial games often lack content analysis. While investigating the effects of "prosocial games," previous studies have often used games with purely prosocial objectives based on real-world standards. However, the objectives are what players are "supposed to do" according to the designer, and they are not necessarily what players intend to do in the game. In *Lemmings* (DMA Design, 1991), used by Greitemeyer and Osswald (2009), players may be saving the Lemmings because that is the objective of the game; however, their intention is not to save a specific Lemming. The shortcoming of these studies is that they do not consider in-game behaviors that might emerge from game-specific rules and designs (Salen & Zimmerman, 2004). Therefore, it is necessary to look at how prosocial behavior emerges in games.

Most existing game content analyses focus on depictions of violence and sexual expressions (Dietz, 1998; Thompson & Haninger, 2001). While violence and gender roles are important topics considering the possible impact of games as agents of socialization, content analyses on positive behavior are also needed. There are attempts on looking at the inclusion of specific contents in serious games, i.e., games with an educational or medical purpose (e.g., Payne, Moxley, & MacDonald, 2015). However, content analyses on positive behavior in commercial games are rare.

This research focuses on digital games and the interaction between a game and its player. Specifically, it investigates prosocial player behavior in the virtual world of games, with a multidimensional approach that considers the situational contexts and players' interpretations of such behaviors.

LITERATURE REVIEW: PROSOCIAL BEHAVIOR

This research adopts Eisenberg's definition of prosocial behavior: "helping, sharing, and other seemingly intentional and voluntary positive behaviors for which the motive is unspecified, unknown, or not altruistic" (Eisenberg, 1982, p. 6). In the field of psychology, the definition of prosocial behavior had been inconsistent among researchers. Often, altruism is discussed as a closely related concept. However, Hawley (2014) provides a clear picture of the difference between altruistic behavior and prosocial behavior. Prosocial behavior is a broader term that refers to intentional acts that benefit others. Altruistic behavior is a type of prosocial behavior that is motivated by concern for others. The definition of prosocial behavior is not concerned with the motive or the context of the behavior; however, prosocial behavior may be categorized according to kinds of situational context.

The definition yields the development of a multidimensional measure of prosocial behavior (Carlo, Hausmann, Christiansen, & Randall, 2003), which categorizes prosocial behavior into six types (public, emotional, dire, anonymous, altruistic, and compliant) based on the situational context in which prosocial behavior is exhibited. (1) Public prosocial behavior is behavior that is "intended to benefit others enacted in the presence of others" (Carlo et al., 2003, p.113). (2) Emotional prosocial behavior is behavior that is "intended to benefit others enacted under emotionally evocative situations" (Carlo et al., 2003, p. 113). (3) Dire prosocial behavior is "helping others under emergency or crisis situations" (Carlo et al., 2003, p. 113). (4) Compliant prosocial behavior is "helping others when asked to" (Carlo et al., 2003, p. 113). (5) Anonymous is "the tendency to help others without other people's knowledge" (Carlo et al., 2003, p. 113). (6) Altruistic prosocial behavior is "helping others when there is little or no perceived potential for a direct, explicit reward to the self" (Carlo et al., 2003, p. 113). Adopting a multidimensional perspective is considered important in studies of prosocial behavior in media in general. Coyne and Smith (2014) note that, currently, content analyses focusing on prosocial behavior in media lack a multidimensional perspective, while studies in developmental studies adopt such a perspective. Developmental studies of prosocial behavior recognize that prosocial behavior of different dimensions in terms of situational contexts and motives may have different mechanisms of socialization. Thus, different types of prosocial behavior should be separately studied.

PROSOCIAL BEHAVIOR IN VARIOUS SITUATIONAL CONTEXTS IN GAMES

The following research investigated specific examples of prosocial behavior in games through content analysis, which clarified that prosocial behaviors exhibited in six different situational contexts observed in the real world were all also evident in games. Among the 27 games analyzed, 22 games (81%) contained at least one depiction of a kind of prosocial behavior. Analyzed games scored an average frequency of 3.59 incidents (26 minutes) of prosocial behaviors in an hour of gameplay. Studies are often concerned about violent and sexual content in games. However, considering the results of a previous study on violence in E-rated (for everyone) games in 2001 (Thompson & Haninger, 2001) that found 64% of games involved violence for an average of 30.7% of gameplay, there are as much positive contents in games as negative contents despite the focus on the latter.

The effects of different situational contexts on prosocial behavior in games was observed through a survey and an experiment. The survey results clarified that the playtime of games with frequent depictions of prosocial behavior (*Paper Mario: Sticker Star* (Nintendo, 2012), *Pokémon Ranger* (Pokémon,

2006), *Dragon Quest IX: Sentinels of the Starry Skies* (Square Enix, 2009), *Hamtaro: Ham-Hams Unite!* (Nintendo, 2001), *Monster Hunter Diary Poka Poka Airu Village* (Capcom, 2010), *Tomodachi Collection* (Nintendo, 2009), *The Legend of Zelda: Phantom Hourglass* (Nintendo, 2007), *Super Mario Sunshine* (Nintendo, 2002), and *Luigi's Mansion: Dark Moon* (Nintendo, 2013)) was marginally correlated with players' prosocial tendencies. Furthermore, depictions of different types of prosocial behavior were related to different types of prosocial tendencies of players. However, in the experiment that used a game with frequent depictions of prosocial behavior, *Dragon Quest IX: Sentinels of the Starry Skies* (Square Enix, 2009), versus a neutral game, *Inazuma Eleven: Blizzard* (LEVEL-5, 2009), although the scores of prosocial tendencies of the experiment group seemed to have increased, statistically significant changes were not observed in players' prosocial tendencies.

It is considered that games, like other media, affect their audience. It is important to focus not only on negative contents but also on the positive contents to promote the positive effects of media. Games can be considered as a significant socializing agent as many children and adolescents play games. Bar-Tal and Raviv (1982) noted that television may work as a socializing agent and the main teaching techniques it can use are modeling and use of story contents. Games, in addition to what television can offer, can utilize role-playing and reinforcement techniques. Thus, if used properly, games can work as an effective agent of socialization to teach prosocial behavior.

However, it is important to see how players interpret behavior or depictions of behavior. For example, prosocial behavior is often accompanied with violence in games. To save allies, a player may have to slay a monster. If it were not for saving allies, the player might not have tried to slay the monster. This incident may be interpreted as helping allies or hurting the monster. In this vein, how a player interprets what happens in games and the motive of the behavior are important.

DIGITAL GAMES AS MEDIA

Digital games are differentiated from traditional media by their interactivity. The interactivity of digital games attracts people and familiarizes players with new technologies. The history of digital games is also the history of new media technologies. Digital games have always been used to diffuse a new media technology. For example, people easily associate virtual reality (VR) and augmented reality (AR) with digital games, because these technologies were introduced to the public through digital games. VR attractions in shopping malls usually feature shooting or racing games, and the public became familiar with AR through Pokémon GO (Niantic, 2016). The first digital game, Spacewar! (1962) was developed on Programmed Data Processor-1 (PDP-1) in Massachusetts Institute of Technology for the annual open house to attract the visitors who came to see the computer—rare at that time. It was a success and ended up being distributed by DEC, the manufacturer of the computer. Later, it was published as an arcade game by Nolan Bushnell (1971). However, interactivity alone is not what attracts people. In the case of *Spacewar!*, before the game, several interactive programs (not games) had been written to attract visitors. However, they failed to attract as many people as *Spacewar!* did. There is something more to digital games than interactivity that attracts people. Digital games are digitalized games, and this leads to a discussion of play, another context in which games are discussed.

DIGITAL GAMES AS PLAY

Although digital games have originated from and been affected by other media technologies, they are founded in play. Games and play are closely related, as apparent in some languages where the same word is used to describe them (e.g., "jeu" in French and "spiel" in German). *Homo Ludens* (Huizinga, 1938/1950) is one of earliest texts that addresses the importance of play in culture. Play is neither developed by a certain civilization nor a unique phenomenon of humanity; it is an irreducible, universal concept that exists on its own. According to Huizinga, "play is non-seriousness" (p. 5). It happens outside the "ordinary" life. He later comes up with the concept of the "the magic circle" (Salen & Zimmerman, 2004) that separates the space and time of a game from that of the real world. *Man, Play, and Games* (Caillois, 1958/1900) is directly affected by *Homo Ludens*. Caillois expands Huizinga's work on the importance of play in the development of civilization. According to Caillois, play is a free, separate, uncertain, unproductive, rule-governed, and make-believe activity (p. 40). He introduces *paidia* and *ludus*; every type of play exists on a continuum between *paidia* and *ludus*. *Paidia* is one extreme of the spectrum where no rules exist; and *ludus* is the other extreme where players are bound by formalized rules. Although the distinction between *paidia* and *ludus* is comparable to the distinction between play and games, recently, it has been recognized that play and games are not completely separate in terms of rules. All plays and games have some of both *paidic* and *ludic* elements (Egenfeldt-Nielsen, Smith, & Tosca, 2013).

GAMEPLAY: RULES, GOALS, AND THE GAME WORLD

What is a game? This research adopts Juul's definition that is based on the definitions of these predecessors; it defines a game as "a rule-based system with a variable and quantifiable outcome, where different outcomes are assigned different values, the player exerts effort in order to influence the outcome, the player feels emotionally attached to the outcome, and the consequences of the activity are negotiable" (2005, p. 36). A game consists of players, rules, and quantifiable outcomes. As shown in the definition, in the discussion of games in the context of play, it is important to look at the interactions among the components of the system, not just the game itself. Juul describes such aspect of games with the concept of *gameplay:* "the way the game is actually played" (2005, p. 83). It is different from the game itself, as it is a result of the interaction between the rules of the game, players' goals, and players' competencies or repertoires.

Rules drive player behavior in digital games. Egenfeldt-Nielsen, Smith, and Tosca (2013) define rules as "an imperative governing the interaction of game objects and the possible outcome of this interaction." Similarly, Juul (2005) states that rules specify limitations and affordances of player actions in games. Rules may control player behavior by constraining player actions. Rules also afford player actions by defining their consequences.

Goals are an essential component of any game. Goals also drive player behaviors in games. The goal of a game does not have to be explicitly designed by the game's designer. Whether short-term or long-term, small or big, goals drive players to continue playing the game and to behave in a certain way. Salen and Zimmerman (2004) describe the role of goals in a game as a drive of "the pleasure of a player." They see the role of big goals as providing players with pleasure and the role of small goals as keeping them going. Goals are also related to the experience of "flow" (Csikszentmihalyi, 1990) in games, in a discussion regarding the enjoyment of playing games. Goals may also engage players in the game narrative. They are used by the designer to guide players to the narrative which the designer wants them to follow. A congruent goal gives the reason to follow game instructions.

Game world is used here to distinguish the real world from the world of a game. However, it does not imply that what happens in the game world is not real. Although hardware, such as a screen, seems to separate the fictional world from the real world, the players outside the fictional world still follow the rules of the game. Players are not only playing in the imaginary fictional world of the game but also playing games under certain rules in the real world (Juul, 2005). Juul discusses digital games in terms of rules and fiction which respectively correspond to the real and unreal parts of digital games. Here, it is suggested that two boundaries can be drawn around digital games: a concrete one between the fictional world and the physical world, and an abstract one between the game and the non-game. Game world implies the world where gameplay takes place. As such, the game world is the place of interaction between the game and the player.

PLAYER BEHAVIOR IN GAMES

Studies on violence and prosocial behavior in games and their effects reference a learning model derived from social cognitive theory, to explain the effects. However, violent and prosocial behaviors are mainly conducted by the players themselves, via their characters. That is, players are not simply exposed to these behaviors; they are actively involved in them. A seemingly violent or prosocial behavior may be motivated by an unexpected interpretation of the situation, and its consequences may have different meanings for different players. For example, when a player exhibits violent behavior toward a monster character, the meaning of the behavior differs for those who did it to help one's teammates, to relieve frustration, or to test their strength. Violence with prosocial motives may be interpreted by the player as a prosocial behavior by means of violence. When considering behavior in games, it is important to observe the situational context of behaviors and how that behavior is interpreted by players.

As seen above, a motive is an important aspect of prosocial behavior that is affected by the interpretation of the situation and that affects the meaning of the behavior. In the current research, empathy is specifically considered when looking at the motives of prosocial behaviors in games, as it is the main motive of prosocial behavior in the real world as noted in the previous section. Empathy and its relationship with prosocial behavior in games are rarely investigated in previous studies. In games, players may feel empathy toward characters and be motivated to help them as they would in the real world. Disregarding the emotional motives of prosocial behavior may lead to the problems of overlooking player differences due to disregarding emotionally motivated prosocial behavior and overcounting unintentional behavior as prosocial behavior.

INTERPRETATIONS OF PLAYERS

Player actions are driven by the rules of a game. However, players do not fully immerse themselves in the game so as to be entirely controlled by the rules. They are aware that they are playing the game, because they are consciously following the rules. Bateson's theory of metacommunication (1955), which is communication about communication, helps explain how players understand that what is happening in games are not real, yet, at the same time, they interpret it as meaningful. Similarly, as mentioned earlier, Juul (2005) states that "a video game is half-real," as players play in the fictional world of the game while playing under the rules in the real world. Players would not be surprised to find that there are some parts of the fictional world that they cannot access. The actions are bound by the rules of the game, and players understand these boundaries.

Players interpret what is going on during gameplay, according to the different frames they adopt. Fine (1983) studied analog role-playing game players in the late 1970s, using frame analyses to look at the meaning of gameplay among players. Fine based his analysis of players on Goffman's frame analysis (1974). The frame is defined as principles or rules that form the basis of interpretations. During observations and interviews with gamers, Fine identified that they talked about games from three different levels. *Person* level is what everything is based on, since it is comprised of knowledge of the real world. For example, among other players, you may only favor your real friend in the game. At the *player* level, gamers interpret what is going on under the rules of the game. For example, you may regard your friend as an enemy under the rules of the game. At the *character* level, gamers interpret what is going on in the game world with the knowledge available in the game world. For example, in analog fantasy role-playing games, although participants as persons may acknowledge the enemy's physical location, as characters, they may not know where the enemy is until they encounter the enemy in the game. Fine explains that players may rapidly down key or up key while they are playing the game or speaking about the game. Players may switch between different selves throughout the gameplay, yet they may also stay at one level when they are engaged in the game. Players may pretend not to know about the other levels (e.g., they may choose to do something as the character even if they know it is a dangerous action as the player) or they may demonstrate knowledge of the other levels.

Fine also discusses self-playing and role-playing within gameplay. Fine notes that players can be divided into two categories: players who role-play by playing as the characters assigned to them, and players who self-play by playing as they would in the real world. Role-players may dismiss their own characteristics to act and think as if they are the characters in the game. Self-players may play themselves regardless of the traits of the characters. Identification and role-distancing are also discussed as they play an important role in how participants behave in the game and deal with the consequences. For example, by distancing oneself from the role, one can avoid feeling too depressed about failure like the death of the character in the game, so they can still enjoy playing.

EMPATHY IN GAMES

In order for a person to feel empathy or exhibit prosocial behavior, one needs another person. Who are "the others" in games? For example, in multiplayer online games, there are other characters in the game world and other players behind computer screens, connected by a network. Also, there are characters controlled by a computer. Despite its significance, the current research will not differentiate the other player (human) and his or her character (the virtual character), because the focus is on the difference between human-controlled characters and computer-controlled characters.

Prosocial behavior is a social behavior that requires a recipient. In games, that recipient is a character. To help other characters in the game for reasons other than extrinsic motivations such as goals or rewards, players should feel that they want to help. One of the factors that may encourage such a feeling is empathy towards characters. Empathy is one of the main motives of prosocial behavior in the real world. Similarly, in games, if players feel empathy toward characters, they would want to help them, and it may affect their priorities that influence the decision to help.

Empathy is also an important topic in game studies. In previous studies, empathy has been considered as a factor that induces engagement in playing games. Studies on player immersion or engagement explore empathy as a part of involvement in the game. De Kort, Iisselsteijn, and Poels (2007) consider empathy as a subscale of the Social Presence Gaming Questionnaire. In their classification of game engagement, Calleja (2007), and Ermi and Mayra (2005) include affective involvement or imaginative immersion, which concern players' emotional states toward others, affecting the gameplay experience. There are various studies regarding empathy in games and its relationship to prosocial behavior. For example, Happ, Melzer, and Steffgen (2014) examined how empathy toward an in-game character that is provoked prior to the gameplay by means of a text and a video clip affected player behavior after the gameplay. Although consideration was given to player behavior outside the game and not in the game, the study suggests that player empathy toward a virtual character may affect player behavior.

Since prosocial games encourage prosocial behavior in players, further in-depth studies on the factors related to prosocial player behavior must be conducted to promote the positively effective use of games. The following research aims to provide an initial model of the process of prosocial behavior in games. To this end, it examines prosocial behavior in games from two aspects: in-game situations and players' internal processes. Specifically, it will observe the cognitive process of players' interpretations of gameplay; and clarify the relationship between prosocial behavior in games and the frames of meaning with regard to players' interpretations and motives.

THE COGNITIVE ASPECT OF PLAYER BEHAVIOR IN GAMES

Using Fine's perspective on role-playing in games, this study investigates how players interpret what is going on in the game while playing *Terraria* (2011), a 2D sandbox game developed by Re-Logic, in an attempt to discuss how it affects the relationship of the participants with in-game characters and their behavior toward the characters. A two-participant case study was conducted to identify the kinds of frames of meaning that were adopted by the participant-players during gameplay and their relationship with players' interpretations and behaviors. The cognitive processes of participants were examined using the think-aloud protocol during gameplays and in the follow-up interviews.

In the think-aloud protocols and interviews, players' expressions revealed the different frames they adopted during gameplay. They thought aloud mostly about what is happening in the game from the character's perspective. However, on some occasions, they appeared to be aware of the real world. While speaking from the character level in the game world, players referred to the time and place of the game world, or the narrative setting of the game. While speaking from the player level in the real world, they referred to what is going on in the game from the meta-character level, in terms of the character's capabilities or where the character can go according to the rules of the game. Also, they sometimes talked about what they are doing or can do as a player in the real-world setting. Physical constraints such as the ability to rapidly press a button were mentioned during gameplay. From the person level, players talked about themselves in the real-world setting; however, talking from the person level was rarely observed. Players also switched from one frame to another in a short time. They quickly switched frames to interpret what was going on during gameplay, which is consistent with previous findings on coaching behavior of game players (Harrop, Gibbs, & Carter, 2013). For example, one participant said, "fourteen minutes have passed (since the beginning of the play). It is becoming dark." At first, she was referring to the time in real life and then to the time of day in the game world. Also, a few minutes later she said, "I wonder what time it is now. That is why I need more silver (to make a watch)." The other participant said, "I want iron. Making ingots with iron and making tools with them, and fighting monsters with those, and then more digging, is the theory of this game (what you are supposed to do), I think." While the participant might be talking about what she wanted to do as a character, she was aware of what the game expects the players to do.

Each participant developed a different kind of relationship with their characters and other characters. Participants were similar in the way that they distanced themselves from the character according to their needs as observed in their reaction to the death of their characters. However, they empathized differently with other characters. Participant A mentioned in the interview that she empathized with other characters during gameplay, sometimes with the other PC and at other times with NPCs. Participant B did not appear to empathize with other characters at all. She seemed to avoid contact with them. She stated that she first thought other NPCs were fellow PCs, so she tried not to interact with them. She seemed to regard other characters as utilities for success in the game.

Regarding prosocial behavior, Participant A tried to save an NPC from a monster's attack in the earlier part of the play. In the later part of the play, such behavior was not evident. When asked about the motives of the behavior in the earlier part and why she stopped helping the NPC, the participant replied that she initially tried to help the NPC because she thought that NPCs could not fight for themselves. She thought that she had to help to keep them alive, which she thought was required to continue the game. However, once she learned that NPCs could attack other characters to protect themselves, she stopped helping. When the participants were asked what they would do if they found out that a character was seeking an item they possessed. The details of the character (e.g., whether it was a PC or NPC) were not specified. Both participants prioritized their personal needs. If they did not urgently need item and the item could be found with little effort, they were willing to give the item to the character requesting it. If the narrative of the game depended on their choices, e.g., if it was necessary to give up the item to proceed with the game, they were willing to give the item away regardless of their priorities. No other aspects, such as how much the other character needed the item, were mentioned.

It seems that prosocial behaviors in games are closely related to players' goals and priorities. In real life, personal goals and priorities influence prosocial actions; however, emotional responses such as empathy are considered the main motive of the antecedent prosocial behaviors that are antecedent to other motives. In games, a player's goal may be the main motive underlying many behaviors, prosocial or not. In this study, the question's focusing on the decision to give away an item or not might have provoked the participants to focus on the rules as players. If the focus were on details such as what kind of character needs the item, their interpretations might have been different. According to Fine, when gamers adopt the player level, they are more concerned about the rules of the game rather than the role-playing aspect of the game.

Based on the study results, it can be assumed that players' in-game behaviors are affected by the frames of meaning they adopt. Specifically, the frames of meaning affect the interpretation of situational contexts in games. Different interpretations may invoke different emotional or cognitive responses and accordingly affect a player's behavior. As for prosocial behavior, how a player perceives the recipients of prosocial behavior, his or her relationship with the recipient, may invoke different responses. It was revealed during the interviews that if participants are aware of gains and losses, they will be concerned more about their priorities as players. However, gameplay may induce empathy toward the recipient, or it may induce a feeling of obligation. Players would help in either case, yet the underlying motives would be different (Figure 1).

When examining the mechanism of player behavior in games, it is important to look at intention and motives. Fine's perspective may explain the different effects on or behaviors of players in games. It is also helpful in explaining the negative experiences of gameplay. For example, players interpreting from different levels, where the rules are not shared with other participants, may result in conflicts such as trolling. Further research is necessary to expand the discussion.

Figure 1. How same behavior may result from different motives

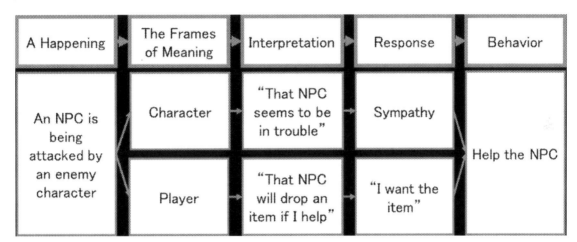

THE PROCESS OF PROSOCIAL BEHAVIOR IN GAMES

This survey study was conducted to observe the motives of prosocial behaviors and their relationship with the frames of meaning adopted by players. Previous research based on social cognitive theory demonstrates that depictions in games may affect player behavior. However, there are mixed opinions about the effects of games on players (e.g., discussions on violence in games, Ferguson, 2015; Boxer, Groves, & Docherty, 2015). In Study 1, it was posited that all six different kinds of prosocial behavior that are observed in the real world were depicted in popular games, their relationship with prosocial tendencies was found to be only partially significant, and their effects were not significant. A possible explanation for this is that the meaning of prosocial behavior depicted or exhibited by players in games is different for each player. Considering from the player's perspective, a prosocial behavior may either be an altruistic behavior motivated by empathy or an egoistic behavior driven by rules and goals of the game. Furthermore, as discussed in Study 2-1, depending on the adopted frame, interpretations of the same situation may invoke different emotional or cognitive responses in players. In other words, the motives of prosocial behavior in a game world may depend on how players interpret the situation and the goals of the game. This study looks at how frames of meaning influence motives of prosocial behaviors in games. With the aim to clarify the relationship between the frames adopted for interpretation and the motives of prosocial behaviors in the game, the survey conducted focused on the role of empathy, which is considered as the main motive of prosocial behaviors and compared how it worked for players who adopt the player-frame versus the character-frame.

To clarify how empathy relates to prosocial behaviors exhibited in a game, this study focuses on the frames of meaning adopted by players and their relation to empathy toward other characters and other motives of prosocial behaviors. In addition, the study investigates differences in prosocial behaviors toward non-player characters (NPCs), player characters (PCs), and a person, to see how differently a situation is interpreted by those who adopt the player-frame versus the character-frame. Following hypotheses were proposed:

Firstly, since players who mainly play as characters (hereafter, **character-players**) base their interpretations on the game world, they would perceive NPCs as social agents. However, those who play as players (hereafter, **player-players**) would perceive NPCs as virtual beings. The level of empathy toward NPCs would differ between the two groups of players. Specifically, character-players would be more empathetic toward NPCs than player-players. Character-players would perceive PCs in the same way as NPCs. However, for player-players, an NPC would be considered a virtual being in the game, while a PC would be perceived as the other human player in the real world. PCs would be considered as "others" in terms of social agents. Thus, the level of empathy toward a PC would not differ between character-players and player-players.

Since NPCs and PCs are perceived in a similar way by character-players, their levels of empathy toward a PC or NPC would not be different. However, player-players would perceive NPCs and PCs differently. That is, NPCs would be perceived as virtual beings and PCs as human beings. Therefore, their levels of empathy toward NPCs and PCs, and their motives of prosocial behaviors would differ. That is, player-players would be more empathetic toward PCs than NPCs.

H1-1: The level of empathy of character-players toward NPCs would be higher than that of player-players, but the level of empathy toward PCs would not differ between character-players and player-players.

H1-2: Character-players would have the same level of empathy toward NPCs and PCs, but player-players would have a higher level of empathy towards PCs.

Secondly, some prosocial behavior in games would be motivated by empathy. However, character-players would be more likely than player-players to empathize with and help other characters in games, because they are more aware of what is going on in the game world than they are of the game rules. Also, their motives would be comparatively similar for prosocial behaviors toward NPCs and PCs, for they are perceived similarly. On the other hand, player-players would be more likely to have goal-oriented motives for helping characters in games, because they are more aware of the game rules than they are of the game world. However, player-players would have different motives for helping NPCs and PCs because they perceive NPCs and PCs differently.

H2-1: Some prosocial behavior in games would be motivated by empathy.

H2-2: Motives of prosocial behaviors would differ between character-players and player-players in both situations of helping NPC and PC.

H2-3: The similarity between the motives of prosocial behaviors of character-players toward both NPCs and PCs would be higher compared to that of player-players.

Thirdly, the frequency of prosocial behavior would not differ depending on whether the character being helped is a PC or NPC, or on the frame of meaning that players adopt. Since prosocial behavior in games could also be motivated by factors such as game design and gameplay in addition to empathy, the frequency of prosocial behavior would not differ.

H3: The frequencies of prosocial behavior in games would not differ between different types of recipients of prosocial behaviors nor between different frames of meaning that players adopt.

Lastly, since empathy is considered to be an important motive of prosocial behaviors in the real world, and since game elements such as rules, stories, and rewards drive different behaviors in the game, motives of prosocial behaviors would be different in games than those in the real world.

H4: The motives of prosocial behaviors in games would be different in games than those in the real world, and the effects of empathy would be stronger in the real world.

These five hypotheses were tested through a survey.

H1-1 and H1-2 regarding the levels of empathy were not supported. It was expected that the level of empathy of character-players toward NPCs would be higher than that of player-players and that character-players and player-players would have the same level of empathy toward PCs. Also, it was expected that the level of empathy of character-players toward NPCs and PCs would not be different, and the level of empathy of player-players toward PCs would be higher than that toward NPCs. However, the levels of all three types of empathy toward NPCs and PCs were not different for character-players and player-players. In comparing the level of empathy for different types of recipients of prosocial behaviors, only the level of cognitive empathy differed between that toward NPCs and PCs for both character-players and player-players. The cognitive empathy levels of both character-players and player-players toward PCs were significantly higher than those toward NPCs. However, levels of emotional empathy and personal distress did not differ between NPCs or PCs, nor between character-players and player-players.

H2-1, which stated prosocial behaviors in games would be motivated by empathy, was partially supported. Emotional empathy and personal distress were predictors of prosocial behavior toward NPCs and PCs, while cognitive empathy was not. H2-2 and H2-3 were supported. It was expected that character-players and player-players' motives of prosocial behaviors toward NPCs would be different. Figure 2 shows the results of the correspondence analysis of the responses of character-players in the NPC situation ("character-NPC"), player-players in the NPC situation ("player-NPC"), character-players in the PC situation ("character-PC"), and player-players in the PC situation ("player-PC"). For example, "character-NPC" in the upper left quadrant indicates where the responses of character-players in the NPC situation are located in reference to the words in blue in the same quadrant. The two axes divide the types of recipient of prosocial behaviors and the frames of meaning. The first axis delineates the situations where the recipient is an NPC (on the left) from where it is a PC (on the right). The second axis separates character-players (on the top) from player-players (on the bottom). The distance between the responses of character-players on prosocial behaviors toward NPCs and PCs is closer than that of player-players, which indicates that the responses of character-players are comparatively similar in the two situations while the responses of player-players are comparatively distinct in the two situations.

Figure 2. The results of the correspondence analysis of responses regarding helping in games

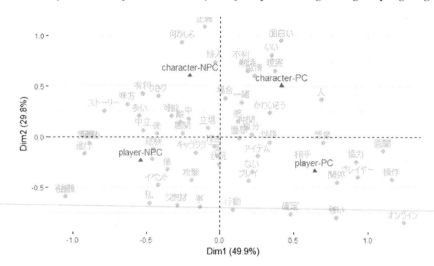

In the situation where an NPC were being attacked, the responses of character-players frequently included words such as "ally," "story," and "advantageous" which indicate that a reward was expected, as well as "empathize" which indicates an emotional response. Similarly, in the situation where players were to help PCs, the motives of character-players included words such as "emotion" and "sympathetic" which indicate empathy toward the character, as well as "expectation" which indicates an expectation of rewards or reciprocity. When player-players were to help an NPC, the motives included phrases such as "event" and "scenario" which indicate that player-players were concerned about advancing in the game; however, in the situation where players were to help a PC, the responses of player-players included phrases such as "the other person," "relationship," and "cooperation" which indicate that they were concerned about the other players.

The frames of meaning moderated the effect of emotional empathy on prosocial behavior. There was a significant difference between the regression coefficients of emotional empathy of character-players and player-players toward NPCs ($t(194) = 2.471$, $p < .05$). The regression coefficients of emotional empathy were higher for character-players. The multivariate logistic regression model (Table 1, Figure 3) supports a mixed effect of the frames of meaning and emotional empathy. The main effects of emotional empathy and the dummy variable indicate that whether players are character-players or player-players, the greater their emotional empathy toward NPCs, the more they demonstrate helpful actions. Furthermore, player-players are more likely to help. However, the level of emotional empathy of character-players has more of an impact on prosocial behavior than those of player-players. As seen in Figure 3a, most character-players with low emotional empathy responded that they would not help, and those with high emotional empathy responded that they would help. Figure 3b shows that most player-players responded that they would help regardless of their level of empathy, so the probability of helping, as expected by the logistic regression model, is high (over 50%) even when the level of emotional empathy is the lowest. On the other hand, not all player-players with high emotional empathy responded that they would help.

Table 1. Coefficients of logistic regression on helping behavior toward NPCs

N = 198	Multivariate model with an interaction variable	
	β	95% CI
(Intercept)	-3.328**	[-5.44, -1.62]
	(0.957)	
Level of interpretation	3.025**	[0.98, 5.37]
	(1.105)	
Emotional empathy	1.7086**	[1.01, 2.62]
	(0.404)	
Level of interpretation × Emotional empathy	-1.1155*	[-2.10, -0.30]
	(0.452)	
Nagelkerke R-sq.	.291	
AIC	184.45	
Chi-square	42.876**	
Note Inside the brackets are standard errors. *p < .05, **p < .01.		

Figure 3. The difference in the impact of emotional empathy on prosocial behavior between (a) character-players and (b) player-players. The red lines indicate how the logistic regression models expect the probabilities of helping to change as the levels of empathy change.

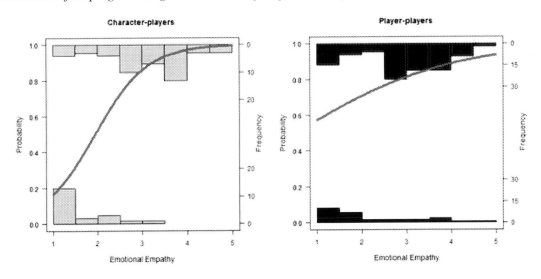

In the hypothetical situation where a PC were being attacked, different kinds of empathy motivated prosocial behavior of character-players and player-players. The helping behaviors of both character-players and player-players were motivated by empathy toward PCs. However, there is a difference between the most fitted models of prosocial behaviors toward PCs. The level of emotional empathy predicts prosocial behavior for both groups. Furthermore, for player-players, less personal distress in a situation means that they are more likely to help; however, a low level of personal distress does not predict prosocial behavior for character-players. The multivariable model demonstrates the main effect of emotional empathy, which means that whether players are character-players or player-players, the greater their emotional empathy, the more they are likely to help. Regarding the interaction effect of the frames of meaning and personal distress, personal distress alone does not predict helpful actions; however, player-players with low personal distress are more likely to help.

H3 stated that the frequency of prosocial behavior in games would not depend on the types of recipients of prosocial behavior and the frames of meaning that players adopt. Most participants would help in all situations whether they are character-players, player-players, or others. The hypothesis was supported as the proportion of those responded that they would help did not differ between the participants of different frames of meaning (Fisher's exact test, $p > 0.22$) and also between different situations, except for the case where there were more player-players who did not to help a person but an NPC or PC than who helped person but not NPC or PC (McNemar's Chi-squared test, $p < .05$).

H4 stated that the motives of prosocial behaviors in games and in the real world would be different and that the effects of empathy would be stronger in the real world. This hypothesis was supported. Figure 4 shows the relationship for each situation and the words used in the responses of helpers. The figure clearly shows that the responses on the motives to help are different for each situation. The first axis divides the game world situation (on the left) and the real-world situation (on the right), and the second axis divides the kind of recipient of prosocial behavior—PCs at the top and NPCs at the bottom. For the situation where NPCs were attacked, responses for the reason to help frequently included words such as "unfolding," "progress," and "event." For the situation where PCs were being attacked, responses included words such as "cooperation," "relationship," and "sympathetic." For the real-world situation where a person were attacked, responses included words such as "ignore," "regret," and "police."

Regarding how empathy motivated prosocial behavior, cognitive empathy does not predict prosocial behavior in any situation. Emotional empathy and personal distress predict prosocial behavior in the real-world situation for all kinds of players. Personal distress predicts prosocial behavior in the real-world situation only for character-players, whereas for player-players, it predicts prosocial behavior toward PCs in the game world situation and prosocial behavior toward a person in the real-world situation.

Figure 4. The results of the correspondence analysis of responses for different situations

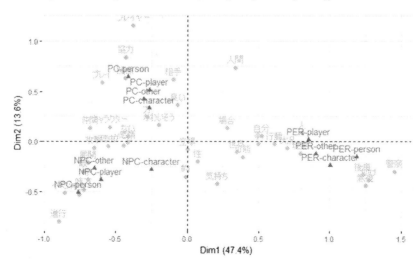

This study aimed to clarify how empathy and other factors motivate prosocial behaviors in games in relation to frames of meaning. Although frames of meaning have no effect on the level of empathy, it does affect how different types of empathy motivate prosocial behaviors of a game player. Frames of meaning may not directly affect how players respond to a certain situation, but they do affect how the response works in motivating a certain behavior. Emotional empathy toward NPCs has more impact on prosocial behavior of character-players than that of player-players. Personal distress toward PCs has no impact on prosocial behavior of character-players but impacts the prosocial behavior of player-players. Emotional empathy and personal distress toward people in the real world have an impact on prosocial behaviors of all kinds of players.

Character-players' prosocial behaviors toward PCs is similar to their prosocial behaviors toward NPCs. Contrastingly, player-players' prosocial behaviors toward PCs is similar to their prosocial behaviors toward people in real life in terms of the underlying motives. It seems that they draw lines between what they perceive as a character in the game and a person in the real world differently than character-players do (Figure 5). The figure shows the boundary between what is a game and what is not in terms of players' perspectives. The borderline between the real world and the game world is defined by a player's interpretation of the game based on frames of meaning.

Figure 5. The difference in the perception of the game world. The border between the game world and the real world differs for player-players and character-players

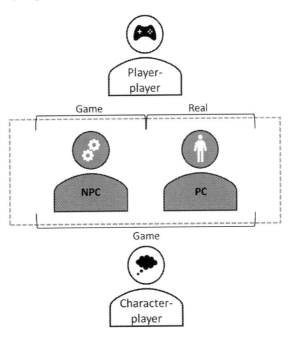

It is similar to the model proposed by Fine (1983), yet different in its structure. Fine tried to explain the frames having an embedding structure in which a character level is the innermost level, and a person level is the outermost level. However, the frames seem rather parallel, and players may directly adopt the character frame without necessarily going through the player frame. I propose a model to examine the game world and its boundary. This model challenges the current view of the boundary of the game world and the real world by considering players' perspectives of the game world. The model attempts to integrate existing views on the boundary between game worlds and the real world, to provide new insights for future studies.

THE MODEL OF PROCESS OF PROSOCIAL BEHAVIOR IN GAMES

Figure 6 shows the model of the process of prosocial behavior in games from the perspective of the player. NPCs requesting players to find an item for them is a common request for prosocial behavior in the genre of role-playing games. For example, a mayor of a town may ask the player to bring a herb that can be found in the dangerous forest near the town, because he needs to prepare a certain medicine for his wife (but he has to stay home to take care of his wife.) Whether a player perceives the situation as an earnest request by a man in the game world or as a part of the repertoire of the genre depends on how the player interprets the game. The interpretation also affects how the player's response to the situation affects their subsequent behaviors. The player may feel emotional empathy for the mayor, or the player may feel obliged to accept the request expecting that this will advance the story of the game. It is likely that the player will help, and the behavior may be motivated by emotional empathy or expectation of progress in the game. The model clearly demonstrates that observing the content of games is not enough, and the player's perspective is also important in examining player behavior in games.

Figure 6. The process of prosocial behavior in games

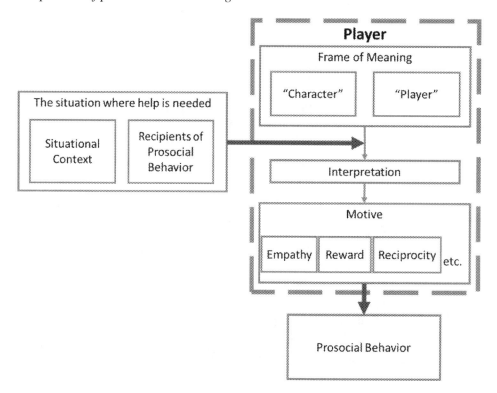

Figure 7. What happens between game and player during gameplay

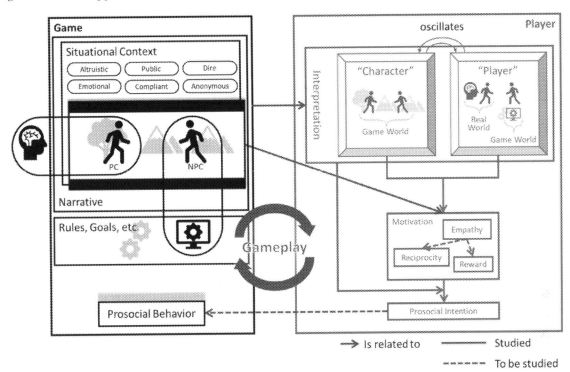

Figure 7 shows what happens when a player plays a game based on the model, providing the answer to the question presented at the very beginning of the research. When the player plays the game, s/he will adopt a frame of meaning to interpret what is happening in the game. During gameplay, the player will encounter a scene where prosocial behavior may be exhibited. The prosocial behavior may fall into one of the six categories according to the situation: prosocial behavior encouraged by other people or characters watching (public); prosocial behavior when no one is watching (anonymous); prosocial behavior in an emotionally provoking situation (emotional); prosocial behavior in a dire situation (dire); prosocial behavior requested by other people or characters (compliant); and prosocial behavior where no reward is expected (altruistic). Also, the characters involved in the scene may be PCs or NPCs. Behind the scenes, there is a narrative that leads to the specific scene, and game mechanics like rules and goals that afford the behavior of characters in the game. Whether the situational contexts are interpreted as is or otherwise depends on the frame of meaning adopted by a player. The frame determines how a player perceives the game and the space in which the rules apply, and it affects the motivational process of prosocial behavior in the game world. The player who adopts the "character" frame may see the game as a narrative and perceive both PCs and NPCs as a part of the game world. The player who adopts the "player" frame may see the game as a system of game mechanics and players. Such a player may regard PCs as another player in the real world and NPCs as being controlled by the game rules. The player may switch between the two frames. The interpretation based on the adopted frame affects the motivation of prosocial behavior. Some motivational factors of prosocial behavior may be directly affected by the game, such as empathy, an immediate response to the situation. However, how empathy or other motivational factors lead to the prosocial intention is affected by the interpretation. Although it is not explicitly studied in the current research, the prosocial intention may lead to the prosocial behavior in the game, affecting the state of the game. Gameplay is constant interaction between the game and the player, each affecting the state of the other which distinguishes digital games from other entertainment media.

CONCLUSION

The research in this chapter addressed several problems of previous studies on digital games and their effects. First, the empirical studies were based on a concrete definition of prosocial behavior, with a multidimensional perspective, and content analysis was based on this definition. Also, the current research looked at what players actually do in games not what they are designed to do. Furthermore, it contributed to previous studies by looking at prosocial behavior between a player character and other player characters, and between a player character and non-player characters.

The multidimensional perspective on prosocial behavior in games adopted in this research has implications for studies on the effects of games, for it clarifies the mechanism of positive effects of the depiction of prosocial behavior in games. A similar view may apply to studies on the negative effects of the depictions of violence and sexual expressions in games. The current research also has implications for studies on communication in virtual environments. Although limited to looking at prosocial behavior in the game world, this research has implications for prosocial behavior studies, as prosocial behavior in games are not completely different from prosocial behavior in the real world in terms of process and motives. Regarding practical implications, the discussions here may be used to educate young people and their parents about game use at home. The discussions also have implications for game development.

REFERENCES

Adachi, P. J. C., & Willoughby, T. (2011). The effect of violent video games on aggression: Is it more than just the violence? *Aggression and Violent Behavior, 16*(1), 55–62. doi:10.1016/j.avb.2010.12.002

Bar-Tal, D., & Raviv, A. (1982). A cognitive-learning model of helping behavior development: Possible implications and applications. In N. Eisenberg (Ed.), *The development of prosocial behavior* (pp. 199–217). Academic Press. doi:10.1016/B978-0-12-234980-5.50013-4

Bateson, G. (1955). A theory of play and fantasy. *Psychiatric Research Reports, 2*, 39–51. PMID:13297882

Boxer, P., Groves, C. L., & Docherty, M. (2015). Video games do indeed influence children and adolescents' aggression, prosocial behavior, and academic performance: A clearer reading of Ferguson (2015). *Perspectives on Psychological Science, 10*(5), 671–673. doi:10.1177/1745691615592239 PMID:26386004

Bushman, B. J., & Anderson, C. A. (2002). Violent video games and hostile expectations: A test of the General Aggression Model. *Personality and Social Psychology Bulletin, 28*(12), 1679–1686. doi:10.1177/014616702237649

Caillois, R. (1990). *Man, play and games* (M. Tada & M. Tsukazaki, Trans.). Kodansha. (Original work published 1958)

Calleja, G. (2007). Revising immersion: A conceptual model for the analysis of digital game involvement. *Situated Play, Proceedings of DiGRA 2007 Conference*, 83-90.

Carlo, G., Hausmann, A., Chritiansen, S., & Randall, B. A. (2003). Sociocognitive and behavioral correlates of a measure of prosocial tendencies for adolescents. *The Journal of Early Adolescence, 23*(1), 107–134. doi:10.1177/0272431602239132

Chambers, J. H., & Ascione, F. R. (1987). The effects of prosocial and aggressive videogames on children's donating and helping. *The Journal of Genetic Psychology, 148*(4), 499–505. doi:10.1080/00221 325.1987.10532488 PMID:3437274

Coyne, S. M., & Smith, N. J. (2014). Sweetness on the screen: A multidimensional view of prosocial behavior in media. In L. M. Padilla-Walker & G. Carlo (Eds.), *Prosocial development: A multidimensional approach* (pp. 156–177). Oxford University Press. doi:10.1093/acprof:oso/9780199964772.003.0008

Csikszentmihalyi, M. (1990). *Flow: The psychology of optimal experience*. Harper & Row.

De Kort, Y. A. W., Ijsselsteijn, W. A., & Poels, K. (2007). Digital games as social presence technology: Development of the Social Presence in Gaming Questionnaire (SPGQ). *Presence (Cambridge, Mass.), 2007*, 1–9.

Dietz, T. L. (1998). An examination of violence and gender role portrayals in video games: Implications for gender socialization and aggressive behavior. *Sex Roles, 38*(5/6), 425–442. doi:10.1023/A:1018709905920

Dill, K. E., & Dill, J. C. (1998). Video game violence: A review of the empirical literature. *Aggression and Violent Behavior, 3*(4), 407–428. doi:10.1016/S1359-1789(97)00001-3

Egenfeldt-Nielsen, S., Smith, J. H., & Tosca, S. P. (2013). *Understanding video games: the essential introduction* (2nd ed.). Routledge. doi:10.4324/9780203116777

Eisenberg, N. (Ed.). (1982). *The development of prosocial behavior*. Academic Press.

Ermi, L., & Mäyrä, F. (2005). Fundamental components of the gameplay experience: Analysing immersion. *Proceedings of DiGRA 2005 Conference: Changing Views – Worlds in Play.*

Ferguson, C. J. (2015). Do Angry Birds make for angry children? A meta-analysis of video game influences on children's and adolescents' aggression, mental health, prosocial behavior, and academic performance. *Perspectives on Psychological Science, 10*(5), 646–666. doi:10.1177/1745691615592234 PMID:26386002

Fine, G. A. (1983). *Shared fantasy: Role-playing games as social worlds*. The University of Chicago Press.

Funk, J. B., Baldacci, H. B., Pasold, T., & Baumgardner, J. (2004). Violence exposure in real-life, video games, television, movies, and the internet: Is there desensitization? *Journal of Adolescence, 27*(1), 23–39. doi:10.1016/j.adolescence.2003.10.005 PMID:15013258

Gentile, D. A., Anderson, C. A., Yukawa, S., Ihori, N., Saleem, M., Lim, K. M., Shibuya, A., Liau, A. K., Khoo, A., Bushman, B. J., Huesmann, L. R., & Sakamoto, A. (2009). The effects of prosocial video games on prosocial behaviors: International evidence from correlational, longitudinal, and experimental studies. *Personality and Social Psychology Bulletin, 35*(6), 752–763. doi:10.1177/0146167209333045 PMID:19321812

Goffman, E. (1974). *Frame analysis: An essay on the organization of experience*. Harper & Row.

Greitemeyer, T., & Osswald, S. (2009). Prosocial video games reduce aggressive cognitions. *Journal of Experimental Social Psychology, 45*(4), 896–900. doi:10.1016/j.jesp.2009.04.005

Greitemeyer, T., & Osswald, S. (2010). Effects of prosocial video games on prosocial behavior. *Journal of Personality and Social Psychology, 98*(2), 211–221. doi:10.1037/a0016997 PMID:20085396

Happ, C., Melzer, A., & Steffgen, G. (2014). Like the good or bad guy—Empathy in antisocial and prosocial games. *Psychology of Popular Media Culture, 4*(2), 80–96. doi:10.1037/ppm0000021

Harrop, M., Gibbs, M., & Carter, M. (2013). The pretence awareness contexts and oscillating nature of coaching frames. *Proceedings of DiGRA 2013 Conference: DeFragging Game Studies.*

Hawley, P. H. (2014). Evolution, prosocial behavior, and altruism: A roadmap for understanding where the proximate meets the ultimate. In L. M. Padilla-Walker & G. Carlo (Eds.), *Prosocial development: A multidimensional approach* (pp. 43–69). Oxford University Press. doi:10.1093/acprof:oso/9780199964772.003.0003

Huizinga, J. (1950). *Homo ludens, a study of the play-element in culture*. Oxford, UK: Roy. (Original work published 1938)

Juul, J. (2005). Half-real: Video games between real rules and fictional worlds. Cambridge, MA: The MIT Press.

Katada, H. (2019, March 1). *Interview*. Retrieved from https://www.famitsu.com/news/201903/01172506.html

McGonigal, J. (2015). *SuperBetter: A revolutionary approach to getting stronger, happier, braver and more resilient*. Penguin.

Payne, H. E., Moxley, V. B. A., & MacDonald, E. (2015). Health Behavior Theory in physical activity game apps: A content analysis. *JMIR Serious Games, 3*(2), e4. doi:10.2196/games.4187 PMID:26168926

Phelps, J. (2018, March 8). Trump turns spotlight on violent video games in wake of Parkland shootings. *ABC News*. Retrieved from https://abcnews.go.com/Politics/trump-turns-spotlight-violent-video-games-wake-parkland/story?id=53593714

Salen, K., & Zimmerman, E. (2004). *Rules of play: Game design fundamentals*. The MIT Press.

Thompson, K. M., & Haninger, K. (2001). Violence in E-rated video games. *Medicine and the Media, 286*(5), 591–598. PMID:11476663

World Health Organization. (2018, September). *Gaming disorder*. Retrieved from https://www.who.int/features/qa/gaming-disorder/en/

Section 8
Game–Based Learning: Code and Play

Chapter 44
Students as Gamers:
Design, Code, and Play

Polat Şendurur
Ondokuz Mayıs University, Turkey

Emine Sendurur
ⓘ https://orcid.org/0000-0002-0340-6378
Ondokuz Mayis University, Turkey

ABSTRACT

Games have been considered as an important part of child development and can roughly be defined as fictional structures with certain rules to be followed to achieve certain goals. Modern games (ex. Minecraft) sometimes require quite sophisticated skills to move on, and these skills mostly match up with 21st century skills. From this perspective, this chapter tries to explain the relationship between 21st century skills and game playing skills, the design thinking approach where students are game designers, coders, and players.

INTRODUCTION

Games have been considered as entertainment activities of any age in addition to being an important tool for child development. Games can roughly be defined as fictional structures with certain rules, which are required to be followed in order to achieve certain goals within various settings. Games sometimes can serve as formal or informal tools of learning. The ways games are integrated into educational context vary. Such integrations might refer to either an instructional methodology (such as game-based learning) or an instructional material (such as a digital game with curriculum-based goals) or just a cognitive tool (such as interdisciplinary activities embedded into games). Serious games, educational games, game-based pedagogy, gamification, and many other terms have emerged in the literature related to the subject of games in education. Games within the scope of education might not be defined in a unidimensional way, because there are many aspects to be considered. From a broader perspective, the learning outcomes, the

DOI: 10.4018/978-1-7998-7271-9.ch044

sequence of content, the construction of content with game elements, and the relatedness of the cover story can be listed as the main dimensions of adopting games for educational purposes. Although there is not a universal definition of educational games, the following features can be listed to define the term (Shute, Rieber, & van Eck, 2014; Whitton, 2014):

- Conflict or challenge
- Rules of engagement
- Particular goals or outcomes to achieve
- Progression and rewards
- Continuous feedback
- Interaction within the environment
- Compelling storyline
- Separate from the real world
- Played with or against others.

The main aspects of game theory remain the same with complementary educational tools such as well-defined instructional goals based on curricular needs. In the learner-centered paradigm of instruction, games may serve as the main tools of formal learning in addition to being complementary ones. The construction of knowledge and skills through the active involvement is one of the main notions of constructivist paradigm. Since games and active involvement are closely related, this relationship can make the computer science education stronger. Having its motivation from this assumption, the power of digital games will be discussed within the integration boundaries as well as providing the historical evolution of games in education. The potential benefits of digital games while designing, coding, and playing them will be explained in relation to computer science.

BACKGROUND

The history of games in education is not independent from paradigms of education and learning. In the industrial age, automated tasks were highly in demand. In order to improve the knowledge and skills, intense drill-and-practice was required. The behavioristic approach had a specific emphasis on the importance of associations and repetitions to memorize and form the observable behavior. This phenomenon can be observed in early educational game formats. The street games or early educational games did not require specific technological devices as means of playing, but the introduction of such interactive devices as computers changed the way games are played. During the 60s and 70s, early digital games including Spacewar and Pong had become popular, but not within the educational context. Pac-Man, Tetris, Super Mario and Quake were the iconic digital games of the 80s and 90s (Kirriemuir, 2006). During the 80s, many influential advancements had introduced such as PCs. Those were the times of early educational games called edutainment (Whitton, 2014). Token economies, reward, punishment, and reinforcement are the main notions of behaviorism, and they were prevalent in early educational games. They generally had linear structures with well-defined problems and strict solutions/answers requiring memorization or basic operations. The triggers of motivation were generally external, so that the integration of games in education was at the control of teachers.

As the mobile devices became smarter and the Internet became faster and affordable, the number of digital games dramatically increased. Today, the platforms offer variety of games including the educational ones. Moreover, the interaction with games have been evolved into different forms such as playing the with the whole body via augmented reality (AR) technology. Since the 60s, the game industry has been enhancing its opportunities through shifting the focus on different fields, and the education is one of them. According to Egenfeldt-Nielsen (2006), there are three milestones of educational evolution of games:

1.   Edutainment,
2.   Commercial entertainment, and
3.   Research-based educational games.

The edutainment is the combination of education and entertainment, and it is educational but still conveys the aspects of games for fun. On the other hand, they were produced by commercial firms. The researchers, who follow the trends closely, also produced educational games, which are based upon both scientific theories and practices. De Freitas (2018) divides this evolution (see Figure 1) into three periods:

- **Wave 1:** In its early periods, the educators tried to understand how to integrate games into learning situations. Many different definitions were created, and the line of research tried to integrate the game phenomenon into the educational context. There was a conflict between collaboration and competition.
- **Wave 2:** In this period, serious games came into the scene. The violence in commercial games was a hot topic among society. There was a conflict between the games played for fun and the games played not for fun. The 2000s can be called as the era of serious games. The increased research interest of certain fields including military and health brought about the changes in perceptions about the role of the games in education.
- **Wave 3:** In this period, with the advancement of technology, the integration into such different educational contexts as e-learning has become popular. The focus was on the design issues as well as the integration into different contexts of learning. (pp. 75-76).

Figure 1. Evolution of game integration

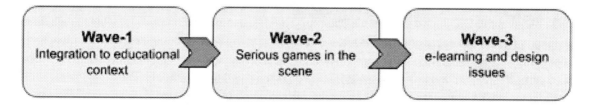

In the light of new Web technologies, especially Web 2.0 brought about new roles or users, who became much more competent since the introduction of Web 2.0 enabled lay people to produce content online, including the games. Scratch platform is one of the crucial Web 2.0 tools facilitating a wide range of content. The capabilities of Web have been developing through Web 3.0 and Web 4.0, which means the web became smarter, so did the games. Therefore, the Wave 3 seems very promising in terms of educational integration because the adaptive learning opportunities, authentic learning context, and rich virtual environments might contribute to the educational games.

The changes in the structure of educational games brought about the issue of integration. If a game is just used for the sake of including a game-based methodology, then it may fail (Gunter, Kenny, & Vick, 2008). The overall design of the educational game can completely become irrelevant from the pedagogical aspects. For example, a game called Math Missions Grades 3-5: The Amazing Arcade Adventure had poor integration of arcade game structure into math learning (Egenfeldt-Nielsen, 2006). Therefore, the genre or other features of game might not guarantee the improved learning. In other words, the way educators link the games and learning experiences might result in significant integration. Whitton (2014) classified these combinations as follows:

- Learning with entertainment games
- Learning with educational games
- Learning inspired by games
- Learning within games
- Learning about games
- Learning from games
- Learning through game creation
- Learning within the game communities (pp. 4-5).

The combinations proposed by Whitton (2014) was not domain-specific, but Shabalina, Malliarakis, Tomos, & Mozelius (2017) offered three perspectives of game-based learning in computer science regardless of any specific game type:

- Learning to program by playing games. Teachers or game developers create the game to be played by students to learn how to program (Shabalina et al., 2017). This perspective is not specific to computer science, i.e., math, languages, social studies, kindergarten, and many other fields benefit from this approach. The scenario changes according to the subject area but the structure of the game remains the same.
- Learning programming through game development. Teachers teach how to develop games, and students learn and develop games (Shabalina et al., 2017). This approach is specific to computer science because the students are required to experience certain stages of game development. Such recent tools as Scratch used for this approach have become user-friendly in terms of interfaces in comparison to text-based editors. For this approach, the design tools have become quite rich. There are many game engines providing rich libraries in certain game engines such as Unity.
- Learning to program by the development of games for learning programming. Teachers teach both programming and game development, so that students can develop their own games to be played either by themselves or other students like novice programmers (Shabalina et al., 2017). This approach is promising with regards to collaboration and peer teaching.

In a systematic review, Loras, Sindre, Trætteberg, and Aalberg (2022) reported two important variables in computer science education: (i) educational context and (ii) pedagogical context (see Figure 2). The review revealed that traditional approaches within campus environments are quite prevalent, and the integration of specific approaches are very limited in higher education, but this is not the case for

K-12 (Loras et al., 2022). In other words, the learner-centered paradigm in programming context became evident at the practice of K-12 level in comparison to higher education (see Figure 3). Especially, the introductory programming concepts might be appropriate for the practice of various instructional methods such as game-based learning. When the games are used in programming context, the utilization of text-based codes might be challenging due to the sophisticated structure. Instead, pseudo codes can help beginners in a game (Wong and Yatim, 2018). The abstractness of coding might require the concrete learning experiences, which might be hard to achieve through teacher-centered practices. That's why, the current paradigm values either tool-based or learner-centered approaches in programming instruction. Recent trends including AR practices, robotics, and visual programming might provide learners with much more tangible experiences. Such environments as Scratch have many enablers in terms of game-based practices. In addition to serving as an instructional methodology, certain aspects of games have been borrowed by other methods. For example, CS-Unplugged activities can consist of such aspects as game rules in combination of a scenario.

Figure 2. Educational context vs. pedagogical context in computer science education

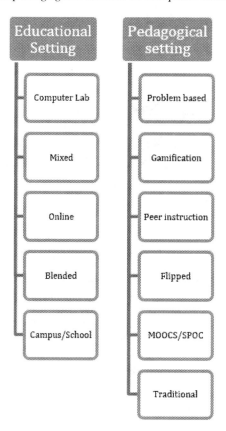

The current paradigm of education leads learners to create their own way of learning (Almeida & Simoes, 2019). The Internet, mobile devices, smart systems, and learning analytics make it easier to learn at their own pace with many alternative content. Today's learners are not the consumers of the content, instead they became the producers thanks to the advancements of Web 2.0. This phenomenon has also affected the way that games are adopted by learners. User-friendly tools welcome novice learners to develop their own games, programs, websites, and so on. For programming education, this means the inclusion of game-based learning that is free from advanced programming knowledge and skills

Figure 3. Paradigm shift in computer science education

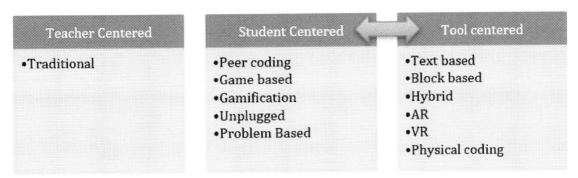

Constructivist approach provided with rich authentic experiences to make the learning meaningful. The design of educational games had been influenced from this paradigm, so the integration of real-world tasks and the triggers of intrinsic motivation had become observed within current games (Whitton, 2014). AR has an important role to create authentic environments. For learning how to code, the authenticity might be crucial because the overall process is an experience of problem solving. The dynamic nature of AR (Klopfer & Squire, 2008), the inclusion of real-time interaction (Azuma, 1997), and the opportunity for natural feedback (Milgram, Takemura, Utsumi, & Kishino, 1995) can be considered as the powerful features of AR. When combined with computer science education, the literature points to the complementary role of AR, but the limited number of resources such as applications or tools is still a barrier (Theodoropoulos & Lepouras, 2021).

The timeline of games in education shows epic trends. It can be concluded that the games in education moved from an isolated form through an integrated form with authentic experiences with technology enhanced practices. The integration of game into educational settings is not free from the game itself, i.e., the instructional design of a commercial game can be quite different from that of educational games. Moreover, the collaborative aspects of current games allow a different way of learning (peer learning / communities of practice / communities of learning / teamwork / collaboration, etc.). Live collaboration tools such as Discord contribute to the creation of these learning communities in informal settings, but in formal education, these issues are still untouched. Finally, there is an emerging paradigm of learning called connectivism. Unlike others, it explains learning as the connection process from various resources. Such games as Minecraft can be viewed as the reflections of this paradigm (Whitton, 2014).

21ST CENTURY SKILLS VS. GAME PLAYING SKILLS

Modern games such as Minecraft may require quite sophisticated skills to move on. The smart phones and other mobile devices have caused people to engage in digital activities regardless of time and place, and therefore the games have been involved into everyday routines of lay people. Existing literature have had a great focus on the potential adverse effects of games. On the other hand, game playing, as a daily routine, also has potential to contribute 21st century skills with research-based evidence. Computational thinking is a recent popular term since it refers to computer-like thinking skills, so that learners become proficient in problem solving. It is a key skill for both computer science education and daily problem solving (Threekunprapa & Yasri, 2020). Such critical 21st century skills as algorithmic thinking can be improved with the help of game-based pedagogy. For example, Stork (2020) reported the utilization of robots for creative thinking skills in combination with coding practices.

The developments in computer science, especially in programming, artificial intelligence (AI), visual computing, networking, and communication have led to the appearance of high-tech games with different genres. Players can find individual solutions to problems, collaborate with other players, and become a member of different communities while engaging in a game environment. For example, in Scratch platform, one might share his/her game with others, then s/he can see analytics and comments, and then explore other projects either to benefit or to comment/contribute. This phenomenon is clearly in line with 21st century skills such as collaboration, creation, communication, critical thinking (Battle for Kids, 2019).

The information age has been evolving into an advanced status. Although this new paradigm does not have a common name (digital age, wisdom age, etc.), there is a consensus on its characteristics. Unlike its predecessors, the available technology is smarter than ever thanks to machine learning, the Internet of Things, artificial intelligence, analytics, and connectedness. As a result, games have become smarter, too. The enhanced capabilities of data processing now enables much more personalized and adaptive experiences for learners including scaffolding via artificial intelligence (De Freitas, 2018). Higher order thinking skills have always been desired by educators, but in the current era it is very crucial because Google knows many things, which means rote memorization is less valuable than ever. Today, Bloom's revised taxonomy of cognitive domain nominated the highest cognitive skill as creativity (Krathwohl & Anderson, 2010). The games can trigger creativity as students design and develop their own games (Shabalina et al., 2017). Moreover, games can enhance computational thinking when designed in an adaptive manner (Hooshyar et al., 2021). Maker games, level development, artefact creation, and game building are among the activities triggering creativity (Whitton, 2014).

One challenge for educators to connect 21st century skills to game playing skills is about the current status of the educational system. The limitations about course hours, one-dimensional learning outcomes, economic factors, and one-teacher commanded learning environment can serve as barriers to educational games (Egenfeldt-Nielsen, 2006; Shabalina, 2017; Shute et al., 2014). Social, structural, and technological barriers can also affect the way of integration (Foster, 2020). For example, if students had restricted access to technological devices, then their game literacies or digital literacies might hinder the learning process. At that point, 21st century skills might become prerequisites. However, being digitally competent might not always guarantee benefitting from games in terms of learning. Collaboration is nominated as one of the key skills of this century, but it can become much more challenging for students while solving problems, completing missions, choosing among alternatives, developing strategies, and creating scenarios during the game-based pedagogies. A good game can enable the improvement of collaborative working skills (Shute et al., 2014).

Self-regulation is another key skill to manage the learning process of oneself. Although distance learning has become popular with Covid-19 pandemic, its roots come from corresponding education, which refers to students' learning via mail services. Today, "anytime and anywhere" notion of distance education affects learning contexts in terms of digital integration. Formal, non-formal, and informal learning had become meshed, and therefore, today students must manage their own learning process. As a result, certain skills such as self-regulation have become important. As students engage in well-designed games, they might have the opportunity to control their own learning. For example, they can assess their progress while playing a game about computer science (Ibrahim et al., 2018; Paiva, Leal, & Queiros, 2020; Shute et al., 2014).

In conclusion, the game context or game-based learning environments can offer many opportunities to develop and improve certain 21st century skills through peer-coding or group project. Furthermore, they can boost creativity when combined with game coding or designing activities; increase motivation; and make the learning process smooth when games are played with the intention of learning.

STUDENTS AS GAME DESIGNERS

This part of the chapter is based upon a design thinking approach, which is also considered to be a part of the 21st century skill set. Design thinking has been adopted by various fields of profession ranging from engineering to information technology. In early paradigms of the field of education, the students were perceived as the receivers of the information. Today, the current paradigm has exchanged the roles of teachers and students (Aslan & Reigeluth, 2013). Students are expected to take responsibility for the learning process, which might mean solving problems, creating artifacts, utilizing tools, and searching for reliable information. In other words, students are not only consumers, but also producers of content. The production process can be attributed as an important part of learning. Hence, games can be used as complementary tools in the learning processes. Unlike earlier versions of game design tools, complementary tools are less challenging in terms of usability. There are lots of opportunities even for beginner level game designers. Open-source software, Web 2.0 tools, and commercial software have introduced a group of features, which can be used to learn while designing. For example, tools like Tinkercad and Sketchup allow learners to design their own virtual worlds, so that they can become ready to be coded in environments like Unity game engines.

Designing a game is quite different from designing a regular instructional material. Even a simple educational game design might include the following:

- User interface
- Interaction tools
- Scenario
- Goals and learning outcomes
- Content (sequence and boundaries)
- Rules
- Tasks, acts, missions and/or challenges
- Motivation tools
- Socialization tools
- Communication tools
- Rewards, levels, punishments, etc.
- Characters
- Algorithm and codes

Designing a good interface can eliminate many risks. The visual design principles have a general rule of thumb: "Keep it simple, stupid!". As Gestalt theory and cognitive load theory suggest, the visual perception can be affected by distracting agents such as moving elements. The key point is to include content related elements and to eliminate the unrelated ones, so that the cognitive effort can be engaged in the learning task. The students as game designers should be aware of this notion of visual design. The design of interaction tools should meet universal standards. For example, WASD keys are popular shortcuts for intense gamers. This habit should be considered by the designer. Otherwise, the satisfaction of users, which is one of the usability standard requirements, might be in danger. While creating the scenario of the game, the students can find a space to demonstrate their creativity. The teacher can provide scaffolds or give courage them to think outside of the box, which is closely related to 21st century skills. Once students are asked to think about the game, they need to consider the overall goal and learning outcomes. For a student, it might not be as easy to understand, but the teacher can divide them into smaller parts, and by doing so, students may not feel overwhelmed. In the case of students as game designers, the content can be given to the students directly, and then they can arrange it rather than creating it from scratch. This might also be a good opportunity for teachers to create a collaborative environment for students by encouraging group work. In two different studies, the observations were positive when students were assigned to design their own games about coding and finally, they were played by novice programming students (Mozelius & Olsson, 2017; Olsson & Mozelius, 2017). The environment used for designing the game might have restrictions, that's why rules, communication, socialization, and motivation tools can be arranged within the limits of the design tool. Algorithm is at the heart of any computer software and designing an algorithm might not be easy for novice learners. Therefore, analyzing the learners before starting the design tasks might contribute to the overall design process. Designing is a kind of creative act, so designing an instruction to make students game designers might result in challenges in terms of instructional design. The role of the teacher as a facilitator can eliminate the challenges.

STUDENTS AS GAME CODERS

This part of the chapter will cover tools for game coding in relation to 21st century skills. Computational thinking (CT), as Wing (2006) defined, includes reformulation of problems into smaller portions that are easier to solve. Since CT appears as a composition of thinking skills such as problem solving, algorithmic thinking, pattern recognition, etc., coding or programming is considered as a fundamental instrument to improve CT skills of learners. Games, with their distinguishing features, could serve as a subject to coding. The environment, rules and objects are interconnected with logical relationships in games and leaners can gain the opportunity to build games, which are the products of their own imagination. The coding process can be facilitated through the game elements, so that learning how to code becomes meaningful (Mathrahani, Chistian, & Ponder-Sutton, 2016). From this perspective, games can be considered as a tool to contribute higher order thinking skills via enabling learners to code their games.

Since the second half of the twentieth century, several programming languages and environments have been utilized as educational coding tools. Some of them are also used for game coding and gamification related purposes. Logo, BASIC, Pascal, Python, and Scratch are some examples of programming languages from the continuum of game coding history. In this section, some of these examples will be explained in relation to learners' game coding experiences in addition to 3D game coding environments like OpenSimulator.

LOGO-Pioneer of Game Coding

Scratch is probably the best-known programming environment used for introductory computer science education in schools. Scratch, which was developed at the MIT Media Lab in 2004 and has continued to evolve since then is widespread all over the world and has its roots can be traced back to the LOGO.

LOGO is a programming language developed by Wally Feurzeig, Seymour Papert, and Cynthia Solomon in the late 60s. Its main aim is to teach kids the abstract programing concepts and enable them to construct their own computer programs. LOGO started to become widespread in the 70s with the increasing use of personal computers (LOGO Foundation, 2015). Basically, LOGO includes programming commands controlling a "Turtle". The Turtle sometimes becomes a robotic turtle, and sometimes becomes an icon on the screen. The users move the turtle by the programming commands. There are several different versions of LOGO today. LOGO foundation groups the LOGO programing environments under three categories. First group is named as "traditional LOGO" and MSWLogo and UCBLogo are two examples under this category. Classic LOGO software mostly carries the basic features of the first version. Programmers create their codes on a text-based editor and output of each code line appears immediately. Another category of LOGO programming environments allows users to code multiple turtles so that the category is called Massively Parallel LOGO. StarLOGO and NetLOGO can be given as examples of Massive Parallel LOGO environments. The last category is "Block Programming". Scratch is the best describing example of this category. Instead of writing codes on a text editor, this type of LOGO version uses building blocks in different colors and shapes. Each block has a programming function. The color and shape provide visual clues and these visual clues reduce syntax errors so that programers can code without paying attention to syntax of their program.

LOGO is also compatible with some hardware. LOGO foundation lists that hardware as Sensor Boards (e.g. MakeyMakey), Micro Controllers (e.g. Arduino, and micro:bit), Plug&Play Robotic Systems (e.g. Lego Mindstorms, and Wex), and Self-Contained Robots (e.g. Beebot, and Mbot). Self-Contained Robots are very similar to the original turtle. Other hardware mostly enables the user to create and code their own system designs.

Since the first creation of the first version in 1967, LOGO has been integrated in many educational environments for different educational purposes. Paperts' influential book "Mindstorm" contributed to the integration of LOGO and programming in educational settings. Variety of learning situations were met with practical solutions in his book (Papert, 1981). In addition, he constituted the theoretical foundations. According to Papert, working with computers provides learners with the ability to construct their own microworlds. They can control and play with all elements of that microworld. The separation of the learning process and what is being learned, which is considered a mistake by Piaget, can be overcome by the help of a microworld and a transitional object such as LOGO and the Turtle. Learners can manipulate the environment and "learn" during the interaction with the microworld via the transitional object.

In such an environment, a game-like experience could be created. Games have four main structural elements: (i) challenges and goals, (ii) rules, (iii) progression, and (iv) outcomes (Whitten, 2014). Learners can define their own goal and get in action to reach that goal in LOGO, and this is the key function of the environment (Ernest, 1988). LOGO and the instructional activities define the rules. After completing the necessary coding progress in the boundaries of the rules, the learner comes up with a computer program as an outcome. But LOGO cannot guarantee the educational game environment alone. There is a need for an instructional design and the teacher's role comes into focus (Foster, & Shah, 2020). Such environments changed teachers' and student's roles, attitudes, and beliefs (Almeida, & Simoes,

2019). Pea, Kurland, and Hawkins (1985) indicates that teacher support is vital in such environments to foster thinking skills of students. From this perspective, the teacher should design the learning processes with the help of examples, projects, and instruction (Pea, Kurland, & Hawkins, 1985). Indeed, a good instructional design is closely related to a good educational game (Shute et al., 2014).

Scratch, Alice -Successor of LOGO

Programming in text-based environments has aspects that make coding difficult. When students are faced with complex programming courses, they might lose their motivation (Carter, 2006) because of the difficulties to remember syntax, bring algorithms to life, etc. To get rid of those difficulties Scratch provides an opportunity.

Scratch is a block-based online programming tool that allows students to create their own games, animations, interactive digital stories and share them within a community. The tool, which was developed by MIT Media Lab, helps students to develop higher order thinking skills. Students getting more experienced with Scratch can create much more complex projects (Su, Huang, Yang, Ding, & Hsieh, 2015). As a block-based successor of LOGO, Scratch has the ability to utilize interactivity. This feature makes it comfortable to design digital games. Students can define elements of what they imagine, define the challenges and rules, designate the progression, and then decide the outcomes at the end.

Alice-Object Oriented Programing

From a digital game perspective, another important concept is open to be constructed by learners. Overmars (2004) indicates that everything in a digital game can be considered as an object. That's why, defining the elements in a digital game actually means defining the objects in coding. Alice with its object-oriented structure enables educators to create game design activities including object-oriented programing (OOP) as supported in the literature (Wong & Yatim, 2018).

Similar to Scratch, Alice is a block-based programming tool used to create animations, digital stories and digital games. It offers a 3D environment. The elements in Alice's environment are defined as objects. User determines the objects and defines their properties. The context of Alice provides is helpful to understand classes, objects, methods, and events (Anniroot, & De Villiers, 2012).

Unity, and OpenSimulator-Open-Source Game Engines

The opportunities and tools to give students the role of game designers have been increasing parallel to the developments in digital technologies and software. Game engines are one of those opportunities. Unity as an open-source game engine enables users to create both 2D and 3D games. "Functions and attributes, intelligence and metric measurements can be done with Unity 3D encoding" Buyuksalih et al., 2017, p. 162). It also supports OOP. Since it has much more complex structure than Scratch and Alice, it appeals to different target groups such as high school students and engineering students. OpenSimulator is another game engine used to create 3D virtual environments. It supports multi-user environments. It is originally based on "Second Life" protocols. The distinguishing feature of OpenSimulator is that users can share their virtual environments with others online.

Game Editor and PyGame-C Programing and Python

Some game construction environments are used to start to learn fundamental programming languages. Game Editor and Pygame can be given as examples to game design for learning programing. Game editor is an open-source software. Users create games by coding in the C programming language. Differently, PyGame is not a software. It is a Python library including a number of Python constructs. The game screen is called a surface in PyGame, and the surface is refreshed a number of times in a second. This structure needs to approach game design from a different perspective. The designer basically tries to define the places of the game objects in a theoretical endless loop. The restrictive environment has the potential to improve computational thinking and foster the learning OOP.

Game development in the field of programming education has been flourishing as an emergent field of research and practice. This might not always mean developing it from scratch, but fixing, changing, checking, executing the source code. There are lots of models, approaches, and practices in the literature. 3I-approach is one of them. In their specific focus on programming language teaching, Shabalina, Vorobkalov, Kataev, and Tarasenko (2009) advised that the introduction of course materials into the game itself, the interpretation of solutions within the game context, and the influence of learning on the game results should be ensured. In such approaches, the programming languages can be located into the game as the main content, so that the flow of the game depends on the performance of the students as programmers. In this case, the students are both the coders and the players. In the literature, there are lots of studies aiming to make students learn how to code with the help of C++ (Shabalina et al., 2009), C (Ibrahim et al., 2018), Java (Xinogalos & Tryfou, 2021), and etc.

STUDENTS AS GAME PLAYERS

The traditional pedagogical approaches might not result in successful integration because a well-structured curriculum might not totally fit the adaptive nature of games. De Freitas (2018) argued that education is in a transformation because of web-based technologies, and digitalization. This transformation will end with a new paradigm of learning including "student developed pedagogy, AI scaffolded learning, leveling points and awards instead of assessment, unique learning patterns, adaptive learning, hidden curriculum, and blended learning" (De Freitas, p. 77). From this point of view, this chapter is shaped around the future learning paradigm where students are game players. However, playing a game might not always guarantee the deep involvement. In their comparison of playing a game vs. being at play, Shute et al. (2014) discussed the importance of paradigm shift to trigger play deeper.

Playing educational games can contribute to knowledge and skill development. In their study Shabalina et al. (2009) designed Graviman within the scope of computer science, and they observed positive changes in motivation in addition to knowledge and skills. Another potential contribution of games can be about attitudes towards such abstract subject areas as math (Cankaya & Karamete, 2009). Moreover, games can be seen as an enjoyable way to learn something (Ibrahim et al., 2018). Once students experience the fun way of learning, they can embrace the games as a dominant learning approach (Ibrahim et al., 2018).

The current paradigm of education emphasizes on the social aspects of learning, and therefore the instructional design approaches connecting students as game coders and players might result in positive learning outcomes. For example, students can create programming games for other students to learn how to program (Shabalina et al., 2017) as they enjoy socially interacting with one another (Lui & Au,

2018). Creating a friendly but competitive environment can enhance the social power of games (Cagiltay, Ozcelik & Ozcelik, 2015, Paiva et al., 2020).

One challenge about playing games is related to the power of context. Their effects can diminish when played at home or without any guidance of teachers. Derboven, Zaman, Geerts, and De Groof (2016) explored the students' home context, during which students seek ways to eliminate or avoid the educational aspects of the games. Therefore, the instructional design should be sensitive to context. Another challenge is about game literacy of teachers, because today's students play games much more often than their teachers (Gunter et al., 2008), which might result in skill gaps. For example, students can explore the shortcuts, or they can complete the levels quicker than expected or they can skip the important parts, or they can just get bored due to comparing the educational game with the commercial ones. The existence of excessive gamers is also a challenge for teachers (Gunter et al., 2008) because their expectations can be high, so their motivation can be affected in a negative way.

Flow theory (see Figure 4) explains how to keep balance between the play or not to play (Csikszentmihalyi, 1990; 2013). If it is too hard to complete, then the player can give up because they might think they do not have the necessary skillset to achieve the goal of the game. If it is too easy to complete, then there is also the risk of quitting, because the player does not feel the challenge. Smoothness of the flow and good connections among instructional elements can trigger higher order thinking skills during an educational game playing experience (Gunter et al., 2008).

Figure 4. Flow theory of Csikszentmihalyi

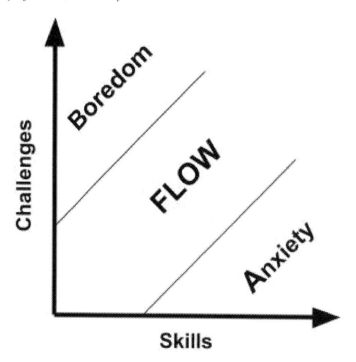

In order to achieve smoothness of the flow and good connections among instructional elements, Csikszentmihalyi (1990) lists eight components:

- Completable task
- Concentration
- Clear goals
- Immediate feedback
- Deep involvement
- Sense of control
- Less self-awareness during, but more after the experience
- Altered sense of duration and time.

Considering an educational game context, this list can be adopted as follows:

- The programming task should be level-sensitive (introductory, basic, advanced, etc.)
- The design of the interface should lead the full concentration of the game content rather than the problematic interaction with the interface
- The goals should be connected to the learning outcomes and clearly stated at the beginning of the missions
- Informative feedback should be provided whenever student needs
- The tasks should be cognitively engaging to ensure the deep involvement
- The interface and scenario design should leave space for user control, and allow going back and forth whenever needed
- The overall flow of the tasks should encourage self-awareness as well as self-assessment
- The overall scenario should not be boring so that students do not consider time and duration.

While playing games, the learners can learn a lot through the flow channel. High levels of engagement while coding in combination of a game-based context can enhance programming skills (Mathrani et al., 2016). In this way, the negative attitudes of students towards programming can be eliminated.

SOLUTIONS AND RECOMMENDATIONS

The integration of digital games has been discussed within game-based learning context. On the contrary to the bad reputation of commercial digital games, the proposed perspective, such as coding a game, can enhance learning in a game-based context. Designing a game has many potential contributions to 21st century skills including creativity. Coding a game requires multiple literacies including computer literacy, and therefore can turn the learning experience into production as a result of direct involvement of game creation through coding, solving problems, engaging in algorithms, etc. However, it might become a challenge for a novice coder. In this case, instead of direct coding by oneself, studying as a group can enrich the learning experience. Playing a game seems less efficient way of learning in comparison to either designing or coding a game. The challenge related to playing games is about keeping the flow. If the level of the game does not fit into the learner's needs, then the learning experience might become a nightmare for users. This form of integration might require a detailed pre-investigation of learners' current state of knowledge, skills, attitudes, and so on.

FUTURE RESEARCH DIRECTIONS

In the history of instructional technologies, any media with innovative features had been perceived as the panacea for all educational problems. Radio, television, and computers had all resulted in similar bad luck caused by the ignorance of integration of them into educational context. The core of the paradigm change, on the other hand, is closely related to the methodology itself. In other words, if the right technology is utilized in line with the needs of context, learners, content, etc., then the learning can become efficient. That's why, the practice of game-based learning in relation to computer science might become successful as long as it meets the mentioned needs. Such engagements as coding can remain abstract and sophisticated if the needs of beginners are ignored, or vice versa. Today's technologies provide with advanced utilities such as interaction through eye movements. These improved features facilitate to achieve authentic learning experiences. Instead of linear scenarios, there are much more complicated and multi-dimensional versions. Thanks to the open source environments, the creation of games has become easier and accessible for anyone interested in gaming. These kinds of experiences can be named as informal learning experiences, which should be understood through further studies due to the challenge nature of the process. The current studies have been focusing on the effects of games on success and motivation, but other dimensions such as contributions to language learning, design thinking, coding, and so on have not been discovered in detail. Moreover, the game-based learning has been discussed as an instructional method, but the overall integration of digital games into specific learning context including computer science has not been discussed from instructional design perspective. The games as cognitive tools of programming language learning process should be studied with the collaboration of other fields, so that the interdisciplinary practices can become much more concrete. The pedagogy of computer science is still in its infancy, and therefore the game-based learning through designing, coding, and playing can improve the pedagogical practices. The further studies can generate models or frameworks for guiding the game integration process within computer science education.

CONCLUSION

Educational games require the consideration of multi-dimensional design issues ranging from interface to pedagogy. For games to be fit into the intended usage, game developers, script writers, and even instructional designers might work in a collaborative manner (Cagiltay et al., 2015) because the prescriptive guidance is one of the factors hindering the integration process (Shute et al., 2014). The decision on how to integrate computer science into games or vice versa is critical because putting the content into a game is not an integration at all. Having an eclectic perspective can eliminate such challenges as technical obstacles. One might need to combine the traditional instructional design practice with the current perspectives of computer science education (Shabalina et al., 2017). The context matters for instructional design of games. At home, at school, with/without guidance, and mobility context should be taken into account to specify the strategies of the game scenario, otherwise intended outputs should not be met. In addition to context, usability of the games might play important roles for the integration process because learnability is a key aspect of user experience. The user should neither pay effort to learn the interface nor read long instructions about the game. Both from cognitive load theory and human-computer interaction practices, ensuring a good interface and instruction can lead to effective learning.

REFERENCES

Almeida, F., & Simoes, J. (2019). The role of serious games, gamification and Industry 4.0 tools in the Education 4.0 paradigm. *Contemporary Educational Technology*, *10*(2), 120–136. doi:10.30935/cet.554469

Anniroot, J., & De Villiers, M. R. (2012). *Study of Alice: A visual environment for teaching object-oriented programming*. Academic Press.

Aslan, S., & Reigeluth, C. M. (2013). Educational technologists: Leading change for a new paradigm of education. *TechTrends*, *57*(5), 18–24. doi:10.100711528-013-0687-4

Azuma, R. T. (1997). A survey of augmented reality. *Presence (Cambridge, Mass.)*, *6*(4), 355–385. doi:10.1162/pres.1997.6.4.355

Battle for Kids. (2019). *Framework for 21st Century Learning*. http://static.battelleforkids.org/documents/p21/P21_Framework_Brief.pdf

Buyuksalih, I., Bayburt, S., Buyuksalih, G., Baskaraca, A. P., Karim, H., & Rahman, A. A. (2017). 3D modelling and visualization based on the unity game engine—advantages and challenges. *ISPRS Annals of Photogrammetry, Remote Sensing & Spatial Information Sciences*, 4.

Cagiltay, N. E., Ozcelik, E., & Ozcelik, N. S. (2015). The effect of competition on learning in games. *Computers & Education*, *87*, 35–41. doi:10.1016/j.compedu.2015.04.001

Cankaya, S., & Karamete, A. (2009). The effects of educational computer games on students' attitudes towards mathematics course and educational computer games. *Procedia: Social and Behavioral Sciences*, *1*(1), 145–149. doi:10.1016/j.sbspro.2009.01.027

Carter, L. (2006). Why students with an apparent aptitude for computer science don't choose to major in computer science. *ACM SIGCSE Bulletin*, *38*(1), 27–31. doi:10.1145/1124706.1121352

Childs, M. (2010). *Learners' experience of presence in virtual worlds* (Doctoral dissertation). University of Warwick.

Csikszentmihalyi, M. (1990). *Flow: The psychology of optimal experience* (Vol. 1990). Harper & Row.

Csikszentmihalyi, M. (2013). *Flow: The psychology of happiness*. Random House.

De Freitas, S. (2018). Are games effective learning tools? A review of educational games. *Journal of Educational Technology & Society*, *21*(2), 74–84.

Derboven, J., Zaman, B., Geerts, D., & De Grooff, D. (2016). Playing educational math games at home: The Monkey Tales case. *Entertainment Computing*, *16*, 1–14. doi:10.1016/j.entcom.2016.05.004

Egenfeldt-Nielsen, S. (2006). Overview of research on the educational use of video games. *Nordic Journal of Digital Literacy*, *1*(03), 184–214. doi:10.18261/ISSN1891-943X-2006-03-03

Ernest, P. (1988). What's the use of LOGO? *Mathematics in School*, *17*(1), 16–20.

Foster, A., & Shah, M. (2020). Principles for advancing game-based learning in teacher education. *Journal of Digital Learning in Teacher Education*, *36*(2), 84–95. doi:10.1080/21532974.2019.1695553

Gunter, G. A., Kenny, R. F., & Vick, E. H. (2008). Taking educational games seriously: Using the RETAIN model to design endogenous fantasy into standalone educational games. *Educational Technology Research and Development*, *56*(5), 511–537. doi:10.100711423-007-9073-2

Hayes, E. R., & Games, I. A. (2008). Making computer games and design thinking: A review of current software and strategies. *Games and Culture*, *3*(3-4), 309–332. doi:10.1177/1555412008317312

Heintz, S., & Law, E. L. C. (2018). Digital educational games: Methodologies for evaluating the impact of game type. *ACM Transactions on Computer-Human Interaction*, *25*(2), 1–47. doi:10.1145/3177881

Hooshyar, D., Pedaste, M., Yang, Y., Malva, L., Hwang, G. J., Wang, M., Lim, H., & Delev, D. (2021). From gaming to computational thinking: An adaptive educational computer game-based learning approach. *Journal of Educational Computing Research*, *59*(3), 383–409. doi:10.1177/0735633120965919

Ibrahim, R., Rahim, N. Z. A., Ten, D. W. H., Yusoff, R., Maarop, N., & Yaacob, S. (2018). Student's opinions on online educational games for learning programming introductory. *International Journal of Advanced Computer Science and Applications*, *9*(6), 332–340. doi:10.14569/IJACSA.2018.090647

Keller, J. M. (1998). Using the ARCS process in CBI and distance education. In M. Theall (Ed.), *Motivation in teaching and learning: New directions for teaching and learning*. Jossey-Bass.

Kirriemuir, J. (2006). A history of digital games. In J. Rutter & J. Bryce (Eds.), *Understanding Digital Games* (pp. 21–36). Sage Publications. doi:10.4135/9781446211397.n2

Klopfer, E., & Squire, K. (2008). Environmental Detectives—The development of an augmented reality platform for environmental simulations. *Educational Technology Research and Development*, *56*(2), 203–228. doi:10.100711423-007-9037-6

Krathwohl, D. R., & Anderson, L. W. (2010). Merlin C. Wittrock and the revision of Bloom's taxonomy. *Educational Psychologist*, *45*(1), 64–65. doi:10.1080/00461520903433562

LOGO Foundation. (2015). *Logo History*. https://el.media.mit.edu/logo-foundationl

Lorås, M., Sindre, G., Trætteberg, H., & Aalberg, T. (2022). Study Behavior in Computing Education-A Systematic Literature Review. *ACM Transactions on Computing Education*, *22*(1), 1–28. doi:10.1145/3469129

Lui, R., & Au, C. H. (2018). IS educational game: Adoption in teaching search engine optimization (SEO). *Journal of Computer Information Systems*.

Mathrani, A., Christian, S., & Ponder-Sutton, A. (2016). PlayIT: Game based learning approach for teaching programming concepts. *Journal of Educational Technology & Society*, *19*(2), 5–17.

Milgram, P., & Kishino, F. (1994). A taxonomy of mixed reality visual displays. *IEICE Transactions on Information and Systems*, *77*, 1321–1329.

Milgram, P., Takemura, H., Utsumi, A., & Kishino, F. (1995, December). Augmented reality: A class of displays on the reality-virtuality continuum. In *Telemanipulator and telepresence technologies* (Vol. 2351, pp. 282–292). International Society for Optics and Photonics. doi:10.1117/12.197321

Mozelius, P., & Olsson, M. (2017, October). Learning to program by building learning games. In *European Conference on Games Based Learning* (pp. 448-455). Academic Conferences International Limited.

Olsson, M., & Mozelius, P. (2017). Learning to Program by Playing Learning Games. In *11th European Conference on Games Based Learning 2017, Graz, Austria, 5-6 October, 2017* (Vol. 11, pp. 498-506). Academic Conferences and Publishing International Limited.

Overmars, M. (2004). Teaching computer science through game design. *Computer*, *37*(4), 81–83. doi:10.1109/MC.2004.1297314

Paiva, J. C., Leal, J. P., & Queirós, R. (2020). Fostering programming practice through games. *Information (Basel)*, *11*(11), 498. doi:10.3390/info11110498

Pea, R. D., Kurland, D. M., & Hawkins, J. (1985). *Logo and the development of thinking skills*. Academic Press.

Shabalina, O., Malliarakis, C., Tomos, F., & Mozelius, P. (2017). Game-based learning for learning to program: from learning through play to learning through game development. In *11th European Conference on Games Based Learning 2017, Graz, Austria, 5-6 October 2017* (Vol. 11, pp. 571-576). Academic Conferences and Publishing International Limited.

Shabalina, O., Malliarakis, C., Tomos, F., Mozelius, P., Balan, O. C., & Alimov, A. (2016) Game-Based Learning as a Catalyst for Creative Learning. *Proceedings of the 9th ECGBL*.

Shabalina, O., Vorobkalov, P., Kataev, A., & Tarasenko, A. (2009). 3I-approach for IT educational games development. In *Proceedings of the European Conference on Games-based Learning* (pp. 339-344). Academic Press.

Shute, V. J., Rieber, L., & Van Eck, R. (2012). Games... and... learning. In R. A. Reiser & J. V. Dempsey (Eds.), Trends and issues in instructional design and technology (3rd ed., pp. 321–332). Academic Press.

Skarbez, R., Smith, M., & Whitton, M. C. (2021). Revisiting Milgram and Kishino's Reality-Virtuality Continuum. *Frontiers in Virtual Reality*, *2*, 27. doi:10.3389/frvir.2021.647997

Stork, M. G. (2020). Supporting twenty-first century competencies using robots and digital storytelling. *Journal of Formative Design in Learning*, *4*(1), 43–50. doi:10.100741686-019-00039-w

Su, A. Y. S., Huang, C. S. J., Yang, S. J. H., Ding, T. J., & Hsieh, Y. Z. (2015). Effects of annotations and homework on learning achievement: An empirical study of Scratch programming pedagogy. *Journal of Educational Technology & Society*, *18*(4), 331–343.

Theodoropoulos, A., & Lepouras, G. (2021). Augmented Reality and programming education: A systematic review. *International Journal of Child-Computer Interaction*, *30*, 100335. doi:10.1016/j.ijcci.2021.100335

Threekunprapa, A., & Yasri, P. (2020). Unplugged Coding Using Flowblocks for Promoting Computational Thinking and Programming among Secondary School Students. *International Journal of Instruction*, *13*(3), 207–222. doi:10.29333/iji.2020.13314a

Whitton, N. (2014). *Digital games and learning: Research and theory*. Routledge. doi:10.4324/9780203095935

Wing, J. M. (2006). Computational thinking. *Communications of the ACM*, *49*(3), 33–35. doi:10.1145/1118178.1118215

Wong, Y. S., & Yatim, M. H. M. (2018, July). A Propriety Multiplatform Game-Based Learning Game to Learn Object-Oriented Programming. In *2018 7th International Congress on Advanced Applied Informatics (IIAI-AAI)* (pp. 278-283). IEEE. 10.1109/IIAI-AAI.2018.00060

Xinogalos, S., & Tryfou, M. M. (2021). Using Greenfoot as a Tool for Serious Games Programming Education and Development. *International Journal of Serious Games*, *8*(2), 67–86. doi:10.17083/ijsg.v8i2.425

Zheng, Y. (2019). 3D Course Teaching Based on Educational Game Development Theory-Case Study of Game Design Course. *International Journal of Emerging Technologies in Learning*, *14*(2), 54. doi:10.3991/ijet.v14i02.9985

ADDITIONAL READING

Boldbaatar, N., & Şendurur, E. (2019). Developing educational 3D games with StarLogo: The role of backwards fading in the transfer of programming experience. *Journal of Educational Computing Research*, *57*(6), 1468–1494. doi:10.1177/0735633118806747

Chou, T. L., Tang, K. Y., & Tsai, C. C. (2021). A Phenomenographic Analysis of College Students' Conceptions of and Approaches to Programming Learning: Insights From a Comparison of Computer Science and Non-Computer Science Contexts. *Journal of Educational Computing Research*, *59*(7). doi:10.1177/0735633121995950

Gee, J. P. (2003). What video games have to teach us about learning and literacy. *Computers in Entertainment*, *1*(1), 20–20. doi:10.1145/950566.950595

Gee, J. P. (2013). Games for learning. *Educational Horizons*, *91*(4), 16–20. doi:10.1177/0013175X1309100406

Laamarti, F., Eid, M., & El Saddik, A. (2014). An overview of serious games. *International Journal of Computer Games Technology*.

Myers, R. D., & Reigeluth, C. M. (2016). Designing games for learning. In *Instructional-Design Theories and Models* (Vol. 4, pp. 221–258). Routledge.

Wake, J. D., Guribye, F., & Wasson, B. (2018). Learning through collaborative design of location-based games. *International Journal of Computer-Supported Collaborative Learning*, *13*(2), 167–187. doi:10.100711412-018-9278-x

Whitton, N. (2014). *Digital games and learning: Research and theory*. Routledge. doi:10.4324/9780203095935

Wronowski, M., Urick, A., Wilson, A. S., Thompson, W., Thomas, D., Wilson, S., Elizondo, F. J., & Ralston, R. (2020). Effect of a serious educational game on academic and affective outcomes for statistics instruction. *Journal of Educational Computing Research, 57*(8), 2053–2084. doi:10.1177/0735633118824693

KEY TERMS AND DEFINITIONS

Coding: Process to develop a computer program by using a computer-based programing language.

Computer Science: The study about computers and any other information processors including hardware, software, algorithms and any other data and information modeling processes.

Digital Game: Games integrated into and played in digital environments.

Educational Games: Games produced to be used within learning environments.

Game Coding: Process to develop a digital game by using a computer-based programing language.

Game Designing: Process to decide on elements of games including rules, objectives, level of interaction, visualization, and other design elements.

Game-Based Learning: Learning by playing games which are developed to reach predefined learning outcomes.

Chapter 45
Learning Coding Through Gaming

Janna Jackson Kellinger
University of Massachusetts, Boston, USA

ABSTRACT

This chapter begins by arguing that computational thinking and coding should be included as two more C's in the Partnership for 21st Century Learning's list of essential skills. It does so by examining how coding and computational thinking can be used to manipulate people. It argues that gaming uses all the C's, including the two new ones proposed. It then explores connections between playing video games and computer programming. It claims that game-based learning would be an optimal way to leverage these connections to teach coding and describes ways in which to do so, including specific challenges that could be included in game-based learning and a sequence of introducing them so students can "level up." It briefly examines different coding games and describes ways in which educators can create their own coding games. It concludes by arguing that educators can make the connections between gamer thinking and computational thinking visible, use games designed to teach coding, or create their own coding games to take advantage of near transfer.

INTRODUCTION

When I was a high school English teacher, one of my students approached me very excited because she had seen the average salary of a computer programmer. She said that is what she wanted to become because she was very good at Excel. Clearly she did not understand the difference between being a consumer and being a producer of technology. In his book, *Program or be Programmed*, Rushkoff (2010) concedes that in the 21st century you can get away without learning how to code, but that, "You do, however, have to learn that programming exists" (p. 8). Rushkoff (2010) clarifies that he wants people to learn about programming not necessarily to become computer programmers, but as "critical thinkers" about technology. Keeshin (2021) and Jiang, et al. (2019) all argue that coding, or "algoRithms", should be added to Reading, wRiting, and aRithmetic as one of the foundational Rs in education. In

DOI: 10.4018/978-1-7998-7271-9.ch045

the 21st century, understanding how technology works, including how technology is programmed, is an essential life skill.

Coding is also a very promising and lucrative career. The U.S. Bureau of Labor and Statistics predicts that jobs in this field will grow 11% over the next ten years. (Klein, 2021). Computer programmers currently earn twice the median salary of all other occupations (Klein, 2021). Unfortunately, access to computer science courses is a barrier for far too many black and brown students, with 60% of black students reporting that they want to take courses in computer science but only 42% reporting that they have (Klein, 2021). Hispanic students have similar numbers (61% and 44%) as do students who live in poverty (59% and 37%) (Klein, 2021). There is also a gender gap with stereotypes and discrimination discouraging female students from pursuing computer science (Klein, 2021). Increasing opportunities for all students, but particularly for marginalized and underserved students, will not only provide pathways to the field of computer science, but will also help diversify the field. In addition, having a basic understanding of coding is becoming a requirement for more and more jobs.

21ST CENTURY SKILLS

The Partnership for 21st Century Skills established in 2001 brought together educators, business leaders, and policy makers to explore and advocate for skills students will need to survive and thrive in their education, careers, and life in the technology-driven world of the 21st century. They organized their framework around four C's essential for success in the 21st century: Critical Thinking, Communication, Collaboration, and Creativity. I propose that two more C's be added: Computational Thinking and Coding.

Computational thinking is a term attributed to Wing (2006), which she defines as involving, "solving problems, designing systems, and understanding human behavior, by drawing on the concepts fundamental to computer science" (p. 33). Vaidyanathan (2016) describes this type of thinker as:

One who collects data and analyzes it to understand the problem. That person then decomposes (breaks it down) into simpler problems. Instead of solving only that problem, you look for patterns, remove details and abstract so you can solve all problems of that type. You define the steps to solve the problem (the algorithm) and if possible, build a model to simulate, test and debug the solution.

Coders uses computational thinking to program a computer. However, Wing (2006) makes it clear that computational thinking applies to much more than just coding, including everyday activities such as packing a backpack ("prefetching and caching"), retracing steps to find a lost item ("backtracking"), choosing the shortest line at the grocery store ("performance modeling for multi-server systems") (Wing, 2006, p. 34). While Wing (2006) and Vaidyanathan (2016) both argue that computational thinking is a fundamental skill for the 21st century, they also both agree that not everyone needs to become a coder.

I also am not proposing that every student become a computer programmer. However, a basic understanding of how coding works, of the strategies behind coding, and how they can be applied outside of coding is imperative in a world where disinformation flows too freely. Personalized algorithms tailor what we see online, creating our own internet worlds that people mistakenly believe are what everyone sees, what Pariser (2011) calls "filter bubbles". A lack of understanding in these areas can create devastating consequences, from a pop-up window hoax leading to senior citizens being scammed out of their life savings to people refusing to get vaccinated against deadly diseases based on social media memes to conspiracy theories about an election being stolen swirling around on the internet leading to an insurrection that threatened the lives of legislators in the oldest continuous democracy. Rushkoff's 2010 concern that a lack of understanding of how coding works could lead to sheeple, i.e. people who follow others like sheep, expressed in the title of his book *Program or be Programmed,* and Pariser's warnings in 2011 about internet "filter bubbles" were very prescient of the current disinformation age.

Listing these now six C's is a convenient way to promote these thinking skills, however, these six C's are not mutually exclusive. In fact, I would argue that coding encompasses all of them. Coding, at its basic level, is *communication*—communication between humans and machines; machines and humans; and humans and humans—particularly since most coding projects involve teams that not only have to communicate, but also have to *collaborate*. Coding involves figuring out the best ways, i.e. *critical thinking*, to get a machine to do what you want by using *computational thinking*—decomposition, pattern recognition, abstraction, and so forth. This all comes down to solving problems in order to produce something that is useful and/or entertaining which involves a high level of *creativity*.

GAMING AND 21ST CENTURY SKILLS

So, the question that follows, then, is if coding is an essential skill for the 21st century, what are the best ways to teach it? Many of the same skills involved in coding—pattern recognition, problem-solving, hypothesis testing, decomposition—are used by gamers to play video games. When I ask my children how they figured something out in a video game, they say, "Because we know how video game designers think." What they often mean is that they identified patterns, tested a hypothesis and learned from the feedback, examined objects and their attributes and behaviors, broke tasks down into their component parts, and used a variety of different strategies to solve problems—all skills that coders use as well. Blending the two—teaching coding through gaming—can promote near transfer, allowing students to be able to apply the skills they use in gaming to coding.

Evidence based on studying gamers themselves suggests that gaming does promote these 21st century C's:

Surveys of gamers show that they have an increased appetite for risk, a greater comfort with failure, a stronger desire for social affiliations, a preference for challenges, a capacity for independent problem solving, and a desire to be involved in meaningful work when compared with nongamers (Beck & Wade, 2004).

Others have come to similar conclusions, describing gamers as active problem solvers who take risks and see mistakes as "opportunities for reflection and learning" while exhibiting "persistence [and] . . . attention to detail" (Klopfer, et al., 2009, p. 1). Gee (2007) describes gamers as taking advantage of "cross functional affiliation" by working with other gamers who have complementary skill sets. These are all skills Freidman (2007) and Wagner (2008) assert are fundamental to excelling in a 21st century workforce where challenges are often tackled by ad hoc groups whose members have a variety of skills to bring to the table. These are also the same skills employed by programmers.

Indeed, many have capitalized on these similarities to teach coding and computational thinking through games. Some have done so using "unplugged" methods, such as board games and physical games such as sports, dance challenges, and childhood games (Berland, 2011; Menon, et al., 2019).

These "unplugged" approaches largely happen at younger grade levels (Bell, et al., 1998; Lee, et al., 2020). Coding, at its core, is crafting a set of directions for the computer to follow. By having students "be" the computer, these unplugged methods tap into a fundamental aspect of games: following a set of rules. Pick up any board game, and they almost always include a set of directions. Physical games, board games where tokens are moved around a board, and card games where cards are passed from player to player, utilize Bruner's (1961) primary approach to teaching—kinesthetic learning. These types of games involve finding the best strategy, just like coders aim for "elegant" code, i.e. efficient programming that uses the fewest lines of code. Unplugged approaches to teach coding leverage the similarities between coding and game-playing.

Others have examined the role that video games can play in teaching coding and computational thinking. For example, Weintrop, et al. (2016) examined the iterative design, i.e. building, testing, and refining, involved in construction and management simulation games. In Combefis' et al., (2016) meta-analysis of studies on using games to teach computers science, they found that games increase motivation and learning. In one study, the use of games increased pass rates by 11% (Combefis, 2016). Lee, et al. (2014) compared teaching computational thinking through paper-based games versus a computer-designed game and found that students were able to articulate algorithms, or common problem-solving formulas, better after playing a computer-designed game, however, they attributed that to the teaching aspect of the game as students had to teach a virtual avatar how to play the games. In addition to playing games, building games themselves have been used to teach coding concepts. This occurs not just at the college level (Burns, 2008; deLaet, et al., 2005; Dolgopolovas, 2018), but also in elementary (Lee, et al., 2020), middle (Nouri, et al., 2018), and high school (Combefis, 2016). Playing, designing, and building games involve following directions and creating your own set of directions, i.e. coding.

Whether playing or designing board games or computer games, there are certain features that researchers have suggested increase engagement, motivation, and learning. One point of emphasis in most of these students is the role of collaboration in helping students refine and articulate their thinking (Sharma, 2018; Harteveld, et al., 2013). Story-based games help establish context and increase engagement (Harteveld, et al., 2013). Puzzle games that require problem-solving were almost universally acknowledged as the key to fostering computational thinking (Jiang, et al, 2019; Harteveld, et al., 2013; Lee, et al., 2014). Hypothesis testing that capitalizes on the feedback loop was another essential component found in the literature (Harteveld, et al., 2013). Teaching others further solidifies learning (Lee, et al., 2014). Most of these attributes are also used when coding, particularly in the workforce, where teams of coders work together to refine and test products.

GAMES, VIDEO GAMES, AND CODING

While not everyone defines themselves as a gamer, almost everyone has played games—whether they be board games, card games, sports, or any other kinds of games. Games in this broad sense capitalize on all of the 21st century skills identified by the Partnership on 21st Century Skills: communication, collaboration, critical thinking, and yes, even in very rule-driven games, creativity, by figuring out work-arounds and actions not prohibited by the rules. For example, one high school basketball team won a close game by having a player get down on all fours and bark like a dog to distract the other team while the other teammates sunk the winning basket. Certain games can foster creativity such as *Pictionary* where players have to draw the target word they are trying to get their teammates to guess. Games are uniquely positioned to foster all of the 21ˢᵗ century skills.

In order to explore how games can be used to teach coding, however, we have to be clear on what a game is. A lot has been written about what constitutes a game, but Kapp's (2012) description of games covers most elements and contains an algorithm that applies to a wide variety of games:

A player gets caught up in playing a game because the instant feedback and constant interaction are related to the challenge of the game, which is defined by the rules, which all work within the system to provoke an emotional reaction and, finally, result in a quantifiable outcome within an abstract version of a larger system. (p. 9)

In my 2017 book, I argue that the element of fun is missing from his, and others, lists of game essentials. However, it is the component that, on the surface, appears contradictory to fun—that of rules—that I want to focus on. McGonagil (2011) uses a common sport to illustrate the necessity of rules to game-making—that of golf. The goal of golf is to get a ball into a hole. However, without the rule of having to hit that ball with a club from a long distance away, that goal can be achieved simply by placing a ball in a hole. It is the rules that set up the challenge that constitute a game. The game world where these rules apply Huizinga (1955/2006) calls, "the magic circle." Without the rules, the game of golf would be no fun.

Adams (2010) points out that one key difference between games in general and video games in particular is that video games do not come with a rule book like conventional games do. Instead, players discover the rules through testing the limits of the video game as the machine enforces the rules by giving the player feedback, like a referee. Adams (2010) contends that this allows players to:

No longer . . . think about the game as a game. A player contemplating an action can simply try it, without having to read the rules to see whether the game permits it. This lets players become much more deeply immersed in the game, to see it not as a temporary artificial environment with arbitrary rules, but as an alternate universe of which the player is a part. (p. 15)

This supports Pelletier and Oliver (2006) findings in their study of gamers in action that, "gamers developed and revised rules and strategies for game playing based on hypothesis testing and actively worked to resolve 'cognitive dissonance'" (quoted from Kellinger, 2017, p. 16). In other words, an essential part of playing video games is discovering what constitutes the borders of the "magic circle" through experimentation.

Coding at its most fundamental level is giving a set of instructions, called commands, to a computer or other type of technology that the computer or other technological device then executes. In other words, defining the rules by which a program operates. Most, but not all, video games involve game players giving a set of instructions, or commands, to an avatar—a character whose actions are determined by a human—that the avatar then executes. Often this involves interacting with agents—characters whose actions are determined by a computer. While the agents, or non-playable characters (NPCs), are programmed prior to gameplay by the people who coded the game, the avatars are "programmed" in the moment by the people playing the game. The commands the avatars can execute are determined by the video game designers, but the order in which they execute them and the objects and NPCs players interact with using those actions are determined by the player. In essence, video game players are programmers. They are coding their avatar in the game to do what they want it to do via an interface—either a game controller or a computer keyboard or sometimes their own body, e.g. with Wii or Kinect—typically by using a set of kinesthetic symbols, e.g. pressing a certain key or moving a joystick in a certain way or even by manipulating their own body. While computer programmers use words and punctuation as their symbols which then get translated into the machine language of ones and zeros, video game players use a pre-programmed set of action symbols in order to code a character, or sometimes objects, on the fly. Video game players are real-time coders.

Even though not everyone defines themselves as a gamer, statistics show that gaming is pervasive, particularly among teenagers. According to the Pew Research Center (2018), 90% of teenagers play video games. The ubiquity of video game devices—from cell phones to computers to consoles—led to a prediction of a 5.6% growth for overall users (Gilbert, 2020). The Pew Research Center (2018) survey found that the most popular types of video games among all users are puzzle and strategy games, i.e. games that promote critical and computational thinking. The popularity of gaming combined with the similarities between the skill sets used by gamers and coders suggests that game-based learning is fertile pedagogy for teaching coding.

COMPUTATIONAL THINKING AND GAMER THINKING

While it is impossible to identify every skill used in videogames—particularly because there are so many different types of video games from first-person shooter to racing games to casual puzzle games to construction and management simulation games—there are some general skills that are used in most games. The kinds of thinking used to figure out or "decode" games, such as pattern recognition and problem-solving, are very similar to the kinds of thinking used to program those very games and, really, to program anything.

Sequencing

One of the more basic elements of the computational thinking behind coding is sequencing, or placing items in a specific order. As programmers quickly learn, if commands are not in the proper order, things go awry. Sequencing is also fundamental to gaming. A common game technique is to find items in a certain order, where one item allows access to the next and so forth until the final item unlocks the next level. Often tasks have to be done in a certain order in video games in order to be able to do the next task. Most video games are built on sequencing as players have to "level up," or move through levels in a certain order with each level requiring a harder and harder skill level to beat it, until the final boss level—the level where all skills are necessary to win the game. With the exception of construction and management simulation games like *SimCity,* most video games require players to move through levels in order. In some cases, challenges involve players having to discover some of those sequences on their own.

Sequencing is the fundamental goal of many coding toys and games geared towards younger children as well. One company developed a caterpillar for kids to use to learn coding where each segment represented a different command—stop, right, left, go. Kids then placed the segments in the proper order to get the caterpillar to do what they wanted it to do. Other beginner games used to teach coding, such as *Kodable*, start with a limited set of commands that the user then has to put in the proper order in order to achieve a goal, in this case guiding an alien through a maze. Because sequencing is so fundamental to learning coding, dancing, which is essentially learning different moves in a set order, is a common way to teach coding to beginners with programs like *danceLogic* (Duncan, 2019) and *Dance Party* on Code.org. Teachers can have their students play "Mix-up-itis", a term from a *Doc McStuffins* game, where they give students the commands needed to achieve a coding goal in a random order and students have to put them in the correct order to get the computer or a robot to achieve a goal. Giving students the commands first allows students to focus solely on sequencing so they can think through what order makes the most sense. By capitalizing on foundational similarities between coding and gaming, games can use sequencing to teach coding.

Decomposition

While the sequencing examples above involved giving students the commands, the next step should be for students to come up with the commands on their own. To do so, students need to break a task down into subtasks. Decomposition—or breaking a larger goal into its component steps—is another foundational coding—and gaming—skill. Johnson (2005) describes how gamers "telescope," or prioritize short-term and long-term goals by putting them in order. In fact, often the most important game skill in many video games is figuring out what the larger goal is and the smaller goals needed in order to get to that final goal, or boss level.

Video games are getting more and more sophisticated so that often it is not just one player who has to use decomposition to break tasks down, but multiple players, each with their own skill set, have to figure out how to use their skills together to accomplish a goal. In other words, *collaborate*. For example, in the video game *Brothers: A Tale of Two Sons*, the younger brother is smaller and can fit between bars and into small spaces whereas the older one is stronger and can lift things the other one cannot, including lifting the younger brother. Often, the younger one has to squeeze into a small space or be lifted by the older brother to a higher space to unlock it so the older one can enter and use his strength to lift something. A similar dynamic takes place in *Luigi's Mansion 3* where Gooigi can ooze between the grills on pipes and enter areas Luigi cannot in order to do something to allow Luigi access where Luigi can then perform his task. This type of collaboration is taken to a whole new level in Multi-player Massive Online Role-playing Games (MMORPGs) where players choose different roles for their avatars, each with different strengths, and have to work cooperatively in guilds in order to defeat enemies and overcome other challenges.

Coding is essentially decomposition—taking a large goal and breaking it into smaller and smaller goals down to the command level. For large programs, project managers will group tasks and farm them out to different coders to the point where a systems engineer is needed to coordinate all the parts, for example to make sure the same naming conventions or units of measurement are used, so that all the parts "fit together" into one complete program. In fact, an older version of the coding game *Code Combat* inadvertently demonstrated the importance of this as each level used a different name for the same object. Establishing a destination and coding an avatar to get to that destination is a common first problem to teach decomposition, whether it be Karel the Robot in the *Gentle Introduction to Programming* books, an alien in a maze like in *Kodable*, or a monkey that has to retrieve bananas in *Code Monkey*. Because a set of directions to get somewhere involves decomposition and decomposition is essentially what coding is, having players program an avatar to reach a destination on a map can be a good next skill after sequencing a pre-set list of commands. Capitalizing on the decomposition needed in video game playing and using it to teach coding is likely to promote near transfer.

Looping

In video games, it is common for an action to have to be done a certain number of times in order for a task to be completed. For example, an enemy might only be defeated after it is hit a certain number of times. In coding, when executing a series of commands, sometimes those commands are repeated. Instead of listing a command over and over again, or even using "ditto", coders use loops to tell the computer to do something a certain number of times, e.g. "For X number of times, do Y." Just like in video games, this can be more than just one command. For example, in a video game, a player might have to execute a series of actions—say a punch and then a kick—a certain number of times to defeat an opponent. Same with coding. A loop can contain multiple commands. This involves identifying patterns in order to realize when using a loop is a more efficient way to code. Whether or not a command is inside or outside a loop and before or after a loop can make or break a computer program, just like executing an action in the wrong place alters gameplay. Having students identify repeated patterns such as repeated turns when programming an avatar to follow directions or repeated dance moves or even taking decomposition to a finer grain of detail by programming an avatar to take multiple steps or walk up a set of stairs can introduce students to looping. Making this connection between video games and coding can help learners understand how looping is used in computer programming.

Conditions

One of the key skills in video game playing is figuring out when to execute actions. Different conditions call for different actions. Sometimes these conditions have to do with the setting. For example, gameplay might be different when it is night versus when it is daytime. Sometimes they have to do with encountering an NPC or object. Sometimes conditions are dependent on the current task at hand. Just as in video games, in computer programming, different conditions can call for different actions. While players can often see or hear what the different conditions are in a video game, because computer programming is removed from the execution, coders have to write conditional statements to test the conditions. Essentially, computer programmers are writing out the thought processes that video gamers have. To do so, both computer programmers and video gamers use If/Then statements—If a certain condition is true, then execute these actions and, in some cases, if this condition is false (ELSE), execute these other commands. A more complicated conditional statement may involve Boolean Logic—if these two conditions are true (AND), if this condition is absent (NOT), or if this condition or this other condition is true (OR). Making this type of thinking visible when playing video games can help transfer this to coding.

Sid Meier, the designer of *Civilization*, famously said that games are, "a series of interesting decisions" (quoted by Prensky 2011, p. 272). Without decisions, a game is not a game, it is just a story. Translating this mental decision-making into IF/THEN/ELSE decision trees can make this explicit for students. Games often use dialogue trees where players have to decide what their avatar will say in reaction to an NPC. The avatar's response then determines what happens next. Embedded decision trees in games allows students to explore and trace the different paths, particularly if a game is replayed. The decision trees themselves make a game replayable as players have different game experiences depending on their choices. Making these different paths explicit by using IF/THEN/ELSE language can introduce students to branching logic.

Conditional Looping

While some loops repeat for a constant number of times, sometimes actions need to take place over and over again until something happens or only when something happens—for both computer programmers and for gamers. For example, a video game player, or rather their avatar, might keep shooting arrows until a target is hit. In this case, the avatar shoots arrows UNTIL the target is hit. However, it could be that the avatar only has a certain number of arrows so it could be until the target is hit OR until the avatar runs out of arrows. Because the number of arrows might differ depending on how many have been used or how many the avatar has picked up or bought, the number of times is not a constant but rather a variable. Computer scientists use a simple formula with variables: $X=X+1$ or, in our arrow case, $X=X-1$ UNTIL $X=0$, within the loop to keep track. Our video game player would likely mentally keep track of this countdown or consult the information on the screen if it is displayed. The two conditions—hitting the target OR running out of arrows—have two different outcomes, another IF/THEN/ELSE scenario.

To keep track of all the paths where IF/THEN/ELSE statements and WHEN/UNTIL loops might lead, computer programmers sometimes use flow charts. Video game players create mental flow charts as they play, adding and modifying them as the game progresses. When they replay a game, they rely on the flow chart they have already created and even make other choices to explore other paths and fill out the missing parts of the flow chart. In fact, some players will even make mistakes on purpose to see what happens. The mental processes of video game players resemble those of flowcharts created by computer programmers. For our beginner coders, having a challenge where they have to program an avatar to search and find something is a perfect opportunity to introduce conditional looping since they have to program their avatar to sweep a location by systematically searching until the target item is found. Making this apparent and applying it to coding, ideally all within the same game world, can help promote transfer.

Algorithms

In video games, the core game mechanic is, "the repeated action that improves throughout the game through practice" (Kellinger, 2017, p. 162). While there may be several skills involved in video game play, these skills are almost always repeated, otherwise, if the player just performed each skill once, there would be no learning, or "leveling up." In fighting games, the core game mechanic is fighting, or putting together a sequence of actions such as punching and kicking in a certain order to defeat the enemy. In racing games, the core game mechanic is moving the vehicle both in terms of forward movement and side-to-side movement. In puzzle games, it is finding and using clues to solve a puzzle. Whatever the core game mechanic is, the player does it over and over again with each level adding a layer of difficulty.

In coding, when a sequence of commands is used throughout a program, instead of typing them out every single time they are used, programmers use *functions*, or commands bundled together and given a name, and then that name is used to signal to the computer to go to the glossary of functions that the programmer has created, find the one named, and execute those commands. This requires a level of abstraction—or recognizing when a sequence of actions can be applied to another task.

At the beginning of playing a video game, executing a series of commands takes intentional thought. However, as the game player practices this algorithm of actions, these functions become automatic. It is as if the brain has created a glossary of functions that the video game player accesses at the right moments. Sometimes this becomes so automatic, the player uses muscle memory to progress in a game.

Sometimes players play so many games, they can use their glossary of functions in a new game by tweaking the functions from an old game to fit the new game.

I would argue that this is the key difference between someone who plays video games and a gamer, that of abstraction—the ability to apply strategies used in one video game to another. Like my children said, "knowing how video game designers think." I even had this transfer occur in real life. In one of the *Myst* adventure games, I got stuck because I could not figure out that you had to close the doors to access hidden tunnels. When I finally figured it out, it was this "aha" moment that stuck in my brain. Clearly the designers had "engineer[ed a] 'memorable moment'" (Squire, 2011, p. 89). Later, when I rented a friend's condominium, I could tell from walking around the outside that it was bigger than what I was seeing on the inside. I went back into her place, closed the front door, only to reveal that behind it was the entryway to the master bedroom. A classic example of applying an algorithm to a new situation is using the strategy of a soldiers attacking a target from different angles to avoid triggering mines and applying that to the problem of a doctor needing to use such a large dose of radiation on a tumor that it would destroy healthy cells in its path. You could call this function, "Split_attack_from_different_angles." Storing these mental functions, recognizing when they apply, and deploying them resembles coders using functions. Programming codifies the same tasks that gamers store mentally. Building these opportunities in a coding game—to apply one set of tasks to a new situation—can help teach students not only what functions are and how to use them, but also how to use abstraction to identify when one strategy can be used in another situation.

Attributes and Behaviors

Object-Oriented Programming involves assigning objects, or nouns, certain attributes, adjectives if you will, to objects as well as defining a list of behaviors, or verbs, that that object can perform. A "child" of a "parent" object inherits these attributes and behaviors which then can be modified. In video games, objects and NPCs have defined attributes and behaviors that sometimes can be transformed based on actions in the game. Avatars too have attributes and behaviors. Choosing attributes and behaviors for an avatar from a pre-determined list can be a feature of a video game. These attributes and behaviors can be ornamental, can designate the level or role of an avatar, but also can sometimes determine gameplay and even success.

In many ways, playing a video game is like object-oriented programming, except in games, the game player "probes" (Johnson, 2005) the game to find out what the attributes and behaviors are of various objects. The big exception is construction and management simulation games like *SimCity* and sandbox games like *Minecraft* where players set their own goals and can choose attributes and behaviors of objects. In some cases, instead of inheritance where attributes and behaviors are directly passed down to children, players build up by combining objects to build up their behaviors. The game *Little Alchemy* has recombination as its core game mechanic. Players start off with earth, air, fire, and water and combine them to create new items, for example fire and earth make a volcano. Essential to both coding and gaming is the use of objects' attributes and behaviors to achieve a goal. Providing opportunities for students to define the attributes and behaviors, whether it be of an avatar or an object, can be used to introduce students to concepts behind object-oriented programming.

Debugging

Hypothesis testing is at the core of playing video games. Players develop a hypothesis about how to achieve success, try it, and, if they are not successful, try something else. An essential element in this loop is feedback, or how the player knows if they are successful or not. When a computer programmer writes a program, they do not know if they are successful until they try it out and get feedback. Executing a program, or part of a program, receiving feedback, and then making changes if that feedback is not what was expected is called debugging. Sometimes computer programmers add something to a program that they later remove in order to help them find problems in the code. For example, they might make the value of a variable visible on the screen so they can track how that variable changes over the course of a program. A lot of video games do this for the player by including a heads-up display or some other means of keeping track of health, success, money, inventory, or other variables within the game. This allows the player to receive a finer level of detail as feedback in their hypothesis testing loop.

Iterative Design

While debugging tests the validity of a program—does the computer do what the programmer intended— iterative design tests a program against its users—does the program have the effect on the users that the programmer intended. Iterative design involves playtesting a program, often via focus groups or other means, to get user feedback. While iterative design is not a necessary component of programming, it does help optimize the success of the program with its users. In gaming, players can play alone with no one privy to their gameplay except themselves, however, more and more a culture is developing around game playing where friends watch each other play, either in-person or online, and gamers even record themselves playing and post their gameplay on a video platform such as *YouTube*. This then garners feedback on gameplay which can improve the efficiency of gameplay of the original video game player and of others. New platforms such as *Twitch* and *Discord* have been designed specifically for sharing video game playing with others. Jenkins, et al. (2009) writes about this "participatory culture" that technology, and specifically games, has created, describing gaming culture as, "Instead of thinking as an autonomous problem solver, the player becomes part of a social and technological system that is generating and deploying information at a rapid pace" (p. 37). In other words, game players become more than just a cog in a machine, but rather programmers working together to create synergy.

CODING GAMES

There are many COTS (commercial, off the shelf) games and free educational games that teach coding. Some are more open-ended simulation type games like *The Pack* where the player explores an environment and must employ coding skills to survive whereas others are goal-oriented and prescriptive in their teaching of coding, like *Code Monkey* where the user has to learn to write code in order for the monkey to retrieve bananas to more story-based coding games like *May's Journey* and *Code Combat*. You could even argue the book series *Secret Coders,* where the characters learn coding and the reader has to create code to solve problems, is a coding game in print form. What all of them have in common is the building of coding skills through leveling up, or, in Gee's (2007) words, "a series of well-ordered problems" (p. 35).

However, educators can also take more control over what is taught by creating their own coding games in order to tailor the learning to their particular students. With the plethora of free game creation tools and the ability to repurpose common tools to create games, many opportunities exist for educators to create their own coding games. For example, using the Learning Management System (LMS) *Blackboard*, I created a semester-long asynchronous coding game for my Coding for Non-coders class. The course begins with the following scenario:

Groggily you come to. You try to move but you realize you are handcuffed and gagged. Slowly you remember being ambushed in your lab and being knocked out by a large person with a chair. "They must be trying to get my new invention," you think. You suspected that once word got out, bad actors would want to get their hands on this powerful new tool, you just didn't think it would happen this quickly. You know you must prevent them at all costs. After all, whoever controls this new technological invention can rule the world.

Students are immediately immersed in the game-story as they are faced with a pressing problem. As they play the game, they come to realize this new invention is the ability to mentally code technology, which comes in handy since they are handcuffed and gagged. They then have to mentally code their robot Sparky to save them, and thus save humanity, by preventing this invention from getting into the hands of evildoers.

By using the free block-based programming platform *Scratch,* students are then able to code Sparky to do certain tasks like find the keys to the handcuffs, figure out the keycode on the door of the lab, walk up an unknown number of steps, and so forth, all via mini-games I created in *Scratch*. When these tasks are successfully completed, the answers to quiz questions in *Blackboard* are revealed. For example, when students successfully code Sparky to find the keys to the handcuffs, Sparky plays a song in celebration. The name of the song is the answer to the quiz question in *Blackboard*. These gates are not labeled as quizzes, but rather are "stealth assessments" (Shute, 2011), in other words, disguised by being a part of the game story. In this way, students can perform tasks outside of *Blackboard* but still use the *Blackboard* platform to create gates so students can only level up to the next problem once they have solved the previous one. This game-based learning format to teach coding has resulted in students reporting being "addicted" and "hooked" to this "engaging" class.

Coding games do not have to be this elaborate, however. For example, in my 2017 book about game-based teaching, I frame the book with a game story that also serves to teach coding concepts, a technique you could call Trojan Horse teaching. I do so by building off the *Choose Your Own Adventure* type of storytelling where readers actively make choices as they read. In doing so, I introduce the concepts of IF/THEN/ELSE branching, Boolean logic, and conditional looping. Software tools to create branched narratives such as *Twine* or survey creators like *GoogleForms* that allow designers create multiple choice questions that "go to section based on answer" or even *Powerpoint* with its internal linking which allows creators to embed multiple links within one slide that each lead to a different slide can be used to create games that not only teach coding but enact coding concepts as well. Having students create a flowchart in their "After Action Review," or debriefing session, can introduce another coding technique.

There are some essentials to game-based learning, particularly when it comes to teaching coding, a skill that can easily lead to frustration. One commonality in coding games—both those made by others and teacher created ones—is leveling up—increasing the difficulty level of the skills required as a player progresses through a game. This leveling up is controlled by gating later material in the game. In order to unlock the gate, players must demonstrate the have mastered the current skill being taught, similar to Skinner's (1953) mastery learning. In this way, game-based teaching adjusts the game to the player's Zone of Proximal Development (ZPD) (Vygotsky, 1978), or challenge zone, what Prensky (2006) terms "adaptivity." Czikszentmihalyi (1990) discusses how being in this challenge zone, where skills are not so easy that the learner gets bored and are not so hard that the learner gets frustrated, contributes to what he calls flow, or the total immersion into an activity where the outside world disappears. In other words, to truly be consumed in Huizinga's "magic circle."

Vygotsky (1978) explains that in order for learners to shift their ZPD to a higher level, the teacher's role is to provide scaffolding. Designing your game-based course so that students can revise and resubmit allows for this scaffolding to be used for learning because students get a chance to apply the scaffolding instead of one and done assignments where teacher feedback hardly ever gets used like in traditional schooling. Having an unlimited number of attempts for "stealth assessments" (Shute, 2011)—whether it be for assignments or for quizzes disguised as part of the game story such as an interview for a job or a coding a robot—mimics video games where players' avatars can die, but can also respawn and try again. However, in order for these retries to be educational and not just trial and error, there must be feedback, perhaps from an NPC or the reaction of an object in the game, to let the player know they did something right or wrong and to gently guide them without telling them, such as a series of more and more direct hints the more wrong attempts are made. Learning by gaming does not come from games telling players what to do, but rather from "performance before competence" (Cazden, 1981)—trying something first, failing, and then learning from failing. It is this aspect of game-based learning that gives students the context and the motivation to "pull" information instead of having it "pushed" on them like in a traditional learning model (Rabone, 2013, p. 2). Just like looping in coding, game-based learning should involve iteration.

What I have described above could be done with a series of tasks or, "well-ordered problems" (Gee, 2007, p. 35). However, I would argue that that would not constitute a game. The most essential ingredient in creating an immersive game is the game-story. A game-story, a story where the player-controlled protagonist, or avatar, has a goal that the player has options for trying to reach either through a decision tree or more open-ended actions, provides the context, motivation, and fun that comprise a game. Stories are also prime vehicles for learning. For example, Brown (2000) describes how Xerox technicians eschewed the service manual in favor of stories of experiences from other Xerox technicians, which the company then capitalized on by providing walkie-talkies and then a website to exchange stories. They found that by doing so, technician knowledge increased by 300%. By embedding learning challenges with feedback cycles that increase in difficulty within the context of a story, game-based learning can be used with almost any subject. In the case of learning to code, the parallels between coding and gaming can be exploited to make game-based learning an even stronger pedagogical tool.

CONCLUSION

Although only an n of 2, when I asked my children about the coding games they have played, the first word they said was "fun"—the element I said was missing in the lists of game components by Kapp (2012), McGonigal (2011), and others. While engagement and motivation do not guarantee learning, certainly being "addicted" to a class can spur students to persist, take risks, and learn from their mistakes. The proof of learning in my game-based Coding for Non-Coders class came from taking students who defined themselves as non-coders, one of whom stated she had tried to learn several times before but with little success, to being able to code their own games by the end of the semester.

Repurposing common tools as game creation devices allows teachers, instructors, and professors to create their own means of teaching the 21ˢᵗ century skill of coding through game-based learning and, in doing so, also teach the other C's of critical thinking, communication, collaboration, creativity, and computational thinking. Not only is game-based learning a highly motivational and engaging way to do so, games themselves can also teach these same skills. In this era where even cars are coded to drive themselves, it is essential that all students learn the fundamentals of coding so they can understand how machines are manipulated and how machines can manipulate them. Whether using a COTS video game to make coding concepts explicit, using a game specifically designed to teach coding, or creating your own coding game, capitalizing on the similarities between coding and gaming is an efficient and elegant way to teach coding.

REFERENCES

Adams, E. (2010). *Fundamentals of game design*. New Riders.

Beck, J. C., & Wade, M. (2004). *Got game: How the gamer generation is reshaping business forever*. Harvard Business Press.

Bell, T., Witten, I., & Fellows, M. (1998). Computer science unplugged … off-line activities and games for all ages. Academic Press.

Berland, M., & Lee, V. R. (2011). Collaborative strategic board games as a site for distributed computational thinking. *International Journal of Game-Based Learning*, *1*(2), 65–81. doi:10.4018/ijgbl.2011040105

Brown, J. S. (2000, March/April). Growing up digital: How the web changes work, education, and the ways people learn. *Change*, *32*(2), 10–20. doi:10.1080/00091380009601719

Bruner, J. S. (1961). The act of discovery. *Harvard Educational Review*, *31*(1), 21–32.

Burns, B. (2008). Teaching the computer science of computer games. *Journal of Computing Sciences in Colleges*, *23*(3), 154–161.

Cazden, C. (1981). Performance before competence: Assistance to child discourse in the zone of proximal development. *The Quarterly Newsletter of the Laboratory of Comparative Human Cognition*, *3*, 5–8.

Combefis, S., Beresnevicius, G., & Dagiene, V. (2016). Learning programming through games and contests: Overview, characterization, and discussion. *Olympiads in Informatics*, *10*(1), 39–60. doi:10.15388/ioi.2016.03

Czikszentmihalyi, M. (1990). *Flow: The psychology of optimal experience*. Harper & Row.

deLaet, V., Kuffner, J., Slattery, M., & Sweedyk, E. (2005). *Computers games and CS education: Why and How*. Paper presented at SIGCSE, St. Louis, MO.

Dolgopolovas, V., Jevsikova, T., & Dagiene, V. (2018). From Android games to coding in C—An approach to motivate novice engineering students to learn programming. *Computer Applications in Engineering Education, 26*(1), 75–90. doi:10.1002/cae.21862

Duncan, J. (2019). Tech with a twist. Innovative youth programming combines coding with dance. *CBS News*. Retrieved 9/13/21 from https://www.cbsnews.com/news/dancelogic-innovative-youth-program-combines-coding-and-dance-2019-06-20/

Friedman, T. (2007). *The world is flat: A brief history of the twenty-first century*. Picador.

Gee, J. P. (2007). *Good video games plus good learning*. Peter Lang. doi:10.3726/978-1-4539-1162-4

Gilbert, N. (2020). *Number of gamers worldwide: Demographics, statistics, and predictions*. Finances Online. Retrieved 9/14/21 from https://financesonline.com/number-of-gamers-worldwide/

Harteveld, C., Smith, G., Carmichael, G., Gee, E., & Stewart-Gardiner, C. (2013). A design- focused analysis of games that teach computer science. *Journal of Computing Sciences in Colleges, 28*(6), 90–97.

Huizinga, J. (1955/2006). Nature and significance of play as a cultural phenomenon from Homo Ludens: A study of the play element in culture. In The Game Designer Reader: A Rules of Play Anthology (pp. 96-120). Cambridge, MA: MIT Press.

Jenkins, H. (2009). *Confronting the challenges of participatory culture: Media education for the 21st century*. MacArthur Foundation.

Jiang, X., Huang, X., Harteveld, C., & Fung, A. (2019). *The Computational Puzzle Design Framework*. Presented at the Association for Computing Machinery, San Luis Obispo, CA.

Johnson, S. (2005). *Everything bad is good for you: How today's popular culture is actually making us smarter*. Riverhead Books.

Kapp, K. (2012). *The Gamification of Learning and Instruction: Game-Based Methods and Strategies for Training and Education*. Pfeiffer.

Keeshin, J. (2021). *Read, write, code. A friendly introduction to the world of coding and why it's the new literacy*. Lioncrest Publishing.

Kellinger, J. (2017). *A guide to designing curricular games: How to 'game' the system*. Springer.

Klein, A. (2021). There aren't enough computer science classes for all the kids who want to take them. *Education Week*. Retrieved (from https://www.edweek.org/teaching-learning/there-arent-enough-computer-science-classes-for-all-the-kids-who-want-to-take-them/2021/09

Klopfer, E., Osterweil, S., & Salen, K. (2009). *Moving learning games forward: Obstacles, opportunities, and openness*. The Education Arcade at MIT.

Lee, T. Y., Mauriello, M., Ahn, J., & Bederson, B. (2014). CTArcade: Computational thinking with games in school-aged children. *International Journal of Child-Computer Interaction, 2*, 26–33.

Lee, V., Poole, F., Clarke-Midura, J., Recker, M., & Rasmussen, M. (2020). *Introducing coding through tabletop board games and their digital instantiations across elementary classrooms and school libraries.* Paper presented at SIGCSE, Portland. OR.

McGonigal, J. (2011). *Reality is broken: Why games make us better and how they can change the world.* Penguin Books.

Menon, D., Romero, M., & Viéville, T. (2019). Computational thinking development and assessment through tabletop escape games. *International Journal of Serious Games*, *6*(4), 3–18.

Nouri, J., Norén, E., & Skog, K. (2018). Learning programming by playing and coding games in K-9. *INTED 2018 : Proceedings*, 7990–7995.

Pariser, E. (2011). *The filter bubble: How the new personalized web is changing what we read and how we think.* Penguin Books.

Pelletier, C., & Oliver, M. (2006). Learning to play in digital games. *Learning, Media and Technology*, *31*(4), 329–342.

Prensky, M. (2006). *Don't bother me Mom—I'm learning!* Paragon House.

Prensky, M. (2011). Comments on research comparing games to other instructional methods. In S. Tobias & J. D. Fletcher (Eds.), *Computer games and instruction* (pp. 251–280). Information Age.

Rabone, D. (2013). How 'game mechanics" can revitalize education. *eSchoolNews.* http://www.eschool-news.com/2013/02/12/how-game-mechanics-can-revitalize- education/3/

Rushkoff, D. (2011). *Program or be programmed: Ten commands for a digital age.* Soft Skull Press.

Sharma, K., Papavlasopoulou, S., & Giannakos, M. (2019). Coding games and robots to enhance computational thinking: How collaboration and engagement moderate attitudes. *International Journal of Child-Computer Interaction*, *21*, 65–76.

Shute, V. (2011). Stealth assessment in computer-based games to support learning. In S. Tobias & J. D. Fletcher (Eds.), *Computer games and instruction* (pp. 503–524). Information Age Publishers.

Skinner, B. F. (1953). *Science and Human Behavior.* The Free Press.

Squire, K. (2011). *Video games and learning: Teaching and participatory culture in the digital age.* Teachers College Press.

Vaidyanathan, S. (2016). What's the difference between coding and computational thinking? *EdSurge.* Retrieved 9/14/2021 from https://www.edsurge.com/news/2016-08-06-what-s-the-difference-between-coding-and-computational-thinking

Vygotsky, L. (1978). *Mind in society.* Harvard University Press.

Wagner, T. (2008). Rigor redefined: Even our "best" schools are failing to prepare students for 21st-century careers and citizenship. *Educational Leadership*, *2*(66), 20–25.

Weintrop, D., Holbert, N., Horn, M., & Wilensky, U. (2016). Computational thinking in constructionist video games. *International Journal of Game-Based Learning*, *6*(1), 1–17.

Wing, J. (2006, March). Computational thinking. *Communications of the ACM, 49*(3), 33–36.

ADDITIONAL READING

Gee, J. P. (2007). *Good video games plus good learning*. Peter Lang. doi:10.3726/978-1-4539-1162-4

Kellinger, J. (2017). *A guide to designing curricular games: How to 'game' the system*. Springer. doi:10.1007/978-3-319-42393-7

Pariser, E. (2011). *The filter bubble: How the new personalized web is changing what we read and how we think*. Penguin Books.

Rushkoff, D. (2011). *Program or be programmed: Ten commands for a digital age*. Soft Skull Press.

Schell, J. (2008). *The art of game design: A book of lenses*. Morgan Kaufmann. doi:10.1201/9780080919171

Wing, J. (2006, March). Computational thinking. *Communications of the ACM, 49*(3), 33–36. doi:10.1145/1118178.1118215

KEY TERMS AND DEFINITIONS

Algorithms: Algorithms are a repeated set of actions that can be applied in multiple situations.

Avatars: Avatars are on-screen characters, whether animal, human, zombie, or object, that are controlled in real time by a human, as opposed to agents which are pre-programmed by a human and controlled by computer code, often in response to avatars' actions.

Coding: Coding, also called computer programming, consists of composing a series of commands with the expectation that a computer or some other sort of technology will later execute those commands.

Computational Thinking: Computational thinking comprises the types of strategies used to code computers and can be applied outside of computer programming with the goal of efficiency and elegance, i.e., doing a lot with a little.

Decomposition: Decomposition involves breaking a task into its component parts, often, like Russian nesting dolls, into smaller and smaller sized tasks in order to make coding manageable.

Functions: Functions are when coders separate out an algorithm from the main code and give that algorithm a name that they then use to call up that function over and over again as it is used throughout the computer program.

Game: A game is play, or experimenting with something by testing its boundaries within a rule set, that has an end goal.

Leveling Up: Leveling up is when someone, or something, masters a skill and then moves to higher level of challenge.

Object-Oriented Programming: Object-oriented programming refers to programming languages where coders define objects by their attributes and behaviors and can then use those objects to build other objects.

Sequencing: Sequencing means placing items in an order that accomplishes a goal.

Chapter 46

Using Custom–Built, Small–Scale Educational Solutions to Teach Qualitative Research Literacy:
No Code, Code, and Complex Applications

Geraldine Bengsch
Kings College London, UK

ABSTRACT

This chapter considers ways in which educators can create their own educational applications to integrate into their teaching. It is argued that interactive uses of technology can aid student engagement and encourage uptake of skills presented to them. Today, tools available allow everyone to create not only static websites, but also functional applications. It is possible to get started without knowing how to code, empowering anyone with an interest in technology to become a creator. While these no and low code solutions may come with some restrictions, they may encourage users to explore more traditional ways to engage with code and its possibilities for teaching. The chapter aims to encourage readers to look at technology as a creative practice to include into their teaching. It suggests strategies to help readers select the most appropriate tool for their projects.

INTRODUCTION

This chapter describes the potential for interactive, custom-built solutions in higher education in teaching qualitative research methods. Gamification has been of increased interest for increasing student engagement and motivation (Aldemir, Celik, & Kaplan, 2018; Tan & Hew, 2016; Tsay, Kofinas, & Luo, 2018). However, gamification does not solely rely on features such as rewards and badges, but rather aims to create an environment that stimulates learning and the acquisition of competencies (Torres-Toukoumidis, Rodríguez, & Rodríguez, 2018; Yıldırım & Şen, 2019). In this sense, the aim is to create multimodal

DOI: 10.4018/978-1-7998-7271-9.ch046

learning experiences that support student learning and competence in conducting research. Learning and teaching can be personal, practice-based and integrated to fit students as digital citizens (Keppell, 2014). Societies are changing and reveal mismatches between education and work reality (Azivov, Atamuratova, Holova, Kamalova, Akobiova, & Oltiev, 2020). This also affects pedagogical models and how they are applied in the classroom (Carvalho &Yeoman, 2018). However, the incorporation of technology may be limited to repetitive activities, such as reading from the screen or ticking boxes, calling for more creative applications of resources available (Kirschner, 2005). The chapter illustrates how applications can be constructed using a variety of tools. It shows examples of basic to more advanced applications to use in qualitative research method courses, constructed with no code and code-based tools. The chapter uses several example applications the author created to discuss considerations when creating custom-built teaching tools.

Background

Digital competence connects traditional education with requirements of today's society, integrating proactive and creative learning strategies into established approaches to improve instruction (Burianová & Turčáni, 2016; Fernández-Batanero, Montenegro-Rueda, Fernández-Cerero, & García-Martínez, 2020; Okoye, Nganji, & Hosseini, 2020). Instructional media for applied research activities have been used to teach modules online (Snelson, 2019). However, educators often lack the skill to build engaging education tools and often disagree on new teaching methods (Federici, Molinas, Sergi, Lussu, & Gola, 2019; Safapour, Kermanshachi, & Taneja, 2019; Taneja, Safapour, & Kermanshachi, 2018). Yet, tools available today allow to create flexible solutions to meet specific needs of students and material. Creating and maintaining apps often does not require expert knowledge, but rather an interest in technology (Boller, 2017; Nganji, 2018). However, support of management and appreciation of the time necessary to develop skills and resources need to be provided (Smith, 2012). There are no-code, low-code, and more code-intensive tools to choose from. The intended use of the app to be created aids naturally in selecting the appropriate tool (Luterbach & Hubbell, 2015; Saia, Nelson, Young, Parham, & Vandegrift, 2021).

Subjects such as research methods can often be perceived as abstract concepts that lack the connection to the students' interest in the field they are studying; custom-built solutions can aid in constructing authentic learning interactions (Keppell, 2014). These apps can add a layer of personalisation to the learning process and empower the user (Ballard & Butler, 2011; Stewart, McKee, 2009). The approach can encourage students to engage with teaching materials outside of the classroom. This aids a level of control over their learning for the student (McLoughlin & Lee, 2010). Students can use the tools to make them fit their own interests and learning speed (Holmes, Anastopoulou, Schaumburg, & Mavrikis, 2008). It also provides an additional way of presenting content to students, which may appeal to a diverse audience and individual needs. Digital approaches, including self-regulated personalisation using specific apps, allow students from different backgrounds, both educational and cultural, to cater the learning to their goals and abilities (Dillon, 2020; Melzer & Schoop, 2019; O'Donnell, Lawless, Sharp, & Wade, 2015). As such, it aims to create an additional layer of instructive material to promote a positive experience with the content (Fizgerald, Jones, Kucikova, & Scanlon, 2018). Algorithm based instruction, such as the use of recommender technology can further personalise students' learning journey to develop their competencies (Hulpuş, Hayes, & Fradin, 2014). Ultimately, this shift in focus on learner autonomy requires a change or adaptation of teaching practice (De Freitas & Neumann, 2009). A successful implementation of these apps may allow for greater learner autonomy, not only with regards to time and distance, but also for continued engagement beyond the duration of the course (Sampson & Karagiannidis, 2002).

The skills discussed in this chapter are applicable to research and work in academia on a more general level (Bermingham, Prendergast, Boland, O'Rawe, & Ryan, 2016; Camp & Wheaton, 2014; Seeger, 2018). Working with code, programming and the development of functional apps teaches the deconstruction of complex problems and its logic (Popat & Starkey, 2019; Tuomi, Multisilta, Saarikoski, & Suominen, 2018). More specifically, the ability to work within the constraints of a language or framework can influence perceptions of general literacy and its instruction (Burke, O'Byrne, & Kafai, 2016).

APPS IN QUALITATIVE RESEARCH LITERACY INSTRUCTION

This section presents different approaches to creating interactive applications, using a range of technologies. It uses some of the solutions created by the author used in qualitative research courses at various education levels. Starting with familiar programmes, it shows that custom apps to support student learning can be made without high levels of commitment. Instead, it allows educators to imagine new solutions to invent for their teaching. "Playing around" with these tools can be highly liberating and encourage educators to revise their teaching materials in new ways. These apps are not meant to replace teaching materials, but rather to use technology for developing helpful apps that encourage students to engage with their learning on an additional level. It creates another way to tell a story through teaching (Erwig, 2017).

Coding approaches may seem intimidating at first but allow for highly flexible apps for teaching support to be developed. As such, they allow for a contemporary blend of traditional approaches to teaching qualitative research methods with requirements of today's world and students' reality. Research literacy is not solely bound to the classroom, but an important life skill for students. Pen and paper are traditionally sufficient to "do" qualitative research; however, the unstructured nature of the data can make it difficult for students to apply methods they have been introduced to. Active learning can be presented in the form of custom applications that guide students through the taught content. The activities can be constructed to be worked with in class or outside, in groups or for individual students, much like traditional approaches.

No and Low Code Approaches to Creating Applications

Programming and coding come with a significant entry barrier, with a myriad of languages and platforms to choose from. However, creating interactive and engaging application is no longer reserved for software engineers. No code and low code tools exist to allow users to create functional apps using graphic user interfaces, instead of coding. Interactive solutions do not solely have to be internet based; indeed, even presentation tools like Microsoft PowerPoint or Apple's Keynote can be used to design engaging guides, workbooks, and resource packs (Anwar et al., 2020; Marcovitz, 2012; Matheson, Abt-Perkins, & Snedden, 2002).

Figure 1 is an example of how a presentation can be structured with hyperlinks to allow students to use slides for their review. Presentations can be converted into PDF format and retain their hyperlinked content. This solution can be highly useful in creating interactive readings for student revision. The aim here is to entice students to engage with the material they are presented with. However, module guides and other material can be overwhelming for students if they are not clear on how the information is structured for them (Butcher, Davies, & Highton, 2019). As a result, they may lose key information, especially if the content is dispersed across different documents and location. The example here was created for a first-year undergraduate module. The aim was to create a comprehensive guide that connects students directly to complementary information. Links embedded in the presentation are presented visually as tabs and buttons to make the usage self-explanatory. Links connect content both within the presentation, and also link to external content, making it a central component within the course.

Figure 1. Screenshot of an interactive Microsoft PowerPoint presentation created by the author

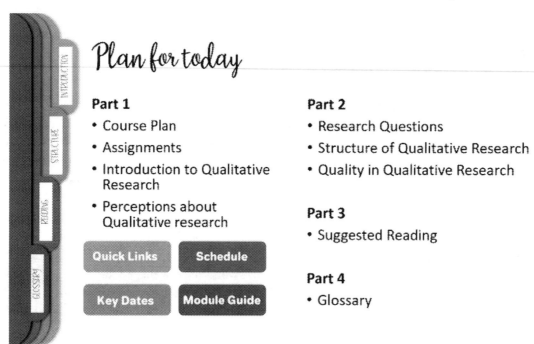

Presentation software is flexible and can be used to create interactive content with custom user interfaces. However not all media can be used in interactive documents, videos are no longer supported in PDFs, so a guide that is to contain embedded media in a portable format may be created in a format, such as EPUB or MOBI (Adobe InDesign is one of the tools that allows to create such documents (Boukhechba & Bouhania, 2019)). PowerPoint can be a powerful introduction to creating interactive solutions, even more so when it can remain in its native format and "hosted" on a shared machine for students to interact with. This "kiosk mode" in PowerPoint can be used to create presentations that act like webpages which students can explore. However, this particular part of the technology is somewhat deprecated and newer versions of PowerPoint no longer allow for presentations to be save directly in this "kiosk mode". Still, PowerPoint is a surprisingly powerful tool to begin creating personalised, interactive teaching materials using a familiar graphic user interface (GUI).

Spotlight Application 1: Interactive Guide to NVivo in Adobe Captivate

There are no-code tools developed specifically for creating educational content. Adobe Captivate is such a software that allows users to create interactive applications that can be integrated into Learning Management Systems (LMS). As an example, users can implement quizzes and revision activities into videos which are tracked by the LMS. Such functionality is often built into different LMs, however, content created there is often locked into the environment it was created in, making it difficult for educators to adapt their resources for other courses.

In the example here, Adobe Captivate was used to create an interactive guide to explain the qualitative research analysis software NVivo (Jackson, 2003). In software demonstrations, it is easy for students to get lost in the details, making it difficult for them to become comfortable in working with the software, especially when learning it in a lecture environment (Bong, 2002; Roberts, Breen, & Symes, 2013). This example shows students basic operations so they can replicate the steps presented to them in class without a wordy script. The application was created for a research method course for Master level students (Silver & Rivers, 2016).

Figure 2. Screenshot of author's interactive guide created in Adobe Captivate

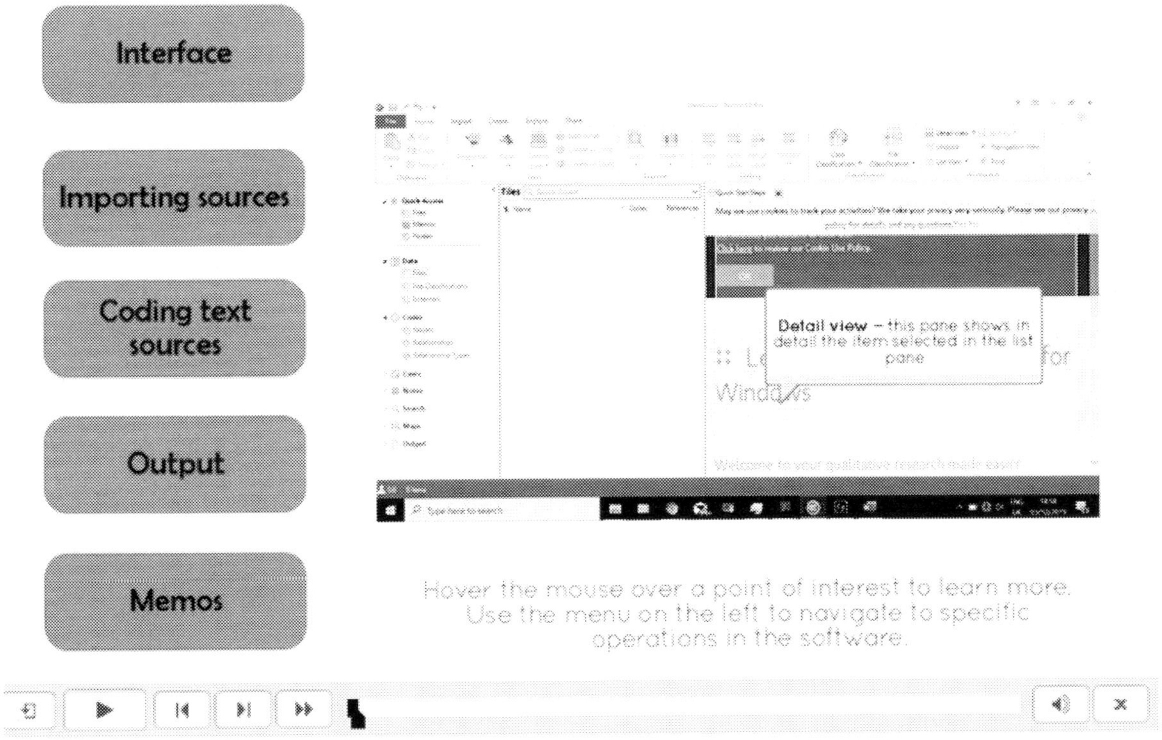

Figure 2 shows the description of the interface. Students can hover over the point of interest to see definitions and explanations. The guide also covers key functions, such as importing sources into the programme, coding, and taking notes. The functions may seem simple; this is part of the design. Students are often exposed to a complex software, such as NVivo in this case, in a short amount of time that can leave them overwhelmed when they need to return to use it. The guide here aims to be a non-threatening reminder of base functions, so that students can concentrate on using the software (Carvajal, 2002). It combines written instructions with pictures, overlays, and animations to cater for different learning styles and student requirements. Student can choose which part they wish to engage with, there is no specific start or endpoint to the guide, which means that it is not bound to a common sentiment of having to complete something, but rather a guide that invites students to return to the material.

Pros and Cons of No/Low Code Approaches:

- **Pros:**
  - Able to use familiar technology to create interactive applications
  - Possibility to practice algorithmic thinking
  - Low level of investment
  - Can be easily integrated into LMS
- **Cons:**
  - Due to its nature, more rigid than code-based solutions
  - Dissemination to students may be restricted
  - Some programs may be expensive

Coding Approaches to Creating Applications

In the Social Sciences, educators have often already encountered tools that can be used to create engaging applications for students to scaffold their learning. Researchers are commonly somewhat familiar with a spreadsheet programme, such as Microsoft Excel. Microsoft Excel has become a powerful tool with a complete programming language to even conduct machine learning tasks (Martino, 2019; Zhang, 2020). Microsoft's *Visual Basic for Applications* language (VBA) allows educators to work with a programming language in a familiar environment (Hasana & Alifiani, 2019). In qualitative research methods, a spreadsheet can be a useful tool for students to keep a record of their reading. Undergraduate students often realise that they need a way to structure their reading, but citation managers might be too intimidating to use and not provide the scaffolding needed for students (Salem & Fehrmann, 2013). Students may also feel that their assignments are not complex enough to justify learning a how to use a designated reference management program (Kuglitsch & Burge, 2016). This intermediary step was created to help students develop information management literacy (Zakharov & Maybee, 2019).

Figure 3 shows a simple reading list manager that introduces students to keeping track of their reading. The entry form was created using VBA to encourage students to practice entering data in a structured way, similar to working with data bases. The in-built development interface can be accessed through the *Developer* tab which may need to be added to the Ribbon if it is not visible by default (see Figure 3). The spreadsheet is set up with additional options that allows students to filter their reading list alphabetically for all the individual options. The aim was to create an engaging experience for the end users. This template was created for a second-year undergraduate course on qualitative methods. The assignment on the module is a critical review of a qualitative article. Some students limit their review to finding flaws, instead of generating a fair view on the work. The table encourages students to take notes on their module reading to reinforce the terms introduced to them and their ability to use them when working with literature. The app considers the motivation of its end users, and the interface was created to reflect this. Once a basic template is created, it can be adapted for many other uses, including administrative lists.

Figure 3. Screenshot of data entry form for an interactive reading list in Microsoft Excel created by the author

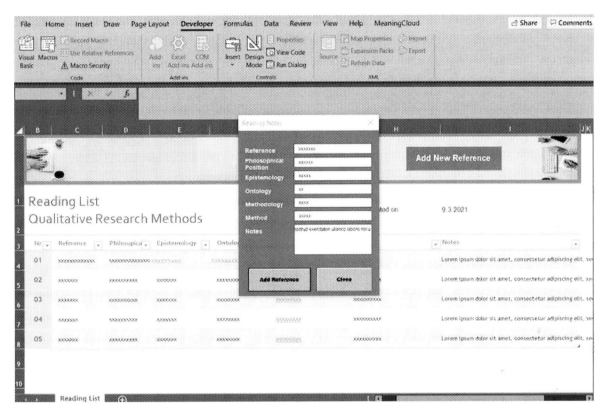

Spotlight Application 2: Observation Practice Web App

One of the restrictions using a standalone software programme to create an application is that it cannot be made available to many students in the same way that a website can be accessed. For such applications, a more traditional approach may be better suitable. A key skill to develop in qualitative research literacy is management of data, and the understanding of the form it can come in (MacQueen & Milstein, 1999; Mulhall, 2003).

Here, the author used HTML/CSS and JavaScript to create an interactive web app to allow students to practice observation and taking field notes of videos. Students often struggle not only with the concepts presented in research methods, but also how to structure their work (Musante & DeWalt, 2010). In this example, students are guided to practice taking notes useful for an observational project. The data is converted to a CSV document which can be imported into software such as Excel or NVivo to continue their analysis. The app was created for the same qualitative research method course as mentioned above.

When creating the app, the focus was placed on the main goal it was to accomplish. Here, creating a structured form for students to practice observing social life (Aktinson & Hammersley, 1998). The app went through several iterations in which additional features where added. The app allows students to take notes based on a random video, accessed through an API service, or to upload their own video to work with. In addition, students can take screenshots of points of interests throughout their videos. As a result, the app has a second usage: it doubles as a rather convenient tool to record screenshots with timestamps for other research projects. In the author's experience, such somewhat unexpected uses are quite common when developing apps. While working on an app, new features and alternative usage cases may arise. For this app, a second observational form was created in which students can reflect on their structured observational notes. Unlike the first form, the student's writing is downloaded in TXT format, thus, remains unstructured. Students are exposed to notes in two different formats to work with and experience what a processing of it may look like.

Figure 4. Screenshot of data entry form on the author's web app "ObserveIt"

Figure 4 shows the data entry form for students to take their notes in. The web app is a companion app to a chapter the author has written on teaching qualitative observations. The chapter includes further instructions on the categories. In addition, it is structured like a website, so that there is instructions and other information present on the site. This was deemed as important, as the app is likely to change and develop beyond the scope of the purpose presented in the original chapter.

Figure 5. Screenshot of data imported into Microsoft Excel

	A	B	C	D	E	F	G	H
1	Title	Hotel reception	four star h	Germany				
2	Date	9/9/2021						
3	Appearance	Receptionist: fema	Guest: couple; dressed casually					
4	Verbal behaviour	Receptionist leads	male cust	both guests nod and reply to receptionists talk				
5	Physical behaviour	Receptionist provi	receptionist gestures to relevant points of interest; guests follc					
6	Personal space	interaction visually	individuals share the reception desk throughout the conversati					
7	Human traffic	Other people are c	others explicitly mark their presence as not part of the ongoing					
8	People who stand out							
9								
10								

The data is exported in CSV format and can be imported into a spreadsheet program, such as Microsoft Excel, as shown in Figure 5. The comma separated value format that the original data is created allows for structured note taking, where every comma creates a new cell within a topic and under a certain header. How students choose to continue with the data is up to them. The data can be coded and manipulated in a program like Excel or prepared to be used in another program (Bree & Gallagher, 2016; Meyer & Avery, 2009).

The screenshot in Figure 6 shows the data transposed in Excel and imported into NVivo. Based on the preparation in Excel, it is possible to import the data as individual cases with certain, desired attributes (Jackson & Bazeley, 2019). The resulting columns and the contained text can be coded in the program (see screenshot).

The tool has been deployed and is usable in teaching. However, this does not mean that it is finished or to remain unchanged. It is always possible to tinker with the current version and to add, change, or remove features. This allows for apps to be developed according to current coding skill level or time available. The application can grow with its creator. The technology used is highly flexible and well supported. Libraries and packages exist for a wide range of uses and can be introduced into a program, often with little effort. This reduces the amount of code that needs to be generated from scratch. One such library is used in the *ObserveIt* app to annotate and draw on screenshots taken during observation. These packages can transform the usability of any app and extend the way it can be interacted with.

Not only the technology is flexible when working with code, but also the working environment. Principally, only a text editor is needed to create applications. However, there are a variety of free integrated development environments (IDEs) that have extra functionalities, such as automatic code completion and error logging (Škorić, Pein, & Orehovački, 2016). These also can make working with different types of frameworks, such as React or Node.js easier. Software such as Adobe Dreamweaver combine code with a visual element that can help a beginner as they provide immediate feedback. However, not all technology may be compatible with it. Tutorials can provide both in-depth and accessible examples of what is possible to create with a chosen program.

Figure 6. Screenshot of data imported into NVivo

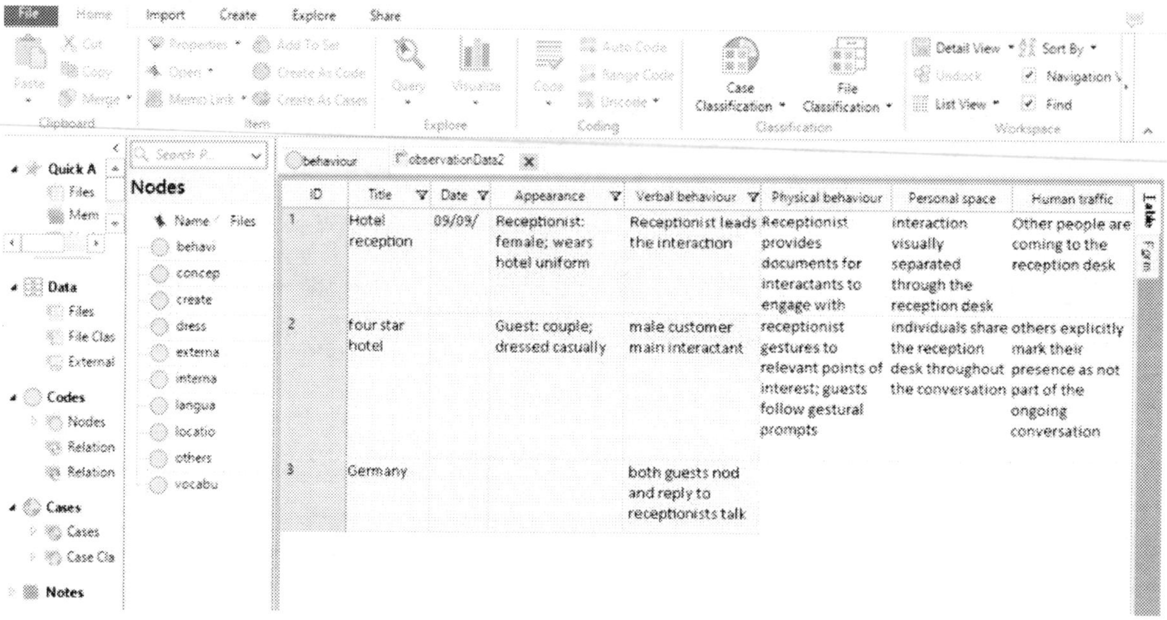

Pros and Cons of Code-Based Approaches

- **Pros:**
  - Highly flexible to customize application
  - Can be embedded into LMS to a degree (static webpages)
  - Can published on the web, no restriction to an LMS or a singular course
  - Mostly open-source, free programs
- **Cons:**
  - Medium to high level of investment
  - Dynamic webpages (using JavaScript) may not be easily embeddable into LMS
  - Deciding on which technology to learn and use can be overwhelming

Complex Applications with Machine Learning

Qualitative research method analysis is often supported using computer programs that help researchers organise their work. However, students often wonder why the programs do not do the analysis in the same way that statistical programs produce an output (Blismas & Dainty, 2003). The technology for automatic analysis of texts certainly exists and technology constantly improves, yet is still far from perfect. This can make for the creation of applications that encourage students to consider technology, ethics, and their impact on everyday life. Students are exposed to data and the story that is told with it daily in their life. Research literacy is an important skill in today's world, and this also includes the ability to engage with qualitative and textual data. Visualisations can help students interpret complex data (Brooker, Sharrock, & Greiffenhagen, 2019), however, they also need to be able to judge the quality and accuracy of the analysis presented. Qualitative research method courses need to teach the methods inherent in the paradigm. At the same time, teaching needs to be relevant to today's concerns and representation of data. This may not always be possible with what is considered a traditional approach in qualitative analysis. Using concepts such as Artificial Intelligence, Machine and Deep Learning open new approaches to understanding and teaching research literacy.

Spotlight Application 3: Thematic Analysis Practice with Machine Learning

In this approach, Python was used to create the beginning of a Machine Learning supported application. Students often struggle to identify themes in the data they are working with (Vaughn & Turner, 2016). In this example, students develop codes for a piece of text and check them against a topic modelling algorithm in the app. This further encourages students to contemplate what computers are capable of and to what extent they are useful in qualitative data analysis – or not. The aim here would be to create an environment in which students can engage with data that has been pre-analysed to see whether their own way of thinking is comparable to the ideas constructed through a model. This skill is not solely important in the classroom, but for students to confidently interact with representations of texts generated by machine learning that they encounter outside of their degree.

Figure 7. Screenshot of topic model; "#coronavirus" Instagram posts

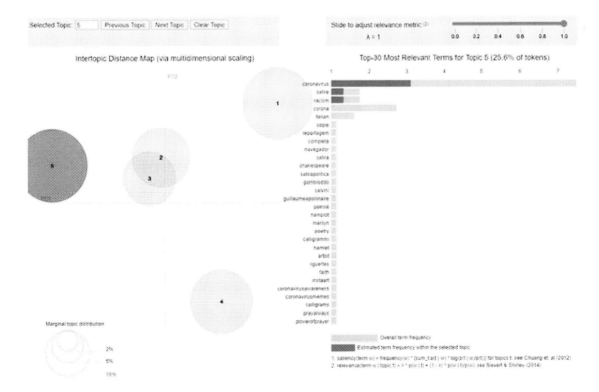

Figure 7 shows a prototype for an app integrating machine learning to teach qualitative research literacy. The interactive visualisation is based on Latent Dirichlet Allocation (LDA), a popular algorithm used to extract topics from texts through topic modelling based on Machine Learning (Wallach, Murray, Salakhutdinov, & Mimno, 2009). It is situated in Natural Language Processing (NLP) that allows for dealing with textual data through computer algorithms (Deng & Liu, 2018; Sarkar, 2016). Here, the model created with the interactive Python package *pyLDAvis* has been set to displaying five topics from the data, but this could be developed into an app where the number of topics can be set by the user. The circles show the topic importance, with the distance between them representing the similarity between them. The histogram displays the 30 most relevant terms within the selected topic. The example in Figure 7 shows captions for the hashtag "coronavirus" on Instagram in January 2020, where "memes" were identified as a topic. The data set was collected by the author. The author has used this model to engage both undergraduate and postgraduate students in discussions on reflexivity and credibility in qualitative research (Woods, Macklin, & Lewis, 2016).

Such a model could be implemented into a variety of tools to encourage students to engage with qualitative data analysis. A simple app could be built using an all-Python framework like *Streamlit*, or it could be integrated into a web app, like the one mentioned previously, so that students can upload their own texts and data. Features could allow students to upload their own texts, or fetch a random text, e.g., a news article, using an API. The basic approach to using machine learning in teaching qualitative research literacy does not end with topic modelling. It is up to the educator to imagine and create their vision through code: models could be used for extractive or abstractive summarisation, sentiment analysis, entity recognition and other NLP tasks (Aggarwal, 2018; Sarkar, 2016). The app could be created as a dashboard that allows students to explore the text through various approaches. Through working with the models in such an app, students could be encouraged to experience how far machine learning has come – or not. This further develops opportunities to engage students with current ethical debates surrounding data and its analysis.

Pros and Cons of Complex Code-Based Approaches:

- **Pros:**
  - Able to create highly complex applications
  - Highly customizable
  - Mostly free, open-source programs
  - Data science can be used as a method for research projects
- **Cons:**
  - Specialist knowledge required
  - May require additional knowledge about data science
  - High level of investment required

SOLUTIONS AND RECOMMENDATIONS

Educators in the social sciences have access to new tools that help them deal with a rapidly changing world, including their teaching (Brooker, 2019). A mix of low and high investment technology allows educators to choose an approach that works best for them and best for their intended use. Creating custom built applications is based on a highly flexible approach. An application does not to have a lot of features to be useful to students. Instead, time investment does not need to be high to begin creating. The app does not need to be fixed, but can be changed, updated, and extended as the need arises – and based on student feedback and evolution of personal teaching practice. Creating an app can be an extension of existing teaching activities that enhances an existing curriculum to engage students in and outside the classroom. Purpose built applications do not need to be innovative but should instead fit the context in which they are to be used. While there are many technologies that a creator can choose from, they all have their place and do not need to compete with each other. It is not necessary to utilise or use all of them. Instead, they should harmonise with the approach in which they are to exist. Complexity of an approach does not dictate the outcome of the app's usability. A simple app may be what is best suited to create learning opportunities. The aim of these apps should be to enhance students' experience with their course and to help them build and retain knowledge. As an educator, it allows to create a solution that fits the exact needs of an approach. It reflects the teaching philosophy. While some of technology mentioned in this chapter is rather expensive, a considerable amount is completely free, and the creator retains all of the copyright for the code of the app. Approaches are flexible and the application can be changed depending on the users' needs throughout its lifecycle. An educator can use their own solutions as templates to build additional apps.

Steps in Creating Your Custom-Built App:

1. Identify an opportunity for a purpose-built application:
    Effective teaching is based on relevant activities. Consider a current issue in your teaching that could be addressed with a new approach.
2. Consider different approaches:
    No code, code, or complex application? Contemplate your current skills and knowledge. How does this fit to your initial idea? Code or no-code approach?
3. Define aim:
    What is the purpose of the app? What should users get out of using the product? How is the app going to scaffold student learning and your teaching? What should students be able to do after engaging with your app?
4. **Find inspiration:** How do you imagine your application? What do applications that already exist in the area look like? What kind of features are common? Are they online or offline approaches? Websites like contain a wealth of ideas on modern user interfaces (UI) for inspiration.
5. Consider needs and wants:
    What is the key feature that addresses your principle aim of your application? In a first iteration, you want to aim to create a "Minimum Viable Product" (MVP), that is, a basic functionable app that users can interact with. Additional features can always be added at a later point. Keep a list of functionalities you may want to implement in the future.
6. Create base app:
    Begin building your application in your chosen technology. This step can be overwhelming. Make yourself detailed notes about the steps that need to be completed to help you structure this process. This will also help highlight if there are additional things you need to learn during development. If there are aspects that you are unsure of, consider replacing them with a placeholder and return to them

at a later stage. You can often create a workable product without implementing everything at once. Websites like www.stackoverflow.com can help answer specific questions on coding technologies.

7. Deploy app and test it:

Once you have something functioning, consider making it available and have potential users engage with it to provide you with feedback for further development. Your students and your network can help you finetune your work. Services such as Netlify can be used to host applications for free.

8. Continue development:

Revisit your application after some time to refine your work and add new features. Creating a feature-rich piece of software takes time; consider keeping it simple and ensure that the functionality is working before you "prettify" it.

FUTURE DIRECTIONS

Technology has always been an important aspect of teaching and assisting students learn. Creating flexible apps for teaching provides an additional avenue to share teaching expertise with other educators. The approaches discussed in this chapter are not integrated into a static system. This means that the applications and their underlying code can be shared with others beyond a singular course, in an open-source approach. Sharing the code base on platforms such as GitHub also makes it possible to allow others to contribute to the application. This also encourages networking and sharing of practices across classrooms. Qualitative research literacy is arguably changing though technology in society. Educators have the opportunity to shape students' perception and appreciation of a qualitative approach to analysis of data. Technology can generate new opportunities for students to create interactive experiences in their learning.

CONCLUSION

The abundance of tools available today allows educators to personalise their teaching to suit their students' needs. Creating applications is no longer reserved for software engineers. The process consists of breaking down complex problems into smaller ones (Elliott, 2019; Zingaro, 2021) – a notion that researchers are familiar with through working with projects. Platforms for development are available that remove barriers to make custom-built tools. For some of the no code solutions, no interest in technology is needed to get started. As discussed in this chapter, the intended purpose of the app will inform the type of technology needed. In the end, what can be created is down to the user's creativity. Apps developed according to the principles in this chapter are extendable, reusable and convertible to new teaching scenarios. A custom-built solution can be targeted to the students' needs, the educator's teaching style and fit a specific aim in teaching. They do not need to be complex to create teachable moments for students and to engage them in their learning. Instead, they can help in connecting students to the story that data tells and letting them be part of the narrative (Erwig, 2017). Purpose built applications are an opportunity to take an active part in shaping the story that qualitative data and its literacy tells.

REFERENCES

Aggarwal, C. C. (2018). Neural networks and deep learning. Springer, 10, 978-973.

Aktinson, P., & Hammersley, M. (1998). Ethnography and participant observation. In *Strategies of Qualitative Inquiry* (pp. 248–261). Sage.

Aldemir, T., Celik, B., & Kaplan, G. (2018). A qualitative investigation of student perceptions of game elements in a gamified course. *Computers in Human Behavior, 78*, 235–254. doi:10.1016/j.chb.2017.10.001

Anwar, Z., Kahar, M. S., Rawi, R. D. P., Nurjannah, N., Suaib, H., & Rosalina, F. (2020). Development of interactive video based powerpoint media In mathematics learning. *Journal of Educational Science and Technology, 6*(2), 167–177. doi:10.26858/est.v6i2.13179

Avizov, S. R., Atamuratova, T. I., Holova, S. A., Kamalova, F. R., Akobirova, L. H., & Oltiev, A. T. (2020). Traditional requirements and innovative learning models in the higher education context. *European Journal of Molecular & Clinical Medicine, 7*(2), 872–885.

Ballard, J., & Butler, P. (2011). Personalised Learning: Developing a Vygotskian Framework for E-learning. *International Journal of Technology, Knowledge and Society, 7*(2), 21–36. doi:10.18848/1832-3669/CGP/v07i02/56198

Bermingham, N., Prendergast, M., Boland, T., O'Rawe, M., & Ryan, B. (2016). Developing mobile apps for improving the orientation experience of first-year third-level students. *Proceedings of 8th Annual International conference on Education and New Learning Technologies.* 10.21125/edulearn.2016.0137

Blismas, N. G., & Dainty, A. R. (2003). Computer-aided qualitative data analysis: Panacea or paradox? *Building Research and Information, 31*(6), 455–463. doi:10.1080/0961321031000108816

Boller, S. (2017). "Appily ever after": How to create your own library mobile app through easy to use, low cost technology. *Library Hi Tech News, 34*(10), 7–10. doi:10.1108/LHTN-09-2017-0069

Bong, S. A. (2002). *Debunking myths in qualitative data analysis.* Paper presented at the Forum Qualitative Sozialforschung/Forum: Qualitative Social Research.

Boukhechba, H., & Bouhania, B. (2019). Adaptation of instructional design to promote learning in traditional EFL classrooms: Adobe Captivate for e-learning content. *International Journal of Education and Development Using Information and Communication Technology, 15*(4), 151–164.

Bree, R. T., & Gallagher, G. (2016). Using Microsoft Excel to code and thematically analyse qualitative data: A simple, cost-effective approach. *All Ireland Journal of Higher Education, 8*(2).

Brooker, P. D. (2019). Programming with Python for Social Scientists. *Sage (Atlanta, Ga.).*

Brooker, P. D., Sharrock, W., & Greiffenhagen, C. (2019). Programming visuals, visualising programs. *Science & Technology Studies, 32*(1), 21–42.

Burianová, M., & Turčáni, M. (2016). Non-traditional education using smart devices. *DIVAI, 2016.*

Burke, Q., O'Byrne, W. I., & Kafai, Y. B. (2016). Computational participation: Understanding coding as an extension of literacy instruction. *Journal of Adolescent & Adult Literacy*, *59*(4), 371–375. doi:10.1002/jaal.496

Butcher, C., Davies, C., & Highton, M. (2019). *Designing learning: From module outline to effective teaching*. Routledge. doi:10.4324/9780429463822

Camp, R. J., & Wheaton, J. M. (2014). Streamlining field data collection with mobile apps. *Eos (Washington, D.C.)*, *95*(49), 453–454. doi:10.1002/2014EO490001

Carvajal, D. (2002). *The artisan's tools. Critical issues when teaching and learning CAQDAS*. Paper presented at the Forum Qualitative Sozialforschung/Forum: Qualitative Social Research.

Carvalho, L., & Yeoman, P. (2018). Framing learning entanglement in innovative learning spaces: Connecting theory, design and practice. *British Educational Research Journal*, *44*(6), 1120–1137. doi:10.1002/berj.3483

De Freitas, S., & Neumann, T. (2009). The use of 'exploratory learning' for supporting immersive learning in virtual environments. *Computers & Education*, *52*(2), 343–352. doi:10.1016/j.compedu.2008.09.010

Deng, L., & Liu, Y. (2018). *Deep learning in natural language processing*. Springer. doi:10.1007/978-981-10-5209-5

Dillon, J. D. (2020). More than netflix: The real potential of personalised learning. *Training & Development*, *47*(2), 20–23.

Elliott, E. (2019). *Composing software: An exploration of functional programming and object composition in JavaScript*. Leanpub.

Erwig, M. (2017). *Once upon an algorithm: How stories explain computing*. MIT Press. doi:10.7551/mitpress/10786.001.0001

Federici, S., Molinas, J., Sergi, E., Lussu, R., & Gola, E. (2019). Rapid and easy prototyping of multimedia tools for education. *Proceedings of the World Conference on Media and Mass Communication*. 10.17501/24246778.2019.5102

Fernández-Batanero, J. M., Montenegro-Rueda, M., Fernández-Cerero, J., & García-Martínez, I. (2020). Digital competences for teacher professional development. Systematic review. *European Journal of Teacher Education*, 1–19. doi:10.1080/02619768.2020.1827389

Hasana, S. N., & Alifiani, A. (2019). Multimedia development using visual basic for application (VBA) to improve students' learning motivation in studying mathematics of economics. *Indonesian Journal of Mathematics Education*, *2*(1), 34–42. doi:10.31002/ijome.v2i1.1230

Holmes, W., Anastopoulou, S., Schaumburg, H., & Mavrikis, M. (2018). *Technology-enhanced personalised learning: Untangling the evidence*. Robert Bosch Stiftung GmbH.

Hulpuş, I., Hayes, C., & Fradinho, M. O. (2014). A framework for personalised Learning-plan recommendations in Game-based learning. In *Recommender Systems for Technology Enhanced Learning* (pp. 99–122). Springer. doi:10.1007/978-1-4939-0530-0_5

Jackson, K. (2003). Blending technology and methodology: A shift toward creative instruction of qualitative methods with NVivo. *Qualitative Research Journal.*

Jackson, K., & Bazeley, P. (2019). Qualitative data analysis with NVivo. *Sage (Atlanta, Ga.).*

Keppell, M. (2014). Personalised learning strategies for higher education. In *The future of learning and teaching in next generation learning spaces.* Emerald Group Publishing Limited. doi:10.1108/S1479-362820140000012001

Kirschner, P. A. (2005). Learning in innovative learning environments. *Computers in Human Behavior, 21*(4), 547–554. doi:10.1016/j.chb.2004.10.022

Kuglitsch, R. Z., & Burge, P. (2016). Beyond the first year: Supporting sophomores through information literacy outreach. *College & Undergraduate Libraries, 23*(1), 79–92. doi:10.1080/10691316.2014.944636

Luterbach, K. J., & Hubbell, K. R. (2015). Capitalizing on app development tools and technologies. *TechTrends, 59*(4), 62–70. doi:10.100711528-015-0872-8

MacQueen, K. M., & Milstein, B. (1999). A systems approach to qualitative data management and analysis. *Field Methods, 11*(1), 27–39. doi:10.1177/1525822X9901100103

Marcovitz, D. M. (2012). *Powerful PowerPoint for educators: Using Visual Basic for applications to make PowerPoint interactive.* Abc-Clio.

Martino, J. C. R. (2019). *Hands-on machine learning with Microsoft Excel 2019: Build complete data analysis flows, from data collection to visualization.* Packt Publishing Ltd.

Matheson, V. A., Abt-Perkins, D., & Snedden, D. (2002). *Making PowerPoint interactive with hyperlinks.* Paper presented at the poster session presented at the annual American Economic Association Convention, Atlanta, GA.

McLoughlin, C., & Lee, M. J. (2010). Personalised and self regulated learning in the Web 2.0 era: International exemplars of innovative pedagogy using social software. *Australasian Journal of Educational Technology, 26*(1). Advance online publication. doi:10.14742/ajet.1100

Melzer, P. (2019). Personalising the IS classroom–insights on course design and implementation. In *A conceptual framework for personalised learning* (pp. 77–100). Springer Gabler. doi:10.1007/978-3-658-23095-1_4

Meyer, D. Z., & Avery, L. M. (2009). Excel as a qualitative data analysis tool. *Field Methods, 21*(1), 91–112. doi:10.1177/1525822X08323985

Mulhall, A. (2003). In the field: Notes on observation in qualitative research. *Journal of Advanced Nursing, 41*(3), 306–313. doi:10.1046/j.1365-2648.2003.02514.x PMID:12581118

Musante, K., & DeWalt, B. R. (2010). *Participant observation: A guide for fieldworkers.* Rowman Altamira.

Nganji, J. T. (2018). Towards learner-constructed e-learning environments for effective personal learning experiences. *Behaviour & Information Technology, 37*(7), 647–657. doi:10.1080/0144929X.2018.1470673

O'Donnell, E., Lawless, S., Sharp, M., & Wade, V. P. (2015). A review of personalised e-learning: Towards supporting learner diversity. *International Journal of Distance Education Technologies, 13*(1), 22–47. doi:10.4018/ijdet.2015010102

Okoye, K., Nganji, J. T., & Hosseini, S. (2020). Learning analytics for educational innovation: A systematic mapping study of early indicators and success factors. *International Journal of Computer Information Systems and Industrial Management Applications, 12*, 138–154.

Popat, S., & Starkey, L. (2019). Learning to code or coding to learn? A systematic review. *Computers & Education, 128*, 365–376. doi:10.1016/j.compedu.2018.10.005

Roberts, L. D., Breen, L. J., & Symes, M. (2013). Teaching computer-assisted qualitative data analysis to a large cohort of undergraduate students. *International Journal of Research & Method in Education, 36*(3), 279–294. doi:10.1080/1743727X.2013.804501

Safapour, E., Kermanshachi, S., & Taneja, P. (2019). A review of nontraditional teaching methods: Flipped classroom, gamification, case study, self-learning, and social media. *Education Sciences, 9*(4), 273. doi:10.3390/educsci9040273

Saia, S. M., Nelson, N. G., Young, S. N., Parham, S., & Vandegrift, M. (2021). *Ten simple rules for researchers who want to develop web apps.* Academic Press.

Salem, J., & Fehrmann, P. (2013). Bibliographic management software: A focus group study of the preferences and practices of undergraduate students. *Public Services Quarterly, 9*(2), 110–120. doi:10.1080/15228959.2013.785878

Sampson, D., & Karagiannidis, C. (2002). Personalised learning: Educational, technological and standarisation perspective. *Digital Education Review*, (4), 24–39.

Sarkar, D. (2016). *Text analytics with python.* Springer. doi:10.1007/978-1-4842-2388-8

Seeger, C. J. (2018). Open-source mapping: Landscape perception, participatory design and user-generated content; collecting user-generated walking and biking route preference data through repurposed apps, custom coding, and open-source mapping tools. In *Codify* (pp. 149–154). Routledge. doi:10.4324/9781315647791-14

Silver, C., & Rivers, C. (2016). The CAQDAS Postgraduate Learning Model: An interplay between methodological awareness, analytic adeptness and technological proficiency. *International Journal of Social Research Methodology, 19*(5), 593–609. doi:10.1080/13645579.2015.1061816

Škorić, I., Pein, B., & Orehovački, T. (2016). *Selecting the most appropriate web IDE for learning programming using AHP.* Paper presented at the 39th International Convention on Information and Communication Technology, Electronics and Microelectronics (MIPRO). 10.1109/MIPRO.2016.7522263

Smith, K. (2012). Lessons learnt from literature on the diffusion of innovative learning and teaching practices in higher education. *Innovations in Education and Teaching International, 49*(2), 173–182. doi:10.1080/14703297.2012.677599

Snelson, C. (2019). Teaching qualitative research methods online: A scoping review of the literature. *Qualitative Report, 24*(11), 2799–2814. doi:10.46743/2160-3715/2019.4021

Stewart, I., & McKee, W. (2009). Review of pedagogical research into technology to support inclusive personalised learning. *Engineering Education, 4*(2), 62–69. doi:10.11120/ened.2009.04020062

Tan, M., & Hew, K. F. (2016). Incorporating meaningful gamification in a blended learning research methods class: Examining student learning, engagement, and affective outcomes. *Australasian Journal of Educational Technology, 32*(5). Advance online publication. doi:10.14742/ajet.2232

Taneja, P., Safapour, E., & Kermanshachi, S. (2018). *Innovative higher education teaching and learning techniques: Implementation trends and assessment approaches.* Paper presented at the 2018 ASEE Annual Conference & Exposition. 10.18260/1-2--30669

Torres-Toukoumidis, Á., Rodríguez, L. M. R., & Rodríguez, A. P. (2018). Ludificación y sus posibilidades en el entorno de blended learning: Revisión documental [Gamification and its possibilities in blended learning: Literature review]. *RIED. Revista Iberoamericana de Educación a Distancia, 21*(1), 95–111. doi:10.5944/ried.21.1.18792

Tsay, C. H.-H., Kofinas, A., & Luo, J. (2018). Enhancing student learning experience with technology-mediated gamification: An empirical study. *Computers & Education, 121*, 1–17. doi:10.1016/j.compedu.2018.01.009

Tuomi, P., Multisilta, J., Saarikoski, P., & Suominen, J. (2018). Coding skills as a success factor for a society. *Education and Information Technologies, 23*(1), 419–434. doi:10.100710639-017-9611-4

Vaughn, P., & Turner, C. (2016). Decoding via coding: Analyzing qualitative text data through thematic coding and survey methodologies. *Journal of Library Administration, 56*(1), 41–51. doi:10.1080/01930826.2015.1105035

Wallach, H. M., Murray, I., Salakhutdinov, R., & Mimno, D. (2009). Evaluation methods for topic models. *Proceedings of the 26th annual international conference on machine learning.* 10.1145/1553374.1553515

Woods, M., Macklin, R., & Lewis, G. K. (2016). Researcher reflexivity: Exploring the impacts of CAQDAS use. *International Journal of Social Research Methodology, 19*(4), 385–403. doi:10.1080/13645579.2015.1023964

Yıldırım, İ., & Şen, S. (2019). The effects of gamification on students' academic achievement: A meta-analysis study. *Interactive Learning Environments*, 1–18. doi:10.1080/10494820.2019.1636089

Zakharov, W., & Maybee, C. (2019). Bridging the gap: Information literacy and learning in online undergraduate courses. *Journal of Library & Information Services in Distance Learning, 13*(1-2), 215–225. doi:10.1080/1533290X.2018.1499256

Zhang, Y. (2020). *Teach machine learning with Excel.* Paper presented at the 2020 ASEE Virtual Annual Conference Content Access. 10.18260/1-2--35268

Zingaro, D. (2021). *Learn to code by solving problems: A Python programming primer.* No Starch Press.

ADDITIONAL READING

Beazley, D., & Jones, B. K. (2013). *Python cookbook: Recipes for mastering Python 3.* O'Reilly Media, Inc.

Dale, K. (2016). *Data visualization with Python and JavaScript: Scrape, clean, explore & transform your data.* O'Reilly Media, Inc.

Danjou, J. (2019). *Serious Python: Black-belt advice on deployment.* No Starch Press.

Downey, A. (2012). *Think Python: How to think like a computer scientist.* O'Reilly Media, Inc.

Glassner, A. (2021). *Deep learning: A visual approach.* No Starch Press.

Hammond, M. (2020). *Python for linguists.* Cambridge University Press. doi:10.1017/9781108642408

Haverbeke, M. (2018). *Eloquent JavaScript: A modern introduction to programming.* No Starch Press.

Jurafsky, D., & Martin, J. H. (2020). *Speech and Language Processing* (3rd ed.). Stanford University and University of Colorado at Boulder.

Matthes, E. (2019). *Python crash course: A hands-on, project-based introduction to programming.* No Starch Press.

Mayer, C., Schroeder, A., & Ward, A. M. (2021). *Python dash.* No Starch Press.

Sweigart, A. (2020). *Automate the boring stuff with Python: Practical programming for total beginners* (2nd ed.). No Starch Press.

Thomas, S. A. (2015). *Data visualization with JavaScript.* No Starch Press.

Zingaro, D. (2020). *Algorithmic thinking: A problem-based introduction.* No Starch Press.

KEY TERMS AND DEFINITIONS

Application (App): Computer or software application. A computer program to carry out a specific task for a specific purpose. Designed for an end user.

Application Programming Interface (API): A software service that allows two programmes to transmit data between each other. Allows to access other company's data or software to enhance functionality and features in another app without having to create it from scratch.

Deployment: Software deployment. Activities that make software available to use on a device. Low and no code environments often have integrated deployment solutions. Other free services include Netlify and Heroku.

Graphical User Interface (GUI): A form of user interface using graphical icons and menus.

HTML and CSS: "hypertext markup language" and "cascading style sheets" are core technologies in building web pages. HTML is the standard markup language to display text in browsers that defines the structure of a site. CSS is a style sheet language that describes the presentation of a web site.

Integrated Development Environment (IDE): A software environment with comprehensive facilities for software development, including source code editor, build automation tools and debugger. Examples include Visual Studio Code, PyCharm, and Sublime Text.

JavaScript (JS): A high-level scripting language used to add interactivity to a web page. Allows to dynamically update content, interact with content, animate images, or control media.

Learning Management System (LMS): Software application for educational, training and development courses. Allows for administration, tracking and documentation of courses. Examples include BlackBoard and Moodle.

Low Code: Development platform or environment that allows the creation of applications through a graphical user interface, allowing for a visual approach to software development. Adobe Dreamweaver combines a GUI with writing actual code in a simplified manner. Thunkable, for example, uses drag-and-drop to create mobile apps using code chanks.

Machine Learning: Computer algorithms which improve through the use of data, without following explicit instructions. Part of artificial intelligence.

No Code: Software development approach that requires non to little programming skills. Some services allow to convert familiar formats, such as Google Sheets ("sheet2site"), into a functionable website without writing any code.

Topic Model: A type of statistical model in machine learning to uncover abstract themes in a collection of texts.

What You See Is What You Get (WYSIWYG): Editor that displays the document exactly as it would appear in the finished product. Original examples include word processing software such as Microsoft word, and code editors, such as Adobe Dreamweaver.

Section 9

Virtual Teaching and Project–Oriented Game–Based Learning

Chapter 47
Project–Oriented Game–Based Learning:
Managers From Fairytales

Pavlo Brin
https://orcid.org/0000-0001-7374-3727
National Technical University "Kharkiv Polytechnic Institute", Ukraine

Mariia Shypilova
Great Wall School, China

ABSTRACT

In this chapter, the authors investigate the potential of project-oriented game-based learning in making students of educational institutes more engaged and gain a deep understanding of the curriculum content. The literature review presents the main definitions and benefits of project-oriented game-based learning, followed by its contribution to improving the performance of students' training. The results of the research are based on testing the main statements of project-oriented game-based learning empirically – if it really can provide additional value for learners in higher education. The empirical data have been collected based on Ukrainian case study and allow the authors to prove the influence of project-oriented game-based learning on increasing students' engagement, satisfaction, performance, and improving learning outcomes. The main idea of the teaching project was to take as an object of the research a character from a fairytale and analyze its managerial activities. The chapter also analyzes the e-learning instruments which can be used in remote teaching.

INTRODUCTION

Today world is becoming more volatile and unpredictable; and no doubts education is being affected by the general trends of human development. And the role of education in the constantly changing environment is quite specific and important: to create those people of the future, who will be able to handle new tasks and overcome difficulties. In human-centered modern educational system a person with necessary

DOI: 10.4018/978-1-7998-7271-9.ch047

knowledge and skills is the main outcome, which is the basis for the critically important goal-setting. Complex and fundamental approach to the goal-setting before starting an educational process or implementing reforms in education on all the levels should consider what exactly modern and prepared for global trends actors must be able to do. For that reason, we would like to emphasize 21st century skills list, many researchers have come to.

The first set of the necessary skills to be mentioned are "4Cs" learning skills which are: Critical thinking, Creativity, Collaboration and Communication (Chiruguru, 2020; Halvorsen A., 2018).

Endless flows and variety of sources of information issued every day to the world demand to analyze it and check if it is truthful and reliable enough to make adequate decisions. Also, it is hard to imagine problems solving process without looking at them from different points of view and using cross-disciplinary approach, which refer to critical thinking. In order to exchange and share information effectively, create new senses and concepts, modern people should be really good communicators (offline and online), which means not only presenting information, but gathering it in a proper way. For this reason, in multinational societies and teams better understanding other people and cultures is another key skill, as well as ability to collaborate and be an effective team-member in order to reach a goal. In such collaboration with other creators, new products and ideas become the consistent result.

So, a critical thinker and problems solver with developed communication and collaboration skills, who is able to create new ideas, products and senses is the very outcome education should be aiming to produce by the end of the studying process. More than that, this person is a life-long-learner, who's able to self-develop respectively to the variety of situations.

Another aspect of 21st century skills related to the fact of informational era continuation, which makes people to have at least basic Information, Media and Technology literacy skills. Information literacy involves ability to understand, remember, analyze, evaluate, apply and create information. Consuming and producing information in different ways are inevitable skills that people should have nowadays. Media literacy means understanding the ways of producing and distributing the information (including such new forms as social networks, podcasts, blogs and vlogs). To realize the previously mentioned opportunities given by informational revolution one should be able to use the newest technological updates (web sites, search engines, virtual worlds, wikis, message boards etc.)

Combination of the previously listed learning and literacy skills together with flexibility, agility and adaptation attitudes as well as leadership and initiative are essential in fast-changing and unpredictable social and economic reality.

And new expected outcomes of studying suppose new approaches to educational process. That is why sagacious educational institutions have already implemented Project Based Learning (PBL) as the way to achieve the necessary skills development. For increasing the effectiveness of PBL it can be used mixed with Game Based Learning (GBL) which can add new positive results for educational process.

The general purpose of the research is to prove the positive contribution of PBL and GBL to the students' performance, therefore structure of the paper was divided into the following steps:

- Describing the skills needed to be trained by modern education;
- Analyzing PBL as the instrument of developing the mentioned skills;
- Discovering possible additional impact of mixing PBL with elements of GBL;
- Comparing the students' performance before and after using GBL to prove the positive impact PBL and GBL on students' results.

LITERATURE REVIEW

Project Based Learning: The Main Characteristics

Numerous applied and theoretical works indicate that PBL is directed to the 21st century learning and literacy skills development. Defining the purpose of the research we need to specify that by PBL we understand a broad category which includes such general elements (processes) as: (1) designing and/ or creating a product (tangible one, performance or event); (2) solving a real-world problem (simulated or fully authentic); (3) investigating a topic to find an answer to an open-ended question. Although the educators point to some differences between *Project*-based and *Problem*-based learning: length, number of subjects studied, scenarios and steps (Larmer, 2015), on our mind, it makes sense to expand PBL to P5BL (Problem-Project-Process-Product-People Based Learning), which corresponds better to the real content of the approach, since all the elements are represented in its realization in the experienced by the authors cases. The literature review on Project-Based Learning inside language education (Mohamad & Tamer, 2021), indicates the increasing interest to the method among language educators in 21 countries around the world within last 10 years, proves that the "...benefits of PBL that have been reported in mainstream education have also been confirmed in the context of language education". It was admitted that a big number of papers were concentrated on PBL usage in higher education and there is still lack of such interest in primary and secondary education. Also, the review discovered that "...while several language-related areas have been addressed, such outcomes as self-confidence, critical thinking, communication, reading and writing skills "are still marginally researched". Thereafter, we will consider other educators findings about different aspects, manifestations and results of PBL application in various educational institutions around the world.

The study in the engineering field in Indonesian university (Nurtanto et al., 2020) revealed that PBL classes serve as "forms of learning innovation" for students' literacy and character movements and that such kind of innovations can be applied to similar competencies. According to the results observed in the class of 34 students with ages 19-22 years old within action research with the Elliot action model carried out in two cycles: successfully implemented literacy movement increased by 19.1%; character values improved student behavior by 14.8%; and strengthening competency in the curriculum by 11.3%.

Another research on PBL and Project-Based Assessment Tasks (PBAT) implementation compared it with standard tests-based assessment practices (Hantzopoulos et al., 2021) states that PBATs in the American focus schools played a significant role in "... cultivating transformative human rights educational practices". The authors believe that PBAT "... has the potential to transform pedagogy, instruction, and school culture in positive ways, larger social, political, and economic forces still undergird this process, as well as the specific contexts and histories in which each school is situated". Although it is obviously impossible to replace one system of assessment by another one in a simple and fast way at the moment, but the use of constant unfolding PBATs is seen in higher standards and rich and effective instruction development as wells as in establishing a culture that humanizes schools, "revitalizes their culture in positive ways and creates a climate of dignity for the young people". These conclusions may encourage educational institutions to take the PBL approach into account "as a necessary part of school reform and education policy".

The PBL as an educational strategy has both benefits (first of all for the students) and difficulties and challenges (mostly for educators). The literature and surveys say about students' reports on "much more inviting and friendlier exchange between the academic and student which promulgates the theory-practice gap" (Wells et al., 2009). We support the idea and can add that looking deeper into the 4Cs learning skills, literacy and life skills necessary in the new socio-economic reality, whatever discipline students study in whatever age PBL (P5BL) they can:

1. Gain project management skills;
2. Learn empathy toward others which is important for better communication skills;
3. Develop strategic thinking from an idea to the final product;
4. Become researchers and investigators instead of copying teacher's samples and following teacher's priorities;
5. Learn to be adaptive and more flexible to reach the goals;
6. Go deeper to the learning process, if the project is really interesting;
7. Think outside the box to solve problems appearing during the project;
8. Learn to take risks and responsibility, working in a real, not ideal, world.

Moreover, some educators put forward and confirm the hypothesis about PBL's impact on learners' cultural awareness (Mohamad, 2021) in their study cases. Despite some limitations it was found that PBL is "… a useful tool for incorporating cultures". We cannot agree more, relying on our teaching experience in PBL. For example, we observed many of these points and skills improvement among Chinese secondary school English learners within one studying year of PBL implementation. Most Bilingual Program Grade 7 students of Great Wall School became more confident English speakers and writers taking part in International friendship project (distant online communication in English with a foreign learner, which lasted for one school year and involved absolutely different categories of students into such oral communication), Students' digest project (writing articles for a newspaper on definite topics in a "students' editorial boards"), which developed not only writing skills, but creative thinking, cooperation in teams, time-management and other learning and literacy skills. It was clear that the students were satisfied with the results of their work. Also, larger scale projects in Grade 8 Group A ("My Hero" - posters and speeches about heroic people and their contribution to human development and humanism, "Young writers" – writing a students' tales book "The power of bravery") helped the students to become more confident and satisfied with the process and the results of their learning. It also proves that even in China with its highly competitive labor market and therefore really tough tests-oriented education programmes there is some place for PBL educational innovations supported by communication and cooperation with international partners.

Language learning is only one of many other spheres, in which teachers use PBL. There are a lot of various subjects to apply PBL in with positive effect for the students' skills development. For example, Susanti mentions that "the analysis results based on the random-effect estimation model showed that the overall effect size of PBL use on students' mathematical communication skills was 0.791 (95% confidence interval, and 0.168 standard error)" (Susanti et al., 2020).

In order to strengthen students' learning and literacy skills, teachers combine PBL with other progressive educational methods and apply it to diverse modern subjects. For example, Mutakinati L., Anwari I. and Yoshisuke K. investigated the learners' critical thinking skill by using STEM (Science, Technology, Engineering, and Mathematics) education through Project Based Learning in Japanese middle school (Mutakinati et al., 2018). It should be admitted that such interdisciplinary activities as STEM and STEAM (Science, Technology, Engineering, the *Arts*, and Mathematics) are really favorable for PBL realization and give a wide range of opportunities for successful results. More findings were revealed by the newest study (Resaba & Gayeta, 2021) on the basis of public Senior High schools. Reading it we can notice that PBL is used successfully in STEM teaching. So, the PBL resource and approach can be combined with and utilized in other progressive methods of teaching.

Based on the results of another research (Ernawati et al., 2020) on using PBL in Physics studying in combination with EiE (Engineering is Elementary) it was concluded that students who carried out the learning process PBL model and EiE approach had higher level of creativity than students who carried out conventional learning (one of the topics was studied and it was the limitation of the research).

One more research organized in Indonesia (Anazifa & Djukri, 2017) reveals that "… project-based learning and problem-based learning affect student's creativity and critical thinking". It also states that "there is a difference effect of project-based learning and problem-based learning on student's creativity, and there is no difference effect of project-based learning and problem-based learning on student's critical thinking". Analyzing students' perception of PBL model researchers concluded that most of the participants of the educational process based on PBL reported about satisfaction when the project is done, challenging learning experience, training creative thinking skills, project management skills and culture of cooperation (Surahman et al., 2019).

The study of Ukrainian researchers on teachers' perception of PBL implementation indicates a high level of interest in modern educational approaches among teachers of engineering specialties (Lutsenko et al., 2018; Brin et al., 2020). At the same time, most respondents admitted the lack of practically oriented materials. Most of the study participants have positive attitude to the introduction of PBL in the process of the students of engineering specialties training. Educators state that PBL implementation is possible for various types of educational activities, which allows integrating PBL into the current system of the training future engineers flexibly. Teachers who have a scientific degree and more than 10 years of teaching experience are among those who most actively implement innovative approaches, which is due to the combination of practical experience gained and the active position of teachers.

Of course, PBL organization and realization causes some challenges for the teachers, who need to be rather facilitators than tutors. Among such drawbacks are:

1. PBL is much more time-consuming than traditional teaching and instructing in preparation part, realization and concluding part. A teacher needs to be creative and self-developing life-long-learner to offer really engaging, interesting and useful in all terms projects. It takes time and efforts.
2. The method requires careful planning to guide students so that required subject specific standards are met. It can take many turns through student research and may need coming back to the goals and content standards intended to be learned.
3. For some reasons most facilitators contract their PBL programmes to integrate a modified delivery approach which often will include much more guided interaction by facilitators than the PBL approach originally allows.

There are also some challenges and obstacles to PBL implementation at the level of educational institutions (schools and universities) to enable the transition toward this new curriculum. One of the studies (Aldabbus, 2018) revealed that not all the participants were able to apply PBL for the reasons of being reluctant and not confident enough to use the method. Most pre-service teachers had difficulties in classroom time-management - projects took more than the expected time. Also, it was challenging to design valid and reliable assessment tools that require students to demonstrate their understanding. The students who faced PBL for the first time had not enough necessary skills of collaboration. Another problem indicated was that some schools did not offer the required facilities and were not ready to shift to PBL because of various constraints such as time, noise and lack of financial support.

The result of Indonesian researchers (Cintang N., et al. 2018) states that the obstacles are caused "by the fact that the teachers have never attended any specific training on the implementation of project-based learning." And those teachers who do not have any understanding or strategy decide not to implement project-based learning at all.

Interdisciplinarity provides some challenges, too. At the organizational level, educational institutions must overcome "monodisciplinary structures regarding different time schedules, curricula designs, and examination regulations in each university department". At the level of a team, "both lecturers and students must solve interdisciplinary conflicts originating in discipline-based differences in teaching and knowledge traditions". Finally, at the individual level, both lecturers and students need to overcome individual discipline-based prejudices as well as personal profession centricity" (Braßler, 2020).

Different educational systems and organized in different way educational processes cause additional difficulties. For example, within Chinese system of education there are such limitations and challenges as: large number of the students in each class (40 - 45 people) and lack of time for the students to have some preparations or do some actions for projects realization (in most boarding schools the schedule is really tight and students are always busy with classes, activities or other subjects self-study). Also, the system is highly tests-oriented and the students' attention and learning habits are directed on completing the standard tests.

Still, in spite of the difficulties, the implementation of the PBL method, undoubtedly, promotes a progressive shift from teacher-centered to student-centered teaching and contributes to students' competence and skills development. The features of PBL which allow the approach to achieve the goals and studying process outcomes corresponding to 21st century necessary skills are the following:

1. The key idea is that students learn things by doing, which means they transform theoretical points into practice, going through real life tasks;
2. The "real world" task is another crucial part of PBL, which provides connection between academic environment and external social, environmental and political realities;
3. Teacher's role changes from a distributor of knowledge to a facilitator, mentor or a process manager. It requires additional training and preparation from teachers to be the right one person at the right place with clear and suitable instructions, so called "guide-on-the-side" (Harmer, 2014);
4. Collaboration and group work is one of the central characteristic of PBL, which supports development of further professional skills (refer to 21st century learning skills of communication, cooperation), behaviours and also social networks;
5. Final product of students' teams is one more unit, which deserves attention. The form of a product can vary depending on the discipline but there should be a definite result to present it and share with the target audience. This finishing part of a project is substantial for the reason of encouraging and motivating moment of completion of the task, achieving the goal and demonstrating it to the world.
6. Interdisciplinarity with many opportunities for collective knowledge creation. According to a German specialist Braßlc, who investigated this phenomenon in the higher educational institutions (HEI), "regarding the organizational level, HEIs can support collective knowledge creation about PBL by providing interdisciplinary structures such as learning spaces, in-house training, and question-naires regarding PBL across all university departments. With an interdisciplinary approach at the

team level, lecturers as well as students can collectively learn and reflect, whether PBL experts or nov¬ices, in an interdisciplinary PBL setting. At the individual level, interdisciplinary student-to-student and lecturer-to-lecturer learning can enhance personal knowledge building about PBL and, in turn, activate further change agents toward additional PBL implementation." (Braßler, 2020). This way an interdisciplinary approach helps to implement PBL by "using economies of scale across university departments, sharing workload and responsibility across lecturers, and activating contributions across students from different disciplinary backgrounds" (Braßler, 2020), which may input to effective reforming of educational institutions.

From Project Based Learning to Game Based Learning

PBL is strongly related to the 4Cs skills development and, as we could understand from the case studies above, it can be successfully combined with other approaches and methods of teaching. The current case study demonstrates combination of PBL with Game-based learning (GBL) which has transformed into Project-oriented Game-based learning.

According to one of the definitions GBL refers to the use of video games to support teaching and learning, which has some key principles and mechanisms of application (Perrotta et al., 2013). Another group of educators defines GBL as "the integration of actual games into the learning process - usually to teach a specific skill or meet a specific objective. This method gives learners the opportunity to become immersed in the learning process and to have fun while doing so". Among the principles of GBL there are intrinsic motivation, goal-oriented learning, self-reliance and autonomy, experiential learning through enjoyment and fun. The mechanisms working in GBL are: rules or requiring decision making; clear but challenging goals, a fictional setting ("fantasy"), progressive difficulty levels, interaction and student control, immediate and constructive feedback and social connection between people, which allow to share experience. Using GBL methodology helps "… to accomplish the desired goals - the leader competencies identification: Coach (coaching team members); Facilitator (developing the skills of team members); Mindset Changer (promoting creativity, eliminate resistances); Communicator (feeding back team and individual performance); and, Motivator (motivating using a combination of intrinsic and extrinsic rewards)." (Sousa & Rocha, 2019). Besides aiming the necessary skills development another aspect educators should consider while implementing new methods – students' motivation, engagement and satisfaction of the process of learning which play vital role in self-development and adaptation during further life-long-learning. Noroozi, Dehghanzadeh and Talaee proved that GBL affects argumentation skills as the outcome (Noroozi et al., 2020). Anastasiadis, Lampropoulos and Siakas consider digital game-based learning approach as an educational instrument "… which can boost students' wellbeing and self-esteem, help them improve their soft skills, develop their critical thinking, decision-making and problem-solving skills, as well as maintain a healthy mental and psychological balance". Under the proper application digital game-based learning may be used as an effective tool for facilitation and enhancing students' learning. GBL improves interaction, communication and cooperation and promotes learning motivation, engagement "as well as induce eager and active participation in lessons" (Anastasiadis et al., 2018).

Important factors of the actual use of digital games in teachers' educational practice are teachers' perceptions and experiences. The findings of the research on teachers' perception of the value of game-based learning (Huizenga et al., 2017) showed that teachers who use games in class "… perceived student engagement and cognitive learning outcomes as effects of the use of games in formal teaching settings". Also, "motivation to learn and the acquisition of general skills were also mentioned as an effect of playing or creating game, but less than engagement or learning a subject'. Also, we should admit that teaching practices we intend to describe and analyze in this work, prove the impact to the forming of the necessary skills and positive effect to the students' performance.

Research Hypothesis

The conducted literature review leads us to conclude that despite the growing practical interests to PBL and GBL and its significant theoretical background there is still a crucial need to test these approaches more carefully and understand better its benefits and limitations in different academic and organizational context.

The purpose of the study is to test the main statements of PBL and GBL empirically - whether it really can provide additional value for different types of learners in education. Therefore, the following hypothesis were set up (fig.1):

Figure 1. The set of hypotheses of the research
Source: Authors' elaboration

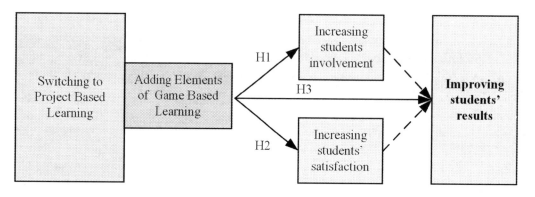

Hypothesis #1: PBL mixed with GBL increases students' involvement in an educational process.
Hypothesis #2: PBL mixed with GBL increases students' satisfaction with the educational system and course materials.
Hypothesis #3: PBL mixed with GBL leads to better students' performance.

To prove (or disprove) the hypothesis we propose to consider the same course within the framework of teaching programs 073 Management, within which teaching was initially conducted according to the traditional scheme (lectures plus case studies), at the next stage, the training was transferred to a project basis, and at the next stage, elements of game-based learning were added to the course.

MATERIALS AND METHODS

Sample

To analyze the set research questions we have chosen course Fundamentals of Management, which is delivered at bachelor level of English Taught Programme at National Technical University "Kharkiv Polytechnic Institute', Kharkiv, Ukraine. The main topics within the course are the following: history and main milestones of the development of contemporary management; internal and external environment of organizations; the main managerial functions (planning, organizing, motivating, controlling); managerial linking processes (communication and decision making); leadership in management. After the course the students are supposed to be skilled in: conducting analysis of business environment; using SMART-approach to objectives setting process, crafting a company's strategy based on sustainable competitive advantage; creating an effective organizational structure; using modern theories of motivating and effective incentives; using techniques of preliminary, concurrent, and post action controlling; using of IT quantitive support of decision-making process. The course is a part of obligatory subjects of the English Taught Programme 073 Management; it is delivered during the second year of study.

By 2020 the course was delivered in the following manner: students were provided with the presentations of the subject's theoretical framework during lectures, case studies and practical issues were discussed during workshops; students were required to take tests twice within the semester. The final grade was set as the average between the grade after case study activities and the grade after the tests.

When delivering the course tutors always faced problems connected with the fact that some part of the students were not involved into course activities (or involved at the low level), some part of the students just performed minimal task for the grade 3E (minimal grade in Ukraine), another ones pass the exam after the session also only for 3E grade. It is valuable to note, that the problem is connected not only with the course, the same situation could be seen also on other subjects of the programme. Therefore, the main intent of the subject's tutors was to use advanced educational technologies and increase students' interest toward the subject and educational process generally. For solving the mentioned problem, it was proposed to reorganize the course within two steps, to add project orientation of the course at the first stage and game elements on the second stage.

In 2020 68 students of bachelor level of study and in 2021 75 students were involved into the project, during 2010-2019 years the course Fundamentals of Management was delivered approximately to 850 students. Students' performance in 2020 and in 2021 was compared with the average performance over last years. We also compared students' attendance of classes (which was optional for students). In 2020 and 20021 a survey was also conducted to assess students' satisfaction with the course Fundamentals of Management.

During the previous years, this course Fundamentals of Management was taught according to the traditional method of teaching (Fig. 2): the students were given by lectures, during practice it was case study discussions.

When the course was switched to PBL (fig.3), during the first week of classes students had to choose an object of the research (a real company in Ukraine and a manager within the company), then every week students had to use the provided theoretical instruments to develop some elements of managerial functions for the object of the research. In addition to cases discussion students presented these elements during workshops. During the last week of the semester students had to present their projects as a whole, thereafter in the process of preparation, they once again had to read and rethink all the theoretical information regarding the course. Usually, students chose companies connected with goods production and a manager from top-management level or a manager connected with production (however, as far there was no recommendations, sometimes students chose other managers connected with financial, marketing, HR, R&D spheres of the company. The students had to explain on the example of the taken manager elements of planning, organizing and motivating, conduct analysis of internal and external environment of the organization, set ten objects (supported with tasks) for different functional spheres of the company and craft a functional strategy for the manager's department.

Figure 2. The way of delivering fundamentals of management in traditional way, after using PBL with further adding elements of GBL
Source: authors' elaboration

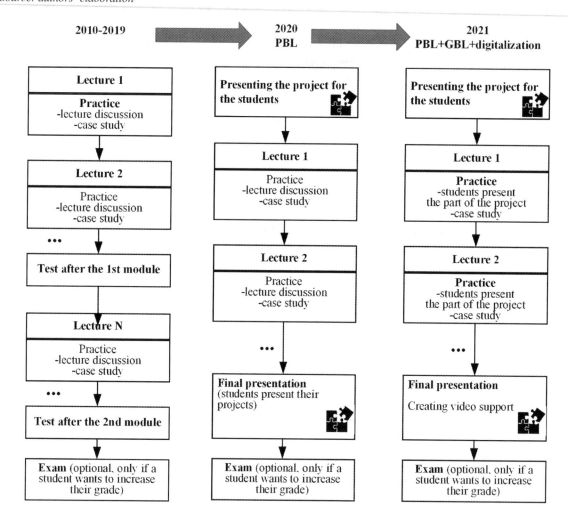

Next academic year, when the course was switched to PBL with elements of GBL, students were able to choose among the two following alternatives (fig 3): (1) the first alternative was to complete the course paper at the basis of a company and a manager within the company (like it was during the previous academic year); (2) the second alternative was to take as an object of the research any character from a fairytale or from a movie and then to analyze he (she, it) as a manager. In the second alternative the tasks were connected with the following: to find and describe some fitches of main managerial functions (planning, organizing, motivating and controlling in the activities of the character; to describe values, aptitudes and attitudes of the character; to analyze the external environment of the character, to formulate a set of objectives for the character using the SMART technology; to describe any project of the character using Gantt's chart.

Figure 3. Tasks within switching the course fundamentals of management to PLL and GBL basis
Source: Authors' elaboration

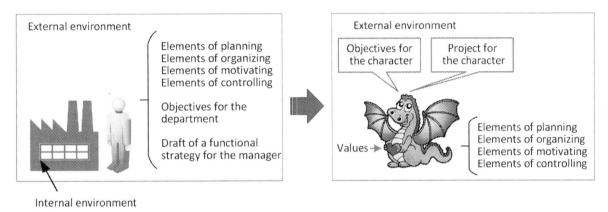

Among the characters which were chosen by the students as the objects of their research were Albus Dumbledore, Sponge Bob, Puss In Boots, Scrooge McDuck, Baby Boss, Headmistress Alfea, Lion King, Mr. Crabs, Manny from "Ice Age", Skipper, Optimus Prime, Mickey Mouse, Kosem Sultan, Lisa Simpson, Mike Wazowski, Tinker Bell, Santa Claus, Kung Fu Panda and many other characters.

It was rather interesting, that ***nobody*** from the students chose the first alternative (to analyze a real company and a manager within the company), everybody wrote their papers at the basis of characters from fairytales. This fact can be also taken into account as empirical evidence of positive correlation between GBL and students' involvement into learning process.

The Influence from Covid-19 Pandemic: Digitalization of the Educational Process

Digitalization of all sides of society, including education, is evidence of the onset of digital reality. The traditional education system was based on the concept of knowledge transfer, involving personal communication between a student and a teacher in one place. Modern digital technologies make it possible to change this process, and if initially the digitalization of education was aimed at increasing its efficiency, then the conditions of the pandemic made the digitalization process not a desirable, but a necessary characteristic. We strongly believe that the COVID -19 pandemic will inevitably pass during next years. But the pandemic has brought significant changes to the contemporary world, international economic relations, modern technologies, and certainly educational process. In its lessons, modern educational institutions have to be changed both in the field of organizing of the educational process, i.e. the provision of communication between lecturers and students by remote communicational technologies. The traditional training system (i.e., delivering lectures in class rooms) that worked effectively in offline training has been found to be ineffective in delivering online training in the contemporary pandemic conditions.

It is valuable to add that the course was delivered in COVID -19 pandemic conditions, thereafter all teaching activities were conducted remotely. Generally, students did not like this way of cooperating because of lack of alive communications, however, in this situation all the instruments of digitalization with the help of e-learning instruments were used (fig 4). Taking into account mentioned within the course Fundamentals of Management the students got the important skills and experience of working in virtual project teams which will be definitely beneficial in our new world after pandemic COVID-19.

Figure 4. The main e-learning instruments used in the project of switching the course fundamentals of management to PLL and GBL basis
Source: authors' elaboration

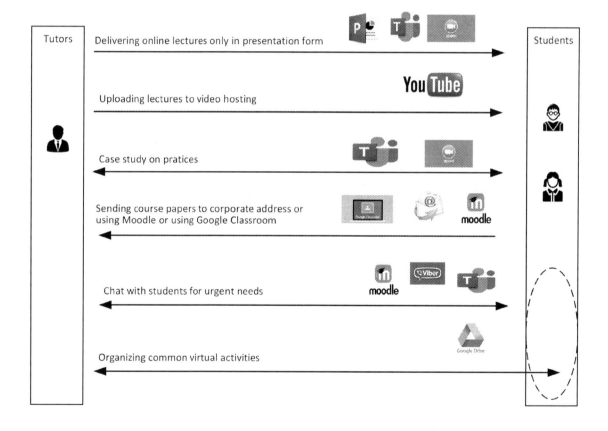

At the end of the course Fundamentals of Management the students had to prepare video support for their presentations, the best students' works is presented in pdf and video form (Fundamentals of Management, 2021); after the course the video presentations were uploaded to the YouTube video service.

RESULTS AND DISCUSSION

To evaluate students' involvement into educational process (to prove or disprove H1) within the course Fundamentals of Management we have assessed their attendance in 2020 when the course was switched to PBL basis in 2021 when GBL component was added to the learning process; the results were compared with the average level for the previous 10 years, the results are shown in the figure 5.

Figure 5. Increasing the students' involvement with the course fundamentals of management after using PBL with further adding elements of GBL
Source: authors' elaboration

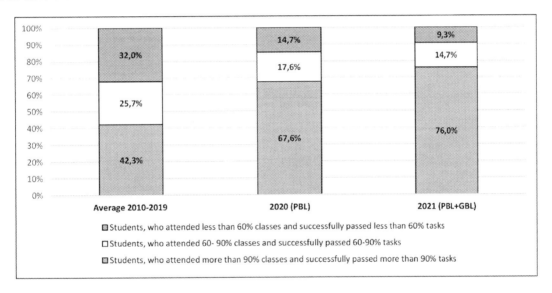

Based on the obtained results, we assume that the proportion of students who regularly attended classes in 2020 and 2021 increased significantly, at the last stage only about 1 student out 10 missed the classes. Taking into account the mentioned we can state that H1 has been proved: the usage of PBL technology, especially with elements of GBL really leads to increasing of the students' involvement into the learning process.

Assessment of students' satisfaction with the course (to prove or disprove H2) was carried out by using the survey method (Fig. 6). After the course students were asked to answer on several questions anonymously. It must be mentioned that the students were asked after the setting grades procedure, thereafter they evaluated the course Fundamentals of Management generally.

In previous years such an assessment was not carried out, in this case, there is no basis for comparisons, however, as it can be seen, only approximately one student out of ten is dissatisfied with the course Fundamentals of Management when PBL element was added, and only approximately one student out of twenty was dissatisfied with the course Fundamentals of Management when GBL was added, which is a very high level of students' satisfaction. Furthermore, when GBL element was added (in 2021), students' satisfaction became almost full. Taking into account the mentioned above we can state that H2 has been proved: the usage of PBL approach with elements of GBL really leads to increasing of the students' satisfaction with the learning process.

Figure 6. Students' satisfaction with the course fundamentals of management after using PBL with further adding elements of GBL
Source: authors' elaboration

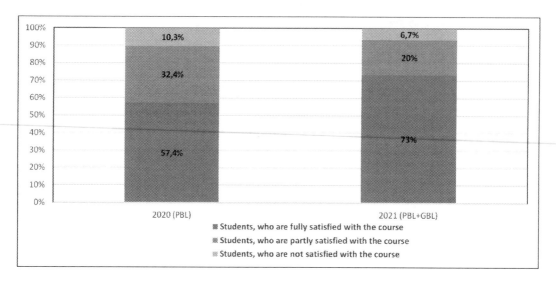

Assessment of changes in students' performance (to prove or disprove H3) was carried out by comparing the performance rate in 2020 and in 2021 with the average performance rate over the previous 10 years of study. The obtained results (fig. 6) shows that the share of excellent and good grades was increased significantly after the implementing of PBL approach in 2020 and PBL+GBL approach in 2021, which indicates a positive correlation between the usage of PBL and GBL with students' performance.

Figure 7. Increasing the students' success after implementing PBL with further adding elements of GBL withing the course fundamentals of management
Source: Authors' elaboration

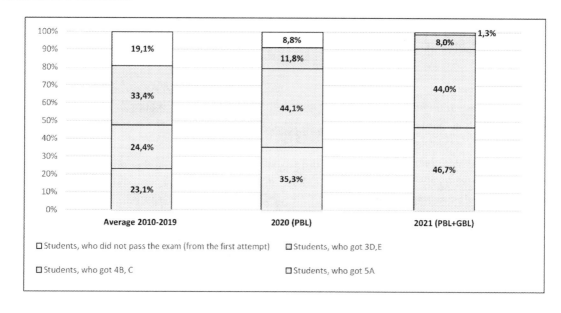

Thus, all three hypotheses can be considered as proven, PBL mixed with GBL really increases students' motivation, their involvement in the learning process and significantly increases students' performance.

SOLUTIONS AND RECOMMENDATIONS

The present theoretical and applied research allows us to conclude that Project-based learning (PBL) (by which we mean Project-Problem-Process-Product-Person-based learning (P5BL) since this educational strategy contains and realized through all 5 elements) is taken by the researchers and practicing teachers as one of the effective approaches to teach students develop their 4Cs learning and literacy skills of 21st century. The results of PBL application to different disciplines (from STEAM/STEM and Language learning to Engineering and Management) in different countries (from Asia to Europe and the USA) and different levels of educational institutions (from primary and middle schools to universities) state that the students not only develop the subject skills more successfully, but at the same time improve their life skills and demonstrate higher motivation, satisfaction of learning and better performance. PBL combination with other methods, like Game-based learning, strengthens the positive effect of the approach. And although there is a range of obstacles and challenges, which teachers face at different levels of current educational system, there are many arguments for progressiveness and perspective of PBL for the educational model of the future due to modern global social and economic trends.

FUTURE RESEARCH DIRECTIONS

The mentioned in the study experience of PBL and GBL realization in conditions of Ukrainian educational system, which has specific characteristics of studying process organization, objectives of studying and respective teaching and learning approaches calls for deeper investigation of the results within longer period of time and bigger number of participants. International PBL and GBL teaching and its effect for Chinese students' literacy and learning skills development is also of great interest of the authors. Comparison of PBL realization in Ukraine and in China may be another direction of scientific cooperation.

CONCLUSION

In modern society it is definitely not enough to use traditional methods of teaching, nowadays responsible education process must include elements of PBL and GBL which can help students to train skills of 21 century.

This study empirically revealed the positive influence of PBL approach with further adding the elements of GBL on the students' involvement into the learning process because in such way students are trained to use gained knowledge and skills and to solve problems. The results also prove a high level of students' satisfaction from participating in such projects that ultimately leads to improving the quality of their learning. In addition, the important fact confirmed in the study is that the project form of work allows not only to improve students' professional knowledge and skills, but also helps teachers to reveal their pedagogical abilities.

REFERENCES

Aldabbus, S. (2018). Project-based learning: Implementation & challenges. *International Journal of Education, Learning and Development, 6*(3), 71–79.

Anastasiadis, T., Lampropoulos, G., & Siakas, K. (2018). Digital Game-based Learning and Serious Games in Education. *International Journal of Advances in Scientific Research and Engineering, 4*(12), 139–144. Advance online publication. doi:10.31695/IJASRE.2018.33016

Anazifa, R. D., & Djukri, S. (2017). Project-based learning and problem-based learning: Are they effective to improve student's thinking skills? *Journal Pendidikan IPA Indonesia, 6*(2), 346–355. doi:10.15294/jpii.v6i2.11100

Braßler, M. (2020). The Role of Interdisciplinarity in Bringing PBL to traditional Universities: Opportunities and Challenges on the Organizational, Team and Individual Level. *The Interdisciplinary Journal of Problem-Based Learning, 14*(2). Advance online publication. doi:10.14434/ijpbl.v14i2.28799

Brin, P., Krasnokutska, N., Polančič, G., & Kous, K. (2020). Project-Based Intercultural Collaborative Learning for Social Responsibility: The Ukrainian-Slovenian Experience. In Handbook of Research on Enhancing Innovation in Higher Education Institutions (pp. 566-586). IGI Global. doi:10.4018/978-1-7998-2708-5.ch024

Chang, C. Y., & Hwang, G. J. (2019). Trends in digital game-based learning in the mobile era: A systematic review of journal publications from 2007 to 2016. *International Journal of Mobile Learning and Organization, 13*(1), 68–90. doi:10.1504/IJMLO.2019.096468

Chang, Y.-H., Hwang, J.-H., Fang, R.-J., & Lu, Y.-T. (2017). A Kinect- and Game-Based Interactive Learning System. *Journal of Mathematics Science and Technology Education, 13*(8), 4897–4914. doi:10.12973/eurasia.2017.00972a

Chen, C. H., Liu, G. Z., & Hwang, G. J. (2016). Interaction between gaming and multistage guiding strategies on students' field trip mobile learning performance and motivation'. *British Journal of Educational Technology, 47*(6), 1032–1050. doi:10.1111/bjet.12270

Chiruguru, S. (2018). *The Essential Skills of 21st Century Classroom (4Cs)*. Louisiana Computer Using Educators.

Cintang, N., Setyowati, D. L., & Handayani, S. S. D. (2018). The Obstacles and Strategy of Project Based Learning Implementation in Elementary School. *Journal of Education and Learning, 12*(1), 7–15. doi:10.11591/edulearn.v12i1.7045

Fundamentals of Management. (2021). *Students' reports on Fundamentals of Management* https://drive.google.com/drive/folders/1fhtTOTTeuWS-zzt7a31Eirbh7UQKQFsw?usp=sharing

Geo-politics and international power. (2017). *European Parliamentary Research Service European Parliament*. https://www.europarl.europa.eu/RegData/etudes/STUD/2017/603263/EPRS_STU(2017)603263_EN.pdf

Halim, A., & Syukri, M. (2020). Integration of Problem Based Learning (PBL) and Engineering is Elementary (EiE) to improve students' creativity. *Journal of Physics: Conference Series, 1460*(1), 012117.

Halvorsen, A. (2018). *21st Century Skills and the "4Cs" in the English Language Classroom*, University of Oregon. https://creativecommons.org/licenses/by/4.0/

Hantzopoulos, M., Rivera-McCutchen, R. L., & Tyner-Mullings, A. R. (2021). Reframing School Culture Through Project-Based Assessment Tasks: Cultivating Transformative Agency and Humanizing Practices in NYC Public Schools. *Teachers College Record, 123*(4), 1–38. doi:10.1177/016146812112300404

Harmer, N. (2014). *Project-based learning. Literature review. School of Geography, Earth and Environmental Sciences.* Plymouth University.

Huizenga, J. C., ten Dam, G. T. M., Voogt, J. M., & Admiraal, W. F. (2017). Teacher perceptions of the value of game-based learning in secondary education. *Computers & Education, 110*, 105–115. doi:10.1016/j.compedu.2017.03.008

Hwang, G. J., Wu, P. H., & Chen, C. C. (2012). An online game approach for improving students' learning performance in web-based problem-solving activities. *Computers & Education, 59*(4), 1246–1256. doi:10.1016/j.compedu.2012.05.009

Israel, M. (2017) *Game-based learning and gamification. Guidance from the experts.* White paper.

Kapp, K. M. (2012). *The gamification of learning and instruction: game-based methods and strategies for training and education.* John Wiley & Sons.

Karacalli, S., & Korur, F. (2014). *The Effects of project-based learning on students' academic achievement, attitude, and retention of knowledge: The subject of electricity in our lives.* https://onlinelibrary.wiley.com/doi/abs/10.1111/ssm.12071

Keesey, C. (2011). Engagement, immersion, and learning cultures: Project planning and decision making for virtual world training programs. In *Global Business: Concepts, Methodologies, Tools and Applications* (pp. 121–134). IGI Global. doi:10.4018/978-1-60960-587-2.ch109

Larmer, J. (2015). *Project-Based Learning vs. Problem-Based Learning vs. X-BL.* https://www.edutopia.org/blog/pbl-vs-pbl-vs-xbl-john-larmer

Mohamad, A. (2021). The Impact of Project-Based Learning on Students' Cultural Awareness. *International Journal of Language and Literary Studies, 3*(2), 54–80. Advance online publication. doi:10.36892/ijlls.v3i2.601

Mohamad, A., & Tamer, Y. (2021). A review of literature on Project-Based Learning inside language education. *Turkish Online Journal of English Language Teaching, 6*(2), 79–105.

Mutakinati L., Anwari I., & Yoshisuke K. (2018). Analysis of students' critical thinking skill of middle school through STEM education project-based learning. *Journal Pendidikan IPA Indonesia, 7*(1), 54-65. doi:10.15294/jpii.v7i1.10495

Noroozi, O., Dehghanzadeh, H., & Talaee, E. (2020). A systematic review on the impacts of game-based learning on argumentation skills. *Entertainment Computing*, *35*, 100369. Advance online publication. doi:10.1016/j.entcom.2020.100369

Nurtanto, M., Fawaid, M., & Sofyan, H. (2020). Problem Based Learning (PBL) in Industry 4.0: Improving Learning Quality through Character-Based Literacy Learning and Life Career Skill (LL-LCS). *Journal of Physics: Conference Series*, *1573*, 012006. doi:10.1088/1742-6596/1573/1/012006

Perrotta, C., Featherstone, G., Aston, H., & Houghton, E. (2013). *Game-based Learning: Latest Evidence and Future Directions Innovation in Education*. NFER.

Resaba, M. L., & Gayeta, N. E. (2021). Utilization of Project - Based Learning (PBL) Resources in Senior High School. *International Multidisciplinary Research Journal, 3*(2).

Sousa, M., & Costa, E. (2014). Game based learning improving leadership skills. *EAI Endorsed Transactions on Serious Games*, *3*(3), e2. Advance online publication. doi:10.4108g.1.3.e2

Sousa, M. J., & Rocha, Á. (2019). Leadership styles and skills developed through game-based learning. *Journal of Business Research*, *94*, 360–366. doi:10.1016/j.jbusres.2018.01.057

Surahman,, E., & Kuswandi,, D., Sulthoni, W. A., & Zufar, Z. (2019). Students' Perception of Project-Based Learning Model in Blended Learning Mode Using Sipejar. *Advances in Social Science, Education and Humanities Research*, 372.

Susanti, N., Juandi, D., & Maximus Tamur, M. (2020). The Effect of Problem-Based Learning (PBL) Model On Mathematical Communication Skills of Junior High School Students – A Meta-Analysis Study. *Journal Theory dan Aplikasi Matematika*, *4*(2), 145-154. doi:10.31764/jtam.v4i2.2481

Wells, S. H., Warelow, P. J., & Jackson, K. L. (2009). Problem based learning (PBL): A conundrum. *Contemporary Nurse*, *33*(2), 191–201. Advance online publication. doi:10.5172/conu.2009.33.2.191 PMID:19929163

ADDITIONAL READING

Altbach, P. G., Reisberg, L., & Rumbley, L. E. (2019). *Trends in global higher education: Tracking an academic revolution*. BRILL.

Brin, P., Krasnokutska, N., Polančič, G., & Kous, K. (2020). Project-Based Intercultural Collaborative Learning for Social Responsibility: The Ukrainian-Slovenian Experience. In Handbook of Research on Enhancing Innovation in Higher Education Institutions (pp. 566-586). IGI Global.

Brin, P., Polančič, G., & Huber, J. (2014). *Business - IT alignment: report on bilateral student projects*. Maribor: Faculty of Electrical Engineering and Computer Science. https://dk.um.si/IzpisGradiva.php?id=54941

Brin, P., Prokhorenko, E., Huber, J., & Polančič, G. (2012) Designing of international project outsourcing in educational process. *V: EICL conference proceedings, Crimea, Ukraine, October 1-2, 2012. International conference "E-internationalization for Collaborative Learning"*.

Mandic, D., Lalic, N., & Bandjur, V. (2010). Managing innovations in education. In *Proceedings of the 9th WSEAS international conference on Artificial intelligence, knowledge engineering and data bases* (pp. 231-236). World Scientific and Engineering Academy and Society (WSEAS).

Martín-Gutiérrez, J., Mora, C. E., Añorbe-Díaz, B., & González-Marrero, A. (2017). Virtual technologies trends in education. *Eurasia Journal of Mathematics, Science and Technology Education*, *13*(2), 469–486.

KEY TERMS AND DEFINITIONS

Collaborative Learning: The educational approach to common learning that requires responsibility and common efforts from all participants and leads to shared values for them.

E-Learning 2.0: The educational technique which means collaborative learning of people situated in different places connected by Web 2.0 instruments.

Educational Project: The activity to create a particularly unique value for participants of educational process over a period of time.

Game-Based Learning: The educational strategy that uses the idea of a playing game to reach specific learning objectives.

Management: The process of planning, organizing, motivating, and controlling in order to formulate and attain organizational objectives.

Project-Based Learning: The educational approach which leads learners to solving a real-life problem.

Chapter 48
Virtual Training for Scuba Divers

Anacleto Correia
https://orcid.org/0000-0002-7248-4310
Naval Academy, Portugal

Pedro B. Água
https://orcid.org/0000-0003-1886-9938
Naval Aacdemy, Portugal

ABSTRACT

Virtual reality (VR) is a technology that is becoming more common for applications in the field of education and training. VR can be used to create simulated two- and three-dimensional scenarios, promoting interactions between the user and the environment, which allows experiencing virtual training situations very close to real actions. The aim of this text is to describe the development of a teaching and training tool using VR technology for scuba divers' operations within the aquatic context for enhancing critical thinking. To this end, a survey of requirements based on real procedures was carried out in order to transpose them into a synthetic environment. After the construction of the artefact, it was tested and evaluated by qualified users, and the results are promising.

INTRODUCTION

Activities in aquatic environment can be considered a type of high-risk missions, as they involve actions in extreme situations. Therefore, it is extremely important that those involved in these operations have acute skills and are adequately trained in critical thinking for the execution of such actions. Scuba divers are individuals that carry out several kinds of underwater tasks and specialized aquatic jobs. Training professionals involved in such activities by means of using VR not only serves as practice, but also safeguards from risks to the physical integrity and to their life. Therefore, for those involved to be able to perform the appropriate actions for this type of mission, a high level of critical thinking training on the procedures to be executed is paramount.

DOI: 10.4018/978-1-7998-7271-9.ch048

The training in real situations requires adequate meteorological and logistical conditions, involving costs that, without prejudice to keep the operational performance, should be minimized. In this sense, this study intends to propose a virtual training environment that allows divers responsible for risky actions, to practice and train the critical thinking and correspondent procedures in a virtual endeavour, being an alternative to training carried out in real conditions. Hence, the main objective of this study was the conception and development of a virtual environment as a serious game for learning purposes. This serious game has the intention to provide scuba divers a simulated training environment, in order to make possible to develop critical thinking and practice the procedures to be carried out in aquatic and marine operations.

This chapter is organised as follows. In the first section, the motivation for the work and its objective is laid down. The next section describes the used methodology to develop the study. The third section describes the problem domain. In the fourth section, it was performed the survey of some main techniques needed to implement the solution. The developed solution is described in the solution building section. The final section summarizes the conclusions.

METHODOLOGY

For the development of this work and an associated artifact, the chosen research methodology was the *Design Science Research* (DSR) (Michalos & Simon, 1970; Vaishnavi & Kuechler, 2004), justified by the need to follow a systematic set of steps to design, build and validate the intended artifact (Wieringa, 2009). Using the selected research method, the research was guided by a practical problem, with the intention of solving it. However, other practical problems and questions did arise, initiating a regulatory cycle. This cycle is composed of four phases: (i) *Problem Investigation,* (ii) *Solution Development,* (iii) *Solution Validation*, and (iv) *Implantation.*

The aim of the *Problem Investigation* phase is to understand the problem and study its context. In the present text, this phase was carried out in the sections named as *Background* and *Literature Review*. In the section *Background* the institutional context and the real training environment of the scuba divers was surveyed. In the section *Literature Review*, the methods and technologies used in the creation of the synthetic environment were elicited.

The phase *Solution Development* refers to the construction of the synthetic environment, being inserted in section five. In this section the construction process of the final solution was explained, making reference to the strategy adopted and the solutions that were used after the study performed in the previous phase. The section concludes with the description of the development of the final solution. In the phase *Solution Validation*, the results of the work after the tests were performed are analysed. For the assessment of the final product, a sample of users did the training in the synthetic environment and answered a questionnaire. Finally, as for the *Implantation* phase, it depends on further iteration of the current solution, and is not described within the scope of this work.

BACKGROUND

Diving may be done for leisure, or professional reasons. Scuba diving is a dangerous and difficult activity, and because of that there are numerous safety procedures to be adequately followed. Scuba divers are qualified professionals specialised in diving operations, that are able to carry out maritime rescue missions among other tasks.

Before a diver training session may take place there are mandatory preparations, which include the planning of the specific mission, in terms of logistics and operationality. Five days is usually the ideal time period for the realization of a scuba divers training aimed at a specific operation. Preparation generally takes one day with the need for coordination among the various involved entities, together with the provision of material and diving mixes. Three days are dedicated to training/diving and the last day to the maintenance and improvement of material. The main objective of divers' training is to become familiar with the procedures, maintenance of qualifications and proficiency of the divers as a working team, so that in real situations, the divers are ready to successfully execute the missions they are assigned. To this end, diver teams need to be prepared for orientation in debris environments, know the procedures for approaching and entry into confined spaces, together with some secondary tasks to enhance the training. These tasks can be, for example, the search and recovery of victims or equipment, previously placed in strategic underwater locations.

The limitations to the accomplishment of the training of the scuba divers are generally the following: (i) meteorological and oceanographic conditions: this is the main factor for the accomplishment or not of a specific training. If the conditions are not adequate, the dive or training will not take place in order not to put the divers at risk; (ii) costs: there are high associated costs for the realization of a divers training in real environment conditions; and (iii) dependence of means: referring to the means of onboard embarkation of the divers, because if the intended boat is not available for the accomplishment of the mission, the training cannot take place.

LITERATURE REVIEW

The way humans perceive reality results from the processing carried out by the brain after a perception of the world is apprehended by the senses (Fleming et al., 2017). By manipulating the senses, it is possible to act on the brain, shaping, or even recreating, the perceived reality. Immersive technologies, such as virtual reality (Suh & Prophet, 2018), which recreate the physical world with a digital and simulated reality, take advantage of this plasticity of the reality as perceived by the brain. Virtual Reality (VR) is a technology capable of replacing a user's real-life environment with a simulated world that is sensorially configured and structured for a particular reality. Virtual reality has the advantage of allowing the user to control the environment in which the he or she lives, as it allows for changing the brain connections in the desired directions (Alqithami, 2021).

Serious games result from the evolution of traditional leisure games, with nobler goals, such as, the support of military training, educational activities, health assessment, and therapeutic rehabilitation (McCallum, 2012; Pasquier et al., 2016; Klaassen et al., 2018; Barba et al., 2019; Araiza, Keane, L. Beaudry, & Kaufman, 2020). The design of this type of games has been researched in order to define the appropriate attributes for its implementation (Landers, 2014; Baptista & Oliveira, 2019). A taxonomy of games (Alqithami, 2021) classifies them into cooperative and non-cooperative games. In cooperative games, players work together to achieve common goals (e.g., building alliances) which somehow can exempt players from ongoing commitments and even contradict the purpose of the game (Alabdulakareem & Jamjoom, 2020). As for non-cooperative games (e.g., stochastic games), players mutually challenge themselves with each of them trying to maximize their usefulness and obtain greater rewards when compared with the competitors. The use of game theory enable the discovery of an optimal player's strategy when his or her strategy depends on the opponents moves (Yannakakis & Togelius, 2018).

In this work, the design of the serious game, supported by virtual reality, was considered from a non-cooperative deterministic perspective. In order to allow the player to have self-confidence and intentionally progress to succeed in the game, one relied on technologies and methods used for the construction of the synthetic solution, such as Gamification. After surveying the main gamification *frameworks*, they were compared and the most suitable one was selected to be used in this study: the *Octalysis* system. The *Octalysis* system has its focus on the user, through eight fundamental elements, which are critical for the creation of motivation, be it intrinsic or extrinsic. Extrinsic motivation is the will to fulfil a goal or obtain something, whereas in intrinsic motivation there is no tangible goal or objective and the activity is rewarding by itself, corresponding to higher levels when considering the Maslow pyramid with its scale of human motivations. The fundamental elements (FE) associated with creativity, self-expression and social dynamics are linked to extrinsic motivation, and the fundamental elements associated with logic, analytical thinking and possession linked to intrinsic motivation (Chou, 2019). The *Meaning* element is directly associated with the *extra motivation* parameter, creating in the user the feeling that he or she is accomplishing something greater than themselves. The *Octalysis* system also advocates, by means of the *Social Influence* element, that motivation can be created through the relationship among users, either through *relationship* or *competition*. For the fundamental elements to work out and be possible to motivate the users, it is mandatory that the users have the will to perform the action (*will*) and be given the freedom to do so (*autonomy*).

SOLUTION DEVELOPMENT

Solution Design

Gamification Process Design

Based on the study of the elements of game *design* - components, mechanics and dynamics – the requirements were defined to take such elements into account and to be inserted in the synthetic environment. The *components* used were: the *avatar*, the *mission* and the scoring *points*. The *avatar* component was chosen because of the need for the interactive environment to have a main character (the *avatar*): a diver in the first-person perspective. For each level, a *mission* was established in order promote in the user the feeling of accomplishing something bigger than himself or herself. During the accomplishment of the missions there are secondary tasks to be performed, for which scoring *points* are awarded to the user (component *points*). The *mechanics* used in the creation of the synthetic environment were: *cooperation and competition*, *challenges* and *victory*. The *cooperation and competition* mechanics were justified by the need to motivate users through competition among themselves, something which is associated to the scoring *points* component. The *challenges* are associated to the *mission* component, since, with the accomplishment of those challenges (proposed tasks), it is ensured that the mission will be fulfilled.

A sense of achievement will therefore be created, thus justifying the *victory* mechanics. The *dynamics* defined were: *progression*, *restrictions* and *emotions*. In the synthetic environment to be created, the user must have the notion of being progressing with the help of scoring *points* and *challenges*, since by accomplishment the proposed challenges, he or she will receive a corresponding score. To perform the tasks, in the operations assigned area, the user will be conditioned to a confined environment (*restriction* dynamic). The *emotion* dynamic will be induced to the user by means of the claustrophobic feeling given by the compartments, the pressure of the scarcity of time available to accomplish the mission, and the relief feeling, associated to the *victory* mechanic, with the conclusion of the assigned mission.

The *Octalysis-Meaning* element was used to assign missions to the user, generating the psychological need to perform them, in order to fulfil his function, and being associated with the *mission* component and the *emotions* dynamic. The user will have a feeling of progression throughout the mission by means of conquering points associated with the performed tasks (scoring *points* component and *challenges* mechanics), materializing the *Octalysis-Accomplisment* element. To develop the motivation for the training of maritime life-saving procedures, the *Octalysis-Social Influence* element was used. This element, together with the scoring system, allows divers to compare results among themselves by making use of the scoring *points* component, the *cooperation and competition* mechanics and the *progression* dynamics. The *Octalysis-Scarcity* element is used when the user cannot get what he or she wants immediately due to some posed difficulties. This element is induced into the synthetic environment by the increase of the difficulty associated with the levels (*challenge* mechanics). In order to arise the curiosity and suspense in the user (dynamic *emotions*), compartments were created in order to search within the synthetic environment, not knowing what the user might find within such confined spaces, thus addressing the element *Octalysis-Unpredictability*. The fundamental element *Octalysis-Avoidance*, motivates the user by raising the fear of losing something (dynamic *emotions*). This feature is transferred to the synthetic environment through the recovery of victims, the main mission of level 1, and with the contamination of the water in the machine space putting the user at danger. The *Empowerment* element is explored by giving the user freedom for searching the compartments and find innovative solutions for the assigned rescue challenge. The *Ownership* element motivate the user through the accumulation of virtual goods correspondent to each level he or she accomplishes.

Design of the Virtual Reality Environment

The Virtual Reality Environment (VRE) do consist of four levels, each corresponding to a specific mission with increasing levels of difficulty. The accomplishment of each mission involves the performing of some specific tasks. The main mission of each level is the following: (i) level 1: save a victim; (ii) level 2: collect an object to be safe with secret content; (iii) level 3: collect a special tool in the ship's workshop; iv) level 4: stop the fuel spill in a ship's engine room.

For the development of the VRE a ship sinking scenario was created. The general rules established for the execution of the operations within the Virtual Reality Environment were the following: (i) all compartments of the ship have to be searched; (ii) the diver has to enter by the ship's bridge; (iii) in order to avoid decompression, it was established that the time for the execution of each level will last for a maximum of 10 minutes; (iv) as a support to the diver, the available time for the execution of the mission will always be displayed on the screen; (v) as the trainee accomplishes the tasks, he or she receives adequate scoring points according to the established criteria; (vi) after the conclusion of the various tasks, the passage to the next level occurs when the user deliberately collides with a colourful sphere; (vii) to support the user, there are display windows that supply essential information for the accomplishment of the missions; (viii) if the user does not accomplish the tasks in the stipulated time, the mission will abort and will not be concluded.

Based on the defined rules, and the main missions associated with the four levels and scoring system, a *storyboard* was created for each level, with its sketch being carried out by means of diagrams. Firstly, the story was planned using several different levels, in order to implement the missions for each corresponding level. As the used method was a non-linear one, only the main scenes were elaborated according to the tasks for each level. Afterwards, important information was added to each scene, such as the following: time, mission, place of action, procedures to be performed, scoring system and the fundamental elements of the *Octalysis* framework used in each scene. These elements are associated with the game *design elements*.

The first level starts with the diver positioned outside the ship, sitting on the support vessel. When the user dives, he or she will head to the ship, where one will have several hazards (as for example, loose cables). When the user reaches the ship, he or she will have to open the bridge door using a tool. When he or she completes this task and enters the ship's bridge, the user will find several items, as for instance navigation tools, scattered about and eventually he or she will later find the victim to be rescued. . The assigned mission of rescuing the victim located at the ship's bridge, induces pressure and *stress* into the user. By accomplishing the tasks at this level, the user will receive scoring points, which will make him or her feel accomplished. By starting outside the sunken ship, the user does not know what he may find inside such ship, thus creating a sense of suspense and curiosity in the user. The user knows that the victim's recovery depends on him, so he is motivated by the fear of not being able to accomplish the mission in due time. Procedures for rescuing the victim, exploring and searching for the best entrance in a confined space were inserted into this level. With these tasks, it was intended to induce *stress* in the user and sensations as close to reality as possible, which the user would feel if he or her were doing training in a real environment.

Building the Solution

In the construction of the virtual environment, it was used a non-immersive type implementation, since the artifact is still in a prototype state. Therefore, users experience the synthetic environment, having as peripherals or interfacing devices the monitor and the keyboard. As the interaction between the user and the environment is greater in the immersive type (Barfield & Blitz, 2018), the realism of the synthetic environment is increased by means of the use of the main character in the maybe first-person perspective (aka *first person shooter*), providing a greater sensation of interaction between the user and the synthetic environment. The character (*avatar*), the main figure built in the solution, implements several functions, such as jumping from the boat, swimming and running. In order to train the procedures of diving in confined spaces, a model of a ship was created by using 3D modelling (Figure 1). To decorate its interior, chairs, doors, stairs, books, beds, cupboards, sofas and kitchen materials were added, in order to make such environment more realistic. For the elaboration of the several different levels in the *Unity* platform, three-dimensional objects were modelled when modelling the ship and the surrounding environment.

After modelling the scenario (the main character, the ship and the area), the virtual environment was programmed to take into account the interactions between the user and the environment. To obtain the four different levels of difficulty, four scenes were created on the *Unity* platform. For the user to have the necessary information before interacting with the solution, a main menu was developed and made accessible to the user. In this menu the user is provided with information about the general training scenario, the virtual environment controls and the missions established for each level. During the completion of each level, the time limit decreases from a pre-set fixed value of 10 minutes, inducing pressure on the user. If the user fails to complete the mission within the allocated time, a new screen informs the user that he or she could not complete the assigned mission, giving him or her the possibility to restart the virtual environment.

Figure 1. Virtual reality environment: ship and scenery

As an example, the scenario within the Virtual Reality Environment for Level 1 is described (see Figure 2). It begins with the diver sitting on the support boat and ready to carry out the assigned mission. To instruct the user about the specific actions to be performed, each level has an informative panel referring to the mission which is always accessible to the user. This informative panel shows the mission goals and the tasks to be performed at this level, as well as the commands to be used (Figure 2.a). In the used platform, the used metaphor for the interaction between the user and the objects is the collision with them. The solution was therefore programmed so that when there is a collision between the diver and one of the strategically placed spherical balloons, some scoring points would be awarded to the user, with the updated scoring appearing on the screen. Besides the mentioned spheres, other instruments exist that allow the attribution of scoring points to the user. The recovery of these instruments is the main task of each different level.

In level 1, for example, the relevant instruments are the cables, the crowbar and the victim (symbolized by a blue sphere). It is intended that the diver trains the entry into the confined space, so cables have been placed at the entrance of the ship, which the user will have to cut. To enter into the ship, the diver will have to open the door with the crowbar. The awarding of scoring points for this task happens when the user collides with the hatch wielding the crowbar. Finally, to complete the main mission of level 1, the user will have to recover the victim placed within the sunken ship. To accomplish this mission, the user will have to collide with the blue sphere near the victim, receiving a message which signals the completion of the assigned task. To give the user a sense of progress, a panel will display the tools that remain to be collected in order to complete the mission. As the user collects the tools, they will appear on the panel (Figure 2.b). After completing the four tasks within level 1, the user can proceed to the next level by colliding with the glowing sphere on the ship's bridge, which signals the change of scene and the passage to the next level (Figure 2.b).

Figure 2. (a) Panel with instructions related to level 1; (b) Virtual Reality Environment with scenario after completion of level 1

On completion of all four levels a screen congratulates the user on their successful in the accomplishment of the mission he or her were assigned. The scoreboard informs the user how successful he or her has been, showing the time taken per level and the final score. After completing the mission, the user has the possibility, to restart the training to improve the score or to exit the virtual environment.

Solution Validation

The Virtual Reality Environment validation phase for the developed solution was the last one performed within the regulatory cycle of the DSR methodology. To this end, a questionnaire was prepared with the aim of evaluating the solution. The questionnaire is composed of several sections in order to collect data from the sample of respondents, specifically: the demographics of the sample, the degree of knowledge of VR technology, the evaluation of the usefulness (Table 1) and usability (Table 2) of the VR solution. Various types of questions were presented, specifically multiple-choice, Likert scale, true-false and free-response questions. Table 1 synthetize the questions placed to the respondents, as well as the attained results.

The sample of respondents was intentional, i.e., a non-probabilistic sample, which was governed by the criteria of convenience and availability of respondents. The respondents, belonged to an organization that has divers with meaningful assignment to diving operations. They were asked to respond to the questionnaire only after having accomplished all the missions proposed by in the Virtual Reality Environment.

The demographic of the sample concluded that from the 35 people who answered the questionnaire, 85.7% were male, with 91.4% under 24 years. From the respondents, 93.8% revealed at least basic knowledge in aquatic rescue missions and 51.4% had participated in a maritime rescue operation. 40% of the respondents revealed little or no knowledge about VR/AR technology. However, VR/AR technology was not unfamiliar to 85.7% of the respondents, although only 74.3% had some familiarity with VR/AR training/teaching solutions, and only 40% knew the difference between AR and VR. Among the areas found more amenable for applying VR/AR by the respondents are: Education & training (86%), Military/Emergency systems (83%), Games (80%), Engineering (66%), Sport (66%), and Medicine & health (63%).

Concerning the evaluation of specific characteristics of the VR solution, it was concluded through the sample responses that: the way the solution defines the mission to be accomplish by the trainee is classified as good/great (for 57.1% of the respondents); the solution provides information to be followed in good/great detail (for 68.6%); the motivation induced by the solution to perform the tasks is good/great (for 51.4%); The way the solution is used is good/great (for 57.1%); the capability of solution trigger emotions during actions is classified as good/great (for 51.4%); the solution's capability for providing detailed context of the action is classified as good/great (for 71.4%); the solution's capability to allow the development of trainees skills is classified as good/great (for 68.6%); and the way the solution adheres to real situations is classified as good/great (for 62.9%).

Table 1. Survey questions

Question	Relevant figures
Demographic profile	
Gender is: male	85.7%
Age is: under 24	91.4%
At least basic knowledge about marine rescue training	93.8%
Participation in maritime rescue training situations	51.4%
Knowledge of Virtual/Augmented Reality technology	
Knowledge of VR/AR technology is: little/no	40%
Familiarity with VR/AR applications is: some to great	85.7%
Familiarity with VR/AR training solutions is: some to great	74.3%
Know the difference between VR and AR: yes	40%
What are the areas more amenable for applying VR/AR?	
Education & training (86%), Military/ Emergency (83%), ...	
Specific evaluation of the Virtual Reality solution	
The way the solution defines the mission to accomplish is: good/great	57.1%
The way the solution provides the information to be followed is: good/great	68.6%
The way the solution motivates the trainee to perform the tasks is: good/great	51.4%
The way the solution is used is: good/great	57.1%
The way the solution arouses emotions during actions is: good/great	51.4%
The way the solution provides the context of the action is: good/great	71.4%
The way the solution allows the development of trainees' skills is: good/great	68.6%
The way the solution adheres to real situations is: good/great	62.9%
Global evaluation of the Virtual Reality solution	
Benefit of training before performing in the real environment is: good/great	77.1%
Degree of realism in relation to a real scenario is: good/great	31.4%
Easiness of use of the solution is: good/great	60.0%
Global assessment of the quality of the solution is: good/great	62.9%
The training innovation with the solution is: good/great	71.4%
The motivation for learning with the solution for trainees is: good/great	88.6%
The potential of VR to improve teaching and training is: good/great	85.7%

Regarding the evaluation of the global characteristics of the VR solution the sample concluded that: the benefit of virtual training before performing in real environment is good/great (for 77.1% of the respondents); the degree of realism in relation to a real scenario is good/great (for 31.4%); the easiness of use of the solution is good/great (for 60.0%); the global assessment of the quality of the solution is good/great (for 62.9%); the training innovation with the solution is good/great (for 71.4%); the motivation for learning with the solution for trainees is good/great (for 88.6%); and the potential of VR to improve teaching and training is good/great (for 85.7%).

For measuring the usability level of the developed solution, it was also used the *System Usability Scale* (SUS). The SUS (Jeff Sauro, 2012) consists of a ten-item questionnaire considering a Likert scale of five response options (from 1-Strongly disagree to 5-Strongly agree) to assess the solution's characteristics of: (i) effectiveness; (ii) efficiency; and (iii) satisfaction. Table 2 shows the percentage of responses chosen for the 4 and 5 options in each questionnaire item. The final SUS score of 63 for the VR solution was attained by averaging the scores of all users. A SUS score below 65 is considered below average (McLellan et al., 2012), so, in terms of usability, there is yet work to do to improve the usability of the built Virtual Reality Environment.

As an overall evaluation the respondents concluded that the use of the Virtual Reality Environment is advantageous for training aquatic rescue situations and that its degree of realism is reasonable, although there is still room for improvement concerning the usability of the developed solution. The respondents agreed that the training concept demonstrated by the solution is innovative and likely to contribute to the improvement of rescue procedures training.

Table 2. System usability scale evaluation

Evaluation of the usability of the proposed solution	
I will use this solution often	51.4%
The solution created is unnecessarily complex	17.1%
The solution is easy to use	51.4%
I would need help from a person with technical knowledge to use the solution	11.4%
The various functions of the solution are very well integrated	31.4%
The solution has a lot of inconsistency	57.1%
The solution is easy to learn	57.1%
The solution is confusing to use	51.4%
I felt confident using the solution	60.0%
I would need to study the topic before being able to use the solution	20.0%

CONCLUSION

This text the development of a Virtual Reality Environment aimed to provide a training tool for scuba divers use, so they could develop critical thinking and learn rescue procedures in a simulated aquatic environment without the limitations, risks and constraints of the physical environments. The solution was developed by means of use of a gamification framework and a *storybording* process, so that divers could put in practice the rescue procedures and feel stimuli and sensations close to those they could feel in a real underwater environment. The synthetic environment was developed in the *Unity* platform by means of implementing game design elements, and the *Octalysis framework*.

The study concluded that generally the use of the Virtual Reality Environment is advantageous for training aquatic rescue situations and that its degree of realism is reasonable, although there is still room for improvement. The respondents agreed that the training concept demonstrated by the present solution is innovative and likely to contribute to the improvement of rescue procedures skills, although the need to further develop the usability of the Virtual Reality solution may be improved. Although the prototype was developed and tested in a desktop PC, the final solution is intended to be deployed in standalone head-mounted displays.

REFERENCES

Alabdulakareem, E., & Jamjoom, M. (2020). Computer-assisted learning for improving ADHD individuals' executive functions through gamified interventions: A review. Entertainment Computing. doi:10.1016/j.entcom.2020.100341

Alqithami, S. (2021). A serious-gamification blueprint towards a normalized attention. *Brain Informatics*, *8*(1), 6. Advance online publication. doi:10.118640708-021-00127-3 PMID:33856585

Araiza, P., Keane, T. L., Beaudry, J., & Kaufman, J. (2020). Immersive Virtual Reality Implementations in Developmental Psychology. *The International Journal of Virtual Reality: a Multimedia Publication for Professionals*. Advance online publication. doi:10.20870/IJVR.2020.20.2.3094

Baptista, G., & Oliveira, T. (2019). Gamification and serious games: A literature meta-analysis and integrative model. Computers in Human Behavior. doi:10.1016/j.chb.2018.11.030

Barba, M. C., Covino, A., de Luca, V., De Paolis, L. T., D'Errico, G., Di Bitonto, P., Di Gestore, S., Magliaro, S., Nunnari, F., Paladini, G. I., Potenza, A., & Schena, A. (2019). *BRAVO: A gaming environment for the treatment of ADHD*. Lecture Notes in Computer Science. doi:10.1007/978-3-030-25965-5_30

Barfield, W., & Blitz, M. J. (2018). Research handbook on the law of virtual and augmented reality. In Research Handbook on the Law of Virtual and Augmented Reality. doi:10.4337/9781786438591

Fleming, T. M., Bavin, L., Stasiak, K., Hermansson-Webb, E., Merry, S. N., Cheek, C., Lucassen, M., Lau, H. M., Pollmuller, B., & Hetrick, S. (2017). Serious games and gamification for mental health: Current status and promising directions. *Frontiers in Psychiatry*, *7*. Advance online publication. doi:10.3389/fpsyt.2016.00215 PMID:28119636

Klaassen, R., Bul, K. C. M., Op Den Akker, R., Van Der Burg, G. J., Kato, P. M., & Di Bitonto, P. (2018). *Design and evaluation of a pervasive coaching and gamification platform for young diabetes patients*. Sensors. doi:10.339018020402

Landers, R. N. (2014). Developing a Theory of Gamified Learning: Linking Serious Games and Gamification of Learning. *Simulation & Gaming*, *45*(6), 752–768. Advance online publication. doi:10.1177/1046878114563660

McCallum, S. (2012). Gamification and serious games for personalized health. *Studies in Health Technology and Informatics*. Advance online publication. doi:10.3233/978-1-61499-069-7-85 PMID:22942036

McLellan, S., Muddimer, A., & Peres, S. (2012). The effect of experience on system usability scale ratings. *Journal of Usability Studies*.

Michalos, A. C., & Simon, H. A. (1970). The Sciences of the Artificial. *Technology and Culture, 11*(1), 118. Advance online publication. doi:10.2307/3102825

Pasquier, P., Mérat, S., Malgras, B., Petit, L., Queran, X., Bay, C., Boutonnet, M., Jault, P., Ausset, S., Auroy, Y., Perez, J. P., Tesnière, A., Pons, F., & Mignon, A. (2016). A serious game for massive training and assessment of french soldiers involved in forward combat casualty care (3d-sc1): Development and deployment. *JMIR Serious Games, 4*(1), e5. Advance online publication. doi:10.2196/games.5340 PMID:27194369

Sauro. (2012). *System Usability Scale. In Measuring Usability With The System Usability Scale*. SUS.

Suh, A., & Prophet, J. (2018). The state of immersive technology research: A literature analysis. *Computers in Human Behavior, 86*, 77–90. Advance online publication. doi:10.1016/j.chb.2018.04.019

Vaishnavi, V. & Kuechler, B. (2004). Design Science Research in Information Systems Overview of Design Science Research. *Ais*.

Wieringa, R. (2009). Design science as nested problem solving. *Proceedings of the 4th International Conference on Design Science Research in Information Systems and Technology, DESRIST '09*. 10.1145/1555619.1555630

Yannakakis, G. N., & Togelius, J. (2018). Artificial intelligence and games. Artificial Intelligence and Games. doi:10.1007/978-3-319-63519-4

ADDITIONAL READING

Arnaldi, B., Guitton, P., & Moreau, G. (2017). Virtual Reality and Augmented Reality: Myths and Realities. Virtual Reality and Augmented Reality: Myths and Realities. doi:10.1002/9781119341031

Elmqaddem, N. (2019). Augmented Reality and Virtual Reality in education. Myth or reality? *International Journal of Emerging Technologies in Learning*. doi:10.3991/ijet.v14i03.9289

Huang, S. (2019, September). Augmented reality and virtual reality: The power of AR and VR for business. *Information Technology & Tourism, 21*(3), 457–459. Advance online publication. doi:10.100740558-019-00149-y

Jerald, J. (2015). *The VR book: Human-centered design for virtual reality*. Morgan & Claypool. doi:10.1145/2792790

Murray, J. W. (2020). *Building Virtual Reality with Unity and SteamVR*. CRC Press. doi:10.1201/9780429295850

Pangilinan, E., Lukas, S., & Mohan, V. (2019). *Creating augmented and virtual realities: theory and practice for next-generation spatial computing*. O'Reilly Media, Inc.

Sala, N. (2020). *Virtual Reality*. Augmented Reality, and Mixed Reality in Education., doi:10.4018/978-1-7998-4960-5.ch003

KEY TERMS AND DEFINITIONS

Augmented Reality (AR): An enhanced version of the real world that is achieved through the overlay of digital visual elements, sound, or other sensory stimuli delivered via technology.

Gamification: The process of enhance systems, services, organizations, and activities to create similar experiences to those experienced when playing games in order to motivate and engage users.

Head-Mounted Display (HMD): A display device, worn on the head or as part of a helmet, that has a small display optic in front of one (monocular HMD) or each eye (binocular HMD). An HMD has many uses including gaming, aviation, engineering, and medicine.

Scuba Diving: An underwater swimming activity involving the use of self-contained underwater breathing apparatus.

Serious Game: Games that have another purpose besides entertainment. They are entertaining, engaging, and immersive, combining learning strategies, knowledge and structures, and game elements to teach specific skills, knowledge, and attitudes.

Simulated Reality: The hypothesis that reality could be simulated to a degree indistinguishable from "true" reality.

Storyboard: A series of panels on which a set of sketches is arranged depicting consecutively the important changes of scene and action in a series of shots.

Usability: The quality of a user's experience when interacting with products or systems, including websites, software, devices, or applications. Usability is about effectiveness, efficiency, and the overall satisfaction of the user.

Virtual Reality (VR): A simulated experience that can be like or completely different from the real world.

Compilation of References

Aarsand, P. (2010). Young boys playing digital games. *Nordic Journal of Digital Literacy*, 5(1), 38–55. doi:10.18261/ISSN1891-943X-2010-01-04

Aarseth, E. (2001). Computer Game Studies, Year One. *Game Studies Journal*, 1(1). Retrieved from http://www.gamestudies.org/0101/editorial.html

Aarseth, E. (2002). The Dungeon and the Ivory Tower: Vive La Difference ou Liaison Dangereuse? *Game Studies Journal*, 2(1). Retrieved from http://www.gamestudies.org/0102/editorial.html

Aarseth, E. (2015). Meta-Game Studies. *Game Studies Journal*, 15(1). Retrieved from http://gamestudies.org/1501/articles/editorial

Abadia Correa, J., Ortiz Paez, L., & Peña Castiblicanco, N. (2021). *Development of a Training Game to Provide Awareness in Cybersecurity to the Staff of the Aviation Military School "Marco Fidel Suárez" of the Colombian Air Force in the city of Cali*. Academic Press.

Abbitt, J. T. (2011). An Investigation of the Relationship between Self-Efficacy Beliefs about Technology Integration and Technological Pedagogical Content Knowledge (TPACK) among Preservice Teachers. *Journal of Digital Learning in Teacher Education*, 27(4), 134–143. doi:10.1080/21532974.2011.10784670

Abbott, D. (2019). Game-based learning for postgraduates: An empirical study of an educational game to teach research skills. *Higher Education Pedagogies*, 4(1), 80–104. doi:10.1080/23752696.2019.1629825

Abrams, S. S. (2009). A gaming frame of mind: Digital contexts and academic implications. *Educational Media International*, 46(4), 335–347. doi:10.1080/09523980903387480

Abrams, S. S. (2016). Emotionally crafted experiences: Layering literacies in Minecraft. *The Reading Teacher*, 70(4), 501–506. doi:10.1002/trtr.1515

Abt, C. (1970). *Serious Games*. The Viking Press.

Acker, A., & Pecker, J. C. (1990). Public misconceptions about astronomy. In *International Astronomical Union Colloquium* (Vol. 105, pp. 229-238). Cambridge University Press. 10.1017/S025292110008684X

Acks, A. (2017, August 1). *Tolkien's Map and The Messed Up Mountains of Middle-earth*. https://www.tor.com/2017/08/01/tolkiens-map-and-the-messed-up-mountains-of-middle-earth/

Adachi, P. J. C., & Willoughby, T. (2011). The effect of violent video games on aggression: Is it more than just the violence? *Aggression and Violent Behavior*, 16(1), 55–62. doi:10.1016/j.avb.2010.12.002

Adams, C. (2017). *The Disadvantages of using games as a Learning tool*. Academic Press.

Adams, E. (2010). *Fundamentals of game design*. New Riders.

Adjibolosoo, S. (2000). *Pillars of economic growth and sustained human-centred development.* Paper presented at the International Institute for Human Factor Development Conference, Harare, Zimbabwe.

Adjibolosoo, S. (1993). The human factor in development. *Scandinavian Journal of Development Alternatives, 12*(4), 139–149.

Adjibolosoo, S. (1994). The human factor and the failure of economic development and policies in Africa. In F. Ezeala-Harrison & S. Adjibolosoo (Eds.), *Perspectives on Economic Development in Africa.* Praeger Publishers.

Adjibolosoo, S. (1995). *The significance of the human factor in African economic development.* Praeger.

Adjibolosoo, S. (1998). *Global development the human factor way.* Praeger.

Adjibolosoo, S. (1999). *Rethinking development theory and policy. A human factor critiques.* Praeger.

Adom, D., Hussain, E. K., & Joe, A. A. (2018). Theoretical and Conceptual Framework: Mandatory Ingredients. *International Journal of Scientific Research, 7*(1), 93–98.

Adorno, T., & Horkheimer, M. (1972). *The dialectic of the enlightenment.* Herder and Herder.

Aggarwal, C. C. (2018). Neural networks and deep learning. Springer, 10, 978-973.

Aghlara, L., & Tamjid, N. H. (2011). The effect of digital games on Iranian children's vocabulary retention in foreign language acquisition. *Procedia: Social and Behavioral Sciences, 29,* 552–560. doi:10.1016/j.sbspro.2011.11.275

Aguiar, A. L., & Aguiar, C. (2020). Classroom composition and quality in early childhood education: A systematic review. *Children and Youth Services Review, 115*(May), 105086. doi:10.1016/j.childyouth.2020.105086

Aguilera & Martínez. (2017). Gamification, a didactic strategy in higher education. *Edulearn17 Proceedings,* 6761-6771.

Agustin-Llach, M. P., & Canga Alonso, A. (2016). Vocabulary growth in young CLIL and traditional EFL learners: Evidence from research and implications for education. *International Journal of Applied Linguistics, 26*(2), 211–217. doi:10.1111/ijal.12090

Ahissar, M., Nahum, M., Nelken, I., & Hochstein, S. (2009). Reverse hierarchies and sensory learning. *Philosophical Transactions of the Royal Society of London. Series B, Biological Sciences, 364*(1515), 285–299. doi:10.1098/rstb.2008.0253 PMID:18986968

Ahmad, F., Ahmed, Z., & Muneeb, S. (2021). Effect of gaming mode upon the players' cognitive performance during brain games play: An exploratory research. *International Journal of Game-Based Learning, 11*(1), 67–76. Advance online publication. doi:10.4018/IJGBL.2021010105

Ahmad, M. I., Mubin, O., Shahid, S., & Orlando, J. (2019). Robot's adaptive emotional feedback sustains children's social engagement and promotes their vocabulary learning: A long-term child–robot interaction study. *Adaptive Behavior, 27*(4), 243–266. doi:10.1177/1059712319844182

Ahmad, M., Mubin, O., & Escudero, P. (2015, October). Using adaptive mobile agents in games-based scenarios to facilitate foreign language word learning. In *Proceedings of the 3rd International Conference on Human-Agent Interaction* (pp. 255-257). 10.1145/2814940.2814990

Ahsan, M. T., Sharma, U., & Deppeler, J. M. (2012). Challenges to prepare pre-service teachers for inclusive education in Bangladesh: Beliefs of higher educational institutional heads. *Asia Pacific Journal of Education, 32*(2), 241–257. doi:10.1080/02188791.2012.655372

Airaksinen, T., Halinen, I., & Linturi, H. (2016). Futuribles of learning 2030 - Delphi supports the reform of the core curricula in Finland. *European Journal of Futures Research, 5*(1), 2. doi:10.100740309-016-0096-y

Aires, L. (2015). *Paradigma Qualitativo e Práticas de Investigação Educacional*. Universidade Aberta.

Akçayır, M., Dündar, H., & Akçayır, G. (2016). What makes you a digital native? Is it enough to be born after 1980? *Computers in Human Behavior*, *60*, 435–440. doi:10.1016/j.chb.2016.02.089

Aktinson, P., & Hammersley, M. (1998). Ethnography and participant observation. In *Strategies of Qualitative Inquiry* (pp. 248–261). Sage.

Al Bailey Apps. (2021). *Phonics town* (Version1.01) [Mobile app]. http://itunes.apple.com

Al Fatta, H., Maksom, Z., & Zakaria, M. H. (2019). Game-based learning and gamification: Searching for definitions. *International Journal of Simulation: Systems, Science & Technology*, *19*, 10–5013.

Alabdulakareem, E., & Jamjoom, M. (2020). Computer-assisted learning for improving ADHD individuals' executive functions through gamified interventions: A review. Entertainment Computing. doi:10.1016/j.entcom.2020.100341

Al-Alwani, A. E. (2010, August). Barriers to effective use of information technology in science education. *International Conference on Enterprise Information Systems and Web Technologies (EISWT)*, 42–49.

Alam, M. J. (2019). Dilemma of Parental Aspiration for Children with Special Needs in Early Childhood Education (ECE) Settings: The Case of Bangladesh. *Asia-Pacific Journal of Research in Early Childhood Education*, *13*(3), 25–43. doi:10.17206/apjrece.2019.13.3.25

Alam, M. J. (2020). Who Chooses School? Understanding Parental Aspirations for Child Transition from Home to Early Childhood Education (ECE) Institutions in Bangladesh. In S. Tatalović Vorkapić & J. LoCasale-Crouch (Eds.), *Supporting Children's Well-Being During Early Childhood Transition to School* (pp. 85–107). IGI Global. doi:10.4018/978-1-7998-4435-8

Alaswad, Z., & Nadolny, L. (2015). Designing for game-based learning: The effective integration of technology to support learning. *Journal of Educational Technology Systems*, *43*(4), 389–402. doi:10.1177/0047239515588164

Alberti, J. (2008). The game of reading and writing: How video games reframe our understanding of literacy. *Computers and Composition*, *25*(3), 258–269. doi:10.1016/j.compcom.2008.04.004

Albirini, A. (2006). Teachers' attitudes toward information and communication technologies: The case of Syrian EFL teachers. *Computers & Education*, *47*(4), 373–398. doi:10.1016/j.compedu.2004.10.013

Aldabbus, S. (2018). Project-based learning: Implementation & challenges. *International Journal of Education, Learning and Development*, *6*(3), 71–79.

Aldemir, T., Celik, B., & Kaplan, G. (2018). A qualitative investigation of student perceptions of game elements in a gamified course. *Computers in Human Behavior*, *78*, 235–254. doi:10.1016/j.chb.2017.10.001

Aldosemani, T. (2019). Inservice Teachers' Perceptions of a Professional Development Plan Based on SAMR Model: A Case Study. *The Turkish Online Journal of Educational Technology*, *18*(3), 46–53.

Aldrich, C. (2003). *Simulations and the future of learning*. Pfeiffer.

Alemi, M., & Haeri, N. S. (2017, October). How to Develop Learners' Politeness: A Study of RALL's Impact on Learning Greeting by Young Iranian EFL Learners. In *2017 5th RSI International Conference on Robotics and Mechatronics (ICRoM)* (pp. 88-94). IEEE. 10.1109/ICRoM.2017.8466206

Alemi, M., Meghdari, A., Basiri, N., & Taheri, A. (2015). The Effect of Applying Humanoid Robots as Teacher Assistants to Help Iranian Autistic Pupils Learn English as a Foreign Language. In *Social Robotics* (pp. 1–10). Lecture Notes in Computer Science. Springer International Publishing.

Alemi, M., Meghdari, A., & Ghazisaedy, M. (2014). Employing humanoid robots for teaching English language in Iranian junior high-schools. *International Journal of HR; Humanoid Robotics, 11*(03), 1450022. doi:10.1142/S0219843614500224

Alessi, S. M., & Trollip, S. R. (1984). *Computer-based instruction: Methods and development*. Prentice-Hall.

Alessi, S. M., & Trollip, S. R. (2001). *Multimedia for learning: Methods and development*. Allyn & Bacon.

Alexander, A., & Ho, T. (2015). Gaming worlds: Secondary students creating an interactive Video game. *Art Education, 68*(1), 28–36. doi:10.1080/00043125.2015.11519303

Alexander, B. (2008). *The globalization of addiction: A study in poverty of the spirit*. Oxford University Press.

Alexander, J. (2009). Gaming, student literacies, and the composition classroom: Some possibilities for transformation. *College Composition and Communication, 61*(1), 35–63.

Alexander, S. (2010). *Flexible Learning in Higher Education*. International Encyclopedia of Education., doi:10.1016/B978-0-08-044894-7.00868-X

Alhashmi, M., Mubin, O., & Baroud, R. (2021). Examining the use of robots as teacher assistants in UAE classrooms: Teacher and student perspectives. *Journal of Information Technology Education*, 245–261. https://doi-org.ezproxy.uws.edu.au/10.28945/4749

Alhassan, R. (2017). Exploring the relationship between Web 2.0 tools self-efficacy and teachers' use of these tools in their teaching. *Journal of Education and Learning, 6*(4), 217–228. doi:10.5539/jel.v6n4p217

Alismail, H. A., & McGuire, P. (2015). 21st century standards and curriculum: Current research and practice. *Journal of Education and Practice, 6*(6), 150–154.

Al-Khatib, K., Wachsmuth, H., Lang, K., Herpel, J., Hagen, M., & Stein, B. (2018). *Modeling Deliberative Argumentation Strategies on Wikipedia*. https://scholar.googleusercontent.com/scholar?q=cache:sOSvXuDA-IAJ:scholar.google.com/&hl=en&as_sdt=2005&sciodt=0,5

Alkind Taylor, A. S., & Backlund, P. (2012). Making the Implicit Explicit: Game-based Training Practices from an Instructor Perspective. In *6th European Conference on Games Based Learning (ECGBL'12)* (pp. 1-10). Cork, Ireland: European Conference on Games Based Learning.

All, A., Nunez Castellar, E. P., & Van Looy, J. (2014). Measuring effectiveness in digital game-based learning: A methodological review. *International Journal of Serious Games, 1*(2), 3–20. doi:10.17083/ijsg.v1i2.18

All, A., Nuñez Castellar, E. P., & Van Looy, J. (2015). Assessing the effectiveness of digital game-based learning: Best practices. *Computers & Education, 92-93*, 90–103. doi:10.1016/j.compedu.2015.10.007

Allal-Chérif, O., & Makhlouf, M. (2016). Using serious games to manage knowledge: The SECI model perspective. *Journal of Business Research, 69*(5), 1539–1543. doi:10.1016/j.jbusres.2015.10.013

Allery, L. (2014). Make use of educational games. *Education for Primary Care, 25*(1), 65–66. doi:10.1080/14739879.2014.11494245 PMID:24423808

Alligator Apps. (2014). *Preschool matching game: Rhyming Words* [Mobile app]. http://itunes.apple.com

Alloway, N., Freebody, P., Gilbert, P., & Muspratt, S. (2002). Boys, literacy and schooling: Expanding the repertoires of practice. Commonwealth of Australia, Department of Education, Science and Training.

Allsop, Y., & Jesse, J. (2015). Teachers' Experience and Reflections on Game-Based Learning in the Primary Classroom: Views from England and Italy. *International Journal of Game-Based Learning, 5*(1), 1–17. doi:10.4018/ijgbl.2015010101

Almeida, F. (2020). Adoption of a Serious Game in the Developing of Emotional Intelligence Skills. *European Journal of Investigation in Health, Psychology and Education, 10*(1), 30–43. doi:10.3390/ejihpe10010004 PMID:34542467

Almeida, F., & Simoes, J. (2019). The role of serious games, gamification and Industry 4.0 tools in the Education 4.0 paradigm. *Contemporary Educational Technology, 10*(2), 120–136. doi:10.30935/cet.554469

Al-Qallaf, C. L., & Al-Mutairi, A. S. (2016). Digital literacy and digital content supports learning: The impact of blogs on teaching English as a foreign language. *The Electronic Library*.

Alqithami, S. (2021). A serious-gamification blueprint towards a normalized attention. *Brain Informatics, 8*(1), 6. Advance online publication. doi:10.118640708-021-00127-3 PMID:33856585

Al-Samarraie, H., Teo, T., & Abbas, M. (2013). Can structured representation enhance students' thinking skills for better understanding of E-learning content? *Computers & Education, 69*, 463–473. doi:10.1016/j.compedu.2013.07.038

Alsawaier, R. S. (2018). The effect of gamification on motivation and engagement. *International Journal of Information and Learning Technology, 35*(1), 56–79. doi:10.1108/IJILT-02-2017-0009

Al-Senaidi, S., Lin, L., & Poirot, J. (2009). Barriers to adopting technology for teaching and learning in Oman. *Computers & Education, 53*(3), 575–590. doi:10.1016/j.compedu.2009.03.015

AlShaiji, O. A. (2015). Video games promote Saudi children's English vocabulary retention. *Education, 136*(2), 123–132.

Alt, D., & Raichel, N. (2020). Enhancing perceived digital literacy skills and creative self-concept through gamified learning environments: Insights from a longitudinal study. *International Journal of Educational Research, 101*, 101561.

Alvermann, D. E. (Ed.). (2005). *Adolescents and literacies in a digital world* (3rd ed.). Peter Lang.

Alvermann, D., & Xu, S. (2003). Children's everyday literacies: Intersections of popular culture and language arts instruction. *Language Arts, 81*(2), 145–154.

Alves, F. (2014). *Gamification - Como criar experiências de aprendizagem engajadoras. Um guia completo*. DVS Editora.

Alyaz, Y., & Genc, Z. S. (2016). Digital game-based language learning in foreign language teacher education. *Turkish Online Journal of Distance Education, 17*(4), 130–146. doi:10.17718/tojde.44375

Alzubi, T., Fernández, R., Flores, J., Duran, M., & Cotos, J. M. (2018). Improving the Working Memory During Early Childhood Education Through the Use of an Interactive Gesture Game-Based Learning Approach. *IEEE Access: Practical Innovations, Open Solutions, 6*, 53998–54009. doi:10.1109/ACCESS.2018.2870575

American Educational Research Association, American Psychological Association, & National Council on Measurement in Education. (2014). *Standards for educational and psychological testing*. American Educational Research Association.

American Library Association. (2000). *Information literacy competency standards for higher education*. https://repository.arizona.edu/handle/10150/105645

American Library Association. (n.d.). *Games and literacy: the connection between literacy and gaming*. Games & Gaming Round Table: A Round Table of the American Library Association. Retrieved from https://www.ala.org/gamert/games-

Amirnuddin, P. S., Mohamed, A. A. A., & Ahmad, M. H. (2020). Transforming Legal Education In The Era Of Fourth Industrial Revolution. *Current Law Journal, 2*, ix–xxiv.

Amirnuddin, P. S., & Turner, J. T. (2020). Learning Law using Augmented Reality and Neuro-Linguistic Programming. In P. Kumar, M. J. Keppell, & C. L. Lim (Eds.), *Preparing 21st Century Teachers for Teach Less, Learn More (TLLM) Pedagogies* (pp. 259–278). IGI Global. doi:10.4018/978-1-7998-1435-1.ch015

An Educator's Guide to Cyberbullying. (2011, Apr. 10). Senate.gov

Ananiadou, K., & Claro, M. (2009). 21st century skills and competences for new millennium learners in OECD countries. *OECD Education Working Papers, 4.*

Ananiadou, K., & Claro, M. (2009). *21st Century Skills and Competences for New Millennium Learners in OECD Countries.* OECD Education Working Papers, 41. OECD Publishing. doi:10.1787/19939019

Anastasiadis, T., Lampropoulos, G., & Siakas, K. (2018). Digital game-based learning and serious games in education. *International Journal of Advances in Scientific Research and Engineering, 4*(12), 139–144. doi:10.31695/IJASRE.2018.33016

Anazifa, R. D., & Djukri, S. (2017). Project-based learning and problem-based learning: Are they effective to improve student's thinking skills? *Journal Pendidikan IPA Indonesia, 6*(2), 346–355. doi:10.15294/jpii.v6i2.11100

Anderson, A., Barham, N., & Northcote, M. (2013). Using the TPACK framework to unite disciplines in online learning. *Australasian Journal of Educational Technology, 29*(4), 549–565. doi:10.14742/ajet.24

Anderson, J. L., & Barnett, M. (2013). Learning physics with digital game simulations in middle school science. *Journal of Science Education and Technology, 22*(6), 914–926. doi:10.100710956-013-9438-8

And-literacy. (n.d.). https://www.ala.org/gamert/games-and-literacy

Andone, D., Dron, J., Boyne, C., & Pemberton, L. (2005). Digital Students and Their Use Of Elearning Enviroments. *IADIS International Conference on WWW/Internet.*

Angeli, C., & Valanides, N. (2009). Epistemological and methodological issues for the conceptualization, development, and assessment of ICT-TPCK: Advances in technological pedagogical content knowledge (TPCK). *Computers & Education, 52*(1), 154–168. doi:10.1016/j.compedu.2008.07.006

Angell, C., Guttersrud, Ø., Henriksen, E. K., & Isnes, A. (2004). Physics: Frightful, but fun. Pupils' and teachers' views of physics and physics teaching. *Science Education, 88*(5), 683-706.

Anniroot, J., & De Villiers, M. R. (2012). *Study of Alice: A visual environment for teaching object-oriented programming.* Academic Press.

Antonaci, A., Klemke, R., & Specht, M. (2019). The Effects of Gamification in Online Learning Environments: A Systematic Literature Review. *Informatics (MDPI), 6*(3), 32. doi:10.3390/informatics6030032

Anwar, Z., Kahar, M. S., Rawi, R. D. P., Nurjannah, N., Suaib, H., & Rosalina, F. (2020). Development of interactive video based powerpoint media In mathematics learning. *Journal of Educational Science and Technology, 6*(2), 167–177. doi:10.26858/est.v6i2.13179

Anyaegbu, R., Ting, W., & Li, Y. (2012). Serious game motivation in an EFL classroom in Chinese primary school. *The Turkish Online Journal of Educational Technology, 11*(1), 154–164.

Araiza, P., Keane, T. L., Beaudry, J., & Kaufman, J. (2020). Immersive Virtual Reality Implementations in Developmental Psychology. *The International Journal of Virtual Reality: a Multimedia Publication for Professionals.* Advance online publication. doi:10.20870/IJVR.2020.20.2.3094

Arango-Lopez, J., Collazos, C. A., Velas, F. L. G., & Moreira, F. (2018). Using pervasive games as learning tools in educational contexts: A systematic review. *International Journal of Learning Technology, 13*(2), 93–114. doi:10.1504/IJLT.2018.092094

Arbitration/Requests/Case/German war effort. (2019a). In *Wikipedia.* https://en.wikipedia.org/w/index.php?title=Wikipedia:Arbitration/Requests/Case/German_war_effort&oldid=886462669

Archambault, L. M., & Barnett, J. H. (2010). Revisiting technological pedagogical content knowledge: Exploring the TPACK framework. *Computers & Education*, *55*(4), 1656–1662. doi:10.1016/j.compedu.2010.07.009

Ariffin, M. M. (2012). Towards digital game-based learning (DGBL) in higher education (HE): The educators' perception. *Developing Country Studies*, *2*(11), 228–236.

Armstrong, S. J. (2011). From the editors: Continuing our quest for meaningful impact on management practice. Academy of Management Learning & Education, 10(2), 181-7.

Arnab, S., Clarke, S., & Morini, L. (2019). Co-creativity through play and game design thinking. *Electronic Journal of E-Learning*, *17*(3), 184–198. doi:10.34190/JEL.17.3.002

Arnett, J. (2002). The psychology of globalization. *The American Psychologist*, *57*(10), 774–783. doi:10.1037/0003-066X.57.10.774 PMID:12369500

Artigue, M. (2002). Learning mathematics in a CAS environment: The genesis of a reflection about instrumentation and the dialectics between technical and conceptual work. *International Journal of Computers for Mathematical Learning*, *7*(3), 245–274. doi:10.1023/A:1022103903080

Asadullah, M., & Chaudhury, N. (2015). The Dissonance between schooling and learning: Evidence from rural Bangladesh. *Comparative Education Review*, *59*(3), 447–472. doi:10.1086/681929

Asai, K., Sugimoto, Y., & Billinghurst, M. (2010). Exhibition of lunar surface navigation system facilitating collaboration between children and parents in science museum. In *Proceedings of the 9th ACM SIGGRAPH Conference on Virtual-Reality Continuum and its Applications in Industry* (pp. 119-124). 10.1145/1900179.1900203

Asal, V., & Blake, E. (2006). Creating simulations for political science education. *Journal of Political Science Education*, *2*(1), 1–18. doi:10.1080/15512160500484119

Asay, M. (2009, 14 January). *Shirky: Problem is filter failure, not info overload.* clnet. Accessed from https://www.cnet.com/news/shirky-problem-is-filter-failure-not-info-overload/

Asch, F. (2015). *Popcorn.* Aladdin.

Ashkanasy, N. M. (2006). Introduction: Arguments for a more grounded approach in management education. *Academy of Management Learning & Education*, *5*(2), 207–208. doi:10.5465/amle.2006.21253785

Ashrafuzzaman, M. (2021). *Impact of Facebook Usage on University Students' Academic Performance.* Unpublished Research Report, Bangabandhu Sheikh Mujibur Rahman Digital University, Bangladesh (BDU).

Aslan, S., & Reigeluth, C. M. (2013). Educational technologists: Leading change for a new paradigm of education. *TechTrends*, *57*(5), 18–24. doi:10.100711528-013-0687-4

AssistiveWare. (2020). *Pictello* (Version 3.7.2) [Mobile app]. http://itunes.apple.com

Association of College and Research Libraries (ACRL). (2015, February 9). *Framework for Information Literacy for Higher Education.* Association of College & Research Libraries (ACRL). https://www.ala.org/acrl/standards/ilframework

Ataíde, A., Souto, I., & Pereira, A. (2019). School Problems and Teachers' Collaboration: Before a Collaborative Problem Solving Program. *Education and New Developments*, *1*(July), 222–226. doi:10.36315/2019v1end047

Atashrouz, B., Pakdaman, S. H., & Asgari, A. (2008). Prediction of academic achievement from attachment rate. *ZtF. Zeitschrift für Familienforschung*, *4*(2), 193–203.

Attard, A., Di Iorio, E., Geven, K., & Santa, R. (2010). Time for a new paradigm in education: student-centred learning. In A. Attard (Ed.), *Student-centred Learning Toolkit* (pp. 1-4). European Students Union. https://www.esu-online.org/wp-content/uploads/2016/07/100814-SCL.pdf

Aufderheide, P. (1993). *Media literacy: A report of the national leadership conference on media literacy*. Aspen Institute.

Avizov, S. R., Atamuratova, T. I., Holova, S. A., Kamalova, F. R., Akobirova, L. H., & Oltiev, A. T. (2020). Traditional requirements and innovative learning models in the higher education context. *European Journal of Molecular & Clinical Medicine, 7*(2), 872–885.

Axelrod, L., & Hone, K. (2006). Affectemes and allaffects: A novel approach to coding user emotional expression during interactive experiences. *Behaviour & Information Technology, 25*(2), 159–173. doi:10.1080/01449290500331164

Ayastuy, M. D., Torres, D., & Fernández, A. (2021). Adaptive Gamification in Collaborative systems, a systematic mapping study. *Computer Science Review, 39*, 100333.

Ayres, L., & Narum, L. (2019). The promise of brain plasticity – overcoming language, learning and reading problems. *The Promise of Brain Plasticity-Overcoming Language*. Retrieved from: https://www.tarnowcenter.com/tarnow-articles/28-tarnow-articles/article-desc/584-the-promise-of-brain-plasticity-overcoming-language,-learning,-and-reading-problems.html

Azam, A., Qiang, F., Abbas, S. A., & Abdullah, M. I. (2013). Structural equation modeling (SEM) based trust analysis of Muslim consumers in the collective religion affiliation model in e-commerce. *Journal of Islamic Marketing, 4*(2), 134–149. doi:10.1108/17590831311329278

Azevedo, J., Padrão, P., Gregório, M. J., Almeida, C., Moutinho, N., Lien, N., & Barros, R. (2019). A web-based gamification program to improve nutrition literacy in families of 3-to 5-year-old children: The Nutriscience Project. *Journal of Nutrition Education and Behavior, 51*(3), 326–334. doi:10.1016/j.jneb.2018.10.008 PMID:30579894

Azim, F., & Ahmed, S. S. (2010). Exploring mathematics teachers' beliefs in secondary schools of Bangladesh. *Teacher's World, 35-36*, 41–53.

Azim, F., & Rahman, M. M. S. (2015). Mobile embedded self-study materials for CPD: The use of English language for teachers (EL4T) in Bangladesh. In G. Pickering & P. Gunashekar (Eds.), *Innovation in English Language Teacher Education*. British Council.

Azman, H., & Farhana Dollsaid, N. (2018). Applying Massively Multiplayer Online Games (MMOGs) in EFL Teaching. *Arab World English Journal, 9*(4), 3–18. doi:10.24093/awej/vol9no4.1

Azuma, R. T. (1997). A survey of augmented reality. *Presence (Cambridge, Mass.), 6*(4), 355–385. doi:10.1162/pres.1997.6.4.355

Baboo, S & Raja, V. (2017). Impact of playing and watching videogames on classroom attention, problem-solving and prosocial behavior of school children, *IDC International Journal, 4*(3).

Bachmair, B., & Bazalgette, C. (2007). The European Charter for media literacy: Meaning and potential. *Research in Comparative and İnternational Education, 2*(1), 80-87.

Backhouse, J. (2013). What makes lecturers in higher education use emerging technologies in their teaching? *Knowledge Management & E-Learning, 5*(3), 345–358. http://www.kmel-journal.org/ojs/index.php/online-publication/article/view/216/218

Baden, D., & Higgs, M. (2015). Challenging the perceived wisdom of management theories and practice. *Academy of Management Learning & Education, 14*(4), 539–555. doi:10.5465/amle.2014.0170

Bado, N. (2019). Game-based learning pedagogy: A review of the literature. *Interactive Learning Environments*, 1–13. doi:10.1080/10494820.2019.1683587

Bado, N., & Franklin, T. (2014). Cooperative Game-based Learning in the English as a Foreign Language Classroom. *Issues and Trends in Educational Technology*, 2(2). Advance online publication. doi:10.2458/azu_itet_v2i2_bado

Baek, Y., & Touati, A. (2017). Exploring how individual traits influence enjoyment in a mobile learning game. *Computers in Human Behavior*, 69, 347–357. doi:10.1016/j.chb.2016.12.053

Baek, Y., & Whitton, N. (2013). *Digital Game Based Learning: Methods, Models and Strategies*. IGI Global. doi:10.4018/978-1-4666-2848-9

Baer, A. (2014, April 15). *Keeping Up With... Digital Writing in the College Classroom*. Association of College & Research Libraries (ACRL). https://www.ala.org/acrl/publications/keeping_up_with/digital_writing

Baharom, S. N., Tan, W. H., & Idris, M. Z. (2014). Emotional design for games: The roles of emotion and perception in game design process. *1st International Symposium on Simulation & Serious Games*, 978-981. 10.3850/978-981-09-0463-0_015

Baid, H., & Lambert, N. (2010). Enjoyable learning: The role of humour, games, and fun activities in nursing and midwifery education. *Nurse Education Today*, 30(6), 548–552. doi:10.1016/j.nedt.2009.11.007 PMID:20044181

Bainbridge, W. S. (2018). Computer Simulation for Space-Oriented Strategic Thinking. In *Computer Simulations of Space Societies* (pp. 113–139). Springer. doi:10.1007/978-3-319-90560-0_5

Baker, F. (2010). Media literacy: 21 st century literacy skills. In H. H. Jacobs (Ed.), Curriculum 21 essential education for a changing world (pp. 133–152). Academic Press.

Baldy, E. (2007). A new educational perspective for teaching gravity. *International Journal of Science Education*, 29(14), 1767–1788. doi:10.1080/09500690601083367

Balkibekov, K., Meiirbekov, S., Tazhigaliyeva, N., & Sandygulova, A. (2016, August). Should robots win or lose? Robot's losing playing strategy positively affects child learning. In *2016 25th IEEE International Symposium on Robot and Human Interactive Communication (RO-MAN)* (pp. 706-711). IEEE. 10.1109/ROMAN.2016.7745196

Ballard, J., & Butler, P. (2011). Personalised Learning: Developing a Vygotskian Framework for E-learning. *International Journal of Technology, Knowledge and Society*, 7(2), 21–36. doi:10.18848/1832-3669/CGP/v07i02/56198

Bal, S. (2018). Using Quizziz.com to enhance pre intermediate students' vocabulary knowledge. *International Journal of Language Academy*, 6(3), 295–303. doi:10.18033/ijla.3953

Bampasidis, G. (2019). Ψηφιακά παιχνίδια σε συσκευές κινητής τεχνολογίας και κίνδυνοι δημιουργίας επιστημονικών παρανοήσεων: Παραδείγματα από την Αεροδιαστημική Επιστήμη και την Τεχνολογία [Digital games in portable devices and the dangers of creating misconceptions: Examples from Aerospace science and Technology]. *Astrolavos, 32*.

Banfield, J., & Wilkerson, B. (2014). Increasing student intrinsic motivation and self-efficacy through gamification pedagogy. *Contemporary Issues in Education Research (Online)*, 7(4), 291–298. doi:10.19030/cier.v7i4.8843

Baptista, G., & Oliveira, T. (2019). Gamification and serious games: A literature meta-analysis and integrative model. Computers in Human Behavior. doi:10.1016/j.chb.2018.11.030

Barab, S. A., Warren, S. J., Zuiker, S., Hickey, D., Ingram-Goble, A., & Dodge, T. (2006). *Transfer of Learning in Complex Learning Environments*. Paper presented at the American Educational Research Association Annual Meeting, San Francisco, CA.

Barab, S. A., Scott, B., Siyahhan, S., Goldstone, R., Ingram-Goble, A., Zuiker, S. J., & Warren, S. (2009). Transformational play as a curricular scaffold: Using videogames to support science education. *Journal of Science Education and Technology*, *18*(4), 305–320. doi:10.100710956-009-9171-5

Barab, S., Ingram-Goble, A., & Warren, S. (2009). Conceptual play spaces. In R. E. Ferdig (Ed.), *Hand-book of Research on Effective Electronic Gaming in Education* (pp. 989–1009). IGI Global. doi:10.4018/978-1-59904-808-6.ch057

Barack, L. (2013). A Minecraft library scores big. *School Library Journal*, *59*(9), 14.

Barba, M. C., Covino, A., de Luca, V., De Paolis, L. T., D'Errico, G., Di Bitonto, P., Di Gestore, S., Magliaro, S., Nunnari, F., Paladini, G. I., Potenza, A., & Schena, A. (2019). *BRAVO: A gaming environment for the treatment of ADHD*. Lecture Notes in Computer Science. doi:10.1007/978-3-030-25965-5_30

Barbas, H. (2000). Connections underlying the synthesis of cognition, memory, and emotion in primate prefrontal cortices. *Brain Research Bulletin*, *52*(5), 319–330. doi:10.1016/S0361-9230(99)00245-2 PMID:10922509

Bardin, L. (2011). *Análise de conteúdo*. Coimbra: Edições 70.

Barfield, W., & Blitz, M. J. (2018). Research handbook on the law of virtual and augmented reality. In Research Handbook on the Law of Virtual and Augmented Reality. doi:10.4337/9781786438591

Barkley, J. E., Lepp, A., & Glickman, E. L. (2017). "Pokémon Go!" may promote walking, discourage sedentary behavior in college students. *Games for Health Journal*, *6*(3), 165–170. doi:10.1089/g4h.2017.0009 PMID:28628384

Barko, T., & Sadler, T. D. (2013). Practicality in virtuality: Finding student meaning in video game education. *Journal of Science Education and Technology*, *22*(2), 124–132. doi:10.100710956-012-9381-0

Barlett, C. P., Anderson, C. A., & Swing, E. L. (2009). Video game effects—Confirmed, suspected, and speculative: A review of the evidence. *Simulation & Gaming*, *40*(3), 377–403. doi:10.1177/1046878108327539

Barna, B., & Fodor, S. (2018). *An Empirical Study on the Use of Gamification on IT Courses at Higher Education. In Advances in Intelligent Systems and Computing* (Vol. 715). Springer. doi:10.1007/978-3-319-73210-7_80

Barnes & Noble College. (2015). *Getting to Know Gen Z – Exploring Middle and High Schoolers' Expectations for Higher Education*. https://www.bncollege.com/wp-content/uploads/2015/10/Gen-Z-Research-Report-Final.pdf

Barnett, L., Harvey, C., & Gatzidis, C. (2018). First Time User Experiences in mobile games: An evaluation of usability. *Entertainment Computing*, *27*, 82–88. doi:10.1016/j.entcom.2018.04.004

Barnett, T., Bass, K., & Brown, G. (1996). Religiosity, ethical ideology, and intentions to report a peer's wrongdoing. *Journal of Business Ethics*, *15*(11), 1161–1174. doi:10.1007/BF00412815

Barreto, J. (2018). *Faraday Museum augmented reality app Extended Play at Faraday Museum*. Retrieved October 4, 2021, from, https://joxnds4.wixsite.com/jbarretoportefolio/copia-leapmotion-game-for-kids

Bar-Tal, D., & Raviv, A. (1982). A cognitive-learning model of helping behavior development: Possible implications and applications. In N. Eisenberg (Ed.), *The development of prosocial behavior* (pp. 199–217). Academic Press. doi:10.1016/B978-0-12-234980-5.50013-4

Bas, G. (2010). effects of multiple intelligences instruction strategy on students achievement levels and attitudes towards English lesson. *Cypriot Journal of Educational Sciences*, *5*(3).

Bates, T. (2015). *Teaching in the digital age*. BC Open Textbooks. Retrieved from https://opentextbc.ca/teachingina-digitalage/

Bateson, G. (1955). A theory of play and fantasy. *Psychiatric Research Reports*, *2*, 39–51. PMID:13297882

Battle for Kids. (2019). *Framework for 21st Century Learning*. http://static.battelleforkids.org/documents/p21/P21_Framework_Brief.pdf

Baudrillard, J. (2004). Full Screen. İstanbul: Yapı Kredi Yayınları.

Baumann, J., & Graves, M. (2010). What is academic vocabulary? *Journal of Adolescent & Adult Literacy*, *54*(1), 4–12. doi:10.1598/JAAL.54.1.1

Bawden, D., & Robinson, L. (2002). Promoting literacy in a digital age: Approaches to training for information literacy. *Learned Publishing*, *15*(4), 297–301. doi:10.1087/095315102760319279

BaxterR. J.HoldernessD. K.JrWoodD. A. (2016). The effects of gamification on corporate compliance training: A field experiment of true office anti-corruption training programs. *Social Science Research Network*. doi:10.2139/ssrn.2766683

Bayeck, R. Y. (2020). Examining board gameplay and learning: A multidisciplinary review of recent research. *Simulation & Gaming*, *51*(4), 411–431. doi:10.1177/1046878119901286

Beach, R., Appleman, D., Hynds, S., & Wilhelm, J. (2006). *Teaching literature to adolescents*. Lawrence Erlbaum Association.

Beard, C., & Wilson, J. P. (2013). *Experiential learning: a handbook for education, training and coaching* (3rd ed.). Kogan Page Limited.

Beard, R. L., Salas, E., & Prince, C. (1995). Enhancing transfer of training: Using role-play to foster teamwork in the cockpit. *The International Journal of Aviation Psychology*, *5*(2), 131–143. doi:10.120715327108ijap0502_1 PMID:11540253

Beavis, C. (2012). Video games in the classroom: Developing digital literacies. *Practically Primary*, *17*(1), 17–20.

Beavis, C. (2013). Multiliteracies in the wild: Learning from computer games. In G. Merchant, J. Gillen, J. Marsh, & J. Davies (Eds.), *Virtual literacies: Interactive spaces for children and young people* (pp. 57–74). Routledge.

Beavis, C. (2014). Games as text, games as action: Video games in the English classroom. *Journal of Adolescent & Adult Literacy*, *57*(6), 433–439. doi:10.1002/jaal.275

Beavis, C., Dezuanni, M., & O'Mara, J. (Eds.). (2017). *Serious Play: Literacy, Learning and Digital Games*. Routledge. doi:10.4324/9781315537658

Beavis, C., Muspratt, S., & Thompson, R. (2015). 'Computer games can get your brain working': Student experience and perceptions of digital games in the classroom. *Learning, Media and Technology*, *40*(1), 21–42. doi:10.1080/17439884.2014.904339

Beavis, C., & O'Mara, J. A. (2010). *Computer games–pushing at the boundaries of literacy. Australian Journal of Language and Literacy, 33(1), 65-76*. http://hdl.handle.net/10072/37372

Becker, K. (2008). *The invention of good games: Understanding learning design in commercial video games* (PhD thesis). University of Calgary.

Becker, K. (2007). Digital game - based learning once removed : Teaching teachers. *British Journal of Educational Technology. SIG-GLUE Special Issue on Game-Based Learning*, *38*(3), 478–488. doi:10.1111/j.1467-8535.2007.00711.x

Beck, I., McKeown, M., & Kucan, L. (2013). *Bringing Words to Life: Robust Vocabulary Instruction* (2nd ed.). Guilford Press.

Beck, J. C., & Wade, M. (2004). *Got game: How the gamer generation is reshaping business forever*. Harvard Business Press.

Beetham, H., & Sharpe, R. (Eds.). (2007). *Rethinking pedagogy for a digital age: Designing and delivering e-learning*. Routledge., doi:10.4324/9780203961681

Beetham, H., & Sharpe, R. (Eds.). (2013). *Rethinking pedagogy for a digital age: Designing for 21st century learning* (Vol. 711). Routledge. doi:10.4324/9780203078952

Beggs, T. (2000). Influences and Barriers to the Adoption of Instructional Technology. *Mid-South Instructional Technology Conference*, 14.

Begum, M., & Farooqui, S. (2008). School based assessment: Will it really change the education scenario in Bangladesh? *International Education Studies, 1*(2), 45–53. doi:10.5539/ies.v1n2p45

Behnke, K. A. (2015). *Gamification in Introductory Computer Science* (Doctoral dissertation). University of Colorado Boulder.

Bell, T., Witten, I., & Fellows, M. (1998). Computer science unplugged … off-line activities and games for all ages. Academic Press.

Bellanca, J., & Brandt, R. (Eds.). (2010). *21ˢᵗ Century skills: Rethinking how students learn*. Solution Tree Press.

Bell, M., Smith-Robbins, S., & Withnail, G. (2010). This is not a game – Social virtual worlds, fun, and learning. In *Researching learning in virtual worlds* (pp. 177–191). Springer., doi:10.1007/978-1-84996-047-2_10

Bellotti, F., Kapralos, B., Lee, K., Moreno-Ger, P., & Berta, R. (2013). Assessment in and of serious games: An overview. *Advances in Human-Computer Interaction, 2013*, 1–11. Advance online publication. doi:10.1155/2013/136864

Belova & Zomada. (2020). Innovating Higher Education via Game-Based Learning on Misconceptions. *Education Sciences*, (10), 221.

Benbow, J., Mizrachi, A., Oliver, D., & Said-Moshiro, L. (2007). *Large Class Sizes in the Developing World : What Do We Know and What Can We Do?* (Cooperative Agreement No. GDG-A_00-03-00006-00; Issue October). https://pdf.usaid.gov/pdf_docs/PNADK328.pdf

Benford, S., Magerkurth, C., & Ljungstrand, P. (2005). Bridging the physical and digital in pervasive gaming. *Communications of the ACM, 48*(3), 54–57. doi:10.1145/1047671.1047704

Bengu, E., Abrignani, E., Sabuncuoglu, I., & Yilmaz, C. (2020). Rethinking higher education for the emerging needs of society. *Global Solutions Summit 2020 Edition, 5*(1), 178-187.

Bennani, S., Maalel, A., & Ben Ghezala, H. (2020). Age-learn: Ontology-based representation of personalized gamification in e-learning. In Procedia Computer Science (Vol. 176, pp. 1005–1014). doi:10.1016/j.procs.2020.09.096

Bennett, D., Yábar, D. P. B., & Saura, J. R. (2017). University Incubators May Be Socially Valuable, but How Effective Are They? A Case Study on Business Incubators at Universities. In *Entrepreneurial Universities* (pp. 165–177). Springer International Publishing. doi:10.1007/978-3-319-47949-1_11

Bennett, N., & Lemoine, G. J. (2014). What a difference a word makes: Understanding threats to performance in a VUCA world. *Business Horizons, 57*(3), 311–317. doi:10.1016/j.bushor.2014.01.001

Bereczki, E. O., & Kárpáti, A. (2021). Technology-enhanced creativity: A multiple case study of digital technology-integration expert teachers' beliefs and practices. *Thinking Skills and Creativity, 39*, 39. doi:10.1016/j.tsc.2021.100791

Bergstrom, I., & Lotto, R. B. (2015). Code Bending: A new creative coding practice. *Leonardo, 48*(1), 25–31. doi:10.1162/LEON_a_00934

Berkling, K., & Neubehler, K. (2019). Boosting Student Performance with Peer Reviews; Integration and Analysis of Peer Reviews in a Gamified Software Engineering Classroom. In *2019 IEEE Global Engineering Education Conference (EDUCON)* (pp. 253-262). IEEE. 10.1109/EDUCON.2019.8725247

Berland, M., & Lee, V. R. (2011). Collaborative strategic board games as a site for distributed computational thinking. *International Journal of Game-Based Learning, 1*(2), 65–81. doi:10.4018/ijgbl.2011040105

Bermingham, N., Prendergast, M., Boland, T., O'Rawe, M., & Ryan, B. (2016). Developing mobile apps for improving the orientation experience of first-year third-level students. *Proceedings of 8th Annual International conference on Education and New Learning Technologies*. 10.21125/edulearn.2016.0137

Bernik, A., Vusić, D., & Milković, M. (2019). Evaluation of Gender Differences Based on Knowledge Adaptation in the Field of Gamification and Computer Science. *International Journal of Emerging Technologies in Learning, 14*(8), 220. doi:10.3991/ijet.v14i08.9847

Besser, A., Flett, G. L., & Zeigler-Hill, V. (2020). Adaptability to a Sudden Transition to Online Learning During the COVID-19 Pandemic: Understanding the Challenges for Students. *Scholarship of Teaching and Learning in Psychology*. Advance online publication. doi:10.1037tl0000198

Bevan, D., & Kipka, C. (2012). Experiential learning and management education. *Journal of Management Development, 31*(3), 193–197. doi:10.1108/02621711211208943

Bhatia, H. K., & Ilyas, Z. (2016). Barriers of ICT Integration in Teaching Learning. *Jamia Journal of Education, 3*(1). Retrieved from https://www.researchgate.net/profile/Harjeet_Bhatia/publication/319272961_Jamia_Journal_of_Education_An_International_Biannual_Publication_Volume_3_Number_1_November_2016

Bhatti, N. (2019). CAI and conventional method for retention of mathematics: An experimental study. *Journal of Physics: Conference Series, 1157*(3), 032079. doi:10.1088/1742-6596/1157/3/032079

Bianchini, S., & Verhagen, E. (Ed.). (2016). Practicable, From Participation to interaction in Contemporary Art. MIT Press.

Bicen, H., & Kocakoyun, S. (2018). Perceptions of Students for Gamification Approach. *International Journal of Emerging Technologies in Learning, 13*(02), 72–93. doi:10.3991/ijet.v13i02.7467

Bignoux, S., & Sund, K. J. (2018). Tutoring executives online: What drives perceived quality? *Behaviour & Information Technology, 37*(7), 703–713. doi:10.1080/0144929X.2018.1474254

Bilici, İ. E. (2011). *Türkiye'de ortaöğretimde medya okuryazarlığı dersi için bir model önerisi. Erciyes Üniversitesi. Doktora Tezi.*

Bilton, N. (2013, September 16). Minecraft, a child's obsession, finds use as an educational tool. *The New York Times, 162*(56261), B8.

Bingimlas, K. A. (2009). Barriers to the successful integration of ICT in teaching and learning environments: A review of the literature. *Eurasia Journal of Mathematics, Science and Technology Education, 5*(3), 235–245. doi:10.12973/ejmste/75275

Binkley, M., Erstad, O., Herman, J., Raizen, S., Ripley, M., Miller-Ricci, M., & Rumble, M. (2012). Defining twenty-first century skills. In P. Griffin & E. Care (Eds.), *Assessment and Teaching of 21st Century Skills: Methods and Approach* (pp. 17–66). Springer. doi:10.1007/978-94-007-2324-5_2

Bíró, G. I. (2014). Didactics 2.0: A pedagogical analysis of gamification theory from a comparative perspective with a special view to the Components of Learning. *Procedia: Social and Behavioral Sciences, 141*, 148–151. doi:10.1016/j.sbspro.2014.05.027

Bissoloti, K., Nogueira, H. G., & Pereira, A. T. C. (2014). *Potencialidades das mídias sociais e da gamificação na educação a distância.* Available at: https://seer.ufrgs.br/renote/article/view/53511/33027

Bista, S. K., Nepal, S., Colineau, N., & Paris, C. (2012). Using Gamification in an online community. In *Collaborative Computing: Networking, Applications, and Worksharing (CollaborateCom), 2012 8th International Conference on* (pp. 611-618). IEEE.

Black, P., & Wiliam, D. (2009). Developing the theory of formative assessment. *Educational Assessment, Evaluation and Accountability, 21*(1), 5-31.

Black, J., Bryant, J., & Thompson, S. (1997). *Introduction to Media Communication* (5th ed.). Mc Grw Hill Company.

Black, P. (2015). Formative assessment – an optimistic but incomplete vision. *Assessment in Education: Principles, Policy & Practice, 22*(1), 161–177. doi:10.1080/0969594X.2014.999643

Black, P., & Wiliam, D. (2006). Developing a Theory of Formative Assessment. In J. Gardner (Ed.), *Assessment and Learning* (pp. 81–100). SAGE.

Black, P., & Wiliam, D. (2018). Classroom assessment and pedagogy. *Assessment in Education: Principles, Policy & Practice, 25*(6), 551–575. doi:10.1080/0969594X.2018.1441807

Blanco-Herrera, J. A., Gentile, D. A., & Rokkum, J. N. (2019). Video games can increase creativity, but with caveats. *Creativity Research Journal, 31*(2), 119–131. doi:10.1080/10400419.2019.1594524

Blau, I., Shamir-Inbal, T., & Avdiel, O. (2020). How does the pedagogical design of a technology-enhanced collaborative academic course promote digital literacies, self-regulation, and perceived learning of students? *The Internet and Higher Education, 45*, 100722. doi:10.1016/j.iheduc.2019.100722

Blickle, G. (1998). Personality traits, learning stratigies, and performance. *European Journal of Personality, 10*(5), 337–352. doi:10.1002/(SICI)1099-0984(199612)10:5<337::AID-PER258>3.0.CO;2-7

Blikstad-Balas, M. (2013). *Redefining School Literacy. Prominent Literacy Practices. Across Subjects in Upper Secondary School.* University of Oslo. Retrieved May 01, 2019 from https://www.duo.uio.no/bitstream/handle/10852/38160/1/dravhandling-blikstad-balas.pdf

Blikstein, P., Kabayadondo, Z., Martin, A., & Fields, D. (2017). An assessment instrument of technological literacies in makerspaces and FabLabs. *Journal of Engineering Education, 106*(1), 149–175. doi:10.1002/jee.20156

Blismas, N. G., & Dainty, A. R. (2003). Computer-aided qualitative data analysis: Panacea or paradox? *Building Research and Information, 31*(6), 455–463. doi:10.1080/0961321031000108816

Blok, H., Oostdam, R., Otter, M. E., & Overmaat, M. (2002). Computer-assisted instruction in support of beginning reading instruction: A review. *Review of Educational Research, 72*(1), 101–130. doi:10.3102/00346543072001101

Blooket. (n.d.). Retrieved October 26, 2021, from https://www.blooket.com/play

Blum, D. (1997). *Sex on the brain: The biological differences between men and women.* Viking.

Blunch, N. H., & Das, M. B. (2015). Changing norms about gender inequality in education: Evidence from Bangladesh. *Demographic Research, 32*(6), 183–218. doi:10.4054/DemRes.2015.32.6

Blunt, R. (n.d.). *Does Game-Based Learning Work? Results from Three Recent Studies*. Academic Press.

Boakye, N. A., & Linden, M. M. (2018). Extended strategy-use instruction to improve students' reading proficiency in a content subject. *Reading and Writing*, *9*(1), 1–9.

Board Game Geek. (n.d.). https://boardgamegeek.com/boardgame/27710/catan-dice-game

Bobbit, L. M., Inks, S. A., Kemp, K. J., & Mayo, D. T. (2000). Integrating marketing courses to enhance team-based experiential learning. *Journal of Marketing Education*, *22*(1), 15–24. doi:10.1177/0273475300221003

Boekaerts, M. (2010). The crucial role of motivation and emotion in classroom learning. In H. Humont, D. Istance, & F. Benavides (Eds.), *The Nature of Learning: Using Research to Inspire Practice* (pp. 91–112). Centre for Educational Research and Innovation. doi:10.1787/9789264086487-6-en

Bogdan, R., & Biklen, S. (1994). *Investigação Qualitativa em Educação*. Porto Editora.

Bögels, S. M., van Oosten, A., Muris, P., & Smulders, D. (2001). Familial correlates of social anxiety in children and adolescents. *Behaviour Research and Therapy*, *39*(3), 273–287. doi:10.1016/S0005-7967(00)00005-X PMID:11227809

Bogliolo, A. (2018). *Coding in your classroom now*. Giunti.

Bogopa, D. L. (2012). The importance of indigenous games: The selected cases of indigenous games in South Africa. *Indilinga*, *11*(2), 245–256.

Bogost, I. (2007). *Persuasive Games: The Expressive Power of Videogames*. MIT Press. doi:10.7551/mitpress/5334.001.0001

Boller, S. (2017). "Appily ever after": How to create your own library mobile app through easy to use, low cost technology. *Library Hi Tech News*, *34*(10), 7–10. doi:10.1108/LHTN-09-2017-0069

Bolliger, D. U., Mills, D., White, J., & Kohyama, M. (2015). Japanese Students' Perceptions of Digital Game Use for English-Language Learning in Higher Education. *Journal of Educational Computing Research*, *53*(3), 384–408. doi:10.1177/0735633115600806

Bond, L. (2015). *Mathimagicians Quest: Applying game design concepts to Education to increase school engagement for students with emotional and behavioral disabilities* (Doctoral dissertation).

Bond, M., Marín, V. I., Dolch, C., Bedenlier, S., & Zawacki-Richter, O. (2018). Digital transformation in German higher education: Student and teacher perceptions and usage of digital media. *Int J Educ Technol High Educ*, *15*(1), 48. doi:10.118641239-018-0130-1

Boney, C. R., & Sternberg, R. J. (2011). Learning to think critically. In R. E. Mayer & P. A. Alexander (Eds.), *Handbook of research on learning and instruction* (pp. 166–196). Routledge., doi:10.4324/9780203839089

Bong, S. A. (2002). *Debunking myths in qualitative data analysis*. Paper presented at the Forum Qualitative Sozialforschung/Forum: Qualitative Social Research.

Bonk, C. J., & Zhang, K. (2006). Introducing R2D2 model: Online learning for the diverse learners of this world. *Distance Education*, *27*(2), 249–264. doi:10.1080/01587910600789670

Book Creator. (2021). *Book creator* [Online software]. https://bookcreator.com/2021/07/

Boonsamuan, S., & Nobaew, B. (2016). Key factor to improve Adversity Quotient in children through mobile game-based learning. In *2016 International Symposium on Intelligent Signal Processing and Communication Systems (ISPACS)* (pp. 1-6). IEEE. 10.1109/ISPACS.2016.7824759

Borko, H., Whitcomb, J., & Liston, D. (2009). Wicked Problems and Other Thoughts on Issues of Technology and Teacher Learning. *Journal of Teacher Education, 60*(1), 3–7. doi:10.1177/0022487108328488

Bottentuit, J. B. Jr. (2012). Do Computador ao Tablet: Vantagens Pedagógicas na Utilização de Dispositivos Móveis na Educação. *Revista Educaonline, 6*, 125–149.

Boukhechba, H., & Bouhania, B. (2019). Adaptation of instructional design to promote learning in traditional EFL classrooms: Adobe Captivate for e-learning content. *International Journal of Education and Development Using Information and Communication Technology, 15*(4), 151–164.

Bourdieu, P. (1986). The forms of capital. In J. Richardson (Ed.), *Handbook of theory and research for the sociology of education* (pp. 241–258). Greenwood Press.

Bourgonjon, J., De Grove, F., De Smet, C., Van Looy, J., Soetaert, R., & Valcke, M. (2013). Acceptance of Game-Based Learning by Secondary School Teachers. *Computers & Education, 67*, 21–35. doi:10.1016/j.compedu.2013.02.010

Bourgonjon, J., & Hanghoi, T. (2011). What does it mean to be a game literate teacher? Interviews with teachers who translate games into educational practice. *Proceedings of the European Conference on Games-Based Learning, 67*–73.

Bourgonjon, J., Valcke, M., Soetaert, R., & Schellens, T. (2010). Students' perceptions about the use of video games in the classroom. *Computers & Education, 54*(4), 1145–1156. doi:10.1016/j.compedu.2009.10.022

Bovermann, K., Weidlich, J., & Bastiaens, T. (2018). Online learning readiness and attitudes towards gaming in gamified online learning – a mixed methods case study. *International Journal of Educational Technology in Higher Education, 15*(1), 0–17. doi:10.1186/s41239-018-0107-0

Bovermann, K., & Bastiaens, T. J. (2020). Towards a motivational design? Connecting gamification user types and online learning activities. *Research and Practice in Technology Enhanced Learning, 15*(1), 1–18. doi:10.118641039-019-0121-4

Bowman, S. (2020). *Educating the Digital Native: Teaching Students in a Binge-Watching World*. Faculty Focus.

Boxer, P., Groves, C. L., & Docherty, M. (2015). Video games do indeed influence children and adolescents' aggression, prosocial behavior, and academic performance: A clearer reading of Ferguson (2015). *Perspectives on Psychological Science, 10*(5), 671–673. doi:10.1177/1745691615592239 PMID:26386004

Boyd, D. (2008). *Taken out of context: American teen sociality in networked publics* (PhD Dissertation). University of California-Berkeley.

Boyd, D., & Ellison, N. (2007). Social network sites: Definition, history, and scholarship. *Journal of Computer-Mediated Communication, 13*(1), 210–230. doi:10.1111/j.1083-6101.2007.00393.x

Boydell, K. (2007). *Ethical issues in conducting qualitative research. Research ethics lecture series. Department of psychiatry*. University of Toronto.

Boyle, E. A., Hainey, T., Connolly, T. M., Gray, G., Earp, J., Ott, M., Lim, T., Ninaus, M., Ribeiro, C., & Pereira, J. (2016). An update to the systematic literature review of empirical evidence of the impacts and outcomes of computer games and serious games. *Computer Education, 94*, 178–192. doi:10.1016/j.compedu.2015.11.003

Bozalek, V., Ng'ambi, D., & Gachago, D. (2013). Transforming teaching with emerging technologies: Implications for higher education institutions. *South African Journal of Higher Education, 27*(2), 419–436. https://open.uct.ac.za/handle/11427/9844

Bozarth, M. A. (1994). Pleasure systems in the brain. *Pleasure: The politics and the reality*, 5-14.

Bozkurt, A., & Durak, G. (2018). A Systematic Review of Gamification Research: In Pursuit of Homo Ludens. *International Journal of Game-Based Learning*, 8(3), 15–33. doi:10.4018/IJGBL.2018070102

Braßler, M. (2020). The Role of Interdisciplinarity in Bringing PBL to traditional Universities: Opportunities and Challenges on the Organizational, Team and Individual Level. *The Interdisciplinary Journal of Problem-Based Learning*, 14(2). Advance online publication. doi:10.14434/ijpbl.v14i2.28799

Breakout edu. (n.d.). Retrieved October 26, 2021, from https://platform.breakoutedu.com/login

Bree, R. T., & Gallagher, G. (2016). Using Microsoft Excel to code and thematically analyse qualitative data: A simple, cost-effective approach. *All Ireland Journal of Higher Education, 8*(2).

Breweston, P., & Millward, L. (2001). *Organizational research methods.* Sage. doi:10.4135/9781849209533

Bridges in Mathematics. (2012). *Grade 1 Assessments and Scoring Checklists, Common Core State Standards.* Bridges in Mathematics. https://bridges1.mathlearningcenter.org/files/media/Bridges_GrK-5_Assmnt/GR1-YearlongAssessment-0512w.pdf

Bridget, B., & Andrea, T. (2011). Do avatars dream of electronic picket lines?: The blurring of work and play in virtual environments. *Information Technology & People*, 24(1), 26–45. doi:10.1108/09593841111109404

Bridle, J. (2019). *New Dark Ages, Technology and the End of the Future.* Verso.

Brin, P., Krasnokutska, N., Polančič, G., & Kous, K. (2020). Project-Based Intercultural Collaborative Learning for Social Responsibility: The Ukrainian-Slovenian Experience. In Handbook of Research on Enhancing Innovation in Higher Education Institutions (pp. 566-586). IGI Global. doi:10.4018/978-1-7998-2708-5.ch024

Bring your learning resources to life! (n.d.). *Wakelet for Educators.* Retrieved October 26, 2021, from https://learn.wakelet.com/

Brom, C., Preuss, M., & Klement, D. (2011). Are educational computer micro-games engaging and effective for knowledge acquisition at high schools? A quasi-experimental study. *Computer Education*, 57(3), 1971–1988. Advance online publication. doi:10.1016/j.compedu.2011.04.007

Brook, C., & Pedler, M. (2020). Action learning in academic management education: A state of the field review. *International Journal of Management Education*, 18(3), 100415. doi:10.1016/j.ijme.2020.100415

Brooker, P. D. (2019). Programming with Python for Social Scientists. *Sage (Atlanta, Ga.).*

Brooker, P. D., Sharrock, W., & Greiffenhagen, C. (2019). Programming visuals, visualising programs. *Science & Technology Studies*, 32(1), 21–42.

Brooks, R., Gupta, A., Jayadeva, S., & Abrahams, J. (2020). Students' views about the purpose of higher education: A comparative analysis of six European countries. *Higher Education Research & Development*, 1–14. Advance online publication. doi:10.1080/07294360.2020.1830039

Brosch, T., Scherer, K. R., Grandjean, D. M., & Sander, D. (2013). The impact of emotion on perception, attention, memory, and decision-making. *Swiss Medical Weekly*, 143, 13786. doi:10.4414mw.2013.13786 PMID:23740562

Brown, D., Standen, P., Saridaki, M., Shopland, N., Roinioti, E., Evett, L., & Smith, P. (2013). *Engaging Students with Intellectual Disabilities through Games Based Learning and Related Technologies.* Paper presented at the Universal Access in Human-Computer Interaction. Applications and Services for Quality of Life, Berlin, Germany. 10.1007/978-3-642-39194-1_66

Brown, S. (2008). *Play is More Than Just Fun*. Retrieved January 18, 2020, from https://www.ted.com/talks/stuart_brown_play_is_more_than_just_fun

Brown, A., & Whiteside, S. (2008). Relations among perceived parental rearing behaviors, attachment style, and worry in anxious children. *Journal of Anxiety Disorders*, 22(2), 263–272. doi:10.1016/j.janxdis.2007.02.002 PMID:17383852

Brown, C. L., Comunale, M. A., Wigdahl, B., & Urdaneta-Hartmann, S. (2018). Current climate for digital game-based learning of science in further and higher education. *FEMS Microbiology Letters*, 365(21), fny237. Advance online publication. doi:10.1093/femsle/fny237 PMID:30260380

Brownell, C. J. (2021). Writing as a Minecrafter: Exploring How Children Blur Worlds of Play in the Elementary English Language Arts Classroom. *Teachers College Record*, 123(3), 1–19. doi:10.1177/016146812112300306

Brown, J. S. (2000). Growing Up Digital. *Change*, 32(2), 10–11. http://www.johnseelybrown.com/Growing_up_digital.pdf

Brown, J. S. (2000, March/April). Growing up digital: How the web changes work, education, and the ways people learn. *Change*, 32(2), 10–20. doi:10.1080/00091380009601719

Brown, J. S., Collins, A., & Duguid, P. (1989). Situated Cognition and the Culture of Learning. *Educational Researcher*, 18(1), 32–42. doi:10.3102/0013189X018001032

Brown, S. L. (2009). *Play: How it shapes the brain, opens the imagination, and invigorates the soul*. Penguin.

Bruce, C. (2002). Information literacy as a catalyst for educational change: A background paper. In P. Danahar (Ed), *Lifelong Learning: Whose responsibility and what is your contribution? Proceedings of The 3rd International Lifelong Learning Conference* (pp. 8-19). Queensland University of Technology. Retrieved from http://eprints.qut.edu.au/4977/1/4977_1.pdf

Brull, S., & Finlayson, S. (2016). Importance of gamification in increasing learning. *Journal of Continuing Education in Nursing*, 47(8), 372–375. doi:10.3928/00220124-20160715-09 PMID:27467313

Brundha, M. P., & Akshaya, K. (n.d.). *Use of crazy card games in understanding pathology-research*. Academic Press.

Bruner, J. (1979). On knowing: Essays for the left hand (expanded edition). Harvard University Press.

Bruner, J. K. (1976). Play, Thought and Language. *Peabody Journal of Education*, 60(3), 60-69.

Bruner, J. (1986). *Actual minds, possible worlds*. Harvard University Press. doi:10.4159/9780674029019

Bruner, J. (1996). *The culture of education*. Harvard University Press.

Bruner, J. S. (1961). The act of discovery. *Harvard Educational Review*, 31(1), 21–32.

Bruns, A. (2008). *Blogs, Wikipedia, Second Life, and beyond: From production to produsage* (Vol. 45). Peter Lang.

Bryce, J. (1921). *Modern democracies*. Macmillan and Co., Ltd.

Buabeng-Andoh, C. (2012, Apr 30). Factors influencing teachers' adoption and integration of information and communication technology into teaching: A review of the literature. *International Journal of Education and Development using ICT*, 8(1), 136–155. Retrieved from https://www.learntechlib.org/p/188018/

Buabeng-Andoh, C. (2019). Factors that influence teachers' pedagogical use of ICT in secondary schools: A case of Ghana. *Contemporary Educational Technology*, 10(3), 272–288. doi:10.30935/cet.590099

Bubou, G. M., & Job, G. C. (2020). Individual innovativeness, self-efficacy and e-learning readiness of students of Yenagoa study centre, National Open University of Nigeria. *Journal of Research in Innovative Teaching & Learning*. doi:10.1108/JRIT-12-2019-0079

Buchner, J., & Zumbach, J. (2020). Augmented Reality in Teacher Education. a Framework To Support Teachers' Technological Pedagogical Content Knowledge. *Italian Journal of Educational Technology, 28*(2), 106–120. doi:10.17471/2499-4324/1151

Buckingham, D. (2013). Challenging concepts: Learning in the media classroom. In Current Perspectives on Media Education (pp. 1-14). London: Routledge.

Buckingham, D. (2016). Defining digital literacy. *Nordic Journal of Digital Literacy,* 21-34.

Buckingham, D. (2007). *Beyond technology: Children's learning in the age of digital culture. Polity.*

Buckingham, D. (2008). *Youth, identity, and digital media (The John D. and Catherine T. MacArthur Foundation series on digital media and learning).* The MIT Press.

Buckingham, D. (2010). Defining digital literacy. In *Medienbildung in neuen Kulturräumen* (pp. 59–71). VS Verlag für Sozialwissenschaften. doi:10.1007/978-3-531-92133-4_4

Buckless, F. A., Krawczyk, K., & Showalter, D. S. (2014). Using virtual worlds to simulate real-world audit procedures. *Issues in Accounting Education, 29*(3), 389–417. doi:10.2308/iace-50785

Buckley, P., & Doyle, E. (2017). Individualising Gamification: An investigation of the impact of learning styles and personality traits on the efficacy of Gamification using a prediction market. *Computers & Education, 106*, 43–55. doi:10.1016/j.compedu.2016.11.009

Burianová, M., & Turčáni, M. (2016). Non-traditional education using smart devices. *DIVAI, 2016.*

Burke, Q., O'Byrne, W. I., & Kafai, Y. B. (2016). Computational participation: Understanding coding as an extension of literacy instruction. *Journal of Adolescent & Adult Literacy, 59*(4), 371–375. doi:10.1002/jaal.496

Burn, A., & Durran, J. (2007). *Media Literacy in Schools: Practice, Production and Progression.* Paul Chapman Publishing.

Burnett, M., Poxnick, B., & Stevens, J. (2007) *Are You Smarter Than a 5th Grader* [Game Show Series]. Fox.

Burnett, C. (2010). Personal digital literacies versus classroom literacies: Investigating pre-service teachers' digital lives in and beyond the classroom. In V. Carrington & M. Robinson (Eds.), *Digital literacies: Social learning and classroom practices* (pp. 115–129). SAGE.

Burnett, C., & Hollander, W. J. (2004). The South African indigenous games research project of 2001/2002. *S.A. Journal for Research in Sport Physical Education and Recreation, 26*(1), 9–23. doi:10.4314ajrs.v26i1.25873

Burns, B. (2008). Teaching the computer science of computer games. *Journal of Computing Sciences in Colleges, 23*(3), 154–161.

Bushman, B. J., & Anderson, C. A. (2002). Violent video games and hostile expectations: A test of the General Aggression Model. *Personality and Social Psychology Bulletin, 28*(12), 1679–1686. doi:10.1177/014616702237649

Butcher, C., Davies, C., & Highton, M. (2019). *Designing learning: From module outline to effective teaching.* Routledge. doi:10.4324/9780429463822

Butler, M. (2006). *Unlocking the groove: Rhythm, meter, and musical design in electronic dance music.* Indiana University Press.

Butts, A. (1938). *Scrabble* [Board Game]. Hasbro.

Buyuksalih, I., Bayburt, S., Buyuksalih, G., Baskaraca, A. P., Karim, H., & Rahman, A. A. (2017). 3D modelling and visualization based on the unity game engine—advantages and challenges. *ISPRS Annals of Photogrammetry, Remote Sensing & Spatial Information Sciences, 4*.

Bwire, A. M., Nyagisere, M. S., Masingila, J. O., & Ayot, H. (Eds.). (2015). *Proceedings of the 4th International Conference on Education*. Academic Press.

Byrne, B. M. (2016). *Structural equation modeling with AMOS: Basic concepts, applications, and programming*. Routledge. doi:10.4324/9781315757421

Byun, J., & Loh, C. S. (2015). Audial engagement: Effects of game sound on learner engagement in digital game-based learning environments. *Computers in Human Behavior, 46*, 129–138. doi:10.1016/j.chb.2014.12.052

C21 Canada. (2017). *The Spiral Playbook. Leading with an inquiring mindset in school systems and schools*. Canadians for 21st Century Learning and Innovation.

Cachia, R., Ferrari, A., & Punie, Y. (2010). Creative Learning and Innovative Teaching. Final Report on the Study on Creativity and Innovation in Education in the EU Member States. *JRC Scientific Technical Reports*, 1-55.

Cagiltay, N. E., Ozcelik, E., & Ozcelik, N. S. (2015). The effect of competition on learning in games. *Computers & Education, 87*, 35–41. doi:10.1016/j.compedu.2015.04.001

Cahill, G. (n.d.). *Why game-based learning?* The Learning Counsel.

Caillois, R. (1990). *Man, play and games* (M. Tada & M. Tsukazaki, Trans.). Kodansha. (Original work published 1958)

Callaghan, N. (2016). Investigating the role of Minecraft in educational learning environments. *Educational Media International, 53*(4), 244–260. doi:10.1080/09523987.2016.1254877

Calleja, G. (2007). Revising immersion: A conceptual model for the analysis of digital game involvement. *Situated Play, Proceedings of DiGRA 2007 Conference*, 83-90.

Call, K., Riedel, A., Hein, K., McLoyd, V., Petersen, A., & Kipke, M. (2002). Adolescent health and well-being in the twenty first century: A global perspective. *Journal of Research on Adolescence, 12*(1), 69–98. doi:10.1111/1532-7795.00025

Calvo-Ferrer, J. R. (2017). Educational games as stand-alone learning tools and their motivational effect on L 2 vocabulary acquisition and perceived learning gains. *British Journal of Educational Technology, 48*(2), 264–278. doi:10.1111/bjet.12387

Cam, L., & Tran, T. M. T. (2017). An evaluation of using games in teaching English grammar for first year English-majored students at Dong Nai Technology University. *International Journal of Learning, Teaching and Educational Research, 16*(7), 55-71.

Camacho Vásquez, G., & Ovalle, J. C. (2019). The Influence of Video Games on Vocabulary Acquisition in a Group of Students from the BA in English Teaching. *GIST Education and Learning Research Journal, 19*, 172–192. doi:10.26817/16925777.707

Cameron, K. E., & Bizo, L. A. (2019). Use of the game-based learning platform KAHOOT! To facilitate learner engagement in Animal Science students. *Research in Learning Technology, 27*(0), 27. doi:10.25304/rlt.v27.2225

Cameron, S. (2011). Whether and where to enroll? Choosing a primary school in the slums of urban Dhaka, Bangladesh. *International Journal of Educational Development, 31*(4), 357–366. doi:10.1016/j.ijedudev.2011.01.004

Camp, R. (2018). *Blank Slate* [Board Game]. USAopoly.

Campbell, B. (1990). What is literacy? Acquiring and using literacy skills. *Australasian Public Libraries and Information Services, 3*(3), 149–152.

Campbell, D. T., & Stanley, J. C. (1963). *Experimental and quasi-experimental design for research.* Cengage Learning.

Campbell, H. (2013). *Digital religion: Understanding religious practice in new media worlds.* Routledge Taylor and Francis Group.

Camp, R. J., & Wheaton, J. M. (2014). Streamlining field data collection with mobile apps. *Eos (Washington, D.C.), 95*(49), 453–454. doi:10.1002/2014EO490001

CananA. (2014) *Philosophy of new media.* Accessed from http://philosophyofnewmedia.com/

Cankaya, S., & Karamete, A. (2009). The effects of educational computer games on students' attitudes towards mathematics course and educational computer games. *Procedia: Social and Behavioral Sciences, 1*(1), 145–149. doi:10.1016/j.sbspro.2009.01.027

Cantoni, L., & Di Blas, N. (2006). Comunicazione. *Teoria e pratiche,* 6.

Cappuccio, M. L., Sandoval, E. B., Mubin, O., Obaid, M., & Velonaki, M. (2021). Robotics Aids for Character Building: More than Just Another Enabling Condition. *International Journal of Social Robotics, 13,* 1–5. doi:10.100712369-021-00756-y

Carbonaro, M., Szafron, D., Cutumisu, M., & Schaeffer, J. (2010). Computer-game construction: A gender-neutral attractor to Computing Science. *Computers & Education, 55*(3), 1098–1111. doi:10.1016/j.compedu.2010.05.007

Cardador, T. M., Northcraft, B. G., & Whicker, J. (2016). A theory of work gamification: Something old, something new, something borrowed, something cool? *Human Resource Management Review.*

Cardinot, A., & Fairfield, J. A. (2019). Game-based learning to engage students with physics and astronomy using a board game. *International Journal of Game-Based Learning, 9*(1), 42–57. doi:10.4018/IJGBL.2019010104

Carenys, J., & Moya, S. (2016). Digital game-based learning in accounting and business education. *Accounting Education, 25*(6), 598–651. doi:10.1080/09639284.2016.1241951

Carlo, G., Hausmann, A., Chritiansen, S., & Randall, B. A. (2003). Sociocognitive and behavioral correlates of a measure of prosocial tendencies for adolescents. *The Journal of Early Adolescence, 23*(1), 107–134. doi:10.1177/0272431602239132

Carretero Gomez, S., Vuorikari, R., & Punie, Y. (2017). *DigComp 2.1: The Digital Competence Framework for Citizens with eight proficiency levels and examples of use. EUR 28558 EN.* Publications Office of the European Union.

Carretero, S., Vuorikari, R. & Punie, Y. (2017). *DigComp 2.1: The Digital Competence Framework for Citizens with eight proficiency levels and examples of use.* EUR 28558 EN, Publications Office of the European Union. doi:10.2760/38842

Carrington, V. (2001). Literacy instruction: A Bourdieuian perspective. In P. Freebody, S. Muspratt, & B. Dwyer (Eds.), *Difference, silence, and textual practice: Studies in critical literacy* (pp. 265–285). Hampton Press, Inc.

Carrington, V., & Luke, A. (1997). Literacy and Bourdieu's sociological theory: A reframing. *Language and Education, 11*(2), 96–112. doi:10.1080/09500789708666721

Carroll, J. M. (1982). The adventure of getting to know a computer. *IEEE Computer, 15*(11).

Carter, L. (2006). Why students with an apparent aptitude for computer science don't choose to major in computer science. *ACM SIGCSE Bulletin, 38*(1), 27–31. doi:10.1145/1124706.1121352

Carter, M. S., & Mahoney, M. C. (2020). Gamification and Training the Technical Workforce. *The Marine Corps Gazette.*

Carter, M., Gibbs, M., & Harrop, M. (2014). Drafting an army: The playful pastime of warhammer 40,000. *Games and Culture, 9*(2), 122–147. doi:10.1177/1555412013513349

Carvajal, D. (2002). *The artisan's tools. Critical issues when teaching and learning CAQDAS.* Paper presented at the Forum Qualitative Sozialforschung/Forum: Qualitative Social Research.

Carvalho, L. F. S. (2015). *Utilização de Dispositivos Móveis na aprendizagem da Matemática no 3o Ciclo.* Dissertação de Mestrado em Tecnologias de Informação e Comunicação na Educação. Universidade Portucalense. Departamento de Inovação, Ciência e Tecnologia.

Carvalho, L., & Yeoman, P. (2018). Framing learning entanglement in innovative learning spaces: Connecting theory, design and practice. *British Educational Research Journal, 44*(6), 1120–1137. doi:10.1002/berj.3483

Casañ-Pitarch, R. (2018). An approach to digital game-based learning: Video-games principles and applications in foreign language learning. *Journal of Language Teaching and Research, 9*(6), 1147–1159. doi:10.17507/jltr.0906.04

Castaneda, D. A., & Cho, M. H. (2016). Use of a game-like application on a mobile device to improve accuracy in conjugating Spanish verbs. *Computer Assisted Language Learning, 29*(7), 1195–1204. doi:10.1080/09588221.2016.1197950

Castells, M. (1999). *La Era de la información: economiá, sociedad y cultura.* Siglo Veintiuno Editores.

Castells, M. (2010). *The rise of the network society. The Information age: Economy, society, and culture* (2nd ed., Vol. 1). Wiley-Blackwell.

Castilhos, D. (2018). *Gamification and active methodologies at university: The case of teaching learning strategy in law.* doi:10.21125/iceri.2018.0220

Castro, K. A. C., Sibo, Í. P. H., & Ting, I. (2018a). Assessing gamification effects on E-learning platforms: An experimental case. *Communications in Computer and Information Science, 870*, 3–14. doi:10.1007/978-3-319-95522-3_1

Castronova, E. (2008). *Exodus to the virtual world: How online fun is changing reality.* Palgrave Macmillan.

Castronova, E., & Knowles, I. (2015). Modding board games into serious games: The case of Climate Policy. *International Journal of Serious Games, 2*(3), 41–62.

Catts, R., & Lau, J. (2008). *Towards information literacy indicators.* Academic Press.

Cavallo, A., Robaldo, A., Ansovini, F., Carmosino, I., & De Gloria, A. (2017). *Gamification of a System for Real-Time Monitoring of Posture. In eHealth 360.* Springer International Publishing.

Cazden, C. (1981). Performance before competence: Assistance to child discourse in the zone of proximal development. *The Quarterly Newsletter of the Laboratory of Comparative Human Cognition, 3*, 5–8.

Cazden, C., Cope, B., Fairclough, N., & Gee, J. (1996). A pedagogy of multiliteracies: Designing Social Futures. *Harvard Educational Review, 66*(1), 60–92. doi:10.17763/haer.66.1.17370n67v22j160u

CCSS. (2010). *Common core state standards initiative.* Retrieved May 6, 2015, from http://www.corestandards.org/the-standards

CDC. (2020, February 11). *COVID-19 Vaccination.* Centers for Disease Control and Prevention. https://www.cdc.gov/coronavirus/2019-ncov/vaccines/distributing/steps-ensure-safety.html

Celik, I., Sahin, I., & Akturk, A. O. (2014). Analysis of the relations among the components of technological pedagogical and content knowledge (TPACK): A structural equation model. *Journal of Educational Computing Research, 51*(1), 1–22. doi:10.2190/EC.51.1.a

Center for Media Literacy. (n.d.). *CML MediaLit Kit*. Retrieved May 15, 2011 from http://www. medialit.org/bp_mlk.html

Chafouleas, S. M., Riley-Tillman, T. C., & Christ, T. J. (2009). Direct Behavior Rating (DBR): An emerging method for assessing social behavior within a tiered intervention system. *Assessment for Effective Intervention, 34*(4), 201–213. doi:10.1177/1534508409340391

Chai, C. S., Koh, J. H., & Tsai, C. C. (2011). Exploring the factor structure of the constructs of technological, pedagogical, content knowledge (TPACK). *The Asia-Pacific Education Researcher, 20*(3), 595–603.

Chai, C. S., Koh, J. H., Tsai, C. C., & Tan, L. L. (2011). Modeling primary school pre-service teachers' Technological Pedagogical Content Knowledge (TPACK) for meaningful learning with information and communication technology (ICT). *Computers & Education, 57*(1), 1184–1193. doi:10.1016/j.compedu.2011.01.007

Chall, J. S. (1996). *Stages of Reading Development*. Harcourt Brace College Publishers.

Chambers, J. H., & Ascione, F. R. (1987). The effects of prosocial and aggressive videogames on children's donating and helping. *The Journal of Genetic Psychology, 148*(4), 499–505. doi:10.1080/00221325.1987.10532488 PMID:3437274

Chan, K. H. W., Wan, K., & King, V. (2021). *Performance over enjoyment? Effect of game-based learning on learning outcome and flow experience*. doi:10.3389/feduc.2021.660376

Chang, M., & Gu, X. (2018). The role of executive function in linking fundamental motor skills and reading proficiency in socioeconomically disadvantaged kindergarteners. *Learning and Individual Differences, 61*(December), 250–255. doi:10.1016/j.lindif.2018.01.002

Chang, M., Lachance, D., Lin, F., Al-Shamali, F., & Chen, N. S. (2015). Enhancing Orbital Physics Learning Performance through a Hands-on Kinect Game. *Egitim ve Bilim, 40*(180).

Chang, C. C., Liang, C., Chou, P.-N., & Lin, G.-Y. (2017). Is game-based learning better in flow experience and various types of cognitive load than non-game-based learning? Perspective from multimedia and media richness. *Computers in Human Behavior, 71*, 218–227. doi:10.1016/j.chb.2017.01.031

Chang, C.-Y., & Hwang, G.-J. (2019). Trends in digital game-based learning in the mobile era: Asystematic review of journal publications from 2007 to 2016. *Int. J. Mobile Learning and Organisation, 13*(1), 68–90. doi:10.1504/IJMLO.2019.096468

Chang, Y.-H., Hwang, J.-H., Fang, R.-J., & Lu, Y.-T. (2017). A Kinect- and Game-Based Interactive Learning System. *Journal of Mathematics Science and Technology Education, 13*(8), 4897–4914. doi:10.12973/eurasia.2017.00972a

Chapman, J. R., & Rich, P. J. (2018). Does educational gamification improve students' motivation? If so, which game elements work best? *Journal of Education for Business, 93*(7), 314–321. doi:10.1080/08832323.2018.1490687

Chapter 6. (2006). *Understandings of Literacy*. Education for All Global Monitoring Report. Retrieved May 02, 2019 from http://www.unesco.org/education/GMR2006/full/chapt6_eng.pdf

Chasek, P. S. (2005). Power politics, diplomacy and role playing: Simulating the UN Security Council's response to terrorism. *International Studies Perspectives, 6*(1), 1–19. doi:10.1111/j.1528-3577.2005.00190.x

Chatzimichali, E. (2020). *A comparative analysis between science curricula for primary school from 17 countries regarding the subject of astronomy* [Συγκριτική μελέτη της παρουσίας της αστρονομίας στα αναλυτικά προγράμματα της πρωτοβάθμιας εκπαίδευσης 17 χωρών προερχομένων από τις 5 ηπείρους] (Master's thesis). National & Kapodistrian University of Athens. Retrieved from https://pergamos.lib.uoa.gr/uoa/dl/frontend/el/browse/2916920

Chaudhary, A. G. (2010). Educational gaming: An effective tool for learning and social change in India. *Journal of Creative Communications*, *5*(3), 135–152. doi:10.1177/0973258612471244

Chaudhury, T. A., & Karim, Z. (2014). CLT approach in developing English reading skills in tertiary levels in Bangladesh. *Asian Journal of Education and e-Learning*, *2*(1), 47-55.

Chaves, M. (2010). SSSR Presidential Address Rain Dances in the Dry Season: Overcoming the Religious Congruence Fallacy. *Journal for the Scientific Study of Religion*, *49*(1), 1–14. doi:10.1111/j.1468-5906.2009.01489.x

Chavez, V., & Soep, E. (2005). Youth radio and the pedagogy of collegiality. *Harvard Educational Review*, *75*(4), 409–434. doi:10.17763/haer.75.4.827u365446030386

Chayko, M. (2018). Süper Bağ(lantı)lı. Çev. Berkan Bayındır, Deniz Yengin ve Tamer Bayrak. İstanbul: Der Kitabevi.

Cheatsheet—MediaWiki. (n.d.). Retrieved June 1, 2021, from https://www.mediawiki.org/wiki/Cheatsheet

Checa-Romero, M., & Pascual Gómez, I. (2018). Minecraft and machinima in action: Development of creativity in the classroom. *Technology, Pedagogy and Education*, *27*(5), 625–637. doi:10.1080/1475939X.2018.1537933

Chee, Y. S., Mehrotra, S., & Ong, J. C. (2014). Facilitating dialog in the game-based learning classroom: Teacher challenges reconstructing professional identity. *Digital Culture & Education*, *6*(4), 298–316.

Chen, D., & Wu, J. (2010). *Deconstructing new media: From computer literacy to new media literacy.* Paper presented at the 8th international conference on education and information systems, Technologies and Applications, Orlando, FL.

Chen, D., Wu, J., & Wang, Y. (2011). *Unpacking new media literacy.* Retrieved on December 3, 2012, from www.iiisci.org/journal/CV\$/sci/pdfs/OL508KR.pdf

Chen, S., Huang, F., Zeng, W., Dong, N., Wu, X., & Tang, Y. (2019). Robots can teach knowledge but can't cultivate values? *China Educational Technology*, (2), 29-35.

Chen, C. H., Huang, K., & Liu, J. H. (2020). Inquiry-Enhanced Digital Game-Based Learning: Effects on Secondary Students' Conceptual Understanding in Science, Game Performance, and Behavioral Patterns. *The Asia-Pacific Education Researcher*, *29*(4), 319–330. doi:10.100740299-019-00486-w

Chen, C. H., Liu, G. Z., & Hwang, G. J. (2016). Interaction between gaming and multistage guiding strategies on students' field trip mobile learning performance and motivation'. *British Journal of Educational Technology*, *47*(6), 1032–1050. doi:10.1111/bjet.12270

Chen, C. H., Wang, K. C., & Lin, Y. H. (2015). The Comparison of Solitary and Collaborative Modes of Game-Based Learning on Students' Science Learning and Motivation. *Journal of Educational Technology & Society*, *18*(2), 237–248.

Chen, C. M., & Chung, C. J. (2008). Personalized mobile English vocabulary learning system based on item response theory and learning memory cycle. *Computers & Education*, *51*(2), 624–645. doi:10.1109/ICSMC.2006.384727

Cheng, C. W. (2012). The system and self-reference of the app economy: The case of angry birds. *Westminster Papers in Communication & Culture*, *9*(1).

Cheng, M. T., Chen, J. H., Chu, S. J., & Chen, S. Y. (2015). The use of serious games in science education: a review of selected empirical research from 2002 to 2013. *Journal of Computers in Education, 2*(3), 353-375.

Cheng, C. H., & Su, C. H. (2012). A Game-based learning system for improving student's learning effectiveness in system analysis course. *Procedia: Social and Behavioral Sciences*, *31*, 669–675. doi:10.1016/j.sbspro.2011.12.122

Chen, H. J. H., & Yang, T. Y. C. (2013). The impact of adventure video games on foreign language learning and the perceptions of learners. *Interactive Learning Environments*, *21*(2), 129–141. doi:10.1080/10494820.2012.705851

Chen, N. S., Quadir, B., & Teng, D. C. (2011). Integrating book, digital content and robot for enhancing elementary school students' learning of English. *Australasian Journal of Educational Technology*, *27*(3). Advance online publication. doi:10.14742/ajet.960

Chen, S. W., Yang, C. H., Huang, K. S., & Fu, S. L. (2019). Digital games for learning energy conservation: A study of impacts on motivation, attention, and learning outcomes. *Innovations in Education and Teaching International*, *56*(1), 66–76. doi:10.1080/14703297.2017.1348960

Chen, S. Y., & Chang, Y. M. (2020). The impacts of real competition and virtual competition in digital game-based learning. *Computers in Human Behavior*, *104*(2), 106171. doi:10.1016/j.chb.2019.106171

Chen, S., Husnaini, S. J., & Chen, J.-J. (2020). Effects of games on students' emotions of learning science and achievement in chemistry. *International Journal of Science Education*, *42*(13), 2224–2245. doi:10.1080/09500693.2020.1817607

Chen, S., Zhang, S., Qi, G. Y., & Yang, J. (2020). Games Literacy for Teacher Education : Towards the Implementation of Game-based Learning. *Journal of Educational Technology & Society*, *23*(2), 77–92.

Chen, Y. C. (2017). Empirical Study on the Effect of Digital Game-Based Instruction on Students' Learning Motivation and Achievement. *Eurasia Journal of Mathematics, Science and Technology Education*, *13*(7). Advance online publication. doi:10.12973/eurasia.2017.00711a

Chess, S. (2020). *Play Like a Feminist*. MIT Press. doi:10.7551/mitpress/12484.001.0001

Chetouani, M., Vanden Abeele, V., Leuven, K., Carmen Moret-Tatay, B., Lopes, S., Magalhães, P., Pereira, A., Martins, J., Magalhães, C., Chaleta, E., & Rosário, P. (2018). Games Used With Serious Purposes: A Systematic Review of Interventions in Patients With Cerebral Palsy. *Frontiers in Psychology*, *9*, 1712. doi:10.3389/fpsyg.2018.01712 PMID:30283377

Cheung, G. W., & Rensvold, R. B. (2002). Evaluating goodness-of-fit indexes for testing measurement invariance. *Structural Equation Modeling*, *9*(2), 233–255. doi:10.1207/S15328007SEM0902_5

Chien-Pen, C., Neien-Tzu, H., & Yi-Jeng, H. (2004). *Life education based on game learning strategy for vocational education students in Taiwan*. http://163.21.114.214/ezfiles/0/1000/img/4/20130527-d17.pdf

Childs, M. (2010). *Learners' experience of presence in virtual worlds* (Doctoral dissertation). University of Warwick.

Chinaka, G. (2017). *Factors affecting the adoption and integration of ICT as a pedagogical tool in rural primary schools* (Dissertation). Midlands State University.

Chinyoka, K. (2014). Causes of school drop-out among ordinary level learners in a resettlement area in Masvingo, Zimbabwe. *Journal of Emerging Trends in Educational Research and Policy Studies*, *5*(3), 294–300.

Chiong, C., Ree, J., Takeuchi, L., & Erickson, I. (2012). *Print books vs e-books. Comparing parent-child co-reading on print, basic and enhanced e-book platforms*. The Joan Ganz Cooney Center at Sesame Workshop. http://www.joanganzcooneycenter.org/wp-content/uploads/2012/07/jgcc_ebooks_ quickreport.pdf

Chiruguru, S. (2018). *The Essential Skills of 21st Century Classroom (4Cs)*. Louisiana Computer Using Educators.

Chivaura, V., & Mararike, C. (1998). *The human factor approach to development in Africa*. University of Zimbabwe Publications.

Cho, M. H., & Castañeda, D. A. (2019). Motivational and affective engagement in learning Spanish with a mobile application. *System*, *81*, 90–99. doi:10.1016/j.system.2019.01.008

Chong, D. Y. K. (2019). Benefits and challenges with gamified multimedia physiotherapy case studies: A mixed-method study. *Archives of Physiotherapy*, *9*(1), 7. doi:10.118640945-019-0059-2 PMID:31139434

Chou, Y-k. (n.d.) *Wordpress*. Retrieved from https://yukaichou.com/gamification-examples/octalysis-complete-gamification-framework/

Choudaha, R. (2008). *Competency-based curriculum for a master's program in Service Science, Management and Engineering (SSME): An online Delphi study* [Dissertation Thesis]. University of Denver, Proquest Dissertation Publishing.

Chowdhury, F. D. (2010). Dowry, women, and law in Bangladesh. *International Journal of Law, Policy and the Family*, *24*(2), 198–221. doi:10.1093/lawfam/ebq003

Chowdhury, R., & Sarkar, M. (2018). Education in Bangladesh: Changing contexts and emerging realities. In R. Chowdhury, M. Sarkar, F. Mojumder, & M. M. Roshid (Eds.), *Engaging in Educational Research: Revisiting Policy and Practice in Bangladesh* (Vol. 44, pp. 1–18). Springer. doi:10.1007/978-981-13-0708-9_1

Chu, S. K. W., Tang, Q., Chow, K., & Tse, S. K. (2007). *A study on inquiry-based learning in a primary school through librarian-teacher partnerships*. Academic Press.

Chuang, T. Y., Liu, E. Z., & Shiu, W. Y. (2015). Game-based creativity assessment system: The application of fuzzy theory. *Multimedia Tools and Applications*, *74*(21), 9141–9155. doi:10.100711042-014-2070-7

Chun, E., & Evans, A. (2009). Bridging the diversity divide: Globalization and reciprocal empowerment in higher education. *ASHE Higher Education Report*, *35*(1). https://onlinelibrary.wiley.com/doi/10.1002/aehe.3501

Chung-Yuan, H., Meng-Jung, T., Yu-Hsuan, C., & Liang, J. C. (2017). Surveying in-service teachers' beliefs about game-based learning and perceptions of technological pedagogical and content knowledge of games. *Journal of Educational Technology & Society*, *20*(1), 134.

Chu, S. K. W., & Kennedy, D. M. (2011). Using online collaborative tools for groups to co-construct knowledge. *Online Information Review*, *35*(4), 581–597. doi:10.1108/14684521111161945

Chu, S. K. W., Reynolds, R. B., Tavares, N. J., Notari, M., & Lee, C. W. Y. (2017). *Assessment Instruments for Twenty-First Century Skills. In 21st Century Skills Development Through Inquiry-Based Learning*. Springer Singapore.

Chye, C., & Nakajima, T. (2012). Game based approach to learn martial arts for beginners. *18th IEEE International Conference on Embedded and Real-Time Computing Systems and Applications*, 482-485. 10.1109/RTCSA.2012.37

Cintang, N., Setyowati, D. L., & Handayani, S. S. D. (2018). The Obstacles and Strategy of Project Based Learning Implementation in Elementary School. *Journal of Education and Learning*, *12*(1), 7–15. doi:10.11591/edulearn.v12i1.7045

Clapper, T. C. (2018). Serious games are not all serious. *Simulation & Gaming*, *49*(4), 375–377. doi:10.1177/1046878118789763

Clark, D., Nelson, B., Sengupta, P., & Angelo, C. D. (2009). *Rethinking science learning through digital games and simulations: Genres, examples, and evidence*. Academic Press.

Clark, D. B., Sengupta, P., Brady, C. E., Martinez-Garza, M. M., & Killingsworth, S. S. (2015). Disciplinary integration of digital games for science learning. *International Journal of STEM Education*, *2*(1), 1–21. doi:10.118640594-014-0014-4

Clark, D. B., Tanner-Smith, E. E., & Killingsworth, S. S. (2016). Digital games, design, and learning: A systematic review and meta-analysis. *Review of Educational Research*, *86*(1), 79–122. doi:10.3102/0034654315582065 PMID:26937054

Clarke, S., Peel, D. J., Arnab, S., Morini, L., Keegan, H., Wood, O., Morini, L., & Wood, O. (2017). *escapED : A Framework for Creating Educational Escape Rooms and Interactive Games For Higher / Further Education*. Academic Press.

Clark, J. W., & Dawson, L. E. (1996). Personal religiousness and ethical judgements: An empirical analysis. *Journal of Business Ethics*, *15*(3), 359–372. doi:10.1007/BF00382959

Clark, K. R. (2015). The effects of the flipped model of instruction on student engagement and performance in the secondary mathematics classroom. *The Journal of Educators Online*, *12*(1), 91–114. doi:10.9743/JEO.2015.1.5

Claymier, B. (2014). Integrating stem into the elementary curriculum. *Children's Technology & Engineering*, *18*(3), 5.

Cleveland-Innes, M., & Wilton, D. (2018). *Guide to Blended Learning*. Commonwealth of Learning. Retrieved from http://oasis.col.org/handle/11599/3095

Cobb, T. (2007). Computing the vocabulary demands of L2 reading. *Language Learning & Technology*, *11*(3), 38–63.

Cobo, C., Zucchetti, A., Kass-Hanna, J., & Lyons, A. (2019). *Leaving no one behind: Measuring the multidimensionality of digital literacy in the age of AI and other transformative technologies*. Academic Press.

Cohen, N. (2021, September 7). One Woman's Mission to Rewrite Nazi History on Wikipedia. *Wired*. https://www.wired.com/story/one-womans-mission-to-rewrite-nazi-history-wikipedia/

Cohen, J. (1992). A power primer. *Psychological Bulletin*, *112*(1), 155–159. doi:10.1037/0033-2909.112.1.155 PMID:19565683

Cojocariu, V. M., & Boghian, I. (2014). Teaching the relevance of game-based learning to preschool and primary teachers. *Procedia: Social and Behavioral Sciences*, *142*, 640–646. doi:10.1016/j.sbspro.2014.07.679

Cole, H., & Griffiths, M. D. (2007). Social interactions in massively multiplayer online role-playing gamers. *Cyberpsychology & Behavior*, *10*(4), 575–583. doi:10.1089/cpb.2007.9988 PMID:17711367

Coleman, T. E., & Money, A. G. (2020). Student-centred digital game–based learning: A conceptual framework and survey of the state of the art. *Higher Education*, *79*(3), 415–457. doi:10.100710734-019-00417-0

Cole, R., & Snider, B. (2017a). Rolling the Dice on Global Supply Chain Sustainability: A Total Cost of Ownership Simulation. *INFORMS Transactions on Education*, *20*(3), 165–176. doi:10.1287/ited.2019.0225

Cole, S. W., Yoo, D. J., & Knutson, B. (2012). Interactivity and reward-related neural activation during a serious videogame. *PLoS One*, *7*(3), e33909. doi:10.1371/journal.pone.0033909 PMID:22442733

Collins, A., & Halverson, R. (2009). *Rethinking education in the age of technology: The digital revolution and schooling in America*. Teachers College Press.

Combefis, S., Beresnevicius, G., & Dagiene, V. (2016). Learning programming through games and contests: Overview, characterization, and discussion. *Olympiads in Informatics*, *10*(1), 39–60. doi:10.15388/ioi.2016.03

Comber, B., & Nixon, H. (2005). Children re-read and re-write their neighbourhoods: Critical literacies and identity work. In J. Evans (Ed.), *Literacy moves on: Using popular culture, new technologies and critical literacy in the primary classroom* (pp. 127–148). Heinemann.

Comeron, L. (2008). *Teaching Languages to Young Learners* (10th ed.). Cambridge Universty Press.

Common Sense Media. (2021). *Introduction to the TPACK model*. https://www.commonsense.org/education/videos/introduction-to-the-tpack-model

Commonwealth of Learning (COL). (2017). *MOOC on Introduction to Technology-Enabled Learning*. Commonwealth of Learning and Athabasca University.

Computer Literacy Skills. (n.d.). Retrieved May 01, 2019 from https://mdk12.msde.maryland.gov/instruction/curriculum/technology_literacy/computerliteracyskills.pdf

Conejero, A., & Rueda, M. (2017). Early Development of Executive Attention. *Journal of Child and Adolescent Behavior*, *05*(02), 341. doi:10.4172/2375-4494.1000341

Conger, S. (2016). Gamification of Service Desk Work. *The Impact of ICT on Work*, (November), 1–220. doi:10.1007/978-981-287-612-6

Connell, R. (1996). Teaching the boys: New research on masculinity, and gender strategies for schools. *Teachers College Record*, *98*(2), 206–235.

Connell, R. S., & Mileham, P. J. (2006). Student assistant training in a small academic library. *Public Services Quarterly*, *2*(2–3), 69–84. doi:10.1300/J295v02n02_06

Connell, R. W. (2000). *The men and the boys*. Polity.

Connolly, T. M., Boyle, E. A., Macarthur, E., Hainey, T., & Boyle, J. M. (2012). A systematic literature review of empirical evidence on computer games and serious games. *Computers & Education*, *59*(2), 661–686. doi:10.1016/j.compedu.2012.03.004

Conroy, S. J., & Emerson, T. L. N. (2004). Business ethics and religion: Religiosity as a predictor of ethical awareness among students. *Journal of Business Ethics*, *50*(4), 383–396. doi:10.1023/B:BUSI.0000025040.41263.09

Consalvo, M. (2012). Confronting toxic gamer culture: a challenge for feminist game studies scholars. Ada: A Journal of Gender, New Media, and Technology, 1. doi:10.7264/N33X84KH

Considine, D., Horton, J., & Moorman, G. (2009). Teaching And Reaching The Millenial Generation Through Media Literacy. *Journal of Adolescent and Adult Literacy, 52*(6), 471-481.

Cope, B., & Kalantzis, M. (2016). *A pedagogy of multiliteracies: Learning by design*. Palgrave Macmillan UK. Retrieved from https://books.google.ca/books?id=N6GkCgAAQBAJ

Cope, B., & Kalantzis, M. (2000). Introduction: Multiliteracies: the beginnings of an ideas. In B. Cope & M. Kalantzis (Eds.), *Multliteracies: Literacy learning and the design of social futures* (pp. 3–8). MacMillan Publishers.

Cope, B., & Kalantzis, M. (2009). "Multiliteracies": New literacies, new learning. *Pedagogies*, *4*(3), 164–195. doi:10.1080/15544800903076044

Cope, B., & Kalantzis, M. (2013). "Multiliteracies": New Literacies, New Learning. In M. Hawkins (Ed.), *Framing Languages and Literacies: Socially Situated Views and Perspectives* (pp. 115–145). Routledge. doi:10.4324/9780203070895-13

Cope, B., & Kalantzis, M. (2015). *The things you do to know: An introduction to the pedagogy of multiliteracies*. Springer.

Cope, B., & Kalantzis, M. (Eds.). (2000). *Multiliteracies: Literacy learning and the design of social futures*. Routledge.

Cope, B., Kalantzis, M., & Smith, A. (2018). Pedagogies and Literacies, Disentangling the Historical Threads: An Interview with Bill Cope and Mary Kalantzis. *Theory into Practice*, *57*(1), 5–11. doi:10.1080/00405841.2017.1390332

Corlett, J. T., & Mokgwathi, M. M. (1986). Play, games, sport preferences of Tswana children. In *Sport, culture, society. International historical and sociological perspectives. Proceedings of the VIII Commonwealth and International Conference on Sport, Physical Education, Dance, Recreation and Health. Conference'86 Glasgow, 18-23 July* (pp. 253-261). E. & FN Spon.

Cornellà, P., Estebanell, M., & Brusi, D. (2020). Gamificación y aprendizaje basado en juegos. Consideraciones generales y algunos ejemplos para la Enseñanza de la Geología. *Enseñanza de las Ciencias de la Tierra, 28*(1), 5–19.

Correia, V. (2017). *Design and the Culture of Participation in the Era of Digital Media* (PhD Thesis). Faculdade de Ciências Sociais e Humanas (FCSH), Universidade Nova de Lisboa, Lisbon, Portugal.

Costa, M. C., Manso, A., & Patrício, J. (2020). Design of a mobile augmented reality platform with game-based learning purposes. *Information (Basel), 11*(3), 127. doi:10.3390/info11030127

Costello, R. (2020). Gamification Strategies for Retention, Motivation, and Engagement in Higher Education: Emerging Research and Opportunities. IGI Global.

Costello, R., & Shaw, N. (2014). Personalised Learning Environments, HEA STEM (Computing): Learning Technologies Workshop. University of Hull.

Costello, R. (2017). *Research on Scientific and Technological Developments in Asia. In Socio-economic challenges facing the Asia and Pacific region in Higher Education. IGI Global.*

Costello, R., & Lambert, M. (2018). Motivational influences for Higher Education (HE) Students. *International Journal of Online Pedagogy and Course Design, 9*(1), 3.

Costello, R., & Lambert, M. (2019). Pokémon GO as a Cognitive and Societal Development Tool for Personalised Learning. *International Journal of End-User Computing and Development, 8*(1), 1–30. doi:10.4018/IJEUCD.2019010101

Costello, R., Lambert, M., & Smith, L. (2021). An innovative approach of using Mobile Gaming to bridge, anxiety, depression & isolation. *International Journal of Adult Vocational Education and Technology.*

Cote, A. C. (2020). *Gaming Sexism, Gender and Identity in the Era of Casual Video Games.* New York University Press. doi:10.18574/nyu/9781479838523.001.0001

Cotton, V., & Patel, M. S. (2019). Gamification use and design in popular health and fitness mobile applications. *American Journal of Health Promotion, 33*(3), 448–451. doi:10.1177/0890117118790394 PMID:30049225

Couse, L. J., & Chen, D. W. (2010). A Tablet Computer for Young Children? Exploring Its Viability for Early Childhood Education. *Journal of Research on Technology in Education, 43*(1), 75–98. doi:10.1080/15391523.2010.10782562

Covax: How many Covid vaccines have the US and the other G7 countries pledged? (2021, June 11). *BBC News.* https://www.bbc.com/news/world-55795297

Cowan, K. (2017). Digital Languages: Multimodal meaning-making in Reggio-inspired early years education. In Digi-LitEY: The Digital and Multimodal Practices of Young Children, Short Term Scientific Mission—Final Report. Academic Press. http://digilitey.eu/wp-content/uploads/2015/09/ElisabeteBarros-STSM-FinalReport_FI-1.pdf

Cowan, K. (2019). Digital meaning making: Reggio Emilia-inspired practice in Swedish preschools. *Media Education Research Journal, 8*(2), 11–29.

Cowen, T. (2013). *Average is over: Powering America beyond the age of the great stagnation.* Dutton.

Coyle, D. (2007). Content and language integrated learning: Towards a connected research agenda for CLIL pedagogies. *International Journal of Bilingual Education and Bilingualism, 10*(5), 543–562. doi:10.2167/beb459.0

Coyle, D., Hood, P., & Marsh, D. (2010). *CLIL - content and language integrated learning.* Cambridge University Press. doi:10.1017/9781009024549

Coyne, S. M., & Smith, N. J. (2014). Sweetness on the screen: A multidimensional view of prosocial behavior in media. In L. M. Padilla-Walker & G. Carlo (Eds.), *Prosocial development: A multidimensional approach* (pp. 156–177). Oxford University Press. doi:10.1093/acprof:oso/9780199964772.003.0008

Cózar-Gutiérrez, R., & Sáez-López, J. M. (2016). Game-based learning and gamification in initial teacher training in the social sciences: An experiment with minecraftedu. *International Journal of Educational Technology in Higher Education, 13*(1), 2. doi:10.118641239-016-0003-4

Craft, J. L. (2013). A Review of the Empirical Ethical Decision-Making Literature: 2004–2011. *Journal of Business Ethics, 117*(2), 221–259. doi:10.100710551-012-1518-9

Craig, S. D., Graesser, A. C., Sullins, J., & Gholson, B. (2004). Affect and Learning: An Exploratory Look into the Role of Affect in Learning with AutoTutor. *Journal of Educational Media, 29*(3), 241–250. doi:10.1080/1358165042000283101

Create unforgettable experiences. (n.d.). *GooseChase*. Retrieved October 26, 2021, from https://www.goosechase.com/

Creswell, J. W. (2003). *Research design: qualitative, quantitative, and mixed method approaches*. Sage Publications.

Creswell, J. W. (2007). *Qualitative inquiry & research design: Choosing among five approaches*. Sage Publications.

Creswell, J. W. (2014). *Research design: qualitative, quantitative, and mixed methods approaches* (4th ed.). SAGE Publications.

Creswell, J. W., & Poth, C. N. (2017). *Qualitative inquiry and research design: Choosing among five approaches*. Sage.

Crews, A. (2011). Getting Teachers on" Board. *Knowledge Quest, 40*(1), 10.

Crocco, F., Offenholley, K., & Hernandez, C. (2016). A Proof-of-Concept Study of Game-Based Learning in Higher Education. *Simulation & Gaming, 47*(4), 403–422. doi:10.1177/1046878116632484

Crookall, D. (2010). Serious games, debriefing, and simulation/gaming as a discipline. *Simulation & Gaming, 41*(6), 898–920. doi:10.1177/1046878110390784

Croxton, D., & Kortemeyer, G. (2018). Informal physics learning from video games: A case study using gameplay videos. *Physics Education, 53*(1), 015012. doi:10.1088/1361-6552/aa8eb0

Csikszentmihalyi, M. (1975). *Beyond boredom and anxiety. Experiencing flow in work and play*. Jossey-Bass.

Csikszentmihalyi, M. (1990). *Flow*. Harper & Row.

Csikszentmihalyi, M. (1990). *Flow: The psychology of optimal experience*. Harper and Row.

Csikszentmihalyi, M. (1990). *Flow: The Psychology of Optimal Experience*. Harper.

Csikszentmihalyi, M. (1996). *Creativity. Flow and the psychology of discovery and invention*. Harper Perennial.

Csikszentmihalyi, M. (1997). *Finding flow*. Basic Books.

Csikszentmihalyi, M. (2000). Positive psychology: An introduction. *The American Psychologist, 55*(1), 5–14. doi:10.1037/0003-066X.55.1.5 PMID:11392865

Csikszentmihalyi, M. (2013). *Flow: The psychology of happiness*. Random House.

Csikszentmihalyi, M., & Csikszentmihalyi, I. (1988). *Optimal experience: Psychological studies of flow in consciousness*. Cambridge University Press. doi:10.1017/CBO9780511621956

Csikszentmihalyi, M., Rathunde, K., & Whalen, S. (1993). *Talented teenagers*. Cambridge University Press.

Cudeck, R., & Browne, M. W. (1983). Cross-validation of covariance structures. *Multivariate Behavioral Research*, *18*(2), 147–167. doi:10.120715327906mbr1802_2 PMID:26781606

Culatta, B., Hall-Kenyon, K., & Bingham, G. (2016). *Five Questions Everyone Should Ask Before Choosing Early Literacy Apps*. The Joan Ganz Cooney Center at Sesame Workshop. https://www.joanganzcooneycenter.org/2016/01/07/five-questions-everyone-should-ask-before-choosing-early-literacy-apps/

Culatta, B., Black, S., & Hall-Kenyon, K. (2013). *Systematic and Engaging Early Literacy: Instruction and intervention*. Plural Publishing, Inc.

Culatta, B., Hall, K., Kovarsky, D., & Theodore, G. (2007). Contextualized approach to language and literacy instruction. *Communication Disorders Quarterly*, *28*(4), 216–235. doi:10.1177/1525740107311813

Culatta, R. (2021). *Digital for Good: Raising Kids to Thrive in an Online World*. Harvard Business Review Press.

Culatta, R., Culatta, B., Frost, M., & Buzzell, K. (2004). Project SEEL: Part II. Using technology to enhance early literacy instruction in Spanish. *Communication Disorders Quarterly*, *25*(2), 89–96. doi:10.1177/15257401040250020601

Cummings, Mason, & Baur. (2017). Active Learning Strategies for Online and Blended Learning Environments. Flipped Instruction: Breakthroughs in Research and Practice, 88–116.

Cushen, W. E. (1955). War games and operations research. *Philosophy of Science*, *2*(4), 309–320. doi:10.1086/287446

Cutrer, W. B., Miller, B., Pusic, M. V., Mejicano, G., Mangrulkar, R. S., Gruppen, L. D., & Moore, D. E. Jr. (2017). Fostering the development of master adaptive learners: A conceptual model to guide skill acquisition in medical Education. *Academic Medicine*, *92*(1), 70–75. doi:10.1097/ACM.0000000000001323 PMID:27532867

Dabbagh, N., Benson, A. D., Denham, A., Joseph, R., & Zgheib, M. A. G. (2015). *Learning Technologies and Globalization Pedagogical Frameworks and Applications*. Academic Press.

Dabbagh, N., Benson, A. D., Denham, A., Joseph, R., Al-Freih, M., Zgheib, G., Fake, H., & Guo, Z. (2016). *Learning Technologies and Globalization; Pedagogical Frameworks and Applications*. Springer. https://link.springer.com/10.1007/978-3-319-22963-8

Dadheech, A. (n.d.). *The Importance of Game Based Learning in Modern Education*. Knowledge Review. Retrieved from https://theknowledgereview.com/importance-game-based-learning-modern-education/

Dahlgren, P. (2007). *Young citizens and new media: Learning from democratic participation*. Routledge.

Dale, L., & Tanner, R. (2012). *CLIL activities: A resource for subject and language teachers*. Cambridge University Press.

Dale, S. (2014). Gamification: Making work fun, or making fun of work? *Business Information Review*, *31*(2), 82–90. doi:10.1177/0266382114538350

Dalton, B., & Proctor, C. P. (2007). Reading as thinking: Integrating strategy instruction in a universally designed digital literacy environment. *Reading comprehension strategies: Theories, interventions, and technologies*, 423-442.

Dalton-Puffer, C. (2007). *Discourse in content and language integrated learning (CLIL) classrooms*. John Benjamins Publishing Company. doi:10.1075/lllt.20

Daly, E. (2012). Explore, create, survive. *School Library Journal*, *58*(5), 24–25.

Damásio, A. (2021). *Deus Cérebro. Maquinaria das emoções*. Retrieved January 18, 2020, from https://www.rtp.pt/play/p8309/deus-cerebro

Daniele, V. (2021). Socioeconomic inequality and regional disparities in educational achievement: The role of relative poverty. *Intelligence, 84*(October), 101515. doi:10.1016/j.intell.2020.101515

Danka, I. (2020). Motivation by gamification: Adapting motivational tools of massively multiplayer online role-playing games (MMORPGs) for peer-to-peer assessment in connectivist massive open online courses (cMOOCs). *International Review of Education, 66*(1), 75–92. doi:10.100711159-020-09821-6

Darling-Hammond, L., Schachner, A., & Edgerton, A. K. (2020). Restarting and reinventing school: Learning in the time of COVID and beyond. Palo Alto, CA: Learning Policy Institute.

Darrow, C.D. (2006). *Monopoly: the property trading board game* [Board Game]. Hasbro/Parker.

Daspit, J. J., & D'Souza, D. E. (2012). Using the community of inquiry framework to introduce wiki environments in blended-learning pedagogies: Evidence from a business capstone course. *Academy of Management Learning & Education, 11*(4), 666–683. doi:10.5465/amle.2010.0154

Davidson, M., & Hobbs, J. (2013). Delivering reading intervention to the poorest children: The case of Liberia and EGRA-Plus, a primary grade reading assessment and intervention. *International Journal of Educational Development, 33*(3), 283–293. doi:10.1016/j.ijedudev.2012.09.005

Davis, F. D. (1993). *User acceptance of information technology: system characteristics, user perceptions and behavioral impacts.* Academic Press.

Davis, F. (1989). Perceived usefulness, perceived ease of use, and user acceptance of information technology. *Management Information Systems Quarterly, 13*(3), 319–340. doi:10.2307/249008

Davis, F. D., Bagozzi, R. P., & Warshaw, P. R. (1989). User Acceptance of Computer-Technology - A Comparison of 2 Theoretical-Models. *Management Science, 35*(8), 982–1003. doi:10.1287/mnsc.35.8.982

Davis, F. D., Bagozzi, R. P., & Warshaw, P. R. (1992). Extrinsic and intrinsic motivation to use computers in the workplace. *Journal of Applied Social Psychology, 22*(14), 1111–1132. doi:10.1111/j.1559-1816.1992.tb00945.x

Davis, M. H., & Gaskell, M. G. (2009). A complementary systems account of word learning: Neural and behavioural evidence. *Philosophical Transactions of the Royal Society of London. Series B, Biological Sciences, 364*(1536), 3773–3800. doi:10.1098/rstb.2009.0111 PMID:19933145

Dawson, S. (2008). A study of the relationship between student social networks and sense of community. *Journal of Educational Technology & Society, 11*(3), 224–238.

Day, E. A., Arthur, W. Jr, & Gettman, D. (2001). Knowledge structures and the acquisition of a complex skill. *The Journal of Applied Psychology, 86*(5), 1022–1033. doi:10.1037/0021-9010.86.5.1022 PMID:11596796

De Coninck, K., Valcke, M., Ophalvens, I., & Vanderlinde, R. (2019). Bridging the theory-practice gap in teacher education: The design and construction of simulation-based learning environments. In *Kohärenz in der Lehrerbildung* (pp. 263–280). Springer VS. doi:10.1007/978-3-658-23940-4_17

De Freitas, S. (2006). *Learning in immersive worlds: A review of game-based learning.* Academic Press.

De Freitas, S. (2006). *Learning in immersive worlds: A review of game-based learning.* IJSC.

De Freitas, S. (2018). Are games effective learning tools? A review of educational games. *Journal of Educational Technology & Society, 21*(2), 74–84.

De Freitas, S., & Neumann, T. (2009). The use of 'exploratory learning' for supporting immersive learning in virtual environments. *Computers & Education, 52*(2), 343–352. doi:10.1016/j.compedu.2008.09.010

De Gloria, A., Bellotti, F., & Berta, R. (2014). Serious games for education and training. *International Journal of Serious Games*, *1*(1). Advance online publication. doi:10.17083/ijsg.v1i1.11

de Jong, M. T., & Bus, A. G. (2002). Quality of book-reading matters for emergent readers: An experiment with the same book in a regular or electronic format. *Journal of Educational Psychology*, *94*(1), 145–155. doi:10.1037/0022-0663.94.1.145

De Kort, Y. A. W., Ijsselsteijn, W. A., & Poels, K. (2007). Digital games as social presence technology: Development of the Social Presence in Gaming Questionnaire (SPGQ). *Presence (Cambridge, Mass.)*, *2007*, 1–9.

de Sousa Borges, S., Durelli, V. H., Reis, H. M., & Isotani, S. (2014). A systematic mapping on Gamification applied to Education. In *Proceedings of the 29th Annual ACM Symposium on Applied Computing* (pp. 216-222). ACM. 10.1145/2554850.2554956

de Temple, J. M., & Snow, C. E. (2001). Conversations about literacy: Social mediation of psycholinguistic activity. In L. Verhoeven & C. Snow (Eds.), *Literacy and motivation: Reading engagement in individuals and groups* (pp. 71–94). Lawrence Erlbaum Associates.

DeCoito, I., & Richardson, T. (2016). Focusing on integrated STEM concepts in a digital game. In M. Urban & D. Falvo (Eds.), *Improving K-12 STEM Education* (pp. 1–23).

Dede, C. (2005b). Planning for neomillennial learning styles: Implications for investments in technology and faculty. In *Educating the net generation*. EDUCAUSE. https://www.educause.edu/research-and-publications/books/educating-net-generation/planning-neomillennial-learning-styles-implications-investments-tech

Dede, C. (2005a). Planning for neomillennial learning styles: Shifts in students' learning style will prompt a shift to active construction of knowledge through mediated immersion. *EDUCAUSE Quarterly*, *28*(1), 7–12. https://er.educause.edu/-/media/files/article-downloads/eqm0511.pdf

deHaan, J. (2019). Teaching language and literacy with games: What? How? Why? *Ludic Language Pedagogy*, *1*, 1–57.

DeHaan, J., Reed, W. M., & Kuwanda, K. (2010). The effect of interactivity with a music video game on second language vocabulary recall. *Language Learning & Technology*, *14*(2), 74–94.

deLaet, V., Kuffner, J., Slattery, M., & Sweedyk, E. (2005). *Computers games and CS education: Why and How*. Paper presented at SIGCSE, St. Louis, MO.

Dellos, R. (2015). *Kahoot! A digital game resource for learning*. Academic Press.

Delors, J. (1996). *Learning: The treasure within*. Paris: UNESCO. Retrieved May 11, 2015 from https://unesdoc.unesco.org/images/0010/001095/109590eo.pdf

de-Marcos, L., Domínguez, A., Saenz-de-Navarrete, J., & Pagés, C. (2014). An empirical study comparing gamification and social networking on e-learning. *Computers & Education*, *75*, 82–91. doi:10.1016/j.compedu.2014.01.012

Demarin, V., & Morovic, S. (2014). Neuroplasticity. *Periodicum Biologorum*, *116*(2), 209–211. https://hrcak.srce.hr/126369

Demkah, M., & Bhargava, D. (2019, February). Gamification in Education: A Cognitive Psychology Approach to Cooperative and Fun Learning. In *2019 Amity International Conference on Artificial Intelligence (AICAI)* (pp. 170-174). IEEE. 10.1109/AICAI.2019.8701264

Deng, L., & Liu, Y. (2018). *Deep learning in natural language processing*. Springer. doi:10.1007/978-981-10-5209-5

Denning, P. J., Flores, F., & Flores, G. (2011). Pluralistic coordination. In M. M. Cruz-Cunha, V. H. Varvalho, & P. Tavares (Eds.), *Business, technological, and social dimensions of computer games: Multidisciplinary developments* (pp. 416–431). Information Science Reference. doi:10.4018/978-1-60960-567-4.ch025

Department of Basic Education. (2017). *SACMEQ IV project in South Africa: A study of the conditions of schooling and quality of education.* http://www.sacmeq.org/sites/default/files/sacmeq/publications/sacmeq_iv_project_in_south_africa_report.pdf

Department of Education. (2004, September 2). White Paper on e-Education: Transforming Learning and Teaching through Information and Communication Technologies (ICTs). *Government Gazette,* (26734), 3 - 46.

Department of Educational Planning and Research Services. (2017). *SACMEQ IV project in Botswana: A study of the conditions of schooling and quality of education.* http://www.sacmeq.org/sites/default/files/sacmeq/publications/final_saqmeq_iv_report_botswana-compressed.pdf

Derboven, J., Zaman, B., Geerts, D., & De Grooff, D. (2016). Playing educational math games at home: The Monkey Tales case. *Entertainment Computing, 16,* 1–14. doi:10.1016/j.entcom.2016.05.004

Deterding, S. (2014). The Ambiguity of Games: Histories and Discourses of a Gameful World. In S. P. Walz & S. Deterding (Eds.), *The Gameful World: Approaches, Issues, Applications* (pp. 23–64). MIT Press.

Deterding, S., Dixon, D., Khaled, R., & Nacke, L. (2011, September). From game design elements to gamefulness: defining "gamification". In *Proceedings of the 15th international academic MindTrek conference: Envisioning future media environments* (pp. 9-15). 10.1145/2181037.2181040

Deterding, S., Sicart, M., Nacke, L., O'Hara, K., & Dixon, D. (2011). Gamification using game-design elements in non-gaming contexts. In *CHI'11 Extended Abstracts on Human Factors in Computing Systems* (pp. 2425–2428). ACM. doi:10.1145/1979742.1979575

Dewar, T. (1996). *Adult learning online.* http://www.cybercorp.net/ ~tammy/lo/oned2.html

Dewey, J. (1934). Art as experience. Academic Press.

Dewey, J. (1934). *Art as Experience.* Capricorn Books.

Dewey, J. (1963). *Experience and education.* Collier Books.

Dhamija, A., & Dhamija, D. (2020). Impact of Innovative and Interactive Instructional Strategies on Student Classroom Participation. In M. Montebello (Ed.), Handbook of Research on Digital Learning (pp. 20-37). IGI Global. doi:10.4018/978-1-5225-9304-1.ch002

Dhamija, A., Sharma, R., & Dhamija, D. (2020). Emergence of EdTech Products in South Asia: A Comparative Analysis. In S. Ikuta (Ed.), *Handbook of Research on Software for Gifted and Talented School Activities in K-12 Classrooms* (pp. 303–327). IGI Global. doi:10.4018/978-1-7998-1400-9.ch014

Dias, J. (2017). Teaching operations research to undergraduate management students: The role of gamification. *International Journal of Management Education, 15*(1), 98–111. doi:10.1016/j.ijme.2017.01.002

DiasSoeiro, J. (2021). Studying Wine in Non-Wine-Producing Countries: How Are Southeast Asian Students Coping With Their Learning? In C. Kahl (Ed.), Higher Education Challenges in South-East Asia (pp. 99-117). IGI Global. doi:10.4018/978-1-7998-4489-1.ch005

Dicheva, D., Dichev, C., Agre, G., & Angelova, G. (2015). Gamification in education: A systematic mapping study. *Journal of Educational Technology & Society, 18*(3), 75–88. https://www.jstor.org/stable/jeductechsoci.18.3.75

Dickey, M. D. (2007). Game design and learning: A conjectural analysis of how massively multiple online role-playing games (MMORPGs) foster intrinsic motivation. *Educational Technology Research and Development, 55*(3), 253–273. doi:10.100711423-006-9004-7

Dickey, M. D. (2010). Murder on Grimm Isle: The impact of game narrative design in an educational game-based learning environment. *British Journal of Educational Technology*. Advance online publication. doi:10.1111/j.1467-8535.2009.01032.x

Diedrich, J., Benedek, M., Jauk, E., & Neubauer, A. (2015). Are Creative Ideas Novel and Useful? *Psychology of Aesthetics, Creativity, and the Arts, 9*(1), 35–40. doi:10.1037/a0038688

Dietz, T. L. (1998). An examination of violence and gender role portrayals in video games: Implications for gender socialization and aggressive behavior. *Sex Roles, 38*(5/6), 425–442. doi:10.1023/A:1018709905920

Digital Literacy. (n.d.). Retrieved May 01, 2019 from https://www.deakin.edu.au/__data/assets/pdf_file/0008/1237742/digital-literacy.pdf

Digital Skills Country Action Plan Methodological Guidebook Part 2. (2021). *Digital Skills: The Why, the What and the How*. Retrieved from https://thedocs.worldbank.org/en/doc/a4a6a0b2de23c53da91bf4f97c315bee-0200022021/original/DSCAP-Guidebook-Part2.pdf

Dill, K. E., & Dill, J. C. (1998). Video game violence: A review of the empirical literature. *Aggression and Violent Behavior, 3*(4), 407–428. doi:10.1016/S1359-1789(97)00001-3

Dillon, J. D. (2020). More than netflix: The real potential of personalised learning. *Training & Development, 47*(2), 20–23.

Dillon, L., & Dillon, D. (2002). *Rap a tap tap: Here's Bojangles—Think of that!* Blue Sky Press.

Dinan Thompson, M., Meldrum, K., & Sellwood, J. (2014). '… it is not just a game': Connecting with culture through Traditional Indigenous Games. *American Journal of Educational Research, 2*(11), 1015–1022.

DiNardo, C. O., & Broussard, M. J. S. (2019). Commercial tabletop games to teach information literacy. *RSR. Reference Services Review, 47*(2), 106–117. doi:10.1108/RSR-10-2018-0066

Ding, D., Guan, C., & Yu, Y. (2017). Game-based learning in tertiary education: A new learning experience for the generation Z. *International Journal of Information and Education Technology (IJIET), 7*(2), 148–152. doi:10.18178/ijiet.2017.7.2.857

Ding, J., Shan, R., Chenmeng, M., Tu, M., Yu, Q., Kong, F., & Zhao, Q. (2021). Are online games a blessing or evil? The moderating role of self-worth. *Thinking Skills and Creativity, 41*, 100915. doi:10.1016/j.tsc.2021.100915

Dingli, A., & Seychell, D. (2015). Who Are the Digital Natives? In *The New Digital Natives*. Springer. doi:10.1007/978-3-662-46590-5_2

Divjak, B., & Tomic, D. (2011). The Impact of Game-Based Learning on the Achievement of Learning Goals and Motivation for Learning Mathematics - Literature Review. *Journal of Information and Organizational Sciences, 35*(1), 15–30.

Dixon, M. L., Thiruchselvam, R., Todd, R., & Christoff, K. (2017). Emotion and the prefrontal cortex: An integrative review. *Psychological Bulletin, 143*(10), 1033–1081. doi:10.1037/bul0000096 PMID:28616997

Dlthewave. (2019). Pro and Con: Has gun violence been improperly excluded from gun articles? In *Wikipedia*. https://en.wikipedia.org/w/index.php?title=Wikipedia:Wikipedia_Signpost/2019-03-31/Op-Ed&oldid=969726090

Doganieri, E. & Munster, B. (2001). *The Amazing Race* [Game Show Series]. CBS.

Dolanbay, H. (2018). Günümüz dünya sorunları bağlamında medya ve etkileri. In Günümüz Dünya Sorunları. Pegem akademi.

Dolanbay, H. (2018). *Sosyal Bilgiler Öğretmen Adaylarına Yönelik Medya Okuryazarlığı Eğitimi Modeli.* Doktora Tezi. Marmara Üniversitesi.

Dolean, D., Melby-Lervåg, M., Tincas, I., Damsa, C., & Lervåg, A. (2019). Achievement gap: Socioeconomic status affects reading development beyond language and cognition in children facing poverty. *Learning and Instruction, 63*(June), 101218. doi:10.1016/j.learninstruc.2019.101218

Dolgopolovas, V., Jevsikova, T., & Dagiene, V. (2018). From Android games to coding in C—An approach to motivate novice engineering students to learn programming. *Computer Applications in Engineering Education, 26*(1), 75–90. doi:10.1002/cae.21862

Domingo, H., & Mashiko, N. (2013). Media literacy education (MLE) in the classroom: A descriptive case study of one exemplary Japanese teacher's mle practices, attitude and perception. Gifu University Curriculum Development Research, 30(1), 13-29.

Donahue, M. J. (1985). Intrinsic and extrinsic religiousness: Review and meta-analysis. *Journal of Personality and Social Psychology, 48*(2), 400–419. doi:10.1037/0022-3514.48.2.400

Donohue, C., & Schomburg, R. (2017). Technology and interactive media in early childhood programs. *Young Children, 72*(4), 72–78.

Donovan, L., Green, T. D., & Mason, C. (2014). Examining the 21st century classroom: Developing an innovation configuration map. *Journal of Educational Computing Research, 50*(2), 161–178. doi:10.2190/EC.50.2.a

Down's Syndrome Association. (2008). *Incidence of Down's Syndrome in the UK.* DSA.

Downing, S. (2005). The social construction of entrepreneurship: Narrative and dramatic processes in the coproduction of organizations and identities. *Entrepreneurship Theory and Practice, 29*(2), 185–204. doi:10.1111/j.1540-6520.2005.00076.x

Draper, S. (2004). *Learning Styles.* www.psy.gla.ac.uk/~steve/lstyles.html

Driver, R. (1989). The construction of scientific knowledge in school classrooms. In R. Millar (Ed.), *Doing science: Images of science in science education* (pp. 83–106). Falmer Press.

Driver, R., Squires, A., Rushworth, P., & Wood-Robinson, V. (2014). *Making sense of secondary science: Research into children's ideas.* Routledge. doi:10.4324/9781315747415

Droogers, A. F., van Harskamp, A., Clarke, P. B., Davie, G., & Versteeg, P. (2006). Playful Religion: Challenges for the Study of Religion. Uitgeverij B.V.

Duffy, T. M., & Cunningham, D. J. (1996). Constructivism: Implications for the design and delivery of instruction. In D. H. Jonassen (Ed.), *Handbook of research for educational communications and technology.* Macmillan Library Reference. doi:10.4324/9781410609519

Duggal, Gupta, & Singh. (2021). Gamification and machine learning inspired approach for classroom engagement and learning. *Mathematical Problems in Engineering.* doi:10.1155/2021/9922775

Duit, R. (1987). Research on students' alternative frameworks in science - topics, theoretical frameworks, consequences for science teaching. In J. Novak (Ed.), *Proceedings of the 2nd International Seminar on Misconceptions and Educational Strategies in science and Mathematics* (pp. 151–162). Ithaca, NY: Cornell University.

Duke, B., Harper, G., & Johnston, M. (1966). *Connectivism as a Learning Theory for the Digital Age.* Academic Press.

Duncan, J. (2019). Tech with a twist. Innovative youth programming combines coding with dance. *CBS News.* Retrieved 9/13/21 from https://www.cbsnews.com/news/dancelogic-innovative-youth-program-combines-coding-and-dance-2019-06-20/

Dunning, J. H. (2000). Regions, globalization, and the knowledge economy: Issues stated. In J. H. Dunning (Ed.), *Regions, globalization, and the knowledge-based economy* (pp. 7–41). Oxford University Press.

Dunn, J., Gray, C., Moffett, P., & Mitchell, D. (2018). 'It's more funner than doing work': Children's perspectives on using tablet computers in the early years of school. *Early Child Development and Care, 188*(6), 819–831. doi:10.1080/03004430.2016.1238824

Dunn, R., Cavanaugh, D., Eberle, B., & Zenhausern, R. (1982). Hemispheric preference: The newest element of learning style. *The American Biology Teacher, 44*(5), 291–294. doi:10.2307/4447506

Dunn, R., Della Valle, J., Dunn, K., Geisert, G., Sinatra, R., & Zenhausern, R. (1986). 'The effects of matching and mismatching students' mobility preferences on recognition and memory tasks'. *The Journal of Educational Research, 79*(5), 267–272. doi:10.1080/00220671.1986.10885690

Dunn, R., Dunn, K., & Price, E. (1989). *The learning style inventory.* Price Systems.

Durak, G., Çankaya, S., & İzmirli, S. (2020). Examining the Turkish universities' distance education systems during the COVID-19 pandemic. *Necatibey Eğitim Fakültesi Elektronik Fen ve Matematik Eğitimi Dergisi., 14*(1), 787–809. doi:10.17522/balikesirnef.743080

Duret, C., & Pons, C. M. (Eds.). (2016). *Contemporary research on intertextuality in video games.* IGI Global. doi:10.4018/978-1-5225-0477-1

Dutta, S., & Smita, M. K. (2020). The Impact of COVID-19 Pandemic on Tertiary Education in Bangladesh: Students' Perspectives. *Open Journal of Social Sciences, 8*(9), 53–68. doi:10.4236/jss.2020.89004

Dwarkan, L. (2017). *SACMEQ IV project in Mauritius: A study of the conditions of schooling and quality of education.* http://www.sacmeq.org/sites/default/files/sacmeq/publications/final_sacmeq_4_report_mauritius.pdf

Dzansi, D. Y., & Amedzo, K. (2014). Integrating ICT into Rural South African Schools: Possible Solutions for Challenges. *International Journal of Educational Sciences, 6*(2), 341–348. doi:10.1080/09751122.2014.11890145

Dzimiri, C., & Mapute, L. (2013). Integration of Information and Communication Technology (ICT) with pedagogy. *IOSR Journal of Humanities and Social Science, 16*(3), 86–92. doi:10.9790/0837-1638692

Eastwood, J. L., & Sadler, T. D. (2013). Teachers' implementation of a game-based biotechnology curriculum. *Computers & Education, 66*(0), 11–24. doi:10.1016/j.compedu.2013.02.003

Ebrahimzadeh, M. (2017). Readers, players, and watchers: EFL students' vocabulary acquisition through digital video games. *English Language Teaching, 10*(2), 1–18. doi:10.5539/elt.v10n2p1

Ebrahimzadeh, M., & Alavi, S. (2016). Motivating EFL students: E-learning enjoyment as a predictor of vocabulary learning through digital video games. *Cogent Education, 3*(1), 1255400. doi:10.1080/2331186X.2016.1255400

Eck, R. V. (2006). Digital Game-Based Learning: It's Not Just the Digital Natives Who Are Restless. *EDUCAUSE Review, 41*(2), 16–30.

Edlund, A. C., Edlund, L. E., & Haugen, S. (Eds.). (2014). *Vernacular Literacies – Past, Present and Future.* Umea University and Royal Skyttean Society. Retrieved May 01, 2019 from http://umu.diva-portal.org/smash/get/diva2:738154/FULLTEXT01.pdf

Educause. (2014). *7 things you should know about games and learning*. Retrieved from https://courses.dcs.wisc.edu/design-teaching/PlanDesign_Fall2016/2-Online-Course-Design/4_Instructional-Materials/resources/SevenThingsGames.pdf

Edwards, A., Edwards, C., Spence, P., Harris, C., & Gambino, A. (2016). Robots in the classroom: Differences in students' perceptions of credibility and learning between "teacher as robot" and "robot as teacher." *Computers in Human Behavior*, *65*, 627–634. doi:10.1016/j.chb.2016.06.005

Edwards, B., Edwards, B. B., Griffiths, S., Reynolds, F. F., Stanford, A., & Woods, M. (2021). The Bryn Celli Ddu Minecraft Experience: A Workflow and Problem-Solving Case Study in the Creation of an Archaeological Reconstruction in Minecraft for Cultural Heritage Education. *Journal on Computing and Cultural Heritage*, *14*(2), 1–16. doi:10.1145/3427913

Edwards, C. P. (2002). Three approaches from Europe: Waldorf, Montessori, and Reggio Emilia. *Early Childhood Research & Practice*, *4*(1), n1.

Egenfeldt Nielsen, S. (2008). Practical Barriers in Using Educational Computer Games. In D. Drew (Ed.), Beyond Fun (pp. 20-26). ETC Press.

Egenfeldt-Nielsen, S. (2018). *Making sweet music: The educational use of computer games*. Center for Computer Games Research: University of Copenhagen. Retrieved from https://www.cs.swarthmore.edu/~turnbull/cs91/f09/paper/MakingSweetMusic.pdf

Egenfeldt-Nielsen, S. (2006). Overview of research on the educational use of video games. *Nordic Journal of Digital Literacy*, *1*(03), 184–214. doi:10.18261/ISSN1891-943X-2006-03-03

Egenfeldt-Nielsen, S. (2007). Third generation educational use of computer games. *Journal of Educational Multimedia and Hypermedia*, *16*(3), 263–281.

Egenfeldt-Nielsen, S., Smith, J. H., & Tosca, S. P. (2013). *Understanding video games: the essential introduction* (2nd ed.). Routledge. doi:10.4324/9780203116777

Eggs, R. (2021). *Fast phonics* (Version 3.0.4) [Mobile app]. https://readingeggs.com/fast-phonics-games/

Egri, C. P. (2013). From the editors: Context matters in management education scholarship. Academy of Management Learning & Education, 12(2), 155-7. doi:10.5465/amle.2013.0140

Ehri, L. C., & McCormick, S. (1998). Phases of word learning: Implications for instruction with delayed and disabled readers. *Reading & Writing Quarterly*, *14*(April), 135–163. doi:10.1080/1057356980140202

Eisenberg, N. (Ed.). (1982). *The development of prosocial behavior*. Academic Press.

Eklund, K. M., Torppa, M., & Lyytinen, H. (2013). Predicting reading disability: Early cognitive risk and protective factors. *Dyslexia (Chichester, England)*, *19*(1), 1–10. doi:10.1002/dys.1447 PMID:23297103

Elbro, C., Rasmussen, I., & Spelling, B. (1996). Teaching reading to disabled readers with language disorders: A controlled evaluation of synthetic speech feedback. *Scandinavian Journal of Psychology*, *37*(2), 140–155. doi:10.1111/j.1467-9450.1996.tb00647.x PMID:8711453

Eleftheria, C. A., Charikleia, P., Iason, C. G., Athanasios, T., & Dimitrios, T. (2013). An innovative augmented reality educational platform using Gamification to enhance lifelong learning and cultural education. In *Information, Intelligence, Systems and Applications (IISA), 2013 Fourth International Conference on* (pp. 1-5). IEEE. 10.1109/IISA.2013.6623724

Elkins, A. J. (2015). Lets Play: Why School Librarians Should Embrace Gaming in the Library. *Knowledge Quest*, *43*(5), 58–63.

Elkins, D. N., Hedstrom, L. J., Hughes, L. L., Leaf, J. A., & Saunders, C. (1988). Toward a humanistic-phenomenological spirituality: Definition, description, and measurement. *Journal of Humanistic Psychology*, *28*(4), 5–18. doi:10.1177/0022167888284002

Elliot, A. J. (1999). Approach and avoidance motivation and achievement goals. *Educational Psychologist*, *34*(3), 169–189. doi:10.120715326985ep3403_3

Elliott, E. (2019). *Composing software: An exploration of functional programming and object composition in JavaScript*. Leanpub.

Elliott, J., & Tsai, C. T. (2008). What might Confucius have to say about action research? *Educational Action Research*, *16*(4), 569–578. doi:10.1080/09650790802445759

Emon, E. K. H., Alif, A. R., & Islam, M. S. (2020). Impact of COVID-19 on the Institutional Education System and its Associated Students in Bangladesh. *Asian Journal of Education and Social Studies*, *11*(2), 34–46. doi:10.9734/ajess/2020/v11i230288

Enakrire, T. R., & Onyenania, O. G. (2007). Causes inhibiting the growth or development of information transfer in Africa: A contextual treatment. *Library Hi Tech News*, *24*(4), 20–28. doi:10.1108/07419050710778491

Encheva, M., Tammaro, A. M., & Kumanova, A. (2020). Games to improve students information literacy skills. *The International Information & Library Review*, *52*(2), 130–138. doi:10.1080/10572317.2020.1746024

Enders, C. K. (2011). Analyzing longitudinal data with missing values. *Rehabilitation Psychology*, *56*(4), 267–288. doi:10.1037/a0025579 PMID:21967118

Eng, D. (2019). *The player experience*. https://www.universityxp.com/blog/2019/9/10/the-player-experience

English, A. R. (2016). John Dewey and the role of the teacher in a globalised world: Imagination, empathy, and "third voice". *Educational Philosophy and Theory*, *48*(10), 1046–1064. doi:10.1080/00131857.2016.1202806

Ennis, L. (2018). *Game-Based Learning: An Instructional Tool, Digital repository*. Iowa State University.

Epic! Creations. (2021). *Epic books for kids* (version 5.31) [Mobile app]. https://www.getepic.com

Epper, R., Derryberry, A., & Jackon, S. (2012). *Game-Based Learning: Developing an Institutional Strategy*. EDUCAUSE Research. http://educause.edu/ecar

Epstein, E. M. (2002). Religion and business–the critical role of religious traditions in management education. *Journal of Business Ethics*, *38*(1-2), 91–96. doi:10.1023/A:1015712827640

Erdem, C. (2019). *Introduction to 21st century skills and education*. Retrieved from https://www.researchgate.net/publication/336148206_Introduction_to_21st_century_skills_and_education

Ērgle, D., & Ludviga, I. (2018). Use of gamification in human resource management: Impact on engagement and satisfaction. *Contemporary Business Management Challenges and Opportunities*, 409–417. doi:10.3846/bm.2018.45

Erickson, F. (1986). Qualitative Methods in Research on Teaching. In M. C. Wittrock (Ed.), *Handbook of Research on Teaching* (pp. 119–161). Macmillan.

Ermi, L., & Mäyrä, F. (2005). Fundamental components of the gameplay experience: Analysing immersion. *Proceedings of DiGRA 2005 Conference: Changing Views – Worlds in Play*.

Ernest, P. (1988). What's the use of LOGO? *Mathematics in School*, *17*(1), 16–20.

Erwig, M. (2017). *Once upon an algorithm: How stories explain computing*. MIT Press. doi:10.7551/mitpress/10786.001.0001

Eryansyah, E., Erlina, E., Fiftinova, F., & Nurweni, A. (2019). EFL Students' Needs of Digital Literacy to Meet the Demands of 21stCentury Skills. *Indonesian Research Journal of Education*, 442–460.

Escudeiro, P., & de Carvalho, C. V. (2013). Game-based language learning. *International Journal of Information and Education Technology (IJIET)*, *3*(6), 643–647. doi:10.7763/IJIET.2013.V3.353

Eseryel, D., Law, V., Ifenthaler, D., Ge, X., & Miller, R. (2014). An investigation of the interrelationships between motivation, engagement, and complex problem solving in game-based learning. *Journal of Educational Technology & Society*, *17*(1), 42–53.

Esmaeili, H., & Woods, P. C. (2016). Calm down buddy! it's just a game: Behavioral patterns observed among teamwork MMO participants in WARGAMING's world of tanks. In *2016 22nd International Conference on Virtual System & Multimedia (VSMM)* (pp. 1-11). IEEE.

Esteves, M., Pereira, A., Veiga, N., Vasco, R., & Veiga, A. (2018). The Use of New Learning Technologies in Higher Education Classroom: A Case Study. In M. Auer, D. Guralnick, & I. Simonics (Eds.), *Teaching and Learning in a Digital World. ICL 2017. Advances in Intelligent Systems and Computing* (Vol. 715). Springer., doi:10.1007/978-3-319-73210-7_59

ET. (2008). 21st century learning: Research, innovation and policy. directions from recent OECD analyses. *OECD/CERI International Conference*.

EU Lifelong Learning Programme. (2011). *Production of Creative Game-Based Learning Scenarios: A Handbook for Teachers*. ProActive. https://bit.ly/3tJVKbq

European Commission (EC) & Gabinete de Comunicacion. (2009). *Study on the current trends and approaches to media literacy in Europe*. Authors.

Evoh, C. (2007). Policy networks and the transformation of secondary education through ICTs in Africa: The prospects and challenges of the NEPAD e-schools initiative. *International Journal of Education and Development Using Information and Communication Technology*, *3*(1), 64–84.

Eyebraingym. (2021). *Key Science*. eyebraingym. Retrieved from: https://www.eyebraingym.com/key-science/

Facer, K. (2011). *Learning futures: Education, technology and social change*. Routledge. doi:10.4324/9780203817308

Fachada, N. (2018). Teaching database concepts to video game design e development students. *Revista Lusófona de Educação*, *40*(40), 151–165. doi:10.24140/issn.1645-7250.rle40.10

Faculdade de Belas-Artes da Universidade de Lisboa. (2021). Retrieved October 4, 2021, from, http://www.belasartes.ulisboa.pt/

Fadel, C. (2008). *21st century skills: How can you prepare students for the new global economy?* https://www.oecd.org/site/educeri21st/40756908.pdf

Fadel, C., & Trilling, B. (2012). *21st Century Skills, Learning for Life in our Times*. Wiley.

Fahuzan, K., & Santosa, R. H. (2018). Gender Differences in Motivation to Learn Math Using Role Play Game in Smartphone. *Journal of Physics: Conference Series*, *1097*(1), 1–7. doi:10.1088/1742-6596/1097/1/012130

Fandiño Parra, Y. (2013). 21st century skills and the English foreign language classroom: A call for more awareness in Colombia. *Gist Education and Learning Research Journal*, *7*, 190–208.

Fang, X. Y., Dai, L. Q., Fang, C., & Deng, L. (2006). The relationship between parent-adolescent communication problems and adolescents' social adjustments. *Xinli Fazhan Yu Jiaoyu*, 2247–2252.

Fang, Y., Chen, K., & Huang, Y. (2016). Emotional reactions of different interface formats: Comparing digital and traditional board games. *Advances in Mechanical Engineering*, 8(3), 1–8. doi:10.1177/1687814016641902

Fani, T., & Ghaemi, F. (2011). Implications of Vygotsky's Zone of Proximal Development (ZPD) in Teacher Education: ZPTD and Self-scaffolding. *Procedia: Social and Behavioral Sciences*, 29, 1549–1554. doi:10.1016/j.sbspro.2011.11.396

Farber, M. (2015). *Gamify your classroom: A field guide to game-based learning*. Peter Lang. doi:10.3726/978-1-4539-1459-5

Favia, A., Comins, N. F., Thorpe, G. L., & Batuski, D. J. (2014). A direct examination of college student misconceptions in astronomy: A new instrument. *J. Rev. Astron. Educ. Outreach*, 1(1), A21–A39.

February, P. J. (2018). *Teaching and learning to read in Afrikaans: Teacher competence and computer-assisted support*. University of Jyväskylä. http://urn.fi/URN:ISBN:978-951-39-7515-9

Federici, S., Molinas, J., Sergi, E., Lussu, R., & Gola, E. (2019). Rapid and easy prototyping of multimedia tools for education. *Proceedings of the World Conference on Media and Mass Communication*. 10.17501/24246778.2019.5102

Fedorov, A. (2003). Media Education and Media Literacy: Experts' Opinions. A Media Education Curriculum for Teachers in the Mediterranean, UNESCO.

Felix, J. W., & Johnson, R. T. (1993). Learning from video games. *Computers in the Schools*, 9(2-3), 119–134. doi:10.1300/J025v09n02_11

Felten, P. (2008). *Visual Literacy*. Retrieved May 02, 2019 from http://one2oneheights.pbworks.com/f/Felten,P.(2008).Visual%20Literacy.pdf

Felton, E. L., & Sims, R. R. (2005). Teaching business ethics: Targeted outputs. *Journal of Business Ethics*, 60(4), 377–391. doi:10.100710551-004-8206-3

Ferguson, C. J. (2015). Do Angry Birds make for angry children? A meta-analysis of video game influences on children's and adolescents' aggression, mental health, prosocial behavior, and academic performance. *Perspectives on Psychological Science*, 10(5), 646–666. doi:10.1177/1745691615592234 PMID:26386002

Fernández-Batanero, J. M., Montenegro-Rueda, M., Fernández-Cerero, J., & García-Martínez, I. (2020). Digital competences for teacher professional development. Systematic review. *European Journal of Teacher Education*, 1–19. doi:10.1080/02619768.2020.1827389

Fernández, E., Ordóñez, E., Morales, B., & López, J. (2019). *La competencia digital en la docencia universitaria*. Octaedro.

Fernando, M., & Chowdhury, R. M. M. I. (2010). The relationship between spiritual well-being and ethical orientations in decision making: An empirical study with business executives in Australia. *Journal of Business Ethics*, 95(2), 211–225. doi:10.100710551-009-0355-y

Ferreiro-González, M., Amores-Arrocha, A., Espada-Bellido, E., Aliano-Gonzalez, M. J., Vázquez-Espinosa, M., González-De-Peredo, A. V., Sancho-Galán, P., Álvarez-Saura, J. Á., Barbero, G. F., & Cejudo-Bastante, C. (2019). Escape ClassRoom: Can You Solve a Crime Using the Analytical Process? *Journal of Chemical Education*, 96(2), 267–273. doi:10.1021/acs.jchemed.8b00601

Fhkps, B., Ho, W., Leung, E., Li, P., Mok, B., Shek, V., & Shek, E. (2021). Nurturing leadership qualities under COVID-19: Student perceptions of the qualities and effectiveness of online teaching and learning on leadership development. *International Journal of Child and Adolescent Health*, 14(1), 89–100.

Fichten, C. S., Asuncion, J., & Scapin, R. (2014). Digital Technology, Learning, and Postsecondary Students with Disabilities: Where We've Been and Where We're Going. *Journal of Postsecondary Education and Disability, 27*(4), 369–379.

Field, A. (2013). *Discovering statistics using IBM SPSS Statistics: And sex and drugs and rock 'n' roll* (4th ed.). Sage Publications.

Figueiredo, A. D. (2020). *Which School for Citizenship?* Retrieved January 14, 2020, from https://adfig.com/pt/?p=630

Filipe, A. (2019). Design of a Learning Framework for Open Mobile Applications. *Educ. foco. Juiz de Fora, 24*(1), 529-530.

Fine, G. A. (2002). *Shared Fantasy*. University of Chicago Press. https://press.uchicago.edu/ucp/books/book/chicago/S/bo5949823.html

Fine, G. A. (1983). *Shared fantasy: Role-playing games as social worlds*. The University of Chicago Press.

Finn, P. J. (1999). *Literacy with an attitude: Educating working-class children in their own self-interest*. State University of New York Press.

Fischer, H., Heinz, M., Schlenker, L., & Follert, F. (2016). Gamifying higher education. beyond badges, points and leaderboards. *Knowledge Communities in Online Education and, Visual Knowledge Management - Proceedings of 19th Conference GeNeMe 2016, as Part of IFKAD 2016,* 93–104.

Fischer, E., & Hänze, M. (2020). How do university teachers' values and beliefs affect their teaching? *Educational Psychology, 40*(3), 296–317. doi:10.1080/01443410.2019.1675867

Fishbach, A., Eyal, T., & Finkelstein, S. R. (2010). How positive and negative feedback motivate goal pursuit. *Social and Personality Psychology Compass, 4*(8), 517–530. doi:10.1111/j.1751-9004.2010.00285.x

Fitzgerald, M., Danaia, L., & McKinnon, D. H. (2019). Barriers inhibiting inquiry-based science teaching and potential solutions: Perceptions of positively inclined early adopters. *Research in Science Education, 49*(2), 543–566. doi:10.100711165-017-9623-5

Fitz-Walter, Z. J. (2015). Achievement unlocked: Investigating the design of effective gamification experiences for mobile applications and devices. School of Information Systems; Science & Engineering Faculty, Queensland University of Technology.

Flanagan, M. (2009). *Critical Play, Radical Game Design*. MIT Press. doi:10.7551/mitpress/7678.001.0001

Fleming, N. D., & Mills, C. (1992). Not Another Inventory, Rather a Catalyst for Reflection. *To Improve the Academy, 11*(1), 137-144.

Fleming, T. M., Bavin, L., Stasiak, K., Hermansson-Webb, E., Merry, S. N., Cheek, C., Lucassen, M., Lau, H. M., Pollmuller, B., & Hetrick, S. (2017). Serious games and gamification for mental health: Current status and promising directions. *Frontiers in Psychiatry, 7*. Advance online publication. doi:10.3389/fpsyt.2016.00215 PMID:28119636

Flores-Morador, F. (2013). *The beam in the eye: ICT, school and broken technologies* [La viga en el ojo: los nuevos medios de comunicación, la escuela y las tecnologías rotas]. Academic Press.

Floridi, L. (2014). *The Fourth Revolution: How the infosphere is reshaping human reality*. Oxford University Press.

Fong, C. J., Kim, Y., Davis, C. W., Hoang, T. V., & Kim, Y. W. (2017). A meta-analysis on critical thinking and community college student achievement. *Thinking Skills and Creativity, 26*, 71-83. .2017.06.002 doi:10.1016/j.tsc

Forbes. (2019). *Research Report Shows How Much Time We Spend Gaming*. Retrieved from https://www.forbes.com/sites/kevinanderton/2019/03/21/research-report-shows-how-much-time-we-spend-gaming-infographic/#1a9602d13e07

Ford, H., & Wajcman, J. (2017). 'Anyone can edit', not everyone does: Wikipedia's infrastructure and the gender gap. *Social Studies of Science, 47*(4), 511–527. doi:10.1177/0306312717692172 PMID:28791929

Forsyth, D. R., O'Boyle, E. H. Jr, & McDaniel, M. A. (2008). East meets west: A meta-analytic investigation of cultural variations in idealism and relativism. *Journal of Business Ethics, 83*(4), 813–833. doi:10.100710551-008-9667-6

Fortier, M. (2019). *The Power of a Gamified Classroom, Technology and Curriculum.* Retrieved from https://techand-curr2019.pressbooks.com/chapter/gamified-classroom/

Foster, A., & Shah, M. (2015). The Play Curricular Activity Reflection Discussion Model for Game-Based Learning. *Journal of Research on Technology in Education, 47*(2), 71–88. doi:10.1080/15391523.2015.967551

Foster, A., & Shah, M. (2020). Principles for Advancing Game-Based Learning in Teacher Education. *Journal of Digital Learning in Teacher Education, 36*(2), 84–95. doi:10.1080/21532974.2019.1695553

Fraillon, J., Ainley, J., Schulz, W., Duckworth, D., & Friedman, T. (2019). *IEA international computer and information literacy study 2018 assessment framework.* Springer Nature. doi:10.1007/978-3-030-19389-8

Francescato, D., Porcelli, R., Mebane, M., Cuddetta, M., Klobas, J., & Renzi, P. (2006). Evaluation of the efficacy of collaborative learning in face-to-face and computer-supported university contexts. *Computers in Human Behavior, 22*(2), 163–176. doi:10.1016/j.chb.2005.03.001

Franciosi, S. J., Yagi, J., Tomoshige, Y., & Ye, S. (2016). The effect of a simple simulation game on long-term vocabulary retention. *CALICO Journal, 33*(3), 355–379. doi:10.1558/cj.v33i2.26063

Francis, M. K., Wormington, S. V., & Hulleman, C. (2019). The Costs of Online Learning: Examining Differences in Motivation and Academic Outcomes in Online and Face-to-Face Community College Developmental Mathematics Courses. *Frontiers in Psychology, 10*(September), 1–12. doi:10.3389/fpsyg.2019.02054 PMID:31551886

Franklin, R. M. (2004). *Moral Literacy: The Knowledge of Truth, Justice, Goodness and Interdependence.* Retrieved May 02, 2019 from https://c.ymcdn.com/sites/www.sais.org/resource/resmgr/imported/HC%2004%20Franklin.pdf

Fred Rogers Center for Early Learning and Children's Media at Saint Vincent College. (2012). *A framework for quality in digital media for young children: Considerations for parents, educators, and media creators.* https://cmhd.northwestern.edu/wp-content/uploads/2015/10/Framework_Statement_2-April_2012-Full_Doc-Exec_Summary-1.pdf

Fredricks, J. A., Blumenfeld, P. C., & Paris, A. H. (2004). School engagement: Potential of the concept, state of the evidence. *Review of Educational Research, 74*(1), 59–109. https://doi.org/10.3102/00346543074001059

Freeman, A., Adams Becker, S., Cummins, M., Davis, A., & Hall Giesinger, C. (2017). *New Media Consortium (NMC)/Consortium of School Networking (CoSN) Horizon Report: 2017 K–12.* The New Media Consortium.

Freire, P. (1996). *Pedagogy of the oppressed* (New rev. ed). Penguin Books.

Freire, P., & Macedo, D. (1987). *Literacy: Reading the word and the world.* Bergin and Garvey.

Freire, P., & Macedo, D. (1987). *Literacy: Reading the Word and the World.* Bergin Garvey.

Freitas, S. de. (2006). *Learning in Immersive worlds: A review of game-based learning.* Academic Press.

Friedman, T. (2007). *The world is flat: A brief history of the twenty-first century.* Picador.

Frossard, F. (2013). *Fostering teachers' creativity through the creation of GBL scenarios* [Doctoral thesis, Universitat de Barcelona]. Departament de Didàctica i Organització Educativa. http://hdl.handle.net/10803/130831

Frost, J. L., Wortham, S. C., & Reifel, S. (2012). *Play and child development* (4th ed.). Pearson Education Inc.

Fucci, M. (2015, July 9). *The Digital Competence Framework 2.0*. EU Science Hub - European Commission. https://ec.europa.eu/jrc/en/digcomp/digital-competence-framework

Fulks, A., & Lord, B. (2016). Leveling up in a gamified classroom. *AMLE Magazine, 3*(6), 41.

Fülöp, M. (2009). Happy and Unhappy Competitors: What Makes the Difference? *Psihologijske Teme, 18*(2), 345–367.

Fundamentals of Management. (2021). *Students' reports on Fundamentals of Management* https://drive.google.com/drive/folders/1fhtTOTTeuWS-zzt7a31Eirbh7UQKQFsw?usp=sharing

Funk, J. B., Baldacci, H. B., Pasold, T., & Baumgardner, J. (2004). Violence exposure in real-life, video games, television, movies, and the internet: Is there desensitization? *Journal of Adolescence, 27*(1), 23–39. doi:10.1016/j.adolescence.2003.10.005 PMID:15013258

Gainer, J. (2007). Social critique and pleasure: Critical media literacy with popular culture texts. *Language Arts, 85*(2), 106–115.

Gains, P., & Parkes, A. (2012). *Report on the development, implementation and findings of the EGRA pilot in Hardap, Kavango and Oshikoto regions: November 2011-May 2012*. Academic Press.

Gallahue, D. L., & Donnelly, F. C. (2003). Movement skill acquisition. In *Developmental Physical Education for all Children* (4th ed.). Human Kinetics.

Galletta, D. F., Ahuja, M., Hartman, A., Teo, T., & Graham Peace, A. (1995). Social influence and end-user training. *Communications of the ACM, 38*(7), 70–79. doi:10.1145/213859.214800

Galloway, A. R. (2006). Protocol. *Theory, Culture & Society, 23*(2-3), 317–320. doi:10.1177/026327640602300241

Game Lab. Laboratório de Jogos. (2021). Retrieved October 4, 2021, from, https://labjogos.tecnico.ulisboa.pt/en https://www.facebook.com/LabJogosIST/

GameDevTecnico Students Twitter and Instagram links. (2021). Retrieved October 5, 2021, from, https://twitter.com/gamedevtecnico https://www.instagram.com/p/CGpvQ24KJKM/

GameDevTecnico. (2021). Retrieved October 4, 2021, from, https://gamedev.tecnico.ulisboa.pt/ https://gamedevtecnico.itch.io/

Garcia, M., Rabelo, D., Silva, D., & Amaral, S. (2011). Novas competências docentes frente às tecnologias digitais interativas. *Revista Teoria e Prática de Educação, 14*(1), 79–87.

García-Redondo, P., García, T., Areces, D., Núñez, J. C., & Rodríguez, C. (2019). Serious Games and Their Effect Improving Attention in Students with Learning Disabilities. *International Journal of Environmental Research and Public Health, 16*(14), 2480. doi:10.3390/ijerph16142480 PMID:31336804

Gardner, H., & Hatch, T. (1990). *Multiple intelligences go to school: educational implications of the theory of multiple intelligences*. Center for Children and Technology Technical Report. www.edc.org/cct/ccthome/reports/tr4.html

Gardner, H. (1983). *Frames of Mind: The Theory of Multiple Intelligences*. Basic Books.

Gardner, H. (1993). *Multiple Intelligences: The Theory in Practice*. Basic Books.

Garrido, P. C., Miraz, G. M., Ruiz, I. L., & Gomez-Nieto, M. (2011). *Use of NFC- based pervasive games for encouraging learning and student motivation*. doi:10.1109/NFC.2011.13

Garris, P. A., Collins, L. B., Jones, S. R., & Wightman, R. M. (1993). Evoked extracellular dopamine in vivo in the medial prefrontal cortex. *Journal of Neurochemistry, 61*(2), 637–647. doi:10.1111/j.1471-4159.1993.tb02168.x PMID:8336146

Garris, R., Ahlers, R., & Driskell, J. E. (2002). Games, motivation and learning: A research and practice model. *Simulation & Gaming*, *33*(4), 441–467. doi:10.1177/1046878102238607

Garvey, C. (1990). *Play*. Harvard University Press.

Gatti, L., Ulrich, M., & Seele, P. (2019). Education for sustainable development through business simulation games: An exploratory study of sustainability gamification and its effects on students' learning outcomes. *Journal of Cleaner Production*, *207*, 667–678. doi:10.1016/j.jclepro.2018.09.130

Gauquier, E., & Schneider, J. (2013). Minecraft programs in the library: If you build it they will come. *Young Adult Library Services*, *11*(2), 17–19.

Gay, G. (2010). *Culturally responsive teaching: Theory, research, and practice*. Teachers College Press.

Geck, C. (2007). The generation Z connection: Teaching information literacy to the newest net generation. In E. Rosenfeld & D. V. Loertscher (Eds.), *Toward a 21st-century school library media program* (pp. 236–248). Scarecrow Press.

Gee, J. P. (2008). Learning and games. In K. Salen (Ed.) The Ecology of Games: Connecting Youth, Games, and Learning. John D. and Catherine T. MacArthur Foundation Series on Digital Media and Learning. Cambridge, MA: The MIT Press. 10.1162/dmal.9780262693646.021

Gee, J. P. (2010). A situated-sociocultural approach to literacy and technology. *The New Literacies: Multiple Perspectives on Research and Practice*, 165–193.

Gee, J. P., & Hayes, E. (2012). Nurturing affinity spaces and game-based learning. *Games, learning, and society: Learning and meaning in the digital age, 123*, 1-40.

Gee, J. P., & Hayes, E. R. (2010). Passionate affinity groups. In Women and Gaming (pp. 105-123). Palgrave Macmillan. doi:10.1057/9780230106734_6

Gee, J. (1996). *Social linguistics and literacies: Ideology in discourses*. Falmer.

Gee, J. P. (2003). *What Video Games Have to Teach Us about Learning and Literacy*. Palgrave Macmillan. doi:10.1145/950566.950595

Gee, J. P. (2005). Learning by design: Good video games as learning machines. *E-Learning and Digital Media*, *2*(1), 5–16. doi:10.2304/elea.2005.2.1.5

Gee, J. P. (2007). *Good Video Games and Good Learning: Collected Essays on Video Games, Learning and Literacy*. P. Lang. doi:10.3726/978-1-4539-1162-4

Gee, J. P. (2007). *What video games have to teach us about learning and literacy?* Palgrave Macmillan.

Gee, J. P. (2009). *New digital media and learning as an emerging area and "worked examples" as one way forward*. MIT Press. doi:10.7551/mitpress/8563.001.0001

Gee, J. P. (2013). Games for learning. *Educational Horizons*, *91*(4), 16–20. doi:10.1177/0013175X1309100406

Gee, J. P. (2014). *Collected essays on learning and assessment in the digital world. The Learner series*. Common Ground. doi:10.18848/978-1-61229-424-7/CGP

Gee, J. P. (2014). *What video games have to teach us about learning and literacy*. MacMillan.

Gee, J. P. (2017). Affinity spaces and 21st-century learning. *Educational Technology*, 27–31.

Gee, J. P., & Hayes, E. R. (2010). *The Sims and 21ˢᵗ century learning*. Palgrave Macmillan., doi:10.1057/9780230106734

Gee, J. P., Hull, G., & Lankshear, C. (2019). *The New Work Order: Behind the Language of the New Capitalism.* Routledge. doi:10.4324/9780429496127

Gee, J., & Hayes, E. (2012). Nurturing affinity spaces and game-based learning. In C. Steinkuehler, K. Squire, & S. A. Barab (Eds.), *Games, learning, and society: Learning and meaning in the digital age* (pp. 129–153). Cambridge University Press. doi:10.1017/CBO9781139031127.015

Gender Action, Mutual Learning Workshop on Gender and Digitalization. (2021). *Interactive Multimedia Experiences in Higher Education: Gaming, Augmented and Virtual Reality, and Research.* Retrieved October 4, 2021, from https://genderaction.eu/exploratory-mutual-learning-workshop-on-gender-and-digitalization/

Generate tables in MediaWiki format—TablesGenerator.com. (n.d.). Retrieved June 1, 2021, from https://www.tables-generator.com/mediawiki_tables

Genoni, M., Bhatta, S., & Sharma, U. (2019). Equity in education outcomes and spending in Bangladesh: Evidence from household income and expenditure surveys. *Bangladesh Development Studies, 42*(2/3), 217–262. https://www.jstor.org/stable/27031112

Gentile, D. A., Anderson, C. A., Yukawa, S., Ihori, N., Saleem, M., Lim, K. M., Shibuya, A., Liau, A. K., Khoo, A., Bushman, B. J., Huesmann, L. R., & Sakamoto, A. (2009). The effects of prosocial video games on prosocial behaviors: International evidence from correlational, longitudinal, and experimental studies. *Personality and Social Psychology Bulletin, 35*(6), 752–763. doi:10.1177/0146167209333045 PMID:19321812

Gentry, J., & McAdams, L. (2013). Digital Story Expressions: Blending Best Practices in Literacy and Technology with Middle School Students. In *Proceedings of Society for Information Technology and Teacher Education International Conference* (pp.4253-4257). Chesepake, VA: AACE. http://www.editlib.org/p/48794

Geo-politics and international power. (2017). *European Parliamentary Research Service European Parliament.* https://www.europarl.europa.eu/RegData/etudes/STUD/2017/603263/EPRS_STU(2017)603263_EN.pdf

Georgiou, G. K., Hirvonen, R., Liao, C.-H., Manolitsis, G., Parrila, R., & Nurmi, J.-E. (2011). The role of achievement strategies on literacy acquisition across languages. *Contemporary Educational Psychology, 36*(2), 130–141. doi:10.1016/j.cedpsych.2011.01.001

Gerber, H. R. (2012). *Can education be gamified? Examining gamification, education, and the future.* Charles Town, WV: White paper for the American Public University System (APUS).

Gerber, H. R., Abrams, S. S., Onwuegbuzie, A. J., & Benge, C. L. (2014). From Mario to FIFA: What qualitative case study research suggests about games-based learning in a US classroom. *Educational Media International, 51*(1), 16–34. doi:10.1080/09523987.2014.889402

Gerber, H. R., & Price, D. P. (2013). Fighting baddies and collecting bananas: Teachers' perceptions of games-based literacy learning. *Educational Media International, 50*(1), 51–62. doi:10.1080/09523987.2013.777182

Geroimenko, V. (2019). Concluding Remarks: From Pokémon GO to Serious Augmented Reality Games. *Augmented Reality Games, 2*, 305.

Ghavifekr, S., Razak, A. Z., Ghani, M. F., Ran, N. Y., Meixi, Y., & Tengyue, Z. (2014). ICT integration in education: Incorporation for teaching & learning improvement. *Malaysian Online Journal of Educational Technology, 2*(2), 24–45.

Ghetti, S., & Bunge, S. A. (2012). Neural changes underlying the development of episodic memory during middle childhood. *Developmental Cognitive Neuroscience, 2*(4), 381–395. doi:10.1016/j.dcn.2012.05.002 PMID:22770728

Giddens, A. (1991). *Modernity and self-identity: Self and society in the late modern age.* Stanford University Press.

Giddings, J., & Weinberg, J. (2020). Experiential Legal Education. Stepping Back to See the Future. In C. Denvir (Ed.), *Modernizing Legal Education* (pp. 38–56). Cambridge University Press. doi:10.1017/9781108663311.004

Gilbert, N. (2020). *Number of gamers worldwide: Demographics, statistics, and predictions*. Finances Online. Retrieved 9/14/21 from https://financesonline.com/number-of-gamers-worldwide/

Gilbert, A., Tait-MCutcheon, S., & Knewstubb, B. (2021). Innovative teaching in higher education: Teachers' perceptions of support and constraint. *Innovations in Education and Teaching International*, *58*(2), 123–134. doi:10.1080/14703297.2020.1715816

Gilboy, M. B., Heinerichs, S., & Pazzaglia, G. (2015). Enhancing student engagement using the flipped classroom. *Journal of Nutrition Education and Behavior*, *47*(1), 109–114. doi:10.1016/j.jneb.2014.08.008 PMID:25262529

Gillispie, L., Martin, F., & Parker, M. (2009). Effects of the Dimension-M 3D Video Gaming Experience on Middle School Student Achievement and Attitude in Mathematics. In *Society for Information Technology & Teacher Education International Conference*. Society for Information Technology & Teacher Education.

Gills, A. S. (2020). *Definition: Digital native*. Teach Target. https://whatis.techtarget.com/definition/digital-native

Gingerich, J. (2012). The *spiraling narrative*. Litreactor LLC. https://litreactor.com/columns/the-spiraling-theme

Giordano, V. A. (2007). A professional development model to promote Internet integration into p-12 teachers' practice: A mixed methods study. *Computers in the Schools*, *24*(3–4), 111–123. doi:10.1300/J025v24n03_08

Giovetti, O. (2020). *How does education affect poverty? It can help end it*. Concern Worldwide. https://www.concernusa.org/story/how-education-affects-poverty/

Girl, R. (2017, February 14). *How to play Love Letter in 3 minutes* [Video]. YouTube. https://www.youtube.com/watch?v=WAiI7G3QdOU

Glock, C. Y., & Stark, R. (1965). *Religion and Society in Tension, Rand McNally Sociology Series*. Rand McNally & Company.

Glock, S., & Kleen, H. (2020). Preservice teachers' attitudes, attributions, and stereotypes: Exploring the disadvantages of students from families with low socioeconomic status. *Studies in Educational Evaluation*, *67*(October), 1–9. doi:10.1016/j.stueduc.2020.100929

Glover, I. (2013). Play As You Learn: Gamification as a Technique for Motivating Learners. *Proceedings of World Conference on Educational Multimedia, Hypermedia and Telemcommunications*, 1999–2008. http://shura.shu.ac.uk/7172/

Glover, I. (2013). Play as you learn: Gamification as a technique for motivating learners. In *Proceedings of World Conference on Educational Multimedia, Hypermedia and Telecommunications*. AACE.

Goffman, E. (1974). *Frame analysis: An essay on the organization of experience*. Harper & Row.

Gomes, C., Pereira, A., & Nobre, A. (2018). *Gamificação no ensino superior online: dois exemplos. LE@D - Laboratório de Educação a Distância e Elearning*. Universidade Aberta.

Gómez-Gonzalvo, F., Molina Alventosa, P., & Devis, J. (2018). Los videojuegos como materiales curriculares: una aproximación a su uso en Educación Física / Video games as curriculum materials: an approach to their use in Physical Education. *Retos*, *34*(34), 305–310. doi:10.47197/retos.v0i34.63440

González, C. S., & Mora, A. (2014). Methodological proposal for Gamification in the computer engineering teaching. *Proceeding Computers in Education (SIIE), 2014 International Symposium on*, 29-34. 10.1109/SIIE.2014.7017700

González-González, C., & Blanco-Izquierdo, F. (2012). Designing social video-games for educational uses. *Computers & Education*, *58*(1), 250–262. doi:10.1016/j.compedu.2011.08.014

Gonzalez, L., & Kardong-Edgren, S. (2017). Deliberate Practice for Mastery Learning in Nursing. *Clinical Simulation in Nursing*, *13*(1), 10–14. doi:10.1016/j.ecns.2016.10.005

Gonzalo-Iglesia, J. L., Lozano-Monterrubio, N., & Prades-Tena, J. (2018). Non Educational board games in university education. Perceptions of students experiencing game-based learning methodologies. *Revista Lusófona de Educação*, *41*(41), 45–62. doi:10.24140/issn.1645-7250.rle41.03

Gooch, D., Vasalou, A., & Benton, L. (2015). Exploring the use of a Gamification Platform to Support Students with Dyslexia. In *Information, Intelligence, Systems and Applications (IISA), 2015, 6th International Conference on* (pp. 1-6). IEEE. 10.1109/IISA.2015.7388001

Gooch, D., Vasalou, A., Benton, L., & Khaled, R. (2016). *Using Gamification to motivate students with dyslexia.* doi:10.1145/2858036.2858231

Goodman, S. (2003). *Teaching youth media: A critical guide to literacy, video production, and social change.* Teachers College Press.

Goodson, M. (1976). *Family Feud* [Game Show Series]. ABC.

Goosen, L. (2018a). Sustainable and Inclusive Quality Education Through Research Informed Practice on Information and Communication Technologies in Education. In L. Webb (Ed.), *Proceedings of the 26th Conference of the Southern African Association for Research in Mathematics, Science and Technology Education (SAARMSTE)* (pp. 215 - 228). Gabarone: University of Botswana.

Goosen, L. (2019c). Information Systems and Technologies Opening New Worlds for Learning to Children with Autism Spectrum Disorders. Smart Innovation, Systems and Technologies, 111, 134-143. doi:10.1007/978-3-030-03577-8_16

Goosen, L. (2019d). Innovative Technologies and Learning in a Massive Open Online Course. In L. Rønningsbakk, T.-T. Wu, F. E. Sandnes, & Y.-M. Huang (Eds.), Lecture Notes in Computer Science (Vol. 11937, pp. 653–662). Springer. doi:10.1007/978-3-030-35343-8_69

Goosen, L., & Van der Merwe, R. (2015). e-Learners, Teachers and Managers at e-Schools in South Africa. In C. Watson (Ed.), *Proceedings of the 10th International Conference on e-Learning (ICEL)* (pp. 127 - 134). Nassau: Academic Conferences and Publishing International.

Goosen, L., & Van der Merwe, R. (2017). Keeping ICT in Education Community Engagement Relevant: Infinite Possibilities? Communications in Computer and Information Science, 730, 113 - 127. doi:10.1007/978-3-319-69670-6_8

Goosen, L., & Van Heerden, D. (2013). Project-Based Assessment Influencing Pass Rates of an ICT Module at an ODL Institution. In E. Ivala (Ed.), *Proceedings of the 8th International Conference on e-Learning*. Academic Conferences and Publishing.

Goosen, L., & Van Heerden, D. (2017). Beyond the Horizon of Learning Programming with Educational Technologies. In U. I. Ogbonnaya, & S. Simelane-Mnisi (Ed.), *Proceedings of the South Africa International Conference on Educational Technologies* (pp. 78 - 90). Pretoria: African Academic Research Forum.

Goosen, L. (2008). A Brief History of Choosing First Programming Languages. In J. Impagliazzo (Ed.), *History of Computing and Education 3* (Vol. 269, pp. 167–170). Springer. doi:10.1007/978-0-387-09657-5_11

Goosen, L. (2018b). Trans-Disciplinary Approaches to Action Research for e-Schools, Community Engagement, and ICT4D. In T. A. Mapotse (Ed.), *Cross-Disciplinary Approaches to Action Research and Action Learning* (pp. 97–110). IGI Global. doi:10.4018/978-1-5225-2642-1.ch006

Goosen, L. (2018c). Ethical Data Management and Research Integrity in the Context of e-Schools and Community Engagement. In C. Sibinga (Ed.), *Ensuring Research Integrity and the Ethical Management of Data* (pp. 14–45). IGI Global. doi:10.4018/978-1-5225-2730-5.ch002

Goosen, L. (2018d). Ethical Information and Communication Technologies for Development Solutions: Research Integrity for Massive Open Online Courses. In C. Sibinga (Ed.), *Ensuring Research Integrity and the Ethical Management of Data* (pp. 155–173). IGI Global. doi:10.4018/978-1-5225-2730-5.ch009

Goosen, L. (2019a). Research on Technology-Supported Teaching and Learning for Autism. In L. Makewa, B. Ngussa, & J. Kuboja (Eds.), *Technology-Supported Teaching and Research Methods for Educators* (pp. 88–110). IGI Global. doi:10.4018/978-1-5225-5915-3.ch005

Goosen, L. (2019b). Technology-Supported Teaching and Research Methods for Educators: Case Study of a Massive Open Online Course. In L. Makewa, B. Ngussa, & J. Kuboja (Eds.), *Technology-Supported Teaching and Research Methods for Educators* (pp. 128–148). IGI Global. doi:10.4018/978-1-5225-5915-3.ch007

Goosen, L. (2022). Assistive Technologies for Children and Adolescents With Autism Spectrum Disorders. In F. Stasolla (Ed.), *Assistive Technologies for Assessment and Recovery of Neurological Impairments* (pp. 1–24). IGI Global. doi:10.4018/978-1-7998-7430-0.ch001

Goosen, L., Mentz, E., & Nieuwoudt, H. (2007). Choosing the "Best" Programming Language?! In E. Cohen (Ed.), *Proceedings of the 2007 Computer Science and IT Education Conference* (pp. 269-282). Informing Science Press.

Goradia, T. (2018). Role of educational technologies utilizing the TPACK framework and 21st century pedagogies: Academics' perspectives. *IAFOR Journal of Education, 6*(3), 43–61. doi:10.22492/ije.6.3.03

Gorbanev, I., Agudelo-Londoño, S., González, R. A., Cortes, A., Pomares, A., Delgadillo, V., Yepes, F. J., & Muñoz, Ó. (2018). A systematic review of serious games in medical education: Quality of evidence and pedagogical strategy. *Medical Education Online, 23*(1), 1438718. doi:10.1080/10872981.2018.1438718 PMID:29457760

Gordon, G., Spaulding, S., Westlund, J. K., Lee, J. J., Plummer, L., Martinez, M., . . . Breazeal, C. (2016, March). Affective personalization of a social robot tutor for children's second language skills. In *Proceedings of the AAAI conference on artificial intelligence* (Vol. 30, No. 1). https://ojs.aaai.org/index.php/AAAI/article/view/9914

Gough, C. (2019, August 9). *Number of active players of Minecraft worldwide as of October 2018 (in millions)*. Retrieved from https://www.statista.com/statistics/680139/minecraft-active-players-worldwide/

Gouveia, P. (2010). Artes e Jogos Digitais, Estética e Design da Experiência Lúdica. Universitárias Lusófonas.

Gouveia, P. (2014). A possible narration about Portuguese videogames creation. Critical book review: *Videogames in Portugal: History, Technology and Art*, Nelson Zagalo, 2013. *Aniki, Portuguese Journal of the Moving Image, 1*(2), 369-74. doi:10.14591/aniki.v1n2.69

Gouveia, P. (2015). Serious gaming: how gamers are solving real world problems. In *Proceedings of Artech 2015, Seventh International Conference on Digital Arts (Creating Digital e-motions)*. Óbidos

Gouveia, P. (2018). Transmedia experiences that blur the boundaries between the real and the fictional world. In Trends, Experiences, and Perspectives on Immersive Multimedia Experience and Augmented Reality. IGI Global.

Gouveia, P. (2020). The New Media vs. Old Media Trap: How Contemporary Arts Became Playful Transmedia Environments. In Multidisciplinary Perspectives on New Media Art. IGI Global. doi:10.4018/978-1-7998-3669-8.ch002

Gouveia, P., Lima, L., Unterholzner, A., & Carvalho, D. (2021). *O mundo expandido das imagens invisíveis.* Instituto de Estudos Filosóficos, Faculdade de Letras da Universidade de Coimbra.

Gozcu, E., & Caganaga, C. K. (2016). The importance of using games in EFL classrooms. *Cypriot Journal of Educational Sciences, 11*(3), 126–135. doi:10.18844/cjes.v11i3.625

Graber, D., & Mendoza, K. (2012). New Media Literacy Education: A Developmental Approach The national association for media literacy education. *The Journal of Media Literacy Education, 4*(1), 82–92.

Graddol, D. (2006). *English next.* British Council Publications.

Grafstein, A. (2002). A discipline-based approach to information literacy. *Journal of Academic Librarianship, 28*(4), 197–204. doi:10.1016/S0099-1333(02)00283-5

Gray, P. (2013). Free to Learn: Why Unleashing the Instinct to Play Will Make Our Children Happier. *More Self-Reliant, and Better Students for Life, 141.*

Gray, K. L. (2020). *Intersectional Tech, Black Users in Digital Gaming.* Louisiana State University Press.

Greco, A., & Morris, T. (2002). Parental child-rearing style and child social anxiety: Investigation of child perceptions and actual father behavior. *Journal of Psychopathology and Behavioral Assessment, 24*(4), 259–267. doi:10.1023/A:1020779000183

Greene, M. (1995). *Releasing the imagination: Essays on education, the arts, and social change.* Jossey-Bass. doi:10.1080/14452294.2011.11649524

Greene, M. (2001). *Variations on a blue guitar: The Lincoln Centre Institute lectures on aesthetic education.* Teachers College Press.

Greenfield, P. M. (1994). Video games as cultural artefacts. *Journal of Applied Developmental Psychology, 15*(1), 3–12. doi:10.1016/0193-3973(94)90003-5

Greenfield, P. M., Camaioni, L., Ercolani, P., Weiss, L., Lauber, B. A., & Perucchini, P. (1994). Cognitive socialization by computer games in two cultures: Inductive discovery or mastery of an iconic code. *Journal of Applied Developmental Psychology, 15*(1), 59–85. doi:10.1016/0193-3973(94)90006-X

Greipl, S., Klein, E., Lindstedt, A., Kiili, K., Moeller, K., Karnath, H. O., & Ninaus, M. (2021). When the brain comes into play: Neurofunctional correlates of emotions and reward in game-based learning. *Computers in Human Behavior, 125*, 106946. doi:10.1016/j.chb.2021.106946

Greipl, S., Moeller, K., & Ninaus, M. (2020). Potential and limits of game-based learning. *International Journal of Technology Enhanced Learning, 12*(4), 363–389. doi:10.1504/IJTEL.2020.110047

Greitemeyer, T., & Osswald, S. (2009). Prosocial video games reduce aggressive cognitions. *Journal of Experimental Social Psychology, 45*(4), 896–900. doi:10.1016/j.jesp.2009.04.005

Greitemeyer, T., & Osswald, S. (2010). Effects of prosocial video games on prosocial behavior. *Journal of Personality and Social Psychology, 98*(2), 211–221. doi:10.1037/a0016997 PMID:20085396

Griffin, M. (1964). *Jeopardy!* [Game Show Series]. NBC.

Griffith, J. (2014). *Teaching Literacy in the Digital Age: İnspiration For All Levels And Literacies* (M. Gura, Ed.). İnternational Society for Technology in Education.

Griffiths, M. D. (2002). The educational benefits of videogames. *Education for Health, 20*(3), 47–51.

Gros, B. (2010). Game-based learning: A strategy to integrate digital games in schools. In J. Yamamoto, J. Kush, R. Lombard, & C. Hertzog (Eds.), Technology Implementation and Teacher Education: Reflective Models (pp. 365-379). doi:10.4018/978-1-61520-897-5.ch021

Gros, B. (2007). Digital games in education: The design of games-based learning environments. *Journal of Research on Technology in Education, 40*(1), 23–38. doi:10.1080/15391523.2007.10782494

Group, N. P. D. (2020, December 7). *Evolution of entertainment: Spotlight on video games* [Video]. YouTube. https://youtu.be/lrPiK506umQ

Grove, F. De, Cornillie, F., Mechant, P., & Looy, J. Van. (2013). *Tapping into the Field of Foreign Language Learning Games. April 2014.* doi:10.1504/IJART.2013.050690

Grover, S., & Pea, R. (2017). Computational Thinking: A Competency Whose Time Has Come. Computer science education: Perspectives on teaching and learning in school, 19.

Growth Engineering. (2021). *Growth Engineering.* Retrieved from https://www.growthengineering.co.uk/how-to-use-the-octalysis-framework-for-your-gamified-training-programme/

Grubic, N., Badovinac, S., & Johri, A. M. (2020). Student mental health in the midst of the COVID-19 pandemic: A call for further research and immediate solutions. *The International Journal of Social Psychiatry, 66*(5), 517–518. doi:10.1177/0020764020925108 PMID:32364039

Grussendorf, S. (2021). *Game-based Learning.* Retrieved from https://lse.atlassian.net/wiki/spaces/MG2/pages/1427144719/Game-based+learning#Benefits

Guigon, G., Humeau, J., & Vermeulen, M. (2018). A model to design learning escape games: SEGAM. *CSEDU 2018 - Proceedings of the 10th International Conference on Computer Supported Education, 2*(March), 191–197. 10.5220/0006665501910197

Guillemin, M., & Gillam, L. (2010). Ethics, reflexivity, and "ethically important moments" in research. *Qualitative Inquiry, 10*(2), 261–280. doi:10.1177/1077800403262360

Gui, M. (2007). Formal and substantial Internet information skills: The role of socio-demographic differences on the possession of different components of digital literacy. *First Monday, 12*(9). Advance online publication. doi:10.5210/fm.v12i9.2009

Gumulak, S., & Webber, S. (2011). Playing video games: Learning and information literacy. In *Aslib Proceedings.* Emerald Group Publishing Limited. doi:10.1108/00012531111135682

Gündüz, A. Y., & Akkoyunlu, B. (2020). Effectiveness of Gamification in Flipped Learning. *SAGE Open, 10*(4). doi:10.1177/2158244020979837

Güngör, N. (2018). İletişim Kuram ve Yaklaşımlar. Ankara: Siyasal Kitabevi.

Gunter, G. A., Kenny, R. F., & Vick, E. H. (2008). Taking educational games seriously: Using the RETAIN model to design endogeneous fantasy into standalone educational games. *Educational Technology Research and Development, 56*(5-6), 511–537. doi:10.100711423-007-9073-2

Gupta, M., & Boyd, L. (2011). An Excel-based dice game: An integrative learning activity in operations management. *International Journal of Operations & Production Management*, *31*(6), 608–630. doi:10.1108/01443571111131962

Gurian, M., & Stevens, K. (2010a). *Boys and girls learn differently! A guide for teachers and parents*. Jossey-Bass.

Gurian, M., & Stevens, K. (2010b). *The minds of boys: Saving our sons from falling behind in school and life*. Jossey-Bass.

Guthrie, J. T., & Knowles, K. T. (2001). Promoting reading motivation. In L. Verhoeven & C. Snow (Eds.), *Literacy and motivation* (pp. 159–176). Erlbaum.

Guyton, G. (2011). Using Toys to Support Infant-Toddler Learning and Development. *Young Children*, *66*, 50.

Habershon, N. (1993). Metaplan (R): Achieving Two-way Communications. *Journal of European Industrial Training*, *17*(7). doi:10.1108/03090599310042528

Habgood, M. P. J., & Ainsworth, S. E. (2011). Motivating children to learn effectively: Exploring the value of intrinsic integration in educational games. *Journal of the Learning Sciences*, *20*(2), 169–206. doi:10.1080/10508406.2010.508029

Hackbarth, G., Grover, V., & Yi Mun, Y. (2003). Computer playfulness and anxiety: Positive and negative mediators of the system experience effect on perceived ease of use. *Information & Management*, *40*(3), 221–232. doi:10.1016/S0378-7206(02)00006-X

Hainey, T., Connolly, T. M., Stansfield, M., & Boyle, E. A. (2011). Evaluation of a Game to Teach Requirements Collection and Analysis in Software Engineering at Tertiary Education Level. *Computers & Education*, *56*(1), 21–35. doi:10.1016/j.compedu.2010.09.008

Haktanir, A., Watson, J. C., Ermis-Demirtas, H., Karaman, M. A., Freeman, P. D., Kumaran, A., & Streeter, A. (2018). Resilience, academic self-concept, and college adjustment among first-year students. *Journal of College Student Retention*, *38*, 286–297. doi:10.1177/1521025118810666

Hales, A. (2012*). Using Systematic and Engaging Early Literacy instruction and digital books to teach at-risk kindergarteners to read target words* [Unpublished master's thesis]. Brigham Young University, Provo, UT, United States.

Halfaker, A., Kittur, A., & Riedl, J. (2011). Don't bite the newbies: How reverts affect the quantity and quality of Wikipedia work. *Proceedings of the 7th International Symposium on Wikis and Open Collaboration - WikiSym '11*, 163. 10.1145/2038558.2038585

Halim, A., & Syukri, M. (2020). Integration of Problem Based Learning (PBL) and Engineering is Elementary (EiE) to improve students' creativity. *Journal of Physics: Conference Series*, *1460*(1), 012117.

Halinen, I. (2018). The new educational curriculum in Finland. In M. Matthes, L. Pulkkinen, C. Clouder, & B. Heys (Eds.), *Improving the quality of childhood in Europe* (Vol. 7, pp. 75–89). Alliance for Childhood European Network Foundation. https://www.allianceforchildhood.eu/files/Improving_the_quality_of_Childhood_Vol_7/QOC%20V7%20CH06%20DEF%20WEB.pdf

Hall, D., & Ames, R. (1987). *Thinking through Confucius. SUNY Series in Systematic Philosophy*. State University of New York Press.

Halliday, M., & Halliday, M. (1973). *Explorations in the functions of language*. Edward Arnold.

Hallifax, S., Serna, A., Marty, J. C., & Lavou, E. (2019). Adaptive gamification in education: A literature review of current trends and developments. *European Conference on Technology Enhanced Learning (EC-TEL)*, 294-307. 10.1007/978-3-030-29736-7_22

Hallinen, N., Walker, E., Wylie, R., Ogan, A., & Jones, C. (2009). I Was Playing When I Learned: A Narrative Game for French Aspectual Distinctions. *Proc. Workshop Intelligent Educational Games at the 14th Int'l Conf. Artificial Intelligence in Education*, 117-120.

Hall, S., & Gay, P. (1996). *Questions of cultural identity*. Sage.

Hall, T. E., Hughes, C. A., & Filbert, M. (2000). Computer assisted instruction in reading for students with learning disabilities: A research synthesis. *Education & Treatment of Children*, *23*(2), 173–193. http://eric.ed.gov.ezp-prod1.hul.harvard.edu/ERICWebPortal/search/detailmini.jsp?_nfpb=true&_&ERICExtSearch_SearchValue_0=EJ611303&ERICExtSearch_SearchType_0=no&accno=EJ611303

Halvorsen, A. (2018). *21st Century Skills and the "4Cs" in the English Language Classroom*, University of Oregon. https://creativecommons.org/licenses/by/4.0/

Hamann, S. (2001). Cognitive and neural mechanisms of emotional memory. *Trends in Cognitive Sciences*, *5*(9), 394–400. doi:10.1016/S1364-6613(00)01707-1 PMID:11520704

Hamari, J. (2019). Gamification. *The Blackwell encyclopedia of sociology*, 1–3.

Hamari, J., Koivisto, J., & Sarsa, H. (2014). Does gamification work? A literature review of empirical studies on gamification. *2014 47th Hawaii International Conference on System Sciences*, 3025-3034. 10.1109/HICSS.2014.377

Hamari, J., Koivisto, J., & Sarsa, H. (2014, January). Does gamification work? - A literature review of empirical studies on gamification. In *2014 47th Hawaii International Conference on System Sciences* (pp. 3025–3034). New York: IEEE.

Hamari, J., & Nousiainen, T. (2015). Why Do Teachers Use Game-Based Learning Technologies? The Role of Individual and Institutional ICT Readiness. *Hawaii International Conference on System Sciences*. 10.1109/HICSS.2015.88

Hamari, J., Shernoff, D. J., Rowe, E., Coller, B., Asbell-Clarke, J., & Edwards, T. (2016). Challenging games help students learn: An empirical study on engagement, flow and immersion in game-based learning. *Computers in Human Behavior*, *54*, 170–179. doi:10.1016/j.chb.2015.07.045

Hamburger, Y., & Ben-Artzi, E. (2003). Loneliness and Internet use. *Computers in Human Behavior*, *19*(1), 71–80. doi:10.1016/S0747-5632(02)00014-6

Hammerschall, U. (2019). A Gamification Framework for Long-Term Engagement in Education Based on Self Determination Theory and the Transtheoretical Model of Change. In *2019 IEEE Global Engineering Education Conference (EDUCON)* (pp. 95-101). IEEE. 10.1109/EDUCON.2019.8725251

Hamm, J. M., Perry, R. P., Chipperfield, J. G., Parker, P. C., & Heckhausen, J. (2019). A motivation treatment to enhance goal engagement in online learning environments: Assisting failure-prone college students with low optimism. *Motivation Science*, *5*(2), 116–134. doi:10.1037/mot0000107

Hammond, M., & Ross, M. (2014). *The Student Guide to Mooting*. Edinburgh University Press.

Hamzah, W. M., Ali, N., Saman, M., Yusoff, M. H., & Yacob, A. (2015). Influence of Gamification on Students' Motivation in using E-Learning Applications Based on the Motivational Design Model. *International Journal of Emerging Technologies in Learning*, *10*(2), 30–34. doi:10.3991/ijet.v10i2.4355

Hanbidge, A. S., Tin, T., & Sanderson, N. (2018). Information Literacy Skills on the Go: Mobile Learning Innovation. *Journal of Information Literacy*, *12*(1).

Hancock, D., Sirizzotti, M. S., Joe, R., & Martin, R. J. (2019). *Methods and systems for gamification*. U.S. Patent Application No. 15/466,379.

Hanghøj, T., Nielsen, B. L., Skott, C. K., & Ejsing-Duun, S. (2020). Teacher agency and dialogical positions in relation to game-based design activities. *Proceedings of the European Conference on Games-Based Learning*, 234–241. 10.34190/GBL.20.033

Hanse-Himarwa, K. (2015). *State of Education*. Arts and Culture Address.

Hantzopoulos, M., Rivera-McCutchen, R. L., & Tyner-Mullings, A. R. (2021). Reframing School Culture Through Project-Based Assessment Tasks: Cultivating Transformative Agency and Humanizing Practices in NYC Public Schools. *Teachers College Record*, 123(4), 1–38. doi:10.1177/016146812112300404

Hanus, M. D., & Fox, J. (2015). Assessing the effects of Gamification in the Classroom: A longitudinal study on intrinsic motivation, social comparison, satisfaction, effort, and academic performance. *Computers & Education*, 80, 152–161. doi:10.1016/j.compedu.2014.08.019

Happ, C., Melzer, A., & Steffgen, G. (2014). Like the good or bad guy—Empathy in antisocial and prosocial games. *Psychology of Popular Media Culture*, 4(2), 80–96. doi:10.1037/ppm0000021

Haque, M. S., & Akter, T. (2013). Cultural imperialism in English medium schools: A critical insight. *Stamford Journal of English*, 7, 98–128. doi:10.3329je.v7i0.14468

Harada, V. H., & Yoshina, J. M. (2004). *Inquiry learning through librarian-teacher partnerships*. Linworth Publishing.

Hardy, C., & Tolhurst, D. (2014). Epistemological beliefs and cultural diversity matters in management education and learning: A critical review and future directions. *Academy of Management Learning & Education*, 13(2), 265–289. doi:10.5465/amle.2012.0063

Harel, I. E., & Papert, S. E. (1991). *Constructionism*. Ablex Publishing.

Harman, K., Koohang, A., & Paliszkiewicz, J. (2014). Scholarly interest in gamification: A citation network analysis. *Industrial Management & Data Systems*, 114(9), 1438–1452. doi:10.1108/IMDS-07-2014-0208

Harmer, N. (2014). *Project-based learning. Literature review. School of Geography, Earth and Environmental Sciences*. Plymouth University.

Harrop, M., Gibbs, M., & Carter, M. (2013). The pretence awareness contexts and oscillating nature of coaching frames. *Proceedings of DiGRA 2013 Conference: DeFragging Game Studies*.

Hart, A. (2013). *Kindergarteners' incidental learning of words during exposure to systematic and engaging early literacy instruction and digital books* [Unpublished honors thesis]. Brigham Young University, Provo, UT, United States.

Harteveld, C., Smith, G., Carmichael, G., Gee, E., & Stewart-Gardiner, C. (2013). A design- focused analysis of games that teach computer science. *Journal of Computing Sciences in Colleges*, 28(6), 90–97.

Hartman, V. (1995). Teaching and learning style preferences: Transitions through technology. *VCCA Journal*, 9(2), 18–20.

Hartshorne, J. K., & Germine, L. T. (2015). When does cognitive functioning peak. *The asynchronous rise and fall of different cognitive abilities across the life span*, 26, 433-443.

Hartt, M., Hosseini, H., & Mostafapour, M. (2020). Game On: Exploring the Effectiveness of Game-based Learning. *Planning Practice and Research*, 35(5), 589–604. doi:10.1080/02697459.2020.1778859

Harvey, M. M. (2018). *Video games and virtual reality as classroom literature: Thoughts, experiences, and learning with 8th grade middle school students* (Doctoral dissertation). https://digitalrepository.unm.edu/educ_llss_etds/90/

Harvey, M. M., & Marlatt, R. (2020). That was then, this is now: Literacies for the 21st Century classroom. In E. Podovšovnik (Ed.), *Examining the roles of teachers and students in mastering new technologies* (pp. 164–183). IGI Global. doi:10.4018/978-1-7998-2104-5.ch008

Hasana, S. N., & Alifiani, A. (2019). Multimedia development using visual basic for application (VBA) to improve students' learning motivation in studying mathematics of economics. *Indonesian Journal of Mathematics Education, 2*(1), 34–42. doi:10.31002/ijome.v2i1.1230

Hasan, K., Islam, M. S., Shams, A. T., & Gupta, H. (2018). Total quality management (TQM): Implementation in primary education system of Bangladesh. *International Journal of Research in Industrial Engineering, 7*(3), 370–380. doi:10.22105/RIEJ.2018.128170.1041

Hassan, L., Dias, A., & Hamari, J. (2019). How motivational feedback increases user's benefits and continued use: A study on Gamification, quantified-self and social networking. *International Journal of Information Management, 46*, 151–162. doi:10.1016/j.ijinfomgt.2018.12.004

Hassan, M. A., Habiba, U., Majeed, F., & Shoaib, M. (2021). Adaptive gamification in e-learning based on students' learning styles. *Interactive Learning Environments, 29*(4), 545–565. doi:10.1080/10494820.2019.1588745

Hattie, J. (2009). *Visible learning: A synthesis of over 800 meta-analyses relating to achievement*. Routledge.

Hattie, J. A. C. (2008). *Visible Learning: A synthesis of over 800 meta-analyses relating to achievement*. Routledge. doi:10.4324/9780203887332

Hawley, P. H. (2014). Evolution, prosocial behavior, and altruism: A roadmap for understanding where the proximate meets the ultimate. In L. M. Padilla-Walker & G. Carlo (Eds.), *Prosocial development: A multidimensional approach* (pp. 43–69). Oxford University Press. doi:10.1093/acprof:oso/9780199964772.003.0003

Hayak, M., & Avidov-Ungar, O. (2020). The Integration of Digital Game-Based Learning into the Instruction: Teachers' Perceptions at Different Career Stages. *TechTrends, 64*(6), 887–898. doi:10.100711528-020-00503-6

Hayes, E. (2008). Girls, gaming and trajectories of IT expertise. In Beyond Barbie and Mortal Kombat: New perspectives on gender and computer games (pp.138-194). Cambridge MA: The MIT Press.

Hayes, E. R., & Games, I. A. (2008). Making computer games and design thinking: A review of current software and strategies. *Games and Culture, 3*(3-4), 309–332. doi:10.1177/1555412008317312

Hayes, E. R., & Gee, J. P. (2010). No selling the genie lamp: A game literacy practice in The Sims. *E-Learning and Digital Media, 7*(1), 67–78. doi:10.2304/elea.2010.7.1.67

Hebert, C., & Jenson, J. (2019). Digital game-based pedagogies: Developing teaching strategies for game-based learning. *Journal of Interactive Technology and Pedagogy, 15*.

Hébert, C., Jenson, J., & Terzopoulos, T. (2021). Access to technology is the major challenge: Teacher perspectives on barriers to DGBL in K-12 classrooms. *E-Learning and Digital Media, 18*(3), 307–324. doi:10.1177/2042753021995315

Heeter, C. (1992). Being there: The subjective experience of presence. *Presence (Cambridge, Mass.), 1*(2), 262–271. doi:10.1162/pres.1992.1.2.262

Heinich, R., Molenda, M., Russell, J. D., & Smaldino, S. E. (2002). *Instructional media and technologies for learning*. Merrill Prentice Hall.

Heintz, S., & Law, E. L. C. (2018). Digital educational games: Methodologies for evaluating the impact of game type. *ACM Transactions on Computer-Human Interaction, 25*(2), 1–47. doi:10.1145/3177881

Hellerstedt, A., & Mozelius, P. (2019). *Game-based learning - a long history*. https://www.researchgate.net/publication/336460471_Game-based_learning_-_a_long_history

Hennessy, S., Harrison, D., & Wamakote, L. (2010). Teacher Factors Influencing Classroom Use of ICT in Sub-Saharan Africa. *Itupale Online Journal of African Studies, 2*(1), 39–54.

Hergenrader, T. (2018). *Collaborative Worldbuilding for Writers and Gamers*. Bloomsbury Publishing.

Herman, K. C., Prewett, S. L., Eddy, C. L., Savala, A., & Reinke, W. M. (2020). Profiles of middle school teacher stress and coping: Concurrent and prospective correlates. *Journal of School Psychology, 78*, 54–68. doi:10.1016/j.jsp.2019.11.003 PMID:32178811

Herman, S. W. (2015). Spirituality, Inc.: Religion in the American Workplace, by Lake Lambert III. New York: New York University Press, 2009. *Business Ethics Quarterly, 21*(3), 533–537. doi:10.5840/beq201121330

Herodotou, C. (2018). Mobile games and science learning: A comparative study of 4 and 5 years old playing the game Angry Birds. *British Journal of Educational Technology, 49*(1), 6–16. doi:10.1111/bjet.12546

Herodotou, C., Sharples, M., Gaved, M., Kukulska-Hulme, A., Rienties, B., Scanlon, E., & Whitelock, D. (2019, October). Innovative pedagogies of the future: An evidence-based selection. In *Frontiers in Education* (Vol. 4, p. 113). Frontiers. doi:10.3389/feduc.2019.00113

Heron, J., & Reason, P. (2006). The practice of co-operative inquiry: Research 'with'rather than 'on'people. In P. Reason & H. Bradbury (Eds.), *Handbook of action research: Participative inquiry and pratice*. Sage.

Herro, D. C., Lin, L., & Fowler, M. (2017). Meet the (Media) Producers: Artists, Composers, and Gamemakers. *Journal of Applied Research in Higher Education, 9*(1), 40–53. doi:10.1108/JARHE-04-2015-0029

Herzig, P., Strahringer, S., & Ameling, M. (2012). Gamification of ERP systems -Exploring gamification effects on user acceptance constructs. In *Multikonferenz Wirtschaftsinformatik* (pp. 793–804). GITO.

Hess, T., & Gunter, G. (2013). Serious game-based and nongame-based online courses: Learning experiences and outcomes. *British Journal of Educational Technology, 44*(3), 372–385. doi:10.1111/bjet.12024

Hewett, K. J. E. (2014). Jump in! A teacher's journey into Minecraft. *TechEdge Magazine, 2*, 14–17.

Hewett, K., Zeng, G., & Pletcher, B. (2020). The Acquisition of 21 st Century Skills Through Video Games: Minecraft Design Process Models and Their Web of Class Roles. *Simulation & Gaming, 51*(3). doi:10.1177/1046878120904976

Hickey, D., Goble, A. I., & Jameson, E. (2012). Designing Assessments and Assessing Designs in Virtual Educational Environments. *Journal of Science Education and Technology, 18*(2), 187–208. doi:10.100710956-008-9143-1

Higgins, S. (2014). Critical thinking for 21st century education: A cyber-tooth curriculum? *Prospects, 44*(4), 559–574. doi:10.100711125-014-9323-0

Hilton, M. (2015). Preparing students for life and work. *Issues in Science and Technology, 31*(4), 63.

Hinduja, S., & Patchin, J. (2009). *Bullying beyond the schoolyard: Preventing and responding to cyberbullying*. Corwin Press.

Hinebaugh, J. P. (2009). *A board game education*. R&L Education.

Hirsh-Pasek, K., Zosh, J. M., Golinkoff, R. M., Gray, J. H., Robb, M. B., & Kaufman, J. (2015). Putting education in educational apps: Lessons from the science of learning. *Psychological Science in the Public Interest, 16*(1), 3–34. https://doi.org/10.1177/1529100615569721

Hirumi, A., & Stapleton, C. (2009). Applying Pedagogy during Game Development to Enhance Game-Based Learning. *Games: Purpose and Potential in Education*, 127–162. doi:10.1007/978-0-387-09775-6_6

Hisam, A., Mashhadi, S. F., Faheem, M., Sohail, M., Ikhlaq, B., & Iqbal, I. (2018). Does playing video games effect cognitive abilities in Pakistani children? *Pakistan Journal of Medical Sciences*, *34*(6), 1507–1511. doi:10.12669/pjms.346.15532 PMID:30559813

Hmelo-Silver, C. E. (2004). Problem-based learning: What and how do students learn? *Educational Psychology Review*, *16*(3), 235–266. doi:10.1023/B:EDPR.0000034022.16470.f3

Hobbs, R. & Jensen, A. (2009). The past, present and future of media literacy education. *Journal of Media Literacy Education, 1*, 1-11.

Hobbs, R. (1994, Winter). Teaching Media Literacy— Are you hip to this? *Media Studies Journal,* 135-145.

Hobbs, R. (2010). *Digital and Media Literacy: A Plan of Action*. The Aspen Institute.

Hobbs, R. (2010). *Digital media literacy: A plan of action*. The Aspen Institute.

Hochleitner, C., Hochleitner, W., Graf, C., & Tscheligi, M. (2015). A Heuristic Framework for Evaluating User Experience in Games. In Game User Experience Evaluation. Bernhaupt.

Hodges, R. E. (2004). *What is literacy? Selected definitions and essays from "The literacy dictionary: The vocabulary of reading and writing"*. International Reading Assoc.

Hoel, T., & Jernes, M. (2020). Samtalebasert lesing av bildebok-apper: barnehagelærer versus hotspoter [Dialogue-Based Reading of Picture Book Apps: The Kindergarten Teacher Versus Hotspots]. *Norsk Pedagogisk Tidsskrift, 104*(2), 121–133. doi:10.18261/issn.1504-2987-2020-02-04

Hoffman, B., & Nadelson, L. (2010). Motivational engagement and video gaming: A mixed methods study. *Educational Technology Research and Development*, *58*(3), 245–270. doi:10.100711423-009-9134-9

Hofstede, G. (2011). Dimensionalizing cultures: The Hofstede model in context. *Online Readings in Psychology and Culture*, *2*(1). Advance online publication. doi:10.9707/2307-0919.1014

Hogg, M. A., Adelman, J. R., & Blagg, R. D. (2010). Religion in the face of uncertainty: An uncertainty-identity theory account of religiousness. *Personality and Social Psychology Review*, *14*(1), 72–83. doi:10.1177/1088868309349692 PMID:19855094

Ho, J. A. (2010). Ethical perception: Are differences between ethnic groups situation dependent? *Business Ethics (Oxford, England)*, *19*(2), 154–182. doi:10.1111/j.1467-8608.2010.01583.x

Holdcroft, B. (2006). What is religiosity. *Catholic Education: A Journal of Inquiry and Practice, 10*(1).

Holmes, W., Anastopoulou, S., Schaumburg, H., & Mavrikis, M. (2018). *Technology-enhanced personalised learning: Untangling the evidence*. Robert Bosch Stiftung GmbH.

Hommel, B. (2010). Grounding attention in action control: The intentional control of selection. In Effortless attention: A new perspective in the cognitive science of attention and action (pp. 121-140). Academic Press.

Hommel, M. (2010). Video games and learning. *School Library Monthly*, *26*(10), 37–40.

Hood, D., Lemaignan, S., & Dillenbourg, P. (2015, March). When children teach a robot to write: An autonomous teachable humanoid which uses simulated handwriting. In *Proceedings of the Tenth Annual ACM/IEEE International Conference on Human-Robot Interaction* (pp. 83-90). 10.1145/2696454.2696479

Hooshyar, D., Pedaste, M., Yang, Y., Malva, L., Hwang, G. J., Wang, M., Lim, H., & Delev, D. (2021). From gaming to computational thinking: An adaptive educational computer game-based learning approach. *Journal of Educational Computing Research, 59*(3), 383–409. doi:10.1177/0735633120965919

Horkheimer, M. (1982). *Critical theory selected essays.* Continuum Pub.

Hossain, A., & Zeitlyn, B. (2010). *Poverty, equity and access to education in Bangladesh.* CREATE. https://files.eric.ed.gov/fulltext/ED517693.pdf

Hosseini, H., Hartt, M., & Mostafapour, M. (2019). Learning is child's play: Game-based learning in computer science education. *ACM Transactions on Computing Education, 19*(3), 1–18. doi:10.1145/3282844

Howard-Jones, P. A., & Jay, T. (2016). Reward, Learning and Games. *Current Opinion in Behavioral Sciences, 10,* 65–72. doi:10.1016/j.cobeha.2016.04.015

Howard-Jones, P. A., Jay, T., Mason, A., & Jones, H. (2016). Gamification of learning deactivates the default mode network. *Frontiers in Psychology, 6,* 1891. doi:10.3389/fpsyg.2015.01891 PMID:26779054

Howard, T. C. (2001). Telling their side of the story: African-American students' perceptions of culturally relevant teaching. *The Urban Review, 33*(2), 131–149. doi:10.1023/A:1010393224120

Howell, E. (2017). Pokémon GO: Implications for literacy in the classroom. *The Reading Teacher, 70*(6), 729–732. doi:10.1002/trtr.1565

Hoyles, C., & Noss, R. (2003). What can digital technologies take from and bring to research in mathematics education? In A. J. Bishop, M. A. Clements, C. Keitel, J. Kilpatrick, & F. K. S. Leung (Eds.), *Second International Handbook of Mathematics Education* (Vol. 10, pp. 323–349). Springer. doi:10.1007/978-94-010-0273-8_11

Hramiak, A., Boulton, H., & Irwin, B. (2009). Trainee teachers' use of blogs as private reflections for professional development. *Learning, Media and Technology, 34*(3), 259–269. doi:10.1080/17439880903141521

Hsiao, H.-S., Chang, C. S., Lin, C. Y., & Hu, P. M. (2014). Development of children's creativity and manual skills within digital game-based learning environment. *Journal of Computer Assisted Learning, 30*(4), 377–395. doi:10.1111/jcal.12057

Hsieh, M. L., Dawson, P. H., & Yang, S. Q. (2021). The ACRL Framework successes and challenges since 2016: A survey. *Journal of Academic Librarianship, 47*(2), 102306. doi:10.1016/j.acalib.2020.102306

Hsu, C. C., & Sandford, B. A. (2007). The Delphi technique: Making sense of consensus. *Practical Assessment, Research & Evaluation, 12*(1), 1–8. doi:10.7275/pdz9-th90

Hsu, H., & Wang, S. (2010). Using gaming literacies to cultivate new literacies. *Simulation & Gaming, 41*(3), 400–417. doi:10.1177/1046878109355361

Hu & Bentler. (1999). Cutoff criteria for fit indexes in covariance structure analysis: conventional criteria versus new alternatives. *Structural Equation Modeling, 6*(1), 1–55.

Huang, W. H. Y., & Soman, D. (2013). Gamification of education. *Report Series: Behavioural Economics in Action, 29.*

Huang, R., Liu, D., Xu, J., Chen, N., Fan, L., & Zeng, H. (2017). The development status and trend of educational robots. *Modern Educational Technology, 27*(1), 13–20.

Huang, W. H. (2010). Evaluating learners' motivational and cognitive processing in an online game-based learning environment. *Computers in Human Behavior.* Advance online publication. doi:10.1016/j.chb.2010.07.021

Huang, W. H.-Y., & Soman, D. (2013). *A practitioner's guide to gamification of education*. University of Toronto, Rotman School of Management.

Huang, Y. L., Chang, D. F., & Wu, B. (2017). Mobile game-based learning with a mobile app: Motivational effects and learning performance. *Journal of Advanced Computational Intelligence and Intelligent Informatics, 21*(6), 963–970. doi:10.20965/jaciii.2017.p0963

Huang, Y. L., Ho, Y. S., & Chuang, K. Y. (2006). Bibliometric analysis of nursing research in Taiwan 1991-2004. *The Journal of Nursing Research, 14*(1), 75–81. doi:10.1097/01.JNR.0000387564.57188.b4 PMID:16547908

Huang, Y. M., Liang, T. H., Su, Y. N., & Chen, N. S. (2012). Empowering personalized learning with an interactive e-book learning system for elementary school students. *Educational Technology Research and Development, 60*(4), 703–722. doi:10.100711423-012-9237-6

Huber, G. P., & Lewis, K. (2010). Cross-understanding: Implications for group cognition and performance. *Academy of Management Review, 35*(1), 6–26.

Huberman, A. (Host). (2021, February 15). Using Failures, Movement & Balance to Learn Faster. *Huberman Lab* [Audio podcast episode]. https://hubermanlab.com/using-failures-movement-and-balance-to-learn-faster/

Huertas-Abril, C. A. (2020). *Tecnologías para la educación bilingüe*. Peter Lang.

Hu, G. (2005). English language education in China: Policies, progress, and problems. *Language Policy, 4*(1), 5–24. doi:10.100710993-004-6561-7

Huizenga, J. C., ten Dam, G. T. M., Voogt, J. M., & Admiraal, W. F. (2017). Teacher perceptions of the value of game-based learning in secondary education. *Computers & Education, 110*, 105–115. doi:10.1016/j.compedu.2017.03.008

Huizenga, J., Akkerman, S., Admiraal, W., & Dam, G. T. (2009). Mobile game-based learning in secondary education: Engagement, motivation and learning in a mobile city game. *Journal of Computer Assisted Learning, 25*(4), 332–344. doi:10.1111/j.1365-2729.2009.00316.x

Huizinga, J. (1950). *Homo ludens, a study of the play-element in culture*. Oxford, UK: Roy. (Original work published 1938)

Huizinga, J. (1955/2006). Nature and significance of play as a cultural phenomenon from Homo Ludens: A study of the play element in culture. In The Game Designer Reader: A Rules of Play Anthology (pp. 96-120). Cambridge, MA: MIT Press.

Huizinga, J. (1949). *Homo Ludens Ils 86* (1st ed.). Routledge. doi:10.4324/9781315824161

Huizinga, J. (1955). *Homo ludens: A study of the play element in culture*. Routledge.

Huizinga, J., Nachod, H., & Flitner, A. (2006). *Homo ludens: vom Ursprung der Kultur im Spiel*. Rowohlt Taschenbuch Verlag.

Hulpuş, I., Hayes, C., & Fradinho, M. O. (2014). A framework for personalised Learning-plan recommendations in Game-based learning. In *Recommender Systems for Technology Enhanced Learning* (pp. 99–122). Springer. doi:10.1007/978-1-4939-0530-0_5

Humphrey, J. H., & Sullivan, D. D. (1970). *Teaching Slow Learners through Active Games*. Academic Press.

Hung, H. C., & Young, S. S. C. (2015). An Investigation of Game-Embedded Handheld Devices to Enhance English Learning. *Journal of Educational Computing Research, 52*(4), 548–567. doi:10.1177/0735633115571922

Hung, H. T., Yang, J. C., Hwang, G. J., Chu, H. C., & Wang, C. C. (2018). A scoping review of research on digital game-based language learning. *Computers & Education*, *126*, 89–104. doi:10.1016/j.compedu.2018.07.001

Hung, H. T., Yang, J. C., & Tsai, Y. C. (2020). Student Game Design as a Literacy Practice. *Journal of Educational Technology & Society*, *23*(1), 50–63.

Hungi, N., Makuwa, D., Ross, K., Saito, M., Dolata, S., van Capelle, F., Paviot, L., & Vellien, J. (2010). SACMEQ III Project Results: Pupil achievement levels in reading and mathematics. Southern and Eastern African Consortium for Monitoring Educational Quality. doi:10.100711125-005-6819-7

Hung, I. C., Chao, K. J., Lee, L., & Chen, N. S. (2013). Designing a robot teaching assistant for enhancing and sustaining learning motivation. *Interactive Learning Environments*, *21*(2), 156–171. doi:10.1080/10494820.2012.705855

Hunter, J. (2020). *STEAM games are good for learning: A study of teacher professional development in the Philippines.* New orleans, LA: SITE 2020.

Hunt, M. W. (2013). (APP) elite for instruction: 21st-century learners in a video and audio production classroom. *Techniques - American Vocational Association*, *88*(8), 36.

Hurtado, M. F., & González, J. (2017). Necesidades formativas del profesorado de Secundaria para la implementación de experiencias gamificadas en STEM. *Revista de Educación a Distancia, 54*(8), 30–36. https://www.um.es/ead/red/54/fuentes_gonzalez.pdf

Husnaini, S. J., & Chen, S. (2019). Effects of guided inquiry virtual and physical laboratories on conceptual understanding, inquiry performance, inquiry self-efficacy, and enjoyment. *Physical Review. Physics Education Research*, *15*(1), 010119. doi:10.1103/PhysRevPhysEducRes.15.010119

Hussein, G. (2010). The Attitudes of Undergraduate Students towards Motivation and Technology in a Foreign Language Classroom. *International Journal of Learning and Teaching*, *2*(2), 14–24.

Hutchison, A., Beschorner, B., & Schmidt-Crawford, D. (2012). Exploring the use of the iPad for literacy learning. *The Reading Teacher*, *66*(1), 15–23. https://doi.org/ 10.1002/TRTR.01090

Hwang, D., Staley, B., Te Chen, Y., & Lan, J.-S. (2008). Confucian culture and whistle-blowing by professional accountants: An exploratory study. *Managerial Auditing Journal*, *23*(5), 504–526. doi:10.1108/02686900810875316

Hwang, G. J., & Chang, C. Y. (2020). Facilitating decision-making performances in nursing treatments: A contextual digital game-based flipped learning approach. *Interactive Learning Environments*, 1–16. Advance online publication. doi:10.1080/10494820.2020.1765391

Hwang, G. J., Chiu, L. Y., & Chen, C. H. (2015). A contextual game-based learning approach to improving students' inquiry-based learning performance in social studies courses. *Computers & Education*, *81*, 13–25. doi:10.1016/j.compedu.2014.09.006

Hwang, G. J., & Wu, P. H. (2012). Advancements and trends in digital game-based learning research: A review of publications in selected journals from 2001 to 2010. *British Journal of Educational Technology*, *43*(1), E6–E10. doi:10.1111/j.1467-8535.2011.01242.x

Hwang, G. J., Wu, P. H., & Chen, C. C. (2012). An online game approach for improving students' learning performance in web-based problem-solving activities. *Computers & Education, 59*(4), 1246–1256. doi:10.1016/j.compedu.2012.05.009

Iacobucci, D., Posavac, S. S., Kardes, F. R., Schneider, M. J., & Popovich, D. L. (2015). The median split: Robust, refined, and revived. *Journal of Consumer Psychology*, *25*(4), 690–704. doi:10.1016/j.jcps.2015.06.014

Iacono, S., Vallarino, M., & Vercelli, G. (2020). Gamification in corporate training to enhance engagement: An approach. *International Journal of Emerging Technology in Learning*, *15*(17), 69–84. doi:10.3991/ijet.v15i17.14207

IbanezF. C. (2018). https://elearningindustry.com/elearning-authors/felipe-casajus-ibanez

Ibrahim, N. A., Howard, D. P., & Angelidis, J. P. (2008). The relationship between religiousness and corporate social responsibility orientation: Are there differences between business managers and students? *Journal of Business Ethics*, *78*(1-2), 165–174. doi:10.100710551-006-9321-0

Ibrahimoglu, N., Unaldi, I., Samancioglu, M., & Baglibel, M. (2013). The relationship between personality traits and learning styles: A cluster analysis. *Asian Journal of Management Sciences and Education*, *2*(3), 93–108.

Ibrahim, R., & Jaafar, A. (2009). Educational games (EG) design framework: Combination of game design, pedagogy and content modeling. *IEEE International Conference on Electrical Engineering and Informatics*, 293-298. 10.1109/ICEEI.2009.5254771

Ibrahim, R., Masrom, S., Yusoff, R. C. M., Zainuddin, N. M. M., & Rizman, Z. I. (2017). Students' acceptance of Educational Games in Higher Education. *Journal of Fundamental and Applied Sciences*, *9*(3S), 809–829. doi:10.4314/jfas.v9i3s.62

Ibrahim, R., Rahim, N. Z. A., Ten, D. W. H., Yusoff, R., Maarop, N., & Yaacob, S. (2018). Student's opinions on online educational games for learning programming introductory. *International Journal of Advanced Computer Science and Applications*, *9*(6), 332–340. doi:10.14569/IJACSA.2018.090647

Ifenthaler, D., Eseryel, D., & Ge, X. (2012). Assessment for game-based learning. In *Assessment in game-based learning: Foundations, innovations, and perspectives*. Springer-Verlag. doi:10.1007/978-1-4614-3546-4_1

IGDA. (2019). *Developer Satisfaction Survey 2019*. International Game Developers Association.

Immordino-Yang, M. H. (2016). *Emotions, Learning, and the Brain*. W. W. Norton & Company.

Impact of COVID-19 on people's livelihoods, their health and our food systems. (n.d.). Retrieved September 2, 2021, from https://www.who.int/news/item/13-10-2020-impact-of-covid-19-on-people's-livelihoods-their-health-and-our-food-systems

Imray, P., & Hinchcliffe, V. (2013). *Curricula for teaching children and young people with severe or profound and multiple learning difficulties: Practical strategies for educational professionals*. Routledge. doi:10.4324/9781315883298

Information Literacy Competency Standards for Higher Education. (2000). [Brochure]. *Association of College & Research Libraries*. http://hdl.handle.net/10150/105645 https://www.ala.org/ala/acrl/acrlstandards/informationliteracycompetency.htm

Ingram, R. (1990). Self-focused attention in clinical disorders: Review and a conceptual model. *Psychological Bulletin*, *107*(2), 156–176. doi:10.1037/0033-2909.107.2.156 PMID:2181521

Instituto de Geografia e Ordenamento do Território. (2021). Retrieved October 4, 2021, from, http://www.igot.ulisboa.pt/

Instituto Superior Técnico. (2021). Retrieved October 4, 2021, from, https://tecnico.ulisboa.pt/en/

INTEF. (2017). *Common Digital Competence Framework for Teachers*. National Institute of Educational Technologies and Teacher Training, Spanish Ministry of Education, Culture and Sport. https://bit.ly/3pkRJdh

Interactive Technologies Institute. (2021). Retrieved October 5, 2021, from, https://iti.larsys.pt/

International Society for Technology in Education. (2016). *Essential Conditions for Teaching ISTE Standards*. Author.

Iosup, A., & Epema, D. (2014). *An Experience Report on Using Gamification in Technical Higher Education*. Conference paper SIGCSE, Atlanta, GA. 10.1145/2538862.2538899

Irmade, O., & Anisa, N. (2021, March). Research trends of serious games: Bibliometric analysis. []. IOP Publishing.]. *Journal of Physics: Conference Series, 1842*(1), 012036. doi:10.1088/1742-6596/1842/1/012036

Israel, M. (2017) *Game-based learning and gamification. Guidance from the experts.* White paper.

Israel, M., Marino, M., Delisio, L., & Serianni, B. (2014, September). *Supporting content learning through technology for K-12 students with disabilities* (Document No. IC-10). Retrieved from University of Florida, Collaboration for Effective Educator, Development, Accountability, and Reform Center: https://ceedar.education.ufl.edu/tools/innovation-configurations/

Ito, M., Gutierrez, K., Livingstone, S., Penuel, B., Rhodes, J., Salen, K., & Schor, J. (2010). Living and learning with new media: Summary of findings from the digital youth project (The John D. and Catherine T. MacArthur Foundation reports on digital media and learning). MIT Press.

Ito, M. (2008). *Living and learning with new media: summary of findings from the digital youth project.* The John D. and Catherine T. MacArthur Foundation.

Ivus, M., Quan, T., & Snider, N. (2020). *Class, take out your tablets: The impact of technology on learning and teaching in Canada.* Information and Communications Technology Council.

Ivus, M., Quan, T., & Snider, N. (2021). *21st Century Digital Skills: Competencies, Innovations and Curriculum in Canada, Information and Communications Technology Council.* ICTC.

Jaaska, E., Aaltonen, K., & Kujala, J. (2021). Game-Based Learning in Project Sustainability Management Education. *Sustainability, 13*(15), 15. doi:10.3390u13158204

Jackson, E. (2013). Choosing a methodology: philosophical underpinning. *Practitioner Research in Higher Education Journal, 7*(1), 49-62.

Jackson, G.T., & McNemara, D. (2013). *Motivation and Performance in a Game-Based Intelligent Tutoring System.* Academic Press.

Jackson, K. (2003). Blending technology and methodology: A shift toward creative instruction of qualitative methods with NVivo. *Qualitative Research Journal.*

Jackson, K., & Bazeley, P. (2019). Qualitative data analysis with NVivo. *Sage (Atlanta, Ga.).*

Jackson, L. C., O'Mara, J., Moss, J., & Jackson, A. C. (2018). A critical review of the effectiveness of narrative-driven digital educational games. *International Journal of Game-Based Learning, 8*(4), 32–49. doi:10.4018/IJGBL.2018100103

Jagger, S., Siala, H., & Sloan, D. (2015). It's All in the Game: A 3D Learning Model for Business Ethics. *Journal of Business Ethics, 137*(2), 383–403. doi:10.100710551-015-2557-9

Jaipal, K., & Figg, C. (2009). Using video games in science instruction: Pedagogical, social, and concept-related aspects. *Canadian Journal of Science Mathematics and Technology Education, 9*(2), 117–134. doi:10.1080/14926150903047780

Jamaludin, A., & Hung, D. (2017). Problem-solving for STEM learning: Navigating games as narrativized problem spaces for 21st. *Research and Practice in Technology Enhanced Learning, 12*(1), 1–14. doi:10.118641039-016-0038-0 PMID:30613250

Jamaludin, N. F., Wook, T. S. M. T., Noor, S. F. M., & Qamar, F. (2021). Gamification Design Elements to Enhance Adolescent Motivation in Diagnosing Depression. *International Journal of Interactive Mobile Technologies*, *15*(10), 154. doi:10.3991/ijim.v15i10.21137

James, F. (2019). *Everything You Need to Know About Education 4.0*. QS. https://www.qs.com/everything-you-need-to-know-education-40/

James, E., Gaskell, M. G., Weighall, A., & Henderson, L. (2017). Consolidation of vocabulary during sleep: The rich get richer? *Neuroscience and Biobehavioral Reviews*, *77*, 1–13. doi:10.1016/j.neubiorev.2017.01.054 PMID:28274725

James, M. (2020). *The Impact of Game-Based Learning in a Special Education Classroom*. Academic Press.

Jan, M. (2009). *Designing an augmented reality game-based curriculum for argumentation* (Unpublished doctoral dissertation). University of Wisconsin-Madison.

Jan, M., & Tan, E. (2013). Learning in and for the 21st century. Professorial Lecture Series, 4, 13-22.

Jan, M., Chee, Y. S., & Tan, E. M. (2010). Learning science via a science-in-the-making process: The design of a game-based learning curriculum. In S. Martin (Ed.), *iVERG 2010 Proceedings - International Conference on Immersive Technologies for Learning: A multi-disciplinary approach* (pp. 13-25). Stockton, CA: Iverg Publishing.

Jana, M. (2016). Teachers ' Views on Game-based Learning (GBL) as a Teaching Method in Elementary Level Education. *Global Journal for Research Analysis*, *5*(1).

Janebi Enayat, M., & Haghighatpasand, M. (2019). Exploiting adventure video games for second language vocabulary recall: A mixed-methods study. *Innovation in Language Learning and Teaching*, *13*(1), 61–75. doi:10.1080/17501229.2017.1359276

Jang & Ryu. (2011). Exploring game experiences and game leadership in massively multiplayer online role-playing games. *British Journal of Educational Technology, 42*(4), 616-23. . doi:10.1111/j.1467-8535.2010.01064.x

Jan, M., Tan, E. M., & Chen, V. (2015). Issues and Challenges of Enacting Game-Based Learning in Schools. In T. B. Lin, V. Chen, & C. Chai (Eds.), *New Media and Learning in the 21st Century. Education Innovation Series*. Springer. doi:10.1007/978-981-287-326-2_5

Jansz, J. (2005). The emotional appeal of violent video games for adolescent males. *Communication Theory, 15*(3), 219-241. Retrieved from https://onlinelibrary.wiley.com/doi/10.1111/j.1468-2885.2005.tb00334.x/abstract;jsessionid=797D278A2C3BFFD76C1E71DA17729991.f02t02

Jarvis, P. (2009). Learning from everyday life. In P. Jarvis (Ed.), *The Routledge international handbook of lifelong learning* (pp. 19–30). Routledge. doi:10.4324/9780203870549

Jasperson, J. S., Carter, & Zmud. (2005). A comprehensive conceptualization of post-adoptive behaviors associated with information technology enabled work systems. *Management Information Systems Quarterly, 29*(3), 525–557. doi:10.2307/25148694

Jemielniak, D. (2014). *Common Knowledge? An Ethnography of Wikipedia*. Stanford University Press. https://ebookcentral.proquest.com/lib/nuim/detail.action?docID=1680678

Jenkins, B. (2014). Don't quit playing: Video games in the STEM classroom. *Techniques*, *89*(1), 60–61.

Jenkins, H. (2002). Game design as narrative architecture. In P. Harrington & N. Frup-Waldrop (Eds.), *First Person*. MIT Press.

Jenkins, H. (2006). *Convergence culture: Where old and new media collide*. New York University Press.

Jenkins, H. (2006). *Fans, Bloggers, and Gamers: Exploring Participatory Culture.* New York University Press.

Jenkins, H. (2009). *Confronting the challenges of participatory culture: Media education for the 21ˢᵗ century.* MacArthur Foundation.

Jenkins, H., Squire, K., & Tan, P. (2003). Entering the education arcade. *Computers in Entertainment, 1*(1), 17. doi:10.1145/950566.950591

Jewitt, C., Bezemer, J., & O'Halloran, K. (2016). *Introducing multimodality.* Routledge.

Jiang, X., Huang, X., Harteveld, C., & Fung, A. (2019). *The Computational Puzzle Design Framework.* Presented at the Association for Computing Machinery, San Luis Obispo, CA.

Jin, D. Y. (2017). The Emergence of Asian Mobile Games: Definitions, Industries, and Trajectories. *Mobile Gaming in Asia: Politics, Culture and Emerging Technologies*, 3-20.

Jin, G., Tu, M., Kim, T. H., Heffron, J., & White, J. (2018). Evaluation of game-based learning in cybersecurity education for high school students. [EduLearn]. *Journal of Education and Learning, 12*(1), 150–158. doi:10.11591/edulearn. v12i1.7736

Johnson, A. C., & Drougas, A. M. (2002). *Using Goldratt's Game to Introduce Simulation in the Introductory Operations Management Course.* Https://Doi.Org/10.1287/Ited.3.1.20

Johnson, D. W., & Johnson, F. P. (1997). *Joining Together: Group Theory and Group Skills* (6th ed.). Allyn & Bacon.

Johnson, S. (2005). *Everything bad is good for you: How today's popular culture is actually making us smarter.* Riverhead Books.

Johnston, E., & Olson, L. (2015). *The feeling brain: The biology and psychology of emotions.* WW Norton & Company.

Johnston, P. (2012). *Opening minds: Using language to change lives.* Stenhouse.

Jonassen, D. H. (2007). Engaging and supporting problem solving in online learning. *Online Learning Communities*, 109-127.

Jonassen, D. H. (1994). Thinking technology: Toward a constructivist design model. *Educational Technology, 34*(4), 34–37. https://www.learntechlib.org/p/171050/

Jonassen, D. H. (1997). Instructional design models for well-structured and ill-structured problem-solving learning outcomes. *Educational Technology Research and Development, 45*(1), 65–94. doi:10.1007/BF02299613

Jonassen, D. H., & Hung, W. (2012). Problem Solving. In N. M. Seel (Ed.), *Encyclopedia of the Sciences of Learning.* Springer. doi:10.1007/978-1-4419-1428-6_208

Jonassen, D., Campbell, J., & Davidson, M. (1994). Learning with media: Restructuring the debate. *Educational Technology Research and Development, 42*(2), 31–39. doi:10.1007/BF02299089

Jones, A. (2004). *A review of the research literature on barriers to the uptake of ICT by teachers.* London, UK: British Educational Communications and Technology Agency (BECTA). Retrieved from www.becta.org.uk

Jones, V. R. (2014). Teaching STEM: 21st century skills. *Children's Technology & Engineering, 18*(4), 11–13.

Jordan, M. E., Kleinsasser, R. C., & Roe, M. F. (2014). Wicked problems: Inescapable wickedity. *Journal of Education for Teaching, 40*(4), 415–430. doi:10.1080/02607476.2014.929381

Jouriles, E. N., McDonald, R., Kullowatz, A., Rosenfield, D., Gomez, G. S., & Cuevas, A. (2009). Can virtual reality increase the realism of role plays used to teach college women sexual coercion and rape-resistance skills? *Behavior Therapy*, *40*(4), 337–345. doi:10.1016/j.beth.2008.09.002 PMID:19892079

Jude, L. T., Kajura, M. A., & Birevu, M. P. (2014). Adoption of the SAMR model to asses ICT pedagogical adoption: A case of Makerere University. *International Journal of e-Education, e-Business, e- Management Learning*, *4*(2), 106–115.

Juul, J. (2005). Half-real: Video games between real rules and fictional worlds. Cambridge, MA: The MIT Press.

Juul, J. (2005). *Half-real: Video games between real rules and fictional worlds*. MIT Press.

Kader, M. A., & Salam, M. A. (2018). A comprehensive study on service quality and satisfaction level to the English medium education system in Bangladesh. *International Journal of Contemporary Research and Review*, *9*(7), 20850–20866. doi:10.15520/ijcrr/2018/9/07/541

Kafai, Y. B., Burke, Q., & Steinkuehler, C. (2016). *Connected gaming: What making video games can teach us about learning and literacy*. MIT Press. Retrieved from https://books.google.ca/books?id=zPC7DQAAQBAJ

Kafai, Y. B. (1995). *Minds in play: Computer game design as a context for children's learning*. Routledge.

Kahl, C. (2013). A deeper lecturer and student view of a sustainable learning requirement in tertiary education in Malaysia. *International Journal for Cross-Disciplinary Subjects in Education*, *4*(2), 1144–1152. doi:10.20533/ijcdse.2042.6364.2013.0161

Kahoot! for schools - choose plan for higher education. (2021, September 16). *Kahoot!* Retrieved September 11, 2021 from https://kahoot.com/register/pricing-higher-ed/

Kaimara, P., Fokides, E., & Oikonomou, A. (2021). *Potential Barriers to the Implementation of Digital Game-Based Learning in the Classroom: Pre-service Teachers' Views*. Tech Know Learn. doi:10.100710758-021-09512-7

Kalantzis, M., Varnvava-Skoura, G., & Cope, B. (2002). *Learning for the future: New worlds, new literacies, new learning, new people*. Common Ground Publishing. http://www.thelearner.com

Kalantzis, M., & Cope, B. (2012). *Introducing the Learning by Design Project*. University of Illinois.

Kalantzis, M., & Cope, B. (2012). *Literacies*. Cambridge University Press. doi:10.1017/CBO9781139196581

Kalantzis, M., & Cope, B. (2020). After the COVID-19 crisis: Why higher education may (and perhaps should) never be the same. *Access: Contemporary Issues in Education*, *40*(1), 51–55. doi:10.46786/ac20.9496

Kali, Y., McKenney, S., & Sagy, O. (2015). Teachers as designers of technology enhanced learning. *Instructional Science*, *43*(2), 173–179. doi:10.100711251-014-9343-4

Kamarudin, N., Halim, L., Osman, K., & Meerah, T. S. M. (2009). Pengurusan Penglibatan Pelajar dalam Amali Sains [Management of Students' Involvement in Science Practical Work]. *Jurnal Pendidikan Malaysia*, *34*(1), 205–217.

Kamisah, O., Zanaton, H. L., & Lilia, H. (2007). Sikap terhadap sains dan sikap saintifik di kalangan pelajar sains. *Jurnal Pendidikan*, *32*(3), 39–60.

Kamışlı, H. (2019). On primary school teachers' training needs in relation to game-based learning. *International Journal of Curriculum and Instruction*, *11*(2), 285–296.

Kamunya, S., Mirirti, E., Oboko, R., & Maina, E. (2020b). An Adaptive Gamification Model for E-Learning. *2020 IST-Africa Conference, IST-Africa 2020*. https://api.elsevier.com/content/abstract/scopus_id/85094323708

Kamunya, S., Mirirti, E., Oboko, R., & Maina, E. (2020a). An Adaptive Gamification Model for E-Learning. *2020 IST-Africa Conference. IST-Africa, 2020*, 1–10.

Kanai, S. (2012). *Lover Letter* [Board Game]. Alderac Entertainment Group.

Kangas, A. (2017). Global Cities, International Relations and the Fabrication of the World. *Global Society, 31*(4), 531–550. doi:10.1080/13600826.2017.1322939

Kangas, M. (2010a). Creative and playful learning: Learning through game co-creation and games in a playful learning environment. *Thinking Skills and Creativity, 5*(1), 1–15. doi:10.1016/j.tsc.2009.11.001

Kangas, M., Koskinen, A., & Krokfors, L. (2017). A qualitative literature review of educational games in the classroom: The teacher's pedagogical activities. *Teachers and Teaching, 23*(4), 451–470.

Kang, M., Choo, P., & Watters, C. E. (2015). Design for experiencing: Participatory design approach with multidisciplinary perspectives. *Procedia: Social and Behavioral Sciences, 174*, 830–833. doi:10.1016/j.sbspro.2015.01.676

Kankanhalli, A., Taher, M., Cavusoglu, H., & Kim, S. H. (2012). Gamification: A new paradigm for online user engagement. *Thirty Third International Conference on Information Systems*, 1-10.

Kaplan, A., & Haenlein, M. (2010). "Users of the world, unite! The challenges and opportunities of social media" (PDF). *Business Horizons, 53*(1), 61. doi:10.1016/j.bushor.2009.09.003

Kapp, K. (2012). *The gamification of learning and instruction.* Pfeiffer Press.

Kapp, K. (2012). *The Gamification of Learning and Instruction: Game-based Methods and Strategies for Training and Education.* Pfeiffer.

Kapp, K. (2012). *The Gamification of Learning and Instruction: Game-Based Methods and Strategies for Training and Education.* Pfeiffer.

Kapp, K. M. (2012). *The gamification of learning and instruction: game-based methods and strategies for training and education.* Pfeiffer.

Kapur, R. (n.d.). *Significance and Meaning of Academic Literacy.* https://www.researchgate.net/profile/Radhika_Kapur/publication/336982773_Significance_and_Meaning_of_Academic_Literacy/links/5dbd1fc4a6fdcc2128f8ff82/Significance-and-Meaning-of-Academic-Literacy

Karacalli, S., & Korur, F. (2014). *The Effects of project-based learning on students' academic achievement,attitude, and retention of knowledge: The subject of electricity in our lives.* https://onlinelibrary.wiley.com/doi/abs/10.1111/ssm.12071

Karagiannis, S., & Magkos, E. (2021). Engaging Students in Basic Cybersecurity Concepts Using Digital Game-Based Learning: Computer Games as Virtual Learning Environments. In *Advances in Core Computer Science-Based Technologies*. Springer., doi:10.1007/978-3-030-41196-1_4

Karaman, M. A., Vela, J. C., Aguilar, A. A., Saldana, K., & Montenegro, M. C. (2019). Psychometric properties of U.S.-Spanish versions of the grit and resilience scales with a Latinx population. *International Journal for the Advancement of Counseling, 41*(1), 125–136. doi:10.100710447-018-9350-2

Karchmer-Klein, R., & Shinas, V. H. (2012). Guiding principles for supporting new literacies in your classroom. *The Reading Teacher, 65*(5), 288–293. doi:10.1002/TRTR.01044

Karen, H. (1939). *New ways in psychoanalysis.* Norton.

Karpouzis, K., & Yannakakis, G. N. (2016). *Emotion in Games.* Springer. doi:10.1007/978-3-319-41316-7

Kasasa. (2021, July). Boomers, Gen X, Gen Y, Gen Z, and Gen A Explained. *Kasasa.* https://bit.ly/3Bm4x5Z

Katada, H. (2019, March 1). *Interview.* Retrieved from https://www.famitsu.com/news/201903/01172506.html

Kathrani, P. (2020). The Gamification of Written Problem Questions in Law. Reflections on the "Serious Games at Westminster's Project. In C. Denvir (Ed.), *Modernizing Legal Education* (pp. 186–203). Cambridge University Press. doi:10.1017/9781108663311.012

Katz, J., & Mirenda, P. (2002). Including students with developmental disabilities in general education classrooms: Educational benefits. *International Journal of Special Education, 17*(2), 14–24.

Kaushik, V., & Walsh, C. A. (2019). Pragmatism as a research paradigm and its implications for Social Work research. *Social Sciences, 8*(9), 255. Advance online publication. doi:10.3390ocsci8090255

Kay, R. H. (2006). Evaluating strategies used to incorporate technology into preservice education: A review of the literature. *Journal of Research on Technology in Education, 38*(4), 383–408. doi:10.1080/15391523.2006.10782466

Keefe, E. B., & Copeland, S. R. (2011). What is Literacy? The Power of a Definition. *Research and Practice for Persons with Severe Disabilities, 36*(3-4), 92–99. doi:10.2511/027494811800824507

Keesey, C. (2011). Engagement, immersion, and learning cultures: Project planning and decision making for virtual world training programs. In *Global Business: Concepts, Methodologies, Tools and Applications* (pp. 121–134). IGI Global. doi:10.4018/978-1-60960-587-2.ch109

Keeshin, J. (2021). *Read, write, code. A friendly introduction to the world of coding and why it's the new literacy.* Lioncrest Publishing.

Ke, F. (2008). Computer games application within alternative classroom goal structures: Cognitive, metacognitive, and affective evaluation. *Educational Technology Research and Development, 56*(5-6), 539–556. doi:10.100711423-008-9086-5

Ke, F. (2016). Designing and integrating purposeful learning in gameplay: A systematic review. *Educational Technology Research and Development, 64*(2), 219–244. doi:10.100711423-015-9418-1

Keller, J. (2008). An integrative theory of motivation, volition, and performance. *Technol. Instr. Cogn. Learn., 6,* 79–104. https://www.oldcitypublishing.com/journals/ticl-home/ticl-issue-contents/ticl-volume-6-number-2-2008/ticl-6-2-p-79-104/

Keller, J. M. (1998). Using the ARCS process in CBI and distance education. In M. Theall (Ed.), *Motivation in teaching and learning: New directions for teaching and learning.* Jossey-Bass.

Kelley, & Knowles, Han, & Sung. (2019). Creating a 21st century skills survey instrument for high school students. *American Journal of Educational Research, 7*(8), 583–590. doi:10.12691/education-7-8-7

Kellinger, J. J. (2017). Let the Games Begin! Teaching Your Game. In A Guide to Designing Curricular Games (pp. 271-311). Springer International Publishing. doi:10.1007/978-3-319-42393-7_8

Kellinger, J. (2017). *A guide to designing curricular games: How to 'game' the system.* Springer.

Kellner, D. (2001). New Technologies/New Literacies: Reconstructing Education for the new millennium. *International Journal of Technology and Design Education, 11,* 67–81.

Kellner, D. (2002). New media and new literacies: Reconstructing education for the new millennium. In L. Lievrouw & S. Livingston (Eds.), *The handbook of new media* (pp. 90–104). Sage.

Kellner, D., & Share, J. (2005). Toward critical media literacy: Core concepts, debates, organizations, and policy. *Discourse (Abingdon)*, *26*(3), 369–386.

Kempson, E. (2009). *Framework for the development of financial literacy baseline surveys: A first international comparative analysis*. Academic Press.

Kennedy, E. J., & Lawton, L. (1998). Religiousness and business ethics. *Journal of Business Ethics*, *17*(2), 163–175. doi:10.1023/A:1005747511116

Kennedy, J., Baxter, P., Senft, E., & Belpaeme, T. (2016). Social Robot Tutoring for Child Second Language Learning. *The Eleventh ACM/IEEE International Conference on Human Robot Interaction*, 231-238. 10.1109/HRI.2016.7451757

Keppell, M. (2014). Personalised learning strategies for higher education. In *The future of learning and teaching in next generation learning spaces*. Emerald Group Publishing Limited. doi:10.1108/S1479-362820140000012001

Kerim, A., & Genc, B. (2020). Mobile Games Success and Failure: Mining the Hidden Factors. In *2020 7th International Conference on Soft Computing & Machine Intelligence (ISCMI)* (pp. 167-171). IEEE.

Kervin, L., Mantei, J., & Herrington, J. (2009). Using technology in pedagogically responsive ways to support literacy learners. In T. Wee & R. Subramaniam (Eds.), *Handbook on new media literacy at the K-12 level: Issues and Challenges* (pp. 203–215). IGI Global.

Ketonen, R., Salmi, P., & Krimark, P. (Eds.). (2015). Namibia: Literacy Assessment Tools for Grades 1-3 and Special Education. Namibia: Literacy Assessment Tools for Grades 1-3 and Special Education. Grapho Learning training Programme (2012-2014). Niilo Mäki Institute.

Kétyi, A. (2013). Using smart phones in language learning – A pilot study to turn CALL into MALL. In L. Bradley & S. Thouësny (Eds.), *20 Years of EUROCALL: Learning from the Past, Looking to the Future. Proceedings of the 2013 EUROCALL Conference, Évora, Portugal* (pp.129-134). Research-publishing.net. 10.14705/rpnet.2013.000150

Keup, J., & Barefoot, B. (2005). Learning How to be a Successful Student: Exploring the Impact of First-Year Seminars on Student Outcomes. *Journal of the First-Year Experience & Students in Transition*, *17*(1), 11–47.

Khadka, S. (2014). *New Media Multiliteracies, and the globalized classroom*. Syracuse University. Dissertations. https://surface.syr.edu/cgi/viewcontent.cgi?article=1055&context=etd

Khan, A., Ahmad, F. H., & Malik, M. M. (2017). Use of digital game based learning and gamification in secondary school science: The effect on student engagement, learning and gender difference. *Education and Information Technologies*, *22*(6), 2767–2804. doi:10.100710639-017-9622-1

Khan, M. N. U., Rana, E. A., & Haque, M. R. (2014). Reforming the education system in Bangladesh: Reckoning a knowledge-based society. *World Journal of Education*, *4*(4), 1–11. doi:10.5430/wje.v4n4p1

Kickbusch, I., Pelikan, J. M., Apfel, F., & Tsouros, A. D. (Eds.). (2013). *Health Literacy. The Solid Facts*. World Health Organization. Retrieved May 03, 2019 from http://www.euro.who.int/__data/assets/pdf_file/0008/190655/e96854.pdf

Kietzmann, J., & Kristopher, H. (2011). Social media? Get serious! Understanding the functional building blocks of social media. *Business Horizons*, *54*(3), 241–251. doi:10.1016/j.bushor.2011.01.005

Kiili, K., Kiili, C., Ott, M., & Jönkkäri, T. (2012). Towards creative pedagogy: Empowering students to develop games. In *6th European Conference on Games Based Learning*. Academic Press.

Kiili, K. (2005). Content creation challenges and flow experience in educational games: The IT-Emperor case. *The Internet and Higher Education*, *8*(3), 183–198. doi:10.1016/j.iheduc.2005.06.001

Kiili, K. (2005). Digital game- based learning: Towards an experiential gaming model. *The Internet and Higher Education, 8*(1), 13–24. doi:10.1016/j.iheduc.2004.12.001

Kiili, K., Lainema, T., de Freitas, S., & Arnab, S. (2014). Flow framework for analyzing the quality of educational games. *Entertainment Computing, 4*(4), 367–377. doi:10.1016/j.entcom.2014.08.002

Kiili, K., Moeller, K., & Ninaus, M. (2018). Evaluating a Game-Based Training of Rational Number Understanding-In-Game Metrics as Learning Indicators. *Computers & Education*, 13–28. doi:10.1016/j.compedu.2018.01.012

Kim, B. (2012). Harnessing the power of game dynamics: Why, how to, and how not to gamify the library experience. *College & Research Libraries News, 73*(8), 465–469. doi:10.5860/crln.73.8.8811

Kim, S. S., & Malhotra, N. K. (2005). A longitudinal model of continued IS use: An integrative view of four mechanisms underlying postadoption phenomena. *Management Science, 51*(5), 741–755. doi:10.1287/mnsc.1040.0326

Kim, S., Song, K., Lockee, B., & Burton, J. (2018). *Gamification in learning and education: enjoy learning like gaming.* Springer. doi:10.1007/978-3-319-47283-6

Kim, Y., Smith, D., Kim, N., & Chen, T. (2014). Playing with a robot to learn English vocabulary. In *KAERA. Research Forum, 1*(2), 3–8.

Kinect for Windows. (2016). Retrieved September 11, 2021 from http://kinectforwindows.org/

King, D. L., Delfabbro, P. H., Billieux, J., & Potenza, M. N. (2020). Problematic online gaming and the COVID-19 pandemic. *Journal of Behavioral Addictions, 9*(2), 184–186. doi:10.1556/2006.2020.00016 PMID:32352927

King, D., Greaves, F., Exeter, C., & Darzi, A. (2013). 'Gamification': Influencing health behaviours with games. *Journal of the Royal Society of Medicine, 106*(3), 76–78. doi:10.1177/0141076813480996 PMID:23481424

Kipping, P. (2004). Media literacy-An important strategy for building peace. *Peace Magazine.* Retrieved on December 3, 2012, from homes.ieu.edu.tr

Kirchner, E., Alexander, S., & Tötemeyer, A.-J. (2014). The reading habits / behaviour and preferences of African children : The Namibian chapter in collaboration with UNISA. Academic Press.

Kirikkaya, E. B., Işeri, Ş., & Vurkaya, G. (2010). A board game about space and solar system for primary school students. *The Turkish Online Journal of Educational Technology, 9*(2), 1–13.

Kirriemuir, J. (2006). A history of digital games. In J. Rutter & J. Bryce (Eds.), *Understanding Digital Games* (pp. 21–36). Sage Publications. doi:10.4135/9781446211397.n2

Kirriemuir, J., & McFarlane, A. (2004). *Literature review in games and learning* (Vol. 8). Futurelab.

Kirschner, P. A. (2005). Learning in innovative learning environments. *Computers in Human Behavior, 21*(4), 547–554. doi:10.1016/j.chb.2004.10.022

Kiryakova, G., Angelova, N., & Yordanova, L. (2014). Gamification in education. *Proceedings of 9th International Balkan Education and Science Conference.*

Kivunja, C. (2014). Theoretical Perspectives of How Digital Natives Learn. *International Journal of Higher Education, 3*(1), 94–109. doi:10.5430/ijhe.v3n1p94

Kivunja, C. (2018). Distinguishing between theory, theoretical framework, and conceptual framework: A systematic review of lessons from the field. *International Journal of Higher Education, 7*(6), 44–53. doi:10.5430/ijhe.v7n6p44

Klaassen, R., Bul, K. C. M., Op Den Akker, R., Van Der Burg, G. J., Kato, P. M., & Di Bitonto, P. (2018). *Design and evaluation of a pervasive coaching and gamification platform for young diabetes patients*. Sensors. doi:10.339018020402

Klein, A. (2021). There aren't enough computer science classes for all the kids who want to take them. *Education Week*. Retrieved (from https://www.edweek.org/teaching-learning/there-arent-enough-computer-science-classes-for-all-the-kids-who-want-to-take-them/2021/09

Kler, S. (2014). ICT Integration in Teaching and Learning: Empowerment of Education with Technology. *Issues and Ideas in Education*, 2(2), 255–271. doi:10.15415/iie.2014.22019

Klock, A. C. T., Gasparini, I., Pimenta, M. S., & Hamari, J. (2020). Tailored gamification: A review of literature. *International Journal of Human-Computer Studies*, 144, 102495. Advance online publication. doi:10.1016/j.ijhcs.2020.102495

Klopfer, E., Osterweil, S., & Salen, K. (2009). *Moving learning games forward: Obstacles, opportunities, and openness*. The Education Arcade at MIT.

Klopfer, E., & Squire, K. (2008). Environmental Detectives—The development of an augmented reality platform for environmental simulations. *Educational Technology Research and Development*, 56(2), 203–228. doi:10.100711423-007-9037-6

Knauf, H. (2016). Interlaced social worlds: exploring the use of social media in the kindergarten. *Early Years*, 36(3), 254-270. doi:10.1080/09575146.2016.1147424

Knautz, K., Orszullok, L., & Soubusta, S. (2013). Game-based IL instruction–A journey of knowledge in four acts. In *European Conference on Information Literacy* (pp. 366-372). Springer International Publishing. 10.1007/978-3-319-03919-0_48

Knezek, G., & Christensen, R. (2002). Impact of new information technologies on teachers and students. *Education and Information Technologies*, 7(4), 369–376. doi:10.1023/A:1020921807131

Knol, E., & De Vries, P. W. (2011). EnerCities, a serious game to stimulate sustainability and energy conservation: Preliminary results. *eLearning Papers*, 25, 1–10. Retrieved from https://papers.ssrn.com/sol3/papers.cfm?abstract_id=1866206

Knudsen, E. I. (2018). Neural Circuits That Mediate Selective Attention: A Comparative Perspective. *Trends in Neurosciences*, 41(11), 789–805. doi:10.1016/j.tins.2018.06.006 PMID:30075867

Knutson, B., Westdorp, A., Kaiser, E., & Hommer, D. (2000). FMRI visualization of brain activity during a monetary incentive delay task. *NeuroImage*, 12(1), 20–27. doi:10.1006/nimg.2000.0593 PMID:10875899

Kocaman, O., & Cumaoglu, G. K. (2014). The effect of educational software (DENIS) and games on vocabulary learning strategies and achievement. *Eğitim ve Bilim*, 39(176), 305–316. doi:10.15390/EB.2014.3704

Koehler, M. J., Mishra, P., & Cain, W. (2013). What is Technological Pedagogical Content Knowledge (TPACK)? *Journal of Education*, 193(3), 13–19. doi:10.1177/002205741319300303

Koehler, M. J., Mishra, P., Kereluik, K., Shin, T. S., & Graham, C. R. (2014). The technological pedagogical content knowledge framework. In J. M. Spector, M. D. Merrill, J. van Merrienboer, & M. P. Driscoll (Eds.), *Handbook of research on educational communications and technology* (pp. 101–111). Springer. doi:10.1007/978-1-4614-3185-5_9

Koenitz, H., Ferri, G., Haahr, M., Sezen, D., & Sezen, T. I. (Eds.). (2015). *Interactive digital narrative: History, theory and practice*. Routledge. doi:10.4324/9781315769189

Kogan, L., Hellyer, P., Duncan, C., & Schoenfeld-Tacher, R. (2017). A pilot investigation of the physical and psychological benefits of playing Pokémon GO for dog owners. *Computers in Human Behavior*, *76*, 431–437. doi:10.1016/j.chb.2017.07.043

Koivisto, J., & Hamari, J. (2014). Demographic differences in perceived benefits from Gamification. Computers in Human Behavior, 35, 179-188.

Koivisto, J., & Hamari, J. (2019). The Rise of Motivational Information Systems: A Review of Gamification Research. *International Journal of Information Management*, *45*, 191–210. doi:10.1016/j.ijinfomgt.2018.10.013

Kolb, D. A. (1984). Experiential learning: Experience as the source of learning and development, David A. Kolb, Prentice-Hall International, Hemel Hempstead, Herts., 1984. No. of pages: xiii + 256. Journal of Organizational Behavior.

Kolb, D. A., & Kolb, A. Y. (2013). Research on Validity and Educational Applications. *Experience Based Learning Systems, 5.*

Kolb, A. Y., & Kolb, D. A. (2005). Learning Styles and Learning Spaces: Enhancing Experiential Learning in Higher Education. *Academy of Management Learning & Education*, *4*(2), 193–212. doi:10.5465/amle.2005.17268566

Kolb, D. (1984). *Experiential learning as the science of learning and development.* Prentice Hall.

Kolb, D. (1984). *Experiential learning: Experience as the source of learning and development.* Prentice-Hall.

Kolb, L. (2020). *Learning first, Technology second in practice: New strategies, research and tools for student success.* International Society for Technology in Education.

Kong, S. C. (2014). Developing information literacy and critical thinking skills through domain knowledge learning in digital classrooms: An experience of practicing flipped classroom strategy. *Computers & Education*, *78*, 160–173. doi:10.1016/j.compedu.2014.05.009

Korn, O. (2012). Industrial playgrounds: how Gamification helps to enrich work for elderly or impaired persons in production. In *Proceedings of the 4th ACM SIGCHI symposium on Engineering interactive computing systems* (pp. 313-316). ACM. 10.1145/2305484.2305539

Kory, J., & Breazeal, C. (2014, August). Storytelling with robots: Learning companions for preschool children's language development. In *The 23rd IEEE international symposium on robot and human interactive communication* (pp. 643-648). IEEE. 10.1109/ROMAN.2014.6926325

Koster, R. (2004). *Theory of fun for game design.* Paraglyph.

Kotilainen, S. (2009). Promoting youth civic participation with media production: The case of youth choice editorial board. In D. Frau-Meigs & J. Torrent (Eds.), Mapping media education policies in the world: Vision,programmes and challenges. New York: UN-Alliance of Civilization.

Kottek, M., Grieser, J., Beck, C., Rudolf, B., & Rubel, F. (2006). *World map of the Köppen-Geiger climate classification updated.* Academic Press.

Koutromanos, G. (2020). Primary School Students' Perceptions About the Use of Mobile Games in the Classroom. In Mobile Learning Applications in Early Childhood Education (pp. 230-250). IGI Global.

Koutromanos, G., & Avraamidou, L. (2014). The use of mobile games in formal and informal learning environments: A review of the literature. *Educational Media International*, *51*(1), 49–65. doi:10.1080/09523987.2014.889409

Kouwenhoven, W., Howie, S. J., & Plomp, T. (2003). The Role of Needs Assessment in Developing Competence-Based Education in Mozambican Higher Education. *Perspectives in Education*, *21*(1), 34–154.

Kozdras, D., Joseph, C., & Schneider, J. J. (2015). Reading Games: Close Viewing and Guided Playing of Multimedia Texts. *The Reading Teacher*, *69*(3), 331–338. doi:10.1002/trtr.1413

Krathwohl, D. R., & Anderson, L. W. (2010). Merlin C. Wittrock and the revision of Bloom's taxonomy. *Educational Psychologist*, *45*(1), 64–65. doi:10.1080/00461520903433562

Kress, G. R. (2010). *Multimodality: A social semiotic approach to contemporary communication*. Routledge.

Krishnaswamy. (2011). *New media vs traditional media*. Retrieved in Sept 2021, from https://www.scribd.com/document/397697219/New-Media-vs-Traditional-Media

Kritzinger, E., Loock, M., & Goosen, L. (2019). Cyber Safety Awareness – Through the Lens of 21st Century Learning Skills and Game-Based Learning. *Lecture Notes in Computer Science*, *11937*, 477–485. doi:10.1007/978-3-030-35343-8_51

Krouse, R. Z., Ransdell, L. B., Lucas, S. M., & Pritchard, M. E. (2011). Motivation, goal orientation, coaching, and training habits of women ultrarunners. *Journal of Strength and Conditioning Research*, *25*(10), 2835–2842. doi:10.1519/JSC.0b013e318204caa0 PMID:21946910

Krstic, K., Stepanovic-Ilic, I., & Videnovic, M. (2017). Student dropout in primary and secondary education in the Republic of Serbia. *Psiholoska Istrazivanja*, *20*(1), 27–50. doi:10.5937/PsIstra1701027K

Kruger, W. (2012). *Learning to read Afrikaans*. www.homeschooling-curriculum-guide.com

Kubota, T. (2017). *Faculty and students at Stanford argue for increased study of games and interactive media*. Retrieved January 14, 2020, from https://news.stanford.edu/2017/05/03/interest-grows-study-games-interactive-media/

Kucirkova, N. (2018). *How and why to read and create digital books: A guide for primary practitioners*. UCL Press.

Kuglitsch, R. Z. (2015). Teaching for Transfer: Reconciling the Framework with Disciplinary Information Literacy. *Portal (Baltimore, Md.)*, *15*(3), 457–470. doi:10.1353/pla.2015.0040

Kuglitsch, R. Z., & Burge, P. (2016). Beyond the first year: Supporting sophomores through information literacy outreach. *College & Undergraduate Libraries*, *23*(1), 79–92. doi:10.1080/10691316.2014.944636

Kuhlthau, C. C., Caspari, A. K., & Maniotes, L. K. (2007). *Guided inquiry: Learning in the 21st century*. Libraries Unlimited.

Kuhn, J. (2017). Minecraft: Education edition. *CALICO Journal*, *35*(2), 214–223. doi:10.1558/cj.34600

Kuhn, J., & Stevens, V. (2017). Participatory culture as professional development: Preparing teachers to use Minecraft in the classroom. *TESOL Journal*, *8*(4), 753–767. doi:10.1002/tesj.359

Kumar, S. (2017). A river by any other name: Ganga/Ganges and the postcolonial politics of knowledge on Wikipedia. *Information Communication and Society*, *20*(6), 809–824. doi:10.1080/1369118X.2017.1293709

Küng, H. (2015). A Global Ethic in an Age of Globalization. *Business Ethics Quarterly*, *7*(3), 17–32. doi:10.2307/3857310

Kurkovsky, S. (2013). Mobile game development: Improving student engagement and motivation in introductory computing courses. *Journal of Computer Science Education*, *23*(2), 138–157. doi:10.1080/08993408.2013.777236

Kyle, F., Kujala, J., Richardson, U., Lyytinen, H., & Goswami, U. (2013). Assessing the effectiveness of two theoretically motivated computer-assisted reading interventions in the United Kingdom: GG rime and GG phoneme. *Reading Research Quarterly*, *48*(1), 61–76. http://www.learntechlib.org/p/91905. doi:10.1002/rrq.038

La Guardia, D., Gentile, M., Dal Grande, V., Ottaviano, S., & Allegra, M. (2014). A Game based Learning Model for Entrepreneurship Education. *Procedia: Social and Behavioral Sciences*, *141*, 195–199. doi:10.1016/j.sbspro.2014.05.034

Laboratory, H. A. L. (2014). *Super Smash Bros. Melee* [Video game]. Nintendo.

Laborde, C., Kynigos, C., Hollebrands, K., & Strässer, R. (2006). Teaching and learning geometry with technology. In A. Guitiérrez & P. Boero (Eds.), *Handbook of Research on the Psychology of Mathematics Education: Past, Present and Future* (pp. 275–304). Sense Publishers.

Lai, C.-H., Lee, T.-P., Jong, B.-S., & Hsia, Y.-T. (2012). A Research on Applying Game-Based Learning to Enhance the Participation of Student. In Embedded and Multimedia Computing Technology and Service (pp. 311–318). Springer Netherlands. doi:10.1007/978-94-007-5076-0_36

Lai, N. K., Ang, T. F., Por, L. Y., & Liew, C. S. (2018). The impact of play on child development - a literature review. *European Early Childhood Education Research Journal, 26*(5), 625–643. doi:10.1080/1350293X.2018.1522479

Lambert, J. (2013). *Digital storytelling: Capturing lives, creating community* (4th ed.). Routledge. doi:10.4324/9780203102329

Lambrecht, M., Creemers, S., Boute, R., & Leus, R. (2012). Extending the production dice game. *International Journal of Operations & Production Management, 32*(12), 144–3577. doi:10.1108/01443571211284197

Lam, C. M. (2016). Fostering rationality in Asian education. In C. M. Lam & J. Park (Eds.), *Sociological and philosophical perspectives on education in the Asia-Pacific region: issues, concerns and prospects* (Vol. 29, pp. 9–22). Springer. doi:10.1007/978-981-287-940-0_2

Landers, R. N. (2014). Developing a Theory of Gamified Learning:Linking Serious Games and Gamification of Learning. *Simulation & Gaming, 45*(6), 752–768. doi:10.1177/1046878114563660

Landi, N., Malins, J. G., Frost, S. J., Magnuson, J. S., Molfese, P., Ryherd, K., & Pugh, K. R. (2018). Neural representations for newly learned words are modulated by overnight consolidation, reading skill, and age. *Neuropsychologia, 111*, 133–144. doi:10.1016/j.neuropsychologia.2018.01.011 PMID:29366948

Landow, G. (1997). *The convergence of contemporary critical theory and technology.* The Johns Hopkins University Press.

Lane, C. A. (2018). *Multiliteracies meaning-making: How four boys' video gaming experiences influence their cultural knowledge—Two ethnographic cases* (Doctoral Dissertation, Western University). Electronic Thesis and Dissertation Repository. 5303. https://ir.lib.uwo.ca/etd/5303

Lane, C. A. (2018). *Multiliteracies meaning-making: How four boys' video gaming experiences influence their cultural knowledge—Two ethnographic cases.* The University of Western Ontario. Retrieved from https://ir.lib.uwo.ca/cgi/viewcontent.cgi?article=7128&context=etd

Lane, C.-A. (2014, March). How video games affect boys' literacy practices. In *The Robert MacMillan Graduate Research in Education Symposium - Theory to Practice.* Western University.

Lane, C.-A. (2019a). Digitizing Learning: How Video Games Can Be Used as Alternative Pathways to Learning. In Innovative Trends in Flipped Teaching and Adaptive Learning (pp. 138-161). IGI Global.

Lane, C.-A. (2019b). Video Games Support Alternative Classroom Pedagogies to Support Boys' Meaning-Making. In Integrating Digital Technology in Education: School-University-Community Collaboration (pp. 199-224). Information Age.

Lane, C.-A. (2021). Using Digital Technologies in the 21st Century Classroom: How Video Games Support Dynamic Learning Opportunities. In Present and Future Paradigms of Cyberculture in the 21st Century (pp. 109-134). IGI Global.

Lane, C. A. (2021). Using Digital Technologies in the 21st Century Classroom: How Video Games Support Dynamic Learning Opportunities. In C. A. Lane (Ed.), *Present and Future Paradigms of Cyberculture in the 21st Century* (pp. 109–134). IGI Global. doi:10.4018/978-1-5225-8024-9.ch007

Lane, C.-A. (2013). Using Video Technology to Address Boys' Literacy Gap and Connect the Male Voice in Gender Dynamics. *International Journal of Technology and Inclusive Education*, *2*(1), 139–150. doi:10.20533/ijtie.2047.0533.2013.0020

Lane, C.-A. (2016). 'Play, Score, Engage': Finding Ways for Boys to Make the Grade! *Literacy Information and Computer Education Journal*, *7*(4), 2461–2467. doi:10.20533/licej.2040.2589.2016.0327

Lane, H. C., & Yi, S. (2017). Playing with virtual blocks: Minecraft as a learning environment for practice and research. In *Cognitive development in digital contexts* (pp. 145–166). Academic Press. doi:10.1016/B978-0-12-809481-5.00007-9

Langat, A. C. (2015). Barriers Hindering Implementation, Innovation and Adoption of ICT in Primary Schools in Kenya. *International Journal of Innovative Research and Development*, *4*(2), 1–11.

Lankshear, C. (1997). *Changing literacies*. McGraw-Hill Education.

Lankshear, C., & Knobel, M. (2006). *New literacies: Everyday practices and classroom learning*. Open University Press.

Lankshear, C., & Knobel, M. (2011). *New literacies: Everyday practices and social learning* (3rd ed.). McGraw-Hill.

Lan, Y. J., Botha, A., Shang, J., & Jong, M. S. Y. (2018). Guest editorial: Technology enhanced contextual game-based language learning. *Journal of Educational Technology & Society*, *21*(3), 86–89.

Larmer, J. (2015). *Project-Based Learning vs. Problem-Based Learning vs. X-BL*. https://www.edutopia.org/blog/pbl-vs-pbl-vs-xbl-john-larmer

Larose, F., Grenon, V., Morin, M. P., & Hasni, A. (2009). The impact of pre-service field training sessions of the probability of future teachers using ICT in school. *European Journal of Teacher Education*, *32*(3), 289–303. doi:10.1080/02619760903006144

Larson, L. C. (2010). Digital readers: The next chapter in ebook reading and response. *The Reading Teacher*, *64*(1), 15–22. https://doi.org/10.1598/RT.64.1.2

Lasagabaster, D. (2008). Foreign language competence in content and language integrated courses. *The Open Applied Linguistics Journal*, *1*(1), 31–42. doi:10.2174/1874913500801010030

Latorre-Cosculluela, C., Suárez, C., Quiroga, S., Sobradiel-Sierra, N., Lozano-Blasco, R., & Rodríguez-Martínez, A. (2021). Flipped Classroom model before and during COVID-19: Using technology to develop 21st century skills. *Interactive Technology and Smart Education*, *18*(2), 189–204. Advance online publication. doi:10.1108/ITSE-08-2020-0137

Laughey, D. (2010). Medya calışmaları, teoriler ve yaklaşımlar. İstanbul: Kalkedon.

Lauricella, A. R., Robb, M. B., & Wartella, E. (2007). Challenges and suggestions for determining quality in children's media. In D. Lemish (Ed.), The Routledge international handbook of children, adolescents, and media (pp. 425–432). https://doi.org/10.4324/9780203366981.CH52.

Laurillard, D. (2002). *Rethinking university teaching: a framework for the effective use of learning technologies* (2nd ed.). Routledge Falmer. doi:10.4324/9780203160329

Lavender, T. J. (2008). *Homeless: It's no game-measuring the effectiveness of a persuasive videogame*. School of Interactive Arts & Technology-Simon Fraser University.

Lawrence, R., Ching, L. F., & Abdullah, H. (2019). Strengths and Weaknesses of Education 4.0 in the Higher Education Institution. *International Journal of Innovative Technology and Exploring Engineering*, 9(2), 511–519. Advance online publication. doi:10.35940/ijitee.B1122.1292S319

Layton, L., & Brown, E. (2012, Sept. 24). SAT Reading Scores Hit a Four-Decade Low. *The Washington Post*, p. 1.

Leadership Project. (1995). *Adult Learning Principles & Practice*. Sheridan College.

Leander, K., & Ehret, C. (Eds.). (2019). *Affect turn in literacy learning and teaching: Pedagogies, politics, and coming to know*. Routledge. doi:10.4324/9781351256766

Learning games: Make learning awesome! (2021, October 22). *Kahoot!* Retrieved October 26, 2021, from https://kahoot.com/

Learning tools & flashcards, for free. (n.d.). *quizlet*. Retrieved October 26, 2021, from https://quizlet.com/

Leary, M., & Tangney, J. (2003). *Handbook of self and identity*. Guilford Press.

Lederman, L. C. (1984). Debriefing: A critical re-examination of the post-experience analytic process and implications for effective use. *Simulation & Games*, 15(4), 415–431. doi:10.1177/0037550084154002

Ledward, B. C., & Hirata, D. (2011). *An overview of 21st century skills. Summary of 21st century skills for students and teachers*. Kamehameha Schools–Research & Evaluation.

Lee, Cheung, & Chen. (2005). Acceptance of Internet-based learning medium: the role of extrinsic and intrinsic motivation. *Information & Management, 42*(8), 1095-104.

Lee, K. H. (2021). *The educational 'metaverse' is coming*. The Campus. Retrieved from https://www.timeshighereducation.com/campus/educational-metaverse-coming

Lee, V., Poole, F., Clarke-Midura, J., Recker, M., & Rasmussen, M. (2020). *Introducing coding through tabletop board games and their digital instantiations across elementary classrooms and school libraries*. Paper presented at SIGCSE, Portland. OR.

Lee, W. J., Huang, C. W., Wu, C. J., Huang, S. T., & Chen, G. D. (2012). The effects of using embodied interactions to improve learning performance. *2012 IEEE 12th international conference on advanced learning technologies (ICALT)*, 557-559.

Leemkuil, H., & De Jong, T. O. N. (2012). Adaptive advice in learning with a computer-based knowledge management simulation game. *Academy of Management Learning & Education*, 11(4), 653–665. doi:10.5465/amle.2010.0141

Lee, T. Y., Mauriello, M., Ahn, J., & Bederson, B. (2014). CTArcade: Computational thinking with games in school-aged children. *International Journal of Child-Computer Interaction*, 2, 26–33.

Lee, Y. J., & Gerber, H. (2013). It's a WoW World: Second language acquisition and massively multiplayer online gaming. *Multimedia-Assisted Language Learning*, 16(2), 53–70. doi:10.15702/mall.2013.16.2.53

Legaki, N. Z., Xi, N., Hamari, J., & Assimakopoulos, V. (2019, January). Gamification of The Future: An Experiment on Gamifying Education of Forecasting. *Proceedings of the 52nd Hawaii International Conference on System Sciences*. 10.24251/HICSS.2019.219

Leman, K. (2017). *Ellen's Game of Games* [Game Show Series]. NBC.

Lemmon, P. (1985). A school where learning styles make a difference. *Principal*, 64, 26–29.

Lenhard, W., & Lenhard, A. (2016). *Calculation of Effect Sizes*. Psychometrica., doi:10.13140/RG.2.1.3478.4245

Lenhart, A., Kahne, J., Middaugh, E., Macgill, A. R., Evans, C., & Vitak, J. (2008). *Teens, Video Games, and Civics: Teens' Gaming Experiences Are Diverse and Include Significant Social Interaction and Civic Engagement.* Pew internet & American Life Project.

Lenoir, T. (2004). Foreword. In *M.B.N. Hansen, New Philosophy for New Media*. The MIT Press.

Lenormand, M. (2019). The importance of not being Ernest: An archaeology of child's play in Freud's writings (and some implications for psychoanalytic theory and practice). *The International Journal of Psycho-Analysis, 100*(1), 52–76. doi:10.1080/00207578.2018.1489708 PMID:33945712

Leont'ev, A. (1981). The problem of activity in psychology. In J. Wertsch (Ed.), *The concept of activity in Soviet psychology*. Sharpe.

Leung, E., & Pluskwik, E. (2018, June). *Effectiveness of gamification activities in a project-based learning classroom* [Classroom paper presentation]. 2018 ASEE Annual Conference & Exposition, Salt Lake City, UT. https://peer.asee.org/30361

Lewin, K. M. (2007). *Improving access, equity and transitions in Education: Creating a research agenda*. Centre for International Education. http://www.create-rpc.org/pdf_documents/PTA1.pdf

Lewis Ellison, T. (2017). Digital participation, agency, and choice: An African American youth's digital storytelling about Minecraft. *Journal of Adolescent & Adult Literacy, 61*(1), 25–35. doi:10.1002/jaal.645

Li, C. (2017). *Attitudes towards Digital Game-based Learning of Chinese Primary School English Teachers* [Master's thesis]. University of Edinburgh. https://bit.ly/3yew4UR

Li, Z., Zou, D., Xie, H., Wang, F.-L., & Chang, M. (2018). Enhancing Information Literacy in Hong Kong Higher Education through Game-based Learning. *Proceedings of 22nd Global Chinese Conference on Computers in Education (GCCCE 2018)*, 595-598.

Lichty, P. (2019). The Gamification of Augmented Reality Art. In *Augmented Reality Games II* (pp. 225–246). Springer. doi:10.1007/978-3-030-15620-6_10

Liesa-Orús, M., Latorre-Cosculluela, C., Vázquez-Toledo, S., & Sierra-Sánchez, V. (2020). The Technological Challenge Facing Higher Education Professors: Perceptions of ICT Tools for Developing 21st Century Skills. *Sustainability, 12*(13), 5339. doi:10.3390u12135339

Li, K., Peterson, M., & Wang, Q. (2021). Using Community of Inquiry to Scaffold Language Learning in Out-of-School Gaming: A Case Study. *International Journal of Game-Based Learning, 11*(1), 31–56. doi:10.4018/IJGBL.2021010103

Li, M. C., & Tsai, C.-C. (2013). Game-based learning in science education: A review of relevant research. *Journal of Science Education and Technology, 22*(6), 877–898. doi:10.100710956-013-9436-x

Lima, L., & Gouveia, P. (2020). Gender Asymmetries in the Digital Games Sector in Portugal. *DIGRA 2020 Tampere Conference Proceedings*, 1-16.

Lima, L., Gouveia, P., & Pinto, C. (2021). *Gaming in Portugal 2020: Women in Digital Games and the Impact of Covid-19*. Retrieved October 4, 2021, from, https://icswac.weebly.com/program.html

Lima, L., Gouveia, P., Pinto, C., & Cardoso, P. (2021). I Never Imagined That I Would Work in The Digital Game Industry. In *CoG 2021 Proceedings: 3rd IEEE Conference on Games*. University of Copenhagen.

Lin, C. J., & Hwang, G. J. (2018). A flipped classroom approach to supporting gamebased learning activities for EFL business writing course. In *3rd Annual International Seminar on Transformative Education and Educational Leadership (AISTEEL 2018)*. Atlantis Press

Lin, D. T. A., Ganapathy, M., & Kaur, M. (2018). Kahoot! it: Gamification in higher education. *Social Sciences & Humanities, 26*(1), 565–582. https://www.researchgate.net/profile/Debbita-Tan/publication/320182671_Kahoot_It_Gamification_in_Higher_Education/links/5ab3757aa6fdcc1bc0c288fe/Kahoot-It-Gamification-in-Higher-Education.pdf

Lin, Y., & Nguyen, H. (2021). International Students' Perspectives on e-Learning During COVID-19 in Higher Education in Australia: A Study of an Asian Student. *The Electronic Journal of e-Learning, 19*(4), 241-251. doi:10.34190/ejel.19.4.2349

Lincoln, Y., & Guba, G. (1985). *Naturalistic inquiry*. Sage. doi:10.1016/0147-1767(85)90062-8

Linda, K., & Pennington, C. (2016). "Girls Can't Play": The effects of Stereotype Threat on Females' Gaming Performance. *Computers in Human Behavior, 59*, 202–209. doi:10.1016/j.chb.2016.02.020

Linderoth, J., & Sjöblom, B. (2019). Being an Educator and Game Developer: The Role of Pedagogical Content Knowledge in Non-Commercial Serious Games Production. *Simulation & Gaming, 50*(6), 771–788. doi:10.1177/1046878119873023

Lindquist, K. A., Satpute, A. B., Wager, T. D., Weber, J., & Barrett, L. F. (2016). The brain basis of positive and negative affect: Evidence from a meta-analysis of the human neuroimaging literature. *Cerebral Cortex (New York, N.Y.), 26*(5), 1910–1922. doi:10.1093/cercor/bhv001 PMID:25631056

Lingard, B., Martino, W., Mills, M., & Bahr, M. (2002). Addressing the educational needs of boys. Commonwealth of Australia, Department of Education, Science and Training.

Lin, T. J., & Lan, Y. J. (2015). Language learning in virtual reality environments: Past, present, and future. *Journal of Educational Technology & Society, 18*(4), 486–497.

Lin, Y. C., Liu, T. C., Chang, M., & Yeh, S. P. (2009, August). Exploring children's perceptions of the robots. In *International Conference on Technologies for E-Learning and Digital Entertainment* (pp. 512-517). Springer. 10.1007/978-3-642-03364-3_63

Liou, H. H., Yang, S. J., Chen, S. Y., & Tarng, W. (2017). The influences of the 2D image-based augmented reality and virtual reality on student learning. *Journal of Educational Technology & Society, 20*(3), 110–121.

Li, S. C. S., & Huang, W. C. (2016). Lifestyles, innovation attributes, and teachers' adoption of game-based learning: Comparing non-adopters with early adopters, adopters and likely adopters in Taiwan. *Computers & Education, 96*, 29–41. doi:10.1016/j.compedu.2016.02.009

Litzinger, T. A., Lee, S. H., Wise, J. C., & Felder, R. M. (2007). A psychometric study of the index of learning styles. *Journal of Engineering Education, 96*(4), 309–319. doi:10.1002/j.2168-9830.2007.tb00941.x

Liu, Li, & Santhanam. (2013). Digital Games and Beyond: What Happens When Players Compete. *MIS Quarterly, 37*(1), 111-24.

Liu, E. Z. F., & Chen, P.-K. (2013). The Effect of Game-Based Learning on Students' Learning Performance in Science Learning – A Case of "Conveyance Go." *Procedia: Social and Behavioral Sciences, 103*, 1044–1051. doi:10.1016/j.sbspro.2013.10.430

Liu, S. H. (2011). Factors related to pedagogical beliefs of teachers and technology integration. *Computers & Education, 56*(4), 1012–1022. doi:10.1016/j.compedu.2010.12.001

Liu, Y., Fu, Q., & Fu, X. (2009). The interaction between cognition and emotion. *Chinese Science Bulletin, 54*(22), 4102–4116. doi:10.100711434-009-0632-2

Liu, Z., Moon, J., Kim, B., & Dai, C. P. (2020). Integrating additivity in educational games: A combined bibliometric analysis and meta-analysis review. *Educational Technology Research and Development, 68*(4), 1931–1959. doi:10.100711423-020-09791-4

Live learning game show. (n.d.). *Gimkit*. Retrieved October 26, 2021, from https://www.gimkit.com/

Livingstone, S. (2003). The Changing Natüre and Uses of Media Literacy. *European-mediaculture.org*, (4), 1-37.

Livingstone, S. (2004). What is media literacy? *Intermedia, 32*(3), 18-20. Retrieved May 03, 2019 from http://eprints.lse.ac.uk/1027/1/What_is_media_literacy_(LSERO).pdf

Livingstone, S. (2009). *Children and the internet: Great expectations, challenging realities.* Polity Press.

Livstrom, I. C., Szostkowski, A. H., & Roehrig, G. H. (2019). Integrated STEM in practice: Learning from Montessori philosophies and practices. *School Science and Mathematics, 119*(4), 190–202. doi:10.1111sm.12331

Li, Y., Garza, V., Keicher, A., & Popov, V. (2019). Predicting high school teacher use of technology: Pedagogical beliefs, technological beliefs and attitudes, and teacher training. *Technology. Knowledge and Learning, 24*(3), 501–518. doi:10.100710758-018-9355-2

Lo, C. K., & Hew, K. F. (2017). A critical review of flipped classroom challenges in K-12 education: Possible solutions and recommendations for future research. *Research and Practice in Technology Enhanced Learning, 12*(1), 1–22. doi:10.118641039-016-0044-2 PMID:30613253

LOGO Foundation. (2015). *Logo History.* https://el.media.mit.edu/logo-foundationl

Lombard, P. J. P. (2018). *Factors influencing the transition from high school to higher education: a case of the JuniorTukkie programme* [Doctor of Philosophy, University of Pretoria]. https://repository.up.ac.za/bitstream/handle/2263/67771/Lombard_Factors_2018.pdf?sequence=1&isAllowed

Lombardi, G. (2020). The role of unplugged coding activity in developing computational thinking in ages 6-11. In Handbook of Research on tools for teaching computational thinking in P-12 education (pp.184-199). Information Science Publishing.

Longenecker, J. G., McKinney, J. A., & Moore, C. W. (2004). Religious intensity, evangelical Christianity, and business ethics: An empirical study. *Journal of Business Ethics, 55*(4), 371–384. doi:10.100710551-004-0990-2

Lopes & Mesquita. (2015). Evaluation of a gamification methodology in higher education. *Edulearn15 Proceedings*, 6996-7005.

Lopez Frias, F. J. (2019). Bernard Suits' Response to the Question on the Meaning of Life as a Critique of Modernity. *Sport, Ethics and Philosophy, 13*(3-4), 406–418. doi:10.1080/17511321.2018.1550526

Lorås, M., Sindre, G., Trætteberg, H., & Aalberg, T. (2022). Study Behavior in Computing Education-A Systematic Literature Review. *ACM Transactions on Computing Education, 22*(1), 1–28. doi:10.1145/3469129

Lorenzo, G., & Dziuban, C. (2006). *Ensuring the Net Generation is net savvy.* Educause Learning Initiative Paper 2, September 2006 EDUCAUSE Learning Initiative. https://understandingxyz.com/index_htm_files/Net%20Gen%20paper.pdf

Lotherington, H., & Jenson, J. (2011). Teaching multimodal and digital literacy in L2 settings: New literacies, new basics, new pedagogies. *Annual Review of Applied Linguistics, 31*, 226–246. doi:10.1017/S0267190511000110

Lot, M., & Salleh, S. M. (2016). Game-based learning as a platform for formative assessment in principles of account. *Information (Japan)*, *19*(9B), 3971–3976.

Love, K., & Hamston, J. (2003). Teenage boys' leisure reading dispositions: Juggling male youth culture and family cultural capital. *Educational Review*, *55*(2), 161–177.

Loveless, A., & Williamson, B. (2013). *Learning identities in a digital age: Rethinking creativity, education and technology*. Routledge. doi:10.4324/9780203591161

Lowyck, J., Elen, J., & Clarebout, G. (2004). Instructional conceptions: Analysis from an instructional design perspective. *International Journal of Educational Research*, *41*(6), 429–444. doi:10.1016/j.ijer.2005.08.010

Lui, R., & Au, C. H. (2018). IS educational game: Adoption in teaching search engine optimization (SEO). *Journal of Computer Information Systems*.

Luke, C. (2000). Cyber-schooling and technological change: Multiliteracies for new times. In B. Cope & M. Kalantzis (Eds.), 2009 Multiliteracies (pp. 69–91). Macmillan.

Luke, A., & Elkins, J. (2002). Towards a critical, worldly, literacy. *Journal of Adolescent & Adult Literacy*, *45*(18), 668–674.

Lu, L.-C., & Lu, C.-J. (2010). Moral Philosophy, Materialism, and Consumer Ethics: An Exploratory Study in Indonesia. *Journal of Business Ethics*, *94*(2), 193–210. doi:10.100710551-009-0256-0

Luterbach, K. J., & Hubbell, K. R. (2015). Capitalizing on app development tools and technologies. *TechTrends*, *59*(4), 62–70. doi:10.100711528-015-0872-8

Lyman, S. (2017). *Comparison of early literacy iPad applications: Children's engagement* [Unpublished master's thesis]. Brigham Young University, Provo, UT, United States.

Lynch, L., Fawcett, A. J., & Nicolson, R. I. (2000). Computer-assisted reading intervention in a secondary school: An evaluation study. *British Journal of Educational Technology*, *31*(4), 333–348. doi:10.1111/1467-8535.00166

Lytras, M. D., Ruan, D., Tennyson, R. D., Ordonez De Pablos, P., García Peñalvo, F. J., & Rusu, L. (2013). Communications in Computer and Information Science. In Information Systems, E-learning, and Knowledge Management Research (vol. 278). doi:10.1007/978-3-642-35879-1

Lyytinen, H., Erskine, J., Kujala, J., Ojanen, E., & Richardson, U. (2009). In search of a science-based application: A learning tool for reading acquisition. *Scandinavian Journal of Psychology*, *50*(6), 668–675. doi:10.1111/j.1467-9450.2009.00791.x PMID:19930268

Lyytinen, H., Erskine, J., Tolvanen, A., Torppa, M., Poikkeus, A.-M., & Lyytinen, P. (2006). Trajectories of reading development: A follow-up from birth to school age of children with and without risk for dyslexia. *Merrill-Palmer Quarterly*, *52*(3), 514–546. doi:10.1353/mpq.2006.0031

Lyytinen, H., Ronimus, M., Alanko, A., Poikkeus, A., & Taanila, M. (2007). Early identification of dyslexia and the use of computer game-based practice to support reading acquisition. *Nordic Psychology*, *59*(2), 109–126. doi:10.1027/1901-2276.59.2.109

Mac an Ghaill, M. (1994). *The making of men: Masculinities, sexualities and schooling*. Open University Press.

Mac Callum, K., Jeffrey, L., & Na, K. (2014). Factors impacting teachers' adoption of mobile learning. *Journal of Information Technology Education*, *13*. doi:10.28945/1970

MacKay, K. (2015). *Does an iPad change the experience? A look at mother-child book reading interactions* [Unpublished doctoral dissertation]. Brigham Young University, Provo, UT, United States.

MacMurren, H. (1985). *A comparative study of the effects of matching and mismatching sixth-grade students with their learning style preferences for the physical element of intake and their subsequent reading speed and accuracy scores and attitudes* (Doctoral dissertation). St. John's University.

MacQueen, K. M., & Milstein, B. (1999). A systems approach to qualitative data management and analysis. *Field Methods*, *11*(1), 27–39. doi:10.1177/1525822X9901100103

Maddux, C. D., & Lamont, J. D. (2013). *Technology in Eduction: A Twenty-Year Retrospective*. Taylor and Francis. doi:10.4324/9781315821245

Magnan, A., & Ecalle, J. (2006). Audio-visual training in children with reading disabilities. *Computers & Education*, *46*(4), 407–425. doi:10.1016/j.compedu.2004.08.008

Mahar, D., Henderson, R., & Deane, F. (1997). The effects of computer anxiety, state anxiety, and computer experience on users' performance of computer based tasks. *Personality and Individual Differences*, *22*(5), 683–692. doi:10.1016/S0191-8869(96)00260-7

Maican, C., Lixandroiu, R., & Constantin, C. (2016). Interactive.ro – A study of a gamification framework using zero-cost tools. *Computers in Human Behavior*, *61*, 186–197. doi:10.1016/j.chb.2016.03.023

Majid, S., Yeow, C. W., Audrey, C. S. Y., & Shyong, L. R. (2010). *Enriching learning experience through class participation: A students' perspective. 76th IFLA General Conference and Assembly: Satellite Meeting on Cooperation and Collaboration in Teaching and Research*, Gothenburg, Sweden.

Majuri, J., Koivisto, J., & Hamari, J. (2018). Gamification of education and learning: A review of empirical literature. *Proceedings of the 2nd International GamiFIN Conference*. Retrieved from: http://ceur-ws.org/Vol-2186/paper2.pdf

Makuwa, D., Amadhila, L., Shikongo, S., & Dengeinge, R. (2011). Trends in achievement levels of grade 6 Learners in Namibia. *Policy Brief*, *1*.

Malak, M. S. (2013). Inclusive education in Bangladesh: Are pre-service teachers ready to accept students with special educational needs in regular classes? *Disability, CBR and Inclusive Development*, *24*(1), 56–81. doi:10.5463/dcid.v24i1.191

Malegiannaki, I., Daradoumis, T., & Retalis, S. (2021). Using a Story-Driven Board Game to Engage Students and Adults With Cultural Heritage. *International Journal of Game-Based Learning*, *11*(2), 1–19. doi:10.4018/IJGBL.2021040101

Malhotra, N. K., Kim, S. S., & Patil, A. (2006). Common method variance in IS research: A comparison of alternative approaches and a reanalysis of past research. *Management Science*, *52*(12), 1865–1883. doi:10.1287/mnsc.1060.0597

Mallory, S. (2019). To the Mun: Kerbal Space Program as Playful, Educational Experience. In *International Conference on Human-Computer Interaction* (pp. 320-332). Springer. 10.1007/978-3-030-22602-2_24

Malone, T. W., & Lepper, M. R. (1987). Making learning fun: A taxonomy of intrinsic motivations for learning. In R.E. Snow & M.J Farr (Eds.), Aptitude, learning, and instruction volume 3: Conative and affective process analyses (pp. 223-253). Lawrence Erlbaum Associates, Publishers.

Mandel, M., & Long, E. (2017). *A Economia de Aplicativos no Brasil*. Washington, DC: PPI Progressive Policy Institute.

Manikas, A., Gupta, M., & Boyd, L. (2015). Experiential exercises with four production planning and control systems. *International Journal of Production Research*, *53*(14), 4206–4217. doi:10.1080/00207543.2014.985393

Manovich, L. (2001). *The Language of New Media*. MIT Press.

Manovich, L. (2001). *The Language of new media*. The MIT Press.

Mantiri, O., Hibbert, G. K., & Jacobs, J. (2019). Digital literacy in ESL classroom. *Universal Journal of Educational Research, 7*(5), 1301–1305. doi:10.13189/ujer.2019.070515

Manual:Preventing access—MediaWiki. (n.d.). Retrieved June 1, 2021, from https://www.mediawiki.org/wiki/Manual:Preventing_access

Manurung, K. (2012). Creative teachers and effective teaching strategies that motivates learners to learn. *Indonesian Journal of Science Education, 2*(1), 1-8.

Manzano-León, A., Camacho-Lazarraga, P., Guerrero, M. A., Guerrero-Puerta, L., Aguilar-Parra, J. M., Trigueros, R., & Alias, A. (2021). Between Level Up and Game Over: A Systematic Literature Review of Gamification in Education. *Sustainability, 13*(4), 2247. doi:10.3390u13042247

Maqsood, S. (2020). *The Design, Development and Evaluation of a Digital Literacy Game for Preteens* (Doctoral dissertation). Carleton University.

Marcos-García, J. A., Martínez-Monés, A., & Dimitriadis, Y. (2015). DESPRO: A method based on roles to provide collaboration analysis support adapted to the participants in CSCL situations. *Computers & Education, 82*, 335–353. doi:10.1016/j.compedu.2014.10.027

Marcovitz, D. M. (2012). *Powerful PowerPoint for educators: Using Visual Basic for applications to make PowerPoint interactive*. Abc-Clio.

Marczewski, A. (2015). *Game Thinking Decision Tree*. Gamified UK. https://www.gamified.uk/gamification-framework/differences-between-gamification-and-games/game-thinking-decision-trees-small/

Marczewski, A. (2013). *Gamification: A Simple Introduction*. Andrzej Marczewski.

Maree, J. G., Fletcher, L., & Sommerville, J. (2011). Predicting success among prospective first-year students at the University of Pretoria. *South African Journal of Higher Education, 25*(6), 1125–1139.

Maree, K. (2020). Planning a research proposal. In K. Maree (Ed.), *First steps in research* (3rd ed., pp. 25–53). Van Schaik.

Marklund, B. B., & Taylor, A. S. A. (2016). Educational Games in Practice: The challenges involved in conducting a game-based curriculum. *Electronic Journal of e-Learning, 14*(2), 122-135.

Marklund, B. B., & Taylor, A.-S. A. (2015). *Teachers' Many Roles in Game-Based Learning Projects*. The 9th European Conference on Games Based Learning (ECGBL'15), Steinkjer, Norway.

Marklund, B. B., & Alklind Taylor, A. S. (2016). Educational games in practice: The challenges involved in conducting a game-based curriculum. *Electronic Journal of E-Learning, 14*(2), 121–135.

Marklund, B. B., & Taylor, A. S. A. (2015). Teachers' many roles in game-based learning projects. *Proceedings of the European Conference on Games-Based Learning*, 350–367.

Marlatt, R. (2019). Fortnite and the next level discourse: Understanding how gamers cultivate pedagogy in teacher education. *Proceedings from SITE '19: Society for Information Technology and Teacher Education Annual Conference*.

Marone, V. (2016). Playful constructivism: Making sense of digital games for learning and creativity through play, design, and participation. *Journal of Virtual Worlds Research, 9*(3), 1–18. doi:10.4101/jvwr.v9i3.7244

Marquardt, M. (2007). Action learning: resolving real problems in real time. In M. Silberman (Ed.), *The handbook of experiential learning* (pp. 94–110). Pfeiffer.

Marr, B. (2018). *7 Job Skills of The Future (That AIs And Robots Can't Do Better Than Humans)*. Retrieved from: https://www.forbes.com/sites/bernardmarr/2018/08/06/7-job-skills-of-the-future-that-ais-and-robots-cant-do-better-than-humans/#7c1894496c2e

Marshall, M. B. (2020). *White paper: Finding the way through the waves*. Retrieved from: https://www.eyebraingym.com/wp-content/uploads/2021/03/WHITEPAPER-Finding-the-way-through-the-waves-1.0_compressed.pdf

Marshall, M. B., Taukeni, S. G., Haihambo, C. K., Shihako, M., Muruti, R. D., Ligando, G., De Silva, C. & Marshall, M. (2020). Maximizing student's learning success through Lab-on-line. *Addressing multicultural needs in school guidance and counselling*, 262-276.

Marsh, J., & Yamada-Rice, D. (2013). Early literacy in the digital age. In D. Barone & M. Mallette (Eds.), *Best Practices in Early Literacy Instruction* (pp. 79–95). Guilford Press.

Martín del Pozo, M., Gómez-Pablos, V. B., Sánchez-Prieto, J. C., & García-Valcárcel Muñoz-Repiso, A. (2019). Review of Game-Based Learning in Secondary Education: Considering the Types of Video Games. Analysis. *Claves de Pensamiento Contemporáneo, 22*, 1–10.

Martin, J., & Sneegas, G. (2020). *Critical Worldbuilding: Toward a Geographical Engagement with Imagined Worlds*. /paper/Critical-Worldbuilding%3A-Toward-a-Geographical-with-Martin-Sneegas/8a8d4538706af65d8479b11cbd0f-cb135c32ca44

Martin, C. (2012). Video games, identity, and the constellation of information, video games, identity, and the constellation of information. *Bulletin of Science, Technology & Society, 32*(5), 384–392. doi:10.1177/0270467612463797

Martínez Muñoz, M., Jiménez Rodríguez, M. L., & Gutiérrez de Mesa, J. A. (2013). Electrical storm simulation to improve the learning physics process. *Informatics in Education, 12*(2), 191–206. doi:10.15388/infedu.2013.13

Martinez-Garza, M., Clark, D. B., & Nelson, B. C. (2013). Digital games and the US National Research Council's science proficiency goals. *Studies in Science Education, 49*(2), 170–208. doi:10.1080/03057267.2013.839372

Martino, J. C. R. (2019). *Hands-on machine learning with Microsoft Excel 2019: Build complete data analysis flows, from data collection to visualization*. Packt Publishing Ltd.

Martins, A., & Oliveira, L. (2019). Teachers' experiences and practices with game-based learning. *Proceedings of INTED2019 Conference*, 8575-8583. https://bit.ly/3guwMrd

Martin, W., Silander, M., & Rutter, S. (2019). Digital games as sources for science analogies: Learning about energy through play. *Computers & Education, 130*, 1–12. doi:10.1016/j.compedu.2018.11.002

Martí-Parreño, J., Méndez-Ibáñez, E., & Alonso-Arroyo, A. (2016). The use of gamification in education: A bibliometric and text mining analysis. *Journal of Computer Assisted Learning, 32*(6), 663–676. doi:10.1111/jcal.12161

Martí-Parreño, J., Seguí-Mas, D., & Seguí-Mas, E. (2016). Teachers' attitude towards and actual use of gamification. *Procedia: Social and Behavioral Sciences, 228*, 682–688. doi:10.1016/j.sbspro.2016.07.104

Marwick, A., & Ellison, N. (2012). "There isn't wifi in heaven!" Negotiating visibility on Facebook memorial pages. *Broadcast Education Association of Journal of Broadcasting and Electronic Media, 56*(3), 378–400. doi:10.1080/08838151.2012.705197

Massimino, P., Costa, A., Becciani, U., Krokos, M., Bandieramonte, M., Petta, C., Pistagna, C., Riggi, S., Sciacca, E., & Vitello, F. (2013). Learning astrophysics through mobile gaming. *Astronomical Data Analysis Software and Systems XXII, 475*, 113.

Massung, E., Coyle, D., Cater, K. F., Jay, M., & Preist, C. (2013). Using crowdsourcing to support pro-environmental community activism. In *Proceedings of the SIGCHI Conference on Human Factors in Computing Systems* (pp. 371-380). ACM. 10.1145/2470654.2470708

Masterman, L. (2005). *Teaching the Media*. Taylor and Francis.

Masterman, L. (1993). The Media Education Revolution. *Canadian Journal of Educational Communication, 22*(1), 5–14.

Maswahu, I. L. (2012). *Grade 10 dropout predisposition and resilience in one rural and one urban secondary school in the Kizito cluster of the Caprivi education region in Namibia*. University of the Western Cape. http://etd.uwc.ac.za/handle/11394/4494

Matheson, V. A., Abt-Perkins, D., & Snedden, D. (2002). *Making PowerPoint interactive with hyperlinks*. Paper presented at the poster session presented at the annual American Economic Association Convention, Atlanta, GA.

Mathevula, M. D., & Uwizeyimana, D. E. (2014). The challenges facing the integration of ICT in teaching and learning activities in South African Rural Secondary Schools. *Mediterranean Journal of Social Sciences, 5*(20), 1087–1097. doi:10.5901/mjss.2014.v5n20p1087

Mathrani, A., Christian, S., & Ponder-Sutton, A. (2016). PlayIT: Game based learning approach for teaching programming concepts. *Journal of Educational Technology & Society, 19*(2), 5–17.

Mattis, J. S. (2000). African American women's definitions of spirituality and religiosity. *The Journal of Black Psychology, 26*(1), 101–122. doi:10.1177/0095798400026001006

Mavromihales, M., Holmes, V., & Racasan, R. (2019). Game-based learning in mechanical engineering education: Case study of games-based learning application in computer aided design assembly. *International Journal of Mechanical Engineering Education, 47*(2), 156–179.

May, A. (2021). *Gamification, Game-Based Learning, and Student Engagement in Education*. Leadership Education Capstones 55. Retrieved from https://openriver.winona.edu/leadershipeducationcapstones/55

May, E. L., & Abreh, M. K. (2017). Strategies for Achieving ICT Literacy & Proficiency in the Rural Primary and Secondary Schools in Ghana. *Journal of Education & Social Sciences, 5*(2), 114–126. doi:10.20547/jess0521705203

Mayer, R. E. (2002). Multimedia learning. *Psychology of Learning and Motivation, 41*, 85–139. doi:10.1016/S0079-7421(02)80005-6

Mayer, R. E. (2020). Cognitive foundations of game-based learning. In J. L. Plass, R. E. Mayer, & B. D. Homer (Eds.), *Handbook of game-based learning* (pp. 83–110). The MIT Press.

Maynooth Students' Union. (2020). *COVID-19 Survey Results*. https://www.msu.ie/news/article/6013/COVID-19-Survey-Results/

Mayo, M. (2009). Video games: A route to large-scale STEM education? *Science, 323*(5910), 79–82. doi:10.1126cience.1166900 PMID:19119223

Mäyrä, F. (2008). *An introduction to Game Studies: Games in Culture*. Sage.

Mc Gregor, S. L. T., & Murnane, J. A. (2010). Paradigm, methodology and method: Intellectual integrity in consumer scholarship. *International Journal of Consumer Studies, 34*(4), 419–427. doi:10.1111/j.1470-6431.2010.00883.x

McCallum, S. (2012). Gamification and serious games for personalized health. *Studies in Health Technology and Informatics*. Advance online publication. doi:10.3233/978-1-61499-069-7-85 PMID:22942036

McCarthy, M. (2016). Experiential Learning Theory: From Theory To Practice. *Journal of Business & Economics Research, 14*(3), 91–100. doi:10.19030/jber.v14i3.9749

McCarthy, S. (2001). Identity construction in elementary readers and writers. *Reading Research Quarterly, 36*(12), 122–134. doi:10.1598/RRQ.36.2.2

McCauley, V., Davison, K., McHugh, P., Domegan, C., & Grehan, A. (2021). Innovative Education Strategies to Advance Ocean Literacy. In *Ocean Literacy: Understanding the Ocean* (pp. 149–168). Springer. doi:10.1007/978-3-030-70155-0_7

McClelland, J. L., McNaughton, B. L., & O'Reilly, R. C. (1995). Why there are complementary learning systems in the hippocampus and neocortex: Insights from the successes and failures of connectionist models of learning and memory. *Psychological Review, 102*(3), 419–457. doi:10.1037/0033-295X.102.3.419 PMID:7624455

McCoy, L., Lewis, J. H., & Dalton, D. (2016). Gamification and multimedia for medical Education: A landscape review. *Journal of Osteopathic Medicine, 116*(1), 22–34. doi:10.7556/jaoa.2016.003 PMID:26745561

McCreery, M. P., Schrader, P. G., & Krach, S. K. (2011). Navigating Massively Multiplayer Online Games: Evaluating 21st Century Skills for Learning within Virtual Environments. *Journal of Educational Computing Research, 44*(4), 473–493. doi:10.2190/EC.44.4.f

McCrindle, M. (2021). Generation Alpha. Academic Press.

McDaniel, S. W., & Burnett, J. J. (1990). Consumer religiosity and retail store evaluative criteria. *Journal of the Academy of Marketing Science, 18*(2), 101–112. doi:10.1007/BF02726426

McGonigal, J. (2011). *Reality is broken: Why games make us better and how they can change the world*. Penguin Press.

McGonigal, J. (2011). *Reality is Broken: Why Games make us Better and How they can Change the World*. Penguin.

McGonigal, J. (2011). *Reality is Broken: Why Games Make Us Better and How They Can Change the World*. Penguin.

McGonigal, J. (2015). *SuperBetter: A revolutionary approach to getting stronger, happier, braver and more resilient*. Penguin.

McGreevy, S. (2011). Eight weeks to a better brain. *The Harvard Gazette*. https://news.harvard.edu/gazette/story/2011/01/eight-weeks-to-a-better-brain/

McKenney, S. (2005). Technology for curriculum and teacher development: Software to help educators learn while designing teacher guides. *Journal of Research on Technology in Education, 38*(2), 167–190. doi:10.1080/15391523.2005.10782455

McKenzie, B., Brown, J., Casey, D., Cooney, A., Darcy, E., Giblin, S., & Mhórdha, M. N. (2018). From Poetry to Palmerstown: Using Wikipedia to Teach Critical Skills and Information Literacy in A First-Year Seminar. *College Teaching, 66*(3), 140–147. doi:10.1080/87567555.2018.1463504

McKinley Ross, S. (2010). *Hoot Owl Hoot*. Peaceable Kingdom.

McKnight, K., O'Malley, K., Ruzic, R., Horsley, M. K., Franey, J. J., & Bassett, K. (2016). Teaching in a digital age: How educators use technology to improve student learning. *Journal of Research on Technology in Education, 48*(3), 194–211. doi:10.1080/15391523.2016.1175856

McLaren, B. M., Adams, D. M., Mayer, R. E., & Forlizzi, J. (2017). A computer-based game that promotes mathematics learning more than a conventional approach. *International Journal of Game-Based Learning, 7*(1), 36–56. doi:10.4018/IJGBL.2017010103

McLellan, S., Muddimer, A., & Peres, S. (2012). The effect of experience on system usability scale ratings. *Journal of Usability Studies*.

Mcleod, S. (2013). *Kolb-Learning Styles*. simplypsychology.org/learning-kolb.html

McLoughlin, C., & Lee, M. J. (2010). Personalised and self regulated learning in the Web 2.0 era: International exemplars of innovative pedagogy using social software. *Australasian Journal of Educational Technology, 26*(1). Advance online publication. doi:10.14742/ajet.1100

McMahon, C., Johnson, I., & Hecht, B. (2017). The Substantial Interdependence of Wikipedia and Google: A Case Study on the Relationship Between Peer Production Communities and Information Technologies. *Proceedings of the International AAAI Conference on Web and Social Media, 11*(1), Article 1. https://ojs.aaai.org/index.php/ICWSM/article/view/14883

McMorrow, C. (2020). *Coronavirus plunges universities into funding crisis*. https://www.rte.ie/news/2020/0503/1136316-covid-19-universities/

McNamara, D. S., Jackson, G. T., & Graesser, A. C. (2009). Intelligent Tutoring and Games (ITaG). *Proc. Workshop Intelligent Educational Games at the 14th Int'l Conf. Artificial Intelligence in Education*, 1-10.

Mehra, V., & Omidina, F. (2010). Predicting Factors Affecting University Students ' Attitudes To Adopt E-Learning in India Using Technology Acceptance Model. *International Journal on New Trends in Education and Their Implications, 1*(June), 33–43.

Mehrpour, S., & Ghayour, M. (2017). The effect of educational computerized games on learning English spelling among Iranian children. *The Reading Matrix: An International Online Journal, 17*(2), 165–178.

Mehta, S. (2020). Modern teaching methods: Importance and application. *Eduvoice: The Voice of Education Industry*. Retrieved from https://eduvoice.in/modern-teaching-methods/

Mehtab, F. H. (2019). *Constitutional responsibility of the Government of Bangladesh for implementing compulsory primary education: Issues and challenges* [Doctoral dissertation, University of Dhaka]. Dhaka University Institutional Repository.

Mehtälä, S. (2018). *User interface design for children and youth: websites and applications to promote mental health and wellbeing*. Academic Press.

Melzer, P. (2019). Personalising the IS classroom–insights on course design and implementation. In *A conceptual framework for personalised learning* (pp. 77–100). Springer Gabler. doi:10.1007/978-3-658-23095-1_4

Mendez, M., & Boude, O. (2021). Uso de los videojuegos en básica primaria: Una revisión sistemática. *Espacios, 42*(1), 66–80. doi:10.48082/espacios-a21v42n01p06

Menking, A., & Rosenberg, J. (2021). WP:NOT, WP:NPOV, and Other Stories Wikipedia Tells Us: A Feminist Critique of Wikipedia's Epistemology. *Science, Technology & Human Values, 46*(3), 455–479. doi:10.1177/0162243920924783

Menon, D., Romero, M., & Viéville, T. (2019). Computational thinking development and assessment through tabletop escape games. *International Journal of Serious Games, 6*(4), 3–18.

Menon, V., Boyett-Anderson, J. M., & Reiss, A. L. (2005). Maturation of medial temporal lobe response and connectivity during memory encoding. *Brain Research. Cognitive Brain Research, 25*(1), 379–385. doi:10.1016/j.cogbrainres.2005.07.007 PMID:16122916

Mentor Gilmor, D. (2008). *Principles for a new media literacy*. Berkman Center for Internet & Society at Harvard University.

Mentz, E., & Goosen, L. (2007). Are groups working in the Information Technology class? *South African Journal of Education, 27*(2), 329–343.

Merriam, S. (1988). *Case study research in education. A qualitative approach.* Jossey-Bass.

Merriam, S. B., & Tisdell, E. J. (2015). *Qualitative research: A guide to design and implementation* (4th ed.). Jossey-Bass.

Merrill, J., & Merrill, K. (2019). *The Interactive Class.* Elevate Books Edu.

Mertala, P. (2019). Digital technologies in early childhood education – a frame analysis of preservice teachers' perceptions. *Early Child Development and Care, 189*(8), 1228–1241. doi:10.1080/03004430.2017.1372756

Mesko, B., Győrffy, Z., & Kollár, J. (2015). Digital literacy in the medical curriculum: A course with social media tools and Gamification. *JMIR Medical Education, 1*(2), e4411. doi:10.2196/mededu.4411 PMID:27731856

Meyer, D. Z., & Avery, L. M. (2009). Excel as a qualitative data analysis tool. *Field Methods, 21*(1), 91–112. doi:10.1177/1525822X08323985

Meyer, M., & Wood, L. (2017). A critical reflection on the multiple roles required to facilitate mutual learning during service-learning in Creative Arts education. *Teaching in Higher Education, 22*(2), 158–177. doi:10.1080/13562517.2016.1221808

Mezirow, J. (2009). An overview on transformative learning. In K. Illeris (Ed.), *Contemporary Theories of Learning* (pp. 90–105). Routledge. doi:10.4324/9781315147277

Michael, D., & Chen, S. (2006). *Serious games: Games that educate, train, and inform.* Thomson Course Technology.

Michaelson, C. (2016). A novel approach to business ethics education: Exploring how to live and work in the 21st century. *Academy of Management Learning & Education, 15*(3), 588–606. doi:10.5465/amle.2014.0129

Michalos, A. C. (1982). Purpose and policy. *Journal of Business Ethics, 1*(4), 331.

Michalos, A. C., & Simon, H. A. (1970). The Sciences of the Artificial. *Technology and Culture, 11*(1), 118. Advance online publication. doi:10.2307/3102825

Mifsud, C. L., Vella, R., & Camilleri, L. (2013). Attitudes toward and effects of the use of video games in classroom learning with specific reference to literacy attainment. *Research in Education, 90*(1), 32–52. doi:10.7227/RIE.90.1.3

Mihailidis, P. (2011). New Civic Voices & Emerging Media Literacy Landscape. *The Journal of Media Literacy Education, 3*(1), 4–5.

Mikre, F. (2011). The Roles of Information Communication Technologies in Education: Review Article with Emphasis to the Computer and Internet. *Ethiopian Journal of Education and Sciences, 6*(2), 109–126.

Miles, M. B., Huberman, A. M., & Saldaña, J. (2014). *Qualitative data analysis.* Sage.

Milgram, P., & Kishino, F. (1994). A taxonomy of mixed reality visual displays. *IEICE Transactions on Information and Systems, 77*, 1321–1329.

Milgram, P., Takemura, H., Utsumi, A., & Kishino, F. (1995, December). Augmented reality: A class of displays on the reality-virtuality continuum. In *Telemanipulator and telepresence technologies* (Vol. 2351, pp. 282–292). International Society for Optics and Photonics. doi:10.1117/12.197321

Miller, A. (2012). *Kinect in the Classroom.* Retrieved September 15, 2021 from https://www.edutopia.org/blog/kinect-classroom-andrew-miller

Miller, C. (2013). The gamification of education. *Developments in Business Simulation and Experiential Learning, 40*, 196–200. https://absel-ojs-ttu.tdl.org/absel/index.php/absel/article/view/40

Miller, C. (2013). The gamification of education. *Developments in Business Simulation and Experiential Learning, 40.* https://absel-ojs-ttu.tdl.org/absel/index.php/absel/article/view/40/38

Miller, C.T. (2008). Games: Purpose and Potential in Education. *Springer Science, 7.*

Miller, J. Y. (2021). *Digital Literacy: The Impact of a Blended Learning Model on Student Motivation and Achievement* (Doctoral dissertation). Gardner-Webb University.

Miller, M. (2015). *Ditch that textbook.* Dave Burgess Consulting, Inc.

Miller, M., Ridgway, N., & Ridgway, A. (2019). *Don't ditch that tech: Differentiated instruction in a digital world.* Dave Burgess Consulting, Inc.

Milli Eğitim Bakanlığı. (2018). *Medya Okuryazarlığı Dersi Öğretim Programı (Ortaokul ve İmam Hatip Ortaokulu 7 veya 8. Sınıflar).* Temel Eğitim Genel Müdürlüğü.

Mills, K. A. (2015). *Literacy theories for the digital age: Social, critical, multimodal, spatial, material, and sensory lenses.* Multilingual Matters. doi:10.21832/9781783094639

Milovanović, M., Minović, M., Kovačević, I., Minović, J., & Starčević, D. (2009). *Effectiveness of Game-Based Learning: Influence of Cognitive Style.* Paper presented at the Best Practices for the Knowledge Society. Knowledge, Learning, Development and Technology for All, Berlin, Germany.

Miltgen, C. L., & Peyrat-Guillard, D. (2014). Cultural and generational influences on privacy concerns: A qualitative study in seven European countries. *European Journal of Information Systems, 23*(2), 103–125. doi:10.1057/ejis.2013.17

Milton, J., Jonsen, S., Hirst, S., & Lindenburn, S. (2012). Foreign language vocabulary development through activities in an online 3D environment. *Language Learning Journal, 40*(1), 99–112. doi:10.1080/09571736.2012.658229

Minishi-Majanja, M. K. (2007). Integration of ICTs in library and information science education in sub-Saharan Africa. *World library and information congress: 73rd IFLA general conference and council, 19.*

Ministry of Education Arts and Culture & UNICEF Namibia. (2016). *We are the architects of our destiny: Study of positive deviant schools in Namibia.* https://www.unicef.org/namibia/na.MoEAC_-_Positive_Deviant_Schools_Report_(2016)_-_web_quality(1).pdf

Ministry of Education Arts and Culture. (2015). *Final Draft Language Policy for Schools in Namibia: Pre-primary, Grade 1-12.* Windhoek: Ministry of Education Arts and Culture.

Ministry of Education Bangladesh (MoE). (2004). *National Education Commission Report 2003.* http://lib.banbeis.gov.bd/pdf_view.php?book=National%20education%20Commission%20report-2003.pdf

Ministry of Education Bangladesh (MoE). (2010). National. *Educational Policy, 2010.* https://moedu.gov.bd/sites/default/files/files/moedu.portal.gov.bd/page/ad5cfca5_9b1e_4c0c_a4eb_fb1ded9e2fe5/National%20Education%20Policy%202010%20final.pdf

Ministry of Education. (2005). *Curriculum for the Lower Primary Phase: English Version.* Windhoek: Ministry of Education.

Miri, D. H., & Macke, J. (2021). Gamification, Motivation, and Engagement at Work: A Qualitative Multiple Case Study. *European Business Review.* Advance online publication. doi:10.1108/EBR-04-2020-0106

Mishra, P., & Koehler, M. (2009). Too cool for school? No way! Using the TPACK framework: you can have your hot tools and teach with them, too. *Learning & Leading with Technology, 36*(7), 14+. link.gale.com/apps/doc/A199794723/AONE?u=byuprovo&sid=bookmark-AONE&xid=6b0decfc

Mishra, P. (2019). Considering contextual knowledge: The TPACK diagram gets an upgrade. *Journal of Digital Learning in Teacher Education, 35*(2), 76–78. doi:10.1080/21532974.2019.1588611

Mishra, P., & Koehler, J. (2006). Technological pedagogical content knowledge: A new framework for teacher knowledge. *Teachers College Record, 108*(6), 1017–1054. doi:10.1111/j.1467-9620.2006.00684.x

Mishra, P., & Koehler, M. (2006). Technological pedagogical content knowledge: A framework for integrating technology in teachers' knowledge. *Teachers College Record, 108*(6), 1017–1054. https://doi.org/10.1111/j.1467-9620.2006.00684.x

Misra, R., Eyombo, L. B., & Phillips, F. T. (2019). Benefits and Challenges of Using Educational Games. In *Digital Games for Minority Student Engagement: Emerging Research and Opportunities.* doi:10.4018/978-1-5225-3398-6.ch001

Mohamad, A. (2021). The Impact of Project-Based Learning on Students' Cultural Awareness. *International Journal of Language and Literary Studies, 3*(2), 54–80. Advance online publication. doi:10.36892/ijlls.v3i2.601

Mohamad, A. A. A., Amirnuddin, P. S., Ahmad, M. H., & Ramalingam, C. L. (2021). Transforming Legal Education Teaching and Learning: The Remote Communication Technology. *Malayan Law Journal, 2,* cxxxvii.

Mohamad, A., & Tamer, Y. (2021). A review of literature on Project-Based Learning inside language education. *Turkish Online Journal of English Language Teaching, 6*(2), 79–105.

Moher, D., Liberati, A., Tetzlaff, J., & Altman, D. G. (2009). Preferred reporting items for systematic reviews and meta-analyses: The PRISMA statement. *International Journal of Surgery, 8*(5), 336–341. doi:10.1016/j.ijsu.2010.02.007 PMID:20171303

Mojo, *Montra de Jogos* IST. (2017). Retrieved October 5, 2021, from, https://tecnico.ulisboa.pt/en/events/mojo-montra-de-jogos/

Mojo, *Montra de Jogos* IST. (2018). Retrieved October 5, 2021, from, https://tecnico.ulisboa.pt/en/events/mojo-11th-edition/

Mojo, *Montra de Jogos* IST. (2019). Retrieved October 5, 2021, from, https://tecnico.ulisboa.pt/en/events/mojo-2019-12th-edition/

Mojo, *Montra de Jogos* IST. (2020). Retrieved October 5, 2021, from, https://tecnico.ulisboa.pt/en/events/mojo-2020-13th-edition/

Mojo, *Montra de Jogos* IST. (2021). Retrieved October 5, 2021, from, https://labjogos.tecnico.ulisboa.pt/mojo/2021/

Molderez, I., & Fonseca, E. (2018). The efficacy of real-world experiences and service learning for fostering competences for sustainable development in higher education. *Journal of Cleaner Production, 172,* 4397–4410. doi:10.1016/j.jclepro.2017.04.062

Molin, G. (2017). The Role of the Teacher in Game-Based Learning: A Review and Outlook. Serious Games and Edutainment Applications, 649-674. doi:10.1007/978-3-319-51645-5_28

Moloi, T. J. (2015). Using indigenous games to teach problem-solving in mathematics in rural learning ecologies. *Journal of Higher Education in Africa/Revue de l'enseignement supèrieur en Afrique, 13*(1-2), 21-32.

Moloi, T. J., Mosia, M. S., Matabane, M. E., & Sibaya, K. T. (2021). The Use of Indigenous Games to Enhance the Learning of Word Problems in Grade 4 Mathematics: A Case of Kgati. *International Journal of Learning, Teaching and Educational Research, 20*(1), 240–259.

Mølstad, C. E. (2015). State-based curriculum-making: Approaches to local curriculum work in Norway and Finland. *Journal of Curriculum Studies, 47*(4), 441–461. doi:10.1080/00220272.2015.1039067

Monaghan, J. E. (1988). Literacy Instruction and Gender in Colonial New England. *American Quarterly, 40*(1), 18–41. https://doi.org/10.2307/2713140

Monsoï, K. C. (2017). Information Communication and Technology (ICT) diffusion and inequality in Africa. *Journal of Internet and Information Systems, 7*(1), 1–7. doi:10.5897/JIIS2016.0090

Monteiro, T. B. P. (2017). *"História Go": O contributo dos dispositivos móveis para o ensino-aprendizagem nas visitas de estudo. Relatório realizado no âmbito do Mestrado em Ensino de História no 3.o Ciclo do Ensino Básico e Ensino Secundário.* Faculdade de Letras da Universidade do Porto.

Montessori, M. (1948). *The discovery of the child.* Kalakshetra.

Moon, J.-W., & Kim, Y.-G. (2001). Extending the TAM for a World-Wide-Web context. *Information & Management, 38*(4), 217–230. doi:10.1016/S0378-7206(00)00061-6

Moran, J. (2013). A integração das tecnologias na educação. In A Educação que desejamos: novos desafios e como chegar lá (5th ed.). Campinas: Papirus.

Moreno, R., & Mayer, R. (2007). Interactive multimodal learning environments: special issue on interactive learning environments: contemporary issues and trends. *Educational Psychology Review, 19*(3), 309–326. doi:10.100710648-007-9047-2

Morris, B. J., Croker, S., Masnick, A., & Zimmerman, C. (2012). *The emergence of scientific reasoning. In Trends in Cognitive Development.* InTech.

Morris, B. J., Croker, S., Zimmerman, C., Gill, D., & Romig, C. (2013). Gaming science: The "Gamification" of scientific thinking. *Frontiers in Psychology, 4*, 607. doi:10.3389/fpsyg.2013.00607 PMID:24058354

Morris, T. H., & Rohs, M. (2021). The potential for digital technology to support self-directed learning in formal education of children: A scoping review. *Interactive Learning Environments*, 1–14. doi:10.1080/10494820.2020.1870501

Moschovaki, E., Meadows, S., & Pellegrini, A. (2007). Teachers' affective presentation of children's books and young children's display of affective engagement during classroom book reading. *Instituto Superior de Psicologia Aplicada, 22*(4), 405-420. doi:10.1007/BF03173463

Moseley, A., & Whitton, N. (2015). Using games to enhance the student experience. York, UK: Higher Education Academy (HEA).

Moses, A. (2013). What, when, and how electronic media can be used in an early literacy classroom. In D. Barone & M. Mallette (Eds.), *Best Practices in Early Literacy Instruction* (pp. 96–118). Guilford Press.

Moura, A. (2009). *Geração móvel: um ambiente de aprendizagem suportado por tecnologias móveis para a "Geração Polegar".* Universidade do Minho, Centro de Competência.

Mou, S. (2016). Possibilities and challenges of ICT integration in the Bangladesh education system. *Educational Technology, 56*(2), 50–53. http://www.jstor.org/stable/44430461

Mousumi, M. A., & Kusakabe, T. (2017). Proliferating English-Medium schools in Bangladesh and their educational significance among the "Clientele". *Journal of International Development and Cooperation, 23*(1), 1–13. https://ir.lib.hiroshima-u.ac.jp/files/public/4/42488/20170215110511630423/JIDC_23-1_1.pdf

Movellan, J., Eckhardt, M., Virnes, M., & Rodriguez, A. (2009). Sociable robot improves toddler vocabulary skills. *Proceedings of the 4th ACM/IEEE International Conference on Human Robot Interaction*, 307-308. 10.1145/1514095.1514189

Mozelius, P., & Olsson, M. (2017, October). Learning to program by building learning games. In *European Conference on Games Based Learning* (pp. 448-455). Academic Conferences International Limited.

Mozelius, P., Fagerström, A., & Söderquist, M. (2017). Motivating factors and tangential learning for knowledge acquisition in educational games. *Electronic Journal of e-Learning, 15*(4), 343-354.

Mozelius, P., Hernandez, W., Sällström, J., & Hellerstedt, A. (2017). Teacher attitudes toward game-based learning in history education. *International Journal of Information and Communication Technology Education, 6*(4), 27–35. doi:10.1515/ijicte-2017-0017

Mubin, O., Stevens, C. J., Shahid, S., Al Mahmud, A., & Dong, J. J. (2013). A review of the applicability of robots in education. *Journal of Technology in Education and Learning, 1*(209). doi:10.2316/Journal.209.2013.1.209-0015

Mubin, O., Shahid, S., & Bartneck, C. (2013). Robot Assisted Language Learning through Games: A Comparison of Two Case Studies. *Australian Journal of Intelligent Information Processing Systems, 13*(3), 9–14.

Mukwambo, P. (2019). *Quality higher education means more than learning how to work.* The Conversation. https://theconversation.com/quality-higher-education-means-more-than-learning-how-to-work-122820

Mulhall, A. (2003). In the field: Notes on observation in qualitative research. *Journal of Advanced Nursing, 41*(3), 306–313. doi:10.1046/j.1365-2648.2003.02514.x PMID:12581118

Mumtaz, S. (2000). Factors affecting teachers' use of information and communications technology: A review of the literature. *Journal of Information Technology for Teacher Education, 9*(3), 319–342. doi:10.1080/14759390000200096

Mun, Y. (2003). Predicting the use of web-based information systems: Self-efficacy, enjoyment, learning goal orientation, and the technology acceptance model. *International Journal of Human-Computer Studies, 59*(4), 431–449. doi:10.1016/S1071-5819(03)00114-9

Muris, P., Meesters, C., Merckelbach, H., & Hulsenbeck, P. (2000). Worry in children is related to perceived parental rearing and attachment. *Behaviour Research and Therapy, 38*(5), 487–497. doi:10.1016/S0005-7967(99)00072-8 PMID:10816907

Musante, K., & DeWalt, B. R. (2010). *Participant observation: A guide for fieldworkers.* Rowman Altamira.

Mustapha, S. M., Abd Rahman, N. S. N., & Yunus, M. M. (2010). Factors influencing classroom participation: A case study of Malaysian undergraduate students. *Procedia: Social and Behavioral Sciences, 9*, 1079–1084.

Mustar, P. (2009). Technology management education: Innovation and entrepreneurship at MINES ParisTech, a leading French engineering school. *Academy of Management Learning & Education, 8*(3), 418–425.

Mutakinati L., Anwari I., & Yoshisuke K. (2018). Analysis of students' critical thinking skill of middle school through STEM education project-based learning. *Journal Pendidikan IPA Indonesia, 7*(1), 54-65. doi:10.15294/jpii.v7i1.10495

Muthuprasad, T., Aiswarya, S., Aditya, K. S., & Jha, G. K. (2021). Students' perception and preference for online education in India during COVID-19 pandemic. *Social Sciences & Humanities Open, 3*(1), 100101. Advance online publication. doi:10.1016/j.ssaho.2020.100101 PMID:34173507

Mutula, S. (2004). IT diffusion in Sub-Saharan Africa: Implications for developing and managing digital libraries. *New Library World, 105*(7/8), 281–289. doi:10.1108/03074800410551039

Mweli, P. (2018). Indigenous stories and games as approaches to teaching within the classroom. *Understanding Educational Psychology*, 94-101.

Myers, B. (2008). Minds at play. *American Libraries, 39*(5), 54–57.

Mystakidis, S., & Berki, E. (2018). The case of literacy motivation: Playful 3D immersive learning environments and problem-focused Education for blended digital storytelling. *International Journal of Web-Based Learning and Teaching Technologies, 13*(1), 64–79. doi:10.4018/IJWLTT.2018010105

Nadolny, L., Alaswad, Z., Culver, D., & Wang, W. (2017). Designing with game-based learning: Game mechanics from middle school to higher education. *Simulation & Gaming, 48*(6), 814–831. doi:10.1177/1046878117736893

Nagy, Molnár, Szenkovits, Horváth-Czinger, & Szűts. (2018). Gamification and microcontent orientated methodological solutions based on bring-your-own device logic in higher education. *2018 9th IEEE International Conference on Cognitive Infocommunications (Coginfocom),* 385-388. doi:10.1109/CogInfoCom.2018.8639702

Nah, F. F.-H., Zeng, Q., Telaprolu, V. R., Ayyappa, A. P., & Eschenbrenner, B. (2014). Gamification of Education: A Review of Literature. Academic Press.

Nakamura, J., & Csikszentmihalyi, M. (2002). The concept of flow. In C. R. Snyder & S. J. Lopez (Eds.), Handbook of positive psychology (pp. 89–105). Academic Press.

Namibia Statistics Agency. (2013). *Namibia 2011 Population & Housing Census - Main Report.* http://www.nsa.org.na/files/downloads/Namibia 2011 Population and Housing Census Main Report.pdf

Naraghi-Taghi-Off, R., Horst, R., & Dörner, R. (2020). Gamification Mechanics for Playful Virtual Reality Authoring. In STAG (pp. 131-141). Academic Press.

Nath, S. R., & Chowdhury, M. A. R. (2019). *State of primary education in Bangladesh: Progress made, challenges remained.* Campaign for Popular Education.

National Association for the Education of Young Children. (2012). *Technology and interactive media as tools in early childhood programs serving children from birth through age 8.* http://www.naeyc.org/files/naeyc/file/positions/ PS_technology_ WEB2.pdf

National Early Literacy Panel. (2004, December). *The National Early Literacy Panel: Findings from a synthesis of scientific research on early literacy development* [Paper presentation]. The National Reading Conference, San Antonio, TX, United States.

National Education Association. (2010). *Preparing 21st century students for a global society: An educator's guide to the "Four Cs."* National Education Association.

National Governors Association Center for Best Practices & Council of Chief State School Officers. (2010). *Common Core State Standards (English Language Arts).* http://corestandards.org/

National Research Council. (1997). *Science Teaching Reconsidered: A Handbook.* The National Academies Press. doi:10.17226/5287

National Research Council. (2010). *Exploring the Intersection of Science Education and 21st Century Skills: A Workshop Summary.* Washington, DC: National Academies Press.

National Research Council. (2012). *A Framework for K-12 Science Education: Practices, Crosscutting Concepts, and Core Ideas.* National Academies Press.

Navarrete, C. (2013). Creative thinking in digital game design and development: A case study. *Computers & Education, 69,* 320–331. doi:10.1016/j.compedu.2013.07.025

NCTE. (2019). *Definition of Literacy in a Digital Age.* National Council of Teachers of English Position Statements. https://ncte.org/statement/nctes-definition-literacy-digital-age/

NCTM. (2014). *Principles to Actions: Ensuring Mathematical Success For All*. NCTM.

Ndawi, V. E., Thomas, K. A., & Nyaruwata, T. L. (2013). Barriers to Effective Integration of Information and Communication Technology in Harare Secondary Schools. *International Journal of Scientific Research, 2*(9), 211–216.

Nebel, S., Schneider, S., & Rey, G. D. (2015). From duels to classroom competition: Social competition and learning in educational videogames within different group sizes. *Computers in Human Behavior, 55*, 384–398. doi:10.1016/j.chb.2015.09.035

Nebel, S., Schneider, S., & Rey, G. D. (2016). Mining learning and crafting scientific experiments: A literature review on the use of Minecraft in education and research. *Journal of Educational Technology & Society, 19*(2), 355–366.

Neidorf, T., Arora, A., Erberber, E., Tsokodayi, Y., & Mai, T. (2020). *Student misconceptions and errors in Physics and Mathematics: exploring Data from TIMSS and TIMSS Advanced*. Springer Nature. doi:10.1007/978-3-030-30188-0

Nekongo-Nielsen, H., Mbukusa, N. R., & Tjiramba, E. (2015). Investigating factors that lead to school dropout in Namibia. *Namibia CPD Journal for Educators, 2*(1), 99–118. http://journals.unam.edu.na/index.php/NCPDJE/article/view/1282/1109

Nel, C., Dreyer, C., & Klopper, M. (2004). An analysis of the reading profiles of first-year students at Potchefstroom University: A cross-sectional study and a case study. *South African Journal of Education, 24*(1), 95–103.

Nestor, E. (2019). *Undergraduate Curriculum Evaluation*. Maynooth University.

Neumann, M. M., & Neumann, D. L. (2014). Touch screen tablets and emergent literacy. *Early Childhood Education Journal, 42*(4), 231–239. https://www.learntechlib.org/p/152727/

Neutral point of view. (2019b). In *Wikipedia*. https://en.wikipedia.org/w/index.php?title=Wikipedia:Neutral_point_of_view&oldid=901367786

Neville, D. O. (2015). The story in the mind: The effect of 3D gameplay on the structuring of written L2 narratives. *ReCALL, 27*(1), 21–37. doi:10.1017/S0958344014000160

Newbery, R., Lean, J., & Moizer, J. (2016). Evaluating the impact of serious games: The effect of gaming on entrepreneurial intent. *Information Technology & People, 29*(4), 733–749. doi:10.1108/ITP-05-2015-0111

Newbery, R., Lean, J., Moizer, J., & Haddoud, M. (2018). Entrepreneurial identity formation during the initial entrepreneurial experience: The influence of simulation feedback and existing identity. *Journal of Business Research, 85*, 51–59. doi:10.1016/j.jbusres.2017.12.013

Newman, J. (2001). Eye level. In J. Bell & P. Magrs (Eds.), *The creative writing coursebook* (pp. 141–147). Macmillan.

Newton, L. D., & Newton, D. P. (2014). Creativity in 21st-century education. *Prospects, 44*(4), 575–589. doi:10.100711125-014-9322-1

Ney, M., Emin, V., & Earp, J. (2012). Paving the Way to Game Based Learning: A Question Matrix for Teacher Reflection. *Procedia Computer Science, 15*, 17–24. doi:10.1016/j.procs.2012.10.053

Nganji, J. T. (2018). Towards learner-constructed e-learning environments for effective personal learning experiences. *Behaviour & Information Technology, 37*(7), 647–657. doi:10.1080/0144929X.2018.1470673

Nhongo, K. (2014, March 19). Grade 5 NSAT results depressing. *Windhoek Observer*. http://www.observer.com.na/national/3131-grade-5-nsat-results-depressing#

Nicholson, S. (2012). *Strategies for meaningful gamification: Concepts behind transformative play and participatory museums.* Presented at Meaningful Play 2012, Lansing, MI. Retrieved August 22, 2016, from https://scottnicholson.com/pubs/meaningfulstrategies.pdf

Nicholson, R. I., & Fawcett, A. J. (2000). Long-term learning in dyslexic children. *The European Journal of Cognitive Psychology, 12*(3), 357–393. doi:10.1080/09541440050114552

Nicholson, S. (2012). A user-centered theoretical framework for meaningful Gamification. *Games Learning Society, 8*(1), 223–230.

Nicholson, S. (2018). Creating engaging escape rooms for the classroom. *Childhood Education, 94*(1), 44–49. doi:10.1080/00094056.2018.1420363

Niederhauser, D. S., & Stoddart, T. (2001). Teachers' instructional perspectives and use of educational software. *Teaching and Teacher Education, 17*(1), 15–31. doi:10.1016/S0742-051X(00)00036-6

Nielson, K. A., & Powless, M. (2007). Positive and negative sources of emotional arousal enhance long-term word-list retention when induced as long as 30 min after learning. *Neurobiology of Learning and Memory, 88*(1), 40–47. doi:10.1016/j.nlm.2007.03.005 PMID:17467310

Niemeyer, D., & Gerber, H. R. (2015). Maker culture and *Minecraft*: Implications for the future of learning. *Educational Media International, 52*(3), 216–226. doi:10.1080/09523987.2015.1075103

Nieto, J. J., Creus, R., & Giro-i-Nieto, X. (2021). *Unsupervised Skill-Discovery and Skill-Learning in Minecraft.* arXiv preprint arXiv:2107.08398.

Nieto-Escamez, F. A., & Roldán-Tapia, M. D. (2021). Gamification as online teaching strategy during COVID-19: A mini-review. *Frontiers in Psychology, 12*(648552), 648552. Advance online publication. doi:10.3389/fpsyg.2021.648552 PMID:34093334

Ninnes, P. (2011). *Improving Quality and Equity in Education in Namibia: A Trend and Gap Analysis.* Academic Press.

Nkopodi, N., & Mosimege, M. (2009). Incorporating the indigenous game of morabaraba in the learning of mathematics. *South African Journal of Education, 29*(3), 377–392. doi:10.15700aje.v29n3a273

Noble, K. G., Wolmetz, M. E., Ochs, L. G., Farah, M. J., & McCandliss, B. D. (2006). Brain behavior relationships in reading acquisition are modulated by socio-economic factors. *Developmental Science, 9*(6), 642–654. doi:10.1111/j.1467-7687.2006.00542.x PMID:17059461

Nobre, A. (2020). The Pedagogy That Makes the Students Act Collaboratively and Open Educational Practices. In *Personalization and Collaboration in Adaptive E-Learning*. IGI Global. doi:10.4018/978-1-7998-1492-4.ch002

Nobre, A. (2021). Open Educational Practices and Resources in the Higher Education Learning Environment. In *Advancing Online Course Design and Pedagogy for the 21st Century Learning Environment.* IGI Global. doi:10.4018/978-1-7998-5598-9.ch006

Nobre, A., Mouraz, A., Goulão, M.F., Henriques, S., Barros, D., & Moreira, J. A. (2021). Processos de Comunicação Digital no Sistema Educativo Português em Tempos de Pandemia. *Revista Práxis Educacional, 17*(45), 1-19.

Nobre, A. (2021). Educational Practices Resulting From Digital Intelligence. In *Handbook of Research on Teaching With Virtual Environments and AI*. IGI Global., doi:10.4018/978-1-7998-7638-0.ch003.

Nonoo, S. (2019). *Playing Games Can Build 21st-Century Skills.* Research Explains How.

Nordby, A., Øygardslia, K., Sverdrup, U., & Sverdrup, H. (2016). The art of gamification; Teaching sustainability and system thinking by pervasive game development. *The Electronic Journal of e-Learning, 14*(3), 152–168.

Nor, E. B. A., & Eu, L. K. (2014). Hubungan antara sikap, minat, pengajaran guru dan pengaruh rakan sebaya terhadap pencapaian matametik tambahan tingkatan 4. *JuKu:Jurnal Kurikulum & Pengajaran Asia Pasifik, 2*(1), 1–10.

Norman, K. L. (2011). *Assessing the Components of Skill Necessary for Playing Video Games.* Human-Computer Interaction Technical Report 11-11-11. University of Maryland. Available online at: http://hcil2.cs.umd.edu/trs/2011-27/2011-27.pdf

Noroozi, O., Dehghanzadeh, H., & Talaee, E. (2020). A systematic review on the impacts of game-based learning on argumentation skills. *Entertainment Computing, 35*, 100369. doi:10.1016/j.entcom.2020.100369

North Carolina Foundations Task Force. (2013). *North Carolina foundations for early learning and development.* Author.

Northeastern University Innovation Survey. (2014). https://news.northeastern.edu/2014/11/18/generation-z-survey/

Northrop, L., & Killeen, E. (2013). A framework for using iPads to build early literacy skills. *The Reading Teacher, 66*(7), 531–537. https://doi.org/10.1002/TRTR.1155

Nouri, J., Norén, E., & Skog, K. (2018). Learning programming by playing and coding games in K-9. *INTED 2018 : Proceedings*, 7990–7995.

Nousiainen, T., Kangas, M., Rikala, J., & Vesisenaho, M. (2018). Teacher Competencies in Game-Based Pedagogy. *Teaching and Teacher Education, 74*, 85–96. doi:10.1016/j.tate.2018.04.012

Nunziati, G. (1990). Pour construire un dispositif d'évaluation formatrice. *Cahiers Pedagogiques, 280*, 47–62.

Nurazidawati, Tuan Mastura, & Kamisah. (2011). *Pengalaman pembelajaran melalui khidmat komuniti pelajar Sains: Tranformasi dan inovasi dalam pendidikan.* Bangi: Penerbit Universiti Kebangsaan Malaysia.

Nurtanto, M., Fawaid, M., & Sofyan, H. (2020). Problem Based Learning (PBL) in Industry 4.0: Improving Learning Quality through Character-Based Literacy Learning and Life Career Skill (LL-LCS). *Journal of Physics: Conference Series, 1573*, 012006. doi:10.1088/1742-6596/1573/1/012006

Nuutinen, M., Seppänen, M., Smedlund, A., & Kaasinen, E. (2017). *Seeking New Ways of Innovating in Industry-Research Collaboration Practice. Innovating in practice.* Springer International Publishing.

Nxumalo, S. A., & Mncube, D. W. (2018). Using indigenous games and knowledge to decolonise the school curriculum: Ubuntu perspectives. *Perspectives in Education, 36*(2), 103–118. doi:10.18820/2519593X/pie.v36i2.9

O'Bannon, B. W., & Thomas, K. (2014). Teacher perceptions of using mobile phones in the classroom: Age matters! *Computers & Education, 74*, 15–25. doi:10.1016/j.compedu.2014.01.006

O'Brolcháin, F., Jacquemard, T., Monaghan, D., O'Connor, N., Novitzky, P., & Gordijn, B. (2016). The convergence of virtual reality and social networks: Threats to privacy and autonomy. *Science and Engineering Ethics, 22*(1), 1–29. doi:10.100711948-014-9621-1 PMID:25552240

O'Connor, S., Hanlon, P., O'donnell, C. A., Garcia, S., Glanville, J., & Mair, F. S. (2016). Understanding factors affecting patient and public engagement and recruitment to digital health interventions: A systematic review of qualitative studies. *BMC Medical Informatics and Decision Making, 16*(1), 1–15. doi:10.118612911-016-0359-3 PMID:27630020

O'Doherty, J., Kringerlbach, M. L., Rolls, R. T., Hornak, J., & Andrews, C. (2001). Sažetak reprezentacije nagrade i kazne u ljudskoj orbitofrontalnoj korteksu. *Nature Neuroscience, 4*, 95–102. doi:10.1038/82959 PMID:11135651

O'Donnell, E., Lawless, S., Sharp, M., & Wade, V. P. (2015). A review of personalised e-learning: Towards supporting learner diversity. *International Journal of Distance Education Technologies, 13*(1), 22–47. doi:10.4018/ijdet.2015010102

O'Leary, M., & Scully, D. (2018). *The Leaving Certificate programme as preparation for higher education: The views of undergraduates at the end of their first year in university.* The Centre for Assessment Research, Policy and Practice in Education.

Obar, J., & Wildman, S. (2015). Social media definition and the governance challenge: An introduction to the special issue. *Telecommunications Policy, 39*(9), 745–750. doi:10.1016/j.telpol.2015.07.014

Oberg, A. (2011). Comparison of the effectiveness of a call-based approach and a card-based approach to vocabulary acquisition and retention. *CALICO Journal, 29*(1), 118–144. doi:10.11139/cj.29.1.118-144

Oblinger, D. G., & Oblinger, J. L. (Eds.). (2005). Educating the net generation. Boulder, CO: Educause.

Oblinger, D., & Oblinger, J. (Eds.). (2005). *Educating the net generation.* EDUCAUSE. https://www.educause.edu/ir/library/PDF/pub7101.PDF

Oblinger, D. G. (2004). The next generation of educational entertainment. *Journal of Interactive Media in Education, 8*(1), 1–18.

Oblinger, D. G. (2006). Games and Learning. Digital games have the potential to bring play back to the learning experience. *EDUCAUSE Quarterly, 29.*

Oblinger, D. G. (2006). Games and learning: Digital games have the potential to bring play back to the learning experience. *EDUCAUSE Quarterly, 3,* 5–7.

OECD. (2019). *How much time do teachers spend teaching? In Education at a Glance 2019: OECD Indicators.* OECD Publishing. doi:10.1787/62fbb20d-

Oei & Patterson. (2013). Enhancing cognition with video games: a multiple game training study. *Pubmed, 8*(3).

Offenholley, K. H. (2012). Gaming Your Mathematics Course: The Theory and Practice of Games for Learning. *Journal of Humanistic Mathematics, 2,* 79–92. doi:10.5642/ jhummath.201202.07

Ofosu-Ampong, K. (2020). The Shift to Gamification in Education: A Review on Dominant Issues. *Journal of Educational Technology Systems, 49*(1), 113–137. doi:10.1177/0047239520917629

Ohman, A., Lundqvist, D., & Esteves, F. (2001). The face in the crowd effect: An anger superiority effect with schematic stimuli. *Journal of Personality and Social Psychology, 80*(3), 381–396. doi:10.1037/0022-3514.80.3.381 PMID:11300573

Oh, S., So, H. J., & Gaydos, M. (2017). Hybrid augmented reality for participatory learning: The hidden efficacy of multi-user game-based simulation. *IEEE Transactions on Learning Technologies, 11*(1), 115–127. doi:10.1109/TLT.2017.2750673

Ojanen, E., Ronimus, M., Ahonen, T., Chansa-Kabali, T., February, P., Jere-Folotiya, J., Kauppinen, K.-P., Ketonen, R., & Ngorosho, D., Pitknen, M., Puhakka, S., Sampa, F., Walubita, G., Yalukanda, C., Pugh, K., Richardson, U., Serpell, R., & Lyytinen, H. (2015). GraphoGame-A catalyst for multi-level promotion of literacy in diverse contexts. *Frontiers in Psychology, 6*(May). Advance online publication. doi:10.3389/fpsyg.2015.00671 PMID:26113825

Ojo, O., & Adu, E. (2019). The effectiveness of Information and Communication Technologies (ICTs) in teaching and learning in high schools in Eastern Cape Province. *South African Journal of Education, 38*(Supplement 2), 1–11. doi:10.15700aje.v38ns2a1483

Okoye, K., Nganji, J. T., & Hosseini, S. (2020). Learning analytics for educational innovation: A systematic mapping study of early indicators and success factors. *International Journal of Computer Information Systems and Industrial Management Applications, 12*, 138–154.

Olfers, K. J. F., & Band, G. P. H. (2018). Game-based training of flexibility and attention improves task-switch performance: Near and far transfer of cognitive training in an EEG study. *Psychological Research, 82*(1), 186–202. doi:10.100700426-017-0933-z PMID:29260316

Oliveira, L. R., Correia, A. C., Merrelho, A., Marques, A., Pereira, D. J., & Cardoso, V. (2009). Digital games: possibilities and limitations - The spore game case. In T. Bastiaens, J. Dron, & C. Xin (Eds.), *Proceedings of E-Learn: world conference on elearning in corporate, government, healthcare, and higher education* (pp. 3011-3020). Association for the Advancement of Computing in Education.

Olson, C. K. (2010). Children's motivations for video game play in the context of normal development. *Review of General Psychology, 14*(2), 180-187. Retrieved from http://psycnet.apa.org/?&fa=main.doiLanding&doi=10.1037/a0018984

Olson, C. B., Scarcella, R., & Matuchniak, T. (2015). English Learners, Writing, and the Common Core. *The Elementary School Journal, 115*(4), 570–592. https://doi.org/10.1086/681235

Olson, D. (2007). *Jerome Bruner: The cognitive revolution in educational theory.* Continuum International Publishing Group.

Olsson, M., & Mozelius, P. (2017). Learning to Program by Playing Learning Games. In *11th European Conference on Games Based Learning 2017, Graz, Austria, 5-6 October, 2017* (Vol. 11, pp. 498-506). Academic Conferences and Publishing International Limited.

Omer, A. H. (2017). *Implications And Importance Of Game-Based Learning For New Hires, elearning industry.* Retrieved from https://elearningindustry.com/game-based-learning-for-increased-learner-engagement-new-hires

Oprescu, F., Jones, C., & Katsikitis, M. (2014). I PLAY AT WORK—Ten principles for transforming work processes through Gamification. *Frontiers in Psychology, 5*, 5. doi:10.3389/fpsyg.2014.00014 PMID:24523704

Orbit Books. (2011, January 23). *Leviathan Wakes: Part One.* https://www.youtube.com/watch?v=Yu0xJpCy95o

Orey, M. (2010). *Emerging perspectives on learning, teaching, and technology.* Academic Press.

Originator Inc. (2014). *Endless reader* (Version 2.3) [Mobile app]. http://itunes.apple.com

Osanloo, A., & Grant, C. (2016). Understanding, selecting, and integrating a theoretical framework in dissertation research: Creating the blueprint for your "house". *Administrative Issues Journal: Connecting Education, Practice, and Research, 4*(2), 12-26.

Osatuyi, B. (2013). Information sharing on social media sites. *Journal of Computers in Human Behavior, 29*(6), 2622–2631. doi:10.1016/j.chb.2013.07.001

Osborne, J. (2014). Teaching scientific practices: Meeting the challenge of change. *Journal of Science Teacher Education, 25*(2), 177–196. doi:10.100710972-014-9384-1

Osman, K., & Marimuthu, N. (2010). Setting new learning targets for the 21st century science education in Malaysia. *Procedia: Social and Behavioral Sciences, 2*(2), 3737–3741. doi:10.1016/j.sbspro.2010.03.581

Othman, M. N. A., Abdul Rashid, M. A., Ismail, I. R., Abd Aziz, M. F., Norizan, S., & Mohamad Saad, S. A. (2021). Predicting Preferred Learning Styles on Teaching Approaches Among Gen Z Visual Learner. *Turkish Journal of Computer and Mathematics Education, 12*(9), 2969–2978.

Overby, A., & Jones, B. L. (2015). Virtual LEGOs: Incorporating Minecraft into the art education curriculum. *Art Education, 68*(1), 21–27. doi:10.1080/00043125.2015.11519302

Overmars, M. (2004). Teaching computer science through game design. *Computer, 37*(4), 81–83. doi:10.1109/MC.2004.1297314

Overturf, B. J., Montgomery, L. H., & Smith, M. H. (2013). *Word nerds: Teaching all students to learn and love vocabulary*. Stenhouse Publishing.

Oxendine, C., Robinson, J., & Willson, G. (2010). Experiential learning. In M. Orey (Ed.), Emerging perspectives on learning, teaching, and technology. Global Text Project, funded by the Jacob Foundation, Zurich, Switzerland. Creative Commons 3.0 Attribution Licence.

Oyshi, M. T., Saifuzzaman, M., & Tumpa, Z. N. (2018). Gamification in children education: Balloon shooter. *2018 4th International Conference on Computing Communication and Automation (ICCCA)*. 10.1109/CCAA.2018.8777534

Ozdamar-Keskin, N., Ozata, F. Z., Banar, K., & Royle, K. (2015). Examining Digital Literacy Competences and Learning Habits of Open and Distance Learners. *Contemporary Educational Technology, 6*(1), 74–90. doi:10.30935/cedtech/6140

P21 Framework Definitions. (2009). Retrieved from https://files.eric.ed.gov/fulltext/ED519462.pdf

Padgett, R. D., Keup, J. R., & Pascarella, E. T. (2013). The Impact of First-Year Seminars on College Students' Life-long Learning Orientations. *Journal of Student Affairs Research and Practice, 50*(2), 133–151. doi:10.1515/jsarp-2013-0011

Paiva, J. C., Leal, J. P., & Queirós, R. (2020). Fostering programming practice through games. *Information (Basel), 11*(11), 498. doi:10.3390/info11110498

Pala, Ş. M., & Başıbüyük, A. (2021). The Predictive Effect of Digital Literacy, Self-Control and Motivation on the Academic Achievement in the Science, Technology and Society Learning Area. *Technology, Knowledge and Learning,* 1-17.

Palaus, M., Marron, E. M., Viejo-Sobera, R., & Redolar-Ripoll, D. (2017). Neural basis of video gaming: A systematic review. *Frontiers in Human Neuroscience, 11*, 248. doi:10.3389/fnhum.2017.00248 PMID:28588464

Pallavicini, F., Ferrari, A., & Mantovani, F. (2018). Video Games for Well-Being: A Systematic Review on the Application of Computer Games for Cognitive and Emotional Training in the Adult Population. *Frontiers in Psychology, 9*, 2127. doi:10.3389/fpsyg.2018.02127 PMID:30464753

Palomo-Duarte, M., Berns, A., Cejas, A., Dodero, J. M., Caballero, J. A., & Ruiz-Rube, I. (2016). Assessing Foreign Language Learning Through Mobile Game-Based Learning Environments. *International Journal of Human Capital and Information Technology Professionals, 7*(2), 53–67. doi:10.4018/IJHCITP.2016040104

Paluck, E. L., & Green, D. P. (2009). Deference, Dissent, and Dispute Resolution: An Experimental Intervention Using Mass Media to Change Norms and Behavior in Rwanda. *The American Political Science Review, 103*(4), 622-644.

Panagiotarou, A., Stamatiou, Y. C., Pierrakeas, C., & Kameas, A. (2020). Gamification acceptance for learners with different E-skills. *International Journal of Learning. Teaching and Educational Research, 19*(2), 263–278. doi:10.26803/ijlter.19.2.16

Pangrazio, L. (2016). Reconceptualising critical digital literacy. *Discourse (Abingdon), 37*(2), 163–174. doi:10.1080/01596306.2014.942836

Panksepp, J. (2004). *Affective neuroscience: The foundations of human and animal emotions*. Oxford University Press.

Papadakis, S., Kalogiannakis, M., & Zaranis, N. (2017). Designing and creating an educational app rubric for preschool teachers. *Education and Information Technologies, 22*(6), 3147–3165. doi:10.100710639-017-9579-0

Papastergiou, M. (2009a). Digital game-based learning in high school computer science education: Impact on educational effectiveness and student motivation. *Computers & Education*, *52*(1), 1–12. doi:10.1016/j.compedu.2008.06.004

Papert, S. A. (1980). *Mindstorms: Children, computers, and powerful ideas*. Basic books.

Pappas, S. (2020). What do we really know about kids and screens? *Monitor on Psychology*, *51*(3), 42.

Pariser, E. (2011). *The filter bubble: How the new personalized web is changing what we read and how we think*. Penguin Books.

Parker Brothers. (1988). *Scattergories*. Board Game.

Parong, J., Mayer, R. E., Fiorella, L., MacNamara, A., Homer, B. D., & Plass, J. L. (2017). Learning executive function skills by playing focused video games. *Contemporary Educational Psychology*, *51*, 141–151. doi:10.1016/j.cedpsych.2017.07.002

Parrish, S. (Host) (2020, November 24). Forward thinking with Roger Martin. *The Knowledge Project* [Audio podcast episode]. https://www.youtube.com/watch?v=gmn2c5hrUmI&t=1345s

Parry, E., & Urwin, P. (2017). The Evidence Base for Generational Differences: Where Do We Go from Here? *Work, Aging and Retirement*, *3*(2), 140–148. doi:10.1093/workar/waw037

Partnership for 21st Century Learning. (2016). *Framework for 21st century learning*. www.p21.org/about-us/p21-framework

Partnership for 21st Century Learning. (2019). *Framework for 21st Century Learning Definitions*. http://static.battelleforkids.org/documents/p21/P21_Framework_DefinitionsBFK.pdf

Partnership for 21st Century Skills. (2007). *Framework for 21stcentury learning*. Retrieved from: http://www.p21.org/documents/P21_Framework_Definitions.pdf

Partnership for 21st Century Skills. (2011). *21st century skills map*. Partnership for 21st Century Skills.

Parvin, N., & Alam, M. J. (2016). Empowerment of Women to alleviate Poverty through Education in Bangladesh. *Journal of Governance and Innovation*, *2*(2), 49–60. https://osderpublications.com/uploads/1597820877.pdf

Parvin, R., & Haider, M. Z. (2012). Methods and practices of English language teaching in Bangla and English medium schools. *Bangladesh Education Journal*, *11*(1), 51–63.

Pasquier, P., Mérat, S., Malgras, B., Petit, L., Queran, X., Bay, C., Boutonnet, M., Jault, P., Ausset, S., Auroy, Y., Perez, J. P., Tesnière, A., Pons, F., & Mignon, A. (2016). A serious game for massive training and assessment of french soldiers involved in forward combat casualty care (3d-sc1): Development and deployment. *JMIR Serious Games*, *4*(1), e5. Advance online publication. doi:10.2196/games.5340 PMID:27194369

Passarotti, A. M., Sweeney, J. A., & Pavuluri, M. N. (2009). Neural correlates of incidental and directed facial emotion processing in adolescents and adults. *Social Cognitive and Affective Neuroscience*, *4*(4), 387–398. doi:10.1093can/nsp029 PMID:20035016

Pastushenko, O., Hruška, T., & Zendulka, J. (2018). Increasing students' motivation by using virtual learning environments based on gamification mechanics. *ACM International Conference Proceeding Series*, 755–760. 10.1145/3284179.3284310

Patall, E. A., Cooper, H., & Robinson, J. C. (2008). The effects of choice on intrinsic motivation and related outcomes: A meta-analysis of research findings. *Psychological Bulletin*, *134*(2), 270–300. https://doi.org/10.1037/0033-2909.134.2.270

Patil, S. J., Chavan, R. L., & Khandagale, V. S. (2019). Identification of misconceptions in science: Tools, techniques & skills for teachers. *Aarhat Multidisciplinary International Education Research Journal*, *8*(2), 466–472.

Paul, P. (2009). *Game-based Learning or Game-based Teaching?* Academic Press.

Paul, J. (2015). Despite the terrors of typologies: The importance of understanding categories of difference and identity. *Interventions, 17*(2), 174–195. doi:10.1080/1369801X.2014.993332

Payne, H. E., Moxley, V. B. A., & MacDonald, E. (2015). Health Behavior Theory in physical activity game apps: A content analysis. *JMIR Serious Games, 3*(2), e4. doi:10.2196/games.4187 PMID:26168926

Pea, R. D., Kurland, D. M., & Hawkins, J. (1985). *Logo and the development of thinking skills.* Academic Press.

Peachey, A., Gillen, J., Livingstone, D., & Smith-Robbins, S. (Eds.). (2010). *Researching learning in Virtual Worlds.* Springer. doi:10.1007/978-1-84996-047-2

Peake, B. (2015, April 1). WP:THREATENING2MEN: Misogynist Infopolitics and the Hegemony of the Asshole Consensus on English Wikipedia. *Ada New Media.* https://adanewmedia.org/2015/04/issue7-peake/

Pedaste, M., Mäeots, M., Leijen, Ä., & Sarapuu, S. (2012). Improving students' inquiry skills through reflection and self-regulation scaffolds. *Technology, Instruction. Cognition and Learning, 9*(1-2), 81–95.

Pedaste, M., Mäeots, M., Siiman, L. A., De Jong, T., Van Riesen, S. A., Kamp, E. T., Manoli, C. C., Zacharia, Z. E., & Tsourlidaki, E. (2015). Phases of inquiry-based learning: Definitions and the inquiry cycle. *Educational Research Review, 14,* 47–61. doi:10.1016/j.edurev.2015.02.003

Peddycord-Liu, Z., Cateté, V., Vandenberg, J., Barnes, T., Lynch, C. F., & Rutherford, T. (2019). A Field Study of Teachers Using a Curriculum-integrated Digital Game. In *Proceedings of the 2019 CHI Conference on Human Factors in Computing Systems* (pp. 1-12). CHI Conference. 10.1145/3290605.3300658

Pedreira, O., García, F., Brisaboa, N., & Piattini, M. (2015). Gamification in software engineering–A systematic mapping. *Information and Software Technology, 57,* 157–168. doi:10.1016/j.infsof.2014.08.007

Pegrum, M., Bartle, E., & Longnecker, N. (2015). Can creative podcasting promote deep learning? The use of podcasting for learning content in an undergraduate science unit. *British Journal of Educational Technology, 46*(1), 142–152. doi:10.1111/bjet.12133

Peifer, J. L. (2015). The Inter-Institutional Interface of Religion and Business. *Business Ethics Quarterly, 25*(3), 363–391. doi:10.1017/beq.2015.33

Pekrun, R., & Linnenbrink-Garcia, L. (2014). Introduction to emotions in education. In R. Pekrun & L. Linnenbrink-Garcia (Eds.), International handbook of emotions in education (pp. 1–10). Routledge/Taylor & Francis Group.

Pelgrum, W. J. (2001). Obstacles to the integration of ICT in education: Results from a worldwide educational assessment. *Computers & Education, 37*(2), 163–178. doi:10.1016/S0360-1315(01)00045-8

Pellas, N., Fotaris, P., Kazanidis, I., & Wells, D. (2019). Augmenting the learning experience in primary and secondary school education: A systematic review of recent trends in augmented reality game-based learning. *Virtual Reality (Waltham Cross), 23*(4), 329–346. doi:10.100710055-018-0347-2

Pelletier, C., & Oliver, M. (2006). Learning to play in digital games. *Learning, Media and Technology, 31*(4), 329–342.

Peraica, A. (2019). The age of total images: disappearance of a subjective viewpoint in post-digital photography. Amsterdam University Institute of Network Cultures.

Perotta, C., Featherstone, G., Aston, H., & Houghton, E. (2013). *Game-based learning: Latest evidence and future directions.* Academic Press.

Perrotta, C., Featherstone, G., Aston, H., & Houghton, E. (2013). Game-based learning: Latest evidence and future directions. Slough, UK: National Foundation for Educational Research (NFER).

Perrotta, C., Featherstone, G., Aston, H., & Houghton, E. (2013). *Game-based Learning: Latest Evidence and Future Directions Innovation in Education*. NFER.

Perryer, C., Celestine, A. N., Scott-Ladd, B., & Leighton, C. (2016). Enhancing workplace motivation through Gamification: Transferrable lessons from pedagogy. *International Journal of Management Education, 14*(3), 327–335. doi:10.1016/j.ijme.2016.07.001

Persson, M. (2014, February 25). *Minecraft user announcement* [Social media message]. Retrieved from https://twitter.com/notch/status/438444097141882880

Pessoa, L. (2008). On the relationship between cognition and emotion. *Nature Reviews. Neuroscience, 9*(2), 148–158. doi:10.1038/nrn2317 PMID:18209732

Petersen, C. I., Baepler, P., Beitz, A., Ching, P., Gorman, K. S., Neudauer, C. L., Rozaitis, W., Walker, J. D., & Wingert, D. (2020). The Tyranny of Content: "Content Coverage" as a Barrier to Evidence-Based Teaching Approaches and Ways to Overcome It. *CBE Life Sciences Education, 19*(2), ar17. doi:10.1187/cbe.19-04-0079 PMID:32412836

Peters, M. A., Besley, A. C., & Besley, T. (2006). *Building knowledge cultures: Education and development in the age of knowledge capitalism*. Rowman & Littlefield Education.

Peterson, A., Dumont, H., Lafuente, M., & Law, N. (2018). *Understanding innovative pedagogies: Key themes to analyse new approaches to teaching and learning*. Academic Press.

Peterson, M. (2012). Learner interaction in a massively multiplayer online role playing game (MMORPG): A sociocultural discourse analysis. *ReCALL, 24*(3), 361–380. doi:10.1017/S0958344012000195

Peterson, M. (2016). The use of massively multiplayer online role-playing games in CALL: An analysis of research. *Computer Assisted Language Learning, 29*(7), 1181–1194. doi:10.1080/09588221.2016.1197949

Peters, V. A. M., & Vissers, G. A. N. (2009). A simple classification model for debriefing simulation games. *Simulation & Gaming, 35*(1), 70–84. doi:10.1177/1046878103253719

Petranek, C. F. (2000). Written debriefing: The next vital step in learning with simulations. *Simulation & Gaming: An Interdisciplinary Journal, 31*(1), 108–118. doi:10.1177/104687810003100111

Pew Research Center. (2010). *Millennials: Confident. Connected. Open to change*. Retrieved August 15, 2011 from www.pewresearc.org/millennials

Pfeffer, J., & Fong, C. T. (2004). The business school 'business': Some lessons from the US experience. *Journal of Management Studies, 41*(8), 1501–1520. doi:10.1111/j.1467-6486.2004.00484.x

Pham, H. H., Vuong, Q. H., Luong, D. H., Nguyen, T. T., Dinh, V. H., & Ho, M. T. (2021). A bibliometric review of research on international student mobility's in Asia with Scopus dataset between 1984 and 2019. *Scientometrics, 126*(6), 5201–5224. doi:10.100711192-021-03965-4

Phan, K. L., Wager, T., Taylor, S. F., & Liberzon, I. (2002). Functional neuroanatomy of emotion: Embodied persuasion: Fundamental processes by which bodily responses can impact attitudes. *NeuroImage, 16*, 331–348. doi:10.1006/nimg.2002.1087 PMID:12030820

Phellas, C. N., Bloch, A., & Seale, C. (2011). Structured methods: Interviews, questionnaires and observation. In C. Seale (Ed.), *Research Society and Culture* (3rd ed., pp. 181–205). SAGE.

Phelps, J. (2018, March 8). Trump turns spotlight on violent video games in wake of Parkland shootings. *ABC News*. Retrieved from https://abcnews.go.com/Politics/trump-turns-spotlight-violent-video-games-wake-parkland/story?id=53593714

Pho A & Dinscore A. (2015). *Game Based Learning*. Tips and Trends Instructional Technologies.

Pho, A., & Dinscore, A. (2015). *Game-based learning. Tips and Trends*. https://acrl.ala.org/IS/wp-content/uploads/2014/05/spring2015.pdf

Pho, B. A., Dinscore, A., & Badges, D. (2015). *Game-based learning*. Academic Press.

Piaget, J. (1951). *Play, dreams and imitation in childhood*. Heinemann.

Piaget, J. (1953). *Origins of intelligence in the child*. Routledge & Kegan Paul.

Piaget, J. (1954). *Construction of reality in the child*. Routledge & Kegan Paul. doi:10.1037/11168-000

Piaget, J. (1962). *Play Dreams and Imitation in Childhood*. WW Norton.

Piaget, J. (1964). Cognitive development in children: Development and learning. *Journal of Research in Science Teaching*, *2*(3), 176–186. doi:10.1002/tea.3660020306

Piaget, J. (2008). Intellectual evolution from adolescence to adulthood. *Human Development*, *51*(1), 40–47. doi:10.1159/000112531

Piccoli, G., Ahmad, R., & Ives, B. (2001). Web-based virtual learning environments: A research framework and a preliminary assessment of effectiveness in basic IT skills training. *Management Information Systems Quarterly*, *25*(4), 401–426. doi:10.2307/3250989

Pickering, S. J., & Phye, G. D. (2006). *Working Memory and Education*. Elsevier.

Pierce, R., & Stacey, K. (2013). Teaching with new technology: Four 'early majority' teachers. *Journal of Mathematics Teacher Education*, *16*(5), 323–347. doi:10.100710857-012-9227-y

Pietraß, M. (2009). Digital literacy as framing: Suggestions for an interactive approach based on E. Goffman s frame theory. *Nordic Journal of Digital Literacy, 4*(3-4), 131-142.

Pina, A. A., & Harris, B. R. (1993). *Increasing Teachers' Confidence in Using Computers for Education*. Paper presented at the annaul meeting of the Arizona Educational Research Organization, Tucson, AZ.

Pinard, R., de Winter, A., Sarkis, G. J., Gerstein, M. B., Tartaro, K. R., Plant, R. N., Egholm, M., Rothberg, J. M., & Leamon, J. H. (2006). Assessment of whole genome amplification-induced bias through high-throughput, massively parallel whole genome sequencing. *BMC Genomics*, *7*(1), 1–21. doi:10.1186/1471-2164-7-216 PMID:16928277

Pinder, D. P. J. (2016). Exploring the Effects of Game Based Learning in Trinidad and Tobago's Primary Schools: An Examination of In-Service Teachers'. *Perspectives*, 17.

Pink, D. H. (2006). *A whole new mind: Why right-brainers will rule the future*. Riverhead Books.

Pinto, M., & Ferreira, P. (2017). Use of Videogames in Higher Education in Portugal : A Literature Review. In Challenges 2017: Aprender nas nuvens, Learning in the clouds (pp. 605-620). Universidade do Minho – Centro de Competência.

Pirraglia, P., & Kravitz, R. (2012). Social media: New opportunities, new ethical concerns. *Journal of General Internal Medicine*, *28*(2), 165–166. doi:10.100711606-012-2288-x PMID:23225258

Pivec, M., Dziabenko, O., & Schinnerl, I. (2003). Aspects of Game-Based Learning. *Proceedings of I-KNOW3*, 11.

Pivec, M. (2007). Editorial: Play and learn: potentials of game-based learning. *British Journal of Educational Technology, 38*(3), 387–393. doi:10.1111/j.1467-8535.2007.00722.x

Pivec, M., Dziabenko, O., & Schinnerl, I. (2003). *Aspects of game-based learning.* Academic Press.

Pixlr. (n.d.). https://pixlr.com/. *Free photo editor online graphic design.* Academic Press.

Plass, J. L., Perlin, K., & Nordlinger, J. (2010). *The games for learning institute: Research on design patterns for effective educational games.* Paper presented at the Game Developers Conference, San Francisco, CA.

Plass, J. L., Homer, B. D., & Kinzer, C. K. (2015). Foundations of Game-Based Learning. *Educational Psychologist, 50*(4), 258–283. doi:10.1080/00461520.2015.1122533

Plass, J. L., Mayer, R. E., & Homer, B. D. (2020). *Handbook of Game-based Learning.* MIT Press.

Plato. (1943). *The Republic* (R. E. Allen, Trans.). Yale University Press.

Pløhn, T. (2013). Nuclear Mayhem-A Pervasive Game Designed to Support Learning. *Proceedings of the 7th European Conference on Games Based Learning ECGBL 2013, 2.*

Plowman, L., McPake, J., & Stephen, C. (2010). The technologisation of childhood? Young Children and technology in the home. *Children & Society, 24,* 63-74. http://dx.doi.org.erl.lib.byu.edu/10.1111/j.1099-0860.2008.00180.x

Podolefsky, N. S., Perkins, K. K., & Adams, W. K. (2010). Factors promoting engaged exploration with computer simulations. *Physical Review Special Topics. Physics Education Research, 6*(2), 020117. doi:10.1103/PhysRevSTPER.6.020117

Podsakoff, P. M., MacKenzie, S. B., Lee, J.-Y., & Podsakoff, N. P. (2003). Common method biases in behavioral research: A critical review of the literature and recommended remedies. *The Journal of Applied Psychology, 88*(5), 879–903. doi:10.1037/0021-9010.88.5.879 PMID:14516251

Poiroux, J., Dahl-Jørgensen, T., Løyland, M., & Rye, S. (2016). *Using Minecraft to Enhance Collaboration as a 21st Century Skill in Primary Schools.* University of Oslo.

Polikov, V. (2017, March 6). *New Research Proves Game-Based Learning Works—Here's Why That Matters—EdSurge News.* EdSurge. https://www.edsurge.com/news/2017-03-06-new-research-proves-game-based-learning-works-here-s-why-that-matters

Polished Play, L. L. C. (2021). *Puppet Pals* (Version 1.9.8) [Mobile app]. http://itunes.apple.com

Polistina, K. (n.d.). *Cultural Literacy. Understanding and Respect for the Cultural Aspects of Sustainability.* Retrieved May 02, 2019 from http://arts.brighton.ac.uk/__data/assets/pdf_file/0006/5982/Cultural-Literacy.pdf

Polman, de Castro, B. O., & van Aken, M. A. G. (2008). Experimental study of the differential effects of playing versus watching violent video games on children's aggressive behaviour. *Aggressive Behavior, 34*(3), 256–264. doi:10.1002/ab.20245 PMID:18161877

Ponitz, C. C., & Rimm-Kaufman, S. E. (2011). Contexts of reading instruction: Implications for literacy skills and kindergarteners' behavioral engagement. *Early Childhood Research Quarterly, 26*(2), 157–168. https://doi.org/0.1016/j.ecresq.2010.10.002

Popat, S., & Starkey, L. (2019). Learning to code or coding to learn? A systematic review. *Computers & Education, 128,* 365–376. doi:10.1016/j.compedu.2018.10.005

Portier, C., Friedrich, N., & Peterson, S. S. (2019). Play(ful) pedagogical practices for creative collaborative literacy. *The Reading Teacher, 73*(1), 17–27. doi:10.1002/trtr.1795

Postman, N. (2004). Televizyon Öldüren Eğlence. İstanbul: Ayrıntı.

Potocki, A., Magnan, A., & Ecalle, J. (2015). Computerized trainings in four groups of struggling readers: Specific effects on word reading and comprehension. *Research in Developmental Disabilities, 45–46*(April), 83–92. doi:10.1016/j.ridd.2015.07.016

Potter, W. J. (2011). Media Literacy (5th ed.). Sage Publication.

Potter, W. J. (2004). *Theory of Media Literacy A Cognitive Approach.* Sage Publications.

Potts, R. (1991). Spirits in the bottle: Spirituality and alcoholism treatment in African-American communities. *Journal of Training & Practice in Professional Psychology.*

Prandi, C., Nisi, V., Salomoni, P., & Nunes, N. J. (2015). From Gamification to pervasive game in mapping urban accessibility. In *Proceedings of the 11th Biannual Conference on Italian SIGCHI Chapter* (pp. 126-129). ACM 10.1145/2808435.2808449

Prensky, M. (2001). *Digital Game-Based Learning.* McGraw hill.

Prensky, M. (2001). Digital Natives, Digital Immigrants. MCB University Press.

Prensky, M. (2001). Digital datives, digital immigrants, Part II: Do they really think differently? *On the Horizon, 9*(6), 15–24. doi:10.1108/10748120110424843

Prensky, M. (2001a). Digital natives, digital immigrants. *On the Horizon, 9*(5), 1–6. doi:10.1108/10748120110424816

Prensky, M. (2001b). *Digital game-based learning.* McGraw-Hill.

Prensky, M. (2003c). Digital game-based learning. *ACM Computers in Entertainment, 1*(1), 1–4. doi:10.1145/950566.950596

Prensky, M. (2005). Computer games and learning: Digital game-based learning. In J. Raessens & J. Goldstein (Eds.), *Handbook of computer game studies* (pp. 97–122). MIT Press.

Prensky, M. (2006). *Don't bother me Mom—I'm learning!* Paragon House.

Prensky, M. (2011). Comments on research comparing games to other instructional methods. In S. Tobias & J. D. Fletcher (Eds.), *Computer games and instruction* (pp. 251–280). Information Age.

Prensky, M. (2012). Aprendizagem Baseada. In *Jogos Digitais.* Senac São Paulo.

Prensky, M. (2012). *From digital natives to digital wisdom: Hopeful essays for 21st century learning.* Corwin Press. doi:10.4135/9781483387765

Presnsky, M. (2008). Students as designers and creators of educational computer games: Who else? *British Journal of Educational Technology, 39*(6), 1004–1019. doi:10.1111/j.1467-8535.2008.00823_2.x

Prestridge, S., & de Aldama, C. (2016). A Classification framework for exploring technology enabled practice-FramTEP. *Journal of Educational Computing Research, 54*(7), 901–921. doi:10.1177/0735633116636767

Price, P. C., Chiang, I.-C. A., Leighton, D. C., & Cutler, C. (2017). Reliability and validity of measurement. In R. Jhangiani (Ed.), Research methods in psychology. Pressbooks.

Price-Dennis, D., Holmes, K. A., & Smith, E. (2015). Exploring digital literacy practices in an inclusive classroom. *The Reading Teacher, 69*(2), 195–205.

Priyaadharshini, M., Natha Mayil, N., Dakshina, R., Sandhya, S., & Bettina Shirley, R. (2020). Author. *Procedia Computer Science, 172*, 468–472. doi:10.1016/j.procs.2020.05.143

Priyadharshini, M., Nathamayil, N., Dakshina, R., Sandhya, S., & R, B. S. (2020). *Learning analytics : Game-based learning for programming course in higher education.* Academic Press.

Provost, J. A. (1990). *Work, play and type: Achieving balance in your life.* Consulting Psychologist Press.

Pullano, G., Pinotti, F., Valdano, E., Boëlle, P. Y., Poletto, C., & Colizza, V. (2020). Novel coronavirus (2019-nCoV) early-stage importation risk to Europe, January 2020. *Eurosurveillance, 25*(4), 2000057. doi:10.2807/1560-7917. ES.2020.25.4.2000057 PMID:32019667

Puolakanaho, A. (2007). Early prediction of reading and related language and cognitive skills in children with a familial risk for dyslexia. *Jyväskylä Studies in Education, Psychology and Social Research 317.* https://jyx.jyu.fi/dspace/bitstream/handle/123456789/13367/9789513929985.pdf?sequence=1

Putz, L. M., Hofbauer, F., & Mates, M. (2019). A vignette study among order pickers about the acceptance of Gamification. In GamiFIN (pp. 154-166). Academic Press.

Putz, L. M., Hofbauer, F., & Treiblmaier, H. (2020). Can Gamification help to improve Education? Findings from a longitudinal study. *Computers in Human Behavior, 110*, 106392.

Qian, M., & Clark, K. R. (2016). Game-Based Learning and 21st Century Skills: A Review of Recent Research. *Computers in Human Behavior, 63*, 50–58. doi:10.1016/j.chb.2016.05.023

Qualman, E. (2011). *Socialnomics: How social media transforms the way we live and do business.* John Wiley & Sons, Inc.

Quddus, M., Iii, H. B., & White, L. R. (2009). Business ethics: Perspectives from Judaic, Christian, and Islamic scriptures. *Journal of Management, Spirituality & Religion, 6*(4), 323–334. doi:10.1080/14766080903290143

Rabone, D. (2013). How 'game mechanics" can revitalize education. *eSchoolNews.* http://www.eschoolnews.com/2013/02/12/how-game-mechanics-can-revitalize- education/3/

Raftopoulos, M. (2014). Towards gamification transparency: A conceptual framework for the development of responsible gamified enterprise systems. *Journal of Gaming & Virtual Worlds, 6*(2), 159–178. doi:10.1386/jgvw.6.2.159_1

Rahman, I. S., Falkenthal, E., Holzner, L., & Lozano, A. A. (2019). *Studentaffairs.com 2019 virtual case study* [Powerpoint slides]. https://www.studentaffairs.com/Customer-Content/www/CMS/files/VCS/2019/CalPolySanLuisObispo_rahman.pdf

Raman, K., & Yamat, H. (2014). Barriers Teachers Face in Integrating ICT during English Lessons: A Case Study. *Malaysian Online Journal of Educational Technology, 2*(3), 11–19.

Rama, P. S., Black, R. W., Van Es, E., & Warschauer, M. (2012). Affordances for second language learning in World of Warcraft. *ReCALL, 24*(3), 322–338. doi:10.1017/S0958344012000171

Ramirez, D., & Squire, K. (2015). Gamification and learning. In S. P. Walz & S. Deterding (Eds.), *The Gameful World: Approaches, Issues, Applications* (pp. 629–652). MIT Press.

Ranalli, J., & Ritzko, J. (2013). Assessing the impact of video game based design projects in a first year engineering design course. In 2013 IEEE Frontiers in Education Conference (FIE) (pp. 530-534). IEEE. doi:10.1109/FIE.2013.6684880

Randall, N. (2019). A survey of robot-assisted language learning (RALL). *ACM Transactions on Human-Robot Interaction, 9*(1), 1–36. doi:10.1145/3345506

Randolph, J. J., Kangas, M., Ruokamo, H., & Hyvönen, P. (2016). Creative and playful learning on technology-enriched playgrounds: An international investigation. *Interactive Learning Environments, 24*(3), 409–422. doi:10.1080/104948 20.2013.860902

Rankin, Y., Gold, R., & Gooch, B. (2006). 3D Role-Playing Games as Language Learning Tools. *Eurographics, 25*(3), 33–38.

Rao, D., & Stupans, I. (2012). Exploring the potential of role play in higher education: Development of a typology and teacher guidelines. *Innovations in Education and Teaching International, 49*(4), 427–436.

Rao, N., & Sun, J. (2010). Educating Asian adolescents: a developmental perspective. In L. F. Zhang, J. Biggs, & D. Watkins (Eds.), *Learning and development of Asian students: what the 21st Century teacher needs to think about* (pp. 37–59). Pearson.

Raschke, C. A. (2003). *The digital revolution and the coming of the postmodern university*. Routledge. doi:10.4324/9780203451243

Rasheed, R. A., Kamsin, A., & Abdullah, N. A. (2020). Challenges in the online component of blended learning: A systematic review. *Computers & Education, 144*, 103701. doi:10.1016/j.compedu.2019.103701

Ratheeswari, K. (2018). Information Communication Technology in Education. *Journal of Applied and Advanced Research, 3*(S1), 45. doi:10.21839/jaar.2018.v3iS1.169

Rauch, M. (2013). Best practices for using enterprise gamification to engage employees and customers. In *International Conference on Human-Computer Interaction* (pp. 276-283). Springer Berlin Heidelberg. 10.1007/978-3-642-39262-7_31

Raymundo, M. R. D. (2020). Fostering creativity through online creative collaborative group projects. *Asian Association of Open Universities Journal, 15*(1), 97–113. doi:10.1108/AAOUJ-10-2019-0048

Raziunaite, P., Miliunaite, A., Maskeliunas, R., Damasevicius, R., Sidekerskiene, T., & Narkeviciene, B. (2018). Designing an educational music game for digital game based learning: A Lithuanian case study. *2018 41st International Convention on Information and Communication Technology, Electronics and Microelectronics, MIPRO 2018 - Proceedings*, 800–805. 10.23919/MIPRO.2018.8400148

Read the standards. (n.d.). *Common Core State Standards Initiative*. Retrieved October 25, 2021, from http://www.corestandards.org/read-the-standards/

Real, Y. M. (2008). *An assessment of the relationship between creativity and information and media literacy skills of community college students for a selected major* (PhD Thesis). Pepperdine University Graduate School of Education and Psychology.

Redecker, C. (2017). *European Framework for the Digital Competence of Educators*. European Commission.

Redecker, C. (2017). *European Framework for the Digital Competence of Educators: DigCompEdu*. Publications Office of the European Union., doi:10.2760/159770

Regtvoort, A., & van der Leij, A. (2007). Early intervention with children of dyslexic parents: Effects of computer-based reading instruction at home on literacy acquisition. *Learning and Individual Differences, 17*(1), 35–53. doi:10.1016/j.lindif.2007.01.005

Reinders, H. (2012). *Digital games in language learning and teaching*. Palgrave Macmillan. doi:10.1057/9781137005267

Reinhardt, J., & Sykes, J. M. (2012). Conceptualizing digital game-mediated L2 learning and pedagogy: Game-enhanced and game-based research and practice. In H. Reinders (Ed.), *Digital games in language learning and teaching* (pp. 32–49). Palgrave Macmillan. doi:10.1057/9781137005267_3

Resaba, M. L., & Gayeta, N. E. (2021). Utilization of Project - Based Learning (PBL) Resources in Senior High School. *International Multidisciplinary Research Journal, 3*(2).

Research and Market. (2021, June 23). *World Game-Based Learning Market Report 2021-2026.* Retrieved September 4th, 2021, from Globe Newswire: https://www.globenewswire.com/en/news-release/2021/06/23/2251646/28124/en/World-Game-Based-Learning-Market-Report-2021-2026.html

Rest, J. R. (1986). *Moral development: Advances in research and theory.* Praeger publishers.

Reyes, D. L. Jr, & Gaston, T. W. K. (2017). Teaching ethics in business schools: A conversation on disciplinary differences, academic provincialism, and the case for integrated pedagogy. *Academy of Management Learning & Education, 16*(2), 314–336. doi:10.5465/amle.2014.0402

Reynolds, R. (2016). Defining, designing for, and measuring "social constructivist digital literacy" development in learners: A proposed framework. *Educational Technology Research and Development, 64*(4), 735–762. doi:10.100711423-015-9423-4

Reynolds, R., & Harel Caperton, I. (2011). Contrasts in student engagement, meaning-making, dislikes, and challenges in a discovery-based program of game design learning. *Journal of Educational Technology Research and Development, 59*(2), 267–289. doi:10.100711423-011-9191-8

Rice, S. (n.d.). *Game-Based Learning.* Retrieved September 5, 2021, from College STAR: https://www.collegestar.org/modules/game-based-learning

Rice, J. (2007). Assessing higher order thinking in video games. *Journal of Technology and Teacher Education, 15*(1), 87–100.

Richardson, U. (2011). *GRAPHOGAME Report Summary.* European Commission, Community Research and Development Information Service (CORDIS). https://cordis.europa.eu/result/rcn/48026_en.html

Rideout, V., & Robb, M. B. (2019). *The Common Sense census: Media use by tweens and teens.* Common Sense Media.

Rief, S. (2009). *Club cultures: Boundaries, identities and otherness.* Taylor and Francis.

Riemer, V., & Schrader, C. (2015). Learning with quizzes, simulations, and adventures: Students' attitudes, perceptions and intentions to learn with different types of serious games. *Computers & Education, 88*, 160–168. doi:10.1016/j.compedu.2015.05.003

Rijshouwer, E. (2019). *Organizing Democracy: Power concentration and self-organization in the evolution of Wikipedia.* https://repub.eur.nl/pub/113937

Riordan, R. (2005). *The Lightning Thief.* Hyperion Books for Children.

Ritter, J. (2015, June 25). Gamification or game-based learning? What's the difference? *Knowledge Direct: A Learning Management Platform.* https://www.kdplatform.com/gamification-game-based-learning-whats-difference/

Roberts, L. D., Breen, L. J., & Symes, M. (2013). Teaching computer-assisted qualitative data analysis to a large cohort of undergraduate students. *International Journal of Research & Method in Education, 36*(3), 279–294. doi:10.1080/1743727X.2013.804501

Robinson, K. (2006, June). *Ken Robinson: Do schools kill creativity?* [Video file]. Retrieved From https://www.ted.com/talks/ken_robinson_says_schools_kill_creativity?language=en#t201246

Robinson, K. (1998). National Advisory Council for creative and cultural education - NACCCE. *RSA Journal*, (5486), 20.

Robinson, K., & Aronica, L. (2006). *Creative schools: The grassroots revolution that is transforming education*. Penguin Books.

Robinson, M., & Mackey, M. (2006). Assets in the classroom: Comfort and competence with media among teachers present and future. In J. Marsh & E. Millard (Eds.), *Popular literacies, childhood and schooling* (pp. 200–220). Routledge.

Roca, J. C., & Gagné, M. (2008). Understanding e-learning continuance intention in the workplace: A self-determination theory perspective. *Computers in Human Behavior*, *24*(4), 1585–1604. doi:10.1016/j.chb.2007.06.001

Rodrigues, F. L., & Costa, C. J. O. A. (2016). Playing seriously – How gamification and social cues influence bank customers to use gamified e-business applications. *Computers in Human Behavior*, *63*, 392–407. doi:10.1016/j.chb.2016.05.063

Rodrigues, L. F., Costa, C. J., & Oliveira, A. (2017). How does the web game design influence the behavior of e-banking users? *Computers in Human Behavior*, *74*, 163–174. doi:10.1016/j.chb.2017.04.034

Roefsema, P. R., Van Ooyen, A., & Watanabe, T. (2010, February). Perceptual learning rules based on reinforcers and attention. *Trends in Cognitive Sciences*, *14*(2), 64–71. doi:10.1016/j.tics.2009.11.005 PMID:20060771

Rogers-Vaughn. (2012). The social trifecta of human misery and problematical constructions of the self: Implications for formation and supervision. *Reflective Practice (Decatur, Ga.)*, *32*, 206–223.

Rogoff, B. (1990). *Apprenticeship in thinking. Cognitive development in social context*. Oxford University Press.

Romeiro, P., Nunes, F., Santos, P., & Pinto, C. (2020). Atlas do Setor dos Videojogos em Portugal. Edição Sociedade Portuguesa para a Ciência dos Videojogos.

Ronimus, M., Kujala, J., Tolvanen, A., & Lyytinen, H. (2014). Children's engagement during digital game-based learning of reading: The effects of time, rewards, and challenge. *Computers & Education*, *71*, 237–246. doi:10.1016/j.compedu.2013.10.008

Rosa, J. A. (2012). Marketing education for the next four billion: Challenges and innovations. *Journal of Marketing Education*, *34*(1), 44–54.

Rosen, Y., Stoeffler, K., Yudelson, M., & Simmering, V. (2020). Towards Scalable Gamified Assessment in Support of Collaborative Problem-Solving Competency Development in Online and Blended Learning. In *Proceedings of the Seventh ACM Conference on Learning@ Scale* (pp. 369-372). 10.1145/3386527.3405946

Rosling, H. (2020). Factfulness. Edições Círculo de Leitores: Temas e Debates, Lisboa.

Rossi, M., & Scappini, E. (2014). Church Attendance, Problems of Measurement, and Interpreting Indicators: A Study of Religious Practice in the United States, 1975–2010. *Journal for the Scientific Study of Religion*, *53*(2), 249–267. doi:10.1111/jssr.12115

Rotherham, A. J., & Willingham, D. T. (2010). 21st-century" skills. *American Educator*, *17*(1), 17–20.

Roth, S., Schneckenberg, D., & Tsai, C. W. (2015). The ludic drive as innovation driver: Introduction to the Gamification of innovation. *Creativity and Innovation Management*, *24*(2), 300–306. doi:10.1111/caim.12124

Roux, C. J., Burnett, C., & Hollander, W. J. (2008). Curriculum enrichment through indigenous Zulu games. *S.A. Journal for Research in Sport Physical Education and Recreation*, *30*(1), 89–103. doi:10.4314ajrs.v30i1.25985

Rowan, L., & Beavis, C. (2017). Serious outcomes from serious play: Teachers' beliefs about assessment of game-based learning in schools. In C. Beavis, M. Dezuanni, & J. O'Mara (Eds.), *Serious play: literacy, learning and digital games* (pp. 169–185). Routledge. doi:10.4324/9781315537658-16

Rowe, J. P., Shores, L. R., Mott, B. W., & Lester, J. C. (2011). Integrating learning, problem solving, and engagement in narrative-centered learning environments. *International Journal of Artificial Intelligence in Education, 21*(1-2), 115–133.

Rowsell, J., Burke, A., Flewitt, R., Liao, H.-T., Lin, A., Marsh, J., Mills, K., Prinsloo, M., Rowe, D., & Wohlwend, K. (2016). Humanizing digital literacies: A road trip in search of wisdom and insight. Digital Literacy Column. *The Reading Teacher, 70*(1), 121–129. doi:10.1002/trtr.1501

Rowsell, J., & Walsh, M. (2011). Rethinking literacy education in new times: Multimodality, multiliteracies, & new literacies. *Brock Education, 21*(1), 1. doi:10.26522/brocked.v21i1.236

Rowsell, J., & Wohlwend, K. (2016). Free play or tight spaces? Mapping participatory literacies in apps. *The Reading Teacher, 70*(2), 197–205. doi:10.1002/trtr.1490

Rozario, R. B. (2013). New Media and the Traditional Media Platforms: Introspection on the Differences in Technical and Ideological Factors and Audience-integration Patterns between New Media and Traditional Media. *The Arab Journal of the Social Sciences, 12*(3), 43–61.

Rozman, T., & Donath, L. (2019). The Current State of the Gamification in E-Learning. *Mednarodno Inovativno Poslovanje = Journal of Innovative Business and Management, 11*(3), 5–19. doi:10.32015/JIBM/2019-11-3-2

Roztocki, N., Soja, P., & Weistroffer, H. R. (2019). The role of information and communication technologies in socio-economic development: Towards a multi-dimensional framework. *Information Technology for Development, 25*(2), 171–183. doi:10.1080/02681102.2019.1596654

Ruggiero, D. (2013). Video games in the classroom: The teacher point of view. In *Games for learning workshop of the foundations of digital games conference.* http://fdg2013.org/program/workshops/papers/G4L2013/g4l2013_02.pdf

Ruggiero, T. E. (2000). Uses and gratifications theory in the 21st century. *Mass Communication & Society, 3*(1), 3–37. doi:10.1207/S15327825MCS0301_02

Rumeser, D., & Emsley, M. (2019). Can serious games improve project management decision making under complexity? *Project Management Journal, 50*(1), 23–39. doi:10.1177/8756972818808982

Ruotsalainen, M., & Friman, U. (2018). "There Are No Women and They All Play Mercy": Understanding and Explaining (the Lack of) Women's Presence in Esports and Competitive Gaming. *Proceedings of Nordic DIGRA 2018.* http://www.digra.org/wp-content/uploads/digital-library/DiGRA_Nordic_2018_paper_31.pdf

Rushkoff, D. (2011). *Program or be programmed: Ten commands for a digital age.* Soft Skull Press.

Rusman, E., Ternier, S., & Specht, M. (2018). Early second language learning and adult involvement in a real-world context: Design and evaluation of the "ELENA Goes Shopping" mobile game. *Journal of Educational Technology & Society, 21*(3), 90–103.

Russell, G., & Bradley, G. (1997). Teachers' computer anxiety: Implications for professional development. *Education and Information Technologies, 2*(1), 17–30. doi:10.1023/A:1018680322904

Rutten, K., & Soetaert, R. (2012). Narrative and rhetorical approaches to problems of education: Jerome Bruner and Kenneth Burke revisited. *Studies in Philosophy and Education, 32*(4), 327–343. doi:10.100711217-012-9324-5

Rutten, N., Joolingen, W., & Veen, J. T. (2012). The Learning Effects of Computer Simulations in Science Education. *Computers & Education, 58*(1), 136–153. doi:10.1016/j.compedu.2011.07.017

Ryan, R. M., & Deci, E. L. (2000). *Self-Determination Theory and the Facilitation of Intrinsic Motivation, Social Development, and Well-Being. 55*(1), 68–78. (https://www2.deloitte.com/us/en/insights/focus/behavioral-economics/gaming-away-leadership-gap-developing-leaders.html)

Ryan, M. (2014). Story/Worlds/Media: Tuning the instruments of a media-conscious narratology. In M. Ryan & J. Thon (Eds.), *Storyworlds across media: Toward a media-conscious narratology* (pp. 25–49). University of Nebraska Press. doi:10.2307/j.ctt1d9nkdg.6

Ryan, M., & Anstey, M. (2003). Identity and text: Developing self-conscious readers. *Australian Journal of Language and Literacy, 26*(1), 9–22.

Ryan, R. M., & Deci, E. L. (2000). Intrinsic and extrinsic motivations: Classic definitions and new directions. *Contemporary Educational Psychology, 25*(1), 54–67. doi:10.1006/ceps.1999.1020 PMID:10620381

Ryan, R. M., Rigby, C. S., & Przybylski, A. (2006). The motivational pull of video games: A self-determination theory approach. *Motivation and Emotion, 30*(4), 344–360.

Ryan, W. S., & Ryan, R. M. (2019). Toward a social psychology of authenticity: Exploring within-person variation in autonomy, congruence, and genuineness using self-determination theory. *Review of General Psychology, 23*(1), 99–112. doi:10.1037/gpr0000162

Rybakova, K., Rice, M., Moran, C., Zucker, L., McGrail, E., McDermott, M., Loomis, S., Piotrowski, A., Garcia, M., Gerber, H., & Gibbons, T. (2019). A long arc bending towards equity: Tracing almost 20 years of ELA teaching trends. *Contemporary Issues in Technology and Teacher Education, 19*(4), 549-604. https://citejournal.org/volume-19/issue-4-19/english-language-arts/a-long-arc-bending-toward-equity-tracing-almost-20-years-of-ela-teaching-with-technology/

Saadé, R. G., & Kira, D. (2009). Computer anxiety in e-learning: The effect of computer self-efficacy. *Journal of Information Technology Education, 8.*

Sabourin, J., Rowe, J. P., Mott, B. W., & Lester, J. C. (2011). When Off-Task Is On-Task: The Affective Role of Off-Task Behavior in Narrative-Centered Learning Environments. *Proc. 15th Int'l Conf. Artificial Intelligence in Education,* 523-536.

Sabourin, J. L., & Lester, J. C. (2013). Affect and engagement in Game-BasedLearning environments. *IEEE Transactions on Affective Computing, 5*(1), 45–56. doi:10.1109/T-AFFC.2013.27

Sadler, D. R. (1989). Formative assessment and the design of instructional systems. *Instructional Science, 18*(2), 119–144. doi:10.1007/BF00117714

Safapour, E., Kermanshachi, S., & Taneja, P. (2019). A review of nontraditional teaching methods: Flipped classroom, gamification, case study, self-learning, and social media. *Education Sciences, 9*(4), 273. doi:10.3390/educsci9040273

Saia, S. M., Nelson, N. G., Young, S. N., Parham, S., & Vandegrift, M. (2021). *Ten simple rules for researchers who want to develop web apps.* Academic Press.

Sailer, M., Hense, J. U., Mayr, S. K., & Mandl, H. (2017). How gamification motivates: An experimental study of the effects of specific game design elements on psychological need satisfaction. *Computers in Human Behavior, 69,* 371–380.

Sailer, M., Hense, J., Mandl, H., & Klevers, M. (2017). Fostering Development of Work Competencies and Motivation via Gamification. In *Competence-based Vocational and Professional Education* (pp. 795–818). Springer International Publishing. doi:10.1007/978-3-319-41713-4_37

Sailer, M., & Homner, L. (2019). The Gamification of Learning: aMeta-Analysis. *Educational Psychology Review*, *32*(1), 77–112. doi:10.100710648-019-09498-w

Saine, N. L., Lerkkanen, M.-K., Ahonen, T., Tolvanen, A., & Lyytinen, H. (2010a). Predicting word-level reading fluency outcomes in three contrastive groups: Remedial and computer-assisted remedial reading intervention, and mainstream instruction. *Learning and Individual Differences*, *20*(5), 402–414. doi:10.1016/j.lindif.2010.06.004

Sajjadi, P., Broeckhoven, F. V., & Troyer, O. D. (2014). Dynamically Adaptive Educational Games: A New Perspective. *International Conference on Serious Games*. 10.1007/978-3-319-05972-3_8

Salajan, F. D., Schönwetter, D. J., & Cleghorn, B. M. (2010). Student and faculty inter-generational digital divide: Fact or fiction? *Computers & Education*, *55*(3), 1393–1403. doi:10.1016/j.compedu.2010.06.017

Salas, Wildman, & Piccolo. (2009). Using simulation-based training to enhance management education. *Academy of Management Learning & Education*, *8*(4), 559–573.

Saldaña, J. (2016). *The coding manual for qualitative researchers* (3rd ed.). Sage.

Salehi, H. (2017). Effects of using instructional video games on teaching English vocabulary to Iranian pre-intermediate EFL learners. *International Journal of Learning and Change*, *9*(2), 111–130. doi:10.1504/IJLC.2017.084609

Salem, J., & Fehrmann, P. (2013). Bibliographic management software: A focus group study of the preferences and practices of undergraduate students. *Public Services Quarterly*, *9*(2), 110–120. doi:10.1080/15228959.2013.785878

Salen, K., & Zimmerman, E. (2004). *Rules of Play - Game Design Fundamentals*. The MIT Press. https://gamifique. files.wordpress.com/2011/11/1-rules-of-play-game-design-fundamentals.pdf

Salen, K. (2007). Gaming literacies: A game design study in action. *Journal of Educational Multimedia and Hypermedia*, *16*(3), 301–322.

Salen, K., Tekinbaş, K. S., & Zimmerman, E. (2004). *Rules of Play: Game Design Fundamentals*. MIT Press.

Salen, K., & Zimmerman, E. (2004). *Rules of play: Game design fundamentals*. MIT Press.

Sallis, E. (2014). *Total quality management in education*. Routledge., doi:10.4324/9780203417010

Salvador, R. O., Merchant, A., & Alexander, E. A. (2014). Faith and fair trade: The moderating role of contextual religious salience. *Journal of Business Ethics*, *121*(3), 353–371. doi:10.100710551-013-1728-9

Samiee, S., & Chabowski, B. R. (2012). Knowledge structure in international marketing: A multi-method bibliometric analysis. *Journal of the Academy of Marketing Science*, *40*(2), 364–386. doi:10.100711747-011-0296-8

Sample, M., & Schrum, K. (2013). What's Wrong with Writing Essays. In D. Cohen & J. Scheinfeldt (Eds.), *Hacking the Academy: New Approaches to Scholarship and Teaching from Digital Humanities*. University of Michigan Press. https://muse.jhu.edu/chapter/833166

Sampson, D., & Karagiannidis, C. (2002). Personalised learning: Educational, technological and standarisation perspective. *Digital Education Review*, *4*(1), 24–39.

Samuels, S. J., Rasinski, T. V., & Hiebert, E. H. (2011). Eye movements and reading: What teachers need to know. In A. Farstrup & S. J. Samuels (Eds.), *What research has to say about reading instruction* (4th ed.). IRA. doi:10.1598/0829.02

Sánchez, A. D., Del Río, M. D. L. C., & García, J. Á. (2017). Bibliometric analysis of publications on wine tourism in the databases Scopus and WoS. *European Research on Management and Business Economics*, *23*(1), 8–15. doi:10.1016/j. iedeen.2016.02.001

Sánchez-Martín, J., Corrales-Serrano, M., Luque-Sendra, A., & Zamora-Polo, F. (2020). Exit for success. Gamifying science and technology for university students using escape-room. A preliminary approach. *Heliyon, 6*(7), e04340. doi:10.1016/j.heliyon.2020.e04340 PMID:32671257

Sandberg, J., Maris, M., & Hoogendoorn, P. (2014). The added value of a gaming context and intelligent adaptation for a mobile learning application for vocabulary learning. *Computers & Education, 76*, 119–130. doi:10.1016/j. compedu.2014.03.006

Sandford, R., Ulicsak, M., Facer, K., & Rudd, T. (2006). *Teaching with games: Using commercial off-the-shelf computer games in formal education*. Futurelab.

Sanford, K., & Madill, L. (2006). Resistance through video game play: It's a boy thing. *Canadian Journal of Education, 29*(1), 287–306, 344–345. doi:10.2307/20054157

Sanford, K., & Madill, L. (2007). Understanding the power of new literacies through video game play and design. *Canadian Journal of Education, 30*(2), 432–455. doi:10.2307/20466645

San-Martín, S., Jimenez, N., Camarero, C., & San-José, R. (2020). The path between personality, self-efficacy, and shopping regarding games apps. *Journal of Theoretical and Applied Electronic Commerce Research, 15*(2), 59–75. doi:10.4067/S0718-18762020000200105

Santos, E., & Santos, L. (2019). O papel do GeoGebra nas práticas de regulação do ensino da área do paralelogramo. Quadrante, 28(1), 6-26.

Santos, L. (2008). Dilemas e desafios da avaliação reguladora. In L. Menezes, L. Santos, H. Gomes & C. Rodrigues (Eds.), Avaliação em Matemática: Problemas e desafios, (pp. 11-35). Viseu: Secção de Educação Matemática da Sociedade Portuguesa de Ciências de Educação.

Santos, L. (2019). Reflexões em torno da avaliação pedagógica. In M. I. Ortigão, D. Fernandes, T. Pereira, & L. Santos (Orgs.), Avaliar para aprender no Brasil e em Portugal: Perspetivas teóricas, práticas e de desenvolvimento (pp. 165-190). Curitiba: Editora CRV.

Santos, L., & Cai, J. (2016). Curriculum and assessment. In A. Gutiérrez, G. Leder, & P. Boero (Eds.), *The Second Handbook in the Psychology of Mathematics Education* (pp. 153–185). Sense Publishers.

Santos, L., & Pinto, J. (2018). Ensino de conteúdos escolares: A avaliação como Fator estruturante. In *F. Veiga (Coord.), O Ensino como fator de envolvimento numa escola para todos* (pp. 503–539). Climepsi Editores.

Santos, S. A., Trevisan, L. N., Veloso, E. F. R., & Treff, M. A. (2021). Gamification In Training and Development Processes: Perception On Effectiveness And Results. *Revista de Gestão, 28*(2), 133–146. doi:10.1108/REGE-12-2019-0132

Saracho, O. N., & Spodek, B. (1995). Children's play and early childhood education: Insights from history and theory. *Journal of Education, 177*(3), 129–148. doi:10.1177/002205749517700308

Saraç, S., & Tarhan, B. (2021). Preschool teachers' promotion of self-regulated learning in the classroom and role of contextual and teacher-level factors. *International Electronic Journal of Elementary Education, 13*(2), 309–322. doi:10.26822/iejee.2021.192

Sardone, N. B., & Devlin-Scherer, R. (2010). Teacher candidate responses to digital games: 21st-century skills development. *Journal of Research on Technology in Education, 42*(4), 409–425. doi:10.1080/15391523.2010.10782558

Sardone, N. B., & Devlin-Scherer, R. (2016). Let the (Board) Games Begin: Creative Ways to Enhance Teaching and Learning. *The Clearing House: A Journal of Educational Strategies, Issues and Ideas, 89*(6), 215–222. doi:10.1080/0 0098655.2016.1214473

Sargeantston, E. (2021). Why boardgames are so popular. *Mykindofmeeple.* Accessed August 28, 202. https://mykind-ofmeeple.com/why-are-board-games-popular

Sarkar, D. (2016). *Text analytics with python.* Springer. doi:10.1007/978-1-4842-2388-8

Saunders, M., Lewis, P., & Thornhill, A. (2012). *Research methods for business students.* Peason Education.

Saunders, M., Lewis, P., & Thornhill, A. (2019). *Research Methods for Business Students* (8th ed.). Pearson.

Sauro. (2012). *System Usability Scale. In Measuring Usability With The System Usability Scale.* SUS.

Sauve, L., Renaud, L., Kaufman, D., & Marquis, J. S. (2007). Distinguishing between games and simulation: A systematic review. *Journal of Educational Technology & Society, 10*(3), 247–256. http://citeseerx.ist.psu.edu/viewdoc/download?doi=10.1.1.169.5559&rep=rep1&type=pdf

Sawyer, R. K. (2012). *Explaining Creativity: The Science of Human Innovation.* Oxford University Press.

Sax, L. (2005). *Why gender matters.* Doubleday.

Scarlett, J. (2015). Gaming geography: Using Minecraft to teach essential geography skills. In D. Rutledge & D. Slykhuis (Eds.), *Proceedings of SITE 2015 – Society for Information Technology & Education International Conference* (pp. 838-840). Association for the Advancement of Computing in Education (AACE).

Šćepanović, S., Žarić, N., & Matijević, T. (2015, September 24-25). *Gamification in higher education learning - state of the art, challenges and opportunities.* The Sixth International Conference on e-Learning, Belgrade, Serbia. https://elearning.metropolitan.ac.rs/files/pdf/2015/23-Snezana-Scepanovic-Nada-Zaric-Tripo-Matijevic-Gamification-in-higher-education-learning-state-of-the-art-challenges-and-opportunities.pdf

Scharton, H. (2019). *Busting the Myths of the Digital Native.* https://ptaourchildren.org/busting-the-myths-of-the-digital-native/

Schek, E. J., Mantovani, F., Realdon, O., Dias, J., Paiva, A., Schramm-Yavin, S., & Pat-Horenczyk, R. (2017). *Positive Technologies for Promoting Emotion Regulation Abilities in Adolescents. In eHealth 360.* Springer International Publishing.

Scherer, R., Siddiq, F., & Tondeur, J. (2019). The technology acceptance model (TAM): A meta-analytic structural equation modeling approach to explaining teachers' adoption of digital technology in education. *Computers & Education, 128,* 13–35. doi:10.1016/j.compedu.2018.09.009

Scheuer, M. (2009). Foreword. In D. Frau-Meigs & J. Torrent (Eds.), Mapping media education policies in the world: Visions, programmes and challenges (pp. 7–8). New York: The United Nations-Alliance of Civilization.

Schifter, C., & Cipollone, M. (2013). Minecraft as a teaching tool: One case study. In R. McBride & M. Searson (Eds.), *Proceedings of Society for Information Technology & Teacher Education International Conference 2013* (pp. 2951-2955). Chesapeake, VA: Association for the Advancement of Computing in Education (AACE).

Schmidt, D. A., Baran, E., Thompson, A. D., Mishra, P., Koehler, M. J., & Shin, T. S. (2009). Technological Pedagogical Content Knowledge (TPACK): The development and validation of an assessment instrument for preservice teachers. *Journal of Research on Technology in Education, 42*(2), 123–149. doi:10.1080/15391523.2009.10782544

Schmidt-Kraepelin, M., Thiebes, S., Stepanovic, S., Mettler, T., & Sunyaev, A. (2019). Gamification in health behavior change support systems-A synthesis of unintended side effects. In *Proceedings of the 14th International Conference on Wirtschaftsinformatik* (pp. 1032-1046). Academic Press.

Schmithorst, V. J., Holland, S. K., & Plante, E. (2007). Object identification and lexical/semantic access in children: A functional magnetic resonance imaging study of word-picture matching. *Human Brain Mapping, 28*(10), 1060–1074. doi:10.1002/hbm.20328 PMID:17133401

Schneider, M., & Preckel, F. (2017). Variables Associated With Achievement in Higher Education: A Systematic Review of Meta-Analyses. *Psychological Bulletin, 143*(6), 565–600. doi:10.1037/bul0000098 PMID:28333495

Schnotz, W., Fries, S., & Horz, H. (2009). Some motivational aspects of cognitive load theory. In S. Wosnitza, S. A. Karabenick, A. Efklides, & P. Nenniger (Eds.), *Contemporary Motivation Research: From Global to Local Perspectives* (pp. 86–113). Hogrefe.

Schnurr, M. A., De Santo, E., Green, A., & Taylor, A. (2015). Investigating student perceptions of learning within a role-play simulation of the Convention on Biological Diversity. *The Journal of Geography, 114*(3), 94–107. doi:10.10 80/00221341.2014.937738

Schöbel, S., Saqr, M., & Janson, A. (2021). Two decades of game concepts in digital learning environments–A bibliometric study and research agenda. *Computers & Education, 173*, 104296. doi:10.1016/j.compedu.2021.104296

Schoepp, K. (2005). Barriers to Technology Integration in a Technology-Rich Environment. *Learning and Teaching in Higher Education: Gulf Perspectives, 2*(1), 56–79. doi:10.18538/lthe.v2.n1.02

Schrader, C., & Bastiaens, T. (2012). Educational computer games and learning: The relationship between design, cognitive load, emotions and outcomes. *Journal of Interactive Learning Research, 23*, 251–271. https://www.learntechlib.org/primary/p/36201/

Schreyer, J. (2012). Adolescent literacy practices in online social spaces. In New media literacies and participatory culture: Popular culture across borders. Routledge.

Schroedl, C. J., Corbridge, T. C., Cohen, E. R., Fakhran, S. S., Schimmel, D., McGaghie, W. C., & Wayne, D. B. (2012). Use of simulation-based education to improve resident learning and patient care in the medical intensive care unit: A randomized trial. *Journal of Critical Care, 27*(2), 219.e7–219.e13. doi:10.1016/j.jcrc.2011.08.006 PMID:22033049

Schuytema, P. (2008). *Design de Games: uma abordagem prática*. Cengage Learning.

Sea of Roses Game. (2021). Retrieved October 4, 2021, from, https://tecnico.ulisboa.pt/en/news/campus-community/sea-of-roses-wins-second-place-in-international-game-design-contest/ https://store.steampowered.com/app/1581940/Sea_of_Roses/

Seaman, J. E., Allen, I. E., & Jeff Seaman, J. (2018). *Grade Increase: Tracking Distance Education in the United States.* Retrieved from Babson Survey Research Group: https://files.eric.ed.gov/fulltext/ED580852.pdf

Seeger, C. J. (2018). Open-source mapping: Landscape perception, participatory design and user-generated content; collecting user-generated walking and biking route preference data through repurposed apps, custom coding, and open-source mapping tools. In *Codify* (pp. 149–154). Routledge. doi:10.4324/9781315647791-14

Seele, P. (2018). What makes a business ethicist? A reflection on the transition from applied philosophy to critical thinking. *Journal of Business Ethics, 150*(3), 647–656. doi:10.100710551-016-3177-8

Seele, P., & Lock, I. (2017). The game-changing potential of digitalization for sustainability: Possibilities, perils, and pathways. *Sustainability Science, 12*(2), 183–185. doi:10.100711625-017-0426-4

Seemiller, C., & Grace, M. (2017). Generation Z: Educating and engaging the next generation of students. *About Campus: Enriching the Student Learning Experience, 22*(3), 21–26. doi:10.1002/abc.21293

Seeney, M., & Routledge, H. (2009). Drawing Circles in the Sand: Integrating Content into Serious Games. Games-Based Learning Advancements for Multi-Sensory Human Computer Interfaces.

Sefton-Green, J. (2003). *Digital diversions: Youth culture in the age of multimedia*. Routledge Tailor & Francis Group.

Segers, E., & Verhoeven, L. (2003). Effects of vocabulary training by computer in kindergarten. *Journal of Computer Assisted Learning*, *19*(4), 557–566. doi:10.1046/j.0266-4909.2003.00058.x

Seixas, L. R., Gomes, A. S., & Filho, I. J. M. (2016). Effectiveness of gamification in the engagement of students. *Computers in Human Behavior*, *58*, 48–63. doi:10.1016/j.chb.2015.11.021

Selwyn, N., & Bulfin, S. (2016). Exploring school regulation of students' technology use–rules that are made to be broken? *Educational Review*, *68*(3), 274–290. doi:10.1080/00131911.2015.1090401

Sendra, A., Lozano-Monterrubio, N., Prades-Tena, J., & Gonzalo-Iglesia, J. L. (2021). Developing a Gameful Approach as a Tool for Innovation and Teaching Quality in Higher Education. *International Journal of Game-Based Learning*, *11*(1), 53–66. doi:10.4018/IJGBL.2021010104

Sénéchal, M., LeFevre, J.-A., Smith-Chant, B. L., & Colton, K. V. (2001). On refining theoretical models of emergent literacy: The role of empirical evidence. *Journal of School Psychology*, *39*(5), 439–460. https://doi.org/10.1016/S0022-4405(01)00081-4

Sera, L., & Wheeler, E. (2017). Game on: The Gamification of the pharmacy classroom. *Currents in Pharmacy Teaching & Learning*, *9*(1), 155–159. doi:10.1016/j.cptl.2016.08.046 PMID:29180148

Sergeant, A. (2021). *Re:Higher Education's Changing Landscape*. Retrieved from https://www.equantiis.com/thinkslabs/higher-educations-changing-landscape/

Serholt, S., Barendregt, W., Leite, I., Hastie, H., Jones, A., Paiva, A., . . . Castellano, G. (2014, August). Teachers' views on the use of empathic robotic tutors in the classroom. In *The 23rd IEEE International Symposium on Robot and Human Interactive Communication* (pp. 955-960). IEEE. https:// doi:10.1109/ROMAN.2014.6926376

Serrano, K. (2019). *The effect of digital game-based learning on student learning: A literature review*. Academic Press.

Sescousse, G., Caldú, X., Segura, B., & Dreher, J. C. (2013). Processing of primary and secondary rewards: A quantitative meta-analysis and review of human functional neuroimaging studies. *Neuroscience and Biobehavioral Reviews*, *37*(4), 681–696. doi:10.1016/j.neubiorev.2013.02.002 PMID:23415703

Sezen, D. (2011). *Katılımcı Kültürün Oluşumunda Yeni Medya Okuryazarlığı: ABD ve Türkiye Örnekleri* (PhD thesis). İstanbul Üniversitesi Sosyal Bilimler Enstitüsü.

Shabalina, O., Malliarakis, C., Tomos, F., & Mozelius, P. (2017). Game-based learning for learning to program: from learning through play to learning through game development. In *11th European Conference on Games Based Learning 2017, Graz, Austria, 5-6 October 2017* (Vol. 11, pp. 571-576). Academic Conferences and Publishing International Limited.

Shabalina, O., Vorobkalov, P., Kataev, A., & Tarasenko, A. (2009). 3I-approach for IT educational games development. In *Proceedings of the European Conference on Games-based Learning* (pp. 339-344). Academic Press.

Shabalina, O., Malliarakis, C., Tomos, F., Mozelius, P., Balan, O. C., & Alimov, A. (2016) Game-Based Learning as a Catalyst for Creative Learning. *Proceedings of the 9th ECGBL*.

Shaban, A., & Pearson, E. (2019). A Learning Design Framework to Support Children with Learning Disabilities Incorporating Gamification Techniques. In *Extended Abstracts of the 2019 CHI Conference on Human Factors in Computing Systems* (p. LBW0284). ACM. 10.1145/3290607.3312806

Shafer, W. E., & Simmons, R. S. (2011). Effects of organizational ethical culture on the ethical decisions of tax practitioners in mainland China. *Accounting, Auditing & Accountability Journal, 24*(5), 647–668. doi:10.1108/09513571111139139

Shaffer, D. W., Halverson, R., Squire, K. R., & Gee, J. P. (2005). *Video games and the future of learning* (WCER Working Paper No. 2005-4). University of Wisconsin–Madison, Wisconsin Center for Education Research (NJ1).

Shaffer, D. W., Squire, K. R., Halverson, R., & Gee, J. P. (2005). Video games and the future of learning. *Phi Delta Kappan, 87*(2), 105–111. doi:10.1177/003172170508700205

Shaffer, D., & Kipp, K. (2010). *Developmental psychology: Childhood and adolescence* (8th ed.). Wadsworth Cengage Learning.

Shah, A., Kraemer, K. R., Won, C. R., Black, S., & Hasenbein, W. (2018). Developing digital intervention games for mental disorders: A review. *Games for Health Journal, 7*(4), 213–224. doi:10.1089/g4h.2017.0150 PMID:30106642

Shah, D., & McLeod, J. (2009). Communication and political socialization: Challenges and opportunities for research. *Political Communication, 26*(1), 1–10. doi:10.1080/10584600802686105

Shah, D., McLeod, J., & Lee, N. (2009). Communication competence as a foundation for civic competence: Process of socialization into citizenship. *Political Communication, 26*(1), 102–117. doi:10.1080/10584600802710384

Shah, M., & Foster, A. (2015). Developing and Assessing Teachers ' Knowledge of Game-based Learning. *Journal of Technology and Teacher Education, 23*(2), 241–267.

Shan, J., Gong, L., Li, Y., & Yan, H. (2019). The impact of educational robots on student learning outcomes—Based on a meta-analysis of 49 experimental or quasi-experimental research papers. *China Educational Technology*, (5), 76–83.

Shapiro, J. (2014). *MindShift guide to digital games + learning*. Retrieved from https://a.s.kqed.net/pdf/news/MindShift-GuidetoDigitalGamesandLearning.pdf

Share, J., & Thoman, E. (2007). Teaching Democracy a media literacy approach: A media literacy educators' Guide for dilemma decisions. National Center for the Preservation Democracy.

Sharkey, A. (2016). Should we welcome robot teachers? *Ethics and Information Technology, 18*(4), 283–297. doi:10.100710676-016-9387-z

Sharma, K., Papavlasopoulou, S., & Giannakos, M. (2019). Coding games and robots to enhance computational thinking: How collaboration and engagement moderate attitudes. *International Journal of Child-Computer Interaction, 21*, 65–76.

Sharma, S. K., Palvia, S. C. J., & Kumar, K. (2017). Changing the landscape of higher education: From standardized learning to customized learning. *Journal of Information Technology Case and Application Research, 19*(2), 75–80. doi:10.1080/15228053.2017.1345214

Sharp, J. G., & Kuerbis, P. (2006). Children's ideas about the solar system and the chaos in learning science. *Science Education, 90*(1), 124–147. doi:10.1002ce.20126

Sharp, L. A. (2012). Stealth learning: Unexpected learning opportunities through games. *Journal of Institutional Research, 1*, 42–48. doi:10.9743/JIR.2013.6

Shaw, A. (2013). On Not Becoming Gamers: Moving Beyond the Constructed Audience. *Ada: A Journal of Gender, New Media and Technology*, (2).

Sheakley, M. L., Gilbert, G. E., Leighton, K., Hall, M., Callender, D., & Pederson, D. (2016). A brief simulation intervention increasing basic science and clinical knowledge. *Medical Education, 21*(1), 30744. Advance online publication. doi:10.3402/meo.v21.30744 PMID:27060102

Shear, L., Tan, C. K., Patel, D., Trinidad, G., Koh, R., & Png, S. (2014). ICT and Instructional Innovation; The Case of Crescent Girls' School in Singapore. *International Journal of Education and Development Using Information and Communication Technology, 10*(2), 77–88.

Shellman, S. M., & Turan, K. (2006). Do simulations enhance student learning? An empirical evaluation of an IR simulation. *Journal of Political Science Education, 2*(1), 19–32. doi:10.1080/15512160500484168

Shen, C.-Y., & Chu, H.-P. (2014). *The relations between interface design of digital game-based learning systems and flow experience and cognitive load of learners with different levels of prior knowledge.* Paper presented at the International Conference on Cross-Cultural Design. 10.1007/978-3-319-07308-8_55

Shen, C., Sun, Q., Kim, T., Wolff, G., Ratan, R., & Williams, D. (2020). Viral vitriol: Predictors and contagion of online toxicity in World of Tanks. *Computers in Human Behavior, 108*, 106343. doi:10.1016/j.chb.2020.106343

Sheridan & Rowsell. (2010). *Design literacies: Learning and innovation in the digital age.* Routledge.

Shi, Y.-R., & Shih, J.-L. (2015). *Game factors and game-based learning design model.* Academic Press.

Shigwedha, A. N., Nakashole, L., Auala, H., Amakutuwa, H., & Ailonga, I. (2015). *The SACMEQ IV project in Namibia: A study of the conditions of schooling and the quality of primary education in Namibia.* http://www.sacmeq.org/sites/default/files/sacmeq/publications/final_sacmeq_iv_report_namibia-compressed-compressed.pdf

Shirky, C. (2009). *Here comes everybody: The power of organizing without organizations.* Penguin.

Shirky, C. (2010). *Cognitive surplus: Creativity and generosity in a connected age.* Penguin.

Shi, Y.-R., & Shih, J.-L. (2015). Game Factors and Game-Based Learning Design Model. *International Journal of Computer Games Technology, 11*, 11. doi:10.1155/2015/549684

Shmelev, V., Karpova, M., Kogtikov, N., & Dukhanov, A. (2016, October). Students' development of information-seeking skills in a computer-aided quest. In *2016 IEEE Frontiers in Education Conference (FIE)* (pp. 1-4). IEEE.

Shohel, M. M. C., Ashrafuzzaman, M., Ahsan, M. S., Mahmud, A., & Alam, A. S. (2021a). Education in Emergencies, Inequities, and the Digital Divide: Strategies for Supporting Teachers and Students in Higher Education in Bangladesh. In L. Kyei-Blankson, J. Blankson, & E. Ntuli (Eds.), *Handbook of Research on Inequities in Online Education During Global Crises* (pp. 529–553). IGI Global. doi:10.4018/978-1-7998-6533-9.ch027

Shohel, M. M. C., Ashrafuzzaman, M., Alam, A. S., Mahmud, A., Ahsan, M. S., & Islam, T. M. (2021e). Preparedness of Students for Future Teaching and Learning in Higher Education: A Bangladeshi Perspective. In E. Sengupta & P. Blessinger (Eds.), *New Student Literacies amid COVID-19: International Case Studies, Innovations in Higher Education Teaching and Learning* (Vol. 41, pp. 29–56). Emerald Publishing Limited. doi:10.1108/S2055-364120210000041006

Shohel, M. M. C., Ashrafuzzaman, M., Islam, M. T., Shams, S., & Mahmud, A. (2021d). Blended Teaching and Learning in Higher Education: Challenges and Opportunities. In S. Loureiro & J. Guerreiro (Eds.), *Handbook of Research on Developing a Post-Pandemic Paradigm for Virtual Technologies in Higher Education* (pp. 27–50). IGI Global. doi:10.4018/978-1-7998-6963-4.ch002

Shohel, M. M. C., Mahmud, A., Urmee, M. A., Anwar, N., Rahman, M. M., Acharya, D., & Ashrafuzzaman, M. (2021b). Education in Emergencies, Mental Wellbeing and E-Learning. In M. M. C. Shohel (Ed.), *E-learning and digital education in the twenty-first century: Challenges and Prospects* (pp. 1–22). IntechOpen. doi:10.5772/intechopen.97425

Shohel, M. M. C., Sham, S., Ashrafuzzaman, M., Alam, A. T. M., Mamun, A. A., & Kabir, M. M. (2021c). Emergency Remote Teaching and Learning: Digital Competencies and Pedagogical Transformation in Resource-Constrained Contexts. In M. Islam, S. Behera, & L. Naibaho (Eds.), *Handbook of Research on Asian Perspectives of the Educational Impact of COVID-19*. IGI Global.

Shopova, T. (2014). Digital literacy of students and its improvement at the university. *Journal on Efficiency and Responsibility in Education and Science, 7*(2), 26–32. doi:10.7160/eriesj.2014.070201

Shortage of personal protective equipment endangering health workers worldwide. (n.d.). Retrieved September 2, 2021, from https://www.who.int/news/item/03-03-2020-shortage-of-personal-protective-equipment-endangering-health-workers-worldwide

Short, D. (2012). Teaching scientific concepts using a virtual world—Minecraft. *Teaching Science-the Journal of the Australian Science Teachers Association, 58*(3), 55–58.

Shut Up and Sit Down. (n.d.). *Shut Up and Sit Down.* https://www.shutupandsitdown.com/games/

Shute, V. J., Rieber, L., & Van Eck, R. (2012). Games... and... learning. In R. A. Reiser & J. V. Dempsey (Eds.), Trends and issues in instructional design and technology (3rd ed., pp. 321–332). Academic Press.

Shute, V. (2011). Stealth assessment in computer-based games to support learning. In S. Tobias & J. D. Fletcher (Eds.), *Computer games and instruction* (pp. 503–524). Information Age Publishers.

Siala, H., Kutsch, E., & Jagger, S. (2019). Cultural influences moderating learners' adoption of serious 3D games for managerial learning. *Information Technology & People, 33*(2), 424–455. doi:10.1108/ITP-08-2018-0385

Siala, H., O'Keefe, R. M., & Hone, K. S. (2004). The Impact of Religious Affiliation on Trust in the Context of Electronic Commerce. *Interacting with Computers, 16*(1), 7–27. doi:10.1016/j.intcom.2003.11.002

Siddiquei, N. L., & Khalid, R. (2017). Emerging Trends of E- Learning in Pakistan: Past, Present and Future. *International Journal of Law, Humanities &. Social Science, 2*(1), 20–35.

sidebar—How do you make "infoboxes" in mediawiki? (n.d.). *Stack Overflow.* Retrieved June 1, 2021, from https://stackoverflow.com/questions/27801082/how-do-you-make-infoboxes-in-mediawiki

Sider, S., & Maich, K. (2014, February). Assistive technology tools: Supporting literacy learning for all learners in the inclusive classroom. *What Works? Research into Practice, 50*(1), 1-12. Retrieved from https://oere.oise.utoronto.ca/wp-content/uploads/2014/05/WW_TechnologyTools.pdf

Siemens, G. (2005). Connectivism: A learning theory for the digital age. *International Journal of Instructional Technology and Distance Learning., 3*, 3–10.

Silseth, K. (2012). The multivoicedness of game play: Exploring the unfolding of a student's learning trajectory in a gaming context at school. *International Journal of Computer-Supported Collaborative Learning, 7*(1), 63–84. doi:10.100711412-011-9132-x

Silva Dos Santos, L., von Gillern, S., Lockwood, J., & Geluso, J. (2020). Digital mindsets: College-level ESL instructors' perceptions of multimodal technologies and video games for language instruction. *The European Journal of Applied Linguistics and TEFL, 9*(1), 131–152.

Silva, R. D. O. S., Pereira, A. M., Araújo, D. C. S. A. D., Rocha, K. S. S., Serafini, M. R., & De Lyra, D. P. Jr. (2021). Effect of digital serious games related to patient care in pharmacy education: A systematic review. *Simulation & Gaming, 52*(5), 104687812098889. doi:10.1177/1046878120988895

Silva, R., Rodrigues, R., & Leal, C. (2019). Play it again: How gamebased learning improves flow in Accounting and Marketing education. *Accounting Education*. Advance online publication. doi:10.1080/09639284.2019.1647859

Silver, A. (2009). A European approach to media literacy: Moving toward an inclusive knowledge society. In D. Frau-Meigs & J. Torrent (Eds.), Mapping media education policies in the world: Visions, programmes and challenges (pp. 11–13). New York: The United Nations-Alliance of Civilization.

Silverblatt, A. (Ed.). (2014). The Praeger Handbook of Media Literacy. Praeger.

Silver, C., & Rivers, C. (2016). The CAQDAS Postgraduate Learning Model: An interplay between methodological awareness, analytic adeptness and technological proficiency. *International Journal of Social Research Methodology*, *19*(5), 593–609. doi:10.1080/13645579.2015.1061816

Silverman, M. H., Jedd, K., & Luciana, M. (2015). Neural networks involved in adolescent reward processing: An activation likelihood estimation meta-analysis of functional neuroimaging studies. *NeuroImage*, *122*, 427–439. doi:10.1016/j.neuroimage.2015.07.083 PMID:26254587

Simkins, D. W., & Steinkuehler, C. (2008). Critical ethical reasoning and role-play. *Games and Culture*, *3*(3-4), 333–355. doi:10.1177/1555412008317313

Simondon, G. (1989b). *L'individuation psychique et collective*. Aubier.

Simondon, G. (2005). *L'individuation à la lumière des notions de forme et d'information*. Jerome Million.

Simons, M., & Meeus, W., & Sas, J. T. (2017). Measuring media literacy for media education: Development of a questionnaire for teachers competencies. *The Journal of Media Literacy Education*, *9*(1), 99–115.

Sinclair, B. (2021). *Microsoft game revenues up 50% in Q3*. Gameindustry.biz. https://www.gamesindustry.biz/articles/2021-04-27-microsoft-game-revenues-up-50-percent-in-q3

Singer, N. (2012). You've won a badge (and now we know all about you). *New York Times*, 4.

Singer, E. (2013). Play and playfulness, basic features of early childhood education. *European Early Childhood Education Research Journal*, *21*(2), 172–184. doi:10.1080/1350293X.2013.789198

Singhapakdi, A., Marta, J. K., Rallapalli, K. C., & Rao, C. P. (2000). Toward an Understanding of Religiousness and Marketing Ethics: An Empirical Study. *Journal of Business Ethics*, *27*(4), 305–319. doi:10.1023/A:1006342224035

Singhapakdi, A., Vitell, S. J., Lee, D.-J., Nisius, A. M., & Yu, G. B. (2013). The influence of love of money and religiosity on ethical decision-making in marketing. *Journal of Business Ethics*, *114*(1), 183–191. doi:10.100710551-012-1334-2

Sipiyaruk, K., Gallagher, J. E., Hatzipanagos, S., & Reynolds, P. A. (2018). A rapid review of serious games: From healthcare education to dental education. *European Journal of Dental Education*, *22*(4), 243–257. doi:10.1111/eje.12338 PMID:29573165

Sitzmann, T., & Ely, K. (2009). A meta-analytic examination of the effectiveness of computer-based simulation games. Advanced Distributed Learning Technical Report.

Sitzmann, T. (2011). A meta-analytic examination of the instructional effectiveness of computer-based simulation games. *Personnel Psychology*, *64*(2), 489–528. doi:10.1111/j.1744-6570.2011.01190.x

Siu, Dickinson, & Lee. (2000). Ethical evaluations of business activities and personal religiousness. *Teaching Business Ethics*, *4*(3), 239-56.

Skains, L., Rudd, J. A., Casaliggi, C., Hayhurst, E. J., Horry, R., Ross, H., & Woodward, K. (2021). *Using interactive digital narrative in science and health education.* Emerald Publishing Ltd. doi:10.1108/9781839097607

Skarbez, R., Smith, M., & Whitton, M. C. (2021). Revisiting Milgram and Kishino's Reality-Virtuality Continuum. *Frontiers in Virtual Reality, 2*, 27. doi:10.3389/frvir.2021.647997

Skelton, C., & Francis, B. (2011). Successful boys and literacy: Are "literate boys" challenging or repackaging hegemonic masculinity? *Curriculum Inquiry, 41*(4), 456–479. doi:10.1111/j.1467-873X.2011.00559.x

Skinner, B. F. (1953). *Science and Human Behavior.* The Free Press.

Škorić, I., Pein, B., & Orehovački, T. (2016). *Selecting the most appropriate web IDE for learning programming using AHP.* Paper presented at the 39th International Convention on Information and Communication Technology, Electronics and Microelectronics (MIPRO). 10.1109/MIPRO.2016.7522263

Skorton, D., & Bear, A. (2018). *The Integration of the Humanities and Arts with Sciences, Engineering, and Medicine in Higher Education: Branches from the Same Tree.* The National Academies Press. doi:10.17226/24988

Slomka, J. (2014). *Toward transdisciplinary professionalism in the teaching of public health.* Establishing Transdisciplinary Professionalism for Improving Health Outcomes.

Smagorinsky, P. (2007). Vygotsky and the social dynamics of classrooms. *English Journal*, 61–66.

Smagorinsky, P. (2013). What does Vygotsky provide for the 21st-century language arts teacher? *Language Arts, 90*(3), 192–204.

Smale, M. A. (2011). *Learning through quests and contests: Games in information literacy instruction.* Academic Press.

Smiderle, R., Rigo, S.J., Marques, L.B., Coelho, J.A.P.D.M., & Jaques, P.A. (2020). *The impact of gamification on students' learning, engagement and behaviour based on their personality traits.* doi:10.1186/s40561-019-0098-x

Smith, E. M., & Holmes, N. G. (2021). Best practice for instructional labs. *Nature Physics, 17*(6), 662–663. doi:10.103841567-021-01256-6

Smith, K. (2012). Lessons learnt from literature on the diffusion of innovative learning and teaching practices in higher education. *Innovations in Education and Teaching International, 49*(2), 173–182. doi:10.1080/14703297.2012.677599

Smith, K., Mahdavi, J., Carvalho, M., Fisher, S., Russell, S., & Tippett, N. (2008). Cyberbullying: Its nature and impact in secondary school pupils. *Journal of Child Psychology and Psychiatry, and Allied Disciplines, 49*(4), 376–385. doi:10.1111/j.1469-7610.2007.01846.x PMID:18363945

Smith, N., Simpson, S. S., & Huang, C.-Y. (2007). Why managers fail to do the right thing: An empirical study of unethical and illegal conduct. *Business Ethics Quarterly, 17*(4), 633–667. doi:10.5840/beq20071743

Snelson, C. (2019). Teaching qualitative research methods online: A scoping review of the literature. *Qualitative Report, 24*(11), 2799–2814. doi:10.46743/2160-3715/2019.4021

Snoeyink, R., & Ertmer, P. A. (2001). Thrust into Technology: How Veteran Teachers Respond. *Journal of Educational Technology Systems, 30*(1), 85–111. doi:10.2190/YDL7-XH09-RLJ6-MTP1

Snyder, I. (Ed.). (2002). *Silicon literacies.* Routledge.

So & Seo. (2018). *A systematic literature review of game-based learning and gamification.* Routledge.

Socrative. (2021, September 2). *Higher Ed.* Retrieved September 12, 2021 from https://www.socrative.com/higher-ed/

Socrative. (2021a, August 26). *Plans*. Retrieved September 12, 2021 from https://www.socrative.com/plans/

Sogunro, O. A. (2004). Efficacy of role-playing pedagogy in training leaders: Some reflections. *Journal of Management Development, 23*(4), 355–371.

So, H. J., & Brush, T. A. (2008). Student perceptions of collaborative learning, social presence and satisfaction in a blended learning environment: Relationships and critical factors. *Computers & Education, 51*(1), 318–336. doi:10.1016/j.compedu.2007.05.009

Sokal, R. R., & Rohlf, F. J. (2015). *Biometry: Principles and practice of statistics in biological research* (4th ed.). W. H. Freeman.

Sommers, C. (2013). *Primary education in rural Bangladesh: Degrees of access, choice, and participation of the poorest.* CREATE. http://www.create-rpc.org/pdf_documents/PTA75.pdf

Soulé, H., & Warrick, T. (2015). Defining 21st century readiness for all students: What we know and how to get there. *Psychology of Aesthetics, Creativity, and the Arts, 9*(2), 178–186. doi:10.1037/aca0000017

Sousa, M. J., & Rocha, Á. (2019). Leadership styles and skills developed through game-based learning. *Journal of Business Research, 94*, 360–366. doi:10.1016/j.jbusres.2018.01.057

Sousa, M., & Costa, E. (2014). Game based learning improving leadership skills. *EAI Endorsed Transactions on Serious Games, 3*(3), e2. Advance online publication. doi:10.4108g.1.3.e2

Spaull, N., & Taylor, S. (2012). SACMEQ at a glance series. In *Research on Socio-economic Policy (RESEP)*. https://resep.sun.ac.za/index.php/projects

Speak Out! RAUM Residency. (2020). Retrieved October 5, 2021, from, https://raum.pt/en/terhi-marttila https://www.academia.edu/44788195/Speak_Out_a_playful_interactive_artwork_about_migration_with_a_radical_openness_to_the_World

Spector, J. M., Merrill, M. D., Elen, J., & Bishop, M. J. (Eds.). (2014). *Handbook of research on educational communications and technology*. Springer. doi:10.1007/978-1-4614-3185-5

Spichtig, A. N., Hiebert, E. H., Vorstius, C., Pascoe, J. P., Pearson, D. P., & Radach, R. (2016). The Decline of Comprehension-Based Silent Reading Efficiency in the United States: A Comparison of Current Data With Performance in 1960. *Reading Research Quarterly, 51*(2), 239–259. doi:10.1002/rrq.137

Spiegelman, M., & Glass, R. (2008). Gaming and learning: Winning information literacy collaboration. *College & Research Libraries News, 69*(9), 522–547. doi:10.5860/crln.69.9.8058

Spin Master Games. (1991). *Headbanz [Board Game]*. Spin Master Games.

Spires, H. A. (2012). Digital literacies and learning: Designing a path forward. NC State University.

Spradley, J. P. (1979). *The Ethnographic Interview*. The University of Michigan: Holt, Rinehart and Winston.

Squire, K. (2003). Video games in education. *International Journal of Intelligent Simulations and Gaming, 2*(1), 49-62.

Squire, K. (2004). *Replaying history: Learning world history through playing Civilization III* [Unpublished doctoral dissertation]. Indiana University. Retrieved from https://www.academia.edu/1317076/Replaying_history_Learning_world_history_through_playing_Civilization_III

Squire, K. D. (2014). Video-Game Literacy - a Literacy of Expertise. In J. Coiro, M. Knobel, C. Lankshear, & D. Leu (Eds.), The Handbook of Research in New Literacies (pp. 635-670). Routledge.

Squire, K. D. (2021). From virtual to participatory learning with technology during COVID-19. *E-Learning and Digital Media*. doi:10.1177/20427530211022926

Squire, K. D., & Jan, M. (2007). Mad city mystery: Developing scientific argumentation skills with a place-based augmented reality game on handheld computers. *Journal of Science Education and Technology, 16*(1), 5-29. doi:10.1007/s10956-006-9037-z

Squire, K. (2006). From Content to Context: Videogames as Designed Experience. *Educational Researcher, 35*(8), 19–29. doi:10.3102/0013189X035008019

Squire, K. (2008). *Video games literacy: a literacy of expertise.* In J. Coiro, M. Knobel, C. Lankshear, & D. J. Leu (Eds.), *Handbook of Research on New Literacies* (pp. 639–673). Lawrence Erlbaum.

Squire, K. (2011). *Video games and learning: Teaching and participatory culture in the digital age*. Teachers College Press.

Squire, K. D. (2008). Video game–based learning: An emerging paradigm for instruction. *Performance Improvement Quarterly, 21*(2), 7–36. doi:10.1002/piq.20020

Squire, K. D. (2013). Video game-based learning: An emerging paradigm for instruction. *Performance Improvement Quarterly, 26*(1), 101–130. doi:10.1002/piq.21139

Squire, K., & Jenkins, H. (2003). Harnessing the power of games in education. *Insight (American Society of Ophthalmic Registered Nurses), 3*(1), 5–33. PMID:12703249

Stahel, D. (2018). The Battle for Wikipedia: The New Age of 'Lost Victories'? *The Journal of Slavic Military Studies, 31*(3), 396–402. https://doi.org/10.1080/13518046.2018.1487198

Staley, D., & Trikle, D. (2011). The Changing Landscape of Higher Education. *Educase Review*. Retrieved from https://er.educause.edu/articles/2011/2/the-changing-landscape-of-higher-education

Stamper, L. J. (2015). The LandWarNet School, The Army Learning Model, and Appreciative Inquiry: How is a Centralized Training Organization Improved by Introducing Decentralization. Academic Press.

Stansbury, J. A., & Earnest, D. R. (2017). Meaningful gamification in an industrial/organizational psychology course. *Teaching of Psychology, 44*(1), 38–45.

Star Wars opening crawl. (2021). In *Wikipedia*. https://en.wikipedia.org/wiki/Star_Wars_opening_crawl

Starke, M., Harth, M., & Sirianni, F. (2001). Retention, Bonding, and Academic Achievement: Success of a First-Year Seminar. *Journal of the First-Year Experience & Students in Transition, 13*(2), 7–36.

Stark, R., & Glock, C. Y. (1968). *American Piety: The Nature of Religious Commitment*. University of California Press.

Statler, M., Heracleous, L., & Jacobs, C. D. (2011). Serious play as a practice of paradox. *The Journal of Applied Behavioral Science, 47*(2), 236–256. doi:10.1177/0021886311398453

Stats, S. A. (2012). *Census 2011 statistical release*. Statistics South Africa.

Steinbrick, J. E., & Cook, J. W. (2003). Media literacy skills and the "war on terrorism". *The Clearing House, 76*(6), 284-288. https://www.jstor.org/stable/30189852

Steiner, C. (2003). *Emotional Literacy: Intelligence with a Heart*. Retrieved May 03, 2019 from http://emotional-literacy-training.com/wp-content/uploads/2015/09/Steiner-Emotional-Literacy.pdf

Steinkuehler, C. (2004). *The literacy practices of massively multiplayer online gaming*. Paper presented at the American Educational Research Association, San Diego, CA.

Steinkuehler, C. (2006). The mangle of play. *Journal of Adolescent & Adult Literacy, 1*(3), 199–213.

Steinkuehler, C. (2007). Massively multiplayer online gaming as a constellation of literacy practices. *E-Learning and Digital Media, 4*(3), 297–318. doi:10.2304/elea.2007.4.3.297

Steinkuehler, C. (2010). Video games and digital literacies. *Journal of Adolescent & Adult Literacy, 54*(1), 61–63. doi:10.1598/JAAL.54.1.7

Steinkuehler, C. (2011). *The mismeasure of boys: Reading and online videogames.* Wisconsin Center for Education Research, University of Wisconsin.

Steinkuehler, C., & Duncan, S. (2008). Scientific habits of mind in virtual worlds. *Journal of Science Education and Technology, 17*(6), 530–543. doi:10.100710956-008-9120-8

Steinkuehler, C., Squire, K., & Barab, S. A. (2012). *Games, learning, and society: Learning and meaning in the digital age.* Cambridge University Press. doi:10.1017/CBO9781139031127

Steinmaurer, A., Pirker, J., & Christian, G. (2020). sCool - Game Based Learning in STEM Education: A Case Study in Secondary Education. *The Challenges of the Digital Transformation in Education, 917,* 614–625. doi:10.1007/978-3-030-11932-4_58

Stetsenko, A. (2020). Radical-Transformative Agency: Developing a Transformative Activist Stance on a Marxist-Vygotskyan Foundation. In F. Liberali, M. Dafermos, & A. T. Neto (Eds.), *Revisiting Vygotsky for Social Change: Bringing Together Theory and Practice* (pp. 31–62). Peter Lang Inc.

Stetter, M. E., & Hughes, M. T. (2010). Computer-Assisted Instruction to Enhance the Reading Comprehension of .... *Journal of Special Education Technology, 25*(5), 1–16. doi:10.1177/016264341002500401

Stewart, B. (1956). *To Tell the Truth* [Game Show Series]. CBS.

Stewart, B., Rubino, V., Schwartz, C., & Strahan, M. (Producers). (1964). *100,000 Dollar Pyramid* [Game Show Series]. CBS.

Stewart, I., & McKee, W. (2009). Review of pedagogical research into technology to support inclusive personalised learning. *Engineering Education, 4*(2), 62–69. doi:10.11120/ened.2009.04020062

Stigler, J. W., & Hiebert, J. (2009). *The teaching gap: Best ideas from the world's teachers for improving education in the classroom.* Simon and Schuster.

Stiller, K. D., & Schworm, S. (2019). Game-Based Learning of the Structure and Functioning of Body Cells in a Foreign Language: Effects on Motivation, Cognitive Load, and Performance. *Frontiers in Education, 4,* 18. doi:10.3389/feduc.2019.00018

Stone, C. (1993). What is missing in the metaphor of scaffolding? In E. Forman, N. Minick, & C. Stone (Eds.), *Contexts for learning: Sociocultural dynamics in children's development* (pp. 169–183). Oxford University Press.

Stone, C. A. (1998). The Metaphor of Scaffolding: Its Utility for the Field of Learning Disabilities. *Journal of Learning Disabilities, 31*(4), 344–364. doi:10.1177/002221949803100404 PMID:9666611

Storch, S. A., & Whitehurst, G. J. (2002). Oral language and code-related precursors to reading: Evidence from a longitudinal structural model. *Developmental Psychology, 38*(6), 934–947. https://doi.org/10.1037/0012-1649.38.6.934

Storeygard, J., Hamm, J., & Fosnot, C. T. (2010). Determining what children know: Dynamic versus static assessment. In National Council of Teachers of Mathematics (Ed.), Models of Intervention in Mathematics: Reweaving the Tapestry (pp. 45-69). Reston, VA: NCTM.

Stork, M. G. (2020). Supporting twenty-first century competencies using robots and digital storytelling. *Journal of Formative Design in Learning, 4*(1), 43–50. doi:10.100741686-019-00039-w

Stott, A., & Neustadter, C. (2013). *Analysis of Gamification in Education.* Simon Fraser University.

Stoyanov, S. R., Hides, L., Kavanagh, D. J., Zelenko, O., Tjondronegoro, D., & Mani, M. (2015). Mobile app rating scale: A new tool for assessing the quality of health mobile apps. *JMIR mHealth and uHealth, 3*(1), e27. doi:10.2196/mhealth.3422 PMID:25760773

Student's blog link. (2017). Retrieved October 4, 2021, from, https://fbaulgaming.wixsite.com/gaming2017

Student's blog link. (2018). Retrieved October 4, 2021, from, https://fbaulistgaming2018.wixsite.com/fbaul-istgaming2018

Student's blog link. (2019). Retrieved October 4, 2021, from, https://fbaulistgaming2019.wixsite.com/fbaulistgaming2019

Student's blog link. (2020). Retrieved October 4, 2021, from, https://fbaulistgaming2020.wixsite.com/fbaulistgaming2020

Student's blog link. (2021). Retrieved October 4, 2021, from, https://fbaulistgaming2021.wixsite.com/fbaulistgaming2021

Students' testimonies web documentary. (2019). *Mobility and Permanence in Public Space. Narratives of University Students with Different Self-Determination of Gender and Sexual Orientation.* Retrieved October 4, 2021, from http://www.ceg.ulisboa.pt/mpps/#3

Stufft, C. (2016). Videogames and YA literature: Using book groups to layer literacies. *The ALAN Review, 43*(3), 96–102.

Stufft, C. J. (2018). Engaging students in literacy practices through video game book groups. *Literacy Research: Theory, Method, and Practice, 67*(1), 195–210. doi:10.1177/2381336918787191

Stufft, C., & von Gillern, S. (2021). Fostering Multimodal Analyses of Video Games: Reflective Writing in the Middle School. *Journal of Adolescent & Adult Literacy,* jaal.1198. doi:10.1002/jaal.1198

Su, A. Y. S., Huang, C. S. J., Yang, S. J. H., Ding, T. J., & Hsieh, Y. Z. (2015). Effects of annotations and homework on learning achievement: An empirical study of Scratch programming pedagogy. *Journal of Educational Technology & Society, 18*(4), 331–343.

Suarez-Orozco, M. M. (Ed.). (2007). *Learning in the global era: International perspectives on globalization and education.* University of California Press.

Subhash, S., & Cudney, E. A. (2018). Gamified learning in higher education: A systematic review of literature. *Computers in Human Behavior, 87,* 192–206. doi:10.1016/j.chb.2018.05.002

Subhash, S., & Cudney, E. A. (2018). Gamified learning in higher education: A systematic review of the literature. *Computers in Human Behavior, 87,* 192–206. doi:10.1016/j.chb.2018.05.028

Sucena, A., Filipa, A. S., & Viana, F. L. (2016). Early intervention in reading difficulties using the Graphogame software. *Letronica, 9*(2).

Sudsomboon, W. (2007). Construction Of a Competency Based Curriculum Content Framework For Mechanical Technology Education Program on Automotive Technology Subjects. *Proceedings of the ICASE Asian Symposium.*

Suh, A., & Prophet, J. (2018). The state of immersive technology research: A literature analysis. *Computers in Human Behavior, 86,* 77–90. Advance online publication. doi:10.1016/j.chb.2018.04.019

Suh, S., Kim, S. W., & Kim, N. J. (2010). Effectiveness of MMORPG-based instruction in elementary English education in Korea. *Journal of Computer Assisted Learning, 26*(5), 370–378. doi:10.1111/j.1365-2729.2010.00353.x

Sullivan-Carr, M. (2016). *Game-based learning and children with ADHD* (10126186 Ed.D.), Drexel University. Retrieved from https://www.proquest.com/dissertations-theses/game-based-learning-children-with-adhd/docview/1797415951/se-2?accountid=38885

Sundararajan, B. (2020). Role Play Simulation: Using Cases to Teach Business Concepts - Simulations and Student Learning: A transdisciplinary perspective. University of Toronto Press.

Sung, H.-Y., & Hwang, G.-J. (2013). A collaborative game-based learning approach to improving students' learning performance in science courses. *Computers & Education, 63*, 43–51. doi:10.1016/j.compedu.2012.11.019

Sun, H., & Zhang, P. (2008). An exploration of affect factors and their role in user technology acceptance: Mediation and causality. *Journal of the Association for Information Science and Technology, 59*(8), 1252–1263.

Sun, P.-C., Tsai, R. J., Finger, G., Chen, Y.-Y., & Yeh, D. (2008). What drives a successful e-Learning? An empirical investigation of the critical factors influencing learner satisfaction. *Computers & Education, 50*(4), 1183–1202. doi:10.1016/j.compedu.2006.11.007

Surahman,, E., & Kuswandi,, D., Sulthoni, W. A., & Zufar, Z. (2019). Students' Perception of Project-Based Learning Model in Blended Learning Mode Using Sipejar. *Advances in Social Science, Education and Humanities Research, 372*.

Surendeleg, G., Murwa, V., Yun, H.-K., & Kim, Y. S. (2014). The role of gamification in education–a literature review. *Contemporary Engineering Sciences, 7*(29), 1609–1616. doi:10.12988/ces.2014.411217

Susanti, N., Juandi, D., & Maximus Tamur, M. (2020). The Effect of Problem-Based Learning (PBL) Model On Mathematical Communication Skills of Junior High School Students – A Meta-Analysis Study. *Journal Theory dan Aplikasi Matematika, 4*(2), 145-154. doi:10.31764/jtam.v4i2.2481

Susi, T., Johannesson, M., & Backlund, P. (2007). *Serious games: An overview*. DiVA.

Susman, K., & Pavlin, J. (2020). Improvements in Teachers' Knowledge and Understanding of Basic Astronomy Concepts through Didactic Games. *Journal of Baltic Science Education, 19*(6), 1020–1033. doi:10.33225/jbse/20.19.1020

Suvin, C. (2020). *Why should higher education institutions focus on Education 4.0?* Creatix Campus. https://www.creatrixcampus.com/blog/Education-4.0

Sweller, J. (1994). Cognitive load theory, learning difficulty, and instructional design. *Learning and Instruction, 4*(4), 295–312. doi:10.1016/0959-4752(94)90003-5

Swimberghe, K. R., Sharma, D., & Flurry, L. W. (2011). Does a consumer's religion really matter in the buyer–seller dyad? An empirical study examining the relationship between consumer religious commitment, Christian conservatism and the ethical judgment of a seller's controversial business decision. *Journal of Business Ethics, 102*(4), 581–598. doi:10.100710551-011-0829-6

Swimberghe, K., Flurry, L. A., & Parker, J. M. (2011). Consumer religiosity: Consequences for consumer activism in the United States. *Journal of Business Ethics, 103*(3), 453–467. doi:10.100710551-011-0873-2

Syed, J., & Van Buren, H. J. III. (2015). Global Business Norms and Islamic Views of Women's Employment. *Business Ethics Quarterly, 24*(2), 251–276. doi:10.5840/beq201452910

Sylva, K., Melhuish, E., Sammons, P., Siraj-Blatchford, I., & Taggart, B. (Eds.). (2010). *Early childhood matters: Evidence from the effective pre-school and primary education project*. Routledge. doi:10.4324/9780203862063

Szegedine Lengyel, P. (2020). Can the game-based learning come? Virtual classroom in higher education of 21st century. *International Journal of Emerging Technologies in Learning, 15*(112). doi:10.3991/ijet.v15i02.11521

Tachie, S. A., & Galawe, B. F. (2021). The Value of Incorporating Indigenous Games in the Teaching of Number Sentences and Geometric Patterns. *International Journal for Cross-Disciplinary Subjects in Education, 12*(1), 4350–4361. doi:10.20533/ijcdse.2042.6364.2021.0533

Taillandier, F., Micolier, A., Sauce, G., & Chaplain, M. (2021). DOMEGO: A Board Game for Learning How to Manage a Construction Project. *International Journal of Game-Based Learning, 11*(2), 20–37. doi:10.4018/IJGBL.2021040102

Takeuchi, L. M., & Vaala, S. (2014). *Level up learning: A national survey on teaching with digital games.* The Joan Ganz Cooney Center at Sesame Workshop. https://bit.ly/38cRQhp

Takeuchi, L., & Stevens, R. (2011). *The new coviewing: Designing for learning through joint media engagement.* The Joan Ganz Cooney Center at Sesame Workshop. https://www.joanganzcooneycenter.org/wp-content/uploads/2011/12/jgc_coviewing_desktop.pdf

Talib, C. A., Aliyu, F., & Siang, K. H. (2019). Enhancing students' reasoning skills in engineering and technology through game-based learning. *International Journal of Emerging Technologies in Learning, 14*(24), 69-80. doi:10.3991/ijet.v14i24.12117

Tamminen, J., Payne, J. D., Stickgold, R., Wamsley, E. J., & Gaskell, M. G. (2010). Sleep spindle activity is associated with the integration of new memories and existing knowledge. *The Journal of Neuroscience: The Official Journal of the Society for Neuroscience, 30*(43), 14356–14360. doi:10.1523/JNEUROSCI.3028-10.2010 PMID:20980591

Tan Ai Lin, D., Ganapathy, M., & Kaur, M. (2018). Kahoot! It: Gamification in Higher Education. *Pertanika Journal of Social Science & Humanities, 26*(1).

Tan, J., & Biswas, G. (2007). Simulation-based game learning environments: Building and sustaining a fish tank. *IEEE Xplore Digital Library*, 73–80. . doi:10.1109/DIGITEL.2007.44

Tanak, A. (2020). Designing tpack-based course for preparing student teachers to teach science with technological pedagogical content knowledge. *Kasetsart Journal of Social Sciences, 41*(1), 53–59.

Tanaka, F., & Matsuzoe, S. (2012). Children teach a care-receiving robot to promote their learning: Field experiments in a classroom for vocabulary learning. *Journal of Human-Robot Interaction, 1*(1), 78–95. doi:10.5898/JHRI.1.1.Tanaka

Taneja, P., Safapour, E., & Kermanshachi, S. (2018). *Innovative higher education teaching and learning techniques: Implementation trends and assessment approaches.* Paper presented at the 2018 ASEE Annual Conference & Exposition. 10.18260/1-2--30669

Tang, S., Hanneghan, M., & El Rhalibi, A. (2007). *Describing games for learning: terms, scope and learning approaches.* https://www.academia.edu/25962572/Describing_Games_for_Learning_Terms_Scope_and_Learning_Approaches

Tang, S., Hanneghan, M., & Rhalibi, A. (2009). *Introduction to Games-Based Learning.* IGI Global. doi:10.4018/978-1-60566-360-9.ch001

Tanık Önal, N. (2020). Investigation of gifted students' environmental awareness. *International Journal of Curriculum and Instruction, 12*(2), 95–107.

Tan, M., & Hew, K. F. (2016). Incorporating meaningful gamification in a blended learning research methods class: Examining student learning, engagement, and affective outcomes. *Australasian Journal of Educational Technology, 32*(5). Advance online publication. doi:10.14742/ajet.2232

Tanouri, A., Mulcahy, R., & Russell-Bennett, R. (2019). Transformative gamification services for social behavior brand equity: A hierarchical model. *Journal of Service Theory and Practice, 29*(2), 122–141. doi:10.1108/JSTP-06-2018-0140

Tao, Z., Li, H., & Yong, L. (2010). The effect of flow experience on mobile SNS users' loyalty. *Industrial Management & Data Systems, 110*(6), 930–946. doi:10.1108/02635571011055126

Taspinar, B., Schmidt, W., & Schuhbauer, H. (2016). Gamification in education: A board game approach to knowledge acquisition. *Procedia Computer Science, 99*, 101–116. https://doi.org/10.1016/j.procs.2016.09.104

Tate, M. (2013). *Worksheets don't grow dendrites: 20 instructional strategies that engaged the brain.* Corwin.

Taub, M., Sawyer, R., Smith, A., Rowe, J., Azevedo, R., & Lester, J. (2020). The agency effect: The impact of student agency on learning, emotions, and problem-solving behaviors in a game-based learning environment. *Computers & Education, 147*, 103781. doi:10.1016/j.compedu.2019.103781

Taylor, S. E., & Robinson, H. A. (1963). *The relationship of oculomotor efficiency of the beginning reader to his success in learning to read.* Paper presented at the meeting of the American Educational Research Association, Chicago, IL.

Taylor, S., & Yu, D. (2009). The importance of socio-economic status in determining educational achievement in South Africa. *Stellenbosch Economic Working Papers*, 1–65.

Taylor, S.E., Frackenpohl, H. & Pettee, J.L. (1960). Grade level norms for the Components of the Fundamental Reading skill. *EDL Research Information Bulletin, 3*.

Taylor. (2002). *Teaching & learning online: The workers, the lurkers and the shirkers.* USQ.

Taylor, N. (2017). Monitoring, Accountability and Professional Knowledge. In *Monitoring the Quality of Education in Schools* (pp. 43–52). SensePublishers. doi:10.1007/978-94-6300-453-4_4

Taylor, T. L. (2006). Does WoW change everything? How a PvP server, multinational player base, and surveillance mod scene caused me pause. *Games and Culture, 1*(4), 61–63. doi:10.1177/1555412006292615

Tech4Learning. (n.d.). *Creating a 21st century classroom: combining the 3R's and the 4C's.* Author.

Teh, C. L., Fauzy, W. W., & Toh, S. C. (2007). Why use computer games for learning? *1st International Malaysian Educational Technology Convention*, 835-843.

Teichler, U. (2017). Internationalisation Trends in Higher Education and the Changing Role of International Student Mobility. *Journal of international Mobility, 5*, 177-216. doi:10.3917/jim.005.0179

Tejederas, M. (2020). Gamified methodologies in bilingual teacher training. *6th International Conference on Bilingual Education*. https://www.grupo-ebei.es/confbe/2020/

Tercanli, H., Martina, R., Dias, M. F., Wakkee, I., Reuter, J., Amorim, M., Madaleno, M., Magueta, D., Vieira, E., Veloso, C., Figueiredo, C., Vitória, A., Gomes, I., Meireles, G., Daubariene, A., Daunoriene, A., Mortensen, A. K., Zinovyeva, A., Trigueros, I. R., . . . Gutiérrez-Pérez, J. (2021). *Educational Escape Room in Practice: Research, experiences and recommendations.* Academic Press.

The City Reporters. (2013). *REVEALED! Govt plans to read your tweets, Facebook posts, possibly jail you.* Available at http://thecityreporters.com/revealed-govt-plans-to-readyour-tweets-facebook-posts-possibly-jail-you/

The NCES fast facts tools provides quick answers to many education questions. (n.d.). *National Center for Education Statistics.* Retrieved September 2, 2021, from https://nces.ed.gov/fastfacts/display.asp?id=98

The New London Group. (2000). A pedagogy of multiliteracies: Designing social futures. In B. Cope & M. Kalantzis (Eds.), *Multiliteracies: Literacy learning and the design of social futures.* Routledge.

The World Bank. (2020). *Pandemic Threatens to Push 72 Million More Children into Learning Poverty—World Bank outlines a New Vision to ensure that every child learns, everywhere* [Press release]. https://www.worldbank.org/en/news/press-release/2020/12/02/pandemic-threatens-to-push-72-million-more-children-into-learning-poverty-world-bank-outlines-new-vision-to-ensure-that-every-child-learns-everywhere

Theodoropoulos, A., & Lepouras, G. (2021). Augmented Reality and programming education: A systematic review. *International Journal of Child-Computer Interaction, 30*, 100335. doi:10.1016/j.ijcci.2021.100335

Third Rail Games, L. L. C. (2014). *Flying kitchen* (Version 2.02) [Mobile app]. http://itunes.apple.com

Third Rail Games, L. L. C. (2014). *Hideout: Early reading* (Version 2.02) [Mobile app]. http://itunes.apple.com

Thoman, E. (1990, July). New Directions in Media Education. In *An International Conference at the University of Toulouse.* BFI, CLEMI and UNESCO.

Thomas, A. (2018). *TEDx Talk on The Effective Use of Game-Based Learning in Education.* https://www.youtube.com/watch?v=-X1m7tf9cRQ

Thompson, C. G., & von Gillern, S. (2020). Video-game based instruction for vocabulary acquisition with English language learners: A Bayesian meta-analysis. *Educational Research Review, 30*, 100332. doi:10.1016/j.edurev.2020.100332

Thompson, K. M., & Haninger, K. (2001). Violence in E-rated video games. *Medicine and the Media, 286*(5), 591–598. PMID:11476663

Thomson, S. (2018). Achievement at school and socioeconomic background—An educational perspective. *NPJ Science of Learning, 3*(1), 5. Advance online publication. doi:10.103841539-018-0022-0 PMID:30631466

Threekunprapa, A., & Yasri, P. (2020). Unplugged Coding Using Flowblocks for Promoting Computational Thinking and Programming among Secondary School Students. *International Journal of Instruction, 13*(3), 207–222. doi:10.29333/iji.2020.13314a

Tiba, C., Condy, J., & Tunjera, N. (2016). Re-examining factors influencing teachers' adoption and use of technology as a pedagogical tool. In *South Africa International Conference International Conference on Educational Technologies* (pp. 1-11). Pretoria: African Academic Research Forum.

Tillman, A. (2012). *What We See and Why It Matters: How Competency in Visual Literacy Can Enhance Student Learning.* Retrieved May 03, 2019 from https://digitalcommons.iwu.edu/cgi/viewcontent.cgi?article=1008&context=education_honproj

Tkacz, N. (2007). Power, Visibility, Wikipedia. *Southern Review: Communication. Política y Cultura, 40*(2), 5.

Tobias, S., Fletcher, J. D., & Wind, A. P. (2014). *Game-based learning.* 5 doi:10.1007/978-1-4614-3185-

Tobias, S., Fletcher, J. D., & Wind, A. P. (2014). Game-Based Learning. In J. M. Spector, M. D. Merrill, J. Elen, & M. J. Bishop (Eds.), *Handbook of Research on Educational Communications and Technology* (pp. 485–503). Springer. doi:10.1007/978-1-4614-3185-5_38

Tobin, R., & McInnes, A. (2008). Accommodating differences: Variations in differentiated literacy instruction in grade 2/3 classrooms. *Literacy, 42*(1), 3–9. doi:10.1111/j.1467-9345.2008.00470.x

Todorinova, L. (2015). Wikipedia and undergraduate research trajectories. *New Library World, 116*(3/4), 201–212. doi:10.1108/NLW-07-2014-0086

Toh, W., & Kirschner, D. (2020). Self-directed learning in video games, affordances and pedagogical implications for teaching and learning. *Computers & Education, 154*, 1–11. doi:10.1016/j.compedu.2020.103912

Tolks, D., Sailer, M., Dadaczynski, K., Lampert, C., Huberty, J., Paulus, P., & Horstmann, D. (2019). ONYA—The Well-being Game: How to Use Gamification to Promote Wellbeing. *Information (Basel), 10*(2), 58. doi:10.3390/info10020058

Tomin, B., & Jenson, J. (2021). Exploring Science Fictional Futures With Secondary Students: Practicing Critical Literacy. In *Disciplinary Literacy Connections to Popular Culture in K-12 Settings*. IGI Global. doi:10.4018/978-1-7998-4721-2.ch005

Tomlinson, C. A. (2001). *How to differentiate instruction in mixed ability classrooms* (2nd ed.). ASCD.

Töremen, F., Karakuş, M., & Yasan, T. (2009). Total quality management practices in Turkish primary schools. *Quality Assurance in Education, 17*(1), 30–44. doi:10.1108/09684880910929917

Torgesen, J. K., Wagner, R. K., Rashotte, C. A., Herron, J., & Lindamood, P. (2010). Computer assisted instruction to prevent early reading difficulties in students at risk for dyslexia: Outcomes from two instructional approaches. *Annals of Dyslexia, 60*(1), 40–56. doi:10.100711881-009-0032-y PMID:20052566

Torppa, M. (2007). *Pathways to Reading Acquisition: effects of early skills, learning environment and familial risk for dyslexia*. University of Jyväskylä.

Torres-Toukoumidis, Á., Rodríguez, L. M. R., & Rodríguez, A. P. (2018). Ludificación y sus posibilidades en el entorno de blended learning: Revisión documental [Gamification and its possibilities in blended learning: Literature review]. *RIED. Revista Iberoamericana de Educación a Distancia, 21*(1), 95–111. doi:10.5944/ried.21.1.18792

Tough, J. (1977). *The Development of Meaning*. George Allen & Unwin.

Tracey, D., & Morrow, L. (2009). *Best practices for phonics instruction in today's classroom. Sadlier Professional Development Series, 13, 1–22* .

Tractinsky, N., Katz, A. S., & Ikar, D. (2000). What is beautiful is usable. *Interacting with Computers, 13*(2), 127–145. doi:10.1016/S0953-5438(00)00031-X

Trad, R. (2021). *Teachers' and students' experiences using social media as a pedagogical tool within classrooms: A systematic literature review* [Unpublished master's thesis]. https://ir.lib.uwo.ca/etd/7824

Trespalacios, J., Chamberlin, B., & Gallagher, R. R. (2011). Collaboration, engagement & fun: How youth preferences in video gaming can inform 21st century education. *TechTrends, 55*(6), 49–54. doi:10.100711528-011-0541-5

Trilling, B., & Fidel, C. (2009). *21st Century skills: Learning for life in our times*. Jossey-Bass.

Trinidad, M., Ruiz, M., & Calderón, A. (2021). A bibliometric analysis of gamification research. *IEEE Access: Practical Innovations, Open Solutions, 9*, 46505–46544. doi:10.1109/ACCESS.2021.3063986

Troitschanskaia, Z. O., Pant, H., Lautenbach, C., Molerov, D., Toepper, M., & Brückner, S. (2017). *Modeling and Measuring Competencies in Higher Education: Approaches to Challenges in Higher Education Policy and Practice*. Springer. doi:10.1007/978-3-658-15486-8

Tromba, P. (2013). Build engagement and knowledge one block at a time with Minecraft. *Learning and Leading with Technology, 40*(8), 20–23.

Troppo, G. (2015). *The game believes in you: How digital play can make our kids smarter*. St. Martin's Press.

Troussas, C., Krouska, A., & Sgouropoulou, C. (2020). Collaboration and fuzzy-modeled personalization for mobile game-based learning in higher education. *Computers & Education, 144*, 103698. doi:10.1016/j.compedu.2019.103698

Trundle, K. C., & Bell, R. L. (2010). The use of a computer simulation to promote conceptual change: A quasi-experimental study. *Computers & Education, 54*(4), 1078–1088. doi:10.1016/j.compedu.2009.10.012

Trybus, J. (2015). *Game-Based Learning: What it is, Why it Works, and Where it's Going.* New Media Institute. http://www.newmedia.org /game-based-learning--what-it-is-why-it -works-and-where-its-going.html

Tsai, M.-J., Huang, L.-J., Hou, H.-T., Hsu, C.-Y., & Chiou, G.-L. (2016). Visual behavior, flow and achievement in game-based learning. *Computers & Education, 98,* 115–129. doi:10.1016/j.compedu.2016.03.011

Tsay, C. H.-H., Kofinas, A., & Luo, J. (2018). Enhancing student learning experience with technology-mediated gamification: An empirical study. *Computers & Education, 121,* 1–17. doi:10.1016/j.compedu.2018.01.009

Tsekleves, E., Cosmas, J., & Aggoun, A. (2016). Benefits, barriers and guideline recommendations for the implementation of serious games in education for stakeholders and policymakers. *British Journal of Educational Technology, 47*(1), 164–183. doi:10.1111/bjet.12223

Tuber, K. (2007). *Catan Dice* [Board Game]. CatangmbH.

Tuomi, P., Multisilta, J., Saarikoski, P., & Suominen, J. (2018). Coding skills as a success factor for a society. *Education and Information Technologies, 23*(1), 419–434. doi:10.100710639-017-9611-4

Turgut, Y., & Irgin, P. (2009). Young learners' language learning via computer games. *Procedia: Social and Behavioral Sciences, 1*(1), 760–764. doi:10.1016/j.sbspro.2009.01.135

Turkle, S. (1995). *Life on the screen: Identity in the age of the Internet.* Touchstone.

Turner, J., Amirnuddin, P. S., & Singh, H. (2019). University Legal Learning Spaces Effectiveness in Developing Employability Skills of Future Law Graduates. *Malaysian Journal of Learning and Instruction, 16*(1), 49–79. doi:10.32890/mjli2019.16.1.3

Turoff, A., & Cooke, B. (1974). *Boggle [Board Game].* Parker Brothers.

Tüzün, H., Yılmaz-Soylu, M., Karakuş, T., İnal, Y., & Kızılkaya, G. (2009). The effects of computer games on primary school students' achievement and motivation in geography learning. *Computers & Education, 52*(1), 68–77. doi:10.1016/j.compedu.2008.06.008

Tyng, C., Amin, H., Saad, M., & Malik, A. (2017). The Influences of Emotion on Learning and Memory. Front.Ullman, M. T. (2016). The declarative/procedural model: a neurobiological model of language learning, knowledge, and use. In *Neurobiology of language* (pp. 953–968). Academic Press.

Udara, S. W. I., & De Alwis, A. K. (2019). Gamification for Healthcare and Well-being. *Global Journal of Medical Research,* 25–29. doi:10.34257/GJMRKVOL19IS4PG25

Ullman, M. T., & Lovelett, J. T. (2018). Implications of the declarative/procedural model for improving second language learning: The role of memory enhancement techniques. *Second Language Research, 34*(1), 39–65. doi:10.1177/0267658316675195

Umble, E. J., & Umble, M. (2005). The Production Dice Game: An Active Learning Classroom Exercise and Spreadsheet Simulation. *Operations Management Education Review, 1,* 105–122.

Um, E., Plass, J. L., Hayward, E. O., & Homer, B. D. (2012). Emotional design in multimedia learning. *Journal of Educational Psychology, 104*(2), 485–498. doi:10.1037/a0026609

UNESCO Institute for Information Technologies in Education (UNESCO-IITE). (2011). *Digital natives: How do they learn; How to teach them?* Retrieved from https://iite.unesco.org/files/policy_briefs/pdf/en/digital_natives.pdf

UNESCO. (1990). http://www.unesco.org/new/fileadmin/MULTIMEDIA/HQ/CI/CI/pdf/youth_media_education.pdf

UNESCO. (2006). *Cross-national studies of the quality of education: Planning their design and managing their impact* (K. N. Ross & I. J. Genevois, Eds.). International Institute for Educational Planning.

UNESCO. (2018). *Digital skills critical for jobs and social inclusion.* https://en.unesco.org/news/digital-skills-critical-jobs-and-social-inclusion

UNESCO. (2021). *100 million more children under the minimum reading proficiency level due to COVID-19 – UNESCO convenes world education ministers.* Retrieved September 16, 2021 from https://en.unesco.org/news/100-million-more-children-under-minimum-reading-proficiency-level-due-covid-19-unesco-convenes

United Nations. (2020). *UN Secretary-General's policy brief: The impact of COVID-19 on women.* Retrieved January 18, 2020, from https://www.unwomen.org/en/digital-library/publications/2020/04/policy-brief-the-impact-of-covid-19-on-women

United Nations. (2021). *100 million more children fail basic reading skills because of COVID-19.* UN News. Retrieved September 16, 2021, from https://news.un.org/en/story/2021/03/1088392

University of Lisbon. (2021). Retrieved October 4, 2021, from https://www.ulisboa.pt/en

University of Toronto Libraries. (2021, August 25). *Research Guides.* Retrieved September 6, 2021, from https://guides.library.utoronto.ca/c.php?g=448614&p=3508116

Unlock Creativity through game-based learning at higher education. (2021). https://www.un-lock.eu/

Urh, M., Vukovic, G., Jereb, E., & Pintar, R. (2015). The Model for Introduction of Gamification into E-learning in Higher Education. *Procedia - Social and Behavioral Sciences, 197*(March), 388–397. doi:10.1016/j.sbspro.2015.07.154

Uribe-Jongbloed, E., Espinosa-Medina, H. D., & Biddle, J. (2016). Cultural Transduction and intertextuality in video games: An analysis of three international case studies. In C. Duret & C. M. Pons (Eds.), *Contemporary research on intertextuality in video games* (pp. 143–161). IGI Global. doi:10.4018/978-1-5225-0477-1.ch009

Vaala, S., Ly, A., & Levine, M. H. (2015). Getting a read on the app stores: A market scan and analysis of children's literacy apps. *The Joan Ganz Cooney Center at Sesame Workshop.* https://www.joanganzcooneycenter.org/wp-ontent/uploads/2015/12/jgcc_gettingaread.pdf

Vacca, J. S., & Levitt, R. (2011). Using Scaffolding Techniques to Teach a Lesson about the Civil War. *International Journal of Humanities and Social Science, 1*(18), 150–161. www.ijhssnet.com

Vaidyanathan, S. (2016). What's the difference between coding and computational thinking? *EdSurge.* Retrieved 9/14/2021 from https://www.edsurge.com/news/2016-08-06-what-s-the-difference-between-coding-and-computational-thinking

Vaishnavi, V. & Kuechler, B. (2004). Design Science Research in Information Systems Overview of Design Science Research. *Ais.*

Valsiner, J. (1987). *Culture and the Development of Children's Action: A cultural-historical theory of developmental psychology.* John Wiley & Sons.

van Daal, V., & Reitsma, P. (2000). Computer-assisted learning to read and spell: Results from two pilot studies. *Journal of Research in Reading, 23*(2), 181–193. doi:10.1111/1467-9817.00113

Van der Heijden, H. (2004). User acceptance of hedonic information systems. *Management Information Systems Quarterly, 28*(4), 695–704. doi:10.2307/25148660

Van Der Maren, J. M. (1996). Méthodes de Recherche pour l'Education (2a ed.). Bruxelles: De Boeck Université.

Van Dijk, J. A. G. M. (2005). *The deepening Divide: Inequality in the information society.* SAGE Publications. doi:10.4135/9781452229812

Van Eck, R. (2006). Digital Game-Based Learning: It's Not Just the Digital Natives Who Are Restless. *EDUCAUSE*, 17–30.

Van Eck, N. J., & Waltman, L. (2010). Software survey: VOSviewer, a computer program for bibliometric mapping. *Scientometrics*, *84*(2), 523–538. doi:10.100711192-009-0146-3 PMID:20585380

van Ewijk, G., Smakman, M., & Konijn, E. A. (2020, June). Teachers' perspectives on social robots in education: an exploratory case study. In *Proceedings of the Interaction Design and Children Conference* (pp. 273-280). 10.1145/3392063.3394397

Van Heerden, D., & Goosen, L. (2012). Using Vodcasts to Teach Programming in an ODL Environment. *Progressio*, *34*(3), 144–160.

Van Laar, E., Van Deursen, A. J. A. M., Van Dijk, J. A. G. M., & De Haan, J. (2020). Determinants of 21st-Century Skills and 21st-Century Digital Skills for Workers: A Systematic Literature Review. *SAGE Open*, *10*(1), 1–14. doi:10.1177/2158244019900176

Van Rensburg, C. (2013). 'n Perspektief op 'n periode van kontak tussen Khoi en Afrikaans. *Literator*, *34*(2), 1–11. doi:10.4102/lit.v34i2.413

Van Roy, R., & Zaman, B. (2018). Need-Supporting Gamification In Education: An Assessment Of Motivational Effects Over Time. *Computers & Education*, *127*, 283–297. doi:10.1016/j.compedu.2018.08.018

Vandercruysse, S., Vandewaetere, M., & Clarebout, G. (2012). Game-based learning: A review on the effectiveness of educational games. Handbook of research on serious games as educational, business and research tools, 628-647.

Vandercruysse, S., Vandewaetere, M., Cornillie, F., & Clarebout, G. (2013). Competition and students' perceptions in a game-based language learning environment. *Educational Technology Research and Development*, *61*(6), 927–950. doi:10.100711423-013-9314-5

VanSledright, B. A. (2002). Fifth graders investigating history in the classroom: Results from a researcher-practitioner design experiment. *The Elementary School Journal*, *103*(2), 131–160. doi:10.1086/499720

Varghese, N. V. (2014). Globalization and higher education: Changing trends in cross border education. *Analytical Reports in International Education*, *5*(1), 7–20.

Vásquez. (2017). *Maria & Peñafiel, Myriam & Cevallos Cevallos, Andrés & Zaldumbide, Juan & Vásquez, Diego.* Impact of Game-Based Learning on Students in Higher Education. doi:10.21125/edulearn.2017.1942

Vasquez, V. (2003). What Pokemon can teach us about learning and literacy. *Language Arts*, *81*(2), 145–154.

Vaughn, P., & Turner, C. (2016). Decoding via coding: Analyzing qualitative text data through thematic coding and survey methodologies. *Journal of Library Administration*, *56*(1), 41–51. doi:10.1080/01930826.2015.1105035

Veldkamp, A., Daemen, J., Teekens, S., Koelewijn, S., Knippels, M. C. P. J., & van Joolingen, W. R. (2020). Escape boxes: Bringing escape room experience into the classroom. British Journal of Educational Technology, 51(4), 1220–1239. doi:10.1111/bjet.12935

Venkatesh, V. (2000). Determinants of perceived ease of use: Integrating control, intrinsic motivation, and emotion into the technology acceptance model. *Information Systems Research*, *11*(4), 342–365. doi:10.1287/isre.11.4.342.11872

Venkatesh, V., & Bala, H. (2008). Technology acceptance model 3 and a research agenda on interventions. *Decision Sciences*, *39*(2), 273–315. doi:10.1111/j.1540-5915.2008.00192.x

Verhoeven, L., & Snow, C. (Eds.). (2001). *Literacy and motivation: Reading engagement in individuals and groups.* Lawrence Erlbaum Associates.

Vermeulen, L., Bauwel, S. V., & Looy, J. V. (2017). Tracing Female Gamer Identity: An Empirical Study Into gender and Stereotype Threat Perceptions. *Computer in Human Behavior, 71*, 90-98. doi:10.1016/j.chb.2017.01.054

Vesisenaho, M., Dillon, P., & Sari, H.-N. (2017). Creative Improvisations with Information and Communication Technology to Support Learning: A Conceptual and Developmental Framework. *Journal of Teacher Education and Educators*, *6*(3), 229–250.

Vial, M. (2001). *Se former pour évaluer. Pédagogies en développement.* De boeck Université.

Vicente, E., Verdugo, M. A., Gómez-Vela, M., Fernández-Pulido, R., Wehmeyer, M. L., & Guillén, V. M. (2019). Personal characteristics and school contextual variables associated with student self-determination in Spanish context. *Journal of Intellectual & Developmental Disability*, *44*(1), 23–34. doi:10.3109/13668250.2017.1310828

Vitell, S. J. (2009). The Role of Religiosity in Business and Consumer Ethics: A Review of the Literature. *Journal of Business Ethics*, *90*(2), 155–167. doi:10.100710551-010-0382-8

Vitell, S. J., & Paolillo, J. G. P. (2003). Consumer ethics: The role of religiosity. *Journal of Business Ethics*, *46*(2), 151–162. doi:10.1023/A:1025081005272

Vitos, B. (2014). *Experiencing electronic dance floors: A comparative research of techno and psytrance in Melbourne* (Unpublished PhD Thesis). Monash University, Clayton, Australia.

Vivido. (2021). *Management Platform of the National Support Network for Victims of Domestic Violence.* Working together for an Inclusive Europe, EEA Grants Portugal 2020. Retrieved October 4, 2021, from https://vividoproject.wixsite.com/vivido?lang=en

Vlachopoulos, D., & Makri, A. (2017). The effect of games and simulations on higher education: A systematic literature review. *International Journal of Educational Technology in Higher Education*, *14*(22), 22. Advance online publication. doi:10.118641239-017-0062-1

Vogel, J. J., Greenwood-Ericksen, A., Cannon-Bowers, J., & Bowers, C. A. (2006). Using Virtual Reality with and without Gaming Attributes for Academic Achievement. Journal of Research on Technology in Education, 39(1), 105-118.

Vogel, J. J., Vogel, D. S., Cannon-Bowers, J., Bowers, C. A., Muse, K., & Wright, M. (2006). Computer gaming and interactive simulations for learning: A meta-analysis. *Journal of Educational Computing Research*, *34*(3), 229–243. doi:10.2190/FLHV-K4WA-WPVQ-H0YM

von Gillern, S. (2016b). Perceptual, decision-making, and learning processes during video gameplay: An analysis of *Infamous - Second Son* with the Gamer Response and Decision Framework. *Games and Learning Society 2016 Conference Proceedings.*

von Gillern, S. (2016a). The gamer response and decision framework: A tool for understanding video gameplay experiences. *Simulation & Gaming*, *47*(5), 666–683. doi:10.1177/1046878116656644

von Gillern, S. (2018). Games and their embodied learning principles in the classroom: Connecting learning theory to practice. In M. Khosrow-Pour (Ed.), *Gamification in Education: Breakthroughs in Research and Practice* (pp. 554–582). IGI Global. doi:10.4018/978-1-5225-5198-0.ch029 von Gillern, S. (2021). Communication, cooperation, and competition: Examining the literacy practices of esports teams. In M. Harvey & R. Marlatt (Eds.), *Esports research and its integration in education* (pp. 148–167). IGI Global. doi:10.4018/978-1-7998-7069-2.ch009

von Gillern, S., & Alaswad, Z. (2016). Games and game-based learning in instructional design. *The International Journal of Technologies in Learning, 23*(4), 1–7. doi:10.18848/2327-0144/CGP/v23i04/1-7

von Gillern, S., Stufft, C., & Harvey, M. (2021). Integrating video games into the ELA classroom. *Literacy Today, 38*(6), 64–65.

Von Glasersfeld, E. (1995). *Radical constructivism: a way of knowing and learning. studies in mathematics education series: 6.* Falmer Press.

Voogt, J., & McKenney, S. (2017). TPACK in teacher education: Are we preparing teachers to use technology for early literacy? *Technology, Pedagogy and Education, 26*(1), 69–83. https://doi.org/10.1080/1475939X.2016.1174730

Vorster, J., & Goosen, L. (2017). A Framework for University Partnerships Promoting Continued Support of e-Schools. In J. Liebenberg (Ed.), *Proceedings of the 46th Annual Conference of the Southern African Computer Lecturers' Association (SACLA)* (pp. 118 - 126). Magaliesburg: North-West University.

Vuorikari, R. (2016). *DigComp 2.0: The Digital Competence Framework For Citizens. Update Phase 1: the Conceptual Reference Model.* European Commission, Retrieved from https://ec.europa.eu/jrc/en/publication/eur-scientificand-technical-research-reports/digcomp-20-digital-competence-framework-citizens-update-phase-1-conceptualreference-model

Vygotski, L. (1978). *Mind in society: The development of higher psychological processes.* Harvard University Press.

Vygotsky, L. S. (1978). Readings on the development of children. In From Mind and Society (pp. 79-91). Cambridge, MA: Harvard University Press.

Vygotsky, L. (1962). *Thought and language* (E. Hanf-mann & G. Vakar, Trans.). MIT Press. doi:10.1037/11193-000

Vygotsky, L. (1966). Igra i ee rol v umstvennom razvitii rebenka [Play and its role in the mental development of the child]. *Voprosy Psihologii, 12*(6), 62–76.

Vygotsky, L. (1978). *Mind in society.* Harvard University Press. (Original work published 1930)

Vygotsky, L. S. (1978). *Mind in society: Development of higher psychological processes.* Harvard UP.

Vygotsky, L. S. (1978). *Mind in Society: The development of higher mental processes* (M. Cole, V. John-Steiner, S. Scribner, & E. Souberman, Eds.). Harvard University Press.

Vygotsky, L. S. (1978). *Mind in Society: The Development of Higher Psychological Processes (M. Cole, V. John-Steiner* (S. Scribner & E. Souberman, Eds.). Havard University Press.

Wade, R. (1994). Teacher education students' views on class discussion: Implications for fostering critical thinking. *Teaching and Teacher Education, 10*(2), 231–243. doi:10.1016/0742-051X(94)90015-9

Wafula-Kwake, A., & Ocholla, D. N. (2007). The Feasibility of ICT Diffusion amongst African Rural Women: A case study of South Africa and Kenya. *International Journal of Information Ethics, 7*(2), 1–20.

Wagner, C., Graells-Garrido, E., Garcia, D., & Menczer, F. (2016). Women through the glass ceiling: Gender asymmetries in Wikipedia. *EPJ Data Science, 5*(1), 5. https://doi.org/10.1140/epjds/s13688-016-0066-4

Wagner, S. C., & Lawrence Sanders, G. (2001). Considerations in ethical decision-making and software piracy. *Journal of Business Ethics, 29*(1-2), 161–167. doi:10.1023/A:1006415514200

Wagner, T. (2008). Rigor redefined: Even our "best" schools are failing to prepare students for 21st-century careers and citizenship. *Educational Leadership*, 2(66), 20–25.

Wahyuni, S., Mujiyanto, J., Rukmini, D., & Fitriati, S. W. (2020, June). Teachers' Technology Integration Into English Instructions: SAMR Model. In *International Conference on Science and Education and Technology (ISET)* (pp. 546-550). Atlantis Press. 10.2991/assehr.k.200620.109

Wallach, H. M., Murray, I., Salakhutdinov, R., & Mimno, D. (2009). Evaluation methods for topic models. *Proceedings of the 26th annual international conference on machine learning*. 10.1145/1553374.1553515

Walsh, C. (2010). Systems-based literacy practices: Digital games research, gameplay and design. *Australian Journal of Language and Literacy*, *33*(1), 24–40.

Walsh, J. N., O'Brien, M. P., & Costin, Y. (2021). Investigating student engagement with intentional content: An exploratory study of instructional videos. *International Journal of Management Education*, *19*(2), 100505. doi:10.1016/j.ijme.2021.100505

Wang, A. I. (2020, April 17). *Impact of Kahoot! in higher education – research roundup.* Kahoot! Retrieved September 11, 2021 from https://kahoot.com/blog/2020/04/08/kahoot-impact-higher education-research/

Wang, S.-K., & Han, S. (2010). Six C's of motivation. In M. Orey (Ed.), Emerging perspectives on learning, teaching, and technology. Global Text Project, funded by the Jacob Foundation, Zurich, Switzerland. Creative Commons 3.0 Attribution Licence.

Wang, J. Y., Wu, H. K., & Hsu, Y. S. (2017). Using mobile applications for learning: Effects of simulation design, visual-motor integration, and spatial ability on high school students' conceptual understanding. *Computers in Human Behavior*, *66*, 103–113. doi:10.1016/j.chb.2016.09.032

Wang, J., & Rao, N. (2020). What Do Chinese Students Say about Their Academic Motivational Goals-Reasons Underlying Academic Strivings? *Asia Pacific Journal of Education*, *12*, 1–15. doi:10.1080/02188791.2020.1812513

Wang, L. C., & Chen, M. P. (2010). The effects of game strategy and preference-matching on flow experience and programming performance in game-based learning. *Innovations in Education and Teaching International*, *47*(1), 39–52. doi:10.1080/14703290903525838

Wang, L., Gunasti, K., Gopal, R., Shankar, R., & Pancras, J. (2017). The Impact of Gamification on Word-of-Mouth Effectiveness: Evidence from Foursquare. *Proceedings of the 50th Hawaii International Conference on System Sciences*. 10.24251/HICSS.2017.090

Wang, M., & Zheng, X. (2021). Using game-based learning to support learning science: A study with middle school students. *The Asia-Pacific Education Researcher*, *30*(2), 167–176. doi:10.100740299-020-00523-z

Wang, S., Fang, H., Zhang, G., & Ma, T. (2019). Research on a new type of "dual-teacher classroom" supported by artificial intelligence educational robots & on the teaching design and future prospects of "human-machine collaboration". *Journal of Distance Education*, *37*(2), 25–32.

Waraczynski, M. A. (2006). The central extended amygdala network as a proposed circuit underlying reward valuation. *Neuroscience and Biobehavioral Reviews*, *30*(4), 472–496. doi:10.1016/j.neubiorev.2005.09.001 PMID:16243397

Wardoyo, C., Satrio, Y. D., & Ma'ruf, D. (2020). Effectiveness of Game-Based Learning – Learning in Modern Education. *3rd International Research Conference on Economics and Business*, 81–87. 10.18502/kss.v4i7.6844

Wardrip-Fruin. (2009). Better Game Studies Education the Carcassonne Way. *2009 DiGRA '09 - Proceedings of the 2009 DiGRA International Conference: Breaking New Ground: Innovation in Games, Play, Practice and Theory*.

Waris, O., Jaeggi, S. M., Seitz, A. R., Lehtonen, M., Soveri, A., Lukasik, K. M., Söderström, U., Hoffing, R. A. C., & Laine, M. (2019). Video gaming and working memory: A large-scale cross-sectional correlative study. *Computers in Human Behavior*, *97*, 94–103. doi:10.1016/j.chb.2019.03.005 PMID:31447496

Warren, S. J., Dondlinger, M. J., & Barab, S. A. (2008). A MUVE towards PBL writing: Effects of a digital learning environment designed to improve elementary student writing. *Journal of Research on Technology in Education*, *41*(1), 113–140. doi:10.1080/15391523.2008.10782525

Warren, S. J., Dondlinger, M. J., Stein, R., & Barab, S. A. (2009). Educational Game as Supplemental Learning Tool: Benefits, Challenges, and Tensions Arising from Use in an Elementary School Classroom. *Journal of Interactive Learning Research*, *20*(4), 487–505.

Wati, I. F., & Yuniawatika. (2020). Digital Game-Based Learning as A Solution to Fun Learning Challenges During the Covid-19 Pandemic. *Advances in Social Science, Education and Humanities Research*, *508*, 202–210. doi:10.2991/assehr.k.201214.237

Watson, W. R., Yang, S., & Dana, R. (2016). Games in Schools: Teachers' Perceptions of Barriers to Game-based Learning. *Journal of Interactive Learning Research*, *27*(2). https://www.learntechlib.org/primary/p/151749/

Wawro, A. (2017). Why video game devs don't get 'board' of learning from tabletop games. *Game Developer*. https://www.gamedeveloper.com/design/why-video-game-devs-don-t-get-board-of-learning-from-tabletop-games

We are Social. (2021). *Digital 2021. Global Digital Overview*. https://dijilopedi.com/2021-dunya-internet-sosyal-medya-ve-mobil-kullanim-istatistikleri/

Weaver, G. R., & Agle, B. R. (2002). Religiosity and ethical behavior in organizations: A symbolic interactionist perspective. *Academy of Management Review*, *27*(1), 77–97. doi:10.2307/4134370

Webb, M., & Cox, M. (2004). A review of pedagogy related to information and communications technology. *Technology, Pedagogy and Education*, *13*(3), 235–286. doi:10.1080/14759390400200183

Weber, S., & Mitchell, C. (2008). Imaging, keyboarding, and posting identities: Young people and new media technologies. In D. Buckingham (Ed.), Youth, identity, and digital media (pp. 25–48). The MIT Press.

WEF. (2020). *The Future of Jobs Report 2020*. Geneva: World Economic Forum. Retrieved from https://www3.weforum.org/docs/WEF_Future_of_Jobs_2020.pdf

Weibull, L. (1985). Structural factors in gratifications research. *Media gratifications research: Current perspectives*, 123-47.

Wei, C. W., Kao, H. Y., Lu, H. H., & Liu, Y. C. (2018). The effects of competitive gaming scenarios and personalized assistance strategies on English vocabulary learning. *Journal of Educational Technology & Society*, *21*(3), 146–158.

Weintrop, D., Holbert, N., Horn, M., & Wilensky, U. (2016). Computational thinking in constructionist video games. *International Journal of Game-Based Learning*, *6*(1), 1–17.

Weller, M. (2011). *The digital scholar: How technology is transforming scholarly practice*. Bloomsbury Academic. https://www.open.edu/openlearn/ocw/pluginfile.php/731937/mod_resource/content/1/The%20Digital%20Scholar_%20How%20Technology%20Is%20T%20-%20Martin%20Weller.pdf

Wells, S. H., Warelow, P. J., & Jackson, K. L. (2009). Problem based learning (PBL): A conundrum. *Contemporary Nurse*, *33*(2), 191–201. Advance online publication. doi:10.5172/conu.2009.33.2.191 PMID:19929163

Werbach, K. (2014). ReDefining Gamification: A Process Approach. In A. Spagnolli, L. Chittaro, & L. Gamberini (Eds.), *Persuasive Technology* (pp. 266–272). Springer. doi:10.1007/978-3-319-07127-5_23

Werner, J. S., & James, W. T. Jr. (2001). *Communication Theories: Origins, Methods and Uses in the Mass Media*. Addison Wesley Longman, Inc.

Westbrook, N. (2011). Media literacy pedogog: Critical and new /twenty first centries instructions. *E-Learning and Digital Media*, 8(2), 154–164.

Westera, W. (2015). Games are motivating, aren't they? Disputing the arguments for digital game-based learning. *Int. J. Serious Games*, 2(2), 4–17. doi:10.17083/ijsg.v2i2.58

Westrup, U. & Planander, A. (2013). Role-play as a pedagogical method to prepare students for practice: The students' voice. *Ogre utbildning*, 3(3), 199-210.

When will the COVID-19 pandemic end? (n.d.). *McKinsey*. Retrieved September 2, 2021, from https://www.mckinsey.com/industries/healthcare-systems-and-services/our-insights/when-will-the-covid-19-pandemic-end

Whitaker, R. J. (1983). Aristotle is not dead: Student understanding of trajectory motion. *American Journal of Physics*, 51(4), 352–357. doi:10.1119/1.13247

White, K., & McCoy, L. P. (2019). Effects of Game-Based Learning on Attitude and Achievement in Elementary Mathematics Achievement in Elementary Mathematics. Networks. *An Online Journal for Teacher Research*, 21(1), 1–17. Advance online publication. doi:10.4148/2470-6353.1259

Whitton, N. (2012). Game Based Learning. In *Encyclopedia of the Sciences of Learning*. Springer. doi:10.1007/978-1-4419-1428-6_437

Whitton, N. (2014). *Digital games and learning: Research and theory*. Routledge. doi:10.4324/9780203095935

Whitton, N., & Moseley, A. (2012). *Using Games to Enhance Learning and Teaching: A Beginner's Guide*. Routledge. doi:10.4324/9780203123775

Wieringa, R. (2009). Design science as nested problem solving. *Proceedings of the 4th International Conference on Design Science Research in Information Systems and Technology, DESRIST '09*. 10.1145/1555619.1555630

Wikipedia. (n.d.). Retrieved from https://en.wikipedia.org/wiki/gamification

Wilkes, R. E., Burnett, J. J., & Howell, R. D. (1986). On the meaning and measurement of religiosity in consumer research. *Journal of the Academy of Marketing Science*, 14(1), 47–56. doi:10.1007/BF02722112

Wilkinson, P. (2015). *A Brief History of Serious Games*. https://core.ac.uk/download/pdf/157768453.pdf

Wilkinson, P. (2016). A brief history of serious games. *Entertainment computing and serious games*, 17-41.

Wilkinson, R., & Pickett, K. (2009). *The spirit level: Why greater equality makes societies stronger*. Bloomsbury Press.

Williams, J., Ritter, J., & Bullock, S. M. (2012). Understanding the complexity of becoming a teacher educator: Experience, belonging, and practice within a professional learning community. *Studying Teacher Education*, 8(3), 245–260. doi:10.1080/17425964.2012.719130

Wilson, C. (2012). Media and İnformation Literacy: Pedogy and Possibilities. *Comunicar*, 39, 15–22.

Wing, J. M. (2006). Computational Thinking. *Communications of the ACM, 49*(3), 33-35. https://www.cs.cmu.edu/~15110-s13/Wing06-ct.pdf

Wing, J. M. (2008). Computational thinking and thinking about computing. *Philosophical Transactions Series A, Mathematical, Physical, and Engineering Sciences, 366*, 3717-25. . doi:10.1098/rsta.2008.0118

Wing, J. M. (2006). Computational thinking. *Communications of the ACM, 49*(3), 33–35. doi:10.1145/1118178.1118215

Wise, B. W., Ring, J., & Olson, R. K. (2000). Individual differences in gains from computer-assisted remedial reading. *Journal of Experimental Child Psychology, 77*(3), 197–235. doi:10.1006/jecp.1999.2559 PMID:11023657

Witte, J., Westbrook, R., & Witte, M. M. (2017). *Proceedings of the Global Conference on Education and Research.* 10.5038/2572-6374-v1

Wizards of the Coast. (2015). *Dungeons & Dragons Core Rulebook: Dungeon Master's Guide* (1st ed.). Dungeons & Dragons.

Wizards of the Coast. (2021). *Van Richten's Guide to Ravenloft* (1st ed.). Dungeons & Dragons.

Wohlwend, K. E. (2008). *Play as a literacy of possibilities: Expanding meanings in practices, materials, and spaces.* Academic Press.

Wohlwend, K. E. (2017). Who gets to play? Access, popular media and participatory literacies. *Early Years, 37*(1), 62–76. doi:10.1080/09575146.2016.1219699

Wolcott, H. F. (1987). On ethnographic intent. In Interpretive Ethnography on Education: At Home and Abroad. Hillsdale, NJ: Erlbaum.

Wolfe, S., & Flewitt, R. (2010). New technologies, new multimodal literacy practices and young children's metacognitive development. *Cambridge Journal of Education, 40*(4), 387–399. doi:10.1080/0305764X.2010.526589

Wolf, W. (2014). Framings of narrative in literature and the pictorial arts. In M. Ryan & J. Thon (Eds.), *Storyworlds across media: Toward a media-conscious narratology* (pp. 126–150). University of Nebraska Press. doi:10.2307/j.ctt1d9nkdg.10

Wolk, C., & Nikolai, L. A. (1997). Personality types of accounting students and faculty: Comparisons and implications. *Journal of Accounting Education, 15*(1), 1–17. doi:10.1016/S0748-5751(96)00041-3

Wong, Y. S., & Yatim, M. H. M. (2018, July). A Propriety Multiplatform Game-Based Learning Game to Learn Object-Oriented Programming. In *2018 7th International Congress on Advanced Applied Informatics (IIAI-AAI)* (pp. 278-283). IEEE. 10.1109/IIAI-AAI.2018.00060

Wong, E. M., & Li, S. C. (2008). Framing ICT implementation in a context of educational change: A multilevel analysis. *School Effectiveness and School Improvement, 19*(1), 99–120. doi:10.1080/09243450801896809

Wong, J. K. K. (2004). Are the Learning Styles of Asian International Students Culturally or Contextually Based? *International Education Journal, 4*(4), 154–166.

Wong, K. (1996). Video game effect on computer-based learning design. *British Journal of Educational Technology, 27*(September), 230–232. https://doi.org/10.1111/j.1467-8535.1996.tb00690.x

Wood, E. (2009). Media literacy education: Evaluating media literacy education in Colorado Schools (Master's thesis). Faculty of Social Sciences, University of Denver.

Wood, L. C., & Reiners, T. (2012). Gamification in logistics and supply chain education: Extending active learning. In P. Kommers, T. Issa, & P. Isaías (Eds.), *IADIS International Conference on Internet Technologies & Society,* (pp. 101–108). Academic Press.

Woods, M., Macklin, R., & Lewis, G. K. (2016). Researcher reflexivity: Exploring the impacts of CAQDAS use. *International Journal of Social Research Methodology, 19*(4), 385–403. doi:10.1080/13645579.2015.1023964

Woo, J.-C. (2014). Digital game-based learning supports student motivation, cognitive success, and performance outcomes. *Journal of Educational Technology & Society, 17*, 291–307. https://www.j-ets.net/ETS/issues3ebc.html?id=64

Workshop, S. (2021). *Art maker* [Online software]. https://www.sesamestreet.org/art-maker

World Health Organization. (2018, September). *Gaming disorder.* Retrieved from https://www.who.int/features/qa/gaming-disorder/en/

Wouters, Van der Spek, & Van Oostendorp. (2009). Current practices in serious game research: A review from a learning outcomes perspective. In Games-based learning advancements for multi-sensory human computer interfaces: techniques and effective practices. IGI Global.

Wouters, P., Paas, F., & van Merriënboer, J. J. G. (2008). How to optimize learning from animated models: A review of guidelines based on cognitive load. *Review of Educational Research, 78*(3), 645–675. doi:10.3102/0034654308320320

Wouters, P., Van Nimwegen, C., Van Oostendorp, H., & Van Der Spek, E. D. (2013). A meta-analysis of the cognitive and motivational effects of serious games. *Journal of Educational Psychology, 105*(2), 249–265. doi:10.1037/a0031311

Wozney, L., Venkatesh, V., & Abrami, P. C. (2006). Implementing computer technologies: Teachers' perceptions and practices. *Journal of Technology and Teacher Education, 14*(1), 173.

Wu, M. L. (2015). *Teachers' experience, attitudes, self-efficacy and perceived barriers to the use of digital game-based learning: A survey study through the lens of a typology of educational digital games* [Michigan State University]. In ProQuest Dissertations and Theses. https://d.lib.msu.edu/etd/3754

Wu, K., & Huang, P. (2015). Treatment of an anonymous recipient: Solid-waste management simulation game. *Journal of Educational Computing Research, 52*(4), 568–600. doi:10.1177/0735633115585928

Wu, W. C. V., Wang, R. J., & Chen, N. S. (2015). Instructional design using an in-house built teaching assistant robot to enhance elementary school English-as-a-foreign-language learning. *Interactive Learning Environments, 23*(6), 696–714. doi:10.1080/10494820.2013.792844

Xia, Y., & LeTendre, G. (2021). Robots for future classrooms: A cross-cultural validation study of "negative attitudes toward robots scale" in the US context. *International Journal of Social Robotics, 13*(4), 703–714. doi:10.100712369-020-00669-2

Xinogalos, S., & Tryfou, M. M. (2021). Using Greenfoot as a Tool for Serious Games Programming Education and Development. *International Journal of Serious Games, 8*(2), 67–86. doi:10.17083/ijsg.v8i2.425

Xiong, C., Ye, B., Mihailidis, A., Cameron, J. I., Astell, A., Nalder, E., & Colantonio, A. (2020). Sex and gender differences in technology needs and preferences among informal caregivers of persons with dementia. *BMC Geriatrics, 20*(1), 176. https://www.jstor.org/stable/pdf/44430486.pdf?refreqid=excelsior%3a6a06f288b510b457d0a9c16f60991e8d

Xu, F., Buhalis, D., & Weber, J. (2017). Serious games and the gamification of tourism. In *Tourism Management* (Vol. 60, pp. 244–256). 10.1016/j.tourman.2016.11.020

Yang, J. C., Chien, K. H., & Liu, T. C. (2012). A digital game-based learning system for energy education: An energy Conservation PET. *The Turkish Online Journal of Educational Technology, 11*(2), 27–37.

Yang, J. C., & Quadir, B. (2018). Effects of prior knowledge on learning performance and anxiety in an English learning online role-playing game. *Journal of Educational Technology & Society, 21*(3), 174–185.

Yang, Y. H., Xu, W., Zhang, H., Zhang, J. P., & Xu, M. L. (2014). The application of KINECT motion sensing technology in game-oriented study. *International Journal of Emerging Technologies in Learning, 9*(2), 59–63.

Yang, Y.-T. C. (2012). Building virtual cities, inspiring intelligent citizens: Digital games for developing students' problem solving and learning motivation. *Computers & Education, 59*(2), 365–377. doi:10.1016/j.compedu.2012.01.012

Yannakakis, G. N., & Togelius, J. (2018). Artificial intelligence and games. Artificial Intelligence and Games. doi:10.1007/978-3-319-63519-4

Yasin, A. I., Prima, E. C., & Sholihin, H. (2018). Learning Electricity Using Arduino-Android Based Game to Improve STEM Literacy. *Journal of science Learning, 1*(3), 77-94.

Yee, N., Ducheneaut, N., Shiao, H. T., & Nelson, L. (2012). Through the azerothian looking glass: Mapping in-game preferences to real-world demographics. *Proceedings of the SIGCHI Conference on Human Factors in Computing Systems,* 2811-2814. 10.1145/2207676.2208683

Yeşilbağ, S., Korkmaz, Ö., & Çakir, R. (2020). The effect of educational computer games on students' academic achievements and attitudes towards English lesson. *Education and Information Technologies, 25*(2), 1–18. doi:10.100710639-020-10216-1 PMID:32837235

Yeşilyurt, M., Özdemir Balakoğlu, M., & Erol, M. (2020). The impact of environmental education activities on primary school students' environmental awareness and visual expressions. *Qualitative Research in Education, 9*(2), 188–216. doi:10.17583/qre.2020.5115

Yien, J., Hung, C., Hwang, G., & Lin, Y. (2011). A game-based learning approach to improving students' learning achievements in a nutrition course. *The Turkish Online Journal of Educational Technology, 10*(2).

Yi, L., Zhou, Q., Xiao, T., Qing, G., & Mayer, I. (2020). Conscientiousness in Game-Based Learning. *Simulation & Gaming, 51*(5), 712–734. doi:10.1177/1046878120927061

Yıldırım, İ., & Şen, S. (2019). The effects of gamification on students' academic achievement: A meta-analysis study. *Interactive Learning Environments,* 1–18. doi:10.1080/10494820.2019.1636089

Yin, R. (1989). *Case study research, design and methods.* Sage.

Yip, F. W. M., & Kwan, A. C. M. (2006). Online vocabulary games as a tool for teaching and learning English vocabulary. *Educational Media International, 43*(3), 233–249. doi:10.1080/09523980600641445

Yolcu, Ö. (2020). *Yeni medya.* İstanbul Üniversitesi AUZEF. http://auzefkitap.istanbul.edu.tr/kitap/medyaveiletisim_ue/yenimedya.pdf

Youngkyun, B., & Nicola, W. (2013). *Cases on Digital Game Based Learning: Methods, Models & Strategies.* IGI Global.

Young, M. (2014). What is a curriculum and what can it do? *Curriculum Journal, 25*(1), 7–13. doi:10.1080/09585176.2014.902526 PMID:6909418

Young, M. (2017). Quality of literature review and discussion of findings in selected papers on integration of ICT in teaching, role of mentors, and teaching science through science, technology, engineering, and mathematics (STEM). *Educational Research Review, 12*(4), 189–201. doi:10.5897/ERR2016.3088

Young, M. F., Slota, S., Cutter, A. B., Jalette, G., Mullin, G., Lai, B., & Yukhymenko, M. (2012). Our princess is in another castle: A review of trends in serious gaming for education. *Review of Educational Research, 82*(1), 61–89. doi:10.3102/0034654312436980

Young, S. S. C., & Wang, Y. H. (2014). The game embedded CALL system to facilitate English vocabulary acquisition and pronunciation. *Journal of Educational Technology & Society, 17*(3), 239–251.

Youniss, Bales, S., Christmas-Best, V., Diversi, M., McLaughlin, M., & Silbereisen, R. (2002). Youth Civic Engagement in the Twenty-First Century. *Journal of Research on Adolescence, 12*(1), 121–148. doi:10.1111/1532-7795.00027

You, Y. (2020). Learning experience: An alternative understanding inspired by thinking through Confucius. *ECNU Review of Education, 3*(1), 66–87. doi:10.1177/2096531120904247

Yu, S. & Wang, Q. (2019). Analysis of Collaborative Path Development of "AI+Teachers." *e-EducationResearch,* (4), 14-29.

Yu, S. (2018). The future role of AI teachers. *Open Education Research, 24*(1), 6-28.

Yuen, A. H. K., & Ma, W. W. K. (2008). Exploring teacher acceptance of e-learning technology. *Asia-Pacific Journal of Teacher Education, 36*(3), 229–243. doi:10.1080/13598660802232779

Yukselturk, E., Altıok, S., & Başer, Z. (2018). Using game-based learning with kinect technology in foreign language education course. *Journal of Educational Technology & Society, 21*(3), 159–173.

Yun, S., Shin, J., Kim, D., Kim, C. G., Kim, M., & Choi, M. T. (2011, November). Engkey: Tele-education robot. In *International Conference on Social Robotics* (pp. 142-152). Springer. 10.1007/978-3-642-25504-5_15

Yunus, M., & Shahana, S. (2018). New evidence on outcomes of primary education stipend programme in Bangladesh. *Bangladesh Development Studies, 41*(4), 29–55. https://www.jstor.org/stable/27031081

Yuratich, D. (2020). Ratio! A game of judgment: Using game-based learning to teach legal reasoning. *The Law Teacher,* 1–14.

Yusof, M. (2011). *The Dynamics of Student Participation in Classroom: Observation on level and forms of participation.* Paper presented at Learning and Teaching Congress of UKM, Penang, Malaysia.

Zagalo, N. (2013). *Videojogos em Portugal: História, Tecnologia e Arte.* FCA Editora.

Zakharov, A., Tsheko, G., & Carnoy, M. (2016). Do "better" teachers and classroom resources improve student achievement? A causal comparative approach in Kenya, South Africa, and Swaziland. *International Journal of Educational Development, 50,* 108–124. doi:10.1016/j.ijedudev.2016.07.001

Zakharov, W., & Maybee, C. (2019). Bridging the gap: Information literacy and learning in online undergraduate courses. *Journal of Library & Information Services in Distance Learning, 13*(1-2), 215–225. doi:10.1080/1533290X.2018.1499256

Zampa, M. P., & Felipe Mendes, L. C. (2016). Gamificação: uma proposta para redução da evasão e reprovação em disciplinas finais da graduação. *Caderno de estudos em sistemas de informação, 3*(2).

Zapata-Rivera, D., & Bauer, M. (2012). Exploring the Role of Games in Educational Assessment. In M. C. Mayrath, J. Clarke-Midura, D. H. Robinson, & G. Schraw (Eds.), *Technology-Based Assessments for Twenty-First-Century Skills: Theoretical and Practical Implications from Modern Research* (pp. 147–169). Information Age Publishing.

Zawilski, B. (2020, August 31). *Rhetoric and Situations; Like Peanut Butter and Jelly.* Medium. https://medium.com/@bzawilski/rhetoric-and-situations-like-peanut-butter-and-jelly-ddb0d64e8b6c

Zhang, Y. (2020). *Teach machine learning with Excel.* Paper presented at the 2020 ASEE Virtual Annual Conference Content Access. 10.18260/1-2--35268

Zhang, L. F., Biggs, J., & Watkins, D. (Eds.). (2010). *Learning and development of Asian students: what the 21st Century teacher needs to think about.* Pearson.

Zheng, Y. (2019). 3D Course Teaching Based on Educational Game Development Theory-Case Study of Game Design Course. *International Journal of Emerging Technologies in Learning, 14*(2), 54. doi:10.3991/ijet.v14i02.9985

Zhonggen, Y. (2019). A meta-analysis of use of serious games in education over a decade. *International Journal of Computer Games Technology, 17*, 1–8. doi:10.1155/2019/4797032

Zhu, W., Ma, A. (2019). The application status and development path analysis of domestic AI education. *Primary and Middle School Educational Technology, 8*, 99-102.

Ziadat, A. H. (2010). Major factors contributing to environmental awareness among people in a third world country/Jordan. *Environment, Development and Sustainability, 12*(1), 135–145. doi:10.100710668-009-9185-4

Zichermann, G. (2011). *Gamification by design: Implementing game mechanics in web and mobile apps.* O'Reilly Media.

Ziegler, N. (2016). Taking technology to task: Technology-mediated TBLT, performance, and production. *Annual Review of Applied Linguistics, 36*(1), 136–163. doi:10.1017/S0267190516000039

Zingaro, D. (2021). *Learn to code by solving problems: A Python programming primer.* No Starch Press.

Zinnbauer, B. J., Pargament, K. I., Cole, B., Rye, M. S., Butter, E. M., Belavich, T. G., Hipp, K. M., Scott, A. B., & Kadar, J. L. (1997). Religion and spirituality: Unfuzzying the fuzzy. *Journal for the Scientific Study of Religion, 36*(4), 549–564. doi:10.2307/1387689

Živkovi, Ł. (2016). A model of critical thinking as an important attribute for success in the 21st century. *Procedia: Social and Behavioral Sciences, 232*, 102–108. doi:10.1016/j.sbspro.2016.10.034

Zolyomi, A., & Schmalz, M. (2017). Mining for Social Skills: Minecraft in Home and Therapy for Neurodiverse Youth. *Proceedings of the 50th Hawaii International Conference on System Sciences.* 10.24251/HICSS.2017.411

Zubković, B. R., Pahljina-Reinić, R., & Kolić-Vehovec, S. (2017). Predictors of ICT Use in Teaching in Different Educational Domains. *European Journal of Social Sciences Education and Research, 11*(2), 145. doi:10.26417/ejser.v11i2.p145-154

Zupic, I., & Čater, T. (2015). Bibliometric methods in management and organization. *Organizational Research Methods, 18*(3), 429–472. doi:10.1177/1094428114562629

Zusho, A., Anthony, J. S., Hashimoto, N., & Robertson, G. (2014). Do video games provide motivation to learn? In ILearning by playing: Video gaming in education (pp. 69-86). Oxford, UK: Oxford University Press. doi:10.1093/acprof:osobl/9780199896646.003.0006

Zuze, T. L., & Reddy, V. (2014). School resources and the gender reading literacy gap in South African schools. *International Journal of Educational Development, 36*, 100–107. doi:10.1016/j.ijedudev.2013.10.002

About the Contributors

Carol-Ann Lane has a Ph.D. from the University of Western Ontario, in curriculum and applied linguistics, with a cross-disciplinary focus on science & innovation, multiliteracies, gender, and behavioral sciences. She has conducted Canadian studies about biotechnology among teacher candidates. Her master thesis examined impacts of distance learning on cognition and behaviors in higher education. Carol-Ann has taught elementary and secondary divisions for over 7 years and more than 4 years in university settings at the post-graduate level. She is the editor of an international Handbook of Research (two volumes), to be published in early 2022, she is co-authoring articles, she has published three chapters in 2019-20 (sole author) in global university research handbooks, and 13 sole-authored peer-reviewed journal articles. She is currently working on a series of creative nonfiction books. In the past years at UWO and UofT, Carol-Ann's faculty roles included research collaboration with various faculty members on matters such as instructional strategies, improving hybrid learner experiences, especially during the pandemic, addressing long-range program planning for teacher, master level and Phd level candidates. Furthermore, as a committee member, Carol-Ann collaborated on projects, such as program planning, and implementing an online course program for the Professional Education Doctorate degree; Carol-Ann has continued to work over a decade as a research committee member such as Online Teaching and Learning Group by collaborating and improving online pedagogy for higher education.

* * *

Yogendran Abrose is a post graduate student at Universiti Sains Malaysia. He is assisting the current project related with Minecraft-Game Based Learning.

Pedro B. Água is a Professor of General Management at the Portuguese Naval Academy. He has authored several articles and book chapters, while continuing his research in the field of cutting-edge technology, industrialization, innovation and business policy. Professor Água has over twenty-five years of experience across high technology endeavours, from defence to telecommunications and oil and gas industry, combining his extensive professional and business background with teaching. Professor Água holds an MBA from IESE Business School and a Ph.D. in Management and Engineering awarded by the University of Lisbon.

Nur Jahan Ahmad is a senior lecturer at the School of Educational Studies, Universiti Sains Malaysia (USM), Penang. Malaysia. She holds a B.Sc. in Biological Sciences (Hons) from the University of Pittsburgh, a Diploma in Education from the Universiti Sains Malaysia (USM), an M.Sc. in Chemistry from the Universiti Kebangsaan Malaysia (UKM), and a PhD. in Chemistry Education from the

University of Leeds. She was with the Southeast Asian Ministers of Education Organization Regional Centre for Education in Science and Mathematics (SEAMEO RECSAM) in the department of Research and Development. She also had experience working as a teacher in a secondary school and as a lecturer in Penang Teacher Education Institute. In addition, she had experience in training teachers from Southeast Asia, Asia Pacific, Africa, and Maldives. She has coordinated many workshops, capacity-building programs, Professional Learning Community (PLC) programs, and lesson study activities with the in-service teachers. She is an experienced researcher and involved in research related to chemistry education, science education, STEM Education, and curriculum development. She is the external board advisor for publication, editor, writer, and reviewer; and has published articles and books in science, chemistry, and STEM Education.

Atm S. Alam is currently an Assistant Professor at the School of Electronic Engineering and Computer Science, Queen Mary University of London, UK since 2019. He received his BSc (Hon's) degree with First Class in Information and Communication Engineering from the University of Rajshahi, Bangladesh, the M.Sc. degree with Distinction in Telecommunications and Computer Networks Engineering from the London South Bank University, UK, and the Ph.D. degree in Wireless Communications from The Open University, Milton Keynes, UK. Before joining at the Queen Mary University of London, he worked on several European and UK funded projects as a Research Fellow for the 5G Innovation Centre (5GIC), University of Surrey, UK, and University of Bradford, UK. His research interests include the areas of intelligent wireless communications and networks (5G/6G) and, the emerging applications of machine learning in wireless communications for verticals such as smart grids, intelligent transport systems, smart cities/homes, and industrial automation. Dr. Alam is also interested in technology-driven teaching and learning, and he is currently a Fellow of Higher Education Academy (FHEA).

Md Jahangir Alam is an Assistant Professor in the Department of Japanese Studies at University of Dhaka in Bangladesh. His research interest covers a broad spectrum of development discourses, focusing on the Political Economy of Education, International Education Cooperation, Global Cooperation Studies, and Japan-Bangladesh Relations. His experiences embrace collaborating with international and national organizations, especially International Labor Organization (ILO), International Organization for Migration (IOM), United Nations Development Programme (UNDP), The Japan Foundation (JF), and Bangladesh Consulting Services. He has received several international awards and scholarship from academic associations and government organizations, including the Comparative and International Education Society (CIES) and the Japanese Ministry of Education (MEXT), for his outstanding academic and research contributions to international education development. He has over 13 academic publications, including book chapters and journal articles. He holds his Ph.D. in Education Policy with focus on International Education Development from the Graduate School of International Cooperation Studies, Kobe University, Japan.

Daisy Alexander has completed her B.Sc.; LL.B.; LL.M. and PhD from University of Mumbai (formerly University of Bombay) India. She was also part 48th Graduate School of Ecumenical Studies at Bossey, Geneva affiliated to University of Switzerland in Religious Pluralism & Conflict Resolution on a full scholarship. Her Ph.D. was on Surrogacy seeking regulations for the same. She has 27 years of academic experience. She has been active in gender related issues. Her expertise is in Legal Language and Commercial laws.

Menşure Alkış Küçükaydın, PhD, is an Associate Professor of Basic Education at Necmettin Erbakan University in Konya, Turkey. She received her undergraduate degree in Department of Primary Teacher Education from Gazi University, Faculty of Education in 2006. She received her Ph.D degrees in Department of Primary Teacher Education from Gazi University in 2017. Dr. Alkış Küçükaydın's scholarly work focuses on pedagogical content knowledge, the roles of educational technology in learners' scientific practices, use of technology in education, science and technology education in primary and science misconceptions. Alkış Küçükaydın has 3 books that are edited by her at national level. In addition, she has a book, book chapters, articles, papers and projects related to her study field.

Puteri Sofia Amirnuddin is a Senior Law Lecturer, Programme Director and Chief Project Officer for Centre of Industrial Revolution and Innovation (CIRI) at Taylor's University. Puteri Sofia Amirnuddin is a recipient of various awards and accolades for her teaching innovations in teaching law using AR, NLP, and Gamification.

Marlene Amorim is an Assistant professor at the Department of Economics Management and Industrial Engineering at the University of Aveiro and collaborates as an invited professor at the Catholic University in Porto in the field of Service Operations Management. She received her PhD degree in Management from IESE Business School of University of Navarra in Spain. Marlene serves on the editorial board of three international journals and publishes in leading journals in services operations management. She conducts research in the area of Service Operations and Quality, notably in topics related to service process design and customer participation in service delivery.

Daniela Andreini (PhD) is Associate Professor of Marketing and Management at the Department of Management of the University of Bergamo. Daniela's research focuses mainly on B2B and B2C marketing, branding, and consumer behavior. Her articles have appeared in highly ranked journals such as Organization Studies, Journal of Advertising, Family Business Review, Journal of Business Research, Industrial Marketing Management, Journal of Business Ethics, and Journal of Business & Industrial Marketing, Management Decision, Journal of Product & Brand Management, and other academic outlets. Daniela serves in the Editorial Board of several journals including the Journal of Product & Brand Management and Journal of Business Research. She also serves as a reviewer for several highly-ranked international journals.

Md. Ashrafuzzaman is an Assistant Professor in the Department of Education at Bangabandhu Sheikh Mujibur Rahman Digital University, Bangladesh (BDU). He has been working for about eleven years in the field of teaching and educational research with different organizations. In 2014, he received an MPhil degree in English Language Education from the Institute of Education and Research (IER), University of Dhaka (DU). He has also completed his BEd (Hons.) and MEd from IER, DU. He has published research articles in national and international journals. He has researched significant areas such as teachers' training programs, underprivileged children's education (sex workers, transgender, and slum children), English language education, classroom practice, teaching methods and techniques, assessment and feedback practice, and ICT in education.

Farhan Azim currently works across projects nationally and internationally developing psychometrically sound assessments. His research interests include development of novel assessment instruments, online assessments, measurement theory, teachers' capacity building, and better use of student data for teaching. Farhan has previously worked in areas of assessment including assessment of Mathematical problem solving, teachers' assessment literacy, assessment in STEM, etc. He has also worked in research, monitoring and evaluation of large-scale education projects and taught assessment and research related courses at tertiary institutes in the past. His works have been disseminated through refereed journals, book chapters and international academic conferences.

Smitha Baboo is working as an Assistant Professor in the Department of Psychology, CHRIST University, Bangalore, India. Her expertise area is in School/Educational Psychology, Abuse and Victim Studies, Child, Women and Adolescent Psychology. She has completed her two PhD in the field of Education and Psychology. She has completed 15 scientific manuscripts in the reputed national and international peer-reviewed journals, edited 3 books, 9 book chapters and 3 newspaper articles and has been invited as a guest speaker in the seminars and conferences.

Georgios Bampasidis is a postdoctoral researcher at the Pedagogical Department of Primary Education of the National & Kapodistrian University of Athens (NKUA), working on methodologies that aim to import Astronomy and Remote Sensing in Education. He is also a principal member of the scientific team of the Department's Astronomy and Remote Sensing Club. He taught Astronomy and Remote Sensing at the Master's degree courses of Didactics and Public Understanding of Science and Digital Technology of NKUA, Physics Lab with microsensors at STEM specialization courses of postgraduate students at NKUA and Physics lab and Astrophysics lab to undergraduate students of NKUA. He received his PhD in 2012 in Astrophysics from Paris Observatory in conjunction with the National & Kapodistrian University of Athens working extensively with data from the Cassini-Huygens NASA/ESA joint space mission and he still contributes to Planetary Science.

Meltem Huri Baturay received her Bachelor's and Master's degrees in English Language Teaching from Gazi University. She completed her PhD in the field of Computer Education and Instructional Technology at Middle East Technical University. She published many articles in highly reputable international and SSCI indexed journals and worked as a researcher at an action in COST (European Cooperation in Science and Technology) which was supported by the EU Framework Programme Horizon 2020. She also participated in TUBITAK (The Scientific and Technological Research Council of Turkey) and Erasmus+ KA2 projects as a researcher. She studies technology-assisted language teaching, use of Augmented and Virtual Reality at Education, Distance Education, and Design of Multimedia Enriched Teaching Materials. Currently, she is working as a faculty member and the director of the Center for Teaching and Learning at Atılım University.

Geraldine Bengsch is a postdoctoral researcher at the School of Education, Communication and Society King's College London. Her research interests include interpersonal and intercultural interaction. She works with various research methods and enjoys teaching new methods to students. She has received training as a full stack software engineer and aims to incorporate her knowledge into her research and teaching.

Annesha Biswas is a Junior Research Fellow and a Ph.D. Candidate at the Department of Economics, Christ (Deemed to be University), Bengaluru, India. Her research area centers around Entrepreneurship, Gender Economics, and Rural Development. Her current research focuses upon the study of Entrepreneurship culture among Tribal women and discusses the issues and barriers of women's venture into entrepreneurship.

Pavlo Brin was born in 1976 in Kharkiv, Ukraine; in 1998 graduated from NTU "KhPI" (Master degree in Management, Magna cum laude); in 2003 presented PhD thesis; from 2005 Associate professor; from 2019 Professor of Management and Taxation Department. Prepared and published more than 150 research and methodical papers, textbooks, manuals for students and monographs in Economics and Management.

Kristina Buttrey has taught in K-12 education for 18 years and post- graduate education for 6. Her areas of expertise include literacy, Dyslexia, assessment, differentiation, classroom management, and Middle School Education. Dr. Buttrey is an assistant professor at Murray State University in Murray, Kentucky.

Anshita Chelawat received her Master Degree in the field of Human Resources in the year 2010 and since then she is consistently serving the educational community by teaching subjects related to general management and human resources. She has nearly 7 years of teaching experience along with 2 years of additional experience as a content writer. To move up in her professional career, she has qualified UGC NET (National Eligibility Test) 2013, NTA NET- 2019 and SET (Maharashtra). Currently, she is pursuing her Ph.D under SNDT women's university. She writes and presents widely in the field of educational technology, e-learning, Learner motivation, etc.

Karthigai Prakasam Chellaswamy has 20 years of teaching experience for UG and PG degree students. He holds a master degree in commerce from PSG College of Arts and Commerce an autonomous college affiliated with Bharathiar University, Coimbatore, M.Phil from Madurai Kamaraj University and PhD from Bharathidasan University Apart from these he has also completed MBA from Periyar University and also an MHRM from Pondicherry University. He has participated and presented in many National and International conferences, attended various workshops, FDP's and MDP's and also chaired sessions in International & National level conferences. He has published in various national and international journals. He has received the faculty excellence award for the academic year 2009 at New Horizon College, Bangalore. As of date, he has completed 2 Major Research Projects. Currently, he is working as an Associate Professor of Commerce & Coordinator for MCOM at the Central Campus, Christ (Deemed to be University), Bangalore.

Cafer Ahmet Çinar got his Bachelor's from the Department of Computer Education and Instructional Technology, Faculty of Education at Canakkale Onsekiz Mart University. At the moment, he is doing his Masters at the same department. He is an expert on Augmented Reality and doing research studies on the use of Augmented and Virtual Reality in Education.

Anacleto Correia (M) is an Associate Professor and lecturer of Management and Information Systems subjects at the Portuguese Navy Academy. He holds a Ph.D. in Computer Science, an M.Sc. in Statistics and Information Management, a B.Sc. degree in Management, and also a B.Sc. at Portuguese Naval Academy. His research interests are focused on requirements engineering, software engineering, process modeling, data mining, machine learning, and business engineering. He has also more than 20 years of experience in industry-leading projects and architecting large software development projects and is the author of dozens of scientific papers in journals and conference proceedings.

Barbara Culatta is Professor Emerita of Communication Disorders at Brigham Young University. She received her PhD from the University of Pittsburgh and completed a postdoctoral fellowship at Johns Hopkins University. She has written books, articles, and chapters on language and literacy interventions. She received federal grants to conduct language and literacy intervention programs and was the creator of the Systematic and Engaging Early Literacy project.

Tinanjali Dam is a PhD Candidate, Department of Economics, CHRIST (Deemed to be University). Studied Integrated Master's in Economics, Hyderabad Central University.

Ankit Dhamija is an accomplished academician and academic administrator with an experience of more than 13 years. Currently working at Amity Business School, Amity University Haryana, he has a demonstrated history of performing and delivering quality content to students in the capacity of Assistant Professor in the higher education industry. He has contributed in the Institution building through teaching, research and publications, accreditation and ranking, coordinating the examination, curriculum design & development and student mentoring. He has also published research papers in leading indexed journals and presented papers at several International/National Conferences. Also, he has published e-books and book chapters with leading publishers. With strong education professional with Doctorate in Information Technology, Double Masters in Computer Applications (MCA) and Information Technology (M.Tech(IT)) and Bachelors in Commerce, Dr Dhamija is skilled in areas like Academic Research Paper Writing, Database Management Systems, Management Information System, Web Design & Development and Microsoft Office, Python Programming, System Analysis and Design, Computer Networks. He is a master in adopting innovative teaching pedagogy for engaging students in classrooms and getting the best out of them.

Deepika Dhamija is an academician with more than10 years of experience as Assistant Professor in Information Technology domain. She has published more than 20 research papers and book chapters in reputed journal and also presented papers in national/International Conferences. Having Scopus indexed book chapters with leading publishers and also published an e-book. Attended various FDP's, workshops and seminars with highly reputed organizations and Researchers. She is comfortable with blended-teaching learning. Won Best paper award, Young Scientist Award, Woman Researcher Award in different conferences and seminars. She is skilled in teaching the Under Graduate and Post graduate students with the subject-Ecommerce, Database Management System, Computers in Management, Computer Applications in business, Management Information System.

Joaquim Dias Soeiro is currently appointed as Head of School of the School of Hospitality, Tourism and Events at Taylor's University in Malaysia and also a member of the Centre for Research and Innovation in Tourism (CRiT), Taylor's University. He has lived in Malaysia and worked in education for more than a decade and developed his expertise in outcome-based education and experiential learning. He has built his career in Malaysia by benefiting from his education in France and adapting his profile from a multicultural aspect. His current research area focuses on capability development, learning experience and how learning is being constructed while taking into consideration social and cultural involvements.

Hacer Dolanbay is an Assistant Prof. at the Faculty of Education. Her specialization is media and digital literacy, implementation of new approaches in education, and media literacy education at different levels.

Burcu Durmaz is a faculty member at Süleyman Demirel University, Faculty of Education, Department of Mathematics and Science Education. She received her master's and doctorate degrees in mathematics education from Eskişehir Osmangazi University and Uludağ University, respectively. She worked on gifted students' mathematics education in her PhD thesis and post-doctoral research project as a visiting scholar at St. John's University in NY. The author's areas of interest include gifted students' mathematics education, problem solving skills, children's literature and mathematics integration.

Gonca Yangın Ekşi is a Professor in English Language Teaching (ELT) in the Department of Foreign Language Education, Gazi University where she teaches several undergraduate and graduate courses and supervises MA and PhD dissertations. The courses she has offered include Teaching English to Young Learners, Practice Teaching, ICT and CALL, Curriculum development and Materials Evaluation, Language learning theories, and Psychology of the language learner. She received her MA in ELT in Hacettepe University, Department of ELT and she holds her PhD in ELT in Gazi University. She has worked in a number of projects including the national project for the development of the national English curriculum for Primary and Secondary schools. She has managed an Erasmus KA2 Project with distinguished universities in Turkey and abroad. She has published various research articles nationally and internationally focusing on with teaching and learning English as a foreign language. Her research interests include computer-assisted language learning, pre- and inservice teacher education, curriculum and materials development, teaching skills and language components, young learners, use of corpus in language teaching. She has also been working as an editor to ELT Research Journal.

Marta Ferreira Dias has a PhD in Economics from the University of Warwick, UK, a MSc in Economics from the University of Coimbra and a degree in Economics from the University of Coimbra. She is an Assistant Professor in the University of Aveiro, at the Department of Economics, Management, Industrial Engineering and Tourism. She lectures under graduated and graduated courses of Microeconomics, European Economics, Microeconomic Analysis, International Economics and others, Energy Economics and Energy Policy and regulation. Presently, she is a member of the research unit on Competitiveness, Governance and Public Policies (GOVCOPP). She is a member of research teams of the University of Aveiro participating in several European sponsored projects in the fields of Social Economy and Competences for graduates.

Nagarjuna G. is an Assistant Professor in the Department of Tourism Management, School of Business and Management, Bannerghatta Campus, Christ (Deemed to be University). Before starting his academic career, he worked in Holiday Bliss as an executive in tour operations. Later, he joined Christ University as a Research Assistant for the Major Research Project on "An Evaluation of Eco and Sustainable Tourism Practices of Selected Resorts in Karnataka". He holds a doctoral degree in the sustainable tourism practices of Karnataka. He started his full-Time academic career by joining the Department of Tourism Studies in Indian Academy Degree College, later served as an assistant professor at Mount Carmel College, Bangalore. He has presented research and conceptual papers in seminars and conferences at national and international level. He has published articles in acclaimed journals and also participated in research workshops. He was one of the Organizing committee members for a one-day national seminar on 'Tourism and Community Development'. Apart from his research and academic interest, he is also interested in theatrical performance. He is part of the Thaksh Theatrics play group.

Apostolia (Lia) Galani is an Associate Professor at the Department of Primary Education of the National and Kapodistrian University of Athens, Greece, teaching human and physical geography, as well as the educational use of IT in school geography. Her research interests focus on a) the design of teaching-learning sequences in several areas of science and especially in Remote Sensing and astronomy; b) the use of informal sources in science education; c) the teaching of Socio-Scientific Issues concerning climate change; and d) Cultural Geography in education (i.e. difficult past, the notion of the Other). She has participated in a number of EU and national projects and she has authored or co-authored many articles or chapters in Greek and International Journals or books including the Greek Gymnasium geography textbooks.

María García-Molina holds a Degree in Teaching Primary Education, specialization in Teaching English as a Foreign Language and Bilingual Education, by the University of Córdoba (Spain). She was awarded with a research initiation grant (Beca de colaboración destinada a estudiantes universitarios para realizar tareas de investigación en departamentos universitarios) by the Spanish Ministry of Education. Currently, she works as a language assistant in Dortmund (Germany) thanks to a scholarship (Beca de Auxiliar de Conversación) by the Spanish Ministry of Education.

Leila Goosen is a full professor in the Department of Science and Technology Education of the University of South Africa. Prof. Goosen was an Associate Professor in the School of Computing, and the module leader and head designer of the fully online signature module for the College for Science, Engineering and Technology, rolled out to over 92,000 registered students since the first semester of 2013. She also supervises ten Masters and Doctoral students, and has successfully completed supervision of 43 students at postgraduate level. Previously, she was a Deputy Director at the South African national Department of Education. In this capacity, she was required to develop ICT strategies for implementation. She also promoted, coordinated, managed, monitored and evaluated ICT policies and strategies, and drove the research agenda in this area. Before that, she had been a lecturer of Information Technology (IT) in the Department for Science, Mathematics and Technology Education in the Faculty of Education of the University of Pretoria. Her research interests have included cooperative work in IT, effective teaching and learning of programming and teacher professional development.

Patrícia Gouveia is Associate Professor at Lisbon University Fine Arts Faculty [Faculdade de Belas-Artes da Universidade de Lisboa]. Integrated member of ITI – Interactive Technologies Institute/LARSyS, Laboratory for Robotics and Engineering Systems, IST. Co-curator of the Playmode exhibition (MAAT 2016-2019). Works in Multimedia Arts and Design since the nineties. Her research focus on playable media, interactive fiction and digital arts as a place of convergence between cinema, music, games, arts and design. Previously she was Associate Professor at the Interactive Media (Games and Animation) degree at Noroff University College (2014-16) in Kristiansand, Norway. Invited Assistant Professor at FCSH/UNL (2007-14) and Assistant Professor at ULHT (2008-13) both in Lisbon. From 2006 to 2014 Patrícia edited the blog Mouseland. In 2010 she published the book Digital Arts and Games, Aesthetic and Design of Ludic Experience [Artes e Jogos Digitais, Estética e Design da Experiência Lúdica] (ed. Universitárias Lusófonas), a synthesis of her doctoral thesis and some articles she published. More information here: https://fbaul.academia.edu/PatriciaGouveia/CurriculumVitae.

Emily Guetzoian works at the University of California, Los Angeles (UCLA) Anderson School of Management supporting MBA students with global field study projects. She enjoys working with students during their academic journey and providing individualized strategies to support each unique learner. Emily is a proud first-generation college graduate. She holds a BA in sociology and a BA in communication from California State University Channel Islands, an MS in counseling and guidance (college student personnel) from California Lutheran University, and an EdD in higher education leadership from Fresno State University. Her dissertation was a mixed-methods, multi-institutional study examining the academic success, feelings of belonging, and commitment to service of first-generation sorority members. Emily has experience in a variety of higher education areas at public and private institutions, including housing and residential life, summer conferencing, academic advising, field studies, international education, writing centers, tutoring services, student employment and development, clubs and organizations, and new student orientation. She enjoys staying actively involved in professional organizations, particularly in the learning center community, to continually discover new ideas and strategies to support students.

Kendra M. Hall-Kenyon is a professor and department chair in the Department of Teacher Education at Brigham Young University. Hall-Kenyon has spent the last twenty years studying or working in early education. She received her B.A. in Family Science from BYU, and her M.S. and Ph.D. from Columbia University, Teacher's College in Cognitive Studies. Dr. Hall-Kenyon's research focuses on early literacy instruction and assessment and early childhood teacher education.

Cristina A. Huertas-Abril is an Associate Professor in the Faculty of Education at the University of Córdoba (Spain). Her research interests include Computer-Assisted Language Learning (CALL), Bilingual Education, Teaching English as a Foreign Language (TEFL) and teacher training. She has participated in several national and international research projects, and published numerous scientific articles in prestigious journals. Dr Huertas-Abril teaches at Master's level at the UCO and UCA (Spain) and at the Ateneum-University in Gdansk (Poland), has taught both in formal and non-formal contents, and has directed and taught several specialization courses on Bilingual Education, Translation Studies, and Second Language Acquisition. She has presented many papers at different (inter)national conferences around the world like Spain, Germany, Poland, France, Turkey and Bahrein, among others. Moreover, she has had international academic stays in Chile and in the US. She is a member of the Research Group 'Research in Bilingual and Intercultural Education' (HUM-1006), and the co-founder of the Ibero-

American Research Network on Bilingual and Intercultural Education (IBIE). ORCID: https://orcid.org/0000-0002-9057-5224.

Nilofer Hussaini is an Assistant Professor in the Department of Professional Studies, Christ University, Bangalore. Her research interests mainly includes Socio-Economic and Political issues of Emerging Economies She obtained her PhD in Commerce & MBA from (Bihar), India in 2014 and 2004, respectively. She qualified National Eligibility Test for Lectureship in Management, India, in 2005. She has 7 years of teaching experience in commerce and management discipline and is an author of several research articles and a book. She has presented research papers at several International and National Conferences.

Fritz Ilongo is a Psychologist and Counsellor, Senior Lecturer in the University of Eswatini. He recently authored; 'Creative Education – DDV: SEE', Outskirts Press, USA; 'AfroSymbiocity as a Psychology of Conflict and Conflict Resolution in Africa', Cambridge Scholars Publishing, UK; 'Psychology of Religion, Violence, and Conflict Resolution.' Nova Science Publishers, USA; 'Workplace Bullying in African Tertiary Institutions.' Nova Science Publishers, USA.

Sheikh Rashid Bin Islam is a Researcher in Bangladesh Consulting Services, Dhaka, Bangladesh. His research interest lies in Education Policy Management, Curriculum Development, Inclusive and Special Education, Educating Children with Disabilities, and Japanese Education. He has worked on various education research projects, including gender equity, social inequality, social justice, and socio-economic research in Bangladesh. He is trained as an education specialist at the University of Dhaka, Bangladesh, and he has conducted his research with multiple international and national NGOs in Japan, Myanmar, and Bangladesh. He proactively participates in civil society activities and plays a courageous role in the unending struggle against human deprivation and social injustice. Further, he also contributes to youth-focused international and national organizations such as the United Nations Youth and Student Association Bangladesh (UNYSAB) to promote and empower youths for decent work and sustainable career development.

Sunitha Abhay Jain, Professor, School of Law, Christ University, Bengaluru, holds a Doctoral Degree in Law from NLSIU, Bengaluru. She is the coordinator for the LLM Program at School of Law, Christ University, Bengaluru. She holds an LL.B. and LL.M degree from Bangalore University and has specialized in Corporate and Commercial Laws and had secured Second Rank in the University for her BA LLB (Hons.) program. She also completed her Master of Human Rights from Pondicherry University and a Post Graduate Diploma in Cyber Laws from NALSAR, Hyderabad. She has been a full time faculty in law and has a teaching experience of over two decades. She has guided many PG., MPhil & Ph.D. research scholars. She has numerous publications to her credit in the form of book chapters and research articles in reputed Scopus indexed and UGC care listed journals. Has been invited as a resource person by various national and international institutions. She has chaired and presented papers at national and international seminars and conferences.

Sunil John is an Associate Professor at the School of Law Christ University. Dr. Sunil John holds a Bachelors and Masters degree in History from the Madras Christian College, M. Phil in Gender Studies from Hyderabad Central University. He was awarded the EKD Germany and Cadburys Foundations Scholarship to study Conflict Resolution and Peace Building from Woodbrooke Quaker College in

Birmingham, UK. He did his LL.B and LL.M in International Law from the University of Mumbai. He subsequently pursued his P.hD in the Philosophy of Law and Governance from the University of Mumbai. His thesis was on comparative Natural Law theories of Kautilya and Thomas Aquinas. Dr. Sunil John has also pursued Film studies from the Film and Television Institute of India, Pune. He has an experience of working with NGOs and has been teaching for the last 17 years.

Seena Kaithathara is an Assistant Professor, Dept. Statistics, Christ University, Bangalore, India.

Yogesh Kanna Sathyamoorthy is an Assistant Professor of Neurosciences in the Department of Psychology, Christ University. He is teaching biomedical courses to undergraduate and postgraduate students. He has completed his PhD in Neuroscience from University of Madras.

Janna Kellinger is an associate professor in the Curriculum and Instruction department at the University of Massachusetts Boston. She is the author of A Guide to Designing Curricular Games: How to "Game" the System as well as the book chapter, "Coding across the Curriculum." She most recently designed a course-based game for a Coding for Non-Coders class.

Goh Kok Ming is a global Minecraft mentor and Primary Educator in Under-Enrolled School, who loves to integrate Minecraft in teaching and learning. He is also the Winner of International Society for Technology in Education (ISTE) Awards for Games and Stimulations, and Blended and Online Learning Year 2021.

Joseph Varghese Kureethara is heading the Centre for Research at Christ University. He has over sixteen years of experience in teaching and research at CHRIST (Deemed to be University), Bengaluru and has published over 100 articles in the fields of Graph Theory, Number Theory, History, Religious Studies and Sports both in English and Malayalam. Kureethara has co-edited five books including Recent Trends in Signal and Image Processing, Neuro-Systemic Applications in Learning and Data Science and Security, and authored three books. His blog articles, comments, facts and poems have earned about 1.5 lakhs total pageviews. He has delivered invited talks in over thirty conferences and workshops. He is the Mathematics section editor of Mapana Journal of Sciences and member of the Editorial Board and a reviewer of several journals. He has worked as a member of the Board of Studies, Board of Examiners and Management Committee of several institutions. He has supervised 5 PhDs, 12 MPhils and supervising 8 PhDs.

Georgy P. Kurien is the Associate Dean at the School of Business and Management, Christ University, Bengaluru. He teaches MBA students Supply Chain Management and Sustainable Business Management. Before joining academia, Prof Georgy Kurien served in the Indian Army for two decades and retired as a Lieutenant Colonel. He held prestigious military appointments in Command, Instructional and Staff, both during operations and peacetime. Dr Kurien obtained his B.Tech in Mechanical Engineering from Kerala University, M. E. from the University of Pune, Ph D from the M S University of Baroda and PG in Business Management from XLRI Jamshedpur, India. Dr Kurien is also an alumnus and faculty member of the Haggai Institute International. His research interests and publications are in Supply Chain Performance Measurement, Sustainable Business Models and Terramechanics.

Richard Lambert is a Professor in the Department of Educational Leadership at the University of North Carolina at Charlotte, Director of the Center for Educational Measurement and Evaluation, and Editor of NHSA Dialog: A Research-to-Practice Journal for the Early Intervention Field. He earned his Ph.D. in Research, Measurement, and Statistics and Ed.S. in counseling psychology from Georgia State University. He has received over 20 million dollars in funding for research. He serves as the Principal Investigator for an award from the North Carolina Department of Public Instruction entitled "Evaluating the Implementation of a Formative Assessment System in North Carolina Kindergarten Classrooms" and an award from the North Carolina Department of Health and Human Services entitled "Coaching, Mentoring, Performance Evaluation, and Professional Development for BK Licensed Teachers in Non-public School Classrooms". His research interests include formative assessment for young children, applied statistics, and teacher stress and coping. He has served the College Board in the AP Statistics program for 20 years as a Reader, Table Leader, Question Leader, and Rubric Team Member.

Karen Le Rossignol is a Senior Lecturer in creative writing, editing, publishing and freelancing skills in the School of Communication and Creative Arts at Deakin University, Australia. She has extensive experience in developing industry-oriented curriculum and educational digital storyworlds, for which she has received university and national awards. Her work-integrated learning expertise is demonstrated through project-based approaches to editing/publishing and freelancing as applied research across narrative and digital storytelling.

Yixun (Annie) Li is currently an Assistant Professor in the Department of Early Childhood Education at The Education University of Hong Kong. She holds a Ph.D. in Human Development from the University of Maryland, College Park, a Master's degree in Developmental and Educational Psychology from Beijing Normal University, and a Bachelor's degree in Engineering from North China Electric Power University. Her research concentrates on language development and reading acquisition in monolingual and bilingual children and adults, as well as game-based interventions for first and second language learners.

Luciana Lima has a PhD in Psychology from the Faculty of Psychology and Educational Sciences of the University of Porto. Luciana Lima is currently doing post-doctoral studies at the Multimedia Department at the Faculty of Fine Arts of the University of Lisbon with a scholarship from ARDITI, ITI – Interactive Technologies Institute / LARSyS, Laboratory for Robotics and Engineering Systems, IST. She is an effective member of the Portuguese Psychologists Association and her current research interests focus on the intersection between gender, digital games, and gaming culture. Luciana Lima research focus the hegemony of games as interactive and artistic media and their social impacts, with an emphasis on gender equality.

Gaia Lombardi is an Italian Primary School Teacher with over 20 years of experience in teaching Mathematics, Science and English as a Second Language. Expert in CLIL in ages 6-12. Expert in Coding and Computational Thinking; EU Codweek Leading Teacher for Italy. Previous publications: 2006 "L'avventura di crescere insieme. Manuale teorico-pratico per l'asilo nido" (The adventure of growing together. Theorical-practical manual for nursery"), Juiior Edizioni 2020:The Role of Unplugged Coding Activity in Developing Computational Thinking in Ages 6-11" in Kalogiannis, M., & Papadakis, S., Handbook of research on Tools for Teaching Computational Thinking in P-12 Education, Information Science Publishing.

Hannah Luce is a second-year doctoral student in the Educational Research, Measurement, and Evaluation program at the University of North Carolina at Charlotte (UNCC). She received her Bachelor's Degree in Elementary Education from the University of Vermont (UVM) in 2017 and her Master's in Curriculum and Instruction (Literacy) from UVM in 2020. Since beginning her academic career, Hannah has been awarded the Elementary Education Award from the College of Education at UVM and the Herschel and Cornelia Everett Fellowship from the UNCC Graduate School. Hannah currently works for the Center for Educational Measurement and Evaluation at UNCC where she serves as a co-researcher on an implementation fidelity study. She is primarily interested in the following research areas: formative assessment, interrater reliability, and literacy assessment practices.

Marshall M. is an avid student of visual processing, reading and neuro-modulation. She participates in researching cutting-edge resources to improve the foundational skills needed to advance visual intelligence and plays an integral role in the development of these resources. Her intuition in designing functional models and resources to undergird the approaches proven to support student development with visual skills, vocabulary development, and neuromodulation is well respected. Marinda is passionate to help students reach the next level of skills and personal development.

Mara Madaleno has a Ph.D. in Economics from the University of Aveiro. She currently lectures Finance and Economics at the DEGEIT of UA and is the Director of the Master in Economics. She is also vice-Director of the Master in Data Science for Social Sciences. Highly experiment in publications of peer-reviewed and indexed articles, books, book chapters, and conference proceedings publications. Works in the areas of finance, financial markets, energy and environmental economics and works as a collaborator of research projects in the field of the current publication and in her research interest areas.

Jamie Mahoney is an Associate Professor in the Adolescent, Career, and Special Education Department at Murray State University. She teaches Special Education courses for dual certification Learning Behavior Disorder/ Elementary or Middle School undergraduate students and graduate students in the Alt. Cert, Master LBD, and Moderate Severe Disabilities programs. Dr. Mahoney has recently completed the Level 1 Dyslexia Orton Gillingham Certification through DTI. She currently serves on the KYCEC TED board as Past President. She has taught students with various disabilities in the areas of math, reading, and language arts for over 20 years in the elementary public school setting. She is certified in the areas of special education, general education, reading endorsed, assistive technology certified, and educational leadership certified. Her research interests include preparing preservice and inservice teachers to effectively teach students of all abilities using differentiated instruction methods, dyslexia, response to intervention and progress monitoring, increasing student engagement using technology, collaboration and co-teaching methods, and assessment methodologies.

Anand Manivannan works with the Department of Commerce, Christ University, Bangalore, India. He holds a Ph.D. in Commerce from SRM University (SRM Institute of Science and Technology) Chennai, Tamil Nadu. His area of focus is on mystery shopping and mystery shoppers' profession. His doctoral dissertation was on enhancing job satisfaction through motivation and Emotional Intelligence, a study concerning mystery shoppers. His other research focus is on Work-Life Balance, Gig-Economy, Consumer purchase behavior etc. He has presented his research article at AMA American Marketing Association Conference as an extended feather to his cap.

Rick Marlatt is an associate professor of language, literacy, and culture at New Mexico State University where he received the 2020 Digital Learning Initiatives Leading the Way Award. Rick earned his Ph.D. in Educational Studies from the University of Nebraska-Lincoln and his MFA in Creative Writing from the University of California, Riverside. His work in English language arts bridges the fields of teacher education, digital literacies, literature study, and sociocultural theory. His most recent work appears in English Journal, Journal of Education, Action in Teacher Education, and Journal of Adolescent & Adult Literacy. His co-edited book, Esports Research and its Integration in Education, was published in 2021.

Minda Marshall is an educationalist and researcher focussing on visual processing and cognitive development through the processes of reading. She has successfully developed and implemented such solutions for schools, universities, and various other organizations for more than 20 years. Minda serves on the board of the Destiny Group, oversees Mokopane Destiny Academy and is also a director of Lectorsa, a South African company. In addition, she is a co-founder of M3Line. Minda played an integral role in M3line and Lectorsa launching the Eyebraingym in February 2020. Lectorsa is partnering with various Tertiary Institutions, i.e. Stellenbosch University, University Pretoria, University of the Free State, University of Namibia, and public and private schools to assist students in developing their visual processing reading cognitive skills. The Eyebraingym solution results from more than 100,000 case studies and hours of research compiled into a simplistic user friendly, gauged online visual processing, reading and comprehension development system. Her qualifications include a BA degree, various international leadership training programmes, and Occupational Directed Education and Training Practitioning Skills. In addition, she has authored and co-authored articles, academic articles and books. Minda is passionate about educating and empowering teachers, educators, parents and learners to discover their internal strengths to maximize their abilities. In addition, she trains leaders, educators, parents and students around the world.

Brian McKenzie is a gamer and Associate Professor at Maynooth University in Ireland. He has a PhD in history and research interests in critical literacy, gaming and game design, and innovative pedagogy. He has published historical and pedagogical research and contributed to several Dungeons & Dragons publications as a freelance writer for Goodman Games.

Cora-Lynn Munroe-Lynds is a recent graduate from the School of Information Management, with a Master of Information degree. While attending Dalhousie, she published a prize-winning journal article on the public's perceptions of the government during COVID-19. Her research interests include comprehensive literature searches such as scoping review and systematic reviews, content analyses, business intelligence, information literacy, and information ecosystems. For her master's thesis, she conducted a systematic mapping of information literacy in learning outcomes. Last year she joined a team that conducted a scoping review looking at the impact COVID-19 has had on undergraduate medical education. Cora has been and continues to be a guest speaker for the Information in Society course in the School of Information Management at Dalhousie University. She enjoys sharing her knowledge and speaks on information literacy and information ecosystems.

Shabarisha N. is currently working as Assistant Professor in the School of Business and Management, Christ University, for the last 6 years. He took his Master of Commerce degree in 2012 from Kuvempu University, Shimoga. He also obtained PGDHRM from the same University. He has cleared the UGC - National Eligibility Test for Lectureship twice in 2011 and 2012. He has 9 years of teaching experience. He has published a number of articles in the field of finance and accounting. He has also presented a number of research papers at both national and international conferences and seminars etc. He has delivered more than 30 invited talks in the area of Financial Derivatives, International Financial Reporting Standards, and Indian Accounting Standards. His areas of interest are in Empirical finance - asset pricing, volatility modeling, risk management, financial modelling, accounting standards, and cost management.

Larysa Nadolny is an Associate Professor in the School of Education and Human Computer Interaction at Iowa State University. Her research includes examining motivation and engagement in digital learning environments.

Iffat Naomee is a lecturer of Institute and Education and Research (IER), University of Dhaka. She has completed her graduation and post graduation from the same institute and has earned another post graduation degree from University of Worcester, UK. She has been working in the field of education for the past 6 years.

Cathlyn Niranjana Bennett completed her doctoral work in Neuropsychology from the National Institute of Mental Health and Neurosciences, India. Her research interests include Neuropsychological Assessments and Interventions including EEG Neurofeedback. She currently serves as Assistant Professor with the Department of Psychology, Christ University, India.

Ana Nobre, after living and studying in Paris, currently teaches at Universidade Aberta where she has taught since 1998, having previously been a Professor at the Sorbonne University, Paris. She completed a PhD in Didactologie des langues et des Cultures from the University Sorbonne Paris III. She is dedicated to the teaching of foreign languages in eLearning, to digital resources for learning in online environments and recently to the didactic eLearning and gamification in education. She was coordinator of the project "Teaching / learning languages online" and researcher of @ssess project of the Distance Education Laboratory and eLearning (FCT, 2010-2013) where she investigated the problem of digital alternative assessment of orality.

Vasco Nobre, after having worked since 1994 as Commissioner and Executive Director of the OIKOS Space, began his teaching activity at the Open University in October 2009 as a Tutor and in 2012 as a Guest Assistant Professor. He has a PhD in Arts & Media from the Université Sorbonne (Paris) in 2007. He has been a researcher on digital resources for learning in online contexts.

Keiichi Ogawa is a Professor/Department Chair in the Graduate School of International Cooperation Studies at Kobe University in Japan. He is also a Governing Board Member in the UNESCO International Institute for Educational Planning (IIEP). He has served in various graduate schools and international organizations, including Honorary Professor at Kyrgyz National University, Visiting Professor at Columbia University/the University of Dhaka, Affiliate Professor at the University of Hawaii at Manoa/ George Washington University, and Education Economist at the World Bank. His research interest lies in the economics of education, education finance, and education policy. He has worked on development assistance activities in over 30 countries and has authored or co-edited eight books and over 90 journal articles/book chapters. Many of them are issues related to educational development and cooperation in national and international settings. He holds his Ph.D. in Comparative International Education and Economics of Education from Columbia University.

Anand Patil is Associate Professor of Business Studies at the School of Business Studies and Social Sciences, CHRIST (Deemed to be University) Bangalore. He has M.Com and M.Phil to his credit in Commerce and Management. He obtained Ph.D. in Commerce from Shivaji University, Kolhapur, Maharashtra. Accounting and Taxation are his areas of expertise. He has 19 years of experience in teaching at the graduate and postgraduate levels. He has also presented papers at various national and international conferences and published articles in reputed journals. Dr. Anand also has a rich administrative and industry experience where he served as Academic Head for MBA at Magnus School of Business (MSB, ICFAI) Bangalore, Program Director for BBA at Alliance University, Bangalore and as an internal auditor for various educational institutions, banks and joint-stock companies.

Sharon Peck is a professor of literacy and play advocate. Sharon believes in authentic and meaningful instruction for all. Sharon studies play, game-based pedagogy, multimodal language arts, and place and community-based literacy instruction.

Giuseppe Pedeliento (PhD) is Associate Professor of Marketing at the Department of Management of the University of Bergamo. Former visiting lecturer at the Aalto School of Business (Helsinki, Finland), at Johannes Kepler University (Linz, Austria) and visiting scholar at the University of Washington Bothell (Seattle, USA), his research focuses mainly on B2B and B2C marketing and branding, and consumer behavior. His articles have appeared in journals such as Organization Studies, Journal of Advertising, Family Business Review, Journal of Business Research, Industrial Marketing Management, Journal of Business Ethics, Journal of Business & Industrial Marketing, Consumption, Markets & Culture, Journal of Service Theory and Practice, Management Decision, Journal of Product & Brand Management, and in other academic outlets. Giuseppe serves in the Editorial Board of the Journal of Business Research, Journal of Product & Brand Management, Management Decision, and of the Italian Journal of Marketing. He is also an Associate Editor for Pearson Management & Marketing Cases, and serves as a reviewer for several highly-ranked international journals. In 2021 he has been appointed member of the board of directors of the Italian Marketing Association (Società Italiana Marketing, SIM).

Reena Raj is currently presently working as an Assistant Professor in the Department of Business Analytics, CHRIST (Deemed to be University), Bengaluru, Karnataka. She has 20 years of experience including industry, academia and management research. Prof Reena has presented papers in various national and international conferences and published research papers and edited books. She has mentored close to 200 projects across various domains in management. Her areas of interest include Analytics and Decision Sciences and Behavioural Sciences. She has been associated with Christ University for 13 years.

Sreedhara Raman is having Bachelor of Engineering from Kuvempu University, Post Graduate Diploma in Business Management from Indian Institute of Rural management, Jaipur, and Doctor of Philosophy from the University of Mysore. He has around 5 years of corporate experience during which he worked for Zenith Rubbers Limited and Falcon Tyres. He has around 18 years of teaching and research experience. Presently, he is working as Associate Professor at School of Business and Management,

CHRIST (Deemed to be University) in Marketing Specialization, at the Central campus, Bangalore. His core areas of teaching and research are Sales Management, Distribution Management, and Marketing Research and Analytics. He has published research papers in Scopus indexed and UGC approved journals. He has also presented research papers in the International and National conferences.

Jéssica Reuter is Master in Finance and PhD student in Economics and Business Sciences at the University of Aveiro. Researcher at the University of Aveiro. Her research interests include innovation, education, financial market analysis, international finance, behaviour in finance and public policy.

Mohd Ali Samsudin, PhD, is an Associate Professor at School of Educational Studies, Universiti Sains Malaysia (USM). His research interests include Applied Psychometrics and Statistics in Education and Science, Technology, Engineering and Mathematics (STEM) Digital Learning. In the field of Applied Psychometrics, his research focuses on the use of Computerized Adaptive Testing (CAT), as a tool to integrate technology into assessment. As for the Applied Statistic Research. Dr Mohd Ali Samsudin is currently looking into the use of Big Data and Social Network Analysis as well as the emerging trend in data technology for Industrial Revaluation (IR 4.0). In terms of STEM Digital Learning, he is researching the application of Mixed Reality of STEM Learning and the movement of citizen developer among STEM Teachers.

Seema Sant is currently working as an Associate Dean & Professor Human Resources at Vivekanand Education Society Institute of Management Studies and Research (VESIM), Chembur, Mumbai. She is a behavioral certified trainer with extensive academic and industry experience. She has done her MBA (HR) and Ph.D. in Business Administration, Diploma in Training & Development (ISTD). She is also a Certified Trainer for Saville Consulting International Accreditation Programme. She has 24 years of experience working with corporate and academic institutions. Her areas of interest are Organizational Development, Changing Work Culture, Training Effectiveness & Development and HR Analytics.

Elvira Lázaro dos Santos holds a PhD in Education-Mathematic Didactics at the Institute of Education of the University of Lisbon, a Master's in Education and a degree in Mathematics from the Faculty of Sciences of the University of Lisbon. She teaches in both elementary and high schools and has participated in several innovative National and International projects, which include Technologies and Mathematics Education. She has been interested in initial and in-service teacher training, formative assessment and writes Math books for basic education.

Bidisha Sarkar has completed her MBA from ICFAI Business School, India. She has pursued M.Phil and PhD from Christ University, India. Her research area for M.Phil was finance. She explored the area of econometrics-finance in her PhD. She has four years of experience which includes academic and industry. Dr. Sarkar had served several international clients for major and minor research projects. Her area of expertise is the energy sector. She is a social entrepreneur and founder of 'Utthan Foundation' where members serve for youth development. Dr. Sarkar is presently, working with Christ University, India.

Emine Sendurur received her PhD in Computer Education and Instructional Technology from Middle East Technical University, Turkey, in 2012. In 2005, she was hired as a research assistant in the same department. After completing her PhD, she worked as an instructor in Computer Programming department. She recently works as an associate professor doctor in Computer Education and Instructional Technologies department at Ondokuz Mayıs University, Turkey. She teaches courses including instructional design, computer science, learning theories, Internet based programming and human-computer interaction. Her main research interests consist of user experience, informal learning, social networking sites, cognitive load theory, instructional message design, and eye-tracking methodology.

Polat Sendurur received his bachelor degree in Computer Education and Instructional Technology from Middle East Technical University, Turkey, in 2004, and then he was hired as computer science teacher by Turkish Ministry of Education. In 2006, he started to his PhD education and was hired as a research assistant in Computer Education and Instructional Technology from Middle East Technical University. He recently works as an instructor in Computer Education and Instructional Technologies department at Ondokuz Mayıs University, Turkey. He teaches courses including teaching methods, fundamentals of distance education, qualitative research methods in instructional technologies, and introduction to programing. His main research interests consist of technology integration, cognitive tools, computational thinking, and computer science education.

Lee Ann Setzer holds a master's degree in speech-language pathology. She is the project coordinator for Project SEEL (Systematic and Engaging Early Literacy) at Brigham Young University.

M. Mahruf C. Shohel is an academic researcher with special interests in education, childhood studies, international development, technology-enhanced learning and social science research methods. He has written extensively on development issues in the Global South and conducted research on disadvantaged children including socioeconomically deprived children, street children, sex worker's children and displaced refugee children. Currently, he is engaged in the fields of education in emergencies, education for sustainable development and global citizenship, emerging technologies in education, students' learning journeys and their engagement, and teaching and learning in higher education.

Haytham Siala is a Senior Lecturer (Associate Professor) in Digital Marketing at Newcastle University. Haytham received his Ph.D. in Information Systems from Brunel University, UK. His research interests include Social Media & Digital Marketing, Consumer Behavior, Religious Brand Management, Business Ethics and Technology Enhanced Leaning. His research has been published in leading journals such as Business Ethics, Information, Technology and People, Journal of Business Research, and Information System Frontiers.

Constantine-(Kostas) Skordoulis is Professor of Epistemology and Didactical Methodology of Physics at the Department of Primary Education, National and Kapodistrian University of Athens, Greece, where he teaches Physics and Theory of Scientific Knowledge. He is also Coordinator of the Module "History of Science, Epistemology and Didactical Methodology", in the School of Science and Technology of the Hellenic Open University. He has studied Physics at the University of Kent at Canterbury, UK and has a PhD in Quantum Optics from the University of Ioannina. He has worked as a Visiting Researcher at the Universities of Oxford (UK), Jena (Germany) and Groningen (Netherlands) with scholarships from DAAD (Germany) and NWO (Netherlands). He is Effective Member of the International Academy of History of Science and has been Member of the Council of the European Society for History of Science

(2012-14) and Secretary of the Teaching Commission of the Division of History of Science and Technology of the International Union of History and Philosophy of Science (2007-2017).

Carolyn Stufft is an assistant professor of literacy in the Department of Teacher Education at Berry College. Dr. Stufft is a certified ELAR (English/Language Arts/Reading) teacher, Reading Specialist, and Legacy Master Reading Teacher; she has taught grades 4-8 in charter and Title I public schools. Her research interests include the use of digital literacies to promote K-12 students' literacy practices. Her teaching interests include the preparation of pre-service teachers to effectively incorporate digital literacies within the curriculum.

Binod Sundararajan's research interests lie in organizational, professional and business communication; computer-mediated communication; CSCW, CSCL and social network analysis. He conducts research in adoption and diffusion of mediated technologies, use of CMC in such diverse areas as entrepreneurship, justice, teaching and learning, business ethics education, pedagogical approaches, leadership education, collaborative work and learning and management education, and historical data analysis.

Sanjida Akter Tanni is a lecturer at the Institution of Education and Research, Jagannath University, Dhaka, Bangladesh. Her research interests are online learning, distance education, blended learning, teaching-learning strategies, and technology-based education.

Samantha Taylor is focused on leveraging and integrating technology to increase self-reported efficacy in learners and educators. She supports Open Education Resource (OER) initiatives, sharing original pre-class mini-lectures and active-learning materials via her website. Sam hosts a Guest Speaker podcast available on YouTube and Spotify. She teaches cost management and financial reporting at Dalhousie University, and is an educator and lead policy advisor with CPA Western School of Business.

Rendani Tshifhumulo is the Head of the Department of Arts and Social Sciences. She has presented papers nationally and internationally addressing IKS, Myth, Contemporary social problems including health and domestic violence. Dr. Tshifhumulo teaches Sociology from undergraduate to postgraduate level. She has managed to supervise many students at honours, MA and PhD levels. She has written articles, book chapters and edited a book. Her last article is on the travails of COVID 19 survivors.

Livhuwani Daphney Tshikukuvhe is a lecturer at the university of Venda in the department of Indigenous knowledge systems and heritage. She is an Indigenous Knowledge Holder(IKS) practitioner , She hold her masters of arts degree of African studies department in the School of Human and social sciences. she is currently working towards her PhD. She is a supervisor and supervised students in Indigenous knowledge system and heritage department. She is good in organizing community engagement e.g. celebration of heritage and everything related to cultural days , her researches mostly based on how to preserve culture, it can be on indigenous food/traditional food, morals, values, etc. She is a supervisor and supervised students in Indigenous knowledge system and heritage department.

Anna Rebecca Unterholzner attends the Ph.D. in Fine Arts (Multimedia Art Department) at the Fine Arts Faculty at Lisbon University, Portugal. She completed her Master's degree in Modern and Contemporary European Philosophy in 2019 at the Luxembourg University and received her Bachelor's degree in Economics and Social Sciences in 2016 at the Vienna University of Economics and Business, Austria. She is currently a researcher collaborator at two Lisbon University Research Centres: ITI/ LARsyS, Interactive Technologies Institute and CIEBA Center for research and studies in Fine Arts. Anna Unterholzner's research focuses on transdisciplinary art and design territories that merge arts and emotions, neuroaesthetics, gaming, interactive media, and gender equity.

Sharon Varghese is currently working as Assistant Professor in the Department of Statistics, CHRIST University, India and has obtained Ph.D. in Statistics from Pondicherry University, India in 2019. Currently guiding 2 Ph.D. Scholars and 8 M.Sc. students in their research. The research areas are distribution theory, reliability engineering and survival analysis.

Sankar Varma is a Research Scholar in the field of Economics with Christ (Deemed to be University), Bengaluru, Karnataka, India. His area of research interest includes Political Economy, Ecological Economics, Economics of Growth and Development, Cultural Economics and Criticism. He is at present working on contemporary urban development and exclusion. He has his works published in the Economic and Political Weekly (EPW), the Frontline (The Hindu Publishing Group) and various other books and journal platforms both online and physical.

Cláudia Veloso is Professor of Management (Marketing and Finances) at ESTGA - University of Aveiro. She is a researcher at GOVCOPP. She was a Member of the Board of the Centro Hospitalar do Nordeste (ULSNE) and Technical Adviser of the Ministry of Health of Portugal. She participated in 4 R&D projects, published more than 70 publications in peer-reviewed journals, book chapters and proceedings, and won 7 scientific awards.

Sam von Gillern is an Assistant Professor of Literacy Education at the University of Missouri. His primary research interests include digital citizenship and game-based learning in English language arts education.

John R. Woodward hold degrees in theoretical physics, cognitive science, and computer science, all from the University of Birmingham, U.K. Currently, he is with the School of Computer Science and Mathematics at the University of Stirling, He is a member of the Computational Heuristics, Operational Research and Decision Support research group (http://chords.cs.stir.ac.uk/). He was with the European Organization for Nuclear Research (CERN), where he conducted research into particle physics, the Royal Air Force as an Environmental Noise Scientist, and Electronic Data Systems as a Systems Engineer, and has also taught in China, Japan and the UK. He has given tutorials at GECCO, PPSN, and CEC on The Automatic Design of Algorithms, the aim is to generate high-quality algorithms, more cheaply and quickly. He has also organized a workshop at GECCO on this for the past 7 years.

Ahmet Erdost Yastibaş has a Ph.D. degree in English language teaching and has been working as an English language lecturer for more than 11 years. His research interests include technology-enhanced language teaching and foreign language assessment and evaluation.

Lin Zou is a Chinese language teacher at a primary school affiliated with South China Normal University, P.R. China. She graduated with a Master's degree in Teaching Chinese to Speakers of Other Languages in Jinan University, Guangzhou, P.R. China. She was awarded the China National Teaching Achievement Award in 2018. Her research interests center on game-based interventions for early literacy learning.

Index

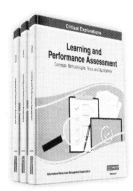
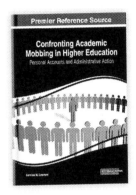

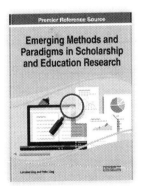

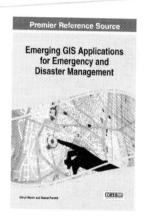
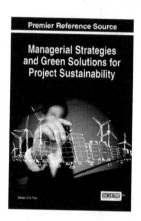

IGI Global Author Services

Providing a high-quality, affordable, and expeditious service, IGI Global's Author Services enable authors to streamline their publishing process, increase chance of acceptance, and adhere to IGI Global's publication standards.

Benefits of Author Services:

- **Professional Service:** All our editors, designers, and translators are experts in their field with years of experience and professional certifications.
- **Quality Guarantee & Certificate:** Each order is returned with a quality guarantee and certificate of professional completion.
- **Timeliness:** All editorial orders have a guaranteed return timeframe of 3-5 business days and translation orders are guaranteed in 7-10 business days.
- **Affordable Pricing:** IGI Global Author Services are competitively priced compared to other industry service providers.
- **APC Reimbursement:** IGI Global authors publishing Open Access (OA) will be able to deduct the cost of editing and other IGI Global author services from their OA APC publishing fee.

Author Services Offered:

English Language Copy Editing
Professional, native English language copy editors improve your manuscript's grammar, spelling, punctuation, terminology, semantics, consistency, flow, formatting, and more.

Scientific & Scholarly Editing
A Ph.D. level review for qualities such as originality and significance, interest to researchers, level of methodology and analysis, coverage of literature, organization, quality of writing, and strengths and weaknesses.

Figure, Table, Chart & Equation Conversions
Work with IGI Global's graphic designers before submission to enhance and design all figures and charts to IGI Global's specific standards for clarity.

Translation
Providing 70 language options, including Simplified and Traditional Chinese, Spanish, Arabic, German, French, and more.

Hear What the Experts Are Saying About IGI Global's Author Services

"Publishing with IGI Global has been an amazing experience for me for sharing my research. The strong academic production support ensures quality and timely completion." – **Prof. Margaret Niess, Oregon State University, USA**

"The service was very fast, very thorough, and very helpful in ensuring our chapter meets the criteria and requirements of the book's editors. I was quite impressed and happy with your service." – **Prof. Tom Brinthaupt, Middle Tennessee State University, USA**

IGI Global
PUBLISHER of TIMELY KNOWLEDGE
www.igi-global.com

Publisher of Peer-Reviewed, Timely, and
Innovative Academic Research Since 1988

IGI Global's Transformative Open Access (OA) Model:
How to Turn Your University Library's Database Acquisitions Into a Source of OA Funding

Well in advance of Plan S, IGI Global unveiled their OA Fee Waiver (Read & Publish) Initiative. Under this initiative, librarians who invest in IGI Global's InfoSci-Books and/or InfoSci-Journals databases will be able to subsidize their patrons' OA article processing charges (APCs) when their work is submitted and accepted (after the peer review process) into an IGI Global journal.

How Does it Work?

Step 1: **Library Invests in the InfoSci-Databases:** A library perpetually purchases or subscribes to the InfoSci-Books, InfoSci-Journals, or discipline/subject databases.

Step 2: **IGI Global Matches the Library Investment with OA Subsidies Fund:** IGI Global provides a fund to go towards subsidizing the OA APCs for the library's patrons.

Step 3: **Patron of the Library is Accepted into IGI Global Journal (After Peer Review):** When a patron's paper is accepted into an IGI Global journal, they option to have their paper published under a traditional publishing model or as OA.

Step 4: **IGI Global Will Deduct APC Cost from OA Subsidies Fund:** If the author decides to publish under OA, the OA APC fee will be deducted from the OA subsidies fund.

Step 5: **Author's Work Becomes Freely Available:** The patron's work will be freely available under CC BY copyright license, enabling them to share it freely with the academic community.

Note: *This fund will be offered on an annual basis and will renew as the subscription is renewed for each year thereafter. IGI Global will manage the fund and award the APC waivers unless the librarian has a preference as to how the funds should be managed.*

Hear From the Experts on This Initiative:

"I'm very happy to have been able to make one of my recent research contributions *freely available* along with having access to the *valuable resources* found within IGI Global's InfoSci-Journals database."

— **Prof. Stuart Palmer,**
Deakin University, Australia

"Receiving the support from IGI Global's OA Fee Waiver Initiative *encourages me to continue my research work without any hesitation.*"

— **Prof. Wenlong Liu**, College of Economics and Management at Nanjing University of Aeronautics & Astronautics, China